Intermediate Accounting

Volume 1
14th edition

Donald E. Kieso PH.D., CPA
Jerry J. Weygandt PH.D., CPA
Terry D. Warfield PH.D.

Department of Accounting
Bergen Community College

To order books or for customer service, please call 1(800)-CALL-WILEY (225-5945).

Printed in the United States of America.

ISBN 978-1-118-11119-2
Printed and bound by Strategic Content Imaging.
10 9 8 7 6 5 4 3 2 1

Brief Contents

INTERNATIONAL ACCOUNTING STANDARDS

Relevant and reliable financial information is a necessity for viable capital markets. Unfortunately, companies outside the United States often prepare financial statements using standards different from U.S. GAAP (or simply GAAP). As a result, international companies, such as **Coca-Cola**, **Microsoft**, and **IBM**, have to develop financial information in different ways. Beyond the additional costs these companies incur, users of the financial statements often must understand at least two sets of accounting standards (understanding one set is hard enough!). It is not surprising, therefore, that there is a growing demand for one set of high-quality international standards.

Presently, there are two sets of rules accepted for international use—**GAAP** and the **International Financial Reporting Standards (IFRS)**, issued by the London-based International Accounting Standards Board (IASB). U.S. companies that list overseas are still permitted to use GAAP, and foreign companies listed on U.S. exchanges are permitted to use IFRS. As you will learn, there are many similarities between GAAP and IFRS.

Already, over 115 countries have adopted IFRS, plus the European Union now requires all listed companies in Europe (over 7,000 companies) to use it. The SEC laid out a roadmap, shown below, by which all U.S. companies might be required to use IFRS by 2015.

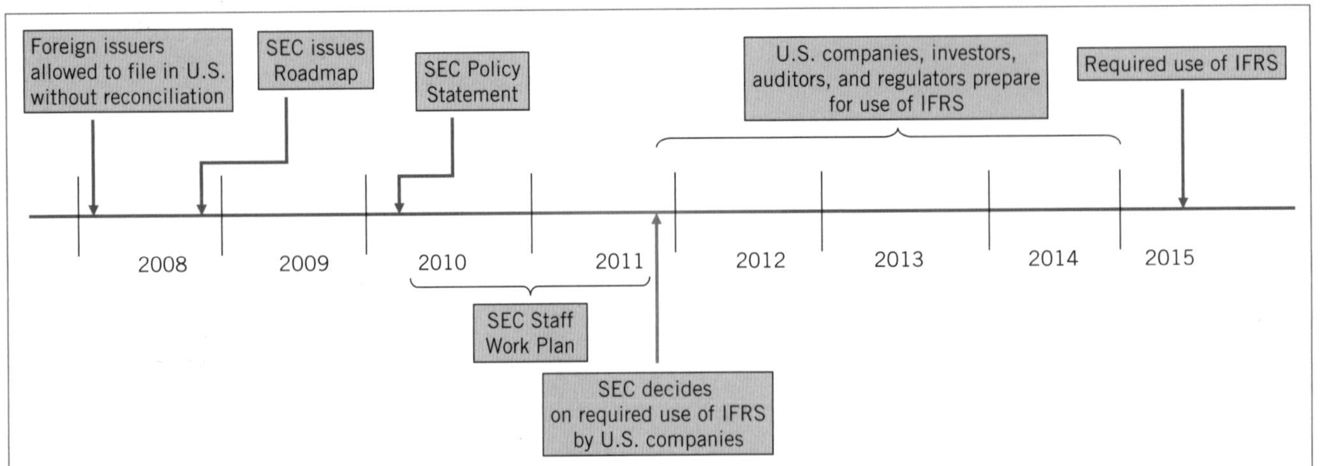

CONVERGENCE OF GAAP AND IFRS

Most parties recognize that global markets will best be served if only one set of accounting standards is used. For example, the FASB and the IASB formalized their commitment to the convergence of GAAP and IFRS by issuing a memorandum of understanding (often referred to as the Norwalk agreement). The two boards agreed to use their best efforts to:

- Make their existing financial reporting standards fully compatible as soon as practicable, and
- Coordinate their future work programs to ensure that once achieved, compatibility is maintained.

As a result of this agreement, the two Boards identified a number of short-term and long-term projects that would lead to convergence.

Because convergence is such an important issue, we provide a discussion of international accounting standards at the end of each chapter called **IFRS Insights**. This feature will help you understand the changes that are taking place in the financial reporting area as we move to one set of international standards. Each IFRS Insights, as shown here, consists of four sections.

An **introduction** typically lists the international accounting pronouncements related to the chapter topic.

The basic accounting and reporting issues related to recognition and measurement of receivables, such as the use of allowance accounts, how to record discounts, use of the allowance method to account for bad debts, and factoring, are similar for both IFRS and GAAP. *IAS 1* ("Presentation of Financial Statements") is the only standard that discusses issues specifically related to cash. *IFRS 7* ("Financial Instruments: Disclosure")

RELEVANT FACTS

- The accounting and reporting related to cash is essentially the same under both IFRS and GAAP. In addition, the definition used for cash equivalents is the same. One difference is that, in general, IFRS classifies bank overdrafts as cash.

Relevant Facts explain similarities and differences of GAAP and IFRS.

About the Numbers generally discusses and provides examples of IFRS applications (in many cases, using real international companies).

ABOUT THE NUMBERS

Impairment Evaluation Process

IFRS provides detailed guidelines to assess whether receivables should be considered uncollectible (often referred to as *impaired*). GAAP does not identify a specific approach. Under IFRS, companies assess their receivables for impairment each reporting period and start the impairment assessment by considering whether objective

ON THE HORIZON

The question of recording fair values for financial instruments will continue to be an important issue to resolve as the Boards work toward convergence. Both the IASB and the FASB have indicated that they believe that financial statements would be more transparent and understandable if companies recorded and reported all financial instruments at fair value. That said, in *IFRS 9*, which was issued in 2009, the IASB

On the Horizon discusses convergence progress and plans related to the accounting topics presented in the chapter.

IFRS Insights also includes *IFRS Self-Test Questions*, as well as *IFRS Concepts and Application*, so students can test their understanding of the material. An *International Financial Reporting Problem*, based on **Marks and Spencer plc**, offers students an opportunity to analyze IFRS-based financial statements.

OTHER INTERNATIONAL COVERAGE

Having a basic understanding of international accounting is becoming ever more important as the profession moves toward convergence of GAAP and international standards. Thus, in addition to the **IFRS Insights** pages discussed above, we continue to include marginal **International Perspectives**, marked with the icon shown here, which we updated throughout to reflect changes in international accounting. These notes describe or compare IFRS as well as accounting practices in other countries with GAAP. This feature helps you to understand that other countries sometimes use different recognition and measurement principles to report financial information.

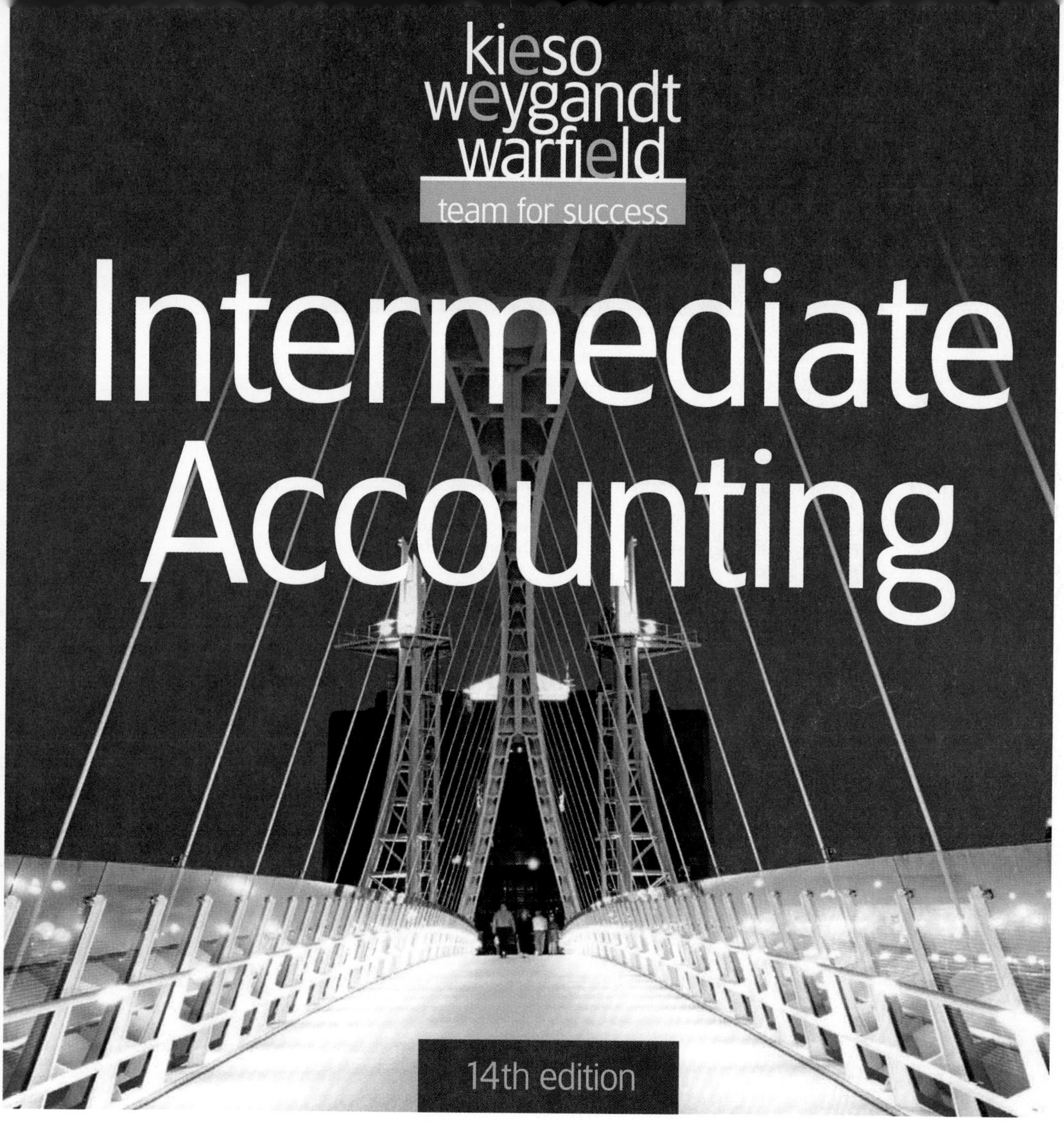

kieso
weygandt
warfield

team for success

Intermediate Accounting

14th edition

Donald E. Kieso PhD, CPA
Northern Illinois University
DeKalb, Illinois

Jerry J. Weygandt PhD, CPA
University of Wisconsin—Madison
Madison, Wisconsin

Terry D. Warfield, PhD
University of Wisconsin—Madison
Madison, Wisconsin

WILEY

John Wiley & Sons, Inc.

Dedicated to
our wives, ***Donna, Enid, and Mary,***
for their love,
support, and encouragement

Vice President & Publisher	George Hoffman
Associate Publisher	Christopher DeJohn
Senior Acquisitions Editor	Michael McDonald
Project Editor	Brian Kamins
Development Editor	Terry Ann Tatro
Production Manager	Dorothy Sinclair
Project Editor	Yana Mermel
Senior Production Editor	Trish McFadden
Associate Director of Marketing	Amy Scholz
Marketing Manager	Karolina Zarychta Honsa
Executive Media Editor	Allie K. Morris
Media Editor	Greg Chaput
Senior Designer	Jim O'Shea
Production Management Services	Ingrao Associates
Creative Director	Harry Nolan
Senior Photo Editor	Mary Ann Price
Senior Editorial Assistant	Jackie Kepping
Cover Photo	Jon Arnold Images/SuperStock, Inc.
Chapter Opener Photo	Paul Fawcett/iStockphoto
Cover Credit	© Gerald Hoberman/Photolibrary

This book was set in Palatino by Aptara®, Inc. and printed and bound by Courier Kendallville.
The cover was printed by Courier Kendallville.

This book is printed on acid-free paper. ∞

ISBN-13 978-0-470-58723-2

Printed in the United States of America

10 9 8 7 6 5 4 3 2 1

Author Commitment

Don Kieso

Donald E. Kieso, PhD, CPA, received his bachelor's degree from Aurora University and his doctorate in accounting from the University of Illinois. He has served as chairman of the Department of Accountancy and is currently the KPMG Emeritus Professor of Accountancy at Northern Illinois University. He has public accounting experience with Price Waterhouse & Co. (San Francisco and Chicago) and Arthur Andersen & Co. (Chicago) and research experience with the Research Division of the American Institute of Certified Public Accountants (New York). He has done post-doctorate work as a Visiting Scholar at the University of California at Berkeley and is a recipient of NIU's Teaching Excellence Award and four Golden Apple Teaching Awards. Professor Kieso is the author of other accounting and business books and is a member of the American Accounting Association, the American Institute of Certified Public Accountants, and the Illinois CPA Society. He has served as a member of the Board of Directors of the Illinois CPA Society, then AACSB's Accounting Accreditation Committees, the State of Illinois Comptroller's Commission, as Secretary-Treasurer of the Federation of Schools of Accountancy, and as Secretary-Treasurer of the American Accounting Association. Professor Kieso is currently serving on the Board of Trustees and Executive Committee of Aurora University, as a member of the Board of Directors of Kishwaukee Community Hospital, and as Treasurer and Director of Valley West Community Hospital. From 1989 to 1993, he served as a charter member of the national Accounting Education Change Commission. He is the recipient of the Outstanding Accounting Educator Award from the Illinois CPA Society, the FSA's Joseph A. Silvoso Award of Merit, the NIU Foundation's Humanitarian Award for Service to Higher Education, a Distinguished Service Award from the Illinois CPA Society, and in 2003 an honorary doctorate from Aurora University.

Jerry Weygandt

Jerry J. Weygandt, PhD, CPA, is Arthur Andersen Alumni Emeritus Professor of Accounting at the University of Wisconsin—Madison. He holds a Ph.D. in accounting from the University of Illinois. Articles by Professor Weygandt have appeared in the *Accounting Review, Journal of Accounting Research, Accounting Horizons, Journal of Accountancy,* and other academic and professional journals. These articles have examined such financial reporting issues as accounting for price-level adjustments, pensions, convertible securities, stock option contracts, and interim reports. Professor Weygandt is author of other accounting and financial reporting books and is a member of the American Accounting Association, the American Institute of Certified Public Accountants, and the Wisconsin Society of Certified Public Accountants. He has served on numerous committees of the American Accounting Association and as a member of the editorial board of the Accounting Review; he also has served as President and Secretary-Treasurer of the American Accounting Association. In addition, he has been actively involved with the American Institute of Certified Public Accountants and has been a member of the Accounting Standards Executive Committee (AcSEC) of that organization. He has served on the FASB task force that examined the reporting issues related to accounting for income taxes and served as a trustee of the Financial Accounting Foundation. Professor Weygandt has received the Chancellor's Award for Excellence in Teaching and the Beta Gamma Sigma Dean's Teaching Award. He is on the board of directors of M & I Bank of Southern Wisconsin. He is the recipient of the Wisconsin Institute of CPA's Outstanding Educator's Award and the Lifetime Achievement Award. In 2001, he received the American Accounting Association's Outstanding Educator Award.

Terry Warfield

Terry D. Warfield, PhD, is the Robert and Monica Beyer Professor of Accounting at the University of Wisconsin—Madison. He received a B.S. and M.B.A. from Indiana University and a Ph.D. in accounting from the University of Iowa. Professor Warfield's area of expertise is financial reporting, and prior to his academic career, he worked for five years in the banking industry. He served as the Academic Accounting Fellow in the Office of the Chief Accountant at the U.S. Securities and Exchange Commission in Washington, D.C. from 1995–1996. Professor Warfield's primary research interests concern financial accounting standards and disclosure policies. He has published scholarly articles in *The Accounting Review, Journal of Accounting and Economics, Research in Accounting Regulation,* and *Accounting Horizons,* and he has served on the editorial boards of *The Accounting Review, Accounting Horizons,* and *Issues in Accounting Education*. He has served as president of the Financial Accounting and Reporting Section, the Financial Accounting Standards Committee of the American Accounting Association (Chair 1995–1996), and on the AAA-FASB Research Conference Committee. He also served on the Financial Accounting Standards Advisory Council of the Financial Accounting Standards Board. Professor Warfield has received teaching awards at both the University of Iowa and the University of Wisconsin, and he was named to the Teaching Academy at the University of Wisconsin in 1995. Professor Warfield has developed and published several case studies based on his research for use in accounting classes. These cases have been selected for the AICPA Professor-Practitioner Case Development Program and have been published in *Issues in Accounting Education*.

for Students

WileyPLUS

WileyPLUS is an innovative, research-based, online environment for effective teaching and learning.

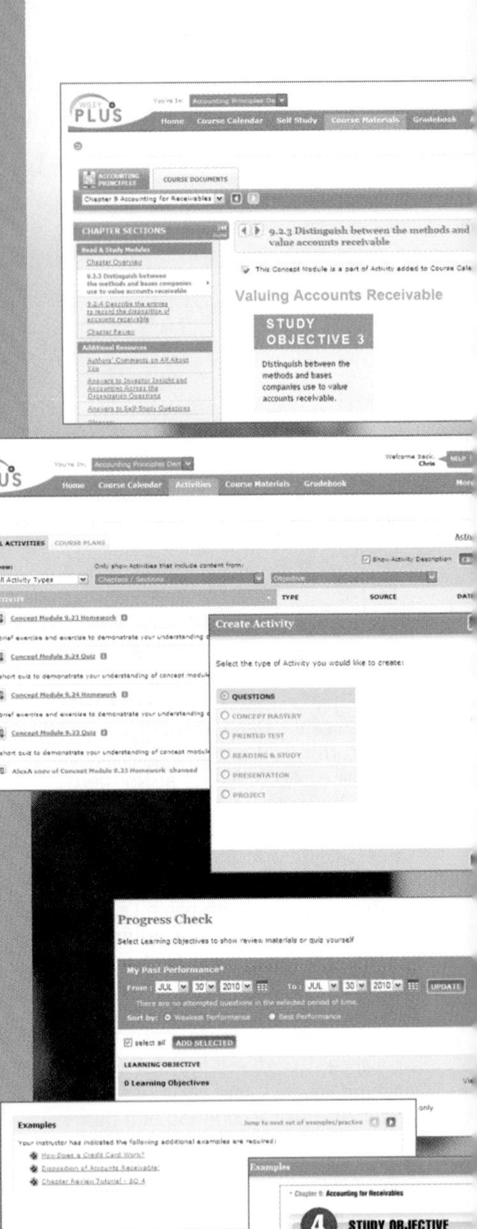

What do STUDENTS receive with *WileyPLUS*?

WileyPLUS increases confidence through an innovative **design** that allows greater **engagement**, which leads to improved learning **outcomes**.

Design

The *WileyPLUS* design integrates relevant resources, including the entire digital textbook, in an easy-to-navigate framework that helps students study more effectively and ensures student engagement. Innovative features, such as calendars and visual progress tracking, as well as a variety of self-evaluation tools, are all designed to improve time-management and increase student confidence.

Engagement

WileyPLUS organizes the textbook content into smaller, more manageable learning units with demonstrable study objectives and outcomes. Related media, examples, and sample practice items are integrated within each section to reinforce the study objectives. Throughout each study session, students can assess progress and gain immediate feedback on strengths and weaknesses in order to ensure they are spending their time most effectively.

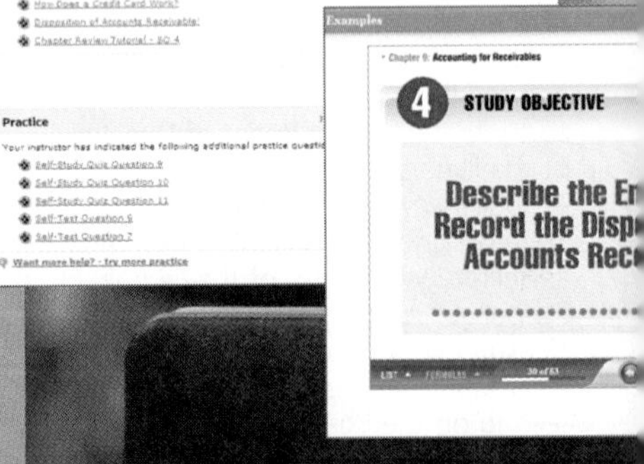

Outcomes

Throughout each study session, students can assess their progress and gain immediate feedback. *WileyPLUS* provides precise reporting of strengths and weaknesses, as well as individualized quizzes, so that students are confident they are spending their time on the right things. With *WileyPLUS*, students always know the exact outcome of their efforts.

With increased confidence, motivation is sustained so students stay on task longer, leading to success.

for Instructors

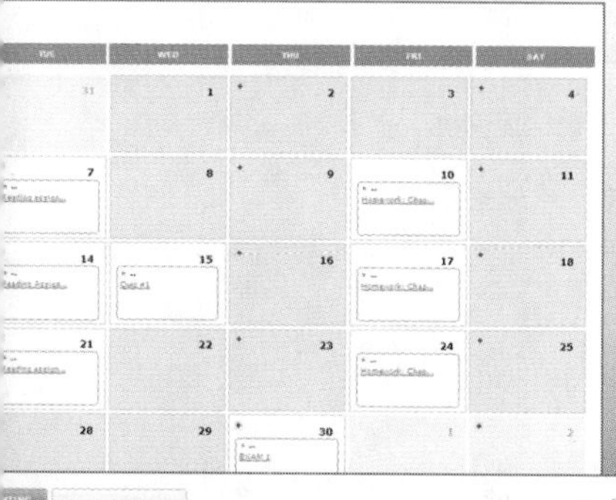

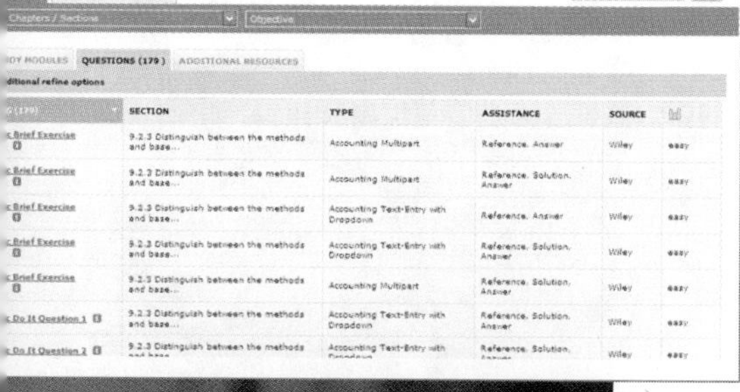

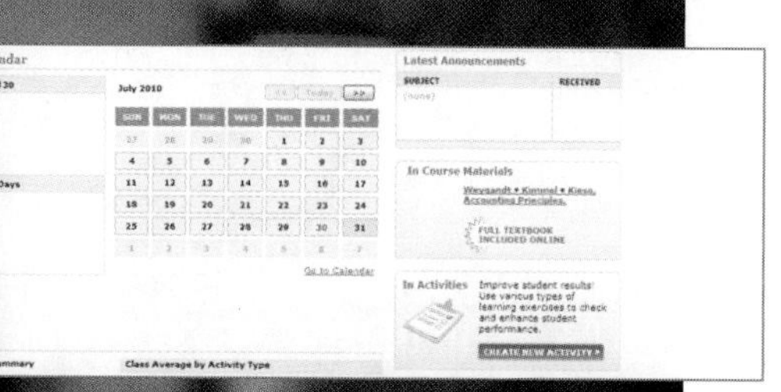

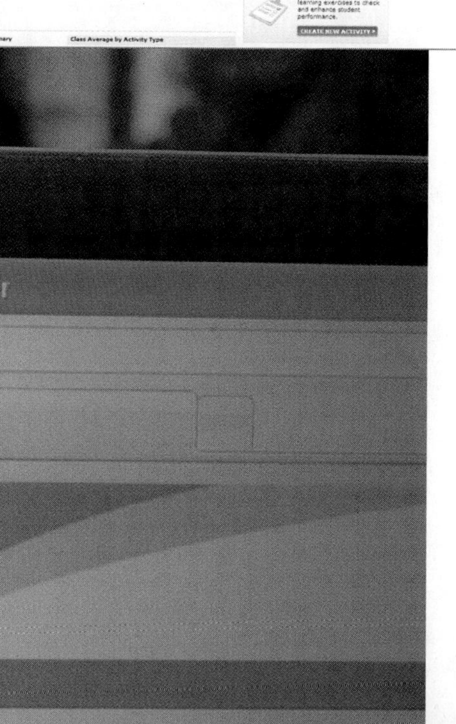

What do INSTRUCTORS receive with *WileyPLUS*?
Support and Insight into Student Progress

WileyPLUS provides reliable, customizable resources that reinforce course goals inside and outside of the classroom, as well as visibility into individual student progress. Pre-created materials and activities help instructors optimize their time.

For class preparation and classroom use:

- Lecture Notes
- PowerPoint Slides
- Tutorials

For assignments and testing:

- Gradable Reading Assignment Questions (embedded with online text)
- Question Assignments: all end-of-chapter problems coded algorithmically with hints, links to text

For course planning: *WileyPLUS* comes with a pre-created **Course Plan** designed by a subject matter expert uniquely for this course. Simple drag-and-drop tools make it easy to assign the course plan as-is or modify it to reflect your course syllabus.

For progress monitoring: *WileyPLUS* provides instant access to reports on trends in class performance, student use of course materials, and progress toward learning objectives, helping inform decisions and drive classroom discussions.

Experience *WileyPLUS* for effective teaching and learning at **www.wileyplus.com**.

Powered by proven technology and built on a foundation of cognitive research, *WileyPLUS* has enriched the education of millions of students, in numerous countries around the world.

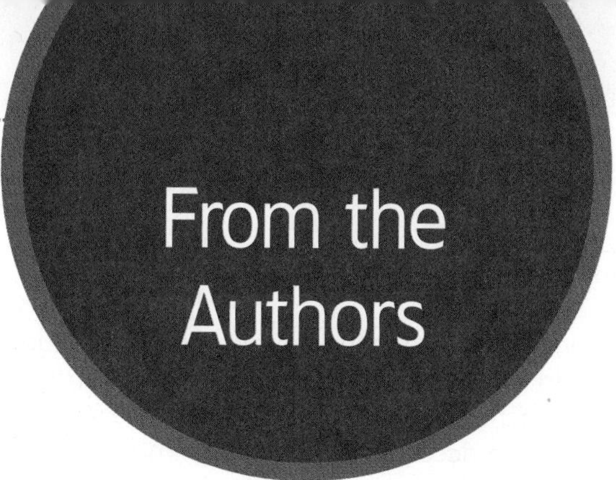

Accounting is the most employable, sought-after major for 2012, according to entry-level job site **CollegeGrad.com**. One reason for this interest is found in the statement by former Secretary of the Treasury and Economic Advisor to the President, Lawrence Summers. He noted that the single-most important innovation shaping our capital markets was the idea of generally accepted accounting principles (GAAP). We agree with Mr. Summers. Relevant and reliable financial information is a necessity for viable capital markets. Without it, our markets would be chaotic, and our standard of living would decrease.

This textbook is the market leader in providing the tools needed to understand what GAAP is and how it is applied in practice. Mastery of this material will be invaluable to you in whatever field you select.

Through many editions, this textbook has continued to reflect the constant changes taking place in the GAAP environment. This edition continues this tradition, which has become even more significant as the financial reporting environment is exploding with major change. Here are three areas of major importance that are now incorporated extensively into this edition of the text.

Convergence of U.S. GAAP and IFRS

As mentioned above, the most important innovation shaping our capital markets was the idea of U.S. GAAP. It might be said that it would be even better if we had one common set of accounting rules for the whole world, which will make it easier for international investors to compare the financial results of companies from different countries. That is happening quickly as U.S. GAAP and international accounting standards are quickly converging toward **International Financial Reporting Standards (IFRS)**, to be used by all companies. And you have the chance to be on the ground floor as we develop for you the similarities and differences in the two systems that ultimately will be one.

> "If this book helps teachers instill in their students an appreciation for the challenges, worth, and limitations of financial reporting, if it encourages students to evaluate critically and understand financial accounting concepts and practice, and if it prepares students for advanced study, professional examinations, and the successful and ethical pursuit of their careers in accounting or business in a global economy, then we will have attained our objectives."

A Fair Value Movement

The FASB believes that fair value information is more relevant to users than historical cost. As a result, there is more information that is being reported on this basis, and even more will occur in the future. The financial press is full of articles discussing how financial institutions must fair value their assets, which has led to massive losses during the recent credit crisis. In addition, additional insight into the reliability related to fair values is being addressed and disclosed to help investors make important capital allocation decisions. As a result, we devote a considerable amount of material that discusses and illustrates fair value concepts in this edition.

A New Way of Looking at Generally Accepted Principles (GAAP)

Learning GAAP used to be a daunting task, as it is comprised of many standards that vary in form, completeness, and structure. Fortunately, the profession has recently developed the Financial Accounting Standards Board Codification (often referred to as the Codification). This Codification provides in one place all the GAAP related to a given topic. This textbook is the first to incorporate this Codification—it will make learning GAAP easier and more interesting!

Intermediate Accounting Works

Intermediate Accounting is the market-leading textbook in providing the tools needed to understand what GAAP is and how it is applied in practice. With this Fourteenth Edition, we strive to continue to provide the material needed to understand this subject area. The book is comprehensive and up-to-date, and provides the instructor with flexibility in the topics to cover. We also include proven pedagogical tools, designed to help students learn more effectively and to answer the changing needs of this course. Page xiv describes all of the learning tools of the textbook in detail.

We are excited about *Intermediate Accounting*, Fourteenth Edition. We believe it meets an important objective of providing useful information to educators and students interested in learning about both GAAP and IFRS. Suggestions and comments from users of this book will be appreciated. Please feel free to e-mail any one of us at *AccountingAuthors@yahoo.com*.

Donald E. Kieso
DeKalb, Illinois

Jerry J. Weygandt
Madison, Wisconsin

Terry D. Warfield
Madison, Wisconsin

WHAT'S NEW?

The Fourteenth Edition expands our emphasis on student learning and improves upon a teaching and learning package that instructors and students have rated the highest in customer satisfaction. Based on extensive reviews, focus groups, and interactions with other intermediate accounting instructors and students, we have developed a number of new pedagogical features and content changes, designed both to help students learn more effectively and to answer the changing needs of the course.

Major Content Revisions

In response to the changing environment, we have significantly revised several chapters.

Chapter 2 Conceptual Framework for Financial Reporting

- Chapter rewritten to reflect latest IASB/FASB work: reliability replaced with faithful representation, fundamental qualities differ, and secondary qualities are now enhancing qualities (and now contain some of the previous primary qualities); the framework now just includes the cost constraint (previously cost-benefit and materiality, materiality now a company-specific aspect of relevance).
- Constraints rewritten per above and prudence/conservatism is discussed as in conflict with the quality of neutrality; as a result, text discussion eliminated, but added a footnote explaining this position.
- Updated discussion of fair value, in light of recent FASB developments. Updated fair value discussions, including discussion of the fair value option, in Chapters 7, 14, and 17.

Chapter 3 The Accounting Information System

- Reduced the number of account titles throughout chapter for simplification.
- Completely new approach to illustrating transaction analysis; each illustration includes Basic Analysis, Equation Analysis, Debit-Credit Analysis, Journal Entry, and Posting sections.

Chapter 5 Balance Sheet and Statement of Cash Flows

- Moved Statement of Cash Flows material before Additional Information section, for improved discussion flow.

Chapter 7 Cash and Receivables

- Reconfigured chapter headings, so chapter now broken into four major sections (cash, accounts receivable, notes receivable, and special issues) instead of just two, for improved readability.
- Rewrote sections on direct write-off and allowance methods, for more current discussion of this material.

Chapter 18 Revenue Recognition

- Updated Current Environment section, with more recent developments in FASB revenue recognition guidelines.
- Revised and updated Revenue Recognition at Point of Sale (e.g., buyback, returns, and bill and hold) section to include new illustrations that demonstrate revenue recognition problems and solutions, as well as discussion on principal-agent relationships and multiple-deliverable arrangements (including an expanded discussion on consignments).

Chapter 23 Statement of Cash Flows

- Revised and updated Section 2: Special Problems in Statement Presentation, to discuss adjustments to net income (depreciation and amortization, losses and gains, stock options, postretirement benefit cost, extraordinary items).

Updated International Financial Reporting Standards (IFRS) Content

As we continue to strive to reflect the constant changes in the accounting environment, we have added new material on International Financial Reporting Standards (IFRS). A new end-of-chapter section, **IFRS Insights**, includes an overview section (Relevant Facts), differences between GAAP and IFRS (About the Numbers), IFRS/GAAP convergence efforts (On the Horizon), and IFRS Self-Test Questions and IFRS Concepts and Application. An international financial reporting problem is also included, based on Marks and Spencer plc (a leading U.K. department store) financial statements, as well as a research case addressing the IFRS literature for each chapter.

Enhanced Homework Material

In each chapter, we have updated Questions, Brief Exercises, Problems, and Concepts for Analysis. In addition, in the Using Your Judgment section, we now offer a new review exercise in each chapter, entitled *Accounting, Analysis, and Principles,* to help students evaluate and analyze information from the chapter. Students review the accounting introduced in the chapter ("Accounting"), consider how the information provided by the accounting is useful to investors and creditors ("Analysis"), and reflect on how the accounting is related to accounting principles and concepts ("Principles"). Such exercises, reinforced with end-of-chapter homework activities, give students the practice they will need to build decision-making skills using the accounting concepts and procedures they are learning. Finally, we have updated the *Professional Simulation* and included it in the textbook.

Chart of Accounts

It is important to always try to eliminate unnecessary barriers to student understanding. Sometimes, the accounting course can seem unnecessarily complicated to students because so many account titles are used. In order to reduce possible confusion, and to keep students focused on those concepts that really matter, in this edition of the textbook we undertook to reduce the number of account titles used. In some chapters, we were able to cut the number of accounts used by more than half.

ENHANCED FEATURES OF THE 14TH EDITION

This edition was also subject to an overall, comprehensive revision to ensure that it is technically accurate, relevant, and up-to-date. We have continued and enhanced many of the features of the 13th Edition of *Intermediate Accounting,* including the following.

Codification

The Codification was introduced in the 13th Edition—the first textbook to do so. The genesis for the Codification is explained in Chapter 1, with all previous references to the FASB literature with references to the Codification throughout the textbook. The complete citations and correspondence to prior FASB literature are presented in the FASB Codification section at the end of the chapter. Each chapter has Codification exercises and a research case (similar to the FARS Cases in the pre-codification editions of *Intermediate Accounting*).

Underlying Concepts

Underlying Concepts

These marginal notes relate topics covered within each chapter back to the conceptual principles introduced in the beginning of the textbook. This continual reinforcement of the essential concepts and principles illustrates how the concepts are applied in practice and helps students understand the *why*, as well as the *how*.

Updated Supplements

All supplements are updated, including newly designed PowerPoint presentations with more review questions, and over 500 new Test bank questions.

Real-World Emphasis

One of the goals of the intermediate accounting course is to orient students to the application of accounting principles and techniques in practice. Accordingly, we have continued our practice of using numerous examples from real companies throughout the textbook. The names of these real companies are highlighted in red. Illustrations and exhibits marked by the icon shown here in the margin are excerpts from actual financial statements of real firms.

What do the numbers mean?

PEPSICO

At the start of each chapter, we have updated and introduced new chapter-opening vignettes to provide an even better real-world context that helps motivate student interest in the chapter topic. Also, throughout the chapters, the "What Do the Numbers Mean?" boxed inserts also provide real-world extensions of the material presented in the textbook. In addition, Appendix 5B contains the 2009 annual report of The Procter & Gamble Company (P&G). The book's companion website contains the 2009 annual reports of The Coca-Cola Company and of PepsiCo, Inc. Problems in the *Using Your Judgment* section involve study of the P&G annual report or comparison of the annual reports of The Coca-Cola Company and PepsiCo. Also, links to many real-company financial reports appear in the company database at the *Gateway to the Profession*.

Currency and Accuracy

Accounting continually changes as its environment changes; an up-to-date book is therefore a necessity. As in past editions, we have strived to make this edition the most up-to-date and accurate textbook available. For the 14th Edition, we added an additional round of accuracy checking.

International Coverage

As discussed above, having a basic understanding of international accounting is becoming ever more important as the profession moves toward convergence of GAAP and international standards. Thus, in addition to the **IFRS Insights** discussed earlier, we continue to include marginal *International Perspectives*, marked with the icon shown here, which we updated throughout to reflect changes in international accounting. These notes describe or compare IFRS and international accounting practices with GAAP. This feature helps students understand that other countries sometimes use different recognition and measurement principles to report financial information.

Streamlined Presentation

We also have continued our efforts to keep the topic coverage of *Intermediate Accounting* in line with the way instructors are *currently* teaching the course. Accordingly, we have moved some optional topics into chapter-end appendices, and we have omitted altogether some topics that formerly were covered in appendices. Details are listed in the specific content changes on pages xii–xiii. We have continued efforts to maintain the readability of the textbook, following the thorough editorial review of the 13th Edition.

Additional Exercises

Our study of the intermediate accounting course indicates the importance of the end-of-chapter Exercises for teaching and practicing important accounting concepts. In the 14th Edition, therefore, we have prepared an additional set of exercises, available at the book's companion website. (Solutions are available at the instructor's portion of the website.) Also, in the 14th Edition, a new Review and Analysis exercise at the book's companion website gives an additional opportunity for students to review the accounting techniques and analysis behind each chapter topic.

Using Your Judgment Section

We have revised and updated the *Using Your Judgment* section at the end of each chapter. Elements included in this section include the following.

- A Financial Reporting Problem, featuring The Procter & Gamble Company.
- A Comparative Analysis Case, featuring The Coca-Cola Company and PepsiCo, Inc., that asks students to compare and contrast the financial reporting for these two companies.
- A Financial Statement Analysis Case that asks students to use the information in published accounting reports to conduct financial analysis.
- A review exercise in each chapter entitled *Accounting, Analysis, and Principles.* As discussed above, this integrated exercise helps students evaluate and analyze information from the chapter.
- A *Professional Research: FASB Codification* case that gives students practice conducting authoritative research using the FASB Codification research system.
- A full presentation of *Professional Simulations*, newly revised for this edition, that model the new computerized CPA exam.

The *Using Your Judgment* assignments are designed to help develop students' critical thinking, analytical, and research skills.

Content Changes by Chapter

Chapter 1 Financial Accounting and Accounting Standards

- Moved "The Challenges Facing Financial Accounting" to later in the chapter, for improved discussion.
- Rewrote "Objective of Financial Reporting" per new conceptual framework guidelines.
- New WDNM box on fair value accounting.

Chapter 2 Conceptual Framework for Financial Reporting

- "Conceptual Framework" rewritten to reflect latest IASB/FASB work: the framework now just includes the cost constraint (previously cost-benefit and materiality, materiality now a company-specific aspect of relevance), reliability replaced with faithful representation, fundamental qualities differ, and secondary qualities are now enhancing qualities (and now contain some of the previous primary qualities).
- Constraints rewritten per above—also, prudence/conservatism now considered to conflict with quality of neutrality, so text discussion eliminated, but added a footnote explaining this position.

Chapter 3 The Accounting Information System

- Reduced the number of account titles throughout chapter, for simplification.
- Completely new approach to illustrating transaction analysis; each illustration includes Basic Analysis, Equation Analysis, Debit-Credit Analysis, Journal Entry, and Posting sections.

Chapter 4 Income Statement and Related Information

- New opening story, "Watch Out for Pro Forma," about the use of pro forma reporting practices and effects and the SEC's response (issuing Regulation G).
- New WDNM boxes: "Four: The Loneliest Number," about managing earnings and the quadrophobia effect, and "Different Income Concepts," about the performance metrics analysts use/create from a company's income statement.

Chapter 5 Balance Sheet and Statement of Cash Flows

- New opening story, "Hey, It Doesn't Balance," about FASB/IASB discussion paper on possible new format of balance sheet (statement of financial position).
- Moved Statement of Cash Flows material before Additional Information section, for improved discussion flow.
- Appendix 5B updated for 2009 **P&G** annual report information.

Chapter 7 Cash and Receivables

- Completely rewritten opening story on **Nortel**.
- Reconfigured chapter headings, so chapter now broken into 4 major sections (cash, accounts receivable, notes receivable, and special issues) instead of just 2, for improved readability.
- New WDNM box, "Deep Pockets," about cash hoarding.
- Rewrote sections on direct write-off and allowance methods, for more current discussion of this material.
- New section on Fair Value Option under Special Issues.
- New detailed footnote on FASB new rules on when a transfer of receivables is recorded as a sale.
- Completed revised WDNM box, "Return to Lender," about debt securities.
- Updated discussion of presentation of receivables.
- Deleted WDNM box in Appendix 7A on consequences of bouncing a check.
- Deleted Background section in Appendix 7B (Impairment of Receivables), as dated.

Chapter 8 Valuation of Inventories: A Cost-Basis Approach

- Rewrote much of the opening story, to incorporate recent information about auto industry slowdown and government bailouts.
- Updated WDNM box on **Wal-Mart**, to include recent information about how it's cutting its supply chain cost.
- New *International Perspective*, to provide latest IFRS views on inventory methods.
- New WDNM box, on possibility and economic consequences of repealing LIFO as acceptable method under GAAP.

Chapter 9 Inventories: Additional Valuation Issues

- Updated opening story, for most recent information about retailers' restocking process, its advantages, and its potential pitfalls.
- In Lower-of-Cost-or-Market section, now use cost-of-goods-sold and loss methods, instead of direct/indirect methods.
- Updated use of real company data throughout chapter.

Chapter 10 Acquisition and Disposition of Property, Plant, and Equipment

- Updated Financial Statement Analysis Case for **Johnson & Johnson**.
- New Professional Simulation exercise.

Chapter 11 Depreciation, Impairments, and Depletion

- New opening story, "Here Come the Write-Offs," about affects (impairment losses) of the 2008 credit crisis.
- New *International Perspective* on component depreciation and depletion.

Chapter 12 Intangible Assets

- New opening story, "Are We There Yet?" about gap between government economic measures and those same measures adjusted for intangible investments.
- New WDNM box, "Impairment Risk," about how goodwill impairments spiked in 2007 and 2008, coinciding with stock market downturn.
- Revised chart on R&D expenditures, to include rationale for specific accounting treatment.

Chapter 13 Current Liabilities and Contingencies

- Updated opening story, "Now You See It, Now You Don't," to provide more of an international perspective of disclosure requirements of contingent liabilities.
- New *International Perspectives* on classification of long-term debt, the IFRS use of the term *provisions,* and how IFRS companies report noncurrent liabilities before current liabilities.

Chapter 14 Long-Term Liabilities

- New opening story, "Bonds versus Notes," about recent trend of companies borrowing more from bond investors than banks; previous opening story now a new WDNM box.
- New section, Fair Value Option, which discusses both measurement and controversy.
- Updated WDNM boxes, "All About Bonds," to replace current discussion with one on 2 different companies, **Wal-Mart** and **Alcoa**, and "How's My Rating?" to incorporate more recent downward trend of S&P ratings.
- New *International Perspectives* on IFRS required use of effective-interest method, how bond issue costs must reduce the carrying amount of the bond, and troubled-debt restructurings.

Chapter 15 Stockholders' Equity

- Updated Reacquisition of Shares section, to discuss recent buyback developments/trend.
- New WDNM boxes, "Not So Good Anymore," about decreased share repurchase activity, and "Dividends Up, Dividends Down," about the recent sharp decrease in companies paying dividends.

Chapter 16 Dilutive Securities and Earnings per Share

- Updated opening story, "Kicking the Habit," about recent trend of companies issuing restricted stock versus stock options.
- New *International Perspectives* on IFRS share-based compensation and employee stock-purchase plans.

Chapter 17 Investments

- New opening story, "What to Do?" about how recent write-down of mortgage-backed securities has led to discussion on how to value financial instruments (e.g., amortized cost, fair value).
- New *International Perspectives* on IFRS classification of debt investments, IFRS valuation of debt investments, and valuation of equity method investments.
- Updated WDNM boxes, "What Is Fair Value?" to include current debate on use of mathematical models as basis for valuations, and "Risky Business" to discuss use of credit default swaps to facilitate sales of mortgage-backed securities.
- New WDNM box, "Who's in Control Here?" about the companies **Molson Coors** and **Lenovo Group**.
- New discussion on FASB/IASB proposal to simplify comprehensive income reporting and the recent amendment to variable-interest entities consolidation rules.

Chapter 18 Revenue Recognition

- Updated Current Environment section, with more recent developments in FASB/IASB revenue recognition policies and guidelines.
- Revised and updated Revenue Recognition at Point of Sale (e.g., buyback, returns, and bill and hold) section, to include new illustrations that demonstrate revenue recognition problems and solutions, as well as discussion on principal-agent relationships and multiple-deliverable arrangements (including an expanded discussion on consignments).

Chapter 19 Accounting for Income Taxes

- New opening story, "How Much Is Enough?" about **Citigroup**'s handling of its deferred tax assets.
- New WDNM box, "Global Tax Rates," about how personal and corporate tax rates vary among countries.

Chapter 20 Accounting for Pensions and Postretirement Benefits

- Updated to reflect all recent data on pensions and postretirement benefits.

Chapter 21 Accounting for Leases

- Updated WDNM box, "Are You Liable?" for international impact on new lease-accounting rule.
- New discussion and illustration of expense front-loading of operating leases if brought on-balance-sheet.

Chapter 22 Accounting Change and Error Analysis

- Updated opening story and charts about types and numbers of recent accounting changes.
- New WDNM box, "Guard the Financial Statements!" about how restatements sometimes occur because of financial fraud.

Chapter 23 Statement of Cash Flows

- Updated opening story, "Show Me the Money!" to discuss how investors analyze companies' free cash flow.
- Revised and updated Section 2: Special Problems in Statement Presentation, to discuss adjustments to net income (depreciation and amortization, losses and gains, stock options, postretirement benefit cost, extraordinary items).

Chapter 24 Full Disclosure in Financial Reporting

- New company note disclosures from more recent annual reports, for example, **Xerox**, **Johnson & Johnson**, **Tootsie Roll Industries**, **Best Buy Co.**, **PepsiCo**, and **Home Depot**.
- New discussion/illustrations in Fraudulent Financial Reporting section.
- New WDNM box, "Disclosure Overload" about six important areas still to be converged between GAAP and IFRS.
- Deleted Appendix 24B, as international coverage now discussed throughout textbook.

Teaching and Learning Supplementary Material

For Instructors

Active-Teaching Aids

In addition to the support instructors receive from *WileyPLUS* and the Wiley Faculty Network, we offer the following useful supplements.

Book's Companion Website. On this website, *www.wiley.com/college/kieso*, instructors will find electronic versions of the Solutions Manual, Test Bank, Instructor's Manual, Computerized Test Bank, and other resources.

Instructor's Resource CD. The Instructor's Resource CD (IRCD) contains an electronic version of all instructor supplements. The IRCD gives instructors the flexibility to access and prepare instructional materials based on their individual needs.

Solutions Manual, Vols. 1 and 2. The Solutions Manual contains detailed solutions to all questions, brief exercises, exercises, and problems in the textbook as well as suggested answers to the questions and cases. The estimated time to complete exercises, problems, and cases is provided.

Solution Transparencies, Vols. 1 and 2. The solution transparencies feature detailed solutions to brief exercises, exercises, problems, and "Using Your Judgment" activities. Transparencies can be easily ordered from the book's companion website.

Instructor's Manual, Vols. 1 and 2. Included in each chapter are lecture outlines with teaching tips, chapter reviews, illustrations, and review quizzes.

Teaching Transparencies. The teaching transparencies are 4-color acetate images of the illustrations found in the Instructor's Manual. Transparencies can be easily ordered from the book's companion website.

Test Bank and Algorithmic Computerized Test Bank. The test bank and algorithmic computerized test bank allow instructors to tailor examinations according to study objectives and learning outcomes, including AACSB, AICPA, and IMA professional standards. Achievement tests, comprehensive examinations, and a final exam are included.

PowerPoint™. The new PowerPoint™ presentations contain a combination of key concepts, images, and problems from the textbook.

WebCT and Desire2Learn. WebCT or Desire2Learn offer an integrated set of course management tools that enable instructors to easily design, develop, and manage Web-based and Web-enhanced courses.

Solutions to Rockford Practice Set and Excel Workbook Templates. Available for download from the book's companion website.

For Students

Active-Learning Aids

Book's Companion Website. On this website, students will find:

- A *B Set of Additional Exercises*
- *Self-Study Tests and Additional Self-Tests*
- A complete *Glossary* of all the key terms used in the text
- A new *Review and Analysis Exercise, with Solution*
- *Financial statements* for The Procter & Gamble Company, The Coca-Cola Company, PepsiCo, and Marks and Spencer plc

Student Study Guide, Vols. 1 and 2. Each chapter of the Study Guide contains a chapter review, chapter outline, and a glossary of key terms. Demonstration problems, multiple-choice, true/false, matching, and other exercises are included.

Problem-Solving Survival Guide, Vols. 1 and 2. This study guide contains exercises and problems that help students develop their intermediate accounting problem-solving skills. Explanations assist in the approach, set-up, and completion of accounting problems. Tips alert students to common pitfalls and misconceptions.

Working Papers, Vols. 1 and 2. The working papers are printed templates that can help students correctly format their textbook accounting solutions. Working paper templates are available for all end-of-chapter brief exercises, exercises, problems, and cases.

Excel Working Papers. The *Excel Working Papers* are Excel templates that students can use to correctly format their textbook accounting solutions.

Excel Primer: Using Excel in Accounting. The online Excel primer and accompanying Excel templates allow students to complete select end-of-chapter exercises and problems identified by a spreadsheet icon in the margin of the textbook.

Rockford Corporation: An Accounting Practice Set. This practice set helps students review the accounting cycle and the preparation of financial statements.

Rockford Corporation: An Accounting Practice Set (General Ledger Software Version). The computerized Rockford practice set is a general ledger software version of the printed practice set.

Gateway to the Profession

The *Gateway to the Profession* resources include the following content.

Professional Resources

Consistent with expanding beyond technical accounting knowledge, the *Gateway to the Profession* materials emphasize certain skills necessary to become a successful accountant or financial manager. The following materials will help students develop needed professional skills.

Financial Statement Analysis Primer. An online primer on financial statement analysis is provided, along with related assignment material. This primer can also be used in conjunction with the database of annual reports of real companies.

Database of Real Companies. Links to more than 20 annual reports of well-known companies, including three international companies, are provided. Assignment material provides some examples of different types of analysis that students can perform.

Writing Handbook. A handbook on professional communications gives students a framework for writing professional materials. This handbook discusses issues such as the top-10 writing problems, strategies for rewriting, how to do revisions, and tips on clarity. This handbook has been class-tested and is effective in helping students enhance their writing skills.

Working in Teams. Recent evaluations of accounting education have identified the need to develop more skills in group problem solving. The *Gateway to the Profession* materials include a second primer dealing with the role that work-groups play in organizations. Information is included on what makes a successful group, how you can participate effectively in the group, and do's and don'ts of group formation.

Ethics in Accounting. The Professional Toolkit contains expanded materials on the role of ethics in the profession, including references to speeches and articles on ethics in accounting, codes of ethics for major professional bodies, and examples and additional case studies on ethics.

Chapter-Level Resources

Also included at the *Gateway to the Profession* are features that help students process and understand the course materials. They are:

Interactive Tutorials. To help students better understand some of the more difficult topics in intermediate accounting, we have developed a number of interactive tutorials that provide expanded discussion and explanation in a visual and narrative context. Topics addressed are the accounting cycle; inventory methods, including dollar-value LIFO; depreciation and impairment of long-lived assets; and interest capitalization.

These tutorials are for the benefit of the student and should require no use of class time on the part of instructors.

Expanded Discussions. The Expanded Discussion section provides additional topics not covered in-depth in the textbook, thereby offering the flexibility to enrich or expand the course.

Spreadsheet Tools. Present value templates are provided. These templates can be used to solve time value of money problems.

Additional Internet Links. A number of useful links related to financial analysis are provided to expand expertise in analyzing real-world reporting.

Acknowledgments

Intermediate Accounting has benefited greatly from the input of focus group participants, manuscript reviewers, those who have sent comments by letter or e-mail, ancillary authors, and proofers. We greatly appreciate the constructive suggestions and innovative ideas of reviewers and the creativity and accuracy of the ancillary authors and checkers.

Fourteenth Edition

Noel Addy
Mississippi State University

Richard Alltizer
University of Central Oklahoma

Paul Bahnson
Boise State University

James Bannister
University of Hartford

Ira Bates
Florida A&M University

Mitra Bathai
Kennesaw State College

Kimberly Brickler
Lindenwood University

Alisa Brink
Virginia Commonwealth University

Helen Brubeck
San Jose State University

Mary Ellen Carter
Boston College

Judson Caskey
University of California, Los Angeles

Bruce Caster
Valdosta State University

Jeff Casterella
Colorado State University

Nancy Christie
Virginia Tech University

Katie Cordova
University of Arizona

Araya Debassay
University of Delaware

Laura Delaune
Louisiana State University

Terry Elliott
Morehead State University

Ed Etter
Eastern Michigan University

Diana Franz
University of Toledo

Lisa Gillespie
Loyola University Chicago

Jodi Gissel
Marquette University

James Gong
University of Illinois at Urbana Chamapaign

Jeff Gramlich
University of Southern Maine

Pamela Graybeal
University of Central Florida

Abo-El-Yazeed Habib
Minnesota State University—Mankato

Penny Hanes
Mercyhurst College

Chuck Harter
Georgia Southern University

John Hassell
IUPUI

Jerry Haugland
Chadron State College

Wendy Heltzer
DePaul University

Kathy Horton
College of DuPage

Marianne James
California State University, Los Angeles

I. Richard Johnson
Utah State University

Mary Keener
University of Tampa

Nathan Kessar
Brooklyn College

Ching-Lih Jan
California State University, Hayward

Steve Lim
Texas Christian University

Tony Lopez
California State University, Fullerton

Hung Yuan Lu
California State University, Fullerton

Ming Lu
Santa Monica College

Stephanie Mason
Hunter College/CUNY

Florence McGovern
Bergen Community College

Paul McKillop
Salve Regina University

David Medved
Thomas Edison State College

Barbara Merino
University of North Texas

Louella Moore
Arkansas State University

Mary Ellen Morris
University of Massachusetts

Derek Oler
Texas Tech University

Sy Pearlman
California State University, Long Beach

Byron Pike
Minnesota State University—Mankato

Catherine Plante
University of New Hampshire

Kevin Poirier
Johnson & Wales University

Pete Poznanski
Cleveland State University

Karl Putnan
University of Texas at El Paso

Krishnamurthy K. Raman
University of North Texas

SD Ray
Arkansas State University

Terry Reilly
Albright College

Jay Rich
Illinois State University

Mark Riley
Northern Illinois University

William Riter
Cornerstone University

Robert Rutledge
Texas State University

Ken Ryack
Northern Kentucky University

Mary Ryan
Bergen Community College

August Saibeni
Consumnes River College

Monica Salomon
University of West Florida

Carol Springer Sargent
Georgia State University

Lewis Shaw
Suffolk University

George Smith
Newman University

Nancy Snow
University of Toledo

Vic Stanton
University of California, Berkeley

Sarah Stanwick
Auburn University

Gina Sturgill
Franklin University

David Sulzen
Ferrum College

Mohsen Nasser Tavakolian
San Francisco State University

Dan Teed
Troy University

Katheren Terrell
University of Central Oklahoma

Brenda Thalacker
Chippewa Valley Technical College

Leslie Turner
Palm Beach Atlantic University

Isabel Wang
Michigan State University

Jeannie Welsh
La Salle University

Wendy Wilson
Southern Methodist University

Suzanne Wright
Penn State University

Yan Xiong
California State University, Sacramento

Yifeng Zhang
State University of New York at Albany

Prior Edition Reviewers

Diana Adcox
University of North Florida

Noel Addy
Mississippi State University

Roberta Allen
Texas Tech University

James Bannister
University of Hartford

Charles Baril
James Madison University

Kathleen Buaer
Midwestern State University

Janice Bell
California State University at Northridge

Larry Bergin
Winona State University

Lynn Bible
University of Nevada, Reno

John C. Borke
University of Wisconsin—Platteville

Tiffany Bortz
University of Texas, Dallas

Lisa Bostick
University of Tampa

Greg Brookins
Santa Monica College

Phillip Buchanan
George Mason University

Tom Buchman
University of Colorado, Boulder

Suzanne M. Busch
California State University—Hayward

Eric Carlsen
Kean College of New Jersey

Tom Carment
Northeastern State University

Tommy Carnes
Western Carolina University

Jeff Custarella
Colorado State University

Robert Cluskey
Tennessee State University

Edwin Cohen
DePaul University

Gene Comiskey
Georgia Tech University

W. Terry Dancer
Arkansas State University

Laura Delaune
Louisiana State University

Lynda Dennis
University of Central Florida

Lee Dexter
Moorhead State University

Judith Doing
University of Arizona

Joanne Duke
San Francisco State University

Richard Dumont
Teikyo Post University

William Dwyer
DeSales University

Claire Eckstein
CUNY—Baruch

Dean S. Eiteman
Indiana University—Pennsylvania

Bob Eskew
Purdue University

Larry R. Falcetto
Emporia State University

Dave Farber
University of Missouri

Richard Fern
Eastern Kentucky University

Richard Fleischman
John Carroll University

Stephen L. Fogg
Temple University

William Foster
New Mexico State University

Clyde Galbraith
West Chester University

Marshall Geiger
University of Richmond

Susan Gill
Washington State University

Harold Goedde
State University of New York at Oneonta

Ellen Goldberg
Northern Virginia Community College

Marty Gosman
Quinnipiac College

Lynford E. Graham
Rutgers University

Donald J. Griffin
Cayuga Community College

Konrad Gunderson
Missouri Western University

Marcia I. Halvorsen
University of Cincinnati

Garry Heesacker
Central Washington University

Kenneth Henry
Florida International University

Julia Higgs
Florida Atlantic University

Wayne M. Higley
Buena Vista University

Judy Hora
University of San Diego

Geoffrey Horlick
St. Francis College

Kathy Hsu
University of Louisiana, Lafayette

Allen Hunt
Southern Illinois University

Marilyn Hunt
University of Central Florida

M. Zarar Iqbal
California Polytechnic State University—San Luis Obispo

Daniel Ivancevich
University of North Carolina at Wilmington

Susan Ivancevich
University of North Carolina at Wilmington

Cynthia Jeffrey
Iowa State University

Scott Jeris
San Francisco State University

James Johnston
Louisiana Tech University

Jeff Jones
University of Texas—San Antonio

Mary Jo Jones
Eastern University

Art Joy
University of South Florida

Celina Jozci
University of South Florida

Ben Ke
Penn State University

Douglas W. Kieso
Aurora University

Paul D. Kimmel
University of Wisconsin—Milwaukee

Martha King
Emporia State University

Florence Kirk
State University of New York at Oswego

Mark Kohlbeck
Florida Atlantic University

Lisa Koonce
University of Texas at Austin

Barbara Kren
University of Wisconsin—Milwaukee

Steve Lafave
Augsburg College

Ellen Landgraf
Loyola University, Chicago

Tom Largay
Thomas College

David B. Law
Youngstown State University

Henry LeClerc
Suffolk Community College—Selden Campus

Patsy Lee
University of Texas—Arlington

Lydia Leporte
Tidewater Community College

Timothy Lindquist
University of Northern Iowa

Ellen Lippman
University of Portland

Barbara Lippincott
University of Tampa

Gary Luoma
University of Southern California

Matt Magilke
University of Utah

Daphne Main
University of New Orleans

Mostafa Maksy
Northeastern Illinois University

Danny Matthews
Midwestern State University

Noel McKeon
Florida Community College

Robert J. Matthews
New Jersey City University

Alan Mayer-Sommer
Georgetown University

Robert Milbrath
University of Houston

James Miller
Gannon University

John Mills
University of Nevada—Reno

Joan Monnin-Callahan
University of Cincinnati

Michael Motes
University of Maryland
University College

Mohamed E. Moustafa
California State University—Long Beach

R.D. Nair
University of Wisconsin—Madison

Ed Nathan
University of Houston

Siva Nathan
Georgia State University

Kermit Natho
Georgia State University

Joseph Nicassio
Westmoreland County Community College

Hugo Nurnberg
CUNY—Baruch

Ann O'Brien
University of Wisconsin—Madison

Anne Oppegard
Augustana College, SD

Patricia Parker
Columbus State Community College

Richard Parker
Olivet College

Obeau S. Persons
Rider University

Ray Pfeiffer
Texas Christian University

Alee Phillips
University of Kansas

Marlene Plumlee
University of Utah

Wing Poon
Montclair State University

Jay Price
Utah State University

Robert Rambo
University of New Orleans

Debbie Rankin
Lincoln University

MaryAnn Reynolds
Western Washington University

Vernon Richardson
University of Arkansas

Richard Riley
West Virginia University

Jeffrey D. Ritter
St. Norbert College

Paul (Jep) Robertson
Henderson State University

Steven Rock
University of Colorado

Larry Roman
Cuyahoga Community College

John Rossi
Moravian College

Bob Rouse
College of Charleston

Tim Ryan
Southern Illinois University

Victoria Rymer
University of Maryland

James Sander
Butler University

John Sander
University of Southern Maine

George Sanders
Western Washington University

Howard Shapiro
Eastern Washington University

Douglas Sharp
Wichita State University

Tim Shea
Foley and Lardner

Jerry Siebel
University of South Florida

Phil Siegel
Florida Atlantic University

John R. Simon
Northern Illinois University

Keith Smith
George Washington University

Pam Smith
Northern Illinois University

Douglas Smith
Samford University

Billy S. Soo
Boston College

Karen Squires
University of Tampa

Carlton D. Stolle
Texas A&M University

William Stout
University of Louisville

Pamela Stuerke
Case Western Reserve University

Ron Stunda
Birmingham Southern College

Eric Sussman
University of California, Los Angeles

Diane L. Tanner
University of North Florida

Gary Taylor
University of Alabama

Gary Testa
Brooklyn College

Lynn Thomas
Kansas State University

Paula B. Thomas
Middle Tennessee State University

Tom Tierney
University of Wisconsin—Madison

Elizabeth Venuti
Hofstra University

James D. Waddington, Jr.
Hawaii Pacific University

Dick Wasson
Southwestern College

Frank F. Weinberg
Golden Gate University

David Weiner
University of San Francisco

Jeannie Welsh
LaSalle University

Shari H. Wescott
Houston Baptist University

Michael Willenborg
University of Connecticut

William H. Wilson
Oregon Health University

Kenneth Wooling
Hampton University

Joni Young
University of New Mexico

Paul Zarowin
New York University

Steve Zeff
Rice University

Special thanks to Kurt Pany, Arizona State University, for his input on auditor disclosure issues, and to Stephen A. Zeff, Rice University, for his comments on international accounting.

In addition, we thank the following colleagues who contributed to several of the unique features of this edition.

Gateway to the Profession and Codification Cases

Jack Cathey
University of North Carolina—Charlotte

Michelle Ephraim
Worcester Polytechnic Institute

Erik Frederickson
Madison, Wisconsin

Jason Hart
Deloitte LLP, Milwaukee

Frank Heflin
Florida State University

Mike Katte
SC Johnson, Racine, WI

Kelly Krieg
E & Y, Milwaukee

Jeremy Kunicki
Walgreens

Courtney Meier
Deloitte LLP, Milwaukee

Andrew Prewitt
KPMG, Chicago

Jeff Seymour
KPMG, Minneapolis

Matt Sullivan
Deloitte LLP, Milwaukee

Matt Tutaj
Deloitte LLP, Chicago

Jen Vaughn
PricewaterhouseCoopers, Chicago

Erin Viel
PricewaterhouseCoopers, Milwaukee

"Working in Teams" Material

Edward Wertheim
Northeastern University

Ancillary Authors, Contributors, Proofers, and Accuracy Checkers

LuAnn Bean
Florida Institute of Technology

Mary Ann Benson
John C. Borke
University of Wisconsin—Platteville

Jack Cathey
University of North Carolina—Charlotte

Jim Emig
Villanova University

Larry Falcetto
Emporia State University

Coby Harmon
University of California, Santa Barbara

Marilyn F. Hunt

Douglas W. Kieso
Aurora University

Mark Kohlbeck
Florida Atlantic University

Maureen Mascha
Marquette University

Barbara Muller
Arizona State University

Jill Misuraca
Middlesex Community College

Yvonne Phang
Borough of Manhattan Community College

John Plouffe
California State Polytechnic University—Pomona

Rex A. Schildhouse
University of Phoenix—San Diego

Lynn Stallworth
Appalachian State University

Sheila Viel
University of Wisconsin—Milwaukee

Dick D. Wasson
Southwestern College, San Diego University

WileyPLUS Developers and Reviewers

Carole Brandt-Fink
Laura McNally
Melanie Yon

Advisory Board

We gratefully acknowledge the following members of the Intermediate Accounting Advisory Board for their advice and assistance with this edition.

Steve Balsam
Temple University

Jack Cathey
University of North Carolina—Charlotte

Uday Chandra
State University of New York at Albany

Ruben Davila
University of Southern California

Doug deVidal
University of Texas—Austin

Dan Givoly
Pennsylvinia State University

Leslie Hodder
University of Indiana—Bloomington

Celina Jozsi
University of South Florida

Jocelyn Kauffunger
University of Pittsburgh

Adam Koch
University of Virginia

Roger Martin
University of Virginia

Linda Nichols
Texas Tech University

Sy Pearlman
California State University—Long Beach

Mark Riley
Northern Illinois University

Pam Smith
Northern Illinois University

Practicing Accountants and Business Executives

From the fields of corporate and public accounting, we owe thanks to the following practitioners for their technical advice and for consenting to interviews.

Mike Crooch
FASB (retired)

Tracy Golden
Deloitte LLP

John Gribble
PricewaterhouseCoopers (retired)

Darien Griffin
S.C. Johnson & Son

Michael Lehman
Sun Microsystems, Inc.

Tom Linsmeier
FASB

Michele Lippert
Evoke.com

Sue McGrath
Vision Capital Management

David Miniken
Sweeney Conrad

Robert Sack
University of Virginia

Clare Schulte
Deloitte LLP

Willie Sutton
Mutual Community Savings Bank, Durham, NC

Lynn Turner
Glass, Lewis, LLP

Rachel Woods
PricewaterhouseCoopers

Arthur Wyatt
Arthur Anderson & Co., and the University of Illinois—Urbana

Finally, we appreciate the exemplary support and professional commitment given us by the development, marketing, production, and editorial staffs of John Wiley & Sons, including the following: George Hoffman, Susan Elbe, Chris DeJohn, Michael McDonald, Amy Scholz, Karolina Zarychta Honsa, Trish McFadden, Brian Kamins, Jackie Kepping, Allie Morris, Greg Chaput, Harry Nolan, and Jim O'Shea. Thanks, too, to Suzanne Ingrao for her production work, to Denise Showers and the staff at Aptara®, Inc. for their work on the textbook, Cyndy Taylor, and to Danielle Urban and the staff at Elm Street Publishing Services for their work on the solutions manual.

We also appreciate the cooperation of the American Institute of Certified Public Accountants and the Financial Accounting Standards Board in permitting us to quote from their pronouncements. We thank The Procter & Gamble Company for permitting us to use its 2009 annual report for our specimen financial statements. We also acknowledge permission from the American Institute of Certified Public Accountants, the Institute of Management Accountants, and the Institute of Internal Auditors to adapt and use material from the Uniform CPA Examinations, the CMA Examinations, and the CIA Examination, respectively.

Suggestions and comments from users of this book will be appreciated. Please feel free to e-mail any one of us at *AccountingAuthors@yahoo.com.*

Donald E. Kieso
Somonauk, Illinois

Jerry J. Weygandt
Madison, Wisconsin

Terry D. Warfield
Madison, Wisconsin

Brief Contents

Contents

Chapter 4

Income Statement and Related Information 158

Watch Out for Pro Forma

Chapter 5

Balance Sheet and Statement of Cash Flows 212

Hey, It Doesn't Balance!

Chapter 6

Accounting and the Time Value of Money 308

Chapter 7

Cash and Receivables 364

Chapter 8

Valuation of Inventories: A Cost-Basis Approach 434

Chapter 9

Inventories: Additional Valuation Issues 492

Chapter 10

Acquisition and Disposition of Property, Plant, and Equipment 554

Chapter 11

Depreciation, Impairments, and Depletion 604

Chapter 12

Intangible Assets 664

Chapter 13

Current Liabilities and Contingencies 720

Chapter 14

Long-Term Liabilities 782

Chapter 15

Stockholders' Equity 842

Chapter 16

Dilutive Securities and Earnings per Share 904

Chapter 17

Investments 974

Chapter 20

Accounting for Pensions and Postretirement Benefits 1208

Where Have All the Pensions Gone?

Chapter 21

Accounting for Leases 1288

More Companies Ask, "Why Buy?"

Chapter 24

Full Disclosure in Financial Reporting 1512

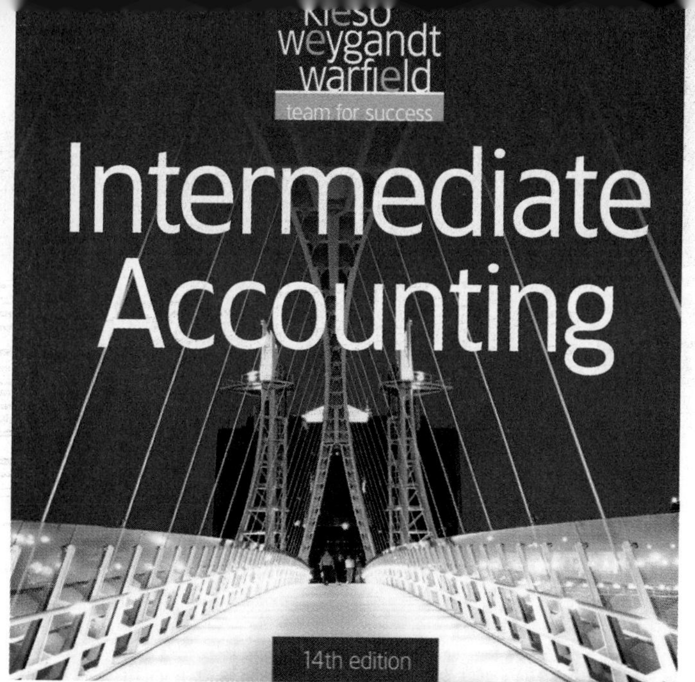

Volume 1: Chapters 1–14

CHAPTER 1

Financial Accounting and Accounting Standards

LEARNING OBJECTIVES

After studying this chapter, you should be able to:

1. Identify the major financial statements and other means of financial reporting.
2. Explain how accounting assists in the efficient use of scarce resources.
3. Identify the objective of financial reporting.
4. Explain the need for accounting standards.
5. Identify the major policy-setting bodies and their role in the standard-setting process.
6. Explain the meaning of generally accepted accounting principles (GAAP) and the role of the Codification for GAAP.
7. Describe the impact of user groups on the rule-making process.
8. Describe some of the challenges facing financial reporting.
9. Understand issues related to ethics and financial accounting.

Thinking Outside the Box

One might take pride in the fact that the U.S. system of financial reporting has long been the most robust and transparent in the world. But most would also comment that we can do better, particularly in light of the many accounting scandals that have occurred at companies like **AIG**, **WorldCom**, and **Lehman Brothers**. So it is time for reevaluation—a time to step back and evaluate whether changes are necessary in the U.S. financial reporting system. In doing so, perhaps it is time to "think outside the box." Here are some thoughts:

1. Today, equity securities are broadly held, with approximately half of American households investing in stocks. This presents a challenge—investors have expressed concerns that **one-size-fits-all financial reports do not meet the needs of the spectrum of investors** who rely on those reports. Many individual investors are more interested in summarized, plain-English reports that are easily understandable; they may not understand all of the underlying detail included in current financial reports. On the other hand, market analysts and other investment professionals may desire information at a far more detailed level than is currently provided. Technology certainly must play a role in delivering the customized level of information that the different types of investors desire.
2. Aside from investors' concerns, companies have expressed concerns with the complexity of our current financial reporting system. Many companies assert that **when preparing financial reports, it is difficult to ensure compliance with the voluminous and complex requirements contained in U.S. GAAP and SEC reporting rules**. In fact, in a recent year almost 10 percent of U.S. public companies restated prior financial reports. This alarmingly high number is a problem because it can be difficult to distinguish between companies with serious underlying problems and those with unintentional misapplications of complex accounting literature. Restatements are costly to companies and can undermine the confidence of investors in the financial reporting system.
3. We also need to look beyond the accounting applied in the basic financial statements and footnotes and consider the broader array of information that investors need to make informed decisions. The U.S. capital markets can run fairly, orderly, and efficiently only through the steady flow of comprehensive and meaningful information. As some have noted, the percentage of a company's market value that can be attributed to accounting book value has declined significantly from the days of a bricks-and-mortar economy. **Thus, we may want to consider a more comprehensive business reporting model, including both financial and nonfinancial key performance indicators.**

IFRS IN THIS CHAPTER

See the **International Perspectives** on pages 8, 9, 18, and 20.

Read the **IFRS Insights** on pages 32–40 for a discussion of:

—International standard-setting organizations

—Hierarchy of IFRS

—International accounting convergence

4. Finally, we must also consider **how to deliver all of this information in a timelier manner**. In the 21st century, in a world where messages can be sent across the world in a blink of an eye, it is ironic that the analysis of financial information is still subject to many manual processes, resulting in delays, increased costs, and errors.

Thus, thinking outside the box to improve financial reporting involves more than simply trimming or reworking the existing accounting literature. In some cases, major change is already underway. For example:

- The FASB and IASB are working on a convergence project, including a reconsideration of the conceptual framework. It is hoped that this project will contribute to less-complex, more-understandable standards.
- Standard-setters are exploring an enhanced business reporting framework, which will result in expanded reporting of key performance indicators.
- The SEC now requires the delivery of financial reports using eXtensible Business Reporting Language (XBRL). Reporting through XBRL allows timelier reporting via the Internet and allows statement users to transform accounting reports to meet their specific needs.

Each of these projects supports "outside the box" thinking on how to improve the quality of financial reporting. They will take the accounting profession beyond the complexity debate to encompass both the usefulness of financial reporting and the most effective delivery of information to investors.

Source: Adapted from Conrad W. Hewitt, "Opening Remarks Before the Initial Meeting of the SEC Advisory Committee on Improvements to Financial Reporting," U.S. Securities and Exchange Commission, Washington, D.C. (August 2, 2007).

PREVIEW OF CHAPTER 1

As our opening story indicates, the U.S. system of financial reporting has long been the most robust and transparent in the world. To ensure that it continues to provide the most relevant and reliable financial information to users, a number of financial reporting issues must be resolved. These issues include such matters as adopting global standards, increasing fair value reporting, using principles-based versus rule-based standards, and meeting multiple user needs. This chapter explains the environment of financial reporting and the many factors affecting it, as follows.

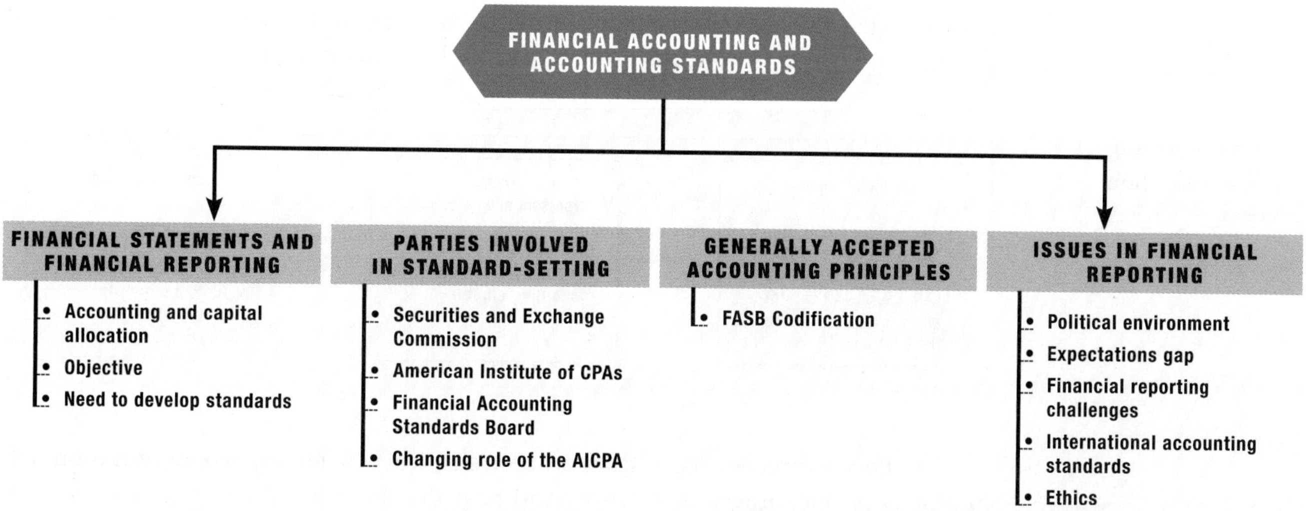

FINANCIAL ACCOUNTING AND ACCOUNTING STANDARDS

FINANCIAL STATEMENTS AND FINANCIAL REPORTING
- Accounting and capital allocation
- Objective
- Need to develop standards

PARTIES INVOLVED IN STANDARD-SETTING
- Securities and Exchange Commission
- American Institute of CPAs
- Financial Accounting Standards Board
- Changing role of the AICPA

GENERALLY ACCEPTED ACCOUNTING PRINCIPLES
- FASB Codification

ISSUES IN FINANCIAL REPORTING
- Political environment
- Expectations gap
- Financial reporting challenges
- International accounting standards
- Ethics

FINANCIAL STATEMENTS AND FINANCIAL REPORTING

LEARNING OBJECTIVE 1
Identify the major financial statements and other means of financial reporting.

The essential characteristics of accounting are (1) the identification, measurement, and communication of financial information about (2) economic entities to (3) interested parties. **Financial accounting** is the process that culminates in the preparation of financial reports on the enterprise for use by both internal and external parties. Users of these financial reports include investors, creditors, managers, unions, and government agencies. In contrast, **managerial accounting** is the process of identifying, measuring, analyzing, and communicating financial information needed by management to plan, control, and evaluate a company's operations.

Financial statements are the principal means through which a company communicates its financial information to those outside it. These statements provide a company's history quantified in money terms. The **financial statements** most frequently provided are (1) the balance sheet, (2) the income statement, (3) the statement of cash flows, and (4) the statement of owners' or stockholders' equity. Note disclosures are an integral part of each financial statement.

Some financial information is better provided, or can be provided only, by means of **financial reporting** other than formal financial statements. Examples include the president's letter or supplementary schedules in the corporate annual report, prospectuses, reports filed with government agencies, news releases, management's forecasts, and social or environmental impact statements. Companies may need to provide such information because of authoritative pronouncement, regulatory rule, or custom. Or they may supply it because management wishes to disclose it voluntarily.

In this textbook, we focus on the development of two types of financial information: (1) the basic financial statements and (2) related disclosures.

Accounting and Capital Allocation

LEARNING OBJECTIVE 2
Explain how accounting assists in the efficient use of scarce resources.

Resources are limited. As a result, people try to conserve them and ensure that they are used effectively. Efficient use of resources often determines whether a business thrives. This fact places a substantial burden on the accounting profession.

Accountants must measure performance accurately and fairly on a timely basis, so that the right managers and companies are able to attract investment capital. For example, relevant and reliable financial information allows investors and creditors to compare the income and assets employed by such companies as **IBM**, **McDonald's**, **Microsoft**, and **Ford**. Because these users can assess the relative return and risks associated with investment opportunities, they channel resources more effectively. Illustration 1-1 shows how this process of capital allocation works.

ILLUSTRATION 1-1
Capital Allocation Process

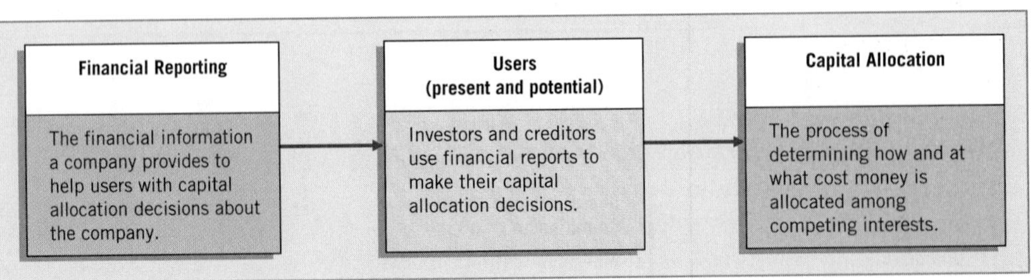

An effective process of capital allocation is critical to a healthy economy. It promotes productivity, encourages innovation, and provides an efficient and liquid market for buying and selling securities and obtaining and granting credit. Unreliable and irrelevant information leads to poor capital allocation, which adversely affects the securities markets.

IT'S THE ACCOUNTING

What do the numbers mean?

"It's the accounting." That's what many investors seem to be saying these days. Even the slightest hint of any accounting irregularity at a company leads to a subsequent pounding of the company's stock price. For example, the *Wall Street Journal* has run the following headlines related to accounting and its effects on the economy.

- Stocks take a beating as accounting woes spread beyond **Enron**.
- Quarterly reports from **IBM** and **Goldman Sachs** sent stocks tumbling.
- **Citi** explains how it hid risk from the public.
- **Bank of America** admits hiding debt.
- Accounting woes at **AIG** take their toll on insurers' shares.

It now has become clear that investors must trust the accounting numbers, or they will abandon the market and put their resources elsewhere. With investor uncertainty, the cost of capital increases for companies who need additional resources. In short, relevant and reliable financial information is necessary for markets to be efficient.

Objective of Financial Reporting

3 LEARNING OBJECTIVE
Identify the objective of financial reporting.

What is the **objective (or purpose) of financial reporting**? The objective of general-purpose financial reporting is to **provide financial information about the reporting entity that is useful to present and potential equity investors, lenders, and other creditors in** decisions about providing resources to the entity. Those decisions involve buying, selling, or holding equity and debt instruments, and providing or settling loans and other forms of credit. Information that is decision-useful to capital providers (investors) may also be helpful to other users of financial reporting who are not investors. Let's examine each of the elements of this objective.[1]

General-Purpose Financial Statements

General-purpose financial statements provide financial reporting information to a wide variety of users. For example, when **Hershey**'s issues its financial statements, these statements help shareholders, creditors, suppliers, employees, and regulators to better understand its financial position and related performance. Hershey's users need this type of information to make effective decisions. To be cost-effective in providing this information, general-purpose financial statements are most appropriate. In other words, general-purpose financial statements provide at the **least cost the most useful information possible**.

Equity Investors and Creditors

The objective of financial reporting **identifies investors and creditors as the primary users for general-purpose financial statements**. Identifying investors and creditors as the primary users provides an important focus of general-purpose financial reporting.

[1]*Statement of Financial Accounting Concepts No. 8*, Chapter 1, "The Objective of General Purpose Financial Reporting," and Chapter 3, "Qualitative Characteristics of Useful Financial Information" (Norwalk, Conn.: FASB, September 2010), par. OB2.

For example, when Hershey issues its financial statements, its primary focus is on investors and creditors because they have the most critical and immediate need for information in financial reports. Investors and creditors need this financial information to assess Hershey's ability to generate net cash inflow and to understand management's ability to protect and enhance the assets of the company, which will be used to generate future net cash inflows. As a result, the primary user groups are not management, regulators, or some other non-investor group.

Entity Perspective

As part of the objective of general-purpose financial reporting, an **entity perspective** is adopted. Companies are viewed as separate and distinct from their owners (present shareholders) using this perspective. The assets of Hershey are viewed as assets of the company and not of a specific creditor or shareholder. Rather, these investors have claims on Hershey's assets in the form of liability or equity claims. The entity perspective is consistent with the present business environment where most companies engaged in financial reporting have substance distinct from their investors (both shareholders and creditors). Thus, a perspective that financial reporting should be focused only on the needs of shareholders—often referred to as the **proprietary perspective**—is not considered appropriate.

DON'T FORGET STEWARDSHIP

What do the numbers mean?

In addition to providing decision-useful information about future cash flows, management also is accountable to investors for the custody and safekeeping of the company's economic resources and for their efficient and profitable use. For example, the management of **Hershey** has the responsibility for protecting its economic resources from unfavorable effects of economic factors, such as price changes, and technological and social changes. Because Hershey's performance in discharging its responsibilities (referred to as its **stewardship** responsibilities) usually affects its ability to generate net cash inflows, financial reporting may also provide decision-useful information to assess management performance in this role.[2]

Decision-Usefulness

Investors are interested in financial reporting because it provides information that is useful for making decisions (referred to as the **decision-usefulness** approach). As indicated earlier, when making these decisions, investors are interested in assessing (1) the company's ability to generate net cash inflows and (2) management's ability to protect and enhance the capital providers' investments. Financial reporting should therefore help investors assess the amounts, timing, and uncertainty of prospective cash inflows from dividends or interest, and the proceeds from the sale, redemption, or maturity of securities or loans. In order for investors to make these assessments, the economic resources of an enterprise, the claims to those resources, and the changes in them must be understood. Financial statements and related explanations should be a primary source for determining this information.

The emphasis on "assessing cash flow prospects" does not mean that the cash basis is preferred over the accrual basis of accounting. Information based on accrual accounting better indicates a company's present and continuing ability to generate favorable

[2]*Statement of Financial Accounting Concepts No. 8,* Chapter 1, "The Objective of General Purpose Financial Reporting," and Chapter 3, "Qualitative Characteristics of Useful Financial Information" (Norwalk, Conn.: FASB, September 2010), paras. OB4–OB10.

cash flows than does information limited to the financial effects of cash receipts and payments.

Recall from your first accounting course the objective of accrual-basis accounting: It ensures that a company records events that change its financial statements in the periods in which the events occur, rather than only in the periods in which it receives or pays cash. Using the accrual basis to determine net income means that a company recognizes revenues when it provides the goods or services rather than when it receives cash. Similarly, it recognizes expenses when it incurs them rather than when it pays them. Under accrual accounting, a company generally recognizes revenues when it makes sales. The company can then relate the revenues to the economic environment of the period in which they occurred. Over the long run, trends in revenues and expenses are generally more meaningful than trends in cash receipts and disbursements.[3]

The Need to Develop Standards

4 LEARNING OBJECTIVE
Explain the need for accounting standards.

The main controversy in setting accounting standards is, "Whose rules should we play by, and what should they be?" The answer is not immediately clear. Users of financial accounting statements have both coinciding and conflicting needs for information of various types. To meet these needs, and to satisfy the stewardship reporting responsibility of management, companies prepare a single set of **general-purpose financial statements**. Users expect these statements to present fairly, clearly, and completely the company's financial operations.

The accounting profession has attempted to develop a set of standards that are generally accepted and universally practiced. Otherwise, each enterprise would have to develop its own standards. Further, readers of financial statements would have to familiarize themselves with every company's peculiar accounting and reporting practices. It would be almost impossible to prepare statements that could be compared.

This common set of standards and procedures is called generally accepted accounting principles (GAAP). The term "generally accepted" means either that an authoritative accounting rule-making body has established a principle of reporting in a given area or that over time a given practice has been accepted as appropriate because of its universal application.[4] Although principles and practices continue to provoke both debate and criticism, most members of the financial community recognize them as the standards that over time have proven to be most useful. We present a more extensive discussion of what constitutes GAAP later in this chapter.

PARTIES INVOLVED IN STANDARD-SETTING

5 LEARNING OBJECTIVE
Identify the major policy-setting bodies and their role in the standard-setting process.

Three organizations are instrumental in the development of financial accounting standards (GAAP) in the United States:

1. Securities and Exchange Commission (SEC)
2. American Institute of Certified Public Accountants (AICPA)
3. Financial Accounting Standards Board (FASB)

[3]As used here, cash flow means "cash generated and used in operations." The term *cash flows* also frequently means cash obtained by borrowing and used to repay borrowing, cash used for investments in resources and obtained from the disposal of investments, and cash contributed by or distributed to owners.

[4]The terms *principles* and *standards* are used interchangeably in practice and throughout this textbook.

Securities and Exchange Commission (SEC)

INTERNATIONAL PERSPECTIVE

The International Organization of Securities Commissions (IOSCO), established in 1987, consists of more than 100 securities regulatory agencies or securities exchanges from all over the world. Collectively, its members represent a substantial proportion of the world's capital markets. The SEC is a member of IOSCO.

External financial reporting and auditing developed in tandem with the growth of the industrial economy and its capital markets. However, when the stock market crashed in 1929 and the nation's economy plunged into the Great Depression, there were calls for increased government regulation of business generally, and especially financial institutions and the stock market.

As a result of these events, the federal government established the **Securities and Exchange Commission (SEC)** to help develop and standardize financial information presented to stockholders. The SEC is a federal agency. It administers the Securities Exchange Act of 1934 and several other acts. Most companies that issue securities to the public or are listed on a stock exchange are required to file audited financial statements with the SEC. In addition, the SEC has broad powers to prescribe, in whatever detail it desires, the accounting practices and standards to be employed by companies that fall within its jurisdiction. The SEC currently exercises oversight over 12,000 companies that are listed on the major exchanges (e.g., the New York Stock Exchange and the Nasdaq).

Public/Private Partnership

At the time the SEC was created, no group—public or private—issued accounting standards. The SEC encouraged the creation of a private standard-setting body because it believed that the private sector had the appropriate resources and talent to achieve this daunting task. As a result, accounting standards have developed in the private sector either through the American Institute of Certified Public Accountants (AICPA) or the Financial Accounting Standards Board (FASB).

The SEC has affirmed its support for the FASB by indicating that financial statements conforming to standards set by the FASB are presumed to have substantial authoritative support. In short, the **SEC requires registrants to adhere to GAAP**. In addition, the SEC indicated in its reports to Congress that "it continues to believe that the initiative for establishing and improving accounting standards should remain in the private sector, subject to Commission oversight."

SEC Oversight

The SEC's partnership with the private sector works well. The SEC acts with remarkable restraint in the area of developing accounting standards. Generally, **the SEC relies on the FASB to develop accounting standards**.

The SEC's involvement in the development of accounting standards varies. In some cases, the SEC rejects a standard proposed by the private sector. In other cases, the SEC prods the private sector into taking quicker action on certain reporting problems, such as accounting for investments in debt and equity securities and the reporting of derivative instruments. In still other situations, the SEC communicates problems to the FASB, responds to FASB exposure drafts, and provides the FASB with counsel and advice upon request.

The SEC's mandate is to establish accounting principles. The private sector, therefore, must listen carefully to the views of the SEC. In some sense, the private sector is the formulator and the implementor of the standards.[5] However, when the private sector

[5]One writer described the relationship of the FASB and SEC and the development of financial reporting standards using the analogy of a pearl. The pearl (a financial reporting standard) "is formed by the reaction of certain oysters (FASB) to an irritant (the SEC)—usually a grain of sand—that becomes embedded inside the shell. The oyster coats this grain with layers of nacre, and ultimately a pearl is formed. The pearl is a joint result of the irritant (SEC) and oyster (FASB); without both, it cannot be created." John C. Burton, "Government Regulation of Accounting and Information," *Journal of Accountancy* (June 1982).

fails to address accounting problems as quickly as the SEC would like, the partnership between the SEC and the private sector can be strained. This occurred in the deliberations on the accounting for business combinations and intangible assets. It is also highlighted by concerns over the accounting for off-balance-sheet special-purpose entities, highlighted in the failure of **Enron** and, more recently, the subprime crises that led to the failure of **IndyMac Bank**.

INTERNATIONAL PERSPECTIVE

The U.S. legal system is based on English common law, whereby the government generally allows professionals to make the rules. The private sector, therefore, develops these rules (standards). Conversely, some countries have followed codified law, which leads to government-run accounting systems.

Enforcement

As we indicated earlier, companies listed on a stock exchange must submit their financial statements to the SEC. If the SEC believes that an accounting or disclosure irregularity exists regarding the form or content of the financial statements, it sends a deficiency letter to the company. Companies usually resolve these deficiency letters quickly. If disagreement continues, the SEC may issue a "stop order," which prevents the registrant from issuing or trading securities on the exchanges. The Department of Justice may also file criminal charges for violations of certain laws. The SEC process, private sector initiatives, and civil and criminal litigation help to ensure the integrity of financial reporting for public companies.

American Institute of Certified Public Accountants (AICPA)

The **American Institute of Certified Public Accountants (AICPA)**, which is the national professional organization of practicing Certified Public Accountants (CPAs), has been an important contributor to the development of GAAP. Various committees and boards established since the founding of the AICPA have contributed to this effort.

Committee on Accounting Procedure

At the urging of the SEC, the AICPA appointed the Committee on Accounting Procedure in 1939. The **Committee on Accounting Procedure (CAP)**, composed of practicing CPAs, issued 51 **Accounting Research Bulletins** during the years 1939 to 1959. These bulletins dealt with a variety of accounting problems. But this problem-by-problem approach failed to provide the needed structured body of accounting principles. In response, in 1959 the AICPA created the Accounting Principles Board.

Accounting Principles Board

The major purposes of the **Accounting Principles Board (APB)** were to (1) advance the written expression of accounting principles, (2) determine appropriate practices, and (3) narrow the areas of difference and inconsistency in practice. To achieve these objectives, the APB's mission was twofold: to develop an overall conceptual framework to assist in the resolution of problems as they become evident and to substantively research individual issues before the AICPA issued pronouncements. The Board's 18 to 21 members, selected primarily from public accounting, also included representatives from industry and academia. The Board's official pronouncements, called **APB Opinions**, were intended to be based mainly on research studies and be supported by reason and analysis. Between its inception in 1959 and its dissolution in 1973, the APB issued 31 opinions.

Unfortunately, the APB came under fire early, charged with lack of productivity and failing to act promptly to correct alleged accounting abuses. Later, the APB tackled numerous thorny accounting issues, only to meet a buzz saw of opposition from industry and CPA firms. It also ran into occasional governmental interference. In 1971, the accounting profession's leaders, anxious to avoid governmental rule-making, appointed a Study Group on Establishment of Accounting Principles. Commonly known as the **Wheat Committee** for its chair Francis Wheat, this group examined the organization and operation of the APB and determined the necessary changes to attain better results. The Study Group submitted its recommendations to the AICPA Council in the spring of 1972. The AICPA Council adopted the recommendations in total, and implemented them by early 1973.

Financial Accounting Standards Board (FASB)

The Wheat Committee's recommendations resulted in the demise of the APB and the creation of a new standard-setting structure composed of three organizations—the Financial Accounting Foundation (FAF), the Financial Accounting Standards Board (FASB), and the Financial Accounting Standards Advisory Council (FASAC). The **Financial Accounting Foundation** selects the members of the FASB and the Advisory Council, funds their activities, and generally oversees the FASB's activities.

The major operating organization in this three-part structure is the **Financial Accounting Standards Board (FASB)**. Its mission is to establish and improve standards of financial accounting and reporting for the guidance and education of the public, which includes issuers, auditors, and users of financial information. The expectations of success and support for the new FASB relied on several significant differences between it and its predecessor, the APB:

1. ***Smaller membership.*** The FASB consists of seven members, replacing the relatively large 18-member APB.
2. ***Full-time, remunerated membership.*** FASB members are well-paid, full-time members appointed for renewable 5-year terms. The APB members volunteered their part-time work.
3. ***Greater autonomy.*** The APB was a senior committee of the AICPA. The FASB is not part of any single professional organization. It is appointed by and answerable only to the Financial Accounting Foundation.
4. ***Increased independence.*** APB members retained their private positions with firms, companies, or institutions. FASB members must sever all such ties.
5. ***Broader representation.*** All APB members were required to be CPAs and members of the AICPA. Currently, it is not necessary to be a CPA to be a member of the FASB.

In addition to research help from its own staff, the FASB relies on the expertise of various task force groups formed for various projects and on the **Financial Accounting Standards Advisory Council (FASAC)**. The FASAC consults with the FASB on major policy and technical issues and also helps select task force members. Illustration 1-2 shows the current organizational structure for the development of financial reporting standards.

Due Process

In establishing financial accounting standards, the FASB relies on two basic premises: (1) The FASB should be responsive to the needs and viewpoints of the entire economic community, not just the public accounting profession. (2) It should operate in full view of the public through a "due process" system that gives interested persons ample opportunity to make their views known. To ensure the achievement of these goals, the FASB follows specific steps to develop a typical FASB Statement of Financial Accounting Standards, as Illustration 1-3 shows.

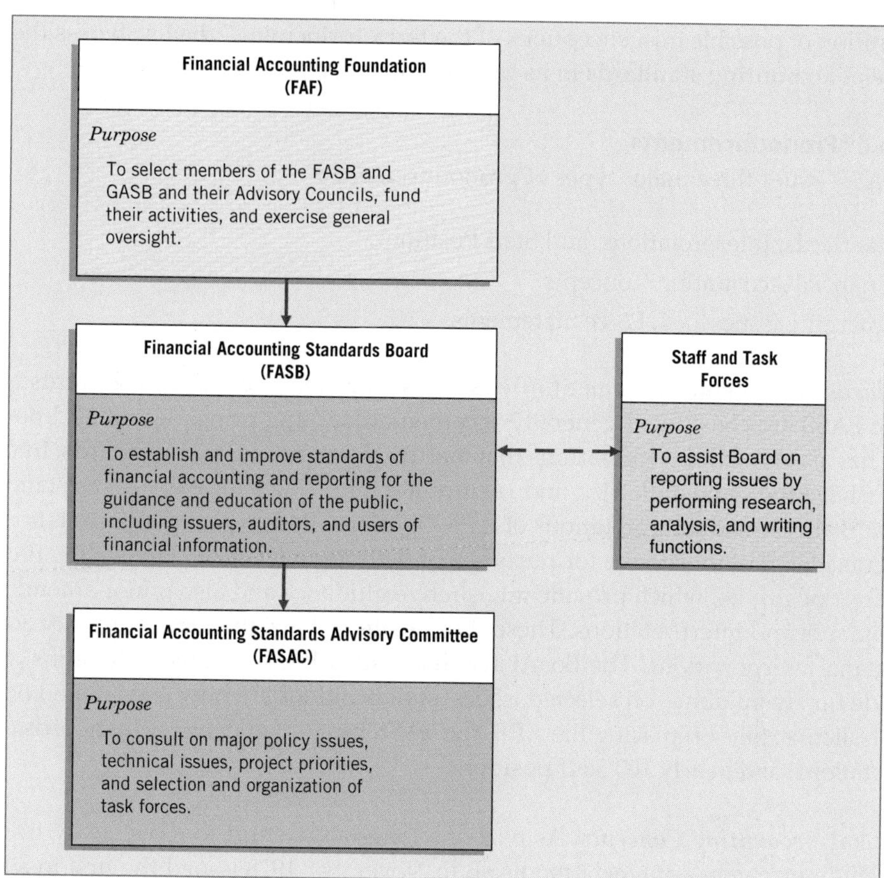

ILLUSTRATION 1-2
Organizational Structure for Setting Accounting Standards

The passage of a new FASB **Standards Statement** requires the support of four of the seven Board members. FASB Statements are considered GAAP and thereby binding in practice. All ARBs and APB Opinions implemented by 1973 (when the FASB formed) continue to be effective until amended or superseded by FASB pronouncements. In

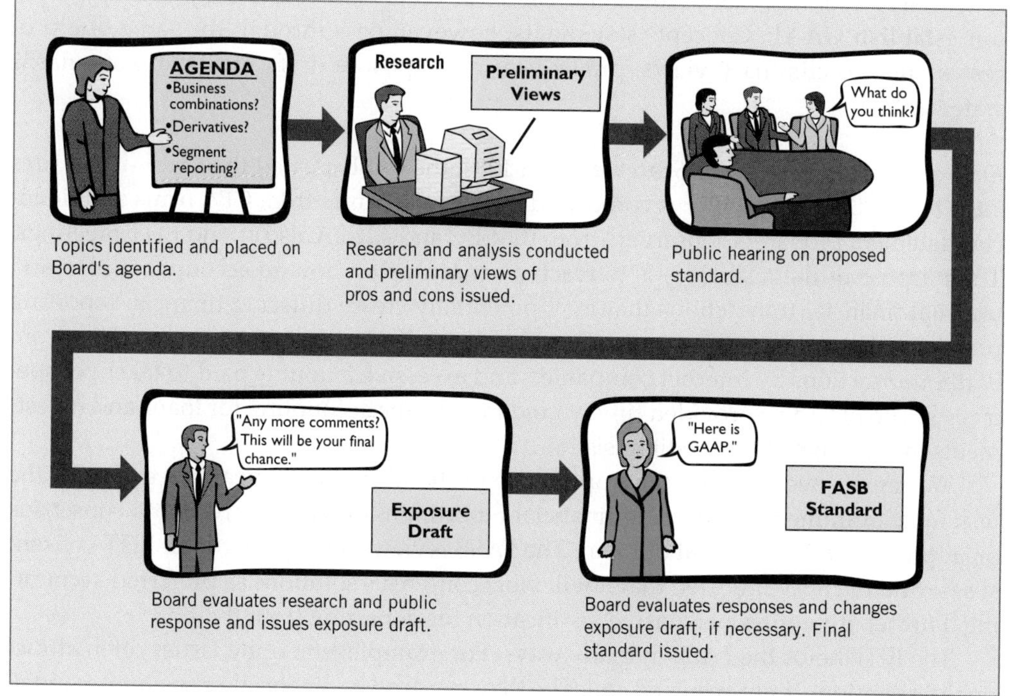

ILLUSTRATION 1-3
The Due Process System of the FASB

recognition of possible misconceptions of the term "principles," the FASB uses the term **financial accounting standards** in its pronouncements.

Types of Pronouncements

The FASB issues three major types of pronouncements:

1. Standards, Interpretations, and Staff Positions.
2. Financial Accounting Concepts.
3. Emerging Issues Task Force Statements.

Standards, Interpretations, and Staff Positions. Financial accounting **standards** issued by the FASB are considered generally accepted accounting principles. In addition, the FASB has also issued **interpretations** that modify or extend existing standards. Interpretations have the same authority, and require the same votes for passage, as standards. The APB also issued interpretations of APB Opinions. Both types of interpretations are now considered authoritative for purposes of determining GAAP. Finally, the FASB issues **staff positions**, which provide interpretive guidance and also minor amendments to standards and interpretations. These staff positions have the same authority as standards and interpretations. The Board also has issued FASB Technical Bulletins, which provide timely guidance on selected issues; staff positions are now used in lieu of technical bulletins. Since replacing the APB, the FASB has issued over 160 standards, 48 interpretations, and nearly 100 staff positions.

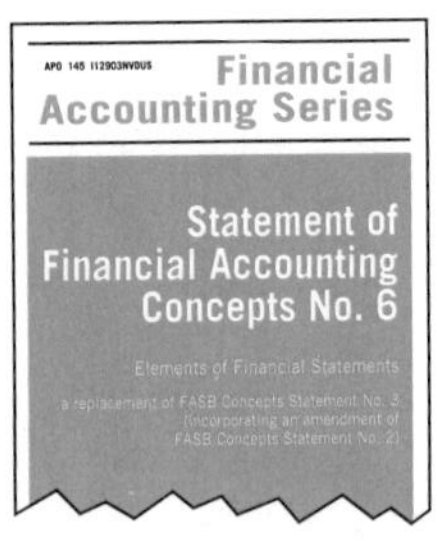

Financial Accounting Concepts. As part of a long-range effort to move away from the problem-by-problem approach, the FASB in November 1978 issued the first in a series of **Statements of Financial Accounting Concepts** as part of its conceptual framework project. (The Concepts Statement can be accessed at *http://www.fasb.org/*.) The series sets forth fundamental objectives and concepts that the Board uses in developing future standards of financial accounting and reporting. The Board intends to form a cohesive set of interrelated concepts—a conceptual framework—that will serve as tools for solving existing and emerging problems in a consistent manner. Unlike a Statement of Financial Accounting Standards, **a Statement of Financial Accounting Concepts does not establish GAAP**. Concepts statements, however, pass through the same due process system (preliminary views, public hearing, exposure draft, etc.) as do standards statements.

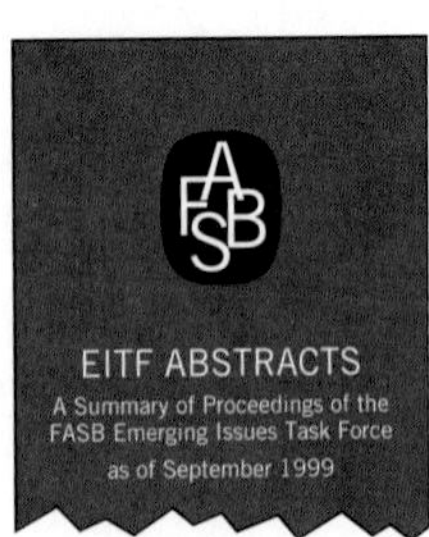

Emerging Issues Task Force Statements. In 1984, the FASB created the **Emerging Issues Task Force (EITF)**. The EITF is comprised of representatives from CPA firms and financial statement preparers. Observers from the SEC and AICPA also attend EITF meetings. The purpose of the task force is to reach a consensus on how to account for new and unusual financial transactions that may potentially create differing financial reporting practices. Examples include accounting for pension plan terminations, revenue from barter transactions by Internet companies, and excessive amounts paid to takeover specialists. The EITF also provided timely guidance for the accounting for loans and investments in the wake of the credit crisis.

We cannot overestimate the importance of the EITF. In one year, for example, the task force examined 61 emerging financial reporting issues and arrived at a consensus on approximately 75 percent of them. The FASB reviews and approves all EITF consensuses. And the SEC indicated that it will view consensus solutions as preferred accounting. Further, it requires persuasive justification for departing from them.

The EITF helps the FASB in many ways. For example, emerging issues often attract public attention. If not resolved quickly, they can lead to financial crises and scandal.

They can also undercut public confidence in current reporting practices. The next step, possible governmental intervention, would threaten the continuance of standard-setting in the private sector. The EITF identifies controversial accounting problems as they arise. The EITF determines whether it can quickly resolve them, or whether to involve the FASB in solving them. In essence, it becomes a "problem filter" for the FASB. Thus, the FASB will hopefully work on more pervasive long-term problems, while the EITF deals with short-term emerging issues.

Changing Role of the AICPA

For several decades, the AICPA provided leadership in developing accounting principles and rules. More than any other organization, it regulated the accounting profession, and developed and enforced accounting practice. When the FASB replaced the Accounting Principles Board, the AICPA established the **Accounting Standards Executive Committee (AcSEC)** as the committee authorized to speak for the AICPA in the area of financial accounting and reporting. It does so through various written communications:

Audit and Accounting Guides summarize the accounting practices of specific industries and provide specific guidance on matters not addressed by the FASB. Examples are accounting for casinos, airlines, colleges and universities, banks, insurance companies, and many others.

Statements of Position (SOP) provide guidance on financial reporting topics until the FASB sets standards on the issue in question. SOPs may update, revise, and clarify audit and accounting guides or provide free-standing guidance.

Practice Bulletins indicate AcSEC's views on narrow financial reporting issues not considered by the FASB.

The role of the AICPA in standard-setting has diminished. The FASB and the AICPA agree that the AICPA and AcSEC no longer will issue authoritative accounting guidance for public companies. Furthermore, while the AICPA has been the leader in developing auditing standards through its **Auditing Standards Board**, the Sarbanes-Oxley Act of 2002 requires the Public Company Accounting Oversight Board to oversee the development of auditing standards. The AICPA will continue to develop and grade the CPA examination, which is administered in all 50 states.

GENERALLY ACCEPTED ACCOUNTING PRINCIPLES

> **6 LEARNING OBJECTIVE**
> Explain the meaning of generally accepted accounting principles (GAAP) and the role of the Codification for GAAP.

Generally accepted accounting principles (GAAP) have substantial authoritative support. The AICPA's Code of Professional Conduct requires that members prepare financial statements in accordance with GAAP. Specifically, Rule 203 of this Code prohibits a member from expressing an unqualified opinion on financial statements that contain a material departure from generally accepted accounting principles.

What is GAAP? The major sources of GAAP come from the organizations discussed earlier in this chapter. It is composed of a mixture of over 2,000 documents that have developed over the last 60 years or so. It includes such items as FASB Standards, Interpretations, and Staff Positions; APB Opinions; and AICPA Research Bulletins. Illustration 1-4 (on page 14) highlights the many different types of documents that comprise GAAP.

ILLUSTRATION 1-4
GAAP Documents

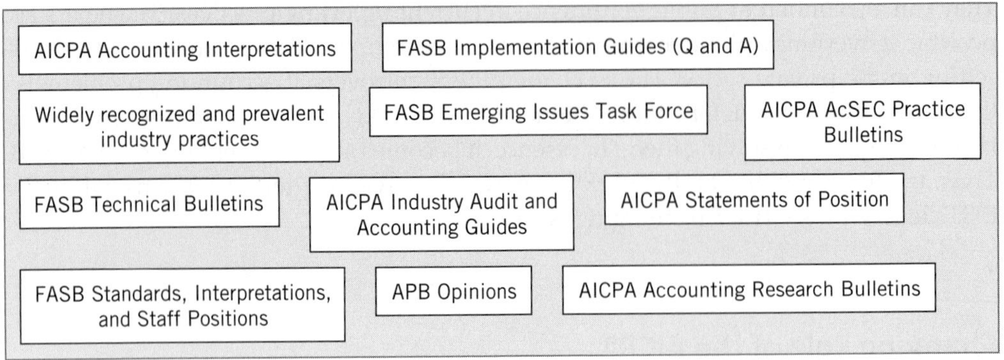

FASB Codification

As might be expected, the documents that comprise GAAP vary in format, completeness, and structure. In some cases, these documents are inconsistent and difficult to interpret. As a result, financial statement preparers sometimes are not sure whether they have the right GAAP; determining what is authoritative and what is not becomes difficult.

In response to these concerns, the FASB developed the **Financial Accounting Standards Board Accounting Standards Codification** (or more simply, "the Codification"). The FASB's primary goal in developing the Codification is to provide in one place all the authoritative literature related to a particular topic. This will simplify user access to all authoritative U.S. generally accepted accounting principles. The Codification changes the way GAAP is documented, presented, and updated. It explains what GAAP is and eliminates nonessential information such as redundant document summaries, basis for conclusions sections, and historical content. In short, the Codification integrates and synthesizes existing GAAP; it does not create new GAAP. It creates one level of GAAP, which is considered authoritative. All other accounting literature is considered non-authoritative.[6]

When the Board approves a new standard, staff position, etc., the results of that process are included in the Codification through an **Accounting Standards Update**. The update is composed of the background and basis for conclusions for the new pronouncement with a common format, regardless of the form in which such guidance may have been issued (e.g., EITF abstracts, FASB staff positions, FASB statements, and FASB interpretations). Accounting Standards Updates are also issued for amendments to the SEC content in the Codification.

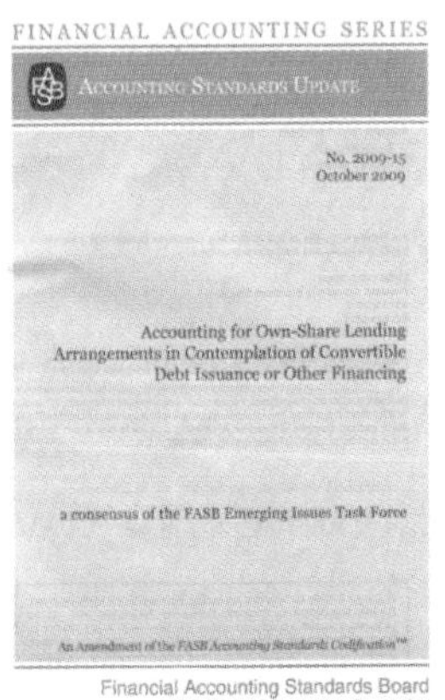

Financial Accounting Standards Board of the Financial Accounting Foundation

To provide easy access to this Codification, the FASB also developed the **Financial Accounting Standards Board Codification Research System (CRS)**. CRS is an online real-time database that provides easy access to the Codification. The Codification and the related CRS provide a topically organized structure, subdivided into topic, subtopics, sections, and paragraphs, using a numerical index system.

For purposes of referencing authoritative GAAP material in this textbook, we will use the Codification framework. Here is an example of how the Codification framework is cited, using Receivables as the example. The purpose of the search shown below is to

[6]The FASB Codification can be accessed at *http://asc.fasb.org/home*. Access to the full functionality of the Codification Research System requires a subscription. Reduced-price academic access is available through the American Accounting Association (see *aaahq.org/FASB/Access.cfm*). Prior to the Codification, the profession relied on *FASB 162*, "The Hierarchy of Generally Accepted Accounting Principles," which defined the meaning of generally accepted accounting principles. In that document, certain documents were deemed more authoritative than others, which led to various levels of GAAP. Fortunately, the Codification does not have different levels of GAAP.

determine GAAP for accounting for loans and trade receivables not held for sale subsequent to initial measurement.

Topic	Go to FASB ASC 310 to access the Receivables topic.
Subtopics	Go to FASB ASC 310-10 to access the Overall Subtopic of the Topic 310.
Sections	Go to FASB ASC 310-10-35 to access the Subsequent Measurement Section of the Subtopic 310-10.
Paragraph	Go to FASB ASC 310-10-35-47 to access the Loans and Trade Receivables not Held for Sale paragraph of Section 310-10-35.

Illustration 1-5 shows the Codification framework graphically.

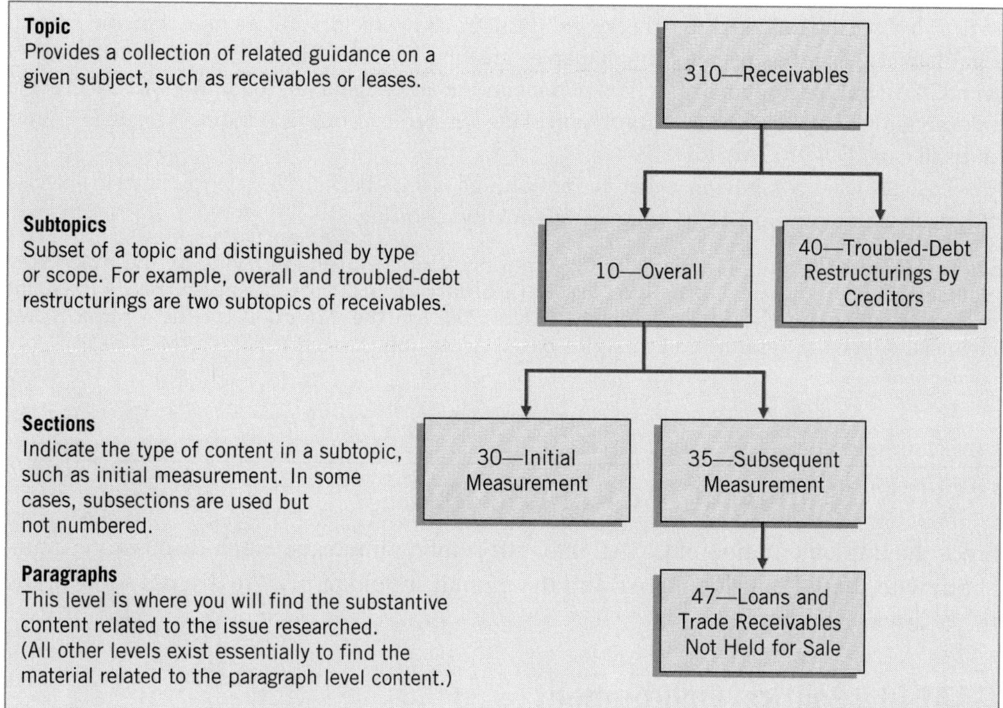

ILLUSTRATION 1-5
FASB Codification Framework

What happens if the Codification does not cover a certain type of transaction or event? In that case, other accounting literature should be considered, such as FASB Concept Statements, international financial reporting standards, and other professional literature. This will happen only rarely.

The expectations for the Codification are high. It is hoped that the Codification will enable users to better understand what GAAP is. As a result, the time to research accounting issues and the risk of noncompliance with GAAP will be reduced, sometimes substantially. In addition, the electronic Web-based format will make updating easier, which will help users stay current with GAAP.[7]

For individuals (like you) attempting to learn GAAP, the Codification will be invaluable. It is an outstanding effort by the profession to streamline and simplify how to determine what GAAP is, which will lead to better financial accounting and reporting. We provide references to the Codification throughout this textbook, using a numbering

[7]To increase the usefulness of the Codification for public companies, relevant authoritative content issued by the SEC is included in the Codification. In the case of SEC content, an "S" precedes the section number.

See the FASB Codification section at the end of each chapter for Codification references and exercises.

system. For example, a bracket with a number, such as [1], indicates that the citation to the FASB Codification can be found in the FASB Codification section at the end of the chapter (immediately before the assignment materials).

YOU HAVE TO STEP BACK

What do the numbers mean?

Should the accounting profession have principles-based standards or rules-based standards? Critics of the profession today say that over the past three decades, standard-setters have moved away from broad accounting principles aimed at ensuring that companies' financial statements are fairly presented.

Instead, these critics say, standard-setters have moved toward drafting voluminous rules that, if technically followed in "check-box" fashion, may shield auditors and companies from legal liability. That has resulted in companies creating complex capital structures that comply with GAAP but hide billions of dollars of debt and other obligations. To add fuel to the fire, the chief accountant of the enforcement division of the SEC recently noted, "One can violate SEC laws and still comply with GAAP."

In short, what he is saying is that it is not enough just to check the boxes. You have to exercise judgment in applying GAAP to achieve high-quality reporting.

Sources: Adapted from S. Liesman, "SEC Accounting Cop's Warning: Playing by the Rules May Not Head Off Fraud Issues," *Wall Street Journal* (February 12, 2002), p. C7. See also "Study Pursuant to Section 108(d) of the Sarbanes-Oxley Act of 2002 on the Adoption by the United States Financial Reporting System of a Principles-Based Accounting System," *SEC* (July 25, 2003).

ISSUES IN FINANCIAL REPORTING

Since the implementation of GAAP may affect many interests, much discussion occurs about who should develop GAAP and to whom it should apply. We discuss some of the major issues below.

GAAP in a Political Environment

LEARNING OBJECTIVE 7
Describe the impact of user groups on the rule-making process.

User groups are possibly the most powerful force influencing the development of GAAP. User groups consist of those most interested in or affected by accounting rules. Like lobbyists in our state and national capitals, user groups play a significant role. **GAAP is as much a product of political action as it is of careful logic or empirical findings.** User groups may want particular economic events accounted for or reported in a particular way, and they fight hard to get what they want. They know that the most effective way to influence GAAP is to participate in the formulation of these rules or to try to influence or persuade the formulator of them.

These user groups often target the FASB, to pressure it to influence changes in the existing rules and the development of new ones.[8] In fact, these pressures have been multiplying. Some influential groups demand that the accounting profession act more quickly and decisively to solve its problems. Other groups resist such action, preferring to implement change more slowly, if at all. Illustration 1-6 shows the various user groups that apply pressure.

[8]FASB board members acknowledged that they undertook many of the Board's projects, such as "Accounting for Contingencies," "Accounting for Pensions," "Statement of Cash Flows," and "Accounting for Derivatives," due to political pressure.

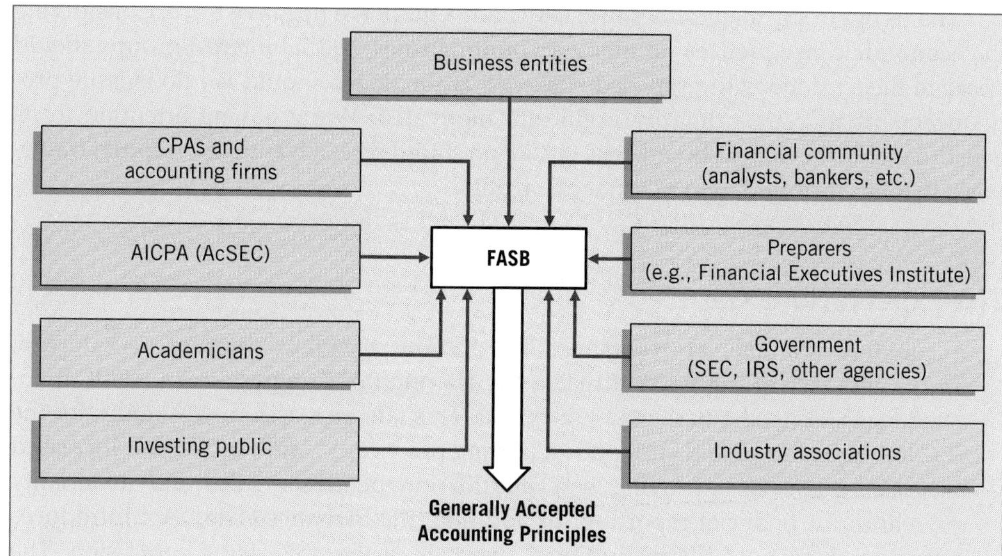

ILLUSTRATION 1-6
User Groups that Influence the Formulation of Accounting Standards

Should there be politics in establishing GAAP for financial accounting and reporting? Why not? We have politics at home; at school; at the fraternity, sorority, and dormitory; at the office; and at church, temple, and mosque. Politics is everywhere. GAAP is part of the real world, and it cannot escape politics and political pressures.

FAIR CONSEQUENCES?

What do the numbers mean?

No recent accounting issue better illustrates the economic consequences of accounting than the current debate over the use of fair value accounting for financial assets. Both the FASB and the International Accounting Standards Board (IASB) have standards requiring the use of fair value accounting for financial assets, such as investments and other financial instruments. Fair value provides the most relevant and reliable information for investors about these assets and liabilities. However, in the wake of the recent credit crisis, some countries, their central banks, and bank regulators want to suspend fair value accounting, based on concerns that use of fair value accounting, which calls for recording significant losses on poorly performing loans and investments, could scare investors and depositors and lead to a "run on the bank."

For example, in 2009, Congress ordered the FASB to change its accounting rules so as to reduce the losses banks reported, as the values of their securities had crumbled. These changes were generally supported by banks. But these changes produced a strong reaction from some investors, with one investor group complaining that the changes would "effectively gut the transparent application of fair value measurement." The group also says suspending fair value accounting would delay the recovery of the banking system.

Such political pressure on accounting standard-setters is not confined to the United States. For example, French President Nicolas Sarkozy is urging his European Union counterparts to back changes to accounting rules and give banks and insurers some breathing space amid the market turmoil. Mr. Sarkozy seeks new regulations, including changes to the mark-to-market accounting rules that have been blamed for aggravating the crisis. It is unclear whether these political pressures will have an effect on fair value accounting, but there is no question that the issue has stirred significant worldwide political debate. In short, the numbers have consequences.

Source: Adapted from Ben Hall and Nikki Tait, "Sarkozy Seeks EU Accounting Change," *The Financial Times Limited* (September 30, 2008), and Floyd Norris, "Banks Are Set to Receive More Leeway on Asset Values," *New York Times* (March 31, 2009).

That is not to say that politics in establishing GAAP is a negative force. Considering the **economic consequences**[9] of many accounting rules, special interest groups should vocalize their reactions to proposed rules. What the Board should *not* do is issue pronouncements that are primarily politically motivated. While paying attention to its constituencies, the Board should base GAAP on sound research and a conceptual framework that has its foundation in economic reality.

The Expectations Gap

INTERNATIONAL PERSPECTIVE

Foreign accounting firms that provide an audit report for a U.S.-listed company are subject to the authority of the accounting oversight board (mandated by the Sarbanes-Oxley Act).

Accounting scandals at companies like **Enron**, **Cendant**, **Sunbeam**, **Rite-Aid**, **Xerox**, and **WorldCom** have attracted the attention of Congress. As a result, it enacted legislation—the **Sarbanes-Oxley Act**. This law increases the resources for the SEC to combat fraud and curb poor reporting practices.[10] And the SEC has increased its policing efforts, approving new auditor independence rules and materiality guidelines for financial reporting. In addition, the Sarbanes-Oxley Act introduces sweeping changes to the institutional structure of the accounting profession. The following are some of the key provisions of the legislation.

- Establishes an oversight board, the **Public Company Accounting Oversight Board (PCAOB)**, for accounting practices. The PCAOB has oversight and enforcement authority and establishes auditing, quality control, and independence standards and rules.
- Implements stronger independence rules for auditors. Audit partners, for example, are required to rotate every five years, and auditors are prohibited from offering certain types of consulting services to corporate clients.
- Requires CEOs and CFOs to personally certify that financial statements and disclosures are accurate and complete, and requires CEOs and CFOs to forfeit bonuses and profits when there is an accounting restatement.
- Requires audit committees to be comprised of independent members and members with financial expertise.
- Requires codes of ethics for senior financial officers.

In addition, Section 404 of the Sarbanes-Oxley Act requires public companies to attest to the effectiveness of their internal controls over financial reporting. **Internal controls** are a system of checks and balances designed to prevent and detect fraud and errors. Most companies have these systems in place, but many have never completely documented them. Companies are finding that it is a costly process but perhaps badly needed. Already, intense examination of internal controls has found lingering problems in the way companies operate. Recently, 424 companies reported deficiencies in internal control.[11] Many problems involved closing the books, revenue recognition deficiencies, reconciling accounts, or dealing with inventory. **SunTrust Bank**, for example, fired three officers after discovering errors in how the company calculates its allowance for bad

[9]*Economic consequences* means the impact of accounting reports on the wealth positions of issuers and users of financial information, and the decision-making behavior resulting from that impact. The resulting behavior of these individuals and groups could have detrimental financial effects on the providers of the financial information. See Stephen A. Zeff, "The Rise of 'Economic Consequences'," *Journal of Accountancy* (December 1978), pp. 56–63. We extend appreciation to Professor Zeff for his insights on this chapter.

[10]*Sarbanes-Oxley Act of 2002,* H. R. Rep. No. 107-610 (2002).

[11]Leah Townsend, "Internal Control Deficiency Disclosures—Interim Alert," *Yellow Card—Interim Trend Alert* (April 12, 2005), Glass, Lewis & Co., LLC.

debts. And Visteon, a car parts supplier, said it found problems recording and managing receivables from its largest customer, Ford Motor.

Will these changes be enough? The expectations gap—what the public thinks accountants *should* do and what accountants think they *can* do—is difficult to close. Due to the number of fraudulent reporting cases, some question whether the profession is doing enough. Although the profession can argue rightfully that accounting cannot be responsible for every financial catastrophe, it must continue to strive to meet the needs of society. However, efforts to meet these needs will become more costly to society. The development of a highly transparent, clear, and reliable system will require considerable resources.

Financial Reporting Challenges

8 LEARNING OBJECTIVE
Describe some of the challenges facing financial reporting.

While our reporting model has worked well in capturing and organizing financial information in a useful and reliable fashion, much still needs to be done. For example, if we move to the year 2022 and look back at financial reporting today, we might read the following.

- ***Nonfinancial measurements.*** Financial reports failed to provide some key performance measures widely used by management, such as customer satisfaction indexes, backlog information, and reject rates on goods purchased.
- ***Forward-looking information.*** Financial reports failed to provide forward-looking information needed by present and potential investors and creditors. One individual noted that financial statements in 2012 should have started with the phrase, "Once upon a time," to signify their use of historical cost and accumulation of past events.
- ***Soft assets.*** Financial reports focused on hard assets (inventory, plant assets) but failed to provide much information about a company's soft assets (intangibles). The best assets are often intangible. Consider Microsoft's know-how and market dominance, Wal-Mart's expertise in supply chain management, and Proctor & Gamble's brand image.
- ***Timeliness.*** Companies only prepared financial statements quarterly and provided audited financials annually. Little to no real-time financial statement information was available.

We believe each of these challenges must be met for the accounting profession to provide the type of information needed for an efficient capital allocation process. We are confident that changes will occur, based on these positive signs:

- Already, some companies voluntarily disclose information deemed relevant to investors. Often such information is nonfinancial. For example, banking companies now disclose data on loan growth, credit quality, fee income, operating efficiency, capital management, and management strategy.
- Initially, companies used the Internet to provide limited financial data. Now, most companies publish their annual reports in several formats on the Web. The most innovative companies offer sections of their annual reports in a format that the user can readily manipulate, such as in an electronic spreadsheet format. Companies also format their financial reports using eXtensible Business Reporting Language (XBRL), which permits quicker and lower-cost access to companies' financial information.
- More accounting standards now require the recording or disclosing of fair value information. For example, companies either record investments in stocks and bonds, debt obligations, and derivatives at fair value, or companies show information related to fair values in the notes to the financial statements.

Changes in these directions will enhance the relevance of financial reporting and provide useful information to financial statement readers.

International Accounting Standards

Former Secretary of the Treasury, Lawrence Summers, has indicated that the single most important innovation shaping the capital markets was the idea of generally accepted accounting principles. He went on to say that we need something similar internationally.

We believe that the Secretary is right. Relevant and reliable financial information is a necessity for viable capital markets. Unfortunately, companies outside the United States often prepare financial statements using standards different from U.S. GAAP (or simply GAAP). As a result, international companies such as **Coca-Cola**, **Microsoft**, and **IBM** have to develop financial information in different ways. Beyond the additional costs these companies incur, users of the financial statements often must understand at least two sets of accounting standards. (Understanding one set is hard enough!) It is not surprising, therefore, that there is a growing demand for one set of high-quality international standards.

INTERNATIONAL PERSPECTIVE

IFRS includes the standards, referred to as International Financial Reporting Standards (IFRS), developed by the IASB. The predecessor to the IASB issued International Accounting Standards (IAS).

Presently, there are two sets of rules accepted for international use—GAAP and the **International Financial Reporting Standards (IFRS)**, issued by the London-based **International Accounting Standards Board (IASB)**. U.S. companies that list overseas are still permitted to use GAAP, and foreign companies listed on U.S. exchanges are permitted to use IFRS. As you will learn, there are many similarities between GAAP and IFRS.

Already over 115 countries use IFRS, and the European Union now requires all listed companies in Europe (over 7,000 companies) to use it. The SEC laid out a roadmap by which all U.S. companies might be required to use IFRS by 2015. Most parties recognize that global markets will best be served if only one set of accounting standards is used. For example, the FASB and the IASB formalized their commitment to the convergence of GAAP and IFRS by issuing a memorandum of understanding (often referred to as the Norwalk agreement). The two boards agreed to use their best efforts to:

- Make their existing financial reporting standards fully compatible as soon as practicable, and
- Coordinate their future work programs to ensure that once achieved, compatibility is maintained.

INTERNATIONAL PERSPECTIVE

The adoption of IFRS by U.S. companies would make it easier to compare U.S. and foreign companies, as well as for U.S. companies to raise capital in foreign markets.

As a result of this agreement, the two Boards identified a number of short-term and long-term projects that would lead to convergence. For example, one short-term project was for the FASB to issue a rule that permits a fair value option for financial instruments. This rule was issued in 2007, and now the FASB and the IASB follow the same accounting in this area. Conversely, the IASB completed a project related to borrowing costs, which makes IFRS consistent with GAAP. Long-term convergence projects relate to such issues as revenue recognition, the conceptual framework, and leases.

Because convergence is such an important issue, we provide a discussion of international accounting standards at the end of each chapter called **IFRS Insights**. This feature will help you understand the changes that are taking place in the financial reporting area as we move to one set of international standards. In addition, throughout the textbook we provide in the margins *International Perspectives* to help you understand the international reporting environment.

Ethics in the Environment of Financial Accounting

LEARNING OBJECTIVE 9

Understand issues related to ethics and financial accounting.

Robert Sack, a noted commentator on the subject of accounting ethics, observed, "Based on my experience, new graduates tend to be idealistic . . . thank goodness for that! Still it is very dangerous to think that your armor is all in place and say to yourself, 'I would have never given in to that.' The pressures don't explode on us; they build, and we often don't recognize them until they have us."

These observations are particularly appropriate for anyone entering the business world. In accounting, as in other areas of business, we frequently encounter ethical dilemmas. Some of these dilemmas are simple and easy to resolve. However, many are not, requiring difficult choices among allowable alternatives.

Companies that concentrate on "maximizing the bottom line," "facing the challenges of competition," and "stressing short-term results" place accountants in an environment of conflict and pressure. Basic questions such as, "Is this way of communicating financial information good or bad?" "Is it right or wrong?" and "What should I do in the circumstance?" cannot always be answered by simply adhering to GAAP or following the rules of the profession. Technical competence is not enough when encountering ethical decisions.

Doing the right thing is not always easy or obvious. The pressures "to bend the rules," "to play the game," or "to just ignore it" can be considerable. For example, "Will my decision affect my job performance negatively?" "Will my superiors be upset?" and "Will my colleagues be unhappy with me?" are often questions business people face in making a tough ethical decision. The decision is more difficult because there is no comprehensive ethical system to provide guidelines.

Gateway to the Profession

Expanded Discussion of Ethical Issues in Financial Reporting

Time, job, client, personal, and peer pressures can complicate the process of ethical sensitivity and selection among alternatives. Throughout this textbook, **we present ethical considerations to help sensitize you** to the type of situations you may encounter in the performance of your professional responsibility.

Conclusion

Bob Herz, former FASB chairman, believes that there are three fundamental considerations the FASB must keep in mind in its rule-making activities: (1) improvement in financial reporting, (2) simplification of the accounting literature and the rule-making process, and (3) international convergence. These are notable objectives, and the Board is making good progress on all three dimensions. Issues such as off-balance-sheet financing, measurement of fair values, enhanced criteria for revenue recognition, and stock option accounting are examples of where the Board has exerted leadership. Improvements in financial reporting should follow.

Also, the Board is making it easier to understand what GAAP is. GAAP has been contained in a number of different documents. The lack of a single source makes it difficult to access and understand generally accepted principles. As discussed earlier, the Codification now organizes existing GAAP by accounting topic regardless of its source (FASB Statements, APB Opinions, and so on). The codified standards are then considered to be GAAP and to be authoritative. All other literature will be considered nonauthoritative.

Finally, international convergence is underway. Some projects already are completed and differences eliminated. Many more are on the drawing board. It appears to be only a matter of time until we will have one set of global accounting standards that will be established by the IASB. The profession has many challenges, but it has responded in a timely, comprehensive, and effective manner.

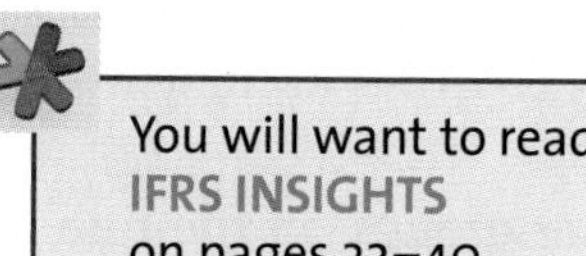

You will want to read the IFRS INSIGHTS on pages 32–40 for discussion of IFRS and the international reporting environment.

SUMMARY OF LEARNING OBJECTIVES

1 Identify the major financial statements and other means of financial reporting. Companies most frequently provide (1) the balance sheet, (2) the income statement, (3) the statement of cash flows, and (4) the statement of owners' or stockholders' equity. Financial reporting other than financial statements may take various forms. Examples include the president's letter and supplementary schedules in the corporate annual report, prospectuses, reports filed with government agencies, news releases, management's forecasts, and descriptions of a company's social or environmental impact.

2 Explain how accounting assists in the efficient use of scarce resources. Accounting provides reliable, relevant, and timely information to managers, investors, and creditors to allow resource allocation to the most efficient enterprises. Accounting also provides measurements of efficiency (profitability) and financial soundness.

3 Identify the objective of financial reporting. The objective of general-purpose financial reporting is to provide financial information about the reporting entity that is useful to present and potential equity investors, lenders, and other creditors in decisions about providing resources to the entity through equity investments and loans or other forms of credit. Information that is decision-useful to investors may also be helpful to other users of financial reporting who are not investors.

4 Explain the need for accounting standards. The accounting profession has attempted to develop a set of standards that is generally accepted and universally practiced. Without this set of standards, each company would have to develop its own standards. Readers of financial statements would have to familiarize themselves with every company's peculiar accounting and reporting practices. As a result, it would be almost impossible to prepare statements that could be compared.

5 Identify the major policy-setting bodies and their role in the standard-setting process. The *Securities and Exchange Commission (SEC)* is a federal agency that has the broad powers to prescribe, in whatever detail it desires, the accounting standards to be employed by companies that fall within its jurisdiction. The *American Institute of Certified Public Accountants (AICPA)* issued standards through its Committee on Accounting Procedure and Accounting Principles Board. The *Financial Accounting Standards Board (FASB)* establishes and improves standards of financial accounting and reporting for the guidance and education of the public.

6 Explain the meaning of generally accepted accounting principles (GAAP) and the role of the Codification for GAAP. Generally accepted accounting principles (GAAP) are those principles that have substantial authoritative support, such as FASB standards, interpretations, and staff positions, APB Opinions and interpretations, AICPA Accounting Research Bulletins, and other authoritative pronouncements. All these documents and others are now classified in one document referred to as the Codification. The purpose of the Codification is to simplify user access to all authoritative U.S. GAAP. The Codification changes the way GAAP is documented, presented, and updated.

7 Describe the impact of user groups on the rule-making process. User groups may want particular economic events accounted for or reported in a particular way, and they fight hard to get what they want. They especially target the FASB to influence changes in existing GAAP and in the development of new rules. Because of the accelerated rate of change and the increased complexity of our economy, these pressures have been multiplying. GAAP is as much a product of political action as it is of careful logic or empirical findings. The IASB is working with the FASB toward international convergence of GAAP.

KEY TERMS

Accounting Principles Board (APB), 9
Accounting Research Bulletins, 9
Accounting Standards Update, 14
accrual-basis accounting, 7
American Institute of Certified Public Accountants (AICPA), 9
APB Opinions, 9
Auditing Standards Board, 13
Committee on Accounting Procedure (CAP), 9
decision-usefulness, 6
Emerging Issues Task Force (EITF), 12
entity perspective, 6
expectations gap, 19
financial accounting, 4
Financial Accounting Standards Board (FASB), 10
Financial Accounting Standards Board Codification (Codification), 14
Financial Accounting Standards Board Codification Research System (CRS), 14
financial reporting, 4
financial statements, 4
generally accepted accounting principles (GAAP), 7
general-purpose financial statements, 5
International Accounting Standards Board (IASB), 20
International Financial Reporting Standards (IFRS), 20
interpretations, 12
objective of financial reporting, 5
Public Company Accounting Oversight Board (PCAOB), 18
Sarbanes-Oxley Act of 2002, 18

8 Describe some of the challenges facing financial reporting. Financial reports fail to provide (1) some key performance measures widely used by management, (2) forward-looking information needed by investors and creditors, (3) sufficient information on a company's soft assets (intangibles), and (4) real-time financial information.

9 Understand issues related to ethics and financial accounting. Financial accountants are called on for moral discernment and ethical decision-making. Decisions sometimes are difficult because a public consensus has not emerged to formulate a comprehensive ethical system that provides guidelines in making ethical judgments.

Securities and Exchange Commission (SEC), *8*
staff positions, *12*
Standards Statement, *11*
Statement of Financial Accounting Concepts, *12*
Wheat Committee, *10*

FASB CODIFICATION

Exercises

Academic access to the FASB Codification is available through university subscriptions, obtained from the American Accounting Association (at *http://aaahq.org/FASB/Access.cfm*), for an annual fee of $150. This subscription covers an unlimited number of students within a single institution. Once this access has been obtained by your school, you should log in (at *http://aaahq.org/ascLogin.cfm*) to prepare responses to the following exercises.

CE1-1 Register for access to the FASB Codification. You will need to enter an email address and provide a password. Familiarize yourself with the resources that are accessible at the FASB Codification homepage.

CE1-2 Click on the "Notice to Participants."

(a) Briefly describe the three main elements that are provided in the module.
(b) What are the primary purposes for development of the Codification?

CE1-3 Briefly describe the purpose and content of the "What's New" link.

Be sure to check the book's companion website for a Review and Analysis Exercise, with solution.

Questions, Brief Exercises, Exercises, Problems, and many more resources are available for practice in WileyPLUS.

QUESTIONS

1. Differentiate broadly between financial accounting and managerial accounting.
2. Differentiate between "financial statements" and "financial reporting."
3. How does accounting help the capital allocation process?
4. What is the objective of financial reporting?
5. Briefly explain the meaning of decision-usefulness in the context of financial reporting.
6. Of what value is a common set of standards in financial accounting and reporting?
7. What is the likely limitation of "general-purpose financial statements"?
8. In what way is the Securities and Exchange Commission concerned about and supportive of accounting principles and standards?
9. What was the Committee on Accounting Procedure, and what were its accomplishments and failings?
10. For what purposes did the AICPA in 1959 create the Accounting Principles Board?
11. Distinguish among Accounting Research Bulletins, Opinions of the Accounting Principles Board, and Statements of the Financial Accounting Standards Board.
12. If you had to explain or define "generally accepted accounting principles or standards," what essential characteristics would you include in your explanation?

13. In what ways was it felt that the statements issued by the Financial Accounting Standards Board would carry greater weight than the opinions issued by the Accounting Principles Board?

14. How are FASB preliminary views and FASB exposure drafts related to FASB "statements"?

15. Distinguish between FASB "statements of financial accounting standards" and FASB "statements of financial accounting concepts."

16. What is Rule 203 of the Code of Professional Conduct?

17. Rank from the most authoritative to the least authoritative, the following three items: FASB Technical Bulletins, AICPA Practice Bulletins, and FASB Standards.

18. The chairman of the FASB at one time noted that "the flow of standards can only be slowed if (1) producers focus less on quarterly earnings per share and tax benefits and more on quality products, and (2) accountants and lawyers rely less on rules and law and more on professional judgment and conduct." Explain his comment.

19. What is the purpose of FASB staff positions?

20. Explain the role of the Emerging Issues Task Force in establishing generally accepted accounting principles.

21. What is the difference between the Codification and the Codification Research System?

22. What are the primary advantages of having a Codification of generally accepted accounting principles?

23. What are the sources of pressure that change and influence the development of GAAP?

24. Some individuals have indicated that the FASB must be cognizant of the economic consequences of its pronouncements. What is meant by "economic consequences"? What dangers exist if politics play too much of a role in the development of GAAP?

25. If you were given complete authority in the matter, how would you propose that GAAP should be developed and enforced?

26. One writer recently noted that 99.4 percent of all companies prepare statements that are in accordance with GAAP. Why then is there such concern about fraudulent financial reporting?

27. What is the "expectations gap"? What is the profession doing to try to close this gap?

28. The Sarbanes-Oxley Act was enacted to combat fraud and curb poor reporting practices. What are some key provisions of this legislation?

29. What are some of the major challenges facing the accounting profession?

30. How are financial accountants challenged in their work to make ethical decisions? Is technical mastery of GAAP not sufficient to the practice of financial accounting?

CONCEPTS FOR ANALYSIS

CA1-1 (FASB and Standard-Setting) Presented below are four statements which you are to identify as true or false. If false, explain why the statement is false.

1. GAAP is the term used to indicate the whole body of FASB authoritative literature.
2. Any company claiming compliance with GAAP must comply with most standards and interpretations but does not have to follow the disclosure requirements.
3. The primary governmental body that has influence over the FASB is the SEC.
4. The FASB has a government mandate and therefore does not have to follow due process in issuing a standard.

CA1-2 (GAAP and Standard-Setting) Presented below are four statements which you are to identify as true or false. If false, explain why the statement is false.

1. The objective of financial statements emphasizes a stewardship approach for reporting financial information.
2. The purpose of the objective of financial reporting is to prepare a balance sheet, an income statement, a statement of cash flows, and a statement of owners' or stockholders' equity.
3. Because they are generally shorter, FASB interpretations are subject to less due process, compared to FASB standards.
4. The objective of financial reporting uses an entity rather than a proprietary approach in determining what information to report.

CA1-3 (Financial Reporting and Accounting Standards) Answer the following multiple-choice questions.

1. GAAP stands for:
   (a) governmental auditing and accounting practices.
   (b) generally accepted attest principles.
   (c) government audit and attest policies.
   (d) generally accepted accounting principles.

2. Accounting standard-setters use the following process in establishing accounting standards:
   (a) Research, exposure draft, discussion paper, standard.
   (b) Discussion paper, research, exposure draft, standard.
   (c) Research, preliminary views, discussion paper, standard.
   (d) Research, discussion paper, exposure draft, standard.
3. GAAP is comprised of:
   (a) FASB standards, interpretations, and concepts statements.
   (b) FASB financial standards.
   (c) FASB standards, interpretations, EITF consensuses, and accounting rules issued by FASB predecessor organizations.
   (d) any accounting guidance included in the FASB Codification.
4. The authoritative status of the conceptual framework is as follows.
   (a) It is used when there is no standard or interpretation related to the reporting issues under consideration.
   (b) It is not as authoritative as a standard but takes precedence over any interpretation related to the reporting issue.
   (c) It takes precedence over all other authoritative literature.
   (d) It has no authoritative status.
5. The objective of financial reporting places most emphasis on:
   (a) reporting to capital providers.
   (b) reporting on stewardship.
   (c) providing specific guidance related to specific needs.
   (d) providing information to individuals who are experts in the field.
6. General-purpose financial statements are prepared primarily for:
   (a) internal users.
   (b) external users.
   (c) auditors.
   (d) government regulators.
7. Economic consequences of accounting standard-setting means:
   (a) standard-setters must give first priority to ensuring that companies do not suffer any adverse effect as a result of a new standard.
   (b) standard-setters must ensure that no new costs are incurred when a new standard is issued.
   (c) the objective of financial reporting should be politically motivated to ensure acceptance by the general public.
   (d) accounting standards can have detrimental impacts on the wealth levels of the providers of financial information.
8. The expectations gap is:
   (a) what financial information management provides and what users want.
   (b) what the public thinks accountants should do and what accountants think they can do.
   (c) what the governmental agencies want from standard-setting and what the standard-setters provide.
   (d) what the users of financial statements want from the government and what is provided.

CA1-4 (Financial Accounting) Omar Morena has recently completed his first year of studying accounting. His instructor for next semester has indicated that the primary focus will be the area of financial accounting.

Instructions

(a) Differentiate between financial accounting and managerial accounting.
(b) One part of financial accounting involves the preparation of financial statements. What are the financial statements most frequently provided?
(c) What is the difference between financial statements and financial reporting?

CA1-5 (Objective of Financial Reporting) Karen Sepan, a recent graduate of the local state university, is presently employed by a large manufacturing company. She has been asked by Jose Martinez, controller, to prepare the company's response to a current Preliminary Views published by the Financial Accounting Standards Board (FASB). Sepan knows that the FASB has a conceptual framework, and she believes that these concept statements could be used to support the company's response to the Preliminary Views. She has prepared a rough draft of the response citing the objective of financial reporting.

Instructions

(a) Identify the objective of financial reporting.
(b) Describe the level of sophistication expected of the users of financial information by the objective of financial reporting.

CA1-6 (Accounting Numbers and the Environment) Hardly a day goes by without an article appearing on the crises affecting many of our financial institutions in the United States. It is estimated that the savings and loan (S&L) debacle of the 1980s, for example, ended up costing $500 billion ($2,000 for every man, woman, and child in the United States). Some argue that if the S&Ls had been required to report their investments at fair value instead of cost, large losses would have been reported earlier, which would have signaled regulators to close those S&Ls and, therefore, minimize the losses to U.S. taxpayers.

Instructions

Explain how reported accounting numbers might affect an individual's perceptions and actions. Cite two examples.

CA1-7 (Need for GAAP) Some argue that having various organizations establish accounting principles is wasteful and inefficient. Rather than mandating accounting rules, each company could voluntarily disclose the type of information it considered important. In addition, if an investor wants additional information, the investor could contact the company and pay to receive the additional information desired.

Instructions

Comment on the appropriateness of this viewpoint.

CA1-8 (AICPA's Role in Rule-Making) One of the major groups involved in the standard-setting process is the American Institute of Certified Public Accountants. Initially, it was the primary organization that established accounting principles in the United States. Subsequently, it relinquished its power to the FASB.

Instructions

(a) Identify the two committees of the AICPA that established accounting principles prior to the establishment of the FASB.

(b) Speculate as to why these two organizations failed. In your answer, identify steps the FASB has taken to avoid failure.

(c) What is the present role of the AICPA in the rule-making environment?

CA1-9 (FASB Role in Rule-Making) A press release announcing the appointment of the trustees of the new Financial Accounting Foundation stated that the Financial Accounting Standards Board (to be appointed by the trustees) "... will become the established authority for setting accounting principles under which corporations report to the shareholders and others" (AICPA news release July 20, 1972).

Instructions

(a) Identify the sponsoring organization of the FASB and the process by which the FASB arrives at a decision and issues an accounting standard.

(b) Indicate the major types of pronouncements issued by the FASB and the purposes of each of these pronouncements.

CA1-10 (Politicization of GAAP) Some accountants have said that politicization in the development and acceptance of generally accepted accounting principles (i.e., rule-making) is taking place. Some use the term "politicization" in a narrow sense to mean the influence by governmental agencies, particularly the Securities and Exchange Commission, on the development of generally accepted accounting principles. Others use it more broadly to mean the compromise that results when the bodies responsible for developing generally accepted accounting principles are pressured by interest groups (SEC, American Accounting Association, businesses through their various organizations, Institute of Management Accountants, financial analysts, bankers, lawyers, and so on).

Instructions

(a) The Committee on Accounting Procedure of the AICPA was established in the mid- to late 1930s and functioned until 1959, at which time the Accounting Principles Board came into existence. In 1973, the Financial Accounting Standards Board was formed and the APB went out of existence. Do the reasons these groups were formed, their methods of operation while in existence, and the reasons for the demise of the first two indicate an increasing politicization (as the term is used in the broad sense) of accounting standard-setting? Explain your answer by indicating how the CAP, the APB, and the FASB operated or operate. Cite specific developments that tend to support your answer.

(b) What arguments can be raised to support the "politicization" of accounting rule-making?

(c) What arguments can be raised against the "politicization" of accounting rule-making?

(CMA adapted)

CA1-11 (Models for Setting GAAP) Presented below are three models for setting GAAP.

1. The purely political approach, where national legislative action decrees GAAP.
2. The private, professional approach, where GAAP is set and enforced by private professional actions only.

3. The public/private mixed approach, where GAAP is basically set by private-sector bodies that behave as though they were public agencies and whose standards to a great extent are enforced through governmental agencies.

Instructions

(a) Which of these three models best describes standard-setting in the United States? Comment on your answer.
(b) Why do companies, financial analysts, labor unions, industry trade associations, and others take such an active interest in standard-setting?
(c) Cite an example of a group other than the FASB that attempts to establish accounting standards. Speculate as to why another group might wish to set its own standards.

CA1-12 (GAAP Terminology) Wayne Rogers, an administrator at a major university, recently said, "I've got some CDs in my IRA, which I set up to beat the IRS." As elsewhere, in the world of accounting and finance, it often helps to be fluent in abbreviations and acronyms.

Instructions

Presented below is a list of common accounting acronyms. Identify the term for which each acronym stands, and provide a brief definition of each term.

(a) AICPA	**(e)** FAF	**(i)** CPA
(b) CAP	**(f)** FASAC	**(j)** FASB
(c) ARB	**(g)** SOP	**(k)** SEC
(d) APB	**(h)** GAAP	**(l)** IASB

CA1-13 (Accounting Organizations and Documents Issued) Presented below are a number of accounting organizations and types of documents they have issued.

Instructions

Match the appropriate document to the organization involved. Note that more than one document may be issued by the same organization. If no document is provided for an organization, write in "0."

Organization	**Document**
1. _____ Accounting Standards Executive Committee	**(a)** Opinions
2. _____ Accounting Principles Board	**(b)** Practice Bulletins
3. _____ Committee on Accounting Procedure	**(c)** Accounting Research Bulletins
4. _____ Financial Accounting Standards Board	**(d)** Financial Accounting Standards
	(e) Statements of Position

CA1-14 (Accounting Pronouncements) Standard-setting bodies have issued a number of authoritative pronouncements. A list is provided on the left, below, with a description of these pronouncements on the right.

Instructions

Match the description to the pronouncements.

1. _____ Staff Positions
2. _____ Interpretations (of the Financial Accounting Standards Board)
3. _____ Statement of Financial Accounting Standards
4. _____ EITF Statements
5. _____ Opinions
6. _____ Statement of Financial Accounting Concepts

(a) Official pronouncements of the APB.
(b) Sets forth fundamental objectives and concepts that will be used in developing future standards.
(c) Primary document of the FASB that establishes GAAP.
(d) Provides additional guidance on implementing or applying FASB Standards or Interpretations.
(e) Provides guidance on how to account for new and unusual financial transactions that have the potential for creating diversity in financial reporting practices.
(f) Represent extensions or modifications of existing standards.

CA1-15 (Rule-Making Issues) When the FASB issues new pronouncements, the implementation date is usually 12 months from date of issuance, with early implementation encouraged. Karen Weller, controller, discusses with her financial vice president the need for early implementation of a rule that would result in a fairer presentation of the company's financial condition and earnings. When the financial vice president

determines that early implementation of the rule will adversely affect the reported net income for the year, he discourages Weller from implementing the rule until it is required.

Instructions

Answer the following questions.

(a) What, if any, is the ethical issue involved in this case?
(b) Is the financial vice president acting improperly or immorally?
(c) What does Weller have to gain by advocacy of early implementation?
(d) Which stakeholders might be affected by the decision against early implementation?

(CMA adapted)

CA1-16 (Securities and Exchange Commission) The U.S. Securities and Exchange Commission (SEC) was created in 1934 and consists of five commissioners and a large professional staff. The SEC professional staff is organized into five divisions and several principal offices. The primary objective of the SEC is to support fair securities markets. The SEC also strives to foster enlightened stockholder participation in corporate decisions of publicly traded companies. The SEC has a significant presence in financial markets, the development of accounting practices, and corporation-shareholder relations, and has the power to exert influence on entities whose actions lie within the scope of its authority.

Instructions

(a) Explain from where the Securities and Exchange Commission receives its authority.
(b) Describe the official role of the Securities and Exchange Commission in the development of financial accounting theory and practices.
(c) Discuss the interrelationship between the Securities and Exchange Commission and the Financial Accounting Standards Board with respect to the development and establishment of financial accounting theory and practices.

(CMA adapted)

CA1-17 (Rule-Making Process) In 1973, the responsibility for developing and issuing rules on accounting practices was given to the Financial Accounting Foundation and, in particular, to an arm of the foundation called the Financial Accounting Standards Board (FASB). The generally accepted accounting principles established by the FASB are enunciated through a publication series entitled *Statements of Financial Accounting Standards*. These statements are issued periodically, and over 160 have been issued. The statements have a significant influence on the way in which financial statements are prepared by U.S. corporations.

Instructions

(a) Describe the process by which a topic is selected or identified as appropriate for study by the Financial Accounting Standards Board (FASB).
(b) Once a topic is considered appropriate for consideration by the FASB, a series of steps is followed before a *Statement of Financial Accounting Standards* is issued. Describe the major steps in the process leading to the issuance of a standard.
(c) Identify at least three other organizations that influence the setting of generally accepted accounting principles (GAAP).

(CMA adapted)

CA1-18 (Financial Reporting Pressures) Presented below is abbreviated testimony from Troy Normand in the **WorldCom** case. He was a manager in the corporate reporting department and is one of five individuals who pleaded guilty. He is testifying in hopes of receiving no prison time when he is ultimately sentenced.

Q. Mr. Normand, if you could just describe for the jury how the meeting started and what was said during the meeting?

A. I can't recall exactly who initiated the discussion, but right away Scott Sullivan acknowledged that he was aware we had problems with the entries, David Myers had informed him, and we were considering resigning.

He said that he respected our concerns but that we weren't being asked to do anything that he believed was wrong. He mentioned that he acknowledged that the company had lost focus quite a bit due to the preparations for the Sprint merger, and that he was putting plans in place and projects in place to try to determine where the problems were, why the costs were so high.

He did say he believed that the initial statements that we produced, that the line costs in those statements could not have been as high as they were, that he believed something was wrong and there was no way that the costs were that high.

I informed him that I didn't believe the entry we were being asked to do was right, that I was scared, and I didn't want to put myself in a position of going to jail for him or the company. He responded that he didn't believe anything was wrong, nobody was going to be going to jail, but that if it later was found to be wrong, that he would be the person going to jail, not me.

He asked that I stay, don't jump off the plane, let him land it softly, that's basically how he put it. And he mentioned that he had a discussion with Bernie Ebbers, asking Bernie to reduce projections going forward and that Bernie had refused.

Q. Mr. Normand, you said that Mr. Sullivan said something about don't jump out of the plane. What did you understand him to mean when he said that?

A. Not to quit.

Q. During this meeting, did Mr. Sullivan say anything about whether you would be asked to make entries like this in the future?

A. Yes, he made a comment that from that point going forward we wouldn't be asked to record any entries, high-level late adjustments, that the numbers would be the numbers.

Q. What did you understand that to be mean, the numbers would be the numbers?

A. That after the preliminary statements were issued, with the exception of any normal transaction, valid transaction, we wouldn't be asked to be recording any more late entries.

Q. I believe you testified that Mr. Sullivan said something about the line cost numbers not being accurate. Did he ask you to conduct any analysis to determine whether the line cost numbers were accurate?

A. No, he did not.

Q. Did anyone ever ask you to do that?

A. No.

Q. Did you ever conduct any such analysis?

A. No, I didn't.

Q. During this meeting, did Mr. Sullivan ever provide any accounting justification for the entry you were asked to make?

A. No, he did not.

Q. Did anything else happen during the meeting?

A. I don't recall anything else.

Q. How did you feel after this meeting?

A. Not much better actually. I left his office not convinced in any way that what we were asked to do was right. However, I did question myself to some degree after talking with him wondering whether I was making something more out of what was really there.

Instructions

Answer the following questions.

(a) What appears to be the ethical issue involved in this case?
(b) Is Troy Normand acting improperly or immorally?
(c) What would you do if you were Troy Normand?
(d) Who are the major stakeholders in this case?

CA1-19 (Economic Consequences) Presented below are comments made in the financial press.

Instructions

Prepare responses to the requirements in each item.

(a) Rep. John Dingell, the ranking Democrat on the House Commerce Committee, threw his support behind the FASB's controversial derivatives accounting standard and encouraged the FASB to adopt the rule promptly. Indicate why a member of Congress might feel obligated to comment on this proposed FASB standard.

(b) In a strongly worded letter to Senator Lauch Faircloth (R-NC) and House Banking Committee Chairman Jim Leach (R-IA), the American Institute of Certified Public Accountants (AICPA) cautioned against government intervention in the accounting standard-setting process, warning that it had the potential of jeopardizing U.S. capital markets. Explain how government intervention could possibly affect capital markets adversely.

CA1-20 (GAAP and Economic Consequences) The following letter was sent to the SEC and the FASB by leaders of the business community.

Dear Sirs:

The FASB has been struggling with accounting for derivatives and hedging for many years. The FASB has now developed, over the last few weeks, a new approach that it proposes to adopt as a final standard. We understand that the Board intends to adopt this new approach as a final standard without exposing it for public comment and debate, despite the evident complexity of the new approach, the speed with which it has been developed and the significant changes to the exposure draft since it was released more than one year ago. Instead, the Board plans to allow only a brief review by selected parties, limited to issues of operationality and clarity, and would exclude questions as to the merits of the proposed approach.

As the FASB itself has said throughout this process, its mission does not permit it to consider matters that go beyond accounting and reporting considerations. Accordingly, the FASB may not have adequately considered the wide range of concerns that have been expressed about the derivatives and hedging proposal, including concerns related to the potential impact on the capital markets, the weakening of companies' ability to manage risk, and the adverse control implications of implementing costly and complex new rules imposed at the same time as other major initiatives, including the Year 2000 issues and a single European currency. We believe that these crucial issues must be considered, if not by the FASB, then by the Securities and Exchange Commission, other regulatory agencies, or Congress.

We believe it is essential that the FASB solicit all comments in order to identify and address all material issues that may exist before issuing a final standard. We understand the desire to bring this process to a prompt conclusion, but the underlying issues are so important to this nation's businesses, the customers they serve and the economy as a whole that expediency cannot be the dominant consideration. As a result, we urge the FASB to expose its new proposal for public comment, following the established due process procedures that are essential to acceptance of its standards, and providing sufficient time to affected parties to understand and assess the new approach.

We also urge the SEC to study the comments received in order to assess the impact that these proposed rules may have on the capital markets, on companies' risk management practices, and on management and financial controls. These vital public policy matters deserve consideration as part of the Commission's oversight responsibilities.

We believe that these steps are essential if the FASB is to produce the best possible accounting standard while minimizing adverse economic effects and maintaining the competitiveness of U.S. businesses in the international marketplace.

Very truly yours,

(This letter was signed by the chairs of 22 of the largest U.S. companies.)

Instructions

Answer the following questions.

(a) Explain the "due process" procedures followed by the FASB in developing a financial reporting standard.

(b) What is meant by the term "economic consequences" in accounting standard-setting?

(c) What economic consequences arguments are used in this letter?

(d) What do you believe is the main point of the letter?

(e) Why do you believe a copy of this letter was sent by the business community to influential members of the U.S. Congress?

USING YOUR JUDGMENT

FINANCIAL REPORTING

Financial Reporting Problem

Beverly Crusher, a new staff accountant, is confused because of the complexities involving accounting standard-setting. Specifically, she is confused by the number of bodies issuing financial reporting standards of one kind or another and the level of authoritative support that can be attached to these reporting standards. Beverly decides that she must review the environment in which accounting standards are set, if she is to increase her understanding of the accounting profession.

Beverly recalls that during her accounting education there was a chapter or two regarding the environment of financial accounting and the development of GAAP. However, she remembers that her instructor placed little emphasis on these chapters.

Instructions

(a) Help Beverly by identifying key organizations involved in accounting rule-making.

(b) Beverly asks for guidance regarding authoritative support. Please assist her by explaining what is meant by authoritative support.

(c) Give Beverly a historical overview of how rule-making has evolved so that she will not feel that she is the only one to be confused.

(d) What authority for compliance with GAAP has existed throughout the history of rule-making?

BRIDGE TO THE PROFESSION

Professional Research

As a newly enrolled accounting major, you are anxious to better understand accounting institutions and sources of accounting literature. As a first step, you decide to explore the FASB Conceptual Framework.

Instructions

If your school has a subscription to the FASB Codification, go to *http://aaahq.org/asclogin.cfm* to log in and access the FASB conceptual framework. When you have accessed the documents, you can use the search tool in your Internet browser to respond to the following items. (Provide paragraph citations.)

(a) What is the objective of financial reporting?

(b) What other means are there of communicating information, besides financial statements?

(c) Indicate some of the users and the information they are most directly concerned with in economic decision-making.

Professional Simulation

In this simulation, you are asked questions regarding accounting principles. Prepare responses to all parts.

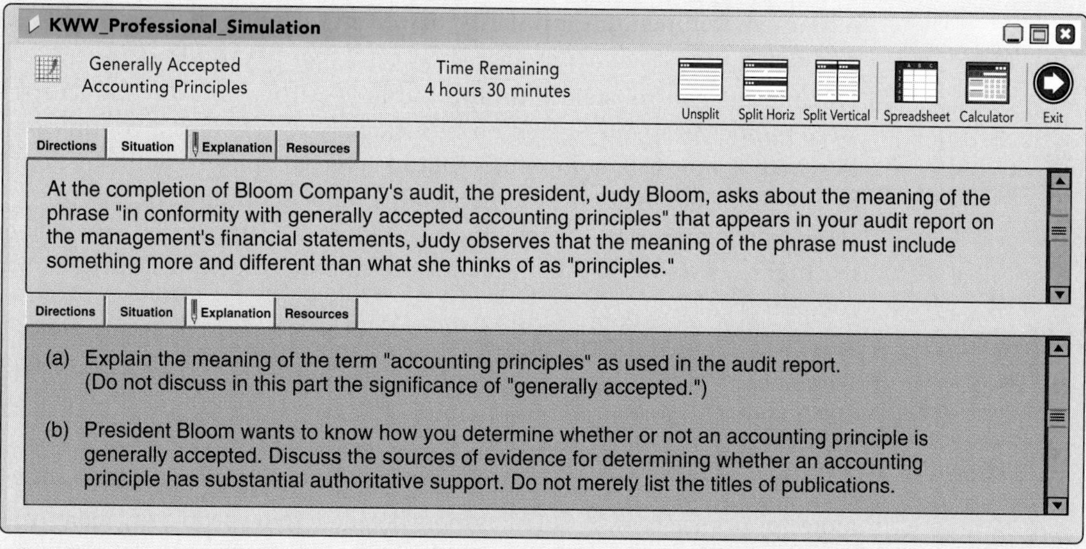

IFRS Insights

Most agree that there is a need for one set of international accounting standards. Here is why:

Multinational corporations. Today's companies view the entire world as their market. For example, Coca-Cola, Intel, and McDonald's generate more than 50 percent of their sales outside the United States, and many foreign companies, such as Toyota, Nestlé, and Sony, find their largest market to be the United States.

Mergers and acquisitions. The mergers between Fiat/Chrysler and Vodafone/Mannesmann suggest that we will see even more such business combinations in the future.

Information technology. As communication barriers continue to topple through advances in technology, companies and individuals in different countries and markets are becoming more comfortable buying and selling goods and services from one another.

Financial markets. Financial markets are of international significance today. Whether it is currency, equity securities (stocks), bonds, or derivatives, there are active markets throughout the world trading these types of instruments.

RELEVANT FACTS

- International standards are referred to as *International Financial Reporting Standards (IFRS)*, developed by the International Accounting Standards Board (IASB). Recent events in the global capital markets have underscored the importance of financial disclosure and transparency not only in the United States but in markets around the world. As a result, many are examining which accounting and financial disclosure rules should be followed.
- U.S standards, referred to as generally accepted accounting principles (GAAP), are developed by the Financial Accounting Standards Board (FASB). The fact that there are differences between what is in this textbook (which is based on U.S. standards) and IFRS should not be surprising because the FASB and IASB have responded to different user needs. In some countries, the primary users of financial statements are private investors; in others, the primary users are tax authorities or central government planners. It appears that the United States and the international standard-setting environment are primarily driven by meeting the needs of investors and creditors.
- The internal control standards applicable to Sarbanes-Oxley (SOX) apply only to large public companies listed on U.S. exchanges. There is a continuing debate as to whether non-U.S. companies should have to comply with this extra layer of regulation. Debate about international companies (non-U.S.) adopting SOX-type standards centers on whether the benefits exceed the costs. The concern is that the higher costs of SOX compliance are making the U.S. securities markets less competitive.
- The textbook mentions a number of ethics violations, such as **WorldCom**, **AIG**, and **Lehman Brothers**. These problems have also occurred internationally, for example, at **Satyam Computer Services** (India), **Parmalat** (Italy), and **Royal Ahold** (the Netherlands).
- IFRS tends to be simpler in its accounting and disclosure requirements; some people say more "principles-based." GAAP is more detailed; some people say more "rules-based." This difference in approach has resulted in a debate about the merits of "principles-based" versus "rules-based" standards.

- The SEC allows foreign companies that trade shares in U.S. markets to file their IFRS financial statements without reconciliation to GAAP.

ABOUT THE NUMBERS

World markets are becoming increasingly intertwined. International consumers drive Japanese cars, wear Italian shoes and Scottish woolens, drink Brazilian coffee and Indian tea, eat Swiss chocolate bars, sit on Danish furniture, watch U.S. movies, and use Arabian oil. The tremendous variety and volume of both exported and imported goods indicates the extensive involvement in international trade—for many companies, the world is their market. To provide some indication of the extent of globalization of economic activity, Illustration IFRS1-1 provides a listing of the top 20 global companies in terms of sales.

ILLUSTRATION IFRS1-1
Global Companies

Rank ($ millions)	Company	Country	Revenues	Rank ($ millions)	Company	Country	Revenues
1	**Wal-Mart Stores**	U.S.	378,799.0	11	**Daimler**	Germany	177,167.1
2	**ExxonMobil**	U.S.	372,824.0	12	**General Electric**	U.S.	176,656.0
3	**Royal Dutch Shell**	Netherlands	355,782.0	13	**Ford Motor**	U.S.	172,468.0
4	**BP**	U.K.	291,438.0	14	**Fortis**	Belgium/Netherlands	164,877.0
5	**Toyota Motor**	Japan	230,200.8	15	**AXA**	France	162,762.3
6	**Chevron**	U.S.	210,783.0	16	**Sinopec**	China	159,259.6
7	**ING Group**	Netherlands	201,516.0	17	**Citigroup**	U.S.	159,229.0
8	**Total**	France	187,279.5	18	**Volkswagen**	Germany	149,054.1
9	**General Motors**	U.S.	182,347.0	19	**Dexia Group**	Belgium	147,648.4
10	**ConocoPhillips**	U.S.	178,558.0	20	**HSBC Holdings**	U.K.	146,500.0

Source: http://money.cnn.com/magazines/fortune/global500/2008/.

As capital markets are increasingly integrated, companies have greater flexibility in deciding where to raise capital. In the absence of market integration, there can be company-specific factors that make it cheaper to raise capital and list/trade securities in one location versus another. With the integration of capital markets, the automatic linkage between the location of the company and location of the capital market is loosening. As a result, companies have expanded choices of where to raise capital, either equity or debt. The move toward adoption of International Financial Reporting Standards has and will continue to facilitate this movement.

International Standard-Setting Organizations

For many years, many nations have relied on their own standard-setting organizations. For example, Canada has the Accounting Standards Board, Japan has the Accounting Standards Board of Japan, Germany has the German Accounting Standards Committee, and the United States has the Financial Accounting Standards Board (FASB). The standards issued by these organizations are sometimes principles-based, rules-based, tax-oriented, or business-based. In other words, they often differ in concept and objective. Starting in 2000, two major standard-setting bodies have emerged as the primary standard-setting bodies in the world. One organization is based in London, United Kingdom, and is called the **International Accounting Standards Board (IASB)**. The IASB issues **International Financial Reporting Standards (IFRS)**, which are used on most foreign exchanges. These standards may also be used by foreign companies listing on U.S. securities exchanges. As indicated earlier, IFRS is presently used in over 115 countries and is rapidly gaining acceptance in other countries as well.

It is generally believed that IFRS has the best potential to provide a common platform on which companies can report and investors can compare financial information. As a result, our discussion focuses on IFRS and the organization involved in developing these standards—the International Accounting Standards Board (IASB). (A detailed discussion of the U.S. system is provided in the chapter.) The two organizations that have a role in international standard-setting are the **International Organization of Securities Commissions (IOSCO)** and the IASB.

International Organization of Securities Commissions (IOSCO)

The International Organization of Securities Commissions (IOSCO) does not set accounting standards. Instead, this organization is dedicated to ensuring that the global markets can operate in an efficient and effective basis. The member agencies (such as from France, Germany, New Zealand, and the U.S. SEC) have resolved to:

- Cooperate to promote high standards of regulation in order to maintain just, efficient, and sound markets.
- Exchange information on their respective experiences in order to promote the development of domestic markets.
- Unite their efforts to establish standards and an effective surveillance of international securities transactions.
- Provide mutual assistance to promote the integrity of the markets by a rigorous application of the standards and by effective enforcement against offenses.

A landmark year for IOSCO was 2005 when it endorsed the IOSCO Memorandum of Understanding (MOU) to facilitate cross-border cooperation, reduce global systemic risk, protect investors, and ensure fair and efficient securities markets. (For more information, go to *http://www.iosco.org/*.)

International Accounting Standards Board (IASB)

The standard-setting structure internationally is composed of four organizations—the International Accounting Standards Committee Foundation, the International Accounting Standards Board (IASB), a Standards Advisory Council, and an International Financial Reporting Interpretations Committee (IFRIC). The trustees of the **International Accounting Standards Committee Foundation (IASCF)** select the members of the IASB and the Standards Advisory Council, fund their activities, and generally oversee the IASB's activities. The IASB is the major operating unit in this four-part structure. Its mission is to develop, in the public interest, a single set of high-quality and understandable IFRS for general-purpose financial statements.

In addition to research help from its own staff, the IASB relies on the expertise of various task force groups formed for various projects and on the **Standards Advisory Council (SAC)**. The SAC consults with the IASB on major policy and technical issues and also helps select task force members. IFRIC develops implementation guidance for consideration by the IASB. Illustration IFRS1-2 shows the current organizational structure for the setting of international standards.

As indicated, the standard-setting structure internationally is very similar to the standard-setting structure in the United States (see Illustration 1-2 on page 11). One notable difference is the size of the Board—the IASB has 14 members, while the FASB has just seven members. The larger IASB reflects the need for broader geographic representation in the international setting.

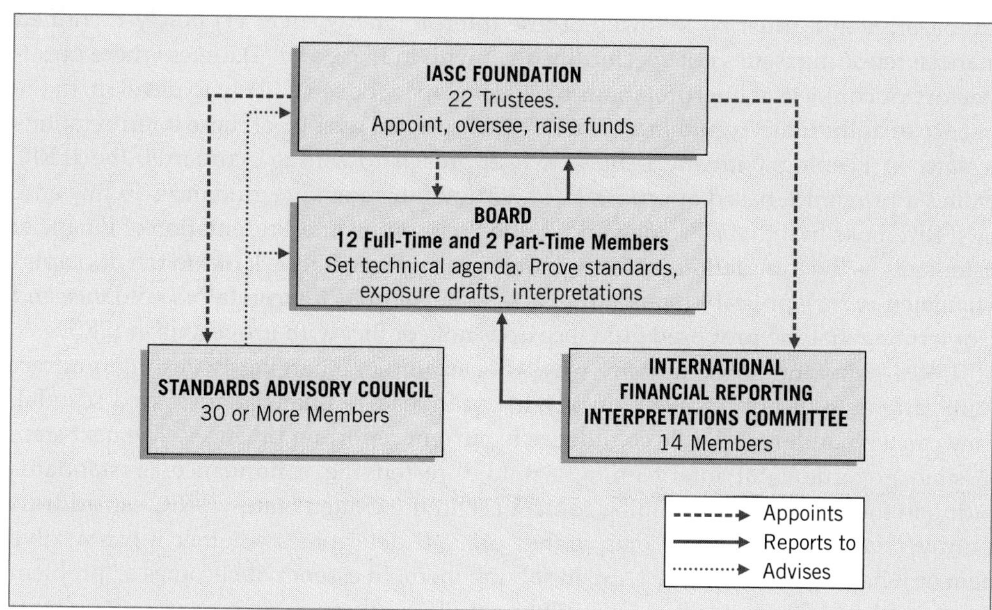

ILLUSTRATION IFRS1-2
International Standard-Setting Structure

Types of Pronouncements

The IASB issues three major types of pronouncements:

1. International Financial Reporting Standards.
2. Framework for financial reporting.
3. International financial reporting interpretations.

International Financial Reporting Standards. Financial accounting standards issued by the IASB are referred to as International Financial Reporting Standards (IFRS). The IASB has issued nine of these standards to date, covering such subjects as business combinations and share-based payments. Prior to the IASB (formed in 2001), standard-setting on the international level was done by the International Accounting Standards Committee, which issued International Accounting Standards (IAS). The committee issued 40 IASs, many of which have been amended or superseded by the IASB. Those still remaining are considered under the umbrella of IFRS.

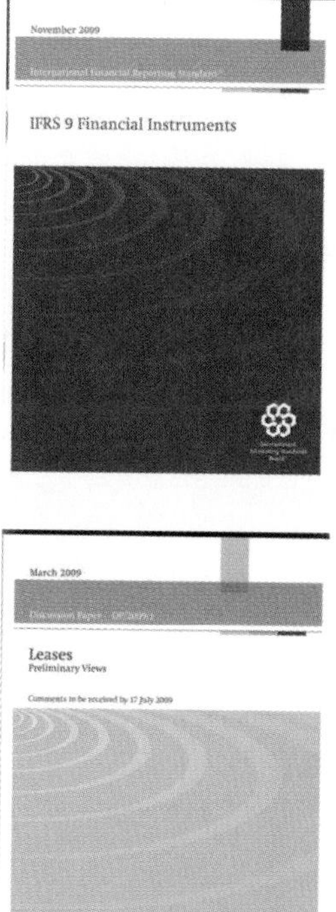

Framework for Financial Reporting. As part of a long-range effort to move away from the problem-by-problem approach, the International Accounting Standards Committee (predecessor to the IASB) issued a document entitled "Framework for the Preparation and Presentation of Financial Statements" (also referred to simply as the Framework). This Framework sets forth fundamental objectives and concepts that the Board uses in developing future standards of financial reporting. The intent of the document is to form a cohesive set of interrelated concepts—a conceptual framework—that will serve as tools for solving existing and emerging problems in a consistent manner. For example, the objective of general-purpose financial reporting discussed earlier is part of this Framework. The Framework and any changes to it pass through the same due process (discussion paper, public hearing, exposure draft, etc.) as an IFRS. However, this Framework is not an IFRS and hence does not define standards for any particular measurement or disclosure issue. Nothing in this Framework overrides any specific international accounting standard.

International Financial Reporting Interpretations. Interpretations issued by the **International Financial Reporting Interpretations Committee (IFRIC)** are also considered

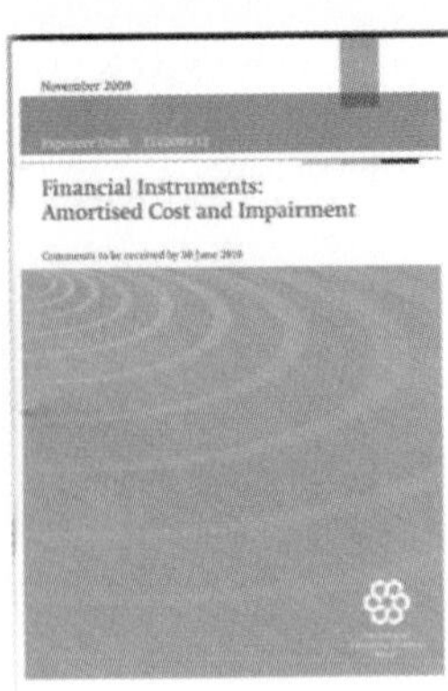

authoritative and must be followed. These interpretations cover (1) newly identified financial reporting issues not specifically dealt with in IFRS, and (2) issues where unsatisfactory or conflicting interpretations have developed, or seem likely to develop, in the absence of authoritative guidance. The IFRIC has issued over 15 of these interpretations to date. In keeping with the IASB's own approach to setting standards, the IFRIC applies a principles-based approach in providing interpretative guidance. To this end, the IFRIC looks first to the Framework for the Preparation and Presentation of Financial Statements as the foundation for formulating a consensus. It then looks to the principles articulated in the applicable standard, if any, to develop its interpretative guidance and to determine that the proposed guidance does not conflict with provisions in IFRS.

IFRIC helps the IASB in many ways. For example, emerging issues often attract public attention. If not resolved quickly, they can lead to financial crises and scandal. They can also undercut public confidence in current reporting practices. The next step, possible governmental intervention, would threaten the continuance of standard-setting in the private sector. Similar to the EITF in the United States, IFRIC can address controversial accounting problems as they arise. It determines whether it can resolve them or whether to involve the IASB in solving them. In essence, it becomes a "problem filter" for the IASB. Thus, the IASB will hopefully work on more pervasive long-term problems, while the IFRIC deals with short-term emerging issues.

Hierarchy of IFRS

Because it is a private organization, the IASB has no regulatory mandate and therefore no enforcement mechanism. Similar to the U.S. setting, in which the Securities and Exchange Commission enforces the use of FASB standards for public companies, the IASB relies on other regulators to enforce the use of its standards. For example, effective January 1, 2005, the European Union required publicly traded member country companies to use IFRS.[12]

Any company indicating that it is preparing its financial statements in conformity with IFRS must use all of the standards and interpretations. The following **hierarchy** is used to determine what recognition, valuation, and disclosure requirements should be used. Companies first look to:

1. International Financial Reporting Standards;
2. International Accounting Standards; and
3. Interpretations originated by the International Financial Reporting Interpretations Committee (IFRIC) or the former Standing Interpretations Committee (SIC).

In the absence of a standard or an interpretation, the following sources in descending order are used: (1) the requirements and guidance in standards and interpretations dealing with similar and related issues; (2) the Framework for financial reporting; and (3) most recent pronouncements of other standard-setting bodies that use a similar conceptual framework to develop accounting standards, other accounting literature, and accepted industry practices, to the extent they do not conflict with the above. The overriding requirement of IFRS is that the financial statements provide a fair presentation (often referred to as a "true and fair view"). Fair representation is assumed to occur if a company follows the guidelines established in IFRS.

[12]Certain changes have been implemented with respect to use of IFRS in the United States. For example, under American Institute of Certified Public Accountants (AICPA) rules, a member of the AICPA can only report on financial statements prepared in accordance with standards promulgated by standard-setting bodies designated by the AICPA Council. In May 2008, the AICPA Council voted to designate the IASB in London as an international accounting standard-setter for purposes of establishing international financial accounting and reporting principles, and to make related amendments to its rules to provide AICPA members with the option to use IFRS.

International Accounting Convergence

The SEC recognizes that the establishment of a single, widely accepted set of high-quality accounting standards benefits both global capital markets and U.S. investors. U.S. investors will make better-informed investment decisions if they obtain high-quality financial information from U.S. companies that are more comparable to the presently available information from non-U.S. companies operating in the same industry or line of business. Thus, the SEC appears committed to move to IFRS, assuming that certain conditions are met. These conditions are spelled out in a document, referred to as the "**Roadmap**" and in a policy statement issued by the SEC in early 2010.[13]

A timeline for potential adoption of IFRS in the United States is shown in Illustration IFRS1-3. As indicated, the SEC has established a very deliberate process, beginning with use of IFRS by foreign companies in U.S. markets, while considering the merits of requiring use of IFRS by U.S. companies.

ILLUSTRATION IFRS1-3
SEC Roadmap

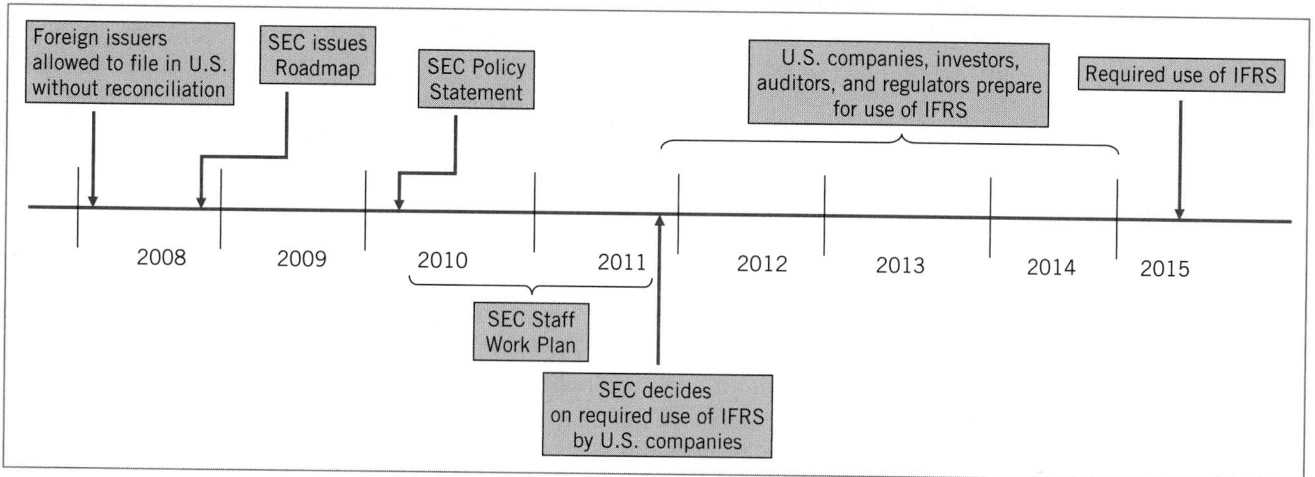

To move to IFRS, the SEC indicates that the international standards must be of high quality and sufficiently comprehensive. To achieve this goal, the IASB and the FASB have set up an extensive work plan to achieve the objective of developing one set of world-class international standards. This work plan actually started in 2002, when an agreement was forged between the two Boards, where each acknowledged their commitment to the development of high-quality, compatible accounting standards that could be used for both domestic and cross-border financial reporting (referred to as the Norwalk Agreement).[14]

At that meeting, the FASB and the IASB pledged to use their best efforts to (1) make their existing financial reporting standards fully compatible as soon as is practicable, and (2) coordinate their future work programs to ensure that once achieved, compatibility is maintained. This document was reinforced in 2006 when the parties issued a memorandum of understanding (MOU) which highlighted three principles:

- Convergence of accounting standards can best be achieved through the development of high-quality common standards over time.

[13]"Roadmap for the Potential Use of Financial Statements Prepared in Accordance with International Financial Reporting Standards by U.S. Issuers," *SEC Release No. 33-8982* (November 14, 2008), and "Statement in Support of Convergence and Global Accounting Standards," *SEC Release Nos. 33-9109; 34-61578* (February 24, 2010).

[14]See *http://www.fasb.org/news/memorandum.pdf.*

- Trying to eliminate differences between two standards that are in need of significant improvement is not the best use of the FASB's and the IASB's resources—instead, a new common standard should be developed that improves the financial information reported to investors.
- Serving the needs of investors means that the Boards should seek convergence by replacing standards in need of improvement with jointly developed new standards.

Subsequently, in 2009 the Boards agreed on a process to complete a number of major projects by 2011, including monthly joint meetings. As part of achieving this goal, it is critical that the process by which the standards are established be independent. And, it is necessary that the standards are maintained, and emerging accounting issues are dealt with efficiently.

The SEC has directed its staff to develop and execute a plan ("Work Plan") to enhance both the understanding of the SEC's purpose and public transparency in this area. Execution of the Work Plan (which addresses such areas as independence of standard-setting, investor understanding of IFRS, and auditor readiness), combined with the completion of the convergence projects of the FASB and the IASB according to their current work plan, will position the SEC to make a decision on required use of IFRS by U.S. issuers. After reviewing the progress related to the Work Plan studies, the SEC will decide, sometime in 2011, whether to mandate the use of IFRS. It is likely that not all companies would be required immediately to change to IFRS, but there would be a transition period in which this would be accomplished.

ON THE HORIZON

The international standard-setting environment shares many common features with U.S. standard-setting. Financial statements prepared according to IFRS have become an important standard around the world for communicating financial information to investors and creditors. The SEC and the FASB are working with their international counterparts to achieve the goal of a single set of high-quality financial reporting standards for use around the world. While there are still many bumps in the road to the establishment of one set of worldwide standards, we are optimistic that this goal can be achieved, which will be of value to all.

IFRS SELF-TEST QUESTIONS

1. IFRS stands for:
   (a) International Federation of Reporting Services.
   (b) Independent Financial Reporting Standards.
   (c) International Financial Reporting Standards.
   (d) Integrated Financial Reporting Services.

2. The major key players on the international side are the:
   (a) IASB and FASB.
   (b) IOSCO and the SEC.
   (c) SEC and FASB.
   (d) IASB and IOSCO.

3. IFRS is comprised of:
   (a) International Financial Reporting Standards and FASB financial reporting standards.
   (b) International Financial Reporting Standards, International Accounting Standards, and international accounting interpretations.
   (c) International Accounting Standards and international accounting interpretations.
   (d) FASB financial reporting standards and International Accounting Standards.

4. The authoritative status of the Framework for the Preparation and Presentation of Financial Statements is as follows:
   (a) It is used when there is no standard or interpretation related to the reporting issues under consideration.
   (b) It is not as authoritative as a standard but takes precedence over any interpretation related to the reporting issue.
   (c) It takes precedence over all other authoritative literature.
   (d) It has no authoritative status.
5. Which of the following statements is *true*?
   (a) The IASB has the same number of members as the FASB.
   (b) The IASB structure has both advisory and interpretation functions, but no trustees.
   (c) The IASB has been in existence longer than the FASB.
   (d) The IASB structure is quite similar to the FASB's, except the IASB has a larger number of board members.

IFRS CONCEPTS AND APPLICATION

IFRS1-1 Who are the two key international players in the development of international accounting standards? Explain their role.

IFRS1-2 What might explain the fact that different accounting standard-setters have developed accounting standards that are sometimes quite different in nature?

IFRS1-3 What is the benefit of a single set of high-quality accounting standards?

IFRS1-4 Briefly describe FASB/IASB convergence process and the principles that guide their convergence efforts.

Financial Reporting Case

IFRS1-5 The following comments were made at an Annual Conference of the Financial Executives Institute (FEI).

There is an irreversible movement towards the harmonization of financial reporting throughout the world. The international capital markets require an end to:

1. The confusion caused by international companies announcing different results depending on the set of accounting standards applied.
2. Companies in some countries obtaining unfair commercial advantages from the use of particular national accounting standards.
3. The complications in negotiating commercial arrangements for international joint ventures caused by different accounting requirements.
4. The inefficiency of international companies having to understand and use a myriad of different accounting standards depending on the countries in which they operate and the countries in which they raise capital and debt. Executive talent is wasted on keeping up to date with numerous sets of accounting standards and the never-ending changes to them.
5. The inefficiency of investment managers, bankers, and financial analysts as they seek to compare financial reporting drawn up in accordance with different sets of accounting standards.

Instructions

(a) What is the International Accounting Standards Board?
(b) What stakeholders might benefit from the use of International Accounting Standards?
(c) What do you believe are some of the major obstacles to convergence?

Professional Research

IFRS1-6 As a newly enrolled accounting major, you are anxious to better understand accounting institutions and sources of accounting literature. As a first step, you decide to explore the IASB's Framework for the Preparation and Presentation of Financial Statements.

Instructions

Access the IASB Framework at the IASB website (*http://eifrs.iasb.org/*). When you have accessed the documents, you can use the search tool in your Internet browser to respond to the following items. (Provide paragraph citations.)

(a) What is the objective of financial reporting?

(b) What other means are there of communicating information, besides financial statements?

(c) Indicate some of the users and the information they are most directly concerned with in economic decision-making.

International Financial Reporting Problem: *Marks and Spencer plc*

IFRS1-7 The financial statements of **Marks and Spencer plc (M&S)** are available at the book's companion website or can be accessed at *http://corporate.marksandspencer.com/documents/ publications/2010/Annual_Report_2010.*

Instructions

Refer to M&S's financial statements and the accompanying notes to answer the following questions.

(a) What is the company's main line of business?

(b) In what countries does the company operate?

(c) What is the address of the company's corporate headquarters?

(d) What is the company's reporting currency?

ANSWERS TO IFRS SELF-TEST QUESTIONS

1. c **2.** d **3.** b **4.** a **5.** d

Remember to check the book's companion website to find additional resources for this chapter.

CHAPTER 2

Conceptual Framework for Financial Reporting

LEARNING OBJECTIVES

After studying this chapter, you should be able to:

1. Describe the usefulness of a conceptual framework.
2. Describe the FASB's efforts to construct a conceptual framework.
3. Understand the objective of financial reporting.
4. Identify the qualitative characteristics of accounting information.
5. Define the basic elements of financial statements.
6. Describe the basic assumptions of accounting.
7. Explain the application of the basic principles of accounting.
8. Describe the impact that constraints have on reporting accounting information.

What Is It?

Everyone agrees that accounting needs a framework—a conceptual framework, so to speak—that will help guide the development of standards. To understand the importance of developing this framework, let's see how you would respond in the following two situations.

Situation 1: "Taking a Long Shot . . ."

To supplement donations collected from its general community solicitation, Tri-Cities United Charities holds an Annual Lottery Sweepstakes. In this year's sweepstakes, United Charities is offering a grand prize of $1,000,000 to a single winning ticket holder. A total of 10,000 tickets have been printed, and United Charities plans to sell all the tickets at a price of $150 each.

Since its inception, the Sweepstakes has attracted area-wide interest, and United Charities has always been able to meet its sales target. However, in the unlikely event that it might fail to sell a sufficient number of tickets to cover the grand prize, United Charities has reserved the right to cancel the Sweepstakes and to refund the price of the tickets to holders.

In recent years, a fairly active secondary market for tickets has developed. This year, buying–selling prices have varied between $75 and $95 before stabilizing at about $90.

When the tickets first went on sale this year, multimillionaire Phil N. Tropic, well-known in Tri-Cities civic circles as a generous but sometimes eccentric donor, bought one of the tickets from United Charities, paying $150 cash.

How would you answer the following questions?

1. Should Phil N. Tropic recognize his lottery ticket as an asset in his financial statements?
2. Assuming that Phil N. Tropic recognizes the lottery ticket as an asset, at what amount should it be reported? Some possible answers are $150, $100, and $90.

IFRS IN THIS CHAPTER

See the **International Perspectives** on pages 45, 56, and 57.

Read the **IFRS Insights** on pages 81–85 for a discussion of:

- Financial statement elements
- Conceptual framework Work Plan

Situation 2: The $20 Million Question

The Hard Rock Mining Company has just completed the first year of operations at its new strip mine, the Lonesome Doe. Hard Rock spent $10 million for the land and $20 million in preparing the site for mining operations. The mine is expected to operate for 20 years. Hard Rock is subject to environmental statutes requiring it to restore the Lonesome Doe mine site on completion of mining operations.

Based on its experience and industry data, as well as current technology, Hard Rock forecasts that restoration will cost about $10 million when it is undertaken. Of those costs, about $4 million is for restoring the topsoil that was removed in preparing the site for mining operations (prior to opening the mine); the rest is directly proportional to the depth of the mine, which in turn is directly proportional to the amount of ore extracted.

How would you answer the following questions?

1. Should Hard Rock recognize a liability for site restoration in conjunction with the opening of the Lonesome Doe Mine? If so, what is the amount of that liability?
2. After Hard Rock has operated the Lonesome Doe Mine for 5 years, new technology is introduced that reduces Hard Rock's estimated future restoration costs to $7 million, $3 million of which relates to restoring the topsoil. How should Hard Rock account for this change in its estimated future liability?

The answer to the questions on the two situations depends on how assets and liabilities are defined and how they should be valued. Hopefully, this chapter will provide you with a framework to resolve questions like these.

Source: Adapted from Todd Johnson and Kim Petrone, *The FASB Cases on Recognition and Measurement*, Second Edition (New York: John Wiley and Sons, Inc., 1996).

PREVIEW OF CHAPTER 2

As our opening story indicates, users of financial statements can face difficult questions about the recognition and measurement of financial items. To help develop the type of financial information that can be used to answer these questions, financial accounting and reporting relies on a conceptual framework. In this chapter, we discuss the basic concepts underlying the conceptual framework as follows.

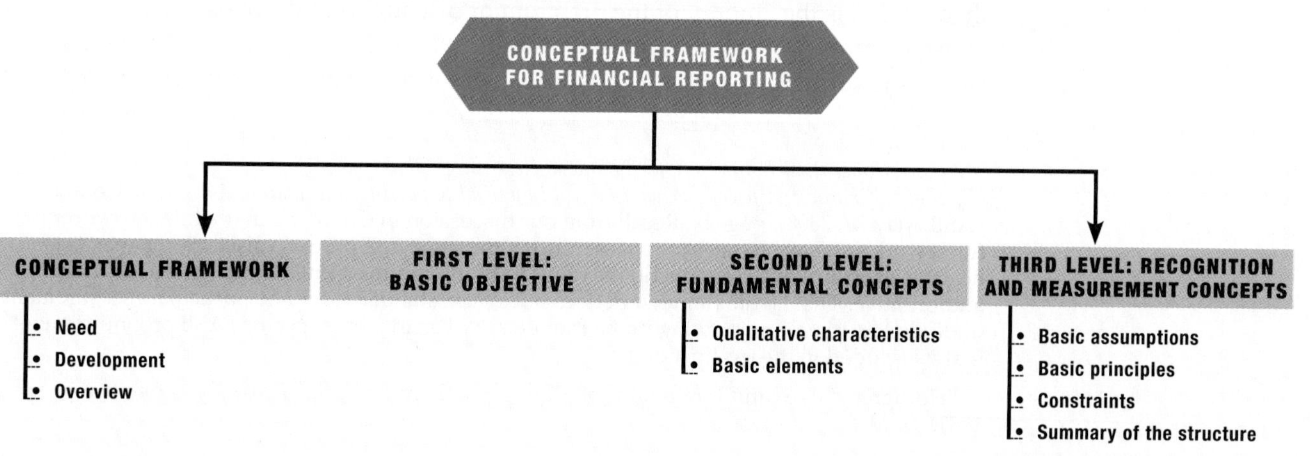

CONCEPTUAL FRAMEWORK

A **conceptual framework** establishes the concepts that underlie financial reporting. A conceptual framework is a coherent system of concepts that flow from an objective. The objective identifies the purpose of financial reporting. The other concepts provide guidance on (1) identifying the boundaries of financial reporting; (2) selecting the transactions, other events, and circumstances to be represented; (3) how they should be recognized and measured; and (4) how they should be summarized and reported.[1]

Need for a Conceptual Framework

LEARNING OBJECTIVE 1
Describe the usefulness of a conceptual framework.

Why do we need a conceptual framework? First, to be useful, rule-making should build on and relate to an established body of concepts. A soundly developed conceptual framework thus enables the FASB to issue **more useful and consistent pronouncements over time; a coherent set of standards should result**. Indeed, without the guidance provided by a soundly developed framework, standard-setting ends up being based on individual concepts developed by each member of the standard-setting body. The following observation by a former standard-setter highlights the problem.

> "As our professional careers unfold, each of us develops a technical conceptual framework. Some individual frameworks are sharply defined and firmly held; others are vague and weakly held; still others are vague and firmly held. . . . At one time or another, most of us have felt the discomfort of listening to somebody buttress a preconceived conclusion by building a convoluted chain of shaky reasoning. Indeed, perhaps on occasion we have voiced such thinking ourselves. . . . My experience . . . taught me many lessons. A major one was that most of us have a natural tendency and an incredible talent for processing new facts in such a way that our prior conclusions remain intact.[2]

In other words, standard-setting that is based on personal conceptual frameworks will lead to different conclusions about identical or similar issues than it did previously. As a result, standards will not be consistent with one another, and past decisions may not be indicative of future ones. Furthermore, the framework should increase financial statement users' understanding of and confidence in financial reporting. It should enhance comparability among companies' financial statements.

Second, as a result of a soundly developed conceptual framework, the profession should be able to more quickly solve new and emerging **practical problems by referring to an existing framework of basic theory**. For example, **Sunshine Mining** sold two issues of bonds. It can redeem them either with $1,000 in cash or with 50 ounces of silver, whichever is worth more at maturity. Both bond issues have a stated interest rate of 8.5 percent. At what amounts should Sunshine or the buyers of the bonds record them? What is the amount of the premium or discount on the bonds? And how should Sunshine amortize this amount, if the bond redemption payments are to be made in silver (the future value of which is unknown at the date of issuance)? Consider that

[1]*Proposed Conceptual Framework for Financial Reporting: Objective of Financial Reporting and Qualitative Characteristics of Decision-Useful Financial Reporting Information* (Norwalk, Conn.: FASB, May 29, 2008), page ix. Recall from our discussion in Chapter 1 that while the conceptual framework and any changes to it pass through the same due process (discussion paper, public hearing, exposure draft, etc.) as do the other FASB pronouncements, the framework is not authoritative. That is, the framework does not define standards for any particular measurement or disclosure issue, and nothing in the framework overrides any specific FASB pronouncement that is included in the Codification.

[2]C. Horngren, "Uses and Limitations of a Conceptual Framework," *Journal of Accountancy* (April 1981), p. 90.

Sunshine cannot know, at the date of issuance, the value of future silver bond redemption payments.

It is difficult, if not impossible, for the FASB to prescribe the proper accounting treatment quickly for situations like this or like those represented in our opening story. Practicing accountants, however, must resolve such problems on a daily basis. How? Through good judgment and with the help of a universally accepted conceptual framework, practitioners can quickly focus on an acceptable treatment.

WHAT'S YOUR PRINCIPLE?

What do the numbers mean?

The need for a conceptual framework is highlighted by accounting scandals such as those at **Enron** and **Lehman Brothers**. To restore public confidence in the financial reporting process, many have argued that regulators should move toward principles-based rules. They believe that companies exploited the detailed provisions in rules-based pronouncements to manage accounting reports, rather than report the economic substance of transactions. For example, many of the off–balance-sheet arrangements of Enron avoided transparent reporting by barely achieving 3 percent outside equity ownership, a requirement in an obscure accounting rule interpretation. Enron's financial engineers were able to structure transactions to achieve a desired accounting treatment, even if that accounting treatment did not reflect the transaction's true nature. Under principles-based rules, hopefully top management's financial reporting focus will shift from demonstrating compliance with rules to demonstrating that a company has attained the objective of financial reporting.

Development of a Conceptual Framework

2 LEARNING OBJECTIVE
Describe the FASB's efforts to construct a conceptual framework.

Over the years, numerous organizations developed and published their own conceptual frameworks, but no single framework was universally accepted and relied on in practice. In 1976, the FASB began to develop a conceptual framework that would be a basis for setting accounting rules and for resolving financial reporting controversies. The FASB has since issued seven Statements of Financial Accounting Concepts that relate to financial reporting for business enterprises.[3] They are as follows.

1. *SFAC No. 1*, "Objectives of Financial Reporting by Business Enterprises," presents the goals and purposes of accounting.
2. *SFAC No. 2*, "Qualitative Characteristics of Accounting Information," examines the characteristics that make accounting information useful.
3. *SFAC No. 3*, "Elements of Financial Statements of Business Enterprises," provides definitions of items in financial statements, such as assets, liabilities, revenues, and expenses.
4. *SFAC No. 5*, "Recognition and Measurement in Financial Statements of Business Enterprises," sets forth fundamental recognition and measurement criteria and guidance on what information should be formally incorporated into financial statements and when.
5. *SFAC No. 6*, "Elements of Financial Statements," replaces *SFAC No. 3* and expands its scope to include not-for-profit organizations.

INTERNATIONAL PERSPECTIVE

The IASB has also issued a conceptual framework. The FASB and the IASB have agreed on a joint project to develop a common and improved conceptual framework. The project is being conducted in phases. Phase A on objectives and qualitative characteristics was issued in 2010.

[3]The FASB also issued a Statement of Financial Accounting Concepts that relates to nonbusiness organizations: "Objectives of Financial Reporting by Nonbusiness Organizations," *Statement of Financial Accounting Concepts No. 4* (December 1980).

6. *SFAC No. 7*, "Using Cash Flow Information and Present Value in Accounting Measurements," provides a framework for using expected future cash flows and present values as a basis for measurement.
7. *SFAC No. 8*, Chapter 1, "The Objective of General Purpose Financial Reporting," and Chapter 3, "Qualitative Characteristics of Useful Financial Information," replaces *SFAC No. 1* and *No. 2*.

Overview of the Conceptual Framework

Illustration 2-1 provides an overview of the FASB's conceptual framework.[4]

ILLUSTRATION 2-1
Framework for Financial Reporting

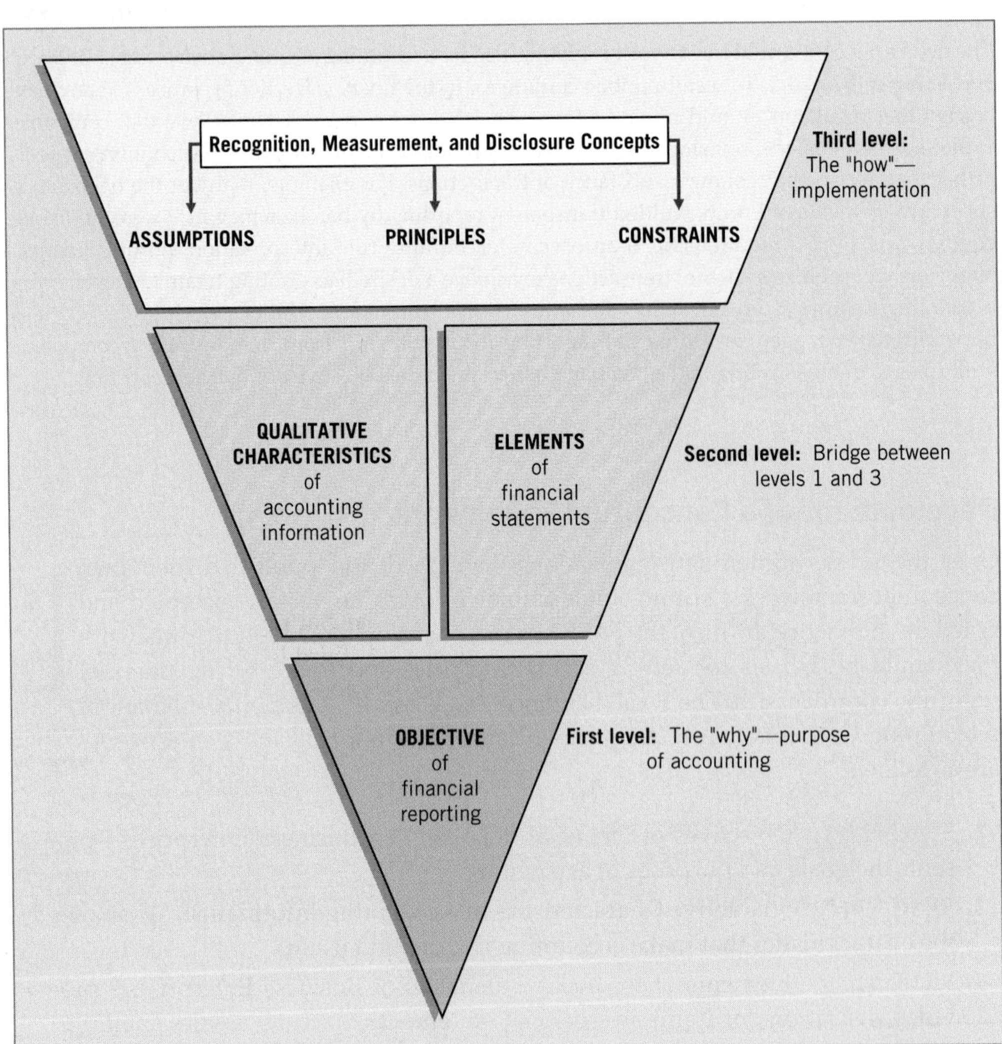

The first level identifies the **objective of financial reporting**—that is, the purpose of financial reporting. The second level provides the **qualitative characteristics** that make accounting information useful and the **elements of financial statements** (assets, liabilities, and so on). The third level identifies the **recognition, measurement, and disclosure** concepts used in establishing and applying accounting standards and the specific concepts to implement the objective. These concepts include assumptions, principles, and constraints that describe the present reporting environment. We examine these three levels of the conceptual framework next.

[4]Adapted from William C. Norby, *The Financial Analysts Journal* (March–April 1982), p. 22.

FIRST LEVEL: BASIC OBJECTIVE

The **objective of financial reporting** is the foundation of the conceptual framework. Other aspects of the framework—qualitative characteristics, elements of financial statements, recognition, measurement, and disclosure—flow logically from the objective. Those aspects of the framework help to ensure that financial reporting achieves its objective.

> **3 LEARNING OBJECTIVE**
> Understand the objective of financial reporting.

The objective of general-purpose financial reporting is to provide financial information about the reporting entity that is **useful to present and potential equity investors, lenders, and other creditors in making decisions about providing resources to the entity**. Those decisions involve buying, selling, or holding equity and debt instruments, and providing or settling loans and other forms of credit. Information that is **decision-useful** to capital providers may also be useful to other users of financial reporting, who are not capital providers.[5]

As indicated in Chapter 1, to provide information to decision-makers, companies prepare general-purpose financial statements. **General-purpose financial reporting** helps users who lack the ability to demand all the financial information they need from an entity and therefore must rely, at least partly, on the information provided in financial reports. However, an implicit assumption is that users need reasonable knowledge of business and financial accounting matters to understand the information contained in financial statements. This point is important. It means that financial statement preparers assume a level of competence on the part of users. This assumption impacts the way and the extent to which companies report information.

SECOND LEVEL: FUNDAMENTAL CONCEPTS

The objective (first level) focuses on the purpose of financial reporting. Later, we will discuss the ways in which this purpose is implemented (third level). What, then, is the purpose of the second level? The second level provides conceptual building blocks that explain the qualitative characteristics of accounting information and define the elements of financial statements.[6] That is, the second level forms a bridge between the **why** of accounting (the objective) and the **how** of accounting (recognition, measurement, and financial statement presentation).

Qualitative Characteristics of Accounting Information

Should companies like **Walt Disney** or **Kellogg's** provide information in their financial statements on how much it costs them to acquire their assets (historical cost basis) or how much the assets are currently worth (fair value basis)? Should **PepsiCo** combine and show as one company the four main segments of its business, or should it report PepsiCo Beverages, Frito Lay, Quaker Foods, and PepsiCo International as four separate segments?

> **4 LEARNING OBJECTIVE**
> Identify the qualitative characteristics of accounting information.

How does a company choose an acceptable accounting method, the amount and types of information to disclose, and the format in which to present it? The answer: By

[5]*Statement of Financial Accounting Concepts No. 8,* "Chapter 1, The Objective of General Purpose Financial Reporting" (Norwalk, Conn.: FASB, September 2010), par. OB2.

[6]*Statement of Financial Accounting Concepts No. 8,* "Chapter 3, Qualitative Characteristics of Useful Financial Information" (Norwalk, Conn.: FASB, September 2010).

determining **which alternative provides the most useful information for decision-making purposes (decision-usefulness)**. The FASB identified the qualitative characteristics of accounting information that distinguish better (more useful) information from inferior (less useful) information for decision-making purposes. In addition, the FASB identified a cost constraint as part of the conceptual framework (discussed later in the chapter). As Illustration 2-2 shows, the characteristics may be viewed as a hierarchy.

ILLUSTRATION 2-2
Hierarchy of Accounting Qualities

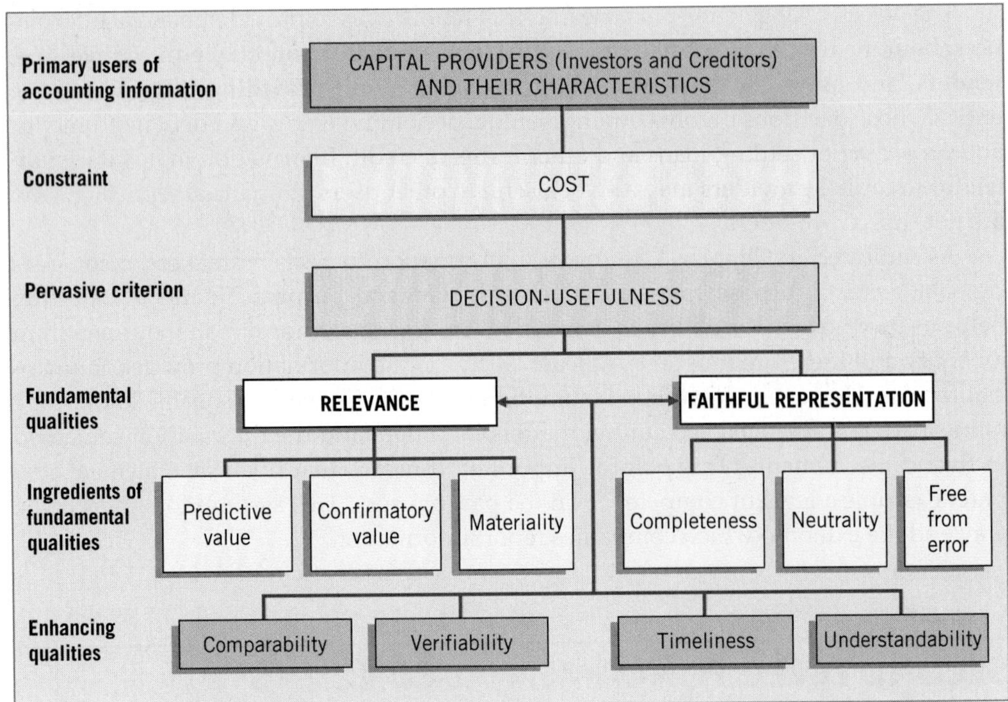

As indicated by Illustration 2-2, qualitative characteristics are either fundamental or enhancing characteristics, depending on how they affect the decision-usefulness of information. Regardless of classification, each qualitative characteristic contributes to the decision-usefulness of financial reporting information. However, providing useful financial information is limited by a pervasive constraint on financial reporting—cost should not exceed the benefits of a reporting practice.

Fundamental Quality—Relevance

Relevance is one of the two fundamental qualities that make accounting information useful for decision-making. Relevance and related ingredients of this fundamental quality are shown below.

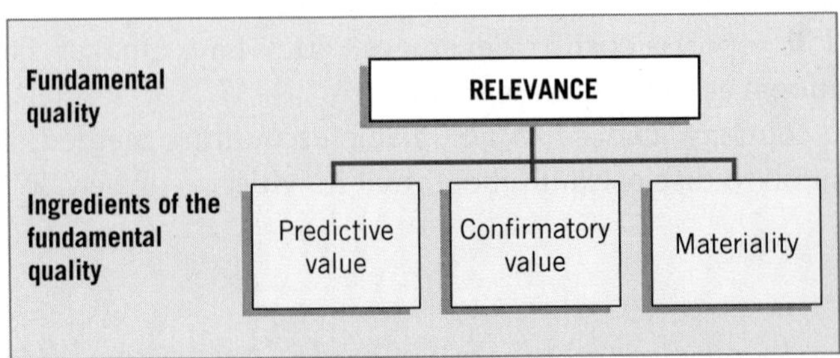

To be relevant, accounting information must be capable of making a difference in a decision. Information with no bearing on a decision is irrelevant. Financial information is capable of making a difference when it has predictive value, confirmatory value, or both.

Financial information has **predictive value** if it has value as an input to predictive processes used by investors to form their own expectations about the future. For example, if potential investors are interested in purchasing common shares in **UPS** (United Parcel Service), they may analyze its current resources and claims to those resources, its dividend payments, and its past income performance to predict the amount, timing, and uncertainty of UPS's future cash flows.

Relevant information also helps users confirm or correct prior expectations; it has **confirmatory value**. For example, when UPS issues its year-end financial statements, it confirms or changes past (or present) expectations based on previous evaluations. It follows that predictive value and confirmatory value are interrelated. For example, information about the current level and structure of UPS's assets and liabilities helps users predict its ability to take advantage of opportunities and to react to adverse situations. The same information helps to confirm or correct users' past predictions about that ability.

Materiality is a company-specific aspect of relevance. Information is material if omitting it or misstating it could influence decisions that users make on the basis of the reported financial information. An individual company determines whether information is material because both the nature and/or magnitude of the item(s) to which the information relates must be considered in the context of an individual company's financial report. Information is *immaterial*, and therefore irrelevant, if it would have no impact on a decision-maker. In short, **it must make a difference** or a company need not disclose it.

Assessing materiality is one of the more challenging aspects of accounting because it requires evaluating both the **relative size and importance** of an item. However, it is difficult to provide firm guidelines in judging when a given item is or is not material. Materiality varies both with relative amount and with relative importance. For example, the two sets of numbers in Illustration 2-3 indicate relative size.

ILLUSTRATION 2-3
Materiality Comparison

	Company A	Company B
Sales	$10,000,000	$100,000
Costs and expenses	9,000,000	90,000
Income from operations	$ 1,000,000	$ 10,000
Unusual gain	$ 20,000	$ 5,000

During the period in question, the revenues and expenses, and therefore the net incomes of Company A and Company B, are proportional. Each reported an unusual gain. In looking at the abbreviated income figures for Company A, it appears insignificant whether the amount of the unusual gain is set out separately or merged with the regular operating income. The gain is only 2 percent of the operating income. If merged, it would not seriously distort the income figure. Company B has had an unusual gain of only $5,000. However, it is relatively much more significant than the larger gain realized by Company A. For Company B, an item of $5,000 amounts to 50 percent of its income from operations. Obviously, the inclusion of such an item in operating income would affect the amount of that income materially. Thus, we see the importance of the **relative size** of an item in determining its materiality.

Companies and their auditors generally adopt the rule of thumb that anything under 5 percent of net income is considered immaterial. However, much can depend on specific rules. For example, one market regulator indicates that a company may use this percentage for an initial assessment of materiality, but it must also consider other factors.[7] For example, companies can no longer fail to record items in order to meet consensus analysts' earnings numbers, preserve a positive earnings trend, convert a loss to a profit or vice versa, increase management compensation, or hide an illegal transaction like a bribe. In other words, **companies must consider both quantitative and qualitative factors in determining whether an item is material.**

Thus, it is generally not feasible to specify uniform quantitative thresholds at which an item becomes material. Rather, materiality judgments should be made in the context of the nature and the amount of an item. Materiality factors into a great many internal accounting decisions, too. Examples of such judgments that companies must make include the amount of classification required in a subsidiary expense ledger, the degree of accuracy required in allocating expenses among the departments of a company, and the extent to which adjustments should be made for accrued and deferred items. Only by **the exercise of good judgment and professional expertise** can reasonable and appropriate answers be found, which is the materiality constraint sensibly applied.

LIVING IN A MATERIAL WORLD

What do the numbers mean?

The first line of defense for many companies caught "cooking the books" had been to argue that a questionable accounting item is immaterial. That defense did not work so well in the wake of accounting meltdowns at Enron and Global Crossing and the tougher rules on materiality issued by the SEC (*SAB 99*).

For example, the SEC alleged in a case against Sunbeam that the company's many immaterial adjustments added up to a material misstatement that misled investors about the company's financial position. More recently, the SEC called for a number of companies, such as Jack in the Box, McDonald's, and AIG, to restate prior financial statements for the effects of incorrect accounting. In some cases, the restatements did not meet traditional materiality thresholds. Don Nicholaisen, then SEC Chief Accountant, observed that whether the amount is material or not-material, some transactions appear to be "flat out intended to mislead investors." In essence he is saying that any wrong accounting for a transaction can represent important information to the users of financial statements.

Responding to new concerns about materiality, blue-chip companies such as IBM and General Electric are providing expanded disclosures of transactions that used to fall below the materiality radar. As a result, some good may yet come from the recent accounting failures.

Source: Adapted from K. Brown and J. Weil, "A Lot More Information Is 'Material' After Enron," *Wall Street Journal Online* (February 22, 2002); S. D. Jones and R. Gibson, "Restaurants Serve Up Restatements," *Wall Street Journal* (January 26, 2005), p. C3; and R. McTauge, "Nicholaisen Says Restatement Needed When Deal Lacks Business Purpose," *Securities Regulation & Law Reporter* (May 9, 2005).

Fundamental Quality—Faithful Representation

Faithful representation is the second fundamental quality that makes accounting information useful for decision-making. Faithful representation and related ingredients of this fundamental quality are shown on the next page.

[7]"Materiality," *SEC Staff Accounting Bulletin No. 99* (Washington, D.C.: SEC, 1999). The auditing profession also adopted this same concept of materiality. See "Audit Risk and Materiality in Conducting an Audit," *Statement on Auditing Standards No. 47* (New York: AICPA, 1983), par. 6.

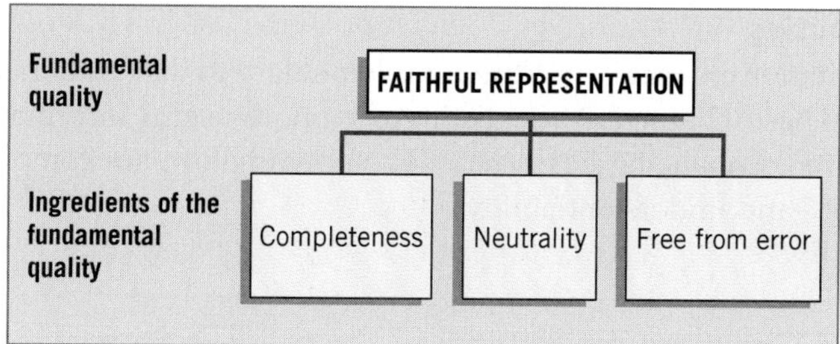

Faithful representation means that the numbers and descriptions match what really existed or happened. Faithful representation is a necessity because most users have neither the time nor the expertise to evaluate the factual content of the information. For example, if **General Motors'** income statement reports sales of $60,510 million when it had sales of $40,510 million, then the statement fails to faithfully represent the proper sales amount. To be a faithful representation, information must be complete, neutral, and free of material error.

Completeness. **Completeness** means that all the information that is necessary for faithful representation is provided. An omission can cause information to be false or misleading and thus not be helpful to the users of financial reports. For example, when **Citigroup** fails to provide information needed to assess the value of its subprime loan receivables (toxic assets), the information is not complete and therefore not a faithful representation of their values.

Neutrality. **Neutrality** means that a company cannot select information to favor one set of interested parties over another. Unbiased information must be the overriding consideration. For example, in the notes to financial statements, tobacco companies such as **R.J. Reynolds** should not suppress information about the numerous lawsuits that have been filed because of tobacco-related health concerns—even though such disclosure is damaging to the company.

Neutrality in rule-making has come under increasing attack. Some argue that the FASB should not issue pronouncements that cause undesirable economic effects on an industry or company. We disagree. Accounting rules (and the standard-setting process) must be free from bias, or we will no longer have credible financial statements. Without credible financial statements, individuals will no longer use this information. An analogy demonstrates the point: Many individuals bet on boxing matches because such contests are assumed not to be fixed. But nobody bets on wrestling matches. Why? Because the public assumes that wrestling matches are rigged. If financial information is biased (rigged), the public will lose confidence and no longer use it.

Free from Error. An information item that is **free from error** will be a more accurate (faithful) representation of a financial item. For example, if **JPMorgan Chase** misstates its loan losses, its financial statements are misleading and not a faithful representation of its financial results. However, faithful representation does not imply total freedom from error. This is because most financial reporting measures involve estimates of various types that incorporate management's judgment. For example, management must estimate the amount of uncollectible accounts to determine bad debt expense. And determination of depreciation expense requires estimation of useful lives of plant and equipment, as well as the residual value of the assets.

Enhancing Qualities

Enhancing qualitative characteristics are complementary to the fundamental qualitative characteristics. These characteristics distinguish more-useful information from less-useful information. Enhancing characteristics, shown below, are comparability, verifiability, timeliness, and understandability.

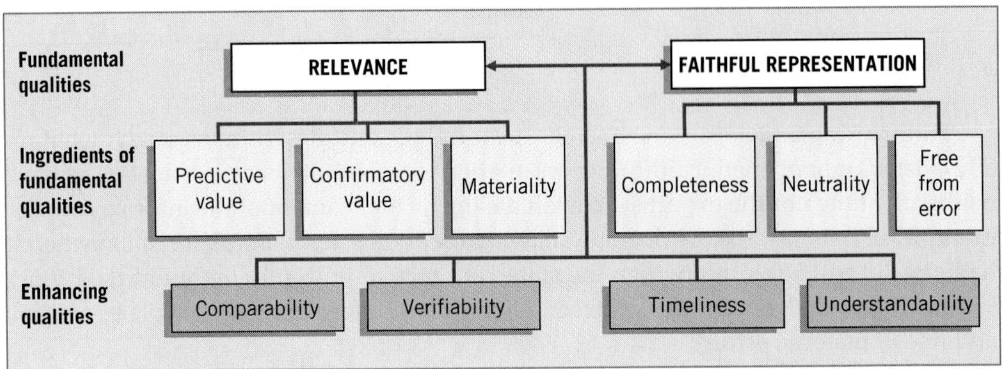

Comparability. Information that is measured and reported in a similar manner for different companies is considered comparable. **Comparability** enables users to identify the real similarities and differences in economic events between companies. For example, historically the accounting for pensions in Japan differed from that in the United States. In Japan, companies generally recorded little or no charge to income for these costs. U.S. companies recorded pension cost as incurred. As a result, it is difficult to compare and evaluate the financial results of **Toyota** or **Honda** to **General Motors** or **Ford**. Investors can only make valid evaluations if comparable information is available.

Another type of comparability, **consistency**, is present when a company applies the same accounting treatment to similar events, from period to period. Through such application, the company shows consistent use of accounting standards. The idea of consistency does not mean, however, that companies cannot switch from one accounting method to another. A company can change methods, but it must first demonstrate that the newly adopted method is preferable to the old. If approved, the company must then disclose the nature and effect of the accounting change, as well as the justification for it, in the financial statements for the period in which it made the change.[8] When a change in accounting principles occurs, the auditor generally refers to it in an explanatory paragraph of the audit report. This paragraph identifies the nature of the change and refers the reader to the note in the financial statements that discusses the change in detail.[9]

Verifiability. **Verifiability** occurs when independent measurers, using the same methods, obtain similar results. Verifiability occurs in the following situations.

1. Two independent auditors count **PepsiCo**'s inventory and arrive at the same physical quantity amount for inventory. Verification of an amount for an asset therefore can occur by simply counting the inventory (referred to as *direct verification*).

[8]Surveys indicate that users highly value consistency. They note that a change tends to destroy the comparability of data before and after the change. Some companies assist users to understand the pre- and post-change data. Generally, however, users say they lose the ability to analyze over time. GAAP guidelines (discussed in Chapter 22) on accounting changes are designed to improve the comparability of the data before and after the change.

[9]These provisions are specified in "Reports on Audited Financial Statements," *Statement on Auditing Standards No. 58* (New York: AICPA, April 1988), par. 34.

2. Two independent auditors compute PepsiCo's inventory value at the end of the year using the FIFO method of inventory valuation. Verification may occur by checking the inputs (quantity and costs) and recalculating the outputs (ending inventory value) using the same accounting convention or methodology (referred to as *indirect verification*).

Timeliness. **Timeliness** means having information available to decision-makers before it loses its capacity to influence decisions. Having relevant information available sooner can enhance its capacity to influence decisions, and a lack of timeliness can rob information of its usefulness. For example, if **Dell** waited to report its interim results until nine months after the period, the information would be much less useful for decision-making purposes.

Understandability. Decision-makers vary widely in the types of decisions they make, how they make decisions, the information they already possess or can obtain from other sources, and their ability to process the information. For information to be useful, there must be a connection (linkage) between these users and the decisions they make. This link, **understandability**, is the quality of information that lets reasonably informed users see its significance. Understandability is enhanced when information is classified, characterized, and presented clearly and concisely.

For example, assume that **GE** issues a three-months' report that shows interim earnings have declined significantly. This interim report provides relevant and faithfully represented information for decision-making purposes. Some users, upon reading the report, decide to sell their shares. Other users, however, do not understand the report's content and significance. They are surprised when GE declares a smaller year-end dividend and the share price declines. Thus, although GE presented highly relevant information that was a faithful representation, it was useless to those who did not understand it.

Thus, users of financial reports are assumed to have a reasonable knowledge of business and economic activities. In making decisions, users also should review and analyze the information with reasonable diligence. Information that is relevant and faithfully represented should not be excluded from financial reports solely because it is too complex or difficult for some users to understand without assistance.[10]

SHOW ME THE EARNINGS!

What do the numbers mean?

The growth of new-economy business on the Internet has led to the development of new measures of performance. When **Priceline.com** splashed on the dot-com scene, it touted steady growth in a measure called "unique offers by users" to explain its heady stock price. To draw investors to its stock, **Drugstore.com** focused on the number of "unique customers" at its website. After all, new businesses call for new performance measures, right?

Not necessarily. In fact, these indicators failed to show any consistent relationship between profits and website visits. Eventually, as the graphs on page 54 show, the profits never materialized, stock prices fell, and the dot-com bubble burst.

[10]*Statement of Financial Accounting Concepts No. 8,* "Chapter 3, Qualitative Characteristics of Useful Financial Information" (Norwalk, Conn.: FASB, September 2010), paras. QC30–QC31.

What do the numbers mean? (continued)

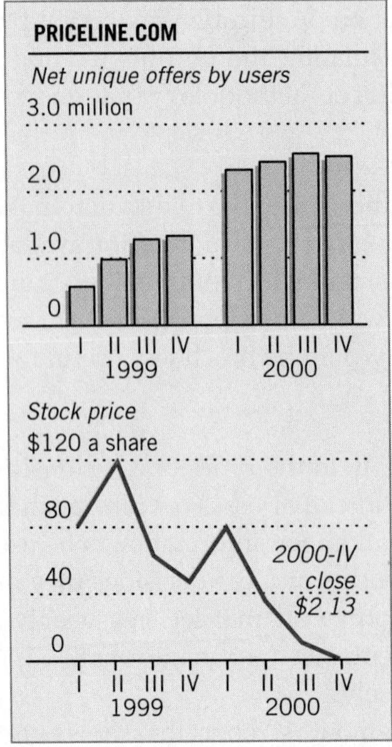

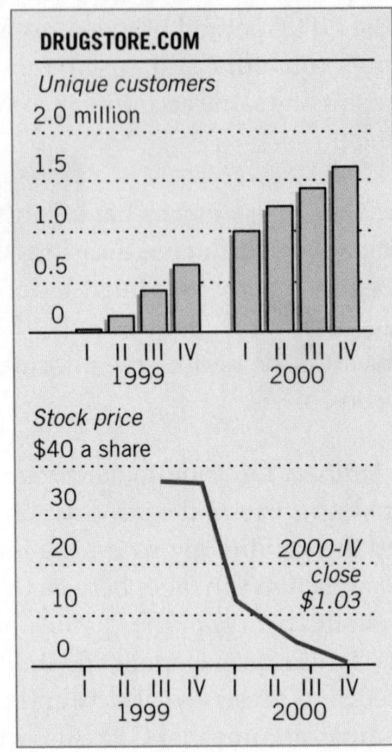

The lesson here: Although the new economy may require some new measures, investors need to be careful not to forget the reliable traditional ones.

Source: Story and graphs adapted from Gretchen Morgenson, "How Did They Value Stocks? Count the Absurd Ways," *New York Times* (March 18, 2001), section 3, p. 1.

Basic Elements

LEARNING OBJECTIVE 5
Define the basic elements of financial statements.

An important aspect of developing any theoretical structure is the body of **basic elements** or definitions to be included in it. Accounting uses many terms with distinctive and specific meanings. These terms constitute the language of business or the jargon of accounting.

One such term is **asset**. Is it merely something we own? Or is an asset something we have the right to use, as in the case of leased equipment? Or is it anything of value used by a company to generate revenues—in which case, should we also consider the managers of a company as an asset?

As this example and the lottery ticket example in the opening story illustrate, it seems necessary, therefore, to develop basic definitions for the elements of financial statements. *Concepts Statement No. 6* defines the ten interrelated elements that most directly relate to measuring the performance and financial status of a business enterprise. We list them on the next page for review and information purposes; you need not memorize these definitions at this point. We will explain and examine each of these elements in more detail in subsequent chapters.

The FASB classifies the elements into two distinct groups. The first group of three elements—assets, liabilities, and equity—describes amounts of resources and claims to resources at a **moment in time**. The other seven elements describe transactions, events, and circumstances that affect a company during a **period of time**. The first class, affected by elements of the second class, provides at any time the cumulative result of all changes. This interaction is referred to as "articulation." That is, key figures in one financial statement correspond to balances in another.

ELEMENTS OF FINANCIAL STATEMENTS

ASSETS. Probable future economic benefits obtained or controlled by a particular entity as a result of past transactions or events.

LIABILITIES. Probable future sacrifices of economic benefits arising from present obligations of a particular entity to transfer assets or provide services to other entities in the future as a result of past transactions or events.

EQUITY. Residual interest in the assets of an entity that remains after deducting its liabilities. In a business enterprise, the equity is the ownership interest.

INVESTMENTS BY OWNERS. Increases in net assets of a particular enterprise resulting from transfers to it from other entities of something of value to obtain or increase ownership interests (or equity) in it. Assets are most commonly received as investments by owners, but that which is received may also include services or satisfaction or conversion of liabilities of the enterprise.

DISTRIBUTIONS TO OWNERS. Decreases in net assets of a particular enterprise resulting from transferring assets, rendering services, or incurring liabilities by the enterprise to owners. Distributions to owners decrease ownership interests (or equity) in an enterprise.

COMPREHENSIVE INCOME. Change in equity (net assets) of an entity during a period from transactions and other events and circumstances from nonowner sources. It includes all changes in equity during a period except those resulting from investments by owners and distributions to owners.

REVENUES. Inflows or other enhancements of assets of an entity or settlement of its liabilities (or a combination of both) during a period from delivering or producing goods, rendering services, or other activities that constitute the entity's ongoing major or central operations.

EXPENSES. Outflows or other using up of assets or incurrences of liabilities (or a combination of both) during a period from delivering or producing goods, rendering services, or carrying out other activities that constitute the entity's ongoing major or central operations.

GAINS. Increases in equity (net assets) from peripheral or incidental transactions of an entity and from all other transactions and other events and circumstances affecting the entity during a period except those that result from revenues or investments by owners.

LOSSES. Decreases in equity (net assets) from peripheral or incidental transactions of an entity and from all other transactions and other events and circumstances affecting the entity during a period except those that result from expenses or distributions to owners.[11]

THIRD LEVEL: RECOGNITION AND MEASUREMENT CONCEPTS

The third level of the framework consists of concepts that implement the basic objective of level one. These concepts explain how companies should recognize, measure, and report financial elements and events. The FASB sets forth most of these in its *Statement of Financial Accounting Concepts No. 5,* "Recognition and Measurement in Financial Statements of Business Enterprises." According to *SFAC No. 5,* to be recognized, an item (event or transaction) must meet the definition of an "element of financial statements" as defined in *SFAC No. 6* and must be measurable. Most aspects of current practice follow these recognition and measurement concepts.

[11]"Elements of Financial Statements," *Statement of Financial Accounting Concepts No. 6* (Stamford, Conn.: FASB, December 1985), pp. ix and x.

The accounting profession continues to use the concepts in *SFAC No. 5* as operational guidelines. Here, we identify the concepts as basic assumptions, principles, and constraints. Not everyone uses this classification system, so focus your attention more on **understanding the concepts** than on how we classify and organize them. These concepts serve as guidelines in responding to controversial financial reporting issues.

LEARNING OBJECTIVE 6
Describe the basic assumptions of accounting.

Basic Assumptions

Four basic assumptions underlie the financial accounting structure: (1) **economic entity**, (2) **going concern**, (3) **monetary unit**, and (4) **periodicity**. We'll look at each in turn.

INTERNATIONAL PERSPECTIVE

Phase D of the conceptual framework convergence project addresses the reporting entity. A final standard is expected in 2011.

Economic Entity Assumption

The economic entity assumption **means that economic activity can be identified with a particular unit of accountability**. In other words, a company keeps its activity separate and distinct from its owners and any other business unit.[12] At the most basic level, the economic entity assumption dictates that Panera Bread Company record the company's financial activities separate from those of its owners and managers. Equally important, financial statement users need to be able to distinguish the activities and elements of different companies, such as General Motors, Ford, and Chrysler. If users could not distinguish the activities of different companies, how would they know which company financially outperformed the other?

The entity concept does not apply solely to the segregation of activities among competing companies, such as Best Buy and Circuit City. An individual, department, division, or an entire industry could be considered a separate entity if we choose to define it in this manner. Thus, **the entity concept does not necessarily refer to a legal entity**. A parent and its subsidiaries are separate **legal** entities, but merging their activities for accounting and reporting purposes does not violate the **economic entity** assumption.[13]

WHOSE COMPANY IS IT?

What do the numbers mean?

The importance of the entity assumption is illustrated by scandals involving W. R. Grace and, more recently, Adelphia. In both cases, senior company employees entered into transactions that blurred the line between the employee's financial interests and those of the company. At Adelphia, among many other self-dealings, the company guaranteed over $2 billion of loans to the founding family. W. R. Grace used company funds to pay for an apartment and chef for the company chairman. As a result of these transactions, these insiders benefitted at the expense of shareholders. Additionally, the financial statements failed to disclose the transactions. Such disclosure would have allowed shareholders to sort out the impact of the employee transactions on company results.

[12]Recently, the FASB has proposed to link the definition of an entity to its financial reporting objective. That is, a reporting entity is described as a circumscribed area of business activity of interest to present and potential equity investors, lenders, and other capital providers. See IASB/FASB *Exposure Draft ED/2010/2: Conceptual Framework for Financial Reporting*. "The Reporting Entity" (March 2010) at *http://www.fasb.org/project/cf_phase-d.shtml*.

[13]The concept of the entity is changing. For example, defining the "outer edges" of companies is now harder. Public companies often consist of multiple public subsidiaries, each with joint ventures, licensing arrangements, and other affiliations. Increasingly, companies form and dissolve joint ventures or customer-supplier relationships in a matter of months or weeks. These "virtual companies" raise accounting issues about how to account for the entity. The FASB (and IASB) is addressing these issues in the entity phase of its conceptual framework project (see *http://www.fasb.org/project/cf_phase-d.shtml*) and in its project on consolidations (see *http://www.iasb.org/Current%20Projects/IASB%20Projects/Consolidation/Consolidation.htm*).

Going Concern Assumption

Most accounting methods rely on the going concern assumption—**that the company will have a long life**. Despite numerous business failures, most companies have a fairly high continuance rate. As a rule, we expect companies to last long enough to fulfill their objectives and commitments.

This assumption has significant implications. The historical cost principle would be of limited usefulness if we assume eventual liquidation. Under a liquidation approach, for example, a company would better state asset values at net realizable value (sales price less costs of disposal) than at acquisition cost. **Depreciation and amortization policies are justifiable and appropriate only if we assume some permanence to the company.** If a company adopts the liquidation approach, the current/noncurrent classification of assets and liabilities loses much of its significance. Labeling anything a fixed or long-term asset would be difficult to justify. Indeed, listing liabilities on the basis of priority in liquidation would be more reasonable.

The going concern assumption applies in most business situations. **Only where liquidation appears imminent is the assumption inapplicable.** In these cases a total revaluation of assets and liabilities can provide information that closely approximates the company's net realizable value. You will learn more about accounting problems related to a company in liquidation in advanced accounting courses.

Monetary Unit Assumption

The monetary unit assumption means that money is the common denominator of economic activity and provides an appropriate basis for accounting measurement and analysis. That is, the monetary unit is the most effective means of expressing to interested parties changes in capital and exchanges of goods and services. **The monetary unit is relevant, simple, universally available, understandable, and useful.** Application of this assumption depends on the even more basic assumption that quantitative data are useful in communicating economic information and in making rational economic decisions.

In the United States, accounting ignores price-level changes (inflation and deflation) and assumes that the unit of measure—the dollar—remains reasonably stable. We therefore use the monetary unit assumption to justify adding 1982 dollars to 2012 dollars without any adjustment. The FASB in *SFAC No. 5* indicated that it expects the dollar, unadjusted for inflation or deflation, to continue to be used to measure items recognized in financial statements. Only if circumstances change dramatically (such as if the United States experiences high inflation similar to that in many South American countries) will the FASB again consider "inflation accounting."

INTERNATIONAL PERSPECTIVE

Due to their experiences with persistent inflation, several South American countries produce "constant-currency" financial reports. Typically, companies in these countries use a general price-level index to adjust for the effects of inflation.

Periodicity Assumption

To measure the results of a company's activity accurately, we would need to wait until it liquidates. Decision makers, however, cannot wait that long for such information. Users need to know a company's performance and economic status on a timely basis so that they can evaluate and compare firms, and take appropriate actions. Therefore, companies must report information periodically.

The periodicity (or time period) assumption implies that a company can divide its economic activities into artificial time periods. These time periods vary, but the most common are monthly, quarterly, and yearly.

The shorter the time period, the more difficult it is to determine the proper net income for the period. A month's results usually prove less verifiable than a quarter's results, and a quarter's results are likely to be less verifiable than a year's results. Investors desire and demand that a company quickly process and disseminate information. Yet the quicker a company releases the information, the more likely the information will include errors. **This phenomenon provides an interesting example of the trade-off between relevance and faithful representation in preparing financial data.**

The problem of defining the time period becomes more serious as product cycles shorten and products become obsolete more quickly. Many believe that, given technology advances, companies need to provide more online, real-time financial information to ensure the availability of relevant information.

LEARNING OBJECTIVE 7
Explain the application of the basic principles of accounting.

Basic Principles of Accounting

We generally use four basic **principles of accounting** to record and report transactions: (1) measurement, (2) revenue recognition, (3) expense recognition, and (4) full disclosure. We look at each in turn.

Measurement Principle

We presently have a "mixed-attribute" system that permits the use of various measurement bases. The most commonly used measurements are based on historical cost and fair value. Here, we discuss each.

Historical Cost. GAAP requires that companies account for and report many assets and liabilities on the basis of acquisition price. This is often referred to as the **historical cost principle**. Historical cost has an important advantage over other valuations: **It is generally thought to be verifiable.**

To illustrate this advantage, consider the problems if companies select current selling price instead. Companies might have difficulty establishing a value for unsold items. Every member of the accounting department might value the assets differently. Further, how often would it be necessary to establish sales value? All companies close their accounts at least annually. But some compute their net income every month. Those companies would have to place a sales value on every asset each time they wished to determine income. Critics raise similar objections against current cost (replacement cost, present value of future cash flows) and any other basis of valuation **except historical cost**.

What about liabilities? Do companies account for them on a cost basis? Yes, they do. Companies issue liabilities, such as bonds, notes, and accounts payable, in exchange for assets (or services), for an agreed-upon price. **This price, established by the exchange transaction, is the "cost" of the liability.** A company uses this amount to record the liability in the accounts and report it in financial statements. Thus, many users prefer historical cost because it provides them with a **verifiable benchmark** for measuring historical trends.

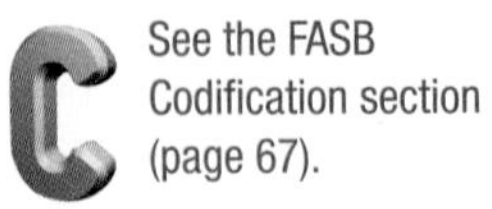
See the FASB Codification section (page 67).

Fair Value. **Fair value** is defined as "the price that would be received to sell an asset or paid to transfer a liability in an orderly transaction between market participants at the measurement date." Fair value is therefore a market-based measure. **[1]** Recently, GAAP has increasingly called for use of fair value measurements in the financial statements. This is often referred to as the **fair value principle**. Fair value information may be more useful than historical cost for certain types of assets and liabilities and in certain industries. For example, companies report many financial instruments, including derivatives, at fair value. Certain industries, such as brokerage houses and mutual funds, prepare their basic financial statements on a fair value basis.

At initial acquisition, historical cost equals fair value. In subsequent periods, as market and economic conditions change, historical cost and fair value often diverge. Thus, fair value measures or estimates often provide more relevant information about the expected future cash flows related to the asset or liability. For example, when long-lived assets decline in value, a fair value measure determines any impairment loss. The FASB believes that fair value information is more relevant to users than historical cost. Fair value measurement, it is argued, provides better insight into the value of a company's asset and liabilities (its financial position) and a better basis for assessing future cash flow prospects.

Recently the Board has taken the additional step of giving companies the option to use fair value (referred to as the **fair value option**) as the basis for measurement of financial assets and financial liabilities. **[2]** The Board considers fair value more relevant than historical cost because it reflects the current cash equivalent value of financial instruments. As a result companies now have the option to record fair value in their accounts for most financial instruments, including such items as receivables, investments, and debt securities.

Use of fair value in financial reporting is increasing. However, measurement based on fair value introduces increased subjectivity into accounting reports, when fair value information is not readily available. To increase consistency and comparability in fair value measures, the FASB established a fair value hierarchy that provides insight into the priority of valuation techniques to use to determine fair value. As shown in Illustration 2-4, the fair value hierarchy is divided into three broad levels.

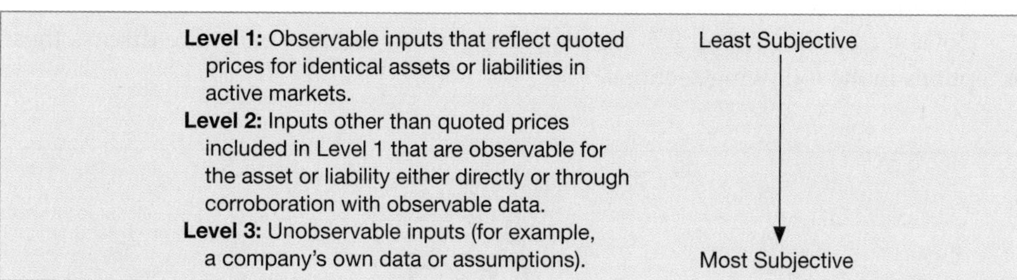

ILLUSTRATION 2-4
Fair Value Hierarchy

As Illustration 2-4 indicates, Level 1 is the least subjective because it is based on quoted prices, like a closing stock price in the *Wall Street Journal*. Level 2 is more subjective and would rely on evaluating similar assets or liabilities in active markets. At the most subjective level, Level 3, much judgment is needed based on the best information available, to arrive at a relevant and representationally faithful fair value measurement.[14]

It is easy to arrive at fair values when markets are liquid with many traders, but fair value answers are not readily available in other situations. For example, how do you value the mortgage assets of subprime lenders, like **Countrywide** and **New Century**, given that the market for these securities has essentially disappeared? A great deal of expertise and sound judgment will be needed to arrive at appropriate answers. GAAP also provides guidance on estimating fair values when market-related data is not available. In general, these valuation issues relate to Level 3 fair value measurements. These measurements may be developed using expected cash flow and present value techniques, as described in *Statement of Financial Accounting Concepts No. 7*, "Using Cash Flow Information and Present Value in Accounting," discussed in Chapter 6.

As indicated above, we presently have a "mixed-attribute" system that permits the use of historical cost and fair value. Although the historical cost principle continues to be an important basis for valuation, recording and reporting of fair value information is increasing. The recent measurement and disclosure guidance should increase consistency and comparability when fair value measurements are used in the financial statements and related notes.

[14]For major groups of assets and liabilities, companies must disclose: (1) the fair value measurement and (2) the fair value hierarchy level of the measurements as a whole, classified by Level 1, 2, or 3. Given the judgment involved, it follows that the more a company depends on Level 3 to determine fair values, the more information about the valuation process the company will need to disclose. Thus, additional disclosures are required for Level 3 measurements; we discuss these disclosures in more detail in subsequent chapters.

Revenue Recognition Principle

A crucial question for many companies is when to recognize revenue. Revenue recognition generally occurs (1) when **realized** or **realizable** and (2) when **earned**. This approach has often been referred to as the **revenue recognition principle**.

A company **realizes** revenues when it exchanges products (goods or services), merchandise, or other assets for cash or claims to cash. Revenues are realizable when assets received or held are readily convertible into cash or claims to cash. Assets are readily convertible when they are salable or interchangeable in an active market at readily determinable prices without significant additional cost.

In addition to the first test (realized or realizable), a company delays recognition of revenues until earned. Revenues are considered **earned** when the company substantially accomplishes what it must do to be entitled to the benefits represented by the revenues.[15] Generally, an objective test, such as a sale, indicates the point at which a company recognizes revenue. The sale provides an objective and verifiable measure of revenue—the sales price. Any basis for revenue recognition short of actual sale opens the door to wide variations in practice. **Recognition at the time of sale provides a uniform and reasonable test.**

However, as Illustration 2-5 shows, exceptions to the rule exist. We discuss these exceptions in the following sections.

ILLUSTRATION 2-5
Timing of Revenue Recognition

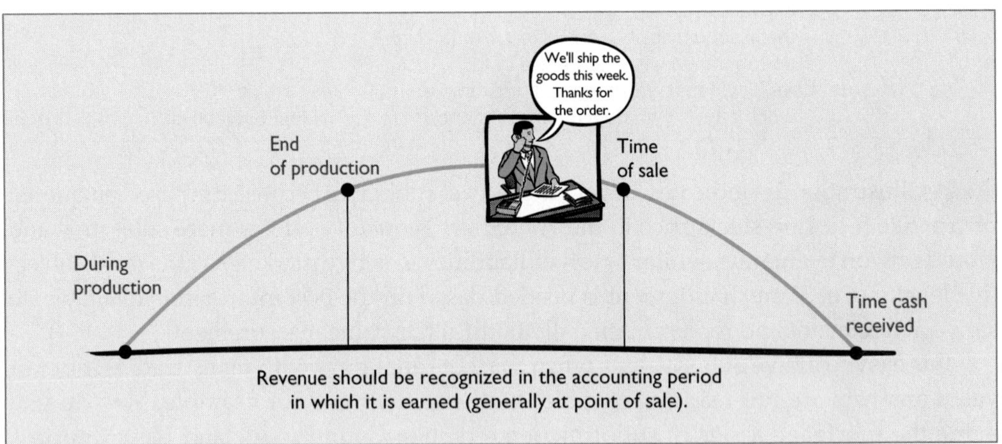

During Production. A company can recognize revenue **before** it completes the job in certain long-term construction contracts. In this method, a company recognizes revenue periodically, based on the percentage of the job it has completed. Although technically a transfer of ownership has not occurred, the earning process is considered substantially completed at various stages of construction. If it is not possible to obtain dependable estimates of cost and progress, then a company delays revenue recognition until it completes the job.

At End of Production. At times, a company may recognize revenue **after completion of the production cycle but before the sale takes place**. This occurs if products or other assets are salable in an active market at readily determinable prices without significant additional cost. An example is the mining of certain minerals. Once a company mines

[15]"Recognition and Measurement in Financial Statements of Business Enterprises," *Statement of Financial Accounting Concepts No. 5* (Stamford, Conn.: FASB, December 1984), par. 83(a) and (b). The FASB and IASB are working on a joint revenue recognition project, which will likely change from revenue recognition criteria based on completing the earnings process to criteria more aligned with changes in assets and liabilities. See *http://www.fasb.org/project/revenue_recognition.shtml.*

the mineral, a ready market at a quoted price exists. The same holds true for some agricultural products.

Upon Receipt of Cash. **Receipt of cash is another basis for revenue recognition.** Companies use the cash-basis approach only when collection is uncertain at the time of sale.

One form of the cash basis is the **installment-sales method**. Here, a company requires payment in periodic installments over a long period of time. Its most common use is in retail, such as for farm and home equipment and furnishings. Companies frequently justify the installment-sales method based on the high risk of not collecting an account receivable. In some instances, this reasoning may be valid. Generally, though, if a sale has been completed, the company should recognize the sale; if bad debts are expected, the company should record them as separate estimates.

To summarize, a company records revenue in the period when realized or realizable and when earned. Normally, this is the date of sale. But circumstances may dictate application of the percentage-of-completion approach, the end-of-production approach, or the receipt-of-cash approach.

Expense Recognition Principle

As indicated in the discussion of financial statement elements, expenses are defined as outflows or other "using up" of assets or incurring of liabilities (or a combination of both) during a period as a result of delivering or producing goods and/or rendering services. It follows then that recognition of expenses is related to net changes in assets and earning revenues. In practice, the approach for recognizing expenses is, "Let the expense follow the revenues." This approach is the **expense recognition principle**.

To illustrate, companies recognize expenses not when they pay wages or make a product, but when the work (service) or the product actually contributes to revenue. Thus, companies tie expense recognition to revenue recognition. That is, by matching **efforts (expenses) with accomplishment (revenues), the expense recognition principle is implemented** in accordance with the definition of expense (outflows or other using up of assets or incurring of liabilities).[16]

Some costs, however, are difficult to associate with revenue. As a result, some other approach must be developed. Often, companies use a "rational and systematic" allocation policy that will approximate the expense recognition principle. This type of expense recognition involves assumptions about the benefits that a company receives as well as the cost associated with those benefits. For example, a company like **Intel** or **Motorola** allocates the cost of a long-lived asset over all of the accounting periods during which it uses the asset because the asset contributes to the generation of revenue throughout its useful life.

Companies charge some costs to the current period as expenses (or losses) simply because they cannot determine a connection with revenue. Examples of these types of costs are officers' salaries and other administrative expenses.

Costs are generally classified into two groups: **product costs** and **period costs**. **Product costs**, such as material, labor, and overhead, attach to the product. Companies carry these costs into future periods if they recognize the revenue from the product in subsequent periods. **Period costs**, such as officers' salaries and other administrative expenses, attach to the period. Companies charge off such costs in the immediate period, even though benefits associated with these costs may occur in the future. Why? Because companies cannot determine a direct relationship between period costs and revenue. Illustration 2-6 (page 62) summarizes these expense recognition procedures.

[16]This approach is commonly referred to as the **matching principle**. However, there is some debate about the conceptual validity of the matching principle. A major concern is that matching permits companies to defer certain costs and treat them as assets on the balance sheet. In fact, these costs may not have future benefits. If abused, this principle permits the balance sheet to become a "dumping ground" for unmatched costs.

ILLUSTRATION 2-6
Expense Recognition

Type of Cost	Relationship	Recognition
Product costs: • Material • Labor • Overhead	Direct relationship between cost and revenue.	Recognize in period of revenue (matching).
Period costs: • Salaries • Administrative costs	No direct relationship between cost and revenue.	Expense as incurred.

Full Disclosure Principle

In deciding what information to report, companies follow the general practice of providing information that is of sufficient importance to influence the judgment and decisions of an informed user. Often referred to as the **full disclosure principle**, it recognizes that the nature and amount of information included in financial reports reflects a series of judgmental trade-offs. These trade-offs strive for (1) sufficient detail to disclose matters that **make a difference** to users, yet (2) sufficient condensation to make the **information understandable**, keeping in mind costs of preparing and using it.

Disclosure is not a substitute for proper accounting. As a former chief accountant of the SEC noted, "Good disclosure does not cure bad accounting any more than an adjective or adverb can be used without, or in place of, a noun or verb." Thus, for example, cash-basis accounting for cost of goods sold is misleading, even if a company discloses accrual-basis amounts in the notes to the financial statements.

Users find information about financial position, income, cash flows, and investments in one of three places: (1) within the main body of financial statements, (2) in the notes to those statements, or (3) as supplementary information.

As discussed in Chapter 1, the **financial statements** are the balance sheet, income statement, statement of cash flows, and statement of owners' equity. They are a structured means of communicating financial information. To be recognized in the main body of financial statements, **an item should meet the definition of a basic element, be measurable with sufficient certainty, and be relevant and reliable.**[17]

The **notes to financial statements** generally amplify or explain the items presented in the main body of the statements. If the main body of the financial statements gives an incomplete picture of the performance and position of the company, the notes should provide the additional information needed. Information in the notes does not have to be quantifiable, nor does it need to qualify as an element. Notes can be partially or totally narrative. Examples of notes include descriptions of the accounting policies and methods used in measuring the elements reported in the statements, explanations of uncertainties and contingencies, and statistics and details too voluminous for inclusion in the statements. The notes can be essential to understanding the company's performance and position.

Supplementary information may include details or amounts that present a different perspective from that adopted in the financial statements. It may be quantifiable information that is high in relevance but low in faithful representation. For example, oil and gas companies typically provide information on proven reserves as well as the related discounted cash flows.

Supplementary information may also include management's explanation of the financial information and its discussion of the significance of that information. For example, many business combinations have produced financing arrangements that demand new accounting and reporting practices and principles. In each of these situations, the same problem must be faced: making sure the company presents enough information to ensure that the **reasonably prudent investor** will not be misled.

We discuss the content, arrangement, and display of financial statements, along with other facets of full disclosure, in Chapters 4, 5, and 24.

[17] *SFAC No. 5*, par. 63.

Constraints

In providing information with the qualitative characteristics that make it useful, companies must consider an overriding factor that limits (constrains) the reporting. This is referred to as the **cost constraint** (the **cost-benefit relationship**). We also review the less-dominant yet important constraint of **industry practices** that is part of the reporting environment.

8 LEARNING OBJECTIVE
Describe the impact that constraints have on reporting accounting information.

Cost Constraint

Too often, users assume that information is free. But preparers and providers of accounting information know that it is not. Therefore, companies must consider the cost constraint (or cost-benefit relationship). They must weigh the costs of providing the information against the benefits that can be derived from using it. Rule-making bodies and governmental agencies use cost-benefit analysis before making final their informational requirements. In order to justify requiring a particular measurement or disclosure, the benefits perceived to be derived from it must exceed the costs perceived to be associated with it.

A corporate executive made the following remark to the FASB about a proposed rule: "In all my years in the financial arena, I have never seen such an absolutely ridiculous proposal. . . . To dignify these 'actuarial' estimates by recording them as assets and liabilities would be virtually unthinkable except for the fact that the FASB has done equally stupid things in the past. . . . For God's sake, use common sense just this once."[18] Although extreme, this remark indicates the frustration expressed by members of the business community about rule-making, and whether the benefits of a given pronouncement exceed the costs.

The difficulty in cost-benefit analysis is that the costs and especially the benefits are not always evident or measurable. The costs are of several kinds: costs of collecting and processing, of disseminating, of auditing, of potential litigation, of disclosure to competitors, and of analysis and interpretation. Benefits to preparers may include greater management control and access to capital at a lower cost. Users may receive better information for allocation of resources, tax assessment, and rate regulation. As noted earlier, benefits are generally more difficult to quantify than are costs.

The recent implementation of the provisions of the Sarbanes-Oxley Act of 2002 illustrates the challenges in assessing costs and benefits of standards. One study estimated the increased costs of complying with the new internal-control standards related to the financial reporting process to be an average of $7.8 million per company. However, the study concluded that ". . . quantifying the benefits of improved more reliable financial reporting is not fully possible."[19]

Despite the difficulty in assessing the costs and benefits of its rules, the FASB attempts to determine that each proposed pronouncement will fill a significant need and that the costs imposed to meet the rule are justified in relation to overall benefits of the resulting information. In addition, the Board seeks input on costs and benefits as part of its due process.[20]

Industry Practices

Another practical consideration is industry practices. **The peculiar nature of some industries and business concerns** sometimes requires departure from basic theory. For

[18]"Decision-Usefulness: The Overriding Objective," *FASB Viewpoints* (October 19, 1983), p. 4.

[19]Charles Rivers and Associates, "Sarbanes-Oxley Section 404: Costs and Remediation of Deficiencies" letter from Deloitte and Touche, Ernst and Young, KPMG, and Pricewaterhouse-Coopers to the SEC (April 11, 2005).

[20]For example, as part of its project on "Share-Based Payment" **[3]**, the Board conducted a field study and surveyed commercial software providers to collect information on the costs of measuring the fair values of share-based compensation arrangements.

example, public-utility companies report noncurrent assets first on the balance sheet to highlight the industry's capital-intensive nature. Agricultural companies often report crops at fair value because it is costly to develop accurate cost figures on individual crops.

Such variations from basic theory are infrequent, yet they do exist. Whenever we find what appears to be a violation of basic accounting theory, we should determine whether some peculiarity of the industry explains the violation before we criticize the procedures followed.[21]

What do the numbers mean?

YOU MAY NEED A MAP

Beyond touting nonfinancial measures to investors (see the "What Do the Numbers Mean?" box on page 53), many companies increasingly promote the performance of their companies through the reporting of various "pro-forma" earnings measures. A recent survey of newswire reports found 36 instances of the reporting of pro-forma measures in just a three-day period.

Pro-forma measures are standard measures (such as earnings) that companies adjust, usually for one-time or nonrecurring items. For example, companies usually adjust earnings for the effects of an extraordinary item. Such adjustments make the numbers more comparable to numbers reported in periods without the unusual item.

However, rather than increasing comparability, it appears that some companies use pro-forma reporting to accentuate the positive in their results. Examples include **Yahoo Inc.** and **Cisco**, which define pro-forma income after adding back payroll tax expense. **Level 8 Systems** transformed an operating loss into a pro-forma profit by adding back expenses for depreciation and amortization of intangible assets.

Lynn Turner, former Chief Accountant at the SEC, calls such earnings measures EBS—"Everything but Bad Stuff." To provide investors a more complete picture of company profitability, not the story preferred by management, the SEC issued Regulation G (REG G). REG G requires companies to reconcile non-GAAP financial measures to GAAP, thereby giving investors a roadmap to analyze adjustments companies make to their GAAP numbers to arrive at pro-forma results.

Sources: Adapted from Gretchen Morgenson, "How Did They Value Stocks? Count the Absurd Ways," *New York Times* (March 18, 2001), section 3, p. 1; and Gretchen Morgenson, "Expert Advice: Focus on Profit," *New York Times* (March 18, 2001), section 3, p. 14. See also SEC Regulation G, "Conditions for Use of Non-GAAP Financial Measures, "Release No. 33–8176 (March 28, 2003).

Summary of the Structure

Illustration 2-7 presents the conceptual framework discussed in this chapter. It is similar to Illustration 2-1, except that it provides additional information for each level. We cannot overemphasize the usefulness of this conceptual framework in helping to understand many of the problem areas that we examine in later chapters.

[21]Sometimes, in practice, it has been acceptable to invoke prudence or conservatism as a justification for an accounting treatment under conditions of uncertainty. **Prudence** or **conservatism** means when in doubt, choose the solution that will be least likely to overstate assets or income and/or understate liabilities or expenses. The framework indicates that prudence or conservatism generally is in conflict with the quality of neutrality. This is because being prudent or conservative likely leads to a bias in the reported financial position and financial performance. In fact, introducing biased understatement of assets (or overstatement of liabilities) in one period frequently leads to overstating financial performance in later periods—a result that cannot be described as prudent. This is inconsistent with neutrality, which encompasses freedom from bias. Accordingly, the framework does not include prudence or conservatism as desirable qualities of financial reporting information. See *Statement of Financial Accounting Concepts No. 8*, "Chapter 3, Qualitative Characteristics of Useful Financial Information" (Norwalk, Conn.: FASB, September 2010), paras. BC3.27–BC3.29.

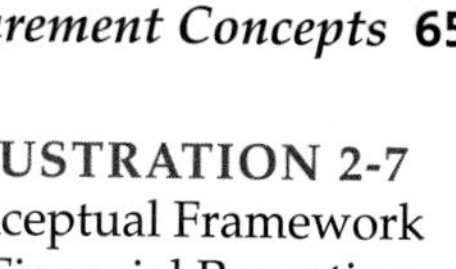

ILLUSTRATION 2-7
Conceptual Framework for Financial Reporting

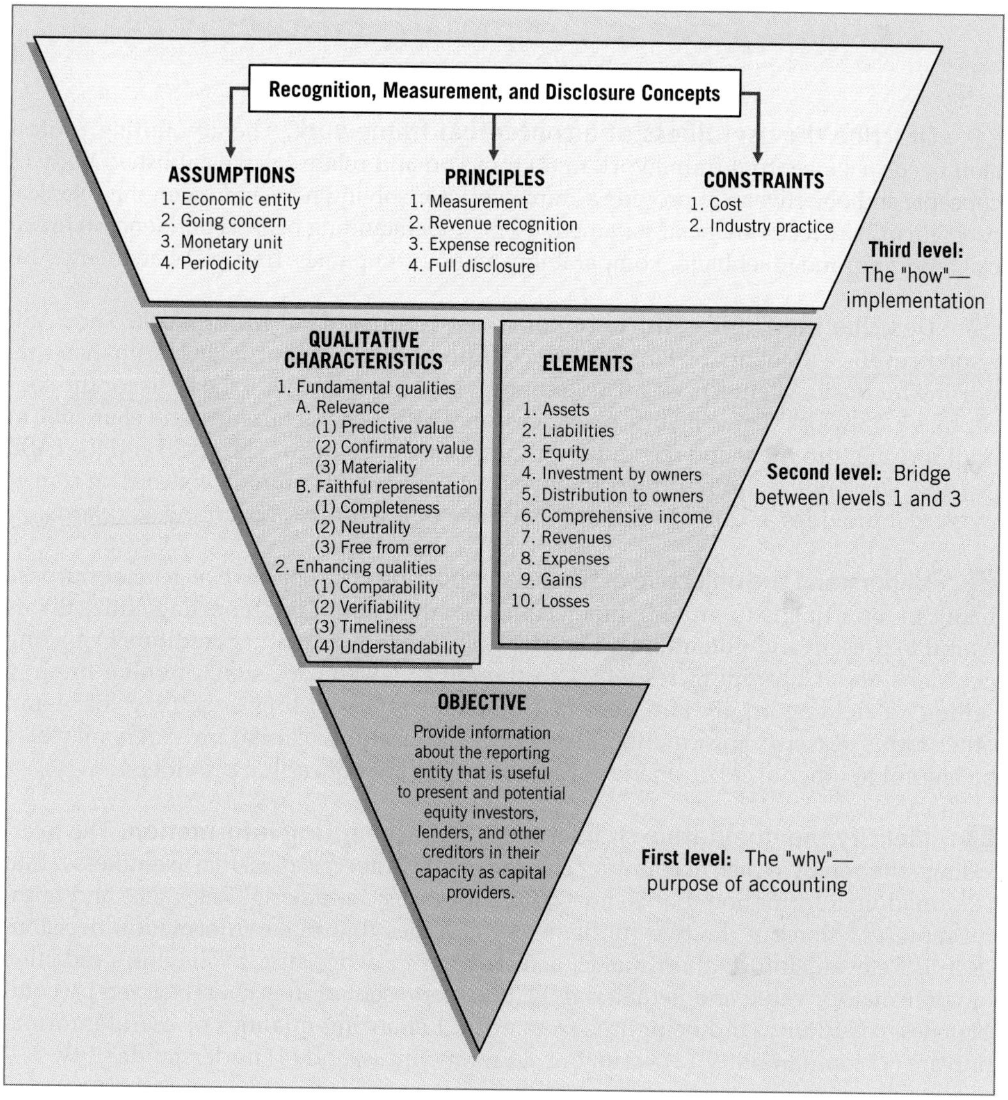

Recognition, Measurement, and Disclosure Concepts

ASSUMPTIONS
1. Economic entity
2. Going concern
3. Monetary unit
4. Periodicity

PRINCIPLES
1. Measurement
2. Revenue recognition
3. Expense recognition
4. Full disclosure

CONSTRAINTS
1. Cost
2. Industry practice

Third level: The "how"—implementation

QUALITATIVE CHARACTERISTICS
1. Fundamental qualities
   A. Relevance
      (1) Predictive value
      (2) Confirmatory value
      (3) Materiality
   B. Faithful representation
      (1) Completeness
      (2) Neutrality
      (3) Free from error
2. Enhancing qualities
   (1) Comparability
   (2) Verifiability
   (3) Timeliness
   (4) Understandability

ELEMENTS
1. Assets
2. Liabilities
3. Equity
4. Investment by owners
5. Distribution to owners
6. Comprehensive income
7. Revenues
8. Expenses
9. Gains
10. Losses

Second level: Bridge between levels 1 and 3

OBJECTIVE
Provide information about the reporting entity that is useful to present and potential equity investors, lenders, and other creditors in their capacity as capital providers.

First level: The "why"—purpose of accounting

You will want to read the **IFRS INSIGHTS** on pages 81–85 for discussion of how IFRS relates to the conceptual framework.

SUMMARY OF LEARNING OBJECTIVES

1 Describe the usefulness of a conceptual framework. The accounting profession needs a conceptual framework to (1) build on and relate to an established body of concepts and objectives, (2) provide a framework for solving new and emerging practical problems, (3) increase financial statement users' understanding of and confidence in financial reporting, and (4) enhance comparability among companies' financial statements.

2 Describe the FASB's efforts to construct a conceptual framework. The FASB issued seven Statements of Financial Accounting Concepts that relate to financial reporting for business enterprises. These concept statements provide the basis for the conceptual framework. They include objectives, qualitative characteristics, and elements. In addition, measurement and recognition concepts are developed. The FASB and the IASB are now working on a joint project to develop an improved common conceptual framework that provides a sound foundation for developing future accounting standards.

3 Understand the objective of financial reporting. The objective of general-purpose financial reporting is to provide financial information about the reporting entity that is **useful to present and potential equity investors, lenders, and other creditors** in making decisions about providing resources to the entity. Those decisions involve buying, selling, or holding equity and debt instruments, and providing or settling loans and other forms of credit. Information that is decision-useful to capital providers may also be helpful to other users of financial reporting who are not capital providers.

4 Identify the qualitative characteristics of accounting information. The overriding criterion by which accounting choices can be judged is decision-usefulness—that is, providing information that is most useful for decision-making. Relevance and faithful representation are the two fundamental qualities that make information decision-useful. Relevant information makes a difference in a decision by having predictive or confirmatory value and is material. Faithful representation is characterized by completeness, neutrality, and being free from error. Enhancing qualities of useful information are (1) comparability, (2) verifiability, (3) timeliness, and (4) understandability.

5 Define the basic elements of financial statements. The basic elements of financial statements are (1) assets, (2) liabilities, (3) equity, (4) investments by owners, (5) distributions to owners, (6) comprehensive income, (7) revenues, (8) expenses, (9) gains, and (10) losses. We define these ten elements on page 55.

6 Describe the basic assumptions of accounting. Four basic assumptions underlying financial accounting are as follows. (1) *Economic entity:* The activity of a company can be kept separate and distinct from its owners and any other business unit. (2) *Going concern:* The company will have a long life. (3) *Monetary unit:* Money is the common denominator by which economic activity is conducted, and the monetary unit provides an appropriate basis for measurement and analysis. (4) *Periodicity:* The economic activities of a company can be divided into artificial time periods.

7 Explain the application of the basic principles of accounting. (1) *Measurement principle:* Existing GAAP permits the use of historical cost, fair value, and other valuation bases. Although the historical cost principle (measurement based on acquisition price) continues to be an important basis for valuation, recording and reporting of fair value information is increasing. (2) *Revenue recognition principle:* A company generally recognizes revenue when (a) realized or realizable and (b) earned. (3) *Expense recognition principle:* As a general rule, companies recognize expenses when the service or the product actually makes its contribution to revenue (commonly referred to as *matching*). (4) *Full disclosure principle:* Companies generally provide information that is of sufficient importance to influence the judgment and decisions of an informed user.

KEY TERMS

 **Describe the impact that constraints have on reporting accounting information.** The constraints and their impact are as follows. (1) *Cost constraint:* The cost of providing the information must be weighed against the benefits that can be derived from using the information. (2) *Industry practices:* Follow the general practices in the company's industry, which sometimes requires departure from basic theory.

revenue recognition principle, *60*
supplementary information, *62*
timeliness, *53*
understandability, *53*
verifiability, *52*

FASB CODIFICATION

FASB Codification References

[1] FASB ASC 820-10. [Predecessor literature: *Statement of Financial Accounting Standards No. 157,* "Fair Value Measurement" (Norwalk, Conn.: FASB, September 2006).]

[2] FASB ASC 825-10-25. [Predecessor literature: "The Fair Value Option for Financial Assets and Liabilities," *Statement of Financial Accounting Standards No. 159* (Norwalk, Conn.: FASB, 2007).]

[3] FASB ASC 718-10. [Predecessor literature: "Share-Based Payment," *Financial Accounting Standards No. 123(R)* (Norwalk, Conn.: FASB, 2004).]

Exercises

If your school has a subscription to the FASB Codification, go to *http://aaahq.org/ascLogin.cfm* to log in and prepare responses to the following. Provide Codification references for your responses.

CE2-1 Access the glossary ("Master Glossary") at the FASB Codification website to answer the following.

(a) What is the definition of fair value?
(b) What is the definition of revenue?
(c) What is the definition of comprehensive income?

CE2-2 Briefly describe how the organization of the FASB Codification corresponds to the elements of financial statements.

CE2-3 How is the constraint of industry practices reflected in the FASB Codification?

Be sure to check the book's companion website for a Review and Analysis Exercise, with solution.

Questions, Brief Exercises, Exercises, Problems, and many more resources are available for practice in WileyPLUS.

QUESTIONS

1. What is a conceptual framework? Why is a conceptual framework necessary in financial accounting?
2. What is the primary objective of financial reporting?
3. What is meant by the term "qualitative characteristics of accounting information"?
4. Briefly describe the two fundamental qualities of useful accounting information.
5. How is materiality (or immateriality) related to the proper presentation of financial statements? What factors and measures should be considered in assessing the materiality of a misstatement in the presentation of a financial statement?
6. What are the enhancing qualities of the qualitative characteristics? What is the role of enhancing qualities in the conceptual framework?

7. According to the FASB conceptual framework, the objective of financial reporting for business enterprises is based on the needs of the users of financial statements. Explain the level of sophistication that the Board assumes about the users of financial statements.

8. What is the distinction between comparability and consistency?

9. Why is it necessary to develop a definitional framework for the basic elements of accounting?

10. Expenses, losses, and distributions to owners are all decreases in net assets. What are the distinctions among them?

11. Revenues, gains, and investments by owners are all increases in net assets. What are the distinctions among them?

12. What are the four basic assumptions that underlie the financial accounting structure?

13. The life of a business is divided into specific time periods, usually a year, to measure results of operations for each such time period and to portray financial conditions at the end of each period.

    (a) This practice is based on the accounting assumption that the life of the business consists of a series of time periods and that it is possible to measure accurately the results of operations for each period. Comment on the validity and necessity of this assumption.

    (b) What has been the effect of this practice on accounting? What is its relation to the accrual system? What influence has it had on accounting entries and methodology?

14. What is the basic accounting problem created by the monetary unit assumption when there is significant inflation? What appears to be the FASB position on a stable monetary unit?

15. The chairman of the board of directors of the company for which you are chief accountant has told you that he has little use for accounting figures based on cost. He believes that replacement values are of far more significance to the board of directors than "out-of-date costs." Present some arguments to convince him that accounting data should still be based on cost.

16. What is the definition of fair value?

17. What is the fair value option? Explain how use of the fair value option reflects application of the fair value principle.

18. Briefly describe the fair value hierarchy.

19. When is revenue generally recognized? Why has that date been chosen as the point at which to recognize the revenue resulting from the entire producing and selling process?

20. Selane Eatery operates a catering service specializing in business luncheons for large corporations. Selane requires customers to place their orders 2 weeks in advance of the scheduled events. Selane bills its customers on the tenth day of the month following the date of service and requires that payment be made within 30 days of the billing date. Conceptually, when should Selane recognize revenue related to its catering service?

21. What is the difference between realized and realizable? Give an example of where the concept of realizable is used to recognize revenue.

22. What is the justification for the following deviations from recognizing revenue at the time of sale?

    (a) Installment sales method of recognizing revenue.

    (b) Recognition of revenue at completion of production for certain agricultural products.

    (c) The percentage-of-completion basis in long-term construction contracts.

23. Mogilny Company paid $135,000 for a machine. The Accumulated Depreciation account has a balance of $46,500 at the present time. The company could sell the machine today for $150,000. The company president believes that the company has a "right to this gain." What does the president mean by this statement? Do you agree?

24. Three expense recognition methods (associating cause and effect, systematic and rational allocation, and immediate recognition) were discussed in the text under the expense recognition principle. Indicate the basic nature of each of these expense recognition methods and give two examples of each.

25. *Statement of Financial Accounting Concepts No. 5* identifies four characteristics that an item must have before it is recognized in the financial statements. What are these four characteristics?

26. Briefly describe the types of information concerning financial position, income, and cash flows that might be provided: (a) within the main body of the financial statements, (b) in the notes to the financial statements, or (c) as supplementary information.

27. In January 2013, Janeway Inc. doubled the amount of its outstanding stock by selling on the market an additional 10,000 shares to finance an expansion of the business. You propose that this information be shown by a footnote on the balance sheet as of December 31, 2012. The president objects, claiming that this sale took place after December 31, 2012, and, therefore, should not be shown. Explain your position.

28. Describe the major constraint inherent in the presentation of accounting information.

29. What are some of the costs of providing accounting information? What are some of the benefits of accounting information? Describe the cost-benefit factors that should be considered when new accounting standards are being proposed.

30. The treasurer of Landowska Co. has heard that conservatism is a doctrine that is followed in accounting and, therefore, proposes that several policies be followed that are conservative in nature. State your opinion with respect to each of the policies listed on the next page.

(a) The company gives a 2-year warranty to its customers on all products sold. The estimated warranty costs incurred from this year's sales should be entered as an expense this year instead of an expense in the period in the future when the warranty is made good.

(b) When sales are made on account, there is always uncertainty about whether the accounts are collectible. Therefore, the treasurer recommends recording the sale when the cash is received from the customers.

(c) A personal liability lawsuit is pending against the company. The treasurer believes there is an even chance that the company will lose the suit and have to pay damages of $200,000 to $300,000. The treasurer recommends that a loss be recorded and a liability created in the amount of $300,000.

(d) The inventory should be valued at "cost or market, whichever is lower" because the losses from price declines should be recognized in the accounts in the period in which the price decline takes place.

BRIEF EXERCISES

4 **BE2-1** Match the qualitative characteristics below with the following statements.

1. Relevance
2. Faithful representation
3. Predictive value
4. Confirmatory value
5. Comparability
6. Completeness
7. Neutrality
8. Timeliness

(a) Quality of information that permits users to identify similarities in and differences between two sets of economic phenomena.
(b) Having information available to users before it loses its capacity to influence decisions.
(c) Information about an economic phenomenon that has value as an input to the processes used by capital providers to form their own expectations about the future.
(d) Information that is capable of making a difference in the decisions of users in their capacity as capital providers.
(e) Absence of bias intended to attain a predetermined result or to induce a particular behavior.

4 **BE2-2** Match the qualitative characteristics below with the following statements.

1. Timeliness
2. Completeness
3. Free from error
4. Understandability
5. Faithful representation
6. Relevance
7. Neutrality
8. Confirmatory value

(a) Quality of information that assures users that information represents the economic phenomena that it purports to represent.
(b) Information about an economic phenomenon that corrects past or present expectations based on previous evaluations.
(c) The extent to which information is accurate in representing the economic substance of a transaction.
(d) Includes all the information that is necessary for a faithful representation of the economic phenomena that it purports to represent.
(e) Quality of information that allows users to comprehend its meaning.

4 **BE2-3** Discuss whether the changes described in each of the cases below require recognition in the CPA's audit report as to consistency. (Assume that the amounts are material.)

(a) The company changed its inventory method to FIFO from weighted-average, which had been used in prior years.
(b) The company disposed of one of the two subsidiaries that had been included in its consolidated statements for prior years.
(c) The estimated remaining useful life of plant property was reduced because of obsolescence.
(d) The company is using an inventory valuation method that is different from those used by all other companies in its industry.

4 **BE2-4** Identify which qualitative characteristic of accounting information is best described in each item below. (Do not use relevance and faithful representation.)

(a) The annual reports of **Best Buy Co.** are audited by certified public accountants.
(b) **Black & Decker** and **Cannondale Corporation** both use the FIFO cost flow assumption.

(c) **Starbucks Corporation** has used straight-line depreciation since it began operations.
(d) **Motorola** issues its quarterly reports immediately after each quarter ends.

4 **BE2-5** Presented below are three different transactions related to materiality. Explain whether you would classify these transactions as material.

(a) Blair Co. has reported a positive trend in earnings over the last 3 years. In the current year, it reduces its bad debt allowance to ensure another positive earnings year. The impact of this adjustment is equal to 3% of net income.
(b) Hindi Co. has an extraordinary gain of $3.1 million on the sale of plant assets and a $3.3 million loss on the sale of investments. It decides to net the gain and loss because the net effect is considered immaterial. Hindi Co.'s income for the current year was $10 million.
(c) Damon Co. expenses all capital equipment under $25,000 on the basis that it is immaterial. The company has followed this practice for a number of years.

5 **BE2-6** For each item below, indicate to which category of elements of financial statements it belongs.

(a) Retained earnings
(b) Sales
(c) Additional paid-in capital
(d) Inventory
(e) Depreciation
(f) Loss on sale of equipment
(g) Interest payable
(h) Dividends
(i) Gain on sale of investment
(j) Issuance of common stock

6 **BE2-7** Identify which basic assumption of accounting is best described in each item below.

(a) The economic activities of **FedEx Corporation** are divided into 12-month periods for the purpose of issuing annual reports.
(b) **Solectron Corporation, Inc.** does not adjust amounts in its financial statements for the effects of inflation.
(c) **Walgreen Co.** reports current and noncurrent classifications in its balance sheet.
(d) The economic activities of **General Electric** and its subsidiaries are merged for accounting and reporting purposes.

7 **BE2-8** Identify which basic principle of accounting is best described in each item below.

(a) **Norfolk Southern Corporation** reports revenue in its income statement when it is earned instead of when the cash is collected.
(b) **Yahoo, Inc.** recognizes depreciation expense for a machine over the 2-year period during which that machine helps the company earn revenue.
(c) **Oracle Corporation** reports information about pending lawsuits in the notes to its financial statements.
(d) **Eastman Kodak Company** reports land on its balance sheet at the amount paid to acquire it, even though the estimated fair value is greater.

7 **BE2-9** Vande Velde Company made three investments during 2012: (1) It purchased 1,000 shares of Sastre Company, a start-up company. Vande Velde made the investment based on valuation estimates from an internally developed model. (2) It purchased 2,000 shares of **GE** stock, which trades on the NYSE. (3) It invested $10,000 in local development authority bonds. Although these bonds do not trade on an active market, their value closely tracks movements in U.S. Treasury bonds. Where will Vande Velde report these investments in the fair value hierarchy?

8 **BE2-10** What accounting constraint is illustrated by the items below?

(a) Greco's Farms, Inc. reports agricultural crops on its balance sheet at fair value.
(b) Rafael Corporation discloses fair value information on its loans because it already gathers this information internally.
(c) Willis Company does not disclose any information in the notes to the financial statements unless the value of the information to financial statement users exceeds the expense of gathering it.
(d) A broker-dealer records all assets and liabilities at fair value.

6 **BE2-11** If the going concern assumption is not made in accounting, discuss the differences in the amounts shown in the financial statements for the following items.

(a) Land.
(b) Unamortized bond premium.
(c) Depreciation expense on equipment.
(d) Merchandise inventory.
(e) Prepaid insurance.

6 7 **BE2-12** What accounting assumption, principle, or constraint would Target Corporation use in each of the
8 situations below?

(a) Target was involved in litigation over the last year. This litigation is disclosed in the financial statements.
(b) Target allocates the cost of its depreciable assets over the life it expects to receive revenue from these assets.
(c) Target records the purchase of a new Dell PC at its cash equivalent price.

5 **BE2-13** Explain how you would decide whether to record each of the following expenditures as an asset or an expense. Assume all items are material.

(a) Legal fees paid in connection with the purchase of land are $1,500.
(b) Eduardo, Inc. paves the driveway leading to the office building at a cost of $21,000.
(c) A meat market purchases a meat-grinding machine at a cost of $3,500.
(d) On June 30, Monroe and Meno, medical doctors, pay 6 months' office rent to cover the month of July and the next 5 months.
(e) Smith's Hardware Company pays $9,000 in wages to laborers for construction on a building to be used in the business.
(f) Alvarez's Florists pays wages of $2,100 for the month an employee who serves as driver of their delivery truck.

EXERCISES

1 3 **E2-1 (Usefulness, Objective of Financial Reporting)** Indicate whether the following statements about the conceptual framework are true or false. If false, provide a brief explanation supporting your position.

(a) Accounting rule-making that relies on a body of concepts will result in useful and consistent pronouncements.
(b) General-purpose financial reports are most useful to company insiders in making strategic business decisions.
(c) Accounting standards based on individual conceptual frameworks generally will result in consistent and comparable accounting reports.
(d) Capital providers are the only users who benefit from general-purpose financial reporting.
(e) Accounting reports should be developed so that users without knowledge of economics and business can become informed about the financial results of a company.
(f) The objective of financial reporting is the foundation from which the other aspects of the framework logically result.

1 3 **E2-2 (Usefulness, Objective of Financial Reporting, Qualitative Characteristics)** Indicate whether the
4 following statements about the conceptual framework are true or false. If false, provide a brief explanation supporting your position.

(a) The fundamental qualitative characteristics that make accounting information useful are relevance and verifiability.
(b) Relevant information only has predictive value, confirmatory value, or both.
(c) Information that is a faithful representation is characterized as having predictive or confirmatory value.
(d) Comparability pertains only to the reporting of information in a similar manner for different companies.
(e) Verifiability is solely an enhancing characteristic for faithful representation.
(f) In preparing financial reports, it is assumed that users of the reports have reasonable knowledge of business and economic activities.

4 8 **E2-3 (Qualitative Characteristics)** *SFAC No. 8* identifies the qualitative characteristics that make accounting information useful. Presented below are a number of questions related to these qualitative characteristics and underlying constraints.

(a) What is the quality of information that enables users to confirm or correct prior expectations?
(b) Identify the pervasive constraint(s) developed in the conceptual framework.
(c) The chairman of the SEC at one time noted, "If it becomes accepted or expected that accounting principles are determined or modified in order to secure purposes other than economic measurement, we assume a grave risk that confidence in the credibility of our financial information system

will be undermined." Which qualitative characteristic of accounting information should ensure that such a situation will not occur? (Do not use representationally faithful.)

(d) Muruyama Corp. switches from FIFO to average cost to FIFO over a 2-year period. Which qualitative characteristic of accounting information is not followed?

(e) Assume that the profession permits the savings and loan industry to defer losses on investments it sells, because immediate recognition of the loss may have adverse economic consequences on the industry. Which qualitative characteristic of accounting information is not followed? (Do not use relevance or representationally faithful.)

(f) What are the two primary qualities that make accounting information useful for decision-making?

(g) Watteau Inc. does not issue its first-quarter report until after the second quarter's results are reported. Which qualitative characteristic of accounting is not followed? (Do not use relevance.)

(h) Predictive value is an ingredient of which of the two primary qualities that make accounting information useful for decision-making purposes?

(i) Duggan, Inc. is the only company in its industry to depreciate its plant assets on a straight-line basis. Which qualitative characteristic of accounting information may not be followed? (Do not use industry practices.)

(j) Roddick Company has attempted to determine the replacement cost of its inventory. Three different appraisers arrive at substantially different amounts for this value. The president, nevertheless, decides to report the middle value for external reporting purposes. Which qualitative characteristic of information is lacking in these data? (Do not use relevance or representational faithfulness.)

4 **E2-4 (Qualitative Characteristics)** The qualitative characteristics that make accounting information useful for decision-making purposes are as follows.

Relevance	Neutrality	Verifiability
Faithful representation	Completeness	Understandability
Predictive value	Timeliness	Comparability
Confirmatory value	Materiality	

Instructions

Identify the appropriate qualitative characteristic(s) to be used given the information provided below.

(a) Qualitative characteristic being employed when companies in the same industry are using the same accounting principles.

(b) Quality of information that confirms users' earlier expectations.

(c) Imperative for providing comparisons of a company from period to period.

(d) Ignores the economic consequences of a standard or rule.

(e) Requires a high degree of consensus among individuals on a given measurement.

(f) Predictive value is an ingredient of this primary quality of information.

(g) Four qualitative characteristics that are related to both relevance and faithful representation.

(h) An item is not recorded because its effect on income would not change a decision.

(i) Neutrality is an ingredient of this primary quality of accounting information.

(j) Two primary qualities that make accounting information useful for decision-making purposes.

(k) Issuance of interim reports is an example of what primary ingredient of relevance?

5 **E2-5 (Elements of Financial Statements)** Ten interrelated elements that are most directly related to measuring the performance and financial status of an enterprise are provided below.

Assets	Distributions to owners	Expenses
Liabilities	Comprehensive income	Gains
Equity	Revenues	Losses
Investments by owners		

Instructions

Identify the element or elements associated with the 12 items below.

(a) Arises from peripheral or incidental transactions.

(b) Obligation to transfer resources arising from a past transaction.

(c) Increases ownership interest.

(d) Declares and pays cash dividends to owners.

(e) Increases in net assets in a period from nonowner sources.

(f) Items characterized by service potential or future economic benefit.

(g) Equals increase in assets less liabilities during the year, after adding distributions to owners and subtracting investments by owners.

(h) Arises from income statement activities that constitute the entity's ongoing major or central operations.

(i) Residual interest in the assets of the enterprise after deducting its liabilities.

(j) Increases assets during a period through sale of product.
(k) Decreases assets during the period by purchasing the company's own stock.
(l) Includes all changes in equity during the period, except those resulting from investments by owners and distributions to owners.

6 7 **E2-6 (Assumptions, Principles, and Constraints)** Presented below are the assumptions, principles, and
8 constraints used in this chapter.

1. Economic entity assumption
2. Going concern assumption
3. Monetary unit assumption
4. Periodicity assumption
5. Historical cost principle
6. Fair value principle
7. Expense recognition principle
8. Full disclosure principle
9. Cost constraint
10. Industry practices

Instructions

Identify by number the accounting assumption, principle, or constraint that describes each situation on the next page. Do not use a number more than once.

(a) Allocates expenses to revenues in the proper period.
(b) Indicates that fair value changes subsequent to purchase are not recorded in the accounts. (Do not use revenue recognition principle.)
(c) Ensures that all relevant financial information is reported.
(d) Rationale why plant assets are not reported at liquidation value. (Do not use historical cost principle.)
(e) Indicates that personal and business record keeping should be separately maintained.
(f) Separates financial information into time periods for reporting purposes.
(g) Permits the use of fair value valuation in certain industries. (Do not use fair value principle.)
(h) Assumes that the dollar is the "measuring stick" used to report on financial performance.

6 7 **E2-7 (Assumptions, Principles, and Constraints)** Presented below are a number of operational guide-
8 lines and practices that have developed over time.

Instructions

Select the assumption, principle, or constraint that most appropriately justifies these procedures and practices. (Do not use qualitative characteristics.)

(a) Fair value changes are not recognized in the accounting records.
(b) Financial information is presented so that investors will not be misled.
(c) Intangible assets are capitalized and amortized over periods benefited.
(d) Repair tools are expensed when purchased.
(e) Agricultural companies use fair value for purposes of valuing crops.
(f) Each enterprise is kept as a unit distinct from its owner or owners.
(g) All significant postbalance sheet events are reported.
(h) Revenue is recorded at point of sale.
(i) All important aspects of bond indentures are presented in financial statements.
(j) Rationale for accrual accounting.
(k) The use of consolidated statements is justified.
(l) Reporting must be done at defined time intervals.
(m) An allowance for doubtful accounts is established.
(n) Goodwill is recorded only at time of purchase.
(o) A company charges its sales commission costs to expense.

7 **E2-8 (Full Disclosure Principle)** Presented below are a number of facts related to Weller, Inc. Assume that no mention of these facts was made in the financial statements and the related notes.

Instructions

Assume that you are the auditor of Weller, Inc. and that you have been asked to explain the appropriate accounting and related disclosure necessary for each of these items.

(a) The company decided that, for the sake of conciseness, only net income should be reported on the income statement. Details as to revenues, cost of goods sold, and expenses were omitted.
(b) Equipment purchases of $170,000 were partly financed during the year through the issuance of a $110,000 notes payable. The company offset the equipment against the notes payable and reported plant assets at $60,000.
(c) Weller has reported its ending inventory at $2,100,000 in the financial statements. No other information related to inventories is presented in the financial statements and related notes.
(d) The company changed its method of valuing inventories from weighted-average to FIFO. No mention of this change was made in the financial statements.

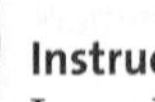

E2-9 (Accounting Principles—Comprehensive) Presented below are a number of business transactions that occurred during the current year for Gonzales, Inc.

Instructions

In each of the situations, discuss the appropriateness of the journal entries in terms of generally accepted accounting principles.

(a) The president of Gonzales, Inc. used his expense account to purchase a new Suburban solely for personal use. The following journal entry was made.

Miscellaneous Expense	29,000	
Cash		29,000

(b) Merchandise inventory that cost $620,000 is reported on the balance sheet at $690,000, the expected selling price less estimated selling costs. The following entry was made to record this increase in value.

Inventory	70,000	
Sales Revenue		70,000

(c) The company is being sued for $500,000 by a customer who claims damages for personal injury apparently caused by a defective product. Company attorneys feel extremely confident that the company will have no liability for damages resulting from the situation. Nevertheless, the company decides to make the following entry.

Loss from Lawsuit	500,000	
Liability for Lawsuit		500,000

(d) Because the general level of prices increased during the current year, Gonzales, Inc. determined that there was a $16,000 understatement of depreciation expense on its equipment and decided to record it in its accounts. The following entry was made.

Depreciation Expense	16,000	
Accumulated Depreciation—Equipment		16,000

(e) Gonzales, Inc. has been concerned about whether intangible assets could generate cash in case of liquidation. As a consequence, goodwill arising from a purchase transaction during the current year and recorded at $800,000 was written off as follows.

Retained Earnings	800,000	
Goodwill		800,000

(f) Because of a "fire sale," equipment obviously worth $200,000 was acquired at a cost of $155,000. The following entry was made.

Equipment	200,000	
Cash		155,000
Sales Revenue		45,000

E2-10 (Accounting Principles—Comprehensive) Presented below is information related to Anderson, Inc.

Instructions

Comment on the appropriateness of the accounting procedures followed by Anderson, Inc.

(a) Depreciation expense on the building for the year was $60,000. Because the building was increasing in value during the year, the controller decided to charge the depreciation expense to retained earnings instead of to net income. The following entry is recorded.

Retained Earnings	60,000	
Accumulated Depreciation—Buildings		60,000

(b) Materials were purchased on January 1, 2012, for $120,000 and this amount was entered in the Materials account. On December 31, 2012, the materials would have cost $141,000, so the following entry is made.

Inventory	21,000	
Gain on Inventories		21,000

(c) During the year, the company purchased equipment through the issuance of common stock. The stock had a par value of $135,000 and a fair value of $450,000. The fair value of the equipment was not easily determinable. The company recorded this transaction as follows.

Equipment	135,000	
Common Stock		135,000

(d) During the year, the company sold certain equipment for $285,000, recognizing a gain of $69,000. Because the controller believed that new equipment would be needed in the near future, she decided to defer the gain and amortize it over the life of any new equipment purchased.

(e) An order for $61,500 has been received from a customer for products on hand. This order was shipped on January 9, 2013. The company made the following entry in 2012.

Accounts Receivable	61,500	
Sales Revenue		61,500

See the book's companion website, www.wiley.com/college/kieso, for a set of B Exercises.

CONCEPTS FOR ANALYSIS

CA2-1 (Conceptual Framework—General) Wayne Cooper has some questions regarding the theoretical framework in which GAAP is set. He knows that the FASB and other predecessor organizations have attempted to develop a conceptual framework for accounting theory formulation. Yet, Wayne's supervisors have indicated that these theoretical frameworks have little value in the practical sense (i.e., in the real world). Wayne did notice that accounting rules seem to be established after the fact rather than before. He thought this indicated a lack of theory structure but never really questioned the process at school because he was too busy doing the homework.

Wayne feels that some of his anxiety about accounting theory and accounting semantics could be alleviated by identifying the basic concepts and definitions accepted by the profession and considering them in light of his current work. By doing this, he hopes to develop an appropriate connection between theory and practice.

Instructions

(a) Help Wayne recognize the purpose of and benefit of a conceptual framework.

(b) Identify any *Statements of Financial Accounting Concepts* issued by FASB that may be helpful to Wayne in developing his theoretical background.

CA2-2 (Conceptual Framework—General) The Financial Accounting Standards Board (FASB) has developed a conceptual framework for financial accounting and reporting. The FASB has issued eight *Statements of Financial Accounting Concepts.* These statements are intended to set forth the objective and fundamentals that will be the basis for developing financial accounting and reporting standards. The objective identifies the goals and purposes of financial reporting. The fundamentals are the underlying concepts of financial accounting that guide the selection of transactions, events, and circumstances to be accounted for; their recognition and measurement; and the means of summarizing and communicating them to interested parties.

The purpose of the statement on qualitative characteristics is to examine the characteristics that make accounting information useful. These characteristics or qualities of information are the ingredients that make information useful and the qualities to be sought when accounting choices are made.

Instructions

(a) Identify and discuss the benefits that can be expected to be derived from the FASB's conceptual framework study.

(b) What is the most important quality for accounting information as identified in the conceptual framework? Explain why it is the most important.

(c) *Statement of Financial Accounting Concepts No. 8* describes a number of key characteristics or qualities for accounting information. Briefly discuss the importance of any three of these qualities for financial reporting purposes.

(CMA adapted)

CA2-3 (Objective of Financial Reporting) Homer Winslow and Jane Alexander are discussing various aspects of the FASB's concepts statement on the objective of financial reporting. Homer indicates that this pronouncement provides little, if any, guidance to the practicing professional in resolving accounting controversies. He believes that the statement provides such broad guidelines that it would be impossible to apply the objective to present-day reporting problems. Jane concedes this point but indicates that the objective is still needed to provide a starting point for the FASB in helping to improve financial reporting.

Instructions

(a) Indicate the basic objective established in the conceptual framework.

(b) What do you think is the meaning of Jane's statement that the FASB needs a starting point to resolve accounting controversies?

CA2-4 (Qualitative Characteristics) Accounting information provides useful information about business transactions and events. Those who provide and use financial reports must often select and evaluate accounting alternatives. The FASB statement on qualitative characteristics of accounting information examines the characteristics of accounting information that make it useful for decision-making. It also points out that various limitations inherent in the measurement and reporting process may necessitate trade-offs or sacrifices among the characteristics of useful information.

Instructions

(a) Describe briefly the following characteristics of useful accounting information.

(1) Relevance
(2) Faithful representation
(3) Understandability
(4) Comparability
(5) Consistency

(b) For each of the following pairs of information characteristics, give an example of a situation in which one of the characteristics may be sacrificed in return for a gain in the other.

(1) Relevance and faithful representation.
(2) Relevance and consistency.
(3) Comparability and consistency.
(4) Relevance and understandability.

(c) What criterion should be used to evaluate trade-offs between information characteristics?

CA2-5 (Revenue and Expense Recognition Principles) After the presentation of your report on the examination of the financial statements to the board of directors of Piper Publishing Company, one of the new directors expresses surprise that the income statement assumes that an equal proportion of the revenue is earned with the publication of every issue of the company's magazine. She feels that the "crucial event" in the process of earning revenue in the magazine business is the cash sale of the subscription. She says that she does not understand why most of the revenue cannot be "recognized" in the period of the sale.

Instructions

(a) List the various accepted times for recognizing revenue in the accounts and explain when the methods are appropriate.

(b) Discuss the propriety of timing the recognition of revenue in Piper Publishing Company's accounts with:

(1) The cash sale of the magazine subscription.
(2) The publication of the magazine every month.
(3) Both events, by recognizing a portion of the revenue with the cash sale of the magazine subscription and a portion of the revenue with the publication of the magazine every month.

CA2-6 (Revenue and Expense Recognition Principles) On June 5, 2011, Argot Corporation signed a contract with Lopez Associates under which Lopez agreed (1) to construct an office building on land owned by Argot, (2) to accept responsibility for procuring financing for the project and finding tenants, and (3) to manage the property for 35 years. The annual net income from the project, after debt service, was to be divided equally between Argot Corporation and Lopez Associates. Lopez was to accept its share of future net income as full payment for its services in construction, obtaining finances and tenants, and management of the project.

By May 31, 2012, the project was nearly completed, and tenants had signed leases to occupy 90% of the available space at annual rentals totaling $4,000,000. It is estimated that, after operating expenses and debt service, the annual net income will amount to $1,500,000.

The management of Lopez Associates believed that (a) the economic benefit derived from the contract with Argot should be reflected on its financial statements for the fiscal year ended May 31, 2012, and directed that revenue be accrued in an amount equal to the commercial value of the services Lopez had rendered during the year, (b) this amount should be carried in contracts receivable, and (c) all related expenditures should be charged against the revenue.

Instructions

(a) Explain the main difference between the economic concept of business income as reflected by Lopez's management and the measurement of income under generally accepted accounting principles.

(b) Discuss the factors to be considered in determining when revenue should be recognized for the purpose of accounting measurement of periodic income.

(c) Is the belief of Lopez's management in accordance with generally accepted accounting principles for the measurement of revenue and expense for the year ended May 31, 2012? Support your opinion by discussing the application to this case of the factors to be considered for asset measurement and revenue and expense recognition.

(AICPA adapted)

CA2-7 (Expense Recognition Principle) An accountant must be familiar with the concepts involved in determining earnings of a business entity. The amount of earnings reported for a business entity is dependent on the proper recognition, in general, of revenue and expense for a given time period. In some situations, costs are recognized as expenses at the time of product sale. In other situations, guidelines have been developed for recognizing costs as expenses or losses by other criteria.

Instructions

(a) Explain the rationale for recognizing costs as expenses at the time of product sale.

(b) What is the rationale underlying the appropriateness of treating costs as expenses of a period instead of assigning the costs to an asset? Explain.

(c) In what general circumstances would it be appropriate to treat a cost as an asset instead of as an expense? Explain.

(d) Some expenses are assigned to specific accounting periods on the basis of systematic and rational allocation of asset cost. Explain the underlying rationale for recognizing expenses on the basis of systematic and rational allocation of asset cost.

(e) Identify the conditions under which it would be appropriate to treat a cost as a loss.

(AICPA adapted)

CA2-8 (Expense Recognition Principle) Accountants try to prepare income statements that are as accurate as possible. A basic requirement in preparing accurate income statements is to record costs and revenues properly. Proper recognition of costs and revenues requires that costs resulting from typical business operations be recognized in the period in which they expired.

Instructions

(a) List three criteria that can be used to determine whether such costs should appear as charges in the income statement for the current period.

(b) As generally presented in financial statements, the following items or procedures have been criticized as improperly recognizing costs. Briefly discuss each item from the viewpoint of matching costs with revenues and suggest corrective or alternative means of presenting the financial information.

(1) Receiving and handling costs.

(2) Cash discounts on purchases.

CA2-9 (Expense Recognition Principle) Daniel Barenboim sells and erects shell houses, that is, frame structures that are completely finished on the outside but are unfinished on the inside except for flooring, partition studding, and ceiling joists. Shell houses are sold chiefly to customers who are handy with tools and who have time to do the interior wiring, plumbing, wall completion and finishing, and other work necessary to make the shell houses livable dwellings.

Barenboim buys shell houses from a manufacturer in unassembled packages consisting of all lumber, roofing, doors, windows, and similar materials necessary to complete a shell house. Upon commencing operations in a new area, Barenboim buys or leases land as a site for its local warehouse, field office, and display houses. Sample display houses are erected at a total cost of $30,000 to $44,000 including the cost of the unassembled packages. The chief element of cost of the display houses is the unassembled packages, inasmuch as erection is a short, low-cost operation. Old sample models are torn down or altered into new models every 3 to 7 years. Sample display houses have little salvage value because dismantling and moving costs amount to nearly as much as the cost of an unassembled package.

Instructions

(a) A choice must be made between (1) expensing the costs of sample display houses in the periods in which the expenditure is made and (2) spreading the costs over more than one period. Discuss the advantages of each method.

(b) Would it be preferable to amortize the cost of display houses on the basis of (1) the passage of time or (2) the number of shell houses sold? Explain.

(AICPA adapted)

CA2-10 (Qualitative Characteristics) Recently, your Uncle Carlos Beltran, who knows that you always have your eye out for a profitable investment, has discussed the possibility of your purchasing some corporate bonds. He suggests that you may wish to get in on the "ground floor" of this deal. The bonds being issued by Neville Corp. are 10-year debentures which promise a 40% rate of return. Neville manufactures novelty/party items.

You have told Neville that, unless you can take a look at its financial statements, you would not feel comfortable about such an investment. Believing that this is the chance of a lifetime, Uncle Carlos has procured a copy of Neville's most recent, unaudited financial statements which are a year old. These statements were prepared by Mrs. Andy Neville. You peruse these statements, and they are quite impressive. The balance sheet showed a debt-to-equity ratio of 0.10 and, for the year shown, the company reported net income of $2,424,240.

The financial statements are not shown in comparison with amounts from other years. In addition, no significant note disclosures about inventory valuation, depreciation methods, loan agreements, etc. are available.

Instructions

Write a letter to Uncle Carlos explaining why it would be unwise to base an investment decision on the financial statements that he has provided to you. Be sure to explain why these financial statements are neither relevant nor representationally faithful.

CA2-11 (Expense Recognition Principle) Anderson Nuclear Power Plant will be "mothballed" at the end of its useful life (approximately 20 years) at great expense. The expense recognition principle requires that expenses be matched to revenue. Accountants Ana Alicia and Ed Bradley argue whether it is better to allocate the expense of mothballing over the next 20 years or ignore it until mothballing occurs.

Instructions

Answer the following questions.

(a) What stakeholders should be considered?
(b) What ethical issue, if any, underlies the dispute?
(c) What alternatives should be considered?
(d) Assess the consequences of the alternatives.
(e) What decision would you recommend?

CA2-12 (Cost Constraint) The AICPA Special Committee on Financial Reporting proposed the following constraints related to financial reporting.

1. Business reporting should exclude information outside of management's expertise or for which management is not the best source, such as information about competitors.
2. Management should not be required to report information that would significantly harm the company's competitive position.
3. Management should not be required to provide forecasted financial statements. Rather, management should provide information that helps users forecast for themselves the company's financial future.
4. Other than for financial statements, management need report only the information it knows. That is, management should be under no obligation to gather information it does not have, or does not need, to manage the business.
5. Companies should present certain elements of business reporting only if users and management agree they should be reported—a concept of flexible reporting.
6. Companies should not have to report forward-looking information unless there are effective deterrents to unwarranted litigation that discourages companies from doing so.

Instructions

For each item, briefly discuss how the proposed constraint addresses concerns about the costs and benefits of financial reporting.

USING YOUR JUDGMENT

FINANCIAL REPORTING

Financial Reporting Problem

The Procter & Gamble Company (P&G)

The financial statements of P&G are presented in Appendix 5B or can be accessed at the book's companion website, **www.wiley.com/college/kieso**.

Instructions

Refer to P&G's financial statements and the accompanying notes to answer the following questions.

(a) Using the notes to the consolidated financial statements, determine P&G's revenue recognition policies. Discuss the impact of trade promotions on P&G's financial statements.

(b) Give two examples of where historical cost information is reported in P&G's financial statements and related notes. Give two examples of the use of fair value information reported in either the financial statements or related notes.

(c) How can we determine that the accounting principles used by P&G are prepared on a basis consistent with those of last year?

(d) What is P&G's accounting policy related to advertising? What accounting principle does P&G follow regarding accounting for advertising? Where are advertising expenses reported in the financial statements?

Comparative Analysis Case

The Coca-Cola Company and PepsiCo, Inc.

Instructions

Go to the book's companion website, and use information found there to answer the following questions related to **The Coca-Cola Company** and **PepsiCo, Inc.**

(a) What are the primary lines of business of these two companies as shown in their notes to the financial statements?

(b) Which company has the dominant position in beverage sales?

(c) How are inventories for these two companies valued? What cost allocation method is used to report inventory? How does their accounting for inventories affect comparability between the two companies?

(d) Which company changed its accounting policies during 2009 which affected the consistency of the financial results from the previous year? What were these changes?

Financial Statement Analysis Case

Wal-Mart

Wal-Mart Stores provided the following disclosure in a recent annual report.

> ***New accounting pronouncement (partial)*** . . . the Securities and Exchange Commission issued Staff Accounting Bulletin No. 101—"Revenue Recognition in Financial Statements" (*SAB 101*). This SAB deals with various revenue recognition issues, several of which are common within the retail industry. As a result of the issuance of this SAB . . . the Company is currently evaluating the effects of the SAB on its method of recognizing revenues related to layaway sales and will make any accounting method changes necessary during the first quarter of [next year].

In response to *SAB 101*, Wal-Mart changed its revenue recognition policy for layaway transactions, in which Wal-Mart sets aside merchandise for customers who make partial payment. Before the change, Wal-Mart recognized all revenue on the sale at the time of the layaway. After the change, Wal-Mart does not recognize revenue until customers satisfy all payment obligations and take possession of the merchandise.

Instructions

(a) Discuss the expected effect on income (1) in the year that Wal-Mart makes the changes in its revenue recognition policy, and (2) in the years following the change.

(b) Evaluate the extent to which Wal-Mart's previous revenue policy was consistent with the revenue recognition principle.

(c) If all retailers had used a revenue recognition policy similar to Wal-Mart's before the change, are there any concerns with respect to the qualitative characteristic of comparability? Explain.

Accounting, Analysis, and Principles

William Murray achieved one of his life-long dreams by opening his own business, The Caddie Shack Driving Range, on May 1, 2012. He invested $20,000 of his own savings in the business. He paid $6,000 cash to have a small building constructed to house the operations and spent $800 on golf clubs, golf balls, and yardage signs. Murray leased 4 acres of land at a cost of $1,000 per month. (He paid the first month's rent in cash.) During the first month, advertising costs totaled $750, of which $150 was unpaid at the end of the month. Murray paid his three nephews $400 for retrieving golf balls. He deposited in the company's bank account all revenues from customers ($4,700). On May 15, Murray withdrew $800 in cash for personal use. On May 31, the company received a utility bill for $100 but did not immediately pay it. On May 31, the balance in the company bank account was $15,100.

Murray is feeling pretty good about results for the first month, but his estimate of profitability ranges from a loss of $4,900 to a profit of $1,650.

Accounting

Prepare a balance sheet at May 31, 2012. Murray appropriately records any depreciation expense on a quarterly basis. How could Murray have determined that the business operated at a profit of $1,650? How could Murray conclude that the business operated at a loss of $4,900?

Analysis

Assume Murray has asked you to become a partner in his business. Under the partnership agreement, after paying him $10,000, you would share equally in all future profits. Which of the two income measures above would be more useful in deciding whether to become a partner? Explain.

Principles

What is income according to GAAP? What concepts do the differences in the three income measures for The Caddie Shack Driving Range illustrate?

BRIDGE TO THE PROFESSION

Professional Research

Your aunt recently received the annual report for a company in which she has invested. The report notes that the statements have been prepared in accordance with "generally accepted accounting principles." She has also heard that certain terms have special meanings in accounting relative to everyday use. She would like you to explain the meaning of terms she has come across related to accounting.

Instructions

If your school has a subscription to the FASB Codification, go to *http://aaahq.org/asclogin.cfm* to log in, access the FASB Statements of Financial Accounting Concepts, and respond to the following items. (Provide paragraph citations.) When you have accessed the documents, you can use the search tool in your Internet browser.

(a) How is "materiality" defined in the conceptual framework?

(b) The concepts statements provide several examples in which specific quantitative materiality guidelines are provided to firms. Identity at least two of these examples. Do you think the materiality guidelines should be quantified? Why or why not?

(c) The concepts statements discuss the concept of "articulation" between financial statement elements. Briefly summarize the meaning of this term and how it relates to an entity's financial statements.

Professional Simulation

In this simulation, you are asked to address questions regarding the FASB conceptual framework. Prepare responses to all parts.

KWW_Professional_Simulation

Conceptual Framework | Time Remaining 4 hours 10 minutes | Unsplit | Split Horiz | Split Vertical | Spreadsheet | Calculator | Exit

Directions | Situation | Explanation | Research | Resources

A friend of yours is one of seven shareholders in a small start-up company. He is evaluating information about the company that was discussed at a recent shareholders' meeting. No mention of these facts was made in the financial statements or the related notes. Given your accounting background, he thought you would know the appropriate treatment of these items.

1. The company is concerned that one of its patents will be worthless in the event of liquidation. As a result, this intangible asset was written off through the following entry.

Retained Earnings	7,000	
Patents		7,000

2. The company is being sued for $15,000 by a customer claiming damages caused by a defective product. The attorney for the company is confident that the company will have no liability for damages. To be safe, the company made the following entry.

Loss from Lawsuit	15,000	
Lawsuit Liability		15,000

3. The company president used her expense account to purchase a new Hummer solely for her personal use. The following entry was made.

Miscellaneous Expense	55,000	
Cash		55,000

Directions | Situation | Explanation | Research | Resources

For each situation, prepare a brief explanation for the appropriate accounting and related disclosure required for each of the items.

Directions | Situation | Explanation | Research | Resources

Your friend had an extensive discussion with other shareholders on the subject of materiality. He argues for a strict quantitative definition of materiality, while the other shareholders believe that both quantitative and qualitative indicators should be considered in evaluating whether an item is material. Using the FASB Codification database, discuss how the conceptual framework defines and operationalizes materiality.

The IASB and the FASB are working on a joint project to develop a common conceptual framework. This framework is based on the existing conceptual frameworks underlying GAAP and IFRS. The objective of this joint project is to develop a conceptual framework that leads to standards that are principles-based and internally consistent and that leads to the most useful financial reporting.

RELEVANT FACTS

- In 2010, the IASB and FASB completed the first phase of a jointly created conceptual framework. In this first phase, they agreed on the objective of financial reporting and a common set of desired qualitative characteristics. These were presented in the Chapter 2 discussion.

- The existing conceptual frameworks underlying GAAP and IFRS are very similar. That is, they are organized in a similar manner (objectives, elements, qualitative characteristics, etc.). There is no real need to change many aspects of the existing frameworks other than to converge different ways of discussing essentially the same concepts.
- The converged framework should be a single document, unlike the two conceptual frameworks that presently exist; it is unlikely that the basic structure related to the concepts will change.
- Both the IASB and FASB have similar measurement principles, based on historical cost and fair value. Although both GAAP and IFRS are increasing the use of fair value to report assets, at this point IFRS has adopted it more broadly. As examples, under IFRS companies can apply fair value to property, plant, and equipment; natural resources; and in some cases intangible assets.
- GAAP has a concept statement to guide estimation of fair values when market-related data is not available (Statement of Financial Accounting Concepts No. 7, "Using Cash Flow Information and Present Value in Accounting"). The IASB is considering a proposal to provide expanded guidance on estimating fair values. See "Discussion Paper on Fair Value Measurement" (London, U.K.: IASB, November 2006).
- The monetary unit assumption is part of each framework. However, the unit of measure will vary depending on the currency used in the country in which the company is incorporated (e.g., Chinese yuan, Japanese yen, and British pound).
- The economic entity assumption is also part of each framework although some cultural differences result in differences in its application. For example, in Japan many companies have formed alliances that are so strong that they act similar to related corporate divisions although they are not actually part of the same company.

ABOUT THE NUMBERS

Financial Statement Elements

While the conceptual framework that underlies IFRS is very similar to that used to develop GAAP, the elements identified and their definitions under IFRS are different. The IASB elements and their definitions are as follows.

> ***Assets.*** A resource controlled by the entity as a result of past events and from which future economic benefits are expected to flow to the entity.
>
> ***Liabilities.*** A present obligation of the entity arising from past events, the settlement of which is expected to result in an outflow from the entity of resources embodying economic benefits. Liabilities may be legally enforceable via a contract or law, but need not be, i.e., they can arise due to normal business practice or customs.
>
> ***Equity.*** A residual interest in the assets of the entity after deducting all its liabilities.
>
> ***Income.*** Increases in economic benefits that result in increases in equity (other than those related to contributions from shareholders). Income includes both revenues (resulting from ordinary activities) and gains.
>
> ***Expenses.*** Decreases in economic benefits that result in decreases in equity (other than those related to distributions to shareholders). Expenses includes losses that are not the result of ordinary activities.

Conceptual Framework Work Plan

The work on the conceptual framework is being done in phases. As indicated in the chart below, final rule (F) of phase A related to objectives and qualitative characteristics has been issued in 2010. A chapter on the reporting entity (phase D) is planned for issuance in 2010. Discussion papers (DPs) related to measurement (phase C) and elements and recognition (phase B) should be issued in 2011.

Conceptual Framework Schedule	2010	2011	Timing not determined
Phase A: Objectives and qualitative characteristics	F		
Phase B: Elements and recognition		DP/F	
Phase C: Measurement		DP/F	
Phase D: Reporting entity	DP	F	
Phase E: Presentation and disclosure			DP
Phase F: Purpose and status			DP
Phase G: Application to not-for-profit entities			DP
Phase H: Remaining issues (Document type not yet determined)			

ON THE HORIZON

The IASB and the FASB face a difficult task in attempting to update, modify, and complete a converged conceptual framework. There are many difficult issues. For example: How do we trade off characteristics such as highly relevant information that is difficult to verify? How do we define control when we are developing a definition of an asset? Is a liability the future sacrifice itself or the obligation to make the sacrifice? Should a single measurement method, such as historical cost or fair value, be used, or does it depend on whether it is an asset or liability that is being measured? We are optimistic that the new document will be a significant improvement over its predecessors and will lead to principles-based standards that help users of the financial statements make better decisions.

IFRS SELF-TEST QUESTIONS

1. Which of the following statements about the IASB and FASB conceptual frameworks is *not* correct?

- **(a)** The IASB conceptual framework does not identify the element *comprehensive income*.
- **(b)** The existing IASB and FASB conceptual frameworks are organized in similar ways.
- **(c)** The FASB and IASB agree that the objective of financial reporting is to provide useful information to investors and creditors.
- **(d)** IFRS does not allow use of fair value as a measurement basis.

2. Which of the following statements is *false*?

- **(a)** The monetary unit assumption is used under IFRS.
- **(b)** Under IFRS, companies may use fair value for property, plant, and equipment.
- **(c)** The FASB and IASB are working on a joint conceptual framework project.
- **(d)** Under IFRS, there are the same number of financial statement elements as in GAAP.

3. Companies that use IFRS:

- **(a)** must report all their assets on the statement of financial position (balance sheet) at fair value.
- **(b)** may report property, plant, and equipment and natural resources at fair value.

(c) may refer to a concept statement on estimating fair values when market data are not available.
(d) may only use historical cost as the measurement basis in financial reporting.

4. The issues that the FASB and IASB must address in developing a common conceptual framework include all of the following *except*:
   (a) Should the characteristic of relevance be traded-off in favor of information that is verifiable?
   (b) Should a single measurement method such as historical cost be used?
   (c) Should the common framework lead to standards that are principles-based or rules-based?
   (d) Should the role of financial reporting focus on stewardship as well as providing information to assist users in decision-making?
5. With respect to the converged FASB/IASB conceptual framework:
   (a) work is being conducted on the framework as a whole, and it will not be issued until all parts are completed.
   (b) no elements of the framework will be issued in 2011.
   (c) work is being conducted on the framework in phases, and completed parts will be issued as completed.
   (d) the framework will not address disclosure issues.

IFRS CONCEPTS AND APPLICATION

IFRS2-1 What two assumptions are central to the IASB conceptual framework?

IFRS2-2 Do the IASB and FASB conceptual frameworks differ in terms of the role of financial reporting? Explain.

IFRS2-3 What are some of the differences in elements in the IASB and FASB conceptual frameworks?

IFRS2-4 What are some of the challenges to the FASB and IASB in developing a converged conceptual framework?

Financial Reporting Case

IFRS2-5 As discussed in Chapter 1, the **International Accounting Standards Board (IASB)** develops accounting standards for many international companies. The IASB also has developed a conceptual framework to help guide the setting of accounting standards. While the FASB and IASB have issued converged concepts statements on the objective and qualitative characteristics, other parts of their frameworks differ. Following is an excerpt of the IASB Framework.

Elements of Financial Statements

Asset: A resource controlled by the enterprise as a result of past events and from which future economic benefits are expected to flow to the enterprise.

Liability: A present obligation of the enterprise arising from past events, the settlement of which is expected to result in an outflow from the enterprise of resources embodying economic benefits.

Equity: The residual interest in the assets of the enterprise after deducting all its liabilities.

Income: Increases in economic benefits during the accounting period in the form of inflows or enhancements of assets or decreases of liabilities that result in increases in equity, other than those relating to contributions from equity participants.

Expenses: Decreases in economic benefits during the accounting period in the form of outflows or depletions of assets or incurrences of liabilities that result in decreases in equity, other than those relating to distributions to equity participants.

Instructions

Briefly discuss the similarities and differences between the FASB and IASB conceptual frameworks as revealed in the above excerpt.

Professional Research

IFRS2-6 Your aunt recently received the annual report for a company in which she has invested. The report notes that the statements have been prepared in accordance with IFRS. She has also heard that certain terms have special meanings in accounting relative to everyday use. She would like you to explain the meaning of terms she has come across related to accounting.

Instructions

Access the IASB Framework at the IASB website (*http://eifrs.iasb.org/*). When you have accessed the documents, you can use the search tool in your Internet browser to prepare responses to the following items. (Provide paragraph citations.)

(a) How is "materiality" defined in the framework?

(b) Briefly discuss how materiality relates to (1) the relevance of financial information, and (2) completeness.

(c) Your aunt observes that under IFRS, the financial statements are prepared on the accrual basis. According to the framework, what does or "accrual basis" mean?

International Financial Reporting Problem: *Marks and Spencer plc*

IFRS2-7 The financial statements of **Marks and Spencer plc (M&S)** are available at the book's companion website or can be accessed at *http://corporate.marksandspencer.com/documents/ publications/2010/Annual_Report_2010.*

Instructions

Refer to M&S's financial statements and the accompanying notes to answer the following questions.

(a) Using the notes to the consolidated financial statements, determine M&S's revenue recognition policies.

(b) Give two examples of where historical cost information is reported in M&S's financial statements and related notes. Give two examples of the use of fair value information reported in either the financial statements or related notes.

(c) How can we determine that the accounting principles used by M&S are prepared on a basis consistent with those of last year?

(d) What is M&S's accounting policy related to refunds and loyalty schemes? Why does M&S include the accounting for refunds and loyalty schemes in its critical accounting estimates and judgments?

ANSWERS TO IFRS SELF-TEST QUESTIONS

1. d **2.** d **3.** b **4.** d **5.** c

Remember to check the book's companion website to find additional resources for this chapter.

CHAPTER

3 The Accounting Information System

LEARNING OBJECTIVES

After studying this chapter, you should be able to:

1. Understand basic accounting terminology.
2. Explain double-entry rules.
3. Identify steps in the accounting cycle.
4. Record transactions in journals, post to ledger accounts, and prepare a trial balance.
5. Explain the reasons for preparing adjusting entries.
6. Prepare financial statements from the adjusted trial balance.
7. Prepare closing entries.

Needed: A Reliable Information System

Maintaining a set of accounting records is not optional. Regulators require that businesses prepare and retain a set of records and documents that can be audited. The U.S. Foreign Corrupt Practices Act, for example, requires public companies to ". . . make and keep books, records, and accounts, which, in reasonable detail, accurately and fairly reflect the transactions and dispositions of the assets. . . ." But beyond these two reasons, a company that fails to keep an accurate record of its business transactions may lose revenue and is more likely to operate inefficiently.

One reason accurate records are not provided is because of economic crime or corruption. It is clear that economic crime remains a persistent and difficult problem for many companies. For example, it was recently estimated that 53 percent of U.S. companies experienced significant economic crime. And its global counterparts are not far behind with a reported rate of 43 percent. In fact, many argue that the rates are even more comparable as U.S. companies often have more stringent internal controls and therefore are more likely to find, report, and discuss crime. Presented below is a chart that indicates U.S. and global companies' perception of the chances of being a victim of economic crime in the near-term future.

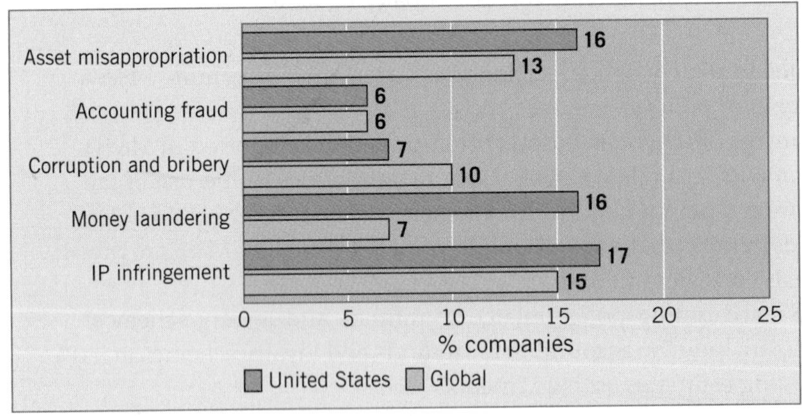

In some of these cases, such as money-laundering or infringement of intellectual property, a sound system of internal controls focused on financial accounting and reporting may not work. Nonetheless, many believe that effective internal control sends a message that a company is serious about finding not only economic crime but also errors or misstatements. As a result, many companies are taking a proactive look as to how they can better prevent both economic crime as well as basic errors in their systems. The chart on the next page indicates the percentage of companies that identified certain factors influencing their decision to implement controls to deter economic crime.

What happens when companies fail to keep an accurate record of its business transactions? Consider **Adecco**, the largest international employment services company, which confirmed existence of weakness in its internal controls systems and Adecco staffing operations in certain countries. Manipulation involved such matters as reconciliation of payroll bank accounts, accounts receivable, and documentation in revenue recognition. These irregularities forced an indefinite delay in the company's income

IFRS IN THIS CHAPTER

Read the **IFRS Insights** on pages 153–157 for a discussion of:

—Accounting system internal controls

—First-time adoption of IFRS

figures, which led to significant decline in share price. Or consider the **Long Island Railroad (LIRR)**, once one of the nation's busiest commuter lines. The LIRR lost money because of poor recordkeeping. It forgot to bill some customers, mistakenly paid some payables twice, and neglected to record redemptions of bonds. Or take **Nortel Networks Corp.**, which overstated and understated its reserve accounts to manage its earnings. It eventually led to the liquidation of the company.

Inefficient accounting also cost the **City of Cleveland**. An audit discovered over 313 examples of dysfunctional accounting, costing taxpayers over $1.3 million. Its poor accounting system resulted in Cleveland's treasurer's ignorance of available cash, which led to missed investment opportunities. Further, delayed recording of pension payments created the false impression of $13 million in the city coffers. The City of Cleveland's bond rating took a hit as a result of these discrepancies.

Even the use of computers is no assurance of accuracy and efficiency. "The conversion to a new system called MasterNet fouled up data processing records to the extent that **Bank of America** was frequently unable to produce or deliver customer statements on a timely basis," said an executive at one of the country's largest banks.

Reasons for Internal Controls

	U.S.	Global
Sarbanes-Oxley Act	99%	84%
U.S. Patriot Act	85	29
Advice from external consultants	63	50
FCPA/OECD Anti-Bribery Convention	38	23
Public discussion/media	38	33
Federal sentencing guidelines	38	29
Incidents of economic crime	31	34
Local legislation	24	51
Bad experience and/or advice from law enforcement	17	36

Although these situations may occur only rarely in large organizations, they illustrate the point: Companies must properly maintain accounts and detailed records or face unnecessary costs.

Source: Adapted from "Economic Crime: People, Culture, and Controls," *The Fourth Biennial Global Economic Crime Survey* (PricewaterhouseCoopers, 2007).

PREVIEW OF CHAPTER 3

As the opening story indicates, a reliable information system is a necessity for all companies. The purpose of this chapter is to explain and illustrate the features of an accounting information system. The content and organization of this chapter are as follows.

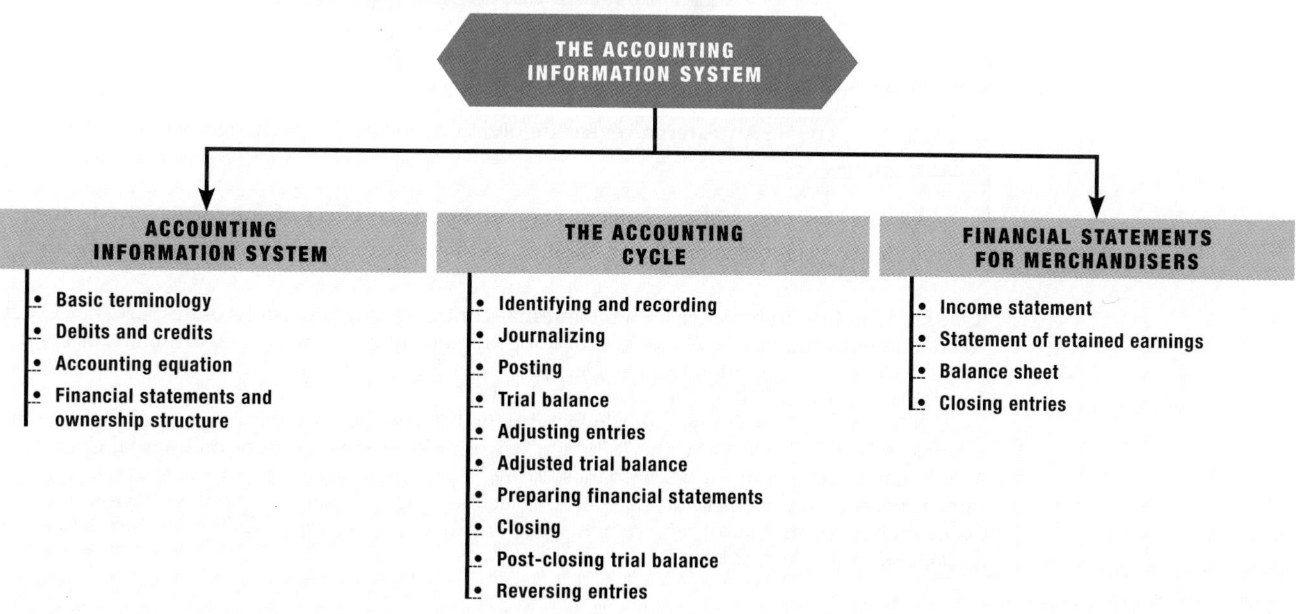

ACCOUNTING INFORMATION SYSTEM

An **accounting information system** collects and processes transaction data and then disseminates the financial information to interested parties. Accounting information systems vary widely from one business to another. Various factors shape these systems: the nature of the business and the transactions in which it engages, the size of the firm, the volume of data to be handled, and the informational demands that management and others require.

As we discussed in Chapters 1 and 2, in response to the requirements of the Sarbanes-Oxley Act of 2002, companies are placing a renewed focus on their accounting systems to ensure relevant and reliable information is reported in financial statements.[1] A good accounting information system helps management answer such questions as:

How much and what kind of debt is outstanding?
Were our sales higher this period than last?
What assets do we have?
What were our cash inflows and outflows?
Did we make a profit last period?
Are any of our product lines or divisions operating at a loss?
Can we safely increase our dividends to stockholders?
Is our rate of return on net assets increasing?

Management can answer many other questions with the data provided by an efficient accounting system. A well-devised accounting information system benefits every type of company.

Basic Terminology

LEARNING OBJECTIVE 1
Understand basic accounting terminology.

Financial accounting rests on a set of concepts (discussed in Chapters 1 and 2) for identifying, recording, classifying, and interpreting transactions and other events relating to enterprises. You therefore need to understand the **basic terminology employed in collecting accounting data.**

BASIC TERMINOLOGY

EVENT. A happening of consequence. An event generally is the source or cause of changes in assets, liabilities, and equity. Events may be external or internal.

TRANSACTION. An **external event** involving a transfer or exchange between two or more entities.

ACCOUNT. A systematic arrangement that shows the effect of transactions and other events on a specific element (asset, liability, and so on). Companies keep a separate account

[1]One study of first compliance with the internal-control testing provisions of the Sarbanes-Oxley Act documented material weaknesses for about 13 percent of companies reporting in 2004 and 2005. L. Townsend, "Internal Control Deficiency Disclosures–Interim Alert," *Yellow Card–Interim Trend Alert* (April 12, 2005), Glass, Lewis & Co., LLC.

In 2006, material weaknesses declined, with just 8.33 percent of companies reporting internal control problems. See K. Pany and J. Zhang, "Current Research Questions on Internal Control over Financial Reporting Under Sarbanes-Oxley," *The CPA Journal* (February 2008), p. 42. At the same time, companies reported a 5.4 percent decline in audit costs to comply with Sarbanes-Oxley internal control audit requirements. See *FEI Audit Fee Survey: Including Sarbanes-Oxley Section 404 Costs* (April 2008).

for each asset, liability, revenue, and expense, and for capital (owners' equity). Because the format of an account often resembles the letter T, it is sometimes referred to as a **T-account.** (See Illustration 3-3, p. 91.)

REAL AND NOMINAL ACCOUNTS. **Real** (permanent) **accounts** are asset, liability, and equity accounts; they appear on the balance sheet. **Nominal** (temporary) **accounts** are revenue, expense, and dividend accounts; except for dividends, they appear on the income statement. Companies periodically close nominal accounts; they do not close real accounts.

LEDGER. The book (or computer printouts) containing the accounts. A **general ledger** is a collection of all the asset, liability, owners' equity, revenue, and expense accounts. A **subsidiary ledger** contains the details related to a given general ledger account.

JOURNAL. The "book of original entry" where the company initially records transactions and selected other events. Various amounts are transferred from the book of original entry, the journal, to the ledger. Entering transaction data in the journal is known as **journalizing.**

POSTING. The process of transferring the essential facts and figures from the book of original entry to the ledger accounts.

TRIAL BALANCE. The list of all open accounts in the ledger and their balances. The trial balance taken immediately after all adjustments have been posted is called an **adjusted trial balance.** A trial balance taken immediately after closing entries have been posted is called a **post-closing** (or **after-closing**) **trial balance.** Companies may prepare a trial balance at any time.

ADJUSTING ENTRIES. Entries made at the end of an accounting period to bring all accounts up to date on an accrual basis, so that the company can prepare correct financial statements.

FINANCIAL STATEMENTS. Statements that reflect the collection, tabulation, and final summarization of the accounting data. Four statements are involved: (1) The **balance sheet** shows the financial condition of the enterprise at the end of a period. (2) The **income statement** measures the results of operations during the period. (3) The **statement of cash flows** reports the cash provided and used by operating, investing, and financing activities during the period. (4) The **statement of retained earnings** reconciles the balance of the retained earnings account from the beginning to the end of the period.

CLOSING ENTRIES. The formal process by which the enterprise reduces all nominal accounts to zero and determines and transfers the net income or net loss to an owners' equity account. Also known as "closing the ledger," "closing the books," or merely "closing."

Debits and Credits

2 LEARNING OBJECTIVE
Explain double-entry rules.

The terms **debit** (Dr.) and **credit** (Cr.) mean left and right, respectively. These terms do not mean increase or decrease, but instead describe *where* a company makes entries in the recording process. That is, when a company enters an amount on the left side of an account, it **debits** the account. When it makes an entry on the right side, it **credits** the account. When comparing the totals of the two sides, an account shows a **debit balance** if the total of the debit amounts exceeds the credits. An account shows a **credit balance** if the credit amounts exceed the debits.

The positioning of debits on the left and credits on the right is simply an accounting custom. We could function just as well if we reversed the sides. However, the United

States adopted the custom, now the rule, of having debits on the left side of an account and credits on the right side, similar to the custom of driving on the right-hand side of the road. This rule applies to all accounts.

The equality of debits and credits provides the basis for the double-entry system of recording transactions (sometimes referred to as double-entry bookkeeping). Under the universally used **double-entry accounting** system, a company records the dual (two-sided) effect of each transaction in appropriate accounts. This system provides a logical method for recording transactions. It also offers a means of proving the accuracy of the recorded amounts. If a company records every transaction with equal debits and credits, then the sum of all the debits to the accounts must equal the sum of all the credits.

Illustration 3-1 presents the basic guidelines for an accounting system. Increases to all asset and expense accounts occur on the left (or debit side) and decreases on the right (or credit side). Conversely, increases to all liability and revenue accounts occur on the right (or credit side) and decreases on the left (or debit side). A company increases stockholders' equity accounts, such as Common Stock and Retained Earnings, on the credit side, but increases Dividends on the debit side.

ILLUSTRATION 3-1
Double-Entry (Debit and Credit) Accounting System

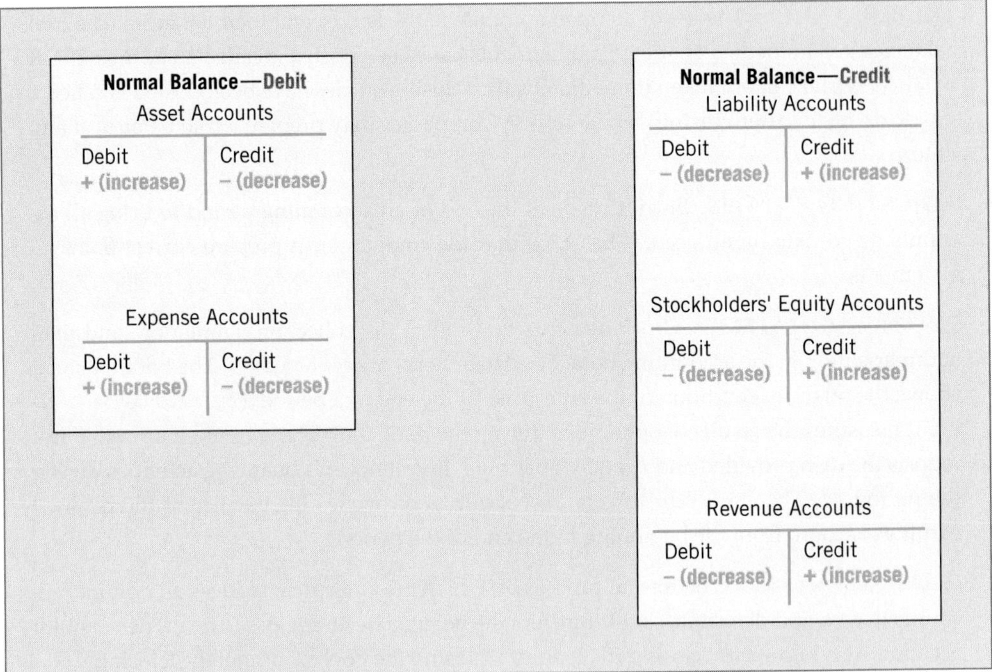

The Accounting Equation

In a double-entry system, for every debit there must be a credit, and vice versa. This leads us, then, to the basic equation in accounting (Illustration 3-2).

ILLUSTRATION 3-2
The Basic Accounting Equation

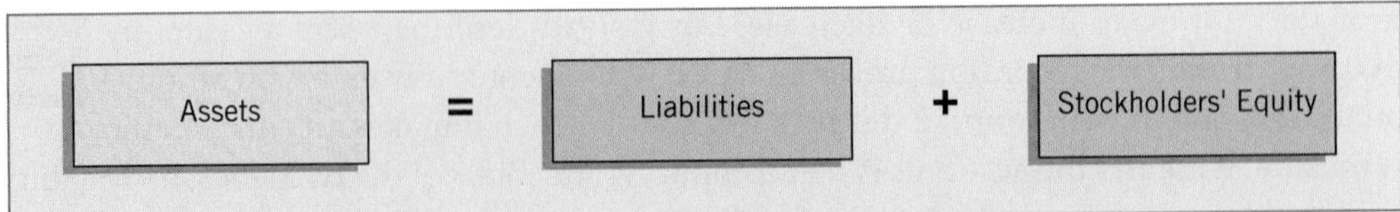

Illustration 3-3 expands this equation to show the accounts that make up stockholders' equity. The figure also shows the debit/credit rules and effects on each type of account. Study this diagram carefully. It will help you understand the fundamentals of the double-entry system. Like the basic equation, the expanded equation must also balance (total debits equal total credits).

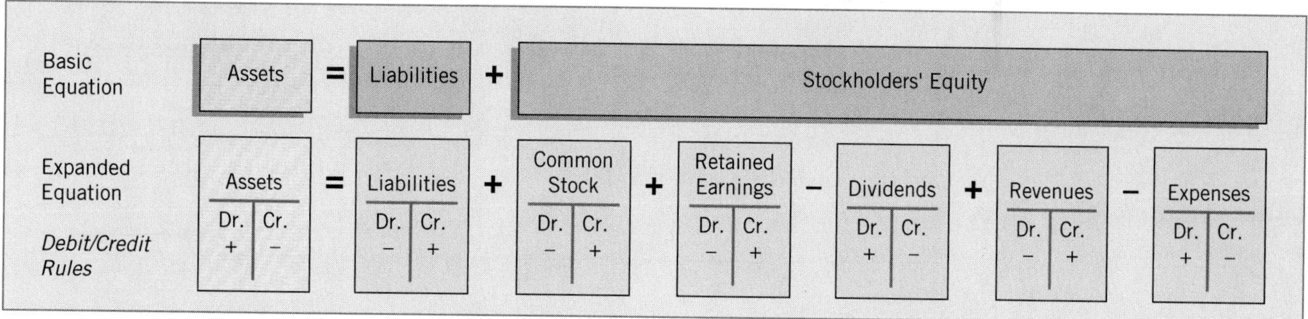

ILLUSTRATION 3-3
Expanded Equation and Debit/Credit Rules and Effects

Every time a transaction occurs, the elements of the accounting equation change. However, the basic equality remains. To illustrate, consider the following eight different transactions for Perez Inc.

1. Owners invest $40,000 in exchange for common stock.

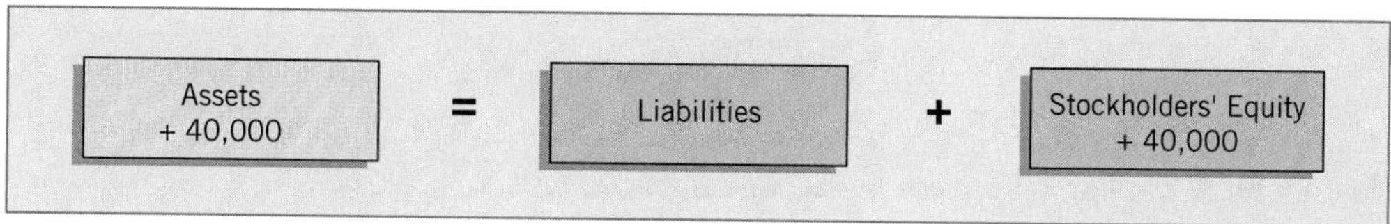

2. Disburse $600 cash for secretarial wages.

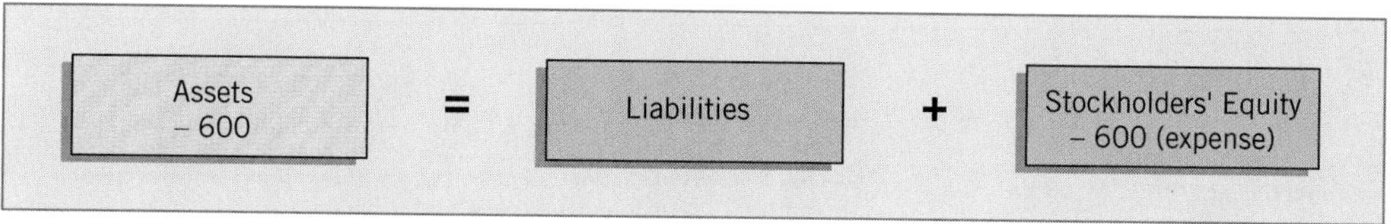

3. Purchase office equipment priced at $5,200, giving a 10 percent promissory note in exchange.

Assets
+ 5,200
=
Liabilities
+5,200
+
Stockholders' Equity

4. Receive $4,000 cash for services rendered.

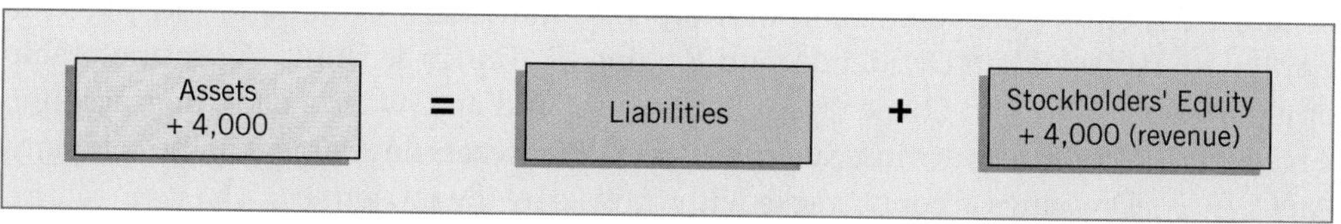

5. Pay off a short-term liability of $7,000.

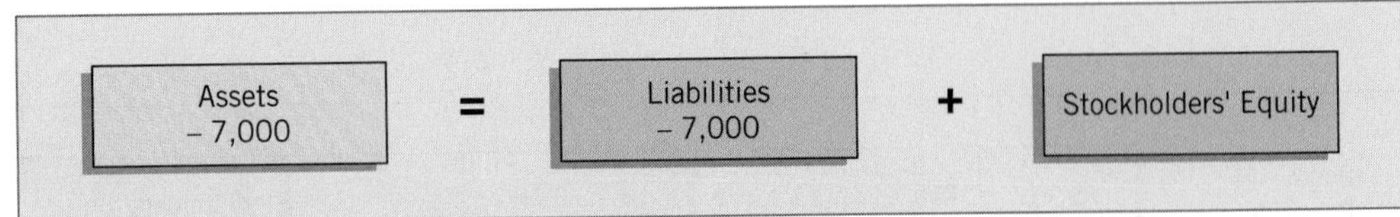

6. Declare a cash dividend of $5,000.

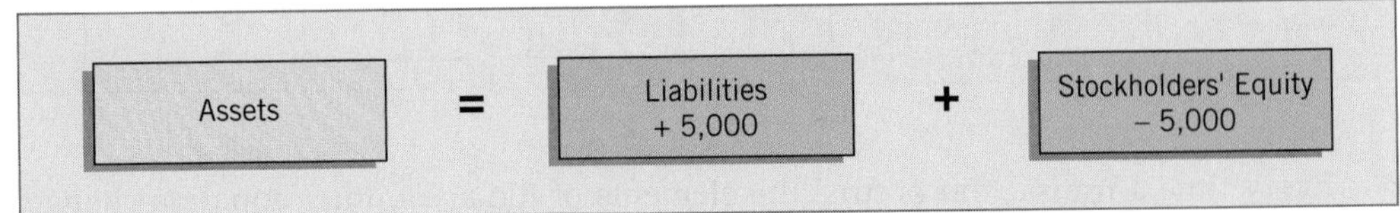

7. Convert a long-term liability of $80,000 into common stock.

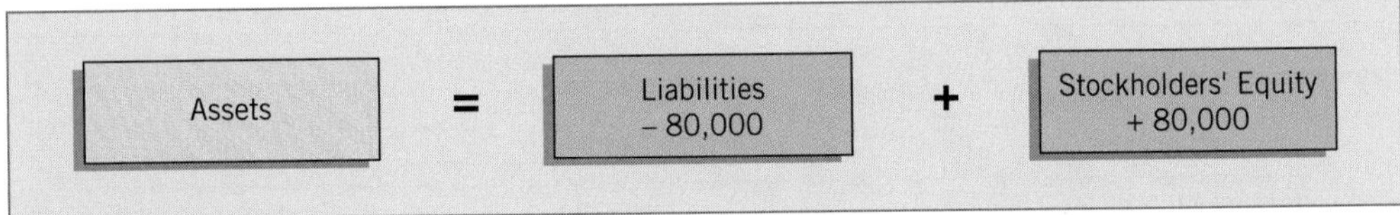

8. Pay cash of $16,000 for a delivery van.

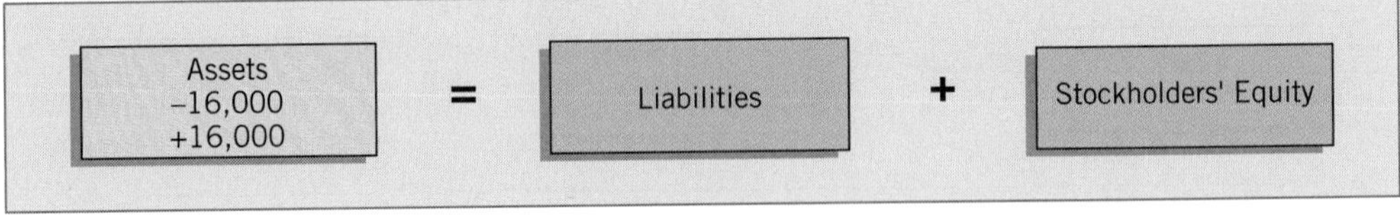

Financial Statements and Ownership Structure

The stockholders' equity section of the balance sheet reports common stock and retained earnings. The income statement reports revenues and expenses. The statement of retained earnings reports dividends. Because a company transfers dividends, revenues, and expenses to retained earnings at the end of the period, a change in any one of these three items affects stockholders' equity. Illustration 3-4 shows the stockholders' equity relationships.

The enterprise's ownership structure dictates the types of accounts that are part of or affect the equity section. A corporation commonly uses Common Stock, Paid-in Capital in Excess of Par, Dividends, and Retained Earnings accounts. A proprietorship or a partnership uses an Owner's Capital account and an Owner's Drawings account. An Owner's Capital account indicates the owner's or owners' investment in the company. An Owner's Drawings account tracks withdrawals by the owner(s).

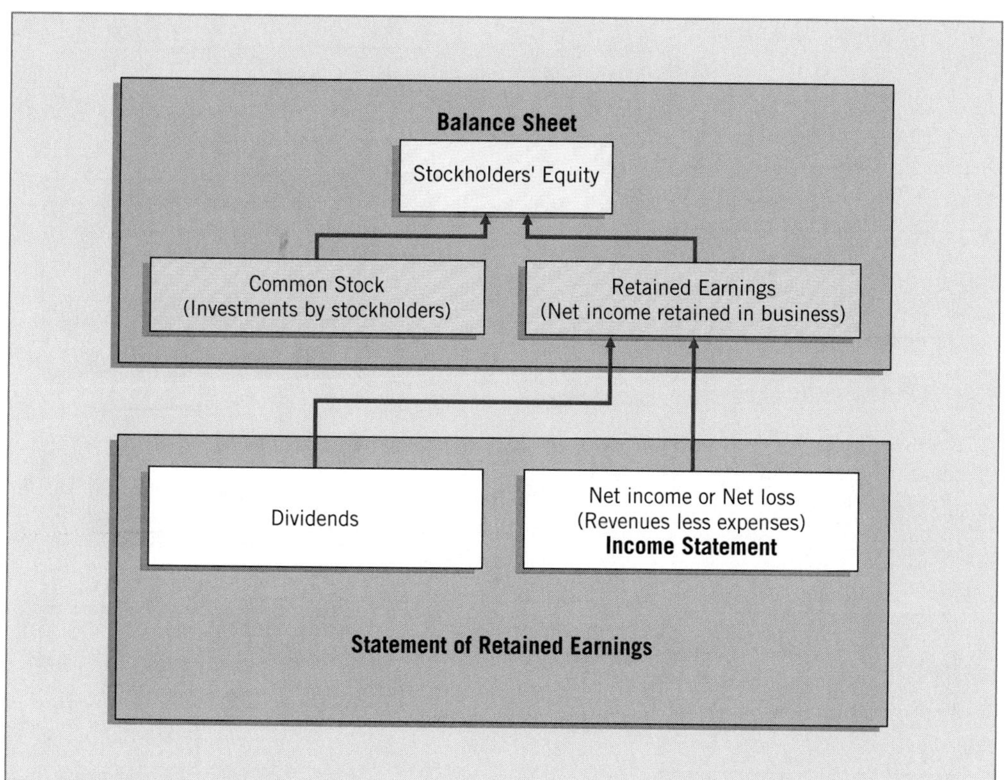

ILLUSTRATION 3-4
Financial Statements and Ownership Structure

Illustration 3-5 summarizes and relates the transactions affecting owners' equity to the nominal (temporary) and real (permanent) classifications and to the types of business ownership.

ILLUSTRATION 3-5
Effects of Transactions on Owners' Equity Accounts

		Ownership Structure			
		Proprietorships and Partnerships		**Corporations**	
Transactions Affecting Owners' Equity	Impact on Owners' Equity	Nominal (Temporary) Accounts	Real (Permanent) Accounts	Nominal (Temporary) Accounts	Real (Permanent) Accounts
Investment by owner(s)	Increase		Capital		Common Stock and related accounts
Revenues earned Expenses incurred Withdrawal by owner(s)	Increase Decrease Decrease	Revenue Expense Drawing	Capital	Revenue Expense Dividends	Retained Earnings

THE ACCOUNTING CYCLE

3 LEARNING OBJECTIVE
Identify steps in the accounting cycle.

Illustration 3-6 (on page 94) shows the steps in the **accounting cycle**. An enterprise normally uses these accounting procedures to record transactions and prepare financial statements.

Identifying and Recording Transactions and Other Events

The first step in the accounting cycle is analysis of transactions and selected other events. The first problem is to determine what to record. Although GAAP provides guidelines, no simple rules exist that state which events a company should record. Although changes

ILLUSTRATION 3-6
The Accounting Cycle

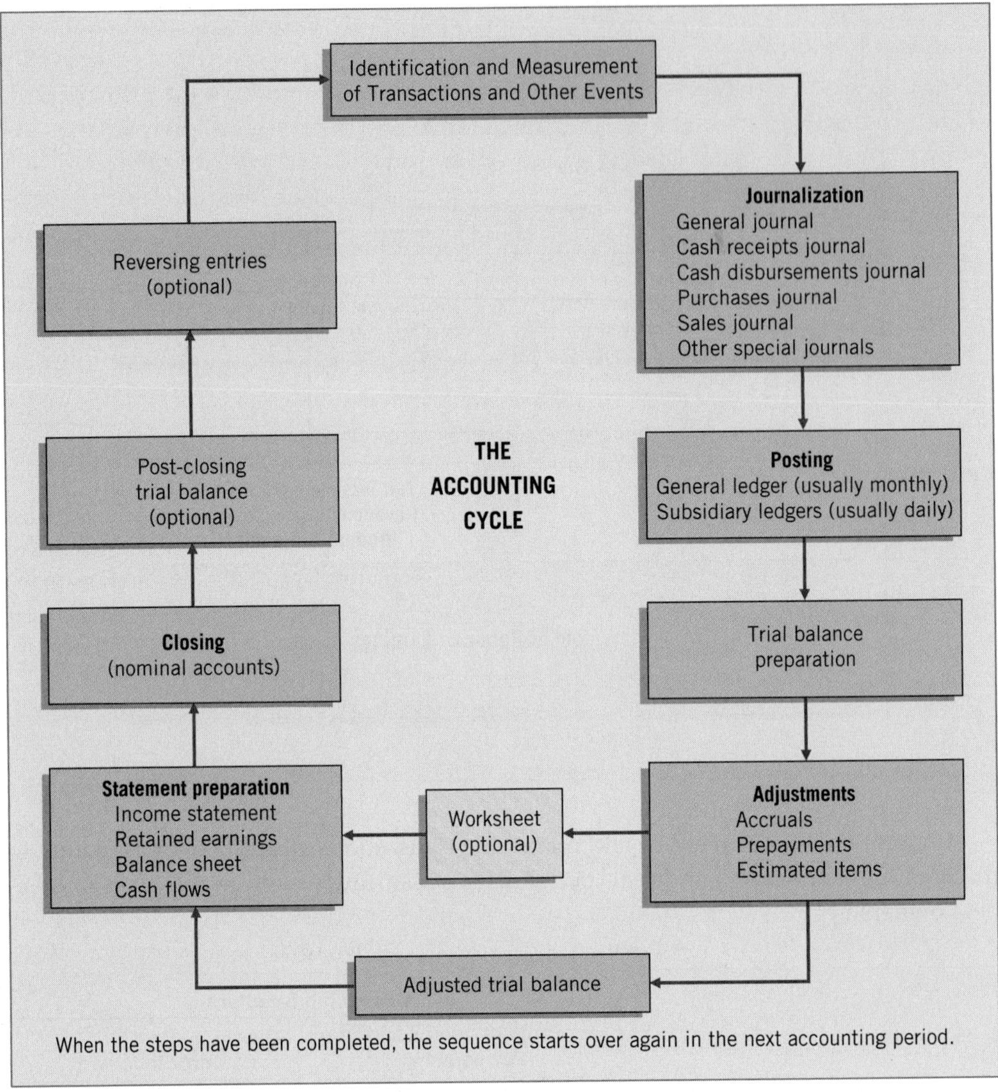

in a company's personnel or managerial policies may be important, the company should not record these items in the accounts. On the other hand, a company should record all cash sales or purchases—no matter how small.

The concepts we presented in Chapter 2 determine what to recognize in the accounts. An item should be recognized in the financial statements if it is an element, is measurable, and is relevant and reliable. Consider human resources. **R. G. Barry & Co.** at one time reported as supplemental data total assets of $14,055,926, including $986,094 for "Net investments in human resources." **AT&T** and **Exxon Mobil Company** also experimented with human resource accounting. Should we value employees for balance sheet and income statement purposes? Certainly skilled employees are an important asset (highly relevant), but the problems of determining their value and measuring it reliably have not yet been solved. Consequently, human resources are not recorded. Perhaps when measurement techniques become more sophisticated and accepted, such information will be presented, if only in supplemental form.

Underlying Concepts

Assets are probable economic benefits controlled by a particular entity as a result of a past transaction or event. Do human resources of a company meet this definition?

The FASB uses the phrase "transactions and other events and circumstances that affect a business enterprise" to describe the sources or causes of changes in an entity's assets, liabilities, and equity.[2] Events are of two types: (1) **External**

[2]"Elements of Financial Statements of Business Enterprises," *Statement of Financial Accounting Concepts No. 6* (Stamford, Conn.: FASB, 1985), pp. 259–260.

events involve interaction between an entity and its environment, such as a transaction with another entity, a change in the price of a good or service that an entity buys or sells, a flood or earthquake, or an improvement in technology by a competitor. (2) **Internal events** occur within an entity, such as using buildings and machinery in operations, or transferring or consuming raw materials in production processes.

Many events have both external and internal elements. For example, hiring an employee, which involves an exchange of salary for labor, is an external event. Using the services of labor is part of production, an internal event. Further, an entity may initiate and control events, such as the purchase of merchandise or use of a machine. Or, events may be beyond its control, such as an interest rate change, theft, or a tax hike.

Transactions are types of external events. They may be an exchange between two entities where each receives and sacrifices value, such as purchases and sales of goods or services. Or, transactions may be transfers in one direction only. For example, an entity may incur a liability without directly receiving value in exchange, such as charitable contributions. Other examples include investments by owners, distributions to owners, payment of taxes, gifts, casualty losses, and thefts.

In short, an enterprise records as many events as possible that affect its financial position. As discussed earlier in the case of human resources, it omits some events because of tradition and others because of complicated measurement problems. Recently, however, the accounting profession shows more receptiveness to accepting the challenge of measuring and reporting events previously viewed as too complex and immeasurable.

Journalizing

4 LEARNING OBJECTIVE
Record transactions in journals, post to ledger accounts, and prepare a trial balance.

A company records in **accounts** those transactions and events that affect its assets, liabilities, and equities. The **general ledger** contains all the asset, liability, and stockholders' equity accounts. An account (see Illustration 3-3, on page 91) shows the effect of transactions on particular asset, liability, equity, revenue, and expense accounts.

In practice, companies do not record transactions and selected other events originally in the ledger. A transaction affects two or more accounts, each of which is on a different page in the ledger. Therefore, in order to have a complete record of each transaction or other event in one place, a company uses a **journal** (also called "the book of original entry"). In its simplest form, a **general journal** chronologically lists transactions and other events, expressed in terms of debits and credits to accounts.

Illustration 3-7 depicts the technique of journalizing, using the first two transactions for Softbyte, Inc. These transactions were:

September 1 Stockholders invested $15,000 cash in the corporation in exchange for shares of stock.
Purchased computer equipment for $7,000 cash.

The J1 indicates these two entries are on the first page of the general journal.

ILLUSTRATION 3-7
Technique of Journalizing

GENERAL JOURNAL				J1
Date	**Account Titles and Explanation**	**Ref.**	**Debit**	**Credit**
2012				
Sept. 1	Cash		15,000	
	Common Stock			15,000
	(Issued shares of stock for cash)			
1	Equipment		7,000	
	Cash			7,000
	(Purchased equipment for cash)			

Gateway to the Profession

Expanded Discussion of Special Journals

Each **general journal entry** consists of four parts: (1) the accounts and amounts to be debited (Dr.), (2) the accounts and amounts to be credited (Cr.), (3) a date, and (4) an explanation. A company enters debits first, followed by the credits (slightly indented). The explanation begins below the name of the last account to be credited and may take one or more lines. A company completes the "Ref." column at the time it posts the accounts.

In some cases, a company uses special journals in addition to the general journal. Special journals summarize transactions possessing a common characteristic (e.g., cash receipts, sales, purchases, cash payments). As a result, using them reduces bookkeeping time.

Posting

The procedure of transferring journal entries to the ledger accounts is called posting. Posting involves the following steps.

1. In the ledger, enter in the appropriate columns of the debited account(s) the date, journal page, and debit amount shown in the journal.
2. In the reference column of the journal, write the account number to which the debit amount was posted.
3. In the ledger, enter in the appropriate columns of the credited account(s) the date, journal page, and credit amount shown in the journal.
4. In the reference column of the journal, write the account number to which the credit amount was posted.

Illustration 3-8 diagrams these four steps, using the first journal entry of Softbyte, Inc. The illustration shows the general ledger accounts in **standard account form**. Some

ILLUSTRATION 3-8
Posting a Journal Entry

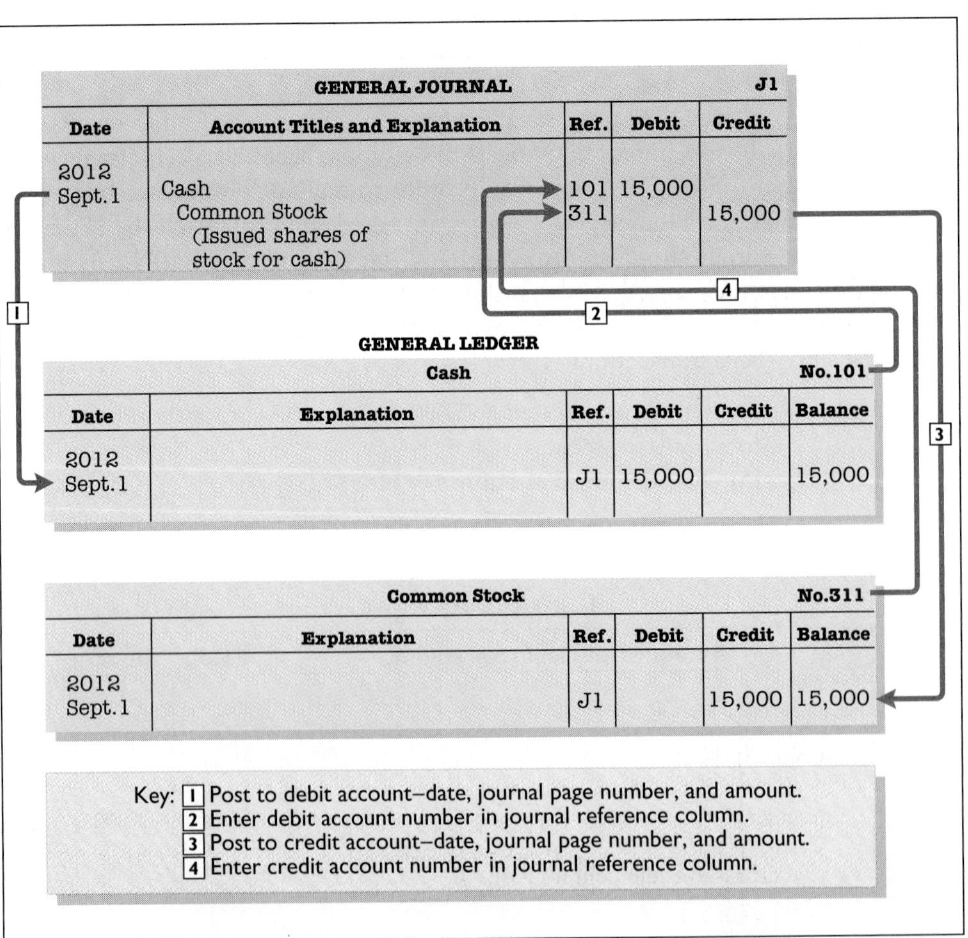

companies call this form the **three-column form of account** because it has three money columns—debit, credit, and balance. The balance in the account is determined after each transaction. The explanation space and reference columns provide special information about the transaction. The boxed numbers indicate the sequence of the steps.

The numbers in the "Ref." column of the general journal refer to the ledger accounts to which a company posts the respective items. For example, the "101" placed in the column to the right of "Cash" indicates that the company posted this $15,000 item to Account No. 101 in the ledger.

The posting of the general journal is completed when a company records all of the posting reference numbers opposite the account titles in the journal. Thus, the number in the posting reference column serves two purposes: (1) It indicates the ledger account number of the account involved. (2) It indicates the completion of posting for the particular item. Each company selects its own numbering system for its ledger accounts. Many begin numbering with asset accounts and then follow with liabilities, owners' equity, revenue, and expense accounts, in that order.

The ledger accounts in Illustration 3-8 show the accounts after completion of the posting process. The reference J1 (General Journal, page 1) indicates the source of the data transferred to the ledger account.

Expanded Example. To show an expanded example of the basic steps in the recording process, we use the October transactions of Pioneer Advertising Agency Inc. Pioneer's accounting period is a month. Illustrations 3-9 through 3-18 show the journal entry and posting of each transaction. For simplicity, we use a T-account form instead of the standard account form. Study the transaction analyses carefully.

The purpose of transaction analysis is (1) to identify the type of account involved, and (2) to determine whether a debit or a credit is required. You should always perform this type of analysis before preparing a journal entry. Doing so will help you understand the journal entries discussed in this chapter as well as more complex journal entries in later chapters. Keep in mind that every journal entry affects one or more of the following items: assets, liabilities, stockholders' equity, revenues, or expenses.

1. October 1: Stockholders invest $100,000 cash in an advertising venture to be known as Pioneer Advertising Agency Inc.

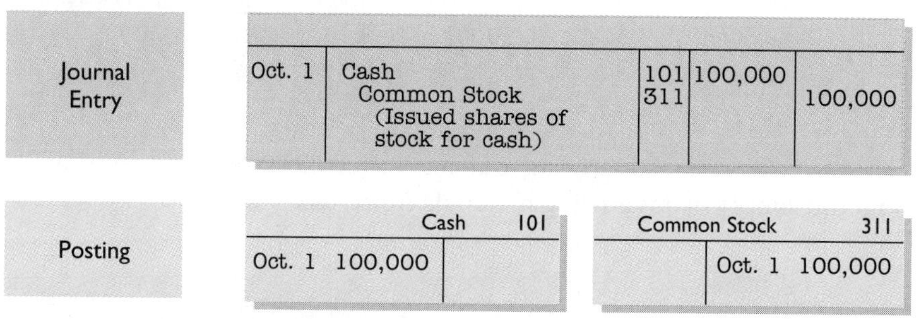

Journal Entry

Date	Account	Ref.	Debit	Credit
Oct. 1	Cash	101	100,000	
	Common Stock	311		100,000
	(Issued shares of stock for cash)			

Posting

Cash 101	
Oct. 1 100,000	

Common Stock 311	
	Oct. 1 100,000

ILLUSTRATION 3-9
Investment of Cash by Stockholders

2. October 1: Pioneer Advertising purchases office equipment costing $50,000 by signing a 3-month, 12%, $50,000 note payable.

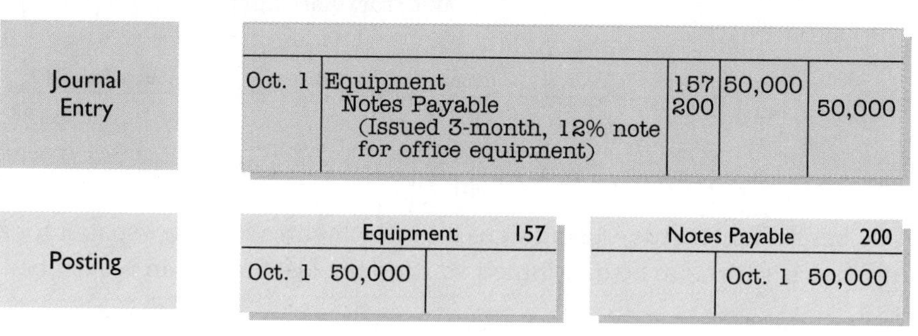

Journal Entry

Date	Account	Ref.	Debit	Credit
Oct. 1	Equipment	157	50,000	
	Notes Payable	200		50,000
	(Issued 3-month, 12% note for office equipment)			

Posting

Equipment 157	
Oct. 1 50,000	

Notes Payable 200	
	Oct. 1 50,000

ILLUSTRATION 3-10
Purchase of Office Equipment

3. October 2: Pioneer Advertising receives a $12,000 cash advance from R. Knox, a client, for advertising services that are expected to be completed by December 31.

ILLUSTRATION 3-11
Receipt of Cash for Future Service

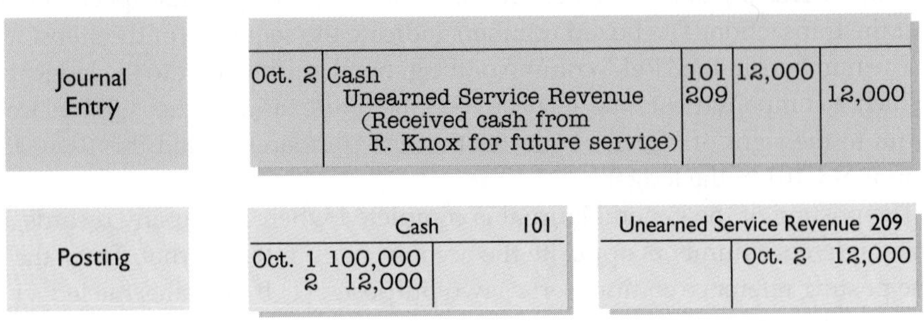

4. October 3: Pioneer Advertising pays $9,000 office rent, in cash, for October.

ILLUSTRATION 3-12
Payment of Monthly Rent

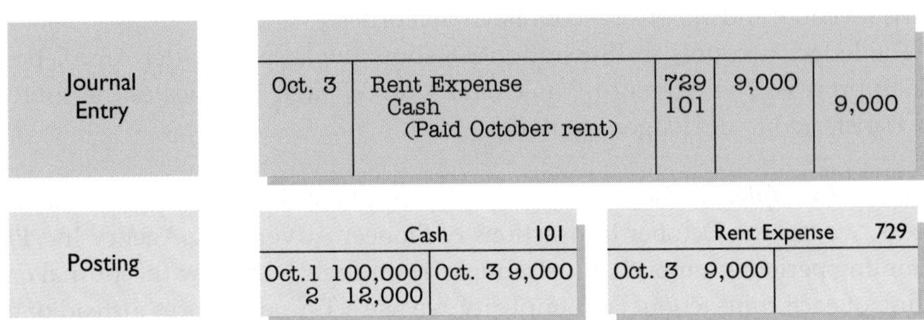

5. October 4: Pioneer Advertising pays $6,000 for a one-year insurance policy that will expire next year on September 30.

ILLUSTRATION 3-13
Payment for Insurance

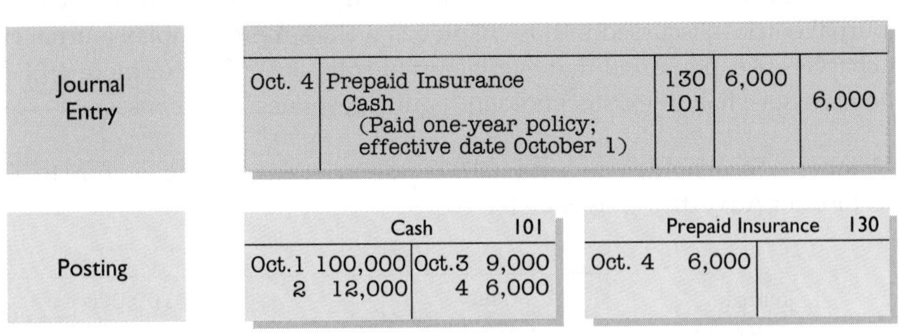

6. October 5: Pioneer Advertising purchases, for $25,000 on account, an estimated 3-month supply of advertising materials from Aero Supply.

ILLUSTRATION 3-14
Purchase of Supplies on Account

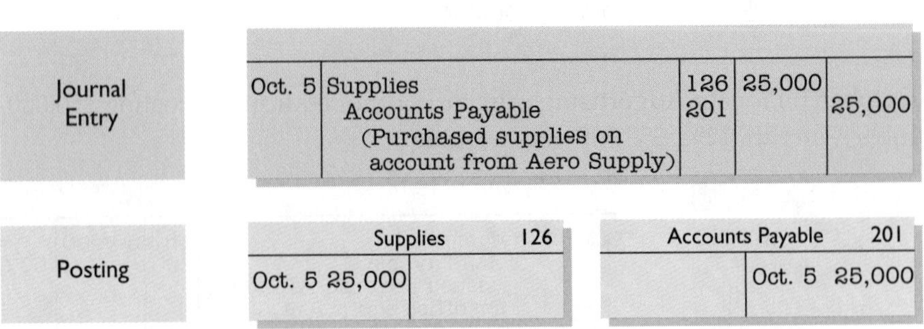

7. October 9: Pioneer Advertising signs a contract with a local newspaper for advertising inserts (flyers) to be distributed starting the last Sunday in November. Pioneer will start work on the content of the flyers in November. Payment of $7,000 is due following delivery of the Sunday papers containing the flyers.

A business transaction has not occurred. There is only an agreement between Pioneer Advertising and the newspaper for the services to be provided in November. Therefore, no journal entry is necessary in October.

ILLUSTRATION 3-15
Signing a Contract

8. October 20: Pioneer Advertising's board of directors declares and pays a $5,000 cash dividend to stockholders.

ILLUSTRATION 3-16
Declaration and Payment of Dividend by Corporation

Journal Entry

Oct. 20	Dividends	332	5,000	
	Cash	101		5,000
	(Declared and paid a cash dividend)			

Posting

Cash		101	
Oct.1	100,000	Oct. 3	9,000
2	12,000	4	6,000
		20	5,000

Dividends		332
Oct. 20	5,000	

9. October 26: Pioneer Advertising pays employee salaries and wages in cash. Employees are paid once a month, every four weeks. The total payroll is $10,000 per week, or $2,000 per day. In October, the pay period began on Monday, October 1. As a result, the pay period ended on Friday, October 26, with salaries and wages of $40,000 being paid.

ILLUSTRATION 3-17
Payment of Salaries and Wages

Journal Entry

Oct. 26	Salaries and Wages Expense	726	40,000	
	Cash	101		40,000
	(Paid salaries to date)			

Posting

Cash		101	
Oct.1	100,000	Oct.3	9,000
2	12,000	4	6,000
		20	5,000
		26	40,000

Salaries and Wages Expense		726
Oct.26	40,000	

10. October 31: Pioneer Advertising receives $28,000 in cash and bills Copa Company $72,000 for advertising services of $100,000 provided in October.

ILLUSTRATION 3-18
Recognize Revenue for Services Provided

Journal Entry

Oct. 31	Cash	101	28,000	
	Accounts Receivable	112	72,000	
	Service Revenue	400		100,000
	(Recognize revenue for services provided)			

Posting

Cash		101	
Oct.1	100,000	Oct.3	9,000
2	12,000	4	6,000
31	28,000	20	5,000
		26	40,000

Accounts Receivable		112
Oct. 31	72,000	

Service Revenue		400	
		Oct. 31	100,000

Trial Balance

A **trial balance** lists accounts and their balances at a given time. A company usually prepares a trial balance at the end of an accounting period. The trial balance lists the accounts in the order in which they appear in the ledger, with debit balances listed in the left column and credit balances in the right column. The totals of the two columns must agree.

The trial balance proves the mathematical equality of debits and credits after posting. Under the double-entry system, this equality occurs when the sum of the debit account balances equals the sum of the credit account balances. A trial balance also uncovers errors in journalizing and posting. In addition, it is useful in the preparation of financial statements. The procedures for preparing a trial balance consist of:

1. Listing the account titles and their balances.
2. Totaling the debit and credit columns.
3. Proving the equality of the two columns.

Illustration 3-19 presents the trial balance prepared from the ledger of Pioneer Advertising Agency Inc. Note that the total debits ($287,000) equal the total credits ($287,000). A trial balance also often shows account numbers to the left of the account titles.

ILLUSTRATION 3-19
Trial Balance (Unadjusted)

PIONEER ADVERTISING AGENCY INC.
TRIAL BALANCE
OCTOBER 31, 2012

	Debit	Credit
Cash	$ 80,000	
Accounts Receivable	72,000	
Supplies	25,000	
Prepaid Insurance	6,000	
Equipment	50,000	
Notes Payable		$ 50,000
Accounts Payable		25,000
Unearned Service Revenue		12,000
Common Stock		100,000
Dividends	5,000	
Service Revenue		100,000
Salaries and Wages Expense	40,000	
Rent Expense	9,000	
	$287,000	$287,000

A trial balance does not prove that a company recorded all transactions or that the ledger is correct. Numerous errors may exist even though the trial balance columns agree. For example, the trial balance may balance even when a company (1) fails to journalize a transaction, (2) omits posting a correct journal entry, (3) posts a journal entry twice, (4) uses incorrect accounts in journalizing or posting, or (5) makes offsetting errors in recording the amount of a transaction. In other words, as long as a company posts equal debits and credits, even to the wrong account or in the wrong amount, the total debits will equal the total credits.

Adjusting Entries

LEARNING OBJECTIVE 5
Explain the reasons for preparing adjusting entries.

In order for a company, like **McDonald's**, to record revenues in the period in which it earns them, and to recognize expenses in the period in which it incurs them, it makes **adjusting entries** at the end of the accounting period. In short, adjustments ensure that McDonald's follows the revenue recognition and expense recognition principles.

The use of adjusting entries makes it possible to report on the balance sheet the appropriate assets, liabilities, and owners' equity at the statement date. Adjusting entries also make it possible to report on the income statement the proper revenues and expenses for the period. However, the trial balance—the first pulling together of the transaction data—may not contain up-to-date and complete data. This occurs for the following reasons.

1. Some events are not journalized daily because it is not expedient. Examples are the consumption of supplies and the earning of wages by employees.
2. Some costs are not journalized during the accounting period because these costs expire with the passage of time rather than as a result of recurring daily transactions. Examples of such costs are building and equipment deterioration and rent and insurance.
3. Some items may be unrecorded. An example is a utility service bill that will not be received until the next accounting period.

Adjusting entries are required every time a company, such as **Coca-Cola**, prepares financial statements. At that time, Coca-Cola must analyze each account in the trial balance to determine whether it is complete and up-to-date for financial statement purposes. The analysis requires a thorough understanding of Coca-Cola's operations and the interrelationship of accounts. Because of this involved process, usually a skilled accountant prepares the adjusting entries. In gathering the adjustment data, Coca-Cola may need to make inventory counts of supplies and repair parts. Further, it may prepare supporting schedules of insurance policies, rental agreements, and other contractual commitments. Companies often prepare adjustments after the balance sheet date. However, they date the entries as of the balance sheet date.

Types of Adjusting Entries

Adjusting entries are classified as either deferrals or accruals. Each of these classes has two subcategories, as Illustration 3-20 shows.

Deferrals	Accruals
1. **Prepaid Expenses.** Expenses paid in cash and recorded as assets **before** they are used or consumed.	3. **Accrued Revenues.** Revenues earned but **not yet received** in cash or recorded.
2. **Unearned Revenues.** Revenues received in cash and recorded as liabilities **before** they are earned.	4. **Accrued Expenses.** Expenses incurred but **not yet paid** in cash or recorded.

ILLUSTRATION 3-20
Classes of Adjusting Entries

We review specific examples and explanations of each type of adjustment in subsequent sections. We base each example on the October 31 trial balance of Pioneer Advertising Agency Inc. (Illustration 3-19). We assume that Pioneer uses an accounting period of one month. Thus, Pioneer will make monthly adjusting entries, dated October 31.

Adjusting Entries for Deferrals

As we indicated earlier, deferrals are either prepaid expenses or unearned revenues. Adjusting entries for deferrals, required at the statement date, record the portion of the deferral that represents the **expense incurred or the revenue earned** in the current accounting period.

If a company does not make an adjustment for these deferrals, the asset and liability are overstated, and the related expense and revenue are understated. For example, in Pioneer's trial balance (Illustration 3-19), the balance in the asset Supplies shows only supplies purchased. This balance is overstated; the related expense account, Supplies Expense, is understated because the cost of supplies used has not been recognized. Thus, the adjusting entry for deferrals will decrease a balance sheet account and increase an income statement account. Illustration 3-21 shows the effects of adjusting entries for deferrals.

ILLUSTRATION 3-21
Adjusting Entries for Deferrals

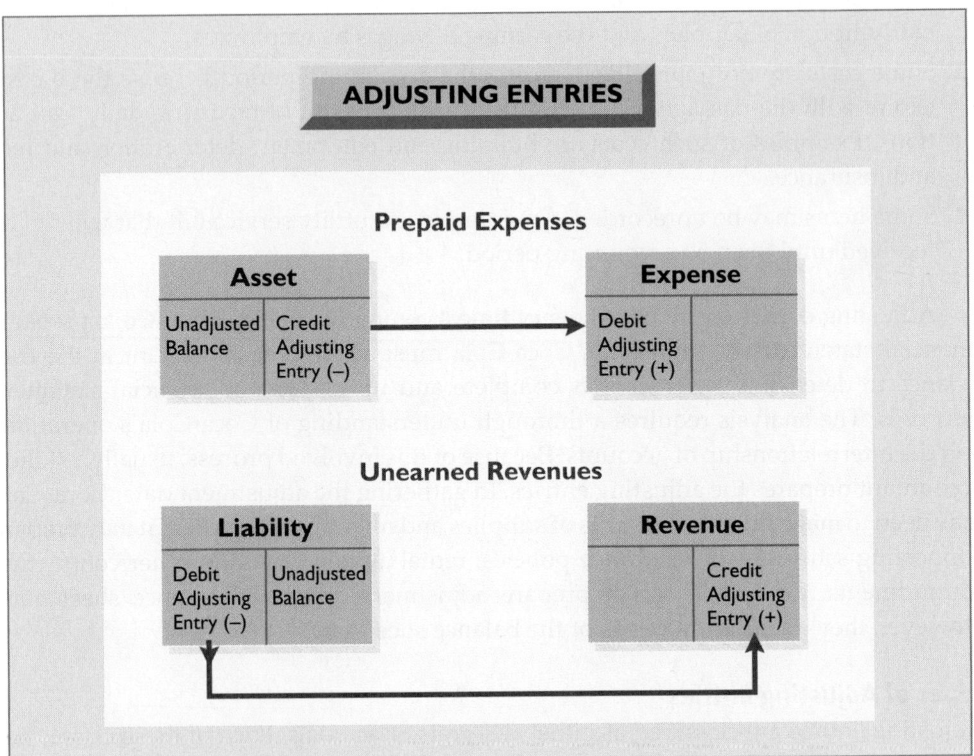

Prepaid Expenses. Assets paid for and recorded before a company uses them are called prepaid expenses. When a company incurs a cost, it debits an asset account to show the service or benefit it will receive in the future. Prepayments often occur in regard to insurance, supplies, advertising, and rent. In addition, companies make prepayments when purchasing buildings and equipment.

Prepaid expenses expire either with the passage of time (e.g., rent and insurance) or **through use and consumption** (e.g., supplies). The expiration of these costs does not require daily recurring entries, an unnecessary and impractical task. Accordingly, a company like **Walgreens** usually postpones the recognition of such cost expirations until it prepares financial statements. At each statement date, Walgreens makes adjusting entries to record the expenses that apply to the current accounting period and to show the unexpired costs in the asset accounts.

As shown above, prior to adjustment, assets are overstated and expenses are understated. Thus, the prepaid expense adjusting entry results in a debit to an expense account and a credit to an asset account.

Supplies. A business enterprise may use several different types of supplies. For example, a CPA firm will use office supplies such as stationery, envelopes, and accounting paper. An advertising firm will stock advertising supplies such as graph paper, video film, and poster paper. Supplies are generally debited to an asset account when they are acquired. Recognition of supplies used is generally deferred until the adjustment process. At that time, a physical inventory (count) of supplies is taken. The difference between the balance in the Supplies (asset) account and the cost of supplies on hand represents the supplies used (expense) for the period.

For example, Pioneer (see Illustration 3-19) purchased advertising supplies costing \$25,000 on October 5. Pioneer therefore debited the asset Supplies. This account shows a balance of \$25,000 in the October 31 trial balance. An inventory count at the close of business on October 31 reveals that \$10,000 of supplies are still on hand. Thus, the cost of supplies used is \$15,000 (\$25,000 − \$10,000). The analysis and adjustment for advertising supplies is summarized in Illustration 3-22.

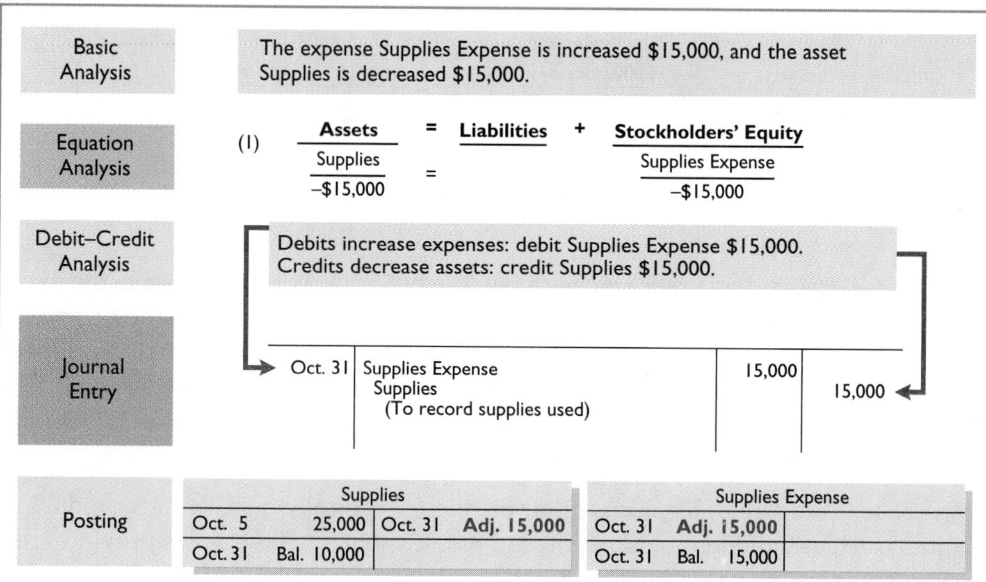

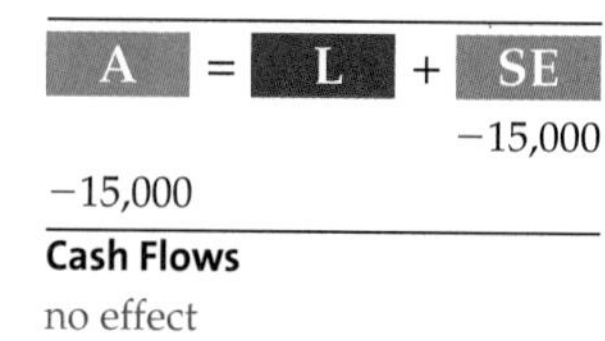

ILLUSTRATION 3-22
Adjustment for Supplies

The asset account Supplies now shows a balance of \$10,000, which equals the cost of supplies on hand at the statement date. In addition, Supplies Expense shows a balance of \$15,000, which equals the cost of supplies used in October. **Without an adjusting entry, October expenses are understated and net income overstated by \$15,000. Moreover, both assets and stockholders' equity are overstated by \$15,000 on the October 31 balance sheet.**

Insurance. Most companies maintain fire and theft insurance on merchandise and equipment, personal liability insurance for accidents suffered by customers, and automobile insurance on company cars and trucks. The extent of protection against loss determines the cost of the insurance (the amount of the premium to be paid). The insurance policy specifies the term and coverage. The minimum term usually covers one year, but three- to five-year terms are available and may offer lower annual premiums. A company usually debits insurance premiums to the asset account Prepaid Insurance when paid. At the financial statement date, it then debits Insurance Expense and credits Prepaid Insurance for the cost that expired during the period.

For example, on October 4, Pioneer paid \$6,000 for a one-year fire insurance policy, beginning October 1. Pioneer debited the cost of the premium to Prepaid Insurance at that time. This account still shows a balance of \$6,000 in the October 31 trial balance. The analysis and adjustment for insurance is summarized in Illustration 3-23 (page 104).

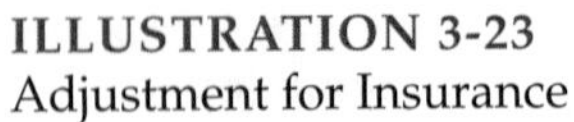

ILLUSTRATION 3-23
Adjustment for Insurance

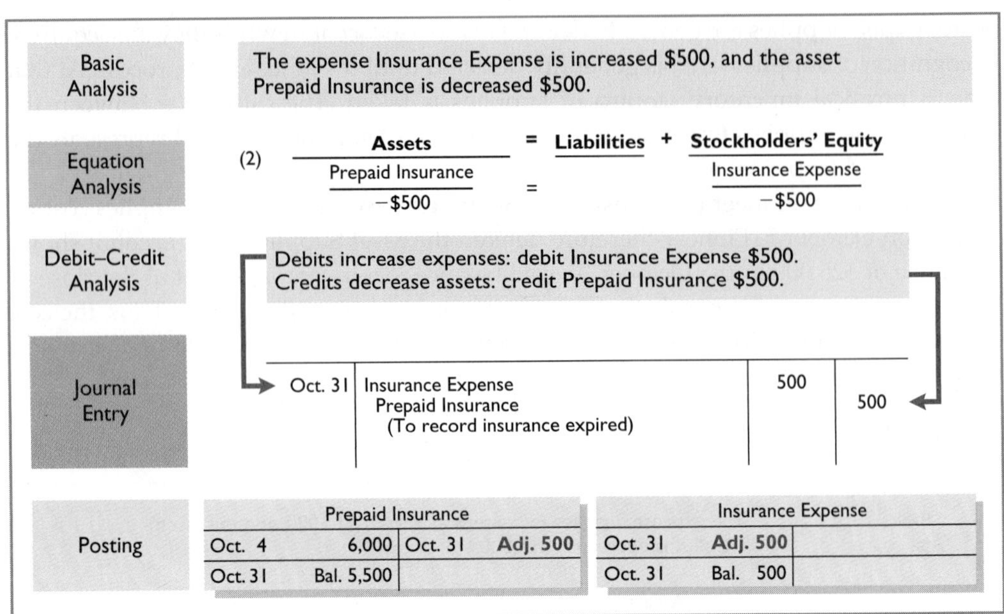

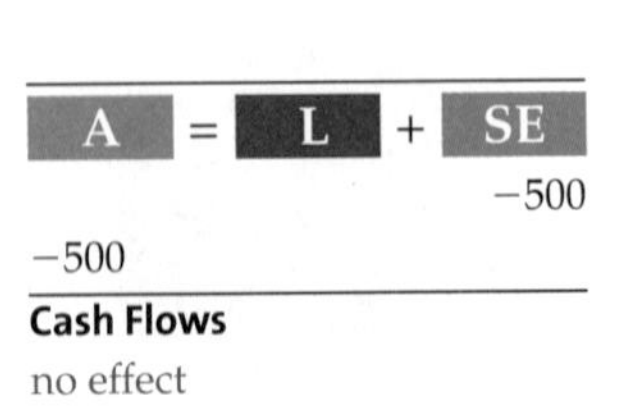

Cash Flows
no effect

The asset Prepaid Insurance shows a balance of $5,500, which represents the unexpired cost for the remaining 11 months of coverage. At the same time, the balance in Insurance Expense equals the insurance cost that expired in October. **Without an adjusting entry, October expenses are understated by $500 and net income overstated by $500. Moreover, both assets and stockholders' equity also are overstated by $500 on the October 31 balance sheet.**

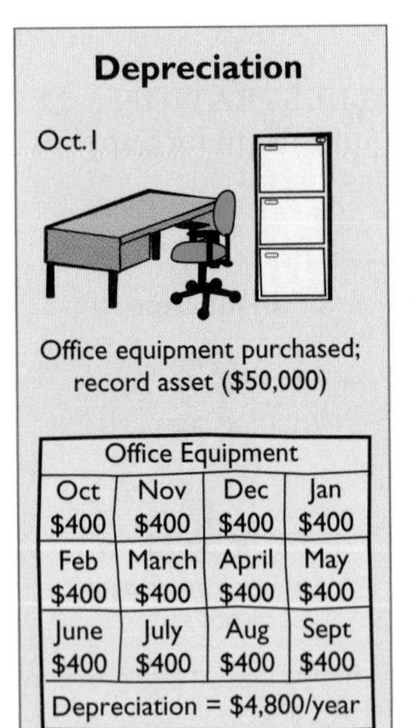

Depreciation. Companies, like **Caterpillar** or **Boeing**, typically own various productive facilities, such as buildings, equipment, and motor vehicles. These assets provide a service for a number of years. The term of service is commonly referred to as the useful life of the asset. Because Caterpillar, for example, expects an asset such as a building to provide service for many years, Caterpillar records the building as an asset, rather than an expense, in the year the building is acquired. Caterpillar records such assets at cost, as required by the historical cost principle.

According to the expense recognition principle, Caterpillar should report a portion of the cost of a long-lived asset as an expense during each period of the asset's useful life. The process of **depreciation** allocates the cost of an asset to expense over its useful life in a rational and systematic manner.

Need for depreciation adjustment. Generally accepted accounting principles (GAAP) view the acquisition of productive facilities as a long-term prepayment for services. The need for making periodic adjusting entries for depreciation is, therefore, the same as we described for other prepaid expenses. That is, a company recognizes the expired cost (expense) during the period and reports the unexpired cost (asset) at the end of the period. The primary causes of depreciation of a productive facility are actual use, deterioration due to the elements, and obsolescence. For example, at the time Caterpillar acquires an asset, the effects of these factors cannot be known with certainty. Therefore, Caterpillar must estimate them. **Thus, depreciation is an estimate rather than a factual measurement of the expired cost.**

To estimate depreciation expense, Caterpillar often divides the cost of the asset by its useful life. For example, if Caterpillar purchases equipment for $10,000 and expects its useful life to be 10 years, Caterpillar records annual depreciation of $1,000.

In the case of Pioneer Advertising, it estimates depreciation on its office equipment to be $4,800 a year (cost $50,000 less salvage value $2,000 divided by useful life of 10 years), or $400 per month. The analysis and adjustment for depreciation is summarized in Illustration 3-24.

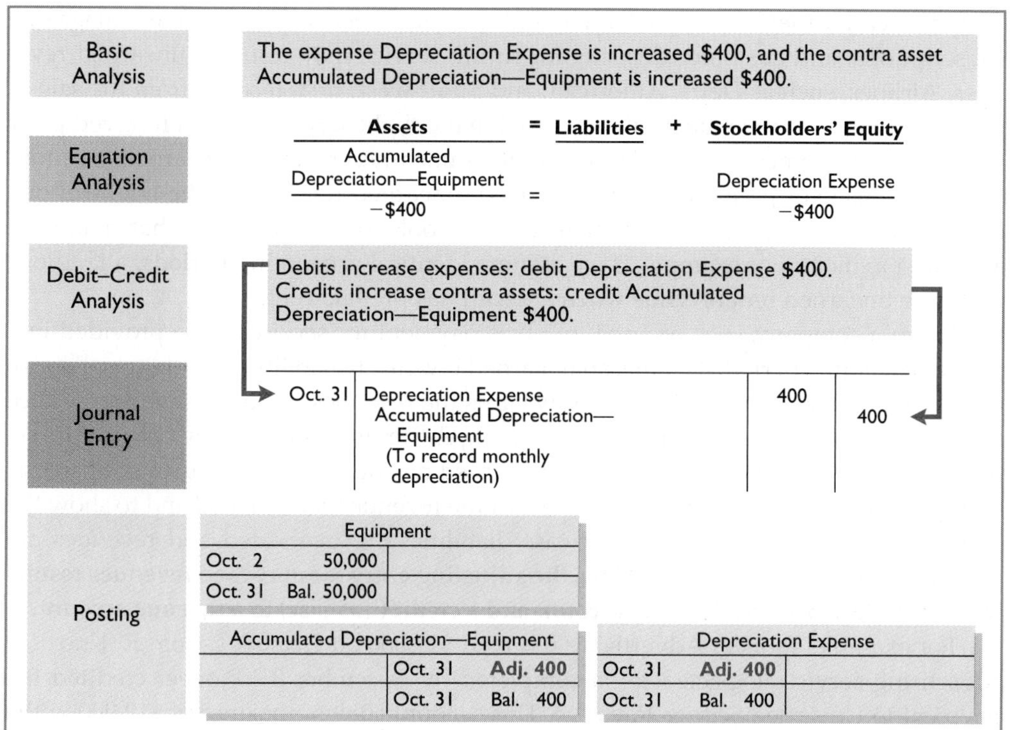

ILLUSTRATION 3-24
Adjustment for Depreciation

A	=	L	+	SE
				−400
−400				

Cash Flows
no effect

The balance in the accumulated depreciation account will increase $400 each month. Therefore, after journalizing and posting the adjusting entry at November 30, the balance will be $800.

Statement presentation. Accumulated Depreciation—Equipment is a contra asset account. A **contra asset account** offsets an asset account on the balance sheet. This means that the accumulated depreciation account offsets the Equipment account on the balance sheet. Its normal balance is a credit. Pioneer uses this account instead of crediting Equipment in order to disclose both the original cost of the equipment and the total expired cost to date. In the balance sheet, Pioneer deducts Accumulated Depreciation—Equipment from the related asset account as follows.

Equipment	$50,000	
Less: Accumulated depreciation—equipment	400	$49,600

ILLUSTRATION 3-25
Balance Sheet Presentation of Accumulated Depreciation

The **book value** of any depreciable asset is the difference between its cost and its related accumulated depreciation. In Illustration 3-25, the book value of the equipment at the balance sheet date is $49,600. Note that the asset's book value generally differs from its fair value because depreciation is not a matter of valuation but rather a means of cost allocation.

Note also that depreciation expense identifies that portion of the asset's cost that expired in October. As in the case of other prepaid adjustments, without this adjusting entry, total assets, total stockholders' equity, and net income are overstated, and depreciation expense is understated.

A company records depreciation expense for each piece of equipment, such as trucks or machinery, and for all buildings. A company also establishes related accumulated depreciation accounts for the above, such as Accumulated Depreciation—Trucks, Accumulated Depreciation—Machinery, and Accumulated Depreciation—Buildings.

Unearned Revenues. Revenues received in cash and recorded as liabilities before a company earns them are called **unearned revenues**. Such items as rent, magazine subscriptions, and customer deposits for future service may result in unearned revenues. Airlines, such as **Delta**, **American**, and **Southwest**, treat receipts from the sale of tickets as unearned revenue until they provide the flight service. Tuition received prior to the start of a semester is another example of unearned revenue. Unearned revenues are the opposite of prepaid expenses. Indeed, unearned revenue on the books of one company is likely to be a prepayment on the books of the company that made the advance payment. For example, if we assume identical accounting periods, a landlord will have unearned rent revenue when a tenant has prepaid rent.

When a company, such as **Intel**, receives payment for services to be provided in a future accounting period, it credits an unearned revenue (a liability) account to recognize the obligation that exists. It subsequently earns the revenues through rendering service to a customer. However, making daily recurring entries to record this revenue is impractical. Therefore, Intel delays recognition of earned revenue until the adjustment process. Then Intel makes an adjusting entry to record the revenue that it earned and to show the liability that remains. In the typical case, liabilities are overstated and revenues are understated prior to adjustment. **Thus, the adjusting entry for unearned revenues results in a debit (decrease) to a liability account and a credit (increase) to a revenue account.**

For example, Pioneer Advertising received $12,000 on October 2 from R. Knox for advertising services expected to be completed by December 31. Pioneer credited the payment to Unearned Service Revenue. This account shows a balance of $12,000 in the October 31 trial balance. Analysis reveals that Pioneer earned $4,000 of these services in October. The analysis and adjustment process for unearned revenue is summarized in Illustration 3-26.

ILLUSTRATION 3-26
Adjustment for Unearned Service Revenue

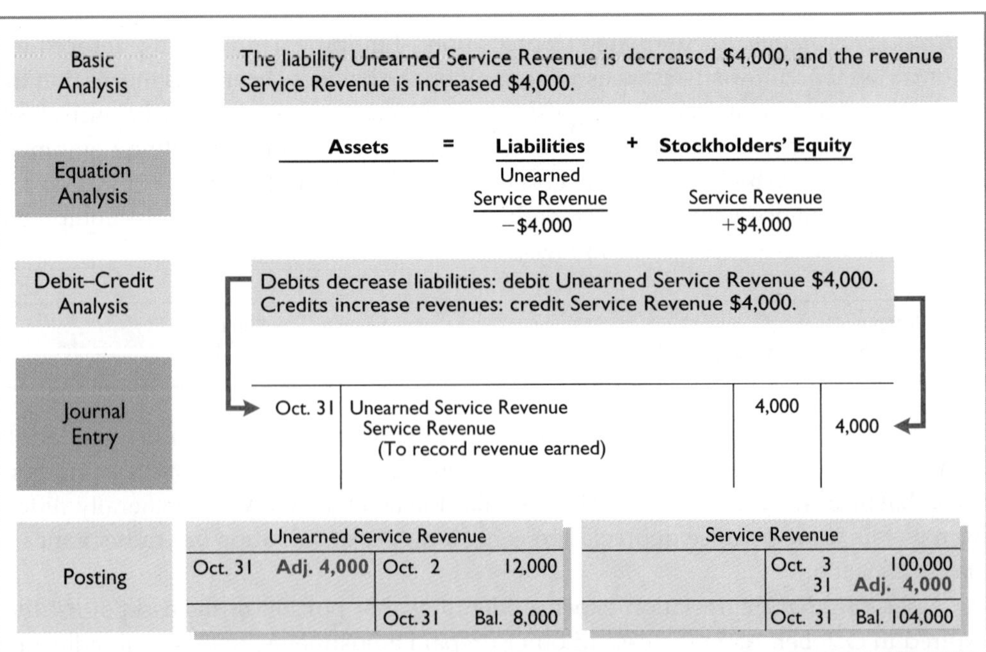

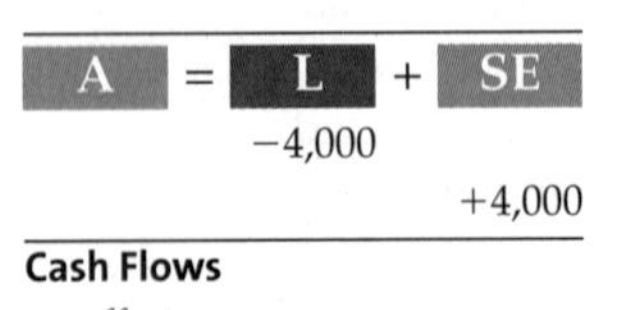

Cash Flows
no effect

The liability Unearned Service Revenue now shows a balance of $8,000, which represents the remaining advertising services expected to be performed in the future. At the same time, Service Revenue shows total revenue earned in October of $104,000. **Without**

this adjustment, revenues and net income are understated by $4,000 in the income statement. Moreover, liabilities are overstated and stockholders' equity are understated by $4,000 on the October 31 balance sheet.

Adjusting Entries for Accruals

The second category of adjusting entries is accruals. Companies make adjusting entries for accruals to record unrecognized revenues earned and expenses incurred in the current accounting period. Without an accrual adjustment, the revenue account (and the related asset account) or the expense account (and the related liability account) are understated. Thus, the adjusting entry for accruals **will increase both a balance sheet and an income statement account**. Illustration 3-27 shows adjusting entries for accruals.

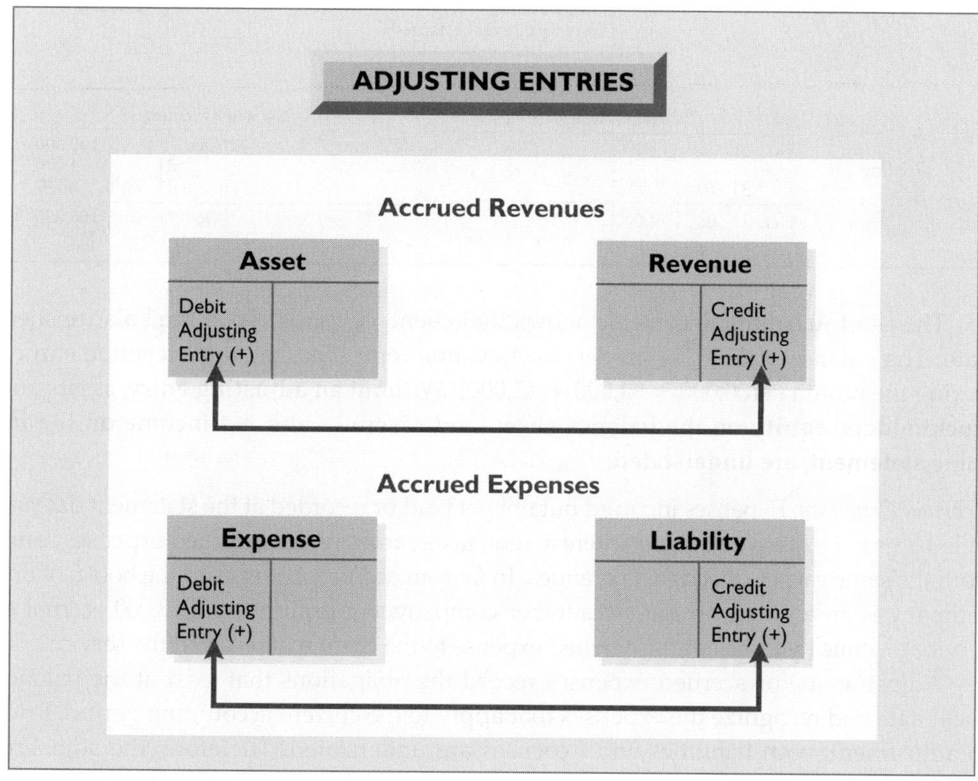

ILLUSTRATION 3-27
Adjusting Entries for Accruals

Accrued Revenues. Revenues earned but not yet received in cash or recorded at the statement date are **accrued revenues**. A company accrues revenues with the passing of time, as in the case of interest revenue and rent revenue. Because interest and rent do not involve daily transactions, these items are often unrecorded at the statement date. Or accrued revenues may result from unbilled or uncollected services that a company performed, as in the case of commissions and fees. A company does not record commissions or fees daily, because only a portion of the total service has been provided.

An adjusting entry shows the receivable that exists at the balance sheet date and records the revenue that a company earned during the period. Prior to adjustment both assets and revenues are understated. Accordingly, **an adjusting entry** for accrued revenues results in a debit (increase) to an asset account and a credit (increase) to a revenue account.

In October, Pioneer earned $2,000 for advertising services that it did not bill to clients before October 31. Pioneer therefore did not yet record these services. The analysis and adjustment for Accounts Receivable and Service Revenue is summarized in Illustration 3-28 (page 108).

ILLUSTRATION 3-28
Accrual Adjustment for Receivable and Revenue Accounts

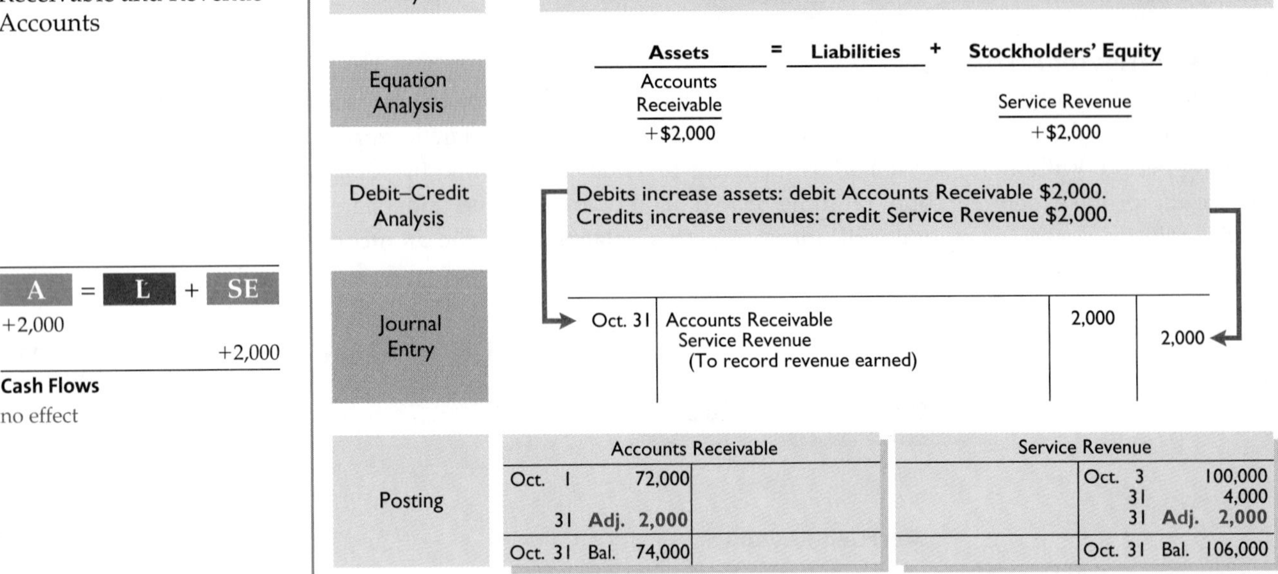

A	=	L	+	SE
+2,000				
				+2,000

Cash Flows
no effect

The asset Accounts Receivable shows that clients owe $74,000 at the balance sheet date. The balance of $106,000 in Service Revenue represents the total revenue earned during the month ($100,000 + $4,000 + $2,000). **Without an adjusting entry, assets and stockholders' equity on the balance sheet, and revenues and net income on the income statement, are understated.**

Accrued Expenses. Expenses incurred but not yet paid or recorded at the statement date are called **accrued expenses**, such as interest, rent, taxes, and salaries. Accrued expenses result from the same causes as accrued revenues. In fact, an accrued expense on the books of one company is an accrued revenue to another company. For example, the $2,000 accrual of service revenue by Pioneer is an accrued expense to the client that received the service.

Adjustments for accrued expenses record the obligations that exist at the balance sheet date and recognize the expenses that apply to the current accounting period. Prior to adjustment, both liabilities and expenses are understated. Therefore, the adjusting entry for accrued expenses results in a debit (increase) to an expense account and a credit (increase) to a liability account.

Accrued interest. Pioneer signed a three-month note payable in the amount of $50,000 on October 1. The note requires interest at an annual rate of 12 percent. Three factors determine the amount of the interest accumulation: (1) the face value of the note; (2) the interest rate, which is always expressed as an annual rate; and (3) the length of time the note is outstanding. The total interest due on Pioneer's $50,000 note at its due date three months' hence is $1,500 ($50,000 × 12% × 3/12), or $500 for one month. Illustration 3-29

ILLUSTRATION 3-29
Formula for Computing Interest

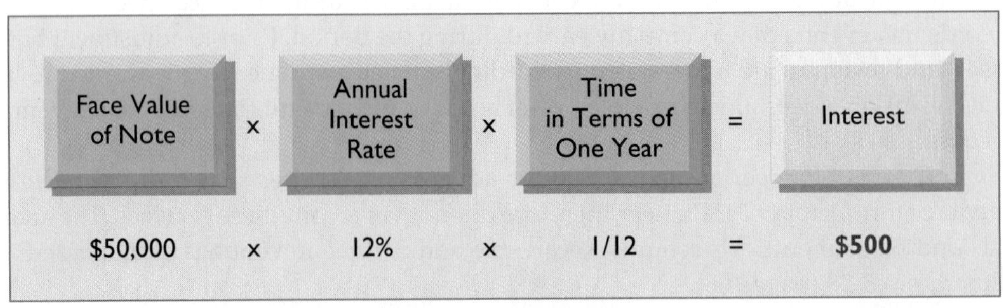

shows the formula for computing interest and its application to Pioneer. Note that the formula expresses the time period as a fraction of a year.

The analysis and adjustment for interest expense is summarized in Illustration 3-30.

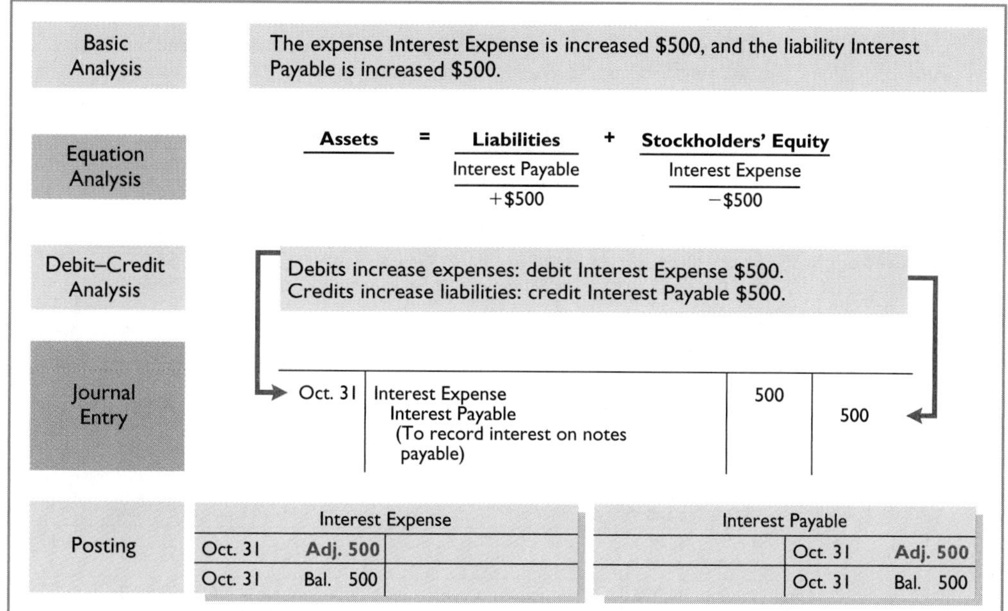

ILLUSTRATION 3-30
Adjustment for Interest

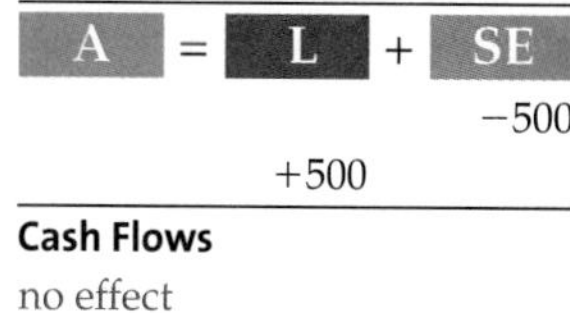

Interest Expense shows the interest charges applicable to the month of October. Interest Payable shows the amount of interest owed at the statement date. Pioneer will not pay this amount until the note comes due at the end of three months. Why does Pioneer use the Interest Payable account instead of crediting Notes Payable? By recording interest payable separately, Pioneer discloses the two types of obligations (interest and principal) in the accounts and statements. **Without this adjusting entry, both liabilities and interest expense are understated, and both net income and stockholders' equity are overstated.**

Accrued salaries and wages. Companies pay for some types of expenses, such as employee salaries and wages, after the services have been performed. For example, Pioneer last paid salaries and wages on October 26. It will not pay salaries and wages again until November 23. However, as shown in the calendar below, three working days remain in October (October 29–31).

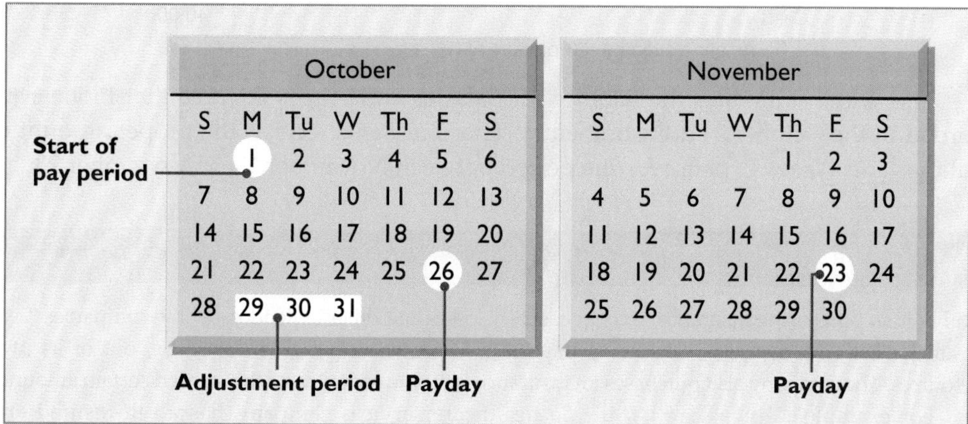

At October 31, the salaries and wages for these days represent an accrued expense and a related liability to Pioneer. The employees receive total salaries and wages of $10,000

for a five-day work week, or $2,000 per day. Thus, accrued salaries and wages at October 31 are $6,000 ($2,000 × 3). The analysis and adjustment process is summarized in Illustration 3-31.

ILLUSTRATION 3-31
Adjustment for Salaries and Wages Expense

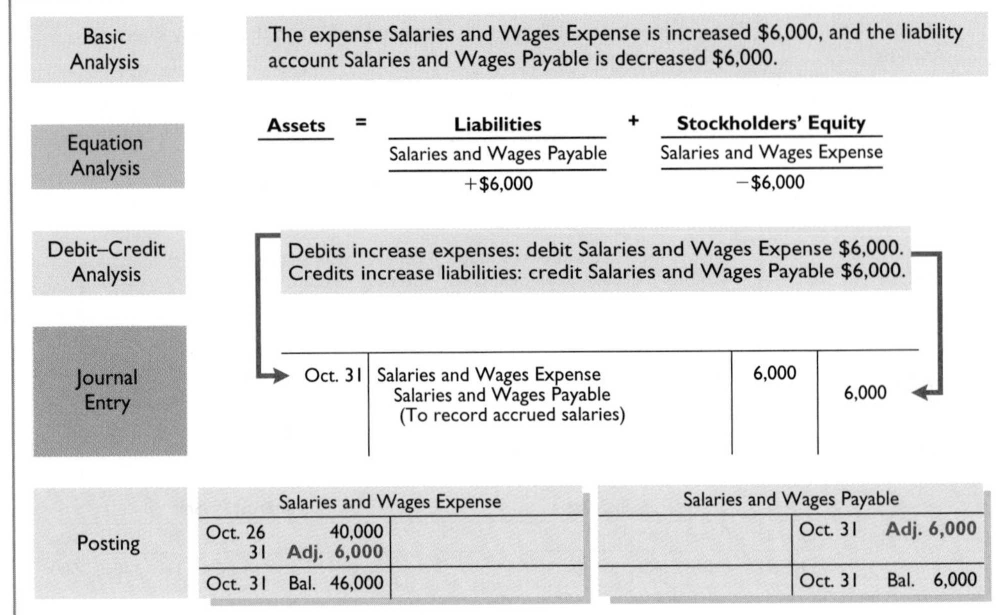

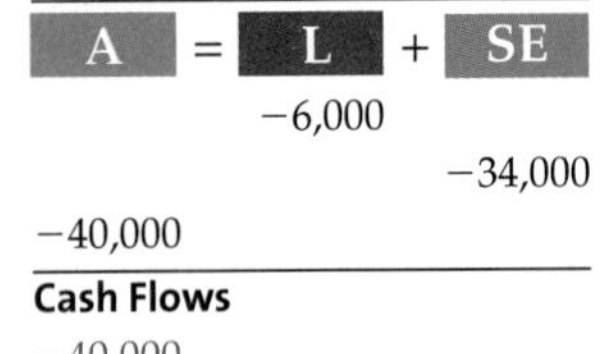

After this adjustment, the balance in Salaries and Wages Expense of $46,000 (23 days × $2,000) is the actual salaries and wages expense for October. The balance in Salaries and Wages Payable of $6,000 is the amount of the liability for salaries and wages owed as of October 31. **Without the $6,000 adjustment for salaries, both Pioneer's expenses and liabilities are understated by $6,000.**

Pioneer pays salaries and wages every four weeks. Consequently, the next payday is November 23, when it will again pay total salaries and wages of $40,000. The payment consists of $6,000 of salaries and wages payable at October 31 plus $34,000 of salaries and wages expense for November (17 working days as shown in the November calendar × $2,000). Therefore, Pioneer makes the following entry on November 23.

A	=	L	+	SE
		−6,000		
				−34,000
−40,000				

Cash Flows
−40,000

Nov. 23		
Salaries and Wages Payable	6,000	
Salaries and Wages Expense	34,000	
Cash		40,000
(To record November 23 payroll)		

This entry eliminates the liability for Salaries and Wages Payable that Pioneer recorded in the October 31 adjusting entry. This entry also records the proper amount of Salaries and Wages Expense for the period between November 1 and November 23.

AM I COVERED?

What do the numbers mean?

Rather than purchasing insurance to cover casualty losses and other obligations, some companies "self-insure." That is, a company decides to pay for any possible claims, as they arise, out of its own resources. The company also purchases an insurance policy to cover losses that exceed certain amounts.

For example, **Almost Family, Inc.**, a healthcare services company, has a self-insured employee health-benefit program. However, Almost Family ran into accounting problems when it failed to record an accrual of the liability for benefits not covered by its back-up insurance policy. This led to restatement of Almost Family's fiscal results for the accrual of the benefit expense.

Bad debts. Proper recognition of revenues and expenses dictates recording bad debts as an expense of the period in which a company earned revenue instead of the period in which the company writes off the accounts or notes. The proper valuation of the receivable balance also requires recognition of uncollectible receivables. Proper recognition and valuation require an adjusting entry.

At the end of each period, a company, such as **General Mills**, estimates the amount of receivables that will later prove to be uncollectible. General Mills bases the estimate on various factors: the amount of bad debts it experienced in past years, general economic conditions, how long the receivables are past due, and other factors that indicate the extent of uncollectibility. To illustrate, assume that, based on past experience, Pioneer reasonably estimates a bad debt expense for the month of $1,600. The analysis and adjustment process for bad debts is summarized in Illustration 3-32.

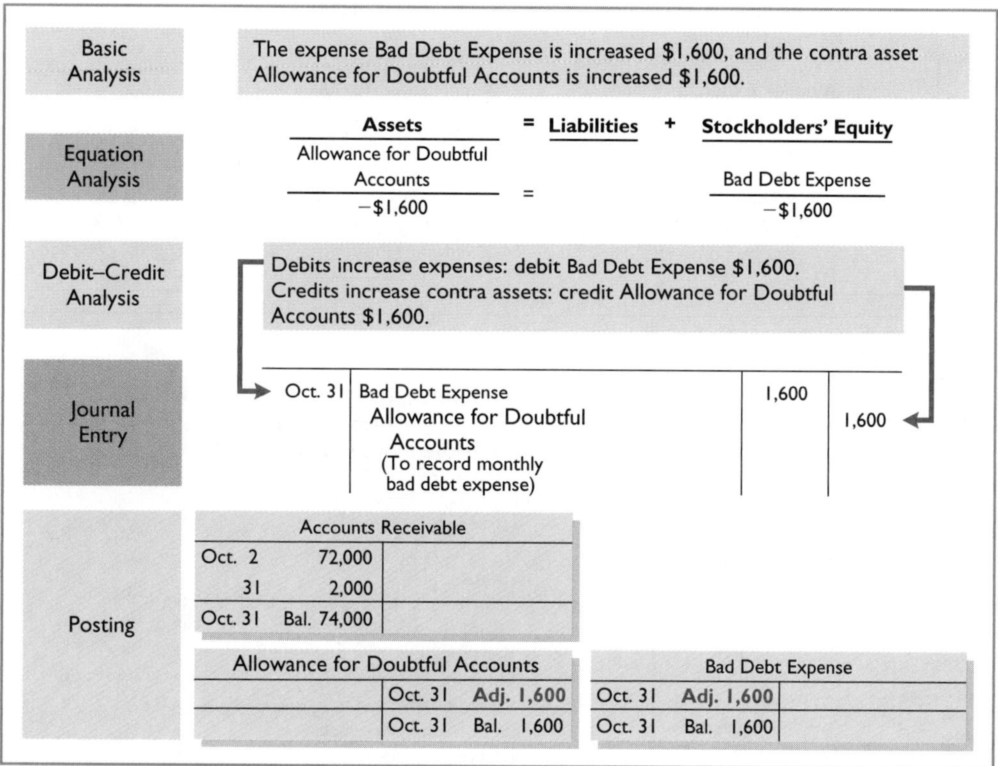

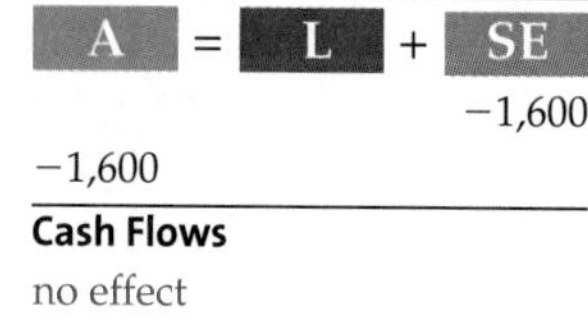

ILLUSTRATION 3-32
Adjustment for Bad Debt Expense

A company often expresses bad debts as a percentage of the revenue on account for the period. Or a company may compute bad debts by adjusting the Allowance for Doubtful Accounts to a certain percentage of the trade accounts receivable and trade notes receivable at the end of the period.

Adjusted Trial Balance

After journalizing and posting all adjusting entries, Pioneer prepares another trial balance from its ledger accounts (shown in Illustration 3-33 on page 112). This trial balance is called an **adjusted trial balance**. It shows the balance of all accounts, including those adjusted, at the end of the accounting period. The adjusted trial balance thus shows the effects of all financial events that occurred during the accounting period.

Preparing Financial Statements

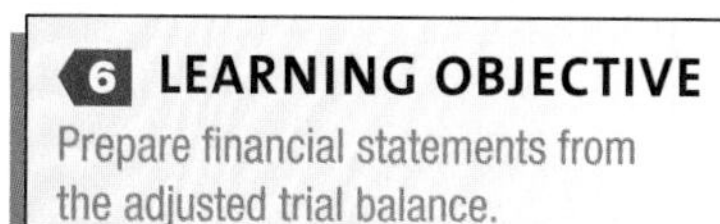

Pioneer can prepare financial statements directly from the adjusted trial balance. Illustrations 3-34 (page 112) and 3-35 (page 113) show the interrelationships of data in the adjusted trial balance and the financial statements.

ILLUSTRATION 3-33
Adjusted Trial Balance

PIONEER ADVERTISING AGENCY INC.
ADJUSTED TRIAL BALANCE
OCTOBER 31, 2012

	Debit	Credit
Cash	$ 80,000	
Accounts Receivable	74,000	
Allowance for Doubtful Accounts		$ 1,600
Supplies	10,000	
Prepaid Insurance	5,500	
Equipment	50,000	
Accumulated Depreciation—Equipment		400
Notes Payable		50,000
Accounts Payable		25,000
Interest Payable		500
Unearned Service Revenue		8,000
Salaries and Wages Payable		6,000
Common Stock		100,000
Dividends	5,000	
Service Revenue		106,000
Salaries and Wages Expense	46,000	
Supplies Expense	15,000	
Rent Expense	9,000	
Insurance Expense	500	
Interest Expense	500	
Depreciation Expense	400	
Bad Debt Expense	1,600	
	$297,500	$297,500

ILLUSTRATION 3-34
Preparation of the Income Statement and Retained Earnings Statement from the Adjusted Trial Balance

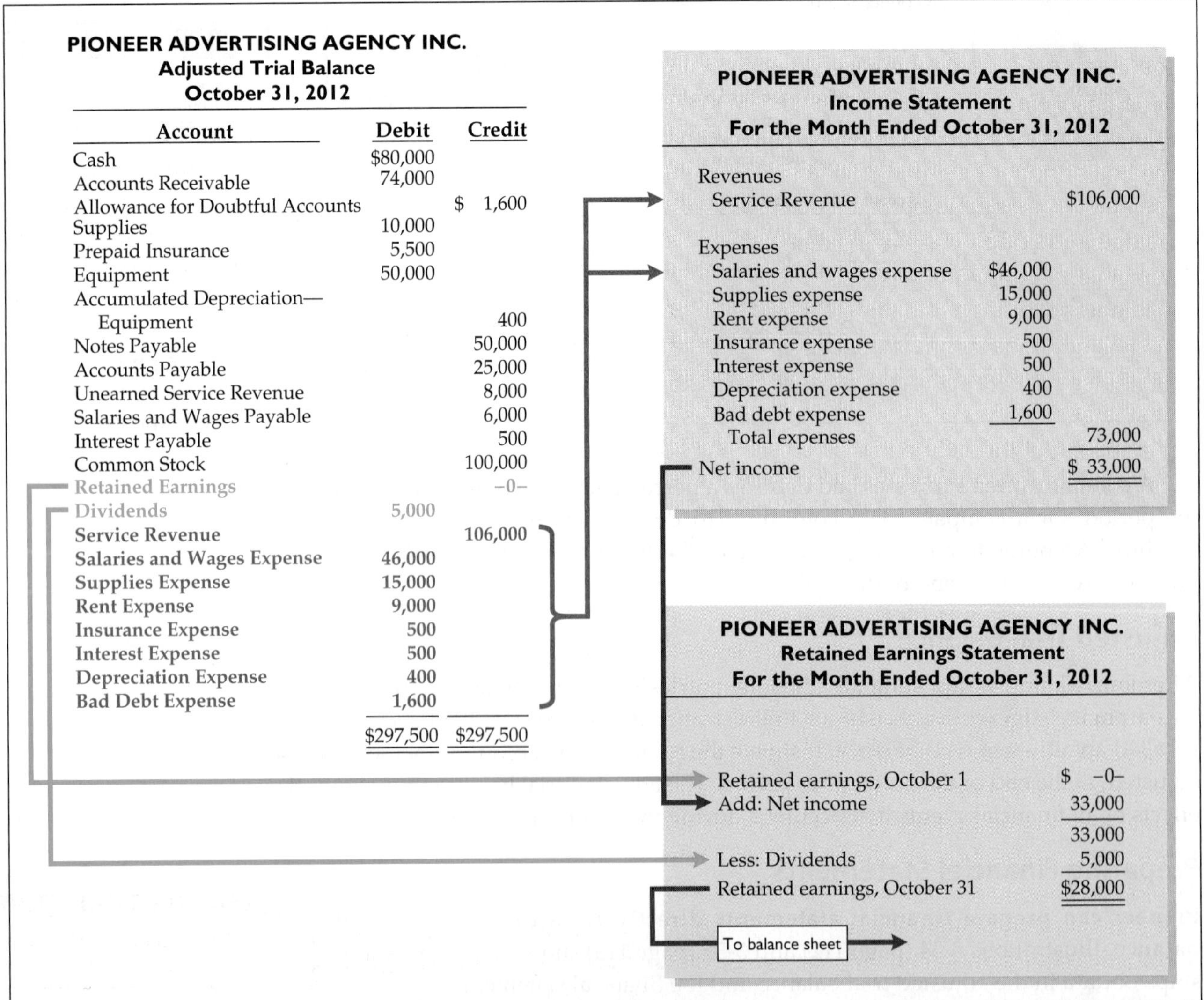

PIONEER ADVERTISING AGENCY INC.
Adjusted Trial Balance
October 31, 2012

Account	Debit	Credit
Cash	$80,000	
Accounts Receivable	74,000	
Allowance for Doubtful Accounts		$ 1,600
Supplies	10,000	
Prepaid Insurance	5,500	
Equipment	50,000	
Accumulated Depreciation—Equipment		400
Notes Payable		50,000
Accounts Payable		25,000
Unearned Service Revenue		8,000
Salaries and Wages Payable		6,000
Interest Payable		500
Common Stock		100,000
Retained Earnings		–0–
Dividends	5,000	
Service Revenue		106,000
Salaries and Wages Expense	46,000	
Supplies Expense	15,000	
Rent Expense	9,000	
Insurance Expense	500	
Interest Expense	500	
Depreciation Expense	400	
Bad Debt Expense	1,600	
	$297,500	$297,500

PIONEER ADVERTISING AGENCY INC.
Income Statement
For the Month Ended October 31, 2012

Revenues		
Service Revenue		$106,000
Expenses		
Salaries and wages expense	$46,000	
Supplies expense	15,000	
Rent expense	9,000	
Insurance expense	500	
Interest expense	500	
Depreciation expense	400	
Bad debt expense	1,600	
Total expenses		73,000
Net income		$ 33,000

PIONEER ADVERTISING AGENCY INC.
Retained Earnings Statement
For the Month Ended October 31, 2012

Retained earnings, October 1	$ –0–
Add: Net income	33,000
	33,000
Less: Dividends	5,000
Retained earnings, October 31	$28,000

PIONEER ADVERTISING AGENCY INC.
Adjusted Trial Balance
October 31, 2012

Account	Debit	Credit
Cash	$80,000	
Accounts Receivable	74,000	
Allowance for Doubtful Accounts		$ 1,600
Supplies	10,000	
Prepaid Insurance	5,500	
Equipment	50,000	
Accumulated Depreciation—Equipment		400
Notes Payable		50,000
Accounts Payable		25,000
Unearned Service Revenue		8,000
Salaries and Wages Payable		6,000
Interest Payable		500
Common Stock		100,000
Retained Earnings		–0–
Dividends	5,000	
Service Revenue		106,000
Salaries and Wages Expense	46,000	
Supplies Expense	15,000	
Rent Expense	9,000	
Insurance Expense	500	
Interest Expense	500	
Depreciation Expense	400	
Bad Debt Expense	1,600	
	$297,500	$297,500

PIONEER ADVERTISING AGENCY INC.
Balance Sheet
October 31, 2012

Assets

Cash		$80,000
Accounts receivable	$74,000	
Less: Allowance	1,600	72,400
Supplies		10,000
Prepaid insurance		5,500
Equipment	50,000	
Less: Accumulated depreciation	400	49,600
Total assets		$217,500

Liabilities and Stockholders' Equity

Liabilities	
Notes payable	$ 50,000
Accounts payable	25,000
Unearned service revenue	8,000
Salaries and wages payable	6,000
Interest payable	500
Total liabilities	89,500
Stockholders' equity	
Common stock	100,000
Retained earnings	28,000
Total liabilities and stockholders' equity	$217,500

Balance at Oct. 31 from Retained Earnings Statement in Illustration 3-34

ILLUSTRATION 3-35
Preparation of the Balance Sheet from the Adjusted Trial Balance

As Illustration 3-34 shows, Pioneer begins preparation of the income statement from the revenue and expense accounts. It derives the retained earnings statement from the retained earnings and dividends accounts and the net income (or net loss) shown in the income statement. As Illustration 3-35 shows, Pioneer then prepares the balance sheet from the asset and liability accounts, the common stock account, and the ending retained earnings balance as reported in the retained earnings statement.

24/7 ACCOUNTING

What do the numbers mean?

To achieve the vision of "24/7 accounting," a company must be able to update revenue, income, and balance sheet numbers every day within the quarter and publish them on the Internet. Such real-time reporting responds to the demand for more timely financial information made available to all investors—not just to analysts with access to company management.

Two obstacles typically stand in the way of 24/7 accounting: having the necessary accounting systems to close the books on a daily basis, and reliability concerns associated with unaudited real-time data. Only a few companies have the necessary accounting capabilities. Cisco Systems, which pioneered the concept of the 24-hour close, is one such company.

Closing

Basic Process

The closing process reduces the balance of nominal (temporary) accounts to zero in order to prepare the accounts for the next period's transactions. In the closing process, Pioneer transfers all of the revenue and expense account balances (income statement items) to a clearing or suspense account called Income Summary. The Income Summary account matches revenues and expenses.

Pioneer uses this clearing account only at the end of each accounting period. The account represents the net income or net loss for the period. It then transfers this amount (the net income or net loss) to an owners' equity account. (For a corporation, the owners' equity account is retained earnings; for proprietorships and partnerships, it is a capital account.) Companies post all such **closing entries** to the appropriate general ledger accounts.

Closing Entries

In practice, companies generally prepare closing entries only at the end of a company's annual accounting period. However, to illustrate the journalizing and posting of closing entries, we will assume that Pioneer Advertising Agency Inc. closes its books monthly. Illustration 3-36 shows the closing entries at October 31.

ILLUSTRATION 3-36
Closing Entries Journalized

GENERAL JOURNAL — J3

Date	Account Titles and Explanation	Debit	Credit
	Closing Entries		
	(1)		
Oct. 31	Service Revenue	106,000	
	Income Summary		106,000
	(To close revenue account)		
	(2)		
31	Income Summary	73,000	
	Supplies Expense		15,000
	Depreciation Expense		400
	Insurance Expense		500
	Salaries and Wages Expense		46,000
	Rent Expense		9,000
	Interest Expense		500
	Bad Debt Expense		1,600
	(To close expense accounts)		
	(3)		
31	Income Summary	33,000	
	Retained Earnings		33,000
	(To close net income to retained earnings)		
	(4)		
31	Retained Earnings	5,000	
	Dividends		5,000
	(To close dividends to retained earnings)		

A couple of cautions about preparing closing entries: (1) Avoid unintentionally doubling the revenue and expense balances rather than zeroing them. (2) Do not close Dividends through the Income Summary account. **Dividends are not expenses, and they are not a factor in determining net income.**

Posting Closing Entries

Illustration 3-37 shows the posting of closing entries and the ruling of accounts. All temporary accounts have zero balances after posting the closing entries. In addition, note that the balance in Retained Earnings represents the accumulated undistributed earnings of Pioneer at the end of the accounting period. Pioneer reports this amount in

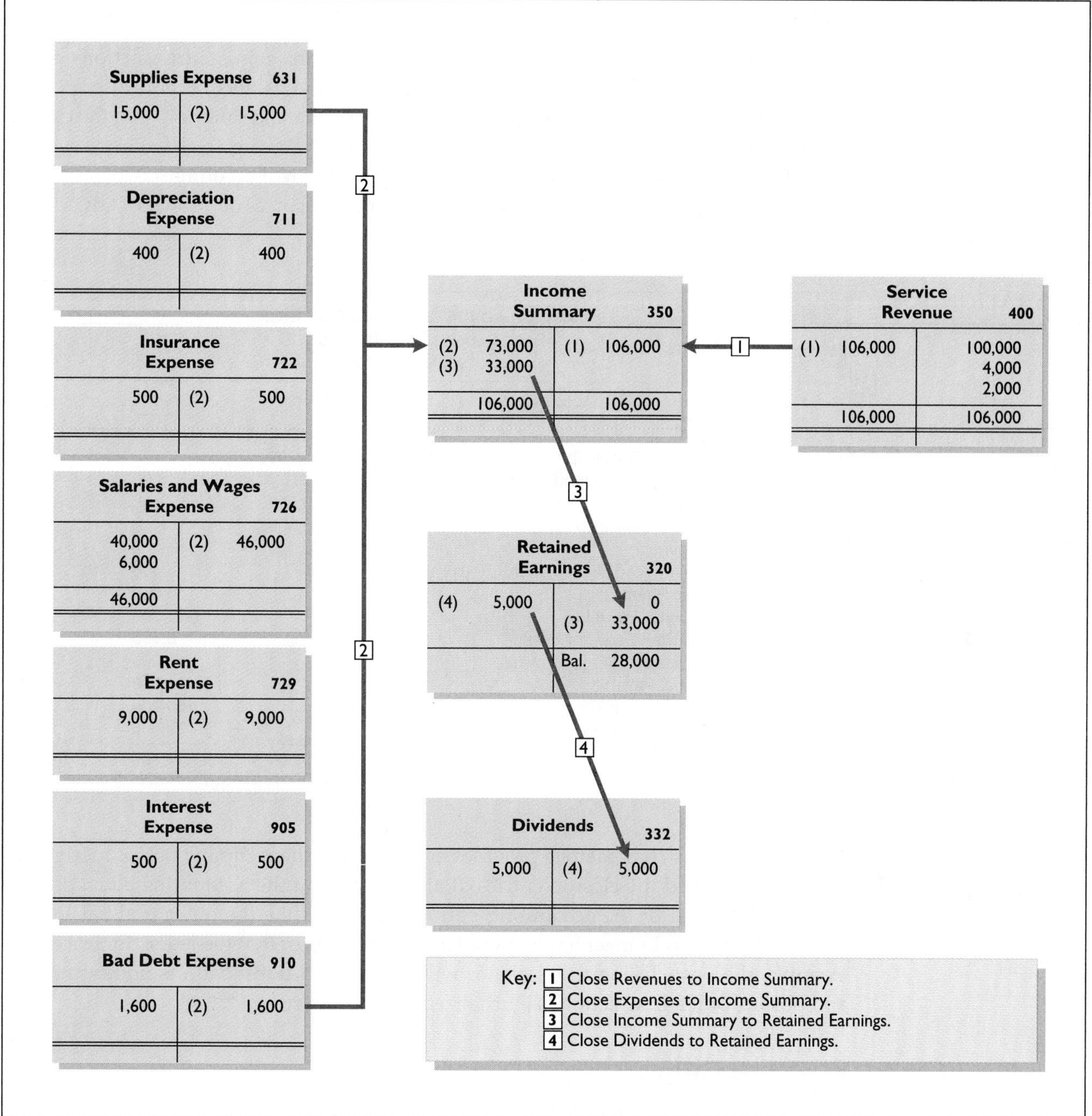

ILLUSTRATION 3-37
Posting of Closing Entries

the balance sheet as the ending amount reported on the retained earnings statement. As noted above, **Pioneer uses the Income Summary account only in closing**. It does not journalize and post entries to this account during the year.

As part of the closing process, Pioneer totals, balances, and double-rules the **temporary accounts**—revenues, expenses, and dividends—as shown in T-account form in Illustration 3-37. It does not close the **permanent accounts**—assets, liabilities, and stockholders' equity (Common Stock and Retained Earnings). Instead, the preparer draws a single rule beneath the current-period entries, and enters beneath the single rules the account balance to be carried forward to the next period. (For example, see Retained Earnings.)

After the closing process, each income statement account and the dividend account are balanced out to zero and are ready for use in the next accounting period.

Post-Closing Trial Balance

Recall that a trial balance is prepared after entering the regular transactions of the period, and that a second trial balance (the adjusted trial balance) occurs after posting the adjusting entries. A company may take a third trial balance after posting the closing entries. The trial balance after closing, called the **post-closing trial balance**, consists only of asset, liability, and owners' equity accounts—the real accounts.

Illustration 3-38 shows the post-closing trial balance of Pioneer Advertising Agency Inc.

ILLUSTRATION 3-38
Post-Closing Trial Balance

PIONEER ADVERTISING AGENCY INC.
POST-CLOSING TRIAL BALANCE
OCTOBER 31, 2012

Account	Debit	Credit
Cash	$ 80,000	
Accounts Receivable	74,000	
Allowance for Doubtful Accounts		$ 1,600
Supplies	10,000	
Prepaid Insurance	5,500	
Equipment	50,000	
Accumulated Depreciation—Equipment		400
Notes Payable		50,000
Accounts Payable		25,000
Unearned Service Revenue		8,000
Salaries and Wages Payable		6,000
Interest Payable		500
Common Stock		100,000
Retained Earnings		28,000
	$219,500	$219,500

A post-closing trial balance provides evidence that the company has properly journalized and posted the closing entries. It also shows that the accounting equation is in balance at the end of the accounting period. However, like the other trial balances, it does not prove that Pioneer has recorded all transactions or that the ledger is correct. For example, the post-closing trial balance will balance if a transaction is not journalized and posted, or if a transaction is journalized and posted twice.

Reversing Entries

After preparing the financial statements and closing the books, a company may reverse some of the adjusting entries before recording the regular transactions of the next period. Such entries are called **reversing entries**. A company makes a reversing entry at the beginning of the next accounting period; this entry is the exact opposite of the related adjusting entry made in the previous period. Making reversing entries is an optional step in the accounting cycle that a company may perform at the beginning of the next accounting period. Appendix 3B discusses reversing entries in more detail.

The Accounting Cycle Summarized

A summary of the steps in the accounting cycle shows a logical sequence of the accounting procedures used during a fiscal period:

1. Enter the transactions of the period in appropriate journals.
2. Post from the journals to the ledger (or ledgers).

3. Take an unadjusted trial balance (trial balance).
4. Prepare adjusting journal entries and post to the ledger(s).
5. Take a trial balance after adjusting (adjusted trial balance).
6. Prepare the financial statements from the second trial balance.
7. Prepare closing journal entries and post to the ledger(s).
8. Take a post-closing trial balance (**optional**).
9. Prepare reversing entries **(optional)** and post to the ledger(s).

A company normally completes all of these steps in every fiscal period.

STATEMENTS, PLEASE

What do the numbers mean?

The use of a worksheet at the end of each month or quarter enables a company to prepare interim financial statements even though it closes the books only at the end of each year. For example, assume that Google closes its books on December 31, but it wants monthly financial statements. To do this, at the end of January, Google prepares an adjusted trial balance (using a worksheet as illustrated in Appendix 3C) to supply the information needed for statements for January.

At the end of February, it uses a worksheet again. Note that because Google did not close the accounts at the end of January, the income statement taken from the adjusted trial balance on February 28 will present the net income for two months. If Google wants an income statement for only the month of February, the company obtains it by subtracting the items in the January income statement from the corresponding items in the income statement for the two months of January and February.

If Google executes such a process daily, it can realize "24/7 accounting" (see the "What Do the Numbers Mean?" box on page 113).

FINANCIAL STATEMENTS FOR A MERCHANDISING COMPANY

Pioneer Advertising Agency Inc. is a service company. In this section, we show a detailed set of financial statements for a merchandising company, Uptown Cabinet Corp. The financial statements, below and on pages 118–119, are prepared from the adjusted trial balance.

Income Statement

The income statement for Uptown is self-explanatory. The income statement classifies amounts into such categories as gross profit on sales, income from operations, income before taxes, and net income. Although earnings per share information is required to be shown on the face of the income statement for a corporation, we omit this item here; it will be discussed more fully later in the text. *For homework problems, do not present earnings per share information unless required to do so.*

Statement of Retained Earnings

A corporation may retain the net income earned in the business, or it may distribute it to stockholders by payment of dividends. In the illustration, Uptown added the net income earned during the year to the balance of retained earnings on January 1, thereby increasing the balance of retained earnings. Deducting dividends of $2,000 results in the ending retained earnings balance of $26,400 on December 31.

ILLUSTRATION 3-39
Income Statement for a Merchandising Company

UPTOWN CABINET CORP. INCOME STATEMENT FOR THE YEAR ENDED DECEMBER 31, 2012			
Net sales			$400,000
Cost of goods sold			316,000
Gross profit on sales			84,000
Selling expenses			
Salaries and wages expense (sales)		$20,000	
Advertising expense		10,200	
Total selling expenses		30,200	
Administrative expenses			
Salaries and wages expense (general)	$19,000		
Depreciation expense—equipment	6,700		
Property tax expense	5,300		
Rent expense	4,300		
Bad debt expense	1,000		
Telephone and Internet expense	600		
Insurance expense	360		
Total administrative expenses		37,260	
Total selling and administrative expenses			67,460
Income from operations			16,540
Other revenues and gains			
Interest revenue			800
			17,340
Other expenses and losses			
Interest expense			1,700
Income before income taxes			15,640
Income tax			3,440
Net income			$ 12,200

ILLUSTRATION 3-40
Statement of Retained Earnings for a Merchandising Company

UPTOWN CABINET CORP. STATEMENT OF RETAINED EARNINGS FOR THE YEAR ENDED DECEMBER 31, 2012	
Retained earnings, January 1	$16,200
Add: Net income	12,200
	28,400
Less: Dividends	2,000
Retained earnings, December 31	$26,400

Balance Sheet

The balance sheet for Uptown is a classified balance sheet. Interest receivable, inventory, prepaid insurance, and prepaid rent are included as current assets. Uptown considers these assets current because they will be converted into cash or used by the business within a relatively short period of time. Uptown deducts the amount of Allowance for Doubtful Accounts from the total of accounts, notes, and interest receivable because it estimates that only $54,800 of $57,800 will be collected in cash.

ILLUSTRATION 3-41
Balance Sheet for a Merchandising Company

UPTOWN CABINET CORP. BALANCE SHEET AS OF DECEMBER 31, 2012			
Assets			
Current assets			
Cash			$ 1,200
Notes receivable	$16,000		
Accounts receivable	41,000		
Interest receivable	800	$57,800	
Less: Allowance for doubtful accounts		3,000	54,800
Inventory			40,000
Prepaid insurance			540
Prepaid rent			500
Total current assets			97,040
Property, plant, and equipment			
Equipment		67,000	
Less: Accumulated depreciation—equipment		18,700	
Total property, plant, and equipment			48,300
Total assets			$145,340
Liabilities and Stockholders' Equity			
Current liabilities			
Notes payable			$ 20,000
Accounts payable			13,500
Property taxes payable			2,000
Income tax payable			3,440
Total current liabilities			38,940
Long-term liabilities			
Bonds payable, due June 30, 2020			30,000
Total liabilities			68,940
Stockholders' equity			
Common stock, $5.00 par value, issued and outstanding, 10,000 shares		$50,000	
Retained earnings		26,400	
Total stockholders' equity			76,400
Total liabilities and stockholders' equity			$145,340

In the property, plant, and equipment section, Uptown deducts the Accumulated Depreciation—Equipment from the cost of the equipment. The difference represents the book or carrying value of the equipment.

The balance sheet shows property taxes payable as a current liability because it is an obligation that is payable within a year. The balance sheet also shows other short-term liabilities such as accounts payable.

The bonds payable, due in 2020, are long-term liabilities. As a result, the balance sheet shows the account in a separate section. (The company paid interest on the bonds on December 31.)

Because Uptown is a corporation, the capital section of the balance sheet, called the stockholders' equity section in the illustration, differs somewhat from the capital section for a proprietorship. Total stockholders' equity consists of the common stock, which is the original investment by stockholders, and the earnings retained in the business. *For homework purposes, unless instructed otherwise, prepare an unclassified balance sheet.*

Closing Entries

Uptown makes closing entries as shown below.

General Journal
December 31, 2012

Interest Revenue	800	
Sales Revenue	400,000	
Income Summary		400,800
(To close revenues to Income Summary)		
Income Summary	388,600	
Cost of Goods Sold		316,000
Salaries and Wages Expense (sales)		20,000
Advertising Expense		10,200
Salaries and Wages Expense (general)		19,000
Depreciation Expense		6,700
Rent Expense		4,300
Property Tax Expense		5,300
Bad Debt Expense		1,000
Telephone and Internet Expense		600
Insurance Expense		360
Interest Expense		1,700
Income Tax Expense		3,440
(To close expenses to Income Summary)		
Income Summary	12,200	
Retained Earnings		12,200
(To close Income Summary to Retained Earnings)		
Retained Earnings	2,000	
Dividends		2,000
(To close Dividends to Retained Earnings)		

You will want to read the IFRS INSIGHTS on pages 153–157 for discussion of IFRS related to information systems.

SUMMARY OF LEARNING OBJECTIVES

1 Understand basic accounting terminology. Understanding the following eleven terms helps in understanding key accounting concepts: (1) Event. (2) Transaction. (3) Account. (4) Real and nominal accounts. (5) Ledger. (6) Journal. (7) Posting. (8) Trial balance. (9) Adjusting entries. (10) Financial statements. (11) Closing entries.

2 Explain double-entry rules. The left side of any account is the debit side; the right side is the credit side. All asset and expense accounts are increased on the left or debit side and decreased on the right or credit side. Conversely, all liability and revenue accounts are increased on the right or credit side and decreased on the left or debit side. Stockholders' equity accounts, Common Stock and Retained Earnings, are increased on the credit side. Dividends is increased on the debit side.

3 Identify steps in the accounting cycle. The basic steps in the accounting cycle are (1) identifying and measuring transactions and other events; (2) journalizing; (3) posting; (4) preparing an unadjusted trial balance; (5) making adjusting entries; (6) preparing an adjusted trial balance; (7) preparing financial statements; and (8) closing.

4 Record transactions in journals, post to ledger accounts, and prepare a trial balance. The simplest journal form chronologically lists transactions and events expressed in terms of debits and credits to particular accounts. The items entered in a general journal must be transferred (posted) to the general ledger. Companies should prepare an unadjusted trial balance at the end of a given period after they have recorded the entries in the journal and posted them to the ledger.

5 Explain the reasons for preparing adjusting entries. Adjustments achieve a proper recognition of revenues and expenses, so as to determine net income for the current period and to achieve an accurate statement of end-of-the-period balances in assets, liabilities, and owners' equity accounts.

6 Prepare financial statements from the adjusted trial balance. Companies can prepare financial statements directly from the adjusted trial balance. The income statement is prepared from the revenue and expense accounts. The statement of retained earnings is prepared from the retained earnings account, dividends, and net income (or net loss). The balance sheet is prepared from the asset, liability, and equity accounts.

7 Prepare closing entries. In the closing process, the company transfers all of the revenue and expense account balances (income statement items) to a clearing account called Income Summary, which is used only at the end of the fiscal year. Revenues and expenses are matched in the Income Summary account. The net result of this matching represents the net income or net loss for the period. That amount is then transferred to an owners' equity account (Retained Earnings for a corporation and capital accounts for proprietorships and partnerships).

KEY TERMS

account, *88*
accounting cycle, *93*
accounting information system, *88*
accrued expenses, *108*
accrued revenues, *107*
adjusted trial balance, *89, 111*
adjusting entry, *89, 100*
balance sheet, *89*
book value, *105*
closing entries, *89, 114*
closing process, *113*
contra asset account, *105*
credit, *89*
debit, *89*
depreciation, *104*
double-entry accounting, *90*
event, *88*
financial statements, *89*
general journal, *95*
general ledger, *89, 95*
income statement, *89*
journal, *89*
journalizing, *89*
ledger, *89*
nominal accounts, *89*
post-closing trial balance, *89, 116*
posting, *89, 96*
prepaid expenses, *102*
real accounts, *89*
reversing entries, *116*
special journals, *96*
statement of cash flows, *89*
statement of retained earnings, *89*
subsidiary ledger, *89*
T-account, *89*
transaction, *88*
trial balance, *89, 100*
unearned revenues, *106*

APPENDIX 3A CASH-BASIS ACCOUNTING VERSUS ACCRUAL-BASIS ACCOUNTING

Most companies use accrual-basis accounting: They recognize revenue when it is earned and expenses in the period incurred, without regard to the time of receipt or payment of cash.

8 LEARNING OBJECTIVE
Differentiate the cash basis of accounting from the accrual basis of accounting.

Some small enterprises and the average individual taxpayer, however, use a strict or modified cash-basis approach. Under the **strict cash basis**, companies record revenue only when they receive cash, and they record expenses only when they disperse cash. Determining income on the cash basis rests upon collecting revenue and paying expenses. The cash basis ignores two principles: the revenue recognition principle and the expense recognition principle. Consequently, cash-basis financial statements are not in conformity with GAAP.

An illustration will help clarify the differences between accrual-basis and cash-basis accounting. Assume that Quality Contractor signs an agreement to construct a garage for $22,000. In January, Quality begins construction, incurs costs of $18,000 on credit, and by the end of January delivers a finished garage to the buyer. In February, Quality collects $22,000 cash from the customer. In March, Quality pays the $18,000 due the creditors. Illustrations 3A-1 and 3A-2 show the net incomes for each month under cash-basis accounting and accrual-basis accounting.

ILLUSTRATION 3A-1
Income Statement—Cash Basis

QUALITY CONTRACTOR
INCOME STATEMENT—CASH BASIS
For the Month of

	January	February	March	Total
Cash receipts	$-0-	$22,000	$ -0-	$22,000
Cash payments	-0-	-0-	18,000	18,000
Net income (loss)	$-0-	$22,000	$(18,000)	$ 4,000

ILLUSTRATION 3A-2
Income Statement—Accrual Basis

QUALITY CONTRACTOR
INCOME STATEMENT—ACCRUAL BASIS
For the Month of

	January	February	March	Total
Revenues	$22,000	$-0-	$-0-	$22,000
Expenses	18,000	-0-	-0-	18,000
Net income (loss)	$ 4,000	$-0-	$-0-	$ 4,000

For the three months combined, total net income is the same under both cash-basis accounting and accrual-basis accounting. The difference is in the **timing** of revenues and expenses. The basis of accounting also affects the balance sheet. Illustrations 3A-3 and 3A-4 show Quality Contractor's balance sheets at each month-end under the cash basis and the accrual basis.

ILLUSTRATION 3A-3
Balance Sheets—Cash Basis

QUALITY CONTRACTOR
BALANCE SHEET—CASH BASIS
As of

	January 31	February 28	March 31
Assets			
Cash	$-0-	$22,000	$4,000
Total assets	$-0-	$22,000	$4,000
Liabilities and Owners' Equity			
Owners' equity	$-0-	$22,000	$4,000
Total liabilities and owners' equity	$-0-	$22,000	$4,000

ILLUSTRATION 3A-4
Balance Sheets—Accrual Basis

QUALITY CONTRACTOR BALANCE SHEET—ACCRUAL BASIS As of	January 31	February 28	March 31
Assets			
Cash	$ -0-	$22,000	$4,000
Accounts receivable	22,000	-0-	-0-
Total assets	$22,000	$22,000	$4,000
Liabilities and Owners' Equity			
Accounts payable	$18,000	$18,000	$-0-
Owners' equity	4,000	4,000	4,000
Total liabilities and owners' equity	$22,000	$22,000	$4,000

Analysis of Quality's income statements and balance sheets shows the ways in which cash-basis accounting is inconsistent with basic accounting theory:

1. The cash basis understates revenues and assets from the construction and delivery of the garage in January. It ignores the $22,000 of accounts receivable, representing a near-term future cash inflow.
2. The cash basis understates expenses incurred with the construction of the garage and the liability outstanding at the end of January. It ignores the $18,000 of accounts payable, representing a near-term future cash outflow.
3. The cash basis understates owners' equity in January by not recognizing the revenues and the asset until February. It also overstates owners' equity in February by not recognizing the expenses and the liability until March.

In short, cash-basis accounting violates the accrual concept underlying financial reporting.

The **modified cash basis** is a mixture of the cash basis and the accrual basis. It is based on the strict cash basis but with modifications that have substantial support, such as capitalizing and depreciating plant assets or recording inventory. This method is often followed by professional services firms (doctors, lawyers, accountants, and consultants) and by retail, real estate, and agricultural operations.[3]

CONVERSION FROM CASH BASIS TO ACCRUAL BASIS

Not infrequently, companies want to convert a cash basis or a modified cash basis set of financial statements to the accrual basis for presentation to investors and creditors. To illustrate this conversion, assume that Dr. Diane Windsor, like many small business owners, keeps her accounting records on a cash basis. In the year 2012, Dr. Windsor received $300,000 from her patients and paid $170,000 for operating expenses, resulting in an excess of cash receipts over disbursements of $130,000 ($300,000 − $170,000). At January 1 and December 31, 2012, she has accounts receivable, unearned service revenue, accrued liabilities, and prepaid expenses as shown in Illustration 3A-5 (page 124).

[3]Companies in the following situations might use a cash or modified cash basis.

(1) A company that is primarily interested in cash flows (for example, a group of physicians that distributes cash-basis earnings for salaries and bonuses).

(2) A company that has a limited number of financial statement users (small, closely held company with little or no debt).

(3) A company that has operations that are relatively straightforward (small amounts of inventory, long-term assets, or long-term debt).

ILLUSTRATION 3A-5
Financial Information Related to Dr. Diane Windsor

	January 1, 2012	December 31, 2012
Accounts receivable	$12,000	$9,000
Unearned service revenue	-0-	4,000
Accrued liabilities	2,000	5,500
Prepaid expenses	1,800	2,700

Service Revenue Computation

To convert the amount of cash received from patients to service revenue on an accrual basis, we must consider changes in accounts receivable and unearned service revenue during the year. Accounts receivable at the beginning of the year represents revenues earned last year that are collected this year. Ending accounts receivable indicates revenues earned this year that are not yet collected. Therefore, to compute revenue on an accrual basis, we subtract beginning accounts receivable and add ending accounts receivable, as the formula in Illustration 3A-6 shows.

ILLUSTRATION 3A-6
Conversion of Cash Receipts to Revenue—Accounts Receivable

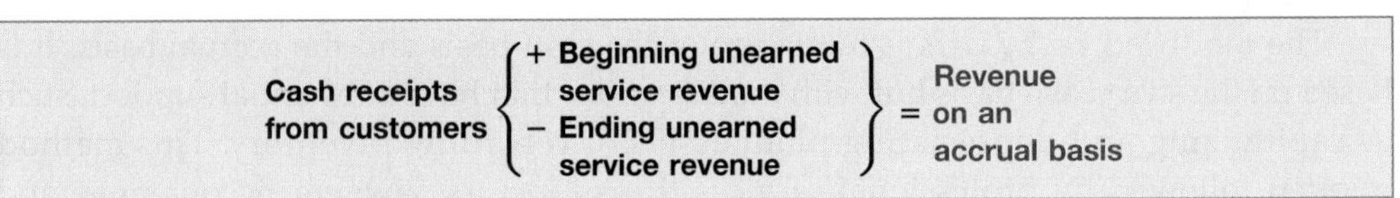

Similarly, beginning unearned service revenue represents cash received last year for revenues earned this year. Ending unearned service revenue results from collections this year that will be recognized as revenue next year. Therefore, to compute revenue on an accrual basis, we add beginning unearned service revenue and subtract ending unearned service revenue, as the formula in Illustration 3A-7 shows.

ILLUSTRATION 3A-7
Conversion of Cash Receipts to Revenue—Unearned Service Revenue

Cash receipts from customers { **+ Beginning unearned service revenue** / **− Ending unearned service revenue** } **= Revenue on an accrual basis**

Therefore, for Dr. Windsor's dental practice, to convert cash collected from customers to service revenue on an accrual basis, we would make the computations shown in Illustration 3A-8.

ILLUSTRATION 3A-8
Conversion of Cash Receipts to Service Revenue

Cash receipts from customers		$300,000
− Beginning accounts receivable	$(12,000)	
+ Ending accounts receivable	9,000	
+ Beginning unearned service revenue	-0-	
− Ending unearned service revenue	(4,000)	(7,000)
Service revenue (accrual)		$293,000

Operating Expense Computation

To convert cash paid for operating expenses during the year to operating expenses on an accrual basis, we must consider changes in prepaid expenses and accrued liabilities. First, we need to recognize as this year's expenses the amount of beginning prepaid expenses. (The cash payment for these occurred last year.) Therefore, to arrive at operating expense on an accrual basis, we add the beginning prepaid expenses balance to cash paid for operating expenses.

Conversely, ending prepaid expenses result from cash payments made this year for expenses to be reported next year. (Under the accrual basis, Dr. Windsor would have deferred recognizing these payments as expenses until a future period.) To convert these cash payments to operating expenses on an accrual basis, we deduct ending prepaid expenses from cash paid for expenses, as the formula in Illustration 3A-9 shows.

ILLUSTRATION 3A-9
Conversion of Cash Payments to Expenses—Prepaid Expenses

Cash paid for operating expenses	+ Beginning prepaid expenses − Ending prepaid expenses	= Expenses on an accrual basis

Similarly, beginning accrued liabilities result from expenses recognized last year that require cash payments this year. Ending accrued liabilities relate to expenses recognized this year that have not been paid. To arrive at expenses on an accrual basis, we deduct beginning accrued liabilities and add ending accrued liabilities to cash paid for expenses, as the formula in Illustration 3A-10 shows.

ILLUSTRATION 3A-10
Conversion of Cash Payments to Expenses—Accrued Liabilities

Cash paid for operating expenses	− Beginning accrued liabilities + Ending accrued liabilities	= Expenses on an accrual basis

Therefore, for Dr. Windsor's dental practice, to convert cash paid for operating expenses to operating expenses on an accrual basis, we would make the computations shown in Illustration 3A-11.

ILLUSTRATION 3A-11
Conversion of Cash Paid to Operating Expenses

Cash paid for operating expenses		$170,000
+ Beginning prepaid expense	$ 1,800	
− Ending prepaid expense	(2,700)	
− Beginning accrued liabilities	(2,000)	
+ Ending accrued liabilities	5,500	2,600
Operating expenses (accrual)		$172,600

This entire conversion can be completed in worksheet form, as shown in Illustration 3A-12.

ILLUSTRATION 3A-12
Conversion of Statement of Cash Receipts and Disbursements to Income Statement

DIANE WINDSOR, D.D.S.
Conversion of Income Statement Data from Cash Basis to Accrual Basis
For the Year 2012

	A	B	C	D	E
1		Cash Basis	Adjustments Add	Deduct	Accrual Basis
2	Collections from customers	$300,000			
3	− Accounts receivable, Jan. 1			$12,000	
4	+ Accounts receivable, Dec. 31		$9,000		
5	+ Unearned service revenue, Jan. 1		—	—	
6	− Unearned service revenue, Dec. 31			4,000	
7	Service revenue				$293,000
8	Disbursement for expenses	170,000			
9	+ Prepaid expenses, Jan. 1		1,800		
10	− Prepaid expenses, Dec. 31			2,700	
11	− Accrued liabilities, Jan. 1			2,000	
12	+ Accrued liabilities, Dec. 31		5,500		
13	Operating expenses				172,600
14	Excess of cash collections over disbursements—cash basis	$130,000			
15	Net income—accrual basis				$120,400

Sheet1 / Sheet2 / Sheet3

Using this approach, we adjust collections and disbursements on a cash basis to revenue and expense on an accrual basis, to arrive at accrual net income. In any conversion from the cash basis to the accrual basis, depreciation or amortization is an additional expense in arriving at net income on an accrual basis.

THEORETICAL WEAKNESSES OF THE CASH BASIS

The cash basis reports exactly when cash is received and when cash is disbursed. To many people that information represents something concrete. Isn't cash what it is all about? Does it make sense to invent something, design it, produce it, market and sell it, if you aren't going to get cash for it in the end? Many frequently say, "Cash is the real bottom line," and also, "Cash is the oil that lubricates the economy." If so, then what is the merit of accrual accounting?

Today's economy is considerably more lubricated by credit than by cash. The accrual basis, not the cash basis, recognizes all aspects of the credit phenomenon. Investors, creditors, and other decision-makers seek timely information about an enterprise's *future* cash flows. Accrual-basis accounting provides this information by reporting the cash inflows and outflows associated with earnings activities as soon as these companies can estimate these cash flows with an acceptable degree of certainty. Receivables and payables are forecasters of future cash inflows and outflows. In other words, accrual-basis accounting aids in predicting future cash flows by reporting transactions and other events with cash consequences at the time the transactions and events occur, rather than when the cash is received and paid.

SUMMARY OF LEARNING OBJECTIVE FOR APPENDIX 3A

8 Differentiate the cash basis of accounting from the accrual basis of accounting. The cash basis of accounting records revenues when cash is received and expenses when cash is paid. The accrual basis recognizes revenue when earned and expenses in the period incurred, without regard to the time of the receipt or payment of cash. Accrual-basis accounting is theoretically preferable because it provides information about future cash inflows and outflows associated with earnings activities as soon as companies can estimate these cash flows with an acceptable degree of certainty. Cash-basis accounting is not in conformity with GAAP.

KEY TERMS

accrual-basis accounting, 121
modified cash basis, 123
strict cash basis, 122

APPENDIX 3B USING REVERSING ENTRIES

LEARNING OBJECTIVE 9
Identify adjusting entries that may be reversed.

Use of reversing entries simplifies the recording of transactions in the next accounting period. The use of reversing entries, however, does not change the amounts reported in the financial statements for the previous period.

ILLUSTRATION OF REVERSING ENTRIES—ACCRUALS

A company most often uses reversing entries to reverse two types of adjusting entries: accrued revenues and accrued expenses. To illustrate the optional use of reversing entries for accrued expenses, we use the following transaction and adjustment data.

1. October 24 (initial salaries and wages entry): Paid $4,000 of salaries and wages incurred between October 10 and October 24.
2. October 31 (adjusting entry): Incurred salaries and wages between October 25 and October 31 of $1,200, to be paid in the November 8 payroll.
3. November 8 (subsequent salaries and wages entry): Paid salaries and wages of $2,500. Of this amount, $1,200 applied to accrued salaries and wages payable at October 31 and $1,300 to salaries and wages payable for November 1 through November 8.

Illustration 3B-1 shows the comparative entries.

Reversing Entries Not Used				Reversing Entries Used			
Initial Salary Entry							
Oct. 24	Salaries and Wages Expense	4,000		Oct. 24	Salaries and Wages Expense	4,000	
	Cash		4,000		Cash		4,000
Adjusting Entry							
Oct. 31	Salaries and Wages Expense	1,200		Oct. 31	Salaries and Wages Expense	1,200	
	Salaries and Wages Payable		1,200		Salaries and Wages Payable		1,200
Closing Entry							
Oct. 31	Income Summary	5,200		Oct. 31	Income Summary	5,200	
	Salaries and Wages Expense		5,200		Salaries and Wages Expense		5,200
Reversing Entry							
Nov. 1	No entry is made.			Nov. 1	Salaries and Wages Payable	1,200	
					Salaries and Wages Expense		1,200
Subsequent Salary Entry							
Nov. 8	Salaries and Wages Payable	1,200		Nov. 8	Salaries and Wages Expense	2,500	
	Salaries and Wages Expense	1,300			Cash		2,500
	Cash		2,500				

ILLUSTRATION 3B-1
Comparison of Entries for Accruals, with and without Reversing Entries

The comparative entries show that the first three entries are the same whether or not the company uses reversing entries. The last two entries differ. The November 1 reversing entry eliminates the $1,200 balance in Salaries and Wages Payable, created by the October 31 adjusting entry. The reversing entry also creates a $1,200 credit balance in the Salaries and Wages Expense account. As you know, it is unusual for an expense account to have a credit balance. However, the balance is correct in this instance. Why? Because the company will debit the entire amount of the first salaries and wages payment in the new accounting period to Salaries and Wages Expense. This debit eliminates the credit balance. The resulting debit balance in the expense account will equal the salaries and wages expense incurred in the new accounting period ($1,300 in this example).

When a company makes reversing entries, it debits all cash payments of expenses to the related expense account. This means that on November 8 (and every payday), the company debits Salaries and Wages Expense for the amount paid without regard to the existence of any accrued salaries and wages payable. Repeating the same entry simplifies the recording process in an accounting system.

ILLUSTRATION OF REVERSING ENTRIES—DEFERRALS

Up to this point, we assumed the recording of all deferrals as prepaid expense or unearned revenue. In some cases, though, a company records deferrals directly in expense or revenue accounts. When this occurs, a company may also reverse deferrals.

To illustrate the use of reversing entries for prepaid expenses, we use the following transaction and adjustment data.

1. December 10 (initial entry): Purchased $20,000 of office supplies with cash.
2. December 31 (adjusting entry): Determined that $5,000 of office supplies are on hand.

Illustration 3B-2 shows the comparative entries.

ILLUSTRATION 3B-2
Comparison of Entries for Deferrals, with and without Reversing Entries

Reversing Entries Not Used				Reversing Entries Used			
Initial Purchase of Supplies Entry							
Dec. 10	Supplies	20,000		Dec. 10	Supplies Expense	20,000	
	Cash		20,000		Cash		20,000
Adjusting Entry							
Dec. 31	Supplies Expense	15,000		Dec. 31	Supplies	5,000	
	Supplies		15,000		Supplies Expense		5,000
Closing Entry							
Dec. 31	Income Summary	15,000		Dec. 31	Income Summary	15,000	
	Supplies Expense		15,000		Supplies Expense		15,000
Reversing Entry							
Jan. 1	No entry			Jan. 1	Supplies Expense	5,000	
					Supplies		5,000

After the adjusting entry on December 31 (regardless of whether using reversing entries), the asset account Supplies shows a balance of $5,000, and Supplies Expense shows a balance of $15,000. If the company initially debits Supplies Expense when it purchases the supplies, it then makes a reversing entry to return to the expense account the cost of unconsumed supplies. The company then continues to debit Supplies Expense for additional purchases of supplies during the next period.

Deferrals are generally entered in real accounts (assets and liabilities), thus making reversing entries unnecessary. This approach is used because it is advantageous for items that a company needs to apportion over several periods (e.g., supplies and parts inventories). However, for other items that do not follow this regular pattern and that may or may not involve two or more periods, a company ordinarily enters them initially in revenue or expense accounts. The revenue and expense accounts may not require adjusting, and the company thus systematically closes them to Income Summary.

Using the nominal accounts adds consistency to the accounting system. It also makes the recording more efficient, particularly when a large number of such transactions occur during the year. For example, the bookkeeper knows to expense invoice items (except for capital asset acquisitions). He or she need not worry whether an item will result in a prepaid expense at the end of the period because the company will make adjustments at the end of the period.

SUMMARY OF REVERSING ENTRIES

We summarize guidelines for reversing entries as follows.

1. All accruals should be reversed.
2. All deferrals for which a company debited or credited the original cash transaction to an expense or revenue account should be reversed.
3. Adjusting entries for depreciation and bad debts are not reversed.

Recognize that reversing entries do not have to be used. Therefore, some accountants avoid them entirely.

SUMMARY OF LEARNING OBJECTIVE FOR APPENDIX 3B

9 Identify adjusting entries that may be reversed. Reversing entries are most often used to reverse two types of adjusting entries: accrued revenues and accrued expenses. Deferrals may also be reversed if the initial entry to record the transaction is made to an expense or revenue account.

APPENDIX 3C USING A WORKSHEET: THE ACCOUNTING CYCLE REVISITED

10 LEARNING OBJECTIVE
Prepare a 10-column worksheet.

In this appendix, we provide an additional illustration of the end-of-period steps in the accounting cycle and illustrate the use of a worksheet in this process. Using a **worksheet** often facilitates the end-of-period (monthly, quarterly, or annually) accounting and reporting process. Use of a worksheet helps a company prepare the financial statements on a more timely basis. How? With a worksheet, a company need not wait until it journalizes and posts the adjusting and closing entries.

A company prepares a worksheet either on columnar paper or within an electronic spreadsheet. In either form, a company uses the worksheet to adjust account balances and to prepare financial statements.

The worksheet does not replace the financial statements. Instead, it is an informal device for accumulating and sorting information needed for the financial statements. Completing the worksheet provides considerable assurance that a company properly handled all of the details related to the end-of-period accounting and statement preparation. The 10-column worksheet in Illustration 3C-1 (on page 130) provides columns for the first trial balance, adjustments, adjusted trial balance, income statement, and balance sheet.

WORKSHEET COLUMNS

Trial Balance Columns

Uptown Cabinet Corp., shown in Illustration 3C-1 (page 130), obtains data for the trial balance from its ledger balances at December 31. The amount for Inventory, $40,000, is the year-end inventory amount, which results from the application of a perpetual inventory system.

Adjustments Columns

After Uptown enters all adjustment data on the worksheet, it establishes the equality of the adjustment columns. It then extends the balances in all accounts to the adjusted trial balance columns.

UPTOWN CABINET CORP.
Ten-Column Worksheet for The Year Ended December 31, 2012

	A	B	C	D	E	F	G	H	I	J	K
1	Accounts	Trial Balance		Adjustments		Adjusted Trial Balance		Income Statement		Balance Sheet	
		Dr.	Cr.	Dr.	Cr.	Dr.	Cr.	Dr.	Cr.	Dr.	Cr.
2	Cash	1,200				1,200				1,200	
3	Notes receivable	16,000				16,000				16,000	
4	Accounts receivable	41,000				41,000				41,000	
5	Allowance for doubtful accounts		2,000		(b) 1,000		3,000				3,000
6	Inventory	40,000				40,000				40,000	
7	Prepaid insurance	900			(c) 360	540				540	
8	Equipment	67,000				67,000				67,000	
9	Accumulated depreciation–equipment		12,000		(a) 6,700		18,700				18,700
10	Notes payable		20,000				20,000				20,000
11	Accounts payable		13,500				13,500				13,500
12	Bonds payable		30,000				30,000				30,000
13	Common stock		50,000				50,000				50,000
14	Retained earnings, Jan. 1, 2012		16,200				16,200				16,200
15	Dividends	2,000				2,000				2,000	
16	Sales revenue		400,000				400,000		400,000		
17	Cost of goods sold	316,000				316,000		316,000			
18	Salaries and wages expense (sales)	20,000				20,000		20,000			
19	Advertising expense	10,200				10,200		10,200			
20	Salaries and wages expense (general)	19,000				19,000		19,000			
21	Telephone and Internet expense	600				600		600			
22	Rent expense	4,800			(e) 500	4,300		4,300			
23	Property tax expense	3,300		(f) 2,000		5,300		5,300			
24	Interest expense	1,700				1,700		1,700			
25	Totals	543,700	543,700								
26	Depreciation expense			(a) 6,700		6,700		6,700			
27	Bad debt expense			(b) 1,000		1,000		1,000			
28	Insurance expense			(c) 360		360		360			
29	Interest receivable			(d) 800		800				800	
30	Interest revenue				(d) 800		800		800		
31	Prepaid rent			(e) 500		500				500	
32	Property taxes payable				(f) 2,000		2,000				2,000
33	Income tax expense			(g) 3,440		3,440		3,440			
34	Income tax payable				(g) 3,440		3,440				3,440
35	Totals			14,800	14,800	557,640	557,640	388,600	400,800		
36	Net income							12,200			12,200
37	Totals							400,800	400,800	169,040	169,040
38											
39											
40											
41											
42											

Sheet1 / Sheet2 / Sheet3

ILLUSTRATION 3C-1
Use of a Worksheet

ADJUSTMENTS ENTERED ON THE WORKSHEET

Items (a) through (g) below serve as the basis for the adjusting entries made in the worksheet for Uptown shown in Illustration 3C-1.

(a) Depreciation of equipment at the rate of 10% per year based on original cost of $67,000.

(b) Estimated bad debts of one-quarter of 1 percent of sales ($400,000).

(c) Insurance expired during the year $360.

(d) Interest accrued on notes receivable as of December 31, $800.

(e) The Rent Expense account contains $500 rent paid in advance, which is applicable to next year.

(f) Property taxes accrued December 31, $2,000.

(g) Income tax payable estimated $3,440.

The adjusting entries shown on the December 31, 2012, worksheet are as follows.

	(a)		
Depreciation Expense		6,700	
Accumulated Depreciation—Equipment			6,700
	(b)		
Bad Debt Expense		1,000	
Allowance for Doubtful Accounts			1,000
	(c)		
Insurance Expense		360	
Prepaid Insurance			360
	(d)		
Interest Receivable		800	
Interest Revenue			800
	(e)		
Prepaid Rent		500	
Rent Expense			500
	(f)		
Property Tax Expense		2,000	
Property Taxes Payable			2,000
	(g)		
Income Tax Expense		3,440	
Income Tax Payable			3,440

Uptown Cabinet transfers the adjusting entries to the Adjustments columns of the worksheet, often designating each by letter. The trial balance lists any new accounts resulting from the adjusting entries, as illustrated on the worksheet. (For example, see the accounts listed in rows 26 through 34 in Illustration 3C-1.) Uptown then totals and balances the Adjustments columns.

Adjusted Trial Balance

The adjusted trial balance shows the balance of all accounts after adjustment at the end of the accounting period. For example, Uptown adds the $2,000 shown opposite the Allowance for Doubtful Accounts in the Trial Balance Cr. column to the $1,000 in the Adjustments Cr. column. The company then extends the $3,000 total to the Adjusted Trial Balance Cr. column. Similarly, Uptown reduces the $900 debit opposite Prepaid Insurance by the $360 credit in the Adjustments column. The result, $540, is shown in the Adjusted Trial Balance Dr. column.

Income Statement and Balance Sheet Columns

Uptown extends all the debit items in the Adjusted Trial Balance columns into the Income Statement or Balance Sheet columns to the right. It similarly extends all the credit items.

The next step is to total the Income Statement columns. Uptown needs the amount of net income or loss for the period to balance the debit and credit columns. The net income of $12,200 is shown in the Income Statement Dr. column because revenues exceeded expenses by that amount.

Uptown then balances the Income Statement columns. The company also enters the net income of $12,200 in the Balance Sheet Cr. column as an increase in retained earnings.

PREPARING FINANCIAL STATEMENTS FROM A WORKSHEET

The worksheet provides the information needed for preparation of the financial statements without reference to the ledger or other records. In addition, the worksheet sorts that data into appropriate columns, which facilitates the preparation of the statements. The financial statements of Uptown Cabinet are shown in Chapter 3, pages 118–119.

KEY TERMS

worksheet, 129

SUMMARY OF LEARNING OBJECTIVE FOR APPENDIX 3C

10 **Prepare a 10-column worksheet.** The 10-column worksheet provides columns for the first trial balance, adjustments, adjusted trial balance, income statement, and balance sheet. The worksheet does not replace the financial statements. Instead, it is an informal device for accumulating and sorting information needed for the financial statements.

Be sure to check the book's companion website for a Review and Analysis Exercise, with solution.

Questions, Brief Exercises, Exercises, Problems, and many more resources are available for practice in WileyPLUS.

Note: All asterisked Questions, Exercises, and Problems relate to material in the appendices to the chapter.

QUESTIONS

1. Give an example of a transaction that results in:

(a) A decrease in an asset and a decrease in a liability.

(b) A decrease in one asset and an increase in another asset.

(c) A decrease in one liability and an increase in another liability.

2. Do the following events represent business transactions? Explain your answer in each case.

(a) A computer is purchased on account.

(b) A customer returns merchandise and is given credit on account.

(c) A prospective employee is interviewed.

(d) The owner of the business withdraws cash from the business for personal use.

(e) Merchandise is ordered for delivery next month.

3. Name the accounts debited and credited for each of the following transactions.

(a) Billing a customer for work done.

(b) Receipt of cash from customer on account.

(c) Purchase of office supplies on account.

(d) Purchase of 15 gallons of gasoline for the delivery truck.

4. Why are revenue and expense accounts called temporary or nominal accounts?

5. Andrea Pafko, a fellow student, contends that the double-entry system means that each transaction must be recorded twice. Is Andrea correct? Explain.

6. Is it necessary that a trial balance be taken periodically? What purpose does it serve?

7. Indicate whether each of the items below is a real or nominal account and whether it appears in the balance sheet or the income statement.

(a) Prepaid Rent.

(b) Salaries and Wages Payable.

(c) Inventory.

(d) Accumulated Depreciation—Equipment.

(e) Equipment.

(f) Service Revenue.

(g) Salaries and Wages Expense.

(h) Supplies.

8. Employees are paid every Saturday for the preceding work week. If a balance sheet is prepared on Wednesday, December 31, what does the amount of wages earned during the first three days of the week (12/29, 12/30, 12/31) represent? Explain.

9. (a) How are the components of revenues and expenses different for a merchandising company? (b) Explain the income measurement process of a merchandising company.

10. What differences are there between the trial balance before closing and the trial balance after closing with respect to the following accounts?

(a) Accounts Payable.

(b) Expense accounts.

(c) Revenue accounts.

(d) Retained Earnings account.

(e) Cash.

11. What are adjusting entries and why are they necessary?

12. What are closing entries and why are they necessary?

13. Jay Hawk, maintenance supervisor for Boston Insurance Co., has purchased a riding lawnmower and accessories to be used in maintaining the grounds around corporate headquarters. He has sent the following information to the accounting department.

Cost of mower and accessories	$4,000	Date purchased	7/1/12
Estimated useful life	5 yrs	Monthly salary of groundskeeper	$1,100
Salvage value	$0	Estimated annual fuel cost	$150

Compute the amount of depreciation expense (related to the mower and accessories) that should be reported on Boston's December 31, 2012, income statement. Assume straight-line depreciation.

14. Midwest Enterprises made the following entry on December 31, 2012.

Interest Expense	10,000	
Interest Payable		10,000
(To record interest expense due on loan from Anaheim National Bank.)		

What entry would Anaheim National Bank make regarding its outstanding loan to Midwest Enterprises? Explain why this must be the case.

***15.** Distinguish between cash-basis accounting and accrual-basis accounting. Why is accrual-basis accounting acceptable for most business enterprises and the cash-basis unacceptable in the preparation of an income statement and a balance sheet?

***16.** When salaries and wages expense for the year is computed, why are beginning accrued salaries and wages subtracted from, and ending accrued salaries and wages added to, salaries and wages paid during the year?

***17.** List two types of transactions that would receive different accounting treatment using (a) strict cash-basis accounting, and (b) a modified cash basis.

***18.** What are reversing entries, and why are they used?

***19.** "A worksheet is a permanent accounting record, and its use is required in the accounting cycle." Do you agree? Explain.

BRIEF EXERCISES

4 **BE3-1** Transactions for Mehta Company for the month of May are presented below. Prepare journal entries for each of these transactions. (You may omit explanations.)

May	1	B.D. Mehta invests $4,000 cash in exchange for common stock in a small welding corporation.
	3	Buys equipment on account for $1,100.
	13	Pays $400 to landlord for May rent.
	21	Bills Noble Corp. $500 for welding work done.

4 **BE3-2** Agazzi Repair Shop had the following transactions during the first month of business as a proprietorship. Journalize the transactions. (Omit explanations.)

Aug.	2	Invested $12,000 cash and $2,500 of equipment in the business.
	7	Purchased supplies on account for $500. (Debit asset account.)
	12	Performed services for clients, for which $1,300 was collected in cash and $670 was billed to the clients.
	15	Paid August rent $600.
	19	Counted supplies and determined that only $270 of the supplies purchased on August 7 are still on hand.

4 5 **BE3-3** On July 1, 2012, Crowe Co. pays $15,000 to Zubin Insurance Co. for a 3-year insurance policy. Both companies have fiscal years ending December 31. For Crowe Co., journalize the entry on July 1 and the adjusting entry on December 31.

4 5 **BE3-4** Using the data in BE3-3, journalize the entry on July 1 and the adjusting entry on December 31 for Zubin Insurance Co. Zubin uses the accounts Unearned Service Revenue and Service Revenue.

4 5 **BE3-5** Assume that on February 1, **Procter & Gamble (P&G)** paid $720,000 in advance for 2 years' insurance coverage. Prepare P&G's February 1 journal entry and the annual adjusting entry on June 30.

4 5 **BE3-6** LaBouche Corporation owns a warehouse. On November 1, it rented storage space to a lessee (tenant) for 3 months for a total cash payment of $2,400 received in advance. Prepare LaBouche's November 1 journal entry and the December 31 annual adjusting entry.

4 5 **BE3-7** Dresser Company's weekly payroll, paid on Fridays, totals $8,000. Employees work a 5-day week. Prepare Dresser's adjusting entry on Wednesday, December 31, and the journal entry to record the $8,000 cash payment on Friday, January 2.

5 **BE3-8** Included in Gonzalez Company's December 31 trial balance is a note receivable of $12,000. The note is a 4-month, 10% note dated October 1. Prepare Gonzalez's December 31 adjusting entry to record $300 of accrued interest, and the February 1 journal entry to record receipt of $12,400 from the borrower.

5 **BE3-9** Prepare the following adjusting entries at August 31 for **Walgreens**.

(a) Interest on notes payable of $300 is accrued.
(b) Services earned but unbilled total $1,400.
(c) Salaries and wages earned by employees of $700 have not been recorded.
(d) Bad debt expense for year is $900.

Use the following account titles: Service Revenue, Accounts Receivable, Interest Expense, Interest Payable, Salaries and Wages Expense, Salaries and Wages Payable, Allowance for Doubtful Accounts, and Bad Debt Expense.

5 **BE3-10** At the end of its first year of operations, the trial balance of Alonzo Company shows Equipment $30,000 and zero balances in Accumulated Depreciation—Equipment and Depreciation Expense. Depreciation for the year is estimated to be $2,000. Prepare the adjusting entry for depreciation at December 31, and indicate the balance sheet presentation for the equipment at December 31.

7 **BE3-11** Side Kicks has year-end account balances of Sales Revenue $808,900; Interest Revenue $13,500; Cost of Goods Sold $556,200; Administrative Expenses $189,000; Income Tax Expense $35,100; and Dividends $18,900. Prepare the year-end closing entries.

8 ***BE3-12** Kelly Company had cash receipts from customers in 2012 of $142,000. Cash payments for operating expenses were $97,000. Kelly has determined that at January 1, accounts receivable was $13,000, and prepaid expenses were $17,500. At December 31, accounts receivable was $18,600, and prepaid expenses were $23,200. Compute (a) service revenue and (b) operating expenses.

9 ***BE3-13** Assume that **Best Buy** made a December 31 adjusting entry to debit Salaries and Wages Expense and credit Salaries and Wages Payable for $4,200 for one of its departments. On January 2, Best Buy paid the weekly payroll of $7,000. Prepare Best Buy's (a) January 1 reversing entry; (b) January 2 entry (assuming the reversing entry was prepared); and (c) January 2 entry (assuming the reversing entry was not prepared).

EXERCISES

4 **E3-1 (Transaction Analysis—Service Company)** Christine Ewing is a licensed CPA. During the first month of operations of her business (a sole proprietorship), the following events and transactions occurred.

April	2	Invested $30,000 cash and equipment valued at $14,000 in the business.
	2	Hired a secretary-receptionist at a salary of $290 per week payable monthly.
	3	Purchased supplies on account $700. (debit an asset account.)
	7	Paid office rent of $600 for the month.
	11	Completed a tax assignment and billed client $1,100 for services rendered. (Use Service Revenue account.)
	12	Received $3,200 advance on a management consulting engagement.
	17	Received cash of $2,300 for services completed for Ferengi Co.
	21	Paid insurance expense $110.
	30	Paid secretary-receptionist $1,160 for the month.
	30	A count of supplies indicated that $120 of supplies had been used.
	30	Purchased a new computer for $5,100 with personal funds. (The computer will be used exclusively for business purposes.)

Instructions

Journalize the transactions in the general journal. (Omit explanations.)

4 **E3-2 (Corrected Trial Balance)** The trial balance of Geronimo Company, shown on the next page, does not balance. Your review of the ledger reveals the following: (a) Each account had a normal balance. (b) The debit footings in Prepaid Insurance, Accounts Payable, and Property Tax Expense were each understated $1,000. (c) A transposition error was made in Accounts Receivable and Service Revenue; the correct

balances for Accounts Receivable and Service Revenue are $2,750 and $6,690, respectively. (d) A debit posting to Advertising Expense of $300 was omitted. (e) A $3,200 cash drawing by the owner was debited to Owner's Capital and credited to Cash.

GERONIMO COMPANY
TRIAL BALANCE
APRIL 30, 2012

	Debit	Credit
Cash	$ 2,100	
Accounts Receivable	2,570	
Prepaid Insurance	700	
Equipment		$ 8,000
Accounts Payable		4,500
Property Taxes Payable	560	
Owner's Capital		11,200
Service Revenue	6,960	
Salaries and Wages Expense	4,200	
Advertising Expense	1,100	
Property Tax Expense		800
	$18,190	$24,500

Instructions

Prepare a correct trial balance.

4 **E3-3 (Corrected Trial Balance)** The following trial balance of Scarlatti Corporation does not balance.

SCARLATTI CORPORATION
TRIAL BALANCE
APRIL 30, 2012

	Debit	Credit
Cash	$ 5,912	
Accounts Receivable	5,240	
Supplies	2,967	
Equipment	6,100	
Accounts Payable		$ 7,044
Common Stock		8,000
Retained Earnings		2,000
Service Revenue		5,200
Office Expense	4,320	
	$24,539	$22,244

An examination of the ledger shows these errors.

1. Cash received from a customer on account was recorded (both debit and credit) as $1,580 instead of $1,850.
2. The purchase on account of a computer costing $1,900 was recorded as a debit to Office Expense and a credit to Accounts Payable.
3. Services were performed on account for a client, $2,250, for which Accounts Receivable was debited $2,250 and Service Revenue was credited $225.
4. A payment of $95 for telephone charges was entered as a debit to Office Expenses and a debit to Cash.
5. The Service Revenue account was totaled at $5,200 instead of $5,280.

Instructions

From this information, prepare a corrected trial balance.

4 **E3-4 (Corrected Trial Balance)** The following trial balance of Oakley Co. does not balance.

OAKLEY CO.
TRIAL BALANCE
JUNE 30, 2012

	Debit	Credit
Cash		$ 2,870
Accounts Receivable	$ 3,231	
Supplies	800	
Equipment	3,800	
Accounts Payable		2,666
Unearned Service Revenue	1,200	
Common Stock		6,000
Retained Earnings		3,000
Service Revenue		2,380
Salaries and Wages Expense	3,400	
Office Expense	940	
	$13,371	$16,916

Each of the listed accounts should have a normal balance per the general ledger. An examination of the ledger and journal reveals the following errors.

1. Cash received from a customer on account was debited for $370, and Accounts Receivable was credited for the same amount. The actual collection was for $730.
2. The purchase of a computer printer on account for $500 was recorded as a debit to Supplies for $500 and a credit to Accounts Payable for $500.
3. Services were performed on account for a client for $890. Accounts Receivable was debited for $890 and Service Revenue was credited for $89.
4. A payment of $65 for telephone charges was recorded as a debit to Office Expense for $65 and a debit to Cash for $65.
5. When the Unearned Service Revenue account was reviewed, it was found that $225 of the balance was earned prior to June 30.
6. A debit posting to Salaries and Wages Expense of $670 was omitted.
7. A payment on account for $206 was credited to Cash for $206 and credited to Accounts Payable for $260.
8. A dividend of $575 was debited to Salaries and Wages Expense for $575 and credited to Cash for $575.

Instructions

Prepare a correct trial balance. (*Note:* It may be necessary to add one or more accounts to the trial balance.)

5 **E3-5 (Adjusting Entries)** The ledger of Chopin Rental Agency on March 31 of the current year includes the following selected accounts before adjusting entries have been prepared.

	Debit	Credit
Prepaid Insurance	$ 3,600	
Supplies	2,800	
Equipment	25,000	
Accumulated Depreciation—Equipment		$ 8,400
Notes Payable		20,000
Unearned Rent Revenue		6,300
Rent Revenue		60,000
Interest Expense	-0-	
Salaries and Wages Expense	14,000	

An analysis of the accounts shows the following.

1. The equipment depreciates $250 per month.
2. One-third of the unearned rent was earned during the quarter.
3. Interest of $500 is accrued on the notes payable.
4. Supplies on hand total $650.
5. Insurance expires at the rate of $300 per month.

Instructions

Prepare the adjusting entries at March 31, assuming that adjusting entries are made quarterly. Additional accounts are: Depreciation Expense, Insurance Expense, Interest Payable, and Supplies Expense. (Omit explanations.)

5 **E3-6 (Adjusting Entries)** Stephen King, D.D.S., opened a dental practice on January 1, 2012. During the first month of operations, the following transactions occurred.

1. Performed services for patients who had dental plan insurance. At January 31, $750 of such services was earned but not yet billed to the insurance companies.
2. Utility expenses incurred but not paid prior to January 31 totaled $520.
3. Purchased dental equipment on January 1 for $80,000, paying $20,000 in cash and signing a $60,000, 3-year note payable. The equipment depreciates $400 per month. Interest is $500 per month.
4. Purchased a one-year malpractice insurance policy on January 1 for $15,000.
5. Purchased $1,600 of dental supplies. On January 31, determined that $400 of supplies were on hand.

Instructions

Prepare the adjusting entries on January 31. (Omit explanations.) Account titles are Accumulated Depreciation—Equipment, Depreciation Expense, Service Revenue, Accounts Receivable, Insurance Expense, Interest Expense, Interest Payable, Prepaid Insurance, Supplies, Supplies Expense, Utilities Expenses, and Accounts Payable.

5 **E3-7 (Analyze Adjusted Data)** A partial adjusted trial balance of Safin Company at January 31, 2012, shows the following.

SAFIN COMPANY
ADJUSTED TRIAL BALANCE
JANUARY 31, 2012

	Debit	Credit
Supplies	$ 900	
Prepaid Insurance	2,400	
Salaries and Wages Payable		$ 800
Unearned Revenue		750
Supplies Expense	950	
Insurance Expense	400	
Salaries and Wages Expense	1,800	
Service Revenue		2,000

Instructions

Answer the following questions, assuming the year begins January 1.

(a) If the amount in Supplies Expense is the January 31 adjusting entry, and $850 of supplies was purchased in January, what was the balance in Supplies on January 1?
(b) If the amount in Insurance Expense is the January 31 adjusting entry, and the original insurance premium was for one year, what was the total premium and when was the policy purchased?
(c) If $2,700 of salaries and wages was paid in January, what was the balance in Salaries and Wages Payable at December 31, 2011?
(d) If $1,600 was received in January for services performed in January, what was the balance in Unearned Service Revenue at December 31, 2011?

5 **E3-8 (Adjusting Entries)** William Bryant is the new owner of Ace Computer Services. At the end of August 2012, his first month of ownership, Bryant is trying to prepare monthly financial statements. Below is some information related to unrecorded expenses that the business incurred during August.

1. At August 31, Bryant owed his employees $2,900 in salaries and wages that will be paid on September 1.
2. At the end of the month, he had not yet received the month's utility bill. Based on past experience, he estimated the bill would be approximately $600.
3. On August 1, Bryant borrowed $60,000 from a local bank on a 15-year mortgage. The annual interest rate is 8%.
4. A telephone bill in the amount of $117 covering August charges is unpaid at August 31.

Instructions

Prepare the adjusting journal entries as of August 31, 2012, suggested by the information above.

5 **E3-9 (Adjusting Entries)** Selected accounts of Leno Company are shown below.

Supplies

Beg. Bal.	800	10/31	470

Accounts Receivable

10/17	2,100		
10/31	1,650		

Salaries and Wages Expense

10/15	800		
10/31	600		

Salaries and Wages Payable

		10/31	600

Unearned Service Revenue

10/31	400	10/20	650

Supplies Expense

10/31	470		

Service Revenue

		10/17	2,100
		10/31	1,650
		10/31	400

Instructions

From an analysis of the T-accounts, reconstruct (a) the October transaction entries, and (b) the adjusting journal entries that were made on October 31, 2012. Prepare explanations for each journal entry.

5 **E3-10 (Adjusting Entries)** Uhura Resort opened for business on June 1 with eight air-conditioned units. Its trial balance on August 31 is as follows.

UHURA RESORT
TRIAL BALANCE
AUGUST 31, 2012

	Debit	Credit
Cash	$ 19,600	
Prepaid Insurance	4,500	
Supplies	2,600	
Land	20,000	
Buildings	120,000	
Equipment	16,000	
Accounts Payable		$ 4,500
Unearned Rent Revenue		4,600
Mortgage Payable		50,000
Common Stock		100,000
Dividends	5,000	
Rent Revenue		86,200
Salaries and Wages Expense	44,800	
Utilities Expenses	9,200	
Maintenance and Repairs Expense	3,600	
	$245,300	$245,300

Other data:

1. The balance in prepaid insurance is a one-year premium paid on June 1, 2012.
2. An inventory count on August 31 shows $650 of supplies on hand.
3. Annual depreciation rates are buildings (4%) and equipment (10%). Salvage value is estimated to be 10% of cost.
4. Unearned Rent Revenue of $3,800 was earned prior to August 31.
5. Salaries of $375 were unpaid at August 31.
6. Rentals of $800 were due from tenants at August 31.
7. The mortgage interest rate is 8% per year.

Instructions

(a) Journalize the adjusting entries on August 31 for the 3-month period June 1–August 31. (Omit explanations.)

(b) Prepare an adjusted trial balance on August 31.

6 **E3-11 (Prepare Financial Statements)** The adjusted trial balance of Cavamanlis Co. as of December 31, 2012, contains the following.

CAVAMANLIS CO.
ADJUSTED TRIAL BALANCE
DECEMBER 31, 2012

Account Titles	Dr.	Cr.
Cash	$18,972	
Accounts Receivable	6,920	
Prepaid Rent Expense	2,280	
Equipment	18,050	
Accumulated Depreciation—Equipment		$ 4,895
Notes Payable		5,700
Accounts Payable		4,472
Common Stock		20,000
Retained Earnings		11,310
Dividends	3,000	
Service Revenue		12,590
Salaries and Wages Expense	6,840	
Rent Expense	2,760	
Depreciation Expense	145	
Interest Expense	83	
Interest Payable		83
	$59,050	$59,050

Instructions

(a) Prepare an income statement.
(b) Prepare a statement of retained earnings.
(c) Prepare a classified balance sheet.

6 **E3-12 (Prepare Financial Statements)** Flynn Design Agency was founded by Kevin Flynn in January 2006. Presented below is the adjusted trial balance as of December 31, 2012.

FLYNN DESIGN AGENCY
ADJUSTED TRIAL BALANCE
DECEMBER 31, 2012

	Dr.	Cr.
Cash	$ 10,000	
Accounts Receivable	21,500	
Supplies	5,000	
Prepaid Insurance	2,500	
Equipment	60,000	
Accumulated Depreciation—Equipment		$ 35,000
Accounts Payable		8,000
Interest Payable		150
Notes Payable		5,000
Unearned Service Revenue		5,600
Salaries and Wages Payable		1,300
Common Stock		10,000
Retained Earnings		3,500
Service Revenue		58,500
Salaries and Wages Expense	12,300	
Insurance Expense	850	
Interest Expense	500	
Depreciation Expense	7,000	
Supplies Expense	3,400	
Rent Expense	4,000	
	$127,050	$127,050

Instructions

(a) Prepare an income statement and a statement of retained earnings for the year ending December 31, 2012, and an unclassified balance sheet at December 31.

(b) Answer the following questions.
   (1) If the note has been outstanding 6 months, what is the annual interest rate on that note?
   (2) If the company paid $17,500 in salaries and wages in 2012, what was the balance in Salaries and Wages Payable on December 31, 2011?

7 **E3-13 (Closing Entries)** The adjusted trial balance of Faulk Company shows the following data pertaining to sales at the end of its fiscal year, October 31, 2012: Sales Revenue $800,000, Freight-out $12,000, Sales Returns and Allowances $24,000, and Sales Discounts $12,000.

Instructions

(a) Prepare the sales revenue section of the income statement.
(b) Prepare separate closing entries for (1) sales revenue and (2) the contra accounts to sales revenue.

7 **E3-14 (Closing Entries)** Presented below is information related to Russell Corporation for the month of January 2012.

Cost of goods sold	$202,000	Salaries and wages expense	$ 61,000
Freight-out	7,000	Sales discounts	8,000
Insurance expense	12,000	Sales returns and allowances	13,000
Rent expense	20,000	Sales revenue	340,000

Instructions

Prepare the necessary closing entries.

6 **E3-15 (Missing Amounts)** Presented below is financial information for two different companies.

	Shabbona Company	Jenkins Company
Sales revenue	$90,000	(d)
Sales returns and allowances	(a)	$ 5,000
Net sales	85,000	90,000
Cost of goods sold	56,000	(e)
Gross profit	(b)	38,000
Operating expenses	15,000	23,000
Net income	(c)	15,000

Instructions

Compute the missing amounts.

7 **E3-16 (Closing Entries for a Corporation)** Presented below are selected account balances for Alistair Co. as of December 31, 2012.

Inventory 12/31/12	$ 60,000	Cost of Goods Sold	$235,700
Common Stock	75,000	Selling Expenses	16,000
Retained Earnings	45,000	Administrative Expenses	38,000
Dividends	18,000	Income Tax Expense	30,000
Sales Returns and Allowances	12,000		
Sales Discounts	15,000		
Sales Revenue	390,000		

Instructions

Prepare closing entries for Alistair Co. on December 31, 2012. (Omit explanations.)

4 **E3-17 (Transactions of a Corporation, Including Investment and Dividend)** Snyder Miniature Golf and Driving Range Inc. was opened on March 1 by Mickey Snyder. The following selected events and transactions occurred during March.

Mar. 1	Invested $60,000 cash in the business in exchange for common stock.
3	Purchased Michelle Wie's Golf Land for $38,000 cash. The price consists of land $10,000; building $22,000; and equipment $6,000. (Make one compound entry.)
5	Advertised the opening of the driving range and miniature golf course, paying advertising expenses of $1,600.
6	Paid cash $1,480 for a one-year insurance policy.
10	Purchased golf equipment for $2,500 from Young Company, payable in 30 days.
18	Received golf fees of $1,200 in cash.
25	Declared and paid a $1,000 cash dividend.
30	Paid wages of $900.
30	Paid Young Company in full.
31	Received $750 of fees in cash.

Snyder uses the following accounts: Cash, Prepaid Insurance, Land, Buildings, Equipment, Accounts Payable, Common Stock, Dividends, Service Revenue, Advertising Expense, and Salaries and Wages Expense.

Instructions

Journalize the March transactions. (Provide explanations for the journal entries.)

8 ***E3-18 (Cash to Accrual Basis)** Corinne Dunbar, M.D., maintains the accounting records of Dunbar Clinic on a cash basis. During 2012, Dr. Dunbar collected $142,600 from her patients and paid $60,470 in expenses. At January 1, 2012, and December 31, 2012, she had accounts receivable, unearned service revenue, accrued expenses, and prepaid expenses as follows. (All long-lived assets are rented.)

	January 1, 2012	December 31, 2012
Accounts receivable	$11,250	$15,927
Unearned service revenue	2,840	4,111
Accrued expenses	3,435	2,108
Prepaid expenses	1,917	3,232

Instructions

Prepare a schedule that converts Dr. Dunbar's "excess of cash collected over cash disbursed" for the year 2012 to net income on an accrual basis for the year 2012.

8 ***E3-19 (Cash and Accrual Basis)** Latta Corp. maintains its financial records on the cash basis of accounting. Interested in securing a long-term loan from its regular bank, Latta Corp. requests you as its independent CPA to convert its cash-basis income statement data to the accrual basis. You are provided with the following summarized data covering 2011, 2012, and 2013.

	2011	2012	2013
Cash receipts from sales:			
On 2011 sales	$290,000	$160,000	$ 30,000
On 2012 sales	–0–	355,000	90,000
On 2013 sales			408,000
Cash payments for expenses:			
On 2011 expenses	185,000	67,000	25,000
On 2012 expenses	40,000[a]	170,000	55,000
On 2013 expenses		45,000[b]	218,000

[a]Prepayments of 2012 expenses.
[b]Prepayments of 2013 expenses.

Instructions

(a) Using the data above, prepare abbreviated income statements for the years 2011 and 2012 on the cash basis.

(b) Using the data above, prepare abbreviated income statements for the years 2011 and 2012 on the accrual basis.

5 9 ***E3-20 (Adjusting and Reversing Entries)** When the accounts of Constantine Inc. are examined, the adjusting data listed below are uncovered on December 31, the end of an annual fiscal period.

1. The prepaid insurance account shows a debit of $6,000, representing the cost of a 2-year fire insurance policy dated August 1 of the current year.
2. On November 1, Rent Revenue was credited for $2,400, representing revenue from a subrental for a 3-month period beginning on that date.
3. Purchase of advertising supplies for $800 during the year was recorded in the Advertising Expense account. On December 31, advertising supplies of $290 are on hand.
4. Interest of $770 has accrued on notes payable.

Instructions

Prepare the following in general journal form.

(a) The adjusting entry for each item.

(b) The reversing entry for each item where appropriate.

10 ***E3-21 (Worksheet)** Presented below are selected accounts for Acevedo Company as reported in the worksheet at the end of May 2012.

	A	B	C	D	E	F	G
1	Accounts	Adjusted Trial Balance Debit	Adjusted Trial Balance Credit	Income Statement Debit	Income Statement Credit	Balance Sheet Debit	Balance Sheet Credit
2	Cash	15,000					
3	Inventory	80,000					
4	Sales Revenue		470,000				
5	Sales Returns and Allowances	10,000					
6	Sales Discounts	5,000					
7	Cost of Goods Sold	250,000					

Sheet1 Sheet2 Sheet3

Instructions

Complete the worksheet by extending amounts reported in the adjusted trial balance to the appropriate columns in the worksheet. Do not total individual columns.

10 ***E3-22 (Worksheet and Balance Sheet Presentation)** The adjusted trial balance for Madrasah Co. is presented in the following worksheet for the month ended April 30, 2012.

MADRASAH CO.
Worksheet (PARTIAL)
For The Month Ended April 30, 2012

	A	B	C	D	E	F	G
		Adjusted Trial Balance		Income Statement		Balance Sheet	
1	Account Titles	Debit	Credit	Debit	Credit	Debit	Credit
2	Cash	$18,972					
3	Accounts Receivable	6,920					
4	Prepaid Rent	2,280					
5	Equipment	18,050					
6	Accumulated Depreciation—Equipment		$4,895				
7	Notes Payable		5,700				
8	Accounts Payable		4,472				
9	Owner's Capital		34,960				
10	Owner's Drawings	6,650					
11	Service Revenue		12,590				
12	Salaries and Wages Expense	6,840					
13	Rent Expense	2,760					
14	Depreciation Expense	145					
15	Interest Expense	83					
16	Interest Payable		83				

Sheet1 / Sheet2 / Sheet3

Instructions

Complete the worksheet and prepare a classified balance sheet.

10 ***E3-23 (Partial Worksheet Preparation)** Letterman Co. prepares monthly financial statements from a worksheet. Selected portions of the January worksheet showed the following data.

LETTERMAN CO.
Worksheet (PARTIAL)
For The Month Ended January 31, 2012

	A	B	C	D	E	F	G
		Trial Balance		Adjustments		Adjusted Trial Balance	
1	Account Title	Debit	Credit	Debit	Credit	Debit	Credit
2	Supplies	3,256			(a) 1,500	1,756	
3	Accumulated Depreciation—Equipment		7,710		(b) 257		7,967
4	Interest Payable		100		(c) 50		150
5	Supplies Expense			(a) 1,500		1,500	
6	Depreciation Expense			(b) 257		257	
7	Interest Expense			(c) 50		50	

Sheet1 / Sheet2 / Sheet3

During February no events occurred that affected these accounts, but at the end of February the following information was available.

(a) Supplies on hand	$515
(b) Monthly depreciation	$257
(c) Accrued interest	$ 50

Instructions

Reproduce the data that would appear in the February worksheet, and indicate the amounts that would be shown in the February income statement.

See the book's companion website, www.wiley.com/college/kieso, for a set of B Exercises.

PROBLEMS

4 6 7 **P3-1 (Transactions, Financial Statements—Service Company)** Listed below are the transactions of Yasunari Kawabata, D.D.S., for the month of September.

Sept.	1	Kawabata begins practice as a dentist and invests $20,000 cash.
	2	Purchases dental equipment on account from Green Jacket Co. for $17,280.
	4	Pays rent for office space, $680 for the month.
	4	Employs a receptionist, Michael Bradley.
	5	Purchases dental supplies for cash, $942.
	8	Receives cash of $1,690 from patients for services performed.
	10	Pays miscellaneous office expenses, $430.
	14	Bills patients $5,820 for services performed.
	18	Pays Green Jacket Co. on account, $3,600.
	19	Withdraws $3,000 cash from the business for personal use.
	20	Receives $980 from patients on account.
	25	Bills patients $2,110 for services performed.
	30	Pays the following expenses in cash: Salaries and wages $1,800; miscellaneous office expenses $85.
	30	Dental supplies used during September, $330.

Instructions

(a) Enter the transactions shown above in appropriate general ledger accounts (use T-accounts). Use the following ledger accounts: Cash, Accounts Receivable, Supplies, Equipment, Accumulated Depreciation—Equipment, Accounts Payable, Owner's Capital, Service Revenue, Rent Expense, Office Expense, Salaries and Wages Expense, Supplies Expense, Depreciation Expense, and Income Summary. Allow 10 lines for the Cash and Income Summary accounts, and 5 lines for each of the other accounts needed. Record depreciation using a 5-year life on the equipment, the straight-line method, and no salvage value. Do not use a drawing account.

(b) Prepare a trial balance.

(c) Prepare an income statement, a statement of owner's equity, and an unclassified balance sheet.

(d) Close the ledger.

(e) Prepare a post-closing trial balance.

5 6 **P3-2 (Adjusting Entries and Financial Statements)** Mason Advertising Agency was founded in January 2008. Presented below are adjusted and unadjusted trial balances as of December 31, 2012.

MASON ADVERTISING AGENCY
TRIAL BALANCE
DECEMBER 31, 2012

	Unadjusted		Adjusted	
	Dr.	Cr.	Dr.	Cr.
Cash	$ 11,000		$ 11,000	
Accounts Receivable	20,000		23,500	
Supplies	8,400		3,000	
Prepaid Insurance	3,350		2,500	
Equipment	60,000		60,000	
Accumulated Depreciation—Equipment		$ 28,000		$ 33,000
Accounts Payable		5,000		5,000
Interest Payable		-0-		150
Notes Payable		5,000		5,000
Unearned Service Revenue		7,000		5,600
Salaries and Wages Payable		-0-		1,300
Common Stock		10,000		10,000
Retained Earnings		3,500		3,500
Service Revenue		58,600		63,500
Salaries and Wages Expense	10,000		11,300	
Insurance Expense			850	
Interest Expense	350		500	
Depreciation Expense			5,000	
Supplies Expense			5,400	
Rent Expense	4,000		4,000	
	$117,100	$117,100	$127,050	$127,050

Instructions

(a) Journalize the annual adjusting entries that were made. (Omit explanations.)

(b) Prepare an income statement and a statement of retained earnings for the year ending December 31, 2012, and an unclassified balance sheet at December 31.

(c) Answer the following questions.

(1) If the note has been outstanding 3 months, what is the annual interest rate on that note?

(2) If the company paid $12,500 in salaries and wages in 2012, what was the balance in Salaries and Wages Payable on December 31, 2011?

5 **P3-3 (Adjusting Entries)** A review of the ledger of Baylor Company at December 31, 2012, produces the following data pertaining to the preparation of annual adjusting entries.

1. Salaries and Wages Payable $0. There are eight employees. Salaries and wages are paid every Friday for the current week. Five employees receive $700 each per week, and three employees earn $600 each per week. December 31 is a Tuesday. Employees do not work weekends. All employees worked the last 2 days of December.

2. Unearned Rent Revenue $429,000. The company began subleasing office space in its new building on November 1. Each tenant is required to make a $5,000 security deposit that is not refundable until occupancy is terminated. At December 31, the company had the following rental contracts that are paid in full for the entire term of the lease.

Date	Term (in months)	Monthly Rent	Number of Leases
Nov. 1	6	$6,000	5
Dec. 1	6	$8,500	4

3. Prepaid Advertising $13,200. This balance consists of payments on two advertising contracts. The contracts provide for monthly advertising in two trade magazines. The terms of the contracts are as shown below.

Contract	Date	Amount	Number of Magazine Issues
A650	May 1	$6,000	12
B974	Oct. 1	7,200	24

The first advertisement runs in the month in which the contract is signed.

4. Notes Payable $60,000. This balance consists of a note for one year at an annual interest rate of 12%, dated June 1.

Instructions

Prepare the adjusting entries at December 31, 2012. (Show all computations).

4 5 6 7 **P3-4 (Financial Statements, Adjusting and Closing Entries)** The trial balance of Bellemy Fashion Center contained the following accounts at November 30, the end of the company's fiscal year.

BELLEMY FASHION CENTER
TRIAL BALANCE
NOVEMBER 30, 2012

	Debit	Credit
Cash	$ 28,700	
Accounts Receivable	33,700	
Inventory	45,000	
Supplies	5,500	
Equipment	133,000	
Accumulated Depreciation—Equipment		$ 24,000
Notes Payable		51,000
Accounts Payable		48,500
Common Stock		90,000
Retained Earnings		8,000
Sales Revenue		757,200
Sales Returns and Allowances	4,200	
Cost of Goods Sold	495,400	
Salaries and Wages Expense	140,000	
Advertising Expense	26,400	
Utilities Expenses	14,000	
Maintenance and Repairs Expense	12,100	
Freight-out	16,700	
Rent Expense	24,000	
	$978,700	$978,700

Adjustment data:

1. Supplies on hand totaled $1,500.
2. Depreciation is $15,000 on the equipment.
3. Interest of $11,000 is accrued on notes payable at November 30.

Other data:

1. Salaries expense is 70% selling and 30% administrative.
2. Rent expense and utilities expense are 80% selling and 20% administrative.
3. $30,000 of notes payable are due for payment next year.
4. Maintenance and repairs expense is 100% administrative.

Instructions

(a) Journalize the adjusting entries.
(b) Prepare an adjusted trial balance.
(c) Prepare a multiple-step income statement and retained earnings statement for the year and a classified balance sheet as of November 30, 2012.
(d) Journalize the closing entries.
(e) Prepare a post-closing trial balance.

5 **P3-5 (Adjusting Entries)** The accounts listed below appeared in the December 31 trial balance of the Savard Theater.

	Debit	Credit
Equipment	$192,000	
Accumulated Depreciation—Equipment		$ 60,000
Notes Payable		90,000
Admissions Revenue		380,000
Advertising Expense	13,680	
Salaries and Wages Expense	57,600	
Interest Expense	1,400	

Instructions

(a) From the account balances listed above and the information given below, prepare the annual adjusting entries necessary on December 31. (Omit explanations.)
- **(1)** The equipment has an estimated life of 16 years and a salvage value of $24,000 at the end of that time. (Use straight-line method.)
- **(2)** The note payable is a 90-day note given to the bank October 20 and bearing interest at 8%. (Use 360 days for denominator.)
- **(3)** In December, 2,000 coupon admission books were sold at $30 each. They could be used for admission any time after January 1.
- **(4)** Advertising expense paid in advance and included in Advertising Expense $1,100.
- **(5)** Salaries and wages accrued but unpaid $4,700.

(b) What amounts should be shown for each of the following on the income statement for the year?
- **(1)** Interest expense.
- **(2)** Admissions revenue.
- **(3)** Advertising expense.
- **(4)** Salaries and wages expense.

5 6 **P3-6 (Adjusting Entries and Financial Statements)** Presented below are the trial balance and the other information related to Yorkis Perez, a consulting engineer.

YORKIS PEREZ, CONSULTING ENGINEER
TRIAL BALANCE
DECEMBER 31, 2012

	Debit	Credit
Cash	$ 29,500	
Accounts Receivable	49,600	
Allowance for Doubtful Accounts		$ 750
Inventory	1,960	
Prepaid Insurance	1,100	
Equipment	25,000	
Accumulated Depreciation—Equipment		6,250
Notes Payable		7,200
Owner's Capital		35,010
Service Revenue		100,000
Rent Expense	9,750	
Salaries and Wages Expense	30,500	
Utilities Expenses	1,080	
Office Expense	720	
	$149,210	$149,210

1. Fees received in advance from clients $6,000.
2. Services performed for clients that were not recorded by December 31, $4,900.
3. Bad debt expense for the year is $1,430.
4. Insurance expired during the year $480.
5. Equipment is being depreciated at 10% per year.
6. Yorkis Perez gave the bank a 90-day, 10% note for $7,200 on December 1, 2012.
7. Rent of the building is $750 per month. The rent for 2012 has been paid, as has that for January 2013.
8. Office salaries and wages earned but unpaid December 31, 2012, $2,510.

Instructions

(a) From the trial balance and other information given, prepare annual adjusting entries as of December 31, 2012. (Omit explanations.)

(b) Prepare an income statement for 2012, a statement of owner's equity, and a classified balance sheet. Yorkis Perez withdrew $17,000 cash for personal use during the year.

5 6 **P3-7 (Adjusting Entries and Financial Statements)** Rolling Hills Golf Inc. was organized on July 1, 2012. Quarterly financial statements are prepared. The trial balance and adjusted trial balance on September 30 are shown here.

ROLLING HILLS GOLF INC.
TRIAL BALANCE
SEPTEMBER 30, 2012

	Unadjusted		Adjusted	
	Dr.	Cr.	Dr.	Cr.
Cash	$ 6,700		$ 6,700	
Accounts Receivable	400		1,000	
Prepaid Rent	1,800		900	
Supplies	1,200		180	
Equipment	15,000		15,000	
Accumulated Depreciation—Equipment				$ 350
Notes Payable		$ 5,000		5,000
Accounts Payable		1,070		1,070
Salaries and Wages Payable				600
Interest Payable				50
Unearned Rent Revenue		1,000		800
Common Stock		14,000		14,000
Retained Earnings		0		0
Dividends	600		600	
Service Revenue		14,100		14,700
Rent Revenue		700		900
Salaries and Wages Expense	8,800		9,400	
Rent Expense	900		1,800	
Depreciation Expense			350	
Supplies Expense			1,020	
Utilities Expenses	470		470	
Interest Expense			50	
	$35,870	$35,870	$37,470	$37,470

Instructions

(a) Journalize the adjusting entries that were made.

(b) Prepare an income statement and a retained earnings statement for the 3 months ending September 30 and a classified balance sheet at September 30.

(c) Identify which accounts should be closed on September 30.

(d) If the note bears interest at 12%, how many months has it been outstanding?

5 6 **P3-8 (Adjusting Entries and Financial Statements)** Vedula Advertising Agency was founded by Murali Vedula in January 2007. Presented on the next page are both the adjusted and unadjusted trial balances as of December 31, 2012.

VEDULA ADVERTISING AGENCY TRIAL BALANCE DECEMBER 31, 2012	Unadjusted		Adjusted	
	Dr.	Cr.	Dr.	Cr.
Cash	$ 11,000		$ 11,000	
Accounts Receivable	16,000		19,500	
Supplies	9,400		6,500	
Prepaid Insurance	3,350		1,790	
Equipment	60,000		60,000	
Accumulated Depreciation—Equipment		$ 25,000		$ 30,000
Notes Payable		8,000		8,000
Accounts Payable		2,000		2,000
Interest Payable		0		560
Unearned Service Revenue		5,000		3,100
Salaries and Wages Payable		0		820
Common Stock		20,000		20,000
Retained Earnings		5,500		5,500
Dividends	10,000		10,000	
Service Revenue		57,600		63,000
Salaries and Wages Expense	9,000		9,820	
Insurance Expense			1,560	
Interest Expense			560	
Depreciation Expense			5,000	
Supplies Expense			2,900	
Rent Expense	4,350		4,350	
	$123,100	$123,100	$132,980	$132,980

Instructions

(a) Journalize the annual adjusting entries that were made.

(b) Prepare an income statement and a retained earnings statement for the year ended December 31, and a classified balance sheet at December 31.

(c) Identify which accounts should be closed on December 31.

(d) If the note has been outstanding 10 months, what is the annual interest rate on that note?

(e) If the company paid $10,500 in salaries and wages in 2012, what was the balance in Salaries and Wages Payable on December 31, 2011?

P3-9 (Adjusting and Closing) Presented below is the trial balance of the Crestwood Golf Club, Inc. as of December 31. The books are closed annually on December 31.

CRESTWOOD GOLF CLUB, INC. TRIAL BALANCE DECEMBER 31	Debit	Credit
Cash	$ 15,000	
Accounts Receivable	13,000	
Allowance for Doubtful Accounts		$ 1,100
Prepaid Insurance	9,000	
Land	350,000	
Buildings	120,000	
Accumulated Depreciation—Buildings		38,400
Equipment	150,000	
Accumulated Depreciation—Equipment		70,000
Common Stock		400,000
Retained Earnings		82,000
Dues Revenue		200,000
Green Fees Revenue		5,900
Rent Revenue		17,600

(Continued)

CRESTWOOD GOLF CLUB, INC.
TRIAL BALANCE
DECEMBER 31

	Debit	Credit
Utilities Expenses	54,000	
Salaries and Wages Expense	80,000	
Maintenance and Repairs Expense	24,000	
	$815,000	$815,000

Instructions

(a) Enter the balances in ledger accounts. Allow five lines for each account.

(b) From the trial balance and the information given below, prepare annual adjusting entries and post to the ledger accounts. (Omit explanations.)

(1) The buildings have an estimated life of 30 years with no salvage value (straight-line method).

(2) The equipment is depreciated at 10% per year.

(3) Insurance expired during the year $3,500.

(4) The rent revenue represents the amount received for 11 months for dining facilities. The December rent has not yet been received.

(5) It is estimated that 12% of the accounts receivable will be uncollectible.

(6) Salaries and wages earned but not paid by December 31, $3,600.

(7) Dues received in advance from members $8,900.

(c) Prepare an adjusted trial balance.

(d) Prepare closing entries and post.

P3-10 (Adjusting and Closing) Presented below is the December 31 trial balance of New York Boutique.

NEW YORK BOUTIQUE
TRIAL BALANCE
DECEMBER 31

	Debit	Credit
Cash	$ 18,500	
Accounts Receivable	32,000	
Allowance for Doubtful Accounts		$ 700
Inventory, December 31	80,000	
Prepaid Insurance	5,100	
Equipment	84,000	
Accumulated Depreciation—Equipment		35,000
Notes Payable		28,000
Common Stock		80,600
Retained Earnings		10,000
Sales Revenue		600,000
Cost of Goods Sold	408,000	
Salaries and Wages Expense (sales)	50,000	
Advertising Expense	6,700	
Salaries and Wages Expense (administrative)	65,000	
Supplies Expense	5,000	
	$754,300	$754,300

Instructions

(a) Construct T-accounts and enter the balances shown.

(b) Prepare adjusting journal entries for the following and post to the T-accounts. (Omit explanations.) Open additional T-accounts as necessary. (The books are closed yearly on December 31.)

(1) Bad debt expense is estimated to be $1,400.

(2) Equipment is depreciated based on a 7-year life (no salvage value).

(3) Insurance expired during the year $2,550.

(4) Interest accrued on notes payable $3,360.

(5) Sales salaries and wages earned but not paid $2,400.

(6) Advertising paid in advance $700.

(7) Office supplies on hand $1,500, charged to Supplies Expense when purchased.

(c) Prepare closing entries and post to the accounts.

8 ***P3-11 (Cash and Accrual Basis)** On January 1, 2012, Norma Smith and Grant Wood formed a computer sales and service enterprise in Soapsville, Arkansas, by investing $90,000 cash. The new company, Arkansas Sales and Service, has the following transactions during January.

1. Pays $6,000 in advance for 3 months' rent of office, showroom, and repair space.
2. Purchases 40 personal computers at a cost of $1,500 each, 6 graphics computers at a cost of $2,500 each, and 25 printers at a cost of $300 each, paying cash upon delivery.
3. Sales, repair, and office employees earn $12,600 in salaries and wages during January, of which $3,000 was still payable at the end of January.
4. Sells 30 personal computers at $2,550 each, 4 graphics computers for $3,600 each, and 15 printers for $500 each; $75,000 is received in cash in January, and $23,400 is sold on a deferred payment basis.
5. Other operating expenses of $8,400 are incurred and paid for during January; $2,000 of incurred expenses are payable at January 31.

Instructions

(a) Using the transaction data above, prepare (1) a cash-basis income statement and (2) an accrual-basis income statement for the month of January.

(b) Using the transaction data above, prepare (1) a cash-basis balance sheet and (2) an accrual-basis balance sheet as of January 31, 2012.

(c) Identify the items in the cash-basis financial statements that make cash-basis accounting inconsistent with the theory underlying the elements of financial statements.

5 6 7 10 ***P3-12 (Worksheet, Balance Sheet, Adjusting and Closing Entries)** Cooke Company has a fiscal year ending on September 30. Selected data from the September 30 worksheet are presented below.

COOKE COMPANY
Worksheet
For The Month Ended September 30, 2012

	A	B	C	D	E
		Trial Balance		Adjusted Trial Balance	
1		Debit	Credit	Debit	Credit
2	Cash	37,400		37,400	
3	Supplies	18,600		4,200	
4	Prepaid Insurance	31,900		3,900	
5	Land	80,000		80,000	
6	Equipment	120,000		120,000	
7	Accumulated Depreciation—Equipment		36,200		42,000
8	Accounts Payable		14,600		14,600
9	Unearned Admissions Revenue		2,700		700
10	Mortgage Payable		50,000		50,000
11	Owner's Capital		109,700		109,700
12	Owner's Drawings	14,000		14,000	
13	Admissions Revenue		278,500		280,500
14	Salaries and Wages Expense	109,000		109,000	
15	Maintenance and Repairs Expense	30,500		30,500	
16	Advertising Expense	9,400		9,400	
17	Utilities Expenses	16,900		16,900	
18	Property Tax Expense	18,000		21,000	
19	Interest Expense	6,000		12,000	
20	Totals	491,700	491,700		
21	Insurance Expense			28,000	
22	Supplies Expense			14,400	
23	Interest Payable				6,000
24	Depreciation Expense			5,800	
25	Property Taxes Payable				3,000
26	Totals			506,500	506,500

Sheet1 / Sheet2 / Sheet3

Instructions

(a) Prepare a complete worksheet.

(b) Prepare a classified balance sheet. (*Note:* $10,000 of the mortgage payable is due for payment in the next fiscal year.)

(c) Journalize the adjusting entries using the worksheet as a basis.

(d) Journalize the closing entries using the worksheet as a basis.

(e) Prepare a post-closing trial balance.

See the book's companion website, www.wiley.com/college/kieso, for a comprehensive problem that illustrates accounting cycle steps for multiple periods.

USING YOUR JUDGMENT

FINANCIAL REPORTING

Financial Reporting Problem

The Procter & Gamble Company (P&G)

The financial statements of **P&G** are presented in Appendix 5B or can be accessed at the book's companion website, **www.wiley.com/college/kieso**.

Instructions

Refer to these financial statements and the accompanying notes to answer the following questions.

(a) What were P&G's total assets at June 30, 2009? At June 30, 2008?

(b) How much cash (and cash equivalents) did P&G have on June 30, 2009?

(c) What were P&G's research and development costs in 2008? In 2009?

(d) What were P&G's revenues in 2008? In 2009?

(e) Using P&G's financial statements and related notes, identify items that may result in adjusting entries for deferrals and accruals.

(f) What were the amounts of P&G's depreciation and amortization expense in 2007, 2008, and 2009?

Comparative Analysis Case

The Coca-Cola Company and PepsiCo, Inc.

Instructions

Go to the book's companion website and use information found there to answer the following questions related to **The Coca-Cola Company** and **PepsiCo, Inc.**

(a) Which company had the greater percentage increase in total assets from 2008 to 2009?

(b) Using the Selected Financial Data section of these two companies, determine their 5-year average growth rates related to net sales and income from continuing operations.

(c) Which company had more depreciation and amortization expense for 2009? Provide a rationale as to why there is a difference in these amounts between the two companies.

Financial Statement Analysis Case

Kellogg Company

Kellogg Company has its headquarters in Battle Creek, Michigan. The company manufactures and sells ready-to-eat breakfast cereals and convenience foods including cookies, toaster pastries, and cereal bars.

Selected data from Kellogg Company's 2009 annual report follows (dollar amounts in millions).

	2009	2008	2007
Sales	$12,575.00	$12,822.00	$11,776.00
Gross profit %	42.87	41.86	43.98
Operating profit	2,001.00	1,953.00	1,868.00
Net cash flow less capital expenditures	1,266.00	806.00	1,031.00
Net earnings	1,208.00	1,146.00	1,102.00

In its annual reports, Kellogg Company has indicated that it plans to achieve sustainability of its operating results with operating principles that emphasize profit-rich, sustainable sales growth, as well as cash flow and return on invested capital. Kellogg believes its steady earnings growth, strong cash flow, and continued investment during a multi-year period demonstrates the strength and flexibility of its business model.

Instructions

(a) Compute the percentage change in sales, operating profit, net cash flow less capital expenditures, and net earnings from year to year for the years presented.

(b) Evaluate Kellogg's performance. Which trend seems most favorable? Which trend seems least favorable? What are the implications of these trends for Kellogg's sustainable performance objectives? Explain.

Accounting, Analysis, and Principles

The Amato Theater is nearing the end of the year and is preparing for a meeting with its bankers to discuss the renewal of a loan. The accounts listed below appeared in the December 31, 2012, trial balance.

	Debit	Credit
Prepaid Advertising	$ 6,000	
Equipment	192,000	
Accumulated Depreciation—Equipment		$ 60,000
Notes Payable		90,000
Unearned Ticket Revenue		17,500
Ticket Revenue		360,000
Advertising Expense	18,680	
Salaries and Wages Expense	67,600	
Interest Expense	1,400	

Additional information is available as follows.

1. The equipment has an estimated useful life of 16 years and a salvage value of $40,000 at the end of that time. Amato uses the straight-line method for depreciation.
2. The note payable is a one-year note given to the bank January 31 and bearing interest at 10%. Interest is calculated on a monthly basis.
3. Late in December 2012, the theater sold 350 coupon ticket books at $50 each. One hundred fifty of these ticket books can be used only for admission any time after January 1, 2013. The cash received was recorded as Unearned Ticket Revenue.
4. Advertising paid in advance was $6,000 and was debited to Prepaid Advertising. The company has used $2,500 of the advertising as of December 31, 2012.
5. Salaries and wages accrued but unpaid at December 31, 2012, were $3,500.

Accounting

Prepare any adjusting journal entries necessary for the year ended December 31, 2012.

Analysis

Determine Amato's income before and after recording the adjusting entries. Use your analysis to explain why Amato's bankers should be willing to wait for Amato to complete its year-end adjustment process before making a decision on the loan renewal.

Principles

Although Amato's bankers are willing to wait for the adjustment process to be completed before they receive financial information, they would like to receive financial reports more frequently than annually or even quarterly. What trade-offs, in terms of relevance and faithful representation, are inherent in preparing financial statements for shorter accounting time periods?

BRIDGE TO THE PROFESSION

Professional Research

Recording transactions in the accounting system requires knowledge of the important characteristics of the elements of financial statements, such as assets and liabilities. In addition, accountants must understand the inherent uncertainty in accounting measures and distinctions between related accounting concepts that are important in evaluating the effects of transactions on the financial statements.

Instructions

If your school has a subscription to the FASB Codification, go to *http://aaahq.org/asclogin.cfm* to log in and provide explanations for the following items. (Provide paragraph citations.) When you have accessed the documents, you can use the search tool in your Internet browser.

(a) The three essential characteristics of assets.

(b) The three essential characteristics of liabilities.

(c) Uncertainty and its effect on financial statements.

(d) The difference between realization and recognition.

Professional Simulation

In this simulation, you are asked to address questions regarding the accounting information system. Prepare responses to all parts.

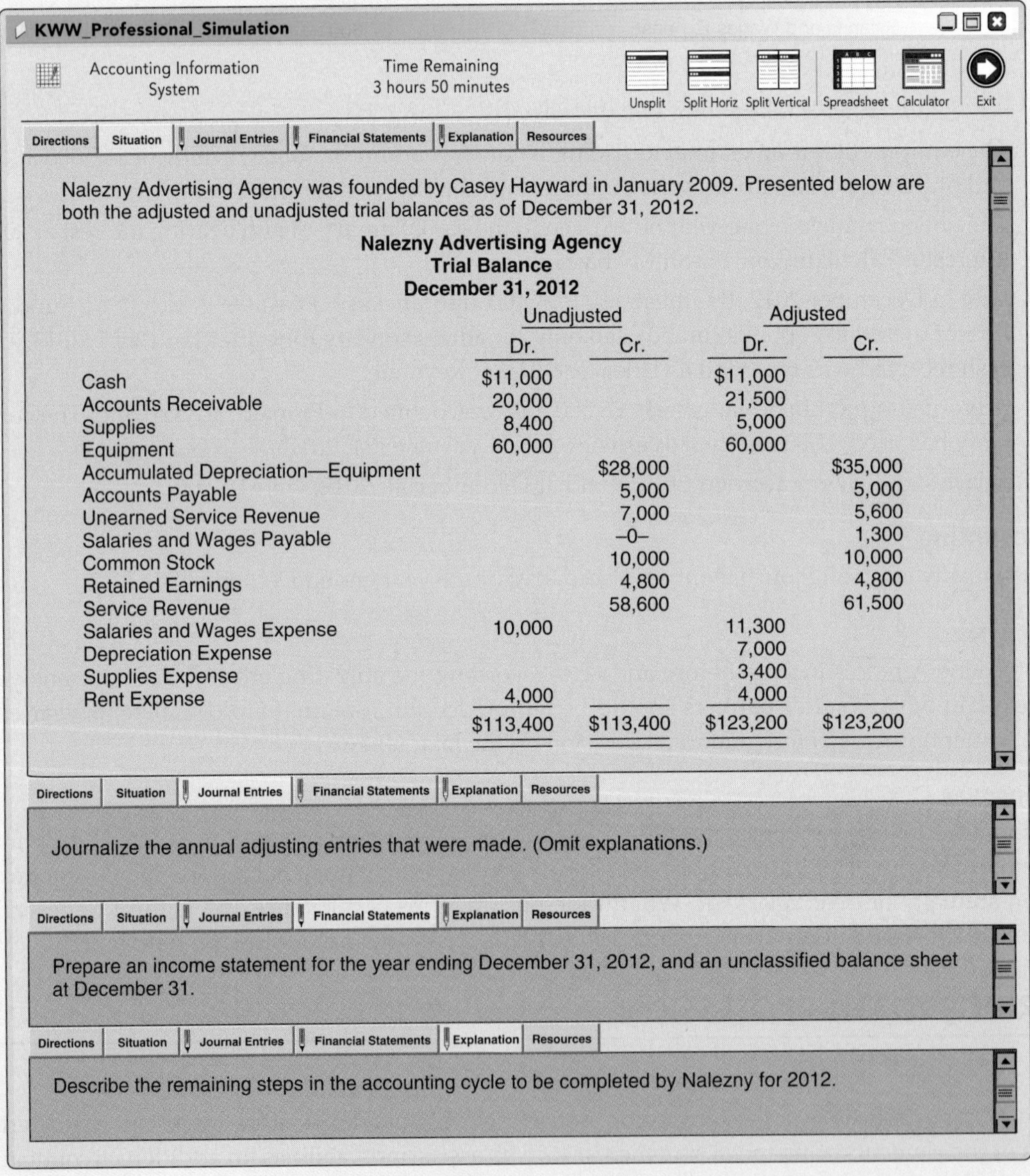

KWW_Professional_Simulation

Accounting Information System

Time Remaining 3 hours 50 minutes

Unsplit | Split Horiz | Split Vertical | Spreadsheet | Calculator | Exit

Directions | Situation | Journal Entries | Financial Statements | Explanation | Resources

Nalezny Advertising Agency was founded by Casey Hayward in January 2009. Presented below are both the adjusted and unadjusted trial balances as of December 31, 2012.

Nalezny Advertising Agency
Trial Balance
December 31, 2012

	Unadjusted		Adjusted	
	Dr.	Cr.	Dr.	Cr.
Cash	$11,000		$11,000	
Accounts Receivable	20,000		21,500	
Supplies	8,400		5,000	
Equipment	60,000		60,000	
Accumulated Depreciation—Equipment		$28,000		$35,000
Accounts Payable		5,000		5,000
Unearned Service Revenue		7,000		5,600
Salaries and Wages Payable		–0–		1,300
Common Stock		10,000		10,000
Retained Earnings		4,800		4,800
Service Revenue		58,600		61,500
Salaries and Wages Expense	10,000		11,300	
Depreciation Expense			7,000	
Supplies Expense			3,400	
Rent Expense	4,000		4,000	
	$113,400	$113,400	$123,200	$123,200

Directions | Situation | Journal Entries | Financial Statements | Explanation | Resources

Journalize the annual adjusting entries that were made. (Omit explanations.)

Directions | Situation | Journal Entries | Financial Statements | Explanation | Resources

Prepare an income statement for the year ending December 31, 2012, and an unclassified balance sheet at December 31.

Directions | Situation | Journal Entries | Financial Statements | Explanation | Resources

Describe the remaining steps in the accounting cycle to be completed by Nalezny for 2012.

As indicated in this chapter, companies must have an effective accounting system. In the wake of accounting scandals at U.S. companies like **Sunbeam**, **Rite-Aid**, **Xerox**, and **WorldCom**, U.S. lawmakers demanded higher assurance on the quality of accounting reports. Since the passage of the Sarbanes-Oxley Act of 2002 (SOX), companies that trade on U.S. exchanges are required to place renewed focus on their accounting systems to ensure accurate reporting.

RELEVANT FACTS

- International companies use the same set of procedures and records to keep track of transaction data. Thus, the material in Chapter 3 dealing with the account, general rules of debit and credit, and steps in the recording process—the journal, ledger, and chart of accounts—is the same under both GAAP and IFRS.
- Transaction analysis is the same under IFRS and GAAP but, as you will see in later chapters, different standards sometimes impact how transactions are recorded.
- Rules for accounting for specific events sometimes differ across countries. For example, European companies rely less on historical cost and more on fair value than U.S. companies. Despite the differences, the double-entry accounting system is the basis of accounting systems worldwide.
- Both the IASB and FASB go beyond the basic definitions provided in this textbook for the key elements of financial statements, that is, assets, liabilities, equity, revenues, and expenses.
- A trial balance under IFRS follows the same format as shown in the textbook. As shown in the textbook, dollar signs are typically used only in the trial balance and the financial statements. The same practice is followed under IFRS, using the currency of the country in which the reporting company is headquartered.
- Internal controls are a system of checks and balances designed to prevent and detect fraud and errors. While most companies have these systems in place, many have never completely documented them nor had an independent auditor attest to their effectiveness. Both of these actions are required under SOX. Enhanced internal control standards apply only to large public companies listed on U.S. exchanges.

ABOUT THE NUMBERS

Accounting System Internal Controls

There is continuing debate over whether foreign issuers should have to comply with this extra layer of regulation.[4] Companies find that internal control review is a costly process but badly needed. One study estimates the cost of compliance for U.S. companies at over $35 billion, with audit fees doubling in the first year of compliance. At the same time, examination of internal controls indicates lingering problems in the way companies operate. One study of first compliance with the internal control testing provisions documented material weaknesses for about 13 percent of companies reporting in 2004 and 2005.

[4]See Greg Ip, Kara Scannel, and Deborah Solomon, "Trade Winds in Call to Deregulate Business, A Global Twist," *Wall Street Journal* (January 25, 2007), p. A1.

Debate about requiring foreign companies to comply with SOX centers on whether the higher costs of a good information system are making the U.S. securities markets less competitive. Presented below are statistics for initial public offerings (IPOs) in the years since the passage of SOX.

Share of IPO proceeds: U.S., Europe, and China (U.S. $, billions)

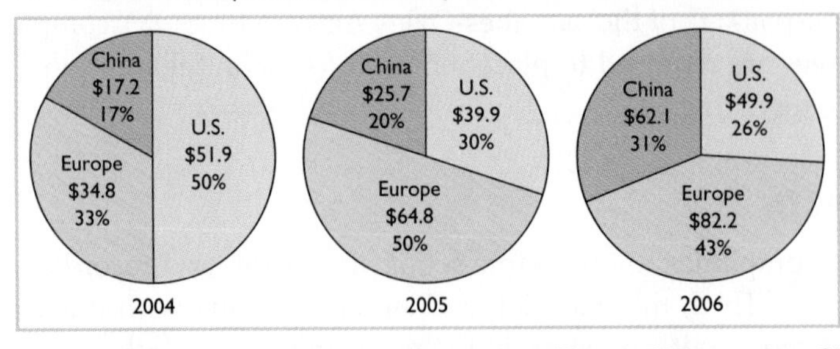

	IPOs	Avg. Size	IPOs	Avg. Size	IPOs	Avg. Size
U.S.	260	$199.7	221	$177.0	236	$211.6
Europe	433	79.5	598	108.4	653	145.7
China	208	82.5	98	260.9	140	444.0

Source: PricewaterhouseCoopers, U.S. IPO Watch: 2006 Analysis and Trends.

Note the U.S. share of IPOs has steadily declined, and some critics of the SOX provisions attribute the decline to the increased cost of complying with the internal control rules. Others, looking at these same trends, are not so sure about SOX being the cause of the relative decline of U.S. IPOs. These commentators argue that growth in non-U.S. markets is a natural consequence of general globalization of capital flows.

First-Time Adoption of IFRS

As discussed in Chapter 1, IFRS is growing in acceptance around the world. For example, recent statistics indicate 40 percent of the Global Fortune 500 companies use IFRS. And the chair of the IASB predicts that IFRS adoption will grow from its current level of 115 countries to nearly 150 countries in the near future.

When countries accept IFRS for use as accepted accounting policies, companies need guidance to ensure that their first IFRS financial statements contain high-quality information. Specifically, *IFRS 1* requires that information in a company's first IFRS statements (1) be transparent, (2) provide a suitable starting point, and (3) have a cost that does not exceed the benefits. As a result, many companies will be going through a substantial conversion process to switch from their reporting standards to IFRS.

The overriding principle in converting to IFRS is full retrospective application of IFRS. Retrospective application—recasting prior financial statements on the basis of IFRS—provides financial statement users with comparable information. As indicated, the objective of the conversion process is to present a set of IFRS statements as if the company always reported using IFRS. To achieve this objective, a company follows these steps:

1. Identify the timing of its first IFRS statements.
2. Prepare an opening balance sheet at the date of transition to IFRS.
3. Select accounting principles that comply with IFRS, and apply these principles retrospectively.
4. Make extensive disclosures to explain the transition to IFRS.

Once a company decides to convert to IFRS, it must decide on the transition date and the reporting date. The transition date is the beginning of the earliest period for which full comparative IFRS information is presented. The reporting date is the closing balance sheet date for the first IFRS financial statements.

To illustrate, assume that FirstChoice Company plans to provide its first IFRS statements for the year ended December 31, 2014. FirstChoice decides to present comparative information for one year only. Therefore, its date of transition to IFRS is January 1, 2013, and its reporting date is December 31, 2014. The timeline for first-time adoption is presented in the following graphic.

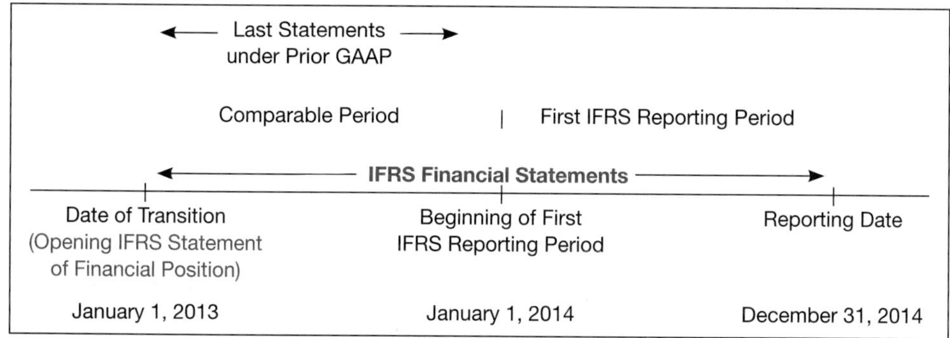

The graphic shows the following.

1. The opening IFRS statement of financial position for FirstChoice on January 1, 2013, serves as the starting point (date of transition) for the company's accounting under IFRS.
2. The first full IFRS statements are shown for FirstChoice for December 31, 2014. In other words, a minimum of two years of IFRS statements must be presented before a conversion to IFRS occurs. As a result, FirstChoice must prepare at least one year of comparative financial statements for 2013 using IFRS.
3. FirstChoice presents financial statements in accordance with GAAP annually to December 31, 2013.

Following this conversion process, FirstChoice provides users of the financial statements with comparable IFRS statements for 2013 and 2014. Upon first-time adoption of IFRS, a company must present at least one year of comparative information under IFRS.

ON THE HORIZON

The basic recording process shown in this textbook is followed by companies around the globe. It is unlikely to change in the future. The definitional structure of assets, liabilities, equity, revenues, and expenses may change over time as the IASB and FASB evaluate their overall conceptual framework for establishing accounting standards. In addition, high-quality international accounting requires both high-quality accounting standards and high-quality auditing. Similar to the convergence of GAAP and IFRS, there is a movement to improve international auditing standards. The International Auditing and Assurance Standards Board (IAASB) functions as an independent standard-setting body. It works to establish high-quality auditing and assurance and quality-control standards throughout the world. Whether the IAASB adopts internal control provisions similar to those in SOX remains to be seen. You can follow developments in the international audit arena at *http://www.ifac.org/iaasb/*.

IFRS SELF-TEST QUESTIONS

1. Which statement is *correct* regarding IFRS?
   (a) IFRS reverses the rules of debits and credits, that is, debits are on the right and credits are on the left.

(b) IFRS uses the same process for recording transactions as GAAP.
(c) The chart of accounts under IFRS is different because revenues follow assets.
(d) None of the above statements are correct.

2. Information in a company's first IFRS statements must:
   (a) have a cost that does not exceed the benefits.
   (b) be transparent.
   (c) provide a suitable starting point.
   (d) All the above.
3. The transition date is the date:
   (a) when a company no longer reports under its national standards.
   (b) when the company issues its most recent financial statement under IFRS.
   (c) three years prior to the reporting date.
   (d) None of the above.
4. When converting to IFRS, a company must:
   (a) recast previously issued financial statements in accordance with IFRS.
   (b) use GAAP in the reporting period but subsequently use IFRS.
   (c) prepare at least three years of comparative statements.
   (d) use GAAP in the transition year but IFRS in the reporting year.
5. The purpose of presenting comparative information in the transition to IFRS is:
   (a) to ensure that the information is reliable.
   (b) in accordance with the Sarbanes-Oxley Act.
   (c) to provide users of the financial statements with information on GAAP in one period and IFRS in the other period.
   (d) to provide users of the financial statements with information on IFRS for at least two periods.

IFRS CONCEPTS AND APPLICATION

IFRS3-1 How is the date of transition and the date of reporting determined in first-time adoption of IFRS?

IFRS3-2 What are the characteristics of high-quality information in a company's first IFRS financial statements?

IFRS3-3 What are the steps to be completed in preparing the opening IFRS statement of financial position?

IFRS3-4 Becker Ltd. is planning to adopt IFRS and prepare its first IFRS financial statements at December 31, 2013. What is the date of Becker's opening balance sheet, assuming one year of comparative information? What periods will be covered in Becker's first IFRS financial statements?

Professional Research

IFRS3-5 Recording transactions in the accounting system requires knowledge of the important characteristics of the elements of financial statements, such as assets and liabilities. In addition, accountants must understand the inherent uncertainty in accounting measures and distinctions between related accounting concepts that are important in evaluating the effects of transactions on the financial statements.

Instructions

Access the IASB Framework at the IASB website (*http://eifrs.iasb.org/*). When you have accessed the documents, you can use the search tool in your Internet browser to respond to the following items. (Provide paragraph citations.)

(a) Provide the definition of an asset and discuss how the economic benefits embodied in an asset might flow to a company.

(b) Provide the definition of a liability and discuss how a company might satisfy a liability.

(c) What is "accrual basis"? How do adjusting entries illustrate application of the accrual basis?

International Financial Reporting Problem: *Marks and Spencer plc*

IFRS3-6 The financial statements of **Marks and Spencer plc (M&S)** are available at the book's companion website or can be accessed at *http://corporate.marksandspencer.com/documents/publications/2010/Annual_Report_2010*.

Instructions

Refer to M&S's financial statements and the accompanying notes to answer the following questions.

(a) What were M&S's total assets at April 3, 2010? At March 28, 2009?

(b) How much cash (and cash equivalents) did M&S have on April 3, 2010?

(c) What were M&S's selling and marketing expenses in 2010? In 2009?

(d) What were M&S's revenues in 2010? In 2009?

(e) Using M&S's financial statements and related notes, identify items that may result in adjusting entries for prepayments and accruals.

(f) What were the amounts of M&S's depreciation and amortization expense in 2009 and 2010?

ANSWERS TO IFRS SELF-TEST QUESTIONS

1. b **2.** d **3.** d **4.** a **5.** d

Remember to check the book's companion website to find additional resources for this chapter.

CHAPTER 4

Income Statement and Related Information

LEARNING OBJECTIVES

After studying this chapter, you should be able to:

1. Understand the uses and limitations of an income statement.
2. Prepare a single-step income statement.
3. Prepare a multiple-step income statement.
4. Explain how to report irregular items.
5. Explain intraperiod tax allocation.
6. Identify where to report earnings per share information.
7. Prepare a retained earnings statement.
8. Explain how to report other comprehensive income.

Watch Out for Pro Forma

Pro forma reporting, in which companies provide investors a choice in reported income numbers, is popular among companies in the S&P 500. For example, in 2008–2009, in addition to income measured according to generally accepted accounting principles (GAAP), nearly 50 percent of S&P 500 companies also reported an income measure that is adjusted for certain items. Companies make these adjustments because they believe the items are not representative of operating results. How do these pro forma numbers compare to GAAP? As shown in the chart below, approximately 30 percent of the S&P 500 companies report pro forma income in excess of operating income in the third quarter of 2009. In general, pro forma profits were 18 percent higher than operating earnings.

Characteristic of pro forma reporting practices is **Amazon.com**. It has adjusted for items such as stock-based compensation, amortization of goodwill and intangibles, impairment charges, and equity in losses of investees. All of these adjustments make pro forma earnings higher than GAAP income. In its earnings announcement, Amazon defended its pro forma reporting, saying that it gives better insight into the fundamental operations of the business.

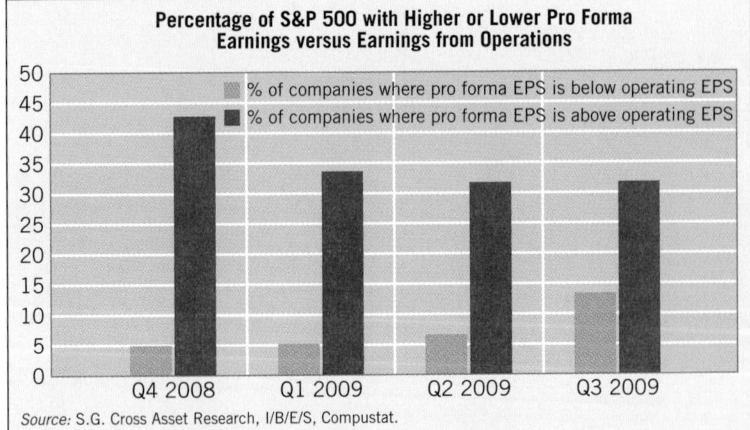

Source: S.G. Cross Asset Research, I/B/E/S, Compustat.

Some raise concerns that companies use pro forma reporting to deflect investor attention from bad news. Skeptics of these practices often note that these adjustments generally lead to higher adjusted net income and, as a result, often report earnings before bad stuff (EBS). In addition, they note that it is difficult to compare these adjusted or pro forma numbers because companies have different views as to what is fundamental to their business.

In many ways, the pro forma reporting practices by companies like Amazon represent implied criticisms of certain financial reporting standards, including how the information is presented on the income statement. In response, the SEC issued Regulation G, which requires companies to reconcile non-GAAP financial measures to GAAP. This regulation provides investors with a roadmap to analyze adjustments companies make to their GAAP numbers to arrive at pro forma results. Regulation G helps investors compare one company's pro forma measures with results reported by another company.

The FASB (and IASB) are working on a joint project on financial statement presentation to address users' concerns about these practices. Users believe too many alternatives exist for classifying and reporting income statement information. They note that information is often highly aggregated and inconsistently presented. As a result, it is difficult to assess the financial performance of the company and compare its results with other companies. This trend toward more transparent income reporting is encouraging, but managers still like pro forma reporting, as indicated by a recent survey in response to the FASB financial statement presentation project. Over 55 percent polled indicated they would continue to practice pro forma reporting, even with a revised income statement format.

Source: A. Stuart, "A New Vision for Accounting: Robert Herz and FASB Are Preparing a Radical New Format for Financial Statements," CFO *Magazine* (February 2008), pp. 49–53. See also SEC Regulation G, *"Conditions for Use of Non-GAAP Financial Measures,"* Release No. 33-8176 (March 28, 2003) and *Compliance & Disclosure Interpretations: Non-GAAP Financial Measures* (January 15, 2010), available at *www.sec.gov/divisions/corpfin/guidance/nongaapinterp.htm.*

IFRS IN THIS CHAPTER

See the **International Perspectives** on pages 169 and 171.

Read the **IFRS Insights** on pages 204–207 for a discussion of:

- Income reporting
- Expense classifications
- Allocations to non-controlling interests

PREVIEW OF CHAPTER 4

As we indicate in the opening story, investors need complete and comparable information on income and its components to assess company profitability correctly. In this chapter, we examine the many different types of revenues, expenses, gains, and losses that affect the income statement and related information, as follows.

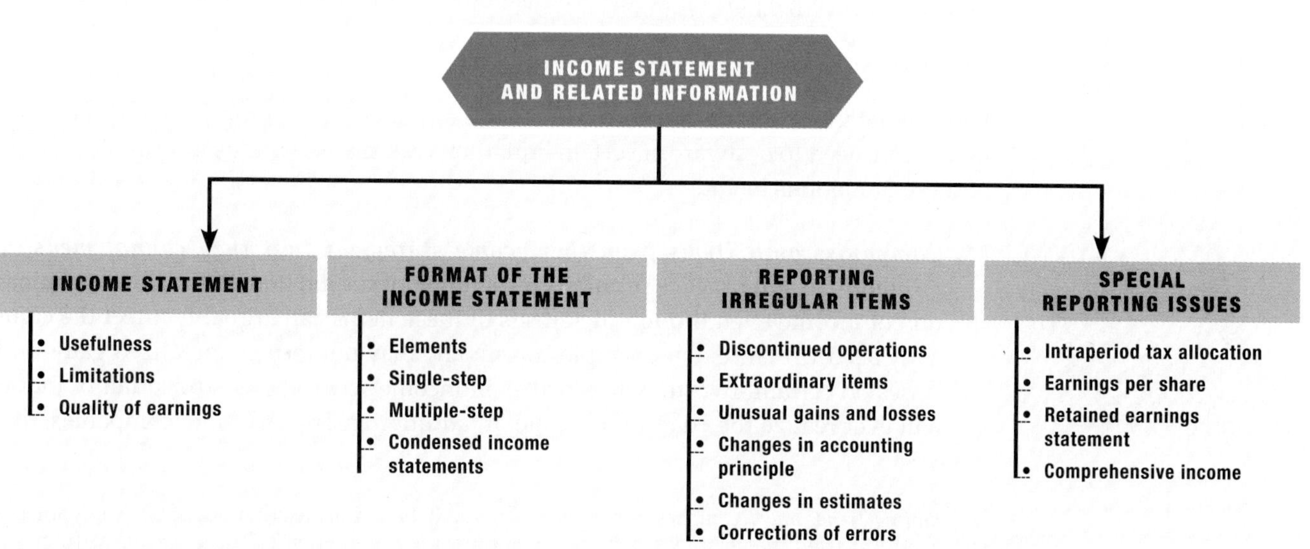

INCOME STATEMENT

LEARNING OBJECTIVE 1
Understand the uses and limitations of an income statement.

The **income statement** is the report that measures the success of company operations for a given period of time. (It is also often called the statement of income or statement of earnings.[1]) The business and investment community uses the income statement to determine profitability, investment value, and creditworthiness. It provides investors and creditors with information that helps them predict the **amounts, timing, and uncertainty of future cash flows.**

Usefulness of the Income Statement

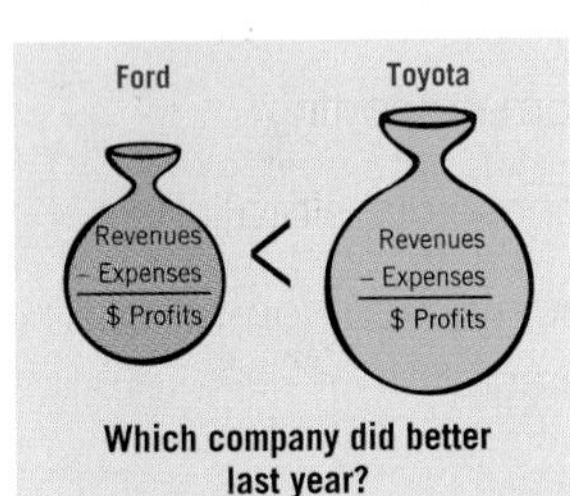

Which company did better last year?

The income statement helps users of financial statements predict future cash flows in a number of ways. For example, investors and creditors use the income statement information to:

1. ***Evaluate the past performance of the company.*** Examining revenues and expenses indicates how the company performed and allows comparison of its performance to its competitors. For example, analysts use the income data provided by **Ford** to compare its performance to that of **Toyota**.

Hmm....Where am I headed?

2. ***Provide a basis for predicting future performance.*** Information about past performance helps to determine important trends that, if continued, provide information about future performance. For example, **General Electric** at one time reported consistent increases in revenues. Obviously past success does not necessarily translate into future success. However, analysts can better predict future revenues, and hence earnings and cash flows, if a reasonable correlation exists between past and future performance.

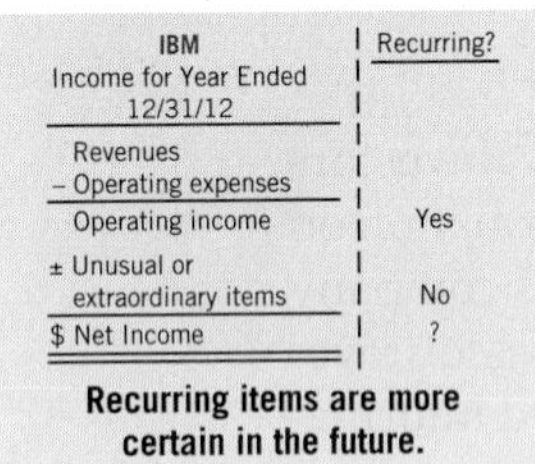

Recurring items are more certain in the future.

3. ***Help assess the risk or uncertainty of achieving future cash flows.*** Information on the various components of income—revenues, expenses, gains, and losses—highlights the relationships among them. It also helps to assess the risk of not achieving a particular level of cash flows in the future. For example, investors and creditors often segregate **IBM**'s operating performance from other nonrecurring sources of income because IBM primarily generates revenues and cash through its operations. Thus, results from continuing operations usually have greater significance for predicting future performance than do results from nonrecurring activities and events.

In summary, information in the income statement—revenues, expenses, gains, and losses—helps users evaluate past performance. It also provides insights into the likelihood of achieving a particular level of cash flows in the future.

Limitations of the Income Statement

Because net income is an estimate and reflects a number of assumptions, income statement users need to be aware of certain limitations associated with its information. Some of these limitations include:

You left something out!

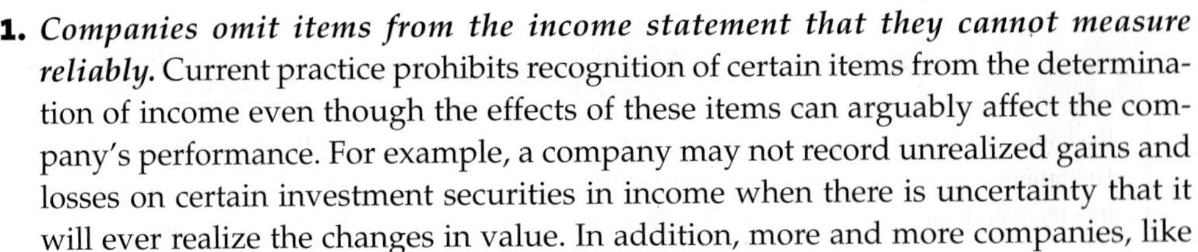

1. ***Companies omit items from the income statement that they cannot measure reliably.*** Current practice prohibits recognition of certain items from the determination of income even though the effects of these items can arguably affect the company's performance. For example, a company may not record unrealized gains and losses on certain investment securities in income when there is uncertainty that it will ever realize the changes in value. In addition, more and more companies, like

[1] *Accounting Trends and Techniques—2010* (New York: AICPA) indicates that out of 500 companies surveyed, 181 used the term *income* in the title of income statements, 242 used *operations* (many companies had net losses), and 70 used *earnings*.

Cisco Systems and **Microsoft**, experience increases in value due to brand recognition, customer service, and product quality. A common framework for identifying and reporting these types of values is still lacking.

2. ***Income numbers are affected by the accounting methods employed.*** One company may depreciate its plant assets on an accelerated basis; another chooses straight-line depreciation. Assuming all other factors are equal, the first company will report lower income. In effect, we are comparing apples to oranges.
3. ***Income measurement involves judgment.*** For example, one company in good faith may estimate the useful life of an asset to be 20 years while another company uses a 15-year estimate for the same type of asset. Similarly, some companies may make optimistic estimates of future warranty costs and bad debt write-offs, which result in lower expense and higher income.

Income Using:
Straight-Line Depreciation
Accelerated Depreciation

Hmm... Is the income the same?

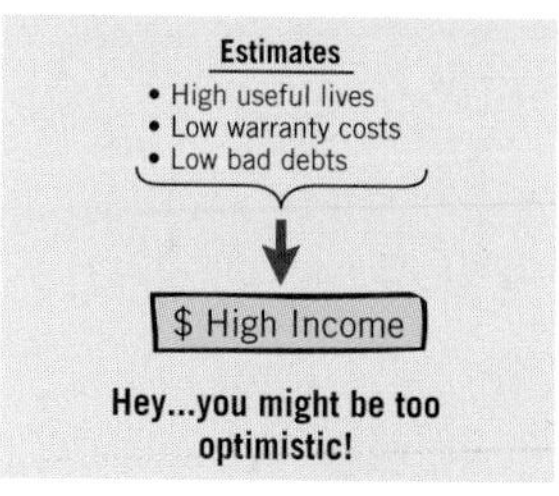

Hey...you might be too optimistic!

In summary, several limitations of the income statement reduce the usefulness of its information for predicting the amounts, timing, and uncertainty of future cash flows.

Quality of Earnings

So far, our discussion has highlighted the importance of information in the income statement for investment and credit decisions, including the evaluation of the company and its managers.[2] Companies try to meet or beat Wall Street expectations so that the market price of their stock and the value of management's stock options increase. As a result, companies have incentives to manage income to meet earnings targets or to make earnings look less risky.

The SEC has expressed concern that the motivations to meet earnings targets may override good business practices. This erodes the quality of earnings and the quality of financial reporting. As indicated by one SEC chairman, "Managing may be giving way to manipulation; integrity may be losing out to illusion."[3] As a result, the SEC has taken decisive action to prevent the practice of earnings management.

What is **earnings management**? It is often defined as the planned timing of revenues, expenses, gains, and losses to smooth out bumps in earnings. In most cases, companies use earnings management to increase income in the current year at the expense of income in future years. For example, they prematurely recognize sales (i.e., before earned) in order to boost earnings. As one commentator noted, ". . . it's like popping a cork in [opening] a bottle of wine before it is ready."

Companies also use earnings management to decrease current earnings in order to increase income in the future. The classic case is the use of "cookie jar" reserves. Companies establish these reserves by using unrealistic assumptions to estimate liabilities for such items as loan losses, restructuring charges, and warranty returns. The companies then reduce these reserves in the future to increase reported income in the future.

Such earnings management negatively affects the **quality of earnings** if it distorts the information in a way that is less useful for predicting future earnings and cash flows. Markets rely on trust. The bond between shareholders and the company must remain strong. Investors or others losing faith in the numbers reported in the financial statements will damage U.S. capital markets. As we mentioned in the opening story, we need heightened scrutiny of income measurement and reporting to ensure the quality of earnings and investors' confidence in the income statement.

[2]In support of the usefulness of income information, accounting researchers have documented an association between the market prices of companies and reported income. See W. H. Beaver, "Perspectives on Recent Capital Markets Research," *The Accounting Review* (April 2002), pp. 453–474.

[3]A. Levitt, "The Numbers Game." Remarks to NYU Center for Law and Business, September 28, 1998 (Securities and Exchange Commission, 1998).

FOUR: THE LONELIEST NUMBER

What do the numbers mean?

Managing earnings up or down adversely affects the quality of earnings. Why do companies engage in such practices? Some recent research concludes that many companies tweak quarterly earnings to meet investor expectations. How do they do it? Research findings indicate that companies tend to nudge their earnings numbers up by a 10th of a cent or two. That lets them round results up to the highest cent, as illustrated in the following chart.

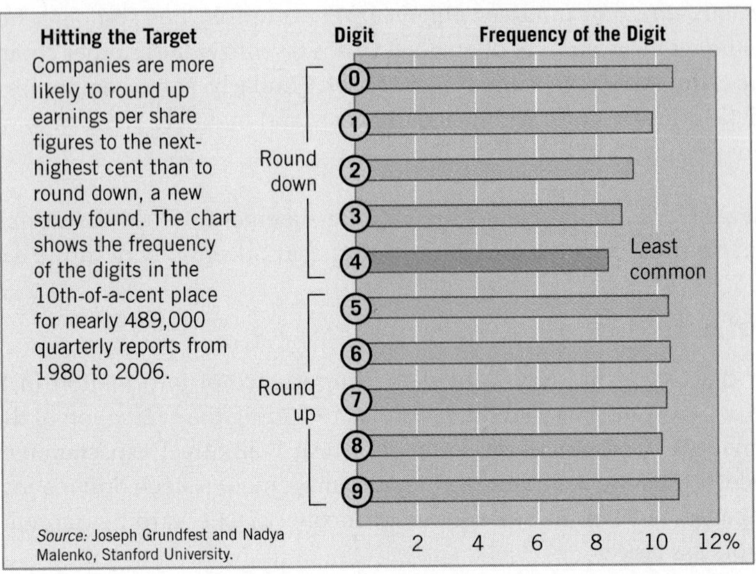

What the research shows is that the number "4" appeared less often in the 10th's place than any other digit and significantly less often than would be expected by chance. This effect is called "quadrophobia." For the typical company in the study, an increase of $31,000 in quarterly net income would boost earnings per share by a 10th of a cent. A more recent analysis of quarterly results for more than 2,600 companies found that rounding up remains more common than rounding down.

A good case study is computer maker **Dell Inc.** It didn't report earnings per share with a "4" in the 10th's place between its 1988 initial public offering and 2006. The likelihood of that happening by random chance is 1 in 2,500. In 2007, Dell restated its results for 2003 through early 2007, reducing its net income by $92 million over the period to correct what it said were errors in the way the company recognized revenue and handled reserve accounts for warranties and other items. Dell said in an SEC filing in 2007 that unnamed executives had adjusted its results after quarters had been completed "so that quarterly performance objectives could be met."

Source: S. Thurm, "For Some Firms, a Case of 'Quadrophobia'," *Wall Street Journal* (February 14, 2010).

FORMAT OF THE INCOME STATEMENT

Elements of the Income Statement

Net income results from revenue, expense, gain, and loss transactions. The income statement summarizes these transactions. This method of income measurement, the **transaction approach**, focuses on the income-related activities that have occurred during the period.[4] The statement can further classify income by customer, product line, or

[4]The most common alternative to the transaction approach is the **capital maintenance approach** to income measurement. Under this approach, a company determines income for the period based on the change in equity, after adjusting for capital contributions (e.g., investments by owners) or distributions (e.g., dividends). The main drawback associated with the capital maintenance approach is that the components of income are not evident in its measurement. The Internal Revenue Service uses the capital maintenance approach to identify unreported income and refers to this approach as the "net worth check."

function, or by operating and nonoperating, continuing and discontinued, and regular and irregular categories.[5] The following lists more formal definitions of income-related items, referred to as the major elements of the income statement.

ELEMENTS OF FINANCIAL STATEMENTS

REVENUES. Inflows or other enhancements of assets of an entity or settlements of its liabilities during a period from delivering or producing goods, rendering services, or other activities that constitute the entity's ongoing major or central operations.

EXPENSES. Outflows or other using-up of assets or incurrences of liabilities during a period from delivering or producing goods, rendering services, or carrying out other activities that constitute the entity's ongoing major or central operations.

GAINS. Increases in equity (net assets) from peripheral or incidental transactions of an entity except those that result from revenues or investments by owners.

LOSSES. Decreases in equity (net assets) from peripheral or incidental transactions of an entity except those that result from expenses or distributions to owners.[6]

Revenues take many forms, such as sales, fees, interest, dividends, and rents. Expenses also take many forms, such as cost of goods sold, depreciation, interest, rent, salaries and wages, and taxes. Gains and losses also are of many types, resulting from the sale of investments or plant assets, settlement of liabilities, write-offs of assets due to impairments or casualty.

The distinction between revenues and gains, and between expenses and losses, depend to a great extent on the typical activities of the company. For example, when **McDonald's** sells a hamburger, it records the selling price as revenue. However, when McDonald's sells land, it records any excess of the selling price over the book value as a gain. This difference in treatment results because the sale of the hamburger is part of McDonald's regular operations. The sale of land is not.

We cannot overemphasize the importance of reporting these elements. Most decision-makers find the *parts* of a financial statement to be more useful than the whole. As we indicated earlier, investors and creditors are interested in predicting the amounts, timing, and uncertainty of future income and cash flows. Having income statement elements shown in some detail and in comparison with prior years' data allows decision-makers to better assess future income and cash flows.

Single-Step Income Statements

2 LEARNING OBJECTIVE
Prepare a single-step income statement.

In reporting revenues, gains, expenses, and losses, companies often use a format known as the **single-step income statement**. The single-step statement consists of just two groupings: revenues and expenses. Expenses are deducted from revenues to arrive at net income or loss, hence the expression "single-step." Frequently companies report income tax separately as the last item before net income to indicate its relationship to income before income tax. Illustration 4-1 (page 164) shows the single-step income statement of Dan Deines Company.

[5]The term "irregular" encompasses transactions and other events that are derived from developments outside the normal operations of the business.

[6]"Elements of Financial Statements," *Statement of Financial Accounting Concepts No. 6* (Stamford, Conn.: FASB, 1985), paras. 78–89.

ILLUSTRATION 4-1
Single-Step Income Statement

DAN DEINES COMPANY INCOME STATEMENT FOR THE YEAR ENDED DECEMBER 31, 2012	
Revenues	
Net sales	$2,972,413
Dividend revenue	98,500
Rent revenue	72,910
Total revenues	3,143,823
Expenses	
Cost of goods sold	1,982,541
Selling expenses	453,028
Administrative expenses	350,771
Interest expense	126,060
Income tax expense	66,934
Total expenses	2,979,334
Net income	$ 164,489
Earnings per common share	$1.74

Companies that use the single-step income statement in financial reporting typically do so because of its simplicity. That is, **the primary advantage of the single-step format lies in its simple presentation and the absence of any implication that one type of revenue or expense item has priority over another**. This format thus eliminates potential classification problems.

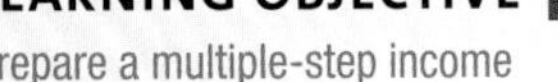

Prepare a multiple-step income statement.

Multiple-Step Income Statements

Some contend that including other important revenue and expense classifications makes the income statement more useful. These further classifications include:

1. ***A separation of operating and nonoperating activities of the company.*** For example, companies often present income from operations followed by sections entitled "Other revenues and gains" and "Other expenses and losses." These other categories include such transactions as interest revenue and expense, gains or losses from sales of long-term assets, and dividends received.
2. ***A classification of expenses by functions, such as merchandising (cost of goods sold), selling, and administration.*** This permits immediate comparison with costs of previous years and with other departments in the same year.

Companies use a **multiple-step income statement** to recognize these additional relationships.[7] This statement separates operating transactions from nonoperating transactions, and matches costs and expenses with related revenues. It highlights certain intermediate components of income that analysts use to compute ratios for assessing the performance of the company.

Intermediate Components of the Income Statement

When a company uses a multiple-step income statement, it may prepare some or all of the following sections or subsections.

[7] *Accounting Trends and Techniques—2010* (New York: AICPA). Of the 500 companies surveyed by the AICPA, 464 employed the multiple-step form, and 76 employed the single-step income statement format. This is a reversal from 1983, when 314 used the single-step form and 286 used the multiple-step form.

INCOME STATEMENT SECTIONS

1. OPERATING SECTION. A report of the revenues and expenses of the company's principal operations.
   (a) **Sales or Revenue Section.** A subsection presenting sales, discounts, allowances, returns, and other related information. Its purpose is to arrive at the net amount of sales revenue.
   (b) **Cost of Goods Sold Section.** A subsection that shows the cost of goods that were sold to produce the sales.
   (c) **Selling Expenses.** A subsection that lists expenses resulting from the company's efforts to make sales.
   (d) **Administrative or General Expenses.** A subsection reporting expenses of general administration.
2. NONOPERATING SECTION. A report of revenues and expenses resulting from secondary or auxiliary activities of the company. In addition, special gains and losses that are infrequent or unusual, but not both, are normally reported in this section. Generally these items break down into two main subsections:
   (a) **Other Revenues and Gains.** A list of the revenues earned or gains incurred, generally net of related expenses, from nonoperating transactions.
   (b) **Other Expenses and Losses.** A list of the expenses or losses incurred, generally net of any related incomes, from nonoperating transactions.
3. INCOME TAX. A short section reporting federal and state taxes levied on income from continuing operations.
4. DISCONTINUED OPERATIONS. Material gains or losses resulting from the disposition of a segment of the business.
5. EXTRAORDINARY ITEMS. Unusual and infrequent material gains and losses.
6. EARNINGS PER SHARE.

Although the content of the operating section is always the same, the organization of the material can differ. The breakdown above uses a **natural expense classification**. Manufacturing concerns and merchandising companies in the wholesale trade commonly use this. Another classification of operating expenses, recommended for retail stores, uses a **functional expense classification** of administrative, occupancy, publicity, buying, and selling expenses.

Usually, financial statements provided to external users have less detail than internal management reports. Internal reports include more expense categories—usually grouped along lines of responsibility. This detail allows top management to judge staff performance. Irregular transactions such as discontinued operations and extraordinary items are reported separately, following income from continuing operations.

Dan Deines Company's statement of income illustrates the multiple-step income statement. This statement, shown in Illustration 4-2 (on page 166), includes items 1, 2, 3, and 6 from the list above.[8] Note that in arriving at net income, the statement presents three subtotals of note:

1. Net sales revenue
2. Gross profit
3. Income from operations

[8]Companies must include *earnings per share* or *net loss per share* on the face of the income statement.

ILLUSTRATION 4-2
Multiple-Step Income Statement

DAN DEINES COMPANY INCOME STATEMENT FOR THE YEAR ENDED DECEMBER 31, 2012			
Sales Revenue			
Sales			$3,053,081
Less: Sales discounts		$ 24,241	
Sales returns and allowances		56,427	80,668
Net sales revenue			2,972,413
Cost of goods sold			1,982,541
Gross profit			989,872
Operating Expenses			
Selling expenses			
Sales salaries and commissions	$202,644		
Sales office salaries	59,200		
Travel and entertainment	48,940		
Advertising expense	38,315		
Freight and transportation-out	41,209		
Shipping supplies and expense	24,712		
Postage and stationery	16,788		
Telephone and Internet expense	12,215		
Depreciation of sales equipment	9,005	453,028	
Administrative expenses			
Officers' salaries	186,000		
Office salaries	61,200		
Legal and professional services	23,721		
Utilities expense	23,275		
Insurance expense	17,029		
Depreciation of building	18,059		
Depreciation of office equipment	16,000		
Stationery, supplies, and postage	2,875		
Miscellaneous office expenses	2,612	350,771	803,799
Income from operations			186,073
Other Revenues and Gains			
Dividend revenue		98,500	
Rent revenue		72,910	171,410
			357,483
Other Expenses and Losses			
Interest on bonds and notes			126,060
Income before income tax			231,423
Income tax			66,934
Net income for the year			$ 164,489
Earnings per common share			$1.74

The disclosure of net sales revenue is useful because Deines reports regular revenues as a separate item. It discloses irregular or incidental revenues elsewhere in the income statement. As a result, analysts can more easily understand and assess trends in revenue from continuing operations.

Similarly, the reporting of gross profit provides a useful number for evaluating performance and predicting future earnings. Statement readers may study the trend in gross profits to determine how successfully a company uses its resources. They also may use that information to understand how competitive pressure affected profit margins.

Finally, disclosing income from operations highlights the difference between regular and irregular or incidental activities. This disclosure helps users recognize that incidental or irregular activities are unlikely to continue at the same level. Furthermore, disclosure of operating earnings may assist in comparing different companies and assessing operating efficiencies.

Condensed Income Statements

In some cases, a single income statement cannot possibly present all the desired expense detail. To solve this problem, a company includes only the totals of expense groups in the statement of income. It then also prepares supplementary schedules to support the totals. This format may thus reduce the income statement itself to a few lines on a single sheet. For this reason, readers who wish to study all the reported data on operations must give their attention to the supporting schedules. For example, consider the income statement shown in Illustration 4-3 for Dan Deines Company. This statement is a condensed version of the more detailed multiple-step statement presented earlier. It is more representative of the type found in practice.

ILLUSTRATION 4-3
Condensed Income Statement

DAN DEINES COMPANY
INCOME STATEMENT
FOR THE YEAR ENDED DECEMBER 31, 2012

Net sales		$2,972,413
Cost of goods sold		1,982,541
Gross profit		989,872
Selling expenses (see Note D)	$453,028	
Administrative expenses	350,771	803,799
Income from operations		186,073
Other revenues and gains		171,410
		357,483
Other expenses and losses		126,060
Income before income tax		231,423
Income tax		66,934
Net income for the year		$ 164,489
Earnings per share		$1.74

Illustration 4-4 shows an example of a supporting schedule, cross-referenced as Note D and detailing the selling expenses.

ILLUSTRATION 4-4
Sample Supporting Schedule

Note D: Selling expenses	
Sales salaries and commissions	$202,644
Sales office salaries	59,200
Travel and entertainment	48,940
Advertising expense	38,315
Freight and transportation-out	41,209
Shipping supplies and expense	24,712
Postage and stationery	16,788
Telephone and Internet expense	12,215
Depreciation of sales equipment	9,005
Total Selling Expenses	$453,028

How much detail should a company include in the income statement? On the one hand, a company wants to present a simple, summarized statement so that readers can readily discover important factors. On the other hand, it wants to disclose the results of all activities and to provide more than just a skeleton report. As we showed above, the income statement always includes certain basic elements, but companies can present them in various formats.

REPORTING IRREGULAR ITEMS

LEARNING OBJECTIVE 4
Explain how to report irregular items.

As the use of a multiple-step or condensed income statement illustrates, GAAP allows flexibility in the presentation of the components of income. However, the FASB developed specific guidelines in two important areas: what to include in income and how to report certain unusual or irregular items.

What should be included in net income has been a controversy for many years. For example, should companies report irregular gains and losses, and corrections of revenues and expenses of prior years, as part of retained earnings? Or should companies first present them in the income statement and then carry them to retained earnings?

This issue is extremely important because the number and magnitude of irregular items are substantial. For example, Illustration 4-5 identifies the most common types and number of irregular items reported in a survey of 500 large companies. Notice that more than 40 percent of the surveyed firms reported restructuring charges, which often contain write-offs and other one-time items. About 16 percent of the surveyed firms reported either an extraordinary item or a discontinued operation charge. And many companies recorded an asset write-down or a gain on a sale of an asset.[9]

ILLUSTRATION 4-5
Number of Irregular Items Reported in a Recent Year by 500 Large Companies

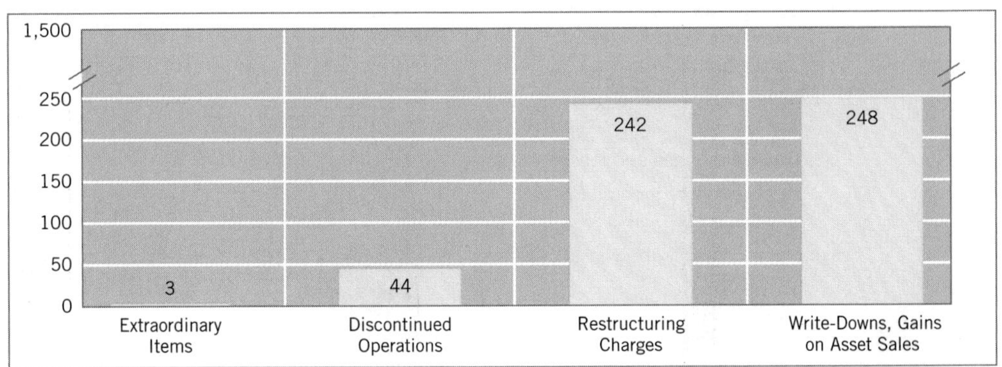

As our opening story discusses, we need consistent and comparable income reporting practices to avoid "promotional" information reported by companies. Developing a framework for reporting irregular items is important to ensure reliable income information.[10] Some users advocate a **current operating performance approach** to income reporting. These analysts argue that the most useful income measure reflects only regular and recurring revenue and expense elements. Irregular items do not reflect a company's future earning power.

In contrast, others warn that a focus on operating income potentially misses important information about a company's performance. Any gain or loss experienced by the company, whether directly or indirectly related to operations, contributes to its long-run profitability. As one analyst notes, "write-offs matter. . . . They speak to the volatility of (past) earnings."[11] As a result, analysts can use some nonoperating items to assess the

[9] *Accounting Trends and Techniques—2010* (New York: AICPA).

[10] The FASB and the IASB are working on a joint project on financial statement presentation, which is studying how to best report income as well as information presented in the balance sheet and the statement of cash flows. See *http://www.fasb.org/project/financial_statement_presentation.shtml.*

[11] D. McDermott, "Latest Profit Data Stir Old Debate Between Net and Operating Income," *Wall Street Journal* (May 3, 1999). A recent survey of 500 large public companies (*Accounting Trends and Techniques—2010* (New York: AICPA)) documented that 248 (almost one-half) of the 500 survey companies reported a write-down of assets (see also Illustration 4-5). This highlights the importance of good reporting for these irregular items.

riskiness of future earnings. Furthermore, determining which items are operating and which are irregular requires judgment. This might lead to differences in the treatment of irregular items and to possible manipulation of income measures.

So, what to do? The accounting profession has **adopted a** modified all-inclusive concept **and requires application of this approach in practice**. This approach indicates that companies record most items, including irregular ones, as part of net income.[12] In addition, companies are required to highlight irregular items in the financial statements so that users can better determine the long-run earning power of the company.

INTERNATIONAL PERSPECTIVE

In many countries, the "modified all-inclusive" income statement approach does not parallel that of the U.S. For example, companies in these countries take some gains and losses directly to owners' equity accounts instead of reporting them on the income statement.

Irregular items fall into six general categories, which we discuss in the following sections:

1. Discontinued operations.
2. Extraordinary items.
3. Unusual gains and losses.
4. Changes in accounting principle.
5. Changes in estimates.
6. Corrections of errors.

ARE ONE-TIME CHARGES BUGGING YOU?

What do the numbers mean?

Which number—net income or income from operations—should an analyst use in evaluating companies that have unusual items? Some argue that operating income better represents what will happen in the future. Others note that special items are often no longer special. For example, one study noted that in 2001, companies in the Standard & Poor's 500 index wrote off items totaling $165 billion—more than in the prior five years combined.

A study by Multex.com and the *Wall Street Journal* indicated that analysts should not ignore these charges. Based on data for companies taking unusual charges from 1996–2001, the study documented that companies reporting the largest unusual charges had more negative stock price performance following the charge, compared to companies with smaller charges. Thus, rather than signaling the end of bad times, these unusual charges indicated poorer future earnings.

In fact, some analysts use these charges to weed out stocks that may be headed for a fall. Following the "cockroach theory," any charge indicating a problem raises the probability of more problems. Thus, investors should be wary of the increasing use of restructuring and other one-time charges, which may bury expenses that signal future performance declines.

Source: Adapted from J. Weil and S. Liesman, "Stock Gurus Disregard Most Big Write-Offs, but They Often Hold Vital Clues to Outlook," *Wall Street Journal Online* (December 31, 2001).

Discontinued Operations

As Illustration 4-5 shows, one of **the most common types of irregular items is discontinued operations**. A discontinued operation occurs when two things happen: (1) a company eliminates the results of operations and cash flows of a *component* from its ongoing operations, and (2) there is no significant continuing involvement in that component after the disposal transaction.

To illustrate a **component**, S. C. Johnson manufactures and sells consumer products. It has several product groups, each with different product lines and brands. For S. C. Johnson,

[12]The FASB issued a statement of concepts that offers some guidance on this topic—"Recognition and Measurement in Financial Statements of Business Enterprises," *Statement of Financial Accounting Concepts No. 5* (Stamford, Conn.: FASB, 1984).

a product group is the lowest level at which it can clearly distinguish the operations and cash flows from the rest of the company's operations. Therefore, each product group is a component of the company. If a component were disposed of, S. C. Johnson would classify it as a discontinued operation.

Here is another example. Assume that Softso Inc. has experienced losses with certain brands in its beauty-care products group. As a result, Softso decides to sell that part of its business. It will discontinue any continuing involvement in the product group after the sale. In this case, Softso eliminates the operations and the cash flows of the product group from its ongoing operations, and reports it as a discontinued operation.

On the other hand, assume Softso decides to remain in the beauty-care business but will discontinue the brands that experienced losses. Because Softso cannot differentiate the cash flows from the brands from the cash flows of the product group as a whole, it cannot consider the brands a component. Softso does not classify any gain or loss on the sale of the brands as a discontinued operation.

Companies report as discontinued operations (in a separate income statement category) the gain or loss from **disposal of a component of a business**. In addition, companies report the **results of operations of a component that has been or will be disposed of** separately from continuing operations. Companies show the effects of discontinued operations net of tax as a separate category, after continuing operations but before extraordinary items. **[1]**

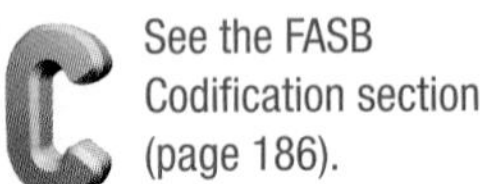
See the FASB Codification section (page 186).

To illustrate, Multiplex Products, Inc., a highly diversified company, decides to discontinue its electronics division. During the current year, the electronics division lost $300,000 (net of tax). Multiplex sold the division at the end of the year at a loss of $500,000 (net of tax). Multiplex shows the information on the current year's income statement as follows.

ILLUSTRATION 4-6
Income Statement Presentation of Discontinued Operations

Income from continuing operations		$20,000,000
Discontinued operations		
Loss from operation of discontinued electronics division (net of tax)	$300,000	
Loss from disposal of electronics division (net of tax)	500,000	800,000
Net income		$19,200,000

Companies use the phrase **"Income from continuing operations"** only when gains or losses on discontinued operations occur.

Extraordinary Items

Extraordinary items are nonrecurring **material** items that differ significantly from a company's typical business activities. The criteria for extraordinary items are as follows.

> Extraordinary items are events and transactions that are distinguished by their unusual nature **and** by the infrequency of their occurrence. Classifying an event or transaction as an extraordinary item requires meeting **both** of the following criteria:
>
> **(a)** ***Unusual nature.*** The underlying event or transaction should possess a high degree of abnormality and be of a type clearly unrelated to, or only incidentally related to, the ordinary and typical activities of the company, taking into account the environment in which it operates.
>
> **(b)** ***Infrequency of occurrence.*** The underlying event or transaction should be of a type that the company does not reasonably expect to recur in the foreseeable future, taking into account the environment in which the company operates. **[2]**

For further clarification, the following gains and losses are not extraordinary items.

(a) Write-down or write-off of receivables, inventories, equipment leased to others, deferred research and development costs, or other intangible assets.

(b) Gains or losses from exchange or translation of foreign currencies, including those relating to major devaluations and revaluations.

(c) Gains or losses on disposal of a component of an entity (reported as a discontinued operation).

(d) Other gains or losses from sale or abandonment of property, plant, or equipment used in the business.

(e) Effects of a strike, including those against competitors and major suppliers.

(f) Adjustment of accruals on long-term contracts. **[3]**

The above items are not considered extraordinary "because they are usual in nature and may be expected to recur as a consequence of customary and continuing business activities."

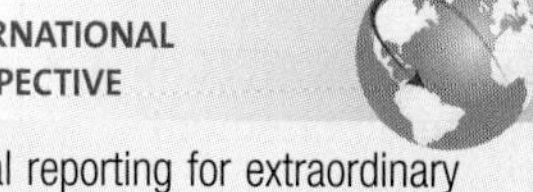

Special reporting for extraordinary items is prohibited under IFRS.

Only rarely does an event or transaction clearly meet the criteria for an extraordinary item.[13] For example, a company classifies gains or losses such as (a) and (d) above as extraordinary if they **resulted directly from a major casualty** (such as an earthquake), **an expropriation**, or a **prohibition under a newly enacted law or regulation**. Such circumstances clearly meet the criteria of unusual and infrequent. For example, **Weyerhaeuser Company** (forest and lumber) incurred an extraordinary item (an approximate $36 million loss) as a result of volcanic activity at Mount St. Helens. The eruption destroyed standing timber, logs, buildings, equipment, and transportation systems covering 68,000 acres.

In determining whether an item is extraordinary, **a company must consider the environment in which it operates**. The environment includes such factors as industry characteristics, geographic location, and the nature and extent of governmental regulations. Thus, the FASB accords extraordinary item treatment to the loss from hail damages to a tobacco grower's crops if hailstorm damage in its locality is rare. On the other hand, frost damage to a citrus grower's crop in Florida does not qualify as extraordinary because frost damage normally occurs there every three or four years.

Similarly, when a company sells the only significant security investment it has ever owned, the gain or loss meets the criteria of an extraordinary item. Another company, however, that has a portfolio of securities acquired for investment purposes would not report such a sales as an extraordinary item. Sale of such securities is part of its ordinary and typical activities.

In addition, considerable judgment must be exercised in determining whether to report an item as extraordinary. For example, the government condemned the forestlands of some paper companies to preserve state or national parks or forests. Is such an event extraordinary, or is it part of a paper company's normal operations? Such determination is not easy. Much depends on the frequency of previous condemnations, the expectation of future condemnations, materiality, and the like.[14]

[13]As indicated earlier, *Accounting Trends and Techniques—2010* (New York: AICPA) indicates that just 3 of the 500 companies surveyed reported an extraordinary item.

[14]Because assessing the materiality of individual items requires judgment, determining what is extraordinary is difficult. However, in making materiality judgments, companies should consider extraordinary items individually, and not in the aggregate. **[4]**

Companies must show extraordinary items net of taxes in a separate section in the income statement, usually just before net income. After listing the usual revenues, expenses, and income taxes, the remainder of the statement shows the following.

ILLUSTRATION 4-7
Income Statement Placement of Extraordinary Items

Income before extraordinary items
Extraordinary items (less applicable income tax of $______)
Net income

For example, Illustration 4-8 shows how **Keystone Consolidated Industries** reported an extraordinary loss.

ILLUSTRATION 4-8
Income Statement Presentation of Extraordinary Items

Keystone Consolidated Industries, Inc.

Income before extraordinary item	$11,638,000
Extraordinary item—flood loss (Note E)	1,216,000
Net income	$10,422,000

Note E: Extraordinary Item. The Keystone Steel and Wire Division's Steel Works experienced a flash flood on June 22. The extraordinary item represents the estimated cost, net of related income taxes of $1,279,000, to restore the steel works to full operation.

EXTRAORDINARY TIMES

What do the numbers mean?

No event better illustrates the difficulties of determining whether a transaction meets the definition of extraordinary than the financial impacts of the terrorist attack on the World Trade Center on September 11, 2001.

To many, this event, which resulted in the tragic loss of lives, jobs, and in some cases entire businesses, clearly meets the criteria for unusual and infrequent. For example, in the wake of the terrorist attack that destroyed the World Trade Center and turned much of lower Manhattan including Wall Street into a war zone, airlines, insurance companies, and other businesses recorded major losses due to property damage, business disruption, and suspension of airline travel and of securities trading.

But, to the surprise of many, the FASB did not permit extraordinary item reporting for losses arising from the terrorist attacks. The reason? After much deliberation, the Emerging Issues Task Force (EITF) of the FASB decided that measurement of the possible loss was too difficult. Take the airline industry as an example: What portion of the airlines' losses after September 11 was related to the terrorist attack, and what portion was due to the ongoing recession? Also, the FASB did not want companies to use the attack as a reason for reporting as extraordinary some losses that had little direct relationship to the attack. Indeed, energy company **AES** and shoe retailer **Footstar**, who both were experiencing profit pressure before 9/11, put some of the blame for their poor performance on the attack.

Source: Julie Creswell, "Bad News Bearers Shift the Blame," *Fortune* (October 15, 2001), p. 44.

Unusual Gains and Losses

Because of the restrictive criteria for extraordinary items, financial statement users must carefully examine the financial statements for items that are **unusual or infrequent but not both**. Recall that companies cannot consider items such as write-downs of inventories and transaction gains and losses from fluctuation of foreign exchange as extraordinary items. Thus, companies sometimes show these items with their normal recurring revenues and expenses. If not material in amount, companies combine these with other items in the income statement. If material, companies must disclose them separately, and report them **above** "Income (loss) before extraordinary items."

For example, **PepsiCo, Inc.** presented an unusual charge in its income statement, as Illustration 4-9 shows.

ILLUSTRATION 4-9
Income Statement Presentation of Unusual Charges

PepsiCo, Inc.
(in millions)

Net sales	$20,917
Costs and expenses, net	
Cost of sales	8,525
Selling, general, and administrative expenses	9,241
Amortization of intangible assets	199
Unusual items (Note 2)	290
Operating income	$ 2,662

Note 2 (Restructuring Charge)

Dispose and write down assets	$183
Improve productivity	94
Strengthen the international bottler structure	13
Net loss	$290

The net charge to strengthen the international bottler structure includes proceeds of $87 million associated with a settlement related to a previous Venezuelan bottler agreement, which were partially offset by related costs.

Restructuring charges, like the one PepsiCo reported, have been common in recent years (see also Illustration 4-5 on page 168). A **restructuring charge** relates to a major reorganization of company affairs, such as costs associated with employee layoffs, plant closing costs, write-offs of assets, and so on. A company should not report a restructuring charge as an extraordinary item because these write-offs are part of a company's ordinary and typical activities.

Companies tend to **report unusual items in a separate section just above "Income from operations before income taxes" and "Extraordinary items,"** especially when there are multiple unusual items. For example, when **General Electric Company** experienced multiple unusual items in one year, it reported them in a separate "Unusual items" section of the income statement below "Income before unusual items and income taxes." *When preparing a multiple-step income statement for homework purposes, you should report unusual gains and losses in the "Other revenues and gains" or "Other expenses and losses" section unless you are instructed to prepare a separate unusual items section.*[15]

In dealing with events that are either unusual or nonrecurring but not both, the profession attempted to prevent a practice that many believed was misleading. Companies often reported such transactions on a net-of-tax basis and prominently displayed the earnings per share effect of these items. Although not captioned "Extraordinary

[15]Many companies report "one-time items." However, some companies take restructuring charges practically every year. **Citicorp** (now **Citigroup**) took restructuring charges six years in a row; **Eastman Kodak Co.** did so five out of six years. Research indicates that the market discounts the earnings of companies that report a series of "nonrecurring" items. Such evidence supports the contention that these elements reduce the quality of earnings. J. Elliott and D. Hanna, "Repeated Accounting Write-offs and the Information Content of Earnings," *Journal of Accounting Research* (Supplement, 1996).

items," companies presented them in the same manner. Some had referred to these as "first cousins" to extraordinary items.

As a consequence, the Board specifically **prohibited a net-of-tax treatment for such items**, to ensure that users of financial statements can easily differentiate extraordinary items—reported net of tax—from material items that are unusual or infrequent, but not both.

Changes in Accounting Principle

Underlying Concepts

Companies can change principles, but they must demonstrate that the newly adopted principle is preferable to the old one. Such changes result in lost consistency from period to period.

Changes in accounting occur frequently in practice because important events or conditions may be in dispute or uncertain at the statement date. One type of accounting change results when a company adopts a different accounting principle. Changes in accounting principle include a change in the method of inventory pricing from FIFO to average cost, or a change in accounting for construction contracts from the percentage-of-completion to the completed-contract method. [5][16]

A company recognizes a change in accounting principle by making a **retrospective adjustment** to the financial statements. Such an adjustment recasts the prior years' statements on a basis consistent with the newly adopted principle. The company records the cumulative effect of the change for prior periods as an adjustment to beginning retained earnings of the earliest year presented.

To illustrate, Gaubert Inc. decided in March 2012 to change from FIFO to weighted-average inventory pricing. Gaubert's income before taxes, using the new weighted-average method in 2012, is $30,000. Illustration 4-10 presents the pretax income data for 2010 and 2011 for this example.

ILLUSTRATION 4-10
Calculation of a Change in Accounting Principle

Year	FIFO	Weighted-Average Method	Excess of FIFO over Weighted-Average Method
2010	$40,000	$35,000	$5,000
2011	30,000	27,000	3,000
Total			$8,000

Illustration 4-11 shows the information Gaubert presented in its comparative income statements, based on a 30 percent tax rate.

ILLUSTRATION 4-11
Income Statement Presentation of a Change in Accounting Principle

	2012	2011	2010
Income before taxes	$30,000	$27,000	$35,000
Income tax	9,000	8,100	10,500
Net income	$21,000	$18,900	$24,500

Thus, under the retrospective approach, the company recasts the prior years' income numbers under the newly adopted method. This approach thus preserves comparability across years.

Changes in Estimates

Estimates are inherent in the accounting process. For example, companies estimate useful lives and salvage values of depreciable assets, uncollectible receivables, inventory obsolescence, and the number of periods expected to benefit from a particular expenditure.

[16]In Chapter 22, we examine in greater detail the problems related to accounting changes.

Not infrequently, due to time, circumstances, or new information, even estimates originally made in good faith must be changed. A company accounts for such **changes in estimates** in the period of change if they affect only that period, or in the period of change and future periods if the change affects both.

To illustrate a change in estimate that affects only the period of change, assume that DuPage Materials Corp. consistently estimated its bad debt expense at 1 percent of credit sales. In 2012, however, DuPage determines that it must revise upward the estimate of bad debts for the current year's credit sales to 2 percent, or double the prior years' percentage. The 2 percent rate is necessary to reduce accounts receivable to net realizable value. Using 2 percent results in a bad debt charge of $240,000, or double the amount using the 1 percent estimate for prior years, DuPage records the provision at December 31, 2012, as follows.

Bad Debt Expense	240,000	
Allowance for Doubtful Accounts		240,000

DuPage includes the entire change in estimate in 2012 income because the change does not affect future periods. **Companies do not handle changes in estimate retrospectively.** That is, such changes are not carried back to adjust prior years. (We examine changes in estimate that affect both the current and future periods in greater detail in Chapter 22.) **Changes in estimate are not considered errors or extraordinary items.**

Corrections of Errors

Errors occur as a result of mathematical mistakes, mistakes in the application of accounting principles, or oversight or misuse of facts that existed at the time financial statements were prepared. In recent years, many companies have corrected for errors in their financial statements. For example, one consulting group noted that over 1,300 companies (10 percent of U.S. public companies) reported error-driven restatements in a recent year. The errors involved such items as improper reporting of revenue, accounting for stock options, allowances for receivables, inventories, and loss contingencies.[17]

Companies must correct errors by making proper entries in the accounts and reporting the corrections in the financial statements. Corrections of errors are treated as **prior period adjustments**, similar to changes in accounting principles. Companies record a correction of an error in the year in which it is discovered. They report the error in the financial statements as an adjustment to the beginning balance of retained earnings. If a company prepares comparative financial statements, it should restate the prior statements for the effects of the error.

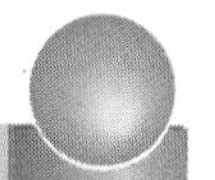

Underlying Concepts

The AICPA Special Committee on Financial Reporting indicates a company's core activities—usual and recurring events—provide the best historical data from which users determine trends and relationships and make their predictions about the future. Therefore, companies should separately display the effects of core and non-core activities.

To illustrate, in 2013, Hillsboro Co. determined that it incorrectly overstated its accounts receivable and sales revenue by $100,000 in 2012. In 2013, Hillsboro makes the following entry to correct for this error (ignore income taxes).

Retained Earnings	100,000	
Accounts Receivable		100,000

Retained Earnings is debited because sales revenue, and therefore net income, was overstated in a prior period. Accounts Receivable is credited to reduce this overstated balance to the correct amount.

[17]While the growth of restatements appears to have slowed, these are still important signals to the market. One study documented a significant increase in the cost of borrowing for companies that report a restatement. See. A. Osterland, "The SarBox: The Bill for Restatements Can Be Costly," *Financial Week* (January 14, 2008).

Summary of Irregular Items

The public accounting profession now tends to accept a modified all-inclusive income concept instead of the current operating performance concept. Except for changes in accounting principle and error corrections, which are charged or credited directly to retained earnings, companies close all other irregular gains or losses or nonrecurring items to Income Summary and include them in the income statement.

Of these irregular items, companies classify **discontinued operations of a component** of a business as a separate item in the income statement, after "Income from continuing operations." Companies show the **unusual, material, nonrecurring items** that significantly differ from the typical or customary business activities in a separate "Extraordinary items" section below "Discontinued operations." They separately disclose other items of a material amount that are of an **unusual or nonrecurring** nature and are **not considered extraordinary**.

Because of the numerous intermediate income figures created by the reporting of these irregular items, readers must carefully evaluate earnings information reported by the financial press. Illustration 4-12 summarizes the basic concepts that we previously discussed. Although simplified, the chart provides a useful framework for determining the treatment of special items affecting the income statement.

ILLUSTRATION 4-12
Summary of Irregular Items in the Income Statement

Type of Situation[a]	Criteria	Examples	Placement on Income Statement
Discontinued operations	Disposal of a component of a business for which the company can clearly distinguish operations and cash flows from the rest of the company's operations.	Sale by diversified company of major division that represents only activities in electronics industry. Food distributor that sells wholesale to supermarket chains and through fast-food restaurants decides to discontinue the division that sells to one of two classes of customers.	Show in separate section after continuing operations but before extraordinary items. (Shown net of tax.)
Extraordinary items	Material, and both unusual and infrequent (nonrecurring).	Gains or losses resulting from casualties, an expropriation, or a prohibition under a new law.	Show in separate section entitled "Extraordinary items." (Shown net of tax.)
Unusual gains or losses, not considered extraordinary	Material; character typical of the customary business activities; unusual or infrequent but not both.	Write-downs of receivables, inventories; adjustments of accrued contract prices; gains or losses from fluctuations of foreign exchange; gains or losses from sales of assets used in business.	Show in separate section above income before extraordinary items. Often reported in "Other revenues and gains" or "Other expenses and losses" section. (Not shown net of tax.)
Changes in principle	Change from one generally accepted accounting principle to another.	Change in the basis of inventory pricing from FIFO to average cost.	Recast prior years' income statements on the same basis as the newly adopted principle. (Shown net of tax.)
Changes in estimates	Normal, recurring corrections and adjustments.	Changes in the realizability of receivables and inventories; changes in estimated lives of equipment, intangible assets; changes in estimated liability for warranty costs, income taxes, and salary payments.	Show change only in the affected accounts. (Not shown net of tax.)
Corrections of errors	Mistake, misuse of facts.	Error in reporting revenue.	Restate prior years' income statements to correct for error. (Shown net of tax.)

[a]This summary provides only the general rules to be followed in accounting for the various situations described above. Exceptions do exist in some of these situations.

SPECIAL REPORTING ISSUES

Intraperiod Tax Allocation

5 LEARNING OBJECTIVE
Explain intraperiod tax allocation.

Companies report irregular items (except for unusual gains and losses) on the income statement or statement of retained earnings net of tax. This procedure is called **intraperiod tax allocation**, that is, allocation within a period. It relates the income tax expense (sometimes referred to as the income tax provision) of the fiscal period to the **specific items** that give rise to the amount of the tax provision.

Intraperiod tax allocation helps financial statement users better understand the impact of income taxes on the various components of net income. For example, readers of financial statements will understand how much income tax expense relates to "income from continuing operations" and how much relates to certain irregular transactions and events. This approach should help users to better predict the amount, timing, and uncertainty of future cash flows. In addition, intraperiod tax allocation discourages statement readers from using pretax measures of performance when evaluating financial results, and thereby recognizes that income tax expense is a real cost.

Companies use intraperiod tax allocation on the income statement for the following items: (1) income from continuing operations, (2) discontinued operations, and (3) extraordinary items. The general concept is "**let the tax follow the income.**"

To compute the income tax expense attributable to "Income from continuing operations," a company would find the income tax expense related to both the revenue and expense transactions used in determining this income. (In this computation, the company does not consider the tax consequences of items excluded from the determination of "Income from continuing operations.") Companies then associate a separate tax effect with each irregular item (e.g., discontinued operations and extraordinary items). Here we look in more detail at calculation of intraperiod tax allocation for extraordinary gains and losses.

Extraordinary Gains

In applying the concept of intraperiod tax allocation, assume that Schindler Co. has income before income tax and extraordinary item of $250,000. It has an extraordinary gain of $100,000 from a condemnation settlement received on one its properties. Assuming a 30 percent income tax rate, Schindler presents the following information on the income statement.

Income before income tax and extraordinary item		$250,000
Income tax		75,000
Income before extraordinary item		175,000
Extraordinary gain—condemnation settlement	$100,000	
Less: Applicable income tax	30,000	70,000
Net income		$245,000

ILLUSTRATION 4-13
Intraperiod Tax Allocation, Extraordinary Gain

Schindler determines the income tax of $75,000 ($250,000 × 30%) attributable to "Income before income tax and extraordinary item" from revenue and expense transactions related to this income. Schindler omits the tax consequences of items excluded from the determination of "Income before income tax and extraordinary item." The company shows a separate tax effect of $30,000 related to the "Extraordinary gain—condemnation settlement."

Extraordinary Losses

To illustrate the reporting of an extraordinary loss, assume that Schindler Co. has income before income tax and extraordinary item of $250,000. It suffers an extraordinary loss from a major casualty of $100,000. Assuming a 30 percent tax rate, Schindler presents the income tax on the income statement as shown in Illustration 4-14. In this case, the loss provides a positive tax benefit of $30,000. Schindler, therefore, subtracts it from the $100,000 loss.

ILLUSTRATION 4-14
Intraperiod Tax Allocation, Extraordinary Loss

Income before income tax and extraordinary item		$250,000
Income tax		75,000
Income before extraordinary item		175,000
Extraordinary item—casualty loss	$100,000	
Less: Applicable income tax reduction	30,000	70,000
Net income		$105,000

Companies may also report the tax effect of an extraordinary item by means of a note disclosure, as illustrated below.

ILLUSTRATION 4-15
Note Disclosure of Intraperiod Tax Allocation

Income before income tax and extraordinary item	$250,000
Income tax	75,000
Income before extraordinary item	175,000
Extraordinary item—casualty loss, less applicable income tax reduction (Note 1)	70,000
Net income	$105,000

Note 1: During the year the Company suffered a major casualty loss of $70,000, net of applicable income tax reduction of $30,000.

Earnings per Share

LEARNING OBJECTIVE 6
Identify where to report earnings per share information.

A company customarily sums up the results of its operations in one important figure: net income. However, the financial world has widely accepted an even more distilled and compact figure as the most significant business indicator—**earnings per share** (EPS).

The computation of earnings per share is usually straightforward. **Earnings per share is net income minus preferred dividends (income available to common stockholders), divided by the weighted average of common shares outstanding.**[18]

To illustrate, assume that Lancer, Inc. reports net income of $350,000. It declares and pays preferred dividends of $50,000 for the year. The weighted-average number of common shares outstanding during the year is 100,000 shares. Lancer computes earnings per share of $3, as shown in Illustration 4-16.

ILLUSTRATION 4-16
Equation Illustrating Computation of Earnings per Share

$$\frac{\text{Net Income} - \text{Preferred Dividends}}{\text{Weighted Average of Common Shares Outstanding}} = \text{Earnings per Share}$$

$$\frac{\$350{,}000 - \$50{,}000}{100{,}000} = \$3$$

[18]In calculating earnings per share, companies deduct preferred dividends from net income if the dividends are declared or if they are cumulative though not declared.

Note that EPS measures the number of dollars earned by each share of common stock. It does not represent the dollar amount paid to stockholders in the form of dividends.

Prospectuses, proxy material, and annual reports to stockholders commonly use the "net income per share" or "earnings per share" ratio. The financial press, statistical services like Standard & Poor's, and Wall Street securities analysts also highlight EPS. Because of its importance, **companies must disclose earnings per share on the face of the income statement**. A company that reports a discontinued operation or an extraordinary item must report per share amounts for these line items either on the face of the income statement or in the notes to the financial statements. **[6]**

To illustrate, consider the income statement for Poquito Industries Inc. shown in Illustration 4-17. Notice the order in which Poquito shows the data, with per share information at the bottom. Assume that the company had 100,000 shares outstanding for the entire year. The Poquito income statement, as Illustration 4-17 shows, is highly condensed. Poquito would need to describe items such as "Unusual charge," "Discontinued operations," and "Extraordinary item" fully and appropriately in the statement or related notes.

ILLUSTRATION 4-17
Income Statement

POQUITO INDUSTRIES INC.
INCOME STATEMENT
FOR THE YEAR ENDED DECEMBER 31, 2012

Sales revenue		$1,420,000
Cost of goods sold		600,000
Gross profit		820,000
Selling and administrative expenses		320,000
Income from operations		500,000
Other revenues and gains		
Interest revenue		10,000
Other expenses and losses		
Loss on disposal of part of Textile Division	$ 5,000	
Unusual charge—loss on sale of investments	45,000	50,000
Income from continuing operations before income tax		460,000
Income tax		184,000
Income from continuing operations		276,000
Discontinued operations		
Income from operations of Pizza Division, less applicable income tax of $24,800	54,000	
Loss on disposal of Pizza Division, less applicable income tax of $41,000	90,000	36,000
Income before extraordinary item		240,000
Extraordinary item—loss from earthquake, less applicable income tax of $23,000		45,000
Net income		$ 195,000
Per share of common stock		
Income from continuing operations		$2.76
Income from operations of discontinued division, net of tax		0.54
Loss on disposal of discontinued operation, net of tax		0.90
Income before extraordinary item		2.40
Extraordinary loss, net of tax		0.45
Net income		$1.95

Many corporations have simple capital structures that include only common stock. For these companies, a presentation such as "Earnings per common share" is appropriate on the income statement. In many instances, however, companies' earnings per share are subject to dilution (reduction) in the future because existing contingencies permit the issuance of additional common shares. **[7]**[19]

[19]We discuss the computational problems involved in accounting for these dilutive securities in earnings per share computations in Chapter 16.

In summary, the simplicity and availability of EPS figures lead to their widespread use. Because of the importance that the public, even the well-informed public, attaches to earnings per share, companies must make the EPS figure as meaningful as possible.

Retained Earnings Statement

LEARNING OBJECTIVE 7
Prepare a retained earnings statement.

Net income increases retained earnings. A net loss decreases retained earnings. Both cash and stock dividends decrease retained earnings. Changes in accounting principles (generally) and prior period adjustments may increase or decrease retained earnings. Companies charge or credit these adjustments (net of tax) to the opening balance of retained earnings. This excludes the adjustments from the determination of net income for the current period.

Companies may show retained earnings information in different ways. For example, some companies prepare a separate retained earnings statement, as Illustration 4-18 shows.

ILLUSTRATION 4-18
Retained Earnings Statement

JUSTIN ROSE, INC.
RETAINED EARNINGS STATEMENT
FOR THE YEAR ENDED DECEMBER 31, 2012

Retained earnings, January 1, as reported		$1,050,000
Correction for understatement of net income in prior period—inventory error (net of tax)		50,000
Retained earnings, January 1, as adjusted		1,100,000
Add: Net income		360,000
		1,460,000
Less: Cash dividends	$100,000	
Stock dividends	200,000	300,000
Retained earnings, December 31		$1,160,000

The reconciliation of the beginning to the ending balance in retained earnings provides information about why net assets increased or decreased during the year. The association of dividend distributions with net income for the period indicates what management is doing with earnings: It may be "plowing back" into the business part or all of the earnings, distributing all current income, or distributing current income plus the accumulated earnings of prior years.[20]

Restrictions of Retained Earnings

Companies often restrict retained earnings to comply with contractual requirements, board of directors' policy, or current necessity. Generally, companies disclose in the notes to the financial statements the amounts of restricted retained earnings. In some cases, companies transfer the amount of retained earnings restricted to an account titled **Appropriated Retained Earnings**. The retained earnings section may therefore report two separate amounts—(1) retained earnings free (unrestricted) and (2) retained earnings appropriated (restricted). The total of these two amounts equals the total retained earnings.

[20]*Accounting Trends and Techniques—2010* (New York: AICPA) indicates that most companies (493 of 500 surveyed) present changes in retained earnings either within the statement of stockholders' equity (490 firms) or in a separate statement of retained earnings (2 firms). Only 2 of the 500 companies prepare a combined statement of income and retained earnings.

DIFFERENT INCOME CONCEPTS

What do the numbers mean?

As mentioned in the opening story, the FASB and the IASB are collaborating on a joint project related to presentation of financial statements. In 2008, these two groups issued an exposure draft that presented examples of what these new financial statements might look like. Recently, they conducted field tests on two groups: preparers and users. Preparers were asked to recast their financial statements and then comment on the results. Users examined the recast statements and commented on their usefulness.

One part of the field test asked analysts to indicate which primary performance metric they use or create from a company's income statement. They were provided with the following options: (a) Net income; (b) Pretax income; (c) Income before interest and taxes (EBIT); (d) Income before interest, taxes, depreciation, and amortization (EBITDA); (e) Operating income; (f) Comprehensive income; and (g) Other. Presented below is a chart that highlights their responses.

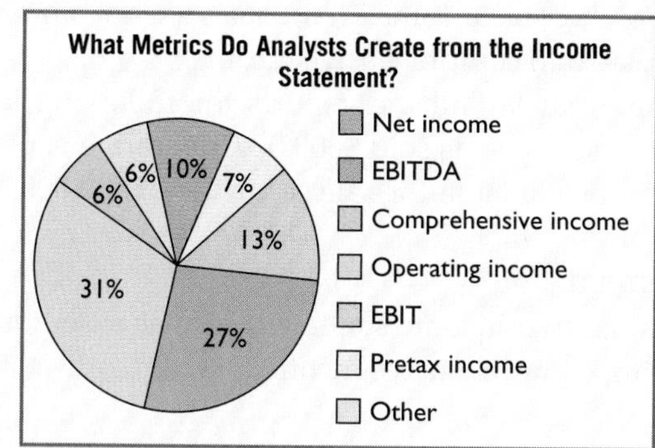

As indicated, Operating income (31%) and EBITDA (27%) were identified as the two primary performance metrics that respondents use or create from a company's income statement. A majority of the respondents identified a primary performance metric that uses net income as its foundation (pretax income would be in this group). Clearly, users and preparers look at more than just the bottom line income number, which supports the common practice of providing subtotals within the income statement.

Source: "FASB-IASB Report on Analyst Field Test Results," Financial Statement Presentation Informational Board Meeting (September 21, 2009).

Comprehensive Income

8 LEARNING OBJECTIVE
Explain how to report other comprehensive income.

Companies generally include in income all revenues, expenses, and gains and losses recognized during the period. These items are classified within the income statement so that financial statement readers can better understand the significance of various components of net income. Changes in accounting principles and corrections of errors are excluded from the calculation of net income because their effects relate to prior periods.

In recent years, there is increased use of fair values for measuring assets and liabilities. Furthermore, possible reporting of gains and losses related to changes in fair value have placed a strain on income reporting. Because fair values are continually changing, some argue that recognizing these gains and losses in net income is misleading. The FASB agrees and has identified a limited number of transactions that should be recorded directly to stockholders equity. One example is unrealized gains and losses on available-for-sale securities.[21] These gains and losses are excluded from net income, thereby reducing volatility in

[21]We further discuss available-for-sale securities in Chapter 17. Additional examples of other comprehensive items are translation gains and losses on foreign currency and unrealized gains and losses on certain hedging transactions.

net income due to fluctuations in fair value. At the same time, disclosure of the potential gain or loss is provided.

Companies include these items that bypass the income statement in a measure called comprehensive income. **Comprehensive income** includes all changes in equity during a period *except* those resulting from investments by owners and distributions to owners. Comprehensive income, therefore, includes the following: all revenues and gains, expenses and losses reported in net income, and all gains and losses that bypass net income but affect stockholders' equity. These items—non-owner changes in equity that bypass the income statement—are referred to as **other comprehensive income.**

The FASB decided that companies must display the components of other comprehensive income in one of three ways: **(1) a second income statement; (2) a combined statement of comprehensive income; or (3) as a part of the statement of stockholders' equity. [8]**[22] Regardless of the format used, companies must add net income to other comprehensive income to arrive at comprehensive income. Companies are not required to report earnings per share information related to comprehensive income.[23]

To illustrate, assume that V. Gill Inc. reports the following information for 2012: sales revenue $800,000; cost of goods sold $600,000; operating expenses $90,000; and an unrealized holding gain on available-for-sale securities of $30,000, net of tax.

Second Income Statement

Illustration 4-19 shows the two-income statement format based on the above information for V. Gill. Reporting comprehensive income in a separate statement indicates that

ILLUSTRATION 4-19
Two-Statement Format: Comprehensive Income

V. GILL INC.
INCOME STATEMENT
FOR THE YEAR ENDED DECEMBER 31, 2012

Sales revenue	$800,000
Cost of goods sold	600,000
Gross profit	200,000
Operating expenses	90,000
Net income	$110,000

V. GILL INC.
COMPREHENSIVE INCOME STATEMENT
FOR THE YEAR ENDED DECEMBER 31, 2012

Net income	$110,000
Other comprehensive income	
Unrealized holding gain, net of tax	30,000
Comprehensive income	$140,000

[22]*Accounting Trends and Techniques—2010* (New York: AICPA) indicates that for the 500 companies surveyed, 492 report comprehensive income. Most companies (400 of 492) include comprehensive income as part of the statement of stockholders' equity. The FASB (and IASB) have a proposal to simplify and improve comparability of comprehensive income reporting. If adopted, all components of comprehensive income will be reported in a continuous financial statement that displays the components of net income and the components of other comprehensive income within comprehensive income; this approach is essentially the combined statement of comprehensive income approach. [Proposed Accounting Standards Update—*Comprehensive Income (Topic 220): Statement of Comprehensive Income* (May 26, 2010).]

[23]A company must display the components of other comprehensive income either (1) net of related tax effects, or (2) before related tax effects, with one amount shown for the aggregate amount of tax related to the total amount of other comprehensive income. Both alternatives must show each component of other comprehensive income, net of related taxes either in the face of the statement or in the notes.

the gains and losses identified as other comprehensive income have the same status as traditional gains and losses. Placing net income as the starting point in the comprehensive income statement highlights the relationship of the statement to the traditional income statement.

Combined Statement of Comprehensive Income

The second approach to reporting other comprehensive income provides a **combined statement** of comprehensive income. In this approach, the traditional net income is a subtotal, with total comprehensive income shown as a final total. The combined statement has the advantage of not requiring the creation of a new financial statement. However, burying net income as a subtotal on the statement is a disadvantage.

Statement of Stockholders' Equity

A third approach reports other comprehensive income items in a **statement of stockholders' equity** (often referred to as statement of changes in stockholders' equity). This statement reports the changes in each stockholder's equity account and in total stockholders' equity during the year. Companies often prepare **in columnar form** the statement of stockholders' equity. In this format, they use columns for each account and for total stockholders' equity.

To illustrate, assume the same information for V. Gill. The company had the following stockholder equity account balances at the beginning of 2012: Common Stock $300,000; Retained Earnings $50,000; and Accumulated Other Comprehensive Income $60,000. No changes in the Common Stock account occurred during the year. Illustration 4-20 shows a statement of stockholders' equity for V. Gill.

ILLUSTRATION 4-20
Presentation of Comprehensive Income Items in Stockholders' Equity Statement

V. GILL INC.
STATEMENT OF STOCKHOLDERS' EQUITY
FOR THE YEAR ENDED DECEMBER 31, 2012

	Total	Comprehensive Income	Retained Earnings	Accumulated Other Comprehensive Income	Common Stock
Beginning balance	$410,000		$ 50,000	$60,000	$300,000
Comprehensive income					
Net income	110,000	$110,000	110,000		
Other comprehensive income					
Unrealized holding gain, net of tax	30,000	30,000		30,000	
Comprehensive income		$140,000			
Ending balance	$550,000		$160,000	$90,000	$300,000

Most companies use the statement of stockholders' equity approach to provide information related to other comprehensive income. Because many companies already provide a statement of stockholders' equity, adding additional columns to display information related to comprehensive income is not costly.

Balance Sheet Presentation

Regardless of the display format used, V. Gill reports the **accumulated other comprehensive income** of $90,000 in the stockholders' equity section of the balance sheet as follows.

ILLUSTRATION 4-21
Presentation of Accumulated Other Comprehensive Income in the Balance Sheet

V. GILL INC.
BALANCE SHEET
AS OF DECEMBER 31, 2012
(STOCKHOLDERS' EQUITY SECTION)

Stockholders' equity	
Common stock	$300,000
Retained earnings	160,000
Accumulated other comprehensive income	90,000
Total stockholders' equity	$550,000

By providing information on the components of comprehensive income, as well as accumulated other comprehensive income, the company communicates information about all changes in net assets.[24] With this information, users will better understand the quality of the company's earnings.

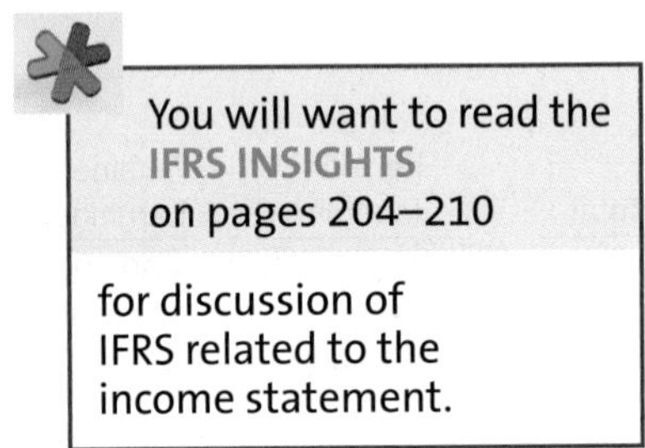

[24]Corrections of errors and changes in accounting principles are not considered other comprehensive income items.

SUMMARY OF LEARNING OBJECTIVES

1 Understand the uses and limitations of an income statement. The income statement provides investors and creditors with information that helps them predict the amounts, timing, and uncertainty of future cash flows. Also, the income statement helps users determine the risk (level of uncertainty) of not achieving particular cash flows. The limitations of an income statement are: (1) The statement does not include many items that contribute to general growth and well-being of a company. (2) Income numbers are often affected by the accounting methods used. (3) Income measures are subject to estimates.

The transaction approach focuses on the activities that occurred during a given period. Instead of presenting only a net change in net assets, it discloses the components of the change. The transaction approach to income measurement requires the use of revenue, expense, loss, and gain accounts.

2 Prepare a single-step income statement. In a single-step income statement, just two groupings exist: revenues and expenses. Expenses are deducted from revenues to arrive at net income or loss—a single subtraction. Frequently, companies report income tax separately as the last item before net income.

3 Prepare a multiple-step income statement. A multiple-step income statement shows two further classifications: (1) a separation of operating results from those obtained through the subordinate or nonoperating activities of the company; and (2) a classification of expenses by functions, such as merchandising or manufacturing, selling, and administration.

4 Explain how to report irregular items. Companies generally include irregular gains or losses or nonrecurring items in the income statement as follows: (1) Discontinued operations of a component of a business are classified as a separate item, after continuing operations. (2) The unusual, material, nonrecurring items that are significantly different from the customary business activities are shown in a separate section for extraordinary items, below discontinued operations. (3) Other items of a material amount that are of an unusual or nonrecurring nature and are not considered extraordinary are separately disclosed as a component of continuing operations. Changes in accounting principle and corrections of errors are adjusted through retained earnings.

5 Explain intraperiod tax allocation. Companies should relate the tax expense for the year to specific items on the income statement to provide a more informative disclosure to statement users. This procedure, intraperiod tax allocation, relates the income tax expense for the fiscal period to the following items that affect the amount of the tax provisions: (1) income from continuing operations, (2) discontinued operations, and (3) extraordinary items.

6 Identify where to report earnings per share information. Because of the inherent dangers of focusing attention solely on earnings per share, the profession concluded that companies must disclose earnings per share on the face of the income statement. A company that reports a discontinued operation or an extraordinary item must report per share amounts for these line items either on the face of the income statement or in the notes to the financial statements.

7 Prepare a retained earnings statement. The retained earnings statement should disclose net income (loss), dividends, adjustments due to changes in accounting principles, error corrections, and restrictions of retained earnings.

8 Explain how to report other comprehensive income. Companies report the components of other comprehensive income in a second statement, a combined statement of comprehensive income, or in a statement of stockholders' equity.

KEY TERMS

accumulated other comprehensive income, *183*
Appropriated Retained Earnings, *180*
capital maintenance approach, *162(n)*
changes in estimates, *175*
comprehensive income, *182*
current operating performance approach, *168*
discontinued operation, *169*
earnings management, *161*
earnings per share, *178*
extraordinary items, *170*
income statement, *160*
intraperiod tax allocation, *177*
irregular items, *169*
modified all-inclusive concept, *169*
multiple-step income statement, *164*
other comprehensive income, *182*
prior period adjustments, *175*
quality of earnings, *161*
single-step income statement, *163*
statement of stockholders' equity, *183*
transaction approach, *162*

FASB CODIFICATION

FASB Codification References

[1] FASB ASC 205-20-45. [Predecessor literature: "Accounting for the Impairment or Disposal of Long-lived Assets," *Statement of Financial Accounting Standards No. 144* (Norwalk, Conn.: FASB, 2001), par. 4.]

[2] FASB ASC 225-20-45-2. [Predecessor literature: "Reporting the Results of Operations," *Opinions of the Accounting Principles Board No. 30* (New York: AICPA, 1973), par. 20.]

[3] FASB ASC 225-20-45-4. [Predecessor literature: "Reporting the Results of Operations," *Opinions of the Accounting Principles Board No. 30* (New York: AICPA, 1973), par. 23, as amended by "Accounting for the Impairment or Disposal of Long-lived Assets," *Statement of Financial Accounting Standards No. 144* (Norwalk, Conn.: FASB, 2001).]

[4] FASB ASC 225-20-45-3. [Predecessor literature: "Reporting the Results of Operations," *Opinions of the Accounting Principles Board No. 30* (New York: AICPA, 1973), par. 24, as amended by "Accounting for the Impairment or Disposal of Long-lived Assets," *Statement of Financial Accounting Standards No. 144* (Norwalk, Conn.: FASB, 2001).]

[5] FASB ASC 250. [Predecessor literature: "Accounting Changes and Error Corrections," *Statement of Financial Accounting Standards No. 154* (Norwalk, Conn.: FASB, 2005).]

[6] FASB ASC 260. [Predecessor literature: "Earnings Per Share," *Statement of Financial Accounting Standards No. 128* (Norwalk, Conn.: FASB, 1996).]

[7] FASB ASC 260-10-10-2. [Predecessor literature: "Earnings Per Share," *Statement of Financial Accounting Standards No. 128* (Norwalk, Conn.: FASB, 1996), par. 11.]

[8] FASB ASC 220. [Predecessor literature: "Reporting Comprehensive Income," *Statement of Financial Accounting Standards No. 130* (Norwalk, Conn.: FASB, 1997).]

Exercises

If your school has a subscription to the FASB Codification, go to *http://aahq.org/asclogin.cfm* to log in and prepare responses to the following. Provide Codification references for your responses.

CE4-1 Access the glossary ("Master Glossary") to answer the following.

(a) What is a change in accounting estimate?

(b) How is a change in accounting principle distinguished from a "change in accounting estimate effected by a change in accounting principle"?

(c) What is the formal definition of comprehensive income?

CE4-2 What distinguishes an item that is "unusual in nature" from an item that is considered "extraordinary"?

CE4-3 Enyart Company experienced a catastrophic loss in the second quarter of the year. The loss meets the criteria for extraordinary item reporting, but Enyart's controller is unsure whether this item should be reported as extraordinary in the second quarter interim report. Advise the controller.

CE4-4 What guidance does the SEC provide for public companies with respect to the reporting of the "effect of preferred stock dividends and accretion of carrying amount of preferred stock on earnings per share"?

An additional Codification case can be found in the Using Your Judgment section, on page 203.

Be sure to check the book's companion website for a Review and Analysis Exercise, with solution.

Questions, Brief Exercises, Exercises, Problems, and many more resources are available for practice in WileyPLUS.

QUESTIONS

1. What kinds of questions about future cash flows do investors and creditors attempt to answer with information in the income statement?
2. How can information based on past transactions be used to predict future cash flows?
3. Identify at least two situations in which important changes in value are not reported in the income statement.
4. Identify at least two situations in which application of different accounting methods or accounting estimates results in difficulties in comparing companies.
5. Explain the transaction approach to measuring income. Why is the transaction approach to income measurement preferable to other ways of measuring income?
6. What is earnings management?
7. How can earnings management affect the quality of earnings?
8. Why should caution be exercised in the use of the net income figure derived in an income statement? What are the objectives of generally accepted accounting principles in their application to the income statement?
9. A *Wall Street Journal* article noted that **Apple** reported higher income than its competitors by using a more aggressive policy for recognizing revenue on future upgrades to its products. Some contend that Apple's quality of earnings is low. What does the term "quality of earnings" mean?
10. What is the major distinction (a) between revenues and gains and (b) between expenses and losses?
11. What are the advantages and disadvantages of the single-step income statement?
12. What is the basis for distinguishing between operating and nonoperating items?
13. Distinguish between the modified all-inclusive income statement and the current operating performance income statement. According to present generally accepted accounting principles, which is recommended? Explain.
14. How should correction of errors be reported in the financial statements?
15. Discuss the appropriate treatment in the financial statements of each of the following.
    - **(a)** An amount of $113,000 realized in excess of the cash surrender value of an insurance policy on the life of one of the founders of the company who died during the year.
    - **(b)** A profit-sharing bonus to employees computed as a percentage of net income.
    - **(c)** Additional depreciation on factory machinery because of an error in computing depreciation for the previous year.
    - **(d)** Rent received from subletting a portion of the office space.
    - **(e)** A patent infringement suit, brought 2 years ago against the company by another company, was settled this year by a cash payment of $725,000.
    - **(f)** A reduction in the Allowance for Doubtful Accounts balance, because the account appears to be considerably in excess of the probable loss from uncollectible receivables.
16. Indicate where the following items would ordinarily appear on the financial statements of Boleyn, Inc. for the year 2012.
    - **(a)** The service life of certain equipment was changed from 8 to 5 years. If a 5-year life had been used previously, additional depreciation of $425,000 would have been charged.
    - **(b)** In 2012, a flood destroyed a warehouse that had a book value of $1,600,000. Floods are rare in this locality.
    - **(c)** In 2012, the company wrote off $1,000,000 of inventory that was considered obsolete.
    - **(d)** An income tax refund related to the 2009 tax year was received.
    - **(e)** In 2009, a supply warehouse with an expected useful life of 7 years was erroneously expensed.
    - **(f)** Boleyn, Inc. changed from weighted-average to FIFO inventory pricing.
17. Indicate the section of a multiple-step income statement in which each of the following is shown.
    - **(a)** Loss on inventory write-down.
    - **(b)** Loss from strike.
    - **(c)** Bad debt expense.
    - **(d)** Loss on disposal of a component of the business.
    - **(e)** Gain on sale of machinery.
    - **(f)** Interest revenue.
    - **(g)** Depreciation expense.
    - **(h)** Material write-offs of notes receivable.
18. Perlman Land Development, Inc. purchased land for $70,000 and spent $30,000 developing it. It then sold the land for $160,000. Sheehan Manufacturing purchased land for a future plant site for $100,000. Due to a change in plans, Sheehan later sold the land for $160,000. Should these two companies report the land sales, both at gains of $60,000, in a similar manner?
19. You run into Greg Norman at a party and begin discussing financial statements. Greg says, "I prefer the single-step income statement because the multiple-step format generally overstates income." How should you respond to Greg?

20. Santo Corporation has eight expense accounts in its general ledger which could be classified as selling expenses. Should Santo report these eight expenses separately in its income statement or simply report one total amount for selling expenses?

21. Cooper Investments reported an unusual gain from the sale of certain assets in its 2012 income statement. How does intraperiod tax allocation affect the reporting of this unusual gain?

22. What effect does intraperiod tax allocation have on reported net income?

23. Neumann Company computed earnings per share as follows.

$$\frac{\text{Net income}}{\text{Common shares outstanding at year-end}}$$

Neumann has a simple capital structure. What possible errors might the company have made in the computation? Explain.

24. Qualls Corporation reported 2012 earnings per share of $7.21. In 2013, Qualls reported earnings per share as follows.

On income before extraordinary item	$6.40
On extraordinary item	1.88
On net income	$8.28

Is the increase in earnings per share from $7.21 to $8.28 a favorable trend?

25. What is meant by "tax allocation within a period"? What is the justification for such practice?

26. When does tax allocation within a period become necessary? How should this allocation be handled?

27. During 2012, Liselotte Company earned income of $1,500,000 before income taxes and realized a gain of $450,000 on a government-forced condemnation sale of a division plant facility. The income is subject to income taxation at the rate of 34%. The gain on the sale of the plant is taxed at 30%. Proper accounting suggests that the unusual gain be reported as an extraordinary item. Illustrate an appropriate presentation of these items in the income statement.

28. On January 30, 2011, a suit was filed against Frazier Corporation under the Environmental Protection Act. On August 6, 2012, Frazier Corporation agreed to settle the action and pay $920,000 in damages to certain current and former employees. How should this settlement be reported in the 2012 financial statements? Discuss.

29. Linus Paper Company decided to close two small pulp mills in Conway, New Hampshire, and Corvallis, Oregon. Would these closings be reported in a separate section entitled "Discontinued operations after income from continuing operations"? Discuss.

30. What major types of items are reported in the retained earnings statement?

31. Generally accepted accounting principles usually require the use of accrual accounting to "fairly present" income. If the cash receipts and disbursements method of accounting will "clearly reflect" taxable income, why does this method not usually also "fairly present" income?

32. State some of the more serious problems encountered in seeking to achieve the ideal measurement of periodic net income. Explain what accountants do as a practical alternative.

33. What is meant by the terms *elements* and *items* as they relate to the income statement? Why might items have to be disclosed in the income statement?

34. What are the three ways that other comprehensive income may be displayed (reported)?

35. How should the disposal of a component of a business be disclosed in the income statement?

BRIEF EXERCISES

2 **BE4-1** Starr Co. had sales revenue of $540,000 in 2012. Other items recorded during the year were:

Cost of goods sold	$330,000
Salaries and wages expense	120,000
Income tax expense	25,000
Increase in value of company reputation	15,000
Other operating expenses	10,000
Unrealized gain on value of patents	20,000

Prepare a single-step income statement for Starr for 2012. Starr has 100,000 shares of stock outstanding.

2 **BE4-2** Brisky Corporation had net sales of $2,400,000 and interest revenue of $31,000 during 2012. Expenses for 2012 were: cost of goods sold $1,450,000; administrative expenses $212,000; selling expenses $280,000; and interest expense $45,000. Brisky's tax rate is 30%. The corporation had 100,000 shares of common stock authorized and 70,000 shares issued and outstanding during 2012. Prepare a single-step income statement for the year ended December 31, 2012.

3 **BE4-3** Using the information provided in BE4-2, prepare a condensed multiple-step income statement for Brisky Corporation.

3 4 **BE4-4** Finley Corporation had income from continuing operations of $10,600,000 in 2012. During 2012, it disposed of its restaurant division at an after-tax loss of $189,000. Prior to disposal, the division operated at a loss of $315,000 (net of tax) in 2012. Finley had 10,000,000 shares of common stock outstanding during 2012. Prepare a partial income statement for Finley beginning with income from continuing operations.

4 5 **BE4-5** Stacy Corporation had income before income taxes for 2012 of $6,300,000. In addition, it suffered an unusual and infrequent pretax loss of $770,000 from a volcano eruption. The corporation's tax rate is 30%. Prepare a partial income statement for Stacy beginning with income before income taxes. The corporation had 5,000,000 shares of common stock outstanding during 2012.

4 **BE4-6** During 2012, Williamson Company changed from FIFO to weighted-average inventory pricing. Pretax income in 2011 and 2010 (Williamson's first year of operations) under FIFO was $160,000 and $180,000, respectively. Pretax income using weighted-average pricing in the prior years would have been $145,000 in 2011 and $170,000 in 2010. In 2012, Williamson Company reported pretax income (using weighted-average pricing) of $180,000. Show comparative income statements for Williamson Company, beginning with "Income before income tax," as presented on the 2012 income statement. (The tax rate in all years is 30%.)

4 **BE4-7** Vandross Company has recorded bad debt expense in the past at a rate of 1½% of net sales. In 2012, Vandross decides to increase its estimate to 2%. If the new rate had been used in prior years, cumulative bad debt expense would have been $380,000 instead of $285,000. In 2012, bad debt expense will be $120,000 instead of $90,000. If Vandross's tax rate is 30%, what amount should it report as the cumulative effect of changing the estimated bad debt rate?

6 **BE4-8** In 2012, Hollis Corporation reported net income of $1,000,000. It declared and paid preferred stock dividends of $250,000. During 2012, Hollis had a weighted average of 190,000 common shares outstanding. Compute Hollis's 2012 earnings per share.

7 **BE4-9** Portman Corporation has retained earnings of $675,000 at January 1, 2012. Net income during 2012 was $1,400,000, and cash dividends declared and paid during 2012 totaled $75,000. Prepare a retained earnings statement for the year ended December 31, 2012.

4 7 **BE4-10** Using the information from BE4-9, prepare a retained earnings statement for the year ended December 31, 2012. Assume an error was discovered: land costing $80,000 (net of tax) was charged to maintenance and repairs expense in 2009.

8 **BE4-11** On January 1, 2012, Richards Inc. had cash and common stock of $60,000. At that date, the company had no other asset, liability, or equity balances. On January 2, 2012, it purchased for cash $20,000 of equity securities that it classified as available-for-sale. It received cash dividends of $3,000 during the year on these securities. In addition, it has an unrealized holding gain on these securities of $4,000 net of tax. Determine the following amounts for 2012: (a) net income; (b) comprehensive income; (c) other comprehensive income; and (d) accumulated other comprehensive income (end of 2012).

EXERCISES

2 **E4-1 (Computation of Net Income)** Presented below are changes in all the account balances of Jackson Furniture Co. during the current year, except for retained earnings.

	Increase (Decrease)		Increase (Decrease)
Cash	$ 69,000	Accounts Payable	$ (51,000)
Accounts Receivable (net)	45,000	Bonds Payable	82,000
Inventory	127,000	Common Stock	125,000
Investments	(47,000)	Paid-in Capital in Excess of Par–Common Stock	13,000

Instructions

Compute the net income for the current year, assuming that there were no entries in the Retained Earnings account except for net income and a dividend declaration of $24,000 which was paid in the current year.

2 **E4-2 (Income Statement Items)** Presented below are certain account balances of Wade Products Co.

Rent revenue	$ 6,500	Sales discounts	$ 7,800
Interest expense	12,700	Selling expenses	99,400
Beginning retained earnings	114,400	Sales revenue	400,000
Ending retained earnings	134,000	Income tax expense	26,600
Dividend revenue	71,000	Cost of goods sold	184,400
Sales returns and allowances	12,400	Administrative expenses	82,500

Instructions
From the foregoing, compute the following: (a) total net revenue, (b) net income, (c) dividends declared during the current year.

2 **E4-3 (Single-Step Income Statement)** The financial records of Dunbar Inc. were destroyed by fire at the end of 2012. Fortunately, the controller had kept certain statistical data related to the income statement as presented below.

1. The beginning merchandise inventory was $92,000 and decreased 20% during the current year.
2. Sales discounts amount to $17,000.
3. 30,000 shares of common stock were outstanding for the entire year.
4. Interest expense was $20,000.
5. The income tax rate is 30%.
6. Cost of goods sold amounts to $500,000.
7. Administrative expenses are 18% of cost of goods sold but only 8% of gross sales.
8. Four-fifths of the operating expenses relate to sales activities.

Instructions
From the foregoing, information, prepare an income statement for the year 2012 in single-step form.

2 3 **E4-4 (Multiple-Step and Single-Step)** Two accountants for the firm of Allen and Wright are arguing about the merits of presenting an income statement in a multiple-step versus a single-step format. The discussion involves the following 2012 information related to Webster Company ($000 omitted).

Administrative expense	
Officers' salaries	$ 4,900
Depreciation of office furniture and equipment	3,960
Cost of goods sold	63,570
Rent revenue	17,230
Selling expense	
Transportation-out	2,690
Sales commissions	7,980
Depreciation of sales equipment	6,480
Sales revenue	96,500
Income tax expense	7,580
Interest expense	1,860

Instructions
(a) Prepare an income statement for the year 2012 using the multiple-step form. Common shares outstanding for 2012 total 40,550 (000 omitted).
(b) Prepare an income statement for the year 2012 using the single-step form.
(c) Which one do you prefer? Discuss.

3 4 **E4-5 (Multiple-Step and Extraordinary Items)** The following balances were taken from the books of Parnevik Corp. on December 31, 2012.

Interest revenue	$ 86,000	Accumulated depreciation—buildings	$ 28,000
Cash	51,000	Notes receivable	155,000
Sales revenue	1,280,000	Selling expenses	194,000
Accounts receivable	150,000	Accounts payable	170,000
Prepaid insurance	20,000	Bonds payable	100,000
Sales returns and allowances	150,000	Office expenses	97,000
Allowance for doubtful accounts	7,000	Accrued liabilities	32,000
Sales discounts	45,000	Interest expense	60,000
Land	100,000	Notes payable	100,000
Equipment	200,000	Loss from earthquake damage (extraordinary item)	120,000
Buildings	140,000		
Cost of goods sold	621,000	Common stock	500,000
Accumulated depreciation—equipment	40,000	Retained earnings	21,000

Assume the total effective tax rate on all items is 34%.

Instructions
Prepare a multiple-step income statement; 100,000 shares of common stock were outstanding during the year.

2 3 **E4-6 (Multiple-Step and Single-Step)** The accountant of Weatherspoon Shoe Co. has compiled the following information from the company's records as a basis for an income statement for the year ended December 31, 2012.

Rent revenue	$ 29,000
Interest expense	18,000
Market appreciation on land above cost	31,000
Salaries and wages expense (sales)	114,800
Supplies (sales)	17,600
Income tax	30,600
Salaries and wages expense (administrative)	135,900
Other administrative expenses	51,700
Cost of goods sold	516,000
Net sales	980,000
Depreciation on plant assets (70% selling, 30% administrative)	65,000
Cash dividends declared	16,000

There were 20,000 shares of common stock outstanding during the year.

Instructions

(a) Prepare a multiple-step income statement.
(b) Prepare a single-step income statement.
(c) Which format do you prefer? Discuss.

2 4 6 **E4-7 (Income Statement, EPS)** Presented below are selected amounts from the records of McGraw Corporation as of December 31, 2012.

Cash	$ 50,000
Administrative expenses	100,000
Selling expenses	80,000
Net sales	540,000
Cost of goods sold	260,000
Cash dividends declared (2012)	20,000
Cash dividends paid (2012)	15,000
Discontinued operations (loss before income taxes)	40,000
Depreciation expense, not recorded in 2011	30,000
Retained earnings, December 31, 2011	90,000
Effective tax rate 30%	

Instructions

(a) Compute net income for 2012.
(b) Prepare a partial income statement beginning with income from continuing operations before income tax, and including appropriate earnings per share information. Assume 20,000 shares of common stock were outstanding during 2012.

3 4 5 6 7 **E4-8 (Multiple-Step Statement with Retained Earnings)** Presented below is information related to Brokaw Corp. for the year 2012.

Net sales	$1,200,000	Write-off of inventory due to obsolescence	$ 80,000
Cost of goods sold	780,000	Depreciation expense omitted by accident in 2011	40,000
Selling expenses	65,000	Casualty loss (extraordinary item) before taxes	50,000
Administrative expenses	48,000	Cash dividends declared	45,000
Dividend revenue	20,000	Retained earnings at December 31, 2011	980,000
Interest revenue	7,000	Effective tax rate of 34% on all items	

Instructions

(a) Prepare a multiple-step income statement for 2012. Assume that 60,000 shares of common stock are outstanding.
(b) Prepare a retained earnings statement for 2012.

6 **E4-9 (Earnings per Share)** The stockholders' equity section of Sosa Corporation appears below as of December 31, 2012.

6% preferred stock, $50 par value, authorized 100,000 shares, outstanding 90,000 shares		$ 4,500,000
Common stock, $1 par, authorized and issued 10 million shares		10,000,000
Additional paid-in capital		20,500,000
Retained earnings	$134,000,000	
Net income	33,000,000	167,000,000
		$202,000,000

Net income for 2012 reflects a total effective tax rate of 34%. Included in the net income figure is a loss of $12,000,000 (before tax) as a result of a major casualty, which should be classified as an extraordinary item. Preferred stock dividends of $270,000 were declared and paid in 2012. Dividends of $1,000,000 were declared and paid to common stockholders in 2012.

Instructions

Compute earnings per share data as it should appear on the income statement of Sosa Corporation.

3 4 **E4-10 (Condensed Income Statement—Periodic Inventory Method)** Presented below are selected ledger
5 6 accounts of Woods Corporation at December 31, 2012.

Cash	$ 185,000	Salaries and wages expense (sales)	$284,000
Inventory	535,000	Salaries and wages expense (office)	346,000
Sales revenue	4,175,000	Purchase returns	15,000
Unearned revenue	117,000	Sales returns and allowances	79,000
Purchases	2,786,000	Transportation-in	72,000
Sales discounts	34,000	Accounts receivable	142,500
Purchase discounts	27,000	Sales commissions	83,000
Selling expenses	69,000	Telephone expense (sales)	17,000
Accounting and legal services	33,000	Utilities expense (office)	32,000
Insurance expense (office)	24,000	Miscellaneous office expenses	8,000
Advertising	54,000	Rent revenue	240,000
Transportation-out	93,000	Extraordinary loss (before tax)	60,000
Depreciation expense (office equipment)	48,000	Interest expense	176,000
Depreciation expense (sales equipment)	36,000	Common stock ($10 par)	900,000

Woods's effective tax rate on all items is 34%. A physical inventory indicates that the ending inventory is $686,000.

Instructions

Prepare a condensed 2012 income statement for Woods Corporation.

7 **E4-11 (Retained Earnings Statement)** McEntire Corporation began operations on January 1, 2009. During its first 3 years of operations, McEntire reported net income and declared dividends as follows.

	Net income	Dividends declared
2009	$ 40,000	$ -0-
2010	125,000	50,000
2011	160,000	50,000

The following information relates to 2012.

Income before income tax	$220,000
Prior period adjustment: understatement of 2010 depreciation expense (before taxes)	$ 25,000
Cumulative decrease in income from change in inventory methods (before taxes)	$ 45,000
Dividends declared (of this amount, $25,000 will be paid on January 15, 2013)	$100,000
Effective tax rate	40%

Instructions

(a) Prepare a 2012 retained earnings statement for McEntire Corporation.

(b) Assume McEntire restricted retained earnings in the amount of $70,000 on December 31, 2012. After this action, what would McEntire report as total retained earnings in its December 31, 2012, balance sheet?

4 5 **E4-12 (Earnings per Share)** At December 31, 2011, Schroeder Corporation had the following stock out-
6 standing.

8% cumulative preferred stock, $100 par, 107,500 shares	$10,750,000
Common stock, $5 par, 4,000,000 shares	20,000,000

During 2012, Schroeder did not issue any additional common stock. The following also occurred during 2012.

Income from continuing operations before taxes	$21,650,000
Discontinued operations (loss before taxes)	3,225,000
Preferred dividends declared	860,000
Common dividends declared	2,200,000
Effective tax rate	35%

Instructions

Compute earnings per share data as it should appear in the 2012 income statement of Schroeder Corporation. (Round to two decimal places.)

4 5 **E4-13 (Change in Accounting Principle)** Zehms Company began operations in 2010 and adopted
6 weighted-average pricing for inventory. In 2012, in accordance with other companies in its industry, Zehms changed its inventory pricing to FIFO. The pretax income data is reported below.

Year	Weighted-Average	FIFO
2010	$370,000	$395,000
2011	390,000	420,000
2012	410,000	460,000

Instructions

(a) What is Zehms's net income in 2012? Assume a 35% tax rate in all years.

(b) Compute the cumulative effect of the change in accounting principle from weighted-average to FIFO inventory pricing.

(c) Show comparative income statements for Zehms Company, beginning with income before income tax, as presented on the 2012 income statement.

3 8 **E4-14 (Comprehensive Income)** Armstrong Corporation reported the following for 2012: net sales $1,200,000; cost of goods sold $720,000; selling and administrative expenses $320,000; and an unrealized holding gain on available-for-sale securities $15,000.

Instructions

Prepare a statement of comprehensive income, using the two-income statement format. Ignore income taxes and earnings per share.

7 8 **E4-15 (Comprehensive Income)** Bryant Co. reports the following information for 2012: sales revenue $750,000; cost of goods sold $500,000; operating expenses $80,000; and an unrealized holding loss on available-for-sale securities for 2012 of $50,000. It declared and paid a cash dividend of $10,000 in 2012.

Bryant Co. has January 1, 2012, balances in common stock $350,000; accumulated other comprehensive income $80,000; and retained earnings $90,000. It issued no stock during 2012.

Instructions

Prepare a statement of stockholders' equity.

2 4 **E4-16 (Various Reporting Formats)** The following information was taken from the records of Gibson
5 6 Inc. for the year 2012: income tax applicable to income from continuing operations $119,000; income tax
7 8 applicable to loss on discontinued operations $25,500; income tax applicable to extraordinary gain $32,300; income tax applicable to extraordinary loss $20,400; and unrealized holding gain on available-for-sale securities $15,000.

Extraordinary gain	$ 95,000	Cash dividends declared	$ 150,000
Loss on discontinued operations	75,000	Retained earnings January 1, 2012	600,000
Administrative expenses	240,000	Cost of goods sold	850,000
Rent revenue	40,000	Selling expenses	300,000
Extraordinary loss	60,000	Sales revenue	1,700,000

Shares outstanding during 2012 were 100,000.

Instructions

(a) Prepare a single-step income statement for 2012.

(b) Prepare a retained earnings statement for 2012.

(c) Show how comprehensive income is reported using the second income statement format.

See the book's companion website, www.wiley.com/college/kieso, for a set of B Exercises.

PROBLEMS

3 4 **P4-1 (Multiple-Step Income, Retained Earnings)** Presented below is information related to Dickinson
5 6 Company for 2012.
7

Retained earnings balance, January 1, 2012	$ 980,000
Sales revenue	25,000,000
Cost of goods sold	16,000,000
Interest revenue	70,000
Selling and administrative expenses	4,700,000
Write-off of goodwill	820,000
Income taxes for 2012	1,244,000
Gain on the sale of investments (normal recurring)	110,000
Loss due to flood damage—extraordinary item (net of tax)	390,000
Loss on the disposition of the wholesale division (net of tax)	440,000
Loss on operations of the wholesale division (net of tax)	90,000
Dividends declared on common stock	250,000
Dividends declared on preferred stock	80,000

Instructions

Prepare a multiple-step income statement and a retained earnings statement. Dickinson Company decided to discontinue its entire wholesale operations and to retain its manufacturing operations. On September 15, Dickinson sold the wholesale operations to Rogers Company. During 2012, there were 500,000 shares of common stock outstanding all year.

P4-2 (Single-Step Income, Retained Earnings, Periodic Inventory) Presented below is the trial balance of Thompson Corporation at December 31, 2012.

THOMPSON CORPORATION
TRIAL BALANCE
DECEMBER 31, 2012

	Debits	Credits
Purchase Discounts		$ 10,000
Cash	$ 189,700	
Accounts Receivable	105,000	
Rent Revenue		18,000
Retained Earnings		160,000
Salaries and Wages Payable		18,000
Sales Revenue		1,100,000
Notes Receivable	110,000	
Accounts Payable		49,000
Accumulated Depreciation—Equipment		28,000
Sales Discounts	14,500	
Sales Returns and Allowances	17,500	
Notes Payable		70,000
Selling Expenses	232,000	
Administrative Expenses	99,000	
Common Stock		300,000
Income Tax Expense	53,900	
Cash Dividends	45,000	
Allowance for Doubtful Accounts		5,000
Supplies	14,000	
Freight-in	20,000	
Land	70,000	
Equipment	140,000	
Bonds Payable		100,000
Gain on Sale of Land		30,000
Accumulated Depreciation—Buildings		19,600
Inventory	89,000	
Buildings	98,000	
Purchases	610,000	
Totals	$1,907,600	$1,907,600

A physical count of inventory on December 31 resulted in an inventory amount of $64,000; thus, cost of goods sold for 2012 is $645,000.

Instructions

Prepare a single-step income statement and a retained earnings statement. Assume that the only changes in retained earnings during the current year were from net income and dividends. Thirty thousand shares of common stock were outstanding the entire year.

P4-3 (Irregular Items) Maher Inc. reported income from continuing operations before taxes during 2012 of $790,000. Additional transactions occurring in 2012 but not considered in the $790,000 are as follows.

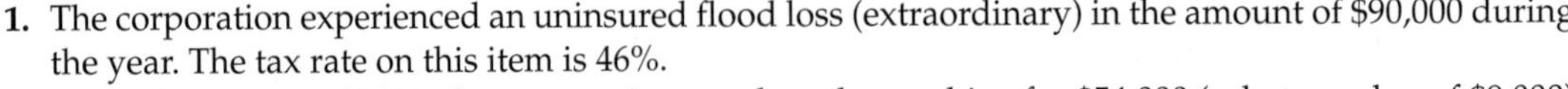

1. The corporation experienced an uninsured flood loss (extraordinary) in the amount of $90,000 during the year. The tax rate on this item is 46%.

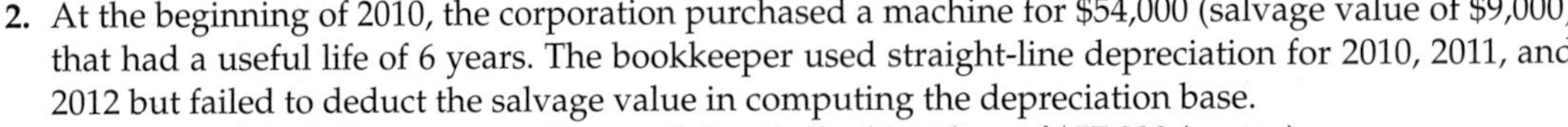

2. At the beginning of 2010, the corporation purchased a machine for $54,000 (salvage value of $9,000) that had a useful life of 6 years. The bookkeeper used straight-line depreciation for 2010, 2011, and 2012 but failed to deduct the salvage value in computing the depreciation base.

3. Sale of securities held as a part of its portfolio resulted in a loss of $57,000 (pretax).
4. When its president died, the corporation realized $150,000 from an insurance policy. The cash surrender value of this policy had been carried on the books as an investment in the amount of $46,000 (the gain is nontaxable).

5. The corporation disposed of its recreational division at a loss of $115,000 before taxes. Assume that this transaction meets the criteria for discontinued operations.
6. The corporation decided to change its method of inventory pricing from average cost to the FIFO method. The effect of this change on prior years is to increase 2010 income by $60,000 and decrease 2011 income by $20,000 before taxes. The FIFO method has been used for 2012. The tax rate on these items is 40%.

Instructions

Prepare an income statement for the year 2012 starting with income from continuing operations before taxes. Compute earnings per share as it should be shown on the face of the income statement. Common shares outstanding for the year are 120,000 shares. (Assume a tax rate of 30% on all items, unless indicated otherwise.)

3 4 **P4-4 (Multiple- and Single-Step Income, Retained Earnings)** The following account balances were
6 7 included in the trial balance of Twain Corporation at June 30, 2012.

Sales revenue	$1,578,500	Depreciation expense (office furniture and equipment)	$ 7,250
Sales discounts	31,150	Property tax expense	7,320
Cost of goods sold	896,770	Bad debt expense (selling)	4,850
Salaries and wages expense (sales)	56,260	Maintenance and repairs expense (administration)	9,130
Sales commissions	97,600	Office expense	6,000
Travel expense (salespersons)	28,930	Sales returns and allowances	62,300
Freight-out	21,400	Dividends received	38,000
Entertainment expense	14,820	Interest expense	18,000
Telephone and Internet expense (sales)	9,030	Income tax expense	102,000
Depreciation expense (sales equipment)	4,980	Depreciation understatement due to error—2009 (net of tax)	17,700
Maintenance and repairs expense (sales)	6,200	Dividends declared on preferred stock	9,000
Miscellaneous selling expenses	4,715	Dividends declared on common stock	37,000
Office supplies used	3,450		
Telephone and Internet expense (administration)	2,820		

The Retained Earnings account had a balance of $337,000 at July 1, 2011. There are 80,000 shares of common stock outstanding.

Instructions

(a) Using the multiple-step form, prepare an income statement and a retained earnings statement for the year ended June 30, 2012.

(b) Using the single-step form, prepare an income statement and a retained earnings statement for the year ended June 30, 2012.

4 5 **P4-5 (Irregular Items)** Presented below is a combined single-step income and retained earnings statement
6 7 for Nerwin Company for 2012.

		(000 omitted)
Net sales		$640,000
Costs and expenses		
Cost of goods sold	$500,000	
Selling, general, and administrative expenses	66,000	
Other, net	17,000	583,000
Income before income tax		57,000
Income tax		19,400
Net income		37,600
Retained earnings at beginning of period, as previously reported	141,000	
Adjustment required for correction of error	(7,000)	
Retained earnings at beginning of period, as restated		134,000
Dividends on common stock		(12,200)
Retained earnings at end of period		$159,400

Additional facts are as follows.

1. "Selling, general, and administrative expenses" for 2012 included a charge of $8,500,000 that was usual but infrequently occurring.
2. "Other, net" for 2012 included an extraordinary item (charge) of $6,000,000. If the extraordinary item (charge) had not occurred, income taxes for 2012 would have been $21,400,000 instead of $19,400,000.

3. "Adjustment required for correction of an error" was a result of a change in estimate (useful life of certain assets reduced to 8 years and a catch-up adjustment made).
4. Nerwin Company disclosed earnings per common share for net income in the notes to the financial statements.

Instructions

Determine from these additional facts whether the presentation of the facts in the Nerwin Company income and retained earnings statement is appropriate. If the presentation is not appropriate, describe the appropriate presentation and discuss its theoretical rationale. (Do not prepare a revised statement.)

4 5 7 **P4-6 (Retained Earnings Statement, Prior Period Adjustment)** Below is the Retained Earnings account for the year 2012 for Acadian Corp.

Retained earnings, January 1, 2012		$257,600
Add:		
Gain on sale of investments (net of tax)	$41,200	
Net income	84,500	
Refund on litigation with government, related to the year 2009 (net of tax)	21,600	
Recognition of income earned in 2011, but omitted from income statement in that year (net of tax)	25,400	172,700
		430,300
Deduct:		
Loss on discontinued operations (net of tax)	35,000	
Write-off of goodwill (net of tax)	60,000	
Cumulative effect on income of prior years in changing from LIFO to FIFO inventory valuation in 2012 (net of tax)	23,200	
Cash dividends declared	32,000	150,200
Retained earnings, December 31, 2012		$280,100

Instructions

(a) Prepare a corrected retained earnings statement. Acadian Corp. normally sells investments of the type mentioned above. FIFO inventory was used in 2012 to compute net income.

(b) State where the items that do not appear in the corrected retained earnings statement should be shown.

4 5 6 **P4-7 (Income Statement, Irregular Items)** Wade Corp. has 150,000 shares of common stock outstanding. In 2012, the company reports income from continuing operations before income tax of $1,210,000. Additional transactions not considered in the $1,210,000 are as follows.

1. In 2012, Wade Corp. sold equipment for $40,000. The machine had originally cost $80,000 and had accumulated depreciation of $30,000. The gain or loss is considered ordinary.
2. The company discontinued operations of one of its subsidiaries during the current year at a loss of $190,000 before taxes. Assume that this transaction meets the criteria for discontinued operations. The loss from operations of the discontinued subsidiary was $90,000 before taxes; the loss from disposal of the subsidiary was $100,000 before taxes.
3. An internal audit discovered that amortization of intangible assets was understated by $35,000 (net of tax) in a prior period. The amount was charged against retained earnings.
4. The company had a gain of $125,000 on the condemnation of much of its property. The gain is taxed at a total effective rate of 40%. Assume that the transaction meets the requirements of an extraordinary item.

Instructions

Analyze the above information and prepare an income statement for the year 2012, starting with income from continuing operations before income tax. Compute earnings per share as it should be shown on the face of the income statement. (Assume a total effective tax rate of 38% on all items, unless otherwise indicated.)

CONCEPTS FOR ANALYSIS

CA4-1 (Identification of Income Statement Deficiencies) O'Malley Corporation was incorporated and began business on January 1, 2012. It has been successful and now requires a bank loan for additional working capital to finance expansion. The bank has requested an audited income statement for the year 2012. The accountant for O'Malley Corporation provides you with the following income statement which O'Malley plans to submit to the bank.

O'MALLEY CORPORATION
INCOME STATEMENT

Sales revenue		$850,000
Dividends		32,300
Gain on recovery of insurance proceeds from earthquake loss (extraordinary)		38,500
		920,800
Less:		
Selling expenses	$101,100	
Cost of goods sold	510,000	
Advertising expense	13,700	
Loss on obsolescence of inventories	34,000	
Loss on discontinued operations	48,600	
Administrative expense	73,400	780,800
Income before income tax		140,000
Income tax		56,000
Net income		$ 84,000

Instructions

Indicate the deficiencies in the income statement presented above. Assume that the corporation desires a single-step income statement.

CA4-2 (Income Reporting Deficiencies) The following represents a recent income statement for **Boeing Company**.

	($ in millions)
Sales	$21,924
Costs and expenses	20,773
Income from operations	1,151
Other income	122
Interest expense	(130)
Earnings before income taxes	1,143
Income taxes	(287)
Net income	$ 856

It includes only *five* separate numbers (two of which are in billions of dollars), *two* subtotals, and the net earnings figure.

Instructions

(a) Indicate the deficiencies in the income statement.

(b) What recommendations would you make to Boeing to improve the usefulness of its income statement?

CA4-3 (Extraordinary Items) Derek Lee, vice president of finance for Atlanta Company, has recently been asked to discuss with the company's division controllers the proper accounting for extraordinary items. Derek Lee prepared the factual situations presented below as a basis for discussion.

1. An earthquake destroys one of the oil refineries owned by a large multinational oil company. Earthquakes are rare in this geographical location.
2. A publicly held company has incurred a substantial loss in the unsuccessful registration of a bond issue.
3. A large portion of a cigarette manufacturer's tobacco crops are destroyed by a hailstorm. Severe damage from hailstorms is rare in this locality.
4. A large diversified company sells a block of shares from its portfolio of securities acquired for investment purposes.
5. A company that operates a chain of warehouses sells the excess land surrounding one of its warehouses. When the company buys property to establish a new warehouse, it usually buys more land than it expects to use for the warehouse with the expectation that the land will appreciate in value. Twice during the past 5 years the company sold excess land.
6. A company experiences a material loss in the repurchase of a large bond issue that has been outstanding for 3 years. The company regularly repurchases bonds of this nature.
7. A railroad experiences an unusual flood loss to part of its track system. Flood losses normally occur every 3 or 4 years.

8. A machine tool company sells the only land it owns. The land was acquired 10 years ago for future expansion, but shortly thereafter the company abandoned all plans for expansion but decided to hold the land for appreciation.

Instructions
Determine whether the foregoing items should be classified as extraordinary items. Present a rationale for your position.

CA4-4 (Earnings Management) Bobek Inc. has recently reported steadily increasing income. The company reported income of $20,000 in 2009, $25,000 in 2010, and $30,000 in 2011. A number of market analysts have recommended that investors buy the stock because they expect the steady growth in income to continue. Bobek is approaching the end of its fiscal year in 2012, and it again appears to be a good year. However, it has not yet recorded warranty expense.

Based on prior experience, this year's warranty expense should be around $5,000, but some managers have approached the controller to suggest a larger, more conservative warranty expense should be recorded this year. Income before warranty expense is $43,000. Specifically, by recording a $7,000 warranty accrual this year, Bobek could report an increase in income for this year and still be in a position to cover its warranty costs in future years.

Instructions
(a) What is earnings management?
(b) Assume income before warranty expense is $43,000 for both 2012 and 2013 and that total warranty expense over the 2-year period is $10,000. What is the effect of the proposed accounting in 2012? In 2013?
(c) What is the appropriate accounting in this situation?

CA4-5 (Earnings Management) Charlie Brown, controller for the Kelly Corporation, is preparing the company's income statement at year-end. He notes that the company lost a considerable sum on the sale of some equipment it had decided to replace. Since the company has sold equipment routinely in the past, Brown knows the losses cannot be reported as extraordinary. He also does not want to highlight it as a material loss since he feels that will reflect poorly on him and the company. He reasons that if the company had recorded more depreciation during the assets' lives, the losses would not be so great. Since depreciation is included among the company's operating expenses, he wants to report the losses along with the company's expenses, where he hopes it will not be noticed.

Instructions
(a) What are the ethical issues involved?
(b) What should Brown do?

CA4-6 (Income Reporting Items) Simpson Corp. is an entertainment firm that derives approximately 30% of its income from the Casino Knights Division, which manages gambling facilities. As auditor for Simpson Corp., you have recently overheard the following discussion between the controller and financial vice president.

VICE PRESIDENT: If we sell the Casino Knights Division, it seems ridiculous to segregate the results of the sale in the income statement. Separate categories tend to be absurd and confusing to the stockholders. I believe that we should simply report the gain on the sale as other income or expense without detail.

CONTROLLER: Professional pronouncements would require that we disclose this information separately in the income statement. If a sale of this type is considered unusual and infrequent, it must be reported as an extraordinary item.

VICE PRESIDENT: What about the walkout we had last month when employees were upset about their commission income? Would this situation not also be an extraordinary item?

CONTROLLER: I am not sure whether this item would be reported as extraordinary or not.

VICE PRESIDENT: Oh well, it doesn't make any difference because the net effect of all these items is immaterial, so no disclosure is necessary.

Instructions
(a) On the basis of the foregoing discussion, answer the following questions: Who is correct about handling the sale? What would be the correct income statement presentation for the sale of the Casino Knights Division?
(b) How should the walkout by the employees be reported?
(c) What do you think about the vice president's observation on materiality?
(d) What are the earnings per share implications of these topics?

CA4-7 (Identification of Income Statement Weaknesses) The following financial statement was prepared by employees of Walters Corporation.

WALTERS CORPORATION
INCOME STATEMENT
YEAR ENDED DECEMBER 31, 2012

Revenues	
Gross sales, including sales taxes	$1,044,300
Less: Returns, allowances, and cash discounts	56,200
Net sales	988,100
Dividends, interest, and purchase discounts	30,250
Recoveries of accounts written off in prior years	13,850
Total revenues	1,032,200
Costs and expenses	
Cost of goods sold, including sales taxes	465,900
Salaries and related payroll expenses	60,500
Rent	19,100
Freight-in and freight-out	3,400
Bad debt expense	27,800
Total costs and expenses	576,700
Income before extraordinary items	455,500
Extraordinary items	
Loss on discontinued styles (Note 1)	71,500
Loss on sale of marketable securities (Note 2)	39,050
Loss on sale of warehouse (Note 3)	86,350
Total extraordinary items	196,900
Net income	$ 258,600
Net income per share of common stock	$2.30

Note 1: New styles and rapidly changing consumer preferences resulted in a $71,500 loss on the disposal of discontinued styles and related accessories.

Note 2: The corporation sold an investment in marketable securities at a loss of $39,050. The corporation normally sells securities of this nature.

Note 3: The corporation sold one of its warehouses at an $86,350 loss.

Instructions

Identify and discuss the weaknesses in classification and disclosure in the single-step income statement above. You should explain why these treatments are weaknesses and what the proper presentation of the items would be in accordance with GAAP.

CA4-8 (Classification of Income Statement Items) As audit partner for Grupo and Rijo, you are in charge of reviewing the classification of unusual items that have occurred during the current year. The following material items have come to your attention.

1. A merchandising company incorrectly overstated its ending inventory 2 years ago. Inventory for all other periods is correctly computed.
2. An automobile dealer sells for $137,000 an extremely rare 1930 S type Invicta which it purchased for $21,000 10 years ago. The Invicta is the only such display item the dealer owns.
3. A drilling company during the current year extended the estimated useful life of certain drilling equipment from 9 to 15 years. As a result, depreciation for the current year was materially lowered.
4. A retail outlet changed its computation for bad debt expense from 1% to ½ of 1% of sales because of changes in its customer clientele.
5. A mining concern sells a foreign subsidiary engaged in uranium mining, although it (the seller) continues to engage in uranium mining in other countries.
6. A steel company changes from the average cost method to the FIFO method for inventory costing purposes.
7. A construction company, at great expense, prepared a major proposal for a government loan. The loan is not approved.
8. A water pump manufacturer has had large losses resulting from a strike by its employees early in the year.

9. Depreciation for a prior period was incorrectly understated by $950,000. The error was discovered in the current year.
10. A large sheep rancher suffered a major loss because the state required that all sheep in the state be killed to halt the spread of a rare disease. Such a situation has not occurred in the state for 20 years.
11. A food distributor that sells wholesale to supermarket chains and to fast-food restaurants (two distinguishable classes of customers) decides to discontinue the division that sells to one of the two classes of customers.

Instructions

From the foregoing information, indicate in what section of the income statement or retained earnings statement these items should be classified. Provide a brief rationale for your position.

CA4-9 (Comprehensive Income) Willie Nelson, Jr., controller for Jenkins Corporation, is preparing the company's financial statements at year-end. Currently, he is focusing on the income statement and determining the format for reporting comprehensive income. During the year, the company earned net income of $400,000 and had unrealized gains on available-for-sale securities of $15,000. In the previous year, net income was $410,000, and the company had no unrealized gains or losses.

Instructions

(a) Show how income and comprehensive income will be reported on a comparative basis for the current and prior years, using the separate income statement format.
(b) Show how income and comprehensive income will be reported on a comparative basis for the current and prior years, using the combined income statement format.
(c) Which format should Nelson recommend?

USING YOUR JUDGMENT

FINANCIAL REPORTING

Financial Reporting Problem

The Procter & Gamble Company (P&G)

The financial statements of P&G are presented in Appendix 5B or can be accessed at the book's companion website, **www.wiley.com/college/kieso**.

Instructions

Refer to P&G's financial statements and the accompanying notes to answer the following questions.

(a) What type of income statement format does P&G use? Indicate why this format might be used to present income statement information.
(b) What are P&G's primary revenue sources?
(c) Compute P&G's gross profit for each of the years 2007–2009. Explain why gross profit decreased in 2009.
(d) Why does P&G make a distinction between operating and nonoperating revenue?
(e) What financial ratios did P&G choose to report in its "Financial Summary" section covering the years 1999–2009?

Comparative Analysis Case

The Coca-Cola Company and PepsiCo, Inc.

Instructions

Go to the book's companion website and use information found there to answer the following questions related to **The Coca-Cola Company** and **PepsiCo, Inc.**

(a) What type of income format(s) is used by these two companies? Identify any differences in income statement format between these two companies.

(b) What are the gross profits, operating profits, and net incomes for these two companies over the 3-year period 2007–2009? Which company has had better financial results over this period of time?

(c) Identify the irregular items reported by these two companies in their income statements over the 3-year period 2007–2009. Do these irregular items appear to be significant?

Financial Statement Analysis Cases

Case 1 Bankruptcy Prediction

The Z-score bankruptcy prediction model uses balance sheet and income information to arrive at a Z-Score, which can be used to predict financial distress:

$$Z = \frac{\text{Working capital}}{\text{Total assets}} \times 1.2 + \frac{\text{Retained earnings}}{\text{Total assets}} \times 1.4 + \frac{\text{EBIT}}{\text{Total assets}} \times 3.3 + \frac{\text{Sales}}{\text{Total assets}} \times .99 + \frac{\text{MV equity}}{\text{Total liabilities}} \times 0.6$$

EBIT is earnings before interest and taxes. MV Equity is the market value of common equity, which can be determined by multiplying stock price by shares outstanding.

Following extensive testing, it has been shown that companies with Z-scores above 3.0 are unlikely to fail; those with Z-scores below 1.81 are very likely to fail. While the original model was developed for publicly held manufacturing companies, the model has been modified to apply to companies in various industries, emerging companies, and companies not traded in public markets.

Instructions

(a) Use information in the financial statements of a company like **Walgreens** or **Deere & Co.** to compute the Z-score for the past 2 years.

(b) Interpret your result. Where does the company fall in the financial distress range?

(c) The Z-score uses EBIT as one of its elements. Why do you think this income measure is used?

Case 2 Dresser Industries

Dresser Industries provides products and services to oil and natural gas exploration, production, transmission and processing companies. A recent income statement is reproduced below. Dollar amounts are in millions.

Sales	$2,697.0
Service revenues	1,933.9
Share of earnings of unconsolidated affiliates	92.4
Total revenues	4,723.3
Cost of sales	1,722.7
Cost of services	1,799.9
Total costs of sales and services	3,522.6
Gross earnings	1,200.7
Selling, engineering, administrative and general expenses	(919.8)
Special charges	(70.0)
Other income (deductions)	
Interest expense	(47.4)
Interest earned	19.1
Other, net	4.8
Earnings before income taxes and other items below	187.4
Income taxes	(79.4)
Minority interest	(10.3)
Earnings from continuing operations	97.7
Discontinued operations	(35.3)
Earnings before extraordinary items	62.4
Extraordinary items	(6.3)
Net earnings	$ 56.1

Instructions

Assume that 177,636,000 shares of stock were issued and outstanding. Prepare the per share portion of the income statement. Remember to begin with "Earnings from continuing operations."

Case 3 P/E Ratios

One of the more closely watched ratios by investors is the price/earnings or P/E ratio. By dividing price per share by earnings per share, analysts get insight into the value the market attaches to a company's earnings. More specifically, a high P/E ratio (in comparison to companies in the same industry) may suggest the stock is overpriced. Also, there is some evidence that companies with low P/E ratios are underpriced and tend to outperform the market. However, the ratio can be misleading.

P/E ratios are sometimes misleading because the E (earnings) is subject to a number of assumptions and estimates that could result in overstated earnings and a lower P/E. Some analysts conduct "revenue analysis" to evaluate the quality of an earnings number. Revenues are less subject to management estimates and all earnings must begin with revenues. These analysts also compute the price-to-sales ratio (PSR = price per share ÷ sales per share) to assess whether a company is performing well compared to similar companies. If a company has a price-to-sales ratio significantly higher than its competitors, investors may be betting on a stock that has yet to prove itself. [*Source:* Janice Revell, "Beyond P/E," *Fortune* (May 28, 2001), p. 174.]

Instructions

(a) Identify some of the estimates or assumptions that could result in overstated earnings.

(b) Compute the P/E ratio and the PSR for **Tootsie Roll** and **Hershey** for 2009.

(c) Use these data to compare the quality of each company's earnings.

Accounting, Analysis, and Principles

Counting Crows Inc. provided the following information for the year 2012.

Retained earnings, January 1, 2012	$ 600,000
Administrative expenses	240,000
Selling expenses	300,000
Sales revenue	1,900,000
Cash dividends declared	80,000
Cost of goods sold	850,000
Extraordinary gain	95,000
Loss on discontinued operations	75,000
Rent revenue	40,000
Unrealized holding gain on available-for-sale securities	17,000
Income tax applicable to continuing operations	187,000
Income tax benefit applicable to loss on discontinued operations	25,500
Income tax applicable to extraordinary gain	32,300
Income tax applicable to unrealized holding gain on available-for-sale securities	2,000

Accounting

Prepare (a) a single step income statement for 2012, (b) a retained earnings statement for 2012, and (c) a statement of comprehensive income using the second income statement format. Shares outstanding during 2012 were 100,000.

Analysis

Explain how a multiple-step income statement format can provide useful information to a financial statement user.

Principles

In a recent meeting with its auditor, Counting Crows' management argued that the company should be able to prepare a pro forma income statement with some one-time administrative expenses reported similar to extraordinary items and discontinued operations. Is such reporting consistent with the qualitative characteristics of accounting information as discussed in the conceptual framework? Explain.

BRIDGE TO THE PROFESSION

Professional Research: FASB Codification

Your client took accounting a number of years ago and was unaware of comprehensive income reporting. He is not convinced that any accounting standards exist for comprehensive income.

Instructions

If your school has a subscription to the FASB Codification, go to *http://aahq.org/asclogin.cfm* to log in and prepare responses to the following. Provide Codification references for your responses.

(a) What authoritative literature addresses comprehensive income? When was it issued?

(b) Provide the definition of comprehensive income.

(c) Define classifications within net income; give examples.

(d) Define classifications within other comprehensive income; give examples.

(e) What are reclassification adjustments?

Professional Simulation

In this simulation, you are asked to compute various income amounts. Assume a tax rate of 30% and 100,000 shares of common stock outstanding during the year. Prepare responses to all parts.

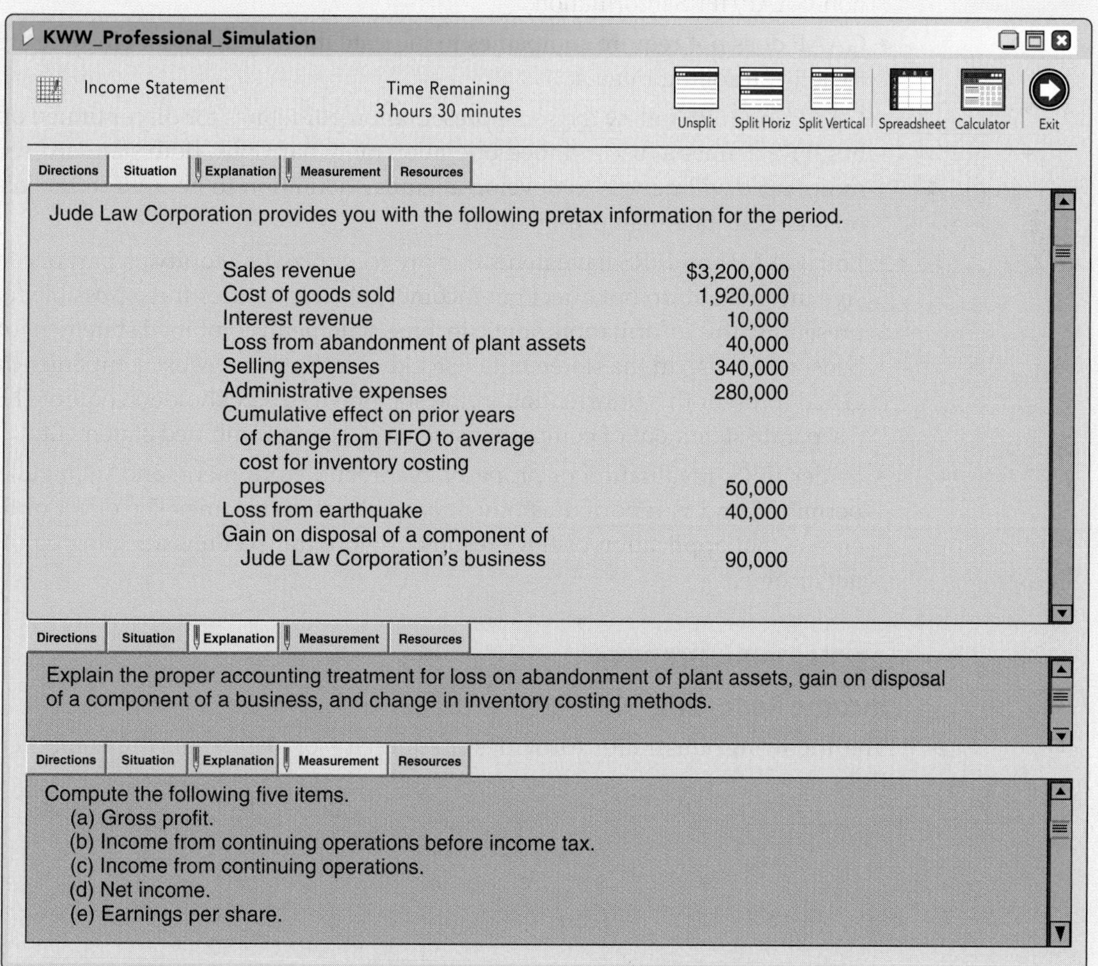

KWW_Professional_Simulation

Income Statement — Time Remaining 3 hours 30 minutes

Directions | Situation | Explanation | Measurement | Resources

Jude Law Corporation provides you with the following pretax information for the period.

Sales revenue	$3,200,000
Cost of goods sold	1,920,000
Interest revenue	10,000
Loss from abandonment of plant assets	40,000
Selling expenses	340,000
Administrative expenses	280,000
Cumulative effect on prior years of change from FIFO to average cost for inventory costing purposes	50,000
Loss from earthquake	40,000
Gain on disposal of a component of Jude Law Corporation's business	90,000

Explain the proper accounting treatment for loss on abandonment of plant assets, gain on disposal of a component of a business, and change in inventory costing methods.

Compute the following five items.
(a) Gross profit.
(b) Income from continuing operations before income tax.
(c) Income from continuing operations.
(d) Net income.
(e) Earnings per share.

IFRS Insights

As in GAAP, the income statement is a required statement for IFRS. In addition, the content and presentation of an IFRS income statement is similar to the one used for GAAP. *IAS 1*, "Presentation of Financial Statements," provides general guidelines for the reporting of income statement information. Subsequently, a number of international standards have been issued that provide additional guidance to issues related to income statement presentation.

RELEVANT FACTS

- Presentation of the income statement under GAAP follows either a single-step or multiple-step format. IFRS does not mention a single-step or multiple-step approach. In addition, under GAAP, companies must report an item as extraordinary if it is unusual in nature and infrequent in occurrence. Extraordinary items are prohibited under IFRS.
- Under IFRS, companies must classify expenses by either nature or function. GAAP does not have that requirement, but the U.S. SEC requires a functional presentation.
- IFRS identifies certain minimum items that should be presented on the income statement. GAAP has no minimum information requirements. However, the SEC rules have more rigorous presentation requirements.
- IFRS does not define key measures like income from operations. SEC regulations define many key measures and provide requirements and limitations on companies reporting non-GAAP/IFRS information.
- GAAP does not require companies to indicate the amount of net income attributable to non-controlling interest.
- GAAP and IFRS follow the same presentation guidelines for discontinued operations, but IFRS defines a discontinued operation more narrowly. Both standard-setters have indicated a willingness to develop a similar definition to be used in the joint project on financial statement presentation.
- Both GAAP and IFRS have items that are recognized in equity as part of comprehensive income but do not affect net income. GAAP provides three possible formats for presenting this information: single income statement, combined statement of comprehensive income, in the statement of stockholders' equity. Most companies that follow GAAP present this information in the statement of stockholders' equity. IFRS allows a separate statement of comprehensive income or a combined statement.
- Under IFRS, revaluation of property, plant, and equipment, and intangible assets is permitted and is reported as other comprehensive income. The effect of this difference is that application of IFRS results in more transactions affecting equity but not net income.

ABOUT THE NUMBERS

Income Reporting

The following illustration provides a summary of the primary income items under IFRS.

Type of Situation	Criteria	Examples	Placement on Income Statement
Sales or service revenues	Revenue arising from the ordinary activities of the company	Sales revenue, service revenue	Sales or revenue section
Cost of goods sold	Expense arising from the cost of inventory sold or services provided	In a merchandising company, Cost of goods sold; in a service company, Cost of services	Deduct from sales (to arrive at gross profit) or service revenue
Selling and administrative expenses	Expenses arising from the ordinary activities of the company	Sales salaries, Freight-out, Rent, Depreciation, Utilities	Deduct from gross profit; if the function-of-expense approach is used, depreciation and amortization expense and labor costs must be disclosed
Other income and expense	Gains and losses and other ancillary revenues and expenses	Gain on sale of long-lived assets, impairment loss on intangible assets, investment revenue, Dividend and interest revenue, Casualty losses	Report as part of income from operations
Financing costs	Separates cost of financing from operating costs	Interest expense	Report in separate section between income from operations and income before income tax
Income tax	Levies imposed by governmental bodies on the basis of income	Taxes computed on income before income tax	Report in separate section between income before income tax and net income
Discontinued operations	A component of a company that has either been disposed of or is classified as held-for-sale	A sale by diversified company of a major division representing its only activities in the electronics industry Food distributor that sells wholesale to supermarkets decides to discontinue the division in a major geographic area	Report gains or losses on discontinued operations net of tax in a separate section between income from continuing operations and net income
Non-controlling interest	Allocation of net income of loss divided between two classes; (1) the majority interest represented by the shareholders who own the controlling interest, and (2) the non-controlling interest (often referred to as the minority interest)	Net profit (loss) attributable to non-controlling shareholders	Report as a separate item below net income or loss as an allocation of the net income or loss (not as an item of income or expense)

As indicated, similar to GAAP, companies report all revenues, gains, expenses, and losses on the income statement and, at the end of the period, close them to Income Summary. They provide useful subtotals on the income statement, such as gross profit, income from operations, income before income tax, and net income. Companies classify discontinued operations of a component of a business as a separate item in the income statement, after "Income from continuing operations." Companies present other income and expense in a separate section, before income from operations. Providing intermediate income figures helps readers evaluate earnings information in assessing the amounts, timing, and uncertainty of future cash flows.

Expense Classifications

Companies are required to present an analysis of expenses classified either by their nature (such as cost of materials used, direct labor incurred, delivery expense, advertising expense, employee benefits, depreciation expense, and amortization expense) or their function (such as cost of goods sold, selling expenses, and administrative expenses).

An advantage of the **nature-of-expense method** is that it is simple to apply because allocations of expense to different functions are not necessary. For manufacturing companies that must allocate costs to the product produced, using a nature-of-expense approach permits companies to report expenses without making arbitrary allocations.

The **function-of-expense method**, however, is often viewed as more relevant because this method identifies the major cost drivers of the company and therefore helps users assess whether these amounts are appropriate for the revenue generated. As indicated, a disadvantage of this method is that the allocation of costs to the varying functions may be arbitrary and therefore the expense classification becomes misleading.

To illustrate these two methods, assume that the accounting firm of Telaris Co. provides audit, tax, and consulting services. It has the following revenues and expenses.

Service revenues	$400,000
Cost of services	
Staff salaries (related to various services performed)	145,000
Supplies expense (related to various services performed)	10,000
Selling expenses	
Advertising costs	20,000
Entertainment expense	3,000
Administrative expenses	
Utilities expense	5,000
Depreciation on building	12,000

If Telaris Co. uses the nature-of-expense approach, its income statement presents each expense item but does not classify the expenses into various subtotals, as follows.

TELARIS CO.
INCOME STATEMENT
FOR THE MONTH OF JANUARY 2012

Service revenues	$400,000
Staff salaries	145,000
Supplies expense	10,000
Advertising costs	20,000
Utilities expense	5,000
Depreciation on building	12,000
Entertainment expense	3,000
Net income	$205,000

If Telaris uses the function-of-expense approach, its income statement is as follows.

TELARIS CO.
INCOME STATEMENT
FOR THE MONTH OF JANUARY 2012

Service revenues	$400,000
Cost of services	155,000
Selling expenses	23,000
Administrative expenses	17,000
Net income	$205,000

The function-of-expense method is generally used in practice although many companies believe both approaches have merit. These companies use the function-of-expense approach on the income statement but provide detail of the expenses (as in the nature-of-expense approach) in the notes to the financial statements. The IASB-FASB discussion paper on financial statement presentation also recommends the dual approach.

Allocation to Non-Controlling Interests

Assume that Boc Hong Company owns more than 50 percent of the ordinary shares of LTM Group. In this case, Boc Hong is called the parent company and LTM Group is referred to as a subsidiary company. Because of Boc Hong's share interest, it has a controlling interest in LTM.

If Boc Hong acquires 100 percent of the shares of LTM, LTM is said to be wholly owned. When Boc Hong's interest in LTM is less than 100 percent, LTM is only partially owned. Under this arrangement, the ownership of LTM is divided into two classes: (1) the majority interest represented by the shareholders who own the controlling interest, and (2) the non-controlling interest (often referred to as the *minority interest*) represented by shareholders who are not part of the controlling group.

If Boc Hong prepares a consolidated income statement that includes LTM, IFRS requires that net income be allocated to the controlling and non-controlling interest. This allocation is reported at the bottom of the income statement after net income. Assuming that Boc Hong's net income of $164,489 is allocated as $120,000 to Boc Hong and $44,489 to the non-controlling interest, the presentation on the income statement is as follows.

Net income	$164,489
Attributable to:	
Shareholders of Boc Hong	$120,000
Non-controlling interest	44,489

These amounts are to be presented as allocations of net income or net loss, not as an item of income or expense.

ON THE HORIZON

The IASB and FASB are working on a project that would rework the structure of financial statements. One stage of this project will address the issue of how to classify various items in the income statement. A main goal of this new approach is to provide information that better represents how businesses are run. The FASB and IASB have issued a proposal to require comprehensive income be reported in a combined statement of comprehensive income. This approach draws attention away from just one number—net income.

IFRS SELF-TEST QUESTIONS

1. Which of the following is *not* reported in an income statement under IFRS?
   (a) Discontinued operations.
   (b) Extraordinary items.
   (c) Cost of goods sold.
   (d) Income tax.

2. Which of the following statements is *correct* regarding income reporting under IFRS?
   (a) IFRS does not permit revaluation of property, plant, and equipment, and intangible assets.
   (b) IFRS provides the same options for reporting comprehensive income as GAAP.
   (c) Companies must classify expenses either by nature or function.
   (d) IFRS provides a definition for all items presented in the income statement.

3. Which statement is *correct* regarding IFRS?
   (a) An advantage of the nature-of-expense method is that it is simple to apply because allocations of expense to different functions are not necessary.
   (b) The function-of-expense approach never requires arbitrary allocations.
   (c) An advantage of the function-of-expense method is that allocation of costs to the varying functions is rarely arbitrary.
   (d) IFRS requires use of the nature-of-expense approach.

4. The non-controlling interest section of the income statement is shown:
   (a) below income from operations.
   (b) above other income and expenses.
   (c) below net income.
   (d) above income tax.

5. Which of the following is *not* an acceptable way of displaying the components of other comprehensive income under IFRS?
   (a) Within the statement of retained earnings.
   (b) Second income statement.
   (c) Combined statement of comprehensive income.
   (d) All of the above are acceptable.

IFRS CONCEPTS AND APPLICATION

IFRS4-1 Explain the difference between the "nature-of-expense" and "function-of-expense" classifications.

IFRS4-2 Discuss the appropriate treatment in the income statement for the following items:
   (a) Loss on discontinued operations.
   (b) Non-controlling interest allocation.

IFRS4-3 Bradshaw Company experienced a loss that was deemed to be both unusual in nature and infrequent in occurrence. How should Bradshaw report this item in accordance with IFRS?

IFRS4-4 Presented below is information related to Viel Company at December 31, 2012, the end of its first year of operations.

Sales revenue	$310,000
Cost of goods sold	140,000
Selling and administrative expenses	50,000
Gain on sale of plant assets	30,000
Unrealized gain on non-trading equity securities	10,000
Interest expense	6,000
Loss on discontinued operations	12,000
Allocation to non-controlling interest	40,000
Dividends declared and paid	5,000

Instructions

Compute the following: (a) income from operations, (b) net income, (c) net income attributable to Viel Company controlling shareholders, (d) comprehensive income, and (e) retained earnings balance at December 31, 2012. (Ignore income taxes.)

IFRS4-5 On the next page is the income statement for a British company, **Avon Rubber plc**. Avon prepares its financial statements in accordance with IFRS.

Avon Rubber plc
Consolidated Income Statement for the Year Ended 30 September

	2009	2008
Continuing operations		
Revenue	91,688	54,606
Cost of sales	68,148	44,476
Gross profit	23,540	10,130
Distribution costs	4,676	3,445
Administrative expenses	16,881	20,496
Other operating income	120	1,225
Operating profit/(loss) from continuing operations	2,103	12,586
Operating profit/(loss) is analysed as:		
Before depreciation, amortization and exceptional items	8,595	686
Depreciation and amortization	3,957	3,419
Operating profit/(loss) before exceptional items	4,638	4,105
Exceptional operating items	2,535	8,481
Finance income	33	27
Finance costs	1,539	1,015
Other finance income	394	1,183
Profit/(loss) before taxation	991	(12,391)
Taxation	1,699	1,259
Profit/(loss) for the year from continuing operations	(708)	(11,132)
Discontinued operations		
Profit/(loss) for the year from discontinued operations	566	(8,337)
Loss for the year	(142)	(19,469)
Earnings/(loss) per share		
Basic	(0.6)p	(68.4)p
Diluted	(0.6)p	(68.4)p
Earnings/(loss) per share from continuing operations		
Basic	(2.6)p	(39.1)p
Diluted	(2.6)p	(39.1)p

Instructions

(a) Review the Avon Rubber income statement and identify at least three differences between the IFRS income statement and an income statement of a U.S. company as presented in the chapter.

(b) Identify any irregular items reported by Avon Rubber. Is the reporting of these irregular items in Avon's income statement similar to reporting of these items in U.S. companies' income statements? Explain.

Professional Research

IFRS4-6 Your client took accounting a number of years ago and was unaware of comprehensive income reporting. He is not convinced that any accounting standards exist for comprehensive income.

Instructions

Access the IFRS authoritative literature at the IASB website (*http://eifrs.iasb.org/*). When you have accessed the documents, you can use the search tool in your Internet browser to respond to the following questions. (Provide paragraph citations.)

(a) What IFRS addresses reporting in the statement of comprehensive income? When was it issued?

(b) Provide the definition of total comprehensive income.

(c) Explain the rationale for presenting additional line items, headings, and subtotals in the statement of comprehensive income.
(d) What items of income or expense may be presented either in the statement of comprehensive income or in the notes?

International Financial Reporting Problem: *Marks and Spencer plc*

IFRS4-7 The financial statements of Marks and Spencer plc (M&S) are available at the book's companion website or can be accessed at *http://corporate.marksandspencer.com/documents/publications/2010/Annual_Report_2010.*

Instructions

Refer to M&S's financial statements and the accompanying notes to answer the following questions.

(a) What type of income statement format does M&S use? Indicate why this format might be used to present income statement information.
(b) What are M&S's primary revenue sources?
(c) Compute M&S's gross profit for each of the years 2009 and 2010. Explain why gross profit increased in 2010.
(d) Why does M&S make a distinction between operating and non-operating profit?
(e) Does M&S report any non-GAAP measures? Explain.

ANSWERS TO IFRS SELF-TEST QUESTIONS

1. b **2.** c **3.** a **4.** c **5.** a

Remember to check the book's companion website to find additional resources for this chapter.

CHAPTER 5

Balance Sheet and Statement of Cash Flows

LEARNING OBJECTIVES

After studying this chapter, you should be able to:

1. Explain the uses and limitations of a balance sheet.
2. Identify the major classifications of the balance sheet.
3. Prepare a classified balance sheet using the report and account formats.
4. Indicate the purpose of the statement of cash flows.
5. Identify the content of the statement of cash flows.
6. Prepare a basic statement of cash flows.
7. Understand the usefulness of the statement of cash flows.
8. Determine which balance sheet information requires supplemental disclosure.
9. Describe the major disclosure techniques for the balance sheet.

Hey, It Doesn't Balance!

A good accounting student knows by now that Total Assets = Total Liabilities + Total Equity. From this equation, we can also determine net assets, which are determined as follows: Total Assets − Total Liabilities = Net Assets. O.K., this is simple so far. But let's look at the new discussion paper by the FASB/IASB on how the statement of financial position (the balance sheet) should be structured.

The statement of financial position is divided into five major parts, with many assets and liabilities netted against one another. Here is the general framework for the new statement of financial position:

BUSINESS
  Operating assets and liabilities
  Investing assets and liabilities
FINANCING
  Financing assets
  Financing liabilities
INCOME TAXES
DISCONTINUED OPERATIONS
EQUITY

The statement does look a bit different than the traditional balance sheet. Let's put some numbers to the statement and see how it works. (See the example on the facing page.)

Well, it does balance—in that net assets equal equity—but isn't it important to know total assets and total liabilities? As some have observed, the statement of financial position will not balance the way we expect it to. That is, assets won't equal liabilities and equity. This is because the assets and liabilities are grouped into the business, financing, discontinued operations, and income taxes categories. This new model raises a number of questions, such as:

- Does separating "business activities from financing activities" provide information that is more decision-useful?
- Does information on income taxes and discontinued operations merit separate categories?

The FASB and IASB are working to get answers to these and other questions about this proposed model. One thing is for sure—adoption of the new financial statements will be a dramatic change but hopefully one for the better.

IFRS IN THIS CHAPTER

- See the **International Perspectives** on pages 231 and 242.
- Read the **IFRS Insights** on pages 301–307 for a discussion of:
  - Classification in the statement of financial position
  - Equity
  - Revaluation equity
  - Fair presentation

STATEMENT OF FINANCIAL POSITION

BUSINESS		
Operating		
Inventories	$ 400,000	
Receivables	200,000	
Total short-term assets		$ 600,000
Property (net)	500,000	
Intangible assets	50,000	
Total long-term assets		550,000
Accounts payable	30,000	
Wages payable	40,000	
Total short-term liabilities		(70,000)
Lease liability	10,000	
Other long-term debt	35,000	
Total long-term liabilities		(45,000)
Net operating assets		**1,035,000**
Investing		
Trading securities	45,000	
Other securities	5,000	
Total investing assets		50,000
TOTAL NET BUSINESS ASSETS		**1,085,000**
FINANCING		
Financing assets		
Cash	30,000	
Total financing assets		30,000
Financing liabilities		
Short- and long-term borrowing	130,000	
Total financing liabilities		(130,000)
NET FINANCING LIABILITIES		**(100,000)**
DISCONTINUED OPERATIONS		
Assets held for sale		420,000
INCOME TAXES		
Deferred income taxes		70,000
NET ASSETS		**$1,475,000**
EQUITY		
Share capital—ordinary	$1,000,000	
Retained earnings	475,000	
TOTAL EQUITY		**$1,475,000**

Sources: Marie Leone and Tim Reason, "How Extreme Is the Makeover?" *CFO Magazine* (March 1, 2009); and *Preliminary Views on Financial Statement Presentation*, FASB/IASB Discussion Paper (October 2008).

PREVIEW OF CHAPTER 5

As the opening story indicates, the FASB and IASB are working to improve the presentation of financial information on the balance sheet, as well as other financial statements. In this chapter, we examine the many different types of assets, liabilities, and equity items that affect the balance sheet and the statement of cash flows. The content and organization of the chapter are as follows.

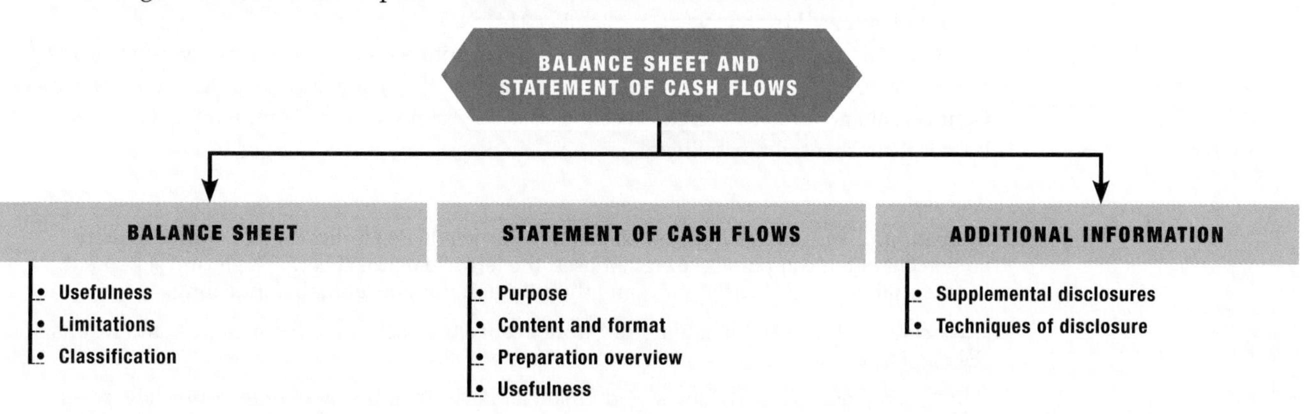

SECTION 1 • BALANCE SHEET

LEARNING OBJECTIVE 1
Explain the uses and limitations of a balance sheet.

The **balance sheet**, sometimes referred to as the **statement of financial position**, reports the assets, liabilities, and stockholders' equity of a business enterprise at a specific date. This financial statement provides information about the nature and amounts of investments in enterprise resources, obligations to creditors, and the owners' equity in net resources.[1] It therefore helps in predicting the amounts, timing, and uncertainty of future cash flows.

USEFULNESS OF THE BALANCE SHEET

By providing information on assets, liabilities, and stockholders' equity, the balance sheet provides a basis for computing rates of return and evaluating the capital structure of the enterprise. Analysts also use information in the balance sheet to assess a company's risk[2] and future cash flows. In this regard, analysts use the balance sheet to assess a company's liquidity, solvency, and financial flexibility.

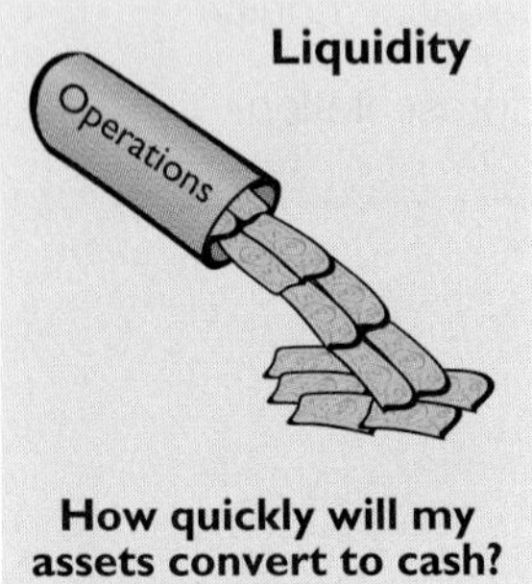

Liquidity describes "the amount of time that is expected to elapse until an asset is realized or otherwise converted into cash or until a liability has to be paid."[3] Creditors are interested in short-term liquidity ratios, such as the ratio of cash (or near cash) to short-term liabilities. These ratios indicate whether a company, like **Amazon**, will have the resources to pay its current and maturing obligations. Similarly, stockholders assess liquidity to evaluate the possibility of future cash dividends or the buyback of shares. In general, the greater Amazon's liquidity, the lower its risk of failure.

GROUNDED

What do the numbers mean?

The terrorist attacks of September 11, 2001, showed how vulnerable the major airlines are to falling demand for their services. Since that infamous date, major airlines have reduced capacity and slashed jobs to avoid bankruptcy. **United Airlines**, **Northwest Airlines**, **US Airways**, and several smaller competitors filed for bankruptcy in the wake of 9/11.

Delta Airlines made the following statements in its annual report issued shortly after 9/11:

> "If we are unsuccessful in further reducing our operating costs . . . we will need to restructure our costs under Chapter 11 of the U.S. Bankruptcy Code. . . . We have substantial liquidity needs and there is no assurance that we will be able to obtain the necessary financing to meet those needs on acceptable terms, if at all."

The financial distress related to the airline industry was not an insider's secret. The airlines' balance sheets clearly revealed their financial inflexibility and low liquidity even before September 11. For example, major airlines such as **Braniff**, **Continental**, **Eastern**, **Midway**, and **America West** declared bankruptcy before September 11.

These financial flexibility challenges have continued, exacerbated by ever-increasing fuel prices and labor costs. Not surprisingly, several of the major airlines (Delta and Northwest, Continental and United) merged recently as a way to build some competitive synergies and to bolster their financial flexibility.

[1]*Accounting Trends and Techniques—2010* (New York: AICPA) indicates that approximately 95 percent of the companies surveyed used the term "balance sheet." The term "statement of financial position" is used infrequently, although it is conceptually appealing.

[2]Risk conveys the unpredictability of future events, transactions, circumstances, and results of the company.

[3]"Reporting Income, Cash Flows, and Financial Position of Business Enterprises," *Proposed Statement of Financial Accounting Concepts* (Stamford, Conn.: FASB, 1981), par. 29.

Solvency refers to the ability of a company to pay its debts as they mature. For example, when a company carries a high level of long-term debt relative to assets, it has lower solvency than a similar company with a low level of long-term debt. Companies with higher debt are relatively more risky because they will need more of their assets to meet their fixed obligations (interest and principal payments).

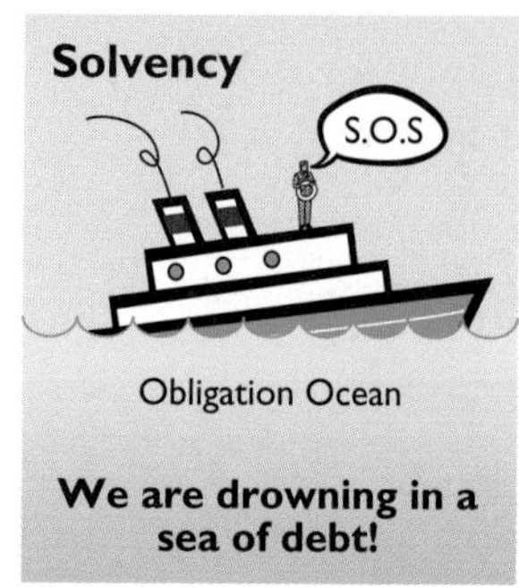

Liquidity and solvency affect a company's **financial flexibility**, which measures the "ability of an enterprise to take effective actions to alter the amounts and timing of cash flows so it can respond to unexpected needs and opportunities."[4] For example, a company may become so loaded with debt—so financially inflexible—that it has little or no sources of cash to finance expansion or to pay off maturing debt. A company with a high degree of financial flexibility is better able to survive bad times, to recover from unexpected setbacks, and to take advantage of profitable and unexpected investment opportunities. Generally, the greater an enterprise's financial flexibility, the lower its risk of failure.

LIMITATIONS OF THE BALANCE SHEET

Some of the major limitations of the balance sheet are:

1. Most assets and liabilities are reported at **historical cost**. As a result, the information provided in the balance sheet is often criticized for not reporting a more relevant fair value. For example, **Georgia-Pacific** owns timber and other assets that may appreciate in value after purchase. Yet, Georgia-Pacific reports any increase only if and when it sells the assets.
2. Companies use **judgments and estimates** to determine many of the items reported in the balance sheet. For example, in its balance sheet, **Dell** estimates the amount of receivables that it will collect, the useful life of its warehouses, and the number of computers that will be returned under warranty.
3. The balance sheet necessarily **omits many items that are of financial value** but that a company cannot record objectively. For example, the knowledge and skill of **Intel** employees in developing new computer chips are arguably the company's most significant assets. However, because Intel cannot reliably measure the value of its employees and other intangible assets (such as customer base, research superiority, and reputation), it does not recognize these items in the balance sheet. Similarly, many liabilities are reported in an "off-balance-sheet" manner, if at all.

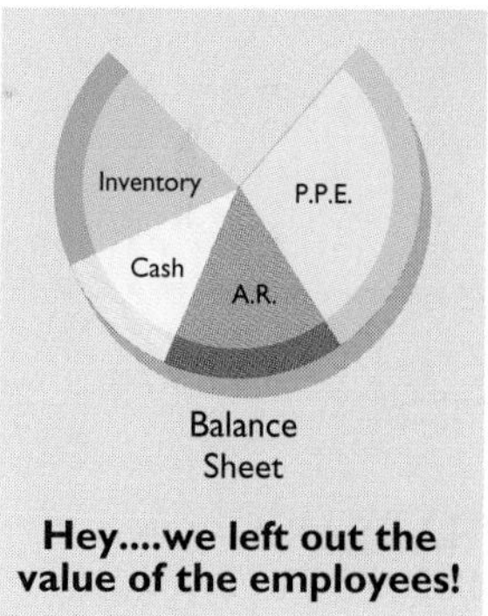

The bankruptcy of **Enron**, the seventh-largest U.S. company at the time, highlights the omission of important items in the balance sheet. In Enron's case, it failed to disclose certain off-balance-sheet financing obligations in its main financial statements.[5]

CLASSIFICATION IN THE BALANCE SHEET

> **2 LEARNING OBJECTIVE**
> Identify the major classifications of the balance sheet.

Balance sheet accounts are **classified**. That is, balance sheets group together similar items to arrive at significant subtotals. Furthermore, the material is arranged so that important relationships are shown.

The FASB has often noted that the parts and subsections of financial statements can be more informative than the whole. Therefore, the FASB discourages

[4]"Reporting Income, Cash Flows, and Financial Position of Business Enterprises," *Proposed Statement of Financial Accounting Concepts* (Stamford, Conn.: FASB, 1981), par. 25.

[5]We discuss several of these omitted items (such as leases and other off-balance-sheet arrangements) in later chapters. See Wayne Upton, Jr., Special Report: *Business and Financial Reporting, Challenges from the New Economy* (Norwalk, Conn.: FASB, 2001).

the reporting of summary accounts alone (total assets, net assets, total liabilities, etc.). Instead, companies should report and classify individual items in sufficient detail to permit users to assess the amounts, timing, and uncertainty of future cash flows. Such classification also makes it easier for users to evaluate the company's liquidity and financial flexibility, profitability, and risk.

To classify items in financial statements, companies group those items with similar characteristics and separate items with different characteristics.[6] For example, companies should report separately:

1. Assets that differ in their **type or expected function** in the company's central operations or other activities. For example, IBM reports merchandise inventories separately from property, plant, and equipment.
2. Assets and liabilities with **different implications for the company's financial flexibility**. For example, a company that uses assets in its operations, like Walgreens, should report those assets separately from assets held for investment and assets subject to restrictions, such as leased equipment.
3. Assets and liabilities with **different general liquidity characteristics**. For example, Boeing Company reports cash separately from inventories.

The three general classes of items included in the balance sheet are assets, liabilities, and equity. We defined them in Chapter 2 as follows.

ELEMENTS OF THE BALANCE SHEET

1. ASSETS. Probable future economic benefits obtained or controlled by a particular entity as a result of past transactions or events.
2. LIABILITIES. Probable future sacrifices of economic benefits arising from present obligations of a particular entity to transfer assets or provide services to other entities in the future as a result of past transactions or events.
3. EQUITY. Residual interest in the assets of an entity that remains after deducting its liabilities. In a business enterprise, the equity is the ownership interest.[7]

Companies then further divide these items into several subclassifications. Illustration 5-1 indicates the general format of balance sheet presentation.

ILLUSTRATION 5-1
Balance Sheet Classifications

Assets	Liabilities and Owners' Equity
Current assets	Current liabilities
Long-term investments	Long-term debt
Property, plant, and equipment	Owners' equity
Intangible assets	Capital stock
Other assets	Additional paid-in capital
	Retained earnings

A company may classify the balance sheet in some other manner, but in practice you usually see little departure from these major subdivisions. A proprietorship or partnership does present the classifications within the owners' equity section a little differently, as we will show later in the chapter.

[6]"Reporting Income, Cash Flows, and Financial Positions of Business Enterprises," *Proposed Statement of Financial Accounting Concepts* (Stamford, Conn.: FASB, 1981), par. 51.

[7]"Elements of Financial Statements of Business Enterprises," *Statement of Financial Accounting Concepts No. 6* (Stamford, Conn.: FASB, 1985), paras. 25, 35, and 49.

Current Assets

Current assets **are cash and other assets a company expects to convert into cash, sell, or consume either in one year or in the operating cycle, whichever is longer.** The operating cycle is the average time between when a company acquires materials and supplies and when it receives cash for sales of the product (for which it acquired the materials and supplies). The cycle operates from cash through inventory, production, receivables, and back to cash. When several operating cycles occur within one year (which is generally the case for service companies), a company uses the one-year period. If the operating cycle is more than one year, a company uses the longer period.

Current assets are presented in the balance sheet in order of liquidity. The five major items found in the current assets section, and their bases of valuation, are shown in Illustration 5-2.

ILLUSTRATION 5-2
Current Assets and Basis of Valuation

Item	Basis of Valuation
Cash and cash equivalents	Fair value
Short-term investments	Generally, fair value
Receivables	Estimated amount collectible
Inventories	Lower-of-cost-or-market
Prepaid expenses	Cost

A company does not report these five items as current assets if it does not expect to realize them in one year or in the operating cycle, whichever is longer. For example, a company excludes from the current assets section cash restricted for purposes other than payment of current obligations or for use in current operations. **Generally, if a company expects to convert an asset into cash or to use it to pay a current liability within a year or the operating cycle, whichever is longer, it classifies the asset as current.**

This rule, however, is subject to interpretation. A company classifies an investment in common stock as either a current asset or a noncurrent asset depending on management's intent. When it has small holdings of common stocks or bonds that it will hold long-term, it should not classify them as current.

Although a current asset is well defined, certain theoretical problems also develop. For example, how is including prepaid expenses in the current assets section justified? The rationale is that if a company did not pay these items in advance, it would instead need to use other current assets during the operating cycle. If we follow this logic to its ultimate conclusion, however, any asset previously purchased saves the use of current assets during the operating cycle and would be considered current.

Another problem occurs in the current-asset definition when a company consumes plant assets during the operating cycle. Conceptually, it seems that a company should place in the current assets section an amount equal to the current depreciation charge on the plant assets, because it will consume them in the next operating cycle. However, this conceptual problem is ignored. This example illustrates that the formal distinction made between some current and noncurrent assets is somewhat arbitrary.

Cash

Cash is generally considered to consist of currency and demand deposits (monies available on demand at a financial institution). **Cash equivalents** are short-term highly liquid investments that will mature within three months or less. Most companies use the caption "Cash and cash equivalents," and they indicate that this amount approximates fair value.

A company must disclose any restrictions or commitments related to the availability of cash. As an example, see the excerpt from the annual report of Alterra Healthcare Corp. in Illustration 5-3 on the next page.

ILLUSTRATION 5-3
Balance Sheet Presentation of Restricted Cash

Alterra Healthcare Corp.

Current assets	
Cash	$18,728,000
Restricted cash and investments (Note 7)	7,191,000

Note 7: Restricted Cash and Investments. Restricted cash and investments consist of certificates of deposit restricted as collateral for lease arrangements and debt service with interest rates ranging from 4.0% to 5.5%.

Alterra Healthcare restricted cash to meet an obligation due currently. Therefore, Alterra included this restricted cash under current assets.

If a company restricts cash for purposes other than current obligations, it excludes the cash from current assets. Illustration 5-4 shows an example of this, from the annual report of **Owens Corning, Inc.**

ILLUSTRATION 5-4
Balance Sheet Presentation of Current and Noncurrent Restricted Cash

Owens Corning, Inc.
(in millions)

Current assets	
Cash and cash equivalents	$ 70
Restricted securities—Fibreboard—current portion (Note 23)	900
Other assets	
Restricted securities—Fibreboard (Note 23)	938

Note 23 (in part). The Insurance Settlement funds are held in and invested by the Fibreboard Settlement Trust (the "Trust") and are available to satisfy Fibreboard's pending and future asbestos related liabilities. . . . The assets of the Trust are comprised of cash and marketable securities (collectively, the "Trust Assets") and are reflected on Owens Corning's consolidated balance sheet as restricted assets. These assets are reflected as current assets or other assets, with each category denoted "Restricted securities—Fibreboard."

Short-Term Investments

Companies group investments in debt and equity securities into three separate portfolios for valuation and reporting purposes:

Held-to-maturity: Debt securities that a company has the positive intent and ability to hold to maturity.

Trading: Debt and equity securities bought and held primarily for sale in the near term to generate income on short-term price differences.

Available-for-sale: Debt and equity securities not classified as held-to-maturity or trading securities.

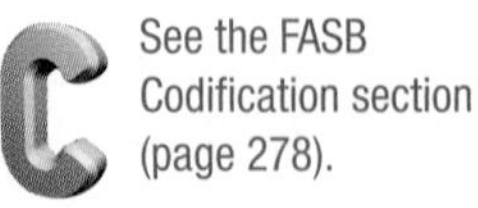

A company should report trading securities (whether debt or equity) as current assets. It classifies individual held-to-maturity and available-for-sale securities as current or noncurrent depending on the circumstances. It should report held-to-maturity securities at amortized cost. All trading and available-for-sale securities are reported at fair value. [1][8]

For example, see Illustration 5-5 on the next page, which is an excerpt from the annual report of **Intuit Inc.** with respect to its available-for-sale investments.

[8]Under the fair value option, companies may elect to use fair value as the measurement basis for selected financial assets and liabilities. For these companies, some of their financial assets (and liabilities) may be recorded at historical cost, while others are recorded at fair value. [2]

ILLUSTRATION 5-5
Balance Sheet Presentation of Investments in Securities

Intuit Inc.
(in thousands)

Assets	
Cash and cash equivalents	$ 170,043
Short-term investments (Note 2)	1,036,758

Note 2 (in part). The following schedule summarizes the estimated fair value of our short-term investments (all available-for-sale):

Corporate notes	$ 50,471
Municipal bonds	931,374
U.S. government securities	54,913

Receivables

A company should clearly identify any anticipated loss due to uncollectibles, the amount and nature of any nontrade receivables, and any receivables used as collateral. Major categories of receivables should be shown in the balance sheet or the related notes. For receivables arising from unusual transactions (such as sale of property, or a loan to affiliates or employees), companies should separately classify these as long-term, unless collection is expected within one year. **Mack Trucks, Inc.** reported its receivables as shown in Illustration 5-6.

ILLUSTRATION 5-6
Balance Sheet Presentation of Receivables

Mack Trucks, Inc.

Current assets	
Trade receivables	
Accounts receivable	$102,212,000
Affiliated companies	1,157,000
Installment notes and contracts	625,000
Total	103,994,000
Less: Allowance for uncollectible accounts	8,194,000
Trade receivables—net	95,800,000
Receivables from unconsolidated financial subsidiaries	22,106,000

Inventories

To present inventories properly, a company discloses the basis of valuation (e.g., lower-of-cost-or-market) and the cost flow assumption used (e.g., FIFO or LIFO). A manufacturing concern (like **Abbott Laboratories**, shown in Illustration 5-7) also indicates the stage of completion of the inventories.

ILLUSTRATION 5-7
Balance Sheet Presentation of Inventories, Showing Stage of Completion

Abbott Laboratories
(in thousands)

Current assets	
Inventories	
Finished products	$ 772,478
Work in process	338,818
Materials	384,148
Total inventories	1,495,444

Note 1 (in part): Inventories. Inventories are stated at the lower-of-cost- (first-in, first-out basis) or-market.

Weyerhaeuser Company, a forestry company and lumber manufacturer with several finished-goods product lines, reported its inventory as shown in Illustration 5-8.

ILLUSTRATION 5-8
Balance Sheet Presentation of Inventories, Showing Product Lines

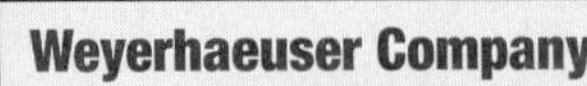

Weyerhaeuser Company

Current assets	
Inventories—at FIFO lower of cost or market	
Logs and chips	$ 68,471,000
Lumber, plywood and panels	86,741,000
Pulp, newsprint and paper	47,377,000
Containerboard, paperboard, containers and cartons	59,682,000
Other products	161,717,000
Total product inventories	423,988,000
Materials and supplies	175,540,000

Prepaid Expenses

A company includes prepaid expenses in current assets if it will receive benefits (usually services) within one year or the operating cycle, whichever is longer.[9] As we discussed earlier, these items are current assets because if they had not already been paid, they would require the use of cash during the next year or the operating cycle. A company reports prepaid expenses at the amount of the unexpired or unconsumed cost.

A common example is the prepayment for an insurance policy. A company classifies it as a prepaid expense because the payment precedes the receipt of the benefit of coverage. Other common prepaid expenses include prepaid rent, advertising, taxes, and office or operating supplies. **Hasbro, Inc.**, for example, listed its prepaid expenses in current assets as shown in Illustration 5-9.

ILLUSTRATION 5-9
Balance Sheet Presentation of Prepaid Expenses

Hasbro, Inc.
(in thousands of dollars)

Current assets	
Cash and cash equivalents	$ 715,400
Accounts receivable, less allowances of $27,700	556,287
Inventories	203,337
Prepaid expenses and other current assets	243,291
Total current assets	$1,718,315

Noncurrent Assets

Noncurrent assets are those not meeting the definition of current assets. They include a variety of items, as we discuss in the following sections.

Long-Term Investments

Long-term investments, often referred to simply as investments, normally consist of one of four types:

1. Investments in securities, such as bonds, common stock, or long-term notes.
2. Investments in tangible fixed assets not currently used in operations, such as land held for speculation.

[9] *Accounting Trends and Techniques—2010* (New York: AICPA) in its survey of 500 annual reports identified 330 companies that reported prepaid expenses.

3. Investments set aside in special funds such as a sinking fund, pension fund, or plant expansion fund. This includes the cash surrender value of life insurance.
4. Investments in nonconsolidated subsidiaries or affiliated companies.

Companies expect to hold long-term investments for many years. They usually present them on the balance sheet just below "Current assets," in a separate section called "Investments." Realize that many securities classified as long-term investments are, in fact, readily marketable. But a company does not include them as current assets unless it **intends to convert them to cash in the short-term**—that is, within a year or in the operating cycle, whichever is longer. As indicated earlier, securities classified as available-for-sale are reported at fair value, and held-to-maturity securities are reported at amortized cost.

Motorola, Inc. reported its investments section, located between "Property, plant, and equipment" and "Other assets," as shown in Illustration 5-10.

ILLUSTRATION 5-10
Balance Sheet Presentation of Long-Term Investments

Motorola, Inc.
(in millions)

Investments	
Equity investments	$ 872
Other investments	2,567
Fair value adjustment to available-for-sale securities	2,487
Total	$5,926

Property, Plant, and Equipment

Property, plant, and equipment are tangible long-lived assets used in the regular operations of the business. These assets consist of physical property such as land, buildings, machinery, furniture, tools, and wasting resources (timberland, minerals). With the exception of land, a company either depreciates (e.g., buildings) or depletes (e.g., timberlands or oil reserves) these assets.

Mattel, Inc. presented its property, plant, and equipment in its balance sheet as shown in Illustration 5-11.

ILLUSTRATION 5-11
Balance Sheet Presentation of Property, Plant, and Equipment

Mattel, Inc.

Property, plant, and equipment	
Land	$ 32,793,000
Buildings	257,430,000
Machinery and equipment	564,244,000
Capitalized leases	23,271,000
Leasehold improvements	74,988,000
	952,726,000
Less: Accumulated depreciation	472,986,000
	479,740,000
Tools, dies and molds, net	168,092,000
Property, plant, and equipment, net	647,832,000

A company discloses the basis it uses to value property, plant, and equipment; any liens against the properties; and accumulated depreciation—usually in the notes to the financial statements.

Intangible Assets

Intangible assets lack physical substance and are not financial instruments (see definition on page 238). They include patents, copyrights, franchises, goodwill, trademarks, trade names, and customer lists. A company writes off (amortizes) limited-life intangible assets over their useful lives. It periodically assesses indefinite-life intangibles (such as goodwill) for impairment. Intangibles can represent significant economic resources, yet financial analysts often ignore them, because valuation is difficult.

PepsiCo, Inc. reported intangible assets in its balance sheet as shown in Illustration 5-12.

ILLUSTRATION 5-12
Balance Sheet Presentation of Intangible Assets

PepsiCo, Inc.
(in millions)

Intangible assets	
Goodwill	$3,374
Trademarks	1,320
Other identifiable intangibles	147
Total intangibles	$4,841

Other Assets

The items included in the section "Other assets" vary widely in practice. Some include items such as long-term prepaid expenses, prepaid pension cost, and noncurrent receivables. Other items that might be included are assets in special funds, deferred income taxes, property held for sale, and restricted cash or securities. A company should limit this section to include only unusual items sufficiently different from assets included in specific categories.

Liabilities

Similar to assets, companies classify liabilities as current or long-term.

Current Liabilities

Current liabilities are the obligations that a company reasonably expects to liquidate either through the use of current assets or the creation of other current liabilities. This concept includes:

1. Payables resulting from the acquisition of goods and services: accounts payable, wages payable, taxes payable, and so on.
2. Collections received in advance for the delivery of goods or performance of services, such as unearned rent revenue or unearned subscriptions revenue.
3. Other liabilities whose liquidation will take place within the operating cycle, such as the portion of long-term bonds to be paid in the current period or short-term obligations arising from the purchase of equipment.

At times, a liability that is payable within the next year is not included in the current liabilities section. This occurs either when the company expects to refinance the debt through another long-term issue [3] or to retire the debt out of noncurrent assets. This approach is used because liquidation does not result from the use of current assets or the creation of other current liabilities.

Companies do not report current liabilities in any consistent order. In general, though, companies most commonly list notes payable, accounts payable, or short-term debt as the first item. Income taxes payable, current maturities of long-term debt, or other current liabilities are commonly listed last. For example, see **Halliburton Company**'s current liabilities section in Illustration 5-13 on the next page.

ILLUSTRATION 5-13
Balance Sheet Presentation of Current Liabilities

Halliburton Company
(in millions)

Current liabilities	
Short-term notes payable	$1,570
Accounts payable	782
Accrued employee compensation and benefits	267
Unearned revenues	386
Income taxes payable	113
Accrued special charges	6
Current maturities of long-term debt	8
Other current liabilities	694
Total current liabilities	3,826

Current liabilities include such items as trade and nontrade notes and accounts payable, advances received from customers, and current maturities of long-term debt. If the amounts are material, companies classify income taxes and other accrued items separately. A company should fully describe in the notes any information about a secured liability—for example, stock held as collateral on notes payable—to identify the assets providing the security.

The excess of total current assets over total current liabilities is referred to as **working capital** (or sometimes **net working capital**). Working capital represents the net amount of a company's relatively liquid resources. That is, it is the liquidity buffer available to meet the financial demands of the operating cycle.

Companies seldom disclose on the balance sheet an amount for working capital. But bankers and other creditors compute it as an indicator of the short-run liquidity of a company. To determine the actual liquidity and availability of working capital to meet current obligations, however, requires analysis of the composition of the current assets and their nearness to cash.

"SHOW ME THE ASSETS!"

What do the numbers mean?

Before the dot-com bubble burst, concerns about liquidity and solvency led creditors of many dot-com companies to demand more assurances that these companies could pay their bills when due. A key indicator for creditors is the amount of working capital. For example, when a report predicted that **Amazon.com**'s working capital would turn negative, the company's vendors began to explore steps that would ensure that Amazon would pay them.

Some vendors demanded that their dot-com customers sign notes stating that the goods shipped to them would serve as collateral for the transaction. Other vendors began shipping goods on consignment—an arrangement whereby the vendor retains ownership of the goods until a third party buys and pays for them.

Another recent bubble in the real estate market created a working capital and liquidity crisis for no less a revered financial institution than **Bear Stearns**. What happened? Bear Stearns was one of the biggest investors in mortgage-backed securities. But when the housing market cooled off and the value of the collateral backing Bear Stearns's mortgage securities dropped dramatically, the market began to question Bear Stearns's ability to meet its obligations. The result: The Federal Reserve stepped in to avert a collapse of the company, backing a bailout plan that guaranteed *$30 billion* of Bear Stearns's investments. This paved the way for a buy-out by **JPMorgan Chase** at $2 per share (later amended to $10 a share)—quite a bargain since Bear Stearns had been trading above $80 a share just a month earlier.

Source: Robin Sidel, Greg Ip, Michael M. Phillips, and Kate Kelly, "The Week That Shook Wall Street: Inside the Demise of Bear Stearns," *Wall Street Journal* (March 18, 2008), p. A1.

Long-Term Liabilities

Long-term liabilities are obligations that a company does not reasonably expect to liquidate within the normal operating cycle. Instead, it expects to pay them at some date beyond that time. The most common examples are bonds payable, notes payable, some deferred income tax amounts, lease obligations, and pension obligations. **Companies classify long-term liabilities that mature within the current operating cycle as current liabilities if payment of the obligation requires the use of current assets.**

Generally, long-term liabilities are of three types:

1. Obligations arising from specific financing situations, such as the issuance of bonds, long-term lease obligations, and long-term notes payable.
2. Obligations arising from the ordinary operations of the company, such as pension obligations and deferred income tax liabilities.
3. Obligations that depend on the occurrence or non-occurrence of one or more future events to confirm the amount payable, or the payee, or the date payable, such as service or product warranties and other contingencies.

Companies generally provide a great deal of supplementary disclosure for long-term liabilities, because most long-term debt is subject to various covenants and restrictions for the protection of lenders.[10]

It is desirable to report any premium or discount separately as an addition to or subtraction from the bonds payable. Companies frequently describe the terms of all long-term liability agreements (including maturity date or dates, rates of interest, nature of obligation, and any security pledged to support the debt) in notes to the financial statements. Illustration 5-14 provides an example of this, taken from an excerpt from The Great Atlantic & Pacific Tea Company's financials.

ILLUSTRATION 5-14
Balance Sheet Presentation of Long-Term Debt

The Great Atlantic & Pacific Tea Company, Inc.

Total current liabilities	$978,109,000
Long-term debt (See note)	254,312,000
Obligations under capital leases	252,618,000
Deferred income taxes	57,167,000
Other non-current liabilities	127,321,000

Note: Indebtedness. Debt consists of:

9.5% senior notes, due in annual installments of $10,000,000	$ 40,000,000
Mortgages and other notes due through 2011 (average interest rate of 9.9%)	107,604,000
Bank borrowings at 9.7%	67,225,000
Commercial paper at 9.4%	100,102,000
	314,931,000
Less: Current portion	(60,619,000)
Total long-term debt	$254,312,000

[10]Companies usually explain the pertinent rights and privileges of the various securities (both debt and equity) outstanding in the notes to the financial statements. Examples of information that companies should disclose are dividend and liquidation preferences, participation rights, call prices and dates, conversion or exercise prices or rates and pertinent dates, sinking fund requirements, unusual voting rights, and significant terms of contracts to issue additional shares. [4]

Owners' Equity

The owners' equity (**stockholders' equity**) section is one of the most difficult sections to prepare and understand. This is due to the complexity of capital stock agreements and the various restrictions on stockholders' equity imposed by state corporation laws, liability agreements, and boards of directors. Companies usually divide the section into three parts:

STOCKHOLDERS' EQUITY SECTION

1. CAPITAL STOCK. The par or stated value of the shares issued.
2. ADDITIONAL PAID-IN CAPITAL. The excess of amounts paid in over the par or stated value.
3. RETAINED EARNINGS. The corporation's undistributed earnings.

For capital stock, companies must disclose the par value and the authorized, issued, and outstanding share amounts. A company usually presents the additional paid-in capital in one amount, although subtotals are informative if the sources of additional capital are varied and material. The retained earnings amount may be divided between the **unappropriated** (the amount that is usually available for dividend distribution) and **restricted** (e.g., by bond indentures or other loan agreements) amounts. In addition, companies show any capital stock reacquired (treasury stock) as a reduction of stockholders' equity.

Illustration 5-15 presents an example of the stockholders' equity section from Quanex Corporation.

ILLUSTRATION 5-15
Balance Sheet Presentation of Stockholders' Equity

Quanex Corporation
(in thousands)

Stockholders' equity	
Preferred stock, no par value, 1,000,000 shares authorized; 345,000 issued and outstanding	$ 86,250
Common stock, $0.50 par value, 25,000,000 shares authorized; 13,638,005 shares issued and outstanding	6,819
Additional paid-in capital	87,260
Retained earnings	57,263
	$237,592

The ownership or stockholders' equity accounts in a corporation differ considerably from those in a partnership or proprietorship. Partners show separately their permanent capital accounts and the balance in their temporary accounts (drawing accounts). Proprietorships ordinarily use a single capital account that handles all of the owner's equity transactions.

Balance Sheet Format

3 LEARNING OBJECTIVE
Prepare a classified balance sheet using the report and account formats.

One common arrangement that companies use in presenting a classified balance sheet is the account form. It lists assets, by sections, on the left side, and liabilities and stockholders' equity, by sections, on the right side. The main disadvantage is the need for a sufficiently wide space in which to present the items side by side. Often, the account form requires two facing pages.

To avoid this disadvantage, the **report form** lists the sections one above the other, on the same page. See, for example, Illustration 5-16, which lists assets, followed by liabilities and stockholders' equity directly below, on the same page.[11]

ILLUSTRATION 5-16
Classified Report Form Balance Sheet

SCIENTIFIC PRODUCTS, INC. BALANCE SHEET DECEMBER 31, 2012			
Assets			
Current assets			
Cash		$ 42,485	
Available-for-sale securities—at fair value		28,250	
Accounts receivable	$165,824		
Less: Allowance for doubtful accounts	1,850	163,974	
Notes receivable		23,000	
Inventories—at average cost		489,713	
Supplies on hand		9,780	
Prepaid expenses		16,252	
Total current assets			$ 773,454
Long-term investments			
Equity investments			87,500
Property, plant, and equipment			
Land—at cost		125,000	
Buildings—at cost	975,800		
Less: Accumulated depreciation	341,200	634,600	
Total property, plant, and equipment			759,600
Intangible assets			
Goodwill			100,000
Total assets			$1,720,554
Liabilities and Stockholders' Equity			
Current liabilities			
Notes payable to banks	$ 50,000		
Accounts payable	197,532		
Accrued interest on notes payable	500		
Income taxes payable	62,520		
Accrued salaries, wages, and other liabilities	9,500		
Deposits received from customers	420		
Total current liabilities			$ 320,472
Long-term debt			
Twenty-year 12% debentures, due January 1, 2020			500,000
Total liabilities			820,472
Stockholders' equity			
Paid in on capital stock			
Preferred, 7%, cumulative			
Authorized, issued, and outstanding, 30,000 shares of $10 par value	300,000		
Common—			
Authorized, 500,000 shares of $1 par value; issued and outstanding, 400,000 shares	400,000		
Additional paid-in capital	37,500	$737,500	
Retained earnings		162,582	
Total stockholders' equity			900,082
Total liabilities and stockholders' equity			$1,720,554

Underlying Concepts

The presentation of balance sheet information meets the objective of financial reporting—to provide information about entity resources, claims to resources, and changes in them.

[11]*Accounting Trends and Techniques—2010* (New York: AICPA) indicates that all of the 500 companies surveyed use either the "report form" (437) or the "account form" (63), sometimes collectively referred to as the "customary form."

Infrequently, companies use other balance sheet formats. For example, companies sometimes deduct current liabilities from current assets to arrive at working capital. Or, they deduct all liabilities from all assets.

WARNING SIGNALS

What do the numbers mean?

Analysts use balance sheet information in models designed to predict financial distress. Researcher E. I. Altman pioneered a bankruptcy-prediction model that derives a "Z-score" by combining balance sheet and income measures in the following equation.

$$Z = \frac{\text{Working capital}}{\text{Total assets}} \times 1.2 + \frac{\text{Retained earnings}}{\text{Total assets}} \times 1.4 + \frac{\text{EBIT}}{\text{Total assets}} \times 3.3$$

$$+ \frac{\text{Sales}}{\text{Total assets}} \times 0.99 + \frac{\text{MV equity}}{\text{Total liabilities}} \times 0.6$$

Following extensive testing, Altman found that companies with Z-scores above 3.0 are unlikely to fail. Those with Z-scores below 1.81 are very likely to fail.

Altman developed the original model for publicly held manufacturing companies. He and others have modified the model to apply to companies in various industries, emerging companies, and companies not traded in public markets.

At one time, the use of Z-scores was virtually unheard of among practicing accountants. Today, auditors, management consultants, and courts of law use this measure to help evaluate the overall financial position and trends of a firm. In addition, banks use Z-scores for loan evaluation. While a low score does not guarantee bankruptcy, the model has been proven accurate in many situations.

Source: Adapted from E. I. Altman and E. Hotchkiss, *Corporate Financial Distress and Bankruptcy,* Third Edition (New York: John Wiley and Sons, 2005).

SECTION 2 • STATEMENT OF CASH FLOWS

Chapter 2 indicated that one of the three basic objectives of financial reporting is "assessing the amounts, timing, and uncertainty of cash flows." The three financial statements we have looked at so far—the income statement, the statement of stockholders' equity, and the balance sheet—each present some information about the cash flows of an enterprise during a period. But they do so to a limited extent. For instance, the income statement provides information about resources provided by operations, but not exactly cash. The statement of stockholders' equity shows the amount of cash used to pay dividends or purchase treasury stock. Comparative balance sheets might show what assets the company has acquired or disposed of and what liabilities it has incurred or liquidated.

Underlying Concepts

The statement of cash flows meets the objective of financial reporting—to help assess the amounts, timing, and uncertainty of future cash flows.

Useful as they are, none of these statements presents a detailed summary of all the cash inflows and outflows, or the sources and uses of cash during the period. To fill this need, the FASB requires the **statement of cash flows** (also called the **cash flow statement**). **[5]**

PURPOSE OF THE STATEMENT OF CASH FLOWS

4 LEARNING OBJECTIVE
Indicate the purpose of the statement of cash flows.

The primary purpose of a statement of cash flows is to provide relevant information about the cash receipts and cash payments of an enterprise during a period. To achieve this purpose, the statement of cash flows reports the following: (1) the cash effects of operations during a period, (2) investing transactions, (3) financing transactions, and (4) the net increase or decrease in cash during the period.[12]

Reporting the sources, uses, and net increase or decrease in cash helps investors, creditors, and others know what is happening to a company's most liquid resource. Because most individuals maintain a checkbook and prepare a tax return on a cash basis, they can comprehend the information reported in the statement of cash flows.

The statement of cash flows provides answers to the following simple but important questions:

1. Where did the cash come from during the period?
2. What was the cash used for during the period?
3. What was the change in the cash balance during the period?

WATCH THAT CASH FLOW

What do the numbers mean?

Investors usually focus on net income measured on an accrual basis. However, information on cash flows can be important for assessing a company's liquidity, financial flexibility, and overall financial performance. The graph below shows **W. T. Grant**'s financial performance over 7 years.

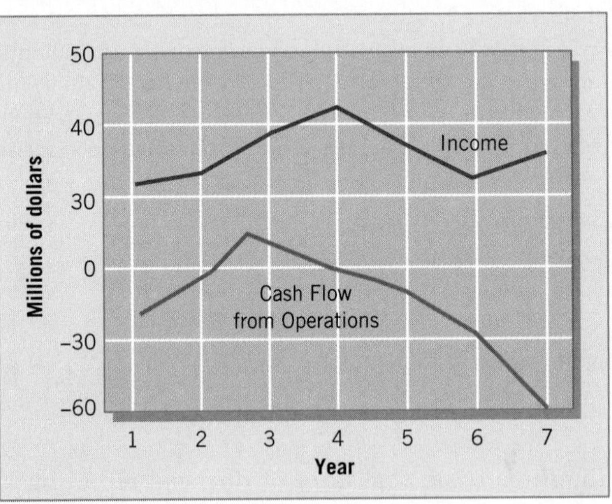

Although W. T. Grant showed consistent profits and even some periods of earnings growth, its cash flow began to "go south" starting in about year 3. The company filed for bankruptcy shortly after year 7. Financial statement readers who studied the company's cash flows would have found early warnings of W. T. Grant's problems. The Grant experience is a classic case, illustrating the importance of cash flows as an early-warning signal of financial problems.

A more recent retailer case is **Target**. Although Target has shown good profits, some are concerned that a bit too much of its sales have been made on credit rather than cash. Why is this a problem? Like W. T. Grant, the earnings of profitable lenders can get battered in future periods if they have to start adding large amounts to their bad-loan reserve to catch up with credit losses. And if losses ramp up on Target-branded credit cards, Target may get hit in this way.

Source: Peter Eavis, "Is Target Corp.'s Credit Too Generous?" *Wall Street Journal* (March 11, 2008), p. C1.

CONTENT AND FORMAT OF THE STATEMENT OF CASH FLOWS

LEARNING OBJECTIVE 5
Identify the content of the statement of cash flows.

Companies classify cash receipts and cash payments during a period into three different activities in the statement of cash flows—operating, investing, and financing activities, defined as follows.

1. **Operating activities** involve the cash effects of transactions that enter into the determination of net income.

[12]The FASB recommends the basis as "cash and cash equivalents." **Cash equivalents** are liquid investments that mature within three months or less.

2. **Investing activities** include making and collecting loans and acquiring and disposing of investments (both debt and equity) and property, plant, and equipment.
3. **Financing activities** involve liability and owners' equity items. They include (a) obtaining resources from owners and providing them with a return on their investment, and (b) borrowing money from creditors and repaying the amounts borrowed.

Illustration 5-17 shows the basic format of the statement of cash flows.

ILLUSTRATION 5-17
Basic Format of Cash Flow Statement

Statement of Cash Flows	
Cash flows from operating activities	$XXX
Cash flows from investing activities	XXX
Cash flows from financing activities	XXX
Net increase (decrease) in cash	XXX
Cash at beginning of year	XXX
Cash at end of year	$XXX

Illustration 5-18 graphs the inflows and outflows of cash classified by activity.

ILLUSTRATION 5-18
Cash Inflows and Outflows

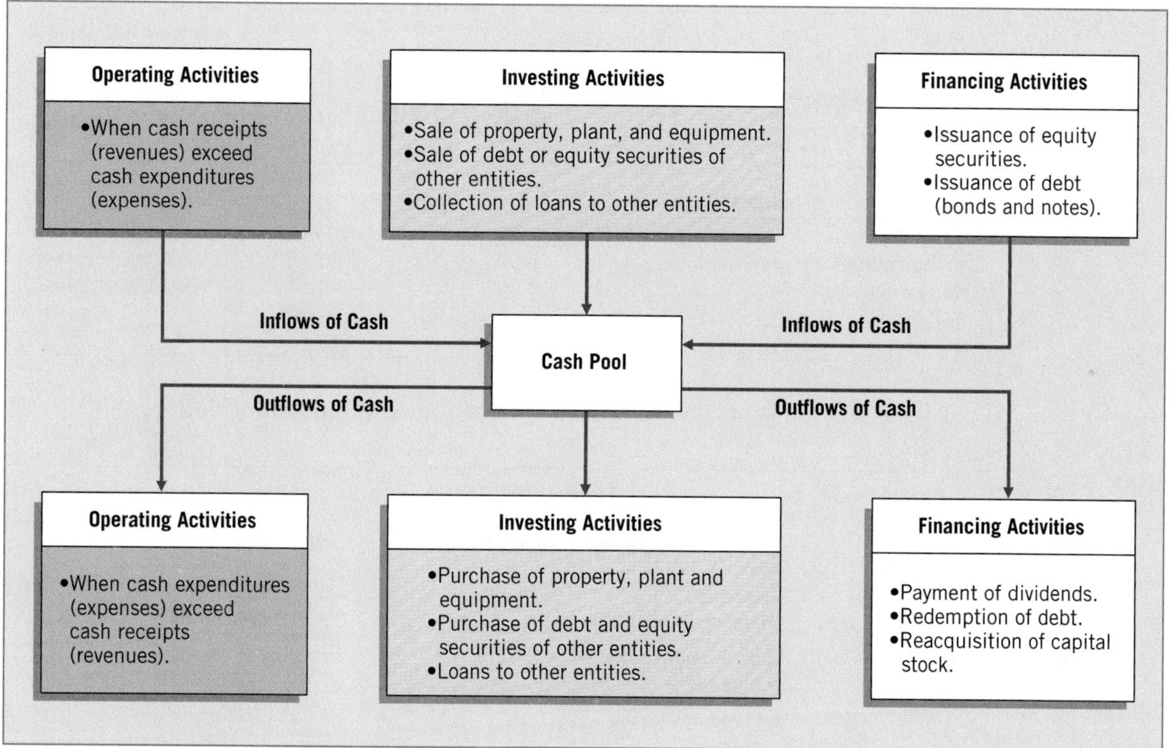

The statement's value is that it helps users evaluate liquidity, solvency, and financial flexibility. As stated earlier, **liquidity** refers to the "nearness to cash" of assets and liabilities. **Solvency** is the firm's ability to pay its debts as they mature. **Financial flexibility** is a company's ability to respond and adapt to financial adversity and unexpected needs and opportunities.

We have devoted Chapter 23 entirely to the detailed preparation and content of the statement of cash flows. The intervening chapters will cover several elements and complex topics that affect the content of a typical statement of cash flows. The presentation in this chapter is introductory—a reminder of the existence of the statement of cash flows and its usefulness.

OVERVIEW OF THE PREPARATION OF THE STATEMENT OF CASH FLOWS

Sources of Information

LEARNING OBJECTIVE 6
Prepare a basic statement of cash flows.

Companies obtain the information to prepare the statement of cash flows from several sources: (1) comparative balance sheets, (2) the current income statement, and (3) selected transaction data.

The following simple example demonstrates how companies use these sources in preparing a statement of cash flows.

On January 1, 2012, in its first year of operations, Telemarketing Inc. issued 50,000 shares of $1 par value common stock for $50,000 cash. The company rented its office space, furniture, and telecommunications equipment and performed marketing services throughout the first year. In June 2012, the company purchased land for $15,000. Illustration 5-19 shows the company's comparative balance sheets at the beginning and end of 2012.

ILLUSTRATION 5-19
Comparative Balance Sheets

TELEMARKETING INC.
BALANCE SHEETS

Assets	Dec. 31, 2012	Jan. 1, 2012	Increase/Decrease
Cash	$31,000	$-0-	$31,000 Increase
Accounts receivable	41,000	-0-	41,000 Increase
Land	15,000	-0-	15,000 Increase
Total	$87,000	$-0-	
Liabilities and Stockholders' Equity			
Accounts payable	$12,000	$-0-	12,000 Increase
Common stock	50,000	-0-	50,000 Increase
Retained earnings	25,000	-0-	25,000 Increase
Total	$87,000	$-0-	

Illustration 5-20 presents the income statement and additional information.

ILLUSTRATION 5-20
Income Statement Data

TELEMARKETING INC.
INCOME STATEMENT
FOR THE YEAR ENDED DECEMBER 31, 2012

Revenues	$172,000
Operating expenses	120,000
Income before income tax	52,000
Income tax	13,000
Net income	$ 39,000

Additional information:
Dividends of $14,000 were paid during the year.

Preparing the Statement of Cash Flows

Preparing the statement of cash flows from these sources involves four steps:

1. Determine the cash provided by (or used in) operating activities.
2. Determine the cash provided by or used in investing and financing activities.
3. Determine the change (increase or decrease) in cash during the period.
4. Reconcile the change in cash with the beginning and the ending cash balances.

Cash provided by operating activities is the excess of cash receipts over cash payments from operating activities. Companies determine this amount by converting net income on an accrual basis to a cash basis. To do so, they add to or deduct from net income those items in the income statement that do not affect cash. This procedure requires that a company analyze not only the current year's income statement but also the comparative balance sheets and selected transaction data.

Analysis of Telemarketing's comparative balance sheets reveals two items that will affect the computation of net cash provided by operating activities:

1. The increase in accounts receivable reflects a noncash increase of $41,000 in revenues.
2. The increase in accounts payable reflects a noncash increase of $12,000 in expenses.

Therefore, to arrive at cash provided by operations, Telemarketing Inc. deducts from net income the increase in accounts receivable ($41,000), and it adds back to net income the increase in accounts payable ($12,000). As a result of these adjustments, the company determines cash provided by operations to be $10,000, computed as shown in Illustration 5-21.

Net income		$39,000
Adjustments to reconcile net income to net cash provided by operating activities:		
Increase in accounts receivable	$(41,000)	
Increase in accounts payable	12,000	(29,000)
Net cash provided by operating activities		$10,000

ILLUSTRATION 5-21
Computation of Net Cash Provided by Operations

Next, the company determines its investing and financing activities. Telemarketing Inc.'s only **investing activity** was the land purchase. It had two **financing activities**: (1) Common stock increased $50,000 from the issuance of 50,000 shares for cash. (2) The company paid $14,000 cash in dividends. Knowing the amounts provided/used by operating, investing, and financing activities, the company determines the **net increase in cash**. Illustration 5-22 presents Telemarketing Inc.'s statement of cash flows for 2012.

INTERNATIONAL PERSPECTIVE

IFRS requires a statement of cash flows. Both IFRS and GAAP specify that the cash flows must be classified as operating, investing, or financing.

TELEMARKETING INC.
STATEMENT OF CASH FLOWS
FOR THE YEAR ENDED DECEMBER 31, 2012

Cash flows from operating activities		
Net income		$39,000
Adjustments to reconcile net income to net cash provided by operating activities:		
Increase in accounts receivable	$(41,000)	
Increase in accounts payable	12,000	(29,000)
Net cash provided by operating activities		10,000
Cash flows from investing activities		
Purchase of land	(15,000)	
Net cash used by investing activities		(15,000)
Cash flows from financing activities		
Issuance of common stock	50,000	
Payment of cash dividends	(14,000)	
Net cash provided by financing activities		36,000
Net increase in cash		31,000
Cash at beginning of year		–0–
Cash at end of year		$31,000

ILLUSTRATION 5-22
Statement of Cash Flows

The increase in cash of $31,000 reported in the statement of cash flows **agrees with** the increase of $31,000 in cash calculated from the comparative balance sheets.

Significant Noncash Activities

Not all of a company's significant activities involve cash. Examples of significant noncash activities are:

1. Issuance of common stock to purchase assets.
2. Conversion of bonds into common stock.
3. Issuance of debt to purchase assets.
4. Exchanges of long-lived assets.

Significant financing and investing activities that do not affect cash are not reported in the body of the statement of cash flows. Rather, these activities are reported in either a separate schedule at the bottom of the statement of cash flows or in separate notes to the financial statements. Such reporting of these noncash activities satisfies the full disclosure principle.

Illustration 5-23 shows an example of a comprehensive statement of cash flows. Note that the company purchased equipment through the issuance of $50,000 of bonds, which is a significant noncash transaction. *In solving homework assignments, you should present significant noncash activities in a separate schedule at the bottom of the statement of cash flows.*

ILLUSTRATION 5-23
Comprehensive Statement of Cash Flows

NESTOR COMPANY
STATEMENT OF CASH FLOWS
FOR THE YEAR ENDED DECEMBER 31, 2012

Cash flows from operating activities		
Net income		$320,750
Adjustments to reconcile net income to net cash provided by operating activities:		
Depreciation expense	$ 88,400	
Amortization of intangibles	16,300	
Gain on sale of plant assets	(8,700)	
Increase in accounts receivable (net)	(11,000)	
Decrease in inventory	15,500	
Decrease in accounts payable	(9,500)	91,000
Net cash provided by operating activities		411,750
Cash flows from investing activities		
Sale of plant assets	90,500	
Purchase of equipment	(182,500)	
Purchase of land	(70,000)	
Net cash used by investing activities		(162,000)
Cash flows from financing activities		
Payment of cash dividend	(19,800)	
Issuance of common stock	100,000	
Redemption of bonds	(50,000)	
Net cash provided by financing activities		30,200
Net increase in cash		279,950
Cash at beginning of year		135,000
Cash at end of year		$414,950
Noncash investing and financing activities		
Purchase of equipment through issuance of $50,000 of bonds		

USEFULNESS OF THE STATEMENT OF CASH FLOWS

7 LEARNING OBJECTIVE
Understand the usefulness of the statement of cash flows.

"Happiness is a positive cash flow" is certainly true. Although net income provides a long-term measure of a company's success or failure, cash is its lifeblood. Without cash, a company will not survive. For small and newly developing companies, cash flow is the single most important element for survival. Even medium and large companies must control cash flow.

Creditors examine the cash flow statement carefully because they are concerned about being paid. They begin their examination by finding net cash provided by operating activities. A high amount indicates that a company is able to generate sufficient cash from operations to pay its bills without further borrowing. Conversely, a low or negative amount of net cash provided by operating activities indicates that a company may have to borrow or issue equity securities to acquire sufficient cash to pay its bills. Consequently, creditors look for answers to the following questions in the company's cash flow statements.

1. How successful is the company in generating net cash provided by operating activities?
2. What are the trends in net cash flow provided by operating activities over time?
3. What are the major reasons for the positive or negative net cash provided by operating activities?

You should recognize that companies can fail even though they report net income. The difference between net income and net cash provided by operating activities can be substantial. Companies such as **W. T. Grant Company** and **Prime Motor Inn**, for example, reported high net income numbers but negative net cash provided by operating activities. Eventually both companies filed for bankruptcy.

In addition, substantial increases in receivables and/or inventory can explain the difference between positive net income and negative net cash provided by operating activities. For example, in its first year of operations Hu Inc. reported a net income of $80,000. Its net cash provided by operating activities, however, was a negative $95,000, as shown in Illustration 5-24.

HU INC.
NET CASH FLOW FROM OPERATING ACTIVITIES

Cash flows from operating activities		
Net income		$ 80,000
Adjustments to reconcile net income to net cash provided by operating activities:		
Increase in receivables	$ (75,000)	
Increase in inventories	(100,000)	(175,000)
Net cash provided by operating activities		$(95,000)

ILLUSTRATION 5-24
Negative Net Cash Provided by Operating Activities

Hu could easily experience a "cash crunch" because it has its cash tied up in receivables and inventory. If Hu encounters problems in collecting receivables, or if inventory moves slowly or becomes obsolete, its creditors may have difficulty collecting on their loans.

Financial Liquidity

Readers of financial statements often assess liquidity by using the **current cash debt coverage ratio**. It indicates whether the company can pay off its current liabilities from its operations in a given year. Illustration 5-25 (page 234) shows the formula for this ratio.

ILLUSTRATION 5-25
Formula for Current Cash Debt Coverage Ratio

$$\frac{\text{Net Cash Provided by Operating Activities}}{\text{Average Current Liabilities}} = \text{Current Cash Debt Coverage Ratio}$$

The higher the current cash debt coverage ratio, the less likely a company will have liquidity problems. For example, a ratio near 1:1 is good: It indicates that the company can meet all of its current obligations from internally generated cash flow.

Financial Flexibility

The **cash debt coverage ratio** provides information on financial flexibility. It indicates a company's ability to repay its liabilities from net cash provided by operating activities, without having to liquidate the assets employed in its operations. Illustration 5-26 shows the formula for this ratio. Notice its similarity to the current cash debt coverage ratio. However, because it uses average total liabilities in place of average current liabilities, it takes a somewhat longer-range view.

ILLUSTRATION 5-26
Formula for Cash Debt Coverage Ratio

$$\frac{\text{Net Cash Provided by Operating Activities}}{\text{Average Total Liabilities}} = \text{Cash Debt Coverage Ratio}$$

The higher this ratio, the less likely the company will experience difficulty in meeting its obligations as they come due. It signals whether the company can pay its debts and survive if external sources of funds become limited or too expensive.

Free Cash Flow

A more sophisticated way to examine a company's financial flexibility is to develop a free cash flow analysis. **Free cash flow** is the amount of discretionary cash flow a company has. It can use this cash flow to purchase additional investments, retire its debt, purchase treasury stock, or simply add to its liquidity. Financial statement users calculate free cash flow as shown in Illustration 5-27.

ILLUSTRATION 5-27
Formula for Free Cash Flow

$$\text{Net Cash Provided by Operating Activities} - \text{Capital Expenditures} - \text{Dividends} = \text{Free Cash Flow}$$

In a free cash flow analysis, we first deduct capital spending, to indicate it is the least discretionary expenditure a company generally makes. (Without continued efforts to maintain and expand facilities, it is unlikely that a company can continue to maintain its competitive position.) We then deduct dividends. Although a company *can* cut its dividend, it usually will do so only in **a financial emergency**. The amount resulting after these deductions is the company's free cash flow. Obviously, the greater the amount of free cash flow, the greater the company's financial flexibility.

Questions that a free cash flow analysis answers are:

1. Is the company able to pay its dividends without resorting to external financing?
2. If business operations decline, will the company be able to maintain its needed capital investment?
3. What is the amount of discretionary cash flow that can be used for additional investment, retirement of debt, purchase of treasury stock, or addition to liquidity?

Illustration 5-28 is a free cash flow analysis using the cash flow statement for Nestor Company (shown in Illustration 5-23 on page 232).

ILLUSTRATION 5-28
Free Cash Flow Computation

NESTOR COMPANY
FREE CASH FLOW ANALYSIS

Net cash provided by operating activities	$411,750
Less: Capital expenditures	(252,500)
Dividends	(19,800)
Free cash flow	$139,450

This computation shows that Nestor has a positive, and substantial, net cash provided by operating activities of $411,750. Nestor's statement of cash flows reports that the company purchased equipment of $182,500 and land of $70,000 for total capital spending of $252,500. Nestor has more than sufficient cash flow to meet its dividend payment and therefore has satisfactory financial flexibility.

As you can see from looking back at Illustration 5-23 (page 232), Nestor used its free cash flow to redeem bonds and add to its liquidity. If it finds additional investments that are profitable, it can increase its spending without putting its dividend or basic capital spending in jeopardy. Companies that have strong financial flexibility can take advantage of profitable investments even in tough times. In addition, strong financial flexibility frees companies from worry about survival in poor economic times. In fact, those with strong financial flexibility often fare better in a poor economy because they can take advantage of opportunities that other companies cannot.

"THERE OUGHT TO BE A LAW"

What do the numbers mean?

As one manager noted, "There ought to be a law that before you can buy a stock, you must be able to read a balance sheet." We agree, and the same can be said for a statement of cash flows.

Krispy Kreme Doughnuts provides an example of how stunning earnings growth can hide real problems. Not long ago the doughnut maker was a glamour stock with a 60 percent earnings per share growth rate and a price-earnings ratio around 70. Seven months later its stock price had dropped 72 percent. What happened? Stockholders alleged that Krispy Kreme may have been inflating its revenues and not taking enough bad debt expense (which inflated both assets and income). In addition, Krispy Kreme's operating cash flow was negative. Most financially sound companies generate positive cash flow.

Following are additional examples of how one rating agency rated the earnings quality of some companies, using some key balance sheet and statement of cash flow measurements.

Earnings-Quality Winners	Company	Earnings-Quality Indicators
	Avon Products	Strong cash flow
	Capital One Financial	Conservatively capitalized
	Ecolab	Good management of working capital
	Timberland	Minimal off-balance-sheet commitments
Earnings-Quality Losers	**Company**	**Earnings-Quality Indicators**
	Ford Motor	High debt and underfunded pension plan
	Kroger	High goodwill and debt
	Ryder System	Negative free cash flow
	Teco Energy	Selling assets to meet liquidity needs

Another rating organization has developed a metric to adjust for shortcomings in amounts reported in the balance sheet. Just as a deteriorating balance sheet and statement of cash flows warn of earnings declines (and falling stock prices), improving balance sheet and cash flow information is a leading indicator of improved earnings.

Source: Adapted from Gretchen Morgenson, "How Did They Value Stocks? Count the Absurd Ways," *New York Times on the Web* (March 18, 2001); K. Badanhausen, J. Gage, C. Hall, and M. Ozanian, "Beyond Balance Sheet: Earnings Quality," *Forbes.com* (January 28, 2005); and Moody's Investors Service, "Why Balance Sheets Fall Short as Indicators of Credit Risk" (October 9, 2009).

SECTION 3 • ADDITIONAL INFORMATION

In both Chapter 4 and this chapter, we have discussed the primary financial statements that all companies prepare in accordance with GAAP. However, the primary financial statements cannot provide the complete picture related to the financial position and financial performance of the company. Additional descriptive information in supplemental disclosures and certain techniques of disclosure expand on and amplify the items presented in the main body of the statements.

SUPPLEMENTAL DISCLOSURES

LEARNING OBJECTIVE 8
Determine which balance sheet information requires supplemental disclosure.

The balance sheet is not complete if a company simply lists the assets, liabilities, and owners' equity accounts. It still needs to provide important supplemental information. This may be information not presented elsewhere in the statement, or it may elaborate on items in the balance sheet. There are normally four types of information that are supplemental to account titles and amounts presented in the balance sheet. They are listed below.

SUPPLEMENTAL BALANCE SHEET INFORMATION

1. CONTINGENCIES. Material events that have an uncertain outcome.
2. ACCOUNTING POLICIES. Explanations of the valuation methods used or the basic assumptions made concerning inventory valuations, depreciation methods, investments in subsidiaries, etc.
3. CONTRACTUAL SITUATIONS. Explanations of certain restrictions or covenants attached to specific assets or, more likely, to liabilities.
4. FAIR VALUES. Disclosures of fair values, particularly for financial instruments.

Underlying Concepts
The basis for including additional information should meet the *full disclosure* principle. That is, the information should be of sufficient importance to influence the judgment of an informed user.

Contingencies

A **contingency** is an existing situation involving uncertainty as to possible gain (gain contingency) or loss (loss contingency) that will ultimately be resolved when one or more future events occur or fail to occur. In short, contingencies are material events with an uncertain future. Examples of gain contingencies are tax operating-loss carryforwards or company litigation against another party. Typical loss contingencies relate to litigation, environmental issues, possible tax assessments, or government investigations. We examine the accounting and reporting requirements involving contingencies more fully in Chapter 13.

Accounting Policies

GAAP recommends disclosure for all significant accounting principles and methods that involve selection from among alternatives or those that are peculiar to a given industry. [6] For instance, companies can compute inventories under several cost flow assumptions (e.g., LIFO and FIFO), depreciate plant and equipment under several accepted methods (e.g., double-declining balance and straight-line), and carry investments at different valuations (e.g., cost, equity, and fair value). Sophisticated users of financial statements know of these possibilities and examine the statements closely to determine the methods used.

Companies must also disclose information about the nature of their operations, the use of estimates in preparing financial statements, certain significant estimates, and vulnerabilities due to certain concentrations. **[7]** Illustration 5-29 shows an example of such a disclosure.

Chesapeake Corporation

Risks and Uncertainties. Chesapeake operates in three business segments which offer a diversity of products over a broad geographic base. The Company is not dependent on any single customer, group of customers, market, geographic area or supplier of materials, labor or services. Financial statements include, where necessary, amounts based on the judgments and estimates of management. These estimates include allowances for bad debts, accruals for landfill closing costs, environmental remediation costs, loss contingencies for litigation, self-insured medical and workers' compensation insurance and determinations of discount and other rate assumptions for pensions and postretirement benefit expenses.

ILLUSTRATION 5-29
Balance Sheet Disclosure of Significant Risks and Uncertainties

Disclosure of significant accounting principles and methods and of risks and uncertainties is particularly useful if given in a separate **Summary of Significant Accounting Policies** preceding the notes to the financial statements or as the initial note.

Contractual Situations

Companies should disclose contractual situations, if significant, in the notes to the financial statements. For example, they must clearly state the essential provisions of lease contracts, pension obligations, and stock option plans in the notes. Analysts want to know not only the amount of the liabilities, but also how the different contractual provisions affect the company at present and in the future.

Companies must disclose the following commitments if the amounts are material: commitments related to obligations to maintain working capital, to limit the payment of dividends, to restrict the use of assets, and to require the maintenance of certain financial ratios. Management must exercise considerable judgment to determine whether omission of such information is misleading. The rule in this situation is, "When in doubt, disclose." It is better to disclose a little too much information than not enough.

WHAT ABOUT YOUR COMMITMENTS?

What do the numbers mean?

Many of the recent accounting scandals related to the nondisclosure of significant contractual obligations. In response, the SEC has mandated that companies disclose contractual obligations in a tabular summary in the management discussion and analysis section of the company's annual report.

Presented below, as an example, is a disclosure from The Procter & Gamble Company.

Contractual Commitments, as of June 30, 2009 (in millions of dollars)

	Total	Less Than 1 Year	1–3 Years	3–5 Years	After 5 Years
Recorded liabilities					
Total debt	$36,631	$16,270	$1,438	$6,091	$12,832
Capital leases	392	46	84	76	186
Other					
Interest payments relating to long-term debt	12,616	1,183	2,469	1,788	7,176
Operating leases[1]	1,620	305	495	378	442
Minimum pension funding[2]	1,499	616	883	—	—
Purchase obligations[3]	3,897	1,258	1,659	681	299
Total contractual commitments	$56,655	$19,678	$7,028	$9,014	$20,935

(1)Operating lease obligations are shown net of guaranteed sublease income.

(2)Represents future pension payments to comply with local funding requirements. The projected payments beyond fiscal year 2010 are not currently determinable.

(3)Primarily reflects future contractual payments under various take-or-pay arrangements entered into as part of the normal course of business.

Fair Values

As we have discussed, fair value information may be more useful than historical cost for certain types of assets and liabilities. This is particularly so in the case of financial instruments. **Financial instruments** are defined as cash, an ownership interest, or a contractual right to receive or obligation to deliver cash or another financial instrument. Such contractual rights to receive cash or other financial instruments are assets. Contractual obligations to pay are liabilities. Cash, investments, accounts receivable, and payables are examples of financial instruments.

Given the expanded use of fair value measurements, as discussed in Chapter 2, GAAP also has expanded disclosures about fair value measurements. **[8]** To increase consistency and comparability in the use of fair value measures, companies follow a fair value hierarchy that provides insight into how to determine fair value. The hierarchy has three levels. **Level 1** measures (the most reliable) are based on observable inputs, such as market prices for identical assets or liabilities. **Level 2** measures (less reliable) are based on market-based inputs other than those included in Level 1, such as those based on market prices for similar assets or liabilities. **Level 3** measures (least reliable) are based on unobservable inputs, such as a company's own data or assumptions.[13]

For major groups of assets and liabilities, companies must make the following fair value disclosures: (1) the fair value measurement and (2) the fair value hierarchy level of the measurements as a whole, classified by Level 1, 2, or 3. Illustration 5-30 provides a disclosure for **Devon Energy** for its assets and liabilities measured at fair value.

ILLUSTRATION 5-30
Disclosure of Fair Values

Devon Energy Corporation

Note 7: Fair Value Measurements (in part). Certain of Devon's assets and liabilities are reported at fair value in the accompanying balance sheets. The following table provides fair value measurement information for such assets and liabilities.

		Fair Value Measurements Using:		
	Total Fair Value	Quoted Prices in Active Markets (Level 1)	Significant Other Observable Inputs (Level 2)	Significant Unobservable Inputs (Level 3)
			(In millions)	
Assets:				
Short-term investments	$ 341	$ 341	$ —	$ —
Investment in Chevron common stock	1,327	1,327	—	—
Financial instruments	8	—	8	—
Liabilities:				
Financial instruments	497	—	497	—
Asset retirement obligation (ARO)	1,300	—	—	1,300

GAAP establishes a fair value hierarchy that prioritizes the inputs to valuation techniques used to measure fair value. As presented in the table above, this hierarchy consists of three broad levels. Level 1 inputs on the hierarchy consist of unadjusted quoted prices in active markets for identical assets and liabilities and have the highest priority. Level 3 inputs have the lowest priority. Devon uses appropriate valuation techniques based on the available inputs to measure the fair values of its assets and liabilities. When available, Devon measures fair value using Level 1 inputs because they generally provide the most reliable evidence of fair value.

[13]Level 3 fair value measurements may be developed using expected cash flow and present value techniques, as described in *Statement of Financial Accounting Concepts No. 7,* "Using Cash Flow Information and Present Value in Accounting," as discussed in Chapter 6.

In addition, companies must provide significant additional disclosure related to Level 3 measurements. The disclosures related to Level 3 are substantial and must identify what assumptions the company used to generate the fair value numbers and any related income effects. Companies will want to use Level 1 and 2 measurements as much as possible. In most cases, these valuations should be very reliable, as the fair value measurements are based on market information. In contrast, a company that uses Level 3 measurements extensively must be carefully evaluated to understand the impact these valuations have on the financial statements.

TECHNIQUES OF DISCLOSURE

Companies should disclose as completely as possible the effect of various contingencies on financial condition, the methods of valuing assets and liabilities, and the company's contracts and agreements. To disclose this pertinent information, companies may use parenthetical explanations, notes, cross reference and contra items, and supporting schedules.

Describe the major disclosure techniques for the balance sheet.

Parenthetical Explanations

Companies often provide additional information by parenthetical explanations following the item. For example, Illustration 5-31 shows a parenthetical explanation of the number of shares issued by **Ford Motor Company** on the balance sheet under "Stockholders' equity."

Ford Motor Company

Stockholders' Equity (in millions)	
Common stock, par value $0.01 per share (1,837 million shares issued)	$18

ILLUSTRATION 5-31
Parenthetical Disclosure of Shares Issued—Ford Motor Company

This additional pertinent balance sheet information adds clarity and completeness. It has an advantage over a note because it brings the additional information into the **body of the statement** where readers will less likely overlook it. Companies, however, should avoid lengthy parenthetical explanations, which might be distracting.

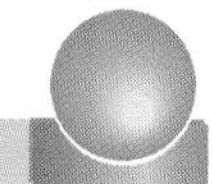

Underlying Concepts

The user-specific quality of *understandability* requires accountants to be careful in describing transactions and events.

Notes

Companies use notes if they cannot conveniently show additional explanations as parenthetical explanations. Illustration 5-32 (page 240) shows how **International Paper Company** reported its inventory costing methods in its accompanying notes.

ILLUSTRATION 5-32
Note Disclosure

International Paper Company

Note 11

Inventories by major category were (millions):

Raw materials	$ 371
Finished pulp, paper and packaging products	1,796
Finished lumber and panel products	184
Operating supplies	351
Other	16
Total inventories	$2,718

The last-in, first-out inventory method is used to value most of International Paper's U.S. inventories. Approximately 70% of total raw materials and finished products inventories were valued using this method. If the first-in, first-out method had been used, it would have increased total inventories balances by approximately $170 million.

Companies commonly use notes to disclose the following: the existence and amount of any preferred stock dividends in arrears, the terms of or obligations imposed by purchase commitments, special financial arrangements and instruments, depreciation policies, any changes in the application of accounting principles, and the existence of contingencies.

Notes therefore must present all essential facts as completely and succinctly as possible. Careless wording may mislead rather than aid readers. Notes should add to the total information made available in the financial statements, not raise unanswered questions or contradict other portions of the statements. The note disclosures in Illustration 5-33 show the presentation of such information.

ILLUSTRATION 5-33
More Note Disclosures

Alberto-Culver Company

Note 3: Long-Term Debt. Various borrowing arrangements impose restrictions on such items as total debt, working capital, dividend payments, treasury stock purchases and interest expense. The company was in compliance with these arrangements and $68 million of consolidated retained earnings was not restricted as to the payment of dividends and purchases of treasury stock.

Consolidated Papers, Inc.

Note 7: Commitments. The company had capital expenditure purchase commitments outstanding of approximately $17 million.

Willamette Industries, Inc.

Note 4: Property, Plant, and Equipment (partial): The company changed its accounting estimates relating to depreciation. The estimated service lives for most machinery and equipment were extended five years. The change was based upon a study performed by the company's engineering department, comparisons to typical industry practices, and the effect of the company's extensive capital investments which have resulted in a mix of assets with longer productive lives due to technological advances. As a result of the change, net income was increased $51,900, or $0.46 per diluted share.

Cross-Reference and Contra Items

Companies "cross-reference" a direct relationship between an asset and a liability on the balance sheet. For example, as shown in Illustration 5-34, on December 31, 2012, a company might show the following entries—one listed among the current assets, and the other listed among the current liabilities.

ILLUSTRATION 5-34
Cross-Referencing and Contra Items

Current Assets (in part)	
Cash on deposit with sinking fund trustee for redemption of bonds payable—see Current liabilities	$800,000

Current Liabilities (in part)	
Bonds payable to be redeemed in 2013—see Current assets	$2,300,000

This cross-reference points out that the company will redeem $2,300,000 of bonds payable currently, for which it has only set aside $800,000. Therefore, it needs additional cash from unrestricted cash, from sales of investments, from profits, or from some other source. Alternatively, the company can show the same information parenthetically.

Another common procedure is to establish contra or adjunct accounts. A **contra account** on a balance sheet reduces either an asset, liability, or owners' equity account. Examples include Accumulated Depreciation and Discount on Bonds Payable. Contra accounts provide some flexibility in presenting the financial information. With the use of the Accumulated Depreciation account, for example, a reader of the statement can see the original cost of the asset as well as the depreciation to date.

An **adjunct account**, on the other hand, increases either an asset, liability, or owners' equity account. An example is Premium on Bonds Payable, which, when added to the Bonds Payable account, describes the total bond liability of the company.

Supporting Schedules

Often a company needs a separate schedule to present more detailed information about certain assets or liabilities, as shown in Illustration 5-35.

ILLUSTRATION 5-35
Disclosure through Use of Supporting Schedules

Property, plant, and equipment	
Land, buildings, equipment, and other fixed assets—net (see Schedule 3)	$643,300

SCHEDULE 3
LAND, BUILDINGS, EQUIPMENT, AND OTHER FIXED ASSETS

	Total	Land	Buildings	Equip.	Other Fixed Assets
Balance January 1, 2012	$740,000	$46,000	$358,000	$260,000	$76,000
Additions in 2012	161,200		120,000	38,000	3,200
	901,200	46,000	478,000	298,000	79,200
Assets retired or sold in 2012	31,700			27,000	4,700
Balance December 31, 2012	869,500	46,000	478,000	271,000	74,500
Depreciation taken to January 1, 2012	196,000		102,000	78,000	16,000
Depreciation taken in 2012	56,000		28,000	24,000	4,000
	252,000		130,000	102,000	20,000
Depreciation on assets retired in 2012	25,800			22,000	3,800
Depreciation accumulated December 31, 2012	226,200		130,000	80,000	16,200
Book value of assets	$643,300	$46,000	$348,000	$191,000	$58,300

Terminology

INTERNATIONAL PERSPECTIVE

Internationally, accounting terminology is a problem. Confusion arises even between nations that share a language. For example, U.S. investors normally think of "stock" as "equity" or "ownership"; to the British, "stocks" means inventory. In the United States, "fixed assets" generally refers to "property, plant, and equipment"; in Britain, the category includes more items.

The account titles in the general ledger do not necessarily represent the best terminology for balance sheet purposes. Companies often use brief account titles and include technical terms that only accountants understand. But many persons unacquainted with accounting terminology examine balance sheets. Thus, balance sheets should contain descriptions that readers will generally understand and clearly interpret.

For example, companies have used the term "reserve" in differing ways: to describe amounts deducted from assets (contra accounts such as accumulated depreciation and allowance for doubtful accounts); as a part of the title of contingent or estimated liabilities; and to describe an appropriation of retained earnings. Because of the different meanings attached to this term, misinterpretation often resulted from its use. Therefore, the profession has recommended that companies use the word reserve only to describe an appropriation of retained earnings. The use of the term in this narrower sense—to describe appropriated retained earnings—has resulted in a better understanding of its significance when it appears in a balance sheet. However, the term "appropriated" appears more logical, and we encourage its use.

For years the profession has recommended that the use of the word **surplus** be discontinued in balance sheet presentations of owners' equity. The use of the terms *capital surplus, paid-in surplus,* and *earned surplus* is confusing. Although condemned by the profession, these terms appear all too frequently in current financial statements.

You will want to read the IFRS INSIGHTS on pages 301–307

for discussion of IFRS related to the balance sheet and statement of cash flows.

SUMMARY OF LEARNING OBJECTIVES

1 Explain the uses and limitations of a balance sheet. The balance sheet provides information about the nature and amounts of investments in a company's resources, obligations to creditors, and owners' equity. The balance sheet contributes to financial reporting by providing a basis for (1) computing rates of return, (2) evaluating the capital structure of the enterprise, and (3) assessing the liquidity, solvency, and financial flexibility of the enterprise.

Three limitations of a balance sheet are: (1) The balance sheet does not reflect fair value because accountants use a historical cost basis in valuing and reporting most assets and liabilities. (2) Companies must use judgments and estimates to determine certain amounts, such as the collectibility of receivables and the useful life of long-term tangible and intangible assets. (3) The balance sheet omits many items that are of financial value to the business but cannot be recorded objectively, such as human resources, customer base, and reputation.

2 Identify the major classifications of the balance sheet. The general elements of the balance sheet are assets, liabilities, and equity. The major classifications of assets are current assets; long-term investments; property, plant, and equipment; intangible assets; and other assets. The major classifications of liabilities are current and long-term liabilities. The balance sheet of a corporation generally classifies owners' equity as capital stock, additional paid-in capital, and retained earnings.

3 Prepare a classified balance sheet using the report and account formats. The report form lists liabilities and stockholders' equity directly below assets on the same page. The account form lists assets, by sections, on the left side, and liabilities and stockholders' equity, by sections, on the right side.

4 Indicate the purpose of the statement of cash flows. The primary purpose of a statement of cash flows is to provide relevant information about a company's cash receipts and cash payments during a period. Reporting the sources, uses, and net change in cash enables financial statement readers to know what is happening to a company's most liquid resource.

5 Identify the content of the statement of cash flows. In the statement of cash flows, companies classify the period's cash receipts and cash payments into three different activities: (1) *Operating activities*: Involve the cash effects of transactions that enter into the determination of net income. (2) *Investing activities*: Include making and collecting loans, and acquiring and disposing of investments (both debt and equity) and of property, plant, and equipment. (3) *Financing activities*: Involve liability and owners' equity items. Financing activities include (a) obtaining capital from owners and providing them with a return on their investment, and (b) borrowing money from creditors and repaying the amounts borrowed.

6 Prepare a basic statement of cash flows. The information to prepare the statement of cash flows usually comes from comparative balance sheets, the current income statement, and selected transaction data. Companies follow four steps to prepare the statement of cash flows from these sources: (1) Determine the cash provided by operating activities. (2) Determine the cash provided by or used in investing and financing activities. (3) Determine the change (increase or decrease) in cash during the period. (4) Reconcile the change in cash with the beginning and ending cash balances.

7 Understand the usefulness of the statement of cash flows. Creditors examine the cash flow statement carefully because they are concerned about being paid. The net cash flow provided by operating activities in relation to the company's liabilities is helpful in making this assessment. Two ratios used in this regard are the current cash debt ratio

KEY TERMS

account form, *225*
adjunct account, *241*
available-for-sale investments, *218*
balance sheet, *214*
cash debt coverage ratio, *234*
contingency, *236*
contra account, *241*
current assets, *217*
current cash debt coverage ratio, *233*
current liabilities, *222*
financial flexibility, *215*
financial instruments, *238*
financing activities, *229*
free cash flow, *234*
held-to-maturity investments, *218*
intangible assets, *222*
investing activities, *229*
liquidity, *214*
long-term investments, *220*
long-term liabilities, *224*
operating activities, *228*
owners' (stockholders') equity, *225*
property, plant, and equipment, *221*
report form, *226*
reserve, *242*
solvency, *215*
statement of cash flows, *227*
trading investments, *218*
working capital, *223*

and the cash debt ratio. In addition, the amount of free cash flow provides creditors and stockholders with a picture of the company's financial flexibility.

8 Determine which balance sheet information requires supplemental disclosure. Four types of information normally are supplemental to account titles and amounts presented in the balance sheet: (1) *Contingencies:* Material events that have an uncertain outcome. (2) *Accounting policies:* Explanations of the valuation methods used or the basic assumptions made concerning inventory valuation, depreciation methods, investments in subsidiaries, etc. (3) *Contractual situations:* Explanations of certain restrictions or covenants attached to specific assets or, more likely, to liabilities. (4) *Fair values:* Disclosures related to fair values, particularly related to financial instruments.

9 Describe the major disclosure techniques for the balance sheet. Companies use four methods to disclose pertinent information in the balance sheet: (1) *Parenthetical explanations:* Parenthetical information provides additional information or description following the item. (2) *Notes:* A company uses notes if it cannot conveniently show additional explanations or descriptions as parenthetical explanations. (3) *Cross-reference and contra items:* Companies "cross-reference" a direct relationship between an asset and a liability on the balance sheet. (4) *Supporting schedules:* Often a company uses a separate schedule to present more detailed information than just the single summary item shown in the balance sheet.

APPENDIX 5A RATIO ANALYSIS—A REFERENCE

USING RATIOS TO ANALYZE PERFORMANCE

LEARNING OBJECTIVE 10
Identify the major types of financial ratios and what they measure.

Analysts and other interested parties can gather qualitative information from financial statements by examining relationships between items on the statements and identifying trends in these relationships. A useful starting point in developing this information is ratio analysis.

A **ratio** expresses the mathematical relationship between one quantity and another. **Ratio analysis** expresses the relationship among pieces of selected financial statement data, in a **percentage**, a **rate**, or a simple **proportion**.

To illustrate, **IBM Corporation** recently had current assets of $46,970 million and current liabilities of $39,798 million. We find the ratio between these two amounts by dividing current assets by current liabilities. The alternative means of expression are:

Percentage: Current assets are 118% of current liabilities.
Rate: Current assets are 1.18 times as great as current liabilities.
Proportion: The relationship of current assets to current liabilities is 1.18:1.

To analyze financial statements, we classify ratios into four types, as follows:

Gateway to the Profession
Expanded Discussion of Financial Statement Analysis

MAJOR TYPES OF RATIOS

LIQUIDITY RATIOS. Measures of the company's short-term ability to pay its maturing obligations.

ACTIVITY RATIOS. Measures of how effectively the company uses its assets.

PROFITABILITY RATIOS. Measures of the degree of success or failure of a given company or division for a given period of time.

COVERAGE RATIOS. Measures of the degree of protection for long-term creditors and investors.

In Chapter 5, we discussed three measures related to the statement of cash flows (the current cash debt coverage and cash debt coverage ratios, and free cash flow). Throughout the remainder of the textbook, we provide ratios to help you understand and interpret the information presented in financial statements. Illustration 5A-1 presents the ratios that we will use throughout the text. You should find this chart helpful as you examine these ratios in more detail in the following chapters. An appendix to Chapter 24 further discusses financial statement analysis.

ILLUSTRATION 5A-1
A Summary of Financial Ratios

Ratio	Formula	Purpose or Use
I. Liquidity		
1. Current ratio	Current assets / Current liabilities	Measures short-term debt-paying ability
2. Quick or acid-test ratio	Cash, marketable securities, and receivables (net) / Current liabilities	Measures immediate short-term liquidity
3. Current cash debt coverage ratio	Net cash provided by operating activities / Average current liabilities	Measures a company's ability to pay off its current liabilities in a given year from its operations
II. Activity		
4. Receivables turnover	Net sales / Average trade receivables (net)	Measures liquidity of receivables
5. Inventory turnover	Cost of goods sold / Average inventory	Measures liquidity of inventory
6. Asset turnover	Net sales / Average total assets	Measures how efficiently assets are used to generate sales
III. Profitability		
7. Profit margin on sales	Net income / Net sales	Measures net income generated by each dollar of sales
8. Rate of return on assets	Net income / Average total assets	Measures overall profitability of assets
9. Rate of return on common stock equity	Net income minus preferred dividends / Average common stockholders' equity	Measures profitability of owners' investment
10. Earnings per share	Net income minus preferred dividends / Weighted shares outstanding	Measures net income earned on each share of common stock
11. Price-earnings ratio	Market price of stock / Earnings per share	Measures the ratio of the market price per share to earnings per share
12. Payout ratio	Cash dividends / Net income	Measures percentage of earnings distributed in the form of cash dividends
IV. Coverage		
13. Debt to total assets	Total debts / Total assets	Measures the percentage of total assets provided by creditors
14. Times interest earned	Income before interest expense and taxes / Interest expense	Measures ability to meet interest payments as they come due
15. Cash debt coverage ratio	Net cash provided by operating activities / Average total liabilities	Measures a company's ability to repay its total liabilities in a given year from its operations
16. Book value per share	Common stockholders' equity / Outstanding shares	Measures the amount each share would receive if the company were liquidated at the amounts reported on the balance sheet
17. Free cash flow	Net cash provided by operating activities − Capital expenditures − Dividends	Measures the amount of discretionary cash flow.

KEY TERMS

activity ratios, 244
coverage ratios, 244
liquidity ratios, 244
profitability ratios, 244
ratio analysis, 244

SUMMARY OF LEARNING OBJECTIVE FOR APPENDIX 5A

10 Identify the major types of financial ratios and what they measure. Ratios express the mathematical relationship between one quantity and another, expressed as a percentage, a rate, or a proportion. *Liquidity* ratios measure the short-term ability to pay maturing obligations. *Activity* ratios measure the effectiveness of asset usage. *Profitability* ratios measure the success or failure of an enterprise. *Coverage* ratios measure the degree of protection for long-term creditors and investors.

APPENDIX 5B SPECIMEN FINANCIAL STATEMENTS: THE PROCTER & GAMBLE COMPANY

The Procter & Gamble Company (P&G) manufactures and markets a range of consumer products in various countries throughout the world. The company markets over 300 branded products in more than 160 countries. It manages its business in five product segments: Fabric and Home Care, Baby and Family Care, Beauty Care, Health Care, and Snacks and Beverages.

The following pages contain the financial statements, accompanying notes, and other information from the 2009 annual report of The Procter & Gamble Company (P&G).

The content and organization of corporate annual reports have become fairly standardized. Excluding the public relations part of the report (pictures, products, etc.), the following are the traditional financial portions of the annual report:

- Letter to the Stockholders
- Financial Highlights
- Management's Discussion and Analysis
- Management Certification of Financial Statements
- Management's Report on Internal Control
- Auditor's Reports
- Financial Statements
- Notes to the Financial Statements
- Supplementary Financial Information (e.g., 10-year financial summary)

You will see examples of most of these standard annual report elements in the following pages (e.g., we do not include the lengthy discussion of P&G products and its Management's Discussion and Analysis). **The complete P&G annual report can be accessed at the book's companion website.**

We do not expect that you will comprehend P&G's financial statements and the accompanying notes in their entirety at your first reading. But we expect that by the time you complete the material in this textbook, your level of understanding and interpretive ability will have grown enormously.

At this point, we recommend that you take 20 to 30 minutes to scan the following statements and notes. Your goal should be to familiarize yourself with the contents and accounting elements. Throughout the following 19 chapters, when you are asked to refer to specific parts of P&G's financial statements, do so! Then, when you have completed reading this book, we challenge you to reread P&G's financials to see how much greater and more sophisticated your understanding of them has become.

P&G has a solid foundation for growth. Our strategies are working. Our billion-dollar and half-billion-dollar brands are among the strongest in the world. P&G's core strengths are those that matter most to winning in our industry. Our relationships with retailers, suppliers and innovation partners are enormous sources of competitive advantage. And the leadership team now in place has been carefully groomed through experience and coaching to lead P&G in the decade ahead. We are building on a rock-solid foundation of continuity. This is one of P&G's greatest advantages.

Bob McDonald
President and Chief Executive Officer

P&G at a Glance

GBU	Reportable Segment	Key Products	Billion-Dollar Brands	Net Sales by GBU(1) (in billions)
BEAUTY	Beauty	Cosmetics, Deodorants, Hair Care, Personal Cleansing, Prestige Fragrances, Skin Care	Head & Shoulders, Olay, Pantene, Wella	**$26.3**
	Grooming	Blades and Razors, Electric Hair Removal Devices, Face and Shave Products, Home Appliances	Braun, Fusion, Gillette, Mach3	
HEALTH AND WELL-BEING	Health Care	Feminine Care, Oral Care, Personal Health Care, Pharmaceuticals	Actonel, Always, Crest, Oral-B	**$16.7**
	Snacks and Pet Care	Pet Food, Snacks	Iams, Pringles	
HOUSEHOLD CARE	Fabric Care and Home Care	Air Care, Batteries, Dish Care, Fabric Care, Surface Care	Ariel, Dawn, Downy, Duracell, Gain, Tide	**$37.3**
	Baby Care and Family Care	Baby Wipes, Bath Tissue, Diapers, Facial Tissue, Paper Towels	Bounty, Charmin, Pampers	

(1) Partially offset by net sales in corporate to eliminate the sales of unconsolidated entities included in business unit results.

2009 NET SALES
(% of total business segments)

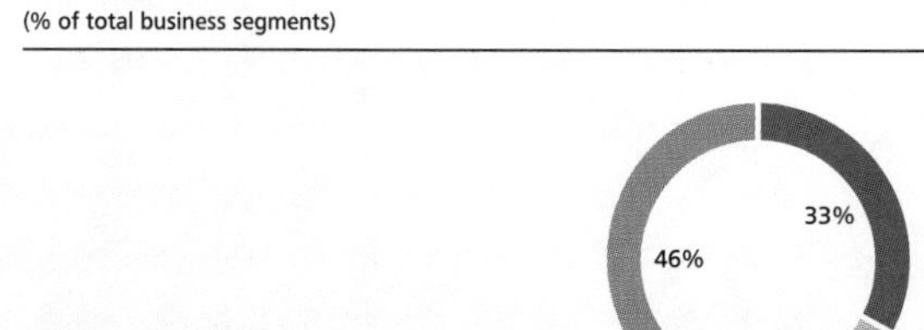

RECOGNITION

P&G is recognized as a leading global company, including a #6 ranking on *Fortune's* "World's Most Admired Companies," the #2 ranking on *Fortune's* "Top Companies for Leaders" survey, the #3 ranking on *Barron's* "World's Most Respected Companies List," a #12 ranking on *Business Week's* list of "World's Most Innovative Companies," named to *Chief Executive* magazine's worldwide survey of the Top 20 Best Companies for Leaders, top rankings on the Dow Jones Sustainability Index from 2000 to 2009, being named to the list of the Global 100 Most Sustainable Corporations in the World, and a consistent #1 ranking within our industry on *Fortune's* Most Admired list for 24 of 25 total years and for 12 years in a row.

P&G's commitment to creating a diverse workplace has been recognized by the National Association for Female Executives (Top 10 Companies for Executive Women), *Working Mother* magazine (100 Best Companies for Working Mothers and Top 20 Best Companies for Multicultural Women), *Black Enterprise* magazine (40 Best Companies for Diversity), and *Diversity Inc.* (Top 50 Companies for Diversity and #3 ranking on the Top 10 Companies for Global Diversity).

Supplier diversity is a fundamental business strategy at P&G. In 2009, P&G spent more than $2 billion with minority- and women-owned businesses. Since 2005, P&G has been a member of the Billion Dollar Roundtable, a forum of 16 corporations that spend more than $1 billion annually with diverse suppliers.

P&G REPORT CARD

Progress Against P&G's Goals and Strategies

GROWTH RESULTS

Average annual	Goals	2009	2001–2009
Organic Sales Growth (1)	**4–6%**	2%	5%
Core Earnings per Share Growth	**10%**	8% (2)	12% (3)
Free Cash Flow Productivity (4)	**90%**	102%	112%

GROWTH STRATEGIES (2001–2009)

Grow from the core: Leading Brands, Big Markets, Top Customers

- Volume up 7%, on average, for P&G's 23 billion-dollar brands (5)
- Volume up 6%, on average, for P&G's top 16 countries (6)
- Volume up 6%, on average, for P&G's top 10 retail customers (6)

Develop faster-growing, higher-margin, more asset-efficient businesses

- Beauty sales more than doubled to $18.8 billion; profits nearly tripled to $2.5 billion
- Health Care sales more than doubled to $13.6 billion; profit increased fourfold to $2.4 billion
- Home Care sales more than doubled; profits more than tripled

Accelerate growth in developing markets and among low-income consumers

- Developing market sales up 15% per year
- Over 40% of total company sales growth from developing markets
- Developing market profit margins comparable to developed-market margins

(1) Organic sales exclude the impacts of acquisitions, divestitures and foreign exchange, which were 6%, on average, in 2001–2009.

(2) Core earnings per share for 2009 excludes a positive $0.14 per share impact from significant adjustments to tax reserves in 2008, a positive $0.68 per share impact from discontinued operations in 2009 and a negative $0.09 per share impact from incremental Folgers-related restructuring charges in 2009.

(3) Core earnings per share for 2001–2009 excludes a negative $0.61 per share impact in 2001 from the Organization 2005 restructuring program charges and amortization of goodwill and intangible assets, positive impacts of $0.06 and $0.68 per share earnings from discontinued operations in 2001 and 2009, respectively and a negative $0.09 per share impact from incremental Folgers-related restructuring charges in 2009.

(4) Free cash flow productivity is the ratio of operating cash flow less capital spending to net earnings. For 2009, we have excluded $2,011 million from net earnings due to the gain on the sale of the Folgers business. Free cash flow productivity in 2009 equals $14,919 million of operating cash flow less $3,238 million in capital spending divided by net earnings of $11,425 million which excludes the Folgers gain. Reconciliations of free cash flow and free cash flow productivity for 2001–2009 are provided on page 48.

(5) Excludes the impact of adding newly acquired billion-dollar brands to the portfolio.

(6) Excludes the impact of adding Gillette.

P&G Growth Strategy: *Touching and improving more consumers' lives in more parts of the world more completely*

WHERE TO PLAY:

1. Grow leading, global brands and core categories
2. Build business with underserved and unserved consumers
3. Continue to grow and develop faster-growing, structurally attractive businesses with global leadership potential

HOW TO WIN:

1. Drive Core P&G Strengths in consumer understanding, brand building, innovation and go to market
2. Simplify, Scale and Execute for competitive advantage
3. Lead change to win with consumers and customers

Financial Highlights

FINANCIAL SUMMARY (UNAUDITED)

Amounts in millions, except per share amounts	2009	2008	2007	2006	2005
Net Sales	**$79,029**	$81,748	$74,832	$66,724	$55,292
Operating Income	**16,123**	16,637	15,003	12,916	10,026
Net Earnings	**13,436**	12,075	10,340	8,684	6,923
Net Earnings Margin from Continuing Operations	**14.3%**	14.4%	13.4%	12.7%	12.0%
Diluted Net Earnings per Common Share from Continuing Operations	**$ 3.58**	$ 3.56	$ 2.96	$ 2.58	$ 2.43
Diluted Net Earnings per Common Share	**4.26**	3.64	3.04	2.64	2.53
Dividends per Common Share	**1.64**	1.45	1.28	1.15	1.03

NET SALES
(in billions of dollars)

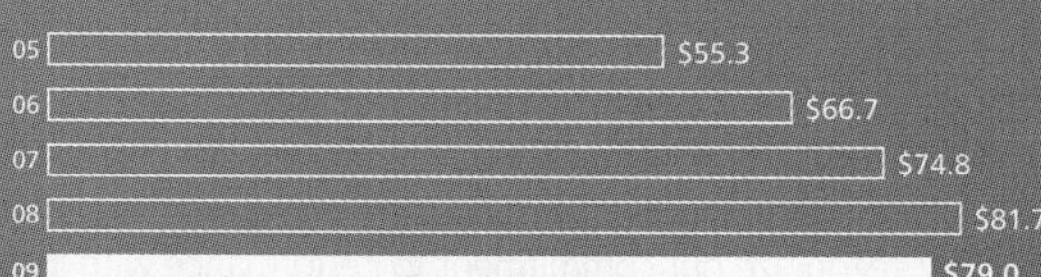

DILUTED NET EARNINGS
(per common share)

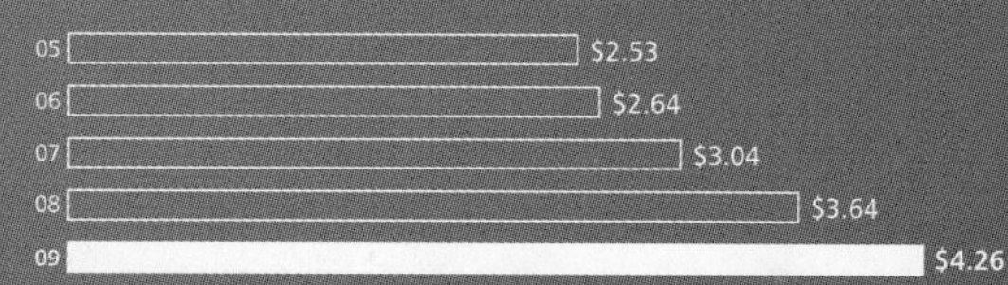

OPERATING CASH FLOW
(in billions of dollars)

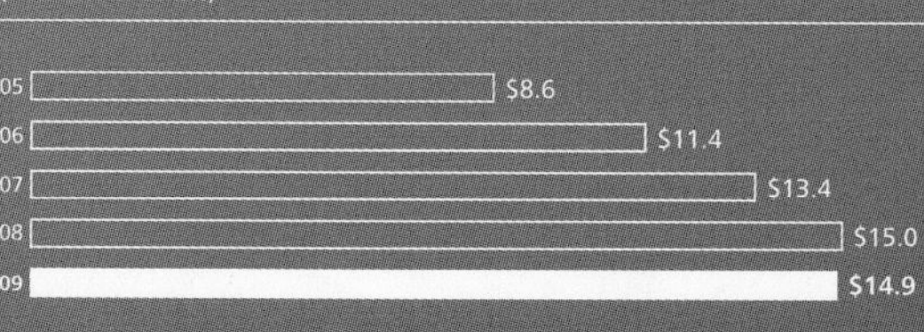

Note: Previous period results have been amended to exclude the results of the Folgers coffee business from continuing operations. For more information refer to Note 12 on page 71.

Management's Responsibility for Financial Reporting

At The Procter & Gamble Company, we take great pride in our long history of doing what's right. If you analyze what's made our company successful over the years, you may focus on our brands, our marketing strategies, our organization design and our ability to innovate. But if you really want to get at what drives our company's success, the place to look is our people. Our people are deeply committed to our Purpose, Values and Principles. It is this commitment to doing what's right that unites us.

This commitment to doing what's right is embodied in our financial reporting. High-quality financial reporting is our responsibility—one we execute with integrity, and within both the letter and spirit of the law.

High-quality financial reporting is characterized by accuracy, objectivity and transparency. Management is responsible for maintaining an effective system of internal controls over financial reporting to deliver those characteristics in all material respects. The Board of Directors, through its Audit Committee, provides oversight. We have engaged Deloitte & Touche LLP to audit our Consolidated Financial Statements, on which they have issued an unqualified opinion.

Our commitment to providing timely, accurate and understandable information to investors encompasses:

Communicating expectations to employees. Every employee—from senior management on down—is required to be trained on the Company's *Worldwide Business Conduct Manual*, which sets forth the Company's commitment to conduct its business affairs with high ethical standards. Every employee is held personally accountable for compliance and is provided several means of reporting any concerns about violations of the *Worldwide Business Conduct Manual*, which is available on our website at www.pg.com.

Maintaining a strong internal control environment. Our system of internal controls includes written policies and procedures, segregation of duties and the careful selection and development of employees. The system is designed to provide reasonable assurance that transactions are executed as authorized and appropriately recorded, that assets are safeguarded and that accounting records are sufficiently reliable to permit the preparation of financial statements conforming in all material respects with accounting principles generally accepted in the United States of America. We monitor these internal controls through control self-assessments conducted by business unit management. In addition to performing financial and compliance audits around the world, including unannounced audits, our Global Internal Audit organization provides training and continuously improves internal control processes. Appropriate actions are taken by management to correct any identified control deficiencies.

Executing financial stewardship. We maintain specific programs and activities to ensure that employees understand their fiduciary responsibilities to shareholders. This ongoing effort encompasses financial discipline in strategic and daily business decisions and brings particular focus to maintaining accurate financial reporting and effective controls through process improvement, skill development and oversight.

Exerting rigorous oversight of the business. We continuously review business results and strategic choices. Our Global Leadership Council is actively involved–from understanding strategies to reviewing key initiatives, financial performance and control assessments. The intent is to ensure we remain objective, identify potential issues, continuously challenge each other and ensure recognition and rewards are appropriately aligned with results.

Engaging our Disclosure Committee. We maintain disclosure controls and procedures designed to ensure that information required to be disclosed is recorded, processed, summarized and reported timely and accurately. Our Disclosure Committee is a group of senior-level executives responsible for evaluating disclosure implications of significant business activities and events. The Committee reports its findings to the CEO and CFO, providing an effective process to evaluate our external disclosure obligations.

Encouraging strong and effective corporate governance from our Board of Directors. We have an active, capable and diligent Board that meets the required standards for independence, and we welcome the Board's oversight. Our Audit Committee comprises independent directors with significant financial knowledge and experience. We review significant accounting policies, financial reporting and internal control matters with them and encourage their independent discussions with external auditors. Our corporate governance guidelines, as well as the charter of the Audit Committee and certain other committees of our Board, are available on our website at www.pg.com.

P&G has a strong history of doing what's right. Our employees embrace our Purpose, Values and Principles. We take responsibility for the quality and accuracy of our financial reporting. We present this information proudly, with the expectation that those who use it will understand our company, recognize our commitment to performance with integrity and share our confidence in P&G's future.

R.A. McDonald
President and Chief Executive Officer

J.R. Moeller
Chief Financial Officer

Management's Report on Internal Control over Financial Reporting

Management is responsible for establishing and maintaining adequate internal control over financial reporting of The Procter & Gamble Company (as defined in Rule 13a-15(f) under the Securities Exchange Act of 1934, as amended). Our internal control over financial reporting is designed to provide reasonable assurance regarding the reliability of financial reporting and the preparation of financial statements for external purposes in accordance with generally accepted accounting principles in the United States of America.

Strong internal controls is an objective that is reinforced through our *Worldwide Business Conduct Manual*, which sets forth our commitment to conduct business with integrity, and within both the letter and the spirit of the law. The Company's internal control over financial reporting includes a Control Self-Assessment Program that is conducted annually by substantially all areas of the Company and is audited by the internal audit function. Management takes the appropriate action to correct any identified control deficiencies. Because of its inherent limitations, any system of internal control over financial reporting, no matter how well designed, may not prevent or detect misstatements due to the possibility that a control can be circumvented or overridden or that misstatements due to error or fraud may occur that are not detected. Also, because of changes in conditions, internal control effectiveness may vary over time.

Management assessed the effectiveness of the Company's internal control over financial reporting as of June 30, 2009, using criteria established in *Internal Control–Integrated Framework* issued by the Committee of Sponsoring Organizations of the Treadway Commission (COSO) and concluded that the Company maintained effective internal control over financial reporting as of June 30, 2009, based on these criteria.

Deloitte & Touche LLP, an independent registered public accounting firm, has audited the effectiveness of the Company's internal control over financial reporting as of June 30, 2009, as stated in their report which is included herein.

R.A. McDonald
President and Chief Executive Officer

J.R. Moeller
Chief Financial Officer

August 14, 2009

Report of Independent Registered Public Accounting Firm

Deloitte.

To the Board of Directors and Stockholders of
The Procter & Gamble Company

We have audited the accompanying Consolidated Balance Sheets of The Procter & Gamble Company and subsidiaries (the "Company") as of June 30, 2009 and 2008, and the related Consolidated Statements of Earnings, Shareholders' Equity, and Cash Flows for each of the three years in the period ended June 30, 2009. These financial statements are the responsibility of the Company's management. Our responsibility is to express an opinion on these financial statements based on our audits.

We conducted our audits in accordance with the standards of the Public Company Accounting Oversight Board (United States). Those standards require that we plan and perform the audit to obtain reasonable assurance about whether the financial statements are free of material misstatement. An audit includes examining, on a test basis, evidence supporting the amounts and disclosures in the financial statements. An audit also includes assessing the accounting principles used and significant estimates made by management, as well as evaluating the overall financial statement presentation. We believe that our audits provide a reasonable basis for our opinion.

In our opinion, such Consolidated Financial Statements present fairly, in all material respects, the financial position of the Company at June 30, 2009 and 2008, and the results of its operations and cash flows for each of the three years in the period ended June 30, 2009, in conformity with accounting principles generally accepted in the United States of America.

As discussed in Note 9 to the Consolidated Financial Statements, the Company adopted new accounting guidance on the accounting for uncertainty in income taxes, effective July 1, 2007.

We have also audited, in accordance with the standards of the Public Company Accounting Oversight Board (United States), the Company's internal control over financial reporting as of June 30, 2009, based on the criteria established in *Internal Control—Integrated Framework* issued by the Committee of Sponsoring Organizations of the Treadway Commission and our report dated August 14, 2009 expressed an unqualified opinion on the Company's internal control over financial reporting.

Deloitte & Touche LLP

Cincinnati, Ohio
August 14, 2009

Report of Independent Registered Public Accounting Firm

Deloitte.

To the Board of Directors and Stockholders of
The Procter & Gamble Company

We have audited the internal control over financial reporting of The Procter & Gamble Company and subsidiaries (the "Company") as of June 30, 2009, based on criteria established in *Internal Control—Integrated Framework* issued by the Committee of Sponsoring Organizations of the Treadway Commission. The Company's management is responsible for maintaining effective internal control over financial reporting and for its assessment of the effectiveness of internal control over financial reporting, included in Management's Report on Internal Control Over Financial Reporting. Our responsibility is to express an opinion on the Company's internal control over financial reporting based on our audit.

We conducted our audit in accordance with the standards of the Public Company Accounting Oversight Board (United States). Those standards require that we plan and perform the audit to obtain reasonable assurance about whether effective internal control over financial reporting was maintained in all material respects. Our audit included obtaining an understanding of internal control over financial reporting, assessing the risk that a material weakness exists, testing and evaluating the design and operating effectiveness of internal control based on the assessed risk, and performing such other procedures as we considered necessary in the circumstances. We believe that our audit provides a reasonable basis for our opinion.

A company's internal control over financial reporting is a process designed by, or under the supervision of, the company's principal executive and principal financial officers, or persons performing similar functions, and effected by the company's board of directors, management, and other personnel to provide reasonable assurance regarding the reliability of financial reporting and the preparation of financial statements for external purposes in accordance with generally accepted accounting principles. A company's internal control over financial reporting includes those policies and procedures that (1) pertain to the maintenance of records that, in reasonable detail, accurately and fairly reflect the transactions and dispositions of the assets of the company; (2) provide reasonable assurance that transactions are recorded as necessary to permit preparation of financial statements in accordance with generally accepted accounting principles, and that receipts and expenditures of the company are being made only in accordance with authorizations of management and directors of the company; and (3) provide reasonable assurance regarding prevention or timely detection of unauthorized acquisition, use, or disposition of the company's assets that could have a material effect on the financial statements.

Because of the inherent limitations of internal control over financial reporting, including the possibility of collusion or improper management override of controls, material misstatements due to error or fraud may not be prevented or detected on a timely basis. Also, projections of any evaluation of the effectiveness of the internal control over financial reporting to future periods are subject to the risk that the controls may become inadequate because of changes in conditions, or that the degree of compliance with the policies or procedures may deteriorate.

In our opinion, the Company maintained, in all material respects, effective internal control over financial reporting as of June 30, 2009, based on the criteria established in *Internal Control — Integrated Framework* issued by the Committee of Sponsoring Organizations of the Treadway Commission.

We have also audited, in accordance with the standards of the Public Company Accounting Oversight Board (United States), the Consolidated Financial Statements of the Company as of and for the year ended June 30, 2009 and our report dated August 14, 2009 expressed an unqualified opinion on those financial statements and included an explanatory paragraph regarding the Company's adoption of new accounting guidance on the accounting for uncertainty in income taxes, effective July 1, 2007.

Deloitte & Touche LLP

Cincinnati, Ohio
August 14, 2009

Consolidated Statements of Earnings

Amounts in millions except per share amounts; Years ended June 30	2009	2008	2007
NET SALES	**$79,029**	$81,748	$74,832
Cost of products sold	**38,898**	39,536	35,659
Selling, general and administrative expense	**24,008**	25,575	24,170
OPERATING INCOME	**16,123**	16,637	15,003
Interest expense	**1,358**	1,467	1,304
Other non-operating income, net	**560**	462	565
EARNINGS FROM CONTINUING OPERATIONS BEFORE INCOME TAXES	**15,325**	15,632	14,264
Income taxes on continuing operations	**4,032**	3,834	4,201
NET EARNINGS FROM CONTINUING OPERATIONS	**11,293**	11,798	10,063
NET EARNINGS FROM DISCONTINUED OPERATIONS	**2,143**	277	277
NET EARNINGS	**$13,436**	$12,075	$10,340
BASIC NET EARNINGS PER COMMON SHARE:			
Earnings from continuing operations	**$ 3.76**	$ 3.77	$ 3.13
Earnings from discontinued operations	**0.73**	0.09	0.09
BASIC NET EARNINGS PER COMMON SHARE	**4.49**	3.86	3.22
DILUTED NET EARNINGS PER COMMON SHARE:			
Earnings from continuing operations	**3.58**	3.56	2.96
Earnings from discontinued operations	**0.68**	0.08	0.08
DILUTED NET EARNINGS PER COMMON SHARE	**4.26**	3.64	3.04
DIVIDENDS PER COMMON SHARE	**$ 1.64**	$ 1.45	$ 1.28

See accompanying Notes to Consolidated Financial Statements.

Consolidated Balance Sheets

Assets

Amounts in millions; June 30	2009	2008
CURRENT ASSETS		
Cash and cash equivalents	**$ 4,781**	$ 3,313
Accounts receivable	**5,836**	6,761
Inventories		
Materials and supplies	**1,557**	2,262
Work in process	**672**	765
Finished goods	**4,651**	5,389
Total inventories	**6,880**	8,416
Deferred income taxes	**1,209**	2,012
Prepaid expenses and other current assets	**3,199**	4,013
TOTAL CURRENT ASSETS	**21,905**	24,515
PROPERTY, PLANT AND EQUIPMENT		
Buildings	**6,724**	7,052
Machinery and equipment	**29,042**	30,145
Land	**885**	889
Total property, plant and equipment	**36,651**	38,086
Accumulated depreciation	**(17,189)**	(17,446)
NET PROPERTY, PLANT AND EQUIPMENT	**19,462**	20,640
GOODWILL AND OTHER INTANGIBLE ASSETS		
Goodwill	**56,512**	59,767
Trademarks and other intangible assets, net	**32,606**	34,233
NET GOODWILL AND OTHER INTANGIBLE ASSETS	**89,118**	94,000
OTHER NONCURRENT ASSETS	**4,348**	4,837
TOTAL ASSETS	**$134,833**	$143,992

See accompanying Notes to Consolidated Financial Statements.

Consolidated Balance Sheets

Liabilities and Shareholders' Equity

Amounts in millions; June 30	2009	2008
CURRENT LIABILITIES		
Accounts payable	**$ 5,980**	$ 6,775
Accrued and other liabilities	**8,601**	11,099
Debt due within one year	**16,320**	13,084
TOTAL CURRENT LIABILITIES	**30,901**	30,958
LONG-TERM DEBT	**20,652**	23,581
DEFERRED INCOME TAXES	**10,752**	11,805
OTHER NONCURRENT LIABILITIES	**9,429**	8,154
TOTAL LIABILITIES	**71,734**	74,498
SHAREHOLDERS' EQUITY		
Convertible Class A preferred stock, stated value $1 per share (600 shares authorized)	**1,324**	1,366
Non-Voting Class B preferred stock, stated value $1 per share (200 shares authorized)	**—**	—
Common stock, stated value $1 per share (10,000 shares authorized; shares issued: 2009—4,007.3, 2008—4,001.8)	**4,007**	4,002
Additional paid-in capital	**61,118**	60,307
Reserve for ESOP debt retirement	**(1,340)**	(1,325)
Accumulated other comprehensive income (loss)	**(3,358)**	3,746
Treasury stock, at cost (shares held: 2009—1,090.3, 2008—969.1)	**(55,961)**	(47,588)
Retained earnings	**57,309**	48,986
TOTAL SHAREHOLDERS' EQUITY	**63,099**	69,494
TOTAL LIABILITIES AND SHAREHOLDERS' EQUITY	**$134,833**	$143,992

See accompanying Notes to Consolidated Financial Statements.

Consolidated Statements of Shareholders' Equity

Dollars in millions/Shares in thousands	Common Shares Outstanding	Common Stock	Preferred Stock	Additional Paid-In Capital	Reserve for ESOP Debt Retirement	Accumulated Other Comprehensive Income	Treasury Stock	Retained Earnings	Total
BALANCE JUNE 30, 2006	3,178,841	$3,976	$1,451	$57,856	$(1,288)	$ (518)	$(34,235)	$35,666	$ 62,908
Net earnings								10,340	10,340
Other comprehensive income:									
Financial statement translation						2,419			2,419
Hedges and investment securities, net of $459 tax						(951)			(951)
Total comprehensive income									$ 11,808
Cumulative impact for adoption of new accounting guidance (1)						(333)			(333)
Dividends to shareholders:									
Common								(4,048)	(4,048)
Preferred, net of tax benefits								(161)	(161)
Treasury purchases	(89,829)						(5,578)		(5,578)
Employee plan issuances	37,824	14		1,167			1,003		2,184
Preferred stock conversions	5,110		(45)	7			38		—
ESOP debt impacts					(20)				(20)
BALANCE JUNE 30, 2007	3,131,946	3,990	1,406	59,030	(1,308)	617	(38,772)	41,797	66,760
Net earnings								12,075	12,075
Other comprehensive income:									
Financial statement translation						6,543			6,543
Hedges and investment securities, net of $1,664 tax						(2,906)			(2,906)
Defined benefit retirement plans, net of $120 tax						(508)			(508)
Total comprehensive income									$ 15,204
Cumulative impact for adoption of new accounting guidance (1)								(232)	(232)
Dividends to shareholders:									
Common								(4,479)	(4,479)
Preferred, net of tax benefits								(176)	(176)
Treasury purchases	(148,121)						(10,047)		(10,047)
Employee plan issuances	43,910	12		1,272			1,196		2,480
Preferred stock conversions	4,982		(40)	5			35		—
ESOP debt impacts					(17)			1	(16)
BALANCE JUNE 30, 2008	3,032,717	4,002	1,366	60,307	(1,325)	3,746	(47,588)	48,986	69,494
Net earnings								**13,436**	**13,436**
Other comprehensive income:									
Financial statement translation						**(6,151)**			**(6,151)**
Hedges and investment securities, net of $452 tax						**748**			**748**
Defined benefit retirement plans, net of $879 tax						**(1,701)**			**(1,701)**
Total comprehensive income									**$ 6,332**
Cumulative impact for adoption of new accounting guidance (1)								**(84)**	**(84)**
Dividends to shareholders:									
Common								**(4,852)**	**(4,852)**
Preferred, net of tax benefits								**(192)**	**(192)**
Treasury purchases	**(98,862)**						**(6,370)**		**(6,370)**
Employee plan issuances	**16,841**	**5**		**804**			**428**		**1,237**
Preferred stock conversions	**4,992**		**(42)**	**7**			**35**		—
Shares tendered for Folgers coffee subsidiary	**(38,653)**						**(2,466)**		**(2,466)**
ESOP debt impacts					**(15)**			**15**	—
BALANCE JUNE 30, 2009	**2,917,035**	**$4,007**	**$1,324**	**$61,118**	**$(1,340)**	**$(3,358)**	**$(55,961)**	**$57,309**	**$ 63,099**

(1) Cumulative impact of adopting new accounting guidance relates to: 2007—defined benefit and post retirement plans; 2008—uncertainty in income taxes; 2009—split-dollar life insurance arrangements.

See accompanying Notes to Consolidated Financial Statements.

Consolidated Statements of Cash Flows

Amounts in millions; Years ended June 30	2009	2008	2007
CASH AND CASH EQUIVALENTS, BEGINNING OF YEAR	**$ 3,313**	$ 5,354	$ 6,693
OPERATING ACTIVITIES			
Net earnings	**13,436**	12,075	10,340
Depreciation and amortization	**3,082**	3,166	3,130
Share-based compensation expense	**516**	555	668
Deferred income taxes	**596**	1,214	253
Gain on sale of businesses	**(2,377)**	(284)	(153)
Change in accounts receivable	**415**	432	(729)
Change in inventories	**721**	(1,050)	(389)
Change in accounts payable, accrued and other liabilities	**(742)**	297	(278)
Change in other operating assets and liabilities	**(758)**	(1,270)	(151)
Other	**30**	(127)	719
TOTAL OPERATING ACTIVITIES	**14,919**	15,008	13,410
INVESTING ACTIVITIES			
Capital expenditures	**(3,238)**	(3,046)	(2,945)
Proceeds from asset sales	**1,087**	928	281
Acquisitions, net of cash acquired	**(368)**	(381)	(492)
Change in investments	**166**	(50)	673
TOTAL INVESTING ACTIVITIES	**(2,353)**	(2,549)	(2,483)
FINANCING ACTIVITIES			
Dividends to shareholders	**(5,044)**	(4,655)	(4,209)
Change in short-term debt	**(2,420)**	2,650	9,006
Additions to long-term debt	**4,926**	7,088	4,758
Reductions of long-term debt	**(2,587)**	(11,747)	(17,929)
Treasury stock purchases	**(6,370)**	(10,047)	(5,578)
Impact of stock options and other	**681**	1,867	1,499
TOTAL FINANCING ACTIVITIES	**(10,814)**	(14,844)	(12,453)
EFFECT OF EXCHANGE RATE CHANGES ON CASH AND CASH EQUIVALENTS	**(284)**	344	187
CHANGE IN CASH AND CASH EQUIVALENTS	**1,468**	(2,041)	(1,339)
CASH AND CASH EQUIVALENTS, END OF YEAR	**$ 4,781**	$ 3,313	$ 5,354

SUPPLEMENTAL DISCLOSURE			
Cash payments for:			
Interest	**$ 1,226**	$ 1,373	$ 1,330
Income Taxes	**3,248**	3,499	4,116
Assets acquired through non-cash capital leases	**8**	13	41
Divestiture of coffee business in exchange for shares of P&G stock	**2,466**	—	—

See accompanying Notes to Consolidated Financial Statements.

Notes to Consolidated Financial Statements

NOTE 1

SUMMARY OF SIGNIFICANT ACCOUNTING POLICIES

Nature of Operations

The Procter & Gamble Company's (the "Company," "we" or "us") business is focused on providing branded consumer goods products of superior quality and value. Our products are sold in more than 180 countries primarily through retail operations including mass merchandisers, grocery stores, membership club stores, drug stores, department stores, salons and high-frequency stores. We have on-the-ground operations in approximately 80 countries.

Basis of Presentation

The Consolidated Financial Statements include the Company and its controlled subsidiaries. Intercompany transactions are eliminated.

Use of Estimates

Preparation of financial statements in conformity with accounting principles generally accepted in the United States of America (U.S. GAAP) requires management to make estimates and assumptions that affect the amounts reported in the Consolidated Financial Statements and accompanying disclosures. These estimates are based on management's best knowledge of current events and actions the Company may undertake in the future. Estimates are used in accounting for, among other items, consumer and trade promotion accruals, pensions, post-employment benefits, stock options, valuation of acquired intangible assets, useful lives for depreciation and amortization, future cash flows associated with impairment testing for goodwill, indefinite-lived intangible assets and long-lived assets, deferred tax assets, uncertain income tax positions and contingencies. Actual results may ultimately differ from estimates, although management does not generally believe such differences would materially affect the financial statements in any individual year. However, in regard to ongoing impairment testing of goodwill and indefinite-lived intangible assets, significant deterioration in future cash flow projections or other assumptions used in valuation models, versus those anticipated at the time of the initial valuations, could result in impairment charges that may materially affect the financial statements in a given year.

Revenue Recognition

Sales are recognized when revenue is realized or realizable and has been earned. Most revenue transactions represent sales of inventory. The revenue recorded is presented net of sales and other taxes we collect on behalf of governmental authorities and includes shipping and handling costs, which generally are included in the list price to the customer. Our policy is to recognize revenue when title to the product, ownership and risk of loss transfer to the customer, which can be on the date of shipment or the date of receipt by the customer. A provision for payment discounts and product return allowances is recorded as a reduction of sales in the same period that the revenue is recognized.

Trade promotions, consisting primarily of customer pricing allowances, merchandising funds and consumer coupons, are offered through various programs to customers and consumers. Sales are recorded net of trade promotion spending, which is recognized as incurred, generally at the time of the sale. Most of these arrangements have terms of approximately one year. Accruals for expected payouts under these programs are included as accrued marketing and promotion in the accrued and other liabilities line item in the Consolidated Balance Sheets.

Cost of Products Sold

Cost of products sold is primarily comprised of direct materials and supplies consumed in the manufacture of product, as well as manufacturing labor, depreciation expense and direct overhead expense necessary to acquire and convert the purchased materials and supplies into finished product. Cost of products sold also includes the cost to distribute products to customers, inbound freight costs, internal transfer costs, warehousing costs and other shipping and handling activity.

Selling, General and Administrative Expense

Selling, general and administrative expense (SG&A) is primarily comprised of marketing expenses, selling expenses, research and development costs, administrative and other indirect overhead costs, depreciation and amortization expense on non-manufacturing assets and other miscellaneous operating items. Research and development costs are charged to expense as incurred and were $2,044 in 2009, $2,212 in 2008, and $2,100 in 2007. Advertising costs, charged to expense as incurred, include worldwide television, print, radio, internet and in-store advertising expenses and were $7,579 in 2009, $8,583 in 2008 and $7,850 in 2007. Non-advertising related components of the Company's total marketing spending include costs associated with consumer promotions, product sampling and sales aids, all of which are included in SG&A, as well as coupons and customer trade funds, which are recorded as reductions to net sales.

Other Non-Operating Income, Net

Other non-operating income, net, primarily includes net divestiture gains and interest and investment income.

Currency Translation

Financial statements of operating subsidiaries outside the United States of America (U.S.) generally are measured using the local currency as the functional currency. Adjustments to translate those statements into U.S. dollars are recorded in other comprehensive income. Currency translation adjustments in accumulated other comprehensive income were gains of $3,333 and $9,484 at June 30, 2009 and 2008, respectively. For subsidiaries operating in highly inflationary economies, the U.S. dollar is the functional currency. Remeasurement adjustments for financial statements in highly inflationary economies and other transactional exchange gains and losses are reflected in earnings.

Amounts in millions of dollars except per share amounts or as otherwise specified.

Cash Flow Presentation

The Statements of Cash Flows are prepared using the indirect method, which reconciles net earnings to cash flow from operating activities. The reconciliation adjustments include the removal of timing differences between the occurrence of operating receipts and payments and their recognition in net earnings. The adjustments also remove cash flows arising from investing and financing activities, which are presented separately from operating activities. Cash flows from foreign currency transactions and operations are translated at an average exchange rate for the period. Cash flows from hedging activities are included in the same category as the items being hedged. Cash flows from derivative instruments designated as net investment hedges are classified as financing activities. Realized gains and losses from non-qualifying derivative instruments used to hedge currency exposures resulting from intercompany financing transactions are also classified as financing activities. Cash flows from other derivative instruments used to manage interest, commodity or other currency exposures are classified as operating activities. Cash payments related to income taxes are classified as operating activities.

Cash Equivalents

Highly liquid investments with remaining stated maturities of three months or less when purchased are considered cash equivalents and recorded at cost.

Investments

Investment securities consist of readily marketable debt and equity securities. Unrealized gains or losses are charged to earnings for investments classified as trading. Unrealized gains or losses on securities classified as available-for-sale are generally recorded in shareholders' equity. If an available-for-sale security is other than temporarily impaired, the loss is charged to either earnings or shareholders' equity depending on our intent and ability to retain the security until we recover the full cost basis and the extent of the loss attributable to the creditworthiness of the issuer. Investments in certain companies over which we exert significant influence, but do not control the financial and operating decisions, are accounted for as equity method investments and are classified as other noncurrent assets. Other investments that are not controlled, and over which we do not have the ability to exercise significant influence, are accounted for under the cost method.

Inventory Valuation

Inventories are valued at the lower of cost or market value. Product-related inventories are primarily maintained on the first-in, first-out method. Minor amounts of product inventories, including certain cosmetics and commodities, are maintained on the last-in, first-out method. The cost of spare part inventories is maintained using the average cost method.

Property, Plant and Equipment

Property, plant and equipment is recorded at cost reduced by accumulated depreciation. Depreciation expense is recognized over the assets' estimated useful lives using the straight-line method. Machinery and equipment includes office furniture and fixtures (15-year life), computer equipment and capitalized software (3- to 5-year lives) and manufacturing equipment (3- to 20-year lives). Buildings are depreciated over an estimated useful life of 40 years. Estimated useful lives are periodically reviewed and, when appropriate, changes are made prospectively. When certain events or changes in operating conditions occur, asset lives may be adjusted and an impairment assessment may be performed on the recoverability of the carrying amounts.

Goodwill and Other Intangible Assets

Goodwill and indefinite-lived brands are not amortized, but are evaluated for impairment annually or when indicators of a potential impairment are present. Our impairment testing of goodwill is performed separately from our impairment testing of individual indefinite-lived intangibles. The annual evaluation for impairment of goodwill and indefinite-lived intangibles is based on valuation models that incorporate assumptions and internal projections of expected future cash flows and operating plans. We believe such assumptions are also comparable to those that would be used by other market-place participants.

We have a number of acquired brands that have been determined to have indefinite lives due to the nature of our business. We evaluate a number of factors to determine whether an indefinite life is appropriate, including the competitive environment, market share, brand history, product life cycles, operating plans and the macroeconomic environment of the countries in which the brands are sold. When certain events or changes in operating conditions occur, an impairment assessment is performed and indefinite-lived brands may be adjusted to a determinable life.

The cost of intangible assets with determinable useful lives is amortized to reflect the pattern of economic benefits consumed, either on a straight-line or accelerated basis over the estimated periods benefited. Patents, technology and other intangibles with contractual terms are generally amortized over their respective legal or contractual lives. Customer relationships and other non-contractual intangible assets with determinable lives are amortized over periods generally ranging from 5 to 40 years. When certain events or changes in operating conditions occur, an impairment assessment is performed and lives of intangible assets with determinable lives may be adjusted.

Fair Values of Financial Instruments

Certain financial instruments are required to be recorded at fair value. The estimated fair values of such financial instruments (including certain debt instruments, investment securities and derivatives) have been determined using market information and valuation methodologies, primarily discounted cash flow analysis. Changes in assumptions or estimation methods could affect the fair value estimates; however, we do not believe any such changes would have a material impact on our financial condition, results of operations or cash flows. Other financial instruments, including cash equivalents, other investments and short-term debt, are recorded at cost, which approximates fair value. The fair values of long-term debt and derivative instruments are disclosed in Note 4 and Note 5, respectively.

Subsequent Events

For the fiscal year ended June 30, 2009, the Company has evaluated subsequent events for potential recognition and disclosure through August 14, 2009, the date of financial statement issuance.

New Accounting Pronouncements and Policies

Other than as described below, no new accounting pronouncement issued or effective during the fiscal year has had or is expected to have a material impact on the Consolidated Financial Statements.

FAIR VALUE MEASUREMENTS

On July 1, 2008, we adopted new accounting guidance on fair value measurements. The new guidance defines fair value, establishes a framework for measuring fair value under U.S. GAAP, and expands disclosures about fair value measurements. It was effective for the Company beginning July 1, 2008, for certain financial assets and liabilities. Refer to Note 5 for additional information regarding our fair value measurements for financial assets and liabilities. The new guidance is effective for non-financial assets and liabilities recognized or disclosed at fair value on a nonrecurring basis beginning July 1, 2009. The Company believes that the adoption of the new guidance applicable to non-financial assets and liabilities will not have a material effect on its financial position, results of operations or cash flows.

DISCLOSURES ABOUT DERIVATIVE INSTRUMENTS AND HEDGING ACTIVITIES

On January 1, 2009, we adopted new accounting guidance on disclosures about derivative instruments and hedging activities. The new guidance impacts disclosures only and requires additional qualitative and quantitative information on the use of derivatives and their impact on an entity's financial position, results of operations and cash flows. Refer to Note 5 for additional information regarding our risk management activities, including derivative instruments and hedging activities.

BUSINESS COMBINATIONS AND NONCONTROLLING INTERESTS IN CONSOLIDATED FINANCIAL STATEMENTS

In December 2007, the Financial Accounting Standards Board issued new accounting guidance on business combinations and non-controlling interests in consolidated financial statements. The new guidance revises the method of accounting for a number of aspects of business combinations and noncontrolling interests, including acquisition costs, contingencies (including contingent assets, contingent liabilities and contingent purchase price), the impacts of partial and step-acquisitions (including the valuation of net assets attributable to non-acquired minority interests) and post-acquisition exit activities of acquired businesses. The new guidance will be effective for the Company during our fiscal year beginning July 1, 2009. The Company believes that the adoption of the new guidance will not have a material effect on its financial position, results of operations or cash flows.

NOTE 2

GOODWILL AND INTANGIBLE ASSETS

The change in the net carrying amount of goodwill by Global Business Unit (GBU) was as follows:

	2009	2008
BEAUTY GBU		
Beauty, beginning of year	**$16,903**	$15,359
Acquisitions and divestitures	**98**	187
Translation and other	**(942)**	1,357
GOODWILL, JUNE 30	**16,059**	16,903
Grooming, beginning of year	**25,312**	24,211
Acquisitions and divestitures	**(246)**	(269)
Translation and other	**(1,066)**	1,370
GOODWILL, JUNE 30	**24,000**	25,312
HEALTH AND WELL-BEING GBU		
Health Care, beginning of year	**8,750**	8,482
Acquisitions and divestitures	**(81)**	(59)
Translation and other	**(265)**	327
GOODWILL, JUNE 30	**8,404**	8,750
Snacks and Pet Care, beginning of year	**2,434**	2,407
Acquisitions and divestitures	**(356)**	(5)
Translation and other	**(23)**	32
GOODWILL, JUNE 30	**2,055**	2,434
HOUSEHOLD CARE GBU		
Fabric Care and Home Care, beginning of year	**4,655**	4,470
Acquisitions and divestitures	**(46)**	(43)
Translation and other	**(201)**	228
GOODWILL, JUNE 30	**4,408**	4,655
Baby Care and Family Care, beginning of year	**1,713**	1,623
Acquisitions and divestitures	**(7)**	(34)
Translation and other	**(120)**	124
GOODWILL, JUNE 30	**1,586**	1,713
GOODWILL, NET, beginning of year	**59,767**	56,552
Acquisitions and divestitures	**(638)**	(223)
Translation and other	**(2,617)**	3,438
GOODWILL, JUNE 30	**56,512**	59,767

The acquisition and divestiture impact during fiscal 2009 in Snacks and Pet Care is primarily due to the divestiture of the Coffee business. The remaining decrease in goodwill during fiscal 2009 is primarily due to currency translation across all GBUs.

Amounts in millions of dollars except per share amounts or as otherwise specified.

Identifiable intangible assets were comprised of:

June 30	2009 Gross Carrying Amount	2009 Accumulated Amortization	2008 Gross Carrying Amount	2008 Accumulated Amortization
INTANGIBLE ASSETS WITH DETERMINABLE LIVES				
Brands	**$ 3,580**	**$1,253**	$ 3,564	$1,032
Patents and technology	**3,168**	**1,332**	3,188	1,077
Customer relationships	**1,853**	**411**	1,947	353
Other	**320**	**210**	333	209
TOTAL	**8,921**	**3,206**	9,032	2,671
BRANDS WITH INDEFINITE LIVES	**26,891**	**—**	27,872	—
TOTAL	**35,812**	**3,206**	36,904	2,671

The amortization of intangible assets for the years ended June 30, 2009, 2008 and 2007 was $648, $649 and $640, respectively. Estimated amortization expense over the next five years is as follows: 2010—$570; 2011—$523; 2012—$489; 2013—$462; and 2014—$429. Such estimates do not reflect the impact of future foreign exchange rate changes.

NOTE 3

SUPPLEMENTAL FINANCIAL INFORMATION

Selected components of current and noncurrent liabilities were as follows:

June 30	2009	2008
ACCRUED AND OTHER LIABILITIES—CURRENT		
Marketing and promotion	**$2,378**	$ 2,760
Compensation expenses	**1,464**	1,527
Accrued Gillette exit costs	**111**	257
Taxes payable	**722**	945
Other	**3,926**	5,610
TOTAL	**8,601**	11,099
OTHER NONCURRENT LIABILITIES		
Pension benefits	**$3,798**	$ 3,146
Other postretirement benefits	**1,516**	512
Unrecognized tax benefits	**2,705**	3,075
Other	**1,410**	1,421
TOTAL	**9,429**	8,154

Gillette Acquisition

On October 1, 2005, we completed our acquisition of The Gillette Company (Gillette) for total consideration of $53.4 billion including common stock, the fair value of vested stock options and acquisition costs. In connection with this acquisition, we recognized an assumed liability for Gillette exit costs of $1.2 billion, including $854 in separation costs related to approximately 5,500 people, $55 in employee relocation costs and $320 in other exit costs. These costs are primarily related to the elimination of selling, general and administrative overlap between the two companies in areas like Global Business Services, corporate staff and go-to-market support, as well as redundant manufacturing capacity. These activities are substantially complete as of June 30, 2009. Total integration plan charges against the assumed liability were $51, $286 and $438 for the years ended June 2009, 2008 and 2007, respectively. A total of $106 and $121 of the liability was reversed during the years ended June 2009 and 2008, respectively, related to underspending on a number of projects that were concluded during the period, which resulted in a reduction of goodwill during those years.

NOTE 4

SHORT-TERM AND LONG-TERM DEBT

June 30	2009	2008
DEBT DUE WITHIN ONE YEAR		
Current portion of long-term debt	**$ 6,941**	$ 1,746
Commercial paper	**5,027**	9,748
Floating rate notes	**4,250**	1,500
Other	**102**	90
TOTAL	**16,320**	13,084

The weighted average short-term interest rates were 2.0% and 2.7% as of June 30, 2009 and 2008, respectively, including the effects of interest rate swaps discussed in Note 5.

June 30	2009	2008
LONG-TERM DEBT		
Floating rate note due July 2009	**$ 1,750**	$ 1,750
Floating rate note due August 2009	**1,500**	1,500
6.88% USD note due September 2009	**1,000**	1,000
Floating rate note due March 2010	**750**	—
2% JPY note due June 2010	**522**	467
4.88% EUR note due October 2011	**1,411**	1,573
3.38% EUR note due December 2012	**1,975**	2,203
4.60% USD note due January 2014	**2,000**	—
4.50% EUR note due May 2014	**2,116**	2,360
4.95% USD note due August 2014	**900**	900
3.50% USD note due February 2015	**750**	—
4.85% USD note due December 2015	**700**	700
5.13% EUR note due October 2017	**1,552**	1,731
4.70% USD note due February 2019	**1,250**	—
4.13% EUR note due December 2020	**846**	944
9.36% ESOP debentures due 2009–2021[(1)]	**896**	934
4.88% EUR note due May 2027	**1,411**	1,573
6.25% GBP note due January 2030	**832**	993
5.50% USD note due February 2034	**500**	500
5.80% USD note due August 2034	**600**	600
5.55% USD note due March 2037	**1,400**	1,400
Capital lease obligations	**392**	407
All other long-term debt	**2,540**	3,792
Current portion of long-term debt	**(6,941)**	(1,746)
TOTAL	**20,652**	23,581

(1) Debt issued by the ESOP is guaranteed by the Company and must be recorded as debt of the Company as discussed in Note 8.

Long-term weighted average interest rates were 4.9% and 4.5% as of June 30, 2009 and 2008, respectively, including the effects of interest rate swaps and net investment hedges discussed in Note 5.

The fair value of the long-term debt was $21,514 and $23,276 at June 30, 2009 and 2008, respectively. Long-term debt maturities during the next five years are as follows: 2010—$6,941; 2011—$47; 2012—$1,474; 2013—$2,013; and 2014—$4,154.

The Procter & Gamble Company fully and unconditionally guarantees the registered debt and securities issued by its 100% owned finance subsidiaries.

NOTE 5

RISK MANAGEMENT ACTIVITIES AND FAIR VALUE MEASUREMENTS

As a multinational company with diverse product offerings, we are exposed to market risks, such as changes in interest rates, currency exchange rates and commodity prices. We evaluate exposures on a centralized basis to take advantage of natural exposure netting and correlation. To the extent we choose to manage volatility associated with the net exposures, we enter into various financial transactions which we account for using the applicable accounting guidance for derivative instruments and hedging activities. These financial transactions are governed by our policies covering acceptable counterparty exposure, instrument types and other hedging practices.

At inception, we formally designate and document qualifying instruments as hedges of underlying exposures. We formally assess, both at inception and at least quarterly, whether the financial instruments used in hedging transactions are effective at offsetting changes in either the fair value or cash flows of the related underlying exposure. Fluctuations in the value of these instruments generally are offset by changes in the fair value or cash flows of the underlying exposures being hedged. This offset is driven by the high degree of effectiveness between the exposure being hedged and the hedging instrument. The ineffective portion of a change in the fair value of a qualifying instrument is immediately recognized in earnings. The amount of ineffectiveness recognized is immaterial for all periods presented.

Credit Risk Management

We have counterparty credit guidelines and generally enter into transactions with investment grade financial institutions. Counterparty exposures are monitored daily and downgrades in credit rating are reviewed on a timely basis. Credit risk arising from the inability of a counterparty to meet the terms of our financial instrument contracts generally is limited to the amounts, if any, by which the counterparty's obligations to us exceed our obligations to the counterparty. We have not incurred and do not expect to incur material credit losses on our risk management or other financial instruments.

Certain of the Company's financial instruments used in hedging transactions are governed by industry standard netting agreements with counterparties. If the Company's credit rating were to fall below the levels stipulated in the agreements, the counterparties could demand either collateralization or termination of the arrangement. The aggregate fair value of the instruments covered by these contractual features that are in a net liability position as of June 30, 2009 was $288 million. The Company has never been required to post any collateral as a result of these contractual features.

Amounts in millions of dollars except per share amounts or as otherwise specified.

Interest Rate Risk Management

Our policy is to manage interest cost using a mixture of fixed-rate and variable-rate debt. To manage this risk in a cost-efficient manner, we enter into interest rate swaps in which we agree to exchange with the counterparty, at specified intervals, the difference between fixed and variable interest amounts calculated by reference to an agreed-upon notional amount.

Interest rate swaps that meet specific accounting criteria are accounted for as fair value and cash flow hedges. There were no fair value hedging instruments at June 30, 2009 or June 30, 2008. For cash flow hedges, the effective portion of the changes in fair value of the hedging instrument is reported in other comprehensive income (OCI) and reclassified into interest expense over the life of the underlying debt. The ineffective portion, which is not material for any year presented, is immediately recognized in earnings.

Foreign Currency Risk Management

We manufacture and sell our products in a number of countries throughout the world and, as a result, are exposed to movements in foreign currency exchange rates. The purpose of our foreign currency hedging program is to manage the volatility associated with short-term changes in exchange rates.

To manage this exchange rate risk, we have historically utilized a combination of forward contracts, options and currency swaps. As of June 30, 2009, we had currency swaps with maturities up to five years, which are intended to offset the effect of exchange rate fluctuations on intercompany loans denominated in foreign currencies and are therefore accounted for as cash flow hedges. The Company has also utilized forward contracts and options to offset the effect of exchange rate fluctuations on forecasted sales, inventory purchases and intercompany royalties denominated in foreign currencies. The effective portion of the changes in fair value of these instruments is reported in OCI and reclassified into earnings in the same financial statement line item and in the same period or periods during which the related hedged transactions affect earnings. The ineffective portion, which is not material for any year presented, is immediately recognized in earnings.

The change in value of certain non-qualifying instruments used to manage foreign exchange exposure of intercompany financing transactions, income from international operations and other balance sheet items subject to revaluation is immediately recognized in earnings, substantially offsetting the foreign currency mark-to-market impact of the related exposure. The net earnings impact of such instruments was a $1,047 loss in 2009 and gains of $1,397 and $56 in 2008 and 2007, respectively.

Net Investment Hedging

We hedge certain net investment positions in major foreign subsidiaries. To accomplish this, we either borrow directly in foreign currencies and designate all or a portion of foreign currency debt as a hedge of the applicable net investment position or enter into foreign currency swaps that are designated as hedges of our related foreign net investments. Changes in the fair value of these instruments are immediately recognized in OCI to offset the change in the value of the net investment being hedged. Currency effects of these hedges reflected in OCI were an after-tax gain of $964 in 2009 and $2,951 loss in 2008. Accumulated net balances were a $4,059 and a $5,023 after-tax loss as of June 30, 2009 and 2008, respectively.

Commodity Risk Management

Certain raw materials used in our products or production processes are subject to price volatility caused by weather, supply conditions, political and economic variables and other unpredictable factors. To manage the volatility related to anticipated purchases of certain of these materials, we use futures and options with maturities generally less than one year and swap contracts with maturities up to five years. These market instruments generally are designated as cash flow hedges. The effective portion of the changes in fair value for these instruments is reported in OCI and reclassified into earnings in the same financial statement line item and in the same period or periods during which the hedged transactions affect earnings. The ineffective and non-qualifying portions, which are not material for any year presented, are immediately recognized in earnings.

Insurance

We self insure for most insurable risks. In addition, we purchase insurance for Directors and Officers Liability and certain other coverage in situations where it is required by law, by contract, or deemed to be in the interest of the Company.

Fair Value Hierarchy

New accounting guidance on fair value measurements for certain financial assets and liabilities requires that assets and liabilities carried at fair value be classified and disclosed in one of the following three categories:

Level 1: Quoted market prices in active markets for identical assets or liabilities.

Level 2: Observable market-based inputs or unobservable inputs that are corroborated by market data.

Level 3: Unobservable inputs reflecting the reporting entity's own assumptions or external inputs from inactive markets.

In valuing assets and liabilities, we are required to maximize the use of quoted market prices and minimize the use of unobservable inputs. We calculate the fair value of our Level 1 and Level 2 instruments based on the exchange traded price of similar or identical instruments where available or based on other observable instruments. The fair value of our Level 3 instruments is calculated as the net present value of expected cash flows based on externally provided inputs. These calculations take into consideration the credit risk of both the Company and our counterparties. The Company has not changed its valuation techniques in measuring the fair value of any financial assets and liabilities during the period.

The following table sets forth the Company's financial assets and liabilities as of June 30, 2009 that are measured at fair value on a recurring basis during the period, segregated by level within the fair value hierarchy:

At June 30	Level 1	Level 2	Level 3	2009	2008
Assets at fair value:					
Investment securities	$ —	$174	$38	**$212**	$ 282
Derivatives relating to:					
Foreign currency hedges	—	—	—	—	4
Other foreign currency instruments (1)	—	300	—	**300**	190
Net investment hedges	—	83	—	**83**	26
Commodities	3	25	—	**28**	229
Total assets at fair value (2)	3	582	38	**623**	731
Liabilities at fair value:					
Derivatives relating to:					
Foreign currency hedges	—	103	—	**103**	37
Other foreign currency instruments (1)	—	39	—	**39**	33
Net investment hedges	—	85	—	**85**	1,210
Interest rate	—	13	—	**13**	17
Commodities	2	96	3	**101**	—
Total liabilities at fair value (3)	2	336	3	**341**	1,297

(1) The other foreign currency instruments are comprised of non-qualifying foreign currency financial instruments.

(2) All derivative assets are presented in prepaid expenses and other current assets or other noncurrent assets with the exception of investment securities which are only presented in other noncurrent assets.

(3) All liabilities are presented in accrued and other liabilities or other noncurrent liabilities.

The table below sets forth a reconciliation of the Company's beginning and ending Level 3 financial assets and liabilities balances for the year ended June 30, 2009.

	Derivatives	Investment Securities
BEGINNING OF YEAR	**$ 17**	**$ 46**
Total gains or (losses) (realized/unrealized) included in earnings (or changes in net assets)	**—**	**(2)**
Total gains or (losses) (realized/unrealized) included in OCI	**(27)**	**(6)**
Net purchases, issuances and settlements	**7**	**—**
Transfers in/(out) of Level 3	**—**	**—**
END OF YEAR	**(3)**	**38**

Amounts in millions of dollars except per share amounts or as otherwise specified.

Disclosures about Derivative Instruments

The fair values and amounts of gains and losses on qualifying and non-qualifying financial instruments used in hedging transactions as of, and for the year ended, June 30, 2009 are as follows:

Derivatives in Cash Flow Hedging Relationships	Notional Amount (Ending Balance)	Fair Value Asset (Liability)	Amount of Gain or (Loss) Recognized in OCI on Derivative (Effective Portion)	Amount of Gain or (Loss) Reclassified from Accumulated OCI into Income (Effective Portion)(1)
		June 30	June 30	Twelve Months Ended June 30
Interest rate contracts	$4,000	$ (13)	$ 18	$ (56)
Foreign currency contracts	690	(103)	26	(66)
Commodity contracts	503	(73)	(62)	(170)
Total	5,193	(189)	(18)	(292)

Derivatives in Net Investment Hedging Relationships	Notional Amount (Ending Balance)	Fair Value Asset (Liability)	Amount of Gain or (Loss) Recognized in OCI on Derivative (Effective Portion)	Amount of Gain or (Loss) Recognized in Income on Derivative (Ineffective Portion and Amount Excluded from Effectiveness Testing)(1)
		June 30	June 30	Twelve Months Ended June 30
Net investment hedges	$2,271	$(2)	$(2)	$(5)
Total	2,271	(2)	(2)	(5)

Derivatives Not Designated as Hedging Instruments	Notional Amount (Ending Balance)	Fair Value Asset (Liability)	Amount of Gain or (Loss) Recognized in Income on Derivative(1)
		June 30	Twelve Months Ended June 30
Foreign currency contracts	$12,348	$261	$(1,047)
Commodity contracts	—	—	(5)
Total	12,348	261	(1,052)

(1) The gain or loss reclassified from accumulated OCI into income is included in the consolidated statement of earnings as follows: interest rate contracts in interest expense, foreign currency contracts in SG&A and interest expense, commodity contracts in cost of products sold and net investment hedges in interest expense.

During the next 12 months, the amount of the June 30, 2009 OCI balance that will be reclassified to earnings is expected to be immaterial. In addition, the total notional amount of contracts outstanding at the end of the period is indicative of the level of the Company's derivative activity during the period.

Amounts in millions of dollars except per share amounts or as otherwise specified.

NOTE 6

EARNINGS PER SHARE

Net earnings less preferred dividends (net of related tax benefits) are divided by the weighted average number of common shares outstanding during the year to calculate basic net earnings per common share. Diluted net earnings per common share are calculated to give effect to stock options and other stock-based awards (see Note 7) and assume conversion of preferred stock (see Note 8).

Net earnings and common shares used to calculate basic and diluted net earnings per share were as follows:

Years ended June 30	2009	2008	2007
NET EARNINGS FROM CONTINUING OPERATIONS	**$11,293**	$11,798	$10,063
Preferred dividends, net of tax benefit	**(192)**	(176)	(161)
NET EARNINGS FROM CONTINUING OPERATIONS AVAILABLE TO COMMON SHAREHOLDERS	**11,101**	11,622	9,902
Preferred dividends, net of tax benefit	**192**	176	161
DILUTED NET EARNINGS FROM CONTINUING OPERATIONS	**11,293**	11,798	10,063
Net earnings from discontinued operations	**2,143**	277	277
NET EARNINGS	**13,436**	12,075	10,340

Shares in millions; Years ended June 30	2009	2008	2007
Basic weighted average common shares outstanding	**2,952.2**	3,080.8	3,159.0
Effect of dilutive securities			
Conversion of preferred shares (1)	**139.2**	144.2	149.6
Exercise of stock options and other unvested equity awards (2)	**62.7**	91.8	90.0
DILUTED WEIGHTED AVERAGE COMMON SHARES OUTSTANDING	**3,154.1**	3,316.8	3,398.6

(1) Despite being included currently in diluted net earnings per common share, the actual conversion to common stock occurs pursuant to the repayment of the ESOPs' obligations through 2035.

(2) Approximately 92 million in 2009, 40 million in 2008 and 41 million in 2007 of the Company's outstanding stock options were not included in the diluted net earnings per share calculation because the options were out of the money or to do so would have been antidilutive (i.e., the total proceeds upon exercise would have exceeded the market value of the underlying common shares).

NOTE 7

STOCK-BASED COMPENSATION

We have stock-based compensation plans under which we annually grant stock option and restricted stock awards to key managers and directors. Exercise prices on options granted have been and continue to be set equal to the market price of the underlying shares on the date of the grant. The key manager stock option awards granted since September 2002 are vested after three years and have a 10-year life. The key manager stock option awards granted from July 1998 through August 2002 vested after three years and have a 15-year life. Key managers can elect to receive up to 50% of the value of their option award in restricted stock units (RSUs). Key manager RSUs are vested and settled in shares of common stock five years from the grant date. The awards provided to the Company's directors are in the form of restricted stock and RSUs. In addition to our key manager and director grants, we make other minor stock option and RSU grants to employees for which the terms are not substantially different.

A total of 229 million shares of common stock were authorized for issuance under stock-based compensation plans approved by shareholders in 2001 and 2003, of which 12 million remain available for grant. An additional 20 million shares of common stock available for issuance under a plan approved by Gillette shareholders in 2004 were assumed by the Company in conjunction with the acquisition of Gillette. A total of 10 million of these shares remain available for grant under this plan.

Total stock-based compensation expense for stock option grants was $460, $522 and $612 for 2009, 2008 and 2007, respectively. The total income tax benefit recognized in the income statement for these stock-based compensation arrangements was $126, $141 and $163 for 2009, 2008 and 2007, respectively. Total compensation cost for restricted stock, RSUs and other stock-based grants, was $56, $33 and $56 in 2009, 2008 and 2007, respectively.

In calculating the compensation expense for stock options granted, we utilize a binomial lattice-based valuation model. Assumptions utilized in the model, which are evaluated and revised, as necessary, to reflect market conditions and experience, were as follows:

Years ended June 30	2009	2008	2007
Interest rate	**0.7–3.8%**	1.3–3.8%	4.3–4.8%
Weighted average interest rate	**3.6%**	3.4%	4.5%
Dividend yield	**2.0%**	1.9%	1.9%
Expected volatility	**18–34%**	19–25%	16–20%
Weighted average volatility	**21%**	20%	19%
Expected life in years	**8.7**	8.3	8.7

Amounts in millions of dollars except per share amounts or as otherwise specified.

Because lattice-based option valuation models incorporate ranges of assumptions for inputs, those ranges are disclosed in the preceding table. Expected volatilities are based on a combination of historical volatility of our stock and implied volatilities of call options on our stock. We use historical data to estimate option exercise and employee termination patterns within the valuation model. The expected life of options granted is derived from the output of the option valuation model and represents the average period of time that options granted are expected to be outstanding. The interest rate for periods within the contractual life of the options is based on the U.S. Treasury yield curve in effect at the time of grant.

A summary of options outstanding under the plans as of June 30, 2009, and activity during the year then ended is presented below:

Options in thousands	Options	Weighted Avg. Exercise Price	Weighted Avg. Remaining Contractual Life in Years	Aggregate Intrinsic Value (in millions)
Outstanding, beginning of year	337,177	$48.25		
Granted	37,623	50.30		
Exercised	(16,199)	39.45		
Canceled	(1,284)	57.62		
OUTSTANDING, END OF YEAR	357,317	48.83	6.3	$2,084
EXERCISABLE	259,362	44.93	5.4	1,984

The weighted average grant-date fair value of options granted was $11.67, $15.91 and $17.29 per share in 2009, 2008 and 2007, respectively. The total intrinsic value of options exercised was $434, $1,129 and $894 in 2009, 2008 and 2007, respectively. The total grant-date fair value of options that vested during 2009, 2008 and 2007 was $537, $532 and $552, respectively. We have no specific policy to repurchase common shares to mitigate the dilutive impact of options; however, we have historically made adequate discretionary purchases, based on cash availability, market trends and other factors, to satisfy stock option exercise activity.

At June 30, 2009, there was $524 of compensation cost that has not yet been recognized related to stock awards. That cost is expected to be recognized over a remaining weighted average period of 2.0 years.

Cash received from options exercised was $639, $1,837 and $1,422 in 2009, 2008 and 2007, respectively. The actual tax benefit realized for the tax deductions from option exercises totaled $146, $318 and $265 in 2009, 2008 and 2007, respectively.

NOTE 8

POSTRETIREMENT BENEFITS AND EMPLOYEE STOCK OWNERSHIP PLAN

We offer various postretirement benefits to our employees.

Defined Contribution Retirement Plans

We have defined contribution plans which cover the majority of our U.S. employees, as well as employees in certain other countries. These plans are fully funded. We generally make contributions to participants' accounts based on individual base salaries and years of service. Total global defined contribution expense was $364, $290, and $273 in 2009, 2008 and 2007, respectively.

The primary U.S. defined contribution plan (the U.S. DC plan) comprises the majority of the balances and expense for the Company's defined contribution plans. For the U.S. DC plan, the contribution rate is set annually. Total contributions for this plan approximated 15% of total participants' annual wages and salaries in 2009, 2008 and 2007.

We maintain The Procter & Gamble Profit Sharing Trust (Trust) and Employee Stock Ownership Plan (ESOP) to provide a portion of the funding for the U.S. DC plan, as well as other retiree benefits. Operating details of the ESOP are provided at the end of this Note. The fair value of the ESOP Series A shares allocated to participants reduces our cash contribution required to fund the U.S. DC plan.

Defined Benefit Retirement Plans and Other Retiree Benefits

We offer defined benefit retirement pension plans to certain employees. These benefits relate primarily to local plans outside the U.S. and, to a lesser extent, plans assumed in the Gillette acquisition covering U.S. employees.

We also provide certain other retiree benefits, primarily health care and life insurance, for the majority of our U.S. employees who become eligible for these benefits when they meet minimum age and service requirements. Generally, the health care plans require cost sharing with retirees and pay a stated percentage of expenses, reduced by deductibles and other coverages. These benefits are primarily funded by ESOP Series B shares, as well as certain other assets contributed by the Company.

Obligation and Funded Status. We use a June 30 measurement date for our defined benefit retirement plans and other retiree benefit plans. The following provides a reconciliation of benefit obligations, plan assets and funded status of these plans:

	Pension Benefits[1]		Other Retiree Benefits[2]	
Years ended June 30	2009	2008	2009	2008
CHANGE IN BENEFIT OBLIGATION				
Benefit obligation at beginning of year[3]	**$10,095**	$ 9,819	**$ 3,553**	$ 3,558
Service cost	**214**	263	**91**	95
Interest cost	**551**	539	**243**	226
Participants' contributions	**15**	14	**55**	58
Amendments	**47**	52	**—**	(11)
Actuarial (gain) loss	**456**	(655)	**186**	(232)
Acquisitions (divestitures)	**(3)**	(7)	**(17)**	2
Curtailments and settlements	**3**	(68)	**—**	(3)
Special termination benefits	**3**	1	**16**	2
Currency translation and other	**(867)**	642	**27**	67
Benefit payments	**(498)**	(505)	**(226)**	(209)
BENEFIT OBLIGATION AT END OF YEAR[3]	**10,016**	10,095	**3,928**	3,553
CHANGE IN PLAN ASSETS				
Fair value of plan assets at beginning of year	**7,225**	7,350	**3,225**	3,390
Actual return on plan assets	**(401)**	(459)	**(678)**	(29)
Acquisitions (divestitures)	**—**	—	**—**	—
Employer contributions	**657**	507	**18**	21
Participants' contributions	**15**	14	**55**	58
Currency translation and other	**(688)**	318	**(4)**	1
ESOP debt impacts[4]	**—**	—	**4**	(7)
Benefit payments	**(498)**	(505)	**(226)**	(209)
FAIR VALUE OF PLAN ASSETS AT END OF YEAR	**6,310**	7,225	**2,394**	3,225
FUNDED STATUS	**(3,706)**	(2,870)	**(1,534)**	(328)

(1) Primarily non-U.S.-based defined benefit retirement plans.

(2) Primarily U.S.-based other postretirement benefit plans.

(3) For the pension benefit plans, the benefit obligation is the projected benefit obligation. For other retiree benefit plans, the benefit obligation is the accumulated postretirement benefit obligation.

(4) Represents the net impact of ESOP debt service requirements, which is netted against plan assets for Other Retiree Benefits.

	Pension Benefits		Other Retiree Benefits	
Years ended June 30	2009	2008	2009	2008
CLASSIFICATION OF NET AMOUNT RECOGNIZED				
Noncurrent assets	**$ 133**	$ 321	**$ —**	$ 200
Current liability	**(41)**	(45)	**(18)**	(16)
Noncurrent liability	**(3,798)**	(3,146)	**(1,516)**	(512)
NET AMOUNT RECOGNIZED	**(3,706)**	(2,870)	**(1,534)**	(328)
AMOUNTS RECOGNIZED IN ACCUMULATED OTHER COMPREHENSIVE INCOME (AOCI)				
Net actuarial loss	**1,976**	715	**1,860**	578
Prior service cost (credit)	**227**	213	**(152)**	(175)
NET AMOUNTS RECOGNIZED IN AOCI	**2,203**	928	**1,708**	403
CHANGE IN PLAN ASSETS AND BENEFIT OBLIGATIONS RECOGNIZED IN ACCUMULATED OTHER COMPREHENSIVE INCOME (AOCI)				
Net actuarial loss—current year	**1,335**	361	**1,309**	226
Prior service cost (credit)—current year	**47**	52	**—**	(11)
Amortization of net actuarial loss	**(29)**	(9)	**(2)**	(7)
Amortization of prior service (cost) credit	**(14)**	(14)	**23**	21
Settlement/Curtailment cost	**—**	(32)	**—**	(2)
Currency translation and other	**(64)**	19	**(25)**	24
TOTAL CHANGE IN AOCI	**1,275**	377	**1,305**	251
NET AMOUNTS RECOGNIZED IN PERIODIC BENEFIT COST AND AOCI	**1,616**	609	**1,088**	33

The underfunding of pension benefits is primarily a function of the different funding incentives that exist outside of the U.S. In certain countries, there are no legal requirements or financial incentives provided to companies to pre-fund pension obligations. In these instances, benefit payments are typically paid directly from the Company's cash as they become due.

Amounts in millions of dollars except per share amounts or as otherwise specified.

The accumulated benefit obligation for all defined benefit retirement pension plans was $8,637 and $8,750 at June 30, 2009 and June 30, 2008, respectively. Pension plans with accumulated benefit obligations in excess of plan assets and plans with projected benefit obligations in excess of plan assets consist of the following:

	Accumulated Benefit Obligation Exceeds the Fair Value of Plan Assets		Projected Benefit Obligation Exceeds the Fair Value of Plan Assets	
Years ended June 30	2009	2008	2009	2008
Projected benefit obligation	**$6,509**	$5,277	**$9,033**	$7,987
Accumulated benefit obligation	**5,808**	4,658	**7,703**	6,737
Fair value of plan assets	**3,135**	2,153	**5,194**	4,792

Net Periodic Benefit Cost. Components of the net periodic benefit cost were as follows:

	Pension Benefits			Other Retiree Benefits		
Years ended June 30	2009	2008	2007	2009	2008	2007
Service cost	**$ 214**	$ 263	$ 279	**$ 91**	$ 95	$ 85
Interest cost	**551**	539	476	**243**	226	206
Expected return on plan assets	**(473)**	(557)	(454)	**(444)**	(429)	(407)
Prior service cost (credit) amortization	**14**	14	13	**(23)**	(21)	(22)
Net actuarial loss amortization	**29**	9	45	**2**	7	2
Curtailment and settlement gain	**6**	(36)	(176)	**—**	(1)	(1)
GROSS BENEFIT COST (CREDIT)	**341**	232	183	**(131)**	(123)	(137)
Dividends on ESOP preferred stock	**—**	—	—	**(86)**	(95)	(85)
NET PERIODIC BENEFIT COST (CREDIT)	**341**	232	183	**(217)**	(218)	(222)

Pursuant to plan revisions adopted during 2007, Gillette's U.S. defined benefit retirement pension plans were frozen effective January 1, 2008, at which time Gillette employees in the U.S. moved into the Trust and ESOP. This revision resulted in a $154 curtailment gain for the year ended June 30, 2007.

Amounts expected to be amortized from accumulated other comprehensive income into net period benefit cost during the year ending June 30, 2010, are as follows:

	Pension Benefits	Other Retiree Benefits
Net actuarial loss	$92	$ 19
Prior service cost (credit)	15	(21)

Assumptions. We determine our actuarial assumptions on an annual basis. These assumptions are weighted to reflect each country that may have an impact on the cost of providing retirement benefits. The weighted average assumptions for the defined benefit and other retiree benefit calculations, as well as assumed health care trend rates, were as follows:

	Pension Benefits		Other Retiree Benefits	
Years ended June 30	2009	2008	2009	2008
ASSUMPTIONS USED TO DETERMINE BENEFIT OBLIGATIONS (1)				
Discount rate	**6.0%**	6.3%	**6.4%**	6.9%
Rate of compensation increase	**3.7%**	3.7%	**—**	—
ASSUMPTIONS USED TO DETERMINE NET PERIODIC BENEFIT COST (2)				
Discount rate	**6.3%**	5.5%	**6.9%**	6.3%
Expected return on plan assets	**7.4%**	7.4%	**9.3%**	9.3%
Rate of compensation increase	**3.7%**	3.1%	**—**	—
ASSUMED HEALTH CARE COST TREND RATES				
Health care cost trend rates assumed for next year	—	—	**8.5%**	8.6%
Rate to which the health care cost trend rate is assumed to decline (ultimate trend rate)	—	—	**5.0%**	5.1%
Year that the rate reaches the ultimate trend rate	—	—	**2016**	2015

(1) Determined as of end of year.

(2) Determined as of beginning of year and adjusted for acquisitions.

Several factors are considered in developing the estimate for the long-term expected rate of return on plan assets. For the defined benefit retirement plans, these include historical rates of return of broad equity and bond indices and projected long-term rates of return obtained from pension investment consultants. The expected long-term rates of return for plan assets are 8%–9% for equities and 5%–6% for bonds. For other retiree benefit plans, the expected long-term rate of return reflects the fact that the assets are comprised primarily of Company stock. The expected rate of return on Company stock is based on the long-term projected return of 9.5% and reflects the historical pattern of favorable returns.

Assumed health care cost trend rates could have a significant effect on the amounts reported for the other retiree benefit plans. A one-percentage point change in assumed health care cost trend rates would have the following effects:

	One-Percentage Point Increase	One-Percentage Point Decrease
Effect on total of service and interest cost components	$ 58	$ (46)
Effect on postretirement benefit obligation	549	(447)

Amounts in millions of dollars except per share amounts or as otherwise specified.

Plan Assets. Our target asset allocation for the year ended June 30, 2009, and actual asset allocation by asset category as of June 30, 2009 and 2008, were as follows:

	Target Asset Allocation	
Asset Category	Pension Benefits	Other Retiree Benefits
Equity securities (1)	45%	93%
Debt securities	55%	7%
TOTAL	100%	100%

	Asset Allocation at June 30			
	Pension Benefits		Other Retiree Benefits	
Asset Category	2009	2008	2009	2008
Equity securities (1)	**42%**	45%	**93%**	96%
Debt securities	**51%**	50%	**7%**	4%
Cash	**6%**	3%	—	—
Real estate	**1%**	2%	—	—
TOTAL	**100%**	100%	**100%**	100%

(1) Equity securities for other retiree plan assets include Company stock, net of Series B ESOP debt, of $2,084 and $2,809 as of June 30, 2009 and 2008, respectively.

Our investment objective for defined benefit retirement plan assets is to meet the plans' benefit obligations, while minimizing the potential for future required Company plan contributions. The investment strategies focus on asset class diversification, liquidity to meet benefit payments and an appropriate balance of long-term investment return and risk. Target ranges for asset allocations are determined by matching the actuarial projections of the plans' future liabilities and benefit payments with expected long-term rates of return on the assets, taking into account investment return volatility and correlations across asset classes. Plan assets are diversified across several investment managers and are generally invested in liquid funds that are selected to track broad market equity and bond indices. Investment risk is carefully controlled with plan assets rebalanced to target allocations on a periodic basis and continual monitoring of investment managers' performance relative to the investment guidelines established with each investment manager.

Cash Flows. Management's best estimate of cash requirements for the defined benefit retirement plans and other retiree benefit plans for the year ending June 30, 2010, is approximately $616 and $24, respectively. For the defined benefit retirement plans, this is comprised of $178 in expected benefit payments from the Company directly to participants of unfunded plans and $438 of expected contributions to funded plans. For other retiree benefit plans, this is comprised of expected contributions that will be used directly for benefit payments. Expected contributions are dependent on many variables, including the variability of the market value of the plan assets as compared to the benefit obligation and other market or regulatory conditions. In addition, we take into consideration our business investment opportunities and resulting cash requirements. Accordingly, actual funding may differ significantly from current estimates.

Total benefit payments expected to be paid to participants, which include payments funded from the Company's assets, as discussed above, as well as payments from the plans, are as follows:

Years ending June 30	Pension Benefits	Other Retiree Benefits
EXPECTED BENEFIT PAYMENTS		
2010	$ 499	$ 184
2011	496	201
2012	507	217
2013	525	232
2014	552	247
2015–2019	3,096	1,453

Employee Stock Ownership Plan

We maintain the ESOP to provide funding for certain employee benefits discussed in the preceding paragraphs.

The ESOP borrowed $1.0 billion in 1989 and the proceeds were used to purchase Series A ESOP Convertible Class A Preferred Stock to fund a portion of the U.S. DC plan. Principal and interest requirements of the borrowing were paid by the Trust from dividends on the preferred shares and from advances provided by the Company. The original borrowing of $1.0 billion has been repaid in full, and advances from the Company of $178 remain outstanding at June 30, 2009. Each share is convertible at the option of the holder into one share of the Company's common stock. The dividend for the current year was equal to the common stock dividend of $1.64 per share. The liquidation value is $6.82 per share.

In 1991, the ESOP borrowed an additional $1.0 billion. The proceeds were used to purchase Series B ESOP Convertible Class A Preferred Stock to fund a portion of retiree health care benefits. These shares, net of the ESOP's debt, are considered plan assets of the Other Retiree Benefits plan discussed above. Debt service requirements are funded by preferred stock dividends, cash contributions and advances provided by the Company, of which $266 is outstanding at June 30, 2009. Each share is convertible at the option of the holder into one share of the Company's common stock. The dividend for the current year was equal to the common stock dividend of $1.64 per share. The liquidation value is $12.96 per share.

Our ESOP accounting practices are consistent with current ESOP accounting guidance, including the permissible continuation of certain provisions from prior accounting guidance. ESOP debt, which is guaranteed by the Company, is recorded as debt (see Note 4) with an offset to the Reserve for ESOP Debt Retirement, which is presented within Shareholders' Equity. Advances to the ESOP by the Company are recorded as an increase in the Reserve for ESOP Debt Retirement. Interest incurred on the ESOP debt is recorded as interest expense. Dividends on all preferred shares, net of related tax benefits, are charged to retained earnings.

Amounts in millions of dollars except per share amounts or as otherwise specified.

The series A and B preferred shares of the ESOP are allocated to employees based on debt service requirements, net of advances made by the Company to the Trust. The number of preferred shares outstanding at June 30 was as follows:

Shares in thousands	2009	2008	2007
Allocated	**56,818**	58,557	60,402
Unallocated	**16,651**	18,665	20,807
TOTAL SERIES A	**73,469**	77,222	81,209
Allocated	**20,991**	21,134	21,105
Unallocated	**42,522**	43,618	44,642
TOTAL SERIES B	**63,513**	64,752	65,747

For purposes of calculating diluted net earnings per common share, the preferred shares held by the ESOP are considered converted from inception.

In connection with the Gillette acquisition, we assumed the Gillette ESOP, which was established to assist Gillette employees in financing retiree medical costs. These ESOP accounts are held by participants and must be used to reduce the Company's other retiree benefit obligations. Such accounts reduced our obligation by $171 at June 30, 2009.

NOTE 9

INCOME TAXES

Income taxes are recognized for the amount of taxes payable for the current year and for the impact of deferred tax liabilities and assets, which represent future tax consequences of events that have been recognized differently in the financial statements than for tax purposes. Deferred tax assets and liabilities are established using the enacted statutory tax rates and are adjusted for any changes in such rates in the period of change.

Earnings from continuing operations before income taxes consisted of the following:

Years ended June 30	2009	2008	2007
United States	**$ 9,064**	$ 8,696	$ 8,692
International	**6,261**	6,936	5,572
TOTAL	**15,325**	15,632	14,264

The provision for income taxes on continuing operations consisted of the following:

Years ended June 30	2009	2008	2007
CURRENT TAX EXPENSE			
U.S. federal	**$1,867**	$ 860	$2,511
International	**1,316**	1,546	1,325
U.S. state and local	**253**	214	112
	3,436	2,620	3,948
DEFERRED TAX EXPENSE			
U.S. federal	**577**	1,267	231
International and other	**19**	(53)	22
	596	1,214	253
TOTAL TAX EXPENSE	**4,032**	3,834	4,201

A reconciliation of the U.S. federal statutory income tax rate to our actual income tax rate on continuing operations is provided below:

Years ended June 30	2009	2008	2007
U.S. federal statutory income tax rate	**35.0%**	35.0%	35.0%
Country mix impacts of foreign operations	**-6.9%**	-6.8%	-4.5%
Income tax reserve adjustments	**-1.2%**	-3.2%	-0.3%
Other	**-0.6%**	-0.5%	-0.7%
EFFECTIVE INCOME TAX RATE	**26.3%**	24.5%	29.5%

Income tax reserve adjustments represent changes in our net liability for unrecognized tax benefits related to prior year tax positions.

Tax benefits credited to shareholders' equity totaled $556 and $1,823 for the years ended June 30, 2009 and 2008, respectively. These primarily relate to the tax effects of net investment hedges, excess tax benefits from the exercise of stock options and the impacts of certain adjustments to pension and other retiree benefit obligations recorded in shareholders' equity.

We have undistributed earnings of foreign subsidiaries of approximately $25 billion at June 30, 2009, for which deferred taxes have not been provided. Such earnings are considered indefinitely invested in the foreign subsidiaries. If such earnings were repatriated, additional tax expense may result, although the calculation of such additional taxes is not practicable.

On July 1, 2007, we adopted new accounting guidance on the accounting for uncertainty in income taxes. The adoption of the new guidance resulted in a decrease to retained earnings as of July 1, 2007, of $232, which was reflected as a cumulative effect of a change in accounting principle, with a corresponding increase to the net liability for unrecognized tax benefits. The impact primarily reflects the accrual of additional statutory interest and penalties as required by the new accounting guidance, partially offset by adjustments to existing unrecognized tax benefits to comply with measurement principles. The implementation of the new guidance also resulted in a reduction in our net tax liabilities for uncertain tax positions related to prior acquisitions accounted for under purchase accounting, resulting in an $80 decrease to goodwill. Additionally, the Company historically classified unrecognized tax benefits in current taxes payable. As a result of the adoption of the new guidance, unrecognized tax benefits not expected to be paid in the next 12 months were reclassified to other noncurrent liabilities.

A reconciliation of the beginning and ending liability for unrecognized tax benefits is as follows:

	2009	2008
BEGINNING OF YEAR	**$2,582**	$2,971
Increases in tax positions for prior years	**116**	164
Decreases in tax positions for prior years	**(485)**	(576)
Increases in tax positions for current year	**225**	375
Settlements with taxing authorities	**(172)**	(260)
Lapse in statute of limitations	**(68)**	(200)
Currency translation	**(195)**	108
END OF YEAR	**2,003**	2,582

The Company is present in over 150 taxable jurisdictions, and at any point in time, has 50–60 audits underway at various stages of completion. We evaluate our tax positions and establish liabilities for uncertain tax positions that may be challenged by local authorities and may not be fully sustained, despite our belief that the underlying tax positions are fully supportable. Unrecognized tax benefits are reviewed on an ongoing basis and are adjusted in light of changing facts and circumstances, including progress of tax audits, developments in case law, and closing of statute of limitations. Such adjustments are reflected in the tax provision as appropriate. The Company has made a concerted effort to bring its audit inventory to a more current position. We have done this by working with tax authorities to conduct audits for several open years at once. We have tax years open ranging from 1997 and forward. We are generally not able to reliably estimate the ultimate settlement amounts until the close of the audit. While we do not expect material changes, it is possible that the amount of unrecognized benefit with respect to our uncertain tax positions will significantly increase or decrease within the next 12 months related to the audits described above. At this time we are not able to make a reasonable estimate of the range of impact on the balance of unrecognized tax benefits or the impact on the effective tax rate related to these items.

Included in the total liability for unrecognized tax benefit at June 30, 2009 is $1,381 that, if recognized, would impact the effective tax rate in future periods.

We recognize accrued interest and penalties related to unrecognized tax benefits in income tax expense. As of June 30, 2009 and 2008, we had accrued interest of $636 and $656 and penalties of $100 and $155, respectively, that are not included in the above table. During the fiscal years ended June 30, 2009 and 2008, we recognized $119 and $213 in interest and $(4) and $35 in penalties, respectively.

Deferred income tax assets and liabilities were comprised of the following:

June 30	2009	2008
DEFERRED TAX ASSETS		
Pension and postretirement benefits	**$ 1,395**	$ 633
Stock-based compensation	**1,182**	1,082
Unrealized loss on financial and foreign exchange transactions	**577**	1,274
Loss and other carryforwards	**439**	482
Goodwill and other intangible assets	**331**	267
Accrued marketing and promotion expense	**167**	125
Accrued interest and taxes	**120**	123
Fixed assets	**114**	100
Inventory	**97**	114
Advance payments	**15**	302
Other	**885**	1,048
Valuation allowances	**(104)**	(173)
TOTAL	**5,218**	5,377
DEFERRED TAX LIABILITIES		
Goodwill and other intangible assets	**11,922**	12,371
Fixed assets	**1,654**	1,847
Other	**146**	151
TOTAL	**13,722**	14,369

Net operating loss carryforwards were $1,428 and $1,515 at June 30, 2009 and 2008, respectively. If unused, $462 will expire between 2010 and 2029. The remainder, totaling $966 at June 30, 2009, may be carried forward indefinitely.

NOTE 10

COMMITMENTS AND CONTINGENCIES

Guarantees

In conjunction with certain transactions, primarily divestitures, we may provide routine indemnifications (e.g., indemnification for representations and warranties and retention of previously existing environmental, tax and employee liabilities) which terms range in duration and in some circumstances are not explicitly defined. The maximum obligation under some indemnifications is also not explicitly stated and, as a result, the overall amount of these obligations cannot be reasonably estimated. Other than obligations recorded as liabilities at the time of divestiture, we have not made significant payments for these indemnifications. We believe that if we were to incur a loss on any of these matters, the loss would not have a material effect on our financial position, results of operations or cash flows.

In certain situations, we guarantee loans for suppliers and customers. The total amount of guarantees issued under such arrangements is not material.

Off-Balance Sheet Arrangements

We do not have off-balance sheet financing arrangements, including variable interest entities, that have a material impact on our financial statements.

Purchase Commitments

We have purchase commitments for materials, supplies, services and property, plant and equipment as part of the normal course of business. Commitments made under take-or-pay obligations are as follows: 2010—$1,258; 2011—$872; 2012—$787; 2013—$525; 2014—$156; and $299 thereafter. Such amounts represent future purchases in line with expected usage to obtain favorable pricing. Approximately 43% of our purchase commitments relate to service contracts for information technology, human resources management and facilities management activities that have been outsourced to third-party suppliers. Due to the proprietary nature of many of our materials and processes, certain supply contracts contain penalty provisions for early termination. We do not expect to incur penalty payments under these provisions that would materially affect our financial position, results of operations or cash flows.

Operating Leases

We lease certain property and equipment for varying periods. Future minimum rental commitments under noncancelable operating leases are as follows: 2010—$305; 2011—$272; 2012—$223; 2013—$202; 2014—$176; and $442 thereafter. Operating lease obligations are shown net of guaranteed sublease income.

Litigation

We are subject to various legal proceedings and claims arising out of our business which cover a wide range of matters such as governmental regulations, antitrust and trade regulations, product liability, patent and trademark matters, income taxes and other actions.

As previously disclosed, the Company is subject to a variety of investigations into potential competition law violations in Europe, including investigations initiated in the fourth quarter of fiscal 2008 by the European Commission with the assistance of national authorities from a variety of countries. We believe these matters involve a number of other consumer products companies and/or retail customers. The Company's policy is to comply with all laws and regulations, including all antitrust and competition laws, and to cooperate with investigations by relevant regulatory authorities, which the Company is doing. Competition and antitrust law inquiries often continue for several years and, if violations are found, can result in substantial fines. In other industries, fines have amounted to hundreds of millions of dollars. At this point, no significant formal claims have been made against the Company or any of our subsidiaries in connection with any of the above inquiries.

In response to the actions of the European Commission and national authorities, the Company has launched its own internal investigations into potential violations of competition laws, some of which are ongoing. The Company has identified violations in certain European countries and appropriate actions are being taken. It is still too early for us to reasonably estimate the fines to which the Company will be subject as a result of these competition law issues. However, the ultimate resolution of these matters will likely result in fines or other costs that could materially impact our income statement and cash flows in the period in which they are accrued and paid, respectively. As these matters evolve the Company will, if necessary, recognize the appropriate reserves.

With respect to other litigation and claims, while considerable uncertainty exists, in the opinion of management and our counsel, the ultimate resolution of the various lawsuits and claims will not materially affect our financial position, results of operations or cash flows.

We are also subject to contingencies pursuant to environmental laws and regulations that in the future may require us to take action to correct the effects on the environment of prior manufacturing and waste disposal practices. Based on currently available information, we do not believe the ultimate resolution of environmental remediation will have a material adverse effect on our financial position, results of operations or cash flows.

NOTE 11

SEGMENT INFORMATION

Through fiscal 2009, we were organized under three GBUs as follows:

- The Beauty GBU includes the Beauty and the Grooming businesses. The Beauty business is comprised of cosmetics, deodorants, prestige fragrances, hair care, personal cleansing and skin care. The Grooming business includes blades and razors, electric hair removal devices, face and shave products and home appliances.
- The Health and Well-Being GBU includes the Health Care and the Snacks and Pet Care businesses. The Health Care business includes feminine care, oral care, personal health care and pharmaceuticals. The Snacks and Pet Care business includes pet food and snacks.
- The Household Care GBU includes the Fabric Care and Home Care as well as the Baby Care and Family Care businesses. The Fabric Care and Home Care business includes air care, batteries, dish care, fabric care and surface care. The Baby Care and Family Care business includes baby wipes, bath tissue, diapers, facial tissue and paper towels.

Under U.S. GAAP, we have six reportable segments: Beauty; Grooming; Health Care; Snacks and Pet Care; Fabric Care and Home Care; and Baby Care and Family Care. The accounting policies of the businesses are generally the same as those described in Note 1. Differences between these policies and U.S. GAAP primarily reflect: income taxes, which are reflected in the businesses using applicable blended statutory rates; the recording of fixed assets at historical exchange rates in certain high-inflation economies; and the treatment of certain unconsolidated investees. Certain unconsolidated investees are managed as integral parts of our business units for management reporting purposes.

Accordingly, these partially owned operations are reflected as consolidated subsidiaries in segment results, with 100% recognition of the individual income statement line items through before-tax earnings. Eliminations to adjust these line items to U.S. GAAP are included in Corporate. In determining after-tax earnings for the businesses, we eliminate the share of earnings applicable to other ownership interests, in a manner similar to minority interest and apply statutory tax rates. Adjustments to arrive at our effective tax rate are also included in Corporate.

Corporate includes certain operating and non-operating activities that are not reflected in the operating results used internally to measure and evaluate the businesses, as well as eliminations to adjust management reporting principles to U.S. GAAP. Operating activities in Corporate include the results of incidental businesses managed at the corporate level along with the elimination of individual revenues and expenses generated by certain unconsolidated investees discussed in the preceding paragraph over which we exert significant influence, but do not control. Operating elements also include certain employee benefit costs, the costs of certain restructuring-type activities to maintain a competitive cost structure, including manufacturing and workforce rationalization, and other general Corporate items. The non-operating elements in Corporate primarily include interest expense, divestiture gains and interest and investing income. In addition, Corporate includes the historical results of certain divested businesses. Corporate assets primarily include cash, investment securities and all goodwill.

The Company had net sales in the U.S. of $31.1 billion, $31.3 billion and $30.3 billion for the years ended June 30, 2009, 2008 and 2007, respectively. Assets in the U.S. totaled $71.9 billion and $73.8 billion as of June 30, 2009 and 2008, respectively.

Our largest customer, Wal-Mart Stores, Inc. and its affiliates, accounted for 15% of consolidated net sales in 2009, 2008 and 2007.

Global Segment Results		Net Sales	Earnings from Continuing Operations Before Income Taxes	Net Earnings from Continuing Operations	Depreciation and Amortization	Total Assets	Capital Expenditures
BEAUTY GBU							
BEAUTY	2009	**$18,789**	**$ 3,367**	**$ 2,531**	**$ 465**	**$ 11,330**	**$ 530**
	2008	19,515	3,528	2,730	454	12,260	465
	2007	17,889	3,440	2,611	419	11,140	431
GROOMING	2009	**7,543**	**2,091**	**1,492**	**710**	**26,192**	**290**
	2008	8,254	2,299	1,679	739	27,406	305
	2007	7,437	1,895	1,383	729	27,767	314
HEALTH AND WELL-BEING GBU							
HEALTH CARE	2009	**13,623**	**3,685**	**2,435**	**435**	**9,373**	**397**
	2008	14,578	3,746	2,506	441	10,597	450
	2007	13,381	3,365	2,233	439	9,512	374
SNACKS AND PET CARE	2009	**3,114**	**388**	**234**	**100**	**1,382**	**72**
	2008	3,204	409	261	102	1,651	78
	2007	2,985	381	244	121	1,570	94
HOUSEHOLD CARE GBU							
FABRIC CARE AND HOME CARE	2009	**23,186**	**4,663**	**3,032**	**578**	**12,457**	**808**
	2008	23,714	5,060	3,411	599	13,708	763
	2007	21,355	4,636	3,119	567	12,113	706
BABY CARE AND FAMILY CARE	2009	**14,103**	**2,827**	**1,770**	**570**	**7,363**	**902**
	2008	13,898	2,700	1,728	612	8,102	763
	2007	12,726	2,291	1,440	671	7,731	769
CORPORATE (1)	2009	**(1,329)**	**(1,696)**	**(201)**	**224**	**66,736**	**239**
	2008	(1,415)	(2,110)	(517)	181	70,268	222
	2007	(941)	(1,744)	(967)	135	68,181	257
TOTAL COMPANY	2009	**79,029**	**15,325**	**11,293**	**3,082**	**134,833**	**3,238**
	2008	81,748	15,632	11,798	3,128	143,992	3,046
	2007	74,832	14,264	10,063	3,081	138,014	2,945

(1) The Corporate reportable segment includes the total assets and capital expenditures of the Coffee business prior to the divestiture in November 2008.

Amounts in millions of dollars except per share amounts or as otherwise specified.

NOTE 12

DISCONTINUED OPERATIONS

In November 2008, the Company completed the divestiture of our Coffee business through the merger of its Folgers coffee subsidiary into The J.M. Smucker Company (Smucker) in an all-stock reverse Morris Trust transaction. In connection with the merger, 38.7 million shares of common stock of the Company were tendered by shareholders and exchanged for all shares of Folgers common stock, resulting in an increase of treasury stock of $2,466. Pursuant to the merger, a Smucker subsidiary merged with and into Folgers and Folgers became a wholly owned subsidiary of Smucker. The Company recorded an after-tax gain on the transaction of $2,011, which is included in Net Earnings from Discontinued Operations in the Consolidated Statement of Earnings for the year ended June 30, 2009.

The Coffee business had historically been part of the Company's Snacks, Coffee and Pet Care reportable segment, as well as the coffee portion of our away-from-home business which is included in the Fabric Care and Home Care reportable segment. In accordance with the applicable accounting guidance for the impairment or disposal of long-lived assets, the results of Folgers are presented as discontinued operations and, as such, have been excluded from both continuing operations and segment results for all years presented. Following is selected financial information included in Net Earnings from Discontinued Operations for the Coffee business:

Years Ended June 30	2009	2008	2007
Net Sales	**$ 668**	$1,754	$1,644
Earnings from discontinued operation	**212**	446	447
Income tax expense	**(80)**	(169)	(170)
Gain on sale of discontinued operation	**1,896**	—	—
Deferred tax benefit on sale	**115**	—	—
Net earnings from discontinued operations	**2,143**	277	277

NOTE 13

QUARTERLY RESULTS (UNAUDITED)

Quarters Ended		Sept 30	Dec 31	Mar 31	Jun 30	Total Year
NET SALES	2008–2009	**$21,582**	**$20,368**	**$18,417**	**$18,662**	**$79,029**
	2007–2008	19,799	21,038	20,026	20,885	81,748
OPERATING INCOME	2008–2009	**4,569**	**4,251**	**3,730**	**3,573**	**16,123**
	2007–2008	4,298	4,590	4,013	3,736	16,637
GROSS MARGIN	2008–2009	**50.8%**	**51.6%**	**50.3%**	**50.3%**	**50.8%**
	2007–2008	53.2%	52.3%	51.7%	49.4%	51.6%
NET EARNINGS:						
Earnings from continuing operations	2008–2009	**$ 3,275**	**$ 2,962**	**$ 2,585**	**$ 2,471**	**$11,293**
	2007–2008	3,004	3,194	2,650	2,950	11,798
Earnings from discontinued operations	2008–2009	**73**	**2,042**	**28**	—	**2,143**
	2007–2008	75	76	60	66	277
Net earnings	2008–2009	**3,348**	**5,004**	**2,613**	**2,471**	**13,436**
	2007–2008	3,079	3,270	2,710	3,016	12,075
DILUTED NET EARNINGS PER COMMON SHARE:						
Earnings from continuing operations	2008–2009	**$ 1.01**	**$ 0.94**	**$ 0.83**	**$ 0.80**	**$ 3.58**
	2007–2008	0.90	0.96	0.80	0.90	3.56
Earnings from discontinued operations	2008–2009	**0.02**	**0.64**	**0.01**	—	**0.68**
	2007–2008	0.02	0.02	0.02	0.02	0.08
Diluted net earnings per common share	2008–2009	**1.03**	**1.58**	**0.84**	**0.80**	**4.26**
	2007–2008	0.92	0.98	0.82	0.92	3.64

Amounts in millions of dollars except per share amounts or as otherwise specified.

Financial Summary (Unaudited)

Amounts in millions, except per share amounts	2009	2008	2007	2006	2005	2004	2003	2002	2001	2000	1999
Net Sales	**$ 79,029**	$ 81,748	$ 74,832	$ 66,724	$55,292	$50,128	$42,133	$38,965	$37,855	$38,545	$36,710
Gross Margin	**40,131**	42,212	39,173	34,549	28,213	25,709	20,570	18,547	16,473	17,854	16,394
Operating Income	**16,123**	16,637	15,003	12,916	10,026	9,019	6,931	5,672	3,976	5,457	5,885
Net Earnings from Continuing Operations	**11,293**	11,798	10,063	8,478	6,648	5,930	4,554	3,663	2,437	3,225	3,513
Net Earnings from Discontinued Operations	**2,143**	277	277	206	275	226	234	247	175	138	170
Net Earnings	**13,436**	12,075	10,340	8,684	6,923	6,156	4,788	3,910	2,612	3,363	3,683
Net Earnings Margin from Continuing Operations	**14.3%**	14.4%	13.4%	12.7%	12.0%	11.8%	10.8%	9.4%	6.4%	8.4%	9.6%
Basic Net Earnings per Common Share:											
Earnings from continuing operations	**$ 3.76**	$ 3.77	$ 3.13	$ 2.72	$ 2.59	$ 2.25	$ 1.71	$ 1.36	$ 0.89	$ 1.19	$ 1.28
Earnings from discontinued operations	**0.73**	0.09	0.09	0.07	0.11	0.09	0.09	0.10	0.07	0.05	0.07
Basic Net Earnings per Common Share	**4.49**	3.86	3.22	2.79	2.70	2.34	1.80	1.46	0.96	1.24	1.35
Diluted Net Earnings per Common Share:											
Earnings from continuing operations	**$ 3.58**	$ 3.56	$ 2.96	$ 2.58	$ 2.43	$ 2.12	$ 1.62	$ 1.30	$ 0.86	$ 1.13	$ 1.21
Earnings from discontinued operations	**0.68**	0.08	0.08	0.06	0.10	0.08	0.08	0.09	0.06	0.04	0.06
Diluted Net Earnings per Common Share	**4.26**	3.64	3.04	2.64	2.53	2.20	1.70	1.39	0.92	1.17	1.27
Dividends per Common Share	**1.64**	1.45	1.28	1.15	1.03	0.93	0.82	0.76	0.70	0.64	0.57
Restructuring Program Charges (1)	**$ —**	$ —	$ —	$ —	$ —	$ —	$ 751	$ 958	$ 1,850	$ 814	$ 481
Research and Development Expense	**2,044**	2,212	2,100	2,060	1,926	1,782	1,641	1,572	1,751	1,880	1,709
Advertising Expense	**7,579**	8,583	7,850	7,045	5,850	5,401	4,406	3,696	3,654	3,828	3,471
Total Assets	**134,833**	143,992	138,014	135,695	61,527	57,048	43,706	40,776	34,387	34,366	32,192
Capital Expenditures	**3,238**	3,046	2,945	2,667	2,181	2,024	1,482	1,679	2,486	3,018	2,828
Long-Term Debt	**20,652**	23,581	23,375	35,976	12,887	12,554	11,475	11,201	9,792	9,012	6,265
Shareholders' Equity	**63,099**	69,494	66,760	62,908	18,475	18,190	17,025	14,415	12,560	12,673	12,352

(1) Restructuring program charges, on an after-tax basis, totaled $538, $706, $1,475, $688 and $285 for 2003, 2002, 2001, 2000 and 1999, respectively, related to a multi-year restructuring plan initiated in 1999 concurrent with the reorganization of our business units from geographic into product-based Global Business Units.

Shareholder Return Performance Graphs

FIVE-YEAR CUMULATIVE TOTAL RETURN

The following graph compares the cumulative total return of P&G's common stock for the 5-year period ending June 30, 2009, against the cumulative total return of the S&P 500 Stock Index and the S&P 500 Consumer Staples Index. The graph and tables assume $100 was invested on June 30, 2004, and that all dividends were reinvested. The benchmark of "Composite Group" has been replaced by the S&P 500 Consumer Staples Index as the more relevant line of business comparison to P&G's operations. The Composite Group results are still provided in this transition year, and are comprised of the S&P Household Products Index, the S&P Paper Products Index, the S&P Personal Products Index, the S&P Health Care Index and the S&P Food Index, all weighted based on P&G's current fiscal year revenues. Further, the Dow Jones Industrial Average will no longer be shown after this year, as a "broad market" index as the S&P 500 satisfies this comparison.

COMPARISON OF FIVE-YEAR CUMULATIVE TOTAL RETURN

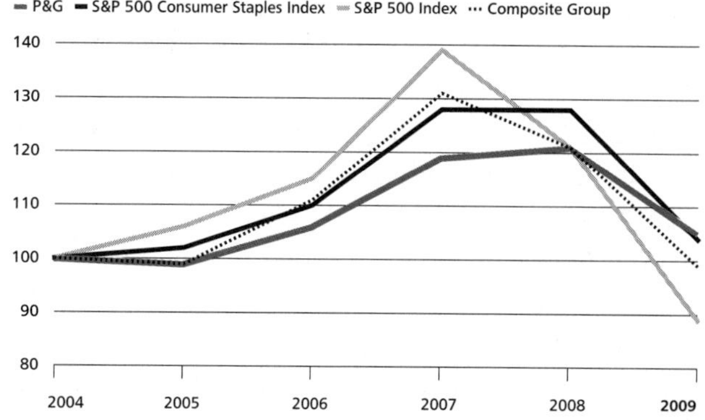

Company Name/Index	2004	2005	2006	2007	2008	2009
	Cumulative Value of $100 Investment, through June 30					
P&G	$100	$ 99	$106	$119	$121	**$105**
S&P 500 Consumer Staples Index	100	102	110	128	128	**104**
S&P 500 Index	100	106	115	139	121	**89**
DJIA	100	101	112	138	119	**92**
Composite Group	100	99	111	131	121	**99**

DIVIDEND HISTORY

P&G has paid dividends without interruption since its incorporation in 1890 and has increased dividends each year for the past 53 fiscal years. P&G's compound annual dividend growth rate is 9.5% over the last 53 years.

DIVIDENDS PER SHARE (split-adjusted)

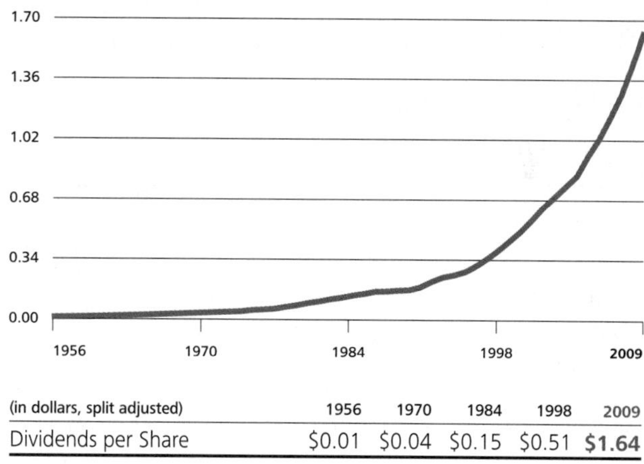

(in dollars, split adjusted)	1956	1970	1984	1998	2009
Dividends per Share	$0.01	$0.04	$0.15	$0.51	**$1.64**

The paper utilized in the printing of this annual report is certified by SmartWood to the FSC Standards, which promotes environmentally appropriate, socially beneficial and economically viable management of the world's forests. The paper contains a mix of pulp that is derived from FSC certified well-managed forests; post-consumer recycled paper fibers and other controlled sources.

Design: VSA Partners, Inc.

FASB CODIFICATION

FASB Codification References

[1] FASB ASC 320-10-35-1. [Predecessor literature: "Accounting for Certain Investments in Debt and Equity Securities," *Statement of Financial Accounting Standards No. 115* (Norwalk, Conn.: FASB, 1993).]

[2] FASB ASC 825-10-25-1. [Predecessor literature: "The Fair Value Option for Financial Assets and Liabilities, Including an Amendment of FASB Statement No. 115," *Statement of Financial Accounting Standards No. 159* (Norwalk, Conn.: FASB, February 2007).]

[3] FASB ASC 470-10-05-6. [Predecessor literature: "Classification of Short-term Obligations Expected to Be Refinanced," *Statement of Financial Accounting Standards No. 6* (Stamford, Conn.: FASB, 1975).]

[4] FASB ASC 505-10-50. [Predecessor literature: "Disclosure of Information about Capital Structure," *Statement of Financial Accounting Standards No. 129* (Norwalk: FASB, 1997), par. 4).]

[5] FASB ASC 230-10-05. [Predecessor literature: "Statement of Cash Flows," *Statement of Financial Accounting Standards No. 95* (Stamford, Conn.: FASB, 1987).]

[6] FASB ASC 235-10-05. [Predecessor literature: "Disclosure of Accounting Policies," *Opinions of the Accounting Principles Board No. 22* (New York: AICPA, 1972).]

[7] FASB ASC 275-10-05. [Predecessor literature: "Disclosure of Certain Significant Risks and Uncertainties," *Statement of Position 94-6* (New York: AICPA, 1994).]

[8] FASB ASC 820-10-15. [Predecessor literature: "Fair Value Measurement," *Statement of Financial Accounting Standards No. 157* (Norwalk, Conn.: FASB, September 2006).]

Exercises

If your school has a subscription to the FASB Codification, go to *http://aaahq.org/asclogin.cfm* to log in and prepare responses to the following. Provide Codification references for your responses.

CE5-1 Access the Codification glossary ("Master Glossary") to answer the following.

(a) What is the definition provided for current assets?

(b) What is the definition of an intangible asset? In what section of the Codification are intangible assets addressed?

(c) What are cash equivalents?

(d) What are financing activities?

CE5-2 What guidance does the Codification provide on the classification of current liabilities?

CE5-3 What guidance does the Codification provide concerning the format of accounting disclosures?

CE5-4 What are the objectives related to the statement of cash flows?

An additional Codification case can be found in the Using Your Judgment section, on page 299.

Be sure to check the book's companion website for a Review and Analysis Exercise, with solution.

Questions, Brief Exercises, Exercises, Problems, and many more resources are available for practice in WileyPLUS.

QUESTIONS

1. How does information from the balance sheet help users of the financial statements?
2. What is meant by solvency? What information in the balance sheet can be used to assess a company's solvency?
3. A recent financial magazine indicated that the airline industry has poor financial flexibility. What is meant by financial flexibility, and why is it important?
4. Discuss at least two situations in which estimates could affect the usefulness of information in the balance sheet.
5. Perez Company reported an increase in inventories in the past year. Discuss the effect of this change on the current ratio (current assets ÷ current liabilities). What does this tell a statement user about Perez Company's liquidity?
6. What is meant by liquidity? Rank the following assets from one to five in order of liquidity.
   (a) Goodwill.
   (b) Inventory.
   (c) Buildings.
   (d) Short-term investments.
   (e) Accounts receivable.
7. What are the major limitations of the balance sheet as a source of information?
8. Discuss at least two items that are important to the value of companies like **Intel** or **IBM** but that are not recorded in their balance sheets. What are some reasons why these items are not recorded in the balance sheet?
9. How does separating current assets from property, plant, and equipment in the balance sheet help analysts?
10. In its December 31, 2012, balance sheet Oakley Corporation reported as an asset, "Net notes and accounts receivable, $7,100,000." What other disclosures are necessary?
11. Should available-for-sale securities always be reported as a current asset? Explain.
12. What is the relationship between current assets and current liabilities?
13. The New York Knicks, Inc. sold 10,000 season tickets at $2,000 each. By December 31, 2012, 16 of the 40 home games had been played. What amount should be reported as a current liability at December 31, 2012?
14. What is working capital? How does working capital relate to the operating cycle?
15. In what section of the balance sheet should the following items appear, and what balance sheet terminology would you use?
   (a) Treasury stock (recorded at cost).
   (b) Checking account at bank.
   (c) Land (held as an investment).
   (d) Sinking fund.
   (e) Unamortized premium on bonds payable.
   (f) Copyrights.
   (g) Pension fund assets.
   (h) Premium on capital stock.
   (i) Long-term investments (pledged against bank loans payable).
16. Where should the following items be shown on the balance sheet, if shown at all?
   (a) Allowance for doubtful accounts receivable.
   (b) Merchandise held on consignment.
   (c) Advances received on sales contract.
   (d) Cash surrender value of life insurance.
   (e) Land.
   (f) Merchandise out on consignment.
   (g) Franchises.
   (h) Accumulated depreciation of plant and equipment.
   (i) Materials in transit—purchased f.o.b. destination.
17. State the generally accepted accounting principle applicable to the balance sheet valuation of each of the following assets.
   (a) Trade accounts receivable.
   (b) Land.
   (c) Inventories.
   (d) Trading securities (common stock of other companies).
   (e) Prepaid expenses.
18. Refer to the definition of assets on page 216. Discuss how a leased building might qualify as an asset of the lessee (tenant) under this definition.
19. Kathleen Battle says, "Retained earnings should be reported as an asset, since it is earnings which are reinvested in the business." How would you respond to Battle?
20. The creditors of Chester Company agree to accept promissory notes for the amount of its indebtedness with a proviso that two-thirds of the annual profits must be applied to their liquidation. How should these notes be reported on the balance sheet of the issuing company? Give a reason for your answer.
21. What is the purpose of a statement of cash flows? How does it differ from a balance sheet and an income statement?
22. The net income for the year for Genesis, Inc. is $750,000, but the statement of cash flows reports that the cash provided by operating activities is $640,000. What might account for the difference?

23. Net income for the year for Carrie, Inc. was $750,000, but the statement of cash flows reports that cash provided by operating activities was $860,000. What might account for the difference?

24. Differentiate between operating activities, investing activities, and financing activities.

25. Each of the following items must be considered in preparing a statement of cash flows. Indicate where each item is to be reported in the statement, if at all. Assume that net income is reported as $90,000.

(a) Accounts receivable increased from $34,000 to $39,000 from the beginning to the end of the year.

(b) During the year, 10,000 shares of preferred stock with a par value of $100 a share were issued at $115 per share.

(c) Depreciation expense amounted to $14,000, and bond premium amortization amounted to $5,000.

(d) Land increased from $10,000 to $30,000.

26. Sergey Co. has net cash provided by operating activities of $1,200,000. Its average current liabilities for the period are $1,000,000, and its average total liabilities are $1,500,000. Comment on the company's liquidity and financial flexibility, given this information.

27. Net income for the year for Tanizaki, Inc. was $750,000, but the statement of cash flows reports that cash provided by operating activities was $860,000. Tanizaki also reported capital expenditures of $75,000 and paid dividends in the amount of $30,000. Compute Tanizaki's free cash flow.

28. What is the purpose of a free cash flow analysis?

29. What are some of the techniques of disclosure for the balance sheet?

30. What is a "Summary of Significant Accounting Policies"?

31. What types of contractual obligations must be disclosed in great detail in the notes to the balance sheet? Why do you think these detailed provisions should be disclosed?

32. What is the profession's recommendation in regard to the use of the term "surplus"? Explain.

BRIEF EXERCISES

3 **BE5-1** Harding Corporation has the following accounts included in its December 31, 2012, trial balance: Accounts Receivable $110,000; Inventory $290,000; Allowance for Doubtful Accounts $8,000; Patents $72,000; Prepaid Insurance $9,500; Accounts Payable $77,000; Cash $30,000. Prepare the current assets section of the balance sheet, listing the accounts in proper sequence.

3 **BE5-2** Koch Corporation's adjusted trial balance contained the following asset accounts at December 31, 2012: Cash $7,000; Land $40,000; Patents $12,500; Accounts Receivable $90,000; Prepaid Insurance $5,200; Inventory $30,000; Allowance for Doubtful Accounts $4,000; Equity Investments (trading) $11,000. Prepare the current assets section of the balance sheet, listing the accounts in proper sequence.

3 **BE5-3** Included in Outkast Company's December 31, 2012, trial balance are the following accounts: Prepaid Rent $5,200; Debt Investments $56,000; Unearned Fees $17,000; Land (held for investment) $39,000; Notes Receivable (long-term) $42,000. Prepare the long-term investments section of the balance sheet.

3 **BE5-4** Lowell Company's December 31, 2012, trial balance includes the following accounts: Inventory $120,000; Buildings $207,000; Accumulated Depreciation—Equipment $19,000; Equipment $190,000; Land (held for investment) $46,000; Accumulated Depreciation—Buildings $45,000; Land $71,000; Timberland $70,000. Prepare the property, plant, and equipment section of the balance sheet.

3 **BE5-5** Crane Corporation has the following accounts included in its December 31, 2012, trial balance: Equity Investments (trading) $21,000; Goodwill $150,000; Prepaid Insurance $12,000; Patents $220,000; Franchises $130,000. Prepare the intangible assets section of the balance sheet.

3 **BE5-6** Patrick Corporation's adjusted trial balance contained the following asset accounts at December 31, 2012: Prepaid Rent $12,000; Goodwill $50,000; Franchise Fees Receivable $2,000; Franchises $47,000; Patents $33,000; Trademarks $10,000. Prepare the intangible assets section of the balance sheet.

3 **BE5-7** Thomas Corporation's adjusted trial balance contained the following liability accounts at December 31, 2012: Bonds Payable (due in 3 years) $100,000; Accounts Payable $72,000; Notes Payable (due in 90 days) $22,500; Salaries and Wages Payable $4,000; Income Taxes Payable $7,000. Prepare the current liabilities section of the balance sheet.

3 **BE5-8** Included in Adams Company's December 31, 2012, trial balance are the following accounts: Accounts Payable $220,000; Pension Asset/Liability $375,000; Discount on Bonds Payable $29,000; Unearned Revenue $41,000; Bonds Payable $400,000; Salaries and Wages Payable $27,000; Interest Payable $12,000; Income Taxes Payable $29,000. Prepare the current liabilities section of the balance sheet.

3 **BE5-9** Use the information presented in BE5-8 for Adams Company to prepare the long-term liabilities section of the balance sheet.

3 **BE5-10** Hawthorn Corporation's adjusted trial balance contained the following accounts at December 31, 2012: Retained Earnings $120,000; Common Stock $750,000; Bonds Payable $100,000; Paid-in Capital in Excess of Par—Common Stock $200,000; Goodwill $55,000; Accumulated Other Comprehensive Loss $150,000. Prepare the stockholders' equity section of the balance sheet.

3 **BE5-11** Stowe Company's December 31, 2012, trial balance includes the following accounts: Investment in Common Stock $70,000; Retained Earnings $114,000; Trademarks $31,000; Preferred Stock $152,000; Common Stock $55,000; Deferred Income Taxes $88,000; Paid-in Capital in Excess of Par—Common Stock $174,000. Prepare the stockholders' equity section of the balance sheet.

6 **BE5-12** Keyser Beverage Company reported the following items in the most recent year.

Net income	$40,000
Dividends paid	5,000
Increase in accounts receivable	10,000
Increase in accounts payable	7,000
Purchase of equipment (capital expenditure)	8,000
Depreciation expense	4,000
Issue of notes payable	20,000

Compute net cash provided by operating activities, the net change in cash during the year, and free cash flow.

6 **BE5-13** Ames Company reported 2012 net income of $151,000. During 2012, accounts receivable increased by $13,000 and accounts payable increased by $9,500. Depreciation expense was $44,000. Prepare the cash flows from operating activities section of the statement of cash flows.

6 **BE5-14** Martinez Corporation engaged in the following cash transactions during 2012.

Sale of land and building	$191,000
Purchase of treasury stock	40,000
Purchase of land	37,000
Payment of cash dividend	95,000
Purchase of equipment	53,000
Issuance of common stock	147,000
Retirement of bonds	100,000

Compute the net cash provided (used) by investing activities.

6 **BE5-15** Use the information presented in BE5-14 for Martinez Corporation to compute the net cash used (provided) by financing activities.

7 **BE5-16** Using the information in BE5-14, determine Martinez's free cash flow, assuming that it reported net cash provided by operating activities of $400,000.

EXERCISES

2 3 **E5-1 (Balance Sheet Classifications)** Presented below are a number of balance sheet accounts of Cunningham, Inc.

(a) Investment in Preferred Stock.
(b) Treasury Stock.
(c) Common Stock.
(d) Dividends Payable.
(e) Accumulated Depreciation—Equipment.
(f) Construction in Process.
(g) Petty Cash.
(h) Interest Payable.
(i) Deficit.
(j) Equity Investments (trading).
(k) Income Tax Payable.
(l) Unearned Subscription Revenue.
(m) Work in Process.
(n) Vacation Wages Payable.

Instructions
For each of the accounts above, indicate the proper balance sheet classification. In the case of borderline items, indicate the additional information that would be required to determine the proper classification.

2 3 **E5-2 (Classification of Balance Sheet Accounts)** Presented below are the captions of Nikos Company's balance sheet.

(a) Current assets.
(b) Investments.
(c) Property, plant, and equipment.
(d) Intangible assets.
(e) Other assets.
(f) Current liabilities.
(g) Non-current liabilities.
(h) Capital stock.
(i) Additional paid-in capital.
(j) Retained earnings.

Instructions

Indicate by letter where each of the following items would be classified.

1. Preferred stock.
2. Goodwill.
3. Salaries and wages payable.
4. Accounts payable.
5. Buildings.
6. Equity investments (trading).
7. Current portion of long-term debt.
8. Premium on bonds payable.
9. Allowance for doubtful accounts.
10. Accounts receivable.
11. Cash surrender value of life insurance.
12. Notes payable (due next year).
13. Supplies.
14. Common stock.
15. Land.
16. Bond sinking fund.
17. Inventory.
18. Prepaid insurance.
19. Bonds payable.
20. Income tax payable.

2 3 **E5-3 (Classification of Balance Sheet Accounts)** Assume that Masters Enterprises uses the following headings on its balance sheet.

(a) Current assets.
(b) Investments.
(c) Property, plant, and equipment.
(d) Intangible assets.
(e) Other assets.
(f) Current liabilities.
(g) Long-term liabilities.
(h) Capital stock.
(i) Paid-in capital in excess of par.
(j) Retained earnings.

Instructions

Indicate by letter how each of the following usually should be classified. If an item should appear in a note to the financial statements, use the letter "N" to indicate this fact. If an item need not be reported at all on the balance sheet, use the letter "X."

1. Prepaid insurance.
2. Stock owned in affiliated companies.
3. Unearned subscriptions revenue.
4. Advances to suppliers.
5. Unearned rent revenue.
6. Preferred stock.
7. Additional paid-in capital on preferred stock.
8. Copyrights.
9. Petty cash fund.
10. Sales tax payable.
11. Accrued interest on notes receivable.
12. Twenty-year issue of bonds payable that will mature within the next year. (No sinking fund exists, and refunding is not planned.)
13. Machinery retired from use and held for sale.
14. Fully depreciated machine still in use.
15. Accrued interest on bonds payable.
16. Salaries that company budget shows will be paid to employees within the next year.
17. Discount on bonds payable. (Assume related to bonds payable in No. 12.)
18. Accumulated depreciation—buildings.

2 3 **E5-4 (Preparation of a Classified Balance Sheet)** Assume that Gulistan Inc. has the following accounts at the end of the current year.

1. Common Stock.
2. Discount on Bonds Payable.
3. Treasury Stock (at cost).
4. Notes Payable (short-term).
5. Raw Materials.
6. Preferred Stock Investments (long-term).
7. Unearned Rent Revenue.
8. Work in Process.
9. Copyrights.
10. Buildings.
11. Notes Receivable (short-term).
12. Cash.
13. Salaries and Wages Payable.
14. Accumulated Depreciation—Buildings.
15. Cash Restricted for Plant Expansion.
16. Land Held for Future Plant Site.
17. Allowance for Doubtful Accounts—Accounts Receivable.
18. Retained Earnings.
19. Paid-in Capital in Excess of Par—Common Stock.
20. Unearned Subscriptions Revenue.
21. Receivables—Officers (due in one year).
22. Finished Goods.
23. Accounts Receivable.
24. Bonds Payable (due in 4 years).

Instructions

Prepare a classified balance sheet in good form. (No monetary amounts are necessary.)

3 **E5-5 (Preparation of a Corrected Balance Sheet)** Bruno Company has decided to expand its operations. The bookkeeper recently completed the balance sheet presented on the next page in order to obtain additional funds for expansion.

BRUNO COMPANY BALANCE SHEET DECEMBER 31, 2012	
Current assets	
Cash	$260,000
Accounts receivable (net)	340,000
Inventories (lower-of-average-cost-or-market)	401,000
Equity investments (trading)—at cost (fair value $120,000)	140,000
Property, plant, and equipment	
Buildings (net)	570,000
Office equipment (net)	160,000
Land held for future use	175,000
Intangible assets	
Goodwill	80,000
Cash surrender value of life insurance	90,000
Prepaid expenses	12,000
Current liabilities	
Accounts payable	135,000
Notes payable (due next year)	125,000
Pension obligation	82,000
Rent payable	49,000
Premium on bonds payable	53,000
Long-term liabilities	
Bonds payable	500,000
Stockholders' equity	
Common stock, $1.00 par, authorized 400,000 shares, issued 290,000	290,000
Additional paid-in capital	180,000
Retained earnings	?

Instructions

Prepare a revised balance sheet given the available information. Assume that the accumulated depreciation balance for the buildings is $160,000 and for the office equipment, $105,000. The allowance for doubtful accounts has a balance of $17,000. The pension obligation is considered a long-term liability.

3 **E5-6 (Corrections of a Balance Sheet)** The bookkeeper for Garfield Company has prepared the following balance sheet as of July 31, 2012.

GARFIELD COMPANY BALANCE SHEET AS OF JULY 31, 2012			
Cash	$ 69,000	Notes and accounts payable	$ 44,000
Accounts receivable (net)	40,500	Long-term liabilities	75,000
Inventory	60,000	Stockholders' equity	155,500
Equipment (net)	84,000		$274,500
Patents	21,000		
	$274,500		

The following additional information is provided.

1. Cash includes $1,200 in a petty cash fund and $12,000 in a bond sinking fund.
2. The net accounts receivable balance is comprised of the following three items: (a) accounts receivable—debit balances $52,000; (b) accounts receivable—credit balances $8,000; (c) allowance for doubtful accounts $3,500.
3. Merchandise inventory costing $5,300 was shipped out on consignment on July 31, 2012. The ending inventory balance does not include the consigned goods. Receivables in the amount of $5,300 were recognized on these consigned goods.
4. Equipment had a cost of $112,000 and an accumulated depreciation balance of $28,000.
5. Taxes payable of $9,000 were accrued on July 31. Garfield Company, however, had set up a cash fund to meet this obligation. This cash fund was not included in the cash balance, but was offset against the taxes payable amount.

Instructions

Prepare a corrected classified balance sheet as of July 31, 2012, from the available information, adjusting the account balances using the additional information.

3 **E5-7 (Current Assets Section of the Balance Sheet)** Presented below are selected accounts of Aramis Company at December 31, 2012.

Finished Goods	$ 52,000	Cost of Goods Sold	$2,100,000
Unearned Revenue	90,000	Notes Receivable	40,000
Equipment	253,000	Accounts Receivable	161,000
Work in Process	34,000	Raw Materials	187,000
Cash	42,000	Supplies Expense	60,000
Equity Investments (short-term)	31,000	Allowance for Doubtful Accounts	12,000
Customer Advances	36,000	Licenses	18,000
Cash Restricted for Plant Expansion	50,000	Additional Paid-in Capital	88,000
		Treasury Stock	22,000

The following additional information is available.

1. Inventories are valued at lower-of-cost-or-market using LIFO.
2. Equipment is recorded at cost. Accumulated depreciation, computed on a straight-line basis, is $50,600.
3. The short-term investments have a fair value of $29,000. (Assume they are trading securities.)
4. The notes receivable are due April 30, 2014, with interest receivable every April 30. The notes bear interest at 6%. (*Hint:* Accrue interest due on December 31, 2012.)
5. The allowance for doubtful accounts applies to the accounts receivable. Accounts receivable of $50,000 are pledged as collateral on a bank loan.
6. Licenses are recorded net of accumulated amortization of $14,000.
7. Treasury stock is recorded at cost.

Instructions

Prepare the current assets section of Aramis Company's December 31, 2012, balance sheet, with appropriate disclosures.

2 **E5-8 (Current vs. Long-term Liabilities)** Pascal Corporation is preparing its December 31, 2012, balance sheet. The following items may be reported as either a current or long-term liability.

1. On December 15, 2012, Pascal declared a cash dividend of $2.00 per share to stockholders of record on December 31. The dividend is payable on January 15, 2013. Pascal has issued 1,000,000 shares of common stock, of which 50,000 shares are held in treasury.
2. At December 31, bonds payable of $100,000,000 are outstanding. The bonds pay 10% interest every September 30 and mature in installments of $25,000,000 every September 30, beginning September 30, 2013.
3. At December 31, 2011, customer advances were $12,000,000. During 2012, Pascal collected $30,000,000 of customer advances, and advances of $25,000,000 were earned.

Instructions

For each item above, indicate the dollar amounts to be reported as a current liability and as a long-term liability, if any.

2 3 **E5-9 (Current Assets and Current Liabilities)** The current assets and current liabilities sections of the balance sheet of Agincourt Company appear as follows.

AGINCOURT COMPANY
BALANCE SHEET (PARTIAL)
DECEMBER 31, 2012

Cash		$ 40,000	Accounts payable	$ 61,000
Accounts receivable	$89,000		Notes payable	67,000
Less: Allowance for doubtful accounts	7,000	82,000		$128,000
Inventory		171,000		
Prepaid expenses		9,000		
		$302,000		

The following errors in the corporation's accounting have been discovered:

1. January 2013 cash disbursements entered as of December 2012 included payments of accounts payable in the amount of $35,000, on which a cash discount of 2% was taken.
2. The inventory included $27,000 of merchandise that had been received at December 31 but for which no purchase invoices had been received or entered. Of this amount, $10,000 had been received on consignment; the remainder was purchased f.o.b. destination, terms 2/10, n/30.
3. Sales for the first four days in January 2013 in the amount of $30,000 were entered in the sales book as of December 31, 2012. Of these, $21,500 were sales on account and the remainder were cash sales.
4. Cash, not including cash sales, collected in January 2013 and entered as of December 31, 2012, totaled $35,324. Of this amount, $23,324 was received on account after cash discounts of 2% had been deducted; the remainder represented the proceeds of a bank loan.

Instructions

(a) Restate the current assets and current liabilities sections of the balance sheet in accordance with good accounting practice. (Assume that both accounts receivable and accounts payable are recorded gross.)

(b) State the net effect of your adjustments on Agincourt Company's retained earnings balance.

2 3 **E5-10 (Current Liabilities)** Mary Pierce is the controller of Arnold Corporation and is responsible for the preparation of the year-end financial statements. The following transactions occurred during the year.

(a) On December 20, 2012, an employee filed a legal action against Arnold for $100,000 for wrongful dismissal. Management believes the action to be frivolous and without merit. The likelihood of payment to the employee is remote.

(b) Bonuses to key employees based on net income for 2012 are estimated to be $150,000.

(c) On December 1, 2012, the company borrowed $900,000 at 8% per year. Interest is paid quarterly.

(d) Credit sales for the year amounted to $10,000,000. Arnold's expense provision for doubtful accounts is estimated to be 2% of credit sales.

(e) On December 15, 2012, the company declared a $2.00 per share dividend on the 40,000 shares of common stock outstanding, to be paid on January 5, 2013.

(f) During the year, customer advances of $160,000 were received; $50,000 of this amount was earned by December 31, 2012.

Instructions

For each item above, indicate the dollar amount to be reported as a current liability. If a liability is not reported, explain why.

3 **E5-11 (Balance Sheet Preparation)** Presented below is the adjusted trial balance of Abbey Corporation at December 31, 2012.

	Debits	Credits
Cash	$?	
Supplies	1,200	
Prepaid Insurance	1,000	
Equipment	48,000	
Accumulated Depreciation—Equipment		$ 9,000
Trademarks	950	
Accounts Payable		10,000
Salaries and Wages Payable		500
Unearned Service Revenue		2,000
Bonds Payable (due 2017)		9,000
Common Stock		10,000
Retained Earnings		20,000
Service Revenue		10,000
Salaries and Wages Expense	9,000	
Insurance Expense	1,400	
Rent Expense	1,200	
Interest Expense	900	
Total	$?	$?

Additional information:

1. Net loss for the year was $2,500.
2. No dividends were declared during 2012.

Instructions

Prepare a classified balance sheet as of December 31, 2012.

3 **E5-12 (Preparation of a Balance Sheet)** Presented below is the trial balance of Vivaldi Corporation at December 31, 2012.

	Debits	Credits
Cash	$ 197,000	
Sales		$ 7,900,000
Debt Investments (trading) (cost, $145,000)	153,000	
Cost of Goods Sold	4,800,000	
Debt Investments (long-term)	299,000	
Equity Investments (long-term)	277,000	
Notes Payable (short-term)		90,000
Accounts Payable		455,000
Selling Expenses	2,000,000	
Investment Revenue		63,000
Land	260,000	
Buildings	1,040,000	
Dividends Payable		136,000
Accrued Liabilities		96,000
Accounts Receivable	435,000	
Accumulated Depreciation—Buildings		352,000
Allowance for Doubtful Accounts		25,000
Administrative Expenses	900,000	
Interest Expense	211,000	
Inventory	597,000	
Extraordinary Gain		80,000
Notes Payable (long-term)		900,000
Equipment	600,000	
Bonds Payable		1,000,000
Accumulated Depreciation—Equipment		60,000
Franchises	160,000	
Common Stock ($5 par)		1,000,000
Treasury Stock	191,000	
Patents	195,000	
Retained Earnings		78,000
Paid-in Capital in Excess of Par		80,000
Totals	$12,315,000	$12,315,000

Instructions

Prepare a balance sheet at December 31, 2012, for Vivaldi Corporation. Ignore income taxes.

5 **E5-13 (Statement of Cash Flows—Classifications)** The major classifications of activities reported in the statement of cash flows are operating, investing, and financing. Classify each of the transactions listed below as:

1. Operating activity—add to net income.
2. Operating activity—deduct from net income.
3. Investing activity.
4. Financing activity.
5. Reported as significant noncash activity.

The transactions are as follows.

(a) Issuance of capital stock.
(b) Purchase of land and building.
(c) Redemption of bonds.
(d) Sale of equipment.
(e) Depreciation of machinery.
(f) Amortization of patent.
(g) Issuance of bonds for plant assets.
(h) Payment of cash dividends.
(i) Exchange of furniture for office equipment.
(j) Purchase of treasury stock.
(k) Loss on sale of equipment.
(l) Increase in accounts receivable during the year.
(m) Decrease in accounts payable during the year.

6 **E5-14 (Preparation of a Statement of Cash Flows)** The comparative balance sheets of Connecticut Inc. at the beginning and the end of the year 2012 appear on the next page.

CONNECTICUT INC.
BALANCE SHEETS

Assets	Dec. 31, 2012	Jan. 1, 2012	Inc./Dec.
Cash	$ 45,000	$ 13,000	$32,000 Inc.
Accounts receivable	91,000	88,000	3,000 Inc.
Equipment	39,000	22,000	17,000 Inc.
Less: Accumulated depreciation—equipment	(17,000)	(11,000)	6,000 Inc.
Total	$158,000	$112,000	
Liabilities and Stockholders' Equity			
Accounts payable	$ 20,000	$ 15,000	5,000 Inc.
Common stock	100,000	80,000	20,000 Inc.
Retained earnings	38,000	17,000	21,000 Inc.
Total	$158,000	$112,000	

Net income of $34,000 was reported, and dividends of $13,000 were paid in 2012. New equipment was purchased and none was sold.

Instructions

Prepare a statement of cash flows for the year 2012.

6 7 **E5-15 (Preparation of a Statement of Cash Flows)** Presented below is a condensed version of the comparative balance sheets for Sondergaard Corporation for the last two years at December 31.

	2012	2011
Cash	$157,000	$ 78,000
Accounts receivable	180,000	185,000
Investments	52,000	74,000
Equipment	298,000	240,000
Less: Accumulated depreciation—equipment	(106,000)	(89,000)
Current liabilities	134,000	151,000
Capital stock	160,000	160,000
Retained earnings	287,000	177,000

Additional information:

Investments were sold at a loss (not extraordinary) of $7,000; no equipment was sold; cash dividends paid were $50,000; and net income was $160,000.

Instructions

(a) Prepare a statement of cash flows for 2012 for Sondergaard Corporation.
(b) Determine Sondergaard Corporation's free cash flow.

6 7 **E5-16 (Preparation of a Statement of Cash Flows)** A comparative balance sheet for Orozco Corporation is presented below.

	December 31	
Assets	2012	2011
Cash	$ 63,000	$ 22,000
Accounts receivable	82,000	66,000
Inventory	180,000	189,000
Land	71,000	110,000
Equipment	270,000	200,000
Accumulated depreciation—equipment	(69,000)	(42,000)
Total	$597,000	$545,000
Liabilities and Stockholders' Equity		
Accounts payable	$ 34,000	$ 47,000
Bonds payable	150,000	200,000
Common stock ($1 par)	214,000	164,000
Retained earnings	199,000	134,000
Total	$597,000	$545,000

Additional information:

1. Net income for 2012 was $105,000.
2. Cash dividends of $40,000 were declared and paid.
3. Bonds payable amounting to $50,000 were retired through issuance of common stock.

Instructions

(a) Prepare a statement of cash flows for 2012 for Orozco Corporation.
(b) Determine Orozco Corporation's current cash debt coverage ratio, cash debt coverage ratio, and free cash flow. Comment on its liquidity and financial flexibility.

3 6 **E5-17 (Preparation of a Statement of Cash Flows and a Balance Sheet)** Chekov Corporation's balance sheet at the end of 2011 included the following items.

Current assets	$235,000	Current liabilities	$150,000
Land	30,000	Bonds payable	100,000
Buildings	120,000	Common stock	180,000
Equipment	90,000	Retained earnings	44,000
Accum. depr.—buildings	(30,000)	Total	$474,000
Accum. depr.—equipment	(11,000)		
Patents	40,000		
Total	$474,000		

The following information is available for 2012.

1. Net income was $55,000.
2. Equipment (cost $20,000 and accumulated depreciation $8,000) was sold for $9,000.
3. Depreciation expense was $4,000 on the building and $9,000 on equipment.
4. Patent amortization was $2,500.
5. Current assets other than cash increased by $25,000. Current liabilities increased by $13,000.
6. An addition to the building was completed at a cost of $27,000.
7. A long-term investment in stock was purchased for $16,000.
8. Bonds payable of $50,000 were issued.
9. Cash dividends of $25,000 were declared and paid.
10. Treasury stock was purchased at a cost of $11,000.

Instructions

(Show only totals for current assets and current liabilities.)

(a) Prepare a statement of cash flows for 2012.
(b) Prepare a balance sheet at December 31, 2012.

6 7 **E5-18 (Preparation of a Statement of Cash Flows, Analysis)** The comparative balance sheets of Menachem Corporation at the beginning and end of the year 2012 appear below.

MENACHEM CORPORATION
BALANCE SHEETS

Assets	Dec. 31, 2012	Jan. 1, 2012	Inc./Dec.
Cash	$ 22,000	$ 13,000	$ 9,000 Inc.
Accounts receivable	106,000	88,000	18,000 Inc.
Equipment	37,000	22,000	15,000 Inc.
Less: Accumulated depreciation—equipment	(17,000)	(11,000)	6,000 Inc.
Total	$148,000	$112,000	
Liabilities and Stockholders' Equity			
Accounts payable	$ 20,000	$ 15,000	5,000 Inc.
Common stock	100,000	80,000	20,000 Inc.
Retained earnings	28,000	17,000	11,000 Inc.
Total	$148,000	$112,000	

Net income of $34,000 was reported, and dividends of $23,000 were paid in 2012. New equipment was purchased and none was sold.

Instructions

(a) Prepare a statement of cash flows for the year 2012.

(b) Compute the current ratio (current assets ÷ current liabilities) as of January 1, 2012, and December 31, 2012, and compute free cash flow for the year 2012.

(c) In light of the analysis in (b), comment on Menachem's liquidity and financial flexibility.

See the book's companion website, www.wiley.com/college/kieso, for a set of B Exercises.

PROBLEMS

3 **P5-1 (Preparation of a Classified Balance Sheet, Periodic Inventory)** Presented below is a list of accounts in alphabetical order.

Accounts Receivable	Land
Accumulated Depreciation—Buildings	Land for Future Plant Site
Accumulated Depreciation—Equipment	Loss from Flood
Advances to Employees	Notes Payable (due next year)
Advertising Expense	Patents
Allowance for Doubtful Accounts	Payroll Taxes Payable
Bond Sinking Fund	Pension Obligations
Bonds Payable	Petty Cash
Buildings	Preferred Stock
Cash in Bank	Premium on Bonds Payable
Cash on Hand	Paid-in Capital in Excess of Par—Preferred Stock
Cash Surrender Value of Life Insurance	Prepaid Rent
Commission Expense	Purchases
Common Stock	Purchase Returns and Allowances
Copyrights	Retained Earnings
Debt Investments (trading)	Sales
Dividends Payable	Sales Discounts
Equipment	Salaries and Wages Expense (sales)
Gain on Sale of Equipment	Salaries and Wages Payable
Interest Receivable	Transportation-in
Inventory—Beginning	Treasury Stock (at cost)
Inventory—Ending	Unearned Subscriptions Revenue

Instructions

Prepare a classified balance sheet in good form. (No monetary amounts are to be shown.)

3 **P5-2 (Balance Sheet Preparation)** Presented below are a number of balance sheet items for Montoya, Inc., for the current year, 2012.

Goodwill	$ 125,000	Accumulated depreciation—equipment	$ 292,000
Payroll taxes payable	177,591	Inventory	239,800
Bonds payable	300,000	Rent payable (short-term)	45,000
Discount on bonds payable	15,000	Income tax payable	98,362
Cash	360,000	Rent payable (long-term)	480,000
Land	480,000	Common stock, $1 par value	200,000
Notes receivable	445,700	Preferred stock, $10 par value	150,000
Notes payable (to banks)	265,000	Prepaid expenses	87,920
Accounts payable	490,000	Equipment	1,470,000
Retained earnings	?	Equity investments (trading)	121,000
Income taxes receivable	97,630	Accumulated depreciation—buildings	270,200
Unsecured notes payable (long-term)	1,600,000	Buildings	1,640,000

Instructions

Prepare a classified balance sheet in good form. Common stock authorized was 400,000 shares, and preferred stock authorized was 20,000 shares. Assume that notes receivable and notes payable are short-term, unless stated otherwise. Cost and fair value of equity investments (trading) are the same.

3 **P5-3 (Balance Sheet Adjustment and Preparation)** The adjusted trial balance of Eastwood Company and other related information for the year 2012 are presented on the next page.

EASTWOOD COMPANY
ADJUSTED TRIAL BALANCE
DECEMBER 31, 2012

	Debits	Credits
Cash	$ 41,000	
Accounts Receivable	163,500	
Allowance for Doubtful Accounts		$ 8,700
Prepaid Insurance	5,900	
Inventory	208,500	
Equity Investments (long-term)	339,000	
Land	85,000	
Construction in Process (building)	124,000	
Patents	36,000	
Equipment	400,000	
Accumulated Depreciation—Equipment		240,000
Discount on Bonds Payable	20,000	
Accounts Payable		148,000
Accrued Expenses		49,200
Notes Payable		94,000
Bonds Payable		200,000
Common Stock		500,000
Paid-in Capital in Excess of Par—Common Stock		45,000
Retained Earnings		138,000
	$1,422,900	$1,422,900

Additional information:

1. The LIFO method of inventory value is used.
2. The cost and fair value of the long-term investments that consist of stocks and bonds is the same.
3. The amount of the Construction in Progress account represents the costs expended to date on a building in the process of construction. (The company rents factory space at the present time.) The land on which the building is being constructed cost $85,000, as shown in the trial balance.
4. The patents were purchased by the company at a cost of $40,000 and are being amortized on a straight-line basis.
5. Of the discount on bonds payable, $2,000 will be amortized in 2013.
6. The notes payable represent bank loans that are secured by long-term investments carried at $120,000. These bank loans are due in 2013.
7. The bonds payable bear interest at 8% payable every December 31, and are due January 1, 2023.
8. 600,000 shares of common stock of a par value of $1 were authorized, of which 500,000 shares were issued and outstanding.

Instructions

Prepare a balance sheet as of December 31, 2012, so that all important information is fully disclosed.

3 **P5-4 (Preparation of a Corrected Balance Sheet)** Presented below and on the next page is the balance sheet of Kishwaukee Corporation as of December 31, 2012.

KISHWAUKEE CORPORATION
BALANCE SHEET
DECEMBER 31, 2012

Assets	
Goodwill (Note 2)	$ 120,000
Buildings (Note 1)	1,640,000
Inventory	312,100
Land	950,000
Accounts receivable	170,000
Treasury stock (50,000 shares)	87,000
Cash on hand	175,900
Assets allocated to trustee for plant expansion	
Cash in bank	70,000
Debt investments (held-to-maturity)	138,000
	$3,663,000

Equities	
Notes payable (Note 3)	$ 600,000
Common stock, authorized and issued, 1,000,000 shares, no par	1,150,000
Retained earnings	858,000
Appreciation capital (Note 1)	570,000
Income tax payable	75,000
Reserve for depreciation recorded to date on the building	410,000
	$3,663,000

Note 1: Buildings are stated at cost, except for one building that was recorded at appraised value. The excess of appraisal value over cost was $570,000. Depreciation has been recorded based on cost.

Note 2: Goodwill in the amount of $120,000 was recognized because the company believed that book value was not an accurate representation of the fair value of the company. The gain of $120,000 was credited to Retained Earnings.

Note 3: Notes payable are long-term except for the current installment due of $100,000.

Instructions

Prepare a corrected classified balance sheet in good form. The notes above are for information only.

3 **P5-5 (Balance Sheet Adjustment and Preparation)** Presented below is the balance sheet of Sargent Corporation for the current year, 2012.

SARGENT CORPORATION
BALANCE SHEET
DECEMBER 31, 2012

Current assets	$ 485,000	Current liabilities	$ 380,000
Investments	640,000	Long-term liabilities	1,000,000
Property, plant, and equipment	1,720,000	Stockholders' equity	1,770,000
Intangible assets	305,000		$3,150,000
	$3,150,000		

The following information is presented.

1. The current assets section includes: cash $150,000, accounts receivable $170,000 less $10,000 for allowance for doubtful accounts, inventories $180,000, and unearned revenue $5,000. Inventories are stated on the lower-of-FIFO-cost-or-market.
2. The investments section includes: the cash surrender value of a life insurance contract $40,000; investments in common stock, short-term (trading) $80,000 and long-term (available-for-sale) $270,000; and bond sinking fund $250,000. The cost and fair value of investments in common stock are the same.
3. Property, plant, and equipment includes: buildings $1,040,000 less accumulated depreciation $360,000; equipment $450,000 less accumulated depreciation $180,000; land $500,000; and land held for future use $270,000.
4. Intangible assets include: a franchise $165,000; goodwill $100,000; and discount on bonds payable $40,000.
5. Current liabilities include: accounts payable $140,000; notes payable—short-term $80,000 and long-term $120,000; and taxes payable $40,000.
6. Long-term liabilities are composed solely of 7% bonds payable due 2020.
7. Stockholders' equity has: preferred stock, no par value, authorized 200,000 shares, issued 70,000 shares for $450,000; and common stock, $1.00 par value, authorized 400,000 shares, issued 100,000 shares at an average price of $10. In addition, the corporation has retained earnings of $320,000.

Instructions

Prepare a balance sheet in good form, adjusting the amounts in each balance sheet classification as affected by the information given above.

3 6 7 **P5-6 (Preparation of a Statement of Cash Flows and a Balance Sheet)** Lansbury Inc. had the balance sheet shown on the next page at December 31, 2011.

LANSBURY INC.
BALANCE SHEET
DECEMBER 31, 2011

Cash	$ 20,000	Accounts payable	$ 30,000
Accounts receivable	21,200	Notes payable (long-term)	41,000
Investments	32,000	Common stock	100,000
Plant assets (net)	81,000	Retained earnings	23,200
Land	40,000		$194,200
	$194,200		

During 2012, the following occurred.

1. Lansbury Inc. sold part of its investment portfolio for $15,000. This transaction resulted in a gain of $3,400 for the firm. The company classifies its investments as available-for-sale.
2. A tract of land was purchased for $18,000 cash.
3. Long-term notes payable in the amount of $16,000 were retired before maturity by paying $16,000 cash.
4. An additional $20,000 in common stock was issued at par.
5. Dividends of $8,200 were declared and paid to stockholders.
6. Net income for 2012 was $32,000 after allowing for depreciation of $11,000.
7. Land was purchased through the issuance of $30,000 in bonds.
8. At December 31, 2012, Cash was $32,000, Accounts Receivable was $41,600, and Accounts Payable remained at $30,000.

Instructions

(a) Prepare a statement of cash flows for 2012.
(b) Prepare an unclassified balance sheet as it would appear at December 31, 2012.
(c) How might the statement of cash flows help the user of the financial statements? Compute two cash flow ratios.

P5-7 (Preparation of a Statement of Cash Flows and Balance Sheet) Aero Inc. had the following balance sheet at December 31, 2011.

AERO INC.
BALANCE SHEET
DECEMBER 31, 2011

Cash	$ 20,000	Accounts payable	$ 30,000
Accounts receivable	21,200	Bonds payable	41,000
Investments	32,000	Common stock	100,000
Plant assets (net)	81,000	Retained earnings	23,200
Land	40,000		$194,200
	$194,200		

During 2012, the following occurred.

1. Aero liquidated its available-for-sale investment portfolio at a loss of $5,000.
2. A tract of land was purchased for $38,000.
3. An additional $30,000 in common stock was issued at par.
4. Dividends totaling $10,000 were declared and paid to stockholders.
5. Net income for 2012 was $35,000, including $12,000 in depreciation expense.
6. Land was purchased through the issuance of $30,000 in additional bonds.
7. At December 31, 2012, Cash was $70,200, Accounts Receivable was $42,000, and Accounts Payable was $40,000.

Instructions

(a) Prepare a statement of cash flows for the year 2012 for Aero.
(b) Prepare the balance sheet as it would appear at December 31, 2012.
(c) Compute Aero's free cash flow and the current cash debt coverage ratio for 2012.
(d) Use the analysis of Aero to illustrate how information in the balance sheet and statement of cash flows helps the user of the financial statements.

CONCEPTS FOR ANALYSIS

CA5-1 (Reporting the Financial Effects of Varied Transactions) In an examination of Arenes Corporation as of December 31, 2012, you have learned that the following situations exist. No entries have been made in the accounting records for these items.

1. The corporation erected its present factory building in 1997. Depreciation was calculated by the straight-line method, using an estimated life of 35 years. Early in 2012, the board of directors conducted a careful survey and estimated that the factory building had a remaining useful life of 25 years as of January 1, 2012.
2. An additional assessment of 2011 income taxes was levied and paid in 2012.
3. When calculating the accrual for officers' salaries at December 31, 2012, it was discovered that the accrual for officers' salaries for December 31, 2011, had been overstated.
4. On December 15, 2012, Arenes Corporation declared a cash dividend on its common stock outstanding, payable February 1, 2013, to the common stockholders of record December 31, 2012.

Instructions

Describe fully how each of the items above should be reported in the financial statements of Arenes Corporation for the year 2012.

CA5-2 (Current Asset and Liability Classification) Below are the titles of a number of debit and credit accounts as they might appear on the balance sheet of Hayduke Corporation as of October 31, 2012.

Debits	Credits
Interest Receivable on U.S. Government Securities	Preferred Stock
Notes Receivable	11% First Mortgage Bonds, due in 2017
Petty Cash Fund	Preferred Cash Dividend, payable Nov. 1, 2012
Debt Investments (trading)	Allowance for Doubtful Accounts Receivable
Treasury Stock	Federal Income Taxes Payable
Unamortized Bond Discount	Customers' Advances (on contracts to be completed next year)
Cash in Bank	Premium on Bonds Redeemable in 2012
Land	Officers' 2012 Bonus Accrued
Inventory of Operating Parts and Supplies	Accrued Payroll
Inventory of Raw Materials	Notes Payable
Patents	Interest Expense
Cash and U.S. Government Bonds Set Aside for Property Additions	Accumulated Depreciation
Investment in Subsidiary	Accounts Payable
Accounts Receivable:	Paid-in Capital in Excess of Par
U.S. Government Contracts	Accrued Interest on Notes Payable
Regular	8% First Mortgage Bonds, to be redeemed in 2012 out of current assets
Installments—Due Next Year	
Installments—Due After Next year	
Goodwill	
Inventory of Finished Goods	
Inventory of Work in Process	
Deficit	

Instructions

Select the current asset and current liability items from among these debits and credits. If there appear to be certain borderline cases that you are unable to classify without further information, mention them and explain your difficulty, or give your reasons for making questionable classifications, if any.

(AICPA adapted)

CA5-3 (Identifying Balance Sheet Deficiencies) The assets of Fonzarelli Corporation are presented on the next page (000s omitted).

FONZARELLI CORPORATION
BALANCE SHEET (PARTIAL)
DECEMBER 31, 2012

Assets		
Current assets		
Cash		$ 100,000
Unclaimed payroll checks		27,500
Debt investments (trading) (fair value $30,000) at cost		37,000
Accounts receivable (less bad debt reserve)		75,000
Inventory—at lower-of-cost- (determined by the next-in, first-out method) or-market		240,000
Total current assets		479,500
Tangible assets		
Land (less accumulated depreciation)		80,000
Buildings and equipment	$800,000	
Less: Accumulated depreciation	250,000	550,000
Net tangible assets		630,000
Long-term investments		
Stocks and bonds		100,000
Treasury stock		70,000
Total long-term investments		170,000
Other assets		
Discount on bonds payable		19,400
Sinking fund		975,000
Total other assets		994,400
Total assets		$2,273,900

Instructions

Indicate the deficiencies, if any, in the foregoing presentation of Fonzarelli Corporation's assets.

CA5-4 (Critique of Balance Sheet Format and Content) Presented below and on the next page is the balance sheet of Rasheed Brothers Corporation (000s omitted).

RASHEED BROTHERS CORPORATION
BALANCE SHEET
DECEMBER 31, 2012

Assets		
Current assets		
Cash	$26,000	
Marketable securities	18,000	
Accounts receivable	25,000	
Inventory	20,000	
Supplies	4,000	
Stock investment in subsidiary company	20,000	$113,000
Investments		
Treasury stock		25,000
Property, plant, and equipment		
Buildings and land	91,000	
Less: Reserve for depreciation	31,000	60,000
Other assets		
Cash surrender value of life insurance		19,000
Total assets		$217,000
Liabilities and Stockholders' Equity		
Current liabilities		
Accounts payable	$22,000	
Reserve for income taxes	15,000	
Customers' accounts with credit balances	1	$ 37,001
Deferred credits		
Unamortized premium on bonds payable		2,000
Long-term liabilities		
Bonds payable		60,000
Total liabilities		99,001

Common stock		
Common stock, par $5	85,000	
Earned surplus	24,999	
Cash dividends declared	8,000	117,999
Total liabilities and stockholders' equity		$217,000

Instructions

Evaluate the balance sheet presented. State briefly the proper treatment of any item criticized.

CA5-5 (Presentation of Property, Plant, and Equipment) Carol Keene, corporate comptroller for Dumaine Industries, is trying to decide how to present "Property, plant, and equipment" in the balance sheet. She realizes that the statement of cash flows will show that the company made a significant investment in purchasing new equipment this year, but overall she knows the company's plant assets are rather old. She feels that she can disclose one figure titled "Property, plant, and equipment, net of depreciation," and the result will be a low figure. However, it will not disclose the age of the assets. If she chooses to show the cost less accumulated depreciation, the age of the assets will be apparent. She proposes the following.

Property, plant, and equipment, net of depreciation	$10,000,000
rather than	
Property, plant, and equipment	$50,000,000
Less: Accumulated depreciation	(40,000,000)
Net book value	$10,000,000

Instructions

Answer the following questions.

(a) What are the ethical issues involved?

(b) What should Keene do?

CA5-6 (Cash Flow Analysis) The partner in charge of the Kappeler Corporation audit comes by your desk and leaves a letter he has started to the CEO and a copy of the cash flow statement for the year ended December 31, 2012. Because he must leave on an emergency, he asks you to finish the letter by explaining: (1) the disparity between net income and cash flow; (2) the importance of operating cash flow; (3) the renewable source(s) of cash flow; and (4) possible suggestions to improve the cash position.

KAPPELER CORPORATION
STATEMENT OF CASH FLOWS
FOR THE YEAR ENDED DECEMBER 31, 2012

Cash flows from operating activities		
Net income		$100,000
Adjustments to reconcile net income to net cash provided by operating activities:		
Depreciation expense	$ 10,000	
Amortization expense	1,000	
Loss on sale of fixed assets	5,000	
Increase in accounts receivable (net)	(40,000)	
Increase in inventory	(35,000)	
Decrease in accounts payable	(41,000)	(100,000)
Net cash provided by operating activities		–0–
Cash flows from investing activities		
Sale of plant assets	25,000	
Purchase of equipment	(100,000)	
Purchase of land	(200,000)	
Net cash used by investing activities		(275,000)
Cash flows from financing activities		
Payment of dividends	(10,000)	
Redemption of bonds	(100,000)	
Net cash used by financing activities		(110,000)
Net decrease in cash		(385,000)
Cash balance, January 1, 2012		400,000
Cash balance, December 31, 2012		$ 15,000

Date

President Kappeler, CEO
Kappeler Corporation
125 Wall Street
Middleton, Kansas 67458

Dear Mr. Kappeler:

I have good news and bad news about the financial statements for the year ended December 31, 2012. The good news is that net income of $100,000 is close to what we predicted in the strategic plan last year, indicating strong performance this year. The bad news is that the cash balance is seriously low. Enclosed is the Statement of Cash Flows, which best illustrates how both of these situations occurred simultaneously . . .

Instructions

Complete the letter to the CEO, including the four components requested by your boss.

USING YOUR JUDGMENT

FINANCIAL REPORTING

Financial Reporting Problem

The Procter & Gamble Company (P&G)

The financial statements of P&G are presented in Appendix 5B or can be accessed at the book's companion website, **www.wiley.com/college/kieso**.

Instructions

Refer to P&G's financial statements and the accompanying notes to answer the following questions.

(a) What alternative formats could P&G have adopted for its balance sheet? Which format did it adopt?

(b) Identify the various techniques of disclosure P&G might have used to disclose additional pertinent financial information. Which technique does it use in its financials?

(c) In what classifications are P&G's investments reported? What valuation basis does P&G use to report its investments? How much working capital did P&G have on June 30, 2009? On June 30, 2008?

(d) What were P&G's cash flows from its operating, investing, and financing activities for 2009? What were its trends in net cash provided by operating activities over the period 2007 to 2009? Explain why the change in accounts payable and in accrued and other liabilities is added to net income to arrive at net cash provided by operating activities.

(e) Compute P&G's (1) current cash debt coverage ratio, (2) cash debt coverage ratio, and (3) free cash flow for 2009. What do these ratios indicate about P&G's financial condition?

Comparative Analysis Case

The Coca-Cola Company and PepsiCo, Inc.

Instructions

Go to the book's companion website and use information found there to answer the following questions related to **The Coca-Cola Company** and **PepsiCo, Inc.**

(a) What format(s) did these companies use to present their balance sheets?

(b) How much working capital did each of these companies have at the end of 2009? Speculate as to their rationale for the amount of working capital they maintain.

(c) What is the most significant difference in the asset structure of the two companies? What causes this difference?

(d) What are the companies' annual and 5-year (2005–2009) growth rates in total assets and long-term debt?

(e) What were these two companies' trends in net cash provided by operating activities over the period 2007 to 2009?

(f) Compute both companies' (1) current cash debt coverage ratio, (2) cash debt coverage ratio, and (3) free cash flow. What do these ratios indicate about the financial condition of the two companies?

Financial Statement Analysis Cases

Case 1 Uniroyal Technology Corporation

Uniroyal Technology Corporation (UTC), with corporate offices in Sarasota, Florida, is organized into three operating segments. The high-performance plastics segment is responsible for research, development, and manufacture of a wide variety of products, including orthopedic braces, graffiti-resistant seats for buses and airplanes, and a static-resistant plastic used in the central processing units of microcomputers. The coated fabrics segment manufactures products such as automobile seating, door and instrument panels, and specialty items such as waterproof seats for personal watercraft and stain-resistant, easy-cleaning upholstery fabrics. The foams and adhesives segment develops and manufactures products used in commercial roofing applications.

The following items relate to operations in a recent year.

1. Serious pressure was placed on profitability by sharply increasing raw material prices. Some raw materials increased in price 50% during the past year. Cost containment programs were instituted and product prices were increased whenever possible, which resulted in profit margins actually improving over the course of the year.
2. The company entered into a revolving credit agreement, under which UTC may borrow the lesser of $15,000,000 or 80% of eligible accounts receivable. At the end of the year, approximately $4,000,000 was outstanding under this agreement. The company plans to use this line of credit in the upcoming year to finance operations and expansion.

Instructions

(a) Should investors be informed of raw materials price increases, such as described in item 1? Does the fact that the company successfully met the challenge of higher prices affect the answer? Explain.

(b) How should the information in item 2 be presented in the financial statements of UTC?

Case 2 Sherwin-Williams Company

Sherwin-Williams, based in Cleveland, Ohio, manufactures a wide variety of paint and other coatings, which are marketed through its specialty stores and in other retail outlets. The company also manufactures paint for automobiles. The Automotive Division has had financial difficulty. During a recent year, five branch locations of the Automotive Division were closed, and new management was put in place for the branches remaining.

The following titles were shown on Sherwin-Williams's balance sheet for that year.

Accounts payable
Accounts receivable, less allowance
Accrued taxes
Buildings
Cash and cash equivalents
Common stock
Employee compensation payable
Finished goods inventories
Intangibles and other assets
Land
Long-term debt
Machinery and equipment
Other accruals
Other capital
Other current assets
Other long-term liabilities
Postretirement obligations other than pensions
Retained earnings
Short-term investments
Taxes payable
Work in process and raw materials inventories

Instructions

(a) Organize the accounts in the general order in which they would have been presented in a classified balance sheet.

(b) When several of the branch locations of the Automotive Division were closed, what balance sheet accounts were most likely affected? Did the balance in those accounts decrease or increase?

Case 3 Deere & Company

Presented below is the SEC-mandated disclosure of contractual obligations provided by **Deere & Company** in a recent annual report. Deere & Company reported current assets of $27,208 and total current liabilities of $15,922 at year-end. All dollars are in millions.

Aggregate Contractual Obligations

The payment schedule for the company's contractual obligations at year-end in millions of dollars is as follows:

	Total	Less than 1 year	2&3 years	4&5 years	More than 5 years
Debt					
Equipment operations	$ 2,061	$ 130	$ 321		$1,610
Financial Services	19,598	8,515	7,025	$3,003	1,055
Total	21,659	8,645	7,346	3,003	2,665
Interest on debt	3,857	941	1,102	557	1,257
Purchase obligations	3,212	3,172	26	9	5
Operating leases	358	100	120	58	80
Capital leases	29	3	6	4	16
Total	$29,115	$12,861	$8,600	$3,631	$4,023

Instructions

(a) Compute Deere & Company's working capital and current ratio (current assets ÷ current liabilities) with and without the contractual obligations reported in the schedule.

(b) Briefly discuss how the information provided in the contractual obligation disclosure would be useful in evaluating Deere & Company for loans: (1) due in one year, (2) due in five years.

Case 4 Amazon.com

The incredible growth of **Amazon.com** has put fear into the hearts of traditional retailers. Amazon's stock price has soared to amazing levels. However, it is often pointed out in the financial press that it took the company several years to report its first profit. The following financial information is taken from Amazon's recent annual report.

($ in millions)	Current Year	Prior Year
Current assets	$ 3,373	$2,929
Total assets	4,363	3,696
Current liabilities	2,532	1,899
Total liabilities	3,932	3,450
Cash provided by operations	702	733
Capital expenditures	216	204
Dividends paid	0	0
Net income(loss)	190	359
Sales	10,711	8,490

Instructions

(a) Calculate free cash flow for Amazon for the current and prior years, and discuss its ability to finance expansion from internally generated cash. Thus far Amazon has avoided purchasing large warehouses. Instead, it has used those of others. It is possible, however, that in order to increase customer satisfaction the company may have to build its own warehouses. If this happens, how might your impression of its ability to finance expansion change?

(b) Discuss any potential implications of the change in Amazon's cash provided by operations from the prior year to the current year.

Accounting, Analysis, and Principles

Early in January 2013, Hopkins Company is preparing for a meeting with its bankers to discuss a loan request. Its bookkeeper provided the following accounts and balances at December 31, 2012.

	Debit	Credit
Cash	$ 75,000	
Accounts Receivable (net)	38,500	
Inventory	65,300	
Equipment (net)	84,000	
Patents	15,000	
Notes and Accounts Payable		$ 52,000
Notes Payable (due 2014)		75,000
Common Stock		100,000
Retained Earnings		50,800
	$277,800	$277,800

Except for the following items, Hopkins has recorded all adjustments in its accounts.

1. Cash includes $500 petty cash and $15,000 in a bond sinking fund.
2. Net accounts receivable is comprised of $52,000 in accounts receivable and $13,500 in allowance for doubtful accounts.
3. Equipment had a cost of $112,000 and accumulated depreciation of $28,000.
4. On January 8, 2013, one of Hopkins' customers declared bankruptcy. At December 31, 2012, this customer owed Hopkins $9,000.

Accounting

Prepare a corrected December 31, 2012, balance sheet for Hopkins Company.

Analysis

Hopkins' bank is considering granting an additional loan in the amount of $45,000, which will be due December 31, 2013. How can the information in the balance sheet provide useful information to the bank about Hopkins' ability to repay the loan?

Principles

In the upcoming meeting with the bank, Hopkins plans to provide additional information about the fair value of its equipment and some internally generated intangible assets related to its customer lists. This information indicates that Hopkins has significant unrealized gains on these assets, which are not reflected on the balance sheet. What objections is the bank likely to raise about the usefulness of this information in evaluating Hopkins for the loan renewal?

BRIDGE TO THE PROFESSION

Professional Research: FASB Codification

In light of the full disclosure principle, investors and creditors need to know the balances for assets, liabilities, and equity as well as the accounting policies adopted by management to measure the items reported in the balance sheet.

Instructions

If your school has a subscription to the FASB Codification, go to *http://aaahq.org/asclogin.cfm* to log in and prepare responses to the following. Provide Codification references for your responses.

(a) Identify the literature that addresses the disclosure of accounting policies.

(b) How are accounting policies defined in the literature?

(c) What are the three scenarios that would result in detailed disclosure of the accounting methods used?

(d) What are some examples of common disclosures that are required under this statement?

Professional Simulation

The professional simulation for this chapter asks you to address questions related to the balance sheet.

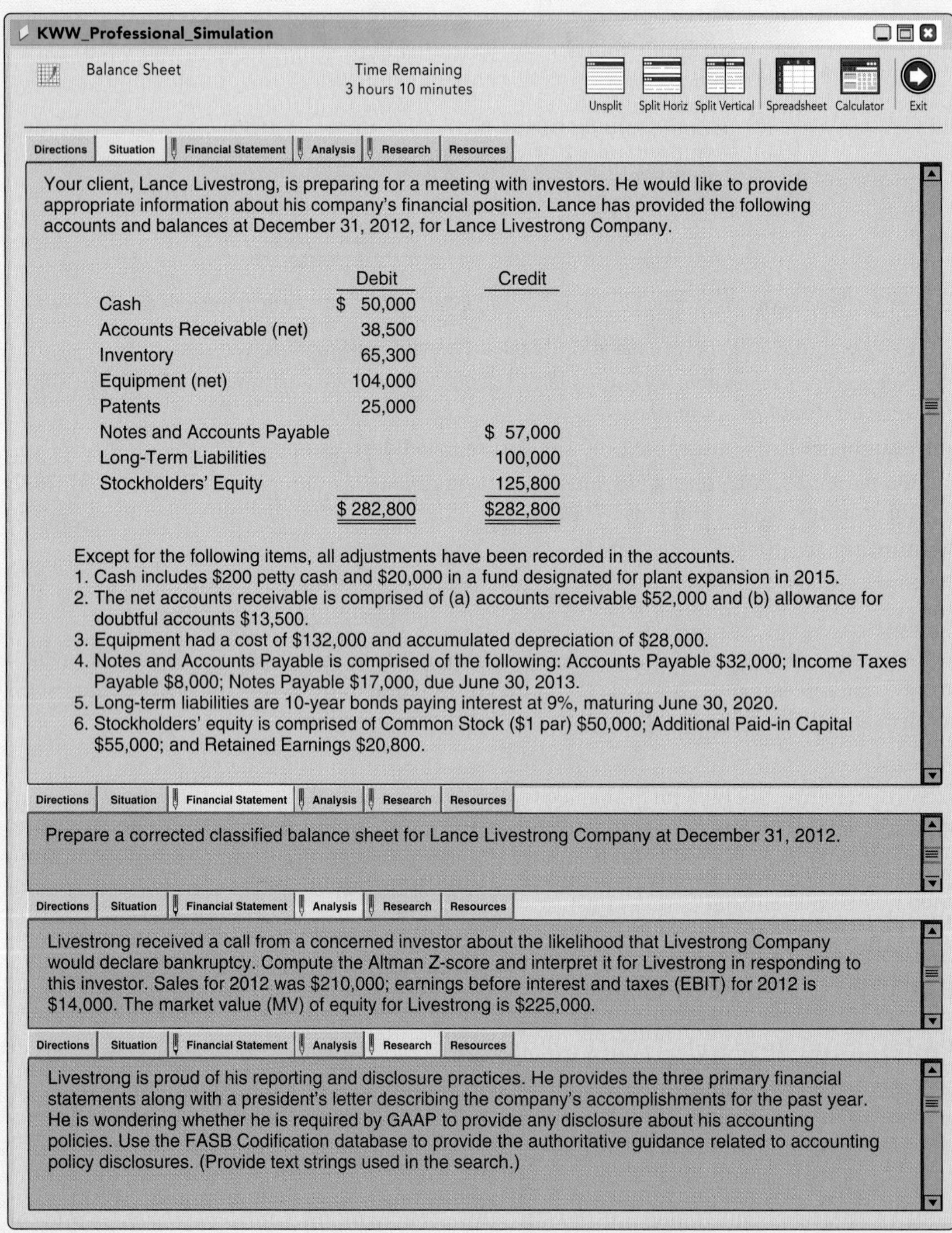

KWW_Professional_Simulation

Balance Sheet

Time Remaining
3 hours 10 minutes

Unsplit | Split Horiz | Split Vertical | Spreadsheet | Calculator | Exit

Directions | Situation | Financial Statement | Analysis | Research | Resources

Your client, Lance Livestrong, is preparing for a meeting with investors. He would like to provide appropriate information about his company's financial position. Lance has provided the following accounts and balances at December 31, 2012, for Lance Livestrong Company.

	Debit	Credit
Cash	$ 50,000	
Accounts Receivable (net)	38,500	
Inventory	65,300	
Equipment (net)	104,000	
Patents	25,000	
Notes and Accounts Payable		$ 57,000
Long-Term Liabilities		100,000
Stockholders' Equity		125,800
	$ 282,800	$282,800

Except for the following items, all adjustments have been recorded in the accounts.

1. Cash includes $200 petty cash and $20,000 in a fund designated for plant expansion in 2015.
2. The net accounts receivable is comprised of (a) accounts receivable $52,000 and (b) allowance for doubtful accounts $13,500.
3. Equipment had a cost of $132,000 and accumulated depreciation of $28,000.
4. Notes and Accounts Payable is comprised of the following: Accounts Payable $32,000; Income Taxes Payable $8,000; Notes Payable $17,000, due June 30, 2013.
5. Long-term liabilities are 10-year bonds paying interest at 9%, maturing June 30, 2020.
6. Stockholders' equity is comprised of Common Stock ($1 par) $50,000; Additional Paid-in Capital $55,000; and Retained Earnings $20,800.

Directions | Situation | Financial Statement | Analysis | Research | Resources

Prepare a corrected classified balance sheet for Lance Livestrong Company at December 31, 2012.

Directions | Situation | Financial Statement | Analysis | Research | Resources

Livestrong received a call from a concerned investor about the likelihood that Livestrong Company would declare bankruptcy. Compute the Altman Z-score and interpret it for Livestrong in responding to this investor. Sales for 2012 was $210,000; earnings before interest and taxes (EBIT) for 2012 is $14,000. The market value (MV) of equity for Livestrong is $225,000.

Directions | Situation | Financial Statement | Analysis | Research | Resources

Livestrong is proud of his reporting and disclosure practices. He provides the three primary financial statements along with a president's letter describing the company's accomplishments for the past year. He is wondering whether he is required by GAAP to provide any disclosure about his accounting policies. Use the FASB Codification database to provide the authoritative guidance related to accounting policy disclosures. (Provide text strings used in the search.)

As in GAAP, the balance sheet and the statement of cash flows are required statements for IFRS. In addition, the content and presentation of an IFRS statement of financial position (balance sheet) and cash flow statement are similar to those used for GAAP. In general, the disclosure requirements related to the balance sheet and the statement of cash flows are much more extensive and detailed in the United States. *IAS 1*, "Presentation of Financial Statements," provides the overall IFRS requirements for balance sheet information. *IAS 7*, "Cash Flow Statements," provides the overall IFRS requirements for cash flow information. IFRS insights on the statement of cash flows are presented in Chapter 23.

RELEVANT FACTS

- IFRS recommends but does not require the use of the title "statement of financial position" rather than balance sheet.
- IFRS requires a classified statement of financial position except in very limited situations. IFRS follows the same guidelines as this textbook for distinguishing between current and noncurrent assets and liabilities. However under GAAP, public companies must follow SEC regulations, which require specific line items. In addition, specific GAAP standards mandate certain forms of reporting this information.
- Under IFRS, current assets are usually listed in the reverse order of liquidity. For example, under GAAP cash is listed first, but under IFRS it is listed last.
- IFRS has many differences in terminology that you will notice in this textbook. For example, in the sample statement of financial position illustrated on page 302, notice in the equity section common stock is called share capital—ordinary.
- Both IFRS and GAAP require disclosures about (1) accounting policies followed, (2) judgments that management has made in the process of applying the entity's accounting policies, and (3) the key assumptions and estimation uncertainty that could result in a material adjustment to the carrying amounts of assets and liabilities within the next financial year. Comparative prior period information must be presented and financial statements must be prepared annually.
- Use of the term "reserve" is discouraged in GAAP, but there is no such prohibition in IFRS.

ABOUT THE NUMBERS

Classification in the Statement of Financial Position

Statement of financial position accounts are **classified**. That is, a statement of financial position groups together similar items to arrive at significant subtotals. Furthermore, the material is arranged so that important relationships are shown. The IASB indicates that the parts and subsections of financial statements are more informative than the whole. Therefore, the IASB discourages the reporting of summary accounts alone (total assets, net assets, total liabilities, etc.).

Instead, companies should report and classify individual items in sufficient detail to permit users to assess the amounts, timing, and uncertainty of future cash flows. Such classification also makes it easier for users to evaluate the company's liquidity and financial flexibility, profitability, and risk. Companies then further divide these items into several sub-classifications. A representative statement of financial position presentation is shown on the next page.

SCIENTIFIC PRODUCTS, INC. STATEMENT OF FINANCIAL POSITION DECEMBER 31, 2012			
Assets			
Non-current assets			
Long-term investments			
Investments in held-for-collection securities		$ 82,000	
Land held for future development		5,500	$ 87,500
Property, plant, and equipment			
Land		125,000	
Buildings	$975,800		
Less: Accumulated depreciation	341,200	634,600	
Total property, plant, and equipment			759,600
Intangible assets			
Capitalized development costs		6,000	
Goodwill		66,000	
Other identifiable intangible assets		28,000	100,000
Total non-current assets			**947,100**
Current assets			
Inventories		489,713	
Prepaid expenses		16,252	
Accounts receivable	165,824		
Less: Allowance for doubtful accounts	1,850	163,974	
Short-term investments		51,030	
Cash and cash equivalents		52,485	
Total current assets			**773,454**
Total assets			**$1,720,554**
Equity and Liabilities			
Equity			
Share capital—preference	$300,000		
Share capital—ordinary	400,000		
Share premium—preference	10,000		
Share premium—ordinary	27,500		
Retained earnings	170,482		
Accumulated other comprehensive income	(8,650)		
Less: Treasury shares	12,750		
Equity attributable to owners	$886,582		
Minority interest	13,500		
Total equity			**$ 900,082**
Non-current liabilities			
Bond liabilities due January 31, 2020	425,000		
Provisions related to pensions	75,000		
Total non-current liabilities		**500,000**	
Current liabilities			
Notes payable	80,000		
Accounts payable	197,532		
Interest payable	20,500		
Salary and wages payable	5,560		
Provisions related to warranties	12,500		
Deposits received from customers	4,380		
Total current liabilities		**320,472**	
Total liabilities			**820,472**
Total equity and liabilities			**$1,720,554**

The statement presented is in "report form" format. Some companies use other statement of financial position formats. For example, companies sometimes deduct current liabilities from current assets to arrive at working capital. Or, they deduct all liabilities from all assets. Some companies report the subtotal *net assets*, which equals total assets minus total liabilities.

Equity

The **equity** (also referred to as **shareholders' equity**) section is one of the most difficult sections to prepare and understand. This is due to the complexity of ordinary and preference share agreements and the various restrictions on equity imposed by corporation laws, liability agreements, and boards of directors. Companies usually divide the section into six parts:

EQUITY SECTION

1. SHARE CAPITAL. The par or stated value of shares issued. It includes ordinary shares (sometimes referred to as *common shares*) and preference shares (sometimes referred to as *preferred shares*).
2. SHARE PREMIUM. The excess of amounts paid-in over the par or stated value.
3. RETAINED EARNINGS. The corporation's undistributed earnings.
4. ACCUMULATED OTHER COMPREHENSIVE INCOME. The aggregate amount of the other comprehensive income items.
5. TREASURY SHARES. Generally, the amount of ordinary shares repurchased.
6. NON-CONTROLLING INTEREST (MINORITY INTEREST). A portion of the equity of subsidiaries not owned by the reporting company.

For ordinary shares, companies must disclose the par value and the authorized, issued, and outstanding share amounts. The same holds true for preference shares. A company usually presents the share premium (for both ordinary and preference shares) in one amount, although subtotals are informative if the sources of additional capital are varied and material. The retained earnings amount may be divided between the **unappropriated** (the amount that is usually available for dividend distribution) and **restricted** (e.g., by bond indentures or other loan agreements) amounts. In addition, companies show any shares reacquired (treasury shares) as a reduction of equity.

Accumulated other comprehensive income (sometimes referred to as *reserves* or *other reserves*) includes such items as unrealized gains and losses on non-trading equity investments and unrealized gains and losses on certain derivative transactions. Non-controlling interest, sometimes referred to as minority interest, is also shown as a separate item (where applicable) as a part of equity.

Delhaize Group presented its equity section as follows.

Delhaize Group
(000,000)

Share capital	€ 50
Share premium	2,725
Treasury shares	(56)
Retained earnings	2,678
Other reserves	(1,254)
Shareholders' equity	4,143
Minority interests	52
Total equity	€4,195

Many companies reporting under IFRS often use the term "reserve" as an all-inclusive catch-all for items such as retained earnings, share premium, and accumulated other comprehensive income.

Revaluation Equity

GAAP and IFRS differ in the IFRS provision for balance sheet revaluations of property, plant, and equipment. Under the *revaluation model*, revaluations are recorded and reported as part of equity. To illustrate, Richardson Company uses IFRS and has property and equipment on an historical cost basis of $2,000,000. At the end of the year, Richardson appraises its property and equipment and determines it had a revaluation increase of $243,000.

Richardson records this revaluation under IFRS with an increase to property and equipment as well as a valuation reserve in equity. A note to the financial statements explains the change in the revaluation equity account from one period to the next, as shown below for Richardson Company, assuming a beginning balance of $11,345,000.

Note 30. Reserves (in part)	
(,000)	2012
Properties Revaluation Reserve	
Balance at beginning of year	$11,345
Increase (decrease) on revaluation of plant and equipment	243
Impairment losses	—
Reversals of impairment losses	—
Balance at end of year	$11,588

Fair Presentation

Companies must present fairly the financial position, financial performance, and cash flows of the company. Fair presentation means the faithful representation of transactions and events using the definitions and recognition criteria in the IASB conceptual framework. It is presumed that the use of IFRS with appropriate disclosure results in financial statements that are fairly presented. In other words, inappropriate use of accounting policies cannot be overcome by explanatory notes to the financial statements. In some rare cases, as indicated in Chapter 2, companies can use a "true and fair" override. This situation develops, for example, when the IFRS for a given company appears to conflict with the objective of financial reporting. This situation might occur when a regulatory body indicates that a specific IFRS may be misleading. As indicated earlier, a true and fair override is highly unlikely in today's reporting environment.

One recent and highly publicized exception is the case of **Société Générale** (SocGen), a French bank. The bank used the true and fair rule to justify reporting losses that occurred in 2008 in the prior year. Although allowed under the true and fair rule, such reporting was questioned because it permitted the bank to "take a bath," that is, record as many losses as possible in 2007, which was already a bad year for the bank. As a result, SocGen's 2008 reports looked better. [See F. Norris, "SocGen Changes Its Numbers," *New York Times* (May 13, 2008).]

ON THE HORIZON

The FASB and the IASB are working on a project to converge their standards related to financial statement presentation. A key feature of the proposed framework is that each of the statements will be organized, in the same format, to separate an entity's financing activities from its operating and investing activities and, further, to separate financing activities into transactions with owners and creditors. Thus, the same classifications used in the statement of financial position would also be used in the statement of comprehensive income and the statement of cash flows. The project has three phases. You can follow the joint financial presentation project at the following link: *http://www.fasb.org/project/financial_statement_presentation.shtml.*

IFRS SELF-TEST QUESTIONS

1. Which of the following statements about IFRS and GAAP accounting and reporting requirements for the balance sheet is *not* correct?
   (a) Both IFRS and GAAP distinguish between current and noncurrent assets and liabilities.
   (b) The presentation formats required by IFRS and GAAP for the balance sheet are similar.
   (c) Both IFRS and GAAP require that comparative information be reported.
   (d) One difference between the reporting requirements under IFRS and those of the GAAP balance sheet is that an IFRS balance sheet may list long-term assets first.

2. Current assets under IFRS are listed generally:
   (a) by importance.
   (b) in the reverse order of their expected conversion to cash.
   (c) by longevity.
   (d) alphabetically.

3. Companies that use IFRS:
   (a) may report all their assets on the statement of financial position at fair value.
   (b) are not allowed to net assets (assets − liabilities) on their statement of financial positions.
   (c) may report noncurrent assets before current assets on the statement of financial position.
   (d) do not have any guidelines as to what should be reported on the statement of financial position.

4. Franco Company uses IFRS and owns property, plant, and equipment with a historical cost of $5,000,000. At December 31, 2011, the company reported a valuation reserve of $690,000. At December 31, 2012, the property, plant, and equipment was appraised at $5,325,000. The valuation reserve will show what balance at December 31, 2012?
   (a) $365,000.
   (b) $325,000.
   (c) $690,000.
   (d) $0.

5. A company has purchased a tract of land and expects to build a production plant on the land in approximately 5 years. During the 5 years before construction, the land will be idle. Under IFRS, the land should be reported as:
   (a) land expense.
   (b) property, plant, and equipment.
   (c) an intangible asset.
   (d) a long-term investment.

IFRS CONCEPTS AND APPLICATION

IFRS5-1 Where can authoritative IFRS guidance be found related to the statement of financial position (balance sheet) and the statement of cash flows?

IFRS5-2 Briefly describe some of the similarities and differences between GAAP and IFRS with respect to statement of financial position (balance sheet) reporting.

IFRS5-3 Briefly describe the convergence efforts related to financial statement presentation.

IFRS5-4 Rainmaker Company prepares its financial statements in accordance with IFRS. In 2012, Rainmaker recorded the following revaluation adjustments related to its buildings and land: The company's building increased in value by $200,000; its land declined by $35,000. How will these revaluation adjustments affect Rainmaker's balance sheet? Will the reporting differ under GAAP? Explain.

International Reporting Case

IFRS5-5 Presented below is the balance sheet for **Tomkins plc**, a British company.

Tomkins plc
Consolidated Balance Sheet
(amounts in £ millions)

Non-current assets	
Goodwill	436.0
Other intangible assets	78.0
Property, plant and equipment	1,122.8
Investments in associates	20.6
Trade and other receivables	81.1
Deferred tax assets	82.9
Post-employment benefit surpluses	1.3
	1,822.7
Current assets	
Inventories	590.8
Trade and other receivables	753.0
Income tax recoverable	49.0
Available-for-sale investments	1.2
Cash and cash equivalents	445.0
	1,839.0
Assets held for sale	11.9
Total assets	3,673.6
Current liabilities	
Bank overdrafts	4.8
Bank and other loans	11.2
Obligations under finance leases	1.0
Trade and other payables	677.6
Income tax liabilities	15.2
Provisions	100.3
	810.1
Non-current liabilities	
Bank and other loans	687.3
Obligations under finance leases	3.6
Trade and other payables	27.1
Post-employment benefit obligations	343.5
Deferred tax liabilities	25.3
Income tax liabilities	79.5
Provisions	19.2
	1,185.5
Total liabilities	1,995.6
Net assets	1,678.0
Capital and reserves	
Ordinary share capital	79.6
Share premium account	799.2
Own shares	(8.2)
Capital redemption reserve	921.8
Currency translation reserve	(93.0)
Available-for-sale reserve	(0.9)
Accumulated deficit	(161.9)
Shareholders' equity	1,536.6
Minority interests	141.4
Total equity	1,678.0

Instructions

(a) Identify at least three differences in balance sheet reporting between British and U.S. firms, as shown in Tomkins' balance sheet.

(b) Review Tomkins' balance sheet and identify how the format of this financial statement provides useful information, as illustrated in the chapter.

Professional Research

IFRS5-6 In light of the full disclosure principle, investors and creditors need to know the balances for assets, liabilities, and equity, as well as the accounting policies adopted by management to measure the items reported in the statement of financial position.

Instructions

Access the IFRS authoritative literature at the IASB website (*http://eifrs.iasb.org/*). When you have accessed the documents, you can use the search tool in your Internet browser to respond to the following questions. (Provide paragraph citations.)

(a) Identify the literature that addresses the disclosure of accounting policies.

(b) How are accounting policies defined in the literature?

(c) What are the guidelines concerning consistency in applying accounting policies?

(d) What are some examples of common disclosures that are required under this statement?

International Financial Reporting Problem:
Marks and Spencer plc

IFRS5-7 The financial statements of **Marks and Spencer plc (M&S)** are available at the book's companion website or can be accessed at *http://corporate.marksandspencer.com/documents/publications/2010/Annual_Report_2010.*

Instructions

Refer to M&S's financial statements and the accompanying notes to answer the following questions.

(a) What alternative formats could M&S have adopted for its statement of financial position? Which format did it adopt?

(b) Identify the various techniques of disclosure M&S might have used to disclose additional pertinent financial information. Which technique does it use in its financials?

(c) In what classifications are M&S's investments reported? What valuation basis does M&S use to report its investments? How much working capital did M&S have on 3 April 2010? On 28 March 2009?

(d) What were M&S's cash flows from its operating, investing, and financing activities for 2010? What were its trends in net cash provided by operating activities over the period 2009 to 2010? Explain why the change in accounts payable and in accrued and other liabilities is added to net income to arrive at net cash provided by operating activities.

(e) Compute M&S's: (1) current cash debt coverage ratio, (2) cash debt coverage ratio, and (3) free cash flow for 2010. What do these ratios indicate about M&S's financial conditions?

ANSWERS TO IFRS SELF-TEST QUESTIONS

1. b **2.** b **3.** c **4.** b **5.** d

Remember to check the book's companion website to find additional resources for this chapter.

CHAPTER

6 Accounting and the Time Value of Money

LEARNING OBJECTIVES

After studying this chapter, you should be able to:

1. Identify accounting topics where the time value of money is relevant.
2. Distinguish between simple and compound interest.
3. Use appropriate compound interest tables.
4. Identify variables fundamental to solving interest problems.
5. Solve future and present value of 1 problems.
6. Solve future value of ordinary and annuity due problems.
7. Solve present value of ordinary and annuity due problems.
8. Solve present value problems related to deferred annuities and bonds.
9. Apply expected cash flows to present value measurement.

The Magic of Interest

Sidney Homer, author of *A History of Interest Rates*, wrote, "$1,000 invested at a mere 8 percent for 400 years would grow to $23 quadrillion—$5 million for every human on earth. But the first 100 years are the hardest." This startling quote highlights the power of time and compounding interest on money. Equally significant, although Homer did not mention it, is the fact that a small difference in the interest rate makes a big difference in the amount of monies accumulated over time.

Taking an example more realistic than Homer's 400-year investment, assume that you had $20,000 in a tax-free retirement account. Half the money is in stocks returning 12 percent, and the other half is in bonds earning 8 percent. Assuming reinvested profits and quarterly compounding, your bonds would be worth $22,080 after 10 years, a doubling of their value. But your stocks, returning 4 percent more, would be worth $32,620, or triple your initial value. The following chart shows this impact.

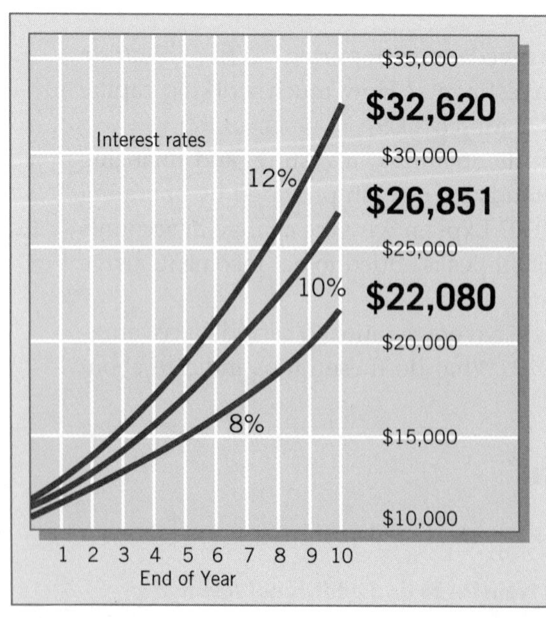

IFRS IN THIS CHAPTER

The time value of money concept is universal and applied the same, regardless of whether a company follows GAAP or IFRS.

Because of interest paid on investments, money received a week from today is not the same as money received today. Business people are acutely aware of this timing factor, and they invest and borrow only after carefully analyzing the relative amounts of cash flows over time.

With the profession's movement toward fair value accounting and reporting, an understanding of present value calculations is imperative. As an example, companies now have the option to report most financial instruments (both assets and liabilities) at fair value. In many cases, a present value computation is needed to arrive at the fair value amount, particularly as it relates to liabilities. In addition, the recent controversy involving the proper impairment charges for mortgage-backed receivables highlights the necessity to use present value methodologies when markets for financial instruments become unstable or nonexistent.

PREVIEW OF CHAPTER 6

As we indicated in the opening story, the timing of the returns on an investment has an important effect on the worth of the investment (asset). Similarly, the timing of debt repayment has an important effect on the value of the debt commitment (liability). As a financial expert, you will be expected to make present and future value measurements and to understand their implications. The purpose of this chapter is to present the tools and techniques that will help you measure the present value of future cash inflows and outflows. The content and organization of the chapter are as follows.

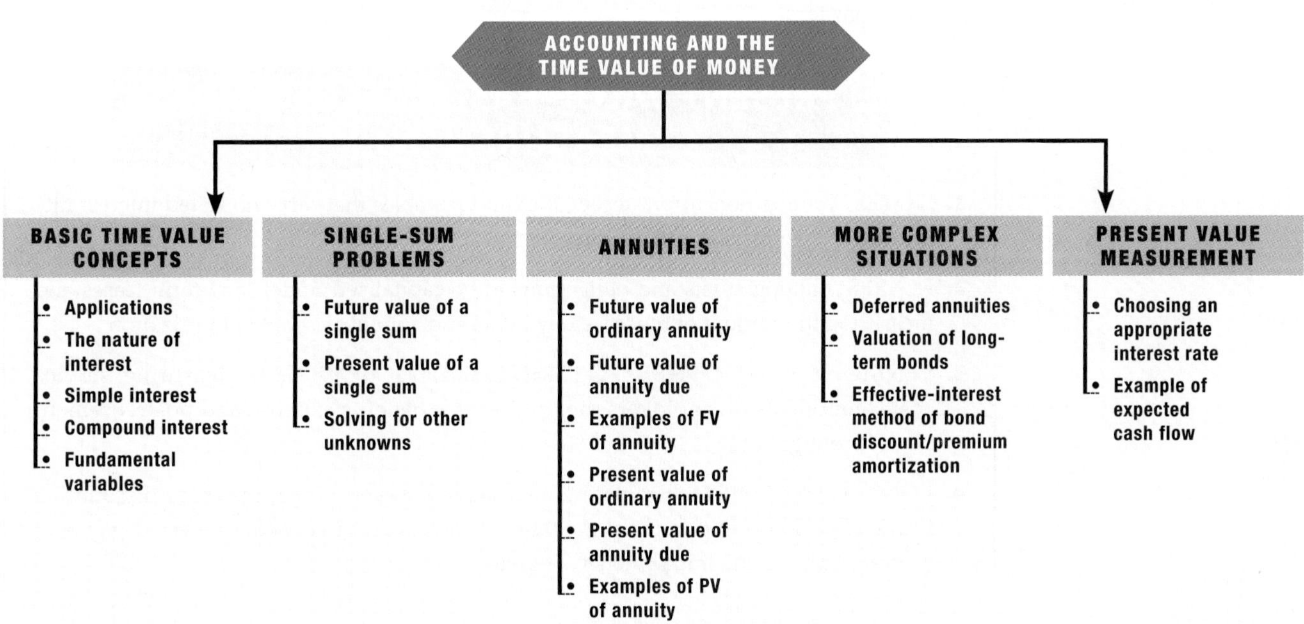

BASIC TIME VALUE CONCEPTS

LEARNING OBJECTIVE 1
Identify accounting topics where the time value of money is relevant.

In accounting (and finance), the phrase **time value of money** indicates a relationship between time and money—that a dollar received today is worth more than a dollar promised at some time in the future. Why? Because of the opportunity to invest today's dollar and receive interest on the investment. Yet, when deciding among investment or borrowing alternatives, it is essential to be able to compare today's dollar and tomorrow's dollar on the same footing—to "compare apples to apples." Investors do that by using the concept of **present value**, which has many applications in accounting.

Applications of Time Value Concepts

Financial reporting uses different measurements in different situations—historical cost for equipment, net realizable value for inventories, fair value for investments. As we discussed in Chapters 2 and 5, the FASB increasingly is requiring the use of fair values in the measurement of assets and liabilities. According to the FASB's recent guidance on fair value measurements, the most useful fair value measures are based on market prices in active markets. Within the fair value hierarchy these are referred to as Level 1. Recall that Level 1 fair value measures are the most reliable because they are based on quoted prices, such as a closing stock price in the *Wall Street Journal*.

However, for many assets and liabilities, market-based fair value information is not readily available. In these cases, fair value can be estimated based on the expected future cash flows related to the asset or liability. Such fair value estimates are generally considered Level 3 (least reliable) in the fair value hierarchy because they are based on unobservable inputs, such as a company's own data or assumptions related to the expected future cash flows associated with the asset or liability. As discussed in the fair value guidance, present value techniques are used to convert expected cash flows into present values, which represent an estimate of fair value. [1]

See the FASB Codification section (page 340).

Because of the increased use of present values in this and other contexts, it is important to understand present value techniques.[1] We list some of the applications of present value-based measurements to accounting topics below; we discuss many of these in the following chapters.

PRESENT VALUE-BASED ACCOUNTING MEASUREMENTS

1. NOTES. Valuing noncurrent receivables and payables that carry no stated interest rate or a lower than market interest rate.
2. LEASES. Valuing assets and obligations to be capitalized under long-term leases and measuring the amount of the lease payments and annual leasehold amortization.
3. PENSIONS AND OTHER POSTRETIREMENT BENEFITS. Measuring service cost components of employers' postretirement benefits expense and postretirement benefits obligation.
4. LONG-TERM ASSETS. Evaluating alternative long-term investments by discounting future cash flows. Determining the value of assets acquired under deferred payment contracts. Measuring impairments of assets.

[1]GAAP addresses present value as a measurement basis for a broad array of transactions, such as accounts and loans receivable [2], leases [3], postretirement benefits [4], asset impairments [5], and stock-based compensation [6].

5. STOCK-BASED COMPENSATION. Determining the fair value of employee services in compensatory stock-option plans.

6. BUSINESS COMBINATIONS. Determining the value of receivables, payables, liabilities, accruals, and commitments acquired or assumed in a "purchase."

7. DISCLOSURES. Measuring the value of future cash flows from oil and gas reserves for disclosure in supplementary information.

8. ENVIRONMENTAL LIABILITIES. Determining the fair value of future obligations for asset retirements.

In addition to accounting and business applications, compound interest, annuity, and present value concepts apply to personal finance and investment decisions. In purchasing a home or car, planning for retirement, and evaluating alternative investments, you will need to understand time value of money concepts.

The Nature of Interest

Interest is payment for the use of money. It is the excess cash received or repaid over and above the amount lent or borrowed (**principal**). For example, Corner Bank lends Hillfarm Company $10,000 with the understanding that it will repay $11,500. The excess over $10,000, or $1,500, represents interest expense for Hillfarm and interest revenue for Corner Bank.

The lender generally states the amount of interest as a rate over a specific period of time. For example, if Hillfarm borrowed $10,000 for one year before repaying $11,500, the rate of interest is 15 percent per year ($1,500 ÷ $10,000). The custom of expressing interest as a percentage rate is an established business practice.[2] In fact, business managers make investing and borrowing decisions on the basis of the rate of interest involved, rather than on the actual dollar amount of interest to be received or paid.

How is the interest rate determined? One important factor is the level of credit risk (risk of nonpayment) involved. Other factors being equal, the higher the credit risk, the higher the interest rate. Low-risk borrowers like **Microsoft** or **Intel** can probably obtain a loan at or slightly below the going market rate of interest. However, a bank would probably charge the neighborhood delicatessen several percentage points above the market rate, if granting the loan at all.

The amount of interest involved in any financing transaction is a function of three variables:

VARIABLES IN INTEREST COMPUTATION

1. PRINCIPAL. The amount borrowed or invested.

2. INTEREST RATE. A percentage of the outstanding principal.

3. TIME. The number of years or fractional portion of a year that the principal is outstanding.

Thus, the following three relationships apply:

- The larger the principal amount, the larger the dollar amount of interest.
- The higher the interest rate, the larger the dollar amount of interest.
- The longer the time period, the larger the dollar amount of interest.

[2]Federal law requires the disclosure of interest rates on an annual basis in all contracts. That is, instead of stating the rate as "1% per month," contracts must state the rate as "12% per year" if it is simple interest or "12.68% per year" if it is compounded monthly.

LEARNING OBJECTIVE 2
Distinguish between simple and compound interest.

Simple Interest

Companies compute **simple interest** on the amount of the principal only. It is the return on (or growth of) the principal for one time period. The following equation expresses simple interest.[3]

$$\text{Interest} = p \times i \times n$$

where

p = principal
i = rate of interest for a single period
n = number of periods

To illustrate, Barstow Electric Inc. borrows $10,000 for 3 years with a simple interest rate of 8% per year. It computes the total interest it will pay as follows.

$$\begin{aligned}\text{Interest} &= p \times i \times n \\ &= \$10{,}000 \times .08 \times 3 \\ &= \$2{,}400\end{aligned}$$

If Barstow borrows $10,000 for 3 months at 8%, the interest is $200, computed as follows.

$$\begin{aligned}\text{Interest} &= \$10{,}000 \times .08 \times 3/12 \\ &= \$200\end{aligned}$$

Compound Interest

John Maynard Keynes, the legendary English economist, supposedly called it magic. Mayer Rothschild, the founder of the famous European banking firm, proclaimed it the eighth wonder of the world. Today, people continue to extol its wonder and its power. The object of their affection? Compound interest.

We compute **compound interest** on principal **and** on any interest earned that has not been paid or withdrawn. It is the return on (or growth of) the principal for two or more time periods. Compounding computes interest not only on the principal but also on the interest earned to date on that principal, assuming the interest is left on deposit.

To illustrate the difference between simple and compound interest, assume that Vasquez Company deposits $10,000 in the Last National Bank, where it will earn simple interest of 9% per year. It deposits another $10,000 in the First State Bank, where it will earn compound interest of 9% per year compounded annually. In both cases, Vasquez will not withdraw any interest until 3 years from the date of deposit. Illustration 6-1 shows the computation of interest Vasquez will receive, as well as its accumulated year-end balance.

ILLUSTRATION 6-1
Simple vs. Compound Interest

Last National Bank

Simple Interest Calculation	Simple Interest	Accumulated Year-end Balance
Year 1 $10,000.00 × 9%	$ 900.00	$10,900.00
Year 2 $10,000.00 × 9%	900.00	$11,800.00
Year 3 $10,000.00 × 9%	900.00	$12,700.00
	$2,700.00	

First State Bank

Compound Interest Calculation	Compound Interest	Accumulated Year-end Balance
Year 1 $10,000.00 × 9%	$ 900.00	$10,900.00
Year 2 $10,900.00 × 9%	981.00	$11,881.00
Year 3 $11,881.00 × 9%	1,069.29	$12,950.29
	$2,950.29	

$250.29 Difference

[3]Business mathematics and business finance textbooks traditionally state simple interest as: I(interest) = P(principal) × R(rate) × T(time).

Note in Illustration 6-1 that simple interest uses the initial principal of $10,000 to compute the interest in all 3 years. **Compound interest uses the accumulated balance (principal plus interest to date) at each year-end to compute interest in the succeeding year.** This explains the larger balance in the compound interest account.

Obviously, any rational investor would choose compound interest, if available, over simple interest. In the example above, compounding provides $250.29 of additional interest revenue. For practical purposes, compounding assumes that unpaid interest earned becomes a part of the principal. Furthermore, the accumulated balance at the end of each year becomes the new principal sum on which interest is earned during the next year.

Compound interest is the typical interest computation applied in business situations. This occurs particularly in our economy, where companies use and finance large amounts of long-lived assets over long periods of time. Financial managers view and evaluate their investment opportunities in terms of a series of periodic returns, each of which they can reinvest to yield additional returns. Simple interest usually applies only to short-term investments and debts that involve a time span of one year or less.

A PRETTY GOOD START

What do the numbers mean?

The continuing debate on Social Security reform provides a great context to illustrate the power of compounding. One proposed idea is for the government to give $1,000 to every citizen at birth. This gift would be deposited in an account that would earn interest tax-free until the citizen retires. Assuming the account earns a modest 5% annual return until retirement at age 65, the $1,000 would grow to $23,839. With monthly compounding, the $1,000 deposited at birth would grow to $25,617.

Why start so early? If the government waited until age 18 to deposit the money, it would grow to only $9,906 with annual compounding. That is, reducing the time invested by a third results in more than a 50% reduction in retirement money. This example illustrates the importance of starting early when the power of compounding is involved.

Compound Interest Tables (see pages 354–363)

3 LEARNING OBJECTIVE
Use appropriate compound interest tables.

We present five different types of compound interest tables at the end of this chapter. These tables should help you study this chapter as well as solve other problems involving interest.

INTEREST TABLES AND THEIR CONTENTS

1. FUTURE VALUE OF 1 *TABLE.* Contains the amounts to which 1 will accumulate if deposited now at a specified rate and left for a specified number of periods. (Table 1)
2. PRESENT VALUE OF 1 *TABLE.* Contains the amounts that must be deposited now at a specified rate of interest to equal 1 at the end of a specified number of periods. (Table 2)
3. FUTURE VALUE OF AN ORDINARY ANNUITY OF 1 *TABLE.* Contains the amounts to which periodic rents of 1 will accumulate if the payments (rents) are invested at the **end** of each period at a specified rate of interest for a specified number of periods. (Table 3)
4. PRESENT VALUE OF AN ORDINARY ANNUITY OF 1 *TABLE.* Contains the amounts that must be deposited now at a specified rate of interest to permit withdrawals of 1 at the **end** of regular periodic intervals for the specified number of periods. (Table 4)
5. PRESENT VALUE OF AN ANNUITY DUE OF 1 *TABLE.* Contains the amounts that must be deposited now at a specified rate of interest to permit withdrawals of 1 at the **beginning** of regular periodic intervals for the specified number of periods. (Table 5)

Illustration 6-2 lists the general format and content of these tables. It shows how much principal plus interest a dollar accumulates to at the end of each of five periods, at three different rates of compound interest.

ILLUSTRATION 6-2
Excerpt from Table 6-1

FUTURE VALUE OF 1 AT COMPOUND INTEREST
(EXCERPT FROM TABLE 6-1, PAGE 355)

Period	9%	10%	11%
1	1.09000	1.10000	1.11000
2	1.18810	1.21000	1.23210
3	1.29503	1.33100	1.36763
4	1.41158	1.46410	1.51807
5	1.53862	1.61051	1.68506

The compound tables rely on basic formulas. For example, the formula to determine the future value factor (*FVF*) for 1 is:

$$FVF_{n,i} = (1 + i)^n$$

where

$FVF_{n,i}$ = future value factor for n periods at i interest
n = number of periods
i = rate of interest for a single period

Gateway to the Profession
Financial Calculator and Spreadsheet Tools

Financial calculators include preprogrammed $FVF_{n,i}$ and other time value of money formulas.

To illustrate the use of interest tables to calculate compound amounts, assume an interest rate of 9%. Illustration 6-3 shows the future value to which 1 accumulates (the future value factor).

ILLUSTRATION 6-3
Accumulation of Compound Amounts

Period	Beginning-of-Period Amount	×	Multiplier $(1 + i)$	=	End-of-Period Amount*	Formula $(1 + i)^n$
1	1.00000		1.09		1.09000	$(1.09)^1$
2	1.09000		1.09		1.18810	$(1.09)^2$
3	1.18810		1.09		1.29503	$(1.09)^3$

*Note that these amounts appear in Table 6-1 in the 9% column.

Throughout our discussion of compound interest tables, note the intentional use of the term **periods** instead of **years**. Interest is generally expressed in terms of an annual rate. However, many business circumstances dictate a compounding period of less than one year. In such circumstances, a company must convert the annual interest rate to correspond to the length of the period. To convert the "annual interest rate" into the "compounding period interest rate," a company **divides the annual rate by the number of compounding periods per year.**

In addition, companies determine the number of periods by **multiplying the number of years involved by the number of compounding periods per year.** To illustrate, assume an investment of $1 for 6 years at 8% annual interest compounded **quarterly**. Using Table 6-1, page 354, read the factor that appears in the 2% column on the 24th row—6 years × 4 compounding periods per year, namely 1.60844, or approximately $1.61. Thus, all compound interest tables use the term **periods**, not **years**, to express the quantity of n. Illustration 6-4 shows how to determine (1) the interest rate per compounding period and (2) the number of compounding periods in four situations of differing compounding frequency.[4]

12% Annual Interest Rate over 5 Years Compounded	Interest Rate per Compounding Period	Number of Compounding Periods
Annually (1)	.12 ÷ 1 = .12	5 years × 1 compounding per year = 5 periods
Semiannually (2)	.12 ÷ 2 = .06	5 years × 2 compoundings per year = 10 periods
Quarterly (4)	.12 ÷ 4 = .03	5 years × 4 compoundings per year = 20 periods
Monthly (12)	.12 ÷ 12 = .01	5 years × 12 compoundings per year = 60 periods

ILLUSTRATION 6-4
Frequency of Compounding

How often interest is compounded can substantially affect the rate of return. For example, a 9% annual interest compounded **daily** provides a 9.42% yield, or a difference of 0.42%. The 9.42% is the **effective yield**.[5] The annual interest rate (9%) is the **stated**, **nominal**, or **face rate**. When the compounding frequency is greater than once a year, the effective-interest rate will always exceed the stated rate.

Illustration 6-5 shows how compounding for five different time periods affects the effective yield and the amount earned by an investment of $10,000 for one year.

Interest Rate	Compounding Periods: Annually	Semiannually	Quarterly	Monthly	Daily
8%	8.00% $800	8.16% $816	8.24% $824	8.30% $830	8.33% $833
9%	9.00% $900	9.20% $920	9.31% $931	9.38% $938	9.42% $942
10%	10.00% $1,000	10.25% $1,025	10.38% $1,038	10.47% $1,047	10.52% $1,052

ILLUSTRATION 6-5
Comparison of Different Compounding Periods

[4]Because interest is theoretically earned (accruing) every second of every day, it is possible to calculate interest that is **compounded continuously**. Using the natural, or Napierian, system of logarithms facilitates computations involving continuous compounding. As a practical matter, however, most business transactions assume interest to be compounded no more frequently than daily.

[5]The formula for calculating the **effective rate**, in situations where the compounding frequency (n) is greater than once a year, is as follows.

$$\text{Effective rate} = (1 + i)^n - 1$$

To illustrate, if the stated annual rate is 8% compounded quarterly (or 2% per quarter), the effective annual rate is:

$$\begin{aligned}\text{Effective rate} &= (1 + .02)^4 - 1 \\ &= (1.02)^4 - 1 \\ &= 1.0824 - 1 \\ &= .0824 \\ &= 8.24\%\end{aligned}$$

LEARNING OBJECTIVE 4
Identify variables fundamental to solving interest problems.

Fundamental Variables

The following four variables are fundamental to all compound interest problems.

FUNDAMENTAL VARIABLES

1. RATE OF INTEREST. This rate, unless otherwise stated, is an annual rate that must be adjusted to reflect the length of the compounding period if less than a year.
2. NUMBER OF TIME PERIODS. This is the number of compounding periods. (A period may be equal to or less than a year.)
3. FUTURE VALUE. The value at a future date of a given sum or sums invested assuming compound interest.
4. PRESENT VALUE. The value now (present time) of a future sum or sums discounted assuming compound interest.

Illustration 6-6 depicts the relationship of these four fundamental variables in a **time diagram**.

ILLUSTRATION 6-6
Basic Time Diagram

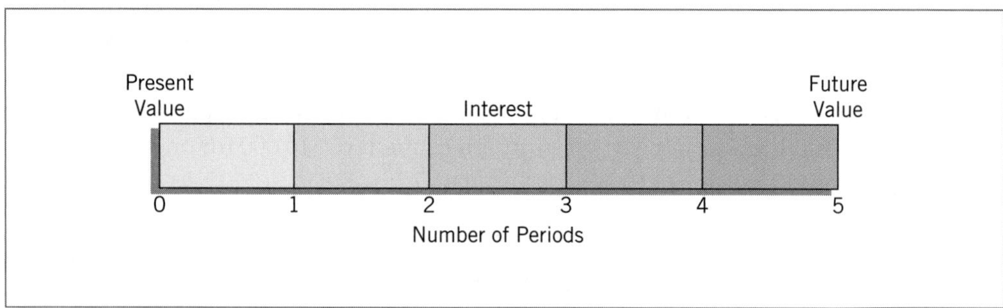

In some cases, all four of these variables are known. However, at least one variable is unknown in many business situations. To better understand and solve the problems in this chapter, we encourage you to sketch compound interest problems in the form of the preceding time diagram.

SINGLE-SUM PROBLEMS

LEARNING OBJECTIVE 5
Solve future and present value of 1 problems.

Many business and investment decisions involve a single amount of money that either exists now or will in the future. Single-sum problems are generally classified into one of the following two categories.

1. Computing the **unknown** future value of a known single sum of money that is invested now for a certain number of periods at a certain interest rate.
2. Computing the **unknown** present value of a known single sum of money in the future that is discounted for a certain number of periods at a certain interest rate.

When analyzing the information provided, determine first whether the problem involves a future value or a present value. Then apply the following general rules, depending on the situation:

- **If solving for a future value**, *accumulate* all cash flows to a future point. In this instance, interest increases the amounts or values over time so that the future value exceeds the present value.

- **If solving for a present value,** *discount* all cash flows from the future to the present. In this case, **discounting** reduces the amounts or values, so that the present value is less than the future amount.

Preparation of time diagrams aids in identifying the unknown as an item in the future or the present. Sometimes the problem involves neither a future value nor a present value. Instead, the unknown is the interest or discount rate, or the number of compounding or discounting periods.

Future Value of a Single Sum

To determine the **future value** of a single sum, multiply the future value factor by its present value (principal), as follows.

$$FV = PV\,(FVF_{n,i})$$

where

$$FV = \text{future value}$$
$$PV = \text{present value (principal or single sum)}$$
$$FVF_{n,i} = \text{future value factor for } n \text{ periods at } i \text{ interest}$$

To illustrate, Bruegger Co. wants to determine the future value of $50,000 invested for 5 years compounded annually at an interest rate of 11%. Illustration 6-7 shows this investment situation in time-diagram form.

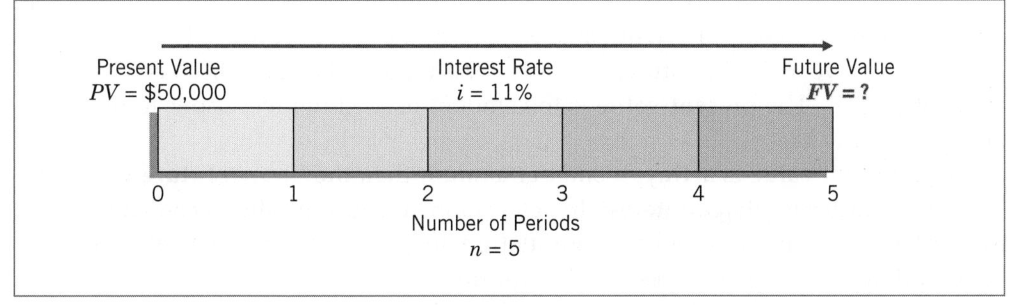

ILLUSTRATION 6-7
Future Value Time Diagram ($n = 5, i = 11\%$)

Using the future value formula, Bruegger solves this investment problem as follows.

$$\begin{aligned}\textbf{Future value} &= PV\,(FVF_{n,i})\\ &= \$50{,}000\,(FVF_{5,11\%})\\ &= \$50{,}000\,(1 + .11)^5\\ &= \$50{,}000\,(1.68506)\\ &= \$84{,}253\end{aligned}$$

To determine the future value factor of 1.68506 in the formula above, Bruegger uses a financial calculator or reads the appropriate table, in this case Table 6-1 (11% column and the 5-period row).

Companies can apply this time diagram and formula approach to routine business situations. To illustrate, assume that **Commonwealth Edison Company** deposited $250 million in an escrow account with **Northern Trust Company** at the beginning of 2012 as a commitment toward a power plant to be completed December 31, 2015. How much will the company have on deposit at the end of 4 years if interest is 10%, compounded semiannually?

With a known present value of $250 million, a total of 8 compounding periods (4×2), and an interest rate of 5% per compounding period ($.10 \div 2$), the company can time-diagram this problem and determine the future value as shown in Illustration 6-8.

ILLUSTRATION 6-8
Future Value Time Diagram (n = 8, i = 5%)

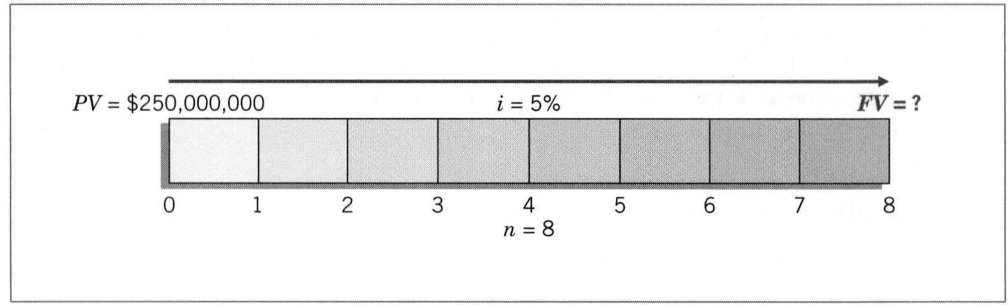

$$\begin{aligned}\text{Future value} &= \$250{,}000{,}000\ (FVF_{8,5\%}) \\ &= \$250{,}000{,}000\ (1 + .05)^8 \\ &= \$250{,}000{,}000\ (1.47746) \\ &= \$369{,}365{,}000\end{aligned}$$

Using a future value factor found in Table 1 (5% column, 8-period row), we find that the deposit of $250 million will accumulate to $369,365,000 by December 31, 2015.

Present Value of a Single Sum

The Bruegger example on page 317 showed that $50,000 invested at an annually compounded interest rate of 11% will equal $84,253 at the end of 5 years. It follows, then, that $84,253, 5 years in the future, is worth $50,000 now. That is, $50,000 is the present value of $84,253. The **present value** is the amount needed to invest now, to produce a known future value.

The present value is always a smaller amount than the known future value, due to earned and accumulated interest. In determining the future value, a company moves forward in time using a process of **accumulation**. In determining present value, it moves backward in time using a process of **discounting**.

As indicated earlier, a "present value of 1 table" appears at the end of this chapter as Table 6-2. Illustration 6-9 demonstrates the nature of such a table. It shows the present value of 1 for five different periods at three different rates of interest.

ILLUSTRATION 6-9
Excerpt from Table 6-2

PRESENT VALUE OF 1 AT COMPOUND INTEREST
(EXCERPT FROM TABLE 6-2, PAGE 357)

Period	9%	10%	11%
1	0.91743	0.90909	0.90090
2	0.84168	0.82645	0.81162
3	0.77218	0.75132	0.73119
4	0.70843	0.68301	0.65873
5	0.64993	0.62092	0.59345

The following formula is used to determine the present value of 1 (present value factor):

$$PVF_{n,i} = \frac{1}{(1 + i)^n}$$

where

$PVF_{n,i}$ = present value factor for n periods at i interest

To illustrate, assuming an interest rate of 9%, the present value of 1 discounted for three different periods is as shown in Illustration 6-10.

Discount Periods	1	÷	$(1 + i)^n$	=	Present Value*	Formula $1/(1 + i)^n$
1	1.00000		1.09		.91743	$1/(1.09)^1$
2	1.00000		$(1.09)^2$		.84168	$1/(1.09)^2$
3	1.00000		$(1.09)^3$		.77218	$1/(1.09)^3$

*Note that these amounts appear in Table 6-2 in the 9% column.

ILLUSTRATION 6-10
Present Value of $1 Discounted at 9% for Three Periods

The present value of any single sum (future value), then, is as follows.

$$PV = FV\,(PVF_{n,i})$$

where

PV = present value

FV = future value

$PVF_{n,i}$ = present value factor for n periods at i interest

To illustrate, what is the present value of $84,253 to be received or paid in 5 years discounted at 11% compounded annually? Illustration 6-11 shows this problem as a time diagram.

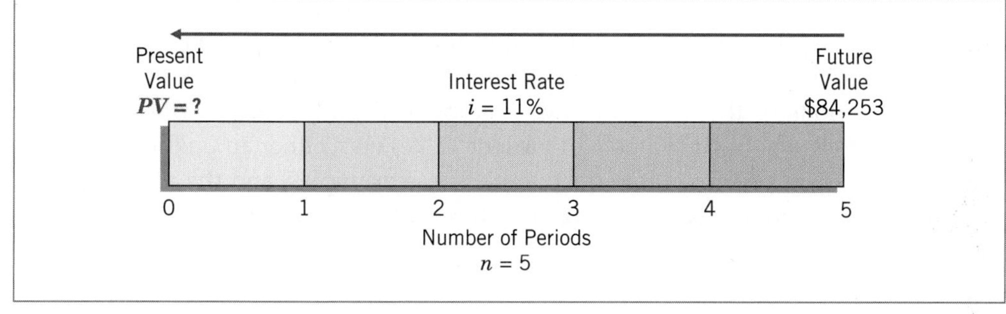

ILLUSTRATION 6-11
Present Value Time Diagram ($n = 5$, $i = 11\%$)

Using the formula, we solve this problem as follows.

$$\begin{aligned}\text{Present value} &= FV\,(PVF_{n,i})\\ &= \$84{,}253\,(PVF_{5,11\%})\\ &= \$84{,}253\left(\frac{1}{(1+.11)^5}\right)\\ &= \$84{,}253\,(.59345)\\ &= \$50{,}000 \text{ (rounded by \$.06)}\end{aligned}$$

To determine the present value factor of 0.59345, use a financial calculator or read the present value of a single sum in Table 6-2 (11% column, 5-period row).

The time diagram and formula approach can be applied in a variety of situations. For example, assume that your rich uncle decides to give you $2,000 for a trip to Europe when you graduate from college 3 years from now. He proposes to finance the trip by investing a sum of money now at 8% compound interest that will provide you with $2,000 upon your graduation. The only conditions are that you graduate and that you tell him how much to invest now.

To impress your uncle, you set up the time diagram in Illustration 6-12 and solve this problem as follows.

ILLUSTRATION 6-12
Present Value Time Diagram ($n = 3, i = 8\%$)

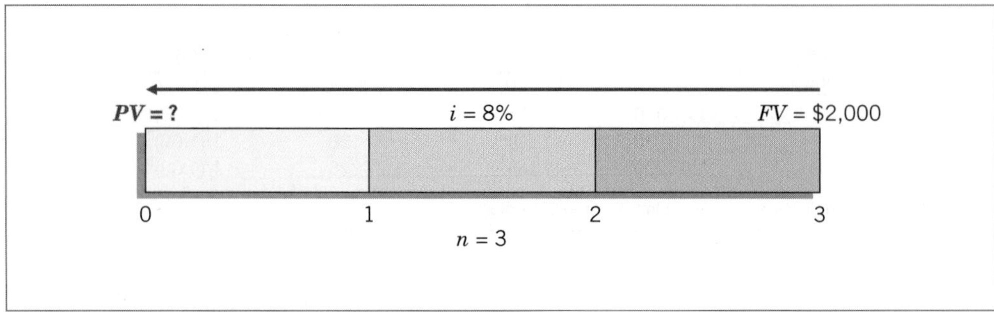

$$\text{Present value} = \$2{,}000\ (PVF_{3,8\%})$$
$$= \$2{,}000\left(\frac{1}{(1+.08)^3}\right)$$
$$= \$2{,}000\ (.79383)$$
$$= \$1{,}587.66$$

Advise your uncle to invest $1,587.66 now to provide you with $2,000 upon graduation. To satisfy your uncle's other condition, you must pass this course (and many more).

Solving for Other Unknowns in Single-Sum Problems

In computing either the future value or the present value in the previous single-sum illustrations, both the number of periods and the interest rate were known. In many business situations, both the future value and the present value are known, but the number of periods or the interest rate is unknown. The following two examples are single-sum problems (future value and present value) with either an unknown number of periods (n) or an unknown interest rate (i). These examples, and the accompanying solutions, demonstrate that knowing any three of the four values (future value, FV; present value, PV; number of periods, n; interest rate, i) allows you to derive the remaining unknown variable.

Example—Computation of the Number of Periods

The Village of Somonauk wants to accumulate $70,000 for the construction of a veterans monument in the town square. At the beginning of the current year, the Village deposited $47,811 in a memorial fund that earns 10% interest compounded annually. How many years will it take to accumulate $70,000 in the memorial fund?

In this illustration, the Village knows both the present value ($47,811) and the future value ($70,000), along with the interest rate of 10%. Illustration 6-13 depicts this investment problem as a time diagram.

ILLUSTRATION 6-13
Time Diagram to Solve for Unknown Number of Periods

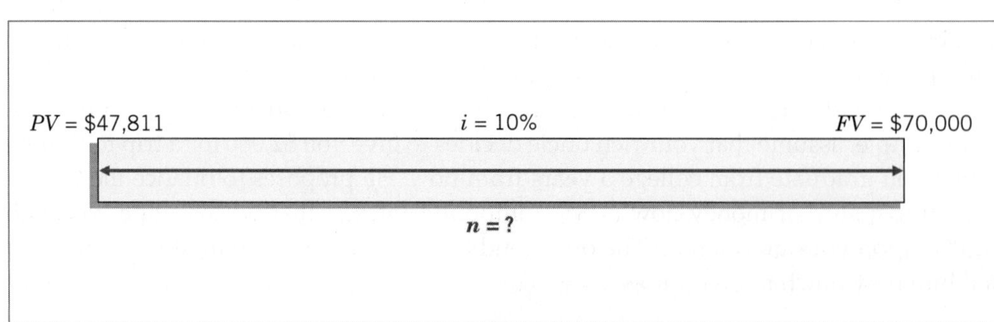

Knowing both the present value and the future value allows the Village to solve for the unknown number of periods. It may use either the future value or the present value formulas, as shown in Illustration 6-14.

Future Value Approach	Present Value Approach
$FV = PV\ (FVF_{n,10\%})$	$PV = FV\ (PVF_{n,10\%})$
$\$70,000 = \$47,811\ (FVF_{n,10\%})$	$\$47,811 = \$70,000\ (PVF_{n,10\%})$
$FVF_{n,10\%} = \frac{\$70,000}{\$47,811} = 1.46410$	$PVF_{n,10\%} = \frac{\$47,811}{\$70,000} = .68301$

ILLUSTRATION 6-14
Solving for Unknown Number of Periods

Using the future value factor of 1.46410, refer to Table 6-1 and read down the 10% column to find that factor in the 4-period row. Thus, it will take 4 years for the $47,811 to accumulate to $70,000 if invested at 10% interest compounded annually. Or, using the present value factor of 0.68301, refer to Table 6-2 and read down the 10% column to find that factor in the 4-period row.

Example—Computation of the Interest Rate

Advanced Design, Inc. needs $1,409,870 for basic research 5 years from now. The company currently has $800,000 to invest for that purpose. At what rate of interest must it invest the $800,000 to fund basic research projects of $1,409,870, 5 years from now?

The time diagram in Illustration 6-15 depicts this investment situation.

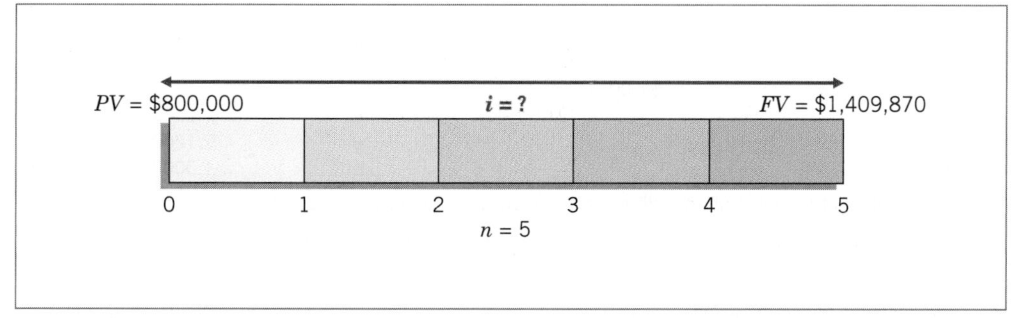

ILLUSTRATION 6-15
Time Diagram to Solve for Unknown Interest Rate

Advanced Design may determine the unknown interest rate from either the future value approach or the present value approach, as Illustration 6-16 shows.

Future Value Approach	Present Value Approach
$FV = PV\ (FVF_{5,i})$	$PV = FV\ (PVF_{5,i})$
$\$1,409,870 = \$800,000\ (FVF_{5,i})$	$\$800,000 = \$1,409,870\ (PVF_{5,i})$
$FVF_{5,i} = \frac{\$1,409,870}{\$800,000} = 1.76234$	$PVF_{5,i} = \frac{\$800,000}{\$1,409,870} = .56743$

ILLUSTRATION 6-16
Solving for Unknown Interest Rate

Using the future value factor of 1.76234, refer to Table 6-1 and read across the 5-period row to find that factor in the 12% column. Thus, the company must invest the $800,000 at 12% to accumulate to $1,409,870 in 5 years. Or, using the present value factor of .56743 and Table 6-2, again find that factor at the juncture of the 5-period row and the 12% column.

ANNUITIES

The preceding discussion involved only the accumulation or discounting of a single principal sum. However, many situations arise in which a series of dollar amounts are paid or received periodically, such as installment loans or sales; regular, partially recovered invested funds; or a series of realized cost savings.

For example, a life insurance contract involves a series of equal payments made at equal intervals of time. Such a process of periodic payment represents the accumulation of a sum of money through an annuity. An **annuity**, by definition, requires the following: (1) periodic payments or receipts (called **rents**) of the same amount, (2) the same-length interval between such rents, and (3) compounding of **interest** once each interval. The **future value of an annuity** is the sum of all the rents plus the accumulated compound interest on them.

Note that the rents may occur at either the beginning or the end of the periods. If the rents occur at the end of each period, an annuity is classified as an **ordinary annuity**. If the rents occur at the beginning of each period, an annuity is classified as an **annuity due**.

Future Value of an Ordinary Annuity

LEARNING OBJECTIVE 6
Solve future value of ordinary and annuity due problems.

One approach to determining the future value of an annuity computes the value to which **each** of the rents in the series will accumulate, and then totals their individual future values.

For example, assume that $1 is deposited at the **end** of each of 5 years (an ordinary annuity) and earns 12% interest compounded annually. Illustration 6-17 shows the computation of the future value, using the "future value of 1" table (Table 6-1) for each of the five $1 rents.

ILLUSTRATION 6-17
Solving for the Future Value of an Ordinary Annuity

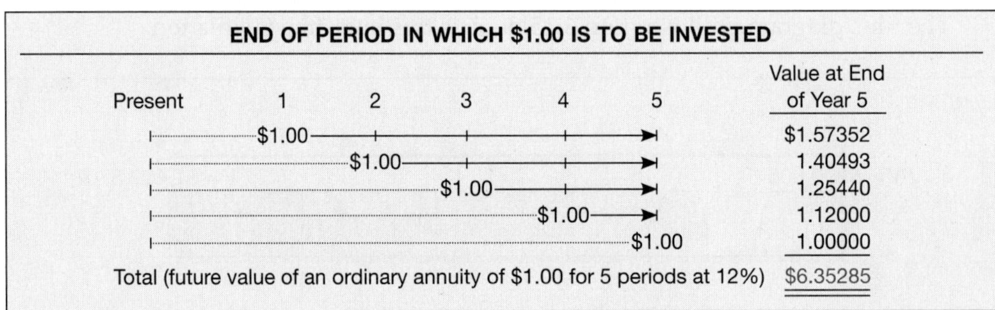

Because an ordinary annuity consists of rents deposited at the end of the period, those rents earn no interest during the period. For example, the third rent earns interest for only two periods (periods four and five). It earns no interest for the third period since it is not deposited until the end of the third period. When computing the future value of an ordinary annuity, the number of compounding periods will always be **one less than the number of rents.**

The foregoing procedure for computing the future value of an ordinary annuity always produces the correct answer. However, it can become cumbersome if the number of rents is large. A formula provides a more efficient way of expressing the future value of an ordinary annuity of 1. This formula sums the individual rents plus the compound interest, as follows:

$$FVF\text{-}OA_{n,i} = \frac{(1 + i)^n - 1}{i}$$

where

$FVF\text{-}OA_{n,i}$ = future value factor of an ordinary annuity
i = rate of interest per period
n = number of compounding periods

For example, $FVF\text{-}OA_{5,12\%}$ refers to the value to which an ordinary annuity of 1 will accumulate in 5 periods at 12% interest.

Using the formula above has resulted in the development of tables, similar to those used for the "future value of 1" and the "present value of 1" for both an ordinary annuity and an annuity due. Illustration 6-18 provides an excerpt from the "future value of an ordinary annuity of 1" table.

FUTURE VALUE OF AN ORDINARY ANNUITY OF 1
(EXCERPT FROM TABLE 6-3, PAGE 359)

Period	10%	11%	12%
1	1.00000	1.00000	1.00000
2	2.10000	2.11000	2.12000
3	3.31000	3.34210	3.37440
4	4.64100	4.70973	4.77933
5	6.10510	6.22780	6.35285*

*Note that this annuity table factor is the same as the sum of the future values of 1 factors shown in Illustration 6-17.

ILLUSTRATION 6-18
Excerpt from Table 6-3

Interpreting the table, if $1 is invested at the end of each year for 4 years at 11% interest compounded annually, the value of the annuity at the end of the fourth year is $4.71 (4.70973 × $1.00). Now, multiply the factor from the appropriate line and column of the table by the dollar amount of **one rent** involved in an ordinary annuity. The result: the accumulated sum of the rents and the compound interest to the date of the last rent.

The following formula computes the future value of an ordinary annuity.

$$\text{Future value of an ordinary annuity} = R(FVF\text{-}OA_{n,\,i})$$

where

$$R = \text{periodic rent}$$

$$FVF\text{-}OA_{n,i} = \text{future value of an ordinary annuity factor for } n \text{ periods at } i \text{ interest}$$

To illustrate, what is the future value of five $5,000 deposits made at the end of each of the next 5 years, earning interest of 12%? Illustration 6-19 depicts this problem as a time diagram.

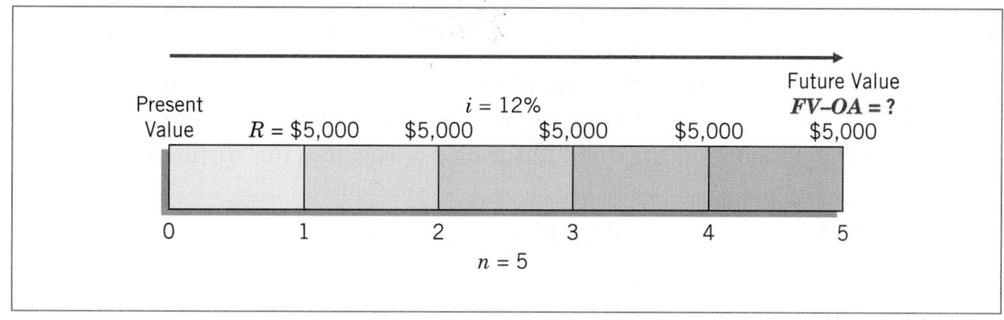

ILLUSTRATION 6-19
Time Diagram for Future Value of Ordinary Annuity ($n = 5$, $i = 12\%$)

Use of the formula solves this investment problem as follows.

$$\begin{aligned}\text{Future value of an ordinary annuity} &= R\,(FVF\text{-}OA_{n,i})\\ &= \$5{,}000\,(FVF\text{-}OA_{5,12\%})\\ &= \$5{,}000\left(\frac{(1+.12)^5-1}{.12}\right)\\ &= \$5{,}000\,(6.35285)\\ &= \$31{,}764.25\end{aligned}$$

To determine the future value of an ordinary annuity factor of 6.35285 in the formula above, use a financial calculator or read the appropriate table, in this case, Table 6-3 (12% column and the 5-period row).

To illustrate these computations in a business situation, assume that Hightown Electronics deposits $75,000 at the end of each 6-month period for the next 3 years, to accumulate enough money to meet debts that mature in 3 years. What is the future value that the company will have on deposit at the end of 3 years if the annual interest rate is 10%? The time diagram in Illustration 6-20 depicts this situation.

ILLUSTRATION 6-20
Time Diagram for Future Value of Ordinary Annuity ($n = 6, i = 5\%$)

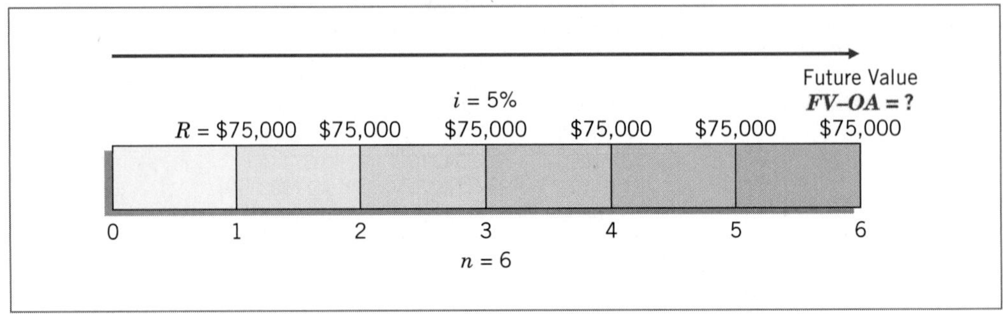

The formula solution for the Hightown Electronics situation is as follows.

$$\text{Future value of an ordinary annuity} = R\,(FVF\text{-}OA_{n,i})$$
$$= \$75{,}000\,(FVF\text{-}OA_{6,5\%})$$
$$= \$75{,}000\left(\frac{(1+.05)^6 - 1}{.05}\right)$$
$$= \$75{,}000\,(6.80191)$$
$$= \$510{,}143.25$$

Thus, six 6-month deposits of $75,000 earning 5% per period will grow to $510,143.25.

Future Value of an Annuity Due

The preceding analysis of an ordinary annuity assumed that the periodic rents occur at the **end** of each period. Recall that an **annuity due** assumes periodic rents occur at the **beginning** of each period. This means an annuity due will accumulate interest during the first period (in contrast to an ordinary annuity rent, which will not). In other words, the two types of annuities differ in the number of interest accumulation periods involved even though the same number of rents occur.

If rents occur at the end of a period (ordinary annuity), in determining the **future value of an annuity** there will be one less interest period than if the rents occur at the beginning of the period (annuity due). Illustration 6-21 shows this distinction.

ILLUSTRATION 6-21
Comparison of the Future Value of an Ordinary Annuity with an Annuity Due

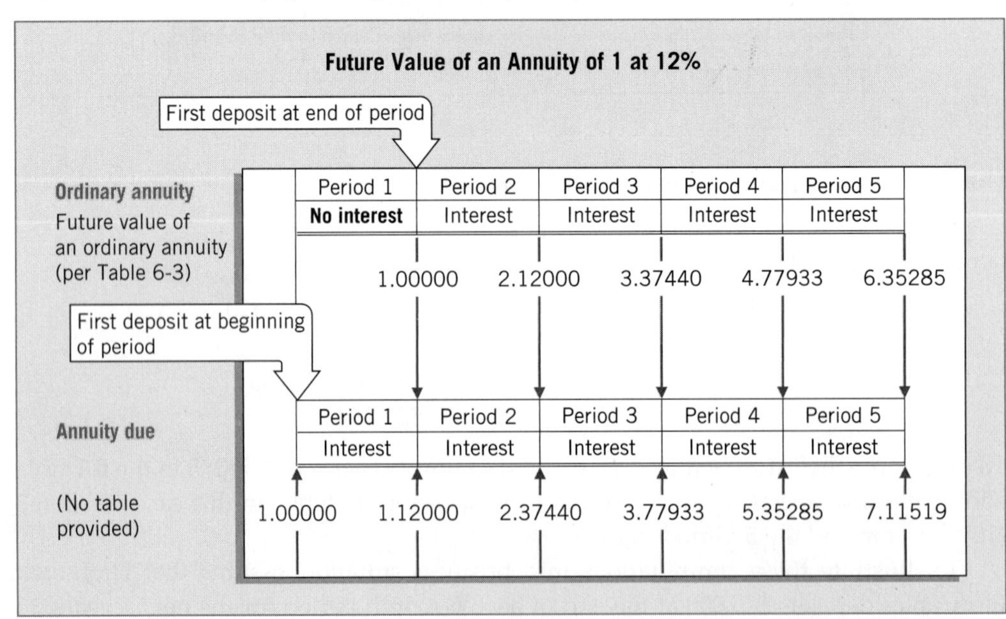

In this example, the cash flows from the annuity due come exactly one period earlier than for an ordinary annuity. As a result, the future value of the annuity due factor is exactly 12% higher than the ordinary annuity factor. For example, the value of an ordinary annuity factor at the end of period one at 12% is 1.00000, whereas for an annuity due it is 1.12000.

To find the future value of an annuity due factor, multiply the future value of an ordinary annuity factor by 1 plus the interest rate. For example, to determine the future value of an annuity due interest factor for 5 periods at 12% compound interest, simply multiply the future value of an ordinary annuity interest factor for 5 periods (6.35285), by one plus the interest rate (1 + .12), to arrive at 7.11519 (6.35285 × 1.12).

To illustrate the use of the ordinary annuity tables in converting to an annuity due, assume that Sue Lotadough plans to deposit $800 a year on each birthday of her son Howard. She makes the first deposit on his tenth birthday, at 6% interest compounded annually. Sue wants to know the amount she will have accumulated for college expenses by her son's eighteenth birthday.

If the first deposit occurs on Howard's tenth birthday, Sue will make a total of 8 deposits over the life of the annuity (assume no deposit on the eighteenth birthday), as shown in Illustration 6-22. Because all the deposits are made at the beginning of the periods, they represent an annuity due.

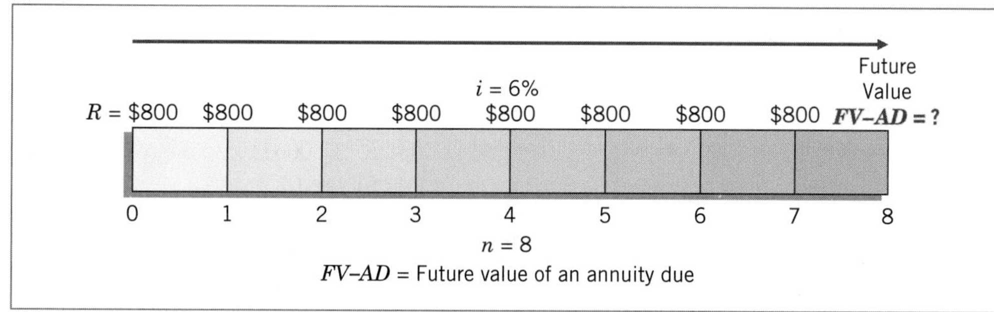

ILLUSTRATION 6-22
Annuity Due Time Diagram

Referring to the "future value of an ordinary annuity of 1" table for 8 periods at 6%, Sue finds a factor of 9.89747. She then multiplies this factor by (1 + .06) to arrive at the future value of an annuity due factor. As a result, the accumulated value on Howard's eighteenth birthday is $8,393.06, as calculated in Illustration 6-23.

ILLUSTRATION 6-23
Computation of Accumulated Value of Annuity Due

1. Future value of an ordinary annuity of 1 for 8 periods at 6% (Table 6-3)	9.89747
2. Factor (1 + .06)	× 1.06
3. Future value of an annuity due of 1 for 8 periods at 6%	10.49132
4. Periodic deposit (rent)	× $800
5. Accumulated value on son's 18th birthday	$8,393.06

Depending on the college he chooses, Howard may have enough to finance only part of his first year of school.

Examples of Future Value of Annuity Problems

The foregoing annuity examples relied on three known values—amount of each rent, interest rate, and number of periods. Using these values enables us to determine the unknown fourth value, future value.

The first two future value problems we present illustrate the computations of (1) the amount of the rents and (2) the number of rents. The third problem illustrates the computation of the future value of an annuity due.

Computation of Rent

Assume that you plan to accumulate $14,000 for a down payment on a condominium apartment 5 years from now. For the next 5 years, you earn an annual return of 8% compounded semiannually. How much should you deposit at the end of each 6-month period?

The $14,000 is the future value of 10 (5 × 2) semiannual end-of-period payments of an unknown amount, at an interest rate of 4% (8% ÷ 2). Illustration 6-24 depicts this problem as a time diagram.

ILLUSTRATION 6-24
Future Value of Ordinary Annuity Time Diagram ($n = 10, i = 4\%$)

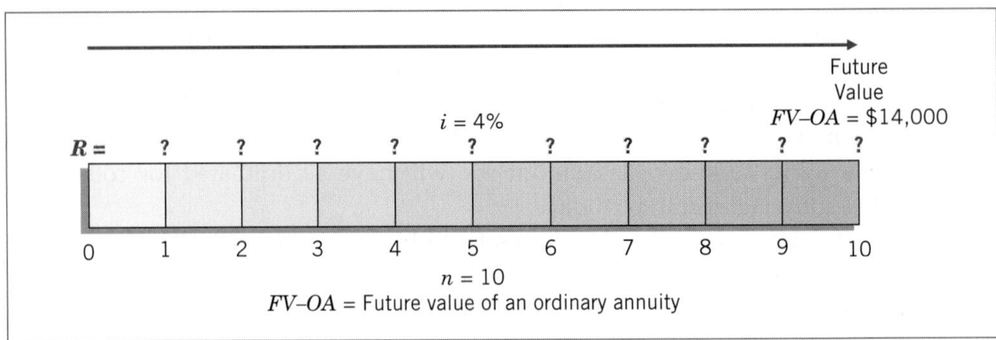

Using the formula for the future value of an ordinary annuity, you determine the amount of each rent as follows.

$$\text{Future value of an ordinary annuity} = R\,(FVF\text{-}OA_{n,i})$$
$$\$14{,}000 = R\,(FVF\text{-}OA_{10,4\%})$$
$$\$14{,}000 = R\,(12.00611)$$
$$R = \$1{,}166.07$$

Thus, you must make 10 semiannual deposits of $1,166.07 each in order to accumulate $14,000 for your down payment.

Computation of the Number of Periodic Rents

Suppose that a company's goal is to accumulate $117,332 by making periodic deposits of $20,000 at the end of each year, which will earn 8% compounded annually while accumulating. How many deposits must it make?

The $117,332 represents the future value of n(?) $20,000 deposits, at an 8% annual rate of interest. Illustration 6-25 depicts this problem in a time diagram.

ILLUSTRATION 6-25
Future Value of Ordinary Annuity Time Diagram, to Solve for Unknown Number of Periods

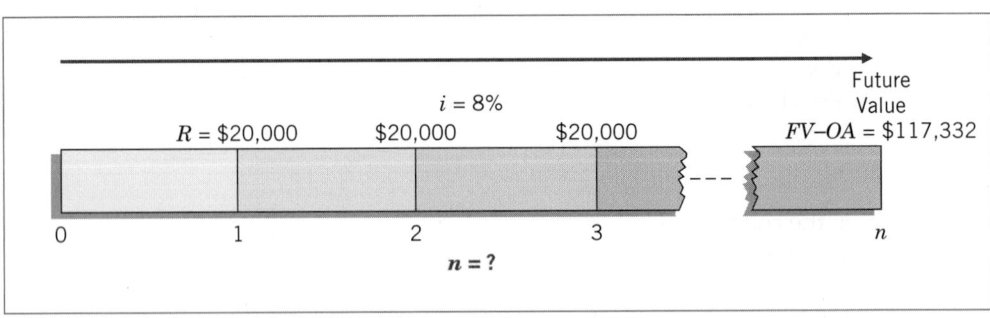

Using the future value of an ordinary annuity formula, the company obtains the following factor.

$$\text{Future value of an ordinary annuity} = R\,(FVF\text{-}OA_{n,i})$$
$$\$117{,}332 = \$20{,}000\,(FVF\text{-}OA_{n,8\%})$$
$$FVF\text{-}OA_{n,8\%} = \frac{\$117{,}332}{\$20{,}000} = 5.86660$$

Use Table 6-3 and read down the 8% column to find 5.86660 in the 5-period row. Thus, the company must make five deposits of $20,000 each.

Computation of the Future Value

To create his retirement fund, Walter Goodwrench, a mechanic, now works weekends. Mr. Goodwrench deposits $2,500 today in a savings account that earns 9% interest. He plans to deposit $2,500 every year for a total of 30 years. How much cash will Mr. Goodwrench accumulate in his retirement savings account, when he retires in 30 years? Illustration 6-26 depicts this problem in a time diagram.

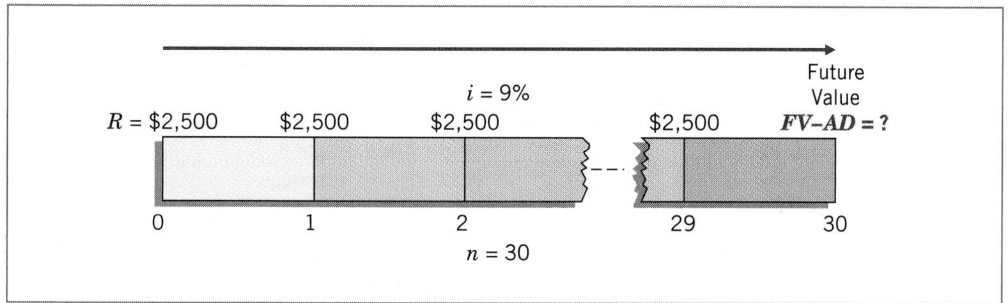

ILLUSTRATION 6-26
Future Value Annuity Due Time Diagram ($n = 30, i = 9\%$)

Using the "future value of an ordinary annuity of 1" table, Mr. Goodwrench computes the solution as shown in Illustration 6-27.

1. Future value of an ordinary annuity of 1 for 30 periods at 9%	136.30754
2. Factor (1 +.09)	× 1.09
3. Future value of an annuity due of 1 for 30 periods at 9%	148.57522
4. Periodic rent	× $2,500
5. Accumulated value at end of 30 years	$371,438

ILLUSTRATION 6-27
Computation of Accumulated Value of an Annuity Due

Present Value of an Ordinary Annuity

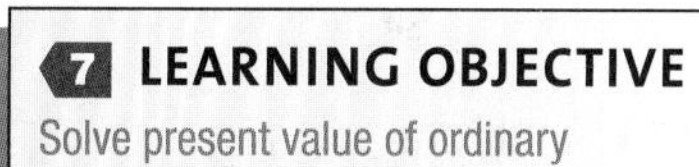

7 LEARNING OBJECTIVE
Solve present value of ordinary and annuity due problems.

The present value of an annuity is **the single sum** that, if invested at compound interest now, would provide for an annuity (a series of withdrawals) for a certain number of future periods. In other words, the present value of an ordinary annuity is the present value of a series of equal rents, to withdraw at equal intervals.

One approach to finding the present value of an annuity determines the present value of each of the rents in the series and then totals their individual present values. For example, we may view an annuity of $1, to be received at the **end** of each of 5 periods, as separate amounts. We then compute each present value using the table of present values (see Table 6-2 on pages 360–361), assuming an interest rate of 12%. Illustration 6-28 shows this approach.

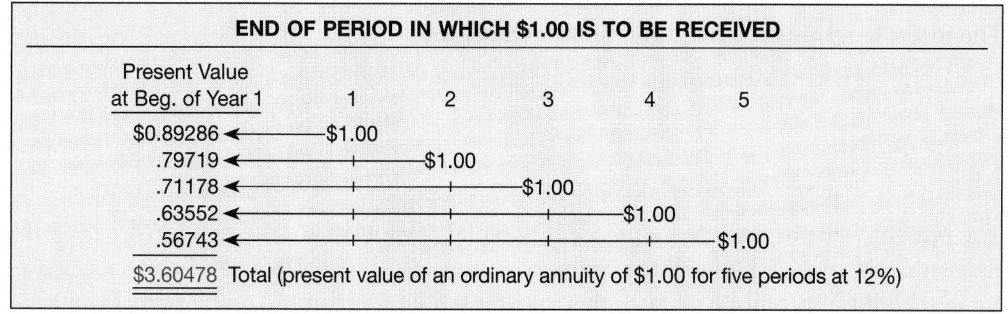

ILLUSTRATION 6-28
Solving for the Present Value of an Ordinary Annuity

This computation tells us that if we invest the single sum of \$3.61 today at 12% interest for 5 periods, we will be able to withdraw \$1 at the end of each period for 5 periods. We can summarize this cumbersome procedure by the following formula.

$$PVF\text{-}OA_{n,i} = \frac{1 - \frac{1}{(1+i)^n}}{i}$$

The expression $PVF\text{-}OA_{n,i}$ refers to the present value of an ordinary annuity of 1 factor for n periods at i interest. Ordinary annuity tables base present values on this formula. Illustration 6-29 shows an excerpt from such a table.

ILLUSTRATION 6-29
Excerpt from Table 6-4

PRESENT VALUE OF AN ORDINARY ANNUITY OF 1
(EXCERPT FROM TABLE 6-4, PAGE 361)

Period	10%	11%	12%
1	0.90909	0.90090	0.89286
2	1.73554	1.71252	1.69005
3	2.48685	2.44371	2.40183
4	3.16986	3.10245	3.03735
5	3.79079	3.69590	3.60478*

*Note that this annuity table factor is equal to the sum of the present value of 1 factors shown in Illustration 6-28.

The general formula for the present value of any ordinary annuity is as follows.

Present value of an ordinary annuity = $R\,(PVF\text{-}OA_{n,i})$

where

R = periodic rent (ordinary annuity)

$PVF\text{-}OA_{n,i}$ = present value of an ordinary annuity of 1 for n periods at i interest

To illustrate with an example, what is the present value of rental receipts of \$6,000 each, to be received at the end of each of the next 5 years when discounted at 12%? This problem may be time-diagrammed and solved as shown in Illustration 6-30.

ILLUSTRATION 6-30
Present Value of Ordinary Annuity Time Diagram

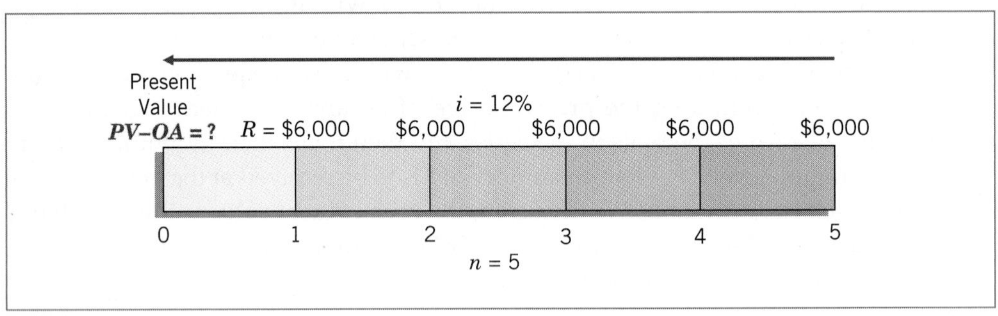

The formula for this calculation is as shown below.

Present value of an ordinary annuity $= R\,(PVF\text{-}OA_{n,i})$
$= \$6{,}000\,(PVF\text{-}OA_{5,12\%})$
$= \$6{,}000\,(3.60478)$
$= \$21{,}628.68$

The present value of the 5 ordinary annuity rental receipts of \$6,000 each is \$21,628.68. To determine the present value of the ordinary annuity factor 3.60478, use a financial calculator or read the appropriate table, in this case Table 6-4 (12% column and 5-period row).

UP IN SMOKE

What do the numbers mean?

Time value of money concepts also can be relevant to public policy debates. For example, several states had to determine how to receive the payments from tobacco companies as settlement for a national lawsuit against the companies for the healthcare costs of smoking.

The **State of Wisconsin** was due to collect 25 years of payments totaling $5.6 billion. The state could wait to collect the payments, or it could sell the payments to an investment bank (a process called *securitization*). If it were to sell the payments, it would receive a lump-sum payment today of $1.26 billion. Is this a good deal for the state? Assuming a discount rate of 8% and that the payments will be received in equal amounts (e.g., an annuity), the present value of the tobacco payment is:

$$\$5.6 \text{ billion} \div 25 = \$224 \text{ million}$$
$$\$224 \text{ million} \times 10.67478^{*} = \$2.39 \text{ billion}$$
$$^{*}PV\text{-}OA(i = 8\%, n = 25)$$

Why would some in the state be willing to take just $1.26 billion today for an annuity whose present value is almost twice that amount? One reason is that Wisconsin was facing a hole in its budget that could be plugged in part by the lump-sum payment. Also, some believed that the risk of not getting paid by the tobacco companies in the future makes it prudent to get the money earlier.

If this latter reason has merit, then the present value computation above should have been based on a higher interest rate. Assuming a discount rate of 15%, the present value of the annuity is $1.448 billion ($5.6 billion ÷ 25 = $224 million; $224 million × 6.46415), which is much closer to the lump-sum payment offered to the State of Wisconsin.

Present Value of an Annuity Due

In our discussion of the present value of an ordinary annuity, we discounted the final rent based on the number of rent periods. In determining the present value of an annuity due, there is always one fewer discount period. Illustration 6-31 shows this distinction.

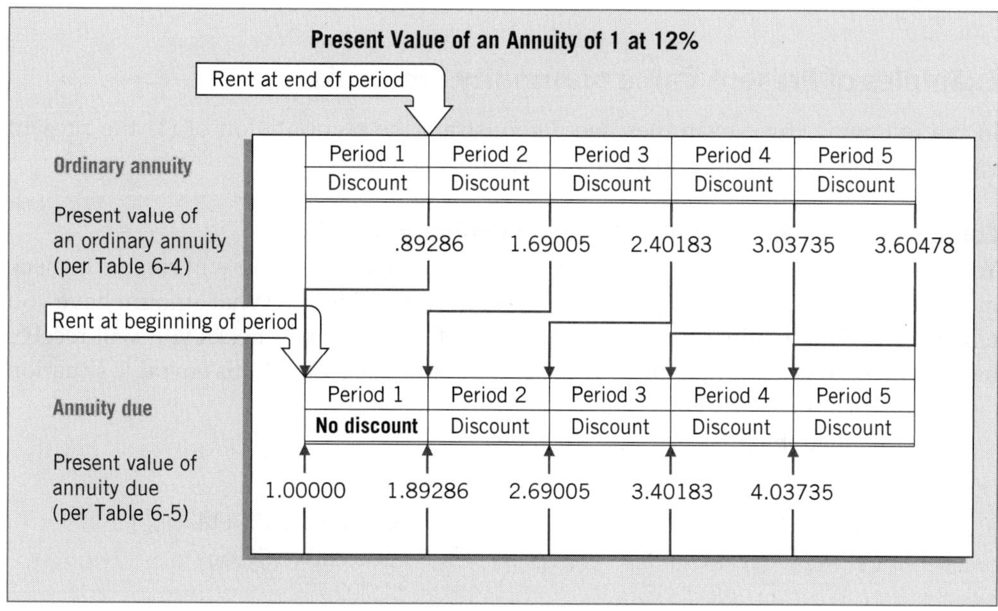

ILLUSTRATION 6-31
Comparison of Present Value of an Ordinary Annuity with an Annuity Due

Because each cash flow comes exactly one period sooner in the present value of the annuity due, the present value of the cash flows is exactly 12% higher than the present value of an ordinary annuity. Thus, **to find the present value of an annuity due factor, multiply the present value of an ordinary annuity factor by 1 plus the interest rate** (that is, $1 + i$).

To determine the present value of an annuity due interest factor for 5 periods at 12% interest, take the present value of an ordinary annuity for 5 periods at 12% interest (3.60478) and multiply it by 1.12 to arrive at the present value of an annuity due, 4.03735 (3.60478 × 1.12). We provide present value of annuity due factors in Table 6-5.

To illustrate, Space Odyssey, Inc., rents a communications satellite for 4 years with annual rental payments of $4.8 million to be made at the beginning of each year. If the relevant annual interest rate is 11%, what is the present value of the rental obligations? Illustration 6-32 shows the company's time diagram for this problem.

ILLUSTRATION 6-32
Present Value of Annuity Due Time Diagram
($n = 4, i = 11\%$)

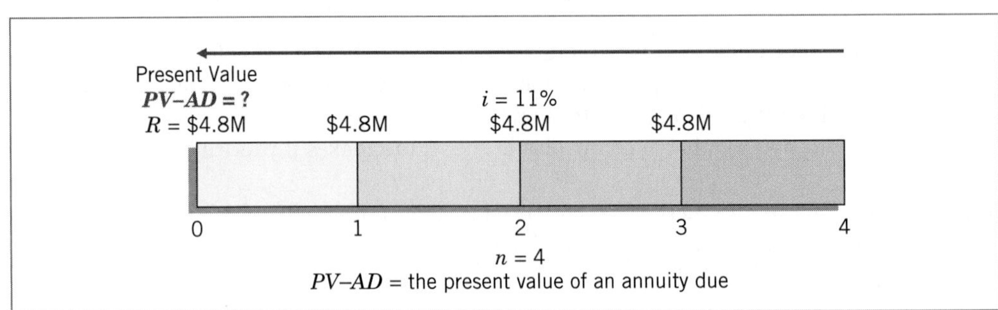

Illustration 6-33 shows the computations to solve this problem.

ILLUSTRATION 6-33
Computation of Present Value of an Annuity Due

1. Present value of an ordinary annuity of 1 for 4 periods at 11% (Table 6-4)	3.10245
2. Factor (1 + .11)	× 1.11
3. Present value of an annuity due of 1 for 4 periods at 11%	3.44372
4. Periodic deposit (rent)	× $4,800,000
5. Present value of payments	$16,529,856

Using Table 6-5 also locates the desired factor 3.44371 and computes the present value of the lease payments to be $16,529,808. (The difference in computations is due to rounding.)

Examples of Present Value of Annuity Problems

In the following three examples, we demonstrate the computation of (1) the present value, (2) the interest rate, and (3) the amount of each rent.

Computation of the Present Value of an Ordinary Annuity

You have just won a lottery totaling $4,000,000. You learn that you will receive a check in the amount of $200,000 at the end of each of the next 20 years. What amount have you really won? That is, what is the present value of the $200,000 checks you will receive over the next 20 years? Illustration 6-34 shows a time diagram of this enviable situation (assuming an appropriate interest rate of 10%).

You calculate the present value as follows:

$$\begin{aligned}\text{Present value of an ordinary annuity} &= R\,(PVF\text{-}OA_{n,i})\\ &= \$200{,}000\,(PVF\text{-}OA_{20,10\%})\\ &= \$200{,}000\,(8.51356)\\ &= \$1{,}702{,}712\end{aligned}$$

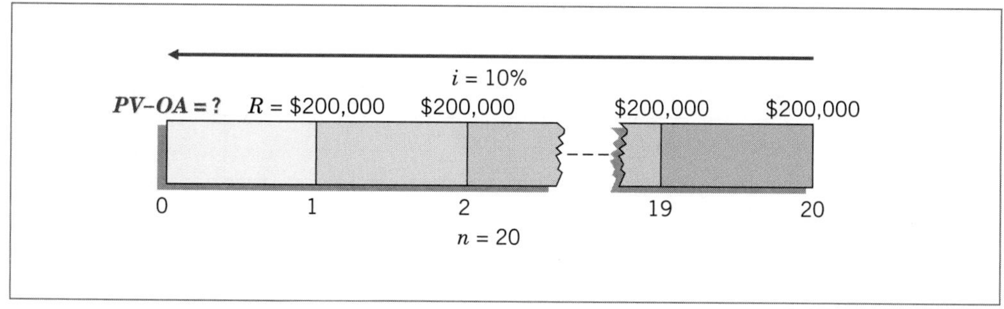

ILLUSTRATION 6-34
Time Diagram to Solve for Present Value of Lottery Payments

As a result, if the state deposits $1,702,712 now and earns 10% interest, it can withdraw $200,000 a year for 20 years to pay you the $4,000,000.

Computation of the Interest Rate

Many shoppers use credit cards to make purchases. When you receive the statement for payment, you may pay the total amount due or you may pay the balance in a certain number of payments. For example, assume you receive a statement from MasterCard with a balance due of $528.77. You may pay it off in 12 equal monthly payments of $50 each, with the first payment due one month from now. What rate of interest would you be paying?

The $528.77 represents the present value of the 12 payments of $50 each at an unknown rate of interest. The time diagram in Illustration 6-35 depicts this situation.

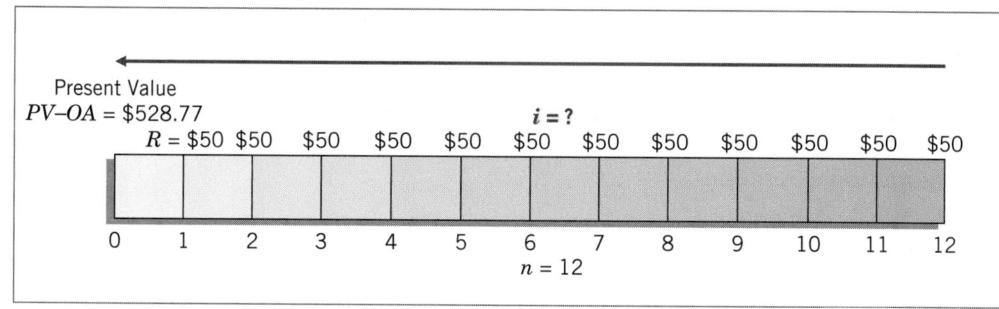

ILLUSTRATION 6-35
Time Diagram to Solve for Effective-Interest Rate on Loan

You calculate the rate as follows.

$$\text{Present value of an ordinary annuity} = R\,(PVF\text{-}OA_{n,i})$$

$$\$528.77 = \$50\,(PVF\text{-}OA_{12,i})$$

$$(PVFOA_{12,i}) = \frac{\$528.77}{\$50} = 10.57540$$

Referring to Table 6-4 and reading across the 12-period row, you find 10.57534 in the 2% column. Since 2% is a monthly rate, the nominal annual rate of interest is 24% (12 × 2%). The effective annual rate is 26.82413% $[(1 + .02)^{12} - 1]$. Obviously, you are better off paying the entire bill now if possible.

Computation of a Periodic Rent

Norm and Jackie Remmers have saved $36,000 to finance their daughter Dawna's college education. They deposited the money in the Bloomington Savings and Loan Association, where it earns 4% interest compounded semiannually. What equal amounts can their daughter withdraw at the end of every 6 months during her 4 college years, without exhausting the fund? Illustration 6-36 (on page 332) shows a time diagram of this situation.

ILLUSTRATION 6-36
Time Diagram for Ordinary Annuity for a College Fund

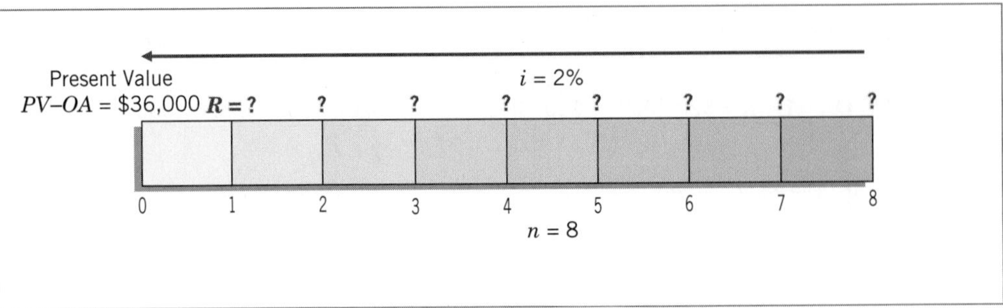

Determining the answer by simply dividing $36,000 by 8 withdrawals is wrong. Why? Because that ignores the interest earned on the money remaining on deposit. Dawna must consider that interest is compounded semiannually at 2% (4% ÷ 2) for 8 periods (4 years × 2). Thus, using the same present value of an ordinary annuity formula, she determines the amount of each withdrawal that she can make as follows.

$$\text{Present value of an ordinary annuity} = R\,(PVF\text{-}OA_{n,i})$$
$$\$36{,}000 = R\,(PVF\text{-}OA_{8,2\%})$$
$$\$36{,}000 = R\,(7.32548)$$
$$R = \$4{,}914.35$$

MORE COMPLEX SITUATIONS

LEARNING OBJECTIVE 8
Solve present value problems related to deferred annuities and bonds.

Solving time value problems often requires using more than one table. For example, a business problem may need computations of both present value of a single sum and present value of an annuity. Two such common situations are:

1. Deferred annuities.
2. Bond problems.

Deferred Annuities

A **deferred annuity** is an annuity in which the rents begin after a specified number of periods. A deferred annuity does not begin to produce rents until two or more periods have expired. For example, "an **ordinary annuity** of six annual rents deferred 4 years" means that no rents will occur during the first 4 years, and that the first of the six rents will occur at the end of the fifth year. "An **annuity due** of six annual rents deferred 4 years" means that no rents will occur during the first 4 years, and that the first of six rents will occur at the beginning of the fifth year.

Future Value of a Deferred Annuity

Computing the future value of a deferred annuity is relatively straightforward. Because there is no accumulation or investment on which interest may accrue, the future value of a deferred annuity is the same as the future value of an annuity not deferred. That is, computing the future value simply ignores the deferred period.

To illustrate, assume that Sutton Corporation plans to purchase a land site in 6 years for the construction of its new corporate headquarters. Because of cash flow problems, Sutton budgets deposits of $80,000, on which it expects to earn 5% annually, only at the end of the fourth, fifth, and sixth periods. What future value will Sutton have accumulated at the end of the sixth year? Illustration 6-37 shows a time diagram of this situation.

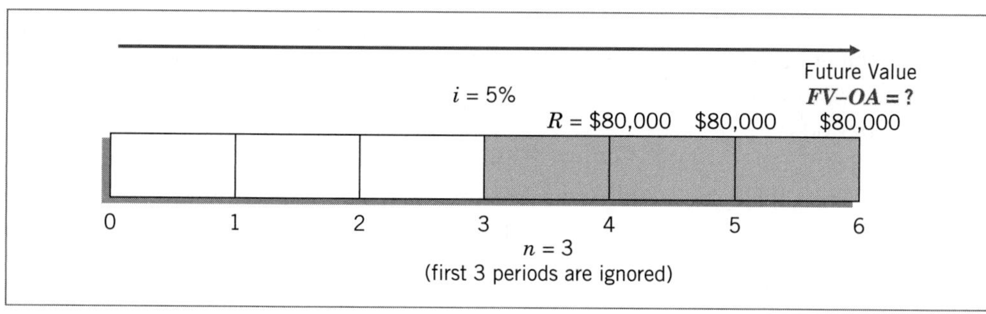

ILLUSTRATION 6-37
Time Diagram for Future Value of Deferred Annuity

Sutton determines the value accumulated by using the standard formula for the future value of an ordinary annuity:

$$
\begin{aligned}
\text{Future value of an ordinary annuity} &= R\,(FVF\text{-}OA_{n,i}) \\
&= \$80{,}000\,(FVF\text{-}OA_{3,5\%}) \\
&= \$80{,}000\,(3.15250) \\
&= \$252{,}200
\end{aligned}
$$

Present Value of a Deferred Annuity

Computing the present value of a deferred annuity must recognize the interest that accrues on the original investment during the deferral period.

To compute the present value of a deferred annuity, we compute the present value of an ordinary annuity of 1 as if the rents had occurred for the entire period. We then subtract the present value of rents that were not received during the deferral period. We are left with the present value of the rents actually received subsequent to the deferral period.

To illustrate, Bob Bender has developed and copyrighted tutorial software for students in advanced accounting. He agrees to sell the copyright to Campus Micro Systems for six annual payments of $5,000 each. The payments will begin 5 years from today. Given an annual interest rate of 8%, what is the present value of the six payments?

This situation is an ordinary annuity of 6 payments deferred 4 periods. The time diagram in Illustration 6-38 depicts this sales agreement.

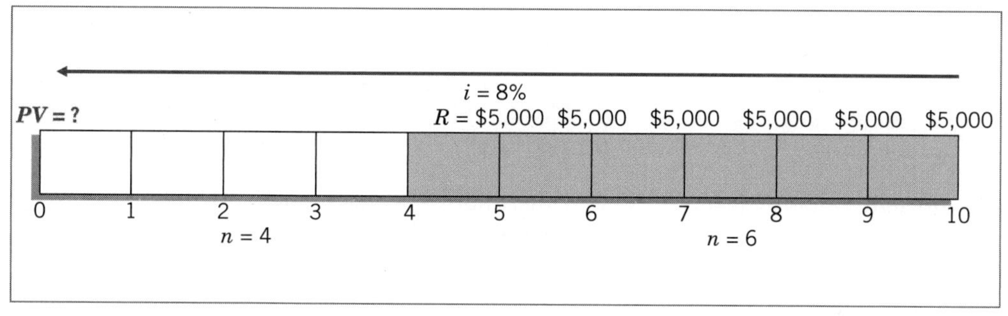

ILLUSTRATION 6-38
Time Diagram for Present Value of Deferred Annuity

Two options are available to solve this problem. The first is to use only Table 6-4, as shown in Illustration 6-39.

1. Each periodic rent		$5,000
2. Present value of an ordinary annuity of 1 for total periods (10) [number of rents (6) plus number of deferred periods (4)] at 8%	6.71008	
3. Less: Present value of an ordinary annuity of 1 for the number of deferred periods (4) at 8%	3.31213	
4. Difference		× 3.39795
5. Present value of six rents of $5,000 deferred 4 periods		$16,989.75

ILLUSTRATION 6-39
Computation of the Present Value of a Deferred Annuity

The subtraction of the present value of an annuity of 1 for the deferred periods eliminates the nonexistent rents during the deferral period. It converts the present value of an ordinary annuity of $1.00 for 10 periods to the present value of 6 rents of $1.00, deferred 4 periods.

Alternatively, Bender can use both Table 6-2 and Table 6-4 to compute the present value of the 6 rents. He can first discount the annuity 6 periods. However, because the annuity is deferred 4 periods, he must treat the present value of the annuity as a future amount to be discounted another 4 periods. The time diagram in Illustration 6-40 depicts this two-step process.

ILLUSTRATION 6-40
Time Diagram for Present Value of Deferred Annuity (2-Step Process)

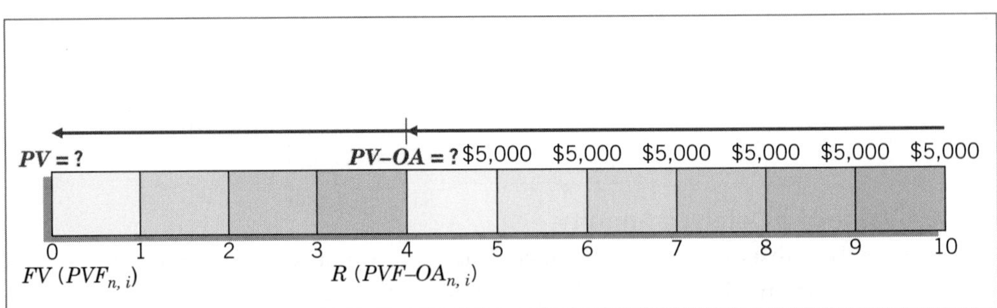

Calculation using formulas would be done in two steps, as follows.

Step 1: Present value of an ordinary annuity $= R\ (PVF\text{-}OA_{n,i})$
$= \$5{,}000\ (PVF\text{-}OA_{6,8\%})$
$= \$5{,}000\ (4.62288)$
(Table 6-4, Present value of an ordinary annuity)
$= \$23{,}114.40$

Step 2: Present value of a single sum $= FV\ (PVF_{n,i})$
$= \$23{,}114.40\ (PVF_{4,8\%})$
$= \$23{,}114.40\ (.73503)$
(Table 6-2, Present value of a single sum)
$= \$16{,}989.78$

The present value of $16,989.78 computed above is the same as in Illustration 6-39, although computed differently. (The $0.03 difference is due to rounding.)

Valuation of Long-Term Bonds

A long-term bond produces two cash flows: (1) periodic interest payments during the life of the bond, and (2) the principal (face value) paid at maturity. At the date of issue, bond buyers determine the present value of these two cash flows using the market rate of interest.

The periodic interest payments represent an annuity. The principal represents a single-sum problem. The current market value of the bonds is the combined present values of the interest annuity and the principal amount.

To illustrate, Alltech Corporation on January 1, 2012, issues $100,000 of 9% bonds due in 5 years with interest payable annually at year-end. The current market rate of interest for bonds of similar risk is 11%. What will the buyers pay for this bond issue?

The time diagram in Illustration 6-41 depicts both cash flows.

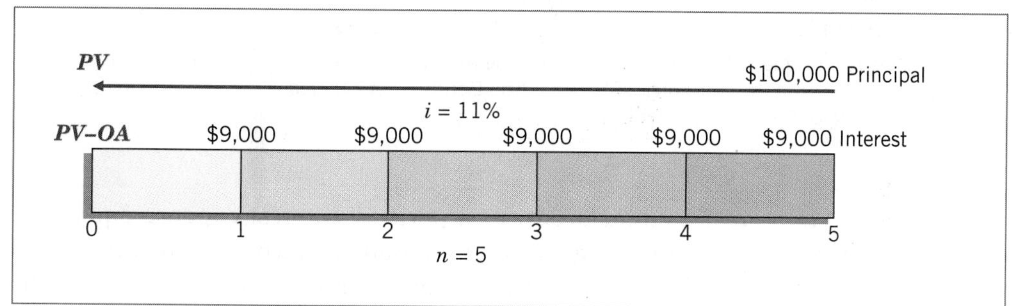

ILLUSTRATION 6-41
Time Diagram to Solve for Bond Valuation

Alltech computes the present value of the two cash flows by discounting at 11% as follows.

1. Present value of the principal: $FV\ (PVF_{5,11\%})$ = $100,000 (.59345)	$59,345.00
2. Present value of the interest payments: $R\ (PVF\text{-}OA_{5,11\%})$ = $9,000 (3.69590)	33,263.10
3. Combined present value (market price)—carrying value of bonds	$92,608.10

ILLUSTRATION 6-42
Computation of the Present Value of an Interest-Bearing Bond

By paying $92,608.10 at date of issue, the buyers of the bonds will realize an effective yield of 11% over the 5-year term of the bonds. This is true because Alltech discounted the cash flows at 11%.

Effective-Interest Method of Amortization of Bond Discount or Premium

In the previous example (Illustration 6-42), Alltech Corporation issued bonds at a discount, computed as follows.

Maturity value (face amount) of bonds		$100,000.00
Present value of the principal	$59,345.00	
Present value of the interest	33,263.10	
Proceeds (present value and cash received)		(92,608.10)
Discount on bonds issued		$ 7,391.90

ILLUSTRATION 6-43
Computation of Bond Discount

Alltech amortizes (writes off to interest expense) the amount of this discount over the life of the bond issue.

The preferred procedure for amortization of a discount or premium is the **effective-interest method**. Under the effective-interest method:

1. The company issuing the bond first computes bond interest expense by multiplying the carrying value of the bonds at the beginning of the period by the effective-interest rate.
2. The company then determines the bond discount or premium amortization by comparing the bond interest expense with the interest to be paid.

Gateway to the Profession
Use of Spreadsheets to Calculate Bond Amortization

Illustration 6-44 depicts the computation of bond amortization.

ILLUSTRATION 6-44
Amortization Computation

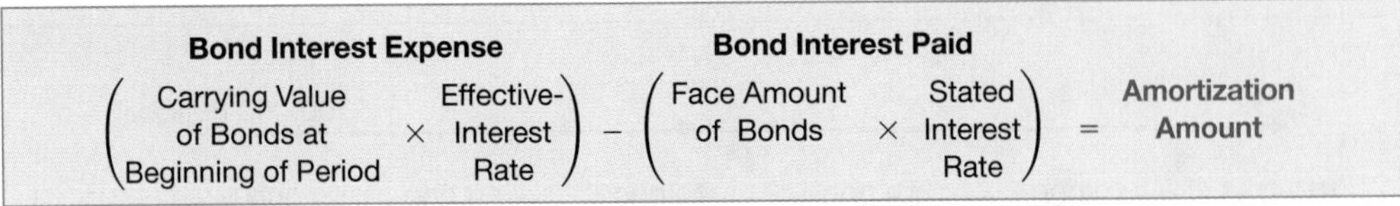

$$\left(\text{Carrying Value of Bonds at Beginning of Period} \times \text{Effective-Interest Rate}\right) - \left(\text{Face Amount of Bonds} \times \text{Stated Interest Rate}\right) = \text{Amortization Amount}$$

(Bond Interest Expense) − (Bond Interest Paid) = Amortization Amount

The effective-interest method produces a periodic interest expense equal to a **constant percentage of the carrying value of the bonds.** Since the percentage used is the effective rate of interest incurred by the borrower at the time of issuance, the effective-interest method results in matching expenses with revenues.

We can use the data from the Alltech Corporation example to illustrate the effective-interest method of amortization. Alltech issued $100,000 face value of bonds at a discount of $7,391.90, resulting in a carrying value of $92,608.10. Illustration 6-45 shows the effective-interest amortization schedule for Alltech's bonds.

ILLUSTRATION 6-45
Effective-Interest Amortization Schedule

SCHEDULE OF BOND DISCOUNT AMORTIZATION
5-YEAR, 9% BONDS SOLD TO YIELD 11%

Date	Cash Interest Paid	Interest Expense	Bond Discount Amortization	Carrying Value of Bonds
1/1/10				$ 92,608.10
12/31/10	$ 9,000[a]	$10,186.89[b]	$1,186.89[c]	93,794.99[d]
12/31/11	9,000	10,317.45	1,317.45	95,112.44
12/31/12	9,000	10,462.37	1,462.37	96,574.81
12/31/13	9,000	10,623.23	1,623.23	98,198.04
12/31/14	9,000	10,801.96	1,801.96	100,000.00
	$45,000	$52,391.90	$7,391.90	

[a]$100,000 × .09 = $9,000
[b]$92,608.10 × .11 = $10,186.89
[c]$10,186.89 − $9,000 = $1,186.89
[d]$92,608.10 + $1,186.89 = $93,794.99

We use the amortization schedule illustrated above for note and bond transactions in Chapters 7 and 14.

PRESENT VALUE MEASUREMENT

LEARNING OBJECTIVE 9
Apply expected cash flows to present value measurement.

In the past, most accounting calculations of present value relied on the most likely cash flow amount. *Concepts Statement No. 7* introduces an **expected cash flow approach.**[6] It uses a range of cash flows and incorporates the probabilities of those cash flows to provide a more relevant measurement of present value.

To illustrate the expected cash flow model, assume that there is a 30% probability that future cash flows will be $100, a 50% probability that they will be $200, and a 20% probability that they will be $300. In this case, the expected cash flow would be $190 [($100 × 0.3) + ($200 × 0.5) + ($300 × 0.2)]. Traditional present value approaches would use the most likely estimate ($200). However, that estimate fails to consider the different probabilities of the possible cash flows.

[6]"Using Cash Flow Information and Present Value in Accounting Measurements," *Statement of Financial Accounting Concepts No. 7* (Norwalk, Conn.: FASB, 2000).

HOW LOW CAN THEY GO?

What do the numbers mean?

Management of the level of interest rates is an important policy tool of the Federal Reserve Bank and its chair, Ben Bernanke. Through a number of policy options, the Fed has the ability to move interest rates up or down, and these rate changes can affect the wealth of all market participants. For example, if the Fed wants to raise rates (because the overall economy is getting overheated), it can raise the *discount rate*, which is the rate banks pay to borrow money from the Fed. This rate increase will factor into the rates banks and other creditors use to lend money. As a result, companies will think twice about borrowing money to expand their businesses. The result will be a slowing economy. A rate cut does just the opposite: It makes borrowing cheaper, and it can help the economy expand as more companies borrow to expand their operations.

Keeping rates low had been the Fed's policy for much of the early years of this decade. The low rates did help keep the economy humming. But these same low rates may have also resulted in too much real estate lending and the growth of a real estate bubble, as the price of housing was fueled by cheaper low-interest mortgage loans. But, as the old saying goes, "What goes up, must come down." That is what real estate prices did, triggering massive loan write-offs, a seizing up of credit markets, and a slowing economy.

So just when a rate cut might help the economy, the Fed's rate-cutting toolbox is empty. As a result, the Fed began to explore other options, such as loan guarantees, to help banks lend more money and to spur the economy out of its recent funk.

Source: J. Lahart, "Fed Might Need to Reload," *Wall Street Journal* (March 27, 2008), p. A6.

Choosing an Appropriate Interest Rate

After determining expected cash flows, a company must then use the proper interest rate to discount the cash flows. The interest rate used for this purpose has three components:

THREE COMPONENTS OF INTEREST

1. PURE RATE OF INTEREST (2%–4%). This would be the amount a lender would charge if there were no possibilities of default and no expectation of inflation.
2. EXPECTED INFLATION RATE OF INTEREST (0%–?). Lenders recognize that in an inflationary economy, they are being paid back with less valuable dollars. As a result, they increase their interest rate to compensate for this loss in purchasing power. When inflationary expectations are high, interest rates are high.
3. CREDIT RISK RATE OF INTEREST (0%–5%). The government has little or no credit risk (i.e., risk of nonpayment) when it issues bonds. A business enterprise, however, depending upon its financial stability, profitability, etc., can have a low or a high credit risk.

The FASB takes the position that after computing the expected cash flows, a company should discount those cash flows by the risk-free rate of return. That rate is defined as **the pure rate of return plus the expected inflation rate**. The Board notes that the expected cash flow framework adjusts for credit risk because it incorporates the probability of receipt or payment into the computation of expected cash flows. Therefore, the rate used to discount the expected cash flows should consider only the pure rate of interest and the inflation rate.

Example of Expected Cash Flow

To illustrate, assume that Al's Appliance Outlet offers a 2-year warranty on all products sold. In 2012, Al's Appliance sold $250,000 of a particular type of clothes dryer. Al's Appliance entered into an agreement with Ralph's Repair to provide all warranty service on the dryers sold in 2012. To determine the warranty expense to record in 2012 and the amount of warranty liability to record on the December 31, 2012, balance sheet, Al's Appliance must measure the fair value of the agreement. Since there is not a ready market for these warranty contracts, Al's Appliance uses expected cash flow techniques to value the warranty obligation.

Based on prior warranty experience, Al's Appliance estimates the expected cash outflows associated with the dryers sold in 2012, as shown in Illustration 6-46.

ILLUSTRATION 6-46
Expected Cash Outflows—Warranties

	Cash Flow Estimate	×	Probability Assessment	=	Expected Cash Flow
2012	$3,800		20%		$ 760
	6,300		50%		3,150
	7,500		30%		2,250
			Total		$6,160
2013	$5,400		30%		$1,620
	7,200		50%		3,600
	8,400		20%		1,680
			Total		$6,900

Applying expected cash flow concepts to these data, Al's Appliance estimates warranty cash outflows of $6,160 in 2012 and $6,900 in 2013.

Illustration 6-47 shows the present value of these cash flows, assuming a risk-free rate of 5 percent and cash flows occurring at the end of the year.

ILLUSTRATION 6-47
Present Value of Cash Flows

Year	Expected Cash Flow	×	PV Factor, $i = 5\%$	=	Present Value
2012	$6,160		0.95238		$ 5,866.66
2013	6,900		0.90703		6,258.51
			Total		$12,125.17

KEY TERMS

annuity, *322*
annuity due, *322*
compound interest, *312*
deferred annuity, *332*
discounting, *317*
effective yield, *315*
effective-interest method, *335*
expected cash flow approach, *336*
face rate, *315*
future value, *316*
future value of an annuity, *322*
interest, *311*
nominal rate, *315*
ordinary annuity, *322*
present value, *316*
principal, *311*
risk-free rate of return, *337*

SUMMARY OF LEARNING OBJECTIVES

1 Identify accounting topics where the time value of money is relevant. Some of the applications of present value–based measurements to accounting topics are: (1) notes, (2) leases, (3) pensions and other postretirement benefits, (4) long-term assets, (5) sinking funds, (6) business combinations, (7) disclosures, and (8) installment contracts.

2 Distinguish between simple and compound interest. See items 1 and 2 in the Fundamental Concepts on page 339.

3 Use appropriate compound interest tables. In order to identify which of the five compound interest tables to use, determine whether you are solving for (1) the future value of a single sum, (2) the present value of a single sum, (3) the future value of a series of sums (an annuity), or (4) the present value of a series of sums (an annuity). In addition, when a series of sums (an annuity) is involved, identify whether these sums are received or paid (1) at the beginning of each period (annuity due) or (2) at the end of each period (ordinary annuity).

4 Identify variables fundamental to solving interest problems. The following four variables are fundamental to all compound interest problems: (1) *Rate of interest:* unless otherwise stated, an annual rate, adjusted to reflect the length of the compounding period if less than a year. (2) *Number of time periods:* the number of compounding periods (a period may be equal to or less than a year). (3) *Future value:* the value at a future date of a given sum or sums invested assuming compound interest. (4) *Present value:* the value now (present time) of a future sum or sums discounted assuming compound interest.

5 Solve future and present value of 1 problems. See items 5(a) and 6(a) in the Fundamental Concepts.

6 Solve future value of ordinary and annuity due problems. See item 5(b) in the Fundamental Concepts.

7 Solve present value of ordinary and annuity due problems. See item 6(b) in the Fundamental Concepts on page 340.

8 Solve present value problems related to deferred annuities and bonds. Deferred annuities are annuities in which rents begin after a specified number of periods. The future value of a deferred annuity is computed the same as the future value of an annuity not deferred. To find the present value of a deferred annuity, compute the present value of an ordinary annuity of 1 as if the rents had occurred for the entire period, and then subtract the present value of rents not received during the deferral period. The current market price of bonds combines the present values of the interest annuity and the principal amount.

9 Apply expected cash flows to present value measurement. The expected cash flow approach uses a range of cash flows and the probabilities of those cash flows to provide the most likely estimate of expected cash flows. The proper interest rate used to discount the cash flows is the risk-free rate of return.

FUNDAMENTAL CONCEPTS

1. SIMPLE INTEREST. Interest on principal only, regardless of interest that may have accrued in the past.

2. COMPOUND INTEREST. Interest accrues on the unpaid interest of past periods as well as on the principal.

3. RATE OF INTEREST. Interest is usually expressed as an annual rate, but when the compounding period is shorter than one year, the interest rate for the shorter period must be determined.

4. ANNUITY. A series of payments or receipts (called rents) that occur at equal intervals of time. Types of annuities:

(a) Ordinary Annuity. Each rent is payable (receivable) at the end of the period.

(b) Annuity Due. Each rent is payable (receivable) at the beginning of the period.

5. FUTURE VALUE. Value at a later date of a single sum that is invested at compound interest.

(a) Future Value of 1 (or value of a single sum). The future value of $1 (or a single given sum), *FV*, at the end of *n* periods at *i* compound interest rate (Table 6-1).

(b) Future Value of an Annuity. The future value of a series of rents invested at compound interest. In other words, the accumulated total that results from a series of equal deposits at regular intervals invested at compound interest. Both deposits and interest increase the accumulation.

(1) Future Value of an Ordinary Annuity. The future value on the date of the last rent (Table 6-3).

(2) Future Value of an Annuity Due. The future value one period after the date of the last rent. When an annuity due table is not available, use Table 6-3 with the following formula.

$$\text{Value of annuity due of 1 for } n \text{ rents} = (\text{Value of ordinary annuity for } n \text{ rents}) \times (1 + \text{interest rate})$$

6. PRESENT VALUE. The value at an earlier date (usually now) of a given future sum discounted at compound interest.

(a) Present Value of 1 (or present value of a single sum). The present value (worth) of $1 (or a given sum), due n periods hence, discounted at i compound interest (Table 6-2).

(b) Present Value of an Annuity. The present value (worth) of a series of rents discounted at compound interest. In other words, it is the sum when invested at compound interest that will permit a series of equal withdrawals at regular intervals.

(1) Present Value of an Ordinary Annuity. The value now of $1 to be received or paid at the end of each period (rents) for n periods, discounted at i compound interest (Table 6-4).

(2) Present Value of an Annuity Due. The value now of $1 to be received or paid at the beginning of each period (rents) for n periods, discounted at i compound interest (Table 6-5). To use Table 4 for an annuity due, apply this formula.

$$\text{Present value of annuity due of 1 for } n \text{ rents} = \text{(Present value of an ordinary annuity of } n \text{ rents)} \times (1 + \text{interest rate})$$

FASB CODIFICATION

FASB Codification References

[1] FASB ASC 820-10. [Predecessor literature: "Fair Value Measurement," *Statement of Financial Accounting Standards No. 157* (Norwalk, Conn.: FASB, September 2006).]

[2] FASB ASC 310-10. [Predecessor literature: "Accounting by Creditors for Impairment of a Loan," *FASB Statement No. 114* (Norwalk, Conn.: FASB, May 1993).]

[3] FASB ASC 840-30-30. [Predecessor literature: "Accounting for Leases," *FASB Statement No. 13* as amended and interpreted through May 1980 (Stamford, Conn.: FASB, 1980).]

[4] FASB ASC 715-30-35. [Predecessor literature: "Employers' Accounting for Pension Plans," *Statement of Financial Accounting Standards No. 87* (Stamford, Conn.: FASB, 1985).]

[5] FASB ASC 360-10-35. [Predecessor literature: "Accounting for the Impairment or Disposal of Long-Lived Assets," *Statement of Financial Accounting Standards No. 144* (Norwalk, Conn.: FASB, 2001).]

[6] FASB ASC 718-10-10. [Predecessor literature: "Accounting for Stock-Based Compensation," *Statement of Financial Accounting Standards No. 123* (Norwalk, Conn: FASB, 1995); and "Share-Based Payment," *Statement of Financial Accounting Standard No. 123(R)* (Norwalk, Conn: FASB, 2004).]

Exercises

If your school has a subscription to the FASB Codification, go to *http://aaahq.org/asclogin.cfm* to log in and prepare responses to the following. Provide Codification references for your responses.

CE6-1 Access the glossary ("Master Glossary") to answer the following.

(a) What is the definition of present value?
(b) Briefly describe the term "discount rate adjustment technique."
(c) Identify the other codification references to present value.

CE6-2 In addition to the list of topics identified in footnote 1 on page 310, identify three areas in which present value is used as a measurement basis. Briefly describe one topic related to:

(a) Assets. (b) Liabilities. (c) Revenues or expenses.

CE6-3 What is interest cost? Briefly describe imputation of interest.

An additional Codification case can be found in the Using Your Judgment section, on page 353.

Be sure to check the book's companion website for a Review and Analysis Exercise, with solution.

Questions, Brief Exercises, Exercises, Problems, and many more resources are available for practice in WileyPLUS.

QUESTIONS

1. What is the time value of money? Why should accountants have an understanding of compound interest, annuities, and present value concepts?
2. Identify three situations in which accounting measures are based on present values. Do these present value applications involve single sums or annuities, or both single sums and annuities? Explain.
3. What is the nature of interest? Distinguish between "simple interest" and "compound interest."
4. What are the components of an interest rate? Why is it important for accountants to understand these components?
5. Presented below are a number of values taken from compound interest tables involving the same number of periods and the same rate of interest. Indicate what each of these four values represents.

   (a) 6.71008. (c) .46319.

   (b) 2.15892. (d) 14.48656.
6. Jose Oliva is considering two investment options for a $1,500 gift he received for graduation. Both investments have 8% annual interest rates. One offers quarterly compounding; the other compounds on a semiannual basis. Which investment should he choose? Why?
7. Regina Henry deposited $20,000 in a money market certificate that provides interest of 10% compounded quarterly if the amount is maintained for 3 years. How much will Regina Henry have at the end of 3 years?
8. Will Smith will receive $80,000 on December 31, 2017 (5 years from now), from a trust fund established by his father. Assuming the appropriate interest rate for discounting is 12% (compounded semiannually), what is the present value of this amount today?
9. What are the primary characteristics of an annuity? Differentiate between an "ordinary annuity" and an "annuity due."
10. Kehoe, Inc. owes $40,000 to Ritter Company. How much would Kehoe have to pay each year if the debt is retired through four equal payments (made at the end of the year), given an interest rate on the debt of 12%? (Round to two decimal places.)
11. The Kellys are planning for a retirement home. They estimate they will need $200,000 4 years from now to purchase this home. Assuming an interest rate of 10%, what amount must be deposited at the end of each of the 4 years to fund the home price? (Round to two decimal places.)
12. Assume the same situation as in Question 11, except that the four equal amounts are deposited at the beginning of the period rather than at the end. In this case, what amount must be deposited at the beginning of each period? (Round to two decimals.)
13. Explain how the future value of an ordinary annuity interest table is converted to the future value of an annuity due interest table.
14. Explain how the present value of an ordinary annuity interest table is converted to the present value of an annuity due interest table.
15. In a book named *Treasure*, the reader has to figure out where a 2.2 pound, 24 kt gold horse has been buried. If the horse is found, a prize of $25,000 a year for 20 years is provided. The actual cost to the publisher to purchase an annuity to pay for the prize is $245,000. What interest rate (to the nearest percent) was used to determine the amount of the annuity? (Assume end-of-year payments.)
16. Alexander Enterprises leases property to Hamilton, Inc. Because Hamilton, Inc. is experiencing financial difficulty, Alexander agrees to receive five rents of $20,000 at the end of each year, with the rents deferred 3 years. What is the present value of the five rents discounted at 12%?
17. Answer the following questions.

   (a) On May 1, 2012, Goldberg Company sold some machinery to Newlin Company on an installment contract basis. The contract required five equal annual payments, with the first payment due on May 1, 2012. What present value concept is appropriate for this situation?

   (b) On June 1, 2012, Seymour Inc. purchased a new machine that it does not have to pay for until May 1, 2014. The total payment on May 1, 2014, will include both principal and interest. Assuming interest at a 12% rate, the cost of the machine would be the total payment multiplied by what time value of money concept?

   (c) Costner Inc. wishes to know how much money it will have available in 5 years if five equal amounts of $35,000 are invested, with the first amount invested immediately. What interest table is appropriate for this situation?

(d) Jane Hoffman invests in a "jumbo" $200,000, 3-year certificate of deposit at First Wisconsin Bank. What table would be used to determine the amount accumulated at the end of 3 years?

18. Recently, Glenda Estes was interested in purchasing a Honda Acura. The salesperson indicated that the price of the car was either $27,600 cash or $6,900 at the end of each of 5 years. Compute the effective-interest rate to the nearest percent that Glenda would pay if she chooses to make the five annual payments.

19. Recently, property/casualty insurance companies have been criticized because they reserve for the total loss as much as 5 years before it may happen. The IRS has joined the debate because it says the full reserve is unfair from a taxation viewpoint. What do you believe is the IRS position?

BRIEF EXERCISES

(Unless instructed otherwise, round answers to the nearest dollar.)

5 **BE6-1** Chris Spear invested $15,000 today in a fund that earns 8% compounded annually. To what amount will the investment grow in 3 years? To what amount would the investment grow in 3 years if the fund earns 8% annual interest compounded semiannually?

5 **BE6-2** Tony Bautista needs $25,000 in 4 years. What amount must he invest today if his investment earns 12% compounded annually? What amount must he invest if his investment earns 12% annual interest compounded quarterly?

5 **BE6-3** Candice Willis will invest $30,000 today. She needs $150,000 in 21 years. What annual interest rate must she earn?

5 **BE6-4** Bo Newman will invest $10,000 today in a fund that earns 5% annual interest. How many years will it take for the fund to grow to $17,100?

6 **BE6-5** Sally Medavoy will invest $8,000 a year for 20 years in a fund that will earn 12% annual interest. If the first payment into the fund occurs today, what amount will be in the fund in 20 years? If the first payment occurs at year-end, what amount will be in the fund in 20 years?

6 **BE6-6** Steve Madison needs $250,000 in 10 years. How much must he invest at the end of each year, at 11% interest, to meet his needs?

5 **BE6-7** John Fillmore's lifelong dream is to own his own fishing boat to use in his retirement. John has recently come into an inheritance of $400,000. He estimates that the boat he wants will cost $300,000 when he retires in 5 years. How much of his inheritance must he invest at an annual rate of 12% (compounded annually) to buy the boat at retirement?

5 **BE6-8** Refer to the data in BE6-7. Assuming quarterly compounding of amounts invested at 12%, how much of John Fillmore's inheritance must be invested to have enough at retirement to buy the boat?

6 **BE6-9** Morgan Freeman is investing $16,380 at the end of each year in a fund that earns 10% interest. In how many years will the fund be at $100,000?

7 **BE6-10** Henry Quincy wants to withdraw $30,000 each year for 10 years from a fund that earns 8% interest. How much must he invest today if the first withdrawal is at year-end? How much must he invest today if the first withdrawal takes place immediately?

7 **BE6-11** Leon Tyler's VISA balance is $793.15. He may pay it off in 12 equal end-of-month payments of $75 each. What interest rate is Leon paying?

7 **BE6-12** Maria Alvarez is investing $300,000 in a fund that earns 8% interest compounded annually. What equal amounts can Maria withdraw at the end of each of the next 20 years?

6 **BE6-13** Adams Inc. will deposit $30,000 in a 12% fund at the end of each year for 8 years beginning December 31, 2012. What amount will be in the fund immediately after the last deposit?

7 **BE6-14** Amy Monroe wants to create a fund today that will enable her to withdraw $25,000 per year for 8 years, with the first withdrawal to take place 5 years from today. If the fund earns 8% interest, how much must Amy invest today?

8 **BE6-15** Clancey Inc. issues $2,000,000 of 7% bonds due in 10 years with interest payable at year-end. The current market rate of interest for bonds of similar risk is 8%. What amount will Clancey receive when it issues the bonds?

7 **BE6-16** Zach Taylor is settling a $20,000 loan due today by making 6 equal annual payments of $4,727.53. Determine the interest rate on this loan, if the payments begin one year after the loan is signed.

7 **BE6-17** Consider the loan in BE6-16. What payments must Zach Taylor make to settle the loan at the same interest rate but with the 6 payments beginning on the day the loan is signed?

EXERCISES

(Unless instructed otherwise, round answers to the nearest dollar. Interest rates are per annum unless otherwise indicated.)

3 **E6-1 (Using Interest Tables)** For each of the following cases, indicate (a) to what rate columns, and (b) to what number of periods you would refer in looking up the interest factor.

1. In a future value of 1 table:

Annual Rate	Number of Years Invested	Compounded
a. 9%	9	Annually
b. 8%	5	Quarterly
c. 10%	15	Semiannually

2. In a present value of an annuity of 1 table:

Annual Rate	Number of Years Involved	Number of Rents Involved	Frequency of Rents
a. 9%	25	25	Annually
b. 8%	15	30	Semiannually
c. 12%	7	28	Quarterly

2 5 **E6-2 (Simple and Compound Interest Computations)** Lyle O'Keefe invests $30,000 at 8% annual interest, leaving the money invested without withdrawing any of the interest for 8 years. At the end of the 8 years, Lyle withdrew the accumulated amount of money.

Instructions

(a) Compute the amount Lyle would withdraw assuming the investment earns simple interest.
(b) Compute the amount Lyle would withdraw assuming the investment earns interest compounded annually.
(c) Compute the amount Lyle would withdraw assuming the investment earns interest compounded semiannually.

5 6 7 **E6-3 (Computation of Future Values and Present Values)** Using the appropriate interest table, answer each of the following questions. (Each case is independent of the others.)

(a) What is the future value of $9,000 at the end of 5 periods at 8% compounded interest?
(b) What is the present value of $9,000 due 8 periods hence, discounted at 11%?
(c) What is the future value of 15 periodic payments of $9,000 each made at the end of each period and compounded at 10%?
(d) What is the present value of $9,000 to be received at the end of each of 20 periods, discounted at 5% compound interest?

6 7 **E6-4 (Computation of Future Values and Present Values)** Using the appropriate interest table, answer the following questions. (Each case is independent of the others).

(a) What is the future value of 20 periodic payments of $5,000 each made at the beginning of each period and compounded at 8%?
(b) What is the present value of $2,500 to be received at the beginning of each of 30 periods, discounted at 10% compound interest?
(c) What is the future value of 15 deposits of $2,000 each made at the beginning of each period and compounded at 10%? (Future value as of the end of the fifteenth period.)
(d) What is the present value of six receipts of $3,000 each received at the beginning of each period, discounted at 9% compounded interest?

7 **E6-5 (Computation of Present Value)** Using the appropriate interest table, compute the present values of the periodic amounts, shown on page 344, due at the end of the designated periods.

(a) $50,000 receivable at the end of each period for 8 periods compounded at 12%.
(b) $50,000 payments to be made at the end of each period for 16 periods at 9%.
(c) $50,000 payable at the end of the seventh, eighth, ninth, and tenth periods at 12%.

5 6 **E6-6 (Future Value and Present Value Problems)** Presented below are three unrelated situations.

7 (a) Ron Stein Company recently signed a lease for a new office building, for a lease period of 10 years. Under the lease agreement, a security deposit of $12,000 is made, with the deposit to be returned at the expiration of the lease, with interest compounded at 10% per year. What amount will the company receive at the time the lease expires?
(b) Kate Greenway Corporation, having recently issued a $20 million, 15-year bond issue, is committed to make annual sinking fund deposits of $620,000. The deposits are made on the last day of each year and yield a return of 10%. Will the fund at the end of 15 years be sufficient to retire the bonds? If not, what will the deficiency be?
(c) Under the terms of his salary agreement, president Juan Rivera has an option of receiving either an immediate bonus of $40,000, or a deferred bonus of $75,000 payable in 10 years. Ignoring tax considerations, and assuming a relevant interest rate of 8%, which form of settlement should Rivera accept?

8 **E6-7 (Computation of Bond Prices)** What would you pay for a $100,000 debenture bond that matures in 15 years and pays $10,000 a year in interest if you wanted to earn a yield of:

(a) 8%? (b) 10%? (c) 12%?

8 **E6-8 (Computations for a Retirement Fund)** Stephen Bosworth, a super salesman contemplating retirement on his fifty-fifth birthday, decides to create a fund on an 8% basis that will enable him to withdraw $25,000 per year on June 30, beginning in 2016 and continuing through 2019. To develop this fund, Stephen intends to make equal contributions on June 30 of each of the years 2012–2015.

Instructions

(a) How much must the balance of the fund equal on June 30, 2015, in order for Stephen Bosworth to satisfy his objective?
(b) What are each of Stephen's contributions to the fund?

5 **E6-9 (Unknown Rate)** Kross Company purchased a machine at a price of $100,000 by signing a note payable, which requires a single payment of $118,810 in 2 years. Assuming annual compounding of interest, what rate of interest is being paid on the loan?

5 **E6-10 (Unknown Periods and Unknown Interest Rate)** Consider the following independent situations.

(a) Mark Yoders wishes to become a millionaire. His money market fund has a balance of $148,644 and has a guaranteed interest rate of 10%. How many years must Mark leave that balance in the fund in order to get his desired $1,000,000?
(b) Assume that Elvira Lehman desires to accumulate $1 million in 15 years using her money market fund balance of $239,392. At what interest rate must Elvira's investment compound annually?

7 **E6-11 (Evaluation of Purchase Options)** Amos Excavating Inc. is purchasing a bulldozer. The equipment has a price of $100,000. The manufacturer has offered a payment plan that would allow Amos to make 10 equal annual payments of $15,582, with the first payment due one year after the purchase.

Instructions

(a) How much total interest will Amos pay on this payment plan?
(b) Amos could borrow $100,000 from its bank to finance the purchase at an annual rate of 8%. Should Amos borrow from the bank or use the manufacturer's payment plan to pay for the equipment?

7 **E6-12 (Analysis of Alternatives)** Brubaker Inc., a manufacturer of high-sugar, low-sodium, low-cholesterol frozen dinners, would like to increase its market share in the Sunbelt. In order to do so, Brubaker has decided to locate a new factory in the Panama City, Florida, area. Brubaker will either buy or lease a site depending upon which is more advantageous. The site location committee has narrowed down the available sites to the following three buildings.

Building A: Purchase for a cash price of $610,000, useful life 25 years.
Building B: Lease for 25 years with annual lease payments of $70,000 being made at the beginning of the year.
Building C: Purchase for $650,000 cash. This building is larger than needed; however, the excess space can be sublet for 25 years at a net annual rental of $6,000. Rental payments will be received at the end of each year. Brubaker Inc. has no aversion to being a landlord.

Instructions

In which building would you recommend that Brubaker Inc. locate, assuming a 12% cost of funds?

8 **E6-13 (Computation of Bond Liability)** Messier Inc. manufactures cycling equipment. Recently, the vice president of operations of the company has requested construction of a new plant to meet the increasing demand for the company's bikes. After a careful evaluation of the request, the board of directors has decided to raise funds for the new plant by issuing $3,000,000 of 11% term corporate bonds on March 1, 2012, due on March 1, 2027, with interest payable each March 1 and September 1. At the time of issuance, the market interest rate for similar financial instruments is 10%.

Instructions

As the controller of the company, determine the selling price of the bonds.

8 **E6-14 (Computation of Pension Liability)** Calder, Inc. is a furniture manufacturing company with 50 employees. Recently, after a long negotiation with the local labor union, the company decided to initiate a pension plan as a part of its compensation plan. The plan will start on January 1, 2012. Each employee covered by the plan is entitled to a pension payment each year after retirement. As required by accounting standards, the controller of the company needs to report the pension obligation (liability). On the basis of a discussion with the supervisor of the Personnel Department and an actuary from an insurance company, the controller develops the following information related to the pension plan.

Average length of time to retirement	15 years
Expected life duration after retirement	10 years
Total pension payment expected each year after retirement for all employees. Payment made at the end of the year.	$800,000 per year

The interest rate to be used is 8%.

Instructions

On the basis of the information above, determine the present value of the pension liability.

5 6 **E6-15 (Investment Decision)** Derek Lee just received a signing bonus of $1,000,000. His plan is to invest this payment in a fund that will earn 6%, compounded annually.

Instructions

(a) If Lee plans to establish the DL Foundation once the fund grows to $1,898,000, how many years until he can establish the foundation?

(b) Instead of investing the entire $1,000,000, Lee invests $300,000 today and plans to make 9 equal annual investments into the fund beginning one year from today. What amount should the payments be if Lee plans to establish the $1,898,000 foundation at the end of 9 years?

6 **E6-16 (Retirement of Debt)** Alex Hardaway borrowed $90,000 on March 1, 2010. This amount plus accrued interest at 12% compounded semiannually is to be repaid March 1, 2020. To retire this debt, Alex plans to contribute to a debt retirement fund five equal amounts starting on March 1, 2015, and for the next 4 years. The fund is expected to earn 10% per annum.

Instructions

How much must be contributed each year by Alex Hardaway to provide a fund sufficient to retire the debt on March 1, 2020?

7 **E6-17 (Computation of Amount of Rentals)** Your client, Wyeth Leasing Company, is preparing a contract to lease a machine to Souvenirs Corporation for a period of 25 years. Wyeth has an investment cost of $421,087 in the machine, which has a useful life of 25 years and no salvage value at the end of that time. Your client is interested in earning an 11% return on its investment and has agreed to accept 25 equal rental payments at the end of each of the next 25 years.

Instructions

You are requested to provide Wyeth with the amount of each of the 25 rental payments that will yield an 11% return on investment.

7 **E6-18 (Least Costly Payoff)** Assume that Sonic Foundry Corporation has a contractual debt outstanding. Sonic has available two means of settlement: It can either make immediate payment of $3,500,000, or it can make annual payments of $400,000 for 15 years, each payment due on the last day of the year.

Instructions

Which method of payment do you recommend, assuming an expected effective-interest rate of 8% during the future period?

7 **E6-19 (Least Costly Payoff)** Assuming the same facts as those in E6-18 except that the payments must begin now and be made on the first day of each of the 15 years, what payment method would you recommend?

9 **E6-20 (Expected Cash Flows)** For each of the following, determine the expected cash flows.

	Cash Flow Estimate	Probability Assessment
(a)	$ 4,800	20%
	6,300	50%
	7,500	30%
(b)	$ 5,400	30%
	7,200	50%
	8,400	20%
(c)	$(1,000)	10%
	3,000	80%
	5,000	10%

9 **E6-21 (Expected Cash Flows and Present Value)** Keith Bowie is trying to determine the amount to set aside so that he will have enough money on hand in 2 years to overhaul the engine on his vintage used car. While there is some uncertainty about the cost of engine overhauls in 2 years, by conducting some research online, Keith has developed the following estimates.

Engine Overhaul Estimated Cash Outflow	Probability Assessment
$200	10%
450	30%
600	50%
750	10%

Instructions

How much should Keith Bowie deposit today in an account earning 6%, compounded annually, so that he will have enough money on hand in 2 years to pay for the overhaul?

9 **E6-22 (Fair Value Estimate)** Killroy Company owns a trade name that was purchased in an acquisition of McClellan Company. The trade name has a book value of $3,500,000, but according to GAAP, it is assessed for impairment on an annual basis. To perform this impairment test, Killroy must estimate the fair value of the trade name. (You will learn more about intangible asset impairments in Chapter 12.) It has developed the following cash flow estimates related to the trade name based on internal information. Each cash flow estimate reflects Killroy's estimate of annual cash flows over the next 8 years. The trade name is assumed to have no residual value after the 8 years. (Assume the cash flows occur at the end of each year.)

Cash Flow Estimate	Probability Assessment
$380,000	20%
630,000	50%
750,000	30%

Instructions

(a) What is the estimated fair value of the trade name? Killroy determines that the appropriate discount rate for this estimation is 8%. Round calculations to the nearest dollar.

(b) Is the estimate developed for part (a) a Level 1 or Level 3 fair value estimate? Explain.

See the book's companion website, www.wiley.com/college/kieso, for a set of B Exercises.

PROBLEMS

(Unless instructed otherwise, round answers to the nearest dollar. Interest rates are per annum unless otherwise indicated.)

P6-1 (Various Time Value Situations) Answer each of these unrelated questions.

(a) On January 1, 2012, Fishbone Corporation sold a building that cost $250,000 and that had accumulated depreciation of $100,000 on the date of sale. Fishbone received as consideration a $240,000 non-interest-bearing note due on January 1, 2015. There was no established exchange price for the building, and the note had no ready market. The prevailing rate of interest for a note of this type on January 1, 2012, was 9%. At what amount should the gain from the sale of the building be reported?

(b) On January 1, 2012, Fishbone Corporation purchased 300 of the $1,000 face value, 9%, 10-year bonds of Walters Inc. The bonds mature on January 1, 2022, and pay interest annually beginning January 1, 2013. Fishbone purchased the bonds to yield 11%. How much did Fishbone pay for the bonds?

(c) Fishbone Corporation bought a new machine and agreed to pay for it in equal annual installments of $4,000 at the end of each of the next 10 years. Assuming that a prevailing interest rate of 8% applies to this contract, how much should Fishbone record as the cost of the machine?

(d) Fishbone Corporation purchased a special tractor on December 31, 2012. The purchase agreement stipulated that Fishbone should pay $20,000 at the time of purchase and $5,000 at the end of each of the next 8 years. The tractor should be recorded on December 31, 2012, at what amount, assuming an appropriate interest rate of 12%?

(e) Fishbone Corporation wants to withdraw $120,000 (including principal) from an investment fund at the end of each year for 9 years. What should be the required initial investment at the beginning of the first year if the fund earns 11%?

P6-2 (Various Time Value Situations) Using the appropriate interest table, provide the solution to each of the following four questions by computing the unknowns.

(a) What is the amount of the payments that Ned Winslow must make at the end of each of 8 years to accumulate a fund of $90,000 by the end of the eighth year, if the fund earns 8% interest, compounded annually?

(b) Robert Hitchcock is 40 years old today and he wishes to accumulate $500,000 by his sixty-fifth birthday so he can retire to his summer place on Lake Hopatcong. He wishes to accumulate this amount by making equal deposits on his fortieth through his sixty-fourth birthdays. What annual deposit must Robert make if the fund will earn 12% interest compounded annually?

(c) Diane Ross has $20,000 to invest today at 9% to pay a debt of $47,347. How many years will it take her to accumulate enough to liquidate the debt?

(d) Cindy Houston has a $27,600 debt that she wishes to repay 4 years from today; she has $19,553 that she intends to invest for the 4 years. What rate of interest will she need to earn annually in order to accumulate enough to pay the debt?

P6-3 (Analysis of Alternatives) Assume that **Wal-Mart Stores, Inc.** has decided to surface and maintain for 10 years a vacant lot next to one of its stores to serve as a parking lot for customers. Management is considering the following bids involving two different qualities of surfacing for a parking area of 12,000 square yards.

Bid A: A surface that costs $5.75 per square yard to install. This surface will have to be replaced at the end of 5 years. The annual maintenance cost on this surface is estimated at 25 cents per square yard for each year except the last year of its service. The replacement surface will be similar to the initial surface.

Bid B: A surface that costs $10.50 per square yard to install. This surface has a probable useful life of 10 years and will require annual maintenance in each year except the last year, at an estimated cost of 9 cents per square yard.

Instructions

Prepare computations showing which bid should be accepted by Wal-Mart. You may assume that the cost of capital is 9%, that the annual maintenance expenditures are incurred at the end of each year, and that prices are not expected to change during the next 10 years.

7 **P6-4 (Evaluating Payment Alternatives)** Howie Long has just learned he has won a $500,000 prize in the lottery. The lottery has given him two options for receiving the payments: (1) If Howie takes all the money today, the state and federal governments will deduct taxes at a rate of 46% immediately. (2) Alternatively, the lottery offers Howie a payout of 20 equal payments of $36,000 with the first payment occurring when Howie turns in the winning ticket. Howie will be taxed on each of these payments at a rate of 25%.

Instructions

Assuming Howie can earn an 8% rate of return (compounded annually) on any money invested during this period, which pay-out option should he choose?

5 7 **P6-5 (Analysis of Alternatives)** Julia Baker died, leaving to her husband Brent an insurance policy contract that provides that the beneficiary (Brent) can choose any one of the following four options.

(a) $55,000 immediate cash.

(b) $4,000 every 3 months payable at the end of each quarter for 5 years.

(c) $18,000 immediate cash and $1,800 every 3 months for 10 years, payable at the beginning of each 3-month period.

(d) $4,000 every 3 months for 3 years and $1,500 each quarter for the following 25 quarters, all payments payable at the end of each quarter.

Instructions
If money is worth 2½% per quarter, compounded quarterly, which option would you recommend that Brent exercise?

8 **P6-6 (Purchase Price of a Business)** During the past year, Stacy McGill planted a new vineyard on 150 acres of land that she leases for $30,000 a year. She has asked you, as her accountant, to assist her in determining the value of her vineyard operation.

The vineyard will bear no grapes for the first 5 years (1–5). In the next 5 years (6–10), Stacy estimates that the vines will bear grapes that can be sold for $60,000 each year. For the next 20 years (11–30), she expects the harvest will provide annual revenues of $110,000. But during the last 10 years (31–40) of the vineyard's life, she estimates that revenues will decline to $80,000 per year.

During the first 5 years, the annual cost of pruning, fertilizing, and caring for the vineyard is estimated at $9,000; during the years of production, 6–40, these costs will rise to $12,000 per year. The relevant market rate of interest for the entire period is 12%. Assume that all receipts and payments are made at the end of each year.

Instructions
Dick Button has offered to buy Stacy's vineyard business by assuming the 40-year lease. On the basis of the current value of the business, what is the minimum price Stacy should accept?

5 6 7 **P6-7 (Time Value Concepts Applied to Solve Business Problems)** Answer the following questions related to Dubois Inc.

(a) Dubois Inc. has $600,000 to invest. The company is trying to decide between two alternative uses of the funds. One alternative provides $80,000 at the end of each year for 12 years, and the other is to receive a single lump-sum payment of $1,900,000 at the end of the 12 years. Which alternative should Dubois select? Assume the interest rate is constant over the entire investment.

(b) Dubois Inc. has completed the purchase of new Dell computers. The fair value of the equipment is $824,150. The purchase agreement specifies an immediate down payment of $200,000 and semiannual payments of $76,952 beginning at the end of 6 months for 5 years. What is the interest rate, to the nearest percent, used in discounting this purchase transaction?

(c) Dubois Inc. loans money to John Kruk Corporation in the amount of $800,000. Dubois accepts an 8% note due in 7 years with interest payable semiannually. After 2 years (and receipt of interest for 2 years), Dubois needs money and therefore sells the note to Chicago National Bank, which demands interest on the note of 10% compounded semiannually. What is the amount Dubois will receive on the sale of the note?

(d) Dubois Inc. wishes to accumulate $1,300,000 by December 31, 2022, to retire bonds outstanding. The company deposits $200,000 on December 31, 2012, which will earn interest at 10% compounded quarterly, to help in the retirement of this debt. In addition, the company wants to know how much should be deposited at the end of each quarter for 10 years to ensure that $1,300,000 is available at the end of 2022. (The quarterly deposits will also earn at a rate of 10%, compounded quarterly.) (Round to even dollars.)

7 **P6-8 (Analysis of Alternatives)** Ellison Inc., a manufacturer of steel school lockers, plans to purchase a new punch press for use in its manufacturing process. After contacting the appropriate vendors, the purchasing department received differing terms and options from each vendor. The Engineering Department has determined that each vendor's punch press is substantially identical and each has a useful life of 20 years. In addition, Engineering has estimated that required year-end maintenance costs will be $1,000 per year for the first 5 years, $2,000 per year for the next 10 years, and $3,000 per year for the last 5 years. Following is each vendor's sale package.

Vendor A: $55,000 cash at time of delivery and 10 year-end payments of $18,000 each. Vendor A offers all its customers the right to purchase at the time of sale a separate 20-year maintenance service contract, under which Vendor A will perform all year-end maintenance at a one-time initial cost of $10,000.

Vendor B: Forty semiannual payments of $9,500 each, with the first installment due upon delivery. Vendor B will perform all year-end maintenance for the next 20 years at no extra charge.

Vendor C: Full cash price of $150,000 will be due upon delivery.

Instructions
Assuming that both Vendors A and B will be able to perform the required year-end maintenance, that Ellison's cost of funds is 10%, and the machine will be purchased on January 1, from which vendor should the press be purchased?

5 7 **P6-9 (Analysis of Business Problems)** James Kirk is a financial executive with McDowell Enterprises. Although James Kirk has not had any formal training in finance or accounting, he has a "good sense" for

numbers and has helped the company grow from a very small company ($500,000 sales) to a large operation ($45 million in sales). With the business growing steadily, however, the company needs to make a number of difficult financial decisions in which James Kirk feels a little "over his head." He therefore has decided to hire a new employee with "numbers" expertise to help him. As a basis for determining whom to employ, he has decided to ask each prospective employee to prepare answers to questions relating to the following situations he has encountered recently. Here are the questions.

(a) In 2011, McDowell Enterprises negotiated and closed a long-term lease contract for newly constructed truck terminals and freight storage facilities. The buildings were constructed on land owned by the company. On January 1, 2012, McDowell took possession of the leased property. The 20-year lease is effective for the period January 1, 2012, through December 31, 2031. Advance rental payments of $800,000 are payable to the lessor (owner of facilities) on January 1 of each of the first 10 years of the lease term. Advance payments of $400,000 are due on January 1 for each of the last 10 years of the lease term. McDowell has an option to purchase all the leased facilities for $1 on December 31, 2031. At the time the lease was negotiated, the fair value of the truck terminals and freight storage facilities was approximately $7,200,000. If the company had borrowed the money to purchase the facilities, it would have had to pay 10% interest. Should the company have purchased rather than leased the facilities?

(b) Last year the company exchanged a piece of land for a non-interest-bearing note. The note is to be paid at the rate of $15,000 per year for 9 years, beginning one year from the date of disposal of the land. An appropriate rate of interest for the note was 11%. At the time the land was originally purchased, it cost $90,000. What is the fair value of the note?

(c) The company has always followed the policy to take any cash discounts on goods purchased. Recently, the company purchased a large amount of raw materials at a price of $800,000 with terms 1/10, n/30 on which it took the discount. McDowell has recently estimated its cost of funds at 10%. Should McDowell continue this policy of always taking the cash discount?

5 7 **P6-10 (Analysis of Lease vs. Purchase)** Dunn Inc. owns and operates a number of hardware stores in the New England region. Recently, the company has decided to locate another store in a rapidly growing area of Maryland. The company is trying to decide whether to purchase or lease the building and related facilities.

Purchase: The company can purchase the site, construct the building, and purchase all store fixtures. The cost would be $1,850,000. An immediate down payment of $400,000 is required, and the remaining $1,450,000 would be paid off over 5 years at $350,000 per year (including interest payments made at end of year). The property is expected to have a useful life of 12 years, and then it will be sold for $500,000. As the owner of the property, the company will have the following out-of-pocket expenses each period.

Property taxes (to be paid at the end of each year)	$40,000
Insurance (to be paid at the beginning of each year)	27,000
Other (primarily maintenance which occurs at the end of each year)	16,000
	$83,000

Lease: First National Bank has agreed to purchase the site, construct the building, and install the appropriate fixtures for Dunn Inc. if Dunn will lease the completed facility for 12 years. The annual costs for the lease would be $270,000. Dunn would have no responsibility related to the facility over the 12 years. The terms of the lease are that Dunn would be required to make 12 annual payments (the first payment to be made at the time the store opens and then each following year). In addition, a deposit of $100,000 is required when the store is opened. This deposit will be returned at the end of the twelfth year, assuming no unusual damage to the building structure or fixtures.

Instructions

Which of the two approaches should Dunn Inc. follow? (Currently, the cost of funds for Dunn Inc. is 10%.)

8 **P6-11 (Pension Funding)** You have been hired as a benefit consultant by Jean Honore, the owner of Attic Angels. She wants to establish a retirement plan for herself and her three employees. Jean has provided the following information: The retirement plan is to be based upon annual salary for the last year before retirement and is to provide 50% of Jean's last-year annual salary and 40% of the last-year annual salary for each employee. The plan will make annual payments at the beginning of each year for 20 years from the date of retirement. Jean wishes to fund the plan by making 15 annual deposits beginning January 1, 2012. Invested funds will earn 12% compounded annually. Information about plan participants as of January 1, 2012, is as follows.

Jean Honore, owner: Current annual salary of $48,000; estimated retirement date January 1, 2037.

Colin Davis, flower arranger: Current annual salary of $36,000; estimated retirement date January 1, 2042.

Anita Baker, sales clerk: Current annual salary of $18,000; estimated retirement date January 1, 2032.

Gavin Bryars, part-time bookkeeper: Current annual salary of $15,000; estimated retirement date January 1, 2027.

In the past, Jean has given herself and each employee a year-end salary increase of 4%. Jean plans to continue this policy in the future.

Instructions

(a) Based upon the above information, what will be the annual retirement benefit for each plan participant? (Round to the nearest dollar.) (*Hint:* Jean will receive raises for 24 years.)

(b) What amount must be on deposit at the end of 15 years to ensure that all benefits will be paid? (Round to the nearest dollar.)

(c) What is the amount of each annual deposit Jean must make to the retirement plan?

8 **P6-12 (Pension Funding)** Craig Brokaw, newly appointed controller of STL, is considering ways to reduce his company's expenditures on annual pension costs. One way to do this is to switch STL's pension fund assets from First Security to NET Life. STL is a very well-respected computer manufacturer that recently has experienced a sharp decline in its financial performance for the first time in its 25-year history. Despite financial problems, STL still is committed to providing its employees with good pension and postretirement health benefits.

Under its present plan with First Security, STL is obligated to pay $43 million to meet the expected value of future pension benefits that are payable to employees as an annuity upon their retirement from the company. On the other hand, NET Life requires STL to pay only $35 million for identical future pension benefits. First Security is one of the oldest and most reputable insurance companies in North America. NET Life has a much weaker reputation in the insurance industry. In pondering the significant difference in annual pension costs, Brokaw asks himself, "Is this too good to be true?"

Instructions

Answer the following questions.

(a) Why might NET Life's pension cost requirement be $8 million less than First Security's requirement for the same future value?

(b) What ethical issues should Craig Brokaw consider before switching STL's pension fund assets?

(c) Who are the stakeholders that could be affected by Brokaw's decision?

7 9 **P6-13 (Expected Cash Flows and Present Value)** Danny's Lawn Equipment sells high-quality lawn mowers and offers a 3-year warranty on all new lawn mowers sold. In 2012, Danny sold $300,000 of new specialty mowers for golf greens for which Danny's service department does not have the equipment to do the service. Danny has entered into an agreement with Mower Mavens to provide all warranty service on the special mowers sold in 2012. Danny wishes to measure the fair value of the agreement to determine the warranty liability for sales made in 2012. The controller for Danny's Lawn Equipment estimates the following expected warranty cash outflows associated with the mowers sold in 2012.

Year	Cash Flow Estimate	Probability Assessment
2013	$2,500	20%
	4,000	60%
	5,000	20%
2014	$3,000	30%
	5,000	50%
	6,000	20%
2015	$4,000	30%
	6,000	40%
	7,000	30%

Instructions

Using expected cash flow and present value techniques, determine the value of the warranty liability for the 2012 sales. Use an annual discount rate of 5%. Assume all cash flows occur at the end of the year.

7 9 **P6-14 (Expected Cash Flows and Present Value)** At the end of 2012, Sawyer Company is conducting an impairment test and needs to develop a fair value estimate for machinery used in its manufacturing operations. Given the nature of Sawyer's production process, the equipment is for special use. (No secondhand market values are available.) The equipment will be obsolete in 2 years, and Sawyer's accountants have developed the following cash flow information for the equipment.

Year	Net Cash Flow Estimate	Probability Assessment
2013	$6,000	40%
	9,000	60%
2014	$ (500)	20%
	2,000	60%
	4,000	20%
	Scrap value	
2014	$ 500	50%
	900	50%

Instructions

Using expected cash flow and present value techniques, determine the fair value of the machinery at the end of 2012. Use a 6% discount rate. Assume all cash flows occur at the end of the year.

9 **P6-15 (Fair Value Estimate)** Murphy Mining Company recently purchased a quartz mine that it intends to work for the next 10 years. According to state environmental laws, Murphy must restore the mine site to its original natural prairie state after it ceases mining operations at the site. To properly account for the mine, Murphy must estimate the fair value of this asset retirement obligation. This amount will be recorded as a liability and added to the value of the mine on Murphy's books. (You will learn more about these asset retirement obligations in Chapters 10 and 13.)

There is no active market for retirement obligations such as these, but Murphy has developed the following cash flow estimates based on its prior experience in mining-site restoration. It will take 3 years to restore the mine site when mining operations cease in 10 years. Each estimated cash outflow reflects an annual payment at the end of each year of the 3-year restoration period.

Restoration Estimated Cash Outflow	Probability Assessment
$15,000	10%
22,000	30%
25,000	50%
30,000	10%

Instructions

(a) What is the estimated fair value of Murphy's asset retirement obligation? Murphy determines that the appropriate discount rate for this estimation is 5%. Round calculations to the nearest dollar.

(b) Is the estimate developed for part (a) a Level 1 or Level 3 fair value estimate? Explain.

USING YOUR JUDGMENT

FINANCIAL REPORTING

Financial Reporting Problem

The Procter & Gamble Company (P&G)

P&G The financial statements and accompanying notes of P&G are presented in Appendix 5B or can be accessed at the book's companion website, **www.wiley.com/college/kieso**.

Instructions

(a) Examining each item in P&G's balance sheet, identify those items that require present value, discounting, or interest computations in establishing the amount reported. (The accompanying notes are an additional source for this information.)

(b) (1) What interest rates are disclosed by P&G as being used to compute interest and present values? (2) Why are there so many different interest rates applied to P&G's financial statement elements (assets, liabilities, revenues, and expenses)?

Financial Statement Analysis Case

Consolidated Natural Gas Company

Consolidated Natural Gas Company (CNG), with corporate headquarters in Pittsburgh, Pennsylvania, is one of the largest producers, transporters, distributors, and marketers of natural gas in North America.

Periodically, the company experiences a decrease in the value of its gas and oil producing properties, and a special charge to income was recorded in order to reduce the carrying value of those assets.

Assume the following information: In 2011, CNG estimated the cash inflows from its oil and gas producing properties to be $375,000 per year. During 2012, the write-downs described above caused the estimate to be decreased to $275,000 per year. Production costs (cash outflows) associated with all these properties were estimated to be $125,000 per year in 2011, but this amount was revised to $155,000 per year in 2012.

Instructions

(Assume that all cash flows occur at the end of the year.)

(a) Calculate the present value of net cash flows for 2011–2013 (three years), using the 2011 estimates and a 10% discount factor.

(b) Calculate the present value of net cash flows for 2012–2014 (three years), using the 2012 estimates and a 10% discount factor.

(c) Compare the results using the two estimates. Is information on future cash flows from oil and gas producing properties useful, considering that the estimates must be revised each year? Explain.

Accounting, Analysis, and Principles

Johnson Co. accepts a note receivable from a customer in exchange for some damaged inventory. The note requires the customer make semiannual installments of $50,000 each for 10 years. The first installment begins six months from the date the customer took delivery of the damaged inventory. Johnson's management estimates that the fair value of the damaged inventory is $670,591.65.

Accounting

(a) What interest rate is Johnson implicitly charging the customer? Express the rate as an annual rate but assume semiannual compounding.

(b) At what dollar amount do you think Johnson should record the note receivable on the day the customer takes delivery of the damaged inventory?

Analysis

Assume the note receivable for damaged inventory makes up a significant portion of Johnson's assets. If interest rates increase, what happens to the fair value of the receivable? Briefly explain why.

Principles

The Financial Accounting Standards Board recently issued an accounting standard that allows companies to report assets such as notes receivable at fair value. Discuss how fair value versus historical cost potentially involves a trade-off of one desired quality of accounting information against another.

BRIDGE TO THE PROFESSION

Professional Research

At a recent meeting of the accounting staff in your company, the controller raised the issue of using present value techniques to conduct impairment tests for some of the company's fixed assets. Some of the more senior members of the staff admitted having little knowledge of present value concepts in this context, but they had heard about a FASB Concepts Statement that may be relevant. As the junior staff in the department, you have been asked to conduct some research of the authoritative literature on this topic and report back at the staff meeting next week.

Instructions

If your school has a subscription to the FASB Codification, go to *http://aaahq.org/asclogin.cfm* to log in and access the FASB Statements of Financial Accounting Concepts. When you have accessed the documents, you can use the search tool in your Internet browser to respond to the following items. (Provide paragraph citations.)

(a) Identify the recent concept statement that addresses present value measurement in accounting.

(b) What are some of the contexts in which present value concepts are applied in accounting measurement?

(c) Provide definitions for the following terms:

(1) Best estimate.

(2) Estimated cash flow (contrasted to expected cash flow).

(3) Fresh-start measurement.

(4) Interest methods of allocation.

Professional Simulation

In this simulation, you are asked to address questions concerning the application of time value of money concepts to accounting problems. Prepare responses to all parts.

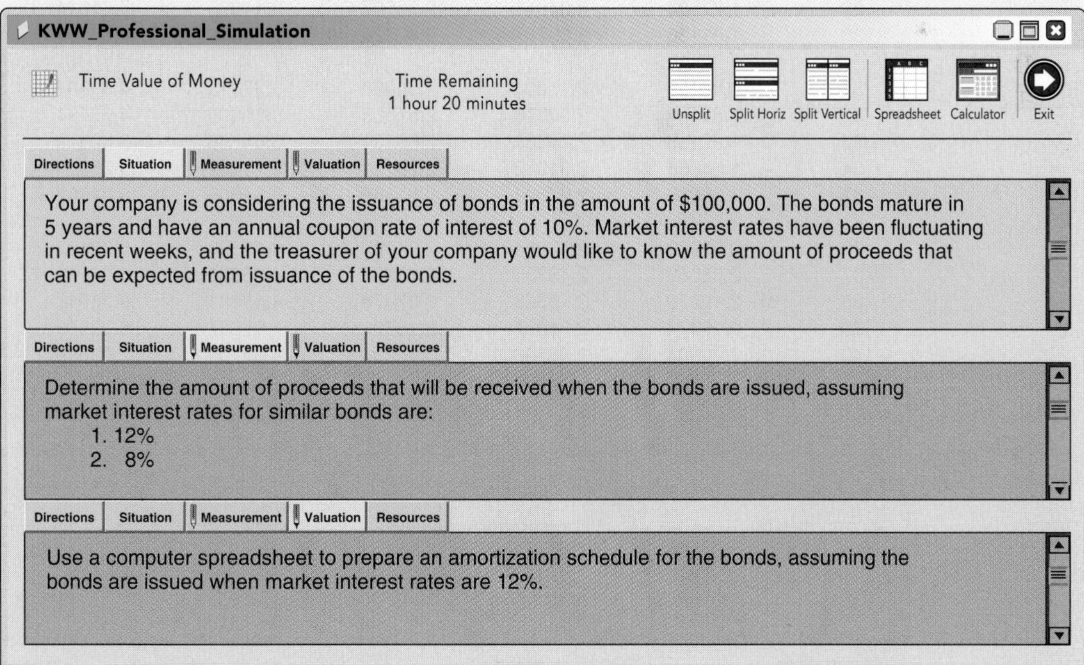

Remember to check the book's companion website to find additional resources for this chapter.

TABLE 6-1 FUTURE VALUE OF 1 (FUTURE VALUE OF A SINGLE SUM)

$$FVF_{n,i} = (1 + i)^n$$

(n) Periods	2%	2½%	3%	4%	5%	6%
1	1.02000	1.02500	1.03000	1.04000	1.05000	1.06000
2	1.04040	1.05063	1.06090	1.08160	1.10250	1.12360
3	1.06121	1.07689	1.09273	1.12486	1.15763	1.19102
4	1.08243	1.10381	1.12551	1.16986	1.21551	1.26248
5	1.10408	1.13141	1.15927	1.21665	1.27628	1.33823
6	1.12616	1.15969	1.19405	1.26532	1.34010	1.41852
7	1.14869	1.18869	1.22987	1.31593	1.40710	1.50363
8	1.17166	1.21840	1.26677	1.36857	1.47746	1.59385
9	1.19509	1.24886	1.30477	1.42331	1.55133	1.68948
10	1.21899	1.28008	1.34392	1.48024	1.62889	1.79085
11	1.24337	1.31209	1.38423	1.53945	1.71034	1.89830
12	1.26824	1.34489	1.42576	1.60103	1.79586	2.01220
13	1.29361	1.37851	1.46853	1.66507	1.88565	2.13293
14	1.31948	1.41297	1.51259	1.73168	1.97993	2.26090
15	1.34587	1.44830	1.55797	1.80094	2.07893	2.39656
16	1.37279	1.48451	1.60471	1.87298	2.18287	2.54035
17	1.40024	1.52162	1.65285	1.94790	2.29202	2.69277
18	1.42825	1.55966	1.70243	2.02582	2.40662	2.85434
19	1.45681	1.59865	1.75351	2.10685	2.52695	3.02560
20	1.48595	1.63862	1.80611	2.19112	2.65330	3.20714
21	1.51567	1.67958	1.86029	2.27877	2.78596	3.39956
22	1.54598	1.72157	1.91610	2.36992	2.92526	3.60354
23	1.57690	1.76461	1.97359	2.46472	3.07152	3.81975
24	1.60844	1.80873	2.03279	2.56330	3.22510	4.04893
25	1.64061	1.85394	2.09378	2.66584	3.38635	4.29187
26	1.67342	1.90029	2.15659	2.77247	3.55567	4.54938
27	1.70689	1.94780	2.22129	2.88337	3.73346	4.82235
28	1.74102	1.99650	2.28793	2.99870	3.92013	5.11169
29	1.77584	2.04641	2.35657	3.11865	4.11614	5.41839
30	1.81136	2.09757	2.42726	3.24340	4.32194	5.74349
31	1.84759	2.15001	2.50008	3.37313	4.53804	6.08810
32	1.88454	2.20376	2.57508	3.50806	4.76494	6.45339
33	1.92223	2.25885	2.65234	3.64838	5.00319	6.84059
34	1.96068	2.31532	2.73191	3.79432	5.25335	7.25103
35	1.99989	2.37321	2.81386	3.94609	5.51602	7.68609
36	2.03989	2.43254	2.89828	4.10393	5.79182	8.14725
37	2.08069	2.49335	2.98523	4.26809	6.08141	8.63609
38	2.12230	2.55568	3.07478	4.43881	6.38548	9.15425
39	2.16474	2.61957	3.16703	4.61637	6.70475	9.70351
40	2.20804	2.68506	3.26204	4.80102	7.03999	10.28572

TABLE 6-1 FUTURE VALUE OF 1

8%	9%	10%	11%	12%	15%	(n) Periods
1.08000	1.09000	1.10000	1.11000	1.12000	1.15000	1
1.16640	1.18810	1.21000	1.23210	1.25440	1.32250	2
1.25971	1.29503	1.33100	1.36763	1.40493	1.52088	3
1.36049	1.41158	1.46410	1.51807	1.57352	1.74901	4
1.46933	1.53862	1.61051	1.68506	1.76234	2.01136	5
1.58687	1.67710	1.77156	1.87041	1.97382	2.31306	6
1.71382	1.82804	1.94872	2.07616	2.21068	2.66002	7
1.85093	1.99256	2.14359	2.30454	2.47596	3.05902	8
1.99900	2.17189	2.35795	2.55803	2.77308	3.51788	9
2.15892	2.36736	2.59374	2.83942	3.10585	4.04556	10
2.33164	2.58043	2.85312	3.15176	3.47855	4.65239	11
2.51817	2.81267	3.13843	3.49845	3.89598	5.35025	12
2.71962	3.06581	3.45227	3.88328	4.36349	6.15279	13
2.93719	3.34173	3.79750	4.31044	4.88711	7.07571	14
3.17217	3.64248	4.17725	4.78459	5.47357	8.13706	15
3.42594	3.97031	4.59497	5.31089	6.13039	9.35762	16
3.70002	4.32763	5.05447	5.89509	6.86604	10.76126	17
3.99602	4.71712	5.55992	6.54355	7.68997	12.37545	18
4.31570	5.14166	6.11591	7.26334	8.61276	14.23177	19
4.66096	5.60441	6.72750	8.06231	9.64629	16.36654	20
5.03383	6.10881	7.40025	8.94917	10.80385	18.82152	21
5.43654	6.65860	8.14028	9.93357	12.10031	21.64475	22
5.87146	7.25787	8.95430	11.02627	13.55235	24.89146	23
6.34118	7.91108	9.84973	12.23916	15.17863	28.62518	24
6.84847	8.62308	10.83471	13.58546	17.00000	32.91895	25
7.39635	9.39916	11.91818	15.07986	19.04007	37.85680	26
7.98806	10.24508	13.10999	16.73865	21.32488	43.53532	27
8.62711	11.16714	14.42099	18.57990	23.88387	50.06561	28
9.31727	12.17218	15.86309	20.62369	26.74993	57.57545	29
10.06266	13.26768	17.44940	22.89230	29.95992	66.21177	30
10.86767	14.46177	19.19434	25.41045	33.55511	76.14354	31
11.73708	15.76333	21.11378	28.20560	37.58173	87.56507	32
12.67605	17.18203	23.22515	31.30821	42.09153	100.69983	33
13.69013	18.72841	25.54767	34.75212	47.14252	115.80480	34
14.78534	20.41397	28.10244	38.57485	52.79962	133.17552	35
15.96817	22.25123	30.91268	42.81808	59.13557	153.15185	36
17.24563	24.25384	34.00395	47.52807	66.23184	176.12463	37
18.62528	26.43668	37.40434	52.75616	74.17966	202.54332	38
20.11530	28.81598	41.14479	58.55934	83.08122	232.92482	39
21.72452	31.40942	45.25926	65.00087	93.05097	267.86355	40

TABLE 6-2 PRESENT VALUE OF 1 (PRESENT VALUE OF A SINGLE SUM)

$$PVF_{n,i} = \frac{1}{(1+i)^n} = (1+i)^{-n}$$

(n) Periods	2%	2½%	3%	4%	5%	6%
1	.98039	.97561	.97087	.96154	.95238	.94340
2	.96117	.95181	.94260	.92456	.90703	.89000
3	.94232	.92860	.91514	.88900	.86384	.83962
4	.92385	.90595	.88849	.85480	.82270	.79209
5	.90573	.88385	.86261	.82193	.78353	.74726
6	.88797	.86230	.83748	.79031	.74622	.70496
7	.87056	.84127	.81309	.75992	.71068	.66506
8	.85349	.82075	.78941	.73069	.67684	.62741
9	.83676	.80073	.76642	.70259	.64461	.59190
10	.82035	.78120	.74409	.67556	.61391	.55839
11	.80426	.76214	.72242	.64958	.58468	.52679
12	.78849	.74356	.70138	.62460	.55684	.49697
13	.77303	.72542	.68095	.60057	.53032	.46884
14	.75788	.70773	.66112	.57748	.50507	.44230
15	.74301	.69047	.64186	.55526	.48102	.41727
16	.72845	.67362	.62317	.53391	.45811	.39365
17	.71416	.65720	.60502	.51337	.43630	.37136
18	.70016	.64117	.58739	.49363	.41552	.35034
19	.68643	.62553	.57029	.47464	.39573	.33051
20	.67297	.61027	.55368	.45639	.37689	.31180
21	.65978	.59539	.53755	.43883	.35894	.29416
22	.64684	.58086	.52189	.42196	.34185	.22751
23	.63416	.56670	.50669	.40573	.32557	.26180
24	.62172	.55288	.49193	.39012	.31007	.24698
25	.60953	.53939	.47761	.37512	.29530	.23300
26	.59758	.52623	.46369	.36069	.28124	.21981
27	.58586	.51340	.45019	.34682	.26785	.20737
28	.57437	.50088	.43708	.33348	.25509	.19563
29	.56311	.48866	.42435	.32065	.24295	.18456
30	.55207	.47674	.41199	.30832	.23138	.17411
31	.54125	.46511	.39999	.29646	.22036	.16425
32	.53063	.45377	.38834	.28506	.20987	.15496
33	.52023	.44270	.37703	.27409	.19987	.14619
34	.51003	.43191	.36604	.26355	.19035	.13791
35	.50003	.42137	.35538	.25342	.18129	.13011
36	.49022	.41109	.34503	.24367	.17266	.12274
37	.48061	.40107	.33498	.23430	.16444	.11579
38	.47119	.39128	.32523	.22529	.15661	.10924
39	.46195	.38174	.31575	.21662	.14915	.10306
40	.45289	.37243	.30656	.20829	.14205	.09722

TABLE 6-2 PRESENT VALUE OF 1

8%	9%	10%	11%	12%	15%	(n) Periods
.92593	.91743	.90909	.90090	.89286	.86957	1
.85734	.84168	.82645	.81162	.79719	.75614	2
.79383	.77218	.75132	.73119	.71178	.65752	3
.73503	.70843	.68301	.65873	.63552	.57175	4
.68058	.64993	.62092	.59345	.56743	.49718	5
.63017	.59627	.56447	.53464	.50663	.43233	6
.58349	.54703	.51316	.48166	.45235	.37594	7
.54027	.50187	.46651	.43393	.40388	.32690	8
.50025	.46043	.42410	.39092	.36061	.28426	9
.46319	.42241	.38554	.35218	.32197	.24719	10
.42888	.38753	.35049	.31728	.28748	.21494	11
.39711	.35554	.31863	.28584	.25668	.18691	12
.36770	.32618	.28966	.25751	.22917	.16253	13
.34046	.29925	.26333	.23199	.20462	.14133	14
.31524	.27454	.23939	.20900	.18270	.12289	15
.29189	.25187	.21763	.18829	.16312	.10687	16
.27027	.23107	.19785	.16963	.14564	.09293	17
.25025	.21199	.17986	.15282	.13004	.08081	18
.23171	.19449	.16351	.13768	.11611	.07027	19
.21455	.17843	.14864	.12403	.10367	.06110	20
.19866	.16370	.13513	.11174	.09256	.05313	21
.18394	.15018	.12285	.10067	.08264	.04620	22
.17032	.13778	.11168	.09069	.07379	.04017	23
.15770	.12641	.10153	.08170	.06588	.03493	24
.14602	.11597	.09230	.07361	.05882	.03038	25
.13520	.10639	.08391	.06631	.05252	.02642	26
.12519	.09761	.07628	.05974	.04689	.02297	27
.11591	.08955	.06934	.05382	.04187	.01997	28
.10733	.08216	.06304	.04849	.03738	.01737	29
.09938	.07537	.05731	.04368	.03338	.01510	30
.09202	.06915	.05210	.03935	.02980	.01313	31
.08520	.06344	.04736	.03545	.02661	.01142	32
.07889	.05820	.04306	.03194	.02376	.00993	33
.07305	.05340	.03914	.02878	.02121	.00864	34
.06763	.04899	.03558	.02592	.01894	.00751	35
.06262	.04494	.03235	.02335	.01691	.00653	36
.05799	.04123	.02941	.02104	.01510	.00568	37
.05369	.03783	.02674	.01896	.01348	.00494	38
.04971	.03470	.02430	.01708	.01204	.00429	39
.04603	.03184	.02210	.01538	.01075	.00373	40

TABLE 6-3 FUTURE VALUE OF AN ORDINARY ANNUITY OF 1

$$\text{FVF-OA}_{n,i} = \frac{(1 + i)^n - 1}{i}$$

(n) Periods	2%	2½%	3%	4%	5%	6%
1	1.00000	1.00000	1.00000	1.00000	1.00000	1.00000
2	2.02000	2.02500	2.03000	2.04000	2.05000	2.06000
3	3.06040	3.07563	3.09090	3.12160	3.15250	3.18360
4	4.12161	4.15252	4.18363	4.24646	4.31013	4.37462
5	5.20404	5.25633	5.30914	5.41632	5.52563	5.63709
6	6.30812	6.38774	6.46841	6.63298	6.80191	6.97532
7	7.43428	7.54743	7.66246	7.89829	8.14201	8.39384
8	8.58297	8.73612	8.89234	9.21423	9.54911	9.89747
9	9.75463	9.95452	10.15911	10.58280	11.02656	11.49132
10	10.94972	11.20338	11.46338	12.00611	12.57789	13.18079
11	12.16872	12.48347	12.80780	13.48635	14.20679	14.97164
12	13.41209	13.79555	14.19203	15.02581	15.91713	16.86994
13	14.68033	15.14044	15.61779	16.62684	17.71298	18.88214
14	15.97394	16.51895	17.08632	18.29191	19.59863	21.01507
15	17.29342	17.93193	18.59891	20.02359	21.57856	23.27597
16	18.63929	19.38022	20.15688	21.82453	23.65749	25.67253
17	20.01207	20.86473	21.76159	23.69751	25.84037	28.21288
18	21.41231	22.38635	23.41444	25.64541	28.13238	30.90565
19	22.84056	23.94601	25.11687	27.67123	30.53900	33.75999
20	24.29737	25.54466	26.87037	29.77808	33.06595	36.78559
21	25.78332	27.18327	28.67649	31.96920	35.71925	39.99273
22	27.29898	28.86286	30.53678	34.24797	38.50521	43.39229
23	28.84496	30.58443	32.45288	36.61789	41.43048	46.99583
24	30.42186	32.34904	34.42647	39.08260	44.50200	50.81558
25	32.03030	34.15776	36.45926	41.64591	47.72710	54.86451
26	33.67091	36.01171	38.55304	44.31174	51.11345	59.15638
27	35.34432	37.91200	40.70963	47.08421	54.66913	63.70577
28	37.05121	39.85980	42.93092	49.96758	58.40258	68.52811
29	38.79223	41.85630	45.21885	52.96629	62.32271	73.63980
30	40.56808	43.90270	47.57542	56.08494	66.43885	79.05819
31	42.37944	46.00027	50.00268	59.32834	70.76079	84.80168
32	44.22703	48.15028	52.50276	62.70147	75.29883	90.88978
33	46.11157	50.35403	55.07784	66.20953	80.06377	97.34316
34	48.03380	52.61289	57.73018	69.85791	85.06696	104.18376
35	49.99448	54.92821	60.46208	73.65222	90.32031	111.43478
36	51.99437	57.30141	63.27594	77.59831	95.83632	119.12087
37	54.03425	59.73395	66.17422	81.70225	101.62814	127.26812
38	56.11494	62.22730	69.15945	85.97034	107.70955	135.90421
39	58.23724	64.78298	72.23423	90.40915	114.09502	145.05846
40	60.40198	67.40255	75.40126	95.02552	120.79977	154.76197

TABLE 6-3 FUTURE VALUE OF AN ORDINARY ANNUITY OF 1

8%	9%	10%	11%	12%	15%	(n) Periods
1.00000	1.00000	1.00000	1.00000	1.00000	1.00000	1
2.08000	2.09000	2.10000	2.11000	2.12000	2.15000	2
3.24640	3.27810	3.31000	3.34210	3.37440	3.47250	3
4.50611	4.57313	4.64100	4.70973	4.77933	4.99338	4
5.86660	5.98471	6.10510	6.22780	6.35285	6.74238	5
7.33592	7.52334	7.71561	7.91286	8.11519	8.75374	6
8.92280	9.20044	9.48717	9.78327	10.08901	11.06680	7
10.63663	11.02847	11.43589	11.85943	12.29969	13.72682	8
12.48756	13.02104	13.57948	14.16397	14.77566	16.78584	9
14.48656	15.19293	15.93743	16.72201	17.54874	20.30372	10
16.64549	17.56029	18.53117	19.56143	20.65458	24.34928	11
18.97713	20.14072	21.38428	22.71319	24.13313	29.00167	12
21.49530	22.95339	24.52271	26.21164	28.02911	34.35192	13
24.21492	26.01919	27.97498	30.09492	32.39260	40.50471	14
27.15211	29.36092	31.77248	34.40536	37.27972	47.58041	15
30.32428	33.00340	35.94973	39.18995	42.75328	55.71747	16
33.75023	36.97371	40.54470	44.50084	48.88367	65.07509	17
37.45024	41.30134	45.59917	50.39593	55.74972	75.83636	18
41.44626	46.01846	51.15909	56.93949	63.43968	88.21181	19
45.76196	51.16012	57.27500	64.20283	72.05244	102.44358	20
50.42292	56.76453	64.00250	72.26514	81.69874	118.81012	21
55.45676	62.87334	71.40275	81.21431	92.50258	137.63164	22
60.89330	69.53194	79.54302	91.14788	104.60289	159.27638	23
66.76476	76.78981	88.49733	102.17415	118.15524	184.16784	24
73.10594	84.70090	98.34706	114.41331	133.33387	212.79302	25
79.95442	93.32398	109.18177	127.99877	150.33393	245.71197	26
87.35077	102.72314	121.09994	143.07864	169.37401	283.56877	27
95.33883	112.96822	134.20994	159.81729	190.69889	327.10408	28
103.96594	124.13536	148.63093	178.39719	214.58275	377.16969	29
113.28321	136.30754	164.49402	199.02088	241.33268	434.74515	30
123.34587	149.57522	181.94343	221.91317	271.29261	500.95692	31
134.21354	164.03699	201.13777	247.32362	304.84772	577.10046	32
145.95062	179.80032	222.25154	275.52922	342.42945	644.66553	33
158.62667	196.98234	245.47670	306.83744	384.52098	765.36535	34
172.31680	215.71076	271.02437	341.58955	431.66350	881.17016	35
187.10215	236.12472	299.12681	380.16441	484.46312	1014.34568	36
203.07032	258.37595	330.03949	422.98249	543.59869	1167.49753	37
220.31595	282.62978	364.04343	470.51056	609.83053	1343.62216	38
238.94122	309.06646	401.44778	523.26673	684.01020	1546.16549	39
259.05652	337.88245	442.59256	581.82607	767.09142	1779.09031	40

TABLE 6-4 PRESENT VALUE OF AN ORDINARY ANNUITY OF 1

$$PVF\text{-}OA_{n,i} = \frac{1 - \frac{1}{(1+i)^n}}{i}$$

(n) Periods	2%	2½%	3%	4%	5%	6%
1	.98039	.97561	.97087	.96154	.95238	.94340
2	1.94156	1.92742	1.91347	1.88609	1.85941	1.83339
3	2.88388	2.85602	2.82861	2.77509	2.72325	2.67301
4	3.80773	3.76197	3.71710	3.62990	3.54595	3.46511
5	4.71346	4.64583	4.57971	4.45182	4.32948	4.21236
6	5.60143	5.50813	5.41719	5.24214	5.07569	4.91732
7	6.47199	6.34939	6.23028	6.00205	5.78637	5.58238
8	7.32548	7.17014	7.01969	6.73274	6.46321	6.20979
9	8.16224	7.97087	7.78611	7.43533	7.10782	6.80169
10	8.98259	8.75206	8.53020	8.11090	7.72173	7.36009
11	9.78685	9.51421	9.25262	8.76048	8.30641	7.88687
12	10.57534	10.25776	9.95400	9.38507	8.86325	8.38384
13	11.34837	10.98319	10.63496	9.98565	9.39357	8.85268
14	12.10625	11.69091	11.29607	10.56312	9.89864	9.29498
15	12.84926	12.38138	11.93794	11.11839	10.37966	9.71225
16	13.57771	13.05500	12.56110	11.65230	10.83777	10.10590
17	14.29187	13.71220	13.16612	12.16567	11.27407	10.47726
18	14.99203	14.35336	13.75351	12.65930	11.68959	10.82760
19	15.67846	14.97889	14.32380	13.13394	12.08532	11.15812
20	16.35143	15.58916	14.87747	13.59033	12.46221	11.46992
21	17.01121	16.18455	15.41502	14.02916	12.82115	11.76408
22	17.65805	16.76541	15.93692	14.45112	13.16300	12.04158
23	18.29220	17.33211	16.44361	14.85684	13.48857	12.30338
24	18.91393	17.88499	16.93554	15.24696	13.79864	12.55036
25	19.52346	18.42438	17.41315	15.62208	14.09394	12.78336
26	20.12104	18.95061	17.87684	15.98277	14.37519	13.00317
27	20.70690	19.46401	18.32703	16.32959	14.64303	13.21053
28	21.28127	19.96489	18.76411	16.66306	14.89813	13.40616
29	21.84438	20.45355	19.18845	16.98371	15.14107	13.59072
30	22.39646	20.93029	19.60044	17.29203	15.37245	13.76483
31	22.93770	21.39541	20.00043	17.58849	15.59281	13.92909
32	23.46833	21.84918	20.38877	17.87355	15.80268	14.08404
33	23.98856	22.29188	20.76579	18.14765	16.00255	14.23023
34	24.49859	22.72379	21.13184	18.41120	16.19290	14.36814
35	24.99862	23.14516	21.48722	18.66461	16.37419	14.49825
36	25.48884	23.55625	21.83225	18.90828	16.54685	14.62099
37	25.96945	23.95732	22.16724	19.14258	16.71129	14.73678
38	26.44064	24.34860	22.49246	19.36786	16.86789	14.84602
39	26.90259	24.73034	22.80822	19.58448	17.01704	14.94907
40	27.35548	25.10278	23.11477	19.79277	17.15909	15.04630

TABLE 6-4 PRESENT VALUE OF AN ORDINARY ANNUITY OF 1

8%	9%	10%	11%	12%	15%	(n) Periods
.92593	.91743	.90909	.90090	.89286	.86957	1
1.78326	1.75911	1.73554	1.71252	1.69005	1.62571	2
2.57710	2.53130	2.48685	2.44371	2.40183	2.28323	3
3.31213	3.23972	3.16986	3.10245	3.03735	2.85498	4
3.99271	3.88965	3.79079	3.69590	3.60478	3.35216	5
4.62288	4.48592	4.35526	4.23054	4.11141	3.78448	6
5.20637	5.03295	4.86842	4.71220	4.56376	4.16042	7
5.74664	5.53482	5.33493	5.14612	4.96764	4.48732	8
6.24689	5.99525	5.75902	5.53705	5.32825	4.77158	9
6.71008	6.41766	6.14457	5.88923	5.65022	5.01877	10
7.13896	6.80519	6.49506	6.20652	5.93770	5.23371	11
7.53608	7.16073	6.81369	6.49236	6.19437	5.42062	12
7.90378	7.48690	7.10336	6.74987	6.42355	5.58315	13
8.24424	7.78615	7.36669	6.98187	6.62817	5.72448	14
8.55948	8.06069	7.60608	7.19087	6.81086	5.84737	15
8.85137	8.31256	7.82371	7.37916	6.97399	5.95424	16
9.12164	8.54363	8.02155	7.54879	7.11963	6.04716	17
9.37189	8.75563	8.20141	7.70162	7.24967	6.12797	18
9.60360	8.95012	8.36492	7.83929	7.36578	6.19823	19
9.81815	9.12855	8.51356	7.96333	7.46944	6.25933	20
10.01680	9.29224	8.64869	8.07507	7.56200	6.31246	21
10.20074	9.44243	8.77154	8.17574	7.64465	6.35866	22
10.37106	9.58021	8.88322	8.26643	7.71843	6.39884	23
10.52876	9.70661	8.98474	8.34814	7.78432	6.43377	24
10.67478	9.82258	9.07704	8.42174	7.84314	6.46415	25
10.80998	9.92897	9.16095	8.48806	7.89566	6.49056	26
10.93516	10.02658	9.23722	8.54780	7.94255	6.51353	27
11.05108	10.11613	9.30657	8.60162	7.98442	6.53351	28
11.15841	10.19828	9.36961	8.65011	8.02181	6.55088	29
11.25778	10.27365	9.42691	8.69379	8.05518	6.56598	30
11.34980	10.34280	9.47901	8.73315	8.08499	6.57911	31
11.43500	10.40624	9.52638	8.76860	8.11159	6.59053	32
11.51389	10.46444	9.56943	8.80054	8.13535	6.60046	33
11.58693	10.51784	9.60858	8.82932	8.15656	6.60910	34
11.65457	10.56682	9.64416	8.85524	8.17550	6.61661	35
11.71719	10.61176	9.67651	8.87859	8.19241	6.62314	36
11.77518	10.65299	9.70592	8.89963	8.20751	6.62882	37
11.82887	10.69082	9.73265	8.91859	8.22099	6.63375	38
11.87858	10.72552	9.75697	8.93567	8.23303	6.63805	39
11.92461	10.75736	9.77905	8.95105	8.24378	6.64178	40

TABLE 6-5 PRESENT VALUE OF AN ANNUITY DUE OF 1

$$\text{PVF-AD}_{n,i} = 1 + \frac{1 - \dfrac{1}{(1+i)^{n-1}}}{i}$$

(n) Periods	2%	2½%	3%	4%	5%	6%
1	1.00000	1.00000	1.00000	1.00000	1.00000	1.00000
2	1.98039	1.97561	1.97087	1.96154	1.95238	1.94340
3	2.94156	2.92742	2.91347	2.88609	2.85941	2.83339
4	3.88388	3.85602	3.82861	3.77509	3.72325	3.67301
5	4.80773	4.76197	4.71710	4.62990	4.54595	4.46511
6	5.71346	5.64583	5.57971	5.45182	5.32948	5.21236
7	6.60143	6.50813	6.41719	6.24214	6.07569	5.91732
8	7.47199	7.34939	7.23028	7.00205	6.78637	6.58238
9	8.32548	8.17014	8.01969	7.73274	7.46321	7.20979
10	9.16224	8.97087	8.78611	8.43533	8.10782	7.80169
11	9.98259	9.75206	9.53020	9.11090	8.72173	8.36009
12	10.78685	10.51421	10.25262	9.76048	9.30641	8.88687
13	11.57534	11.25776	10.95400	10.38507	9.86325	9.38384
14	12.34837	11.98319	11.63496	10.98565	10.39357	9.85268
15	13.10625	12.69091	12.29607	11.56312	10.89864	10.29498
16	13.84926	13.38138	12.93794	12.11839	11.37966	10.71225
17	14.57771	14.05500	13.56110	12.65230	11.83777	11.10590
18	15.29187	14.71220	14.16612	13.16567	12.27407	11.47726
19	15.99203	15.35336	14.75351	13.65930	12.68959	11.82760
20	16.67846	15.97889	15.32380	14.13394	13.08532	12.15812
21	17.35143	16.58916	15.87747	14.59033	13.46221	12.46992
22	18.01121	17.18455	16.41502	15.02916	13.82115	12.76408
23	18.65805	17.76541	16.93692	15.45112	14.16300	13.04158
24	19.29220	18.33211	17.44361	15.85684	14.48857	13.30338
25	19.91393	18.88499	17.93554	16.24696	14.79864	13.55036
26	20.52346	19.42438	18.41315	16.62208	15.09394	13.78336
27	21.12104	19.95061	18.87684	16.98277	15.37519	14.00317
28	21.70690	20.46401	19.32703	17.32959	15.64303	14.21053
29	22.28127	20.96489	19.76411	17.66306	15.89813	14.40616
30	22.84438	21.45355	20.18845	17.98371	16.14107	14.59072
31	23.39646	21.93029	20.60044	18.29203	16.37245	14.76483
32	23.93770	22.39541	21.00043	18.58849	16.59281	14.92909
33	24.46833	22.84918	21.38877	18.87355	16.80268	15.08404
34	24.98856	23.29188	21.76579	19.14765	17.00255	15.23023
35	25.49859	23.72379	22.13184	19.41120	17.19290	15.36814
36	25.99862	24.14516	22.48722	19.66461	17.37419	15.49825
37	26.48884	24.55625	22.83225	19.90828	17.54685	15.62099
38	26.96945	24.95732	23.16724	20.14258	17.71129	15.73678
39	27.44064	25.34860	23.49246	20.36786	17.86789	15.84602
40	27.90259	25.73034	23.80822	20.58448	18.01704	15.94907

TABLE 6-5 PRESENT VALUE OF AN ANNUITY DUE OF 1

8%	9%	10%	11%	12%	15%	(n) Periods
1.00000	1.00000	1.00000	1.00000	1.00000	1.00000	1
1.92593	1.91743	1.90909	1.90090	1.89286	1.86957	2
2.78326	2.75911	2.73554	2.71252	2.69005	2.62571	3
3.57710	3.53130	3.48685	3.44371	3.40183	3.28323	4
4.31213	4.23972	4.16986	4.10245	4.03735	3.85498	5
4.99271	4.88965	4.79079	4.69590	4.60478	4.35216	6
5.62288	5.48592	5.35526	5.23054	5.11141	4.78448	7
6.20637	6.03295	5.86842	5.71220	5.56376	5.16042	8
6.74664	6.53482	6.33493	6.14612	5.96764	5.48732	9
7.24689	6.99525	6.75902	6.53705	6.32825	5.77158	10
7.71008	7.41766	7.14457	6.88923	6.65022	6.01877	11
8.13896	7.80519	7.49506	7.20652	6.93770	6.23371	12
8.53608	8.16073	7.81369	7.49236	7.19437	6.42062	13
8.90378	8.48690	8.10336	7.74987	7.42355	6.58315	14
9.24424	8.78615	8.36669	7.98187	7.62817	6.72448	15
9.55948	9.06069	8.60608	8.19087	7.81086	6.84737	16
9.85137	9.31256	8.82371	8.37916	7.97399	6.95424	17
10.12164	9.54363	9.02155	8.54879	8.11963	7.04716	18
10.37189	9.75563	9.20141	8.70162	8.24967	7.12797	19
10.60360	9.95012	9.36492	8.83929	8.36578	7.19823	20
10.81815	10.12855	9.51356	8.96333	8.46944	7.25933	21
11.01680	10.29224	9.64869	9.07507	8.56200	7.31246	22
11.20074	10.44243	9.77154	9.17574	8.64465	7.35866	23
11.37106.	10.58021	9.88322	9.26643	8.71843	7.39884	24
11.52876	10.70661	9.98474	9.34814	8.78432	7.43377	25
11.67478	10.82258	10.07704	9.42174	8.84314	7.46415	26
11.80998	10.92897	10.16095	9.48806	8.89566	7.49056	27
11.93518	11.02658	10.23722	9.54780	8.94255	7.51353	28
12.05108	11.11613	10.30657	9.60162	8.98442	7.53351	29
12.15841	11.19828	10.36961	9.65011	9.02181	7.55088	30
12.25778	11.27365	10.42691	9.69379	9.05518	7.56598	31
12.34980	11.34280	10.47901	9.73315	9.08499	7.57911	32
12.43500	11.40624	10.52638	9.76860	9.11159	7.59053	33
12.51389	11.46444	10.56943	9.80054	9.13535	7.60046	34
12.58693	11.51784	10.60858	9.82932	9.15656	7.60910	35
12.65457	11.56682	10.64416	9.85524	9.17550	7.61661	36
12.71719	11.61176	10.67651	9.87859	9.19241	7.62314	37
12.77518	11.65299	10.70592	9.89963	9.20751	7.62882	38
12.82887	11.69082	10.73265	9.91859	9.22099	7.63375	39
12.87858	11.72552	10.75697	9.93567	9.23303	7.63805	40

CHAPTER

7 Cash and Receivables

LEARNING OBJECTIVES

After studying this chapter, you should be able to:

1. Identify items considered cash.
2. Indicate how to report cash and related items.
3. Define receivables and identify the different types of receivables.
4. Explain accounting issues related to recognition of accounts receivable.
5. Explain accounting issues related to valuation of accounts receivable.
6. Explain accounting issues related to recognition and valuation of notes receivable.
7. Explain the fair value option.
8. Explain accounting issues related to disposition of accounts and notes receivable.
9. Describe how to report and analyze receivables.

No-Tell Nortel

Nortel Networks filed for bankruptcy in early 2009. Nortel's demise is one of the biggest financial failures in Canadian history. At one time, it accounted for one-third of all equity traded on the Toronto Stock Exchange; in 2000, its shares were as high as $124.50. In 2009, however, those shares were worth just 1.2¢. What happened to Nortel? First, competition was intense, and some bad business decisions were made. As a result, the company was hit very hard by the technology stock price decline in the early 2000s. Second, it became involved in accounting scandals for which eventually three of its executives faced criminal charges.

In one accounting scheme, Nortel managed its bad debt allowance to ensure that executives received additional bonuses. For example, Nortel announced that its net income for 2003 was really half what it originally reported. In addition, the company had understated net income for 2002. How could this happen? One reason: Nortel set up "cookie jar" reserves, using the allowance for doubtful accounts as the cookie jar. As the chart below shows, in 2002, Nortel overestimated the amount of bad debt expense (with a sizable allowance for doubtful accounts).

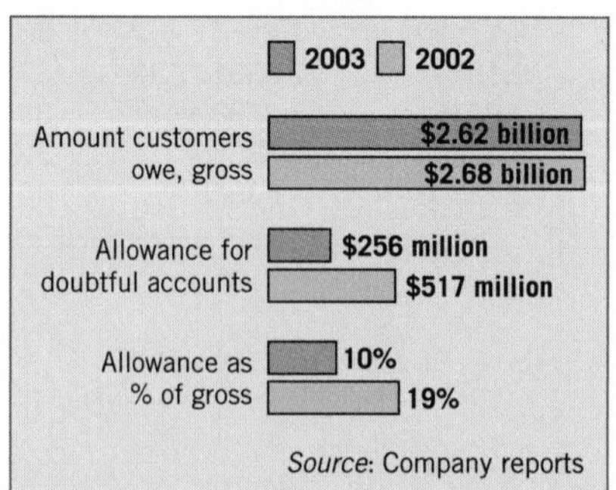

Then, in 2003, Nortel slashed the amount of bad debt expense even though the total money owed by customers remained nearly unchanged. In 2002, its allowance was 19 percent of receivables compared to 10 percent in 2003—quite a difference.

IFRS IN THIS CHAPTER

See the **International Perspectives** on pages 384, 391, and 395.

Read the **IFRS Insights** on pages 428–432 for a discussion of:

—Impairment evaluation

—Recovery of impairment losses

It is difficult to determine if the allowance was too high in 2002 or too low in 2003, or both. Whatever the case, the use of the allowance cookie jar permitted Nortel to report higher operating margins and net income in 2003.

This analysis suggests the importance of looking carefully at the amount of bad debt expense reported in annual reports. Nortel is an example of a nonfinancial company and its issues related to bad debts. In the financial arena, we have been in cardiac arrest. The quality of receivables in the financial sector remains very poor in mid-2009 and will continue to be questionable for some time. As a result, loan-loss allowances have jumped, as evidenced from the chart below for four large financial institutions.

Source: Company reports.

Quite an increase; on average, bank loan-loss allowances are in the 1–2% range.

Source: Adapted from J. Weil, "At Nortel, Warning Signs Existed Months Ago," *Wall Street Journal* (May 18, 2004), p. C3; M. Crittenden, "U.S. Thrifts Set a Record for Loan Loss Provisions," *Wall Street Journal* (May 28, 2008), p. C8; and P. Eavis, "For Wells, Multiple Ruts in the Road," *Wall Street Journal* (July 23, 2009), p. C10.

PREVIEW OF CHAPTER 7

As our opening story indicates, estimating the collectibility of accounts receivable has important implications for accurate reporting of operating profits, net income, and assets. In this chapter, we discuss cash and receivables—two assets that are important to companies as diverse as **Nortel** and **J.P. Morgan**. The content and organization of the chapter are as follows.

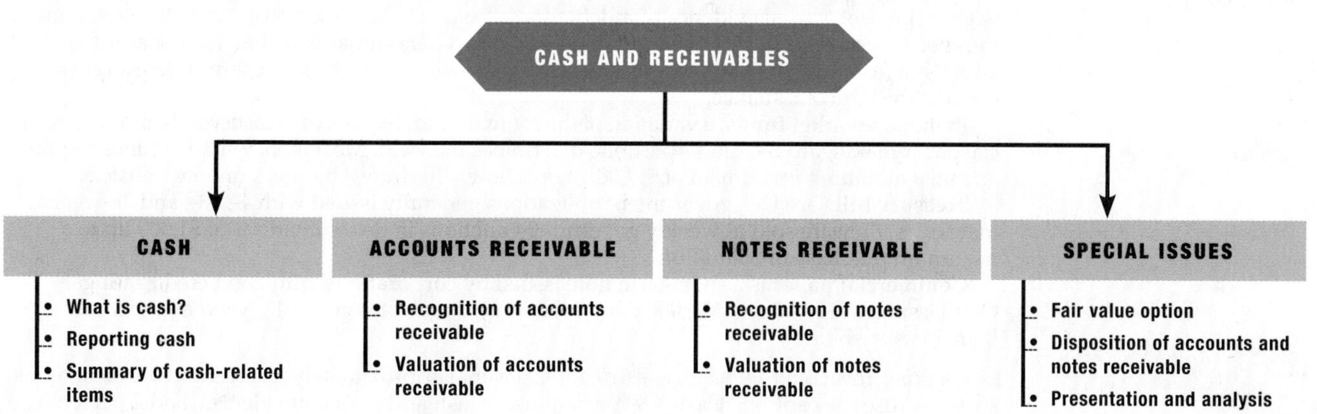

CASH

What Is Cash?

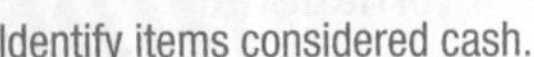

LEARNING OBJECTIVE 1
Identify items considered cash.

Cash, the most liquid of assets, is the standard medium of exchange and the basis for measuring and accounting for all other items. Companies generally classify cash as a current asset. Cash consists of coin, currency, and available funds on deposit at the bank. Negotiable instruments such as money orders, certified checks, cashier's checks, personal checks, and bank drafts are also viewed as cash. What about savings accounts? Banks do have the legal right to demand notice before withdrawal. But, because banks rarely demand prior notice, savings accounts nevertheless are considered cash.

Some negotiable instruments provide small investors with an opportunity to earn interest. These items, more appropriately classified as temporary investments than as cash, include money market funds, money market savings certificates, certificates of deposit (CDs), and similar types of deposits and "short-term paper."[1] These securities usually contain restrictions or penalties on their conversion to cash. Money market funds that provide checking account privileges, however, are usually classified as cash.

Certain items present classification problems: Companies treat **postdated checks and I.O.U.s** as receivables. They also treat **travel advances** as receivables if collected from employees or deducted from their salaries. Otherwise, companies classify the travel advance as a prepaid expense. **Postage stamps on hand** are classified as part of office supplies inventory or as a prepaid expense. Because **petty cash funds and change funds are used** to meet current operating expenses and liquidate current liabilities, companies include these funds in current assets as cash.

Reporting Cash

LEARNING OBJECTIVE 2
Indicate how to report cash and related items.

Although the reporting of cash is relatively straightforward, a number of issues merit special attention. These issues relate to the reporting of:

1. Cash equivalents.
2. Restricted cash.
3. Bank overdrafts.

Cash Equivalents

A current classification that has become popular is "Cash and cash equivalents."[2] Cash equivalents are short-term, highly liquid investments that are both (a) readily convertible to known amounts of cash, and (b) so near their maturity that they present insignificant risk of changes in value because of changes in interest rates. Generally, only investments with

[1]A variety of "short-term paper" is available for investment. For example, **certificates of deposit** (CDs) represent formal evidence of indebtedness, issued by a bank, subject to withdrawal under the specific terms of the instrument. Issued in various denominations, they have maturities anywhere from 7 days to 10 years and generally pay interest at the short-term interest rate in effect at the date of issuance.

In **money-market funds**, a variation of the mutual fund, the mix of Treasury bills and commercial paper making up the fund's portfolio determines the yield. Most money-market funds require an initial minimum investment of $1,000; many allow withdrawal by check or wire transfer.

Treasury bills are U.S. government obligations generally issued with 4-, 13-, and 26-week maturities; they are sold at weekly government auctions in denominations of $1,000 up to a maximum purchase of $5 million.

Commercial paper is a short-term note issued by corporations with good credit ratings. Often issued in $5,000 and $10,000 denominations, these notes generally yield a higher rate than Treasury bills.

[2]*Accounting Trends and Techniques—2010,* indicates that approximately 2 percent of the companies surveyed use the caption "Cash," 89 percent use "Cash and cash equivalents," and 2 percent use a caption such as "Cash and marketable securities" or similar terminology.

original maturities of three months or less qualify under these definitions. Examples of cash equivalents are Treasury bills, commercial paper, and money market funds. Some companies combine cash with temporary investments on the balance sheet. In these cases, they describe the amount of the temporary investments either parenthetically or in the notes.

Most individuals think of cash equivalents as cash. Unfortunately, that is not always the case. Companies like **Kohl's** and **ADC Telecommunications** have found out the hard way and are taking sizable write-downs on cash equivalents. Their losses resulted because they purchased auction-rate notes that declined in value. These notes carry interest rates that usually reset weekly and often have long-maturity dates (as long as 30 years). Companies argued that such notes should be classified as cash equivalents because they can be routinely traded at auction on a daily basis. (In short, they are liquid and risk-free.) Auditors agreed and permitted cash-equivalent treatment even though maturities extended well beyond three months. But when the credit crunch hit, the auctions stopped, and the value of these securities dropped because no market existed. In retrospect, the cash-equivalent classification was misleading.

It now appears likely that the FASB will eliminate the cash-equivalent classification from financial statement presentations altogether. Companies will now report only cash. If an asset is not cash and is short-term in nature, it should be reported as a temporary investment. An interesting moral to this story is that when times are good, some sloppy accounting may work. But in bad times, it quickly becomes apparent that sloppy accounting can lead to misleading and harmful effects for users of the financial statements.

Restricted Cash

Petty cash, payroll, and dividend funds are examples of cash set aside for a particular purpose. In most situations, these fund balances are not material. Therefore, companies do not segregate them from cash in the financial statements. When material in amount, companies segregate **restricted cash** from "regular" cash for reporting purposes. Companies classify restricted cash either in the current assets or in the long-term assets section, depending on the date of availability or disbursement. Classification in the current section is appropriate if using the cash for payment of existing or maturing obligations (within a year or the operating cycle, whichever is longer). On the other hand, companies show the restricted cash in the long-term section of the balance sheet if holding the cash for a longer period of time. Among other potential restrictions, companies need to determine whether any of the cash in accounts outside the United States is restricted by regulations against exportation of currency.

Cash classified in the long-term section is frequently set aside for plant expansion, retirement of long-term debt or, in the case of **International Thoroughbred Breeders**, for entry fee deposits.

ILLUSTRATION 7-1
Disclosure of Restricted Cash

International Thoroughbred Breeders

Restricted cash and investments (See Note)	$3,730,000

Note: Restricted Cash. At year-end, the Company had approximately $3,730,000, which was classified as restricted cash and investments. These funds are primarily cash received from horsemen for nomination and entry fees to be applied to upcoming racing meets, purse winnings held in trust for horsemen, and amounts held for unclaimed ticketholder winnings.

Banks and other lending institutions often require customers to maintain minimum cash balances in checking or savings accounts. The SEC defines these minimum balances, called **compensating balances**, as "that portion of any demand deposit (or any time deposit or certificate of deposit) maintained by a corporation which constitutes support for existing borrowing arrangements of the corporation with a lending institution. Such arrangements would include both outstanding borrowings and the assurance of future credit availability." **[1]**

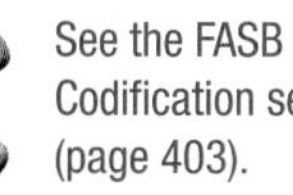

See the FASB Codification section (page 403).

To avoid misleading investors about the amount of cash available to meet recurring obligations, the SEC recommends that companies state separately **legally restricted deposits** held as compensating balances against **short-term** borrowing arrangements among the "Cash and cash equivalent items" in current assets. Companies should classify separately restricted deposits held as compensating balances against **long-term** borrowing arrangements as noncurrent assets in either the investments or other assets sections, using a caption such as "Cash on deposit maintained as compensating balance." In cases where compensating balance arrangements exist without agreements that restrict the use of cash amounts shown on the balance sheet, companies should describe the arrangements and the amounts involved in the notes.

Bank Overdrafts

Bank overdrafts occur when a company writes a check for more than the amount in its cash account. Companies should report bank overdrafts in the current liabilities section, adding them to the amount reported as accounts payable. If material, companies should disclose these items separately, either on the face of the balance sheet or in the related notes.[3]

Bank overdrafts are generally not offset against the cash account. A major exception is when available cash is present in another account in the same bank on which the overdraft occurred. Offsetting in this case is required.

Summary of Cash-Related Items

Cash and cash equivalents include the medium of exchange and most negotiable instruments. If the item cannot be quickly converted to coin or currency, a company separately classifies it as an investment, receivable, or prepaid expense. Companies segregate and classify cash that is unavailable for payment of currently maturing liabilities in the long-term assets section. Illustration 7-2 summarizes the classification of cash-related items.

ILLUSTRATION 7-2
Classification of Cash-Related Items

Classification of Cash, Cash Equivalents, and Noncash Items

Item	Classification	Comment
Cash	Cash	If unrestricted, report as cash. If restricted, identify and classify as current and noncurrent assets.
Petty cash and change funds	Cash	Report as cash.
Short-term paper	Cash equivalents	Investments with maturity of less than 3 months, often combined with cash.
Short-term paper	Temporary investments	Investments with maturity of 3 to 12 months.
Postdated checks and IOU's	Receivables	Assumed to be collectible.
Travel advances	Receivables	Assumed to be collected from employees or deducted from their salaries.
Postage on hand (as stamps or in postage meters)	Prepaid expenses	May also be classified as office supplies inventory.
Bank overdrafts	Current liability	If right of offset exists, reduce cash.
Compensating balances	Cash separately classified as a deposit maintained as compensating balance	Classify as current or noncurrent in the balance sheet. Disclose separately in notes details of the arrangement.

[3]Bank overdrafts usually occur because of a simple oversight by the company writing the check. Banks often expect companies to have overdrafts from time to time and therefore negotiate a fee as payment for this possible occurrence. However, at one time, **E. F. Hutton** (a large brokerage firm) began intentionally overdrawing its accounts by astronomical amounts—on some days exceeding $1 billion—thus obtaining interest-free loans that it could invest. Because the amounts were so large and fees were not negotiated in advance, E. F. Hutton came under criminal investigation for its actions.

DEEP POCKETS

What do the numbers mean?

Many companies are loaded with cash. One major reason for hoarding cash is to make the company more secure in this credit-crunch environment. As one analyst noted, "At times like this, stockholder value goes out the window and it is all about survival. Liquidity is an absolute key component of any business." Another strategy is using the cash to look for deals. **Centrica** and **Cisco** indicate that they are raising cash for purposes of making acquisitions. Others point out that it enables them to continue investing even in the downturn. For example, CEO Steve Jobs of **Apple** noted that during the last downturn related to the dot-com bubble, the iPod was born. The following are some well-known companies that have substantial cash resources, including **Hewlett-Packard (HP)**. Just recently, HP sold for only six times its $11 billion of cash and equivalents.

Company	Industry	Cash ($000,000)	Market Value/ Cash %
Nokia	Technology hardware and equipment	$10,917	3.8
Sony	Technology hardware and equipment	8,646	4.6
Vale	Materials	10,331	5.3
Siemens	Conglomerate	8,450	6.1
Hewlett-Packard	Technology hardware and equipment	11,189	6.2
ExxonMobil	Oil and gas operations	31,437	10.5
Apple	Technology hardware and equipment	7,236	12.5
Johnson & Johnson	Drugs and biotechnology	10,768	13.3
Chevron	Oil and gas operations	9,347	13.9
Microsoft	Software and services	8,346	18.7

Source: Anonymous, "Cheap and Cash Rich," *Forbes* (April 27, 2009).

ACCOUNTS RECEIVABLE

3 LEARNING OBJECTIVE
Define receivables and identify the different types of receivables.

Receivables are claims held against customers and others for money, goods, or services. For financial statement purposes, companies classify receivables as either **current** (short-term) or **noncurrent** (long-term). Companies expect to collect **current receivables** within a year or during the current operating cycle, whichever is longer. They classify all other receivables as **noncurrent**. Receivables are further classified in the balance sheet as either trade or nontrade receivables.

Customers often owe a company amounts for goods bought or services rendered. A company may subclassify these **trade receivables**, usually the most significant item it possesses, into accounts receivable and notes receivable. **Accounts receivable** are oral promises of the purchaser to pay for goods and services sold. They represent "open accounts" resulting from short-term extensions of credit. A company normally collects them within 30 to 60 days. **Notes receivable** are written promises to pay a certain sum of money on a specified future date. They may arise from sales, financing, or other transactions. Notes may be short-term or long-term.

Nontrade receivables arise from a variety of transactions. Some examples of nontrade receivables are:

1. Advances to officers and employees.
2. Advances to subsidiaries.
3. Deposits paid to cover potential damages or losses.
4. Deposits paid as a guarantee of performance or payment.
5. Dividends and interest receivable.
6. Claims against:
   (a) Insurance companies for casualties sustained.
   (b) Defendants under suit.

(c) Governmental bodies for tax refunds.
(d) Common carriers for damaged or lost goods.
(e) Creditors for returned, damaged, or lost goods.
(f) Customers for returnable items (crates, containers, etc.).

Because of the peculiar nature of nontrade receivables, companies generally report them as separate items in the balance sheet. Illustration 7-3 shows the reporting of trade and nontrade receivables in the balance sheets of **Molson Coors Brewing Company** and **Seaboard Corporation.**

Molson Coors Brewing Company
(in thousands)

Current assets	
Cash and cash equivalents	$ 377,023
Accounts and notes receivable	
Trade, less allowance for doubtful accounts of $8,827	758,526
Current notes receivable and other receivables, less allowance for doubtful accounts of $3,181	112,626
Inventories	369,521
Maintenance and operating supplies, less allowance for obsolete supplies of $10,556	34,782
Other current assets, less allowance for advertising supplies of $948	124,336
Total current assets	$1,776,814

Seaboard Corporation
(in thousands)

Current assets		
Cash and cash equivalents		$ 47,346
Short-term investments		286,660
Receivables		
Trade	$251,005	
Due from foreign affiliates	90,019	
Other	$ 26,349	
		367,373
Allowance for doubtful accounts		(8,060)
Net receivables		359,313
Inventories		392,946
Deferred income taxes		19,558
Other current assets		77,710
Total current assets		$1,183,533

ILLUSTRATION 7-3
Receivables Balance Sheet Presentations

The basic issues in accounting for accounts and notes receivable are the same: **recognition, valuation,** and **disposition.** We discuss these basic issues for accounts and notes receivable next.

Recognition of Accounts Receivable

LEARNING OBJECTIVE 4
Explain accounting issues related to recognition of accounts receivable.

In most receivables transactions, the amount to be recognized is the exchange price between the two parties. **The exchange price is the amount due from the debtor** (a customer or a borrower). Some type of business document, often an invoice, serves as evidence of the exchange price. Two factors may complicate the measurement of the exchange price: (1) the availability of discounts (trade and cash discounts), and (2) the length of time between the sale and the due date of payments (the interest element).

Trade Discounts

Prices may be subject to a trade or quantity discount. Companies use such **trade discounts** to avoid frequent changes in catalogs, to alter prices for different quantities purchased, or to hide the true invoice price from competitors.

Trade discounts are commonly quoted in percentages. For example, say your cell phone has a list price of $90, and the manufacturer sells it to **Best Buy** for list less a

30 percent trade discount. The manufacturer then records the receivable at $63 per phone. The manufacturer, per normal practice, simply deducts the trade discount from the list price and bills the customer net.

As another example, **Maxwell House** at one time sold a 10-ounce jar of its instant coffee listing at $5.85 to supermarkets for $5.05, a trade discount of approximately 14 percent. The supermarkets in turn sold the instant coffee for $5.20 per jar. Maxwell House records the receivable and related sales revenue at $5.05 per jar, not $5.85.

Cash Discounts (Sales Discounts)

Companies offer **cash discounts (sales discounts)** to induce prompt payment. Cash discounts generally presented in terms such as 2/10, n/30 (2 percent if paid within 10 days, gross amount due in 30 days), or 2/10, E.O.M., net 30, E.O.M. (2 percent if paid any time before the tenth day of the following month, with full payment due by the thirtieth of the following month).

Companies usually take sales discounts unless their cash is severely limited. Why? A company that receives a 1 percent reduction in the sales price for payment within 10 days, total payment due within 30 days, effectively earns 18.25 percent (.01 ÷ [20/365]), or at least avoids that rate of interest cost.

Companies usually record sales and related sales discount transactions by entering the receivable and sale at the gross amount. Under this method, companies recognize sales discounts only when they receive payment within the discount period. The income statement shows sales discounts as a deduction from sales to arrive at net sales.

Some contend that sales discounts not taken reflect penalties added to an established price to encourage prompt payment. That is, the seller offers sales on account at a slightly higher price than if selling for cash. The cash discount offered offsets the increase. Thus, customers who pay within the discount period actually purchase at the cash price. Those who pay after expiration of the discount period pay a penalty for the delay—an amount in excess of the cash price. Per this reasoning, companies record sales and receivables net. They subsequently debit any discounts not taken to Accounts Receivable and credit to Sales Discounts Forfeited. The entries in Illustration 7-4 show the difference between the gross and net methods.

ILLUSTRATION 7-4
Entries under Gross and Net Methods of Recording Cash (Sales) Discounts

Gross Method			**Net Method**		
Sales of $10,000, terms 2/10, n/30					
Accounts Receivable	10,000		Accounts Receivable	9,800	
Sales Revenue		10,000	Sales Revenue		9,800
Payment on $4,000 of sales received within discount period					
Cash	3,920		Cash	3,920	
Sales Discounts	80		Accounts Receivable		3,920
Accounts Receivable		4,000			
Payment on $6,000 of sales received after discount period					
Cash	6,000		Accounts Receivable	120	
Accounts Receivable		6,000	Sales Discounts Forfeited		120
			Cash	6,000	
			Accounts Receivable		6,000

If using the gross method, a company reports sales discounts as a deduction from sales in the income statement. Proper expense recognition dictates that the company also reasonably estimates the expected discounts to be taken and charges that amount against sales. If using the net method, a company considers Sales Discounts Forfeited as an "Other revenue" item.[4]

Theoretically, the recognition of Sales Discounts Forfeited is correct. The receivable is stated closer to its realizable value, and the net sales figure measures the revenue earned from the sale. As a practical matter, however, companies seldom use the net method because it requires additional analysis and bookkeeping. For example, the net method requires adjusting entries to record sales discounts forfeited on accounts receivable that have passed the discount period.

Nonrecognition of Interest Element

Ideally, a company should measure receivables in terms of their present value, that is, the discounted value of the cash to be received in the future. When expected cash receipts require a waiting period, the receivable face amount is not worth the amount that the company ultimately receives.

To illustrate, assume that **Best Buy** makes a sale on account for $1,000 with payment due in four months. The applicable annual rate of interest is 12 percent, and payment is made at the end of four months. The present value of that receivable is not $1,000 but $961.54 ($1,000 × .96154). In other words, the $1,000 Best Buy receives four months from now is not the same as the $1,000 received today.

Underlying Concepts

Materiality means it must make a difference to a decision-maker. The FASB believes that present value concepts can be ignored for short-term receivables.

Theoretically, any revenue after the period of sale is interest revenue. In practice, companies ignore interest revenue related to accounts receivable because the amount of the discount is not usually material in relation to the net income for the period. The profession specifically excludes from present value considerations "receivables arising from transactions with customers in the normal course of business which are due in customary trade terms not exceeding approximately one year." **[2]**

Valuation of Accounts Receivable

LEARNING OBJECTIVE 5

Explain accounting issues related to valuation of accounts receivable.

Reporting of receivables involves (1) classification and (2) valuation on the balance sheet. Classification involves determining the length of time each receivable will be outstanding. Companies classify receivables intended to be collected within a year or the operating cycle, whichever is longer, as current. All other receivables are classified as long-term.

Companies value and report short-term receivables at net realizable value—the net amount they expect to receive in cash. Determining net realizable value requires estimating both uncollectible receivables and any returns or allowances to be granted.

Uncollectible Accounts Receivable

As one revered accountant aptly noted, the credit manager's idea of heaven probably would be a place where everyone (eventually) paid his or her debts.[5] Unfortunately, this situation often does not occur. For example, a customer may not be able to pay because of a decline in its sales revenue due to a downturn in the economy. Similarly, individuals may be laid off from their jobs or faced with unexpected hospital bills. Companies record credit losses as debits to Bad Debt Expense (or Uncollectible Accounts Expense). Such losses are a normal and necessary risk of doing business on a credit basis.

[4]To the extent that discounts not taken reflect a short-term financing, some argue that companies could use an interest revenue account to record these amounts.

[5]William J. Vatter, *Managerial Accounting* (Englewood Cliffs, N.J.: Prentice-Hall, 1950), p. 60.

Two methods are used in accounting for uncollectible accounts: (1) the direct write-off method and (2) the allowance method. The following sections explain these methods.

Direct Write-Off Method for Uncollectible Accounts

Under the **direct write-off method**, when a company determines a particular account to be uncollectible, it charges the loss to Bad Debt Expense. Assume, for example, that on December 10 Cruz Co. writes off as uncollectible Yusado's $8,000 balance. The entry is:

December 10		
Bad Debt Expense	8,000	
Accounts Receivable (Yusado)		8,000
(To record write-off of Yusado account)		

Under this method, Bad Debt Expense will show only **actual losses** from uncollectibles. The company will report accounts receivable at its gross amount.

Supporters of the **direct write-off-method** (which is often used for tax purposes) contend that it records facts, not estimates. It assumes that a good account receivable resulted from each sale, and that later events revealed certain accounts to be uncollectible and worthless. From a practical standpoint, this method is simple and convenient to apply. But the direct write-off method is theoretically deficient: It usually fails to record expenses in the same period as associated revenues. Nor does it result in receivables being stated at net realizable value on the statement of financial position. **As a result, using the direct write-off method is not considered appropriate, except when the amount uncollectible is immaterial.**

Allowance Method for Uncollectible Accounts

The **allowance method** of accounting for bad debts involves estimating uncollectible accounts at the end of each period. This ensures that companies state receivables on the balance sheet at their net realizable value. **Net realizable value** is the net amount the company expects to receive in cash. The FASB considers the collectibility of receivables a loss contingency. Thus, the allowance method is appropriate in situations where it is probable that an asset has been impaired and that the amount of the loss can be reasonably estimated. [3]

Although estimates are involved, companies can predict the percentage of uncollectible receivables from past experiences, present market conditions, and an analysis of the outstanding balances. Many companies set their credit policies to provide for a certain percentage of uncollectible accounts. (In fact, many feel that failure to reach that percentage means that they are losing sales due to overly restrictive credit policies.) Thus, the FASB requires the allowance method for financial reporting purposes when bad debts are material in amount. This method has three essential features:

1. Companies **estimate** uncollectible accounts receivable. They match this estimated expense **against revenues** in the same accounting period in which they record the revenues.
2. Companies debit estimated uncollectibles to Bad Debt Expense and credit them to Allowance for Doubtful Accounts (a contra-asset account) through an adjusting entry at the end of each period.
3. When companies write off a specific account, they debit actual uncollectibles to Allowance for Doubtful Accounts and credit that amount to Accounts Receivable.

Recording Estimated Uncollectibles. To illustrate the allowance method, assume that Brown Furniture has credit sales of $1,800,000 in 2012. Of this amount, $150,000 remains uncollected at December 31. The credit manager estimates that $10,000 of these sales will be uncollectible. The adjusting entry to record the estimated uncollectibles is:

December 31		
Bad Debt Expense	10,000	
Allowance for Doubtful Accounts		10,000
(To record estimate of uncollectible accounts)		

Brown reports Bad Debt Expense in the income statement as an operating expense. Thus, the estimated uncollectibles are matched with sales in 2012. Brown records the expense in the same year it made the sales.

As Illustration 7-5 shows, the company deducts the allowance account from accounts receivable in the current assets section of the balance sheet.

ILLUSTRATION 7-5
Presentation of Allowance for Doubtful Accounts

BROWN FURNITURE
BALANCE SHEET (PARTIAL)

Current assets		
Cash		$ 15,000
Accounts receivable	$150,000	
Less: Allowance for doubtful accounts	10,000	140,000
Inventory		300,000
Prepaid insurance		25,000
Total current assets		$480,000

Allowance for Doubtful Accounts shows the estimated amount of claims on customers that the company expects will become uncollectible in the future.[6] Companies use a contra account instead of a direct credit to Accounts Receivable because they do not know which customers will not pay. The credit balance in the allowance account will absorb the specific write-offs when they occur. The amount of $140,000 in Illustration 7-5 represents the **net realizable value** of the accounts receivable at the statement date. **Companies do not close Allowance for Doubtful Accounts at the end of the fiscal year.**

Recording the Write-Off of an Uncollectible Account. When companies have exhausted all means of collecting a past-due account and collection appears impossible, the company should write off the account. In the credit card industry, for example, it is standard practice to write off accounts that are 210 days past due.

To illustrate a receivables write-off, assume that the financial vice president of Brown Furniture authorizes a write-off of the $1,000 balance owed by Randall Co. on March 1, 2013. The entry to record the write-off is:

March 1, 2013		
Allowance for Doubtful Accounts	1,000	
Accounts Receivable (Randall Co.)		1,000
(Write-off of Randall Co. account)		

Bad Debt Expense does not increase when the write-off occurs. **Under the allowance method, companies debit every bad debt write-off to the allowance account rather than to Bad Debt Expense.** A debit to Bad Debt Expense would be incorrect because the company has already recognized the expense when it made the adjusting entry for estimated bad debts. Instead, the entry to record the write-off of an uncollectible account reduces both Accounts Receivable and Allowance for Doubtful Accounts.

[6]The account description employed for the allowance account is usually Allowance for Doubtful Accounts or simply Allowance. *Accounting Trends and Techniques—2010,* for example, indicates that approximately 83 percent of the companies surveyed used "allowance" in their description.

Recovery of an Uncollectible Account. Occasionally, a company collects from a customer after it has written off the account as uncollectible. The company makes two entries to record the recovery of a bad debt: (1) It reverses the entry made in writing off the account. This reinstates the customer's account. (2) It journalizes the collection in the usual manner.

To illustrate, assume that on July 1, Randall Co. pays the $1,000 amount that Brown had written off on March 1. These are the entries:

July 1		
Accounts Receivable (Randall Co.)	1,000	
Allowance for Doubtful Accounts		1,000
(To reverse write-off of account)		
Cash	1,000	
Accounts Receivable (Randall Co.)		1,000
(Collection of account)		

Note that the recovery of a bad debt, like the write-off of a bad debt, affects **only balance sheet accounts**. The net effect of the two entries above is a debit to Cash and a credit to Allowance for Doubtful Accounts for $1,000.[7]

Bases Used for Allowance Method. To simplify the preceding explanation, we assumed we knew the amount of the expected uncollectibles. In "real life," companies must estimate that amount when they use the allowance method. Two bases are used to determine this amount: **(1) percentage of sales**, and **(2) percentage of receivables**. Both bases are generally accepted. The choice is a management decision. It depends on the relative emphasis that management wishes to give to expenses and revenues on the one hand or to net realizable value of the accounts receivable on the other. The choice is whether to emphasize income statement or balance sheet relationships. Illustration 7-6 compares the two bases.

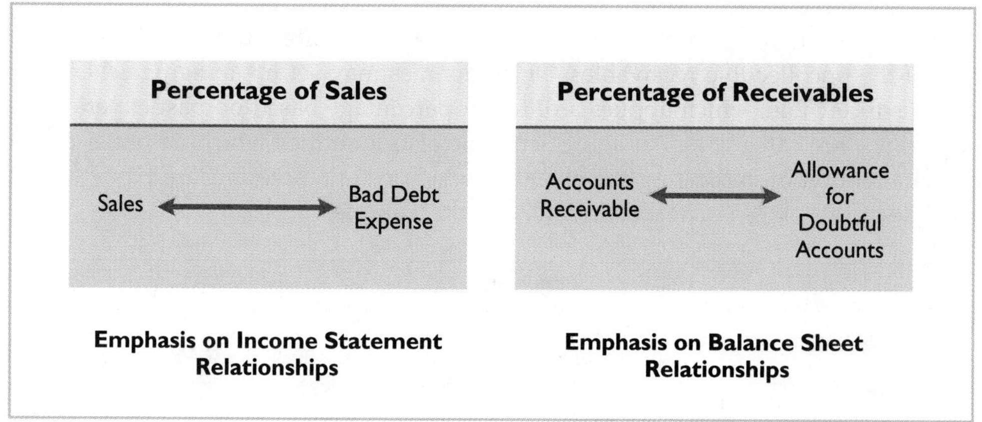

ILLUSTRATION 7-6
Comparison of Bases for Estimating Uncollectibles

The percentage-of-sales basis results in a better matching of expenses with revenues—an income statement viewpoint. The percentage-of-receivables basis produces the better estimate of net realizable value—a balance sheet viewpoint. Under both bases, the company must determine its past experience with bad debt losses.

Underlying Concepts

The percentage-of-sales method illustrates the expense recognition principle, which relates expenses to revenues earned.

Percentage-of-sales (income statement) approach. In the **percentage-of-sales approach**, management estimates what percentage of credit sales will be uncollectible. This percentage is based on past experience and anticipated credit policy.

[7]If using the direct write-off approach, the company debits the amount collected to Cash and credits a revenue account entitled Uncollectible Amounts Recovered, with proper notation in the customer's account.

The company applies this percentage to either total credit sales or net credit sales of the current year. To illustrate, assume that Gonzalez Company elects to use the percentage-of-sales basis. It concludes that 1% of net credit sales will become uncollectible. If net credit sales for 2012 are $800,000, the estimated bad debts expense is $8,000 (1% × $800,000). The adjusting entry is:

December 31		
Bad Debt Expense	8,000	
Allowance for Doubtful Accounts		8,000

After the adjusting entry is posted, assuming the allowance account already has a credit balance of $1,723, the accounts of Gonzalez Company will show the following:

ILLUSTRATION 7-7
Bad Debt Accounts after Posting

Bad Debt Expense			Allowance for Doubtful Accounts	
Dec. 31 Adj.	8,000		Jan. 1 Bal.	1,723
			Dec. 31 Adj.	8,000
			Dec. 31 Bal.	9,723

The amount of bad debt expense and the related credit to the allowance account are unaffected by any balance currently existing in the allowance account. Because the bad debt expense estimate is related to a nominal account (Sales Revenue), any balance in the allowance is ignored. Therefore, the percentage-of-sales method achieves a proper matching of cost and revenues. This method is frequently referred to as the **income statement approach.**

Percentage-of-receivables (balance sheet) approach. Using past experience, a company can estimate the percentage of its outstanding receivables that will become uncollectible, without identifying specific accounts. This procedure provides a reasonably accurate estimate of the receivables' realizable value. But, it does not fit the concept of matching cost and revenues. Rather, it simply reports receivables in the statement of financial position at net realizable value. Hence, it is referred to as the **percentage-of-receivables** (or balance sheet) **approach.**

Companies may apply this method using one **composite rate** that reflects an estimate of the uncollectible receivables. Or, companies may set up an **aging schedule** of accounts receivable, which applies a different percentage based on past experience to the various age categories. An aging schedule also identifies which accounts require special attention by indicating the extent to which certain accounts are past due. The schedule of Wilson & Co. in Illustration 7-8 is an example.

ILLUSTRATION 7-8
Accounts Receivable Aging Schedule

WILSON & CO.
AGING SCHEDULE

Name of Customer	Balance Dec. 31	Under 60 days	60–90 days	91–120 days	Over 120 days
Western Stainless Steel Corp.	$ 98,000	$ 80,000	$18,000		
Brockway Steel Company	320,000	320,000			
Freeport Sheet & Tube Co.	55,000				$55,000
Allegheny Iron Works	74,000	60,000		$14,000	
	$547,000	$460,000	$18,000	$14,000	$55,000

Summary

Age	Amount	Percentage Estimated to Be Uncollectible	Required Balance in Allowance
Under 60 days old	$460,000	4%	$18,400
60–90 days old	18,000	15%	2,700
91–120 days old	14,000	20%	2,800
Over 120 days	55,000	25%	13,750
Year-end balance of allowance for doubtful accounts			$37,650

Wilson reports bad debt expense of $37,650 for this year, assuming that no balance existed in the allowance account.

To change the illustration slightly, **assume that the allowance account had a credit balance of $800 before adjustment**. In this case, Wilson adds $36,850 ($37,650 – $800) to the allowance account, and makes the following entry.

Bad Debt Expense	36,850	
Allowance for Doubtful Accounts		36,850

Wilson therefore states the balance in the allowance account at $37,650. **If the Allowance balance before adjustment had a debit balance of $200**, then Wilson records bad debt expense of $37,850 ($37,650 desired balance + $200 debit balance). In the percentage-of-receivables method, Wilson cannot ignore the balance in the allowance account, because the percentage is related to a real account (Accounts Receivable).

Companies usually do not prepare an aging schedule to determine bad debt expense. Rather, they prepare it as a control device to determine the composition of receivables and to identify delinquent accounts. Companies base the estimated loss percentage developed for each category on previous loss experience and the advice of credit department personnel.

Whether using a composite rate or an aging schedule, the primary objective of the percentage of outstanding receivables method for financial statement purposes is to report receivables in the balance sheet at net realizable value. However, it is deficient in that it may not match the bad debt expense to the period in which the sale takes place.

The allowance for doubtful accounts as a percentage of receivables will vary, depending on the industry and the economic climate. Companies such as **Eastman Kodak**, **General Electric**, and **Monsanto** have recorded allowances ranging from $3 to $6 per $100 of accounts receivable. Other large companies, such as **CPC International** ($1.48), **Texaco** ($1.23), and **USX Corp.** ($0.78), have had bad debt allowances of less than $1.50 per $100. At the other extreme are hospitals that allow for $15 to $20 per $100 of accounts receivable.[8]

Gateway to the Profession

Tutorial on Recording Uncollectible Accounts

Regardless of the method chosen—percentage-of-sales or -receivables—determining the expense associated with uncollectible accounts requires a large degree of judgment. Recent concern exists that, similar to **Nortel** in our opening story, some banks use this judgment to manage earnings. By overestimating the amounts of uncollectible loans in a good earnings year, the bank can "save for a rainy day" in a future period. In future (less-profitable) periods, banks can reduce the overly conservative allowance for loan loss account to increase earnings. In this regard, the SEC brought action against **Suntrust Banks**, requiring a reversal of $100 million of bad debt expense. This reversal increased after-tax profit by $61 million.[9]

[8]Recent statistics indicate that customers have been taking nearly 28 days to pay in full. This is a longer period, compared to 2009 when customers on average paid in 24 days (see Anonymous, *Wall Street Journal* (August 19, 2010), p. B5). A U.S. Department of Commerce study indicated, as a general rule, the following relationships between the age of accounts receivable and their uncollectibility.

30 days or less	4% uncollectible
31–60 days	10% uncollectible
61–90 days	17% uncollectible
91–120 days	26% uncollectible

After 120 days, an approximate 3–4 percent increase in uncollectibles for every 30 days outstanding occurs for the remainder of the first year.

[9]Recall from our earnings management discussion in Chapter 4 that increasing or decreasing income through management manipulation can reduce the quality of financial reports.

What do the numbers mean?

"TOO GENEROUS"?

Target Corp. is one of the few companies that strongly *increased* lending in the face of the ongoing credit crisis. In fact, in a recent quarter, Target had $8.62 billion loans outstanding on its private-label Visa card, an increase of 29 percent over a year earlier. The growth in its credit card business has been the major contributor to Target's recent earnings growth. So what's the problem?

Some fear that Target is lending too much at a time when the economy is slowing. This could lead to earnings problems down the road, especially if Target is growing its credit card business by giving its cards to riskier customers. To gauge the credit-worthiness of borrowers, analysts follow a metric that tracks how much of the loan's principal is paid down each month. A low pay-down proportion indicates that borrowers are having a harder time repaying their credit card debt. Target's pay-down rate has been around 14 percent. In contrast, Discover's pay-down rate was 21 percent. Thus, it looks like Target's borrowers are slower to repay.

Investors should pay attention because Target's earnings could take a hit in the future if, as appears likely, the company will have to increase bad debt expense in order to reserve for these bad loans.

Source: P. Eavis, "Is Target Corp.'s Credit Too Generous?," *Wall Street Journal* (March 11, 2008), p. C1.

NOTES RECEIVABLE

LEARNING OBJECTIVE 

Explain accounting issues related to recognition and valuation of notes receivable.

A note receivable is supported by a formal **promissory note**, a written promise to pay a certain sum of money at a specific future date. Such a note is a negotiable instrument that a **maker** signs in favor of a designated **payee** who may legally and readily sell or otherwise transfer the note to others. Although all notes contain an interest element because of the time value of money, companies classify them as interest-bearing or non-interest-bearing. **Interest-bearing notes** have a stated rate of interest. **Zero-interest-bearing notes** (non-interest-bearing) include interest as part of their face amount. Notes receivable are considered fairly liquid, even if long-term, because companies may easily convert them to cash (although they might pay a fee to do so).

Companies frequently accept notes receivable from customers who need to extend the payment period of an outstanding receivable. Or they require notes from high-risk or new customers. In addition, companies often use notes in loans to employees and subsidiaries, and in the sales of property, plant, and equipment. In some industries (e.g., the pleasure and sport boat industry) notes support all credit sales. The majority of notes, however, originate from lending transactions. The basic issues in accounting for notes receivable are the same as those for accounts receivable: **recognition, valuation, and disposition**.

Recognition of Notes Receivable

Companies generally record short-term notes at face value (less allowances) because the interest implicit in the maturity value is immaterial. A general rule is that notes treated as cash equivalents (maturities of three months or less and easily converted to cash) are not subject to premium or discount amortization.

However, companies should record and report long-term notes receivable at the **present value of the cash they expect to collect**. When the interest stated on an interest-bearing note equals the effective (market) rate of interest, the note sells at face value.[10]

[10]The **stated interest rate**, also referred to as the face rate or the coupon rate, is the rate contracted as part of the note. The **effective-interest rate**, also referred to as the *market rate* or the *effective yield*, is the rate used in the market to determine the value of the note—that is, the discount rate used to determine present value.

When the stated rate differs from the market rate, the cash exchanged (present value) differs from the face value of the note. Companies then record this difference, either a discount or a premium, and amortize it over the life of a note to approximate the effective (market) interest rate. This illustrates one of the many situations in which time value of money concepts are applied to accounting measurement.

Note Issued at Face Value

To illustrate the discounting of a note issued at face value, assume that Bigelow Corp. lends Scandinavian Imports $10,000 in exchange for a $10,000, three-year note bearing interest at 10 percent annually. The market rate of interest for a note of similar risk is also 10 percent. We show the time diagram depicting both cash flows in Illustration 7-9.

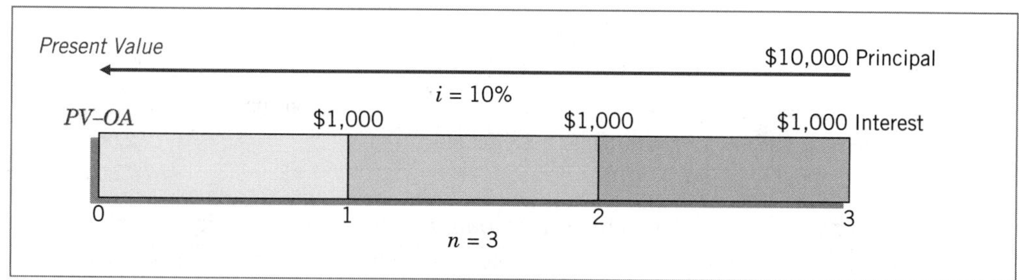

ILLUSTRATION 7-9
Time Diagram for Note Issued at Face Value

Bigelow computes the present value or exchange price of the note as follows.

ILLUSTRATION 7-10
Present Value of Note—Stated and Market Rates the Same

Face value of the note		$10,000
Present value of the principal:		
$10,000 ($PVF_{3,10\%}$) = $10,000 × .75132	$7,513	
Present value of the interest:		
$1,000 ($PVF\text{-}OA_{3,10\%}$) = $1,000 × 2.48685	2,487	
Present value of the note		10,000
Difference		$ -0-

In this case, the present value of the note equals its face value, because the effective and stated rates of interest are also the same. Bigelow records the receipt of the note as follows.

Notes Receivable	10,000	
Cash		10,000

Bigelow recognizes the interest earned each year as follows.

Cash	1,000	
Interest Revenue		1,000

You can use a financial calculator to solve this problem.

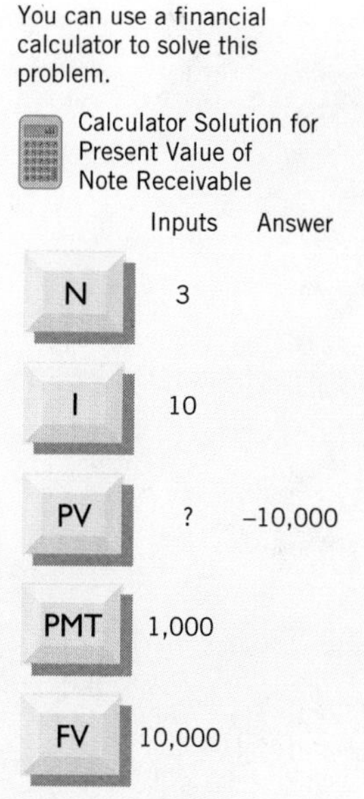

Note Not Issued at Face Value

Zero-Interest-Bearing Notes. If a company receives a zero-interest-bearing note, its present value is the cash paid to the issuer. Because the company knows both the future amount and the present value of the note, it can compute the interest rate. This rate is often referred to as the **implicit interest rate**. Companies record the difference between the future (face) amount and the present value (cash paid) as a discount and amortize it to interest revenue over the life of the note.

To illustrate, Jeremiah Company receives a three-year, $10,000 zero-interest-bearing note, the present value of which is $7,721.80. The implicit rate that equates the total cash to be received ($10,000 at maturity) to the present value of the future cash flows

($7,721.80) is 9 percent (the present value of 1 for three periods at 9 percent is .77218). We show the time diagram depicting the one cash flow in Illustration 7-11.

ILLUSTRATION 7-11
Time Diagram for Zero-Interest-Bearing Note

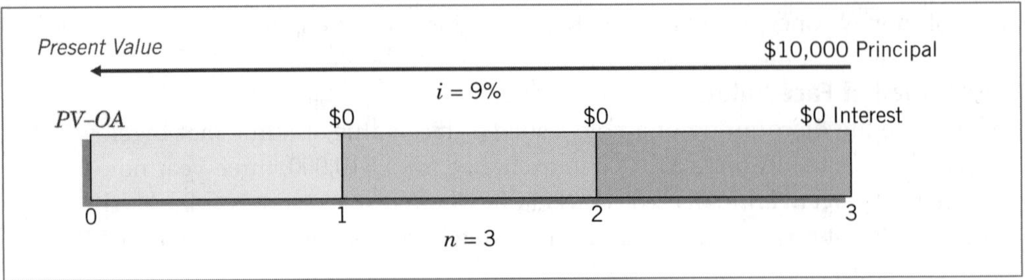

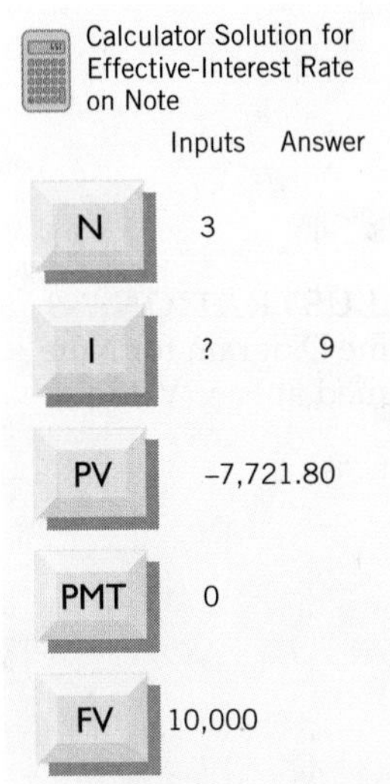

Jeremiah records the transaction as follows.

Notes Receivable	10,000.00	
Discount on Notes Receivable ($10,000 – $7,721.80)		2,278.20
Cash		7,721.80

The Discount on Notes Receivable is a valuation account. Companies report it on the balance sheet as a contra-asset account to notes receivable. They then amortize the discount, and recognize interest revenue annually using the **effective-interest method**. Illustration 7-12 shows the three-year discount amortization and interest revenue schedule.

ILLUSTRATION 7-12
Discount Amortization Schedule—Effective-Interest Method

SCHEDULE OF NOTE DISCOUNT AMORTIZATION
EFFECTIVE-INTEREST METHOD
0% NOTE DISCOUNTED AT 9%

	Cash Received	Interest Revenue	Discount Amortized	Carrying Amount of Note
Date of issue				$ 7,721.80
End of year 1	$ -0-	$ 694.96[a]	$ 694.96[b]	8,416.76[c]
End of year 2	-0-	757.51	757.51	9,174.27
End of year 3	-0-	825.73[d]	825.73	10,000.00
	$ -0-	$2,278.20	$2,278.20	

[a]$7,721.80 × .09 = $694.96
[b]$694.96 – 0 = $694.96
[c]$7,721.80 + $694.96 = $8,416.76
[d]5¢ adjustment to compensate for rounding

Jeremiah records interest revenue at the end of the first year using the effective-interest method as follows.

Discount on Notes Receivable	694.96	
Interest Revenue ($7,721.80 × 9%)		694.96

The amount of the discount, $2,278.20 in this case, represents the interest revenue Jeremiah will receive from the note over the three years.

Interest-Bearing Notes. Often the stated rate and the effective rate differ. The zero-interest-bearing note is one example.

To illustrate a more common situation, assume that Morgan Corp. makes a loan to Marie Co. and receives in exchange a three-year, $10,000 note bearing interest at 10 percent annually. The market rate of interest for a note of similar risk is 12 percent. We show the time diagram depicting both cash flows in Illustration 7-13.

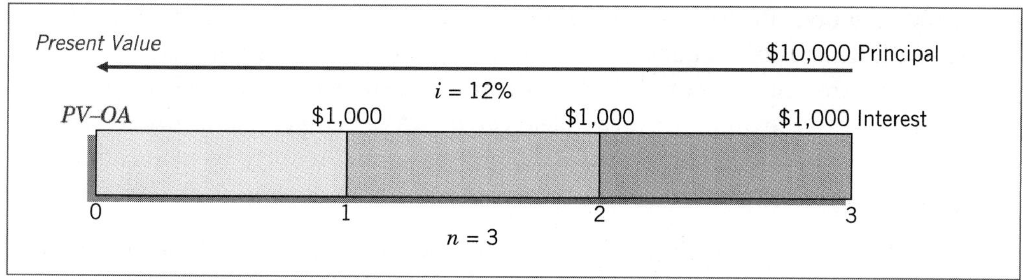

ILLUSTRATION 7-13
Time Diagram for Interest-Bearing Note

Morgan computes the present value of the two cash flows as follows.

ILLUSTRATION 7-14
Computation of Present Value—Effective Rate Different from Stated Rate

Face value of the note		$10,000
Present value of the principal:		
$10,000 ($PVF_{3,12\%}$) = $10,000 × .71178	$7,118	
Present value of the interest:		
$1,000 ($PVF\text{-}OA_{3,12\%}$) = $1,000 × 2.40183	2,402	
Present value of the note		9,520
Difference (Discount)		$ 480

In this case, because the effective rate of interest (12 percent) exceeds the stated rate (10 percent), the present value of the note is less than the face value. That is, Morgan exchanged the note at a **discount**. Morgan records the receipt of the note at a discount as follows.

Notes Receivable	10,000	
Discount on Notes Receivable		480
Cash		9,520

Morgan then amortizes the discount and recognizes interest revenue annually using the **effective-interest method**. Illustration 7-15 shows the three-year discount amortization and interest revenue schedule.

ILLUSTRATION 7-15
Discount Amortization Schedule—Effective-Interest Method

SCHEDULE OF NOTE DISCOUNT AMORTIZATION
EFFECTIVE-INTEREST METHOD
10% NOTE DISCOUNTED AT 12%

	Cash Received	Interest Revenue	Discount Amortized	Carrying Amount of Note
Date of issue				$ 9,520
End of year 1	$1,000[a]	$1,142[b]	$142[c]	9,662[d]
End of year 2	1,000	1,159	159	9,821
End of year 3	1,000	1,179	179	10,000
	$3,000	$3,480	$480	

[a]$10,000 × 10% = $1,000
[b]$9,520 × 12% = $1,142
[c]$1,142 − $1,000 = $142
[d]$9,520 + $142 = $9,662

On the date of issue, the note has a present value of $9,520. Its unamortized discount—additional interest revenue spread over the three-year life of the note—is $480.

At the end of year 1, Morgan receives $1,000 in cash. But its interest revenue is $1,142 ($9,520 × 12%). The difference between $1,000 and $1,142 is the amortized discount, $142. Morgan records receipt of the annual interest and amortization of the discount for the first year as follows (amounts per amortization schedule).

Cash	1,000	
Discount on Notes Receivable	142	
Interest Revenue		1,142

The carrying amount of the note is now $9,662 ($9,520 + $142). Morgan repeats this process until the end of year 3.

When the present value exceeds the face value, the note is exchanged at a premium. Companies record the premium on a note receivable as a debit and amortize it using the effective-interest method over the life of the note as annual reductions in the amount of interest revenue recognized.

Notes Received for Property, Goods, or Services. When a **note is received in exchange for property, goods, or services** in a bargained transaction entered into at arm's length, the stated interest rate is presumed to be fair unless:

1. No interest rate is stated, or
2. The stated interest rate is unreasonable, or
3. The face amount of the note is materially different from the current cash sales price for the same or similar items or from the current market value of the debt instrument. [4]

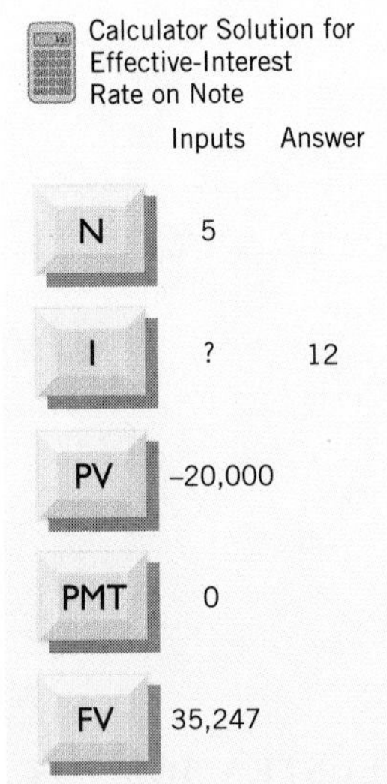

In these circumstances, the company measures the present value of the note by the fair value of the property, goods, or services or by an amount that reasonably approximates the market value of the note.

To illustrate, Oasis Development Co. sold a corner lot to Rusty Pelican as a restaurant site. Oasis accepted in exchange a five-year note having a maturity value of $35,247 and no stated interest rate. The land originally cost Oasis $14,000. At the date of sale, the land had a fair value of $20,000. Given the criterion above, Oasis uses the fair market value of the land, $20,000, as the present value of the note. Oasis therefore records the sale as:

Notes Receivable	35,247	
Discount on Notes Receivable ($35,247 − $20,000)		15,247
Land		14,000
Gain on Disposal of Land ($20,000 − $14,000)		6,000

Oasis amortizes the discount to interest revenue over the five-year life of the note using the effective-interest method.

Choice of Interest Rate

In note transactions, other factors involved in the exchange, such as the fair value of the property, goods, or services, determine the effective or real interest rate. But, if a company cannot determine that fair value, and if the note has no ready market, determining the present value of the note is more difficult. To estimate the present value of a note under such circumstances, the company must approximate an applicable interest rate that may differ from the stated interest rate. This process of interest-rate approximation is called **imputation**. The resulting interest rate is called an **imputed interest rate**.

The prevailing rates for similar instruments, from issuers with similar credit ratings, affect the choice of a rate. Restrictive covenants, collateral, payment schedule, and the existing prime interest rate also impact the choice. A company determines the imputed interest rate when it receives the note. It ignores any subsequent changes in prevailing interest rates.

Valuation of Notes Receivable

Like accounts receivable, companies record and report short-term notes receivable at their net realizable value—that is, at their face amount less all necessary allowances. The primary notes receivable allowance account is Allowance for Doubtful Accounts. The computations and estimations involved in valuing short-term notes receivable and in recording bad debt expense and the related allowance **exactly parallel that for trade accounts receivable**. Companies estimate the amount of uncollectibles by using either a percentage-of-sales revenue or an analysis of the receivables.

Long-term note receivables involve additional estimation problems. For example, the value of a note receivable can change significantly over time from its original cost. That is, with the passage of time, historical numbers become less and less relevant. As discussed in earlier chapters (2, 5, 6), the FASB requires that for financial instruments such as receivables, companies disclose not only their cost but also their fair value in the notes to the financial statements.

Impairments. A note receivable may become impaired. A note receivable is considered **impaired** when it is probable that the creditor will be unable to collect all amounts due (both principal and interest) according to the contractual terms of the receivable. In this case, a loss is recorded for the amount of the impairment. Appendix 7B further discusses impairments of receivables.

ECONOMIC CONSEQUENCES AND WRITE-OFFS

What do the numbers mean?

The massive write-downs that financial firms are posting have begun to spur a backlash among some investors and executives, who are blaming accounting rules for exaggerating the losses and are seeking new, more forgiving ways to value investments.

The rules—which last made headlines back in the Enron era—require companies to value many of the securities they hold at whatever price prevails in the market, no matter how sharply those prices swing.

Some analysts and executives argue this triggers a domino effect. The market falls, forcing banks to take write-offs, pushing the market lower, causing more write-offs. Companies like AIG and Citicorp argue that their write-downs may never actually result in a true charge to the company. It's a sore point because companies feel they are being forced to take big financial hits on holdings that they have no intention of actually selling at current prices.

Companies believe they are strong enough to simply keep the holdings in their portfolios until the crisis passes. Forcing companies to value securities based on what they would fetch if sold today "is an attempt to apply liquidation accounting to a going concern," says one analyst. Bob Herz, FASB chairman, acknowledges the difficulty but notes, "you tell me what a better answer is. . . . Is just pretending that things aren't decreasing in value a better answer? Should you just let everybody say they think it's going to recover?"

Others who favor the use of market values say that for all its imperfections, market value also imposes discipline on companies. "It forces you to realistically confront what's happening to you much quicker, so it plays a useful purpose," said Sen. Jack Reed (D., R.I.), a member of the Senate banking committee.

Japan stands out as an example of how ignoring problems can lead to years-long stagnation. "Look at Japan, where they ignored write-downs at all their financial institutions when loans went bad," said Jeff Mahoney, general counsel at the Council for Institutional Investors.

In addition, companies don't always have the luxury of waiting out a storm until assets recover the long-term value that executives believe exists. Sometimes market crises force their hands. Freddie Mac, for instance, sold $45 billion of assets last fall to help the company meet regulatory capital requirements.

Source: Adapted from David Reilly, "Wave of Write-Offs Rattles Market: Accounting Rules Blasted as Dow Falls; A $600 Billion Toll?" *Wall Street Journal* (March 1, 2008), p. Al.

SPECIAL ISSUES

Three additional special issues for accounting and reporting of receivables relate to the following.

1. Fair value option.
2. Disposition of receivables.
3. Presentation and disclosure.

Fair Value Option

LEARNING OBJECTIVE 7
Explain the fair value option.

INTERNATIONAL PERSPECTIVE

IFRS also has the fair value option.

Recently, the FASB has given companies the option to use fair value as the basis of measurement in the financial statements. [5] The Board believes that fair value measurement for financial instruments provides more relevant and understandable information than historical cost. It considers fair value to be more relevant because it reflects the current cash equivalent value of financial instruments. As a result, companies now have the option to record fair value in their accounts for most financial instruments, including receivables.

If companies choose the **fair value option**, the receivables are recorded at fair value, with unrealized holding gains or losses reported as part of net income. An **unrealized holding gain or loss** is the net change in the fair value of the receivable from one period to another, exclusive of interest revenue. As a result, the company reports the receivable at fair value each reporting date. In addition, it reports the change in value as part of net income.

Companies may elect to use the fair value option at the time the financial instrument is originally recognized or when some event triggers a new basis of accounting (such as when a business acquisition occurs). If a company elects the fair value option for a financial instrument, it must continue to use fair value measurement for that instrument until the company no longer owns this instrument. If the company does not elect the fair value option for a given financial instrument at the date of recognition, it may not use this option on that specific instrument in subsequent periods.

Recording Fair Value Option

Assume that Escobar Company has notes receivable that have a fair value of $810,000 and a carrying amount of $620,000. Escobar decides on December 31, 2012, to use the fair value option for these receivables. This is the first valuation of these recently acquired receivables. Having elected to use the fair value option, Escobar must value these receivables **at fair value in all subsequent periods in which it holds these receivables**. Similarly, if Escobar elects *not* to use the fair value option, it must use its carrying amount for all future periods.

When using the fair value option, Escobar reports the receivables at fair value, with any unrealized holding gains and losses reported as part of net income. The **unrealized holding gain** is the difference between the fair value and the carrying amount at December 31, 2012, which for Escobar is $190,000 ($810,000 − $620,000). At December 31, 2012, Escobar makes an adjusting entry to record the increase in value of Notes Receivable and to record the unrealized holding gain, as follows.

December 31, 2012		
Notes Receivable	190,000	
Unrealized Holding Gain or Loss—Income		190,000

Escobar adds the difference between fair value and the cost of the notes receivable to arrive at the fair value reported on the balance sheet. In subsequent periods, the company will report **any change in fair value** as an unrealized holding gain or loss. For example, if at December 31, 2013, the fair value of the notes receivable is $800,000, Escobar would recognize an unrealized holding loss of $10,000 ($810,000 − $800,000) and reduce the Notes Receivable account.

LEARNING OBJECTIVE 8
Explain accounting issues related to disposition of accounts and notes receivable.

Disposition of Accounts and Notes Receivable

In the normal course of events, companies collect accounts and notes receivable when due and then remove them from the books. However, the growing size and significance of credit sales and receivables has led to changes in this "normal course of events." **In order to accelerate the receipt of cash from receivables, the owner may transfer accounts or notes receivables to another company for cash.**

There are various reasons for this early transfer. First, for competitive reasons, providing sales financing for customers is virtually mandatory in many industries. In the sale of durable goods, such as automobiles, trucks, industrial and farm equipment, computers, and appliances, most sales are on an installment contract basis. Many major companies in these industries have created wholly-owned subsidiaries specializing in receivables financing. For example, Ford has Ford Motor Credit, and John Deere has John Deere Credit.

Second, the **holder** may sell receivables because money is tight and access to normal credit is unavailable or too expensive. Also, a firm may sell its receivables, instead of borrowing, to avoid violating existing lending agreements.

Finally, billing and collection of receivables are often time-consuming and costly. Credit card companies such as MasterCard, Visa, American Express, Diners Club, Discover, and others take over the collection process and provide merchants with immediate cash.

Conversely, some **purchasers** of receivables buy them to obtain the legal protection of ownership rights afforded a purchaser of assets versus the lesser rights afforded a secured creditor. In addition, banks and other lending institutions may need to purchase receivables because of legal lending limits. That is, they cannot make any additional loans but they can buy receivables and charge a fee for this service.

The transfer of receivables to a third party for cash happens in one of two ways:

1. Secured borrowing.
2. Sales of receivables.

Secured Borrowing

A company often uses receivables as collateral in a borrowing transaction. In fact, a creditor often requires that the debtor designate (assign) or pledge[11] receivables as security for the loan. If the loan is not paid when due, the creditor can convert the collateral to cash—that is, collect the receivables.

To illustrate, on March 1, 2012, Howat Mills, Inc. provides (assigns) $700,000 of its accounts receivable to Citizens Bank as collateral for a $500,000 note. Howat Mills continues to collect the accounts receivable; the account debtors are not notified of the arrangement. Citizens Bank assesses a finance charge of 1 percent of the accounts receivable and interest on the note of 12 percent. Howat Mills makes monthly payments to the bank for all cash it collects on the receivables. Illustration 7-16 (page 386) shows the entries for the secured borrowing for Howat Mills and Citizens Bank.

In addition to recording the collection of receivables, Howat Mills must recognize all discounts, returns and allowances, and bad debts. Each month Howat Mills uses the proceeds from the collection of the accounts receivable to retire the note obligation. In addition, it pays interest on the note.[12]

Sales of Receivables

Sales of receivables have increased substantially in recent years. A common type is a sale to a factor. **Factors** are finance companies or banks that buy receivables from businesses

[11]If a company transfers the receivables for custodial purposes, the custodial arrangement is often referred to as a **pledge**.

[12]What happens if Citizens Bank collected the transferred accounts receivable rather than Howat Mills? Citizens Bank would simply remit the cash proceeds to Howat Mills, and Howat Mills would make the same entries shown in Illustration 7-16. As a result, Howat Mills reports these "collaterized" receivables as an asset on the balance sheet.

Howat Mills, Inc.			Citizens Bank		
Transfer of accounts receivable and issuance of note on March 1, 2012					
Cash	493,000		Notes Receivable	500,000	
Interest Expense	7,000*		Interest Revenue		7,000*
Notes Payable		500,000	Cash		493,000
*(1% × $700,000)					
Collection in March of $440,000 of accounts less cash discounts of $6,000 plus receipt of $14,000 sales returns					
Cash	434,000				
Sales Discounts	6,000				
Sales Returns and Allowances	14,000		(No entry)		
Accounts Receivable					
($440,000 + $14,000 = $454,000)		454,000			
Remitted March collections plus accrued interest to the bank on April 1					
Interest Expense	5,000*		Cash	439,000	
Notes Payable	434,000		Interest Revenue		5,000*
Cash		439,000	Notes Receivable		434,000
*($500,000 × .12 × 1/12)					
Collection in April of the balance of accounts less $2,000 written off as uncollectible					
Cash	244,000				
Allowance for Doubtful Accounts	2,000		(No entry)		
Accounts Receivable		246,000*			
*($700,000 − $454,000)					
Remitted the balance due of $66,000 ($500,000 − $434,000) on the note plus interest on May 1					
Interest Expense	660*		Cash	66,660	
Notes Payable	66,000		Interest Revenue		660*
Cash		66,660	Notes Receivable		66,000
*($66,000 × .12 × 1/12)					

ILLUSTRATION 7-16
Entries for Transfer of Receivables—Secured Borrowing

for a fee and then collect the remittances directly from the customers. **Factoring receivables** is traditionally associated with the textile, apparel, footwear, furniture, and home furnishing industries.[13] Illustration 7-17 shows a typical factoring arrangement.

ILLUSTRATION 7-17
Basic Procedures in Factoring

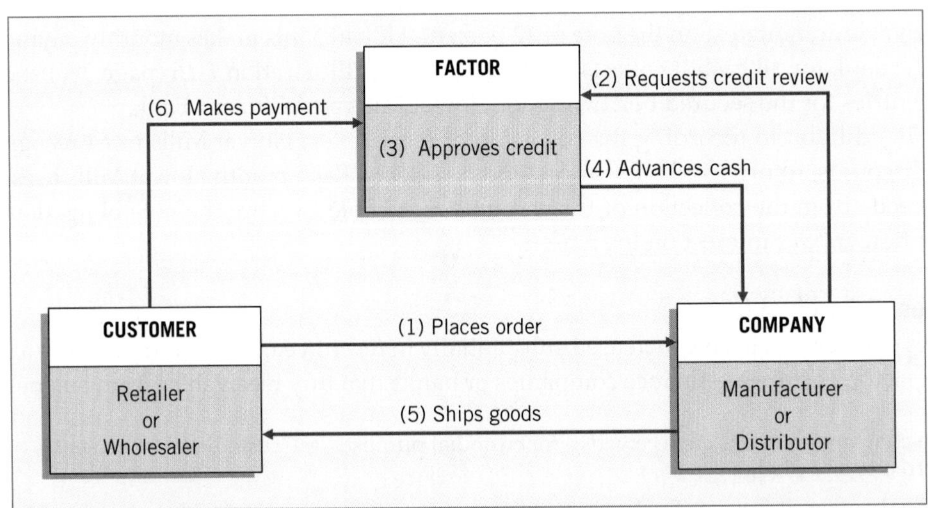

[13]Credit cards like **MasterCard** and **Visa** are a type of factoring arrangement. Typically the purchaser of the receivable charges a ¾–1½ percent commission of the receivables purchased (the commission is 4–5 percent for credit card factoring).

A recent phenomenon in the sale (transfer) of receivables is securitization. **Securitization** takes a pool of assets such as credit card receivables, mortgage receivables, or car loan receivables, and sells shares in these pools of interest and principal payments. This, in effect, creates securities backed by these pools of assets. Virtually every asset with a payment stream and a long-term payment history is a candidate for securitization.

What are the differences between factoring and securitization? Factoring usually involves sale to only one company, fees are high, the quality of the receivables is low, and the seller afterward does not service the receivables. In a securitization, many investors are involved, margins are tight, the receivables are of generally higher quality, and the seller usually continues to service the receivables.

In either a factoring or a securitization transaction, a company sells receivables on either a **without recourse** or a **with recourse** basis.[14]

Sale without Recourse. When buying receivables **without recourse**, the purchaser assumes the risk of collectibility and absorbs any credit losses. The transfer of accounts receivable in a nonrecourse transaction is an outright sale of the receivables both in form (transfer of title) and substance (transfer of control). In nonrecourse transactions, as in any sale of assets, the seller debits Cash for the proceeds and credits Accounts Receivable for the face value of the receivables. The seller recognizes the difference, reduced by any provision for probable adjustments (discounts, returns, allowances, etc.), as a Loss on the Sale of Receivables. The seller uses a Due from Factor account (reported as a receivable) to account for the proceeds retained by the factor to cover probable sales discounts, sales returns, and sales allowances.

To illustrate, Crest Textiles, Inc. factors $500,000 of accounts receivable with Commercial Factors, Inc., on a **without recourse** basis. Crest Textiles transfers the receivable records to Commercial Factors, which will receive the collections. Commercial Factors assesses a finance charge of 3 percent of the amount of accounts receivable and retains an amount equal to 5 percent of the accounts receivable (for probable adjustments). Crest Textiles and Commercial Factors make the following journal entries for the receivables transferred without recourse.

Gateway to the Profession

Comprehensive Illustration of Sale without Recourse

ILLUSTRATION 7-18
Entries for Sale of Receivables without Recourse

Crest Textiles, Inc.		
Cash	460,000	
Due from Factor	25,000*	
Loss on Sale of Receivables	15,000**	
Accounts (Notes) Receivable		500,000

*(5% × $500,000) **(3% × $500,000)

Commercial Factors, Inc.		
Accounts (Notes) Receivable	500,000	
Due to Customer (Crest Textiles)		25,000
Interest Revenue		15,000
Cash		460,000

In recognition of the sale of receivables, Crest Textiles records a loss of $15,000. The factor's net income will be the difference between the financing revenue of $15,000 and the amount of any uncollectible receivables.

Sale with Recourse. For receivables sold **with recourse**, the seller guarantees payment to the purchaser in the event the debtor fails to pay. To record this type of transaction, the seller uses a **financial components approach**, because the seller has a continuing involvement with the receivable. Values are now assigned to such

[14]**Recourse** is the right of a transferee of receivables to receive payment from the transferor of those receivables for (1) failure of the debtors to pay when due, (2) the effects of prepayments, or (3) adjustments resulting from defects in the eligibility of the transferred receivables. **[6]**

components as the recourse provision, servicing rights, and agreement to reacquire. In this approach, each party to the sale only recognizes the assets and liabilities that it controls after the sale.

To illustrate, assume the same information as in Illustration 7-18 for Crest Textiles and for Commercial Factors, except that Crest Textiles sold the receivables on a with-recourse basis. Crest Textiles determines that this recourse liability has a fair value of $6,000. To determine the loss on the sale of the receivables, Crest Textiles computes the net proceeds from the sale as follows.

ILLUSTRATION 7-19
Net Proceeds Computation

Cash received	$460,000	
Due from factor	25,000	$485,000
Less: Recourse liability		6,000
Net proceeds		$479,000

Net proceeds are cash or other assets received in a sale less any liabilities incurred. Crest Textiles then computes the loss as follows.

ILLUSTRATION 7-20
Loss on Sale Computation

Carrying (book) value	$500,000
Net proceeds	479,000
Loss on sale of receivables	$ 21,000

Illustration 7-21 shows the journal entries for both Crest Textiles and Commercial Factors for the receivables sold with recourse.

ILLUSTRATION 7-21
Entries for Sale of Receivables with Recourse

Crest Textiles, Inc.			Commercial Factors, Inc.		
Cash	460,000		Accounts Receivable	500,000	
Due from Factor	25,000		Due to Customer (Crest Textiles)		25,000
Loss on Sale of Receivables	21,000		Interest Revenue		15,000
Accounts (Notes) Receivable		500,000	Cash		460,000
Recourse Liability		6,000			

Gateway to the Profession
Tutorial on the Disposition of Receivables

In this case, Crest Textiles recognizes a loss of $21,000. In addition, it records a liability of $6,000 to indicate the probable payment to Commercial Factors for uncollectible receivables. If Commercial Factors collects all the receivables, Crest Textiles eliminates its recourse liability and increases income. Commercial Factors' net income is the interest revenue of $15,000. It will have no bad debts related to these receivables.

Secured Borrowing versus Sale

The FASB concluded that a sale occurs only if the seller surrenders control of the receivables to the buyer. The following three conditions must be met before a company can record a sale:

1. The transferred asset has been isolated from the transferor (put beyond reach of the transferor and its creditors).

2. The transferees have obtained the right to pledge or exchange either the transferred assets or beneficial interests in the transferred assets.
3. The transferor does not maintain effective control over the transferred assets through an agreement to repurchase or redeem them before their maturity.

If the three conditions are met, a sale occurs. Otherwise, the transferor should record the transfer as a secured borrowing. If sale accounting is appropriate, a company must still consider assets obtained and liabilities incurred in the transaction. Illustration 7-22 shows the rules of accounting for transfers of receivables.

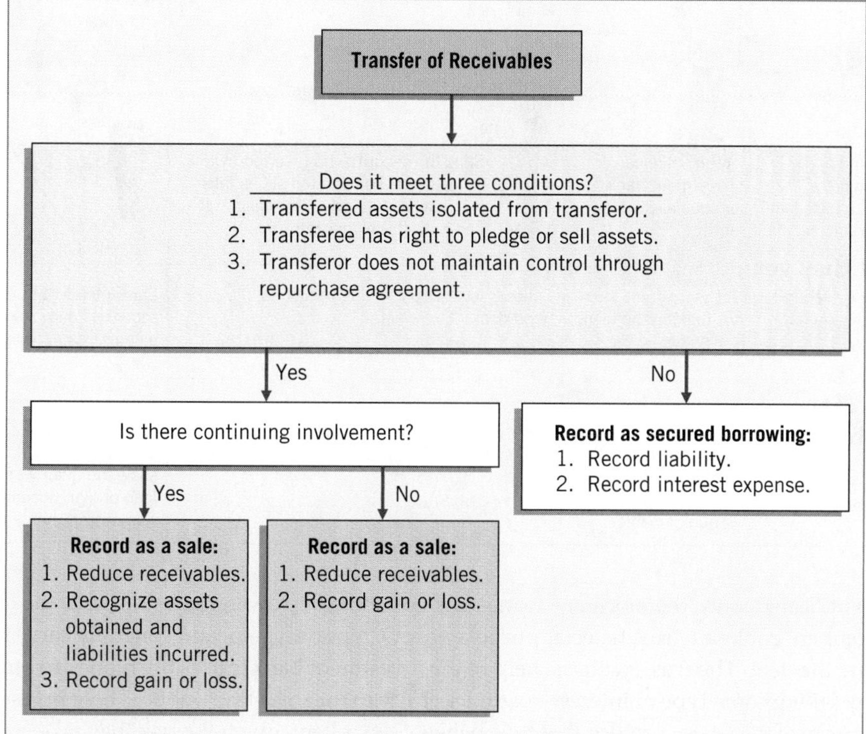

ILLUSTRATION 7-22
Accounting for Transfers of Receivables

As it shows, if there is continuing involvement in a sale transaction, a company must record the assets obtained and liabilities incurred.[15]

[15]In response to the financial crisis, which was partly caused by securitizations gone bad (see the "What Do the Numbers Mean?" box on page 390), the FASB issued new rules to tighten up the conditions when a transfer of receivables is recorded as a sale. The changes in the rules apply primarily to transfers that involve participating interests (which is the case for many securitizations). In order for a transfer with participating interests to be accounted for as a sale, all participating investors must have a pro rata share ownership interest in the transferred asset. That is, all parties to the transfer must receive benefits or be exposed to risks of the transferred assets in proportion to their ownership share. If these criteria are not met (e.g., some investors get paid first or others absorb more losses than others on the transferred receivables), then the transfer is accounted for as a secured borrowing. **[7]** As a result of these new rules, sale treatment for transfers of receivables will be significantly reduced.

RETURN TO LENDER

What do the numbers mean?

It used to be that lenders of mortgages and other types of debt securities carried them on their books as a loan receivable. But thanks to Wall Street, many lenders learned how to package these loans together and sell (securitize) them, and record a gain on the sale. In fact, virtually every asset with a payment stream and a long-term payment history is a candidate for securitization. And, for a while, everyone was happy to be part of the mortgage securitization game. The graphic below illustrates the way the process worked.

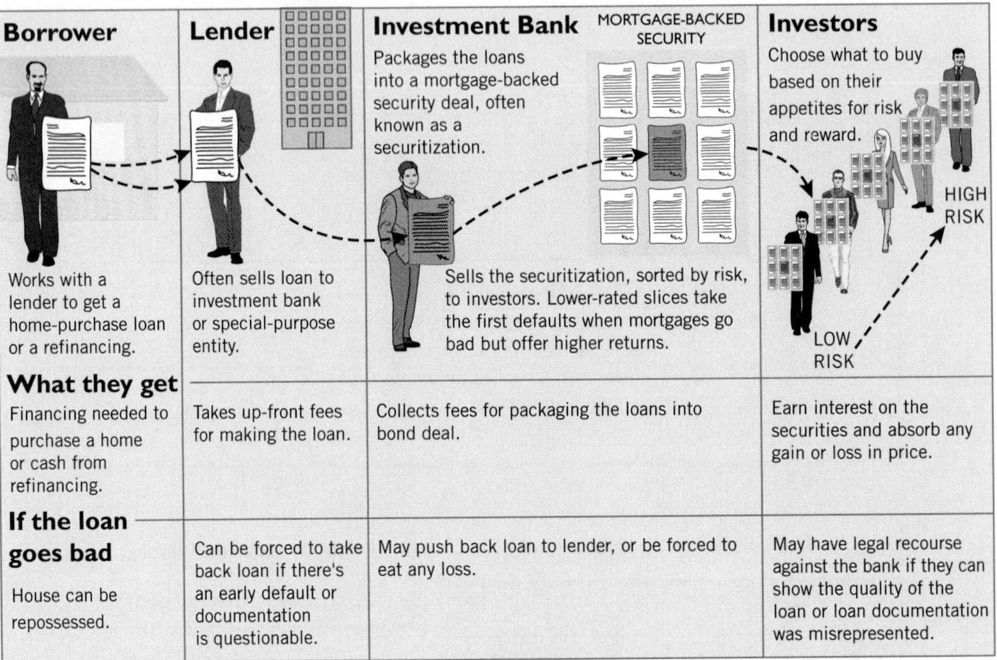

As indicated, once the mortgage loan is signed by the borrower, the lender sells the loans to an investment bank or a trust (special-purpose entity), reports a gain, and generally earns fees for servicing the debt. The trust, with the help of the investment bank, raises the money to buy these loans by selling some type of interest-bearing security to the investing public. These investors are happy because they earn a return that they believe is excellent, given the risk they take.

There were two big problems with these arrangements. First, as indicated in our discussion in the text, the lender has to make sure it does not keep control; otherwise, it cannot sell the receivable *and* receive gain-on-sale treatment. Unfortunately, the accounting rules were loose enough that lenders were able to argue that they do not have control in most cases. Second, lenders realized that lending to subprime borrowers could be very profitable. They focused on these customers because the bank earns a fee for origination of the loan, sells the loans for a gain, and earns servicing revenue—a triple bump to the bottom line. However, when the housing market collapsed, the subprime borrowers could not repay their loans, and the credit markets collapsed. The result was a credit crisis.

So, who loses? Investors, for starters. These investors did not understand the risks they were taking. (And we should note that many of these investors were other financial institutions, who should have known better.) How about the lenders? They claim they sold the loan, and it is no longer their responsibility. But many investors are not ready to let lenders off the hook. They argue that in many of these sales, the lender must take back loans that defaulted unusually fast or contained mistakes or fraud (bogus appraisals, inflated borrower incomes, and other misrepresentations). For example, **Countrywide Financial Corp.**, the largest mortgage lender in the United States, indicated that its liability for such claims increased by nearly $600 million from March 31, 2007, to March 31, 2008.

The moral of the story is that accounting matters. Lenders have strong incentives to want to report upfront gains on sales of loans. But, in most cases, these gains should never have been booked. In response, the FASB has issued new rules to tighten up "gain-on-sale" accounting for securitizations with participating interests (see footnote 15 on page 389). With these new rules, lenders will have to keep the loan on its balance sheet. Under these conditions, lenders would be much less likely to lend so much money to individuals with poor credit ratings.

Source: M. Hudson, "How Wall Street Stoked the Mortgage Meltdown," *Wall Street Journal* (June 27, 2007), p. A10.

What do the numbers mean? (continued)

Presentation and Analysis

Presentation of Receivables

9 LEARNING OBJECTIVE
Describe how to report and analyze receivables.

The general rules in classifying receivables are:

1. Segregate the different types of receivables that a company possesses, if material.
2. Appropriately offset the valuation accounts against the proper receivable accounts.
3. Determine that receivables classified in the current assets section will be converted into cash within the year or the operating cycle, whichever is longer.
4. Disclose any loss contingencies that exist on the receivables.
5. Disclose any receivables designated or pledged as collateral.
6. Disclose the nature of credit risk inherent in the receivables, how that risk is analyzed and assessed in arriving at the allowance for credit losses, and the changes and reasons for those changes in the allowance for credit losses.

With respect to additional disclosures, companies are required to disaggregate based on type of receivable. In response to demands for additional information about credit risk, the FASB recently issued rules for companies to provide the following disclosures about its receivables on a disaggregated basis: (1) a roll-forward schedule of the allowance for doubtful accounts from the beginning of the reporting period to the end of the reporting period, (2) the nonaccrual status of receivables by class of receivables, and (3) impaired receivables by type of receivable. In addition, companies should disclose credit quality indicators and the aging of past due receivables. **[8]**

Companies must disclose concentrations of credit risk for all financial instruments (including receivables). Concentrations of credit risk exist when receivables have common characteristics that may affect their collection. These common characteristics might be companies in the same industry or same region of the country. For example, **Quantum Corporation** reported that sales of its disk drives to its top five customers (including **Hewlett-Packard**) represented nearly 40 percent of its revenues in a recent year. Financial statements users want to know if a substantial amount of receivables from such sales are to customers facing uncertain economic conditions. No numerical guidelines are provided as to what is meant by a "concentration of credit risk."[16]

The assets sections of Colton Corporation's balance sheet in Illustration 7-23 (page 392) show many of the disclosures required for receivables.

[16]Three items should be disclosed with an identified concentration: (1) information on the characteristic that determines the concentration, (2) the amount of loss that could occur upon nonperformance, and (3) information on any collateral related to the receivable. **[9]**

ILLUSTRATION 7-23
Disclosure of Receivables

COLTON CORPORATION
BALANCE SHEET (PARTIAL)
AS OF DECEMBER 31, 2012

Current assets		
Cash and cash equivalents		$ 1,870,250
Accounts and notes receivable (Note 2)	$10,509,673	
Less: Allowance for doubtful accounts	500,226	
	10,009,447	
Advances to subsidiaries due 9/30/12	2,090,000	
Federal income taxes refundable	146,704	
Dividends and interest receivable	75,500	
Other receivables and claims (including debit balances in accounts payable)	174,620	12,496,271
Total current assets		14,366,521
Noncurrent receivables		
Notes receivable from officers and key employees		376,090
Claims receivable (litigation settlement to be collected over four years)		585,000

Segregate different types of receivables

Note 2: Accounts and Notes Receivable. All noncurrent receivables are due within five years from the balance sheet date. Trade receivables that are less than three months past due are not considered impaired. At December 31, the aging analysis of receivables is as follows.

Disclose aging of receivables

			Past Due but Not Impaired				
Amounts ($000)	Total	Neither Past Due or Impaired	<30 days	30–60 days	60–90 days	90–120 days	>120 days
2012	10,510	5,115	2,791	1,582	570	360	92

As at December 31, 2012, trade receivables at initial value of $109 were impaired and fully provided for. The following table summarises movements in the provision for impairment of receivables.

Presentation of impaired receivables

	Total $000
At January 1, 2012	98
Expense for the year	26
Written off	(9)
Recoveries	(6)
At December 31, 2012	109

Disclose collateral arrangements

Certain subsidiaries transferred receivable balances amounting to $1,014 to a bank in exchange for cash during the year ended December 31, 2012. The transaction has been accounted for as a secured borrowing. In case of default under the loan agreement, the borrower has the right to receive the cash flows from the receivables transferred. Without default, the subsidiaries will collect the receivables and assign new receivables as collateral.

INTERNATIONAL PERSPECTIVE

Holding receivables that it will receive in a foreign currency represents risk that the exchange rate may move against the company. This results in a decrease in the amount collected in terms of U.S. dollars. Companies engaged in cross-border transactions often "hedge" these receivables by buying contracts to exchange currencies at specified amounts at future dates.

Analysis of Receivables

Accounts Receivable Turnover Ratio. Analysts frequently compute financial ratios to evaluate the liquidity of a company's accounts receivable. To assess the liquidity of the receivables, they use the **accounts receivable turnover ratio**. This ratio measures the number of times, on average, a company collects receivables during the period. The ratio is computed by dividing net sales by average (net) receivables outstanding during the year. Theoretically, the numerator should include only net credit sales, but this information is frequently unavailable. However, if the relative amounts of credit and cash sales remain fairly constant, the trend indicated by the ratio will still be valid. Barring significant seasonal factors, average receivables outstanding can be computed from the beginning and ending balances of net trade receivables.

To illustrate, **Best Buy** reported 2010 net sales of $49,694 million, its beginning and ending accounts receivable balances were $1,868 million and $2,020 million, respectively. Illustration 7-24 shows the computation of its accounts receivable turnover ratio.

Net Sales / Average Trade Receivables (net)	=	Accounts Receivable Turnover
$49,694 / ($1,868 + $2,020)/2	=	25.6 times, or every 14.3 days (365 ÷ 25.6)

ILLUSTRATION 7-24
Computation of Accounts Receivable Turnover

This information[17] shows how successful the company is in collecting its outstanding receivables. If possible, an aging schedule should also be prepared to help determine how long receivables have been outstanding. A satisfactory accounts receivable turnover may have resulted because certain receivables were collected quickly though others have been outstanding for a relatively long period. An aging schedule would reveal such patterns.

Underlying Concepts

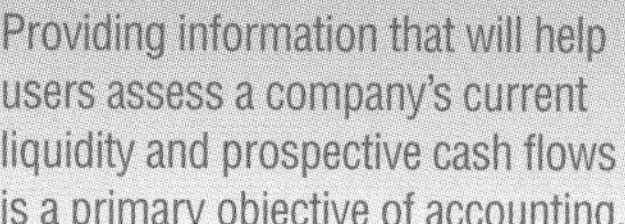

Providing information that will help users assess a company's current liquidity and prospective cash flows is a primary objective of accounting.

Often the accounts receivable turnover is transformed to **days to collect accounts receivable or days outstanding**—an average collection period. In this case, 25.6 is divided into 365 days, resulting in 14.3 days. Companies frequently use the average collection period to assess the effectiveness of a company's credit and collection policies. The general rule is that the average collection period should not greatly exceed the credit term period. That is, if customers are given a 60-day period for payment, then the average collection period should not be too much in excess of 60 days.

You will want to read the IFRS INSIGHTS on pages 428–432 for discussion of IFRS related to cash and receivables.

[17]Several figures other than 365 could be used. A common alternative is 360 days because it is divisible by 30 (days) and 12 (months). *Use 365 days in any homework computations.*

KEY TERMS

accounts receivable, 369
accounts receivable turnover ratio, 392
aging schedule, 376
allowance method, 373
bank overdrafts, 368
cash, 366
cash discounts, 371
cash equivalents, 366
compensating balances, 367
direct write-off method, 373
factoring receivables, 386
fair value option, 384
financial components approach, 387
imputed interest rate, 382
net realizable value, 372, 373
nontrade receivables, 369
notes receivable, 369
percentage-of-receivables approach, 376
percentage-of-sales approach, 375
promissory note, 378
receivables, 369
restricted cash, 367
sales discounts, 371
securitization, 387
trade discounts, 370
trade receivables, 369
unrealized holding gain or loss, 384
with recourse, 387
without recourse, 387
zero-interest-bearing notes, 378

SUMMARY OF LEARNING OBJECTIVES

1 Identify items considered cash. To be reported as "cash," an asset must be readily available for the payment of current obligations and free from contractual restrictions that limit its use in satisfying debts. Cash consists of coin, currency, and available funds on deposit at the bank. Negotiable instruments such as money orders, certified checks, cashier's checks, personal checks, and bank drafts are also viewed as cash. Savings accounts are usually classified as cash.

2 Indicate how to report cash and related items. Companies report cash as a current asset in the balance sheet. The reporting of other related items are: (1) *Restricted cash:* The SEC recommends that companies state separately legally restricted deposits held as compensating balances against short-term borrowing among the "Cash and cash equivalent items" in current assets. Restricted deposits held against long-term borrowing arrangements should be separately classified as noncurrent assets in either the investments or other assets sections. (2) *Bank overdrafts:* Companies should report overdrafts in the current liabilities section and usually add them to the amount reported as accounts payable. If material, these items should be separately disclosed either on the face of the balance sheet or in the related notes. (3) *Cash equivalents:* Companies often report this item together with cash as "Cash and cash equivalents."

3 Define receivables and identify the different types of receivables. Receivables are claims held against customers and others for money, goods, or services. The receivables are classified into three types: (1) current or noncurrent, (2) trade or nontrade, (3) accounts receivable or notes receivable.

4 Explain accounting issues related to recognition of accounts receivable. Two issues that may complicate the measurement of accounts receivable are: (1) The availability of discounts (trade and cash discounts), and (2) the length of time between the sale and the payment due dates (the interest element).

Ideally, companies should measure receivables in terms of their present value—that is, the discounted value of the cash to be received in the future. The profession specifically excludes from the present-value considerations receivables arising from normal business transactions that are due in customary trade terms within approximately one year.

5 Explain accounting issues related to valuation of accounts receivable. Companies value and report short-term receivables at net realizable value—the net amount expected to be received in cash, which is not necessarily the amount legally receivable. Determining net realizable value requires estimating uncollectible receivables.

6 Explain accounting issues related to recognition and valuation of notes receivable. Companies record short-term notes at face value and long-term notes receivable at the present value of the cash they expect to collect. When the interest stated on an interest-bearing note equals the effective (market) rate of interest, the note sells at face value. When the stated rate differs from the effective rate, a company records either a discount or premium. Like accounts receivable, companies record and report short-term notes receivable at their net realizable value. The same is also true of long-term receivables.

7 Explain the fair value option. Companies have the option to record receivables at fair value. Once the fair value option is chosen, the receivable is reported on the balance sheet at fair value, with the change in fair value recorded in income.

8 Explain accounting issues related to disposition of accounts and notes receivable. To accelerate the receipt of cash from receivables, the owner may transfer the receivables to another company for cash in one of two ways: (1) *Secured borrowing:*

A creditor often requires that the debtor designate or pledge receivables as security for the loan. (2) *Sales (factoring) of receivables:* Factors are finance companies or banks that buy receivables from businesses and then collect the remittances directly from the customers. In many cases, transferors may have some continuing involvement with the receivable sold. Companies use a financial components approach to record this type of transaction.

9 Describe how to report and analyze receivables. Companies should report receivables with appropriate offset of valuation accounts against receivables, classify receivables as current or noncurrent, identify pledged or designated receivables, and disclose the credit risk inherent in the receivables. Analysts assess receivables based on turnover and the days outstanding.

APPENDIX 7A CASH CONTROLS

Cash is the asset most susceptible to improper diversion and use. Management faces two problems in accounting for cash transactions: (1) to establish proper controls to prevent any unauthorized transactions by officers or employees, and (2) to provide information necessary to properly manage cash on hand and cash transactions. Yet even with sophisticated control devices, errors can and do happen. For example, the *Wall Street Journal* ran a story entitled "A $7.8 Million Error Has a Happy Ending for a Horrified Bank." The story described how **Manufacturers Hanover Trust Co.** mistakenly overpaid about $7.8 million in cash dividends to its stockholders. (As implied in the headline, most stockholders returned the monies.)

To safeguard cash and to ensure the accuracy of the accounting records for cash, companies need effective **internal control** over cash. Provisions of the Sarbanes-Oxley Act of 2002 call for enhanced efforts to increase the quality of internal control (for cash and other assets). Such efforts are expected to result in improved financial reporting. In this appendix, we discuss some of the basic control issues related to cash.

USING BANK ACCOUNTS

10 LEARNING OBJECTIVE
Explain common techniques employed to control cash.

To obtain desired control objectives, a company can vary the number and location of banks and the types of bank accounts. For large companies operating in multiple locations, the location of bank accounts can be important. Establishing collection accounts in strategic locations can accelerate the flow of cash into the company by shortening the time between a customer's mailing of a payment and the company's use of the cash. Multiple collection centers generally reduce the size of a company's **collection float**. This is the difference between the amount on deposit according to the company's records and the amount of collected cash according to the bank record.

INTERNATIONAL PERSPECTIVE

Multinational corporations often have cash accounts in more than one currency. For financial statement purposes, these corporations typically translate these currencies into U.S. dollars, using the exchange rate in effect at the balance sheet date.

Large, multilocation companies frequently use **lockbox accounts** to collect in cities with heavy customer billing. The company rents a local post office box and authorizes a local bank to pick up the remittances mailed to that box number. The bank empties the box at least once a day and immediately credits the company's account for collections. The greatest advantage of a lockbox is that it accelerates the availability of collected cash. Generally, in a lockbox arrangement the bank microfilms the checks for record purposes and provides the company with a deposit slip, a list of collections, and any customer correspondence. Thus, a lockbox system improves the control over cash and accelerates collection of cash. If the income generated from accelerating the receipt of funds exceeds the cost of the lockbox system, then it is a worthwhile undertaking.

The **general checking account** is the principal bank account in most companies and frequently the only bank account in small businesses. A company deposits in and disburses cash from this account. A company cycles all transactions through it. For example, a company deposits from and disburses to all other bank accounts through the general checking account.

Companies use **imprest bank accounts** to make a specific amount of cash available for a limited purpose. The account acts as a clearing account for a large volume of checks or for a specific type of check. To clear a specific and intended amount through the imprest account, a company transfers that amount from the general checking account or other source. Companies often use imprest bank accounts for disbursing payroll checks, dividends, commissions, bonuses, confidential expenses (e.g., officers' salaries), and travel expenses.

THE IMPREST PETTY CASH SYSTEM

Almost every company finds it necessary to pay small amounts for miscellaneous expenses such as taxi fares, minor office supplies, and employee's lunches. Disbursements by check for such items is often impractical, yet some control over them is important. A simple method of obtaining reasonable control, while adhering to the rule of disbursement by check, is the **imprest system for petty cash** disbursements. This is how the system works:

1. The company designates a petty cash custodian, and gives the custodian a small amount of currency from which to make payments. It records transfer of funds to petty cash as:

Petty Cash	300	
Cash		300

2. The petty cash custodian obtains signed receipts from each individual to whom he or she pays cash, attaching evidence of the disbursement to the petty cash receipt. Petty cash transactions are not recorded until the fund is reimbursed; someone other than the petty cash custodian records those entries.
3. When the supply of cash runs low, the custodian presents to the controller or accounts payable cashier a request for reimbursement supported by the petty cash receipts and other disbursement evidence. The custodian receives a company check to replenish the fund. At this point, the company records transactions based on petty cash receipts.

Supplies Expense	42	
Postage Expense	53	
Miscellaneous Expense	76	
Cash Over and Short	2	
Cash		173

4. If the company decides that the amount of cash in the petty cash fund is excessive, it lowers the fund balance as follows.

Cash	50	
Petty Cash		50

Subsequent to establishment, a company makes entries to the Petty Cash account only to increase or decrease the size of the fund.

A company uses a **Cash Over and Short** account when the petty cash fund fails to prove out. That is, an error occurs such as incorrect change, overpayment of expense, or lost receipt. If cash proves out **short** (i.e., the sum of the receipts and cash in the fund is less than the imprest amount), the company debits the shortage to the Cash Over and

Short account. If cash proves out **over**, it credits the overage to Cash Over and Short. The company closes Cash Over and Short only at the end of the year. It generally shows Cash Over and Short on the income statement as an "Other expense or revenue."

There are usually expense items in the fund except immediately after reimbursement. Therefore, to maintain accurate financial statements, a company must reimburse the funds at the end of each accounting period and also when nearly depleted.

Under the imprest system the petty cash custodian is responsible at all times for the amount of the fund on hand either as cash or in the form of signed receipts. These receipts provide the evidence required by the disbursing officer to issue a reimbursement check. Further, a company follows two additional procedures to obtain more complete control over the petty cash fund:

1. A superior of the petty cash custodian makes surprise counts of the fund from time to time to determine that a satisfactory accounting of the fund has occurred.
2. The company cancels or mutilates petty cash receipts after they have been submitted for reimbursement, so that they cannot be used to secure a second reimbursement.

PHYSICAL PROTECTION OF CASH BALANCES

Not only must a company safeguard cash receipts and cash disbursements through internal control measures, but it must also protect the cash on hand and in banks. Because receipts become cash on hand and disbursements are made from cash in banks, adequate control of receipts and disbursements is part of the protection of cash balances, along with certain other procedures.

Physical protection of cash is so elementary a necessity that it requires little discussion. A company should make every effort to minimize the cash on hand in the office. It should only have on hand a petty cash fund, the current day's receipts, and perhaps funds for making change. Insofar as possible, it should keep these funds in a vault, safe, or locked cash drawer. The company should transmit intact each day's receipts to the bank as soon as practicable. Accurately stating the amount of available cash both in internal management reports and in external financial statements is also extremely important.

Every company has a record of cash received, disbursed, and the balance. Because of the many cash transactions, however, errors or omissions may occur in keeping this record. Therefore, a company must periodically prove the balance shown in the general ledger. It can count cash actually present in the office—petty cash, change funds, and undeposited receipts—for comparison with the company records. For cash on deposit, a company prepares a bank reconciliation—a reconciliation of the company's record and the bank's record of the company's cash.

RECONCILIATION OF BANK BALANCES

At the end of each calendar month the bank supplies each customer with a **bank statement** (a copy of the bank's account with the customer) together with the customer's checks that the bank paid during the month.[18] If neither the bank nor the customer made any errors, if all deposits made and all checks drawn by the customer reached the bank within the same month, and if no unusual transactions occurred that affected either the company's or the bank's record of cash, the balance of cash reported by the bank to the

[18]As we mentioned in Chapter 7, paper checks continue to be used as a means of payment. However, ready availability of desktop publishing software and hardware has created new opportunities for check fraud in the form of duplicate, altered, and forged checks. At the same time, new fraud-fighting technologies, such as ultraviolet imaging, high-capacity barcodes, and biometrics, are being developed. These technologies convert paper documents into electronically processed document files, thereby reducing the risk of fraud.

customer equals that shown in the customer's own records. This condition seldom occurs due to one or more of the reconciling items presented below. Hence, a company expects differences between its record of cash and the bank's record. Therefore, it must reconcile the two to determine the nature of the differences between the two amounts.

RECONCILING ITEMS

1. **DEPOSITS IN TRANSIT.** End-of-month deposits of cash recorded on the depositor's books in one month are received and recorded by the bank in the following month.
2. **OUTSTANDING CHECKS.** Checks written by the depositor are recorded when written but may not be recorded by (may not "clear") the bank until the next month.
3. **BANK CHARGES.** Charges recorded by the bank against the depositor's balance for such items as bank services, printing checks, **not-sufficient-funds (NSF) checks**, and safe-deposit box rentals. The depositor may not be aware of these charges until the receipt of the bank statement.
4. **BANK CREDITS.** Collections or deposits by the bank for the benefit of the depositor that may be unknown to the depositor until receipt of the bank statement. Examples are note collection for the depositor and interest earned on interest-bearing checking accounts.
5. **BANK OR DEPOSITOR ERRORS.** Errors on either the part of the bank or the part of the depositor cause the bank balance to disagree with the depositor's book balance.

A **bank reconciliation** is a schedule explaining any differences between the bank's and the company's records of cash. If the difference results only from transactions not yet recorded by the bank, the company's record of cash is considered correct. But, if some part of the difference arises from other items, either the bank or the company must adjust its records.

A company may prepare two forms of a bank reconciliation. One form reconciles from the bank statement balance to the book balance or vice versa. The other form reconciles both the bank balance and the book balance to a correct cash balance. Most companies use this latter form. Illustration 7A-1 shows a sample of that form and its common reconciling items.

ILLUSTRATION 7A-1
Bank Reconciliation Form and Content

Balance per bank statement (end of period)		$$$
Add: Deposits in transit	$$	
Undeposited receipts (cash on hand)	$$	
Bank errors that understate the bank statement balance	$$	$$
		$$$
Deduct: Outstanding checks	$$	
Bank errors that overstate the bank statement balance	$$	$$
Correct cash balance		$$$
Balance per depositor's books		$$$
Add: Bank credits and collections not yet recorded in the books	$$	
Book errors that understate the book balance	$$	$$
		$$$
Deduct: Bank charges not yet recorded in the books	$$	
Book errors that overstate the book balance	$$	$$
Correct cash balance		$$$

This form of reconciliation consists of two sections: (1) "Balance per bank statement" and (2) "Balance per depositor's books." Both sections end with the same "Correct cash balance." The correct cash balance is the amount to which the books must be adjusted and is the amount reported on the balance sheet. **Companies prepare adjusting journal entries for all the addition and deduction items appearing in the "Balance per depositor's books" section.** Companies should immediately call to the bank's attention any errors attributable to it.

To illustrate, Nugget Mining Company's books show a cash balance at the Denver National Bank on November 30, 2012, of $20,502. The bank statement covering the month of November shows an ending balance of $22,190. An examination of Nugget's accounting records and November bank statement identified the following reconciling items.

1. A deposit of $3,680 that Nugget mailed November 30 does not appear on the bank statement.
2. Checks written in November but not charged to the November bank statement are:

Check #7327	$ 150
#7348	4,820
#7349	31

3. Nugget has not yet recorded the $600 of interest collected by the bank November 20 on Sequoia Co. bonds held by the bank for Nugget.
4. Bank service charges of $18 are not yet recorded on Nugget's books.
5. The bank returned one of Nugget's customer's checks for $220 with the bank statement, marked "NSF." The bank treated this bad check as a disbursement.
6. Nugget discovered that it incorrectly recorded check #7322, written in November for $131 in payment of an account payable, as $311.
7. A check for Nugent Oil Co. in the amount of $175 that the bank incorrectly charged to Nugget accompanied the statement.

Nugget reconciled the bank and book balances to the correct cash balance of $21,044 as shown in Illustration 7A-2.

ILLUSTRATION 7A-2
Sample Bank Reconciliation

NUGGET MINING COMPANY
BANK RECONCILIATION
DENVER NATIONAL BANK, NOVEMBER 30, 2012

Balance per bank statement (end of period)			$22,190
Add: Deposit in transit	(1)	$3,680	
Bank error—incorrect check charged to account by bank	(7)	175	3,855
			26,045
Deduct: Outstanding checks	(2)		5,001
Correct cash balance			$21,044
Balance per books			$20,502
Add: Interest collected by the bank	(3)	$ 600	
Error in recording check #7322	(6)	180	780
			21,282
Deduct: Bank service charges	(4)	18	
NSF check returned	(5)	220	238
Correct cash balance			$21,044

The journal entries required to adjust and correct Nugget's books in early December 2012 are taken from the items in the "Balance per books" section and are as follows.

Cash	600	
Interest Revenue		600
(To record interest on Sequoia Co. bonds, collected by bank)		
Cash	180	
Accounts Payable		180
(To correct error in recording amount of check #7322)		
Office Expense (bank charges)	18	
Cash		18
(To record bank service charges for November)		
Accounts Receivable	220	
Cash		220
(To record customer's check returned NSF)		

Gateway to the Profession

Expanded Discussion of a Four-Column Bank Reconciliation

After posting the entries, Nugget's cash account will have a balance of $21,044. Nugget should return the Nugent Oil Co. check to Denver National Bank, informing the bank of the error.

SUMMARY OF LEARNING OBJECTIVE FOR APPENDIX 7A

KEY TERMS

bank reconciliation, *398*
imprest system for petty cash, *396*
not-sufficient-funds (NSF) checks, *398*

10 Explain common techniques employed to control cash. The common techniques employed to control cash are: (1) *Using bank accounts:* A company can vary the number and location of banks and the types of accounts to obtain desired control objectives. (2) *The imprest petty cash system:* It may be impractical to require small amounts of various expenses be paid by check, yet some control over them is important. (3) *Physical protection of cash balances:* Adequate control of receipts and disbursements is a part of the protection of cash balances. Every effort should be made to minimize the cash on hand in the office. (4) *Reconciliation of bank balances:* Cash on deposit is not available for count and is proved by preparing a bank reconciliation.

APPENDIX 7B IMPAIRMENTS OF RECEIVABLES

LEARNING OBJECTIVE 11
Describe the accounting for a loan impairment.

Companies continually evaluate their receivables to determine their ultimate collectibility. As discussed in the chapter, the FASB considers the collectibility of receivables a *loss contingency*. Thus, the allowance method is appropriate in situations where it is probable that an asset has been impaired and the amount of the loss can be reasonably estimated. Generally, companies start with historical loss rates and modify these rates for changes in economic conditions that could affect a borrower's ability to repay the loan. The discussion in the chapter assumed use of this approach to determine the amount of bad debts to be recorded for a period.

However, for long-term receivables such as loans that are identified as impaired, companies perform an additional impairment evaluation.[19] GAAP has specific rules for

[19]A loan is defined as "a contractual right to receive money on demand or on fixed and determinable dates that is recognized as an asset in the creditor's statement of financial position." For example, accounts receivable with terms exceeding one year are considered loans. **[10]**

measurement and reporting of these impairments. These rules relate to determining the value of these loans and how much loss to recognize if the holder of the loans plans to keep them in hope that the market will recover. More complex rules arise when these loans are sold as part of the securitization process, especially when the original terms of the notes are modified.[20]

IMPAIRMENT MEASUREMENT AND REPORTING

A company considers a loan receivable impaired when it is probable, based on current information and events, that it will not collect all amounts due (both principal and interest). If a loan is determined to be individually impaired, the company should measure the loss due to the **impairment**. This impairment loss is calculated as the difference between the investment in the loan (generally the principal plus accrued interest) and the expected future cash flows discounted at the loan's historical effective interest rate.[21] When using the historical effective loan rate, the value of the investment will change only if some of the legally contracted cash flows are reduced. A company recognizes a loss in this case because the expected future cash flows are now lower. The company ignores interest rate changes caused by current economic events that affect the fair value of the loan. In estimating future cash flows, the creditor should use reasonable and supportable assumptions and projections. **[12]**

Impairment Loss Example

At December 31, 2011, Ogden Bank recorded an investment of $100,000 in a loan to Carl King. The loan has an historical effective-interest rate of 10 percent, the principal is due in full at maturity in three years, and interest is due annually. Unfortunately, King is experiencing financial difficulty and thinks he will have a difficult time making full payment. The loan officer performs a review of the loan's expected future cash flows and utilizes the present value method for measuring the required impairment loss. Illustration 7B-1 shows the cash flow schedule prepared by the loan officer.

ILLUSTRATION 7B-1
Impaired Loan Cash Flows

Dec. 31	Contractual Cash Flow	Expected Cash Flow	Loss of Cash Flow
2012	$ 10,000	$ 5,000	$ 5,000
2013	10,000	5,000	5,000
2014	$110,000	105,000	5,000
Total cash flows	$130,000	$115,000	$15,000

As indicated, this loan is impaired. The expected cash flows of $115,000 are less than the contractual cash flows, including principal and interest, of $130,000. The amount of the impairment to be recorded equals the difference between the recorded investment of $100,000 and the present value of the expected cash flows, as shown in Illustration 7B-2 (on page 402).

[20]Note that the impairment test shown in this appendix only applies to specific loans. However, if the loans are bundled into a security (e.g., the mortgage-backed securities), the impairment test is different. Impairments of securities are measured based on fair value. We discuss this accounting in Chapter 17.

[21]The creditor may also, for the sake of expediency, use the market price of the loan (if such a price is available) or the fair value of the collateral if it is a collateralized loan. **[11]** Recognize that if the value of the investment is based on the historical rate, generally the resultant value will not be equal to the fair value of the loan in subsequent periods. We consider this accounting inconsistent with fair value principles as applied to other financial instruments.

ILLUSTRATION 7B-2
Computation of Impairment Loss

Recorded investment		$100,000
Less: Present value of $100,000 due in 3 years at 10% (Table 6-2); $FV(PVF_{3,10\%})$; ($100,000 × .75132)	$75,132	
Present value of $5,000 interest payable annually for 3 years at 10% $R(PVF\text{-}OA_{3,10\%})$; ($5,000 × 2.48685)	12,434	87,566
Loss on impairment		$ 12,434

The loss due to the impairment is $12,434. Why isn't it $15,000 ($130,000 – $115,000)? Because Ogden Bank must measure the loss at a present-value amount, not at an undiscounted amount, when it records the loss.

LOST IN TRANSLATION

What do the numbers mean?

Floyd Norris, noted financial writer for the *New York Times*, recently wrote in his blog that he attended a conference to discuss the financial crisis in subprime lending. He highlighted, and provided "translations" of, some of the statements he heard at that conference:

- "There is a problem of misaligned incentives."

  Translation: Many parties in the lending process were complicit in not performing due diligence on loans because there were lots of fees to be had if the loans were made, good loans or bad.

- "It is pretty clear that there was a failure in some key assumptions that were supporting our analytics and our models."

  Translation: The rating agencies that evaluated the risk level of these securities made many miscalculations. Some structured finance products that were given superior ratings are no longer worth much.

- "The plumbing of the U.S. economy has been deeply damaged. It is a long window of vulnerability."

  Translation: The U.S. has caused a financial crisis as a result of poor lending practices, and many financial institutions are fighting to survive.

- "I'm glad that this time we did not cause it."

  Translation: Other countries realized they had caused financial crises in the past but were not to blame for the current U.S. financial situation.

- "What you see is what you get. If you don't see it, it will get you."

  Translation: A large number of financial institutions have to take losses on assets that are not reported on their balance sheet. Their continuing interest in some of the loans that they supposedly sold is now coming back to them and they will have to report losses.

Source: Floyd Norris blog, *http://www.norris.blogs.nytimes.com/* (accessed June 2008).

Recording Impairment Losses

Ogden Bank (the creditor) recognizes an impairment loss of $12,434 by debiting Bad Debt Expense for the expected loss. At the same time, it reduces the overall value of the receivable by crediting Allowance for Doubtful Accounts. The journal entry to record the loss is therefore as follows.[22]

[22]In the event of a loan write-off, the company charges the loss against the allowance. In subsequent periods, if revising estimated expected cash flows based on new information, the company adjusts the allowance account and bad debt expense account (either increased or decreased depending on whether conditions improved or worsened) in the same fashion as the original impairment. We use the terms "loss" and "bad debt expense" interchangeably throughout this discussion. Companies should charge losses related to receivables transactions to Bad Debt Expense or the related Allowance for Doubtful Accounts, because they use these accounts to recognize changes in values affecting receivables.

Bad Debt Expense	12,434	
Allowance for Doubtful Accounts		12,434

What entry does Carl King (the debtor) make? The debtor makes no entry because he still legally owes $100,000.

In some cases, debtors like King negotiate a modification in the terms of the loan agreement. In such cases, the accounting entries from Ogden Bank are the same as the situation in which the loan officer must estimate the future cash flows—except that the calculation for the amount of the loss becomes more reliable (because the revised expected cash flow amounts are contractually specified in the loan agreement).[23] The entries related to the debtor in this case often change; they are discussed in Appendix 14A.

SUMMARY OF LEARNING OBJECTIVE FOR APPENDIX 7B

KEY TERM

impairment, *401*

 **Describe the accounting for a loan impairment.** A creditor bases an impairment loan loss on the difference between the present value of the future cash flows (using the historical effective interest rate) and the carrying amount of the note.

FASB CODIFICATION

FASB Codification References

[1] FASB ASC 210-10-S99-1. [Predecessor literature: "Amendments to Regulations S-X and Related Interpretations and Guidelines Regarding the Disclosure of Compensating Balances and Short-Term Borrowing Arrangements," *Accounting Series Release No. 148,* Securities and Exchange Commission (November 13, 1973).]

[2] FASB ASC 835-30-15-3. [Predecessor literature: "Interest on Receivables and Payables," *Opinions of the Accounting Principles Board No. 21* (New York: AICPA, 1971), par. 3(a).]

[3] FASB ASC 310-10-35-8. [Predecessor literature: "Accounting for Contingencies," *Statement of Financial Accounting Standards No. 5* (Stamford, Conn.: FASB, 1975), par. 8.]

[4] FASB ASC 835-30-05. [Predecessor literature: "Interest on Receivables and Payables," *Opinions of the Accounting Principles Board No. 21* (New York: AICPA, 1971), par. 3(a).]

[5] FASB ASC 825-10-25. [Predecessor literature: "The Fair Value Option for Financial Assets and Liabilities—Including an Amendment to FASB No. 115," *Statement of Financial Accounting Standards No. 159* (Norwalk, Conn.: FASB, 2007).]

[6] FASB ASC 860-40 and FASB ASC 860-10-5-15. [Predecessor literature: "Accounting for Transfers and Servicing of Financial Assets and Extinguishments of Liabilities," *Statement of Financial Accounting Standards No. 140* (Stamford, Conn.: FASB, 2000), p. 155.]

[7] FASB ASC 860-10-40. [Predecessor literature: None.]

[8] FASB ASC 310-10-50. [Predecessor literature: None.]

[9] FASB ASC 825-10-50-20 through 22. [Predecessor literature: "Disclosures about Fair Value of Financial Instruments," *Statement of Financial Accounting Standards No. 107* (Norwalk, Conn.: FASB, 1991), par. 15.]

[10] FASB ASC 310-10-35-22. [Predecessor literature: "Accounting by Creditors for Impairment of a Loan," *FASB Statement No. 114* (Norwalk, Conn.: FASB, May 1993).]

[23]Many alternatives are permitted to recognize income by Ogden Bank in subsequent periods. **[13]**

[11] FASB ASC 310-10-35-22. [Predecessor literature: "Accounting by Creditors for Impairment of a Loan," *FASB Statement No. 114* (Norwalk, Conn.: FASB, May 1993), par. 13.]

[12] FASB ASC 310-10-35-26. [Predecessor literature: "Accounting by Creditors for Impairment of a Loan," *FASB Statement No. 114* (Norwalk, Conn.: FASB, May 1993), par. 15.]

[13] FASB ASC 310-10-35-40. [Predecessor literature: "Accounting by Creditors for Impairment of a Loan—Income Recognition and Disclosures," *FASB Statement No. 118* (Norwalk, Conn.: FASB, October 1994).]

Exercises

If your school has a subscription to the FASB Codification, go to *http://aaahq.org/asclogin.cfm* to log in and prepare responses to the following. Provide Codification references for your responses.

CE7-1 Access the glossary ("Master Glossary") to answer the following.

(a) What is the definition of cash?

(b) What is the definition of securitization?

(c) What are the three contexts that give rise to recourse?

CE7-2 Carrie Underwood believes that by establishing a loss contingency for uncollectible receivables, a company provides financial protection against the loss. What does the authoritative literature say about this belief?

CE7-3 In addition to securitizations, what are the other types of transfers of financial assets identified in the Codification?

CE7-4 The controller for Nesheim Construction Company believes that it is appropriate to offset a note payable to Oregon Bank against an account receivable from Oregon Bank related to remodeling services provided to the bank. What is the authoritative guidance concerning the criteria to be met to allow such offsetting?

An additional Codification case can be found in the Using Your Judgment section, on page 426.

Be sure to check the book's companion website for a Review and Analysis Exercise, with solution.

Questions, Brief Exercises, Exercises, Problems, and many more resources are available for practice in WileyPLUS.

Note: All asterisked Questions, Exercises, and Problems relate to material in the appendices to the chapter.

QUESTIONS

1. What may be included under the heading of "cash"?

2. In what accounts should the following items be classified?

(a) Coins and currency.

(b) U.S. Treasury (government) bonds.

(c) Certificate of deposit.

(d) Cash in a bank that is in receivership.

(e) NSF check (returned with bank statement).

(f) Deposit in foreign bank (exchangeability limited).

(g) Postdated checks.

(h) Cash to be used for retirement of long-term bonds.

(i) Deposits in transit.

(j) 100 shares of **Dell** stock (intention is to sell in one year or less).

(k) Savings and checking accounts.

(l) Petty cash.

(m) Stamps.

(n) Travel advances.

3. Define a "compensating balance." How should a compensating balance be reported?

4. Springsteen Inc. reported in a recent annual report "Restricted cash for debt redemption." What section of the balance sheet would report this item?

5. What are the reasons that a company gives trade discounts? Why are trade discounts not recorded in the accounts like cash discounts?

6. What are two methods of recording accounts receivable transactions when a cash discount situation is involved? Which is more theoretically correct? Which is used in practice more of the time? Why?

7. What are the basic problems that occur in the valuation of accounts receivable?

8. What is the theoretical justification of the allowance method as contrasted with the direct write-off method of accounting for bad debts?

9. Indicate how well the percentage-of-sales method and the aging method accomplish the objectives of the allowance method of accounting for bad debts.

10. Of what merit is the contention that the allowance method lacks the objectivity of the direct write-off method? Discuss in terms of accounting's measurement function.

11. Explain how the accounting for bad debts can be used for earnings management.

12. Because of calamitous earthquake losses, Bernstein Company, one of your client's oldest and largest customers, suddenly and unexpectedly became bankrupt. Approximately 30% of your client's total sales have been made to Bernstein Company during each of the past several years. The amount due from Bernstein Company—none of which is collectible—equals 22% of total accounts receivable, an amount that is considerably in excess of what was determined to be an adequate provision for doubtful accounts at the close of the preceding year. How would your client record the write-off of the Bernstein Company receivable if it is using the allowance method of accounting for bad debts? Justify your suggested treatment.

13. What is the normal procedure for handling the collection of accounts receivable previously written off using the direct write-off method? The allowance method?

14. On January 1, 2012, Lombard Co. sells property for which it had paid $690,000 to Sargent Company, receiving in return Sargent's zero-interest-bearing note for $1,000,000 payable in 5 years. What entry would Lombard make to record the sale, assuming that Lombard frequently sells similar items of property for a cash sales price of $640,000?

15. What is "imputed interest"? In what situations is it necessary to impute an interest rate for notes receivable? What are the considerations in imputing an appropriate interest rate?

16. What is the fair value option? Where do companies that elect the fair value option report unrealized holding gains and losses?

17. Indicate three reasons why a company might sell its receivables to another company.

18. When is the financial components approach to recording the transfers of receivables used? When should a transfer of receivables be recorded as a sale?

19. Moon Hardware is planning to factor some of its receivables. The cash received will be used to pay for inventory purchases. The factor has indicated that it will require "recourse" on the sold receivables. Explain to the controller of Moon Hardware what "recourse" is and how the recourse will be reflected in Moon's financial statements after the sale of the receivables.

20. Horizon Outfitters Company includes in its trial balance for December 31 an item for Accounts Receivable $789,000. This balance consists of the following items:

Due from regular customers	$523,000
Refund receivable on prior year's income taxes (an established claim)	15,500
Travel advance to employees	22,000
Loan to wholly owned subsidiary	45,500
Advances to creditors for goods ordered	61,000
Accounts receivable assigned as security for loans payable	75,000
Notes receivable past due plus interest on these notes	47,000
Total	$789,000

Illustrate how these items should be shown in the balance sheet as of December 31.

21. What is the accounts receivable turnover ratio, and what type of information does it provide?

22. You are evaluating Woodlawn Racetrack for a potential loan. An examination of the notes to the financial statements indicates restricted cash at year-end amounts to $100,000. Explain how you would use this information in evaluating Woodlawn's liquidity.

*23. Distinguish among the following: (1) a general checking account, (2) an imprest bank account, and (3) a lockbox account.

*24. What are the general rules for measuring and recognizing gain or loss by both the debtor and the creditor in an impairment?

*25. What is meant by impairment of a loan? Under what circumstances should a creditor recognize an impaired loan?

BRIEF EXERCISES

1 **BE7-1** Kraft Enterprises owns the following assets at December 31, 2012.

Cash in bank—savings account	68,000	Checking account balance	17,000
Cash on hand	9,300	Postdated checks	750
Cash refund due from IRS	31,400	Certificates of deposit (180-day)	90,000

What amount should be reported as cash?

4 **BE7-2** Restin Co. uses the gross method to record sales made on credit. On June 1, 2012, it made sales of $50,000 with terms 3/15, n/45. On June 12, 2012, Restin received full payment for the June 1 sale. Prepare the required journal entries for Restin Co.

4 **BE7-3** Use the information from BE7-2, assuming Restin Co. uses the net method to account for cash discounts. Prepare the required journal entries for Restin Co.

5 **BE7-4** Wilton, Inc. had net sales in 2012 of $1,400,000. At December 31, 2012, before adjusting entries, the balances in selected accounts were: Accounts Receivable $250,000 debit, and Allowance for Doubtful Accounts $2,400 credit. If Wilton estimates that 2% of its net sales will prove to be uncollectible, prepare the December 31, 2012, journal entry to record bad debt expense.

5 **BE7-5** Use the information presented in BE7-4 for Wilton, Inc.

(a) Instead of estimating the uncollectibles at 2% of net sales, assume that 10% of accounts receivable will prove to be uncollectible. Prepare the entry to record bad debt expense.

(b) Instead of estimating uncollectibles at 2% of net sales, assume Wilton prepares an aging schedule that estimates total uncollectible accounts at $24,600. Prepare the entry to record bad debt expense.

6 **BE7-6** Milner Family Importers sold goods to Tung Decorators for $30,000 on November 1, 2012, accepting Tung's $30,000, 6-month, 6% note. Prepare Milner's November 1 entry, December 31 annual adjusting entry, and May 1 entry for the collection of the note and interest.

6 **BE7-7** Dold Acrobats lent $16,529 to Donaldson, Inc., accepting Donaldson's 2-year, $20,000, zero-interest-bearing note. The implied interest rate is 10%. Prepare Dold's journal entries for the initial transaction, recognition of interest each year, and the collection of $20,000 at maturity.

8 **BE7-8** On October 1, 2012, Chung, Inc. assigns $1,000,000 of its accounts receivable to Seneca National Bank as collateral for a $750,000 note. The bank assesses a finance charge of 2% of the receivables assigned and interest on the note of 9%. Prepare the October 1 journal entries for both Chung and Seneca.

8 **BE7-9** Wood Incorporated factored $150,000 of accounts receivable with Engram Factors Inc. on a without-recourse basis. Engram assesses a 2% finance charge of the amount of accounts receivable and retains an amount equal to 6% of accounts receivable for possible adjustments. Prepare the journal entry for Wood Incorporated and Engram Factors to record the factoring of the accounts receivable to Engram.

8 **BE7-10** Use the information in BE7-9 for Wood. Assume that the receivables are sold with recourse. Prepare the journal entry for Wood to record the sale, assuming that the recourse liability has a fair value of $7,500.

8 **BE7-11** Arness Woodcrafters sells $250,000 of receivables to Commercial Factors, Inc. on a with recourse basis. Commercial assesses a finance charge of 5% and retains an amount equal to 4% of accounts receivable. Arness estimates the fair value of the recourse liability to be $8,000. Prepare the journal entry for Arness to record the sale.

8 **BE7-12** Use the information presented in BE7-11 for Arness Woodcrafters but assume that the recourse liability has a fair value of $4,000, instead of $8,000. Prepare the journal entry and discuss the effects of this change in the value of the recourse liability on Arness's financial statements.

9 **BE7-13** The financial statements of **General Mills, Inc.** report net sales of $12,442,000,000. Accounts receivable are $912,000,000 at the beginning of the year and $953,000,000 at the end of the year. Compute General Mills's accounts receivable turnover ratio. Compute General Mills's average collection period for accounts receivable in days.

10 ***BE7-14** Finman Company designated Jill Holland as petty cash custodian and established a petty cash fund of $200. The fund is reimbursed when the cash in the fund is at $15. Petty cash receipts indicate funds were disbursed for office supplies $94 and miscellaneous expense $87. Prepare journal entries for the establishment of the fund and the reimbursement.

10 ***BE7-15** Horton Corporation is preparing a bank reconciliation and has identified the following potential reconciling items. For each item, indicate if it is (1) added to balance per bank statement, (2) deducted from balance per bank statement, (3) added to balance per books, or (4) deducted from balance per books.

(a) Deposit in transit $5,500.
(b) Bank service charges $25.
(c) Interest credited to Horton's account $31.
(d) Outstanding checks $7,422.
(e) NSF check returned $377.

10 ***BE7-16** Use the information presented in BE7-15 for Horton Corporation. Prepare any entries necessary to make Horton's accounting records correct and complete.

11 ***BE7-17** Assume that Toni Braxton Company has recently fallen into financial difficulties. By reviewing all available evidence on December 31, 2012, one of Toni Braxton's creditors, the National American Bank, determined that Toni Braxton would pay back only 65% of the principal at maturity. As a result, the bank decided that the loan was impaired. If the loss is estimated to be $225,000, what entry(ies) should National American Bank make to record this loss?

EXERCISES

1 **E7-1 (Determining Cash Balance)** The controller for Weinstein Co. is attempting to determine the amount of cash and cash equivalents to be reported on its December 31, 2012, balance sheet. The following information is provided.

1. Commercial savings account of $600,000 and a commercial checking account balance of $800,000 are held at First National Bank of Olathe.
2. Money market fund account held at Volonte Co. (a mutual fund organization) permits Weinstein to write checks on this balance, $5,000,000.
3. Travel advances of $180,000 for executive travel for the first quarter of next year (employee to reimburse through salary reduction).
4. A separate cash fund in the amount of $1,500,000 is restricted for the retirement of long-term debt.
5. Petty cash fund of $1,000.
6. An I.O.U. from Marianne Koch, a company customer, in the amount of $150,000.
7. A bank overdraft of $110,000 has occurred at one of the banks the company uses to deposit its cash receipts. At the present time, the company has no deposits at this bank.
8. The company has two certificates of deposit, each totaling $500,000. These CDs have a maturity of 120 days.
9. Weinstein has received a check that is dated January 12, 2013, in the amount of $125,000.
10. Weinstein has agreed to maintain a cash balance of $500,000 at all times at First National Bank of Olathe to ensure future credit availability.
11. Weinstein has purchased $2,100,000 of commercial paper of Sergio Leone Co. which is due in 60 days.
12. Currency and coin on hand amounted to $7,700.

Instructions

(a) Compute the amount of cash and cash equivalents to be reported on Weinstein Co.'s balance sheet at December 31, 2012.
(b) Indicate the proper reporting for items that are not reported as cash on the December 31, 2012, balance sheet.

1 **E7-2 (Determine Cash Balance)** Presented below are a number of independent situations.

Instructions

For each individual situation, determine the amount that should be reported as cash. If the item(s) is not reported as cash, explain the rationale.

1. Checking account balance $925,000; certificate of deposit $1,400,000; cash advance to subsidiary of $980,000; utility deposit paid to gas company $180.
2. Checking account balance $500,000; an overdraft in special checking account at same bank as normal checking account of $17,000; cash held in a bond sinking fund $200,000; petty cash fund $300; coins and currency on hand $1,350.
3. Checking account balance $590,000; postdated check from a customer $11,000; cash restricted due to maintaining compensating balance requirement of $100,000; certified check from customer $9,800; postage stamps on hand $620.
4. Checking account balance at bank $42,000; money market balance at mutual fund (has checking privileges) $48,000; NSF check received from customer $800.
5. Checking account balance $700,000; cash restricted for future plant expansion $500,000; short-term Treasury bills $180,000; cash advance received from customer $900 (not included in checking account balance); cash advance of $7,000 to company executive, payable on demand; refundable deposit of $26,000 paid to federal government to guarantee performance on construction contract.

3 4 **E7-3 (Financial Statement Presentation of Receivables)** Patriot Company shows a balance of $241,140 in the Accounts Receivable account on December 31, 2012. The balance consists of the following.

Installment accounts due in 2013	$23,000
Installment accounts due after 2013	34,000
Overpayments to creditors	2,640
Due from regular customers, of which $40,000 represents accounts pledged as security for a bank loan	89,000
Advances to employees	1,500
Advance to subsidiary company (made in 2010)	91,000

Instructions

Illustrate how the information above should be shown on the balance sheet of Patriot Company on December 31, 2012.

3 4 **E7-4 (Determine Ending Accounts Receivable)** Your accounts receivable clerk, Mary Herman, to whom you pay a salary of $1,500 per month, has just purchased a new Audi. You decided to test the accuracy of the accounts receivable balance of $117,000 as shown in the ledger.

The following information is available for your *first year* in business.

(1) Collections from customers	$198,000
(2) Merchandise purchased	320,000
(3) Ending merchandise inventory	70,000
(4) Goods are marked to sell at 40% above cost	

Instructions

Compute an estimate of the ending balance of accounts receivable from customers that should appear in the ledger and any apparent shortages. Assume that all sales are made on account.

4 **E7-5 (Record Sales Gross and Net)** On June 3, Bolton Company sold to Arquette Company merchandise having a sale price of $2,000 with terms of 2/10, n/60, f.o.b. shipping point. An invoice totaling $90, terms n/30, was received by Arquette on June 8 from John Booth Transport Service for the freight cost. On June 12, the company received a check for the balance due from Arquette Company.

Instructions

(a) Prepare journal entries on the Bolton Company books to record all the events noted above under each of the following bases.
  (1) Sales and receivables are entered at gross selling price.
  (2) Sales and receivables are entered at net of cash discounts.

(b) Prepare the journal entry under basis 2, assuming that Arquette Company did not remit payment until July 29.

4 **E7-6 (Recording Sales Transactions)** Presented below is information from Lopez Computers Incorporated.

July	1	Sold $30,000 of computers to Smallwood Company with terms 3/15, n/60. Lopez uses the gross method to record cash discounts.
	10	Lopez received payment from Smallwood for the full amount owed from the July transactions.
	17	Sold $250,000 in computers and peripherals to The Clark Store with terms of 2/10, n/30.
	30	The Clark Store paid Lopez for its purchase of July 17.

Instructions

Prepare the necessary journal entries for Lopez Computers.

5 **E7-7 (Recording Bad Debts)** Sandel Company reports the following financial information before adjustments.

	Dr.	Cr.
Accounts Receivable	$160,000	
Allowance for Doubtful Accounts		$ 2,000
Sales Revenue (all on credit)		800,000
Sales Returns and Allowances	50,000	

Instructions

Prepare the journal entry to record bad debt expense assuming Sandel Company estimates bad debts at (a) 1% of net sales and (b) 5% of accounts receivable.

5 **E7-8 (Recording Bad Debts)** At the end of 2012, Sorter Company has accounts receivable of $900,000 and an allowance for doubtful accounts of $40,000. On January 16, 2013, Sorter Company determined that its receivable from Ordonez Company of $8,000 will not be collected, and management authorized its write-off.

Instructions

(a) Prepare the journal entry for Sorter Company to write off the Ordonez receivable.

(b) What is the net realizable value of Sorter Company's accounts receivable before the write-off of the Ordonez receivable?

(c) What is the net realizable value of Sorter Company's accounts receivable after the write-off of the Ordonez receivable?

5 **E7-9 (Computing Bad Debts and Preparing Journal Entries)** The trial balance before adjustment of Estefan Inc. shows the following balances.

	Dr.	Cr.
Accounts Receivable	$80,000	
Allowance for Doubtful Accounts	1,750	
Sales, Net Revenue (all on credit)		$580,000

Instructions

Give the entry for estimated bad debts assuming that the allowance is to provide for doubtful accounts on the basis of (a) 4% of gross accounts receivable and (b) 1% of net sales.

5 **E7-10 (Bad-Debt Reporting)** The chief accountant for Dollywood Corporation provides you with the following list of accounts receivable written off in the current year.

Date	Customer	Amount
March 31	E. L. Masters Company	$7,800
June 30	Hocking Associates	9,700
September 30	Amy Lowell's Dress Shop	7,000
December 31	R. Bronson, Inc.	9,830

Dollywood Corporation follows the policy of debiting Bad Debt Expense as accounts are written off. The chief accountant maintains that this procedure is appropriate for financial statement purposes because the Internal Revenue Service will not accept other methods for recognizing bad debts.

All of Dollywood Corporation's sales are on a 30-day credit basis. Sales for the current year total $2,400,000, and research has determined that bad debt losses approximate 2% of sales.

Instructions

(a) Do you agree or disagree with Dollywood's policy concerning recognition of bad debt expense? Why or why not?

(b) By what amount would net income differ if bad debt expense was computed using the percentage-of-sales approach?

5 **E7-11 (Bad Debts—Aging)** Puckett, Inc. includes the following account among its trade receivables.

Alstott Co.

1/1	Balance forward	700	1/28	Cash (#1710)	1,100
1/20	Invoice #1710	1,100	4/2	Cash (#2116)	1,350
3/14	Invoice #2116	1,350	4/10	Cash (1/1 Balance)	255
4/12	Invoice #2412	1,710	4/30	Cash (#2412)	1,000
9/5	Invoice #3614	490	9/20	Cash (#3614 and	890
10/17	Invoice #4912	860		part of #2412)	
11/18	Invoice #5681	2,000	10/31	Cash (#4912)	860
12/20	Invoice #6347	800	12/1	Cash (#5681)	1,250
			12/29	Cash (#6347)	800

Instructions

Age the balance and specify any items that apparently require particular attention at year-end.

4 5 **E7-12 (Journalizing Various Receivable Transactions)** Presented below is information related to Sanford Corp.

8

July 1 Sanford Corp. sold to Legler Co. merchandise having a sales price of $10,000 with terms 2/10, net/60. Sanford records its sales and receivables net.

5 Accounts receivable of $12,000 (gross) are factored with Rothchild Credit Corp. without recourse at a financing charge of 9%. Cash is received for the proceeds; collections are handled by the finance company. (These accounts were all past the discount period.)

9 Specific accounts receivable of $9,000 (gross) are pledged to Rather Credit Corp. as security for a loan of $6,000 at a finance charge of 6% of the amount of the loan. The finance company will make the collections. (All the accounts receivable are past the discount period.)

Dec. 29 Legler Co. notifies Sanford that it is bankrupt and will pay only 10% of its account. Give the entry to write off the uncollectible balance using the allowance method. (*Note:* First record the increase in the receivable on July 11 when the discount period passed.)

Instructions

Prepare all necessary entries in general journal form for Sanford Corp.

8 **E7-13 (Assigning Accounts Receivable)** On April 1, 2012, Prince Company assigns $500,000 of its accounts receivable to the Third National Bank as collateral for a $300,000 loan due July 1, 2012. The assignment agreement calls for Prince Company to continue to collect the receivables. Third National Bank assesses a finance charge of 2% of the accounts receivable, and interest on the loan is 10% (a realistic rate of interest for a note of this type).

Instructions

(a) Prepare the April 1, 2012, journal entry for Prince Company.

(b) Prepare the journal entry for Prince's collection of $350,000 of the accounts receivable during the period from April 1, 2012, through June 30, 2012.

(c) On July 1, 2012, Prince paid Third National all that was due from the loan it secured on April 1, 2012. Prepare the journal entry to record this payment.

5 8 **E7-14 (Journalizing Various Receivable Transactions)** The trial balance before adjustment for Sinatra Company shows the following balances.

	Dr.	Cr.
Accounts Receivable	$82,000	
Allowance for Doubtful Accounts	1,750	
Sales Revenue		$430,000

Instructions

Using the data above, give the journal entries required to record each of the following cases. (Each situation is independent.)

1. To obtain additional cash, Sinatra factors without recourse $20,000 of accounts receivable with Stills Finance. The finance charge is 10% of the amount factored.
2. To obtain a one-year loan of $55,000, Sinatra assigns $65,000 of specific receivable accounts to Ruddin Financial. The finance charge is 8% of the loan; the cash is received and the accounts turned over to Ruddin Financial.
3. The company wants to maintain Allowance for Doubtful Accounts at 5% of gross accounts receivable.
4. The company wishes to increase the allowance account by 1½% of net sales.

8 **E7-15 (Transfer of Receivables with Recourse)** Bryant Inc. factors receivables with a carrying amount of $200,000 to Warren Company for $190,000 on a with recourse basis.

Instructions

The recourse provision has a fair value of $2,000. This transaction should be recorded as a sale. Prepare the appropriate journal entry to record this transaction on the books of Bryant Inc.

8 **E7-16 (Transfer of Receivables with Recourse)** Gringo Corporation factors $250,000 of accounts receivable with Winkler Financing, Inc. on a with recourse basis. Winkler Financing will collect the receivables. The receivables records are transferred to Winkler Financing on August 15, 2012. Winkler Financing assesses a finance charge of 2% of the amount of accounts receivable and also reserves an amount equal to 4% of accounts receivable to cover probable adjustments.

Instructions

(a) What conditions must be met for a transfer of receivables with recourse to be accounted for as a sale?

(b) Assume the conditions from part (a) are met. Prepare the journal entry on August 15, 2012, for Gringo to record the sale of receivables, assuming the recourse liability has a fair value of $3,000.

8 **E7-17 (Transfer of Receivables without Recourse)** SEK Corp. factors $400,000 of accounts receivable with Mays Finance Corporation on a without recourse basis on July 1, 2012. The receivables records are transferred to Mays Finance, which will receive the collections. Mays Finance assesses a finance charge of 1½% of the amount of accounts receivable and retains an amount equal to 4% of accounts receivable to cover sales discounts, returns, and allowances. The transaction is to be recorded as a sale.

Instructions

(a) Prepare the journal entry on July 1, 2012, for SEK Corp. to record the sale of receivables without recourse.

(b) Prepare the journal entry on July 1, 2012, for Mays Finance Corporation to record the purchase of receivables without recourse.

6 **E7-18 (Note Transactions at Unrealistic Interest Rates)** On July 1, 2012, Rentoul Inc. made two sales.

1. It sold land having a fair value of $900,000 in exchange for a 4-year zero-interest-bearing promissory note in the face amount of $1,416,163. The land is carried on Rentoul's books at a cost of $590,000.

2. It rendered services in exchange for a 3%, 8-year promissory note having a face value of $400,000 (interest payable annually).

Rentoul Inc. recently had to pay 8% interest for money that it borrowed from British National Bank. The customers in these two transactions have credit ratings that require them to borrow money at 12% interest.

Instructions

Record the two journal entries that should be recorded by Rentoul Inc. for the sales transactions above that took place on July 1, 2012.

6 7 **E7-19 (Notes Receivable with Unrealistic Interest Rate)** On December 31, 2011, Hurly Co. performed environmental consulting services for Cascade Co. Cascade was short of cash, and Hurly Co. agreed to accept a $300,000 zero-interest-bearing note due December 31, 2013, as payment in full. Cascade is somewhat of a credit risk and typically borrows funds at a rate of 10%. Hurly is much more creditworthy and has various lines of credit at 6%.

Instructions

(a) Prepare the journal entry to record the transaction of December 31, 2011, for the Hurly Co.
(b) Assuming Hurly Co.'s fiscal year-end is December 31, prepare the journal entry for December 31, 2012.
(c) Assuming Hurly Co.'s fiscal year-end is December 31, prepare the journal entry for December 31, 2013.
(d) Assume that Hurly Co. elects the fair value option for this note. Prepare the journal entry at December 31, 2012, if the fair value of the note is $295,000.

9 **E7-20 (Analysis of Receivables)** Presented below is information for Grant Company.

1. Beginning-of-the-year Accounts Receivable balance was $15,000.
2. Net sales (all on account) for the year were $100,000. Grant does not offer cash discounts.
3. Collections on accounts receivable during the year were $80,000.

Instructions

(a) Prepare (summary) journal entries to record the items noted above.
(b) Compute Grant's accounts receivable turnover ratio for the year. The company does not believe it will have any bad debts.
(c) Use the turnover ratio computed in (b) to analyze Grant's liquidity. The turnover ratio last year was 7.0.

8 **E7-21 (Transfer of Receivables)** Use the information for Grant Company as presented in E7-20. Grant is planning to factor some accounts receivable at the end of the year. Accounts totaling $10,000 will be transferred to Credit Factors, Inc. with recourse. Credit Factors will retain 5% of the balances for probable adjustments and assesses a finance charge of 4%. The fair value of the recourse liability is $1,000.

Instructions

(a) Prepare the journal entry to record the sale of the receivables.
(b) Compute Grant's accounts receivable turnover ratio for the year, assuming the receivables are sold, and discuss how factoring of receivables affects the turnover ratio.

10 ***E7-22 (Petty Cash)** McMann, Inc. decided to establish a petty cash fund to help ensure internal control over its small cash expenditures. The following information is available for the month of April.

1. On April 1, it established a petty cash fund in the amount of $200.
2. A summary of the petty cash expenditures made by the petty cash custodian as of April 10 is as follows.

Delivery charges paid on merchandise purchased	$60
Supplies purchased and used	25
Postage expense	40
I.O.U. from employees	17
Miscellaneous expense	36

The petty cash fund was replenished on April 10. The balance in the fund was $12.

3. The petty cash fund balance was increased $100 to $300 on April 20.

Instructions

Prepare the journal entries to record transactions related to petty cash for the month of April.

10 *E7-23 (Petty Cash) The petty cash fund of Teasdale's Auto Repair Service, a sole proprietorship, contains the following.

1. Coins and currency		$ 10.20
2. Postage stamps		7.90
3. An I.O.U. from Richie Cunningham, an employee, for cash advance		40.00
4. Check payable to Teasdale's Auto Repair from Pottsie Weber, an employee, marked NSF		34.00
5. Vouchers for the following:		
Stamps	$ 20.00	
Two Rose Bowl tickets for Nick Teasdale	170.00	
Printer cartridge	14.35	204.35
		$296.45

The general ledger account Petty Cash has a balance of $300.

Instructions

Prepare the journal entry to record the reimbursement of the petty cash fund.

10 *E7-24 (Bank Reconciliation and Adjusting Entries) Kipling Company deposits all receipts and makes all payments by check. The following information is available from the cash records.

June 30 Bank Reconciliation

Balance per bank	$ 7,000
Add: Deposits in transit	1,540
Deduct: Outstanding checks	(2,000)
Balance per books	$ 6,540

Month of July Results

	Per Bank	Per Books
Balance July 31	$8,650	$9,250
July deposits	4,500	5,810
July checks	4,000	3,100
July note collected (not included in July deposits)	1,500	—
July bank service charge	15	—
July NSF check from a customer, returned by the bank (recorded by bank as a charge)	335	—

Instructions

(a) Prepare a bank reconciliation going from balance per bank and balance per book to correct cash balance.
(b) Prepare the general journal entry or entries to correct the Cash account.

10 *E7-25 (Bank Reconciliation and Adjusting Entries) Aragon Company has just received the August 31, 2012, bank statement, which is summarized below.

County National Bank	Disbursements	Receipts	Balance
Balance, August 1			$ 9,369
Deposits during August		$32,200	41,569
Note collected for depositor, including $40 interest		1,040	42,609
Checks cleared during August	$34,500		8,109
Bank service charges	20		8,089
Balance, August 31			8,089

The general ledger Cash account contained the following entries for the month of August.

Cash

Balance, August 1	10,050	Disbursements in August	35,403
Receipts during August	35,000		

Deposits in transit at August 31 are $3,800, and checks outstanding at August 31 total $1,550. Cash on hand at August 31 is $310. The bookkeeper improperly entered one check in the books at $146.50 which was written for $164.50 for supplies (expense); it cleared the bank during the month of August.

Instructions

(a) Prepare a bank reconciliation dated August 31, 2012, proceeding to a correct balance.
(b) Prepare any entries necessary to make the books correct and complete.
(c) What amount of cash should be reported in the August 31 balance sheet?

11 *E7-26 **(Impairments)** On December 31, 2012, Iva Majoli Company borrowed $62,092 from Paris Bank, signing a 5-year, $100,000 zero-interest-bearing note. The note was issued to yield 10% interest. Unfortunately, during 2014, Majoli began to experience financial difficulty. As a result, at December 31, 2014, Paris Bank determined that it was probable that it would receive back only $75,000 at maturity. The market rate of interest on loans of this nature is now 11%.

Instructions

(a) Prepare the entry to record the issuance of the loan by Paris Bank on December 31, 2012.
(b) Prepare the entry, if any, to record the impairment of the loan on December 31, 2014, by Paris Bank.

11 *E7-27 **(Impairments)** On December 31, 2012, Conchita Martinez Company signed a $1,000,000 note to Sauk City Bank. The market interest rate at that time was 12%. The stated interest rate on the note was 10%, payable annually. The note matures in 5 years. Unfortunately, because of lower sales, Conchita Martinez's financial situation worsened. On December 31, 2014, Sauk City Bank determined that it was probable that the company would pay back only $600,000 of the principal at maturity. However, it was considered likely that interest would continue to be paid, based on the $1,000,000 loan.

Instructions

(a) Determine the amount of cash Conchita Martinez received from the loan on December 31, 2012.
(b) Prepare a note amortization schedule for Sauk City Bank up to December 31, 2014.
(c) Determine the loss on impairment that Sauk City Bank should recognize on December 31, 2014.

See the book's companion website, www.wiley.com/college/kieso, for a set of B Exercises.

PROBLEMS

2 **P7-1 (Determine Proper Cash Balance)** Francis Equipment Co. closes its books regularly on December 31, but at the end of 2012 it held its cash book open so that a more favorable balance sheet could be prepared for credit purposes. Cash receipts and disbursements for the first 10 days of January were recorded as December transactions. The information is given below.

1. January cash receipts recorded in the December cash book totaled $45,640, of which $28,000 represents cash sales, and $17,640 represents collections on account for which cash discounts of $360 were given.
2. January cash disbursements recorded in the December check register liquidated accounts payable of $22,450 on which discounts of $250 were taken.
3. The ledger has not been closed for 2012.
4. The amount shown as inventory was determined by physical count on December 31, 2012.

The company uses the periodic method of inventory.

Instructions

(a) Prepare any entries you consider necessary to correct Francis's accounts at December 31.
(b) To what extent was Francis Equipment Co. able to show a more favorable balance sheet at December 31 by holding its cash book open? (Compute working capital and the current ratio.) Assume that the balance sheet that was prepared by the company showed the following amounts:

	Dr.	Cr.
Cash	$39,000	
Accounts receivable	42,000	
Inventory	67,000	
Accounts payable		$45,000
Other current liabilities		14,200

5 **P7-2 (Bad-Debt Reporting)** Presented below are a series of unrelated situations.

1. Halen Company's unadjusted trial balance at December 31, 2012, included the following accounts.

	Debit	Credit
Allowance for doubtful accounts	$4,000	
Net sales		$1,200,000

Halen Company estimates its bad debt expense to be 1½% of net sales. Determine its bad debt expense for 2012.

2. An analysis and aging of Stuart Corp. accounts receivable at December 31, 2012, disclosed the following.

Amounts estimated to be uncollectible	$ 180,000
Accounts receivable	1,750,000
Allowance for doubtful accounts (per books)	125,000

What is the net realizable value of Stuart's receivables at December 31, 2012?

3. Shore Co. provides for doubtful accounts based on 3% of credit sales. The following data are available for 2012.

Credit sales during 2012	$2,400,000
Allowance for doubtful accounts 1/1/12	17,000
Collection of accounts written off in prior years (customer credit was reestablished)	8,000
Customer accounts written off as uncollectible during 2012	30,000

What is the balance in Allowance for Doubtful Accounts at December 31, 2012?

4. At the end of its first year of operations, December 31, 2012, Darden Inc. reported the following information.

Accounts receivable, net of allowance for doubtful accounts	$950,000
Customer accounts written off as uncollectible during 2012	24,000
Bad debt expense for 2012	84,000

What should be the balance in accounts receivable at December 31, 2012, before subtracting the allowance for doubtful accounts?

5. The following accounts were taken from Bullock Inc.'s trial balance at December 31, 2012.

	Debit	Credit
Net credit sales		$750,000
Allowance for doubtful accounts	$ 14,000	
Accounts receivable	310,000	

If doubtful accounts are 3% of accounts receivable, determine the bad debt expense to be reported for 2012.

Instructions

Answer the questions relating to each of the five independent situations as requested.

5 **P7-3 (Bad-Debt Reporting—Aging)** Manilow Corporation operates in an industry that has a high rate of bad debts. Before any year-end adjustments, the balance in Manilow's Accounts Receivable account was $555,000 and the Allowance for Doubtful Accounts had a credit balance of $40,000. The year-end balance reported in the balance sheet for Allowance for Doubtful Accounts will be based on the aging schedule shown below.

Days Account Outstanding	Amount	Probability of Collection
Less than 16 days	$300,000	.98
Between 16 and 30 days	100,000	.90
Between 31 and 45 days	80,000	.85
Between 46 and 60 days	40,000	.80
Between 61 and 75 days	20,000	.55
Over 75 days	15,000	.00

Instructions

(a) What is the appropriate balance for Allowance for Doubtful Accounts at year-end?
(b) Show how accounts receivable would be presented on the balance sheet.
(c) What is the dollar effect of the year-end bad debt adjustment on the before-tax income?

(CMA adapted)

5 **P7-4 (Bad-Debt Reporting)** From inception of operations to December 31, 2012, Fortner Corporation provided for uncollectible accounts receivable under the allowance method: provisions were made monthly at 2% of credit sales; bad debts written off were charged to the allowance account; recoveries of bad debts previously written off were credited to the allowance account; and no year-end adjustments to the allowance account were made. Fortner's usual credit terms are net 30 days.

The balance in Allowance for Doubtful Accounts was $130,000 at January 1, 2012. During 2012, credit sales totaled $9,000,000, interim provisions for doubtful accounts were made at 2% of credit sales, $90,000 of bad debts were written off, and recoveries of accounts previously written off amounted to $15,000. Fortner installed a computer system in November 2012, and an aging of accounts receivable was prepared for the first time as of December 31, 2012. A summary of the aging is as follows.

Classification by Month of Sale	Balance in Each Category	Estimated % Uncollectible
November–December 2012	$1,080,000	2%
July–October	650,000	10%
January–June	420,000	25%
Prior to 1/1/12	150,000	80%
	$2,300,000	

Based on the review of collectibility of the account balances in the "prior to 1/1/12" aging category, additional receivables totaling $60,000 were written off as of December 31, 2012. The 80% uncollectible estimate applies to the remaining $90,000 in the category. Effective with the year ended December 31, 2012, Fortner adopted a different method for estimating the allowance for doubtful accounts at the amount indicated by the year-end aging analysis of accounts receivable.

Instructions

(a) Prepare a schedule analyzing the changes in Allowance for Doubtful Accounts for the year ended December 31, 2012. Show supporting computations in good form. (*Hint:* In computing the 12/31/12 allowance, subtract the $60,000 write-off).

(b) Prepare the journal entry for the year-end adjustment to the Allowance for Doubtful Accounts balance as of December 31, 2012.

(AICPA adapted)

5 **P7-5 (Bad-Debt Reporting)** Presented below is information related to the Accounts Receivable accounts of Gulistan Inc. during the current year 2012.

1. An aging schedule of the accounts receivable as of December 31, 2012, is as follows.

Age	Net Debit Balance	% to Be Applied after Correction Is Made
Under 60 days	$172,342	1%
60–90 days	136,490	3%
91–120 days	39,924*	6%
Over 120 days	23,644	$3,700 definitely uncollectible; estimated remainder uncollectible is 25%
	$372,400	

*The $3,240 write-off of receivables is related to the 91-to-120 day category.

2. The Accounts Receivable control account has a debit balance of $372,400 on December 31, 2012.
3. Two entries were made in the Bad Debt Expense account during the year: (1) a debit on December 31 for the amount credited to Allowance for Doubtful Accounts, and (2) a credit for $3,240 on November 3, 2012, and a debit to Allowance for Doubtful Accounts because of a bankruptcy.
4. Allowance for Doubtful Accounts is as follows for 2012.

Allowance for Doubtful Accounts

Nov. 3	Uncollectible accounts written off	3,240	Jan. 1	Beginning balance	8,750
			Dec. 31	5% of $372,400	18,620

5. A credit balance exists in the Accounts Receivable (60–90 days) of $4,840, which represents an advance on a sales contract.

Instructions

Assuming that the books have not been closed for 2012, make the necessary correcting entries.

3 4 5 **P7-6 (Journalize Various Accounts Receivable Transactions)** The balance sheet of Starsky Company at December 31, 2012, includes the following.

Notes receivable	$ 36,000	
Accounts receivable	182,100	
Less: Allowance for doubtful accounts	17,300	200,800

Transactions in 2012 include the following.

1. Accounts receivable of $138,000 were collected including accounts of $60,000 on which 2% sales discounts were allowed.
2. $5,300 was received in payment of an account which was written off the books as worthless in 2012.
3. Customer accounts of $17,500 were written off during the year.
4. At year-end, Allowance for Doubtful Accounts was estimated to need a balance of $20,000. This estimate is based on an analysis of aged accounts receivable.

Instructions

Prepare all journal entries necessary to reflect the transactions above.

8 **P7-7 (Assigned Accounts Receivable—Journal Entries)** Salen Company finances some of its current operations by assigning accounts receivable to a finance company. On July 1, 2012, it assigned, under guarantee, specific accounts amounting to $150,000. The finance company advanced to Salen 80% of the accounts assigned (20% of the total to be withheld until the finance company has made its full recovery), less a finance charge of ½% of the total accounts assigned.

On July 31, Salen Company received a statement that the finance company had collected $80,000 of these accounts and had made an additional charge of ½% of the total accounts outstanding as of July 31. This charge is to be deducted at the time of the first remittance due Salen Company from the finance company. (*Hint:* Make entries at this time.) On August 31, 2012, Salen Company received a second statement from the finance company, together with a check for the amount due. The statement indicated that the finance company had collected an additional $50,000 and had made a further charge of ½% of the balance outstanding as of August 31.

Instructions

Make all entries on the books of Salen Company that are involved in the transactions above.

(AICPA adapted)

6 **P7-8 (Notes Receivable with Realistic Interest Rate)** On October 1, 2012, Arden Farm Equipment Company sold a pecan-harvesting machine to Valco Brothers Farm, Inc. In lieu of a cash payment Valco Brothers Farm gave Arden a 2-year, $120,000, 8% note (a realistic rate of interest for a note of this type). The note required interest to be paid annually on October 1. Arden's financial statements are prepared on a calendar-year basis.

Instructions

Assuming Valco Brothers Farm fulfills all the terms of the note, prepare the necessary journal entries for Arden Farm Equipment Company for the entire term of the note.

6 **P7-9 (Notes Receivable Journal Entries)** On December 31, 2012, Oakbrook Inc. rendered services to Begin Corporation at an agreed price of $102,049, accepting $40,000 down and agreeing to accept the balance in four equal installments of $20,000 receivable each December 31. An assumed interest rate of 11% is imputed.

Instructions

Prepare the entries that would be recorded by Oakbrook Inc. for the sale and for the receipts and interest on the following dates. (Assume that the effective-interest method is used for amortization purposes.)

(a) December 31, 2012.
(b) December 31, 2013.
(c) December 31, 2014.
(d) December 31, 2015.
(e) December 31, 2016.

6 **P7-10 (Comprehensive Receivables Problem)** Braddock Inc. had the following long-term receivable account balances at December 31, 2011.

Note receivable from sale of division	$1,500,000
Note receivable from officer	400,000

Transactions during 2012 and other information relating to Braddock's long-term receivables were as follows.

1. The $1,500,000 note receivable is dated May 1, 2011, bears interest at 9%, and represents the balance of the consideration received from the sale of Braddock's electronics division to New York Company. Principal payments of $500,000 plus appropriate interest are due on May 1, 2012, 2013, and 2014. The first principal and interest payment was made on May 1, 2012. Collection of the note installments is reasonably assured.
2. The $400,000 note receivable is dated December 31, 2011, bears interest at 8%, and is due on December 31, 2014. The note is due from Sean May, president of Braddock Inc. and is collateralized by 10,000 shares of Braddock's common stock. Interest is payable annually on December 31, and all interest payments were paid on their due dates through December 31, 2012. The quoted market price of Braddock's common stock was $45 per share on December 31, 2012.
3. On April 1, 2012, Braddock sold a patent to Pennsylvania Company in exchange for a $100,000 zero-interest-bearing note due on April 1, 2014. There was no established exchange price for the patent, and the note had no ready market. The prevailing rate of interest for a note of this type at April 1, 2012, was 12%. The present value of $1 for two periods at 12% is 0.797 (use this factor). The patent had a carrying value of $40,000 at January 1, 2012, and the amortization for the year ended December 31, 2012, would have been $8,000. The collection of the note receivable from Pennsylvania is reasonably assured.
4. On July 1, 2012, Braddock sold a parcel of land to Splinter Company for $200,000 under an installment sale contract. Splinter made a $60,000 cash down payment on July 1, 2012, and signed a 4-year 11% note for the $140,000 balance. The equal annual payments of principal and interest on the note will be $45,125 payable on July 1, 2013, through July 1, 2016. The land could have been sold at an

established cash price of $200,000. The cost of the land to Braddock was $150,000. Circumstances are such that the collection of the installments on the note is reasonably assured.

Instructions

(a) Prepare the long-term receivables section of Braddock's balance sheet at December 31, 2012.
(b) Prepare a schedule showing the current portion of the long-term receivables and accrued interest receivable that would appear in Braddock's balance sheet at December 31, 2012.
(c) Prepare a schedule showing interest revenue from the long-term receivables that would appear on Braddock's income statement for the year ended December 31, 2012.

8 9 **P7-11 (Income Effects of Receivables Transactions)** Sandburg Company requires additional cash for its business. Sandburg has decided to use its accounts receivable to raise the additional cash and has asked you to determine the income statement effects of the following contemplated transactions.

1. On July 1, 2012, Sandburg assigned $400,000 of accounts receivable to Keller Finance Company. Sandburg received an advance from Keller of 80% of the assigned accounts receivable less a commission of 3% on the advance. Prior to December 31, 2012, Sandburg collected $220,000 on the assigned accounts receivable, and remitted $232,720 to Keller, $12,720 of which represented interest on the advance from Keller.
2. On December 1, 2012, Sandburg sold $300,000 of net accounts receivable to Wunsch Company for $270,000. The receivables were sold outright on a without-recourse basis.
3. On December 31, 2012, an advance of $120,000 was received from First Bank by pledging $160,000 of Sandburg's accounts receivable. Sandburg's first payment to First Bank is due on January 30, 2013.

Instructions

Prepare a schedule showing the income statement effects for the year ended December 31, 2012, as a result of the above facts.

10 ***P7-12 (Petty Cash, Bank Reconciliation)** Bill Jovi is reviewing the cash accounting for Nottleman, Inc., a local mailing service. Jovi's review will focus on the petty cash account and the bank reconciliation for the month ended May 31, 2012. He has collected the following information from Nottleman's bookkeeper for this task.

Petty Cash

1. The petty cash fund was established on May 10, 2012, in the amount of $250.
2. Expenditures from the fund by the custodian as of May 31, 2012, were evidenced by approved receipts for the following.

Postage expense	$33.00
Mailing labels and other supplies	65.00
I.O.U. from employees	30.00
Shipping charges	57.45
Newspaper advertising	22.80
Miscellaneous expense	15.35

On May 31, 2012, the petty cash fund was replenished and increased to $300; currency and coin in the fund at that time totaled $26.40.

Bank Reconciliation

THIRD NATIONAL BANK
BANK STATEMENT

	Disbursements	Receipts	Balance
Balance, May 1, 2012			$8,769
Deposits		$28,000	
Note payment direct from customer (interest of $30)		930	
Checks cleared during May	$31,150		
Bank service charges	27		
Balance, May 31, 2012			6,522

Nottleman's Cash Account	
Balance, May 1, 2012	$ 8,850
Deposits during May 2012	31,000
Checks written during May 2012	(31,835)

Deposits in transit are determined to be $3,000, and checks outstanding at May 31 total $850. Cash on hand (besides petty cash) at May 31, 2012, is $246.

Instructions

(a) Prepare the journal entries to record the transactions related to the petty cash fund for May.

(b) Prepare a bank reconciliation dated May 31, 2012, proceeding to a correct cash balance, and prepare the journal entries necessary to make the books correct and complete.

(c) What amount of cash should be reported in the May 31, 2012, balance sheet?

10 ***P7-13 (Bank Reconciliation and Adjusting Entries)** The cash account of Aguilar Co. showed a ledger balance of $3,969.85 on June 30, 2012. The bank statement as of that date showed a balance of $4,150. Upon comparing the statement with the cash records, the following facts were determined.

1. There were bank service charges for June of $25.
2. A bank memo stated that Bao Dai's note for $1,200 and interest of $36 had been collected on June 29, and the bank had made a charge of $5.50 on the collection. (No entry had been made on Aguilar's books when Bao Dai's note was sent to the bank for collection.)
3. Receipts for June 30 for $3,390 were not deposited until July 2.
4. Checks outstanding on June 30 totaled $2,136.05.
5. The bank had charged the Aguilar Co.'s account for a customer's uncollectible check amounting to $253.20 on June 29.
6. A customer's check for $90 had been entered as $60 in the cash receipts journal by Aguilar on June 15.
7. Check no. 742 in the amount of $491 had been entered in the cash journal as $419, and check no. 747 in the amount of $58.20 had been entered as $582. Both checks had been issued to pay for purchases of equipment.

Instructions

(a) Prepare a bank reconciliation dated June 30, 2012, proceeding to a correct cash balance.

(b) Prepare any entries necessary to make the books correct and complete.

10 ***P7-14 (Bank Reconciliation and Adjusting Entries)** Presented below is information related to Haselhof Inc.

Balance per books at October 31, $41,847.85; receipts $173,523.91; disbursements $164,893.54. Balance per bank statement November 30, $56,274.20.

The following checks were outstanding at November 30.

1224	$1,635.29
1230	2,468.30
1232	2,125.15
1233	482.17

Included with the November bank statement and not recorded by the company were a bank debit memo for $27.40 covering bank charges for the month, a debit memo for $372.13 for a customer's check returned and marked NSF, and a credit memo for $1,400 representing bond interest collected by the bank in the name of Haselhof Inc. Cash on hand at November 30 recorded and awaiting deposit amounted to $1,915.40.

Instructions

(a) Prepare a bank reconciliation (to the correct balance) at November 30, for Haselhof Inc. from the information above.

(b) Prepare any journal entries required to adjust the cash account at November 30.

11 ***P7-15 (Loan Impairment Entries)** On January 1, 2012, Botosan Company issued a $1,200,000, 5-year, zero-interest-bearing note to National Organization Bank. The note was issued to yield 8% annual interest. Unfortunately, during 2013 Botosan fell into financial trouble due to increased competition. After reviewing all available evidence on December 31, 2013, National Organization Bank decided that the loan was impaired. Botosan will probably pay back only $800,000 of the principal at maturity.

Instructions

(a) Prepare journal entries for both Botosan Company and National Organization Bank to record the issuance of the note on January 1, 2012. (Round to the nearest $10.)

(b) Assuming that both Botosan Company and National Organization Bank use the effective-interest method to amortize the discount, prepare the amortization schedule for the note.

(c) Under what circumstances can National Organization Bank consider Botosan's note to be impaired?

(d) Compute the loss National Organization Bank will suffer from Botosan's financial distress on December 31, 2013. What journal entries should be made to record this loss?

CONCEPTS FOR ANALYSIS

CA7-1 (Bad-Debt Accounting) Simms Company has significant amounts of trade accounts receivable. Simms uses the allowance method to estimate bad debts instead of the direct write-off method. During the year, some specific accounts were written off as uncollectible, and some that were previously written off as uncollectible were collected.

Instructions

(a) What are the deficiencies of the direct write-off method?

(b) What are the two basic allowance methods used to estimate bad debts, and what is the theoretical justification for each?

(c) How should Simms account for the collection of the specific accounts previously written off as uncollectible?

CA7-2 (Various Receivable Accounting Issues) Kimmel Company uses the net method of accounting for sales discounts. Kimmel also offers trade discounts to various groups of buyers.

On August 1, 2012, Kimmel sold some accounts receivable on a without recourse basis. Kimmel incurred a finance charge.

Kimmel also has some notes receivable bearing an appropriate rate of interest. The principal and total interest are due at maturity. The notes were received on October 1, 2012, and mature on September 30, 2014. Kimmel's operating cycle is less than one year.

Instructions

(a) **(1)** Using the net method, how should Kimmel account for the sales discounts at the date of sale? What is the rationale for the amount recorded as sales under the net method?

(2) Using the net method, what is the effect on Kimmel's sales revenues and net income when customers do not take the sales discounts?

(b) What is the effect of trade discounts on sales revenues and accounts receivable? Why?

(c) How should Kimmel account for the accounts receivable factored on August 1, 2012? Why?

(d) How should Kimmel account for the note receivable and the related interest on December 31, 2012? Why?

CA7-3 (Bad-Debt Reporting Issues) Clark Pierce conducts a wholesale merchandising business that sells approximately 5,000 items per month with a total monthly average sales value of $250,000. Its annual bad debt rate has been approximately 1½% of sales. In recent discussions with his bookkeeper, Mr. Pierce has become confused by all the alternatives apparently available in handling the Allowance for Doubtful Accounts balance. The following information has been presented to Pierce.

1. An allowance can be set up (a) on the basis of a percentage of sales or (b) on the basis of a valuation of all past due or otherwise questionable accounts receivable. Those considered uncollectible can be charged to such allowance at the close of the accounting period, or specific items can be charged off directly against (1) Gross Sales or to (2) Bad Debt Expense in the year in which they are determined to be uncollectible.
2. Collection agency and legal fees, and so on, incurred in connection with the attempted recovery of bad debts can be charged to (a) Bad Debt Expense, (b) Allowance for Doubtful Accounts, (c) Legal Expense, or (d) Administrative Expense.
3. Debts previously written off in whole or in part but currently recovered can be credited to (a) Other Revenue, (b) Bad Debt Expense, or (c) Allowance for Doubtful Accounts.

Instructions

Which of the foregoing methods would you recommend to Mr. Pierce in regard to (1) allowances and charge-offs, (2) collection expenses, and (3) recoveries? State briefly and clearly the reasons supporting your recommendations.

CA7-4 (Basic Note and Accounts Receivable Transactions)

Part 1

On July 1, 2012, Wallace Company, a calendar-year company, sold special-order merchandise on credit and received in return an interest-bearing note receivable from the customer. Wallace Company will receive interest at the prevailing rate for a note of this type. Both the principal and interest are due in one lump sum on June 30, 2013.

Instructions

When should Wallace Company report interest revenue from the note receivable? Discuss the rationale for your answer.

Part 2

On December 31, 2012, Wallace Company had significant amounts of accounts receivable as a result of credit sales to its customers. Wallace uses the allowance method based on credit sales to estimate bad debts. Past experience indicates that 2% of credit sales normally will not be collected. This pattern is expected to continue.

Instructions

(a) Discuss the rationale for using the allowance method based on credit sales to estimate bad debts. Contrast this method with the allowance method based on the balance in the trade receivables accounts.

(b) How should Wallace Company report the allowance for doubtful accounts on its balance sheet at December 31, 2012? Also, describe the alternatives, if any, for presentation of bad debt expense in Wallace Company's 2012 income statement.

(AICPA adapted)

CA7-5 (Bad-Debt Reporting Issues) Valasquez Company sells office equipment and supplies to many organizations in the city and surrounding area on contract terms of 2/10, n/30. In the past, over 75% of the credit customers have taken advantage of the discount by paying within 10 days of the invoice date.

The number of customers taking the full 30 days to pay has increased within the last year. Current indications are that less than 60% of the customers are now taking the discount. Bad debts as a percentage of gross credit sales have risen from the 1.5% provided in past years to about 4% in the current year.

The controller has responded to a request for more information on the deterioration in collections of accounts receivable with the report reproduced below.

VALASQUEZ COMPANY
FINANCE COMMITTEE REPORT—ACCOUNTS RECEIVABLE COLLECTIONS
MAY 31, 2013

The fact that some credit accounts will prove uncollectible is normal. Annual bad debt write-offs have been 1.5% of gross credit sales over the past five years. During the last fiscal year, this percentage increased to slightly less than 4%. The current Accounts Receivable balance is $1,600,000. The condition of this balance in terms of age and probability of collection is as follows.

Proportion of Total	Age Categories	Probability of Collection
68%	not yet due	99%
15%	less than 30 days past due	96½%
8%	30 to 60 days past due	95%
5%	61 to 120 days past due	91%
2½%	121 to 180 days past due	70%
1½%	over 180 days past due	20%

Allowance for Doubtful Accounts had a credit balance of $43,300 on June 1, 2012. Valasquez Company has provided for a monthly bad debt expense accrual during the current fiscal year based on the assumption that 4% of gross credit sales will be uncollectible. Total gross credit sales for the 2012–2013 fiscal year amounted to $4,000,000. Write-offs of bad accounts during the year totaled $145,000.

Instructions

(a) Prepare an accounts receivable aging schedule for Valasquez Company using the age categories identified in the controller's report to the finance committee showing:

(1) The amount of accounts receivable outstanding for each age category and in total.

(2) The estimated amount that is uncollectible for each category and in total.

(b) Compute the amount of the year-end adjustment necessary to bring Allowance for Doubtful Accounts to the balance indicated by the age analysis. Then prepare the necessary journal entry to adjust the accounting records.

(c) In a recessionary environment with tight credit and high interest rates:

(1) Identify steps Valasquez Company might consider to improve the accounts receivable situation.

(2) Then evaluate each step identified in terms of the risks and costs involved.

(CMA adapted)

CA7-6 (Sale of Notes Receivable) Corrs Wholesalers Co. sells industrial equipment for a standard 3-year note receivable. Revenue is recognized at time of sale. Each note is secured by a lien on the equipment and has a face amount equal to the equipment's list price. Each note's stated interest rate is below the customer's market rate at date of sale. All notes are to be collected in three equal annual installments beginning one year after sale. Some of the notes are subsequently sold to a bank with recourse, some are subsequently sold without recourse, and some are retained by Corrs. At year end, Corrs evaluates all outstanding notes receivable and provides for estimated losses arising from defaults.

Instructions

(a) What is the appropriate valuation basis for Corrs's notes receivable at the date it sells equipment?

(b) How should Corrs account for the sale, without recourse, of a February 1, 2012, note receivable sold on May 1, 2012? Why is it appropriate to account for it in this way?

(c) At December 31, 2012, how should Corrs measure and account for the impact of estimated losses resulting from notes receivable that it

(1) Retained and did **not** sell?

(2) Sold to bank with recourse?

(AICPA adapted)

CA7-7 (Zero-Interest-Bearing Note Receivable) On September 30, 2011, Rolen Machinery Co. sold a machine and accepted the customer's zero-interest-bearing note. Rolen normally makes sales on a cash basis. Since the machine was unique, its sales price was not determinable using Rolen's normal pricing practices.

After receiving the first of two equal annual installments on September 30, 2012, Rolen immediately sold the note with recourse. On October 9, 2013, Rolen received notice that the note was dishonored, and it paid all amounts due. At all times prior to default, the note was reasonably expected to be paid in full.

Instructions

(a) **(1)** How should Rolen determine the sales price of the machine?

(2) How should Rolen report the effects of the zero-interest-bearing note on its income statement for the year ended December 31, 2011? Why is this accounting presentation appropriate?

(b) What are the effects of the sale of the note receivable with recourse on Rolen's income statement for the year ended December 31, 2012, and its balance sheet at December 31, 2012?

(c) How should Rolen account for the effects of the note being dishonored?

CA7-8 (Reporting of Notes Receivable, Interest, and Sale of Receivables) On July 1, 2012, Moresan Company sold special-order merchandise on credit and received in return an interest-bearing note receivable from the customer. Moresan will receive interest at the prevailing rate for a note of this type. Both the principal and interest are due in one lump sum on June 30, 2013.

On September 1, 2012, Moresan sold special-order merchandise on credit and received in return a zero-interest-bearing note receivable from the customer. The prevailing rate of interest for a note of this type is determinable. The note receivable is due in one lump sum on August 31, 2014.

Moresan also has significant amounts of trade accounts receivable as a result of credit sales to its customers. On October 1, 2012, some trade accounts receivable were assigned to Indigo Finance Company on a non-notification (Moresan handles collections) basis for an advance of 75% of their amount at an interest charge of 8% on the balance outstanding.

On November 1, 2012, other trade accounts receivable were sold on a without-recourse basis. The factor withheld 5% of the trade accounts receivable factored as protection against sales returns and allowances and charged a finance charge of 3%.

Instructions

(a) How should Moresan determine the interest revenue for 2012 on the:

(1) Interest-bearing note receivable? Why?

(2) Zero-interest-bearing note receivable? Why?

(b) How should Moresan report the interest-bearing note receivable and the zero-interest-bearing note receivable on its balance sheet at December 31, 2012?

(c) How should Moresan account for subsequent collections on the trade accounts receivable assigned on October 1, 2012, and the payments to Indigo Finance? Why?

(d) How should Moresan account for the trade accounts receivable factored on November 1, 2012? Why?

(AICPA adapted)

CA7-9 (Accounting for Zero-Interest-Bearing Note) Soon after beginning the year-end audit work on March 10 at Engone Company, the auditor has the following conversation with the controller.

CONTROLLER: The year ended March 31st should be our most profitable in history and, as a consequence, the board of directors has just awarded the officers generous bonuses.

AUDITOR: I thought profits were down this year in the industry, according to your latest interim report.

CONTROLLER: Well, they were down, but 10 days ago we closed a deal that will give us a substantial increase for the year.

AUDITOR: Oh, what was it?

CONTROLLER: Well, you remember a few years ago our former president bought stock in Henderson Enterprises because he had those grandiose ideas about becoming a conglomerate. For 6 years we have not been able to sell this stock, which cost us $3,000,000 and has not paid a nickel in dividends. Thursday we sold this stock to Bimini Inc. for $4,000,000. So, we will have a gain of $700,000 ($1,000,000 pretax) which will increase our net income for the year to $4,000,000, compared with last year's $3,800,000. As far as I know, we'll be the only company in the industry to register an increase in net income this year. That should help the market value of the stock!

AUDITOR: Do you expect to receive the $4,000,000 in cash by March 31st, your fiscal year-end?

CONTROLLER: No. Although Bimini Inc. is an excellent company, they are a little tight for cash because of their rapid growth. Consequently, they are going to give us a $4,000,000 zero-interest-bearing note with payments of $400,000 per year for the next 10 years. The first payment is due on March 31 of next year.

AUDITOR: Why is the note zero-interest-bearing?

CONTROLLER: Because that's what everybody agreed to. Since we don't have any interest-bearing debt, the funds invested in the note do not cost us anything and besides, we were not getting any dividends on the Henderson Enterprises stock.

Instructions

Do you agree with the way the controller has accounted for the transaction? If not, how should the transaction be accounted for?

CA7-10 (Receivables Management) As the manager of the accounts receivable department for Beavis Leather Goods, Ltd., you recently noticed that Kelly Collins, your accounts receivable clerk who is paid $1,200 per month, has been wearing unusually tasteful and expensive clothing. (This is Beavis's first year in business.) This morning, Collins drove up to work in a brand new Lexus.

Naturally suspicious by nature, you decide to test the accuracy of the accounts receivable balance of $192,000 as shown in the ledger. The following information is available for your first year (precisely 9 months ended September 30, 2012) in business.

(1) Collections from customers	$188,000
(2) Merchandise purchased	360,000
(3) Ending merchandise inventory	90,000
(4) Goods are marked to sell at 40% above cost.	

Instructions

Assuming all sales were made on account, compute the ending accounts receivable balance that should appear in the ledger, noting any apparent shortage. Then, draft a memo dated October 3, 2012, to Mark Price, the branch manager, explaining the facts in this situation. Remember that this problem is serious, and you do not want to make hasty accusations.

CA7-11 (Bad-Debt Reporting) Marvin Company is a subsidiary of Hughes Corp. The controller believes that the yearly allowance for doubtful accounts for Marvin should be 2% of net credit sales. The president, nervous that the parent company might expect the subsidiary to sustain its 10% growth rate, suggests that the controller increase the allowance for doubtful accounts to 3% yearly. The president thinks that the lower net income, which reflects a 6% growth rate, will be a more sustainable rate for Marvin Company.

Instructions

(a) Should the controller be concerned with Marvin Company's growth rate in estimating the allowance? Explain your answer.

(b) Does the president's request pose an ethical dilemma for the controller? Give your reasons.

USING YOUR JUDGMENT

FINANCIAL REPORTING

Financial Reporting Problem

The Procter & Gamble Company (P&G)

The financial statements of P&G are presented in Appendix 5B or can be accessed at the book's companion website, **www.wiley.com/college/kieso**.

Instructions

Refer to P&G's financial statements and the accompanying notes to answer the following questions.

(a) What criteria does P&G use to classify "Cash and cash equivalents" as reported in its balance sheet?

(b) As of June 30, 2009, what balances did P&G have in cash and cash equivalents? What were the major uses of cash during the year?

(c) P&G reports no allowance for doubtful accounts, suggesting that bad debt expense is not material for this company. Is it reasonable that a company like P&G would not have material bad debt expense? Explain.

Comparative Analysis Case

The Coca-Cola Company and PepsiCo, Inc.

PEPSICO

Instructions

Go to the book's companion website and use the information found there to answer the following questions related to The Coca-Cola Company and PepsiCo, Inc.

(a) What were the cash and cash equivalents reported by Coca-Cola and PepsiCo at the end of 2009? What does each company classify as cash equivalents?

(b) What were the accounts receivable (net) for Coca-Cola and PepsiCo at the end of 2009? Which company reports the greater allowance for doubtful accounts receivable (amount and percentage of gross receivable) at the end of 2009?

(c) Assuming that all "net operating revenues" (Coca-Cola) and all "net sales" (PepsiCo) were net *credit* sales, compute the accounts receivable turnover ratio for 2009 for Coca-Cola and PepsiCo; also compute the days outstanding for receivables. What is your evaluation of the difference?

Financial Statement Analysis Cases

Case I Occidental Petroleum Corporation

Occidental Petroleum Corporation reported the following information in a recent annual report.

Occidental Petroleum Corporation
Consolidated Balance Sheets
(in millions)

Assets at December 31,	Current year	Prior year
Current assets		
Cash and cash equivalents	$ 683	$ 146
Trade receivables, net of allowances	804	608
Receivables from joint ventures, partnerships, and other	330	321
Inventories	510	491
Prepaid expenses and other	147	307
Total current assets	2,474	1,873
Long-term receivables, net	264	275

Notes to Consolidated Financial Statements

Cash and Cash Equivalents. Cash equivalents consist of highly liquid investments. Cash equivalents totaled approximately $661 million and $116 million at current and prior year-ends, respectively.

Trade Receivables. Occidental has agreement to sell, under a revolving sale program, an undivided percentage ownership interest in a designated pool of non-interest-bearing receivables. Under this program, Occidental serves as the collection agent with respect to the receivables sold. An interest in new receivables is sold as collections are made from customers. The balance sold at current year-end was $360 million.

Instructions

(a) What items other than coin and currency may be included in "cash"?

(b) What items may be included in "cash equivalents"?

(c) What are compensating balance arrangements, and how should they be reported in financial statements?

(d) What are the possible differences between cash equivalents and short-term (temporary) investments?

(e) Assuming that the sale agreement meets the criteria for sale accounting, cash proceeds were \$345 million, the carrying value of the receivables sold was \$360 million, and the fair value of the recourse liability was \$15 million, what was the effect on income from the sale of receivables?

(f) Briefly discuss the impact of the transaction in (e) on Occidental's liquidity.

Case 2 Microsoft Corporation

Microsoft is the leading developer of software in the world. To continue to be successful Microsoft must generate new products, which requires significant amounts of cash. Shown below is the current asset and current liability information from Microsoft's June 30, 2009, balance sheet (in millions). Following the Microsoft data is the current asset and current liability information for **Oracle** (in millions), another major software developer.

Microsoft Corporation
Balance Sheets (partial)
As of June 30
(in millions)

Current assets	2009	2008
Cash and equivalents	\$ 6,076	\$10,339
Short-term investments	25,371	13,323
Accounts receivable	11,192	13,589
Other	6,641	5,991
Total current assets	\$49,280	\$43,242
Total current liabilities	\$27,034	\$29,886

Oracle
Balance Sheets (partial)
As of May 31
(in millions)

Current assets	2009	2008
Cash and equivalents	\$ 8,995	\$ 8,262
Short-term investments	3,629	2,781
Receivables	4,430	5,127
Other current assets	1,527	1,933
Total current assets	\$18,581	\$18,103
Current liabilities	\$ 9,149	\$10,029

Part 1 (Cash and Cash Equivalents)

Instructions

(a) What is the definition of a cash equivalent? Give some examples of cash equivalents. How do cash equivalents differ from other types of short-term investments?

(b) Calculate (1) the current ratio and (2) working capital for each company for 2009 and discuss your results.

(c) Is it possible to have too many liquid assets?

Part 2 (Accounts Receivables)

Microsoft provided the following disclosure related to its accounts receivable.

Allowance for Doubtful Accounts. The allowance for doubtful accounts reflects our best estimate of probable losses inherent in the accounts receivable balance. We determine the allowance based on known troubled accounts, historical experience, and other currently available evidence. Activity in the allowance for doubtful accounts is as follows:

(in millions)

Year Ended June 30	Balance at beginning of period	Charged to costs and expenses	Write-offs and other	Balance at end of period
2007	$142	$ 64	$(89)	$117
2008	117	88	(52)	153
2009	153	360	(62)	451

Instructions

(a) Compute Microsoft's accounts receivable turnover ratio for 2009 and discuss your results. Microsoft had sales revenue of $58,437 million in 2009.

(b) Reconstruct the summary journal entries for 2009 based on the information in the disclosure.

(c) Briefly discuss how the accounting for bad debts affects the analysis in Part 2 (a).

Accounting, Analysis, and Principles

The Flatiron Pub provides catering services to local businesses. The following information was available for The Flatiron for the years ended December 31, 2011 and 2012.

	December 31, 2011	December 31, 2012
Cash	$ 2,000	$ 1,685
Accounts receivable	46,000	?
Allowance for doubtful accounts	550	?
Other current assets	8,500	7,925
Current liabilities	37,000	44,600
Total credit sales	205,000	255,000
Collections on accounts receivable	190,000	228,000

Flatiron management is preparing for a meeting with its bank concerning renewal of a loan and has collected the following information related to the above balances.

1. The cash reported at December 31, 2012, reflects the following items: petty cash $1,575 and postage stamps $110. The Other current assets balance at December 31, 2012, includes the checking account balance of $4,000.
2. On November 30, 2012, Flatiron agreed to accept a 6-month, $5,000 note bearing 12% interest, payable at maturity, from a major client in settlement of a $5,000 bill. The above balances do not reflect this transaction.
3. Flatiron factored some accounts receivable at the end of 2012. It transferred accounts totaling $10,000 to Final Factor, Inc. with recourse. Final Factor will receive the collections from Flatiron's customers and will retain 2% of the balances. Final Factor assesses Flatiron a finance charge of 3% on this transfer. The fair value of the recourse liability is $400. However, management has determined that the amount due from the factor and the fair value of the resource obligation have not been recorded, and neither are included in the balances above.
4. Flatiron charged off uncollectible accounts with balances of $1,600. On the basis of the latest available information, the 2012 provision for bad debts is estimated to be 2.5% of accounts receivable.

Accounting

(a) Based on the above transactions, determine the balance for (1) Accounts Receivable and (2) Allowance for Doubtful Accounts at December 31, 2012.

(b) Prepare the current assets section of The Flatiron's balance sheet at December 31, 2012.

Analysis

(a) Compute Flatiron's current ratio and accounts receivable turnover ratio for December 31, 2012. Use these measures to analyze Flatiron's liquidity. The accounts receivable turnover ratio in 2011 was 4.37.

(b) Discuss how the analysis you did above of Flatiron's liquidity would be affected if Flatiron had transferred the receivables in a secured borrowing transaction.

Principles

What is the conceptual basis for recording bad debt expense based on the percentage-of-receivables at December 31, 2012?

BRIDGE TO THE PROFESSION

Professional Research: FASB Codification

As the new staff person in your company's treasury department, you have been asked to conduct research related to a proposed transfer of receivables. Your supervisor wants the authoritative sources for the following items that are discussed in the securitization agreement.

Instructions

If your school has a subscription to the FASB Codification, go to *http://aaahq.org/asclogin.cfm* to log in and prepare responses to the following. Provide Codification references for your responses.

(a) Identify relevant Codification section that addresses transfers of receivables.

(b) What are the objectives for reporting transfers of receivables?

(c) Provide definitions for the following:

- **(1)** Transfer.
- **(2)** Recourse.
- **(3)** Collateral.

(d) Provide other examples (besides recourse and collateral) that qualify as continuing involvement.

Professional Simulation

In this simulation, you are asked to address various requirements regarding the accounting for receivables. Prepare responses to all parts.

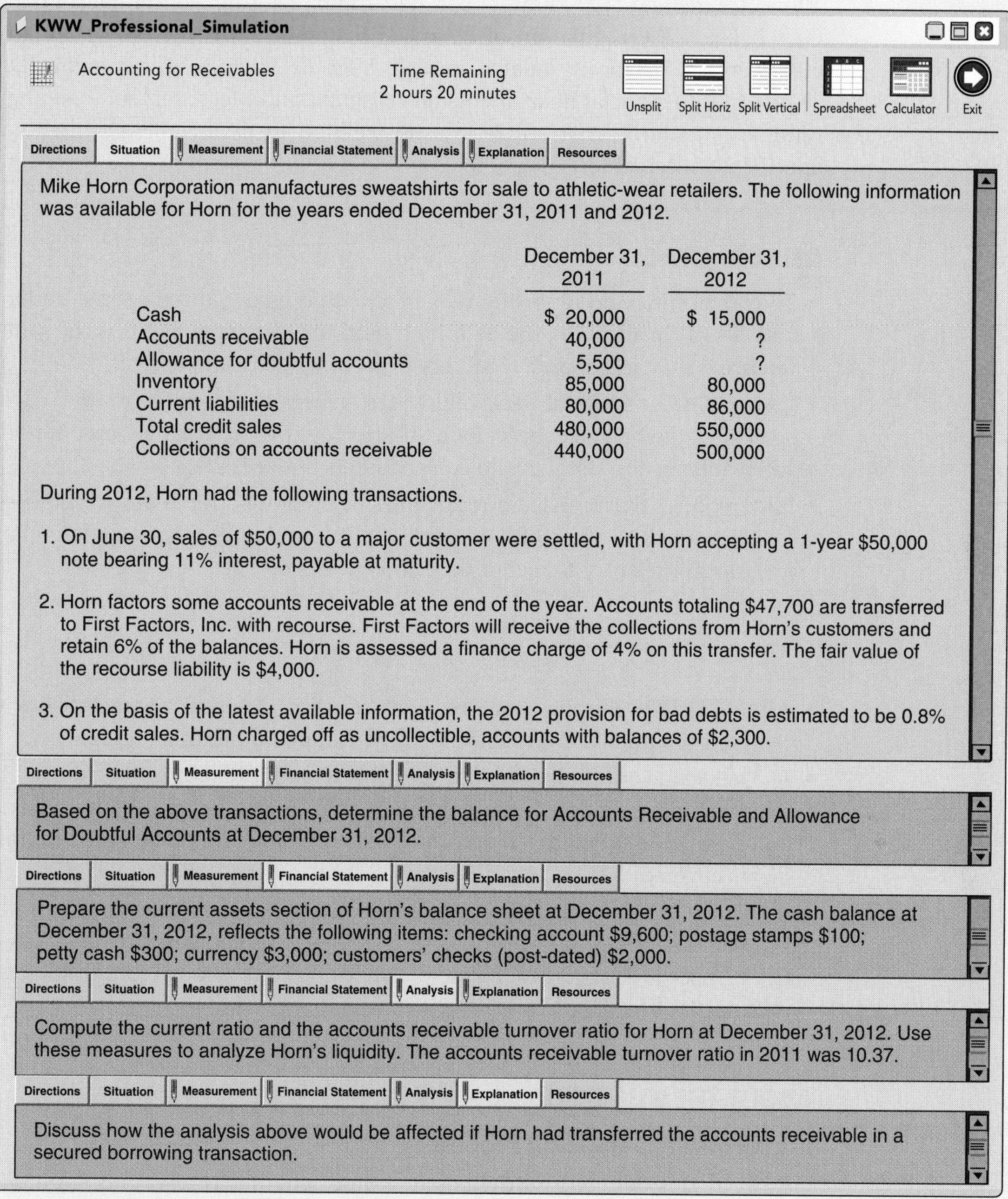

KWW_Professional_Simulation

Accounting for Receivables — Time Remaining 2 hours 20 minutes

Unsplit | Split Horiz | Split Vertical | Spreadsheet | Calculator | Exit

Directions | Situation | Measurement | Financial Statement | Analysis | Explanation | Resources

Mike Horn Corporation manufactures sweatshirts for sale to athletic-wear retailers. The following information was available for Horn for the years ended December 31, 2011 and 2012.

	December 31, 2011	December 31, 2012
Cash	$ 20,000	$ 15,000
Accounts receivable	40,000	?
Allowance for doubtful accounts	5,500	?
Inventory	85,000	80,000
Current liabilities	80,000	86,000
Total credit sales	480,000	550,000
Collections on accounts receivable	440,000	500,000

During 2012, Horn had the following transactions.

1. On June 30, sales of $50,000 to a major customer were settled, with Horn accepting a 1-year $50,000 note bearing 11% interest, payable at maturity.
2. Horn factors some accounts receivable at the end of the year. Accounts totaling $47,700 are transferred to First Factors, Inc. with recourse. First Factors will receive the collections from Horn's customers and retain 6% of the balances. Horn is assessed a finance charge of 4% on this transfer. The fair value of the recourse liability is $4,000.
3. On the basis of the latest available information, the 2012 provision for bad debts is estimated to be 0.8% of credit sales. Horn charged off as uncollectible, accounts with balances of $2,300.

Directions | Situation | Measurement | Financial Statement | Analysis | Explanation | Resources

Based on the above transactions, determine the balance for Accounts Receivable and Allowance for Doubtful Accounts at December 31, 2012.

Directions | Situation | Measurement | Financial Statement | Analysis | Explanation | Resources

Prepare the current assets section of Horn's balance sheet at December 31, 2012. The cash balance at December 31, 2012, reflects the following items: checking account $9,600; postage stamps $100; petty cash $300; currency $3,000; customers' checks (post-dated) $2,000.

Directions | Situation | Measurement | Financial Statement | Analysis | Explanation | Resources

Compute the current ratio and the accounts receivable turnover ratio for Horn at December 31, 2012. Use these measures to analyze Horn's liquidity. The accounts receivable turnover ratio in 2011 was 10.37.

Directions | Situation | Measurement | Financial Statement | Analysis | Explanation | Resources

Discuss how the analysis above would be affected if Horn had transferred the accounts receivable in a secured borrowing transaction.

The basic accounting and reporting issues related to recognition and measurement of receivables, such as the use of allowance accounts, how to record discounts, use of the allowance method to account for bad debts, and factoring, are similar for both IFRS and GAAP. *IAS 1* ("Presentation of Financial Statements") is the only standard that discusses issues specifically related to cash. *IFRS 7* ("Financial Instruments: Disclosure") and *IAS 39* ("Financial Instruments: Recognition and Measurement") are the two international standards that address issues related to financial instruments and more specifically receivables.

RELEVANT FACTS

- The accounting and reporting related to cash is essentially the same under both IFRS and GAAP. In addition, the definition used for cash equivalents is the same. One difference is that, in general, IFRS classifies bank overdrafts as cash.
- Like GAAP, cash and receivables are generally reported in the current assets section of the balance sheet under IFRS. However, companies may report cash and receivables as the last items in current assets under IFRS.
- IFRS requires that loans and receivables be accounted for at amortized cost, adjusted for allowances for doubtful accounts. IFRS sometimes refers to these allowances as *provisions*. The entry to record the allowance would be:

Bad Debt Expense	xxxxxx	
Provision for Doubtful Accounts		xxxxxx

- Although IFRS implies that receivables with different characteristics should be reported separately, there is no standard that mandates this segregation.
- The fair value option is similar under GAAP and IFRS but not identical. The international standard related to the fair value option is subject to certain qualifying criteria not in the U.S. standard. In addition, there is some difference in the financial instruments covered.
- IFRS and GAAP differ in the criteria used to account for transfers of receivables. IFRS is a combination of an approach focused on risks and rewards and loss of control. GAAP uses loss of control as the primary criterion. In addition, IFRS generally permits partial transfers; GAAP does not.

ABOUT THE NUMBERS

Impairment Evaluation Process

IFRS provides detailed guidelines to assess whether receivables should be considered uncollectible (often referred to as *impaired*). GAAP does not identify a specific approach. Under IFRS, companies assess their receivables for impairment each reporting period and start the impairment assessment by considering whether objective evidence indicates that one or more loss events have occurred. Examples of possible loss events are:

- Significant financial problems of the customer.
- Payment defaults.
- Renegotiation of terms of the receivable due to financial difficulty of the customer.

- Measurable decrease in estimated future cash flows from a group of receivables since initial recognition, although the decrease cannot yet be identified with individual assets in the group.

A receivable is considered impaired when a loss event indicates a negative impact on the estimated future cash flows to be received from the customer (*IAS 39*, paragraphs 58–70). The IASB requires that the impairment assessment should be performed as follows.

1. Receivables that are individually significant are considered for impairment separately, if impaired, the company recognizes it. Receivables that are not individually significant may also be assessed individually, but it is not necessary to do so.
2. Any receivable individually assessed that is not considered impaired is included with a group of assets with similar credit-risk characteristics and collectively assessed for impairment.
3. Any receivables **not individually assessed are collectively assessed** for impairment.

To illustrate, assume that Hector Company has the following receivables classified into individually significant and all other receivables.

Individually significant receivables		
Yaan Company	$ 40,000	
Randon Inc.	100,000	
Fernando Co.	60,000	
Blanchard Ltd.	50,000	$250,000
All other receivables		500,000
Total		$750,000

Hector determines that Yaan's receivable is impaired by $15,000, and Blanchard's receivable is totally impaired. Both Randon's and Fernando's receivables are not considered impaired. Hector also determines a composite rate of 2% is appropriate to measure impairment on all other receivables. The total impairment is computed as follows.

Accounts Receivable Impairments		
Individually assessed receivables		
Yaan Company		$15,000
Blanchard Ltd.		50,000
Collectively assessed receivables	$500,000	
Add: Randon Co.	100,000	
Fernando Co.	60,000	
Total collectively assessed receivables	$660,000	
Collectively assessed impairments ($660,00 × 2%)		13,200
Total impairment		$78,200

Hector therefore has an impairment related to its receivables of $78,200. The most controversial part of this computation is that Hector must include in the collective assessment the receivables from Randon and Fernando that were individually assessed and not considered impaired. The rationale for including Randon and Fernando in the collective assessment is that companies often do not have all the information at hand to make an informed decision for individual assessment.

Recovery of Impairment Loss

The accounting for loan impairments is similar between GAAP and IFRS. Subsequent to recording an impairment, events or economic conditions may change such that the extent of the impairment loss decreases (e.g., due to an impairment in the debtor's credit rating). Under IFRS, some or all of the previously recognized impairment loss shall be reversed either directly, with a debit to Accounts Receivable, or by debiting the allowance account and crediting Bad Debt Expense. Such reversals of impairment losses are not allowed under GAAP.

To illustrate, recall the Ogden Bank impairment example of page 402. In that situation, Ogden Bank (the creditor) recognized an impairment loss of $12,434 by debiting Bad Debt Expense for the expected loss. At the same time, it reduced the overall value of the receivable by crediting Allowance for Doubtful Accounts. Ogden made the following entry to record the loss.

Bad Debt Expense	12,434	
Allowance for Doubtful Accounts		12,434

Now, assume that in the year following the impairment recorded by Ogden, Carl King (the borrower) has worked his way out of financial difficulty. Ogden now expects to receive all payments on the loan according to the original loan terms. Based on this new information, the present value of the expected payments is $100,000. Thus, Ogden makes the following entry to reverse the previously recorded impairment.

Allowance for Doubtful Accounts	12,434	
Bad Debt Expense		12,434

Note that the reversal of impairment losses shall not result in carrying amount of the receivable that exceeds the amortized cost that would have been reported had the impairment not been recognized. Under GAAP, reversal of an impairment is not permitted. Rather, the balance of the loan after the impairment becomes the new basis for the loan.

ON THE HORIZON

The question of recording fair values for financial instruments will continue to be an important issue to resolve as the Boards work toward convergence. Both the IASB and the FASB have indicated that they believe that financial statements would be more transparent and understandable if companies recorded and reported all financial instruments at fair value. That said, in *IFRS 9*, which was issued in 2009, the IASB created a split model, where some financial instruments are recorded at fair value, but other financial assets, such as loans and receivables, can be accounted for at amortized cost if certain criteria are met. Critics say that this can result in two companies with identical securities accounting for those securities in different ways. A proposal by the FASB would require that nearly all financial instruments, including loans and receivables, be accounted for at fair value. It has been suggested that *IFRS 9* will likely be changed or replaced as the FASB and IASB continue to deliberate the best treatment for financial instruments. In fact, one member of the IASB said that companies should ignore *IFRS 9* and continue to report under the old standard, because in his opinion, it is extremely likely that it would be changed before the mandatory adoption date of this standard in 2013.

IFRS SELF-TEST QUESTIONS

1. Under IFRS, cash and cash equivalents are reported:

(a) the same as GAAP.

(b) as separate items.

(c) similar to GAAP, except for the reporting of bank overdrafts.
(d) always as the first items in the current assets section.

2. Under IFRS, receivables are to be reported on the balance sheet at:
(a) amortized cost.
(b) amortized cost adjusted for estimated loss provisions.
(c) historical cost.
(d) replacement cost.

3. Which of the following statements is *false*?
(a) Receivables include equity securities purchased by the company.
(b) Receivables include credit card receivables.
(c) Receivables include amounts owed by employees as result of company loans to employees.
(d) Receivables include amounts resulting from transactions with customers.

4. Under IFRS:
(a) the entry to record estimated uncollected accounts is the same as GAAP.
(b) loans and receivables should only be tested for impairment as a group.
(c) it is always acceptable to use the direct write-off method.
(d) all financial instruments are recorded at fair value.

5. Which of the following statements is *true*?
(a) The fair value option requires that some types of financial instruments be recorded at fair value.
(b) The fair value option requires that all noncurrent financial instruments be recorded at amortized cost.
(c) The fair value option allows, but does not require, that some types of financial instruments be recorded at fair value.
(d) The FASB and IASB would like to reduce the reliance on fair value accounting for financial instruments in the future.

IFRS CONCEPTS AND APPLICATION

IFRS7-1 Briefly describe the impairment evaluation process and assessment of receivables on an individual or collective basis.

IFRS7-2 What are some steps taken by both the FASB and IASB to move to fair value measurement for financial instruments? In what ways have some of the approaches differed?

IFRS7-3 On December 31, 2012, Firth Company borrowed $62,092 from Paris Bank, signing a 5-year, $100,000 zero-internet-bearing note. The note was issued to yield 10% interest. Unfortunately, during 2012, Firth began to experience financial difficulty. As a result, at December 31, 2012, Paris Bank determined that it was probable that it would collect only $75,000 at maturity. The market rate of interest on loans of this nature is now 11%.

Instructions

(a) Prepare the entry (if any) to record the impairment of the loan on December 31, 2014, by Paris Bank.
(b) Prepare the entry on March 31, 2015, if Paris learns that Firth will be able to repay the loan under the original terms.

Professional Research

IFRS7-4 As the new staff person in your company's treasury department, you have been asked to conduct research related to a proposed transfer of receivables. Your supervisor wants the authoritative sources for the following items that are discussed in the receivables transfer agreement.

Instructions

Access the IFRS authoritative literature at the IASB website (*http://eifrs.iasb.org/*). When you have accessed the documents, you can use the search tool in your Internet browser to prepare responses to the following items: **(a)** Identify relevant IFRSs that address transfers of receivables. **(b)** What are the objectives for reporting transfers of receivables? **(c)** Provide the definition for "Amortized cost."

International Financial Reporting Problem:
Marks and Spencer plc

IFRS7-5 The financial statements of **Marks and Spencer plc (M&S)** are available at the book's companion website or can be accessed at *http://corporate.marksandspencer.com/documents/publications/2010/Annual_Report_2010.*

Instructions

Refer to M&S's financial statements and the accompanying notes to answer the following questions.

(a) What criteria does M&S use to classify "Cash and cash equivalents" as reported in its statement of financial position?

(b) As of 3 April 2010, what balances did M&S have in cash and cash equivalents? What were the major uses of cash during the year?

(c) What amounts related to trade receivables does M&S report? Does M&S have any past due but not impaired receivables?

ANSWERS TO IFRS SELF-TEST QUESTIONS

1. c **2.** b **3.** a **4.** a **5.** c

Remember to check the book's companion website to find additional resources for this chapter.

CHAPTER 8

Valuation of Inventories: A Cost-Basis Approach

LEARNING OBJECTIVES

After studying this chapter, you should be able to:

1. Identify major classifications of inventory.
2. Distinguish between perpetual and periodic inventory systems.
3. Identify the effects of inventory errors on the financial statements.
4. Understand the items to include as inventory cost.
5. Describe and compare the cost flow assumptions used to account for inventories.
6. Explain the significance and use of a LIFO reserve.
7. Understand the effect of LIFO liquidations.
8. Explain the dollar-value LIFO method.
9. Identify the major advantages and disadvantages of LIFO.
10. Understand why companies select given inventory methods.

Inventories in the Crystal Ball

A substantial increase in inventory may be a leading indicator of an upcoming decline in profit margins. Take the auto industry as an example. Leading up to the recent automobile market slowdown and subsequent government bailouts, automakers' inventories had been growing for several years because the manufacturers liked to run the factories at full capacity, even if they were not selling cars as fast as they could make them. For example, **General Motors (GM)** overproduced and then tried to push the sales with incentives and month-long "blow-out" sales. GM was hoping that the ever-growing market would cover the problem until customer demand grew to the point where the cars were purchased without so many incentives.

Unfortunately, all that was growing was GM inventories. A slowing economy and rising gas prices scared car buyers from the new car lots, especially the sections with low gas-mileage, full-size vehicles and SUVs. Not surprisingly, GM and other automakers responded with discounted prices. For example, the average sticker on a Cadillac DeVille was $54,193, but the net price after incentives was $42,211. This meant that the factory was giving up a substantial amount of profit through rebates, dealer cash, or lease or interest rate subsidies. A similar deal could be had at **Ford**, which was selling Explorers for $25,745 net, a 24 percent reduction for various factory incentives (including free gasoline). But inventories at GM and Ford continued to grow, even with these significant incentives.

A similar swelling inventory problem has occurred for PCs, cell phones, and flat-panel TVs in the recent economic downturn. For example, inventories of chips used to store data in cell phones and music devices surged to $10.2 billion in December 2008, relative to just $3.8 billion in the prior quarter. Like the automakers, chip producers idled factories and had to take some inventory back when retailers could not sell the products in the depressed holiday sales season.

These data concern investors. Here's why: When inventories rise faster than the growth in sales, it is a signal of future declines in profits. That is, when companies face slowing sales and growing inventory, markdowns in prices usually result. These markdowns, in turn, lead to lower sales revenue and income, thereby squeezing profit margins on sales. At the same time, slowing inventory growth

IFRS IN THIS CHAPTER

- See the **International Perspectives** on pages 440, 446, 449, 451, and 464.
- **IFRS Insights** related to inventory are presented in Chapter 9 on pages 545–553.

relative to sales is a good-news signal. These declines indicate that companies are in a good position to deal with a slowing economy, and production cutbacks can be gradual.

Research supporting these observations indicates that increases in retailers' inventories translate into lower prices and lower net income (Bernard and Noel, 1991). Interestingly, the same research found that for manufacturers, only increases in finished goods inventory lead to future profit declines. Increases in raw materials and work in process inventories signal that the company is building its inventory to meet increased demand. Therefore, future sales and income will be higher. These research results reinforce the usefulness of the GAAP requirement for manufacturers to disclose their inventory components on the balance sheet or in related notes.

Sources: Victor Bernard and J. Noel, "Do Inventory Disclosures Predict Sales and Earnings?" *Journal of Accounting, Auditing, and Finance* (March 1991), pp. 145–182; J. Flint, "Inventories: Too Much of a Good Thing," *Forbes.com* (September 21, 2004); Bloomberg News, "Wholesale Inventories Grew Faster in April than Forecasters Expected," *New York Times* (June 7, 2008), p. B3; and Olga Kharif, "Tech: The Shelves Are Groaning," *BusinessWeek* (January 12, 2009), p. 27.

PREVIEW OF CHAPTER 8

As our opening story indicates, information on inventories and changes in inventory helps to predict financial performance. In this chapter, we discuss the basic issues related to accounting and reporting for inventory. The content and organization of the chapter are as follows.

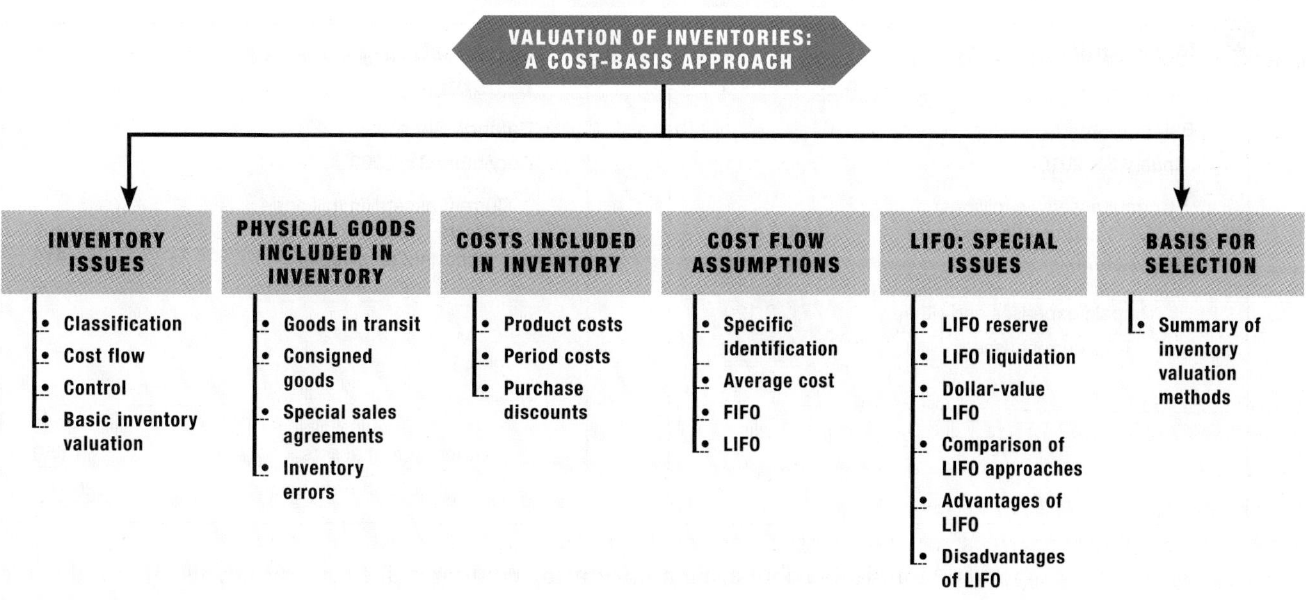

INVENTORY ISSUES

Classification

LEARNING OBJECTIVE 1
Identify major classifications of inventory.

Inventories are asset items that a company holds for sale in the ordinary course of business, or goods that it will use or consume in the production of goods to be sold. The description and measurement of inventory require careful attention. The investment in inventories is frequently the largest current asset of merchandising (retail) and manufacturing businesses.

A **merchandising concern**, such as **Wal-Mart Stores, Inc.**, usually purchases its merchandise in a form ready for sale. It reports the cost assigned to unsold units left on hand as **merchandise inventory**. Only one inventory account, Merchandise Inventory, appears in the financial statements.

Manufacturing concerns, on the other hand, produce goods to sell to merchandising firms. Many of the largest U.S. businesses are manufacturers, such as **Boeing**, **IBM**, **Exxon Mobil**, **Procter & Gamble**, **Ford**, and **Motorola**. Although the products they produce may differ, manufacturers normally have three inventory accounts—Raw Materials, Work in Process, and Finished Goods.

A company reports the cost assigned to goods and materials on hand but not yet placed into production as **raw materials inventory**. Raw materials include the wood to make a baseball bat or the steel to make a car. These materials can be traced directly to the end product.

At any point in a continuous production process some units are only partially processed. The cost of the raw material for these unfinished units, plus the direct labor cost applied specifically to this material and a ratable share of manufacturing overhead costs, constitute the **work in process inventory**.

Companies report the costs identified with the completed but unsold units on hand at the end of the fiscal period as **finished goods inventory**. Illustration 8-1 contrasts the financial statement presentation of inventories of **Wal-Mart** (a merchandising company) with those of **Caterpillar** (a manufacturing company.) The remainder of the balance sheet is essentially similar for the two types of companies.

ILLUSTRATION 8-1
Comparison of Presentation of Current Assets for Merchandising and Manufacturing Companies

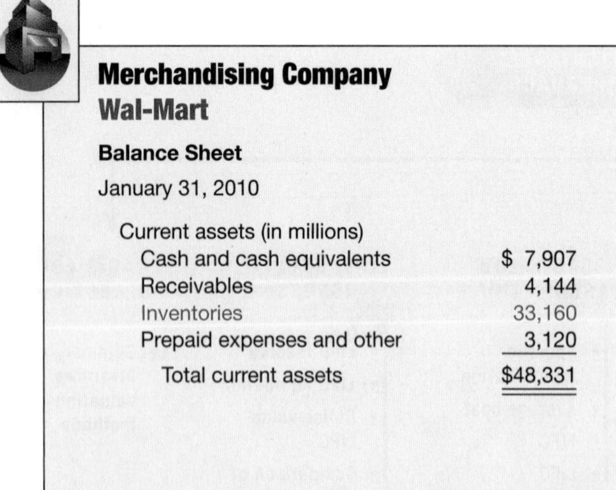

Merchandising Company
Wal-Mart

Balance Sheet
January 31, 2010

Current assets (in millions)	
Cash and cash equivalents	$ 7,907
Receivables	4,144
Inventories	33,160
Prepaid expenses and other	3,120
Total current assets	$48,331

Manufacturing Company
Caterpillar

Balance Sheet
December 31, 2009

Current assets (in millions)		
Cash		$ 4,867
Accounts receivable		13,912
Inventories		
Raw materials	$1,979	
Work in process	656	
Finished goods	3,465	
Supplies	260	
Total inventories		6,360
Other current assets		1,650
Total current assets		$26,789

As indicated above, a manufacturing company, like **Caterpillar**, also might include a Manufacturing or Factory **Supplies Inventory** account. In it, Caterpillar would include such items as machine oils, nails, cleaning material, and the like—supplies that are used in production but are not the primary materials being processed.

Illustration 8-2 shows the differences in the flow of costs through a merchandising company and a manufacturing company.

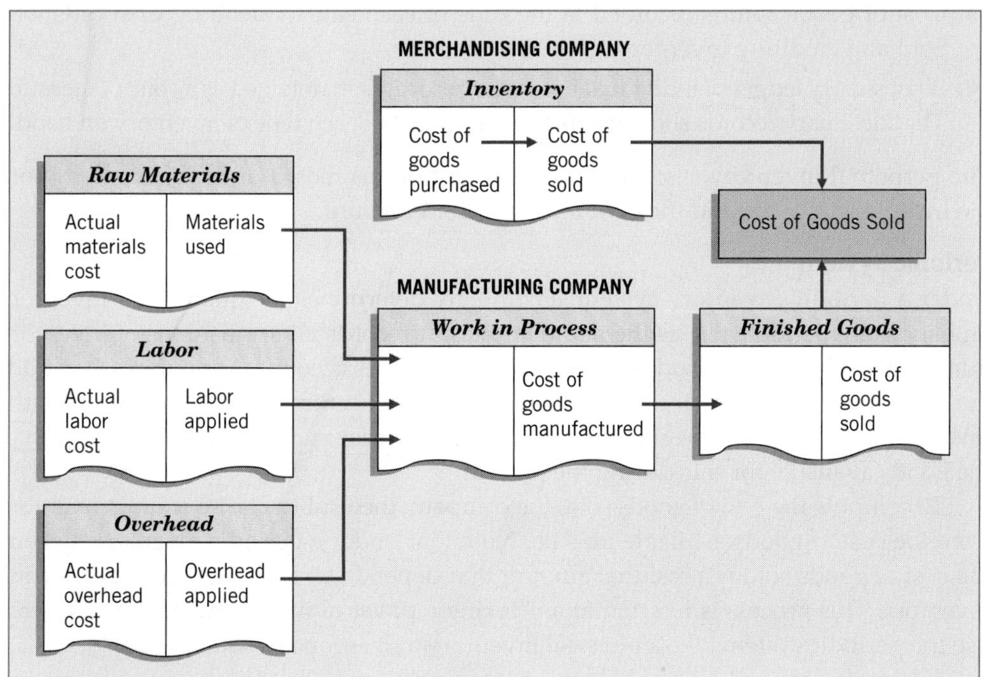

ILLUSTRATION 8-2
Flow of Costs through Manufacturing and Merchandising Companies

Inventory Cost Flow

2 LEARNING OBJECTIVE
Distinguish between perpetual and periodic inventory systems.

Companies that sell or produce goods report inventory and cost of goods sold at the end of each accounting period. The flow of costs for a company is as follows: Beginning inventory plus the cost of goods purchased is the cost of goods available for sale. As goods are sold, they are assigned to cost of goods sold. Those goods that are not sold by the end of the accounting period represent ending inventory. Illustration 8-3 describes these relationships.

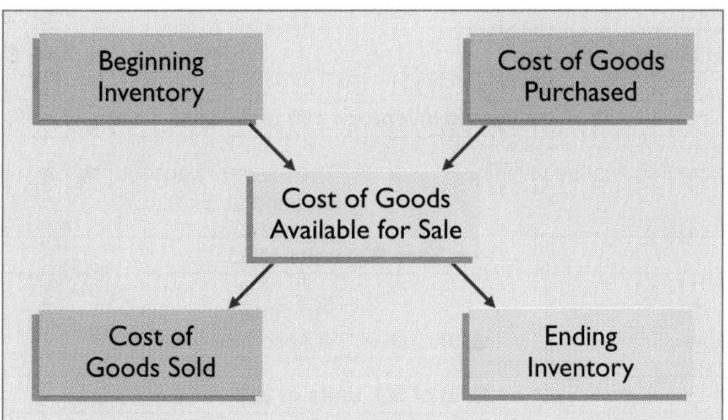

ILLUSTRATION 8-3
Inventory Cost Flow

Companies use one of two types of systems for maintaining accurate inventory records for these costs—the perpetual system or the periodic system.

Perpetual System

A **perpetual inventory system** continuously tracks changes in the Inventory account. That is, a company records all purchases and sales (issues) of goods directly in the Inventory account **as they occur**. The accounting features of a perpetual inventory system are as follows.

1. Purchases of merchandise for resale or raw materials for production are debited to Inventory rather than to Purchases.

2. Freight-in is debited to Inventory, not Purchases. Purchase returns and allowances and purchase discounts are credited to Inventory rather than to separate accounts.
3. Cost of goods sold is recorded at the time of each sale by debiting Cost of Goods Sold and crediting Inventory.
4. A subsidiary ledger of individual inventory records is maintained as a control measure. The subsidiary records show the quantity and cost of each type of inventory on hand.

The perpetual inventory system provides a continuous record of the balances in both the Inventory account and the Cost of Goods Sold account.

Periodic System

Under a periodic inventory system, a company determines the quantity of inventory on hand only periodically, as the name implies. It records all acquisitions of inventory during the accounting period by debiting the Purchases account. A company then adds the total in the Purchases account at the end of the accounting period to the cost of the inventory on hand at the beginning of the period. This sum determines the total cost of the goods available for sale during the period.

To compute the cost of goods sold, the company then subtracts the ending inventory from the cost of goods available for sale. Note that under a periodic inventory system, the cost of goods sold is a residual amount that depends on a physical count of ending inventory. This process is referred to as "taking a physical inventory." Companies that use the periodic system take a physical inventory at least once a year.

Comparing Perpetual and Periodic Systems

To illustrate the difference between a perpetual and a periodic system, assume that Fesmire Company had the following transactions during the current year.

Beginning inventory	100 units at $6 = $600
Purchases	900 units at $6 = $5,400
Sales	600 units at $12 = $7,200
Ending inventory	400 units at $6 = $2,400

Fesmire records these transactions during the current year as shown in Illustration 8-4.

ILLUSTRATION 8-4
Comparative Entries—Perpetual vs. Periodic

Perpetual Inventory System			Periodic Inventory System		
Beginning inventory, 100 units at $6					
The Inventory account shows the inventory on hand at $600.			The Inventory account shows the inventory on hand at $600.		
Purchase 900 units at $6					
Inventory	5,400		Purchases	5,400	
Accounts Payable		5,400	Accounts Payable		5,400
Sale of 600 units at $12					
Accounts Receivable	7,200		Accounts Receivable	7,200	
Sales		7,200	Sales		7,200
Cost of Goods Sold (600 at $6)	3,600		(No entry)		
Inventory		3,600			
End-of-period entries for inventory accounts, 400 units at $6					
No entry necessary.			Inventory (ending, by count)	2,400	
The account, Inventory, shows the ending balance of $2,400 ($600 + $5,400 − $3,600).			Cost of Goods Sold	3,600	
			Purchases		5,400
			Inventory (beginning)		600

When a company uses a perpetual inventory system and a difference exists between the perpetual inventory balance and the physical inventory count, it needs a separate entry to adjust the perpetual inventory account. To illustrate, assume that at the end of the reporting period, the perpetual inventory account reported an inventory balance of $4,000. However, a physical count indicates inventory of $3,800 is actually on hand. The entry to record the necessary write-down is as follows.

Inventory Over and Short	200	
Inventory		200

Perpetual inventory overages and shortages generally represent a misstatement of cost of goods sold. The difference results from normal and expected shrinkage, breakage, shoplifting, incorrect recordkeeping, and the like. Inventory Over and Short therefore adjusts Cost of Goods Sold. In practice, companies sometimes report Inventory Over and Short in the "Other revenues and gains" or "Other expenses and losses" section of the income statement.

Note that a company using the periodic inventory system does not report the account Inventory Over and Short. The reason: The periodic method does not have accounting records against which to compare the physical count. As a result, a company buries inventory overages and shortages in cost of goods sold.

Inventory Control

For various reasons, management is vitally interested in inventory planning and control. Whether a company manufactures or merchandises goods, it needs an accurate accounting system with up-to-date records. It may lose sales and customers if it does not stock products in the desired style, quality, and quantity. Further, companies must monitor inventory levels carefully to limit the financing costs of carrying large amounts of inventory.

In a perfect world, companies would like a continuous record of both their inventory levels and their cost of goods sold. The popularity and affordability of computerized accounting software makes the perpetual system cost-effective for many kinds of businesses. Companies like **Target**, **Best Buy**, and **Sears Holdings** now incorporate the recording of sales with optical scanners at the cash register into perpetual inventory systems.

However, many companies cannot afford a complete perpetual system. But, most of these companies need current information regarding their inventory levels, to protect against stockouts or overpurchasing and to aid in preparation of monthly or quarterly financial data. As a result, these companies use a **modified perpetual inventory system**. This system provides detailed inventory records of increases and decreases in quantities only—not dollar amounts. It is merely a memorandum device outside the double-entry system, which helps in determining the level of inventory at any point in time.

Whether a company maintains a complete perpetual inventory in quantities and dollars or a modified perpetual inventory system, it probably takes a physical inventory once a year. No matter what type of inventory records companies use, they all face the danger of loss and error. Waste, breakage, theft, improper entry, failure to prepare or record requisitions, and other similar possibilities may cause the inventory records to differ from the actual inventory on hand. Thus, **all companies** need periodic verification of the inventory records by actual count, weight, or measurement, with the counts compared with the detailed inventory records. As indicated earlier, a company corrects the records to agree with the quantities actually on hand.

Insofar as possible, companies should take the physical inventory near the end of their fiscal year, to properly report inventory quantities in their annual accounting reports. Because this is not always possible, however, physical inventories taken within two or three months of the year's end are satisfactory, if a company maintains detailed inventory records with a fair degree of accuracy.[1]

STAYING LEAN

What do the numbers mean?

Wal-Mart uses its buying power in the supply chain to purchase an increasing proportion of its goods directly from manufacturers and on a combined basis across geographic borders. Wal-Mart estimates that it saves 5–15% across its supply chain by implementing direct purchasing on a combined basis for the 15 countries in which it operates. Thus, Wal-Mart has a good handle on what products its needs to stock, and it gets the best prices when it purchases.

Wal-Mart also provides a classic example of the use of tight inventory controls. Department managers use a scanner that when placed over the bar code corresponding to a particular item, will tell them how many of the items the store sold yesterday, last week, and over the same period last year. It will tell them how many of those items are in stock, how many are on the way, and how many the neighboring Walmart stores are carrying (in case one store runs out). Wal-Mart's inventory management practices have helped it become one of the top-ranked companies on the Fortune 500 in terms of sales.

Source: J. Birchall, "Walmart Aims to Cut Supply Chain Cost," *Financial Times* (January 4, 2010).

BASIC ISSUES IN INVENTORY VALUATION

Goods sold (or used) during an accounting period seldom correspond exactly to the goods bought (or produced) during that period. As a result, inventories either increase or decrease during the period. Companies must then allocate the cost of all the goods available for sale (or use) between the goods that were sold or used and those that are still on hand. The **cost of goods available for sale or use** is the *sum* of (1) the cost of the goods on hand at the beginning of the period, and (2) the cost of the goods acquired or produced during the period. The **cost of goods sold** is the *difference* between (1) the cost of goods available for sale during the period, and (2) the cost of goods on hand at the end of the period. Illustration 8-5 shows these calculations.

ILLUSTRATION 8-5
Computation of Cost of Goods Sold

Beginning inventory, Jan. 1	$100,000
Cost of goods acquired or produced during the year	800,000
Total cost of goods available for sale	900,000
Ending inventory, Dec. 31	200,000
Cost of goods sold during the year	$700,000

INTERNATIONAL PERSPECTIVE

Who owns the goods, as well as the costs to include in inventory, are essentially accounted for the same under IFRS and GAAP.

Valuing inventories can be complex. It requires determining the following.

1. **The physical goods to include in inventory** (who owns the goods?—goods in transit, consigned goods, special sales agreements).
2. **The costs to include in inventory** (product vs. period costs).
3. **The cost flow assumption to adopt** (specific identification, average cost, FIFO, LIFO, retail, etc.).

We explore these basic issues in the next three sections.

[1]Some companies have developed methods of determining inventories, including statistical sampling, that are sufficiently reliable to make unnecessary an annual physical count of each item of inventory.

PHYSICAL GOODS INCLUDED IN INVENTORY

Technically, a company should record purchases when it obtains legal title to the goods. In practice, however, a company records acquisitions when it receives the goods. Why? Because it is difficult to determine the exact time of legal passage of title for every purchase. In addition, no material error likely results from such a practice if consistently applied. Illustration 8-6 indicates the general guidelines companies use in evaluating whether the seller or buyer reports an item as inventory. Exceptions to the general guidelines can arise for goods in transit and consigned goods.

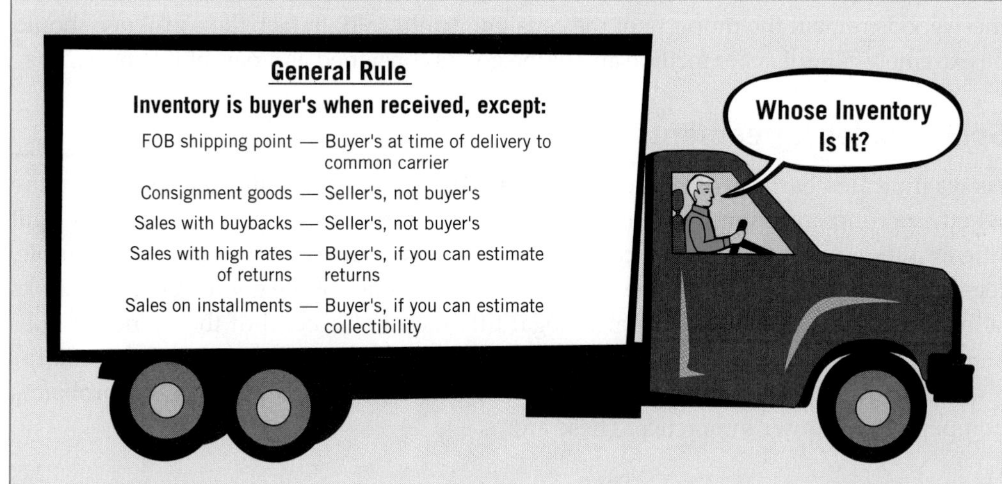

ILLUSTRATION 8-6
Guidelines for Determining Ownership

Goods in Transit

Sometimes purchased merchandise remains in transit—not yet received—at the end of a fiscal period. The accounting for these shipped goods depends on who owns them. For example, a company like **Walgreens** determines ownership by applying the "passage of title" rule. If a supplier ships goods to Walgreens **f.o.b. shipping point**, title passes to Walgreens when the supplier delivers the goods to the common carrier, who acts as an agent for Walgreens. (The abbreviation f.o.b. stands for free on board.) If the supplier ships the goods **f.o.b. destination**, title passes to Walgreens only when it receives the goods from the common carrier. "Shipping point" and "destination" are often designated by a particular location, for example, f.o.b. Denver.

When Walgreens obtains legal title to goods, it must record them as purchases in that fiscal period, assuming a periodic inventory system. Thus, goods shipped to Walgreens f.o.b. shipping point, but in transit at the end of the period, belong to Walgreens. It should show the purchase in its records, because legal title to these goods passed to Walgreens upon shipment of the goods. To disregard such purchases results in understating inventories and accounts payable in the balance sheet, and understating purchases and ending inventories in the income statement.

Consigned Goods

Companies market certain products through a **consignment** shipment. Under this arrangement, a company like Williams' Art Gallery (the consignor) ships various art merchandise to **Sotheby's Holdings** (the consignee), who acts as Williams' agent in selling the **consigned goods**. Sotheby's agrees to accept the goods without any liability, except to exercise due care and reasonable protection from loss or damage, until it sells the goods to a third party. When Sotheby's sells the goods, it remits the revenue, less a selling commission and expenses incurred in accomplishing the sale, to Williams.

Goods out on consignment remain the property of the consignor (Williams in the example above). Williams thus includes the goods in its inventory at purchase price or production cost. Occasionally, and only for a significant amount, the consignor shows the inventory out on consignment as a separate item. Sometimes a consignor reports the inventory on consignment in the notes to the financial statements. For example, **Eagle Clothes, Inc.** reported the following related to consigned goods: "Inventories consist of finished goods shipped on consignment to customers of the Company's subsidiary **April-Marcus, Inc.**"

The consignee makes no entry to the inventory account for goods received. Remember, these goods remain the property of the consignor until sold. In fact, the consignee should be extremely careful *not* to include any of the goods consigned as a part of inventory.

Special Sales Agreements

As we indicated earlier, transfer of legal title is the general guideline used to determine whether a company should include an item in inventory. Unfortunately, transfer of legal title and the underlying substance of the transaction often do not match. For example, legal title may have passed to the purchaser, but the seller of the goods retains the risks of ownership. Conversely, transfer of legal title may not occur, but the economic substance of the transaction is such that the seller no longer retains the risks of ownership.

Three special sales situations are illustrated here to indicate the types of problems companies encounter in practice. These are:

1. Sales with buyback agreement.
2. Sales with high rates of return.
3. Sales on installment.

Sales with Buyback Agreement

Sometimes an enterprise finances its inventory without reporting either the liability or the inventory on its balance sheet. This approach, often referred to as a **product financing arrangement**, usually involves a "sale" with either an implicit or explicit "buyback" agreement.

To illustrate, Hill Enterprises transfers ("sells") inventory to Chase, Inc. and simultaneously agrees to repurchase this merchandise at a specified price over a specified period of time. Chase then uses the inventory as collateral and borrows against it. Chase uses the loan proceeds to pay Hill, which repurchases the inventory in the future. Chase employs the proceeds from repayment to meet its loan obligation.

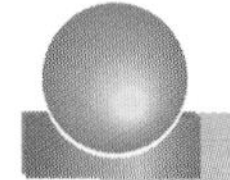

Underlying Concepts

Recognizing revenue at the time the inventory is "parked" violates the revenue recognition principle. This principle requires that the earning process be substantially completed. In this case, the economic benefits remain under the control of the seller.

The essence of this transaction is that Hill Enterprises is financing its inventory—and retaining risk of ownership—even though it transferred to Chase technical legal title to the merchandise. By structuring a transaction in this manner, Hill avoids personal property taxes in certain states. Other advantages of this transaction for Hill are the removal of the current liability from its balance sheet and the ability to manipulate income. For Chase, the purchase of the goods may solve a LIFO liquidation problem (discussed later), or Chase may enter into a similar reciprocal agreement at a later date.

These arrangements are often described in practice as "**parking transactions**." In this situation, Hill simply parks the inventory on Chase's balance sheet for a short period of time. When a repurchase agreement exists at a set price and this price covers all costs of the inventory plus related holding costs, Hill should report the inventory and related liability on its books. **[1]**

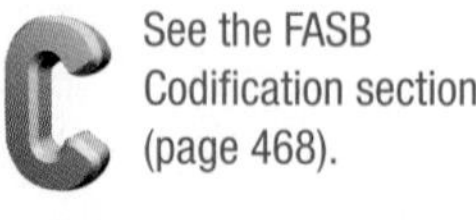

See the FASB Codification section (page 468).

Sales with High Rates of Return

In industries such as publishing, music, toys, and sporting goods, formal or informal agreements often exist that permit purchasers to return inventory for a full or partial refund.

To illustrate, Quality Publishing Company sells textbooks to Campus Bookstores with an agreement that Campus may return for full credit any books not sold. Historically, Campus Bookstores returned approximately 25 percent of the textbooks from Quality Publishing. How should Quality Publishing report its sales transactions?

One alternative is to record the sale at the full amount and establish an estimated sales returns and allowances account until the return period has expired. A second possibility is to not record any sale until circumstances indicate the amount of inventory the buyer will return. The key question is: Under what circumstances should Quality Publishing consider the inventory sold? The answer is that **when Quality Publishing can reasonably estimate the amount of returns**, it should consider the goods sold. Conversely, if returns are unpredictable, Quality Publishing should not consider the goods sold and it should not remove the goods from its inventory. **[2]**

Sales on Installment

"Goods sold on installment" describes any type of sale in which the sale agreement requires payment in periodic installments over an extended period of time. Because the risk of loss from uncollectibles is higher in installment-sale situations than in other sales transactions, the seller sometimes withholds legal title to the merchandise until the buyer has made all the payments.

The question is whether the seller should consider the inventory sold, even though legal title has not passed. The answer is that **the seller should exclude the goods from its inventory if it can reasonably estimate the percentage of bad debts**.

Underlying Concepts

For goods sold on installment, companies should recognize revenues because they have been substantially earned and are reasonably estimable. Collection is not the most critical event if bad debts can be reasonably estimated.

NO PARKING!

What do the numbers mean?

In one of the more elaborate accounting frauds, employees at **Kurzweil Applied Intelligence Inc.** booked millions of dollars in phony inventory sales during a two-year period that straddled two audits and an initial public stock offering. They dummied up phony shipping documents and logbooks to support bogus sales transactions. Then they shipped high-tech equipment, not to customers, but to a public warehouse for "temporary" storage, where some of it sat for 17 months. (Kurzweil still had ownership.)

To foil auditors' attempts to verify the existence of the inventory, Kurzweil employees moved the goods from warehouse to warehouse. To cover the fraudulently recorded sales transactions as auditors closed in, the employees brought back the still-hidden goods, under the pretense that the goods were returned by customers. When auditors uncovered the fraud, the bottom dropped out of Kurzweil's stock.

Similar inventory shenanigans occurred at **Delphi**, which used side-deals with third parties to get inventory off its books and to record sales. The overstatement in income eventually led to a bankruptcy filing for Delphi.

Source: Adapted from "Anatomy of a Fraud," *BusinessWeek* (September 16, 1996), pp. 90–94; and J. McCracken, "Delphi Executives Named in Suit over Inventory Practices," *Wall Street Journal* (May 5, 2005), p. A3.

Effect of Inventory Errors

Items incorrectly included or excluded in determining cost of goods sold through inventory misstatements will result in errors in the financial statements. Let's look at two cases, assuming a periodic inventory system.

Ending Inventory Misstated

LEARNING OBJECTIVE 3
Identify the effects of inventory errors on the financial statements.

What would happen if IBM correctly records its beginning inventory and purchases, but fails to include some items in ending inventory? In this situation, we would have the following effects on the financial statements at the end of the period.

ILLUSTRATION 8-7
Financial Statement Effects of Misstated Ending Inventory

Balance Sheet		Income Statement	
Inventory	Understated	Cost of goods sold	Overstated
Retained earnings	Understated		
Working capital	Understated	Net income	Understated
Current ratio	Understated		

If ending inventory is understated, working capital (current assets less current liabilities) and the current ratio (current assets divided by current liabilities) are understated. If cost of goods sold is overstated, then net income is understated.

To illustrate the effect on net income over a two-year period (2011–2012), assume that Jay Weiseman Corp. understates its ending inventory by $10,000 in 2011; all other items are correctly stated. The effect of this error is to decrease net income in 2011 and to increase net income in 2012. The error is counterbalanced (offset) in 2012 because beginning inventory is understated and net income is overstated. As Illustration 8-8 shows, the income statement misstates the net income figures for both 2011 and 2012, although the *total* for the two years is correct.

ILLUSTRATION 8-8
Effect of Ending Inventory Error on Two Periods

JAY WEISEMAN CORP.
(All Figures Assumed)

	Incorrect Recording		Correct Recording	
	2011	2012	2011	2012
Revenues	$100,000	$100,000	$100,000	$100,000
Cost of goods sold				
Beginning inventory	25,000	20,000	25,000	30,000
Purchased or produced	45,000	60,000	45,000	60,000
Goods available for sale	70,000	80,000	70,000	90,000
Less: Ending inventory	20,000*	40,000	30,000	40,000
Cost of goods sold	50,000	40,000	40,000	50,000
Gross profit	50,000	60,000	60,000	50,000
Administrative and selling expenses	40,000	40,000	40,000	40,000
Net income	$ 10,000	$ 20,000	$ 20,000	$ 10,000
	Total income for two years = $30,000		Total income for two years = $30,000	

*Ending inventory understated by $10,000 in 2011.

If Weiseman *overstates* ending inventory in 2011, the reverse effect occurs: Inventory, working capital, current ratio, and net income are overstated and cost of goods sold is understated. The effect of the error on net income will be counterbalanced in 2012, but the income statement misstates both years' net income figures.

Purchases and Inventory Misstated

Suppose that Bishop Company does not record as a purchase certain goods that it owns and does not count them in ending inventory. The effect on the financial statements (assuming this is a purchase on account) is as follows.

Balance Sheet		Income Statement	
Inventory	Understated	Purchases	Overstated
Retained earnings	No effect	Cost of goods sold	No effect
Accounts payable	Understated	Net income	No effect
Working capital	No effect	Inventory (ending)	Understated
Current ratio	Understated		

ILLUSTRATION 8-9
Financial Statement Effects of Misstated Purchases and Inventory

Omission of goods from purchases and inventory results in an understatement of inventory and accounts payable in the balance sheet; it also results in an understatement of purchases and ending inventory in the income statement. However, the omission of such goods does not affect net income for the period. Why not? Because Bishop understates both purchases and ending inventory by the same amount—the error is thereby offset in cost of goods sold. Total working capital is unchanged, but the current ratio is overstated because of the omission of equal amounts from inventory and accounts payable.

To illustrate the effect on the current ratio, assume that Bishop *understated* accounts payable and ending inventory by $40,000. Illustration 8-10 shows the understated and correct data.

Purchases and Ending Inventory Understated		Purchases and Ending Inventory Correct	
Current assets	$120,000	Current assets	$160,000
Current liabilities	$ 40,000	Current liabilities	$ 80,000
Current ratio	3 to 1	Current ratio	2 to 1

ILLUSTRATION 8-10
Effects of Purchases and Ending Inventory Errors

The understated data indicate a current ratio of 3 to 1, whereas the correct ratio is 2 to 1. Thus, understatement of accounts payable and ending inventory can lead to a "window dressing" of the current ratio. That is, Bishop can make the current ratio appear better than it is.

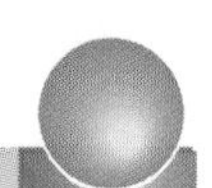

Underlying Concepts

When inventory is misstated, its presentation is not representationally faithful.

If Bishop *overstates* both purchases (on account) and ending inventory, then the effects on the balance sheet are exactly the reverse: The financial statements overstate inventory and accounts payable, and understate the current ratio. The overstatement does not affect cost of goods sold and net income because the errors offset one another. Similarly, working capital is not affected.

We cannot overemphasize the importance of proper inventory measurement in presenting accurate financial statements. For example, **Leslie Fay**, a women's apparel maker, had accounting irregularities that wiped out one year's net income and caused a restatement of the prior year's earnings. One reason: It inflated inventory and deflated cost of goods sold. **Anixter Bros. Inc.** had to restate its income by $1.7 million because an accountant in the antenna manufacturing division overstated the ending inventory, thereby reducing its cost of sales. Similarly, **AM International** allegedly recorded as sold products that were only being rented. As a result, inaccurate inventory and sales figures inappropriately added $7.9 million to pretax income.

COSTS INCLUDED IN INVENTORY

LEARNING OBJECTIVE 4
Understand the items to include as inventory cost.

One of the most important problems in dealing with inventories concerns the dollar amount at which to carry the inventory in the accounts. **Companies generally account for the acquisition of inventories, like other assets, on a cost basis.**

Product Costs

Product costs are those costs that "attach" to the inventory. As a result, a company records product costs in the inventory account. These costs are directly connected with bringing the goods to the buyer's place of business and converting such goods to a salable condition. Such charges include freight charges on goods purchased, other direct costs of acquisition, and labor and other production costs incurred in processing the goods up to the time of sale.

It seems proper also to allocate to inventories a share of any buying costs or expenses of a purchasing department, storage costs, and other costs incurred in storing or handling the goods before their sale. However, because of the practical difficulties involved in allocating such costs and expenses, companies usually exclude these items in valuing inventories.

A manufacturing company's costs include direct materials, direct labor, and manufacturing overhead costs. Manufacturing overhead costs include indirect materials, indirect labor, and various costs, such as depreciation, taxes, insurance, and heat and electricity.

Period Costs

Period costs are those costs that are indirectly related to the acquisition or production of goods. Period costs such as selling expenses and, under ordinary circumstances, general and administrative expenses are therefore not included as part as part of inventory cost.

Yet, conceptually, these expenses are as much a cost of the product as the initial purchase price and related freight charges attached to the product. Why then do companies exclude these costs from inventoriable items? Because companies generally consider selling expenses as more directly related to the cost of goods sold than to the unsold inventory. In addition, period costs, especially administrative expenses, are so unrelated or indirectly related to the immediate production process that any allocation is purely arbitrary.[2]

INTERNATIONAL PERSPECTIVE
GAAP has more detailed rules related to the accounting for inventories, compared to IFRS.

Interest is another period cost. Companies usually expense **interest costs** associated with getting inventories ready for sale. Supporters of this approach argue that interest costs are really a **cost of financing**. Others contend that interest costs incurred to finance activities associated with readying inventories for sale are as much a **cost of the asset** as materials, labor, and overhead. Therefore, they reason, companies should capitalize interest costs.

The FASB ruled that companies should capitalize interest costs related to assets constructed for internal use or assets produced as discrete projects (such as ships or real estate projects) for sale or lease [4].[3] The FASB emphasized that these discrete projects should take considerable time, entail substantial expenditures, and be likely to involve significant amounts of interest cost. A company should not capitalize interest

[2]Companies should not record abnormal freight, handling costs, and amounts of wasted materials (spoilage) as inventory costs. If the costs associated with the actual level of spoilage or product defects are greater than the costs associated with normal spoilage or defects, the company should charge the excess as an expense in the current period. [3]

[3]The reporting rules related to interest cost capitalization have their greatest impact in accounting for long-term assets. We therefore discuss them in Chapter 10.

costs for inventories that it routinely manufactures or otherwise produces in large quantities on a repetitive basis. In this case, the informational benefit does not justify the cost.

Treatment of Purchase Discounts

The use of a **Purchase Discounts** account in a periodic inventory system indicates that the company is reporting its purchases and accounts payable at the gross amount. If a company uses this **gross method**, it reports purchase discounts as a deduction from purchases on the income statement.

Another approach is to record the purchases and accounts payable at an amount **net of the cash discounts**. In this approach, the company records failure to take a purchase discount within the discount period in a Purchase Discounts Lost account. If a company uses this **net method**, it considers purchase discounts lost as a financial expense and reports it in the "Other expenses and losses" section of the income statement. This treatment is considered better for two reasons: (1) It provides a correct reporting of the cost of the asset and related liability. (2) It can measure management inefficiency by holding management responsible for discounts not taken.

To illustrate the difference between the gross and net methods, assume the following transactions.

ILLUSTRATION 8-11
Entries under Gross and Net Methods

Gross Method			Net Method		
Purchase cost $10,000, terms 2/10, net 30					
Purchases	10,000		Purchases	9,800	
Accounts Payable		10,000	Accounts Payable		9,800
Invoices of $4,000 are paid within discount period					
Accounts Payable	4,000		Accounts Payable	3,920	
Purchase Discounts		80	Cash		3,920
Cash		3,920			
Invoices of $6,000 are paid after discount period					
Accounts Payable	6,000		Accounts Payable	5,880	
Cash		6,000	Purchase Discounts Lost	120	
			Cash		6,000

Underlying Concepts

Not using the net method because of resultant difficulties is an example of the application of the cost/benefit constraint.

Many believe that the somewhat more complicated net method is not justified by the resulting benefits. This could account for the widespread use of the less logical but simpler gross method. In addition, some contend that management is reluctant to report in the financial statements the amount of purchase discounts lost.

YOU MAY NEED A MAP

What do the numbers mean?

Does it really matter *where* a company reports certain costs in its income statement, as long as it includes them all as expenses in computing income?

For e-tailers, such as **Amazon.com** or **Drugstore.com**, *where* they report certain selling costs does appear to be important. Contrary to well-established retailer practices, these companies insist on reporting some selling costs—fulfillment costs related to inventory shipping and warehousing—as part of administrative expenses, instead of as cost of goods sold. This practice is allowable within GAAP, *if* applied consistently and adequately disclosed. Although the practice doesn't affect the bottom line, it does make the e-tailers' gross margins look better. For example, at one time Amazon.com reported $265 million of these costs in one quarter. Some experts thought

What do the numbers mean? (continued)

Amazon.com should include those charges in costs of goods sold, which would substantially lower its gross profit, as shown below.

(in millions)

	E-tailer Reporting	Traditional Reporting
Sales	$2,795	$2,795
Cost of goods sold	2,132	2,397
Gross profit	$ 663	$ 398
Gross margin %	24%	14%

Similarly, if **Drugstore.com** and **eToys.com** made similar adjustments, their gross margins would go from positive to negative.

Thus, if you want to be able to compare the operating results of e-tailers to other traditional retailers, it might be a good idea to have a good accounting map in order to navigate their income statements and how they report certain selling costs.

Source: Adapted from P. Elstrom, "The End of Fuzzy Math?" *BusinessWeek,* e.Biz—Net Worth (December 11, 2000). According to GAAP **[5]**, companies must disclose the accounting policy for classifying these selling costs in income.

WHICH COST FLOW ASSUMPTION TO ADOPT?

LEARNING OBJECTIVE 5
Describe and compare the cost flow assumptions used to account for inventories.

During any given fiscal period, companies typically purchase merchandise at several different prices. If a company prices inventories at cost and it made numerous purchases at different unit costs, which cost price should it use? Conceptually, a specific identification of the given items sold and unsold seems optimal. But this measure often proves both expensive and impossible to achieve. Consequently, companies use one of several systematic inventory **cost flow assumptions**.

Indeed, the actual physical flow of goods and the cost flow assumption often greatly differ. **There is no requirement that the cost flow assumption adopted be consistent with the physical movement of goods.** A company's major objective in selecting a method should be to choose the one that, under the circumstances, most clearly reflects periodic income. **[6]**

To illustrate, assume that Call-Mart Inc. had the following transactions in its first month of operations.

Date	Purchases	Sold or Issued	Balance
March 2	2,000 @ $4.00		2,000 units
March 15	6,000 @ $4.40		8,000 units
March 19		4,000 units	4,000 units
March 30	2,000 @ $4.75		6,000 units

From this information, Call-Mart computes the ending inventory of 6,000 units and the cost of goods available for sale (beginning inventory + purchases) of $43,900 [(2,000 @ $4.00) + (6,000 @ $4.40) + (2,000 @ $4.75)]. The question is, which price or prices should it assign to the 6,000 units of ending inventory? The answer depends on which cost flow assumption it uses.

Specific Identification

Specific identification calls for identifying each item sold and each item in inventory. A company includes in cost of goods sold the costs of the specific items sold. It includes in inventory the costs of the specific items on hand. This method may be used only in instances where it is practical to separate physically the different purchases made. As a result, most companies only use this method when handling a relatively small number of costly, easily distinguishable items. In the retail trade this includes some types of jewelry, fur coats, automobiles, and some furniture. In manufacturing it includes special orders and many products manufactured under a job cost system.

To illustrate, assume that Call-Mart Inc.'s 6,000 units of inventory consists of 1,000 units from the March 2 purchase, 3,000 from the March 15 purchase, and 2,000 from the March 30 purchase. Illustration 8-12 shows how Call-Mart computes the ending inventory and cost of goods sold.

ILLUSTRATION 8-12
Specific Identification Method

Date	No. of Units	Unit Cost	Total Cost
March 2	1,000	$4.00	$ 4,000
March 15	3,000	4.40	13,200
March 30	2,000	4.75	9,500
Ending inventory	6,000		$26,700

Cost of goods available for sale (computed in previous section)	$43,900
Deduct: Ending inventory	26,700
Cost of goods sold	$17,200

This method appears ideal. Specific identification matches actual costs against actual revenue. Thus, a company reports ending inventory at actual cost. In other words, **under specific identification the cost flow matches the physical flow of the goods.** On closer observation, however, this method has certain deficiencies.

Some argue that specific identification allows a company to manipulate net income. For example, assume that a wholesaler purchases identical plywood early in the year at three different prices. When it sells the plywood, the wholesaler can select either the lowest or the highest price to charge to expense. It simply selects the plywood from a specific lot for delivery to the customer. A business manager, therefore, can manipulate net income by delivering to the customer the higher- or lower-priced item, depending on whether the company seeks lower or higher reported earnings for the period.

INTERNATIONAL PERSPECTIVE

IFRS indicates specific identification is the preferred inventory method, unless it is impracticable to use.

Another problem relates to the arbitrary allocation of costs that sometimes occurs with specific inventory items. For example, a company often faces difficulty in relating shipping charges, storage costs, and discounts directly to a given inventory item. This results in allocating these costs somewhat arbitrarily, leading to a "breakdown" in the precision of the specific identification method.[4]

Average Cost

As the name implies, the **average cost method** prices items in the inventory on the basis of the average cost of all similar goods available during the period. To illustrate use of the periodic inventory method (amount of inventory computed at the end of the period), Call-Mart computes the ending inventory and cost of goods sold using a **weighted-average method** as follows.

[4]The motion picture industry provides a good illustration of the cost allocation problem. Often actors receive a percentage of net income for a given movie or television program. Some actors, however, have alleged that their programs have been extremely profitable to the motion picture studios but they have received little in the way of profit sharing. Actors contend that the studios allocate additional costs to successful projects to avoid sharing profits.

ILLUSTRATION 8-13
Weighted-Average Method—Periodic Inventory

Date of Invoice	No. Units	Unit Cost	Total Cost
March 2	2,000	$4.00	$ 8,000
March 15	6,000	4.40	26,400
March 30	2,000	4.75	9,500
Total goods available	10,000		$43,900

Weighted-average cost per unit $\frac{\$43,900}{10,000} = \$4.39$

Inventory in units 6,000 units
Ending inventory 6,000 × $4.39 = $26,340

Cost of goods available for sale	$43,900
Deduct: Ending inventory	26,340
Cost of goods sold	$17,560

In computing the average cost per unit, Call-Mart includes the beginning inventory, if any, both in the total units available and in the total cost of goods available.

Companies use the **moving-average method** with perpetual inventory records. Illustration 8-14 shows the application of the average cost method for perpetual records.

ILLUSTRATION 8-14
Moving-Average Method—Perpetual Inventory

Date	Purchased		Sold or Issued	Balance	
March 2	(2,000 @ $4.00)	$ 8,000		(2,000 @ $4.00)	$ 8,000
March 15	(6,000 @ 4.40)	26,400		(8,000 @ 4.30)	34,400
March 19			(4,000 @ $4.30) $17,200	(4,000 @ 4.30)	17,200
March 30	(2,000 @ 4.75)	9,500		(6,000 @ 4.45)	26,700

In this method, Call-Mart computes a **new average unit cost** each time it makes a purchase. For example, on March 15, after purchasing 6,000 units for $26,400, Call-Mart has 8,000 units costing $34,400 ($8,000 plus $26,400) on hand. The average unit cost is $34,400 divided by 8,000, or $4.30. Call-Mart uses this unit cost in costing withdrawals until it makes another purchase. At that point, Call-Mart computes a new average unit cost. Accordingly, the company shows the cost of the 4,000 units withdrawn on March 19 at $4.30, for a total cost of goods sold of $17,200. On March 30, following the purchase of 2,000 units for $9,500, Call-Mart determines a new unit cost of $4.45, for an ending inventory of $26,700.

Companies often use average cost methods for practical rather than conceptual reasons. These methods are simple to apply and objective. They are not as subject to income manipulation as some of the other inventory pricing methods. In addition, proponents of the average cost methods reason that measuring a specific physical flow of inventory is often impossible. Therefore, it is better to cost items on an average-price basis. This argument is particularly persuasive when dealing with similar inventory items.

First-In, First-Out (FIFO)

The **FIFO (first-in, first-out) method** assumes that a company uses goods in the order in which it purchases them. In other words, the FIFO method assumes that **the first goods purchased are the first used** (in a manufacturing concern) **or the first sold** (in a merchandising concern). The inventory remaining must therefore represent the most recent purchases.

To illustrate, assume that Call-Mart uses the periodic inventory system. It determines its cost of the ending inventory by taking the cost of the most recent purchase and working back until it accounts for all units in the inventory. Call-Mart determines its ending inventory and cost of goods sold as shown in Illustration 8-15.

ILLUSTRATION 8-15
FIFO Method—Periodic Inventory

Date	No. Units	Unit Cost	Total Cost
March 30	2,000	$4.75	$ 9,500
March 15	4,000	4.40	17,600
Ending inventory	6,000		$27,100

Cost of goods available for sale	$43,900
Deduct: Ending inventory	27,100
Cost of goods sold	$16,800

If Call-Mart instead uses a perpetual inventory system in quantities and dollars, it attaches a cost figure to each withdrawal. Then the cost of the 4,000 units removed on March 19 consists of the cost of the items purchased on March 2 and March 15. Illustration 8-16 shows the inventory on a FIFO basis perpetual system for Call-Mart.

ILLUSTRATION 8-16
FIFO Method—Perpetual Inventory

Date	Purchased		Sold or Issued	Balance	
March 2	(2,000 @ $4.00)	$ 8,000		2,000 @ $4.00	$ 8,000
March 15	(6,000 @ 4.40)	26,400		2,000 @ 4.00 6,000 @ 4.40	34,400
March 19			2,000 @ $4.00 2,000 @ 4.40 ($16,800)	4,000 @ 4.40	17,600
March 30	(2,000 @ 4.75)	9,500		4,000 @ 4.40 2,000 @ 4.75	27,100

Here, the ending inventory is $27,100, and the cost of goods sold is $16,800 [(2,000 @ 4.00) + (2,000 @ $4.40)].

Notice that in these two FIFO examples, the cost of goods sold ($16,800) and ending inventory ($27,100) are the same. **In all cases where FIFO is used, the inventory and cost of goods sold would be the same at the end of the month whether a perpetual or periodic system is used.** Why? Because the same costs will always be first in and, therefore, first out. This is true whether a company computes cost of goods sold as it sells goods throughout the accounting period (the perpetual system) or as a residual at the end of the accounting period (the periodic system).

One objective of FIFO is to approximate the physical flow of goods. When the physical flow of goods is actually first-in, first-out, the FIFO method closely approximates specific identification. At the same time, it prevents manipulation of income. With FIFO, a company cannot pick a certain cost item to charge to expense.

Another advantage of the FIFO method is that the ending inventory is close to current cost. Because the first goods in are the first goods out, the ending inventory amount consists of the most recent purchases. This is particularly true with rapid inventory turnover. This approach generally approximates replacement cost on the balance sheet when price changes have not occurred since the most recent purchases.

However, the FIFO method fails to match current costs against current revenues on the income statement. A company charges the oldest costs against the more current revenue, possibly distorting gross profit and net income.

Last-In, First-Out (LIFO)

The **LIFO (last-in, first-out) method** matches the cost of the last goods purchased against revenue. If Call-Mart Inc. uses a periodic inventory system, it assumes that **the cost of the total quantity sold or issued during the month comes from the most recent purchases**. Call-Mart prices the ending inventory by using the total units as a basis of computation and disregards the exact dates of sales or issuances. For

INTERNATIONAL PERSPECTIVE

IFRS does not permit LIFO.

example, Call-Mart would assume that the cost of the 4,000 units withdrawn absorbed the 2,000 units purchased on March 30 and 2,000 of the 6,000 units purchased on March 15. Illustration 8-17 shows how Call-Mart computes the inventory and related cost of goods sold, using the periodic inventory method.

ILLUSTRATION 8-17
LIFO Method—Periodic Inventory

Date of Invoice	No. Units	Unit Cost	Total Cost
March 30	2,000	$4.00	$ 8,000
March 15	4,000	4.40	17,600
Ending inventory	6,000		$25,600

Goods available for sale	$43,900
Deduct: Ending inventory	25,600
Cost of goods sold	$18,300

If Call-Mart keeps a perpetual inventory record in quantities and dollars, use of the LIFO method results in **different ending inventory and cost of goods sold amounts than the amounts calculated under the periodic method.** Illustration 8-18 shows these differences under the perpetual method.

ILLUSTRATION 8-18
LIFO Method—Perpetual Inventory

Date	Purchased		Sold or Issued	Balance	
March 2	(2,000 @ $4.00)	$ 8,000		2,000 @ $4.00	$ 8,000
March 15	(6,000 @ 4.40)	26,400		2,000 @ 4.00 6,000 @ 4.40	34,400
March 19			(4,000 @ $4.40) $17,600	2,000 @ 4.00 2,000 @ 4.40	16,800
March 30	(2,000 @ 4.75)	9,500		2,000 @ 4.00 2,000 @ 4.40 2,000 @ 4.75	26,300

The month-end periodic inventory computation presented in Illustration 8-17 (inventory $25,600 and cost of goods sold $18,300) shows a different amount from the perpetual inventory computation (inventory $26,300 and cost of goods sold $17,600). The periodic system matches the total withdrawals for the month with the total purchases for the month in applying the last-in, first-out method. In contrast, the perpetual system matches each withdrawal with the immediately preceding purchases. In effect, the periodic computation assumed that Call-Mart included the cost of the goods that it purchased on March 30 in the sale or issue on March 19.

Gateway to the Profession
Tutorial on Inventory Methods

SPECIAL ISSUES RELATED TO LIFO

LIFO Reserve

LEARNING OBJECTIVE 6
Explain the significance and use of a LIFO reserve.

Many companies use LIFO for tax and external reporting purposes. However, they maintain a FIFO, average cost, or standard cost system for internal reporting purposes. There are several reasons to do so: (1) Companies often base their pricing decisions on a FIFO, average, or standard cost assumption, rather than on a LIFO basis. (2) Recordkeeping on some other basis is easier because the LIFO assumption usually does not approximate the physical flow of the product. (3) Profit-sharing and other bonus arrangements often depend on a non-LIFO inventory assumption. Finally, (4) the use of a pure LIFO system is troublesome for interim periods, which require estimates of year-end quantities and prices.

The difference between the inventory method used for internal reporting purposes and LIFO is the Allowance to Reduce Inventory to LIFO or the **LIFO reserve**. The change in the allowance balance from one period to the next is the **LIFO effect**. The LIFO effect is the adjustment that companies must make to the accounting records in a given year.

To illustrate, assume that Acme Boot Company uses the FIFO method for internal reporting purposes and LIFO for external reporting purposes. At January 1, 2012, the Allowance to Reduce Inventory to LIFO balance is $20,000. At December 31, 2012, the balance should be $50,000. As a result, Acme Boot realizes a LIFO effect of $30,000 and makes the following entry at year-end.

Cost of Goods Sold	30,000	
Allowance to Reduce Inventory to LIFO		30,000

Acme Boot deducts the Allowance to Reduce Inventory to LIFO from inventory to ensure that it states the inventory on a LIFO basis at year-end.

Companies should disclose either the LIFO reserve or the replacement cost of the inventory, as shown in Illustration 8-19. **[7]**

ILLUSTRATION 8-19
Note Disclosures of LIFO Reserve

American Maize-Products Company

Inventories (Note 3)	$80,320,000

Note 3: Inventories. At December 31, $31,516,000 of inventories were valued using the LIFO method. This amount is less than the corresponding replacement value by $3,765,000.

Brown Shoe Company, Inc.
(in thousands)

	Current Year	Previous Year
Inventories, (Note 1)	$365,989	$362,274

Note 1 (partial): Inventories. Inventories are valued at the lower of cost or market determined principally by the last-in, first-out (LIFO) method. If the first-in, first-out (FIFO) cost method had been used, inventories would have been $11,709 higher in the current year and $13,424 higher in the previous year.

COMPARING APPLES TO APPLES

What do the numbers mean?

Investors commonly use the current ratio to evaluate a company's liquidity. They compute the current ratio as current assets divided by current liabilities. A higher current ratio indicates that a company is better able to meet its current obligations when they come due. However, it is not meaningful to compare the current ratio for a company using LIFO to one for a company using FIFO. It would be like comparing apples to oranges, since the two companies measure inventory (and cost of goods sold) differently.

To make the current ratio comparable on an apples-to-apples basis, analysts use the LIFO reserve. The following adjustments should do the trick:

Inventory Adjustment: LIFO inventory + LIFO reserve = FIFO inventory

(For cost of goods sold, deduct the *change* in the LIFO reserve from LIFO cost of goods sold to yield the comparable FIFO amount.)

For **Brown Shoe, Inc.** (see Illustration 8-19), with current assets of $487.8 million and current liabilities of $217.8 million, the current ratio using LIFO is: $487.8 ÷ $217.8 = 2.2. After adjusting for the LIFO effect, Brown's current ratio under FIFO would be: ($487.8 + $11.7) ÷ $217.8 = 2.3.

Thus, without the LIFO adjustment, the Brown Shoe current ratio is understated.

LIFO Liquidation

LEARNING OBJECTIVE 7
Understand the effect of LIFO liquidations.

Up to this point, we have emphasized a **specific-goods approach** to costing LIFO inventories (also called **traditional LIFO** or **unit LIFO**). This approach is often unrealistic for two reasons:

1. When a company has many different inventory items, the accounting cost of tracking each inventory item is expensive.
2. Erosion of the LIFO inventory can easily occur. Referred to as **LIFO liquidation**, this often distorts net income and leads to substantial tax payments.

To understand the LIFO liquidation problem, assume that Basler Co. has 30,000 pounds of steel in its inventory on December 31, 2012, with cost determined on a specific-goods LIFO approach.

Ending Inventory (2012)

	Pounds	Unit Cost	LIFO Cost
2009	8,000	$ 4	$ 32,000
2010	10,000	6	60,000
2011	7,000	9	63,000
2012	5,000	10	50,000
	30,000		$205,000

As indicated, the ending 2012 inventory for Basler comprises costs from past periods. These costs are called **layers** (increases from period to period). The first layer is identified as the base layer. Illustration 8-20 shows the layers for Basler.

ILLUSTRATION 8-20
Layers of LIFO Inventory

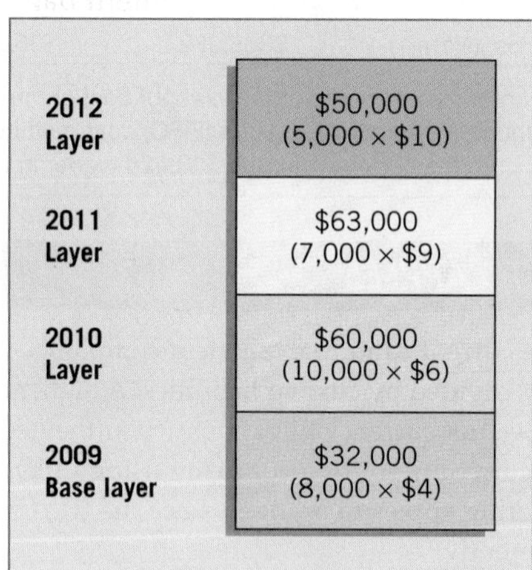

Note the increased price of steel over the 4-year period. In 2013, due to metal shortages, Basler had to liquidate much of its inventory (a LIFO liquidation). At the end of 2013, only 6,000 pounds of steel remained in inventory. Because the company uses LIFO, Basler liquidates the most recent layer, 2012, first, followed by the 2011 layer, and so on. The result: Basler matches costs from preceding periods against sales revenues reported in current dollars. As Illustration 8-21 shows, this leads to a distortion in net income and increased taxable income in the current period. Unfortunately, **LIFO liquidations can occur frequently when using a specific-goods LIFO approach.**

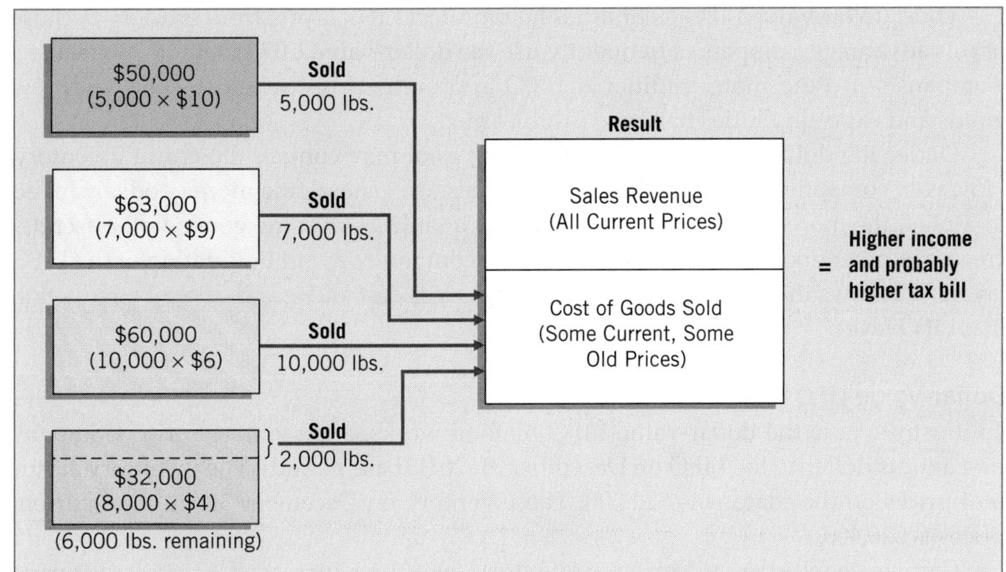

ILLUSTRATION 8-21
LIFO Liquidation

To alleviate the LIFO liquidation problems and to simplify the accounting, companies can combine goods into pools. A **pool** groups items of a similar nature. Thus, instead of only identical units, a company combines, and counts as a group, a number of similar units or products. This method, the **specific-goods pooled LIFO approach**, usually results in fewer LIFO liquidations. Why? Because the reduction of one quantity in the pool may be offset by an increase in another.

The specific-goods pooled LIFO approach eliminates some of the disadvantages of the specific-goods (traditional) accounting for LIFO inventories. This pooled approach, using quantities as its measurement basis, however, creates other problems.

First, most companies continually change the mix of their products, materials, and production methods. As a result, in employing a pooled approach using quantities, companies must continually redefine the pools. This can be time consuming and costly. Second, even when practical, the approach often results in an erosion ("LIFO liquidation") of the layers, thereby losing much of the LIFO costing benefit. Erosion of the layers occurs when a specific good or material in the pool is replaced with another good or material. The new item may not be similar enough to be treated as part of the old pool. Therefore a company may need to recognize any inflationary profit deferred on the old goods as it replaces them.

Dollar-Value LIFO

8 LEARNING OBJECTIVE
Explain the dollar-value LIFO method.

The dollar-value LIFO method overcomes the problems of redefining pools and eroding layers. **The dollar-value LIFO method determines and measures any increases and decreases in a pool in terms of total dollar value, not the physical quantity of the goods in the inventory pool.**

Such an approach has two important advantages over the specific-goods pooled approach. First, companies may include a broader range of goods in a dollar-value LIFO pool. Second, a dollar-value LIFO pool permits replacement of goods that are similar items, similar in use, or interchangeable. (In contrast, a specific-goods LIFO pool only allows replacement of items that are substantially identical.)

Thus, dollar-value LIFO techniques help protect LIFO layers from erosion. Because of this advantage, companies frequently use the dollar-value LIFO method in practice.[5] Companies use the more traditional LIFO approaches only when dealing with few goods and expecting little change in product mix.

Gateway to the Profession

Tutorial on Dollar-Value LIFO

Under the dollar-value LIFO method, one pool may contain the entire inventory. However, companies generally use several pools.[6] In general, the more goods included in a pool, the more likely that increases in the quantities of some goods will offset decreases in other goods in the same pool. Thus, companies avoid liquidation of the LIFO layers. It follows that having fewer pools means less cost and less chance of a reduction of a LIFO layer.[7]

Dollar-Value LIFO Example

To illustrate how the dollar-value LIFO method works, assume that Enrico Company first adopts dollar-value LIFO on December 31, 2011 (base period). The inventory at current prices on that date was $20,000. The inventory on December 31, 2012, at current prices is $26,400.

Can we conclude that Enrico's inventory quantities increased 32 percent during the year ($26,400 ÷ $20,000 = 132%)? First, we need to ask: What is the value of the ending inventory in terms of beginning-of-the-year prices? Assuming that prices have increased 20 percent during the year, the ending inventory at beginning-of-the-year prices amounts to $22,000 ($26,400 ÷ 120%). Therefore, the inventory quantity has increased only 10 percent, or from $20,000 to $22,000 in terms of beginning-of-the-year prices.

The next step is to price this real-dollar quantity increase. This real-dollar quantity increase of $2,000 valued at year-end prices is $2,400 (120% × $2,000). This increment (layer) of $2,400, when added to the beginning inventory of $20,000, totals $22,400 for the December 31, 2012, inventory, as shown below.

First layer—(beginning inventory) in terms of 100	$20,000
Second layer—(2012 increase) in terms of 120	2,400
Dollar-value LIFO inventory, December 31, 2012	$22,400

Note that a layer forms only when the ending inventory at base-year prices exceeds the beginning inventory at base-year prices. And only when a new layer forms must Enrico compute a new index.

[5]A study by James M. Reeve and Keith G. Stanga disclosed that the vast majority of respondent companies applying LIFO use the dollar-value method or the dollar-value retail method to apply LIFO. Only a small minority of companies use the specific-goods (unit LIFO) approach or the specific-goods pooling approach. See J.M. Reeve and K.G. Stanga, "The LIFO Pooling Decision," *Accounting Horizons* (June 1987), p. 27.

[6]The Reeve and Stanga study (ibid.) reports that most companies have only a few pools—the median is six for retailers and three for nonretailers. But the distributions are highly skewed; some companies have 100 or more pools. Retailers that use LIFO have significantly more pools than nonretailers. About a third of the nonretailers (mostly manufacturers) use a single pool for their entire LIFO inventory.

[7]A later study shows that when quantities are increasing, multiple pools over a period of time may produce (under rather general conditions) significantly higher cost of goods sold deductions than a single-pool approach. When a stock-out occurs, a single-pool approach may lessen the layer liquidation for that year, but it may not erase the cumulative cost of goods sold advantage accruing to the use of multiple pools built up over the preceding years. See William R. Coon and Randall B. Hayes, "The Dollar Value LIFO Pooling Decision: The Conventional Wisdom Is Too General," *Accounting Horizons* (December 1989), pp. 57–70.

Comprehensive Dollar-Value LIFO Example

To illustrate the use of the dollar-value LIFO method in a more complex situation, assume that Bismark Company develops the following information.

December 31	Inventory at End-of-Year Prices	÷	Price Index (percentage)	=	End-of-Year Inventory at Base-Year Prices
(Base year) 2009	$200,000		100		$200,000
2010	299,000		115		260,000
2011	300,000		120		250,000
2012	351,000		130		270,000

At December 31, 2009, Bismark computes the ending inventory under dollar-value LIFO as $200,000, as Illustration 8-22 shows.

ILLUSTRATION 8-22
Computation of 2009 Inventory at LIFO Cost

Ending Inventory at Base-Year Prices	Layer at Base-Year Prices		Price Index (percentage)		Ending Inventory at LIFO Cost
$200,000	$200,000	×	100	=	$200,000

At December 31, 2010, a comparison of the ending inventory at base-year prices ($260,000) with the beginning inventory at base-year prices ($200,000) indicates that the quantity of goods (in base-year prices) increased $60,000 ($260,000 − $200,000). Bismark prices this increment (layer) at the 2010 index of 115 percent to arrive at a new layer of $69,000. Ending inventory for 2010 is $269,000, composed of the beginning inventory of $200,000 and the new layer of $69,000. Illustration 8-23 shows the computations.

ILLUSTRATION 8-23
Computation of 2010 Inventory at LIFO Cost

Ending Inventory at Base-Year Prices	Layers at Base-Year Prices			Price Index (percentage)		Ending Inventory at LIFO Cost
$260,000 →	2009	$200,000	×	100	=	$200,000
→	2010	60,000	×	115	=	69,000
		$260,000				$269,000

At December 31, 2011, a comparison of the ending inventory at base-year prices ($250,000) with the beginning inventory at base-year prices ($260,000) indicates a decrease in the quantity of goods of $10,000 ($250,000 − $260,000). If the ending inventory at base-year prices is less than the beginning inventory at base-year prices, **a company must subtract the decrease from the most recently added layer. When a decrease occurs, the company "peels off" previous layers at the prices in existence when it added the layers.** In Bismark's situation, this means that it removes $10,000 in base-year prices from the 2010 layer of $60,000 at base-year prices. It values the balance of $50,000 ($60,000 − $10,000) at base-year prices at the 2010 price index of 115 percent. As a result, it now values this 2010 layer at $57,500 ($50,000 × 115%). Therefore, Bismark computes the ending inventory at $257,500, consisting of the beginning inventory of $200,000 and the second layer of $57,500. Illustration 8-24 (page 458) shows the computations for 2011.

ILLUSTRATION 8-24
Computation of 2011 Inventory at LIFO Cost

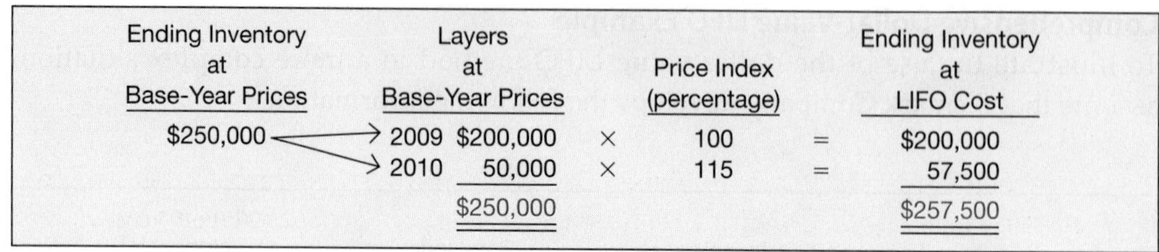

Ending Inventory at Base-Year Prices	Layers at Base-Year Prices			Price Index (percentage)		Ending Inventory at LIFO Cost
$250,000	2009	$200,000	×	100	=	$200,000
	2010	50,000	×	115	=	57,500
		$250,000				$257,500

Note that if Bismark eliminates a layer or base (or portion thereof), it cannot rebuild it in future periods. That is, the layer is gone forever.

At December 31, 2012, a comparison of the ending inventory at base-year prices ($270,000) with the beginning inventory at base-year prices ($250,000) indicates an increase in the quantity of goods (in base-year prices) of $20,000 ($270,000 − $250,000). After converting the $20,000 increase, using the 2012 price index, the ending inventory is $283,500, composed of the beginning layer of $200,000, a 2010 layer of $57,500, and a 2012 layer of $26,000 ($20,000 × 130%). Illustration 8-25 shows this computation.

ILLUSTRATION 8-25
Computation of 2012 Inventory at LIFO Cost

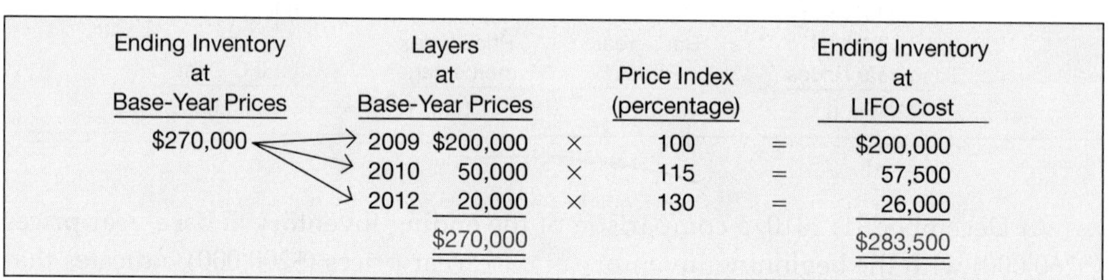

Ending Inventory at Base-Year Prices	Layers at Base-Year Prices			Price Index (percentage)		Ending Inventory at LIFO Cost
$270,000	2009	$200,000	×	100	=	$200,000
	2010	50,000	×	115	=	57,500
	2012	20,000	×	130	=	26,000
		$270,000				$283,500

The ending inventory at base-year prices must always equal the total of the layers at base-year prices. Checking that this situation exists will help to ensure correct dollar-value computations.

Selecting a Price Index

Obviously, price changes are critical in dollar-value LIFO. How do companies determine the price indexes? Many companies use the general price-level index that the federal government prepares and publishes each month. The most popular general external price-level index is the **Consumer Price Index for Urban Consumers** (CPI-U).[8] Companies also use more-specific external price indexes. For instance, various organizations compute and publish daily indexes for most commodities (gold, silver, other metals, corn, wheat, and other farm products). Many trade associations prepare indexes for specific product lines or industries. Any of these indexes may be used for dollar-value LIFO purposes.

When a relevant specific external price index is not readily available, a company may compute its own specific internal price index. The desired approach is to price ending inventory at the most current cost. Therefore, a company that chose to compute its own specific internal price index would ordinarily determine current cost by referring to the actual cost of the goods it most recently had purchased. The price index provides a measure of the change in price or cost levels between the base year and the current year. The company then computes the index for each year after the base year. The general formula for computing the index is as follows.

[8]Indexes may be **general** (composed of several commodities, goods, or services) or **specific** (for one commodity, good, or service). Additionally, they may be **external** (computed by an outside party, such as the government, commodity exchange, or trade association) or **internal** (computed by the enterprise for its own product or service).

ILLUSTRATION 8-26
Formula for Computing a Price Index

$$\frac{\text{Ending Inventory for the Period at Current Cost}}{\text{Ending Inventory for the Period at Base-Year Cost}} = \text{Price Index for Current Year}$$

This approach is generally referred to as the **double-extension method**. As its name implies, the value of the units in inventory is extended at *both* base-year prices and current-year prices.

To illustrate this computation, assume that Toledo Company's base-year inventory (January 1, 2012) consisted of the following.

Items	Quantity	Cost per Unit	Total Cost
A	1,000	$ 6	$ 6,000
B	2,000	20	40,000
January 1, 2012, inventory at base-year costs			$46,000

Examination of the ending inventory indicates that the company holds 3,000 units of Item A and 6,000 units of Item B on December 31, 2012. The most recent actual purchases related to these items were as follows.

Items	Purchase Date	Quantity Purchased	Cost per Unit
A	December 1, 2012	4,000	$ 7
B	December 15, 2012	5,000	25
B	November 16, 2012	1,000	22

Toledo double-extends the inventory as shown in Illustration 8-27.

ILLUSTRATION 8-27
Double-Extension Method of Determining a Price Index

	12/31/12 Inventory at Base-Year Costs			12/31/12 Inventory at Current-Year Costs		
Items	Units	Base-Year Cost per Unit	Total	Units	Current-Year Cost per Unit	Total
A	3,000	$ 6	$ 18,000	3,000	$ 7	$ 21,000
B	6,000	20	120,000	5,000	25	125,000
B				1,000	22	22,000
			$138,000			$168,000

After the inventories are double-extended, Toledo uses the formula in Illustration 8-26 to develop the index for the current year (2012), as follows.

ILLUSTRATION 8-28
Computation of 2012 Index

$$\frac{\text{Ending Inventory for the Period at Current Cost}}{\text{Ending Inventory for the Period at Base-Year Cost}} = \frac{\$168{,}000}{\$138{,}000} = 121.74\%$$

Toledo then applies this index (121.74%) to the layer added in 2012. Note in this illustration that Toledo used the most recent actual purchases to determine current cost; alternatively, it could have used other approaches such as FIFO and average cost. Whichever flow assumption is adopted, a company must use it consistently from one period to another.

Use of the double-extension method is time consuming and difficult where substantial technological change has occurred or where many items are involved. That is, as time passes, the company must determine a new base-year cost for new products, and must keep a base-year cost for each inventory item.[9]

QUITE A DIFFERENCE

What do the numbers mean?

As indicated, significant differences can arise in inventory measured according to current cost and dollar-value LIFO. Let's look at an additional summary example.

Truman Company uses the dollar-value LIFO method of computing its inventory. Inventory for the last three years is as shown below:

Year Ended December 31	Inventory at Current-Year Cost	Price Index
2010	$60,000	100
2011	84,000	105
2012	87,000	116

The values of the 2010, 2011, and 2012 inventories using the dollar-value LIFO method are as follows.

Year	Inventory at End-of-Year Prices	Inventory at Base-Year Prices	Layers at Base-Year Prices	×	Price-Index Layers at LIFO Cost	Dollar-Value LIFO Inventory
2010	$60,000	$60,000 ÷ 100 = $60,000	2010 $60,000	×	100 = $60,000	$60,000
2011	84,000	$84,000 ÷ 105 = $80,000	2010 $60,000	×	100 = $60,000	
			2011 20,000	×	105 = $21,000	$81,000
2012	87,000	$87,000 ÷ 116 = $75,000	2010 $60,000	×	100 = $60,000	
			2011 15,000	×	105 = $15,750	$75,750

Consistent with LIFO costing in times of rising prices, the dollar-value LIFO inventory amount is less than inventory stated at end-of-year prices. The company did not add layers at the 2012 prices. This is because the increase in inventory at end-of-year (current) prices was primarily due to higher prices. Also, establishing the LIFO layers based on price-adjusted dollars relative to base-year layers reduces the likelihood of a LIFO liquidation.

Comparison of LIFO Approaches

We present three different approaches to computing LIFO inventories in this chapter—specific-goods LIFO, specific-goods pooled LIFO, and dollar-value LIFO. As we indicated earlier, the use of the specific-goods LIFO is unrealistic. Most companies have numerous goods in inventory at the end of a period. Costing (pricing) them on a unit basis is extremely expensive and time consuming.

The specific-goods pooled LIFO approach reduces recordkeeping and clerical costs. In addition, it is more difficult to erode the layers because the reduction of one quantity in the pool may be offset by an increase in another. Nonetheless, the pooled approach using quantities as its measurement basis can lead to untimely LIFO liquidations.

As a result, **most companies using a LIFO system employ dollar-value LIFO**. Although the approach appears complex, the logic and the computations are actually quite simple, after determining an appropriate index.

[9]To simplify the analysis, companies may use another approach, initially sanctioned by the Internal Revenue Service for tax purposes. Under this method, a company obtains an index from an outside source or by double-extending only a sample portion of the inventory. For example, the IRS allows all companies to use as their inflation rate for a LIFO pool 80% of the inflation rate reported by the appropriate consumer or producer price indexes prepared by the Bureau of Labor Statistics (BLS). Once the company obtains the index, it divides the ending inventory at current cost by the index to find the base-year cost. Using generally available external indexes greatly simplifies LIFO computations, and frees companies from having to compute internal indexes.

However, problems do exist with the dollar-value LIFO method. The selection of the items to be put in a pool can be subjective.[10] Such a determination, however, is extremely important because manipulation of the items in a pool without conceptual justification can affect reported net income. For example, the SEC noted that some companies have set up pools that are easy to liquidate. As a result, to increase income, a company simply decreases inventory, thereby matching low-cost inventory items to current revenues.

To curb this practice, the SEC has taken a much harder line on the number of pools that companies may establish. In a well-publicized case, **Stauffer Chemical Company** increased the number of LIFO pools from 8 to 280, boosting its net income by $16,515,000 or approximately 13 percent. Stauffer justified the change in its Annual Report on the basis of "achieving a better matching of cost and revenue." The SEC required Stauffer to reduce the number of its inventory pools, contending that some pools were inappropriate and alleging income manipulation.

Major Advantages of LIFO

9 LEARNING OBJECTIVE
Identify the major advantages and disadvantages of LIFO.

One obvious advantage of LIFO approaches is that the LIFO cost flow often approximates the physical flow of the goods in and out of inventory. For instance, in a coal pile, the last coal in is the first coal out because it is on the top of the pile. The coal remover is not going to take the coal from the bottom of the pile! The coal taken first is the coal placed on the pile last.

However, this is one of only a few situations where the actual physical flow corresponds to LIFO. Therefore most adherents of LIFO use other arguments for its widespread use, as follows.

Matching

LIFO matches the more recent costs against current revenues to provide a better measure of current earnings. During periods of inflation, many challenge the quality of non-LIFO earnings, noting that failing to match current costs against current revenues **creates transitory or "paper" profits ("inventory profits")**. Inventory profits occur when the inventory costs matched against sales are less than the inventory replacement cost. This results in understating the cost of goods sold and overstating profit. Using LIFO (rather than a method such as FIFO) matches current costs against revenues, thereby reducing inventory profits.

Tax Benefits/Improved Cash Flow

LIFO's popularity mainly stems from its tax benefits. As long as the price level increases and inventory quantities do not decrease, a deferral of income tax occurs. Why? Because a company matches the items it most recently purchased (at the higher price level) against revenues. For example, when **Fuqua Industries** switched to LIFO, it realized a tax savings of about $4 million. Even if the price level decreases later, the company still temporarily deferred its income taxes. Thus, use of LIFO in such situations improves a company's cash flow.[11]

[10]It is suggested that companies analyze how inventory purchases are affected by price changes, how goods are stocked, how goods are used, and if future liquidations are likely. See William R. Cron and Randall Hayes, ibid., p. 57.

[11]In periods of rising prices, the use of fewer pools will translate into greater income tax benefits through the use of LIFO. The use of fewer pools allows companies to offset inventory reductions on some items and inventory increases in others. In contrast, the use of more pools increases the likelihood of liquidating old, low-cost inventory layers and incurring negative tax consequences. See Reeve and Stanga, ibid., pp. 28–29.

The tax law requires that if a company uses LIFO for tax purposes, it must also use LIFO for financial accounting purposes[12] (although neither tax law nor GAAP requires a company to pool its inventories in the same manner for book and tax purposes). This requirement is often referred to as the **LIFO conformity rule**. Other inventory valuation methods do not have this requirement.

Future Earnings Hedge

With LIFO, future price declines will not substantially affect a company's future reported earnings. The reason: Since the company records the most recent inventory as sold first, there is not much ending inventory at high prices vulnerable to a price decline. Thus LIFO eliminates or substantially minimizes write-downs to market as a result of price decreases. In contrast, inventory costed under FIFO is more vulnerable to price declines, which can reduce net income substantially.

Major Disadvantages of LIFO

Despite its advantages, LIFO has the following drawbacks.

Reduced Earnings

Many corporate managers view the lower profits reported under the LIFO method in inflationary times as a distinct disadvantage. They would rather have higher reported profits than lower taxes. Some fear that investors may misunderstand an accounting change to LIFO, and that the lower profits may cause the price of the company's stock to fall.

Inventory Understated

LIFO may have a distorting effect on a company's balance sheet. The inventory valuation is normally outdated because the oldest costs remain in inventory. This understatement makes the working capital position of the company appear worse than it really is. A good example is Caterpillar, which uses LIFO costing for most of its inventory, valued at $6.4 billion at year-end 2009. Under FIFO costing, Caterpillar's inventories have a value of $9.4 billion—almost 50 percent higher than the LIFO amount.

The magnitude and direction of this variation between the carrying amount of inventory and its current price depend on the degree and direction of the price changes and the amount of inventory turnover. The combined effect of rising product prices and avoidance of inventory liquidations increases the difference between the inventory carrying value at LIFO and current prices of that inventory. This magnifies the balance sheet distortion attributed to the use of LIFO.

Physical Flow

LIFO does not approximate the physical flow of the items except in specific situations (such as the coal pile discussed earlier). Originally companies could use LIFO only in certain circumstances. This situation has changed over the years. Now, physical flow characteristics no longer determine whether a company may employ LIFO.

Involuntary Liquidation/Poor Buying Habits

If a company eliminates the base or layers of old costs, it may match old, irrelevant costs against current revenues. A distortion in reported income for a given period may result, as well as detrimental income tax consequences. For example, in 2009 Caterpillar experienced a LIFO liquidation, resulting in an increased tax bill of $60 million.[13]

[12]Management often selects an accounting procedure because a lower tax results from its use, instead of an accounting method that is conceptually more appealing. Throughout this textbook, we identify accounting procedures that provide income tax benefits to the user.

[13]Companies should disclose the effects on income of LIFO inventory liquidations in the notes to the financial statements. [8]

Because of the liquidation problem, LIFO may cause poor buying habits. A company may simply purchase more goods and match these goods against revenue to avoid charging the old costs to expense. Furthermore, recall that with LIFO, a company may attempt to manipulate its net income at the end of the year simply by altering its pattern of purchases.[14]

One survey uncovered the following reasons why companies reject LIFO.[15]

Reasons to Reject LIFO	Number	% of Total*
No expected tax benefits		
No required tax payment	34	16%
Declining prices	31	15
Rapid inventory turnover	30	14
Immaterial inventory	26	12
Miscellaneous tax related	38	17
	159	74%
Regulatory or other restrictions	26	12%
Excessive cost		
High administrative costs	29	14%
LIFO liquidation–related costs	12	6
	41	20%
Other adverse consequences		
Lower reported earnings	18	8%
Bad accounting	7	3
	25	11%

*Percentage totals more than 100% as some companies offered more than one explanation.

ILLUSTRATION 8-29
Why Do Companies Reject LIFO? Summary of Responses

BASIS FOR SELECTION OF INVENTORY METHOD

10 LEARNING OBJECTIVE
Understand why companies select given inventory methods.

How does a company choose among the various inventory methods? Although no absolute rules can be stated, preferability for LIFO usually occurs in either of the following circumstances: (1) if selling prices and revenues have been increasing faster than costs, thereby distorting income, and (2) in situations where LIFO has been traditional, such as department stores and industries where a fairly constant "base stock" is present (such as refining, chemicals, and glass).[16]

Conversely, LIFO is probably inappropriate in the following circumstances: (1) where prices tend to lag behind costs; (2) in situations where specific identification is traditional, such as in the sale of automobiles, farm equipment, art, and antique jewelry; or (3) where unit costs tend to decrease as production increases, thereby nullifying the tax benefit that LIFO might provide.[17]

[14]For example, **General Tire and Rubber** accelerated raw material purchases at the end of the year to minimize the book profit from a liquidation of LIFO inventories and to minimize income taxes for the year.

[15]Michael H. Granof and Daniel Short, "Why Do Companies Reject LIFO?" *Journal of Accounting, Auditing, and Finance* (Summer 1984), pp. 323–333, Table 1, p. 327.

[16]*Accounting Trends and Techniques—2010* reports that of 666 inventory method disclosures, 176 used LIFO, 325 used FIFO, 147 used average cost, and 18 used other methods. Because of steady or falling raw materials costs and costs savings from electronic data interchange and just-in-time technologies in recent years, many businesses using LIFO no longer experience substantial tax benefits. Even some companies for which LIFO is creating a benefit are finding that the administrative costs associated with LIFO are higher than the LIFO benefit obtained. As a result, some companies are moving to FIFO or average cost.

[17]See Barry E. Cushing and Marc J. LeClere, "Evidence on the Determinants of Inventory Accounting Policy Choice," *The Accounting Review* (April 1992), pp. 355–366, Table 4, p. 363, for a list of factors hypothesized to affect FIFO–LIFO choices.

Tax consequences are another consideration. Switching from FIFO to LIFO usually results in an immediate tax benefit. However, switching from LIFO to FIFO can result in a substantial tax burden. For example, when **Chrysler** changed from LIFO to FIFO, it became responsible for an additional $53 million in taxes that the company had deferred over 14 years of LIFO inventory valuation. Why, then, would Chrysler, and other companies, change to FIFO? The major reason was the profit crunch of that era. Although Chrysler showed a loss of $7.6 million after the switch, the loss would have been $20 million *more* if the company had not changed its inventory valuation from LIFO to FIFO.

It is questionable whether companies should switch from LIFO to FIFO for the sole purpose of increasing reported earnings. Intuitively, one would assume that companies with higher reported earnings would have a higher share valuation (common stock price). However, some studies have indicated that the users of financial data exhibit a much higher sophistication than might be expected. Share prices are the same and, in some cases, even higher under LIFO in spite of lower reported earnings.[18]

The concern about reduced income resulting from adoption of LIFO has even less substance now because the IRS has relaxed the LIFO conformity rule which requires a company employing LIFO for tax purposes to use it for book purposes as well. The IRS has relaxed restrictions against providing non-LIFO income numbers as supplementary information. As a result, companies now provide supplemental non-LIFO disclosures. While not intended to override the basic LIFO method adopted for financial reporting, these disclosures may be useful in comparing operating income and working capital with companies not on LIFO.

For example, **JCPenney, Inc.**, a LIFO user, presented the information in its annual report as shown in Illustration 8-30.

ILLUSTRATION 8-30
Supplemental Non-LIFO Disclosure

JCPenney, Inc.

Some companies in the retail industry use the FIFO method in valuing part or all of their inventories. Had JCPenney used the FIFO method and made no other assumptions with respect to changes in income resulting therefrom, income and income per share from continuing operations would have been:

Income from continuing operations (in millions)	$325
Income from continuing operations per share	$4.63

INTERNATIONAL PERSPECTIVE

Many U.S. companies that have international operations use LIFO for U.S. purposes but use FIFO for their foreign subsidiaries.

Relaxation of the LIFO conformity rule has led some companies to select LIFO as their inventory valuation method because they will be able to disclose FIFO income numbers in the financial reports if they so desire.[19]

Companies often combine inventory methods. For example, **John Deere** uses LIFO for most of its inventories, and prices the remainder using FIFO. **Hershey Foods** follows the same practice. One reason for these practices is that certain product lines can be highly susceptible to deflation instead of inflation. In addition, if the

[18]See, for example, Shyam Sunder, "Relationship Between Accounting Changes and Stock Prices: Problems of Measurement and Some Empirical Evidence," *Empirical Research in Accounting: Selected Studies, 1973* (Chicago: University of Chicago), pp. 1–40. But see Robert Moren Brown, "Short-Range Market Reaction to Changes to LIFO Accounting Using Preliminary Earnings Announcement Dates," *The Journal of Accounting Research* (Spring 1980), which found that companies that do change to LIFO suffer a short-run decline in the price of their stock.

[19]Note that a company can use one variation of LIFO for financial reporting purposes and another for tax without violating the LIFO conformity rule. Such a relaxation has caused many problems because the general approach to accounting for LIFO has been "whatever is good for tax is good for financial reporting."

level of inventory is unstable, unwanted involuntary liquidations may result in certain product lines if using LIFO. Finally, for high inventory turnover in certain product lines, a company cannot justify LIFO's additional recordkeeping and expense. In such cases, a company often uses average cost because it is easy to compute.[20]

Although a company may use a variety of inventory methods to assist in accurate computation of net income, once it selects a pricing method, it must apply it consistently thereafter. If conditions indicate that the inventory pricing method in use is unsuitable, the company must seriously consider all other possibilities before selecting another method. It should clearly explain any change and disclose its effect in the financial statements.

REPEAL LIFO!

What do the numbers mean?

In some situations, use of LIFO can result in significant tax savings for companies. For example, **Sherwin-Williams** estimates its tax bill would increase by $16 million if it were to change from LIFO to FIFO. The option to use LIFO to reduce taxes has become a political issue because of the growing federal deficit. Some are proposing elimination of LIFO (and other tax law changes) to help reduce the federal deficit. Why pick on LIFO? Well, one recent budget estimate indicates that repeal of LIFO would help plug the budget deficit with over $61 billion in additional tax collections. In addition, since IFRS does not permit LIFO, its repeal will contribute to international accounting convergence.

Source: R. Bloom and W. Cenker, "The Death of LIFO?" *Journal of Accountancy* (January 2009), pp. 44–49.

Inventory Valuation Methods—Summary Analysis

The preceding sections of this chapter described a number of inventory valuation methods. Here we present a brief summary of the three major inventory methods to show the effects these valuation methods have on the financial statements. This comparison assumes periodic inventory procedures and the following selected data.

Selected Data

Beginning cash balance		$ 7,000
Beginning retained earnings		$10,000
Beginning inventory:	4,000 units @ $3	$12,000
Purchases:	6,000 units @ $4	$24,000
Sales:	5,000 units @ $12	$60,000
Operating expenses		$10,000
Income tax rate		40%

Illustration 8-31 (page 466) shows the comparative results on net income of the use of average cost, FIFO, and LIFO.

[20]For an interesting discussion of the reasons for and against the use of FIFO and average cost, see Michael H. Granof and Daniel G. Short "For Some Companies, FIFO Accounting Makes Sense," *Wall Street Journal* (August 30, 1982), and the subsequent rebuttal by Gary C. Biddle "Taking Stock of Inventory Accounting Choices," *Wall Street Journal* (September 15, 1982).

ILLUSTRATION 8-31
Comparative Results of Average Cost, FIFO, and LIFO Methods

	Average Cost	FIFO	LIFO
Sales	$60,000	$60,000	$60,000
Cost of goods sold	18,000[a]	16,000[b]	20,000[c]
Gross profit	42,000	44,000	40,000
Operating expenses	10,000	10,000	10,000
Income before taxes	32,000	34,000	30,000
Income taxes (40%)	12,800	13,600	12,000
Net income	$19,200	$20,400	$18,000

[a]4,000 @ $3 = $12,000
6,000 @ $4 = 24,000
$36,000

$36,000 ÷ 10,000 = $3.60
$3.60 × 5,000 = $18,000

[b]4,000 @ $3 = $12,000
1,000 @ $4 = 4,000
$16,000

[c]5,000 @ $4 = $20,000

Notice that gross profit and net income are lowest under LIFO, highest under FIFO, and somewhere in the middle under average cost.

Illustration 8-32 shows the final balances of selected items at the end of the period.

ILLUSTRATION 8-32
Balances of Selected Items under Alternative Inventory Valuation Methods

	Inventory	Gross Profit	Taxes	Net Income	Retained Earnings	Cash
Average Cost	$18,000 (5,000 × $3.60)	$42,000	$12,800	$19,200	$29,200 ($10,000 + $19,200)	$20,200[a]
FIFO	$20,000 (5,000 × $4)	$44,000	$13,600	$20,400	$30,400 ($10,000 + $20,400)	$19,400[a]
LIFO	$16,000 (4,000 × $3) (1,000 × $4)	$40,000	$12,000	$18,000	$28,000 ($10,000 + $18,000)	$21,000[a]

[a]Cash at year-end	=	Beg. Balance	+	Sales	−	Purchases	−	Operating expenses	−	Taxes
Average cost—$20,200	=	$7,000	+	$60,000	−	$24,000	−	$10,000	−	$12,800
FIFO—$19,400	=	$7,000	+	$60,000	−	$24,000	−	$10,000	−	$13,600
LIFO—$21,000	=	$7,000	+	$60,000	−	$24,000	−	$10,000	−	$12,000

LIFO results in the highest cash balance at year-end (because taxes are lower). This example assumes that prices are rising. The opposite result occurs if prices are declining.

SUMMARY OF LEARNING OBJECTIVES

1 Identify major classifications of inventory. Only one inventory account, Inventory, appears in the financial statements of a merchandising concern. A manufacturer normally has three inventory accounts: Raw Materials, Work in Process, and Finished Goods. Companies report the cost assigned to goods and materials on hand but not yet placed into production as raw materials inventory. They report the cost of the raw materials on which production has been started but not completed, plus the direct labor cost applied specifically to this material and a ratable share of manufacturing overhead costs, as work in process inventory. Finally, they report the costs identified with the completed but unsold units on hand at the end of the fiscal period as finished goods inventory.

2 Distinguish between perpetual and periodic inventory systems. A perpetual inventory system maintains a continuous record of inventory changes in the Inventory account. That is, a company records all purchases and sales (issues) of goods

KEY TERMS

average cost method, 449
consigned goods, 441
cost flow assumptions, 448
dollar-value LIFO, 455
double-extension method, 459
finished goods inventory, 436
first-in, first-out (FIFO) method, 450
f.o.b. destination, 441
f.o.b. shipping point, 441
gross method, 447

directly in the Inventory account as they occur. Under a periodic inventory system, companies determine the quantity of inventory on hand only periodically. A company debits a Purchases account, but the Inventory account remains the same. It determines cost of goods sold at the end of the period by subtracting ending inventory from cost of goods available for sale. A company ascertains ending inventory by physical count.

3 Identify the effects of inventory errors on the financial statements. *If the company misstates ending inventory:* (1) In the balance sheet, the inventory and retained earnings will be misstated, which will lead to miscalculation of the working capital and current ratio, and (2) in the income statement the cost of goods sold and net income will be misstated. If the company misstates purchases (and related accounts payable) and inventory: (1) In the balance sheet, the inventory and accounts payable will be misstated, which will lead to miscalculation of the current ratio, and (2) in the income statement, purchases and ending inventory will be misstated.

4 Understand the items to include as inventory cost. Product costs are those costs that attach to the inventory and are recorded in the inventory account. Such charges include freight charges on goods purchased, other direct costs of acquisition, and labor and other production costs incurred in processing the goods up to the time of sale. Period costs are those costs that are indirectly related the acquisition or production of the goods. These changes, such as selling expense and general and administrative expenses, are therefore not included as part of inventory cost.

5 Describe and compare the cost flow assumptions used to account for inventories. (1) *Average cost* prices items in the inventory on the basis of the average cost of all similar goods available during the period. (2) *First-in, first-out* (FIFO) assumes that a company uses goods in the order in which it purchases them. The inventory remaining must therefore represent the most recent purchases. (3) *Last-in, first-out (LIFO)* matches the cost of the last goods purchased against revenue.

6 Explain the significance and use of a LIFO reserve. The difference between the inventory method used for internal reporting purposes and LIFO is referred to as the Allowance to Reduce Inventory to LIFO, or the LIFO reserve. The change in LIFO reserve is referred to as the LIFO effect. Companies should disclose either the LIFO reserve or the replacement cost of the inventory in the financial statements.

7 Understand the effect of LIFO liquidations. LIFO liquidations match costs from preceding periods against sales revenues reported in current dollars. This distorts net income and results in increased taxable income in the current period. LIFO liquidations can occur frequently when using a specific-goods LIFO approach.

8 Explain the dollar-value LIFO method. For the dollar-value LIFO method, companies determine and measure increases and decreases in a pool in terms of total dollar value, not the physical quantity of the goods in the inventory pool.

9 Identify the major advantages and disadvantages of LIFO. The major advantages of LIFO are the following: (1) It matches recent costs against current revenues to provide a better measure of current earnings. (2) As long as the price level increases and inventory quantities do not decrease, a deferral of income tax occurs in LIFO. (3) Because of the deferral of income tax, cash flow improves. Major disadvantages are: (1) reduced earnings, (2) understated inventory, (3) does not approximate physical flow of the items except in peculiar situations, and (4) involuntary liquidation issues.

10 Understand why companies select given inventory methods. Companies ordinarily prefer LIFO in the following circumstances: (1) if selling prices and revenues have been increasing faster than costs and (2) if a company has a fairly constant "base stock." Conversely, LIFO would probably not be appropriate in the following

inventories, *436*
last-in, first-out (LIFO) method, *451*
LIFO effect, *453*
LIFO liquidation, *454*
LIFO reserve, *453*
merchandise inventory, *436*
modified perpetual inventory system, *439*
moving-average method, *450*
net method, *447*
net of the cash discounts, *447*
period costs, *446*
periodic inventory system, *438*
perpetual inventory system, *437*
product costs, *446*
Purchase Discounts, *447*
raw materials inventory, *436*
specific-goods pooled LIFO approach, *455*
specific identification, *448*
weighted-average method, *449*
work in process inventory, *436*

circumstances: (1) if sale prices tend to lag behind costs, (2) if specific identification is traditional, and (3) when unit costs tend to decrease as production increases, thereby nullifying the tax benefit that LIFO might provide.

FASB CODIFICATION

FASB Codification References

[1] FASB ASC 470-40-05. [Predecessor literature: "Accounting for Product Financing Arrangements," *Statement of Financial Accounting Standards No. 49* (Stamford, Conn.: FASB, 1981).]

[2] FASB ASC 605-15-15. [Predecessor literature: "Revenue Recognition When Right of Return Exists," *Statement of Financial Accounting Standards No. 48* (Stamford, Conn.: FASB, 1981).]

[3] FASB ASC 330-10-30-7. [Predecessor literature: "Inventory Costs: An Amendment of ARB No. 43, Chapter 4," *Statement of Financial Accounting Standards No. 151* (Norwalk, Conn.: FASB 2004).]

[4] FASB ASC 835-20-05. [Predecessor literature: "Capitalization of Interest Cost," *Statement of Financial Accounting Standards No. 34* (Stamford, Conn.: FASB, 1979).]

[5] FASB ASC 645-45-05. [Predecessor literature: "Accounting for Shipping and Handling Fees and Costs," *EITF No. 00–10* (2000).]

[6] FASB ASC 330-10-30. [Predecessor literature: "Restatement and Revision of Accounting Research Bulletins," *Accounting Research Bulletin No. 43* (New York: AICPA, 1953), Ch. 4, Statement 4.]

[7] FASB ASC 330-10-S99-1. [Predecessor literature: "AICPA Task Force on LIFO Inventory Problems, *Issues Paper* (New York: AICPA, November 30, 1984), pp. 2–24.]

[8] FASB ASC 330-10-S99-3. [Predecessor literature: "AICPA Task Force on LIFO Inventory Problems, *Issues Paper* (New York: AICPA, November 30, 1984), pp. 36–37.]

Exercises

If your school has a subscription to the FASB Codification, go to *http://aaahq.org/asclogin.cfm* to log in and prepare responses to the following. Provide Codification references for your responses.

CE8-1 Access the glossary ("Master Glossary") to answer the following.

(a) What is the definition provided for inventory?

(b) What is a customer?

(c) Under what conditions is a distributor considered a customer?

(d) What is a product financing arrangement? What inventory measurement issues are raised through these arrangements?

CE8-2 Due to rising fuel costs, your client, **Overstock.com**, is considering adding a charge for shipping and handling costs on products sold through its website. What is the authoritative guidance for reporting these costs?

CE8-3 What guidance does the Codification provide concerning reporting inventories above cost?

CE8-4 What is the nature of the SEC guidance concerning the reporting of LIFO liquidations?

An additional Codification case can be found in the Using Your Judgment section, on page 490.

Be sure to check the book's companion website for a Review and Analysis Exercise, with solution.

Questions, Brief Exercises, Exercises, Problems, and many more resources are available for practice in WileyPLUS.

QUESTIONS

1. In what ways are the inventory accounts of a retailing company different from those of a manufacturing company?
2. Why should inventories be included in (a) a statement of financial position and (b) the computation of net income?
3. What is the difference between a perpetual inventory and a physical inventory? If a company maintains a perpetual inventory, should its physical inventory at any date be equal to the amount indicated by the perpetual inventory records? Why?
4. Mishima, Inc. indicated in a recent annual report that approximately $19 million of merchandise was received on consignment. Should Mishima, Inc. report this amount on its balance sheet? Explain.
5. What is a product financing arrangement? How should product financing arrangements be reported in the financial statements?
6. Where, if at all, should the following items be classified on a balance sheet?
   - **(a)** Goods out on approval to customers.
   - **(b)** Goods in transit that were recently purchased f.o.b. destination.
   - **(c)** Land held by a realty firm for sale.
   - **(d)** Raw materials.
   - **(e)** Goods received on consignment.
   - **(f)** Manufacturing supplies.
7. At the balance sheet date, Clarkson Company held title to goods in transit amounting to $214,000. This amount was omitted from the purchases figure for the year and also from the ending inventory. What is the effect of this omission on the net income for the year as calculated when the books are closed? What is the effect on the company's financial position as shown in its balance sheet? Is materiality a factor in determining whether an adjustment for this item should be made?
8. Define "cost" as applied to the valuation of inventories.
9. Distinguish between product costs and period costs as they relate to inventory.
10. Ford Motor Co. is considering alternate methods of accounting for the cash discounts it takes when paying suppliers promptly. One method suggested was to report these discounts as financial income when payments are made. Comment on the propriety of this approach.
11. Zonker Inc. purchases 500 units of an item at an invoice cost of $30,000. What is the cost per unit? If the goods are shipped f.o.b. shipping point and the freight bill was $1,500, what is the cost per unit if Zonker Inc. pays the freight charges? If these items were bought on 2/10, n/30 terms and the invoice and the freight bill were paid within the 10-day period, what would be the cost per unit?
12. Specific identification is sometimes said to be the ideal method of assigning cost to inventory and to cost of goods sold. Briefly indicate the arguments for and against this method of inventory valuation.
13. FIFO, weighted-average, and LIFO methods are often used instead of specific identification for inventory valuation purposes. Compare these methods with the specific identification method, discussing the theoretical propriety of each method in the determination of income and asset valuation.
14. How might a company obtain a price index in order to apply dollar-value LIFO?
15. Describe the LIFO double-extension method. Using the following information, compute the index at December 31, 2012, applying the double-extension method to a LIFO pool consisting of 25,500 units of product A and 10,350 units of product B. The base-year cost of product A is $10.20 and of product B is $37.00. The price at December 31, 2012, for product A is $21.00 and for product B is $45.60. (Round to two decimal places.)
16. As compared with the FIFO method of costing inventories, does the LIFO method result in a larger or smaller net income in a period of rising prices? What is the comparative effect on net income in a period of falling prices?
17. What is the dollar-value method of LIFO inventory valuation? What advantage does the dollar-value method have over the specific goods approach of LIFO inventory valuation? Why will the traditional LIFO inventory costing method and the dollar-value LIFO inventory costing method produce different inventory valuations if the composition of the inventory base changes?
18. Explain the following terms.
    - **(a)** LIFO layer.
    - **(b)** LIFO reserve.
    - **(c)** LIFO effect.
19. On December 31, 2011, the inventory of Powhattan Company amounts to $800,000. During 2012, the company decides to use the dollar-value LIFO method of costing inventories. On December 31, 2012, the inventory is $1,053,000 at December 31, 2012, prices. Using the December 31, 2011, price level of 100 and the December 31, 2012, price level of 108, compute the inventory value at December 31, 2012, under the dollar-value LIFO method.
20. In an article that appeared in the *Wall Street Journal*, the phrases "phantom (paper) profits" and "high LIFO profits" through involuntary liquidation were used. Explain these phrases.

BRIEF EXERCISES

1 **BE8-1** Included in the December 31 trial balance of Rivera Company are the following assets.

Cash	$ 190,000	Work in process	$200,000
Equipment (net)	1,100,000	Receivables (net)	400,000
Prepaid insurance	41,000	Patents	110,000
Raw materials	335,000	Finished goods	170,000

Prepare the current assets section of the December 31 balance sheet.

2 **BE8-2** Matlock Company uses a perpetual inventory system. Its beginning inventory consists of 50 units that cost $34 each. During June, the company purchased 150 units at $34 each, returned 6 units for credit, and sold 125 units at $50 each. Journalize the June transactions.

4 **BE8-3** Stallman Company took a physical inventory on December 31 and determined that goods costing $200,000 were on hand. Not included in the physical count were $25,000 of goods purchased from Pelzer Corporation, f.o.b. shipping point, and $22,000 of goods sold to Alvarez Company for $30,000, f.o.b. destination. Both the Pelzer purchase and the Alvarez sale were in transit at year-end. What amount should Stallman report as its December 31 inventory?

3 **BE8-4** Bienvenu Enterprises reported cost of goods sold for 2012 of $1,400,000 and retained earnings of $5,200,000 at December 31, 2012. Bienvenu later discovered that its ending inventories at December 31, 2011 and 2012, were overstated by $110,000 and $35,000, respectively. Determine the corrected amounts for 2012 cost of goods sold and December 31, 2012, retained earnings.

5 **BE8-5** Amsterdam Company uses a periodic inventory system. For April, when the company sold 600 units, the following information is available.

	Units	Unit Cost	Total Cost
April 1 inventory	250	$10	$ 2,500
April 15 purchase	400	12	4,800
April 23 purchase	350	13	4,550
	1,000		$11,850

Compute the April 30 inventory and the April cost of goods sold using the average cost method.

5 **BE8-6** Data for Amsterdam Company are presented in BE8-5. Compute the April 30 inventory and the April cost of goods sold using the FIFO method.

5 **BE8-7** Data for Amsterdam Company are presented in BE8-5. Compute the April 30 inventory and the April cost of goods sold using the LIFO method.

8 **BE8-8** Midori Company had ending inventory at end-of-year prices of $100,000 at December 31, 2011; $119,900 at December 31, 2012; and $134,560 at December 31, 2013. The year-end price indexes were 100 at 12/31/11, 110 at 12/31/12, and 116 at 12/31/13. Compute the ending inventory for Midori Company for 2011 through 2013 using the dollar-value LIFO method.

8 **BE8-9** Arna, Inc. uses the dollar-value LIFO method of computing its inventory. Data for the past 3 years follow.

Year Ended December 31	Inventory at Current-Year Cost	Price Index
2011	$19,750	100
2012	22,140	108
2013	25,935	114

Instructions
Compute the value of the 2012 and 2013 inventories using the dollar-value LIFO method.

EXERCISES

4 **E8-1 (Inventoriable Costs)** Presented below is a list of items that may or may not be reported as inventory in a company's December 31 balance sheet.

1. Goods sold on an installment basis (bad debts can be reasonably estimated).
2. Goods out on consignment at another company's store.

3. Goods purchased f.o.b. shipping point that are in transit at December 31.
4. Goods purchased f.o.b. destination that are in transit at December 31.
5. Goods sold to another company, for which our company has signed an agreement to repurchase at a set price that covers all costs related to the inventory.
6. Goods sold where large returns are predictable.
7. Goods sold f.o.b. shipping point that are in transit at December 31.
8. Freight charges on goods purchased.
9. Interest costs incurred for inventories that are routinely manufactured.
10. Materials on hand not yet placed into production by a manufacturing firm.
11. Costs incurred to advertise goods held for resale.
12. Office supplies.
13. Raw materials on which a manufacturing firm has started production, but which are not completely processed.
14. Factory supplies.
15. Goods held on consignment from another company.
16. Costs identified with units completed by a manufacturing firm, but not yet sold.
17. Goods sold f.o.b. destination that are in transit at December 31.
18. Short-term investments in stocks and bonds that will be resold in the near future.

Instructions

Indicate which of these items would typically be reported as inventory in the financial statements. If an item should **not** be reported as inventory, indicate how it should be reported in the financial statements.

4 **E8-2 (Inventoriable Costs)** In your audit of Garza Company, you find that a physical inventory on December 31, 2012, showed merchandise with a cost of $441,000 was on hand at that date. You also discover the following items were all excluded from the $441,000.

1. Merchandise of $61,000 which is held by Garza on consignment. The consignor is the Bontemps Company.
2. Merchandise costing $33,000 which was shipped by Garza f.o.b. destination to a customer on December 31, 2012. The customer was expected to receive the merchandise on January 6, 2013.
3. Merchandise costing $46,000 which was shipped by Garza f.o.b. shipping point to a customer on December 29, 2012. The customer was scheduled to receive the merchandise on January 2, 2013.
4. Merchandise costing $73,000 shipped by a vendor f.o.b. destination on December 30, 2012, and received by Garza on January 4, 2013.
5. Merchandise costing $51,000 shipped by a vendor f.o.b. shipping point on December 31, 2012, and received by Garza on January 5, 2013.

Instructions

Based on the above information, calculate the amount that should appear on Garza's balance sheet at December 31, 2012, for inventory.

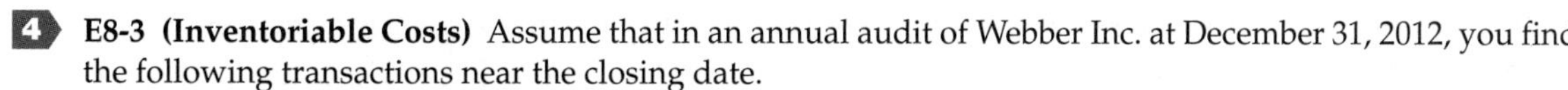

4 **E8-3 (Inventoriable Costs)** Assume that in an annual audit of Webber Inc. at December 31, 2012, you find the following transactions near the closing date.

1. A special machine, fabricated to order for a customer, was finished and specifically segregated in the back part of the shipping room on December 31, 2012. The customer was billed on that date and the machine excluded from inventory although it was shipped on January 4, 2013.
2. Merchandise costing $2,800 was received on January 3, 2013, and the related purchase invoice recorded January 5. The invoice showed the shipment was made on December 29, 2012, f.o.b. destination.
3. A packing case containing a product costing $3,400 was standing in the shipping room when the physical inventory was taken. It was not included in the inventory because it was marked "Hold for shipping instructions." Your investigation revealed that the customer's order was dated December 18, 2012, but that the case was shipped and the customer billed on January 10, 2013. The product was a stock item of your client.
4. Merchandise costing $720 was received on December 28, 2012, and the invoice was not recorded. You located it in the hands of the purchasing agent; it was marked "on consignment."
5. Merchandise received on January 6, 2013, costing $680 was entered in the purchases journal on January 7, 2013. The invoice showed shipment was made f.o.b. supplier's warehouse on December 31, 2012. Because it was not on hand at December 31, it was not included in inventory.

Instructions
Assuming that each of the amounts is material, state whether the merchandise should be included in the client's inventory, and give your reason for your decision on each item.

2 4 **E8-4 (Inventoriable Costs—Perpetual)** Bradford Machine Company maintains a general ledger account for each class of inventory, debiting such accounts for increases during the period and crediting them for decreases. The transactions below relate to the Raw Materials inventory account, which is debited for materials purchased and credited for materials requisitioned for use.

1. An invoice for $8,100, terms f.o.b. destination, was received and entered January 2, 2013. The receiving report shows that the materials were received December 28, 2012.
2. Materials costing $7,300 were returned to the supplier on December 29, 2012, and were shipped f.o.b. shipping point. The return was entered on that date, even though the materials are not expected to reach the supplier's place of business until January 6, 2013.
3. Materials costing $28,000, shipped f.o.b. destination, were not entered by December 31, 2012, "because they were in a railroad car on the company's siding on that date and had not been unloaded."
4. An invoice for $7,500, terms f.o.b. shipping point, was received and entered December 30, 2012. The receiving report shows that the materials were received January 4, 2013, and the bill of lading shows that they were shipped January 2, 2013.
5. Materials costing $19,800 were received December 30, 2012, but no entry was made for them because "they were ordered with a specified delivery of no earlier than January 10, 2013."

Instructions
Prepare correcting general journal entries required at December 31, 2012, assuming that the books have not been closed.

3 4 **E8-5 (Inventoriable Costs—Error Adjustments)** Werth Company asks you to review its December 31, 2012, inventory values and prepare the necessary adjustments to the books. The following information is given to you.

1. Werth uses the periodic method of recording inventory. A physical count reveals $234,890 of inventory on hand at December 31, 2012.
2. Not included in the physical count of inventory is $10,420 of merchandise purchased on December 15 from Browser. This merchandise was shipped f.o.b. shipping point on December 29 and arrived in January. The invoice arrived and was recorded on December 31.
3. Included in inventory is merchandise sold to Bubbey on December 30, f.o.b. destination. This merchandise was shipped after it was counted. The invoice was prepared and recorded as a sale on account for $12,800 on December 31. The merchandise cost $7,350, and Bubbey received it on January 3.
4. Included in inventory was merchandise received from Dudley on December 31 with an invoice price of $15,630. The merchandise was shipped f.o.b. destination. The invoice, which has not yet arrived, has not been recorded.
5. Not included in inventory is $8,540 of merchandise purchased from Minsky Industries. This merchandise was received on December 31 after the inventory had been counted. The invoice was received and recorded on December 30.
6. Included in inventory was $10,438 of inventory held by Werth on consignment from Jackel Industries.
7. Included in inventory is merchandise sold to Sims f.o.b. shipping point. This merchandise was shipped after it was counted. The invoice was prepared and recorded as a sale for $18,900 on December 31. The cost of this merchandise was $11,520, and Sims received the merchandise on January 5.
8. Excluded from inventory was a carton labeled "Please accept for credit." This carton contains merchandise costing $1,500 which had been sold to a customer for $2,600. No entry had been made to the books to reflect the return, but none of the returned merchandise seemed damaged.

Instructions
(a) Determine the proper inventory balance for Werth Company at December 31, 2012.
(b) Prepare any correcting entries to adjust inventory to its proper amount at December 31, 2012. Assume the books have not been closed.

4 **E8-6 (Determining Merchandise Amounts—Periodic)** Two or more items are omitted in each of the following tabulations of income statement data. Fill in the amounts that are missing.

	2011	2012	2013
Sales revenue	$290,000	$?	$410,000
Sales returns and allowances	6,000	13,000	?
Net sales	?	347,000	?
Beginning inventory	20,000	32,000	?
Ending inventory	?	?	?
Purchases	?	260,000	298,000
Purchase returns and allowances	5,000	8,000	10,000
Freight-in	8,000	9,000	12,000
Cost of goods sold	238,000	?	303,000
Gross profit on sales	46,000	91,000	97,000

4 **E8-7 (Purchases Recorded Net)** Presented below are transactions related to Guillen, Inc.

May 10	Purchased goods billed at $20,000 subject to cash discount terms of 2/10, n/60.
11	Purchased goods billed at $15,000 subject to terms of 1/15, n/30.
19	Paid invoice of May 10.
24	Purchased goods billed at $11,500 subject to cash discount terms of 2/10, n/30.

Instructions

(a) Prepare general journal entries for the transactions above under the assumption that purchases are to be recorded at net amounts after cash discounts and that discounts lost are to be treated as financial expense.

(b) Assuming no purchase or payment transactions other than those given above, prepare the adjusting entry required on May 31 if financial statements are to be prepared as of that date.

4 **E8-8 (Purchases Recorded, Gross Method)** Wizard Industries purchased $12,000 of merchandise on February 1, 2012, subject to a trade discount of 10% and with credit terms of 3/15, n/60. It returned $3,000 (gross price before trade or cash discount) on February 4. The invoice was paid on February 13.

Instructions

(a) Assuming that Wizard uses the perpetual method for recording merchandise transactions, record the purchase, return, and payment using the gross method.

(b) Assuming that Wizard uses the periodic method for recording merchandise transactions, record the purchase, return, and payment using the gross method.

(c) At what amount would the purchase on February 1 be recorded if the net method were used?

2 5 **E8-9 (Periodic versus Perpetual Entries)** Chippewas Company sells one product. Presented below is information for January for Chippewas Company.

Jan. 1	Inventory	100 units at $6 each
4	Sale	80 units at $8 each
11	Purchase	150 units at $6.50 each
13	Sale	120 units at $8.75 each
20	Purchase	160 units at $7 each
27	Sale	100 units at $9 each

Chippewas uses the FIFO cost flow assumption. All purchases and sales are on account.

Instructions

(a) Assume Chippewas uses a periodic system. Prepare all necessary journal entries, including the end-of-month closing entry to record cost of goods sold. A physical count indicates that the ending inventory for January is 110 units.

(b) Compute gross profit using the periodic system.

(c) Assume Chippewas uses a perpetual system. Prepare all necessary journal entries.

(d) Compute gross profit using the perpetual system.

3 **E8-10 (Inventory Errors—Periodic)** Thomason Company makes the following errors during the current year. (In all cases, assume ending inventory in the following year is correctly stated.)

1. Both ending inventory and purchases and related accounts payable are understated. (Assume this purchase was recorded and paid for in the following year.)
2. Ending inventory is overstated, but purchases and related accounts payable are recorded correctly.
3. Ending inventory is correct, but a purchase on account was not recorded. (Assume this purchase was recorded and paid for in the following year.)

Instructions

Indicate the effect of each of these errors on working capital, current ratio (assume that the current ratio is greater than 1), retained earnings, and net income for the current year and the subsequent year.

3 **E8-11 (Inventory Errors)** At December 31, 2012, Dwight Corporation reported current assets of $390,000 and current liabilities of $200,000. The following items may have been recorded incorrectly. Dwight uses the periodic method.

1. Goods purchased costing $22,000 were shipped f.o.b. shipping point by a supplier on December 28. Dwight received and recorded the invoice on December 29, 2012, but the goods were not included in Dwight's physical count of inventory because they were not received until January 4, 2013.
2. Goods purchased costing $20,000 were shipped f.o.b. destination by a supplier on December 26. Dwight received and recorded the invoice on December 31, but the goods were not included in Dwight's 2012 physical count of inventory because they were not received until January 2, 2013.
3. Goods held on consignment from Kishi Company were included in Dwight's December 31, 2012, physical count of inventory at $13,000.
4. Freight-in of $3,000 was debited to advertising expense on December 28, 2012.

Instructions

(a) Compute the current ratio based on Dwight's balance sheet.
(b) Recompute the current ratio after corrections are made.
(c) By what amount will income (before taxes) be adjusted up or down as a result of the corrections?

3 **E8-12 (Inventory Errors)** The net income per books of Adamson Company was determined without knowledge of the errors indicated below.

Year	Net Income per Books	Error in Ending Inventory	
2008	$50,000	Overstated	$ 5,000
2009	52,000	Overstated	9,000
2010	54,000	Understated	11,000
2011	56,000	No error	
2012	58,000	Understated	2,000
2013	60,000	Overstated	10,000

Instructions

Prepare a worksheet to show the adjusted net income figure for each of the 6 years after taking into account the inventory errors.

2 5 **E8-13 (FIFO and LIFO—Periodic and Perpetual)** Inventory information for Part 311 of Seminole Corp. discloses the following information for the month of June.

June 1	Balance	300 units @ $10	June 10	Sold	200 units @ $24
11	Purchased	800 units @ $11	15	Sold	500 units @ $25
20	Purchased	500 units @ $13	27	Sold	250 units @ $27

Instructions

(a) Assuming that the periodic inventory method is used, compute the cost of goods sold and ending inventory under (1) LIFO and (2) FIFO.
(b) Assuming that the perpetual inventory method is used and costs are computed at the time of each withdrawal, what is the value of the ending inventory at LIFO?
(c) Assuming that the perpetual inventory method is used and costs are computed at the time of each withdrawal, what is the gross profit if the inventory is valued at FIFO?
(d) Why is it stated that LIFO usually produces a lower gross profit than FIFO?

5 **E8-14 (FIFO, LIFO, and Average Cost Determination)** LoBianco Company's record of transactions for the month of April was as follows.

Purchases		Sales	
April 1 (balance on hand)	600 @ $ 6.00	April 3	500 @ $10.00
4	1,500 @ 6.08	9	1,300 @ 10.00
8	800 @ 6.40	11	600 @ 11.00
13	1,200 @ 6.50	23	1,200 @ 11.00
21	700 @ 6.60	27	900 @ 12.00
29	500 @ 6.79		4,500
	5,300		

Instructions

(a) Assuming that periodic inventory records are kept, compute the inventory at April 30 using (1) LIFO and (2) average cost.

(b) Assuming that perpetual inventory records are kept in both units and dollars, determine the inventory at April 30 using (1) FIFO and (2) LIFO.
(c) Compute cost of goods sold assuming periodic inventory procedures and inventory priced at FIFO.
(d) In an inflationary period, which inventory method—FIFO, LIFO, average cost—will show the highest net income?

5 **E8-15 (FIFO, LIFO, Average Cost Inventory)** Esplanade Company was formed on December 1, 2011. The following information is available from Esplanade's inventory records for Product BAP.

	Units	Unit Cost
January 1, 2012 (beginning inventory)	600	$8.00
Purchases:		
January 5, 2012	1,100	9.00
January 25, 2012	1,300	10.00
February 16, 2012	800	11.00
March 26, 2012	600	12.00

A physical inventory on March 31, 2012, shows 1,500 units on hand.

Instructions

Prepare schedules to compute the ending inventory at March 31, 2012, under each of the following inventory methods.

(a) FIFO. **(b)** LIFO. **(c)** Weighted-average.

5 **E8-16 (Compute FIFO, LIFO, Average Cost—Periodic)** Presented below is information related to radios for the Couples Company for the month of July.

Date	Transaction	Units In	Unit Cost	Total	Units Sold	Selling Price	Total
July 1	Balance	100	$4.10	$ 410			
6	Purchase	800	4.30	3,440			
7	Sale				300	$7.00	$ 2,100
10	Sale				300	7.30	2,190
12	Purchase	400	4.51	1,804			
15	Sale				200	7.40	1,480
18	Purchase	300	4.60	1,380			
22	Sale				400	7.40	2,960
25	Purchase	500	4.58	2,290			
30	Sale				200	7.50	1,500
	Totals	2,100		$9,324	1,400		$10,230

Instructions

(a) Assuming that the periodic inventory method is used, compute the inventory cost at July 31 under each of the following cost flow assumptions.

(1) FIFO.
(2) LIFO.
(3) Weighted-average.

(b) Answer the following questions.

(1) Which of the methods used above will yield the lowest figure for gross profit for the income statement? Explain why.
(2) Which of the methods used above will yield the lowest figure for ending inventory for the balance sheet? Explain why.

2 5 **E8-17 (FIFO and LIFO—Periodic and Perpetual)** The following is a record of Cannondale Company's transactions for Boston Teapots for the month of May 2012.

May 1 Balance 400 units @ $20	May 10 Sale 300 units @ $38
12 Purchase 600 units @ $25	20 Sale 590 units @ $38
28 Purchase 400 units @ $30	

Instructions

(a) Assuming that perpetual inventories are **not** maintained and that a physical count at the end of the month shows 510 units on hand, what is the cost of the ending inventory using (1) FIFO and (2) LIFO?
(b) Assuming that perpetual records are maintained and they tie into the general ledger, calculate the ending inventory using (1) FIFO and (2) LIFO.

5 **E8-18 (FIFO and LIFO, Income Statement Presentation)** The board of directors of Oksana Corporation is considering whether or not it should instruct the accounting department to change from a first-in, first-out (FIFO) basis of pricing inventories to a last-in, first-out (LIFO) basis. The following information is available.

Sales	20,000 units @ $50
Inventory, January 1	6,000 units @ 20
Purchases	6,000 units @ 22
	10,000 units @ 25
	7,000 units @ 30
Inventory, December 31	9,000 units @ ?
Operating expenses	$200,000

Instructions

Prepare a condensed income statement for the year on both bases for comparative purposes.

5 **E8-19 (FIFO and LIFO Effects)** You are the vice president of finance of Mickiewicz Corporation, a retail company that prepared two different schedules of gross margin for the first quarter ended March 31, 2012. These schedules appear below.

	Sales ($5 per unit)	Cost of Goods Sold	Gross Margin
Schedule 1	$150,000	$124,900	$25,100
Schedule 2	150,000	129,600	20,400

The computation of cost of goods sold in each schedule is based on the following data.

	Units	Cost per Unit	Total Cost
Beginning inventory, January 1	10,000	$4.00	$40,000
Purchase, January 10	8,000	4.20	33,600
Purchase, January 30	6,000	4.25	25,500
Purchase, February 11	9,000	4.30	38,700
Purchase, March 17	12,000	4.40	52,800

Peggy Fleming, the president of the corporation, cannot understand how two different gross margins can be computed from the same set of data. As the vice president of finance, you have explained to Ms. Fleming that the two schedules are based on different assumptions concerning the flow of inventory costs, i.e., FIFO and LIFO. Schedules 1 and 2 were not necessarily prepared in this sequence of cost flow assumptions.

Instructions

Prepare two separate schedules computing cost of goods sold and supporting schedules showing the composition of the ending inventory under both cost flow assumptions (assume periodic system).

5 **E8-20 (FIFO and LIFO—Periodic)** Tom Brady Shop began operations on January 2, 2012. The following stock record card for footballs was taken from the records at the end of the year.

Date	Voucher	Terms	Units Received	Unit Invoice Cost	Gross Invoice Amount
1/15	10624	Net 30	50	$20	$1,000
3/15	11437	1/5, net 30	65	16	1,040
6/20	21332	1/10, net 30	90	15	1,350
9/12	27644	1/10, net 30	84	12	1,008
11/24	31269	1/10, net 30	76	11	836
	Totals		365		$5,234

A physical inventory on December 31, 2012, reveals that 110 footballs were in stock. The bookkeeper informs you that all the discounts were taken. Assume that Tom Brady Shop uses the invoice price less discount for recording purchases.

Instructions

(a) Compute the December 31, 2012, inventory using the FIFO method.

(b) Compute the 2012 cost of goods sold using the LIFO method.

(c) What method would you recommend to the owner to minimize income taxes in 2012, using the inventory information for footballs as a guide?

6 **E8-21 (LIFO Effect)** The following example was provided to encourage the use of the LIFO method.

In a nutshell, LIFO subtracts inflation from inventory costs, deducts it from taxable income, and records it in a LIFO reserve account on the books. The LIFO benefit grows as inflation widens the gap between current-year and past-year (minus inflation) inventory costs. This gap is:

	With LIFO	Without LIFO
Revenues	$3,200,000	$3,200,000
Cost of goods sold	2,800,000	2,800,000
Operating expenses	150,000	150,000
Operating income	250,000	250,000
LIFO adjustment	40,000	0
Taxable income	$ 210,000	$ 250,000
Income taxes @ 36%	$ 75,600	$ 90,000
Cash flow	$ 174,400	$ 160,000
Extra cash	$ 14,400	0
Increased cash flow	9%	0%

Instructions

(a) Explain what is meant by the LIFO reserve account.
(b) How does LIFO subtract inflation from inventory costs?
(c) Explain how the cash flow of $174,400 in this example was computed. Explain why this amount may not be correct.
(d) Why does a company that uses LIFO have extra cash? Explain whether this situation will always exist.

5 8 **E8-22 (Alternative Inventory Methods—Comprehensive)** Belanna Corporation began operations on December 1, 2012. The only inventory transaction in 2012 was the purchase of inventory on December 10, 2012, at a cost of $20 per unit. None of this inventory was sold in 2012. Relevant information is as follows.

Ending inventory units		
December 31, 2012		100
December 31, 2013, by purchase date		
December 2, 2013	100	
July 20, 2013	30	130

During the year, the following purchases and sales were made.

Purchases		Sales	
March 15	300 units at $24	April 10	200
July 20	300 units at 25	August 20	300
September 4	200 units at 28	November 18	170
December 2	100 units at 30	December 12	200

The company uses the periodic inventory method.

Instructions

(a) Determine ending inventory under (1) specific identification, (2) FIFO, (3) LIFO, and (4) average cost. (Round unit cost to four decimal places.)
(b) Determine ending inventory using dollar-value LIFO. Assume that the December 2, 2013, purchase cost is the current cost of inventory. (*Hint:* The beginning inventory is the base-layer priced at $20 per unit.)

8 **E8-23 (Dollar-Value LIFO)** Sisko Company has used the dollar-value LIFO method for inventory cost determination for many years. The following data were extracted from Sisko's records.

Date	Price Index	Ending Inventory at Base Prices	Ending Inventory at Dollar-Value LIFO
December 31, 2011	105	$92,000	$92,600
December 31, 2012	?	98,000	99,200

Instructions

Calculate the index used for 2012 that yielded the above results.

8 **E8-24 (Dollar-Value LIFO)** The dollar-value LIFO method was adopted by King Corp. on January 1, 2012. Its inventory on that date was $160,000. On December 31, 2012, the inventory at prices existing on that date amounted to $151,200. The price level at January 1, 2012, was 100, and the price level at December 31, 2012, was 112.

Instructions

(a) Compute the amount of the inventory at December 31, 2012, under the dollar-value LIFO method.

(b) On December 31, 2013, the inventory at prices existing on that date was $195,500, and the price level was 115. Compute the inventory on that date under the dollar-value LIFO method.

8 **E8-25 (Dollar-Value LIFO)** Presented below is information related to Martin Company.

Date	Ending Inventory (End-of-Year Prices)	Price Index
December 31, 2009	$ 80,000	100
December 31, 2010	111,300	105
December 31, 2011	108,000	120
December 31, 2012	122,200	130
December 31, 2013	147,000	140
December 31, 2014	176,900	145

Instructions

Compute the ending inventory for Martin Company for 2009 through 2014 using the dollar-value LIFO method.

8 **E8-26 (Dollar-Value LIFO)** The following information relates to the Choctaw Company.

Date	Ending Inventory (End-of-Year Prices)	Price Index
December 31, 2009	$ 70,000	100
December 31, 2010	88,200	105
December 31, 2011	95,120	116
December 31, 2012	108,000	120
December 31, 2013	100,000	125

Instructions

Use the dollar-value LIFO method to compute the ending inventory for Choctaw Company for 2009 through 2013.

See the book's companion website, www.wiley.com/college/kieso, for a set of B Exercises.

PROBLEMS

4 5 8 **P8-1 (Various Inventory Issues)** The following independent situations relate to inventory accounting.

1. Kim Co. purchased goods with a list price of $175,000, subject to trade discounts of 20% and 10%, with no cash discounts allowable. How much should Kim Co. record as the cost of these goods?
2. Keillor Company's inventory of $1,100,000 at December 31, 2012, was based on a physical count of goods priced at cost and before any year-end adjustments relating to the following items.
   (a) Goods shipped from a vendor f.o.b. shipping point on December 24, 2012, at an invoice cost of $69,000 to Keillor Company were received on January 4, 2013.
   (b) The physical count included $29,000 of goods billed to Sakic Corp. f.o.b. shipping point on December 31, 2012. The carrier picked up these goods on January 3, 2013.
   What amount should Keillor report as inventory on its balance sheet?
3. Zimmerman Corp. had 1,500 units of part M.O. on hand May 1, 2012, costing $21 each. Purchases of part M.O. during May were as follows.

	Units	Units Cost
May 9	2,000	$22.00
17	3,500	23.00
26	1,000	24.00

A physical count on May 31, 2012, shows 2,000 units of part M.O. on hand. Using the FIFO method, what is the cost of part M.O. inventory at May 31, 2012? Using the LIFO method, what is the inventory cost? Using the average cost method, what is the inventory cost?

4. Ashbrook Company adopted the dollar-value LIFO method on January 1, 2012 (using internal price indexes and multiple pools). The following data are available for inventory pool A for the 2 years following adoption of LIFO.

Inventory	At Base-Year Cost	At Current-Year Cost
1/1/12	$200,000	$200,000
12/31/12	240,000	264,000
12/31/13	256,000	286,720

Computing an internal price index and using the dollar-value LIFO method, at what amount should the inventory be reported at December 31, 2013?

5. Donovan Inc., a retail store chain, had the following information in its general ledger for the year 2013.

Merchandise purchased for resale	$909,400
Interest on notes payable to vendors	8,700
Purchase returns	16,500
Freight-in	22,000
Freight-out	17,100
Cash discounts on purchases	6,800

What is Donovan's inventoriable cost for 2013?

Instructions

Answer each of the preceding questions about inventories, and explain your answers.

3 4 **P8-2 (Inventory Adjustments)** Dimitri Company, a manufacturer of small tools, provided the following information from its accounting records for the year ended December 31, 2012.

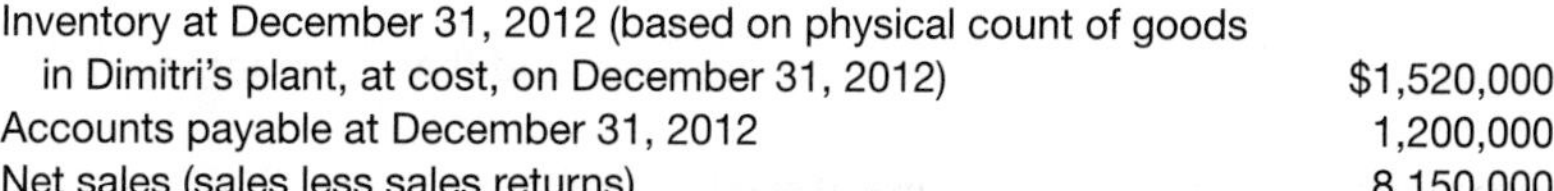

Inventory at December 31, 2012 (based on physical count of goods in Dimitri's plant, at cost, on December 31, 2012)	$1,520,000
Accounts payable at December 31, 2012	1,200,000
Net sales (sales less sales returns)	8,150,000

Additional information is as follows.

1. Included in the physical count were tools billed to a customer f.o.b. shipping point on December 31, 2012. These tools had a cost of $31,000 and were billed at $40,000. The shipment was on Dimitri's loading dock waiting to be picked up by the common carrier.
2. Goods were in transit from a vendor to Dimitri on December 31, 2012. The invoice cost was $76,000, and the goods were shipped f.o.b. shipping point on December 29, 2012.
3. Work in process inventory costing $30,000 was sent to an outside processor for plating on December 30, 2012.
4. Tools returned by customers and held pending inspection in the returned goods area on December 31, 2012, were not included in the physical count. On January 8, 2013, the tools costing $32,000 were inspected and returned to inventory. Credit memos totaling $47,000 were issued to the customers on the same date.
5. Tools shipped to a customer f.o.b. destination on December 26, 2012, were in transit at December 31, 2012, and had a cost of $26,000. Upon notification of receipt by the customer on January 2, 2013, Dimitri issued a sales invoice for $42,000.
6. Goods, with an invoice cost of $27,000, received from a vendor at 5:00 p.m. on December 31, 2012, were recorded on a receiving report dated January 2, 2013. The goods were not included in the physical count, but the invoice was included in accounts payable at December 31, 2012.
7. Goods received from a vendor on December 26, 2012, were included in the physical count. However, the related $56,000 vendor invoice was not included in accounts payable at December 31, 2012, because the accounts payable copy of the receiving report was lost.
8. On January 3, 2013, a monthly freight bill in the amount of $8,000 was received. The bill specifically related to merchandise purchased in December 2012, one-half of which was still in the inventory at December 31, 2012. The freight charges were not included in either the inventory or in accounts payable at December 31, 2012.

Instructions

Using the format shown below, prepare a schedule of adjustments as of December 31, 2012, to the initial amounts per Dimitri's accounting records. Show separately the effect, if any, of each of the eight transactions on the December 31, 2012, amounts. If the transactions would have no effect on the initial amount shown, enter NONE.

	Inventory	Accounts Payable	Net Sales
Initial amounts	$1,520,000	$1,200,000	$8,150,000
Adjustments—increase (decrease)			
1			
2			
3			
4			
5			
6			
7			
8			
Total adjustments			
Adjusted amounts	$	$	$

(AICPA adapted)

4 **P8-3 (Purchases Recorded Gross and Net)** Some of the transactions of Torres Company during August are listed below. Torres uses the periodic inventory method.

August 10	Purchased merchandise on account, $12,000, terms 2/10, n/30.
13	Returned part of the purchase of August 10, $1,200, and received credit on account.
15	Purchased merchandise on account, $16,000, terms 1/10, n/60.
25	Purchased merchandise on account, $20,000, terms 2/10, n/30.
28	Paid invoice of August 15 in full.

Instructions

(a) Assuming that purchases are recorded at gross amounts and that discounts are to be recorded when taken:
   (1) Prepare general journal entries to record the transactions.
   (2) Describe how the various items would be shown in the financial statements.

(b) Assuming that purchases are recorded at net amounts and that discounts lost are treated as financial expenses:
   (1) Prepare general journal entries to enter the transactions.
   (2) Prepare the adjusting entry necessary on August 31 if financial statements are to be prepared at that time.
   (3) Describe how the various items would be shown in the financial statements.

(c) Which of the two methods do you prefer and why?

2 5 **P8-4 (Compute FIFO, LIFO, and Average Cost)** Hull Company's record of transactions concerning part X for the month of April was as follows.

Purchases		Sales	
April 1 (balance on hand)	100 @ $5.00	April 5	300
4	400 @ 5.10	12	200
11	300 @ 5.30	27	800
18	200 @ 5.35	28	150
26	600 @ 5.60		
30	200 @ 5.80		

Instructions

(a) Compute the inventory at April 30 on each of the following bases. Assume that perpetual inventory records are kept in units only. Carry unit costs to the nearest cent.
   (1) First-in, first-out (FIFO).
   (2) Last-in, first-out (LIFO).
   (3) Average cost.

(b) If the perpetual inventory record is kept in dollars, and costs are computed at the time of each withdrawal, what amount would be shown as ending inventory in (1), (2), and (3) above? Carry average unit costs to four decimal places.

 **P8-5 (Compute FIFO, LIFO, and Average Cost)** Some of the information found on a detail inventory card for Slatkin Inc. for the first month of operations is as follows.

Date	Received No. of Units	Received Unit Cost	Issued, No. of Units	Balance, No. of Units
January 2	1,200	$3.00		1,200
7			700	500
10	600	3.20		1,100
13			500	600
18	1,000	3.30	300	1,300
20			1,100	200
23	1,300	3.40		1,500
26			800	700
28	1,600	3.50		2,300
31			1,300	1,000

Instructions

(a) From these data compute the ending inventory on each of the following bases. Assume that perpetual inventory records are kept in units only. Carry unit costs to the nearest cent and ending inventory to the nearest dollar.
  (1) First-in, first-out (FIFO).
  (2) Last-in, first-out (LIFO).
  (3) Average cost.

(b) If the perpetual inventory record is kept in dollars, and costs are computed at the time of each withdrawal, would the amounts shown as ending inventory in (1), (2), and (3) above be the same? Explain and compute. (Round average unit costs to four decimal places.)

P8-6 (Compute FIFO, LIFO, Average Cost—Periodic and Perpetual) Ehlo Company is a multiproduct firm. Presented below is information concerning one of its products, the Hawkeye.

Date	Transaction	Quantity	Price/Cost
1/1	Beginning inventory	1,000	$12
2/4	Purchase	2,000	18
2/20	Sale	2,500	30
4/2	Purchase	3,000	23
11/4	Sale	2,200	33

Instructions

Compute cost of goods sold, assuming Ehlo uses:

(a) Periodic system, FIFO cost flow.
(b) Perpetual system, FIFO cost flow.
(c) Periodic system, LIFO cost flow.
(d) Perpetual system, LIFO cost flow.
(e) Periodic system, weighted-average cost flow.
(f) Perpetual system, moving-average cost flow.

5 **P8-7 (Financial Statement Effects of FIFO and LIFO)** The management of Tritt Company has asked its accounting department to describe the effect upon the company's financial position and its income statements of accounting for inventories on the LIFO rather than the FIFO basis during 2012 and 2013. The accounting department is to assume that the change to LIFO would have been effective on January 1, 2012, and that the initial LIFO base would have been the inventory value on December 31, 2011. Presented below are the company's financial statements and other data for the years 2012 and 2013 when the FIFO method was employed.

	Financial Position as of		
	12/31/11	12/31/12	12/31/13
Cash	$ 90,000	$130,000	$154,000
Accounts receivable	80,000	100,000	120,000
Inventory	120,000	140,000	176,000
Other assets	160,000	170,000	200,000
Total assets	$450,000	$540,000	$650,000
Accounts payable	$ 40,000	$ 60,000	$ 80,000
Other liabilities	70,000	80,000	110,000
Common stock	200,000	200,000	200,000
Retained earnings	140,000	200,000	260,000
Total liabilities and equity	$450,000	$540,000	$650,000

	Income for Years Ended	
	12/31/12	12/31/13
Sales revenue	$900,000	$1,350,000
Less: Cost of goods sold	505,000	756,000
Other expenses	205,000	304,000
	710,000	1,060,000
Income before income taxes	190,000	290,000
Income taxes (40%)	76,000	116,000
Net income	$114,000	$ 174,000

Other data:

1. Inventory on hand at December 31, 2011, consisted of 40,000 units valued at $3.00 each.
2. Sales (all units sold at the same price in a given year):

   2012—150,000 units @ $6.00 each   2013—180,000 units @ $7.50 each

3. Purchases (all units purchased at the same price in given year):

   2012—150,000 units @ $3.50 each   2013—180,000 units @ $4.40 each

4. Income taxes at the effective rate of 40% are paid on December 31 each year.

Instructions

Name the account(s) presented in the financial statements that would have different amounts for 2013 if LIFO rather than FIFO had been used, and state the new amount for each account that is named. Show computations.

(CMA adapted)

8 **P8-8 (Dollar-Value LIFO)** Norman's Televisions produces television sets in three categories: portable, midsize, and flat-screen. On January 1, 2012, Norman adopted dollar-value LIFO and decided to use a single inventory pool. The company's January 1 inventory consists of:

Category	Quantity	Cost per Unit	Total Cost
Portable	6,000	$100	$ 600,000
Midsize	8,000	250	2,000,000
Flat-screen	3,000	400	1,200,000
	17,000		$3,800,000

During 2012, the company had the following purchases and sales.

Category	Quantity Purchased	Cost per Unit	Quantity Sold	Selling Price per Unit
Portable	15,000	$110	14,000	$150
Midsize	20,000	300	24,000	405
Flat-screen	10,000	500	6,000	600
	45,000		44,000	

Instructions

(Round to four decimals.)

(a) Compute ending inventory, cost of goods sold, and gross profit.

(b) Assume the company uses three inventory pools instead of one. Repeat instruction (a).

8 **P8-9 (Internal Indexes—Dollar-Value LIFO)** On January 1, 2012, Bonanza Wholesalers Inc. adopted the dollar-value LIFO inventory method for income tax and external financial reporting purposes. However, Bonanza continued to use the FIFO inventory method for internal accounting and management purposes. In applying the LIFO method, Bonanza uses internal conversion price indexes and the multiple pools approach under which substantially identical inventory items are grouped into LIFO inventory pools. The following data were available for inventory pool no. 1, which comprises products A and B, for the 2 years following the adoption of LIFO.

	FIFO Basis per Records		
	Units	Unit Cost	Total Cost
Inventory, 1/1/12			
Product A	10,000	$30	$300,000
Product B	9,000	25	225,000
			$525,000
Inventory, 12/31/12			
Product A	17,000	36	$612,000
Product B	9,000	26	234,000
			$846,000
Inventory, 12/31/13			
Product A	13,000	40	$520,000
Product B	10,000	32	320,000
			$840,000

Instructions

(a) Prepare a schedule to compute the internal conversion price indexes for 2012 and 2013. Round indexes to two decimal places.

(b) Prepare a schedule to compute the inventory amounts at December 31, 2012 and 2013, using the dollar-value LIFO inventory method.

(AICPA adapted)

8 **P8-10 (Internal Indexes—Dollar-Value LIFO)** Presented below is information related to Kaisson Corporation for the last 3 years.

Item	Quantities in Ending Inventories	Base-Year Cost		Current-Year Cost	
		Unit Cost	Amount	Unit Cost	Amount
December 31, 2011					
A	9,000	$2.00	$18,000	$2.20	$19,800
B	6,000	3.00	18,000	3.55	21,300
C	4,000	5.00	20,000	5.40	21,600
		Totals	$56,000		$62,700
December 31, 2012					
A	9,000	$2.00	$18,000	$2.60	$23,400
B	6,800	3.00	20,400	3.75	25,500
C	6,000	5.00	30,000	6.40	38,400
		Totals	$68,400		$87,300
December 31, 2013					
A	8,000	$2.00	$16,000	$2.70	$21,600
B	8,000	3.00	24,000	4.00	32,000
C	6,000	5.00	30,000	6.20	37,200
		Totals	$70,000		$90,800

Instructions

Compute the ending inventories under the dollar-value LIFO method for 2011, 2012, and 2013. The base period is January 1, 2011, and the beginning inventory cost at that date was $45,000. Compute indexes to two decimal places.

8  **P8-11 (Dollar-Value LIFO)** Richardson Company cans a variety of vegetable-type soups. Recently, the company decided to value its inventories using dollar-value LIFO pools. The clerk who accounts for inventories does not understand how to value the inventory pools using this new method, so, as a private consultant, you have been asked to teach him how this new method works.

He has provided you with the following information about purchases made over a 6-year period.

Date	Ending Inventory (End-of-Year Prices)	Price Index
Dec. 31, 2008	$ 80,000	100
Dec. 31, 2009	111,300	105
Dec. 31, 2010	108,000	120
Dec. 31, 2011	128,700	130
Dec. 31, 2012	147,000	140
Dec. 31, 2013	174,000	145

You have already explained to him how this inventory method is maintained, but he would feel better about it if you were to leave him detailed instructions explaining how these calculations are done and why he needs to put all inventories at a base-year value.

Instructions

(a) Compute the ending inventory for Richardson Company for 2008 through 2013 using dollar-value LIFO.

(b) Using your computation schedules as your illustration, write a step-by-step set of instructions explaining how the calculations are done. Begin your explanation by briefly explaining the theory behind this inventory method, including the purpose of putting all amounts into base-year price levels.

CONCEPTS FOR ANALYSIS

CA8-1 (Inventoriable Costs) You are asked to travel to Milwaukee to observe and verify the inventory of the Milwaukee branch of one of your clients. You arrive on Thursday, December 30, and find that the inventory procedures have just been started. You spot a railway car on the sidetrack at the unloading door and ask the warehouse superintendent, Buck Rogers, how he plans to inventory the contents of the car. He responds, "We are not going to include the contents in the inventory."

Later in the day, you ask the bookkeeper for the invoice on the carload and the related freight bill. The invoice lists the various items, prices, and extensions of the goods in the car. You note that the carload was shipped December 24 from Albuquerque, f.o.b. Albuquerque, and that the total invoice price of the goods in the car was $35,300. The freight bill called for a payment of $1,500. Terms were net 30 days. The bookkeeper affirms the fact that this invoice is to be held for recording in January.

Instructions

(a) Does your client have a liability that should be recorded at December 31? Discuss.

(b) Prepare a journal entry(ies), if required, to reflect any accounting adjustment required. Assume a perpetual inventory system is used by your client.

(c) For what possible reason(s) might your client wish to postpone recording the transaction?

CA8-2 (Inventoriable Costs) Frank Erlacher, an inventory control specialist, is interested in better understanding the accounting for inventories. Although Frank understands the more sophisticated computer inventory control systems, he has little knowledge of how inventory cost is determined. In studying the records of Strider Enterprises, which sells normal brand-name goods from its own store and on consignment through Chavez Inc., he asks you to answer the following questions.

Instructions

(a) Should Strider Enterprises include in its inventory normal brand-name goods purchased from its suppliers but not yet received if the terms of purchase are f.o.b. shipping point (manufacturer's plant)? Why?

(b) Should Strider Enterprises include freight-in expenditures as an inventory cost? Why?

(c) If Strider Enterprises purchases its goods on terms 2/10, net 30, should the purchases be recorded gross or net? Why?

(d) What are products on consignment? How should they be reported in the financial statements?

(AICPA adapted)

CA8-3 (Inventoriable Costs) George Solti, the controller for Garrison Lumber Company, has recently hired you as assistant controller. He wishes to determine your expertise in the area of inventory accounting and therefore asks you to answer the following unrelated questions.

(a) A company is involved in the wholesaling and retailing of automobile tires for foreign cars. Most of the inventory is imported, and it is valued on the company's records at the actual inventory cost plus freight-in. At year-end, the warehousing costs are prorated over cost of goods sold and ending inventory. Are warehousing costs considered a product cost or a period cost?

(b) A certain portion of a company's "inventory" is composed of obsolete items. Should obsolete items that are not currently consumed in the production of "goods or services to be available for sale" be classified as part of inventory?

(c) A company purchases airplanes for sale to others. However, until they are sold, the company charters and services the planes. What is the proper way to report these airplanes in the company's financial statements?

(d) A company wants to buy coal deposits but does not want the financing for the purchase to be reported on its financial statements. The company therefore establishes a trust to acquire the coal deposits. The company agrees to buy the coal over a certain period of time at specified prices. The trust is able to finance the coal purchase and pay off the loan as it is paid by the company for the minerals. How should this transaction be reported?

CA8-4 (Accounting Treatment of Purchase Discounts) Shawnee Corp., a household appliances dealer, purchases its inventories from various suppliers. Shawnee has consistently stated its inventories at the lower of cost (FIFO) or market.

Instructions

Shawnee is considering alternate methods of accounting for the cash discounts it takes when paying its suppliers promptly. From a theoretical standpoint, discuss the acceptability of each of the following methods.

(a) Financial income when payments are made.

(b) Reduction of cost of goods sold for the period when payments are made.

(c) Direct reduction of purchase cost.

(AICPA adapted)

CA8-5 (General Inventory Issues) In January 2012, Susquehanna Inc. requested and secured permission from the commissioner of the Internal Revenue Service to compute inventories under the last-in, first-out (LIFO) method and elected to determine inventory cost under the dollar-value LIFO method. Susquehanna Inc. satisfied the commissioner that cost could be accurately determined by use of an index number computed from a representative sample selected from the company's single inventory pool.

Instructions

(a) Why should inventories be included in (1) a balance sheet and (2) the computation of net income?

(b) The Internal Revenue Code allows some accountable events to be considered differently for income tax reporting purposes and financial accounting purposes, while other accountable events must be reported the same for both purposes. Discuss why it might be desirable to report some accountable events differently for financial accounting purposes than for income tax reporting purposes.

(c) Discuss the ways and conditions under which the FIFO and LIFO inventory costing methods produce different inventory valuations. Do not discuss procedures for computing inventory cost.

(AICPA adapted)

CA8-6 (LIFO Inventory Advantages) Jane Yoakam, president of Estefan Co., recently read an article that claimed that at least 100 of the country's largest 500 companies were either adopting or considering adopting the last-in, first-out (LIFO) method for valuing inventories. The article stated that the firms were switching to LIFO to (1) neutralize the effect of inflation in their financial statements, (2) eliminate inventory profits, and (3) reduce income taxes. Ms. Yoakam wonders if the switch would benefit her company.

Estefan currently uses the first-in, first-out (FIFO) method of inventory valuation in its periodic inventory system. The company has a high inventory turnover rate, and inventories represent a significant proportion of the assets.

Ms. Yoakam has been told that the LIFO system is more costly to operate and will provide little benefit to companies with high turnover. She intends to use the inventory method that is best for the company in the long run rather than selecting a method just because it is the current fad.

Instructions

(a) Explain to Ms. Yoakam what "inventory profits" are and how the LIFO method of inventory valuation could reduce them.

(b) Explain to Ms. Yoakam the conditions that must exist for Estefan Co. to receive tax benefits from a switch to the LIFO method.

CA8-7 (Average Cost, FIFO, and LIFO) Prepare a memorandum containing responses to the following items.

(a) Describe the cost flow assumptions used in average cost, FIFO, and LIFO methods of inventory valuation.

(b) Distinguish between weighted-average cost and moving-average cost for inventory costing purposes.

(c) Identify the effects on both the balance sheet and the income statement of using the LIFO method instead of the FIFO method for inventory costing purposes over a substantial time period when purchase prices of inventoriable items are rising. State why these effects take place.

CA8-8 (LIFO Application and Advantages) Geddes Corporation is a medium-sized manufacturing company with two divisions and three subsidiaries, all located in the United States. The Metallic Division manufactures metal castings for the automotive industry, and the Plastic Division produces small plastic items for electrical products and other uses. The three subsidiaries manufacture various products for other industrial users.

Geddes Corporation plans to change from the lower of first-in, first-out (FIFO) cost or market method of inventory valuation to the last-in, first-out (LIFO) method of inventory valuation to obtain tax benefits. To make the method acceptable for tax purposes, the change also will be made for its annual financial statements.

Instructions

(a) Describe the establishment of and subsequent pricing procedures for each of the following LIFO inventory methods.

(1) LIFO applied to units of product when the periodic inventory system is used.

(2) Application of the dollar-value method to LIFO units of product.

(b) Discuss the specific advantages and disadvantages of using the dollar-value LIFO application as compared to specific goods LIFO (unit LIFO). Ignore income tax considerations.

(c) Discuss the general advantages and disadvantages claimed for LIFO methods.

CA8-9 (Dollar-Value LIFO Issues) Arruza Co. is considering switching from the specific-goods LIFO approach to the dollar-value LIFO approach. Because the financial personnel at Arruza know very little about dollar-value LIFO, they ask you to answer the following questions.

(a) What is a LIFO pool?

(b) Is it possible to use a LIFO pool concept and not use dollar-value LIFO? Explain.

(c) What is a LIFO liquidation?

(d) How are price indexes used in the dollar-value LIFO method?

(e) What are the advantages of dollar-value LIFO over specific-goods LIFO?

CA8-10 (FIFO and LIFO) Harrisburg Company is considering changing its inventory valuation method from FIFO to LIFO because of the potential tax savings. However, the management wishes to consider all of the effects on the company, including its reported performance, before making the final decision.

The inventory account, currently valued on the FIFO basis, consists of 1,000,000 units at $8 per unit on January 1, 2012. There are 1,000,000 shares of common stock outstanding as of January 1, 2012, and the cash balance is $400,000.

The company has made the following forecasts for the period 2012–2014.

	2012	2013	2014
Unit sales (in millions of units)	1.1	1.0	1.3
Sales price per unit	$10	$12	$12
Unit purchases (in millions of units)	1.0	1.1	1.2
Purchase price per unit	$8	$9	$10
Annual depreciation (in thousands of dollars)	$300	$300	$300
Cash dividends per share	$0.15	$0.15	$0.15
Cash payments for additions to and replacement of plant and equipment (in thousands of dollars)	$350	$350	$350
Income tax rate	40%	40%	40%
Operating expenses (exclusive of depreciation) as a percent of sales	15%	15%	15%
Common shares outstanding (in millions)	1	1	1

Instructions

(a) Prepare a schedule that illustrates and compares the following data for Harrisburg Company under the FIFO and the LIFO inventory method for 2012–2014. Assume the company would begin LIFO at the beginning of 2012.

(1) Year-end inventory balances.
(2) Annual net income after taxes.
(3) Earnings per share.
(4) Cash balance.

Assume all sales are collected in the year of sale and all purchases, operating expenses, and taxes are paid during the year incurred.

(b) Using the data above, your answer to (a), and any additional issues you believe need to be considered, prepare a report that recommends whether or not Harrisburg Company should change to the LIFO inventory method. Support your conclusions with appropriate arguments.

(CMA adapted)

CA8-11 (LIFO Choices) Wilkens Company uses the LIFO method for inventory costing. In an effort to lower net income, company president Lenny Wilkens tells the plant accountant to take the unusual step of recommending to the purchasing department a large purchase of inventory at year-end. The price of the item to be purchased has nearly doubled during the year, and the item represents a major portion of inventory value.

Instructions

Answer the following questions.

(a) Identify the major stakeholders. If the plant accountant recommends the purchase, what are the consequences?

(b) If Wilkens Company were using the FIFO method of inventory costing, would Lenny Wilkens give the same order? Why or why not?

USING YOUR JUDGMENT

FINANCIAL REPORTING

Financial Statement Analysis Cases

Case 1 T J International

T J International was founded in 1969 as Trus Joist International. The firm, a manufacturer of specialty building products, has its headquarters in Boise, Idaho. The company, through its partnership in the Trus Joist MacMillan joint venture, develops and manufactures engineered lumber. This product is a high- quality substitute for structural lumber, and uses lower-grade wood and materials formerly considered waste. The company also is majority owner of the Outlook Window Partnership, which is a consortium of three wood and vinyl window manufacturers.

Following is T J International's adapted income statement and information concerning inventories from its annual report.

T J International

Sales	$618,876,000
Cost of goods sold	475,476,000
Gross profit	143,400,000
Selling and administrative expenses	102,112,000
Income from operations	41,288,000
Other expense	24,712,000
Income before income tax	16,576,000
Income taxes	7,728,000
Net income	$ 8,848,000

Inventories. Inventories are valued at the lower of cost or market and include material, labor, and production overhead costs. Inventories consisted of the following:

	Current Year	Prior Year
Finished goods	$27,512,000	$23,830,000
Raw materials and work-in-progress	34,363,000	33,244,000
	61,875,000	57,074,000
Reduction to LIFO cost	(5,263,000)	(3,993,000)
	$56,612,000	$53,081,000

The last-in, first-out (LIFO) method is used for determining the cost of lumber, veneer, Microllam lumber, TJI joists, and open web joists. Approximately 35 percent of total inventories at the end of the current year were valued using the LIFO method. The first-in, first-out (FIFO) method is used to determine the cost of all other inventories.

Instructions

(a) How much would income before taxes have been if FIFO costing had been used to value all inventories?

(b) If the income tax rate is 46.6%, what would income tax have been if FIFO costing had been used to value all inventories? In your opinion, is this difference in net income between the two methods material? Explain.

(c) Does the use of a different costing system for different types of inventory mean that there is a different physical flow of goods among the different types of inventory? Explain.

Case 2 Noven Pharmaceuticals, Inc.

Noven Pharmaceuticals, Inc., headquartered in Miami, Florida, describes itself in a recent annual report as follows.

Noven Pharmaceuticals, Inc.

Noven is a place of ideas—a company where scientific excellence and state-of-the-art manufacturing combine to create new answers to human needs. Our transdermal delivery systems speed drugs painlessly and effortlessly into the bloodstream by means of a simple skin patch. This technology has proven applications in estrogen replacement, but at Noven we are developing a variety of systems incorporating bestselling drugs that fight everything from asthma, anxiety and dental pain to cancer, heart disease and neurological illness. Our research portfolio also includes new technologies, such as iontophoresis, in which drugs are delivered through the skin by means of electrical currents, as well as products that could satisfy broad consumer needs, such as our anti-microbial mouthrinse.

Noven also reported in its annual report that its activities to date have consisted of product development efforts, some of which have been independent and some of which have been completed in conjunction with **Rhone-Poulenc Rorer (RPR)** and **Ciba-Geigy**. The revenues so far have consisted of money received from licensing fees, "milestone" payments (payments made under licensing agreements when certain stages of the development of a certain product have been completed), and interest on its investments. The company expects that it will have significant revenue in the upcoming fiscal year from the launch of its first product, a transdermal estrogen delivery system.

The current assets portion of Noven's balance sheet follows.

Cash and cash equivalents	$12,070,272
Securities held to maturity	23,445,070
Inventory of supplies	1,264,553
Prepaid and other current assets	825,159
Total current assets	$37,605,054

Inventory of supplies is recorded at the lower of cost (first-in, first-out) or net realizable value and consists mainly of supplies for research and development.

Instructions

(a) What would you expect the physical flow of goods for a pharmaceutical manufacturer to be most like: FIFO, LIFO, or random (flow of goods does not follow a set pattern)? Explain.

(b) What are some of the factors that Noven should consider as it selects an inventory measurement method?

(c) Suppose that Noven had $49,000 in an inventory of transdermal estrogen delivery patches. These patches are from an initial production run, and will be sold during the coming year. Why do you think that this amount is not shown in a separate inventory account? In which of the accounts shown is the inventory likely to be? At what point will the inventory be transferred to a separate inventory account?

Case 3 SUPERVALU

SUPERVALU reported the following data in its annual report.

	Feb. 23, 2008	Feb. 28, 2009	Feb. 27, 2010
Total revenues	$44,048	$44,564	$40,597
Cost of sales (using LIFO)	33,943	34,451	31,444
Year-end inventories using FIFO	2,956	2,967	2,606
Year-end inventories using LIFO	2,776	2,709	2,342

(a) Compute SUPERVALU's inventory turnover ratios for 2009 and 2010, using:

(1) Cost of sales and LIFO inventory.

(2) Cost of sales and FIFO inventory.

(b) Some firms calculate inventory turnover using sales rather than cost of goods sold in the numerator. Calculate SUPERVALU's 2009 and 2010 turnover, using:

(1) Sales and LIFO inventory.

(2) Sales and FIFO inventory.

(c) Describe the method that SUPERVALU's appears to use.

(d) State which method you would choose to evaluate SUPERVALU's performance. Justify your choice.

Accounting, Analysis, and Principles

Englehart Company sells two types of pumps. One is large and is for commercial use. The other is smaller and is used in residential swimming pools. The following inventory data is available for the month of March.

	Units	Price per Unit	Total
Residential Pumps			
Inventory at Feb. 28:	200	$ 400	$ 80,000
Purchases:			
March 10	500	$ 450	$225,000
March 20	400	$ 475	$190,000
March 30	300	$ 500	$150,000
Sales:			
March 15	500	$ 540	$270,000
March 25	400	$ 570	$228,000
Inventory at March 31:	500		
Commercial Pumps			
Inventory at Feb. 28:	600	$ 800	$480,000
Purchases:			
March 3	600	$ 900	$540,000
March 12	300	$ 950	$285,000
March 21	500	$1,000	$500,000
Sales:			
March 18	900	$1,080	$972,000
March 29	600	$1,140	$684,000
Inventory at March 31:	500		

Accounting

(a) Assuming Englehart uses a periodic inventory system, determine the cost of inventory on hand at March 31 and the cost of goods sold for March under first-in, first-out (FIFO).

(b) Assume Englehart uses dollar-value LIFO and one pool, consisting of the combination of residential and commercial pumps. Determine the cost of inventory on hand at March 31 and the cost of goods sold for March. Assume Englehart's initial adoption of LIFO is on March 1. Use the double-extension method to determine the appropriate price indices. (*Hint:* The price index for February 28/March 1 should be 1.00.) (Round the index to three decimal places.)

Analysis

(a) Assume you need to compute a current ratio for Englehart. Which inventory method (FIFO or dollar-value LIFO) do you think would give you a more meaningful current ratio?

(b) Some of Englehart's competitors use LIFO inventory costing and some use FIFO. How can an analyst compare the results of companies in an industry, when some use LIFO and others use FIFO?

Principles

Can companies change from one inventory accounting method to another? If a company changes to an inventory accounting method used by most of its competitors, what are the trade-offs in terms of the conceptual framework discussed in Chapter 2 of the text?

BRIDGE TO THE PROFESSION

Professional Research: FASB Codification

In conducting year-end inventory counts, your audit team is debating the impact of the client's right of return policy both on inventory valuation and revenue recognition. The assistant controller argues that there is no need to worry about the return policies since they have not changed in a while. The audit senior wants a more authoritative answer and has asked you to conduct some research of the authoritative literature, before she presses the point with the client.

Instructions

If your school has a subscription to the FASB Codification, go to *http://aaahq.org/asclogin.cfm* to log in and prepare responses to the following. Provide Codification references for your responses.

(a) What is the authoritative guidance for revenue recognition when right of return exists?

(b) When is this guidance important for a company?

(c) Sales with high rates of return can ultimately cause inventory to be misstated. Why are returns allowed? Should different industries be able to make different types of return policies?

(d) In what situations would a reasonable estimate of returns be difficult to make?

Professional Simulation

In this simulation, you are asked to address questions regarding inventory valuation and measurement. Prepare responses to all parts.

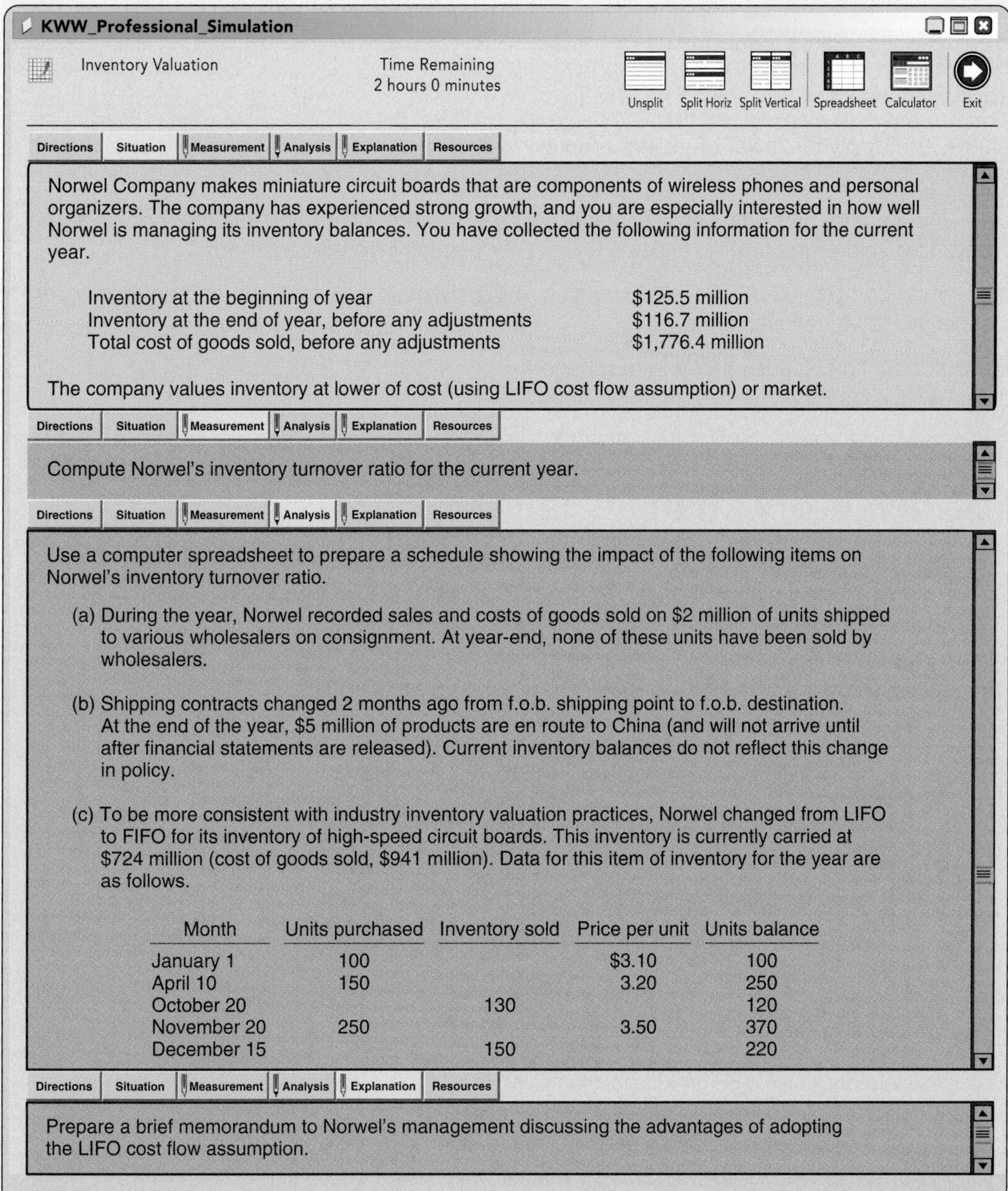

Norwel Company makes miniature circuit boards that are components of wireless phones and personal organizers. The company has experienced strong growth, and you are especially interested in how well Norwel is managing its inventory balances. You have collected the following information for the current year.

Inventory at the beginning of year	$125.5 million
Inventory at the end of year, before any adjustments	$116.7 million
Total cost of goods sold, before any adjustments	$1,776.4 million

The company values inventory at lower of cost (using LIFO cost flow assumption) or market.

Compute Norwel's inventory turnover ratio for the current year.

Use a computer spreadsheet to prepare a schedule showing the impact of the following items on Norwel's inventory turnover ratio.

(a) During the year, Norwel recorded sales and costs of goods sold on $2 million of units shipped to various wholesalers on consignment. At year-end, none of these units have been sold by wholesalers.

(b) Shipping contracts changed 2 months ago from f.o.b. shipping point to f.o.b. destination. At the end of the year, $5 million of products are en route to China (and will not arrive until after financial statements are released). Current inventory balances do not reflect this change in policy.

(c) To be more consistent with industry inventory valuation practices, Norwel changed from LIFO to FIFO for its inventory of high-speed circuit boards. This inventory is currently carried at $724 million (cost of goods sold, $941 million). Data for this item of inventory for the year are as follows.

Month	Units purchased	Inventory sold	Price per unit	Units balance
January 1	100		$3.10	100
April 10	150		3.20	250
October 20		130		120
November 20	250		3.50	370
December 15		150		220

Prepare a brief memorandum to Norwel's management discussing the advantages of adopting the LIFO cost flow assumption.

Remember to check the book's companion website to find additional resources for this chapter.

CHAPTER 9

Inventories: Additional Valuation Issues

LEARNING OBJECTIVES

After studying this chapter, you should be able to:

1. Describe and apply the lower-of-cost-or-market rule.
2. Explain when companies value inventories at net realizable value.
3. Explain when companies use the relative sales value method to value inventories.
4. Discuss accounting issues related to purchase commitments.
5. Determine ending inventory by applying the gross profit method.
6. Determine ending inventory by applying the retail inventory method.
7. Explain how to report and analyze inventory.

What Do Inventory Changes Tell Us?

Department stores face an ongoing challenge: They need to keep enough inventory to meet customer demand, but not to accumulate too much inventory. If demand falls short of expectations, the department store may be forced to reduce prices on its existing inventory, thus losing sales revenue.

For example, the following table shows annual sales and inventory trends for major retailers, compared to the prior year.

Company	Sales	Inventory
Nordstrom	+10.59%	+ 1.73%
Federated Department Stores	+ 2.40%	− 2.95%
JCPenney	+ 3.59%	+ 0.41%
Wal-Mart	+11.63%	+ 9.06%
May Department Stores	+ 8.23%	+13.34%
Target	+11.62%	+18.83%
Best Buy	+17.21%	+25.52%
Sears	−12.22%	+ 4.01%

Source: Company reports.

For over half of these retailers, inventories grew faster than sales from one year to the next—a trend that should raise warning flags for investors. Rising levels of inventories indicate that fewer shoppers are turning out to buy merchandise compared to activity in the prior period. As one analyst remarked, ". . . when inventory grows faster than sales, profits drop." That is, when retailers face slower sales and growing inventory, markdowns in prices are usually not far behind. These markdowns, in turn, lead to lower sales revenue, gross profit, and income.

Bankruptcies of retailers like **Ames Department Stores**, **Montgomery Ward**, and **Circuit City** indicate the consequences of poor inventory management. And more recently, **Kmart**, which filed for bankruptcy and is now part of **Sears Holdings**, was in an inventory "Catch-22." In order to work out

IFRS IN THIS CHAPTER

See the **International Perspectives** on pages 494, 495, and 502.

Read the **IFRS Insights** on pages 545–553 for a discussion of:

—Lower-of-cost-or-net realizable value (LCNRV)

—Agricultural inventory

of bankruptcy, Kmart needed to keep its shelves stocked so that customers would continue to shop in its remaining stores. However, vendors who were worried about Kmart's ability to manage its inventory were reluctant to ship goods without assurances that they would get paid.

Recently, with the economy showing signs of recovery, the reverse dynamic of inventory management has set in. That is, retailers from **Tiffany** to **Home Depot** are starting to restock their shelves. This restocking process has already had a positive impact on the economy's bottom line, with almost two-thirds of the 5.6 percent annual growth in gross domestic product in 2009 being attributed to growth in inventories. Of course, there is a danger to this inventory building. If sales do not increase as much as companies expect, we will be in a discounting and reduced gross profit cycle again. Thus, the inventory balancing act is a never-ending challenge, and investors, creditors, and vendors must keep an eye on information about inventories in the retail industry.

Source: R. Miller and A. Feld, "Key to Recovery: Restocking All Those Shelves," *Bloomberg BusinessWeek* (April 25, 2010), p. 16.

PREVIEW OF CHAPTER 9

As our opening story indicates, information on inventories and changes in inventory helps to predict financial performance—in particular, profits. In this chapter we discuss some of the valuation and estimation concepts that companies use to develop relevant inventory information. The content and organization of the chapter are as follows.

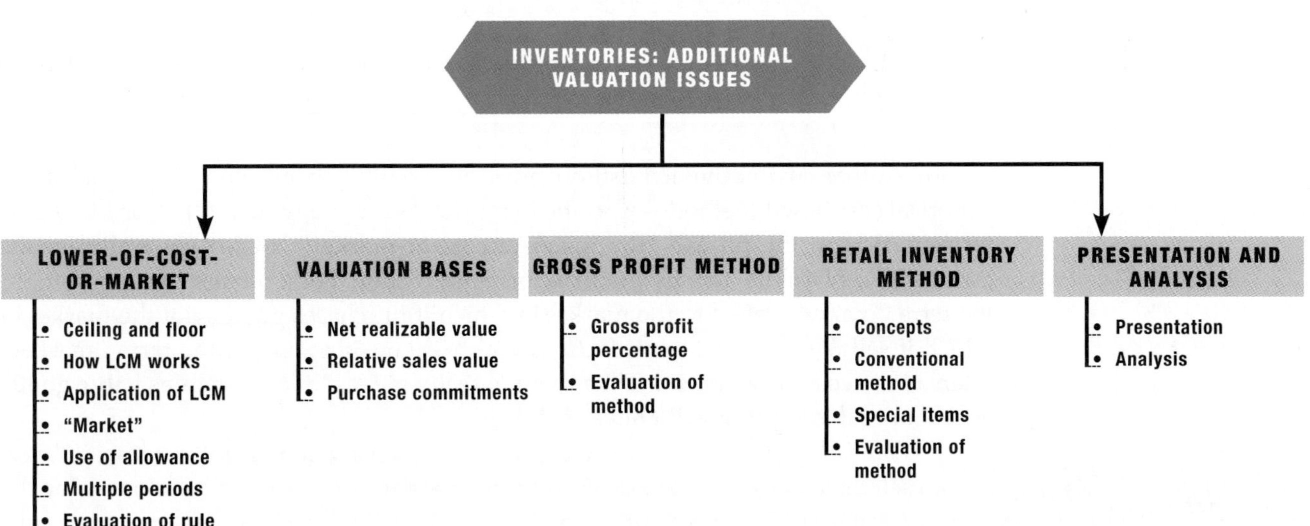

LOWER-OF-COST-OR-MARKET

LEARNING OBJECTIVE 1
Describe and apply the lower-of-cost-or-market rule.

Inventories are recorded at their cost. However, if inventory declines in value below its original cost, a major departure from the historical cost principle occurs. Whatever the reason for a decline—obsolescence, price-level changes, or damaged goods—a company should write down the inventory to market to report this loss. **A company abandons the historical cost principle when the future utility (revenue-producing ability) of the asset drops below its original cost.** Companies therefore **report inventories at the lower-of-cost-or-market** at each reporting period.

Illustration 9-1 shows how **Eastman Kodak** and **Best Buy** reported this information.

ILLUSTRATION 9-1
Lower-of-Cost-or-Market Disclosures

Eastman Kodak
(in millions) As of December 31, 2009

Current Assets	
Inventories, net	$679

Accounting policies (in part)

Inventories

Inventories are stated at the lower of cost or market. The cost of all of the Company's inventories is determined by either the "first in, first out" ("FIFO") or average cost method, which approximates current cost. The Company provides inventory reserves for excess, obsolete or slow-moving inventory based on changes in customer demand, technology developments or other economic factors.

Best Buy
(in millions) February 27, 2010

Current Assets	
Merchandise inventories	$5,486

Summary of Significant Accounting Policies (in part)
Merchandise inventories are recorded at the lower of cost using either the average cost or first-in first-out method, or market.

Recall that **cost** is the acquisition price of inventory computed using one of the historical cost-based methods—specific identification, average cost, FIFO, or LIFO. The term **market** in the phrase "the lower-of-cost-or-market" (LCM) generally means the cost to replace the item by purchase or reproduction. For a retailer like **Nordstrom**, the term "market" refers to the market in which it purchases goods, not the market in which it sells them. For a manufacturer like **William Wrigley Jr.**, the term "market" refers to the cost to reproduce. Thus the rule really means that **companies value goods at cost or cost to replace, whichever is lower.**

INTERNATIONAL PERSPECTIVE

IFRS defines *market* as net realizable value; GAAP defines *market* as replacement cost subject to certain constraints.

For example, say **Target** purchased a **Timex** wristwatch for $30 for resale. Target can sell the wristwatch for $48.95 and replace it for $25. It should therefore value the wristwatch at $25 for inventory purposes under the lower-of-cost-or-market rule. Target can use the lower-of-cost-or-market rule of valuation after applying any of the cost flow methods discussed above to determine the inventory cost.

A departure from cost is justified because **a company should charge a loss of utility against revenues in the period in which the loss occurs**, not in the period of sale. Note also that the lower-of-cost-or-market method is **a conservative approach to inventory valuation**. That is, when doubt exists about the value of an asset, a company should use the lower value for the asset, which also reduces net income.

Ceiling and Floor

Why use replacement cost to represent market value? Because a decline in the replacement cost of an item usually reflects or predicts a decline in selling price. Using replacement cost allows a company to maintain a consistent rate of gross profit on sales (normal profit margin). Sometimes, however, a reduction in the replacement cost of an item fails to indicate a corresponding reduction in its utility. This requires using two additional valuation limitations to value ending inventory—net realizable value and net realizable value less a normal profit margin.

Net realizable value (NRV) is the estimated selling price in the ordinary course of business, less reasonably predictable costs of completion and disposal (often referred to as net selling price). A normal profit margin is subtracted from that amount to arrive at net realizable value less a normal profit margin.

To illustrate, assume that Jerry Mander Corp. has unfinished inventory with a sales value of $1,000, estimated cost of completion and disposal of $300, and a normal profit margin of 10 percent of sales. Jerry Mander determines the following net realizable value.

ILLUSTRATION 9-2
Computation of Net Realizable Value

Inventory—sales value	$1,000
Less: Estimated cost of completion and disposal	300
Net realizable value	700
Less: Allowance for normal profit margin (10% of sales)	100
Net realizable value less a normal profit margin	$ 600

The general lower-of-cost-or-market rule is: A company values inventory at the lower-of-cost-or-market, with market limited to an amount that is not more than net realizable value or less than net realizable value less a normal profit margin. [1]

See the FASB Codification section (page 523).

The upper (ceiling) is the net realizable value of inventory. The lower (floor) is the the net realizable value less a normal profit margin. What is the rationale for these two limitations? Establishing these limits for the value of the inventory prevents companies from over- or understating inventory.

The maximum limitation, **not to exceed the net realizable value (ceiling)**, prevents overstatement of the value of obsolete, damaged, or shopworn inventories. That is, if the replacement cost of an item exceeds its net realizable value, a company should not report inventory at replacement cost. The company can receive only the selling price less cost of disposal. To report the inventory at replacement cost would result in an overstatement of inventory and understatement of the loss in the current period.

To illustrate, assume that Staples paid $1,000 for a color laser printer that it can now replace for $900. The printer's net realizable value is $700. At what amount should Staples report the laser printer in its financial statements? To report the replacement cost of $900 overstates the ending inventory and understates the loss for the period. Therefore, Staples should report the printer at $700.

The minimum limitation (floor) is **not to be less than net realizable value reduced by an allowance for an approximately normal profit margin.** The floor establishes a value below which a company should not price inventory, regardless of replacement cost. It makes no sense to price inventory below net realizable value less a normal margin. This minimum amount (floor) measures what the company can receive for the inventory and still earn a normal profit. Use of a floor deters understatement of inventory and overstatement of the loss in the current period.

INTERNATIONAL PERSPECTIVE

IFRS does not use a ceiling or floor to determine market.

Illustration 9-3 (on page 496) graphically presents the guidelines for valuing inventory at the lower-of-cost-or-market.

ILLUSTRATION 9-3
Inventory Valuation—
Lower-of-Cost-or-Market

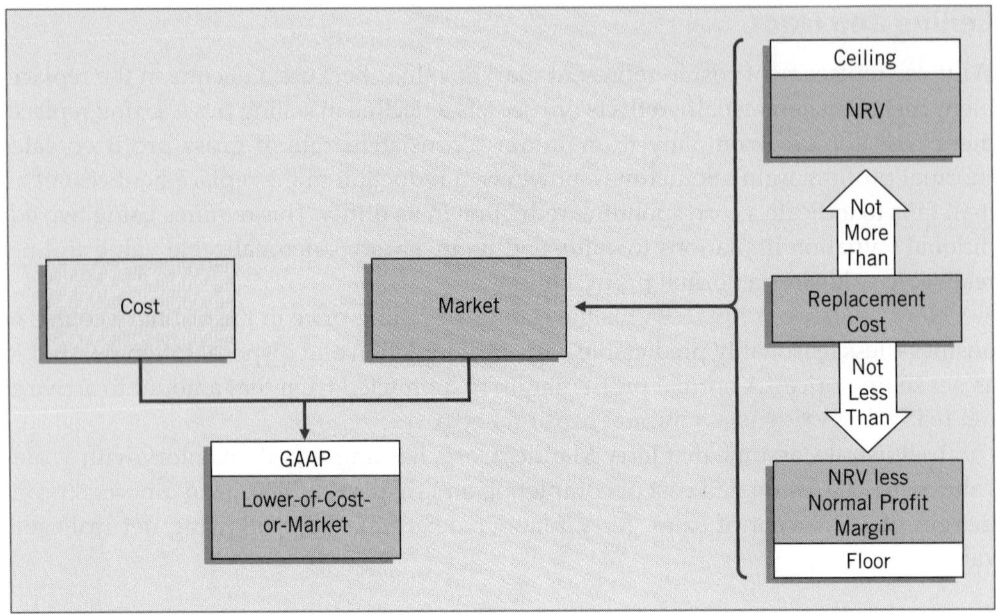

How Lower-of-Cost-or-Market Works

The **designated market value** is the amount that a company compares to cost. It is **always the middle value of three amounts**: replacement cost, net realizable value, and net realizable value less a normal profit margin. To illustrate how to compute designated market value, assume the information relative to the inventory of Regner Foods, Inc., as shown in Illustration 9-4.

ILLUSTRATION 9-4
Computation of
Designated Market Value

Food	Replacement Cost	Net Realizable Value (Ceiling)	Net Realizable Value Less a Normal Profit Margin (Floor)	Designated Market Value
Spinach	$ 88,000	$120,000	$104,000	$104,000
Carrots	90,000	100,000	70,000	90,000
Cut beans	45,000	40,000	27,500	40,000
Peas	36,000	72,000	48,000	48,000
Mixed vegetables	105,000	92,000	80,000	92,000

Designated Market Value Decision:

Spinach	Net realizable value less a normal profit margin is selected because it is the middle value.
Carrots	Replacement cost is selected because it is the middle value.
Cut beans	Net realizable value is selected because it is the middle value.
Peas	Net realizable value less a normal profit margin is selected because it is the middle value.
Mixed vegetables	Net realizable value is selected because it is the middle value.

Regner Foods then compares designated market value to cost to determine the lower-of-cost-or-market. It determines the final inventory value as shown in Illustration 9-5.

The application of the lower-of-cost-or-market rule incorporates only losses in value that occur in the normal course of business from such causes as style changes, shift in demand, or regular shop wear. A company reduces damaged or deteriorated goods to net realizable value. When material, it may carry such goods in separate inventory accounts.

ILLUSTRATION 9-5
Determining Final Inventory Value

Food	Cost	Replacement Cost	Net Realizable Value (Ceiling)	Net Realizable Value Less a Normal Profit Margin (Floor)	Designated Market Value	Final Inventory Value
Spinach	$ 80,000	$ 88,000	$120,000	$104,000	$104,000	$ 80,000
Carrots	100,000	90,000	100,000	70,000	90,000	90,000
Cut beans	50,000	45,000	40,000	27,500	40,000	40,000
Peas	90,000	36,000	72,000	48,000	48,000	48,000
Mixed vegetables	95,000	105,000	92,000	80,000	92,000	92,000
						$350,000

Final Inventory Value:

Spinach	Cost ($80,000) is selected because it is lower than designated market value (net realizable value less a normal profit margin).
Carrots	Designated market value (replacement cost, $90,000) is selected because it is lower than cost.
Cut beans	Designated market value (net realizable value, $40,000) is selected because it is lower than cost.
Peas	Designated market value (net realizable value less a normal profit margin, $48,000) is selected because it is lower than cost.
Mixed vegetables	Designated market value (net realizable value, $92,000) is selected because it is lower than cost.

Methods of Applying Lower-of-Cost-or-Market

In the Regner Foods illustration, we assumed that the company applied the lower-of-cost-or-market rule to each individual type of food. However, companies may apply the lower-of-cost-or-market rule either directly to each item, to each category, or to the total of the inventory. If a company follows a major category or total inventory approach in applying the lower-of-cost-or-market rule, increases in market prices tend to offset decreases in market prices. To illustrate, assume that Regner Foods separates its food products into two major categories, frozen and canned, as shown in Illustration 9-6.

ILLUSTRATION 9-6
Alternative Applications of Lower-of-Cost-or-Market

	Cost	Designated Market	Lower-of-Cost-or-Market by: Individual Items	Major Categories	Total Inventory
Frozen					
Spinach	$ 80,000	$104,000	$ 80,000		
Carrots	100,000	90,000	90,000		
Cut beans	50,000	40,000	40,000		
Total frozen	230,000	234,000		$230,000	
Canned					
Peas	90,000	48,000	48,000		
Mixed vegetables	95,000	92,000	92,000		
Total canned	185,000	140,000		140,000	
Total	$415,000	$374,000	$350,000	$370,000	$374,000

If Regner Foods applied the lower-of-cost-or-market rule to individual items, the amount of inventory is $350,000. If applying the rule to major categories, it jumps to $370,000. If applying LCM to the total inventory, it totals $374,000. Why this difference? When a company uses a major categories or total inventory approach, market values higher than cost offset market values lower than cost. For Regner Foods, using the major categories approach partially offsets the high market value for spinach. Using the total inventory approach totally offsets it.

Companies usually price inventory on an item-by-item basis. In fact, tax rules require that companies use an individual-item basis barring practical difficulties. In addition, the individual-item approach gives the most conservative valuation for balance sheet purposes.[1] Often, a company prices inventory on a total-inventory basis when it offers only one end product (comprised of many different raw materials). If it produces several end products, a company might use a category approach instead. The method selected should be the one that most clearly reflects income. **Whichever method a company selects, it should apply the method consistently from one period to another.**[2]

Recording "Market" Instead of Cost

One of two methods may be used to record the income effect of valuing inventory at market. One method, referred to as the **cost-of-goods-sold method**, debits cost of goods sold for the write-down of the inventory to market. As a result, the company does not report a loss in the income statement because the cost of goods sold already includes the amount of the loss. The second method, referred to as the **loss method**, debits a loss account for the write-down of the inventory to market. We use the following inventory data for Ricardo Company to illustrate entries under both methods.

Cost of goods sold (before adjustment to market)	$108,000
Ending inventory (cost)	82,000
Ending inventory (at market)	70,000

Illustration 9-7 shows the entries for both the cost-of-goods-sold and loss methods, assuming the use of a perpetual inventory system.

ILLUSTRATION 9-7
Accounting for the Reduction of Inventory to Market—Perpetual Inventory System

Cost-of-Goods-Sold Method			Loss Method		
To reduce inventory from cost to market					
Cost of Goods Sold	12,000		Loss Due to Decline of Inventory to Market	12,000	
Inventory		12,000	Inventory		12,000

The cost-of-goods-sold method buries the loss in the Cost of Goods Sold account. The loss method, by identifying the loss due to the write-down, shows the loss separate from Cost of Goods Sold in the income statement.

Illustration 9-8 contrasts the differing amounts reported in the income statement under the two approaches, using data from the Ricardo example.

[1]If a company uses dollar-value LIFO, determining the LIFO cost of an individual item may be more difficult. The company might decide that it is more appropriate to apply the lower-of-cost-or-market rule to the total amount of each pool. The AICPA Task Force on LIFO Inventory Problems concluded that the most reasonable approach to applying the lower-of-cost-or-market provisions to LIFO inventories is to base the determination on reasonable groupings of items. A pool constitutes a reasonable grouping.

[2]Inventory accounting for financial statement purposes can be different from income tax purposes. For example, companies cannot use the lower-of-cost-or-market rule with LIFO for tax purposes. However, companies may use the lower-of-cost-or-market and LIFO for financial accounting purposes.

Cost-of-Goods-Sold Method	
Sales revenue	$200,000
Cost of goods sold (after adjustment to market*)	120,000
Gross profit on sales	$ 80,000
Loss Method	
Sales revenue	$200,000
Cost of goods sold	108,000
Gross profit on sales	92,000
Loss due to decline of inventory to market	12,000
	$ 80,000
*Cost of goods sold (before adjustment to market)	$108,000
Difference between inventory at cost and market ($82,000 − $70,000)	12,000
Cost of goods sold (after adjustment to market)	$120,000

ILLUSTRATION 9-8
Income Statement Presentation—Cost-of-Goods-Sold and Loss Methods of Reducing Inventory to Market

GAAP does not specify a particular account to debit for the write-down. We believe the loss method presentation is preferable because it clearly discloses the loss resulting from a decline in inventory to market.

Underlying Concepts

The income statement under the cost-of-goods-sold method presentation lacks *representational faithfulness*. The cost-of-goods-sold method does not represent what it purports to represent. However, allowing this presentation illustrates the concept of materiality.

Use of an Allowance

Instead of crediting the Inventory account for market adjustments, companies generally use an allowance account, often referred to as the "Allowance to Reduce Inventory to Market." For example, using an allowance account under the loss method, Ricardo Company makes the following entry to record the inventory write-down to market.

Loss Due to Decline of Inventory to Market	12,000	
Allowance to Reduce Inventory to Market		12,000

Use of the allowance account results in reporting both the cost and the market of the inventory. Ricardo reports inventory in the balance sheet as follows.

Inventory (at cost)	$ 82,000
Allowance to reduce inventory to market	(12,000)
Inventory at market	$ 70,000

ILLUSTRATION 9-9
Presentation of Inventory Using an Allowance Account

The use of the allowance under the cost-of-goods-sold or loss method permits both the income statement and the balance sheet to reflect inventory measured at $82,000, although the balance sheet shows a net amount of $70,000. It also keeps subsidiary inventory ledgers and records in correspondence with the control account without changing prices. *For homework purposes, use an allowance account to record market adjustments, unless instructed otherwise.*

With respect to accounting for the allowance in the subsequent period, if the company still has on hand the merchandise in question, it should retain the allowance account. If it does not keep that account, the company will overstate beginning inventory and cost of goods. However, **if the company has sold the goods**, then it should close the account. It then establishes a "new allowance account" for any decline in inventory value that takes place in the current year.[3]

[3]The AICPA Task Force on LIFO Inventory Problems concluded that for LIFO inventories, companies should close the allowance from the prior year and should base the allowance at the end of the year on a new lower-of-cost-or-market computation. **[2]**

Use of an Allowance—Multiple Periods

Underlying Concepts

The inconsistency in the presentation of inventory is an example of the trade-off between *relevancy and reliability*. Market is more relevant than cost, and cost is more reliable than market. Apparently, relevance takes precedence in a down market, and reliability is more important in an up market.

In general, accountants leave the allowance account on the books. They merely adjust the balance at the next year-end to agree with the discrepancy between cost and the lower-of-cost-or-market at that balance sheet date. Thus, if prices are falling, the company records an additional write-down. If prices are rising, the company records an increase in income, as shown in Illustration 9-10.

We can think of the net increase in income as the excess of the credit effect of closing the beginning allowance balance over the debit effect of setting up the current year-end allowance account. Recognizing the increases and decreases has the same effect on net income as closing the allowance balance to beginning inventory or to cost of goods sold.

ILLUSTRATION 9-10
Effect on Net Income of Reducing Inventory to Market

Date	Inventory at Cost	Inventory at Market	Amount Required in Valuation Account	Adjustment of Valuation Account Balance	Effect on Net Income
Dec. 31, 2011	$188,000	$176,000	$12,000	$12,000 inc.	Decrease
Dec. 31, 2012	194,000	187,000	7,000	5,000 dec.	Increase
Dec. 31, 2013	173,000	174,000	0	7,000 dec.	Increase
Dec. 31, 2014	182,000	180,000	2,000	2,000 inc.	Decrease

"PUT IT IN REVERSE"

What do the numbers mean?

The lower-of-cost-or-market rule is designed to provide timely information about the decline in the value of inventory. When the value of inventory declines, income takes a hit in the period of the write-down.

What happens in the periods after the write-down? For some companies, gross margins and bottom lines get a boost when they sell inventory that had been written down in a previous period. For example, as the following table shows, **Vishay Intertechnology**, **Transwitch**, and **Cisco Systems** reported gains from selling inventory that had previously been written down. The table also evaluates how clearly these companies disclosed the effects of the reversal of inventory write-downs.

Company	Gain from reversal	Disclosure
Vishay Intertechnology	Not available	Poor—The semiconductor company did not mention the gain in its earnings announcement. Two weeks later in an SEC filing, Vishay disclosed the gain on the inventory that it had written down.
Transwitch	$600,000	Poor—The company did not mention the gain in its earnings announcement. Three weeks later in an SEC filing, the company disclosed the gain on the inventory that it had written down.
Cisco Systems	$525 million	Good—The networking giant detailed in its earnings release and in SEC filings the gains from selling inventory it had previously written off.

For Transwitch, the reversal of fortunes amounted to 23 percent of net income. The problem is that the $600,000 credit had little to do with the company's ongoing operations, and the company did not do a good job disclosing the effect of the reversal on current-year profitability.

Even when companies do disclose a reversal, it is sometimes hard to determine the impact on income. For example, **Intel** disclosed that it had sold inventory that had been written down in prior periods but did not specify how much reserved inventory was sold.

After the recent accounting scandals, transparency of financial reporting has become a top priority. With better disclosure of the reversals that boost profits in the current period, financial transparency would also get a boost.

Source: S. E. Ante, "The Secret Behind Those Profit Jumps," *BusinessWeek Online* (December 8, 2003).

Evaluation of the Lower-of-Cost-or-Market Rule

The lower-of-cost-or-market rule suffers some conceptual deficiencies:

1. A company recognizes decreases in the value of the asset and the charge to expense in the period in which the loss in utility occurs—not in the period of sale. On the other hand, it recognizes increases in the value of the asset only at the point of sale. This inconsistent treatment can distort income data.
2. Application of the rule results in inconsistency because a company may value the inventory at cost in one year and at market in the next year.
3. Lower-of-cost-or-market values the inventory in the balance sheet conservatively, but its effect on the income statement may or may not be conservative. Net income for the year in which a company takes the loss is definitely lower. Net income of the subsequent period may be higher than normal if the expected reductions in sales price do not materialize.
4. Application of the lower-of-cost-or-market rule uses a "normal profit" in determining inventory values. Since companies estimate "normal profit" based on past experience (which they may not attain in the future), this subjective measure presents an opportunity for income manipulation.

Many financial statement users appreciate the lower-of-cost-or-market rule because they at least know that it prevents overstatement of inventory. In addition, recognizing all losses but anticipating no gains generally results in lower income.

VALUATION BASES

Valuation at Net Realizable Value

2 LEARNING OBJECTIVE
Explain when companies value inventories at net realizable value.

For the most part, companies record inventory at cost or at the lower-of-cost-or-market.[4] However, many believe that for purposes of applying the lower-of-cost-or-market rule, companies should define "market" as **net realizable value** (selling price less estimated costs to complete and sell), rather than as replacement cost. This argument is based on the fact that the amount that companies will collect from this inventory in the future is the net realizable value.[5]

Under limited circumstances, support exists for **recording inventory at net realizable value**, even if that amount is above cost. GAAP permits this exception to the normal recognition rule under the following conditions: (1) when there is a controlled

[4]Manufacturing companies frequently employ a **standardized cost system** that predetermines the unit costs for material, labor, and manufacturing overhead and that values raw materials, work in process, and finished goods inventories at their standard costs. For financial reporting purposes, it is acceptable to price inventories at standard costs if there is no significant difference between the actual costs and standard costs. If there is a significant difference, companies should adjust the inventory amounts to actual cost. In *Accounting Research and Terminology Bulletin, Final Edition*, the profession notes that **"standard costs are acceptable if adjusted at reasonable intervals to reflect current conditions."** Burlington Industries and Hewlett-Packard use standard costs for valuing at least a portion of their inventories.

[5]"The Accounting Basis of Inventories," *Accounting Research Study No. 13* (New York: AICPA, 1973) recommends that companies adopt net realizable value. We also should note that companies frequently fail to apply the rules of lower-of-cost-or-market in practice. For example, companies rarely compute and apply the lower limit—net realizable value less a normal markup—because it is a fairly subjective computation. In addition, companies often do not reduce inventory to market unless its disposition is expected to result in a loss. Furthermore, if the net realizable value of finished goods exceeds cost, companies usually assume that both work in process and raw materials do also. In practice, therefore, authoritative literature [3] is considered a guide, and accountants often exercise professional judgment in lieu of following the pronouncements literally.

market with a quoted price applicable to all quantities, and (2) when no significant costs of disposal are involved. For example, mining companies ordinarily report inventories of certain minerals (rare metals, especially) at selling prices because there is often a controlled market without significant costs of disposal. Similar treatment is given agricultural products that are immediately marketable at quoted prices.

INTERNATIONAL PERSPECTIVE

Similar to GAAP, certain agricultural products and mineral products can be reported at net realizable value using IFRS.

A third reason for allowing valuation at net realizable value is that sometimes it is too difficult to obtain the cost figures. Cost figures are not difficult to determine in, say, a manufacturing plant, where the company combines various raw materials and purchased parts to create a finished product. The manufacturer can use the cost basis to account for various items in inventory, because it knows the cost of each individual component part. The situation is different in a meat-packing plant, however. The "raw material" consists of, say, cattle, each unit of which the company purchases as a whole and then divides into parts that are the products. Instead of one product out of many raw materials or parts, the meat-packing company makes many products from one "unit" of raw material. To allocate the cost of the animal "on the hoof" into the cost of, say, ribs, chuck, and shoulders, is a practical impossibility. It is much easier and more useful for the company to determine the market price of the various products and value them in the inventory at selling price less the various costs necessary to get them to market (costs such as shipping and handling). Hence, because of a peculiarity of the industry, meat-packing companies sometimes carry **inventories at sales price less distribution costs**.

Valuation Using Relative Sales Value

LEARNING OBJECTIVE 3
Explain when companies use the relative sales value method to value inventories.

A special problem arises when a company buys a group of varying units in a single **lump-sum purchase**, also called a **basket purchase**.

To illustrate, assume that Woodland Developers purchases land for $1 million that it will subdivide into 400 lots. These lots are of different sizes and shapes but can be roughly sorted into three groups graded A, B, and C. As Woodland sells the lots, it apportions the purchase cost of $1 million among the lots sold and the lots remaining on hand.

You might wonder why Woodland would not simply divide the total cost of $1 million by 400 lots, to get a cost of $2,500 for each lot. This approach would not recognize that the lots vary in size, shape, and attractiveness. Therefore, to accurately value each unit, the common and most logical practice is to allocate the total among the various units on the basis of their **relative sales value**.

Illustration 9-11 shows the allocation of relative sales value for the Woodland Developers example.

ILLUSTRATION 9-11
Allocation of Costs, Using Relative Sales Value

Lots	Number of Lots	Sales Price per Lot	Total Sales Price	Relative Sales Price	Total Cost	Cost Allocated to Lots	Cost per Lot
A	100	$10,000	$1,000,000	100/250	$1,000,000	$ 400,000	$4,000
B	100	6,000	600,000	60/250	1,000,000	240,000	2,400
C	200	4,500	900,000	90/250	1,000,000	360,000	1,800
			$2,500,000			$1,000,000	

Using the amounts given in the "Cost per Lot" column, Woodland can determine the cost of lots sold and the gross profit as follows.

Lots	Number of Lots Sold	Cost per Lot	Cost of Lots Sold	Sales	Gross Profit
A	77	$4,000	$308,000	$ 770,000	$ 462,000
B	80	2,400	192,000	480,000	288,000
C	100	1,800	180,000	450,000	270,000
			$680,000	$1,700,000	$1,020,000

ILLUSTRATION 9-12
Determination of Gross Profit, Using Relative Sales Value

The ending inventory is therefore $320,000 ($1,000,000 − $680,000).

Woodland also can compute this inventory amount another way. The ratio of cost to selling price for all the lots is $1 million divided by $2,500,000, or 40 percent. Accordingly, if the total sales price of lots sold is, say $1,700,000, then the cost of the lots sold is 40 percent of $1,700,000, or $680,000. The inventory of lots on hand is then $1 million less $680,000, or $320,000.

The petroleum industry widely uses the relative sales value method to value (at cost) the many products and by-products obtained from a barrel of crude oil.

Purchase Commitments—A Special Problem

4 LEARNING OBJECTIVE
Discuss accounting issues related to purchase commitments.

In many lines of business, a company's survival and continued profitability depends on its having a sufficient stock of merchandise to meet customer demand. Consequently, it is quite common for a company to make **purchase commitments**, which are agreements to buy inventory weeks, months, or even years in advance. Generally, the seller retains title to the merchandise or materials covered in the purchase commitments. Indeed, the goods may exist only as natural resources as unplanted seed (in the case of agricultural commodities), or as work in process (in the case of a product).[6]

Usually it is neither necessary nor proper for the buyer to make any entries to reflect commitments for purchases of goods that the seller has not shipped. Ordinary orders, for which the buyer and seller will determine prices at the time of shipment and **which are subject to cancellation**, do not represent either an asset or a liability to the buyer. Therefore the buyer need not record such purchase commitments or report them in the financial statements.

What happens, though, if a buyer enters into a formal, noncancelable purchase contract? Even then, the buyer recognizes no asset or liability at the date of inception, **because the contract is "executory" in nature**: Neither party has fulfilled its part of the contract. However, if material, the buyer should disclose such contract details in a note to its financial statements. Illustration 9-13 shows an example of a purchase commitment disclosure.

Note 1: Contracts for the purchase of raw materials in 2012 have been executed in the amount of $600,000. The market price of such raw materials on December 31, 2011, is $640,000.

ILLUSTRATION 9-13
Disclosure of Purchase Commitment

In the disclosure in Illustration 9-13, the contract price was less than the market price at the balance sheet date. **If the contract price is greater than the market price, and the buyer expects that losses will occur when the purchase is effected, the buyer**

[6]One study noted that about 30 percent of public companies have purchase commitments outstanding, with an estimated value of $725 billion ("SEC Staff Report on Off-Balance Sheet Arrangements, Special Purpose Entities, and Related Issues,") *http://www.sec.gov/news/ studies/ soxoffbalancerpt.pdf,* June 2005). Purchase commitments are popular because the buyer can secure a supply of inventory at a known price. The seller also benefits in these arrangements by knowing how much to produce.

should recognize losses in the period during which such declines in market prices take place. [4]

As an example, at one time many Northwest forest-product companies such as **Boise Cascade**, **Georgia-Pacific**, and **Weyerhaeuser** signed long-term timber-cutting contracts with the **U.S. Forest Service**. These contracts required that the companies pay $310 per thousand board feet for timber-cutting rights. Unfortunately, the market price for timber-cutting rights in the latter part of the year dropped to $80 per thousand board feet. As a result, a number of these companies had long-term contracts that, if fulfilled, would result in substantial future losses.

Underlying Concepts

Reporting the loss is *conservative.* However, reporting the decline in market price is debatable because no asset is recorded. This area demonstrates the need for good definitions of assets and liabilities.

To illustrate the accounting problem, assume that St. Regis Paper Co. signed timber-cutting contracts to be executed in 2013 at a price of $10,000,000. Assume further that the market price of the timber cutting rights on December 31, 2012, dropped to $7,000,000. St. Regis would make the following entry on December 31, 2012.

Unrealized Holding Gain or Loss—Income (Purchase Commitments)	3,000,000	
Estimated Liability on Purchase Commitments		3,000,000

St. Regis would report this unrealized holding loss in the income statement under "Other expenses and losses." And because the contract is to be executed within the next fiscal year, St. Regis would report the Estimated Liability on Purchase Commitments in the current liabilities section on the balance sheet. When St. Regis cuts the timber at a cost of $10 million, it would make the following entry.

Purchases (Inventory)	7,000,000	
Estimated Liability on Purchase Commitments	3,000,000	
Cash		10,000,000

The result of the purchase commitment was that St. Regis paid $10 million for a contract worth only $7 million. It recorded the loss in the previous period—when the price actually declined.

If St. Regis can partially or fully recover the contract price before it cuts the timber, it reduces the Estimated Liability on Purchase Commitments. In that case, it then reports in the period of the price increase a resulting gain for the amount of the partial or full recovery. For example, Congress permitted some of the forest-products companies to buy out of their contracts at reduced prices in order to avoid potential bankruptcies. To illustrate, assume that Congress permitted St. Regis to reduce its contract price and therefore its commitment by $1,000,000. The entry to record this transaction is as follows.

Estimated Liability on Purchase Commitments	1,000,000	
Unrealized Holding Gain or Loss—Income (Purchase Commitments)		1,000,000

If the market price at the time St. Regis cuts the timber is more than $2,000,000 below the contract price, St. Regis will have to recognize an additional loss in the period of cutting and record the purchase at the lower-of-cost-or-market.

Are purchasers at the mercy of market price declines? Not totally. Purchasers can protect themselves against the possibility of market price declines of goods under contract by hedging. In **hedging**, the purchaser in the purchase commitment simultaneously enters into a contract in which it agrees to sell in the future the same quantity of the same (or similar) goods at a fixed price. Thus the company holds a *buy position* in a purchase commitment and a *sell position* in a futures contract in the same commodity. The purpose of the hedge is to offset the price risk of the buy and sell positions: The company will be better off under one contract by approximately (maybe exactly) the same amount by which it is worse off under the other contract.

For example, St. Regis Paper Co. could have hedged its purchase commitment contract with a futures contract for timber rights of the same amount. In that case, its loss of

$3,000,000 on the purchase commitment could have been offset by a $3,000,000 gain on the futures contract.[7]

As easy as this makes it sound, accounting for purchase commitments is still unsettled and controversial. Some argue that companies should report purchase commitments as assets and liabilities at the time they sign the contract.[8] Others believe that the present recognition at the delivery date is more appropriate. *FASB Concepts Statement No. 6* states, "a purchase commitment involves both an item that might be recorded as an asset and an item that might be recorded as a liability. That is, it involves both a right to receive assets and an obligation to pay. . . . If both the right to receive assets and the obligation to pay were recorded at the time of the purchase commitment, the nature of the loss and the valuation account that records it when the price falls would be clearly seen." Although the discussion in *Concepts Statement No. 6* does not exclude the possibility of recording assets and liabilities for purchase commitments, it contains no conclusions or implications about whether companies should record them.[9]

THE GROSS PROFIT METHOD OF ESTIMATING INVENTORY

5 LEARNING OBJECTIVE
Determine ending inventory by applying the gross profit method.

Companies take a physical inventory to verify the accuracy of the perpetual inventory records or, if no records exist, to arrive at an inventory amount. Sometimes, however, taking a physical inventory is impractical. In such cases, companies use substitute measures to approximate inventory on hand.

One substitute method of verifying or determining the inventory amount is the **gross profit method** (also called the **gross margin method**). Auditors widely use this method in situations where they need only an estimate of the company's inventory (e.g., interim reports). Companies also use this method when fire or other catastrophe destroys either inventory or inventory records. The gross profit method relies on three assumptions:

1. The beginning inventory plus purchases equal total goods to be accounted for.
2. Goods not sold must be on hand.
3. The sales, reduced to cost, deducted from the sum of the opening inventory plus purchases, equal ending inventory.

To illustrate, assume that Cetus Corp. has a beginning inventory of $60,000 and purchases of $200,000, both at cost. Sales at selling price amount to $280,000. The gross profit on selling price is 30 percent. Cetus applies the gross profit method as follows.

[7]Appendix 17A provides a complete discussion of hedging and the use of derivatives such as futures.

[8]See, for example, Yuji Ijiri, *Recognition of Contractual Rights and Obligations, Research Report* (Stamford, Conn.: FASB, 1980), who argues that companies should capitalize firm purchase commitments. "Firm" means that it is unlikely that companies can avoid performance under the contract without a severe penalty.

Also, see Mahendra R. Gujarathi and Stanley F. Biggs, "Accounting for Purchase Commitments: Some Issues and Recommendations," *Accounting Horizons* (September 1988), pp. 75–78. They conclude, "Recording an asset and liability on the date of inception for the noncancelable purchase commitments is suggested as the first significant step towards alleviating the accounting problems associated with the issue. At year-end, the potential gains and losses should be treated as contingencies which provides a coherent structure for the reporting of such gains and losses."

[9]"Elements of Financial Statements," *Statement of Financial Accounting Concepts No. 6* (Stamford, Conn.: FASB, 1985), paras. 251–253.

ILLUSTRATION 9-14
Application of Gross Profit Method

Beginning inventory (at cost)		$ 60,000
Purchases (at cost)		200,000
Goods available (at cost)		260,000
Sales (at selling price)	$280,000	
Less: Gross profit (30% of $280,000)	84,000	
Sales (at cost)		196,000
Approximate inventory (at cost)		$ 64,000

The current period's records contain all the information Cetus needs to compute inventory at cost, except for the gross profit percentage. Cetus determines the gross profit percentage by reviewing company policies or prior period records. In some cases, companies must adjust this percentage if they consider prior periods unrepresentative of the current period.[10]

Computation of Gross Profit Percentage

In most situations, the **gross profit percentage** is stated as a percentage of selling price. The previous illustration, for example, used a 30 percent gross profit on sales. Gross profit on selling price is the common method for quoting the profit for several reasons: (1) Most companies state goods on a retail basis, not a cost basis. (2) A profit quoted on selling price is lower than one based on cost. This lower rate gives a favorable impression to the consumer. (3) The gross profit based on selling price can never exceed 100 percent.[11]

In Illustration 9-14, the gross profit was a given. But how did Cetus derive that figure? To see how to compute a gross profit percentage, assume that an article cost $15 and sells for $20, a gross profit of $5. As shown in the computations in Illustration 9-15, this markup is ¼ or 25 percent of retail, and ⅓ or, 33⅓ percent of cost.

ILLUSTRATION 9-15
Computation of Gross Profit Percentage

$$\frac{\textbf{Markup}}{\textbf{Retail}} = \frac{\$5}{\$20} = 25\% \text{ at retail} \qquad \frac{\textbf{Markup}}{\textbf{Cost}} = \frac{\$5}{\$15} = 33\tfrac{1}{3}\% \text{ on cost}$$

Although companies normally compute the gross profit on the basis of selling price, you should understand the basic relationship between markup on cost and markup on

[10]An alternative method of estimating inventory using the gross profit percentage is considered by some to be less complicated than the traditional method. This alternative method uses the standard income statement format as follows. (Assume the same data as in the Cetus example above.)

Sales		$280,000		$280,000
Cost of sales				
Beginning inventory	$ 60,000		$ 60,000	
Purchases	200,000		200,000	
Goods available for sale	260,000		260,000	
Ending inventory	(3) ?		(3) 64,000 Est.	
Cost of goods sold		(2) ?		(2)196,000 Est.
Gross profit on sales (30%)		(1) ?		(1) 84,000 Est.

Compute the unknowns as follows: first the gross profit amount, then cost of goods sold, and finally the ending inventory, as shown below.

(1) $280,000 × 30% = $84,000 (gross profit on sales).
(2) $280,000 − $84,000 = $196,000 (cost of goods sold).
(3) $260,000 − $196,000 = $64,000 (ending inventory).

[11]The terms *gross margin percentage, rate of gross profit,* and *percentage markup* are synonymous, although companies more commonly use *markup* in reference to cost and *gross profit* in reference to sales.

selling price. For example, assume that a company marks up a given item by 25 percent. What, then, is the **gross profit on selling price**? To find the answer, assume that the item sells for $1. In this case, the following formula applies.

$$\begin{aligned} \textbf{Cost + Gross profit} &= \textbf{Selling price} \\ C + .25C &= SP \\ (1 + .25)C &= SP \\ 1.25C &= \$100 \\ C &= \$0.80 \end{aligned}$$

The gross profit equals $0.20 ($1.00 − $0.80). The rate of gross profit on selling price is therefore 20 percent ($0.20/$1.00).

Conversely, assume that the gross profit on selling price is 20 percent. What is the **markup on cost**? To find the answer, again assume that the item sells for $1. Again, the same formula holds:

$$\begin{aligned} \text{Cost + Gross profit} &= \text{Selling price} \\ C + .20SP &= SP \\ C &= (1 - .20)SP \\ C &= .80SP \\ C &= .80(\$1.00) \\ C &= \$0.80 \end{aligned}$$

As in the previous example, the markup equals $0.20 ($1.00 − $0.80). The markup on cost is 25 percent ($0.20/$0.80).

Retailers use the following formulas to express these relationships:

ILLUSTRATION 9-16
Formulas Relating to Gross Profit

$$\textbf{1. Gross profit on selling price} = \frac{\textbf{Percentage markup on cost}}{\textbf{100\% + Percentage markup on cost}}$$

$$\textbf{2. Percentage markup on cost} = \frac{\textbf{Gross profit on selling price}}{\textbf{100\% − Gross profit on selling price}}$$

To understand how to use these formulas, consider their application in the following calculations.

ILLUSTRATION 9-17
Application of Gross Profit Formulas

Gross Profit on Selling Price		Percentage Markup on Cost
Given: 20%	→	$\frac{.20}{1.00 - .20} = 25\%$
Given: 25%	→	$\frac{.25}{1.00 - .25} = 33\frac{1}{3}\%$
$\frac{.25}{1.00 + .25} = 20\%$	←	Given: 25%
$\frac{.50}{1.00 + .50} = 33\frac{1}{3}\%$	←	Given: 50%

Because selling price exceeds cost, and with the gross profit amount the same for both, **gross profit on selling price will always be less than the related percentage based on cost**. Note that companies do not multiply sales by a cost-based markup percentage. Instead, they must convert the gross profit percentage to a percentage based on selling price.

Evaluation of Gross Profit Method

What are the major disadvantages of the gross profit method? One disadvantage is that **it provides an estimate**. As a result, companies must take a physical inventory once a year to verify the inventory. Second, the gross profit method **uses past percentages** in determining the markup. Although the past often provides answers to the future, a current rate is more appropriate. Note that whenever significant fluctuations occur, companies should adjust the percentage as appropriate. Third, companies must be **careful in applying a blanket gross profit rate**. Frequently, a store or department handles merchandise with widely varying rates of gross profit. In these situations, the company may need to apply the gross profit method by subsections, lines of merchandise, or a similar basis that classifies merchandise according to their respective rates of gross profit. The gross profit method is normally unacceptable for financial reporting purposes because it provides only an estimate. GAAP requires a physical inventory as additional verification of the inventory indicated in the records. Nevertheless, GAAP permits the gross profit method to determine ending inventory for interim (generally quarterly) reporting purposes, provided a company discloses the use of this method. Note that the gross profit method will follow closely the inventory method used (FIFO, LIFO, average cost) because it relies on historical records.

THE SQUEEZE

What do the numbers mean?

Managers and analysts closely follow gross profits. A small change in the gross profit rate can significantly affect the bottom line. In 1993, **Apple Computer** suffered a textbook case of shrinking gross profits. In response to pricing wars in the personal computer market, Apple had to quickly reduce the price of its signature Macintosh computers—reducing prices more quickly than it could reduce its costs. As a result its gross profit rate fell from 44 percent in 1992 to 40 percent in 1993. Though the drop of 4 percent seems small, its impact on the bottom line caused Apple's stock price to drop from $57 per share on June 1, 1993, to $27.50 by mid-July 1993. As another example, **Debenham**, the second largest department store in the United Kingdom, experienced a 14 percentage share price decline. The cause? Markdowns on slow-moving inventory reduced its gross profit. On the positive side, an increase in the gross profit rate provides a positive signal to the market. For example, just a 1 percent boost in **Dr. Pepper**'s gross profit rate cheered the market, indicating the company was able to avoid the squeeze of increased commodity costs by raising its prices.

Source: Alison Smith, "Debenham's Shares Hit by Warning," *Financial Times* (July 24, 2002), p. 21; and D. Kardous, "Higher Pricing Helps Boost Dr. Pepper Snapple's Net," *Wall Street Journal Online* (June 5, 2008).

RETAIL INVENTORY METHOD

LEARNING OBJECTIVE 6
Determine ending inventory by applying the retail inventory method.

Accounting for inventory in a retail operation presents several challenges. Retailers with certain types of inventory may use the specific identification method to value their inventories. Such an approach makes sense when a retailer holds significant individual inventory units, such as automobiles, pianos, or fur coats. However, imagine attempting to use such an approach at **Target**, **Home Depot**, **Sears Holdings**, or **Bloomingdale's**—high-volume retailers that have many different types of merchandise. It would be extremely difficult to determine the cost of each sale, to enter cost codes on the tickets, to change the codes to reflect declines in value of the merchandise, to allocate costs such as transportation, and so on.

An alternative is to compile the inventories at retail prices. For most retailers, an observable pattern between cost and price exists. The retailer can then use a formula to convert retail prices to cost. This method is called the **retail inventory method**. **It requires that the retailer keep a record of (1) the total cost and retail value of goods purchased, (2) the total cost and retail value of the goods available for sale, and (3) the**

sales for the period. Use of the retail inventory method is very common. For example, **Safeway** supermarkets uses the retail inventory method, as does **Target Corp.**, **Wal-Mart**, and **Best Buy**.

Here is how it works at a company like **Best Buy**: Beginning with the retail value of the goods available for sale, Best Buy deducts the sales for the period. This calculation determines an estimated inventory (goods on hand) at retail. It next computes the **cost-to-retail ratio** for all goods. The formula for this computation is to divide the cost of total goods available for sale at cost by the total goods available at retail price. Finally, to obtain ending inventory at cost, Best Buy applies the cost-to-retail ratio to the ending inventory valued at retail. Illustration 9-18 shows the retail inventory method calculations for Best Buy (assumed data).

ILLUSTRATION 9-18
Retail Inventory Method

BEST BUY
(current period)

	Cost	Retail
Beginning inventory	$14,000	$ 20,000
Purchases	63,000	90,000
Goods available for sale	$77,000	110,000
Deduct: Sales		85,000
Ending inventory, at retail		$ 25,000

Ratio of cost to retail ($77,000 ÷ $110,000) = 70%
Ending inventory at cost (70% of $25,000) = $17,500

There are different versions of the retail inventory method. These include the **conventional** method (based on lower-of-average-cost-or-market), the **cost** method, the **LIFO retail** method, and the **dollar-value LIFO** retail method. Regardless of which version a company uses, the IRS, various retail associations, and the accounting profession all sanction use of the retail inventory method. One of its advantages is that a company like **Target** can approximate the inventory balance **without a physical count**. However, to avoid a potential overstatement of the inventory, Target makes periodic inventory counts. Such counts are especially important in retail operations where loss due to shoplifting or breakage is common.

The retail inventory method is particularly useful for any type of interim report, because such reports usually need a fairly quick and reliable measure of the inventory. Also, insurance adjusters often use this method to estimate losses from fire, flood, or other type of casualty. This method also acts as a **control device** because a company will have to explain any deviations from a physical count at the end of the year. Finally, the retail method **expedites the physical inventory count** at the end of the year. The crew taking the physical inventory need record only the retail price of each item. The crew does not need to look up each item's invoice cost, thereby saving time and expense.

Retail-Method Concepts

The amounts shown in the "Retail" column of Illustration 9-18 represent the original retail prices, assuming no price changes. In practice, though, retailers frequently mark up or mark down the prices they charge buyers.

For retailers, the term **markup** means an additional markup of the original retail price. (In another context, such as the gross profit discussion on pages 506–507, we often think of markup on the basis of cost.) **Markup cancellations** are decreases in prices of merchandise that the retailer had marked up above the original retail price.

In a competitive market, retailers often need to use **markdowns**, which are decreases in the original sales prices. Such cuts in sales prices may be necessary because of a decrease in the general level of prices, special sales, soiled or damaged goods, overstocking, and market competition. Markdowns are common in retailing these days. **Markdown cancellations** occur when the markdowns are later offset by increases in the prices of goods that the retailer had marked down—such as after a one-day sale, for example. Neither a markup cancellation nor a markdown cancellation can exceed the original markup or markdown.

To illustrate these concepts, assume that Designer Clothing Store recently purchased 100 dress shirts from Marroway, Inc. The cost for these shirts was $1,500, or $15 a shirt. Designer Clothing established the selling price on these shirts at $30 a shirt. The shirts were selling quickly in anticipation of Father's Day, so the manager added a markup of $5 per shirt. This markup made the price too high for customers, and sales slowed. The manager then reduced the price to $32. At this point we would say that the shirts at Designer Clothing have had a markup of $5 and a markup cancellation of $3.

Right after Father's Day, the manager marked down the remaining shirts to a sale price of $23. At this point, an additional markup cancellation of $2 has taken place, and a $7 markdown has occurred. If the manager later increases the price of the shirts to $24, a markdown cancellation of $1 would occur.

Retail Inventory Method with Markups and Markdowns—Conventional Method

Retailers use markup and markdown concepts in developing the proper inventory valuation at the end of the accounting period. To obtain the appropriate inventory figures, companies must give proper treatment to markups, markup cancellations, markdowns, and markdown cancellations.

To illustrate the different possibilities, consider the data for In-Fusion Inc., shown in Illustration 9-19. In-Fusion can calculate its ending inventory at cost under two assumptions, A and B. (We'll explain the reasons for the two later.)

Assumption A: Computes a cost ratio after markups (and markup cancellations) but before markdowns.

Assumption B: Computes a cost ratio after both markups and markdowns (and cancellations).

The computations for In-Fusion are:

Ending inventory at retail × Cost ratio = Value of ending inventory

Assumption A: $12,500 × 53.9% = $6,737.50
Assumption B: $12,500 × 54.7% = $6,837.50

The question becomes: Which assumption and which percentage should In-Fusion use to compute the ending inventory valuation? The answer depends on which retail inventory method In-Fusion chooses.

One approach uses only assumption A (a cost ratio using markups but not markdowns). It approximates the lower-of-average-cost-or-market. We will refer to this approach as the **conventional retail inventory method** or the **lower-of-cost-or-market approach**.

To understand why this method considers only the markups, not the markdowns, in the cost percentage, you must understand how a retail business operates. A markup normally indicates an increase in the market value of the item. On the other hand, a markdown means a decline in the utility of that item. Therefore, to approximate the lower-of-cost-or-market, we would consider markdowns a current loss and so would not include them in calculating the cost-to-retail ratio. Omitting the markdowns

ILLUSTRATION 9-19
Retail Inventory Method with Markups and Markdowns

	Cost	Retail
Beginning inventory	$ 500	$ 1,000
Purchases (net)	20,000	35,000
Markups		3,000
Markup cancellations		1,000
Markdowns		2,500
Markdown cancellations		2,000
Sales (net)		25,000

IN-FUSION INC.

	Cost		Retail
Beginning inventory	$ 500		$ 1,000
Purchases (net)	20,000		35,000
Merchandise available for sale	20,500		36,000
Add: Markups		$3,000	
Less: Markup cancellations		(1,000)	
Net markups			2,000
	20,500		38,000
(A) Cost-to-retail ratio $\frac{\$20,500}{\$38,000} = 53.9\%$			
Deduct:			
Markdowns		2,500	
Less: Markdown cancellations		(2,000)	
Net markdowns			500
	$20,500		37,500
(B) Cost-to-retail ratio $\frac{\$20,500}{\$37,500} = 54.7\%$			
Deduct: Sales (net)			25,000
Ending inventory at retail			$12,500

would make the cost-to-retail ratio lower, which leads to an approximate lower-of-cost-or-market.

An example will make the distinction between the two methods clear: In-Fusion purchased two items for $5 apiece; the original sales price was $10 each. One item was subsequently written down to $2. Assuming no sales for the period, **if markdowns are considered** in the cost-to-retail ratio (assumption B—the **cost method**), we compute the ending inventory in the following way.

ILLUSTRATION 9-20
Retail Inventory Method Including Markdowns—Cost Method

Markdowns Included in Cost-to-Retail Ratio

	Cost	Retail
Purchases	$10	$20
Deduct: Markdowns		8
Ending inventory, at retail		$12

Cost-to-retail ratio $\frac{\$10}{\$12} = 83.3\%$

Ending inventory at cost ($12 × .833) = $10

This approach (the cost method) reflects an **average cost** of the two items of the commodity without considering the loss on the one item. It values ending inventory at $10.

If markdowns are not considered in the cost-to-retail ratio (assumption A—the **conventional retail method**), we compute the ending inventory as follows.

ILLUSTRATION 9-21
Retail Inventory Method Excluding Markdowns—Conventional Method (LCM)

Markdowns Not Included in Cost-to-Retail Ratio

	Cost	Retail
Purchases	$10	$20
Cost-to-retail ratio	$\frac{\$10}{\$20} = 50\%$	
Deduct: Markdowns		8
Ending inventory, at retail		$12

Ending inventory, at cost ($12 × .50) = $6

Under this approach (the conventional retail method, in which markdowns are **not considered**), ending inventory would be $6. The inventory valuation of $6 reflects two inventory items, one inventoried at $5 and the other at $1. It reflects the fact that In-Fusion reduced the sales price from $10 to $2, and reduced the cost from $5 to $1.[12]

To approximate the lower-of-cost-or-market, In-Fusion must establish the **cost-to-retail ratio**. It does this by dividing the cost of goods available for sale by the sum of the original retail price of these goods plus the net markups. This calculation excludes markdowns and markdown cancellations. Illustration 9-22 shows the basic format for the retail inventory method using the lower-of-cost-or-market approach along with the In-Fusion Inc. information.

ILLUSTRATION 9-22
Comprehensive Conventional Retail Inventory Method Format

IN-FUSION INC.

	Cost		Retail
Beginning inventory	$ 500		$ 1,000
Purchases (net)	20,000		35,000
Totals	20,500		36,000
Add: Net markups			
Markups		$3,000	
Markup cancellations		1,000	2,000
Totals	$20,500 ←		→ 38,000
Deduct: Net markdowns			
Markdowns		2,500	
Markdown cancellations		2,000	500
Sales price of goods available			37,500
Deduct: Sales (net)			25,000
Ending inventory, at retail			$12,500

$$\text{Cost-to-retail ratio} = \frac{\text{Cost of goods available}}{\text{Original retail price of goods available, plus net markups}}$$

$$= \frac{\$20,500}{\$38,000} = 53.9\%$$

Ending inventory at lower-of-cost-or-market (53.9% × $12,500) = $6,737.50

[12]This figure is not really market (replacement cost), but it is net realizable value less the normal margin that is allowed. In other words, the sale price of the goods written down is $2, but subtracting a normal margin of 50 percent ($5 cost, $10 price), the figure becomes $1.

Because an averaging effect occurs, an exact lower-of-cost-or-market inventory valuation is ordinarily not obtained, but an adequate approximation can be achieved. In contrast, adding net markups **and** deducting net markdowns yields **approximate cost**.

Special Items Relating to Retail Method

The retail inventory method becomes more complicated when we consider such items as freight-in, purchase returns and allowances, and purchase discounts. In the retail method, we treat such items as follows.

- **Freight costs** are part of the purchase cost.
- **Purchase returns** are ordinarily considered as a reduction of the price at both cost and retail.
- **Purchase discounts and allowances** usually are considered as a reduction of the cost of purchases.

In short, the treatment for the items affecting the cost column of the retail inventory approach follows the computation for cost of goods available for sale.[13]

Note also that **sales returns and allowances** are considered as proper adjustments to gross sales. However, when sales are recorded gross, companies do not recognize **sales discounts**. To adjust for the sales discount account in such a situation would provide an ending inventory figure at retail that would be overvalued.

In addition, a number of special items require careful analysis:

- **Transfers-in** from another department are reported in the same way as purchases from an outside enterprise.
- **Normal shortages** (breakage, damage, theft, shrinkage) should reduce the retail column because these goods are no longer available for sale. Such costs are reflected in the selling price because a certain amount of shortage is considered normal in a retail enterprise. As a result, companies do not consider this amount in computing the cost-to-retail percentage. Rather, to arrive at ending inventory at retail, they show normal shortages as a deduction similar to sales.
- **Abnormal shortages**, on the other hand, are deducted from both the cost and retail columns and reported as a special inventory amount or as a loss. To do otherwise distorts the cost-to-retail ratio and overstates ending inventory.
- **Employee discounts** (given to employees to encourage loyalty, better performance, and so on) are deducted from the retail column in the same way as sales. These discounts should not be considered in the cost-to-retail percentage because they do not reflect an overall change in the selling price.[14]

Illustration 9-23 (page 514) shows some of these concepts. The company, Extreme Sport Apparel, determines its inventory using the conventional retail inventory method.

Evaluation of Retail Inventory Method

Companies like **Gap Inc.**, **Home Depot**, or your local department store use the retail inventory method of computing inventory for the following reasons: (1) to permit the computation of net income without a physical count of inventory, (2) as a control measure in determining inventory shortages, (3) in regulating quantities of merchandise on hand, and (4) for insurance information.

[13]When the purchase allowance is not reflected by a reduction in the selling price, no adjustment is made to the retail column.

[14]Note that if employee sales are recorded gross, no adjustment is necessary for employee discounts in the retail column.

ILLUSTRATION 9-23
Conventional Retail Inventory Method—Special Items Included

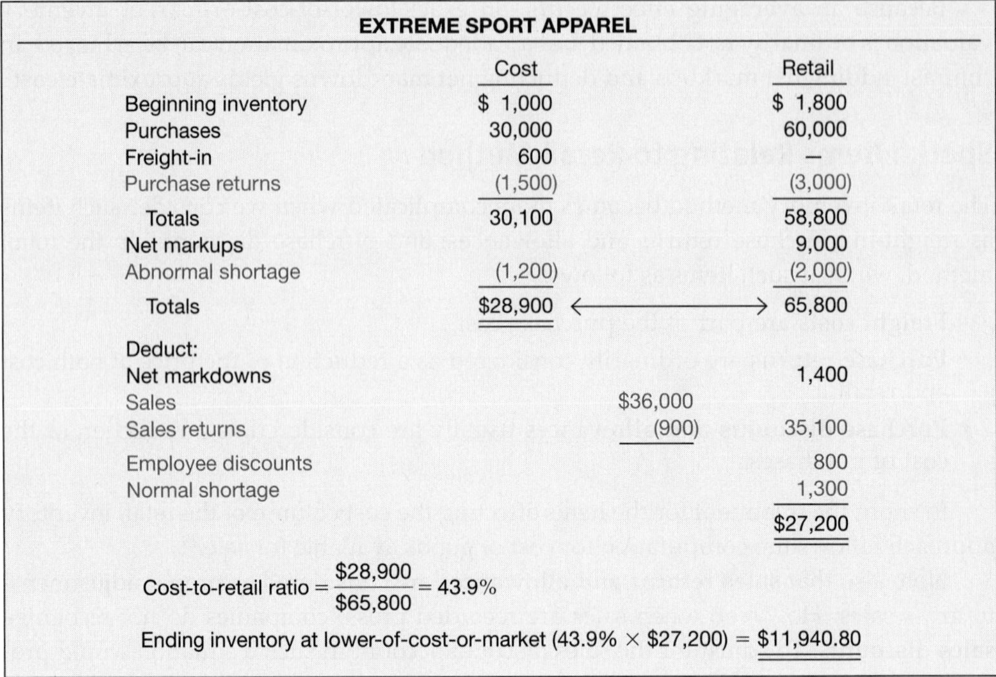

EXTREME SPORT APPAREL

	Cost		Retail
Beginning inventory	$ 1,000		$ 1,800
Purchases	30,000		60,000
Freight-in	600		—
Purchase returns	(1,500)		(3,000)
Totals	30,100		58,800
Net markups			9,000
Abnormal shortage	(1,200)		(2,000)
Totals	$28,900 ⟷		65,800
Deduct:			
Net markdowns			1,400
Sales		$36,000	
Sales returns		(900)	35,100
Employee discounts			800
Normal shortage			1,300
			$27,200

$$\text{Cost-to-retail ratio} = \frac{\$28,900}{\$65,800} = 43.9\%$$

Ending inventory at lower-of-cost-or-market (43.9% × $27,200) = $11,940.80

One characteristic of the retail inventory method is that it **has an averaging effect on varying rates of gross profit**. This can be problematic when companies apply the method to an entire business, where rates of gross profit vary among departments. There is no allowance for possible distortion of results because of such differences. Companies refine the retail method under such conditions by computing inventory separately by departments or by classes of merchandise with similar gross profits. In addition, the reliability of this method assumes that the distribution of items in inventory is similar to the "mix" in the total goods available for sale.

PRESENTATION AND ANALYSIS

Presentation of Inventories

LEARNING OBJECTIVE 7
Explain how to report and analyze inventory.

Accounting standards require financial statement disclosure of the composition of the inventory, inventory financing arrangements, and the inventory costing methods employed. The standards also require the consistent application of costing methods from one period to another.

Manufacturers should report the inventory composition either in the balance sheet or in a separate schedule in the notes. The relative mix of raw materials, work in process, and finished goods helps in assessing liquidity and in computing the stage of inventory completion.

Significant or unusual financing arrangements relating to inventories may require note disclosure. Examples include transactions with related parties, product financing arrangements, firm purchase commitments, involuntary liquidation of LIFO inventories, and pledging of inventories as collateral. Companies should present inventories pledged as collateral for a loan in the current assets section rather than as an offset to the liability.

A company should also report the basis on which it states inventory amounts (lower-of-cost-or-market) and the method used in determining cost (LIFO, FIFO, average cost, etc.). For example, the annual report of **Mumford of Wyoming** contains the following disclosures.

Mumford of Wyoming

ILLUSTRATION 9-24
Disclosure of Inventory Methods

Note A: Significant Accounting Policies

Live feeder cattle and feed—last-in, first-out (LIFO) cost, which is below approximate market	$854,800
Live range cattle—lower of principally identified cost or market	$1,240,500
Live sheep and supplies—lower of first-in, first-out (FIFO) cost or market	$674,000
Dressed meat and by-products—principally at market less allowances for distribution and selling expenses	$362,630

The preceding illustration shows that a company can use different pricing methods for different elements of its inventory. If Mumford changes the method of pricing any of its inventory elements, it must report a change in accounting principle. For example, if Mumford changes its method of accounting for live sheep from FIFO to average cost, it should separately report this change, along with the effect on income, in the current and prior periods. Changes in accounting principle require an explanatory paragraph in the auditor's report describing the change in method.

Fortune Brands, Inc. reported its inventories in its annual report as follows (note the "trade practice" followed in classifying inventories among the current assets).

Fortune Brands, Inc.

ILLUSTRATION 9-25
Disclosure of Trade Practice in Valuing Inventories

Current assets

(in millions)	December 31, 2009
Inventories	
Maturing spirits	$1,243.0
Other raw materials, supplies and work in process	322.7
Finished products	450.9
Total inventories	$2,016.6

Significant Accounting Policies (in part)

Inventories The first-in, first-out (FIFO) inventory method is our principal inventory method across all segments. In accordance with generally recognized trade practice, maturing spirits inventories are classified as current assets, although the majority of these inventories ordinarily will not be sold within one year, due to the duration of aging processes. Inventory provisions are recorded to reduce inventory to the lower of cost or market value for obsolete or slow moving inventory based on assumptions about future demand and marketability of products, the impact of new product introductions, inventory turns, product spoilage and specific identification of items, such as product discontinuance or engineering/material changes.

Analysis of Inventories

As our opening story illustrates, the amount of inventory that a company carries can have significant economic consequences. As a result, companies must manage inventories. But, inventory management is a double-edged sword. It requires constant attention. On the one hand, management wants to stock a great variety and quantity of items. Doing so will provide customers with the greatest selection. However, such an inventory policy may incur excessive carrying costs (e.g., investment, storage, insurance, taxes, obsolescence, and damage). On the other hand, low inventory levels lead to stock-outs, lost sales, and disgruntled customers.

Using financial ratios helps companies to chart a middle course between these two dangers. Common ratios used in the management and evaluation of inventory levels are inventory turnover and a related measure, average days to sell the inventory.

Inventory Turnover Ratio

The **inventory turnover ratio** measures the number of times on average a company sells the inventory during the period. It measures the liquidity of the inventory. To compute inventory turnover, divide the cost of goods sold by the average inventory on hand during the period.

Barring seasonal factors, analysts compute average inventory from beginning and ending inventory balances. For example, in its 2009 annual report **Kellogg Company** reported a beginning inventory of $897 million, an ending inventory of $910 million, and cost of goods sold of $7,184 million for the year. Illustration 9-26 shows the inventory turnover formula and Kellogg Company's 2009 ratio computation below.

ILLUSTRATION 9-26
Inventory Turnover Ratio

$$\text{Inventory Turnover} = \frac{\text{Cost of Goods Sold}}{\text{Average Inventory}} = \frac{\$7{,}184}{(\$910 + \$897)/2} = 7.95 \text{ times}$$

Average Days to Sell Inventory

A variant of the inventory turnover ratio is the **average days to sell inventory**. This measure represents the average number of days' sales for which a company has inventory on hand. For example, the inventory turnover for **Kellogg Company** of 7.95 times divided into 365 is approximately 46 days.

There are typical levels of inventory in every industry. However, companies that keep their inventory at lower levels with higher turnovers than those of their competitors, and that still can satisfy customer needs, are the most successful.

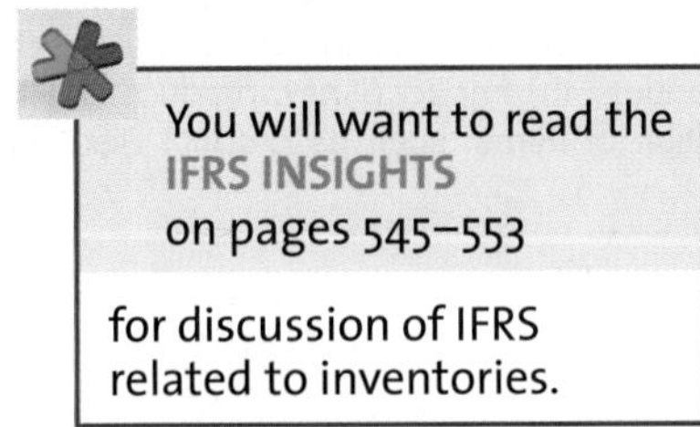
You will want to read the IFRS INSIGHTS on pages 545–553 for discussion of IFRS related to inventories.

SUMMARY OF LEARNING OBJECTIVES

1 **Describe and apply the lower-of-cost-or-market rule.** If inventory declines in value below its original cost, for whatever reason, a company should write down the inventory to reflect this loss. The general rule is to abandon the historical cost principle when the future utility (revenue-producing ability) of the asset drops below its original cost.

2 **Explain when companies value inventories at net realizable value.** Companies value inventory at net realizable value when: (1) there is a controlled market with a quoted price applicable to all quantities, (2) no significant costs of disposal are involved, and (3) the cost figures are too difficult to obtain.

3 **Explain when companies use the relative sales value method to value inventories.** When a company purchases a group of varying units at a single lump-sum price—a so-called basket purchase—the company may allocate the total purchase price to the individual items on the basis of relative sales value.

4 **Discuss accounting issues related to purchase commitments.** Accounting for purchase commitments is controversial. Some argue that companies should report purchase commitment contracts as assets and liabilities at the time the contract is signed. Others believe that recognition at the delivery date is most appropriate. The FASB neither excludes nor recommends the recording of assets and liabilities for purchase commitments, but it notes that if companies recorded such contracts at the time of commitment, the nature of the loss and the valuation account should be reported when the price falls.

5 **Determine ending inventory by applying the gross profit method.** Companies follow these steps to determine ending inventory by the gross profit method: (1) Compute the gross profit percentage on selling price. (2) Compute gross profit by multiplying net sales by the gross profit percentage. (3) Compute cost of goods sold by subtracting gross profit from net sales. (4) Compute ending inventory by subtracting cost of goods sold from total goods available for sale.

6 **Determine ending inventory by applying the retail inventory method.** Companies follow these steps to determine ending inventory by the conventional retail method: (1) To estimate inventory at retail, deduct the sales for the period from the retail value of the goods available for sale. (2) To find the cost-to-retail ratio for all goods passing through a department or firm, divide the total goods available for sale at cost by the total goods available at retail. (3) Convert the inventory valued at retail to approximate cost by applying the cost-to-retail ratio.

7 **Explain how to report and analyze inventory.** Accounting standards require financial statement disclosure of: (1) the composition of the inventory (in the balance sheet or a separate schedule in the notes); (2) significant or unusual inventory financing arrangements; and (3) inventory costing methods employed (which may differ for different elements of inventory). Accounting standards also require the consistent application of costing methods from one period to another. Common ratios used in the management and evaluation of inventory levels are inventory turnover and average days to sell the inventory.

KEY TERMS

average days to sell inventory, *516*
conventional retail inventory method, *510*
cost-of-goods-sold method, *498*
cost-to-retail ratio, *509*
designated market value, *496*
gross profit method, *505*
gross profit percentage, *506*
hedging, *504*
inventory turnover ratio, *516*
loss method, *498*
lower limit (floor), *495*
lower-of-cost-or-market (LCM), *495*
lump-sum (basket) purchase, *502*
markdown, *509*
markdown cancellations, *510*
market (for LCM), *494*
markup, *509*
markup cancellations, *509*
net realizable value (NRV), *495*
net realizable value less a normal profit margin, *495*
purchase commitments, *503*
retail inventory method, *508*
upper limit (ceiling), *495*

APPENDIX 9A LIFO RETAIL METHODS

LEARNING OBJECTIVE 8
Determine ending inventory by applying the LIFO retail methods.

A number of retail establishments have changed from the more conventional treatment to a **LIFO retail method**. For example, the world's largest retailer, **Wal-Mart** uses the LIFO retail method. The primary reason to do so is for the tax advantages associated with valuing inventories on a LIFO basis. In addition, adoption of LIFO results in a better matching of costs and revenues.

The use of LIFO retail is made under two assumptions: (1) stable prices and (2) fluctuating prices.

STABLE PRICES—LIFO RETAIL METHOD

It is much more complex to compute the final inventory balance using a LIFO flow than using the conventional retail method. Under the LIFO retail method, companies like **Wal-Mart** or **Target** consider **both markups and markdowns** in obtaining the proper cost-to-retail percentage. Furthermore, since the LIFO method is concerned only with the additional layer, or the amount that should be subtracted from the previous layer, the beginning inventory is excluded from the cost-to-retail percentage.

A major assumption of the LIFO retail method is that the markups and markdowns apply only to the goods purchased during the current period and not to the beginning inventory. This assumption is debatable and may explain why some companies do not adopt this method.

Illustration 9A-1 presents the major concepts involved in the LIFO retail method applied to the Hernandez Company. Note that, to simplify the accounting, we have assumed that the price level has remained unchanged.

ILLUSTRATION 9A-1
LIFO Retail Method—Stable Prices

	Cost	Retail
Beginning inventory—2012	$ 27,000	$ 45,000
Net purchases during the period	346,500	480,000
Net markups		20,000
Net markdowns		(5,000)
Total (excluding beginning inventory)	346,500 ←→	495,000
Total (including beginning inventory)	$373,500	540,000
Net sales during the period		(484,000)
Ending inventory at retail		$ 56,000

Establishment of cost-to-retail percentage under assumptions of LIFO retail ($346,500 ÷ $495,000) = 70%

Illustration 9A-2 indicates that the inventory is composed of two layers: the beginning inventory and the additional increase that occurred in the inventory this period (2012). When we start the next period (2013), the beginning inventory will be composed of those two layers. If an increase in inventory occurs again, an additional layer will be added.

ILLUSTRATION 9A-2
Ending Inventory at LIFO Cost, 2012—Stable Prices

Ending Inventory at Retail Prices—2012	Layers at Retail Prices			Cost-to-Retail (Percentage)		Ending Inventory at LIFO Cost
$56,000 →	2011	$45,000	×	60%*	=	$27,000
→	2012	11,000	×	70	=	7,700
		$56,000				$34,700

*$27,000 / $45,000 (prior year's cost-to-retail)

However, if the final inventory figure is below the beginning inventory, Hernandez must reduce the beginning inventory starting with the most recent layer. For example, assume that the ending inventory for 2013 at retail is $50,000. Illustration 9A-3 shows the computation of the ending inventory at cost. Notice that the 2012 layer is reduced from $11,000 to $5,000.

ILLUSTRATION 9A-3
Ending Inventory at LIFO Cost, 2013—Stable Prices

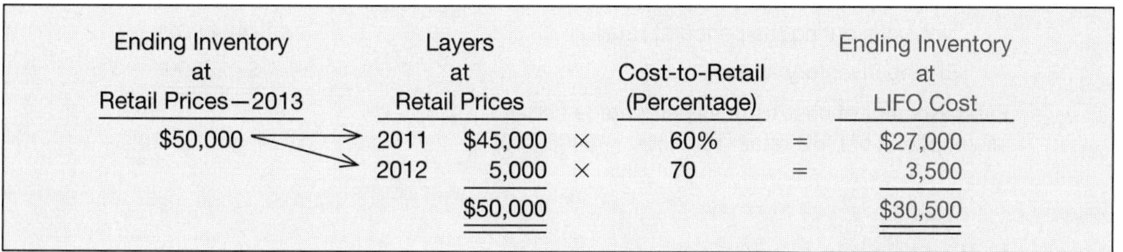

Ending Inventory at Retail Prices—2013	Layers at Retail Prices			Cost-to-Retail (Percentage)		Ending Inventory at LIFO Cost
$50,000 →	2011	$45,000	×	60%	=	$27,000
→	2012	5,000	×	70	=	3,500
		$50,000				$30,500

FLUCTUATING PRICES—DOLLAR-VALUE LIFO RETAIL METHOD

The previous example simplified the LIFO retail method by ignoring changes in the selling price of the inventory. Let us now assume that a change in the price level of the inventories occurs (as is usual). If the price level does change, the company must **eliminate the price change** so as to measure the real increase in inventory, not the dollar increase. This approach is referred to as the **dollar-value LIFO retail method**.

To illustrate, assume that the beginning inventory had a retail market value of $10,000 and the ending inventory had a retail market value of $15,000. Assume further that the price level has risen from 100 to 125. It is inappropriate to suggest that a real increase in inventory of $5,000 has occurred. Instead, the company must deflate the ending inventory at retail, as the computation in Illustration 9A-4 shows.

ILLUSTRATION 9A-4
Ending Inventory at Retail—Deflated and Restated

Ending inventory at retail (deflated) $15,000 ÷ 1.25*	$12,000	
Beginning inventory at retail	10,000	
Real increase in inventory at retail	$ 2,000	
Ending inventory at retail on LIFO basis:		
First layer	$10,000	
Second layer ($2,000 × 1.25)	2,500	$12,500

*1.25 = 125 ÷ 100

This approach is essentially the dollar-value LIFO method discussed in Chapter 8. In computing the LIFO inventory under a dollar-value LIFO approach, the company finds the dollar increase in inventory and deflates it to beginning-of-the-year prices. This indicates whether actual increases or decreases in quantity have occurred. If an increase in quantities occurs, the company prices this increase at the new index, in order to compute the value of the new layer. If a decrease in quantities happens, the company subtracts the increase from the most recent layers to the extent necessary.

The following computations, based on those in Illustration 9A-1 for Hernandez Company, illustrate the differences between the dollar-value LIFO retail method and the regular LIFO retail approach. Assume that the current 2012 price index is 112 (prior year = 100) and that the inventory ($56,000) has remained unchanged. In comparing Illustrations 9A-1 and 9A-5 (see page 520), note that the computations involved in finding the cost-to-retail percentage are exactly the same. However, the dollar-value method determines the increase that has occurred in the inventory in terms of base-year prices.

ILLUSTRATION 9A-5
Dollar-Value LIFO Retail Method—Fluctuating Prices

	Cost	Retail
Beginning inventory—2012	$ 27,000	$ 45,000
Net purchases during the period	346,500	480,000
Net markups		20,000
Net markdowns		(5,000)
Total (excluding beginning inventory)	346,500 ⟷	495,000
Total (including beginning inventory)	$373,500	540,000
Net sales during the period at retail		(484,000)
Ending inventory at retail		$ 56,000

Establishment of cost-to-retail percentage under assumptions of LIFO retail ($346,500 ÷ $495,000) = 70%

A. Ending inventory at retail prices deflated to base-year prices $56,000 ÷ 112 =	$50,000
B. Beginning inventory (retail) at base-year prices	45,000
C. Inventory increase (retail) from beginning of period	$ 5,000

From this information, we compute the inventory amount at cost:

ILLUSTRATION 9A-6
Ending Inventory at LIFO Cost, 2012—Fluctuating Prices

Ending Inventory at Base-Year Retail Prices—2012	Layers at Base-Year Retail Prices			Price Index (percentage)		Cost-to-Retail (percentage)		Ending Inventory at LIFO Cost
$50,000 →	2011	$45,000	×	100%	×	60%	=	$27,000
→	2012	5,000	×	112	×	70	=	3,920
		$50,000						$30,920

As Illustration 9A-6 shows, before the conversion to cost takes place, Hernandez must restate layers of a particular year to the prices in effect in the year when the layer was added.

Note the difference between the LIFO approach (stable prices) and the dollar-value LIFO method as indicated below.

ILLUSTRATION 9A-7
Comparison of Effect of Price Assumptions

	LIFO (stable prices)	LIFO (fluctuating prices)
Beginning inventory	$27,000	$27,000
Increment	7,700	3,920
Ending inventory	$34,700	$30,920

The difference of $3,780 ($34,700 − $30,920) results from an increase in the **price** of goods, not from an increase in the **quantity** of goods.

SUBSEQUENT ADJUSTMENTS UNDER DOLLAR-VALUE LIFO RETAIL

The dollar-value LIFO retail method follows the same procedures in subsequent periods as the traditional dollar-value method discussed in Chapter 8. That is, when a real increase in inventory occurs, Hernandez adds a new layer.

To illustrate, using the data from the previous example, assume that the retail value of the 2013 ending inventory at current prices is $64,800, the 2013 price index is 120 percent of base-year, and the cost-to-retail percentage is 75 percent. In base-year dollars, the ending inventory is therefore $54,000 ($64,800/120%). Illustration 9A-8 shows the computation of the ending inventory at LIFO cost.

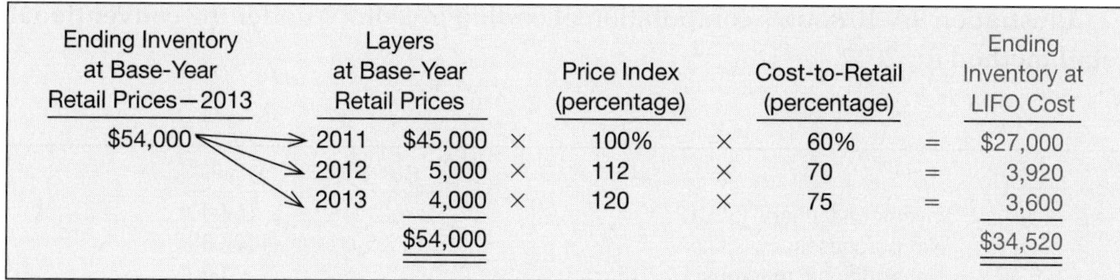

Ending Inventory at Base-Year Retail Prices—2013	Layers at Base-Year Retail Prices			Price Index (percentage)		Cost-to-Retail (percentage)		Ending Inventory at LIFO Cost
$54,000	2011	$45,000	×	100%	×	60%	=	$27,000
	2012	5,000	×	112	×	70	=	3,920
	2013	4,000	×	120	×	75	=	3,600
		$54,000						$34,520

ILLUSTRATION 9A-8
Ending Inventory at LIFO Cost, 2013—Fluctuating Prices

Conversely, when a real decrease in inventory develops, Hernandez "peels off" previous layers at prices in existence when the layers were added. To illustrate, assume that in 2013 the ending inventory in base-year prices is $48,000. The computation of the LIFO inventory is as follows.

Ending Inventory at Base-Year Retail Prices—2013	Layers at Base-Year Retail Prices			Price Index (percentage)		Cost-to-Retail (percentage)		Ending Inventory at LIFO Cost
$48,000	2011	$45,000	×	100%	×	60%	=	$27,000
	2012	3,000	×	112	×	70	=	2,352
		$48,000						$29,352

ILLUSTRATION 9A-9
Ending Inventory at LIFO Cost, 2013—Fluctuating Prices

The advantages and disadvantages of the lower-of-cost-or-market method (conventional retail) versus LIFO retail are the same for retail operations as for non-retail operations. As a practical matter, a company's selection of which retail inventory method to use often involves determining which method provides a lower taxable income. It might appear that retail LIFO will provide the lower taxable income in a period of rising prices. But this is not always the case. LIFO will provide an approximate current cost matching, but it states ending inventory at cost. The conventional retail method may have a large write-off because of the use of the lower-of-cost-or-market approach, which may offset the LIFO current cost matching.

CHANGING FROM CONVENTIONAL RETAIL TO LIFO

Because conventional retail is a lower-of-cost-or-market approach, the company must restate beginning inventory to a cost basis when changing from the conventional retail to the LIFO method.[15] The usual approach is to compute the cost basis from the purchases of the prior year, adjusted for both markups and markdowns.[16]

To illustrate, assume that Hakeman Clothing Store employs the conventional retail method but wishes to change to the LIFO retail method beginning in 2013. The amounts shown by the firm's books are as follows.

	At Cost	At Retail
Inventory, January 1, 2012	$ 5,210	$ 15,000
Net purchases in 2012	47,250	100,000
Net markups in 2012		7,000
Net markdowns in 2012		2,000
Sales in 2012		95,000

[15]Changing from the conventional retail method to LIFO retail represents a change in accounting principle. We provide an expanded discussion of accounting principle changes in Chapter 22.

[16]A logical question to ask is, "Why are only the purchases from the prior period considered and not also the beginning inventory?" Apparently the IRS believes that "the purchases-only approach" provides a more reasonable cost basis. The IRS position is debatable. However, for our purposes, it seems appropriate to use the purchases-only approach.

Illustration 9A-10 shows computation of ending inventory under the **conventional retail method** for 2012.

ILLUSTRATION 9A-10
Conventional Retail Inventory Method

	Cost	Retail
Inventory January 1, 2012	$ 5,210	$ 15,000
Net purchases	47,250	100,000
Net additional markups		7,000
	$52,460	122,000
Net markdowns		(2,000)
Sales		(95,000)
Ending inventory at retail		$ 25,000
Establishment of cost-to-retail percentage ($52,460 ÷ $122,000) =		43%
December 31, 2012, inventory at cost		
Inventory at retail		$ 25,000
Cost-to-retail ratio		× 43%
Inventory at cost under conventional retail		$ 10,750

Hakeman Clothing can then quickly approximate the ending inventory for 2012 under the **LIFO retail method** as shown in Illustration 9A-11.

ILLUSTRATION 9A-11
Conversion to LIFO Retail Inventory Method

December 31, 2012, Inventory at LIFO Cost

	Retail		Ratio		LIFO
Ending inventory	$25,000	×	45%*	=	$11,250

*The cost-to-retail ratio was computed as follows.

$$\frac{\text{Net purchases at cost}}{\text{Net purchases at retail plus markups less markdowns}} = \frac{\$47{,}250}{\$100{,}000 + \$7{,}000 - \$2{,}000} = 45\%$$

The difference of $500 ($11,250 − $10,750) between the LIFO retail method and the conventional retail method in the ending inventory for 2012 is the amount by which the company must adjust beginning inventory for 2013. The entry to adjust the inventory to a cost basis is as follows.

Inventory	500	
Adjustment to Record Inventory at Cost		500

KEY TERMS

dollar-value LIFO retail method, *519*

LIFO retail method, *518*

SUMMARY OF LEARNING OBJECTIVE FOR APPENDIX 9A

8 **Determine ending inventory by applying the LIFO retail methods.** The application of LIFO retail is made under two assumptions: stable prices and fluctuating prices.

Procedures under stable prices: (a) Because the LIFO method is a cost method, both markups and markdowns must be considered in obtaining the proper cost-to-retail percentage. (b) Since the LIFO method is concerned only with the additional layer, or the amount that should be subtracted from the previous layer, the beginning inventory is excluded from the cost-to-retail percentage. (c) The markups and markdowns apply only to the goods purchased during the current period and not to the beginning inventory.

Procedures under fluctuating prices: The steps are the same as for stable prices except that in computing the LIFO inventory under a dollar-value LIFO approach, the dollar increase in inventory is found and deflated to beginning-of-the-year prices. Doing so will determine whether actual increases or decreases in quantity have occurred. If quantities increase, this increase is priced at the new index to compute the new layer. If quantities decrease, the decrease is subtracted from the most recent layers to the extent necessary.

FASB CODIFICATION

FASB Codification References

[1] FASB ASC 330-10-35. [Predecessor literature: "Restatement and Revision of Accounting Research Bulletins," *Accounting Research Bulletin No. 43* (New York: AICPA, 1953), Ch. 4, par. 8).]

[2] FASB ASC 330-10-S99-3. [Predecessor literature: "AICPA Task Force on LIFO Inventory Problems, *Issues Paper* (New York: AICPA, November 30, 1984), pp. 50–55.]

[3] FASB ASC 330-10-35. [Predecessor literature: "Restatement and Revision of Accounting Research Bulletins," *Accounting Research Bulletin No. 43* (New York: AICPA, 1953), Ch. 4.]

[4] FASB ASC 330-10-35-16 through 18. [Predecessor literature: "Restatement and Revision of Accounting Research Bulletins," *Accounting Research Bulletin No. 43* (New York: AICPA, 1953), Ch. 4, par. 16).]

Exercises

If your school has a subscription to the FASB Codification, go to *http://aaahq.org/asclogin.cfm* to log in and prepare responses to the following. Provide Codification references for your responses.

CE9-1 Access the glossary ("Master Glossary") to answer the following.

(a) What is the definition of inventory?

(b) What is the definition of market as it relates to inventory?

(c) What is the definition of net realizable value?

CE9-2 Based on increased competition for one of its key products, Tutaj Company is concerned that it will not be able to sell its products at a price that would cover its costs. Since the company is already having a bad year, the sales manager proposes writing down the inventory to the lowest level possible, so that all the bad news will be in the current year. Explain to the sales manager the rationale for lower-of-cost-or-market adjustments, according to GAAP.

CE9-3 What are the provisions for subsequent measurement of inventory in the context of a hedging transaction?

CE9-4 What is the nature of the SEC guidance concerning inventory disclosures?

An additional Codification case can be found in the Using Your Judgment section, on page 544.

Be sure to check the book's companion website for a Review and Analysis Exercise, with solution.

Questions, Brief Exercises, Exercises, Problems, and many more resources are available for practice in WileyPLUS.

Note: All asterisked Questions, Exercises, and Problems relate to material in the appendix to the chapter.

QUESTIONS

1. Where there is evidence that the utility of inventory goods, as part of their disposal in the ordinary course of business, will be less than cost, what is the proper accounting treatment?

2. Explain the rationale for the ceiling and floor in the lower-of-cost-or-market method of valuing inventories.

3. Why are inventories valued at the lower-of-cost-or-market? What are the arguments against the use of the LCM method of valuing inventories?

4. What approaches may be employed in applying the lower-of-cost-or-market procedure? Which approach is normally used and why?

5. In some instances, accounting principles require a departure from valuing inventories at cost alone. Determine the proper unit inventory price in the following cases.

	Cases				
	1	2	3	4	5
Cost	$15.90	$16.10	$15.90	$15.90	$15.90
Net realizable value	14.50	19.20	15.20	10.40	16.40
Net realizable value less normal profit	12.80	17.60	13.75	8.80	14.80
Market (replacement cost)	14.80	17.20	12.80	9.70	16.80

6. What method(s) might be used in the accounts to record a loss due to a price decline in the inventories? Discuss.

7. What factors might call for inventory valuation at sales prices (net realizable value or market price)?

8. Under what circumstances is relative sales value an appropriate basis for determining the price assigned to inventory?

9. At December 31, 2012, Ashley Co. has outstanding purchase commitments for 150,000 gallons, at $6.20 per gallon, of a raw material to be used in its manufacturing process. The company prices its raw material inventory at cost or market, whichever is lower. Assuming that the market price as of December 31, 2012, is $5.90, how would you treat this situation in the accounts?

10. What are the major uses of the gross profit method?

11. Distinguish between gross profit as a percentage of cost and gross profit as a percentage of sales price. Convert the following gross profit percentages based on cost to gross profit percentages based on sales price: 25% and 33⅓%. Convert the following gross profit percentages based on sales price to gross profit percentages based on cost: 33⅓% and 60%.

12. Adriana Co., with annual net sales of $5 million, maintains a markup of 25% based on cost. Adriana's expenses average 15% of net sales. What is Adriana's gross profit and net profit in dollars?

13. A fire destroys all of the merchandise of Assante Company on February 10, 2012. Presented below is information compiled up to the date of the fire.

Inventory, January 1, 2012	$ 400,000
Sales to February 10, 2012	1,950,000
Purchases to February 10, 2012	1,140,000
Freight-in to February 10, 2012	60,000
Rate of gross profit on selling price	40%

What is the approximate inventory on February 10, 2012?

14. What conditions must exist for the retail inventory method to provide valid results?

15. The conventional retail inventory method yields results that are essentially the same as those yielded by the lower-of-cost-or-market method. Explain. Prepare an illustration of how the retail inventory method reduces inventory to market.

16. (a) Determine the ending inventory under the conventional retail method for the furniture department of Mayron Department Stores from the following data.

	Cost	Retail
Inventory, Jan. 1	$ 149,000	$ 283,500
Purchases	1,400,000	2,160,000
Freight-in	70,000	
Markups, net		92,000
Markdowns, net		48,000
Sales		2,175,000

(b) If the results of a physical inventory indicated an inventory at retail of $295,000, what inferences would you draw?

17. **Deere and Company** reported inventory in its balance sheet as follows:

Inventories	$1,999,100,000

What additional disclosures might be necessary to present the inventory fairly?

18. Of what significance is inventory turnover to a retail store?

*19. What modifications to the conventional retail method are necessary to approximate a LIFO retail flow?

BRIEF EXERCISES

1 2 **BE9-1** Presented below is information related to Rembrandt Inc.'s inventory.

(per unit)	Skis	Boots	Parkas
Historical cost	$190.00	$106.00	$53.00
Selling price	212.00	145.00	73.75
Cost to distribute	19.00	8.00	2.50
Current replacement cost	203.00	105.00	51.00
Normal profit margin	32.00	29.00	21.25

Determine the following: (a) the two limits to market value (i.e., the ceiling and the floor) that should be used in the lower-of-cost-or-market computation for skis; (b) the cost amount that should be used in the lower-of-cost-or-market comparison of boots; and (c) the market amount that should be used to value parkas on the basis of the lower-of-cost-or-market.

1 2 **BE9-2** Floyd Corporation has the following four items in its ending inventory.

Item	Cost	Replacement Cost	Net Realizable Value (NRV)	NRV less Normal Profit Margin
Jokers	$2,000	$2,050	$2,100	$1,600
Penguins	5,000	5,100	4,950	4,100
Riddlers	4,400	4,550	4,625	3,700
Scarecrows	3,200	2,990	3,830	3,070

Determine the final lower-of-cost-or-market inventory value for each item.

1 2 **BE9-3** Kumar Inc. uses a perpetual inventory system. At January 1, 2013, inventory was $214,000 at both cost and market value. At December 31, 2013, the inventory was $286,000 at cost and $265,000 at market value. Prepare the necessary December 31 entry under (a) the cost-of-goods-sold method and (b) the loss method.

3 **BE9-4** Bell, Inc. buys 1,000 computer game CDs from a distributor who is discontinuing those games. The purchase price for the lot is $8,000. Bell will group the CDs into three price categories for resale, as indicated below.

Group	No. of CDs	Price per CD
1	100	$ 5
2	800	10
3	100	15

Determine the cost per CD for each group, using the relative sales value method.

4 **BE9-5** Kemper Company signed a long-term noncancelable purchase commitment with a major supplier to purchase raw materials in 2013 at a cost of $1,000,000. At December 31, 2012, the raw materials to be purchased have a market value of $950,000. Prepare any necessary December 31, 2012, entry.

4 **BE9-6** Use the information for Kemper Company from BE9-5. In 2013, Kemper paid $1,000,000 to obtain the raw materials which were worth $950,000. Prepare the entry to record the purchase.

5 **BE9-7** Fosbre Corporation's April 30 inventory was destroyed by fire. January 1 inventory was $150,000, and purchases for January through April totaled $500,000. Sales for the same period were $700,000. Fosbre's normal gross profit percentage is 35% on sales. Using the gross profit method, estimate Fosbre's April 30 inventory that was destroyed by fire.

6 **BE9-8** Boyne Inc. had beginning inventory of $12,000 at cost and $20,000 at retail. Net purchases were $120,000 at cost and $170,000 at retail. Net markups were $10,000; net markdowns were $7,000; and sales were $147,000. Compute ending inventory at cost using the conventional retail method.

7 **BE9-9** In its 2010 annual report, **Wal-Mart** reported inventory of $33,160 million on January 31, 2010, and $34,511 million on January 31, 2009, cost of sales of $304,657 million for fiscal year 2010, and net sales of $405,046 million. Compute Wal-Mart's inventory turnover and the average days to sell inventory for the fiscal year 2010.

8 ***BE9-10** Use the information for Boyne Inc. from BE9-8. Compute ending inventory at cost using the LIFO retail method.

8 ***BE9-11** Use the information for Boyne Inc. from BE9-8, and assume the price level increased from 100 at the beginning of the year to 115 at year-end. Compute ending inventory at cost using the dollar-value LIFO retail method.

EXERCISES

1 2 **E9-1 (Lower-of-Cost-or-Market)** The inventory of Oheto Company on December 31, 2013, consists of the following items.

Part No.	Quantity	Cost per Unit	Cost to Replace per Unit
110	600	$ 95	$100
111	1,000	60	52
112	500	80	76
113	200	170	180
120	400	205	208
121[a]	1,600	16	14
122	300	240	235

[a]Part No. 121 is obsolete and has a realizable value of $0.50 each as scrap.

Instructions

(a) Determine the inventory as of December 31, 2013, by the lower-of-cost-or-market method, applying this method directly to each item.

(b) Determine the inventory by the lower-of-cost-or-market method, applying the method to the total of the inventory.

1 2 **E9-2 (Lower-of-Cost-or-Market)** Riegel Company uses the lower-of-cost-or-market method, on an individual-item basis, in pricing its inventory items. The inventory at December 31, 2013, consists of products D, E, F, G, H, and I. Relevant per-unit data for these products appear below.

	Item D	Item E	Item F	Item G	Item H	Item I
Estimated selling price	$120	$110	$95	$90	$110	$90
Cost	75	80	80	80	50	36
Replacement cost	120	72	70	30	70	30
Estimated selling expense	30	30	35	35	30	30
Normal profit	20	20	20	20	20	20

Instructions

Using the lower-of-cost-or-market rule, determine the proper unit value for balance sheet reporting purposes at December 31, 2013, for each of the inventory items above.

1 2 **E9-3 (Lower-of-Cost-or-Market)** Sedato Company follows the practice of pricing its inventory at the lower-of-cost-or-market, on an individual-item basis.

Item No.	Quantity	Cost per Unit	Cost to Replace	Estimated Selling Price	Cost of Completion and Disposal	Normal Profit
1320	1,200	$3.20	$3.00	$4.50	$0.35	$1.25
1333	900	2.70	2.30	3.40	0.50	0.50
1426	800	4.50	3.70	5.00	0.40	1.00
1437	1,000	3.60	3.10	3.20	0.45	0.90
1510	700	2.25	2.00	3.25	0.80	0.60
1522	500	3.00	2.70	3.90	0.40	0.50
1573	3,000	1.80	1.60	2.50	0.75	0.50
1626	1,000	4.70	5.20	6.00	0.50	1.00

Instructions

From the information above, determine the amount of Sedato Company's inventory.

1 2 **E9-4 (Lower-of-Cost-or-Market—Journal Entries)** Dover Company began operations in 2012 and determined its ending inventory at cost and at lower-of-cost-or-market at December 31, 2012, and December 31, 2013. This information is presented below.

	Cost	Lower-of-Cost-or-Market
12/31/12	$346,000	$322,000
12/31/13	410,000	390,000

Instructions

(a) Prepare the journal entries required at December 31, 2012, and December 31, 2013, assuming that the inventory is recorded at lower-of-cost-or-market, and a perpetual inventory system. Assume the cost-of-goods-sold method with no allowance used.

(b) Prepare journal entries required at December 31, 2012, and December 31, 2013, assuming that the inventory is recorded at lower-of-cost-or-market, and a perpetual inventory system. Assume the loss method with an allowance used.

(c) Which of the two methods above provides the higher net income in each year?

1 2 **E9-5 (Lower-of-Cost-or-Market—Valuation Account)** Presented below is information related to Knight Enterprises.

	Jan. 31	Feb. 28	Mar. 31	Apr. 30
Inventory at cost	$15,000	$15,100	$17,000	$14,000
Inventory at the lower-of-cost-or-market	14,500	12,600	15,600	13,300
Purchases for the month		17,000	24,000	26,500
Sales for the month		29,000	35,000	40,000

Instructions

(a) From the information, prepare (as far as the data permit) monthly income statements in columnar form for February, March, and April. The inventory is to be shown in the statement at cost, the gain or loss due to market fluctuations is to be shown separately, and a valuation account is to be set up for the difference between cost and the lower-of-cost-or-market.

(b) Prepare the journal entry required to establish the valuation account at January 31 and entries to adjust it monthly thereafter.

1 2 **E9-6 (Lower-of-Cost-or-Market—Error Effect)** LaGreca Company uses the lower-of-cost-or-market method, on an individual-item basis, in pricing its inventory items. The inventory at December 31, 2012, included product X. Relevant per-unit data for product X appear below.

Estimated selling price	$50
Cost	40
Replacement cost	38
Estimated selling expense	14
Normal profit	9

There were 1,000 units of product X on hand at December 31, 2012. Product X was incorrectly valued at $38 per unit for reporting purposes. All 1,000 units were sold in 2013.

Instructions

Compute the effect of this error on net income for 2012 and the effect on net income for 2013, and indicate the direction of the misstatement for each year.

3 **E9-7 (Relative Sales Value Method)** Larsen Realty Corporation purchased a tract of unimproved land for $55,000. This land was improved and subdivided into building lots at an additional cost of $30,000. These building lots were all of the same size but owing to differences in location were offered for sale at different prices as follows.

Group	No. of Lots	Price per Lot
1	9	$3,000
2	15	4,000
3	19	2,000

Operating expenses for the year allocated to this project total $18,200. Lots unsold at the year-end were as follows.

Group 1	5 lots
Group 2	7 lots
Group 3	2 lots

Instructions

At the end of the fiscal year Larsen Realty Corporation instructs you to arrive at the net income realized on this operation to date.

3 **E9-8 (Relative Sales Value Method)** During 2013, Crawford Furniture Company purchases a carload of wicker chairs. The manufacturer sells the chairs to Crawford for a lump sum of $60,000 because it is

discontinuing manufacturing operations and wishes to dispose of its entire stock. Three types of chairs are included in the carload. The three types and the estimated selling price for each are listed below.

Type	No. of Chairs	Estimated Selling Price Each
Lounge chairs	400	$90
Armchairs	300	80
Straight chairs	800	50

During 2013, Crawford sells 200 lounge chairs, 100 armchairs, and 120 straight chairs.

Instructions
What is the amount of gross profit realized during 2013? What is the amount of inventory of unsold straight chairs on December 31, 2013?

4 **E9-9 (Purchase Commitments)** Prater Company has been having difficulty obtaining key raw materials for its manufacturing process. The company therefore signed a long-term noncancelable purchase commitment with its largest supplier of this raw material on November 30, 2013, at an agreed price of $400,000. At December 31, 2013, the raw material had declined in price to $375,000.

Instructions
What entry would you make on December 31, 2013, to recognize these facts?

4 **E9-10 (Purchase Commitments)** At December 31, 2013, Volkan Company has outstanding noncancelable purchase commitments for 40,000 gallons, at $3.00 per gallon, of raw material to be used in its manufacturing process. The company prices its raw material inventory at cost or market, whichever is lower.

Instructions

(a) Assuming that the market price as of December 31, 2013, is $3.30, how would this matter be treated in the accounts and statements? Explain.

(b) Assuming that the market price as of December 31, 2013, is $2.70, instead of $3.30, how would you treat this situation in the accounts and statements?

(c) Give the entry in January 2014, when the 40,000-gallon shipment is received, assuming that the situation given in (b) above existed at December 31, 2013, and that the market price in January 2014 was $2.70 per gallon. Give an explanation of your treatment.

5 **E9-11 (Gross Profit Method)** Each of the following gross profit percentages is expressed in terms of cost.

(a) 20%. **(c)** 33⅓%.
(b) 25%. **(d)** 50%.

Instructions
Indicate the gross profit percentage in terms of sales for each of the above.

5 **E9-12 (Gross Profit Method)** Astaire Company uses the gross profit method to estimate inventory for monthly reporting purposes. Presented below is information for the month of May.

Inventory, May 1	$ 160,000
Purchases (gross)	640,000
Freight-in	30,000
Sales	1,000,000
Sales returns	70,000
Purchase discounts	12,000

Instructions

(a) Compute the estimated inventory at May 31, assuming that the gross profit is 25% of sales.

(b) Compute the estimated inventory at May 31, assuming that the gross profit is 25% of cost.

5 **E9-13 (Gross Profit Method)** Zidek Corp. requires an estimate of the cost of goods lost by fire on March 9. Merchandise on hand on January 1 was $38,000. Purchases since January 1 were $92,000; freight-in, $3,400; purchase returns and allowances, $2,400. Sales are made at 33⅓% above cost and totaled $120,000 to March 9. Goods costing $10,900 were left undamaged by the fire; remaining goods were destroyed.

Instructions

(a) Compute the cost of goods destroyed.

(b) Compute the cost of goods destroyed, assuming that the gross profit is 33⅓% of sales.

5 **E9-14 (Gross Profit Method)** Castlevania Company lost most of its inventory in a fire in December just before the year-end physical inventory was taken. The corporation's books disclosed the following.

Beginning inventory	$170,000	Sales	$650,000
Purchases for the year	450,000	Sales returns	24,000
Purchase returns	30,000	Rate of gross profit on net sales	30%

Merchandise with a selling price of $21,000 remained undamaged after the fire. Damaged merchandise with an original selling price of $15,000 had a net realizable value of $5,300.

Instructions
Compute the amount of the loss as a result of the fire, assuming that the corporation had no insurance coverage.

5 **E9-15 (Gross Profit Method)** You are called by Kevin Garnett of Celtic Co. on July 16 and asked to prepare a claim for insurance as a result of a theft that took place the night before. You suggest that an inventory be taken immediately. The following data are available.

Inventory, July 1	$ 38,000
Purchases—goods placed in stock July 1–15	90,000
Sales—goods delivered to customers (gross)	116,000
Sales returns—goods returned to stock	4,000

Your client reports that the goods on hand on July 16 cost $30,500, but you determine that this figure includes goods of $6,000 received on a consignment basis. Your past records show that sales are made at approximately 25% over cost. Garnett's insurance covers only goods owned.

Instructions
Compute the claim against the insurance company.

5 **E9-16 (Gross Profit Method)** Sliver Lumber Company handles three principal lines of merchandise with these varying rates of gross profit on cost.

Lumber	25%
Millwork	30%
Hardware	40%

On August 18, a fire destroyed the office, lumber shed, and a considerable portion of the lumber stacked in the yard. To file a report of loss for insurance purposes, the company must know what the inventories were immediately preceding the fire. No detail or perpetual inventory records of any kind were maintained. The only pertinent information you are able to obtain are the following facts from the general ledger, which was kept in a fireproof vault and thus escaped destruction.

	Lumber	Millwork	Hardware
Inventory, Jan. 1, 2013	$ 250,000	$ 90,000	$ 45,000
Purchases to Aug. 18, 2013	1,500,000	375,000	160,000
Sales to Aug. 18, 2013	2,050,000	533,000	245,000

Instructions
Submit your estimate of the inventory amounts immediately preceding the fire.

5 **E9-17 (Gross Profit Method)** Presented below is information related to Jerrold Corporation for the current year.

Beginning inventory	$ 600,000	
Purchases	1,500,000	
Total goods available for sale		$2,100,000
Sales		2,300,000

Instructions
Compute the ending inventory, assuming that (a) gross profit is 40% of sales; (b) gross profit is 60% of cost; (c) gross profit is 35% of sales; and (d) gross profit is 25% of cost.

6 **E9-18 (Retail Inventory Method)** Presented below is information related to McKenna Company.

	Cost	Retail
Beginning inventory	$ 58,000	$100,000
Purchases (net)	122,000	200,000
Net markups		20,000
Net markdowns		30,000
Sales		186,000

Instructions
(a) Compute the ending inventory at retail.
(b) Compute a cost-to-retail percentage (round to two decimals) under the following conditions.

(1) Excluding both markups and markdowns.
(2) Excluding markups but including markdowns.
(3) Excluding markdowns but including markups.
(4) Including both markdowns and markups.

(c) Which of the methods in (b) above (1, 2, 3, or 4) does the following?
(1) Provides the most conservative estimate of ending inventory.
(2) Provides an approximation of lower-of-cost-or-market.
(3) Is used in the conventional retail method.

(d) Compute ending inventory at lower-of-cost-or-market (round to nearest dollar).
(e) Compute cost of goods sold based on (d).
(f) Compute gross profit based on (d).

6 **E9-19 (Retail Inventory Method)** Presented below is information related to Kuchinsky Company.

	Cost	Retail
Beginning inventory	$ 200,000	$ 280,000
Purchases	1,425,000	2,140,000
Markups		95,000
Markup cancellations		15,000
Markdowns		35,000
Markdown cancellations		5,000
Sales		2,250,000

Instructions
Compute the inventory by the conventional retail inventory method.

6 **E9-20 (Retail Inventory Method)** The records of Mandy's Boutique report the following data for the month of April.

Sales	$95,000	Purchases (at cost)	$55,000
Sales returns	2,000	Purchases (at sales price)	88,000
Markups	10,000	Purchase returns (at cost)	2,000
Markup cancellations	1,500	Purchase returns (at sales price)	3,000
Markdowns	9,300	Beginning inventory (at cost)	30,000
Markdown cancellations	2,800	Beginning inventory (at sales price)	46,500
Freight on purchases	2,400		

Instructions
Compute the ending inventory by the conventional retail inventory method.

7 **E9-21 (Analysis of Inventories)** The financial statements of General Mills, Inc.'s 2010 annual report disclose the following information.

(in millions)	May 30, 2010	May 31, 2009	May 25, 2008
Inventories	$1,344	$1,347	$1,367

	Fiscal Year	
	2010	2009
Sales	$14,797	$14,691
Cost of goods sold	8,923	9,458
Net income	1,535	1,314

Instructions
Compute General Mills's (a) inventory turnover and (b) the average days to sell inventory for 2010 and 2009.

8 ***E9-22 (Retail Inventory Method—Conventional and LIFO)** Brewster Company began operations on January 1, 2012, adopting the conventional retail inventory system. None of the company's merchandise was marked down in 2012 and, because there was no beginning inventory, its ending inventory for 2012 of $41,100 would have been the same under either the conventional retail system or the LIFO retail system.

On December 31, 2013, the store management considers adopting the LIFO retail system and desires to know how the December 31, 2013, inventory would appear under both systems. All pertinent data regarding purchases, sales, markups, and markdowns are shown on the next page. There has been no change in the price level.

	Cost	Retail
Inventory, Jan. 1, 2013	$ 41,100	$ 60,000
Markdowns (net)		13,000
Markups (net)		22,000
Purchases (net)	150,000	191,000
Sales (net)		167,000

Instructions
Determine the cost of the 2013 ending inventory under both (a) the conventional retail method and (b) the LIFO retail method.

8 ***E9-23 (Retail Inventory Method—Conventional and LIFO)** Robinson Company began operations late in 2012 and adopted the conventional retail inventory method. Because there was no beginning inventory for 2012 and no markdowns during 2012, the ending inventory for 2012 was $14,000 under both the conventional retail method and the LIFO retail method. At the end of 2013, management wants to compare the results of applying the conventional and LIFO retail methods. There was no change in the price level during 2013. The following data are available for computations.

	Cost	Retail
Inventory, January 1, 2013	$14,000	$20,000
Sales		75,000
Net markups		9,000
Net markdowns		2,500
Purchases	55,500	81,000
Freight-in	7,500	
Estimated theft		2,000

Instructions
Compute the cost of the 2013 ending inventory under both (a) the conventional retail method and (b) the LIFO retail method.

8 ***E9-24 (Dollar-Value LIFO Retail)** You assemble the following information for Dillon Department Store, which computes its inventory under the dollar-value LIFO method.

	Cost	Retail
Inventory on January 1, 2012	$222,000	$300,000
Purchases	364,800	480,000
Increase in price level for year		9%

Instructions
Compute the cost of the inventory on December 31, 2012, assuming that the inventory at retail is (a) $294,300 and (b) $359,700.

8 ***E9-25 (Dollar-Value LIFO Retail)** Presented below is information related to Atrium Corporation.

	Price Index	LIFO Cost	Retail
Inventory on December 31, 2012, when dollar-value LIFO is adopted	100	$36,000	$74,500
Inventory, December 31, 2013	110	?	95,150

Instructions
Compute the ending inventory under the dollar-value LIFO method at December 31, 2013. The cost-to-retail ratio for 2013 was 55%.

8 ***E9-26 (Conventional Retail and Dollar-Value LIFO Retail)** Mander Corporation began operations on January 1, 2012, with a beginning inventory of $34,300 at cost and $50,000 at retail. The following information relates to 2012.

	Retail
Net purchases ($108,500 at cost)	$150,000
Net markups	10,000
Net markdowns	5,000
Sales	128,000

Instructions
(a) Assume Mander decided to adopt the conventional retail method. Compute the ending inventory to be reported in the balance sheet.

(b) Assume instead that Mander decides to adopt the dollar-value LIFO retail method. The appropriate price indexes are 100 at January 1 and 110 at December 31. Compute the ending inventory to be reported in the balance sheet.

(c) On the basis of the information in part (b), compute cost of goods sold.

8 ***E9-27 (Dollar-Value LIFO Retail)** Springsteen Corporation adopted the dollar-value LIFO retail inventory method on January 1, 2011. At that time the inventory had a cost of $54,000 and a retail price of $100,000. The following information is available.

	Year-End Inventory at Retail	Current Year Cost—Retail %	Year End Price Index
2011	$121,900	57%	106
2012	138,750	60%	111
2013	126,500	61%	115
2014	162,500	58%	125

The price index at January 1, 2011, is 100.

Instructions

Compute the ending inventory at December 31 of the years 2011–2014. Round to the nearest dollar.

8 ***E9-28 (Change to LIFO Retail)** Mueller Ltd., a local retailing concern in the Bronx, N.Y., has decided to change from the conventional retail inventory method to the LIFO retail method starting on January 1, 2013. The company recomputed its ending inventory for 2012 in accordance with the procedures necessary to switch to LIFO retail. The inventory computed was $210,600.

Instructions

Assuming that Mueller Ltd.'s ending inventory for 2012 under the conventional retail inventory method was $205,000, prepare the appropriate journal entry on January 1, 2013.

See the book's companion website, www.wiley.com/college/kieso, for a set of B Exercises.

PROBLEMS

1 2 **P9-1 (Lower-of-Cost-or-Market)** Remmers Company manufactures desks. Most of the company's desks are standard models and are sold on the basis of catalog prices. At December 31, 2012, the following finished desks appear in the company's inventory.

Finished Desks	A	B	C	D
2012 catalog selling price	$450	$480	$900	$1,050
FIFO cost per inventory list 12/31/12	470	450	830	960
Estimated current cost to manufacture (at December 31, 2012, and early 2013)	460	430	610	1,000
Sales commissions and estimated other costs of disposal	50	60	80	130
2013 catalog selling price	500	540	900	1,200

The 2012 catalog was in effect through November 2012, and the 2013 catalog is effective as of December 1, 2012. All catalog prices are net of the usual discounts. Generally, the company attempts to obtain a 20% gross profit on selling price and has usually been successful in doing so.

Instructions

At what amount should each of the four desks appear in the company's December 31, 2012, inventory, assuming that the company has adopted a lower-of-FIFO-cost-or-market approach for valuation of inventories on an individual-item basis?

1 2 **P9-2 (Lower-of-Cost-or-Market)** Garcia Home Improvement Company installs replacement siding, windows, and louvered glass doors for single-family homes and condominium complexes in northern New Jersey and southern New York. The company is in the process of preparing its annual financial statements for the fiscal year ended May 31, 2012, and Jim Alcide, controller for Garcia, has gathered the following data concerning inventory.

At May 31, 2012, the balance in Garcia's Raw Materials Inventory account was $408,000, and the Allowance to Reduce Inventory to Market had a credit balance of $27,500. Alcide summarized the relevant inventory cost and market data at May 31, 2012, in the schedule below.

Alcide assigned Patricia Devereaux, an intern from a local college, the task of calculating the amount that should appear on Garcia's May 31, 2012, financial statements for inventory under the lower-of-cost-or-market rule as applied to each item in inventory. Devereaux expressed concern over departing from the cost principle.

	Cost	Replacement Cost	Sales Price	Net Realizable Value	Normal Profit
Aluminum siding	$ 70,000	$ 62,500	$ 64,000	$ 56,000	$ 5,100
Cedar shake siding	86,000	79,400	94,000	84,800	7,400
Louvered glass doors	112,000	124,000	186,400	168,300	18,500
Thermal windows	140,000	126,000	154,800	140,000	15,400
Total	$408,000	$391,900	$499,200	$449,100	$46,400

Instructions

(a) (1) Determine the proper balance in the Allowance to Reduce Inventory to Market at May 31, 2012.

(2) For the fiscal year ended May 31, 2012, determine the amount of the gain or loss that would be recorded due to the change in the Allowance to Reduce Inventory to Market.

(b) Explain the rationale for the use of the lower-of-cost-or-market rule as it applies to inventories.

(CMA adapted)

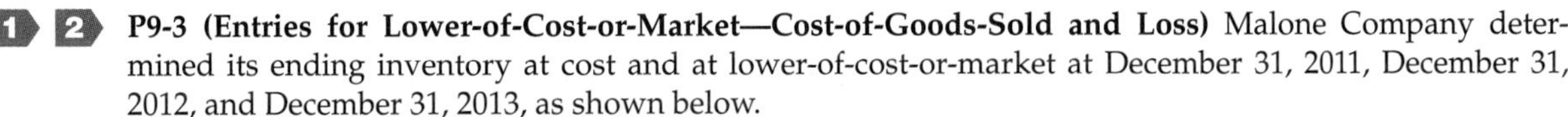

1 2 **P9-3 (Entries for Lower-of-Cost-or-Market—Cost-of-Goods-Sold and Loss)** Malone Company determined its ending inventory at cost and at lower-of-cost-or-market at December 31, 2011, December 31, 2012, and December 31, 2013, as shown below.

	Cost	Lower-of-Cost-or-Market
12/31/11	$650,000	$650,000
12/31/12	780,000	712,000
12/31/13	905,000	830,000

Instructions

(a) Prepare the journal entries required at December 31, 2012, and at December 31, 2013, assuming that a perpetual inventory system and the cost-of-goods-sold method of adjusting to lower-of-cost-or-market is used.

(b) Prepare the journal entries required at December 31, 2012, and at December 31, 2013, assuming that a perpetual inventory is recorded at cost and reduced to lower-of-cost-or-market using the loss method.

5 **P9-4 (Gross Profit Method)** Eastman Company lost most of its inventory in a fire in December just before the year-end physical inventory was taken. Corporate records disclose the following.

Inventory (beginning)	$ 80,000	Sales	$415,000
Purchases	290,000	Sales returns	21,000
Purchase returns	28,000	Gross profit % based on net selling price	35%

Merchandise with a selling price of $30,000 remained undamaged after the fire, and damaged merchandise has a salvage value of $8,150. The company does not carry fire insurance on its inventory.

Instructions

Prepare a formal labeled schedule computing the fire loss incurred. (Do not use the retail inventory method.)

5 **P9-5 (Gross Profit Method)** On April 15, 2013, fire damaged the office and warehouse of Stanislaw Corporation. The only accounting record saved was the general ledger, from which the trial balance on page 534 was prepared.

STANISLAW CORPORATION
TRIAL BALANCE
MARCH 31, 2013

Cash	$ 20,000	
Accounts receivable	40,000	
Inventory, December 31, 2012	75,000	
Land	35,000	
Buildings	110,000	
Accumulated depreciation		$ 41,300
Equipment	3,600	
Accounts payable		23,700
Other accrued expenses		10,200
Common stock		100,000
Retained earnings		52,000
Sales revenue		135,000
Purchases	52,000	
Miscellaneous expense	26,600	
	$362,200	$362,200

The following data and information have been gathered.

1. The fiscal year of the corporation ends on December 31.
2. An examination of the April bank statement and canceled checks revealed that checks written during the period April 1–15 totaled $13,000: $5,700 paid to accounts payable as of March 31, $3,400 for April merchandise shipments, and $3,900 paid for other expenses. Deposits during the same period amounted to $12,950, which consisted of receipts on account from customers with the exception of a $950 refund from a vendor for merchandise returned in April.
3. Correspondence with suppliers revealed unrecorded obligations at April 15 of $15,600 for April merchandise shipments, including $2,300 for shipments in transit (f.o.b. shipping point) on that date.
4. Customers acknowledged indebtedness of $46,000 at April 15, 2013. It was also estimated that customers owed another $8,000 that will never be acknowledged or recovered. Of the acknowledged indebtedness, $600 will probably be uncollectible.
5. The companies insuring the inventory agreed that the corporation's fire-loss claim should be based on the assumption that the overall gross profit rate for the past 2 years was in effect during the current year. The corporation's audited financial statements disclosed this information:

	Year Ended December 31	
	2012	2011
Net sales	$530,000	$390,000
Net purchases	280,000	235,000
Beginning inventory	50,000	66,000
Ending inventory	75,000	50,000

6. Inventory with a cost of $7,000 was salvaged and sold for $3,500. The balance of the inventory was a total loss.

Instructions

Prepare a schedule computing the amount of inventory fire loss. The supporting schedule of the computation of the gross profit should be in good form.

(AICPA adapted)

6 **P9-6 (Retail Inventory Method)** The records for the Clothing Department of Sharapova's Discount Store are summarized below for the month of January.

Inventory, January 1: at retail $25,000; at cost $17,000
Purchases in January: at retail $137,000; at cost $82,500
Freight-in: $7,000
Purchase returns: at retail $3,000; at cost $2,300
Transfers in from suburban branch: at retail $13,000; at cost $9,200
Net markups: $8,000
Net markdowns: $4,000
Inventory losses due to normal breakage, etc.: at retail $400
Sales at retail: $95,000
Sales returns: $2,400

Instructions

(a) Compute the inventory for this department as of January 31, at retail prices.
(b) Compute the ending inventory using lower-of-average-cost-or-market.

6 **P9-7 (Retail Inventory Method)** Presented below is information related to Waveland Inc.

	Cost	Retail
Inventory, 12/31/12	$250,000	$ 390,000
Purchases	914,500	1,460,000
Purchase returns	60,000	80,000
Purchase discounts	18,000	—
Gross sales (after employee discounts)	—	1,410,000
Sales returns	—	97,500
Markups	—	120,000
Markup cancellations	—	40,000
Markdowns	—	45,000
Markdown cancellations	—	20,000
Freight-in	42,000	—
Employee discounts granted	—	8,000
Loss from breakage (normal)	—	4,500

Instructions

Assuming that Waveland Inc. uses the conventional retail inventory method, compute the cost of its ending inventory at December 31, 2013.

6 **P9-8 (Retail Inventory Method)** Fuque Inc. uses the retail inventory method to estimate ending inventory for its monthly financial statements. The following data pertain to a single department for the month of October 2013.

Inventory, October 1, 2013	
At cost	$ 52,000
At retail	78,000
Purchases (exclusive of freight and returns)	
At cost	272,000
At retail	423,000
Freight-in	16,600
Purchase returns	
At cost	5,600
At retail	8,000
Markups	9,000
Markup cancellations	2,000
Markdowns (net)	3,600
Normal spoilage and breakage	10,000
Sales	390,000

Instructions

(a) Using the conventional retail method, prepare a schedule computing estimated lower-of-cost-or-market inventory for October 31, 2013.
(b) A department store using the conventional retail inventory method estimates the cost of its ending inventory as $60,000. An accurate physical count reveals only $47,000 of inventory at lower-of-cost-or-market. List the factors that may have caused the difference between the computed inventory and the physical count.

P9-9 (Statement and Note Disclosure, LCM, and Purchase Commitment) Maddox Specialty Company, a division of Lost World Inc., manufactures three models of gear shift components for bicycles that are sold to bicycle manufacturers, retailers, and catalog outlets. Since beginning operations in 1988, Maddox has used normal absorption costing and has assumed a first-in, first-out cost flow in its perpetual inventory system. The balances of the inventory accounts at the end of Maddox's fiscal year, November 30, 2012, are shown below. The inventories are stated at cost before any year-end adjustments.

Finished goods	$647,000
Work in process	112,500
Raw materials	264,000
Factory supplies	69,000

The following information, shown on page 536, relates to Maddox's inventory and operations.

1. The finished goods inventory consists of the items analyzed below.

	Cost	Market
Down tube shifter		
Standard model	$ 67,500	$ 67,000
Click adjustment model	94,500	89,000
Deluxe model	108,000	110,000
Total down tube shifters	270,000	266,000
Bar end shifter		
Standard model	83,000	90,050
Click adjustment model	99,000	97,550
Total bar end shifters	182,000	187,600
Head tube shifter		
Standard model	78,000	77,650
Click adjustment model	117,000	119,300
Total head tube shifters	195,000	196,950
Total finished goods	$647,000	$650,550

2. One-half of the head tube shifter finished goods inventory is held by catalog outlets on consignment.
3. Three-quarters of the bar end shifter finished goods inventory has been pledged as collateral for a bank loan.
4. One-half of the raw materials balance represents derailleurs acquired at a contracted price 20 percent above the current market price. The market value of the rest of the raw materials is $127,400.
5. The total market value of the work in process inventory is $108,700.
6. Included in the cost of factory supplies are obsolete items with an historical cost of $4,200. The market value of the remaining factory supplies is $65,900.
7. Maddox applies the lower-of-cost-or-market method to each of the three types of shifters in finished goods inventory. For each of the other three inventory accounts, Maddox applies the lower-of-cost-or-market method to the total of each inventory account.
8. Consider all amounts presented above to be material in relation to Maddox's financial statements taken as a whole.

Instructions

(a) Prepare the inventory section of Maddox's balance sheet as of November 30, 2012, including any required note(s).

(b) Without prejudice to your answer to (a), assume that the market value of Maddox's inventories is less than cost. Explain how this decline would be presented in Maddox's income statement for the fiscal year ended November 30, 2012.

(c) Assume that Maddox has a firm purchase commitment for the same type of derailleur included in the raw materials inventory as of November 30, 2012, and that the purchase commitment is at a contracted price 15% greater than the current market price. These derailleurs are to be delivered to Maddox after November 30, 2012. Discuss the impact, if any, that this purchase commitment would have on Maddox's financial statements prepared for the fiscal year ended November 30, 2012.

(CMA adapted)

1 2  **P9-10 (Lower-of-Cost-or-Market)** Fiedler Co. follows the practice of valuing its inventory at the lower-of-cost-or-market. The following information is available from the company's inventory records as of December 31, 2012.

Item	Quantity	Unit Cost	Replacement Cost/Unit	Estimated Selling Price/Unit	Completion & Disposal Cost/Unit	Normal Profit Margin/Unit
A	1,100	$7.50	$8.40	$10.50	$1.50	$1.80
B	800	8.20	7.90	9.40	0.90	1.20
C	1,000	5.60	5.40	7.20	1.15	0.60
D	1,000	3.80	4.20	6.30	0.80	1.50
E	1,400	6.40	6.30	6.70	0.70	1.00

Instructions

Greg Forda is an accounting clerk in the accounting department of Fiedler Co., and he cannot understand why the market value keeps changing from replacement cost to net realizable value to something that he cannot even figure out. Greg is very confused, and he is the one who records inventory purchases and calculates ending inventory. You are the manager of the department and an accountant.

(a) Calculate the lower-of-cost-or-market using the "individual item" approach.

(b) Show the journal entry he will need to make in order to write down the ending inventory from cost to market.

(c) Then write a memo to Greg explaining what designated market value is as well as how it is computed. Use your calculations to aid in your explanation.

8 ***P9-11 (Conventional and Dollar-Value LIFO Retail)** As of January 1, 2012, Aristotle Inc. installed the retail method of accounting for its merchandise inventory.

To prepare the store's financial statements at June 30, 2012, you obtain the following data.

	Cost	Selling Price
Inventory, January 1	$ 30,000	$ 43,000
Markdowns		10,500
Markups		9,200
Markdown cancellations		6,500
Markup cancellations		3,200
Purchases	104,800	155,000
Sales		154,000
Purchase returns	2,800	4,000
Sales returns and allowances		8,000

Instructions

(a) Prepare a schedule to compute Aristotle's June 30, 2012, inventory under the conventional retail method of accounting for inventories.

(b) Without prejudice to your solution to part (a), assume that you computed the June 30, 2012, inventory to be $59,400 at retail and the ratio of cost to retail to be 70%. The general price level has increased from 100 at January 1, 2012, to 108 at June 30, 2012. Prepare a schedule to compute the June 30, 2012, inventory at the June 30 price level under the dollar-value LIFO retail method.

(AICPA adapted)

8 ***P9-12 (Retail, LIFO Retail, and Inventory Shortage)** Late in 2009, Joan Seceda and four other investors took the chain of Becker Department Stores private, and the company has just completed its third year of operations under the ownership of the investment group. Andrea Selig, controller of Becker Department Stores, is in the process of preparing the year-end financial statements. Based on the preliminary financial statements, Seceda has expressed concern over inventory shortages, and she has asked Selig to determine whether an abnormal amount of theft and breakage has occurred. The accounting records of Becker Department Stores contain the following amounts on November 30, 2012, the end of the fiscal year.

	Cost	Retail
Beginning inventory	$ 68,000	$100,000
Purchases	255,000	400,000
Net markups		50,000
Net markdowns		110,000
Sales revenue		320,000

According to the November 30, 2012, physical inventory, the actual inventory at retail is $115,000.

Instructions

(a) Describe the circumstances under which the retail inventory method would be applied and the advantages of using the retail inventory method.

(b) Assuming that prices have been stable, calculate the value, at cost, of Becker Department Stores' ending inventory using the last-in, first-out (LIFO) retail method. Be sure to furnish supporting calculations.

(c) Estimate the amount of shortage, at retail, that has occurred at Becker Department Stores during the year ended November 30, 2012.

(d) Complications in the retail method can be caused by such items as (1) freight-in costs, (2) purchase returns and allowances, (3) sales returns and allowances, and (4) employee discounts. Explain how each of these four special items is handled in the retail inventory method.

(CMA adapted)

8 ***P9-13 (Change to LIFO Retail)** Diderot Stores Inc., which uses the conventional retail inventory method, wishes to change to the LIFO retail method beginning with the accounting year ending December 31, 2012.

Amounts as shown below appear on the store's books before adjustment.

	At Cost	At Retail
Inventory, January 1, 2012	$ 15,800	$ 24,000
Purchases in 2012	116,200	184,000
Markups in 2012		12,000
Markdowns in 2012		5,500
Sales in 2012		175,000

You are to assume that all markups and markdowns apply to 2012 purchases, and that it is appropriate to treat the entire inventory as a single department.

Instructions

Compute the inventory at December 31, 2012, under the following methods.

(a) The conventional retail method.

(b) The last-in, first-out retail method, effecting the change in method as of January 1, 2012. Assume that the cost-to-retail percentage for 2011 was recomputed correctly in accordance with procedures necessary to change to LIFO. This ratio was 59%.

(AICPA adapted)

8 *__P9-14 (Change to LIFO Retail; Dollar-Value LIFO Retail)__ Davenport Department Store converted from the conventional retail method to the LIFO retail method on January 1, 2012, and is now considering converting to the dollar-value LIFO inventory method. During your examination of the financial statements for the year ended December 31, 2013, management requested that you furnish a summary showing certain computations of inventory cost for the past 3 years.

Here is the available information.

1. The inventory at January 1, 2011, had a retail value of $56,000 and cost of $29,800 based on the conventional retail method.
2. Transactions during 2011 were as follows.

	Cost	Retail
Gross purchases	$311,000	$554,000
Purchase returns	5,200	10,000
Purchase discounts	6,000	
Gross sales (after employee discounts)		551,000
Sales returns		9,000
Employee discounts		3,000
Freight-in	17,600	
Net markups		20,000
Net markdowns		12,000

3. The retail value of the December 31, 2012, inventory was $75,600, the cost ratio for 2012 under the LIFO retail method was 61%, and the regional price index was 105% of the January 1, 2012, price level.
4. The retail value of the December 31, 2013, inventory was $62,640, the cost ratio for 2013 under the LIFO retail method was 60%, and the regional price index was 108% of the January 1, 2012, price level.

Instructions

(a) Prepare a schedule showing the computation of the cost of inventory on hand at December 31, 2011, based on the conventional retail method.

(b) Prepare a schedule showing the recomputation of the inventory to be reported on December 31, 2011, in accordance with procedures necessary to convert from the conventional retail method to the LIFO retail method beginning January 1, 2012. Assume that the retail value of the December 31, 2011, inventory was $60,000.

(c) Without prejudice to your solution to part (b), assume that you computed the December 31, 2011, inventory (retail value $60,000) under the LIFO retail method at a cost of $33,300. Prepare a schedule showing the computations of the cost of the store's 2012 and 2013 year-end inventories under the dollar-value LIFO method.

(AICPA adapted)

CONCEPTS FOR ANALYSIS

CA9-1 (Lower-of-Cost-or-Market) You have been asked by the financial vice president to develop a short presentation on the lower-of-cost-or-market method for inventory purposes. The financial VP needs to explain this method to the president because it appears that a portion of the company's inventory has declined in value.

Instructions

The financial VP asks you to answer the following questions.

(a) What is the purpose of the lower-of-cost-or-market method?
(b) What is meant by "market"? (*Hint:* Discuss the ceiling and floor constraints.)
(c) Do you apply the lower-of-cost-or-market method to each individual item, to a category, or to the total of the inventory? Explain.
(d) What are the potential disadvantages of the lower-of-cost-or-market method?

CA9-2 (Lower-of-Cost-or-Market) The market value of Lake Corporation's inventory has declined below its cost. Sheryl Conan, the controller, wants to use the loss method to write down inventory because it more clearly discloses the decline in market value and does not distort the cost of goods sold. Her supervisor, financial vice president Dick Wright, prefers the cost-of-goods-sold method to write down inventory because it does not call attention to the decline in market value.

Instructions

Answer the following questions.

(a) What, if any, is the ethical issue involved?
(b) Is any stakeholder harmed if Dick Wright's preference is used?
(c) What should Sheryl Conan do?

CA9-3 (Lower-of-Cost-or-Market) Ogala Corporation purchased a significant amount of raw materials inventory for a new product that it is manufacturing.

Ogala uses the lower-of-cost-or-market rule for these raw materials. The replacement cost of the raw materials is above the net realizable value, and both are below the original cost.

Ogala uses the average cost inventory method for these raw materials. In the last 2 years, each purchase has been at a lower price than the previous purchase, and the ending inventory quantity for each period has been higher than the beginning inventory quantity for that period.

Instructions

(a) **(1)** At which amount should Ogala's raw materials inventory be reported on the balance sheet? Why?
(2) In general, why is the lower-of-cost-or-market rule used to report inventory?
(b) What would have been the effect on ending inventory and cost of goods sold had Ogala used the LIFO inventory method instead of the average-cost inventory method for the raw materials? Why?

CA9-4 (Retail Inventory Method) Saurez Company, your client, manufactures paint. The company's president, Maria Saurez, has decided to open a retail store to sell Saurez paint as well as wallpaper and other supplies that would be purchased from other suppliers. She has asked you for information about the conventional retail method of pricing inventories at the retail store.

Instructions

Prepare a report to the president explaining the retail method of pricing inventories. Your report should include the following points.

(a) Description and accounting features of the method.
(b) The conditions that may distort the results under the method.
(c) A comparison of the advantages of using the retail method with those of using cost methods of inventory pricing.
(d) The accounting theory underlying the treatment of net markdowns and net markups under the method.

(AICPA adapted)

CA9-5 (Cost Determination, LCM, Retail Method) Olson Corporation, a retailer and wholesaler of national brand-name household lighting fixtures, purchases its inventories from various suppliers.

Instructions

(a) **(1)** What criteria should be used to determine which of Olson's costs are inventoriable?
(2) Are Olson's administrative costs inventoriable? Defend your answer.

(b) **(1)** Olson uses the lower-of-cost-or-market rule for its wholesale inventories. What are the theoretical arguments for that rule?

(2) The replacement cost of the inventories is below the net realizable value less a normal profit margin, which, in turn, is below the original cost. What amount should be used to value the inventories? Why?

(c) Olson calculates the estimated cost of its ending inventories held for sale at retail using the conventional retail inventory method. How would Olson treat the beginning inventories and net markdowns in calculating the cost ratio used to determine its ending inventories? Why?

(AICPA adapted)

CA9-6 (Purchase Commitments) Prophet Company signed a long-term purchase contract to buy timber from the U.S. Forest Service at $300 per thousand board feet. Under these terms, Prophet must cut and pay $6,000,000 for this timber during the next year. Currently, the market value is $250 per thousand board feet. At this rate, the market price is $5,000,000. Jerry Herman, the controller, wants to recognize the loss in value on the year-end financial statements, but the financial vice president, Billie Hands, argues that the loss is temporary and should be ignored. Herman notes that market value has remained near $250 for many months, and he sees no sign of significant change.

Instructions

(a) What are the ethical issues, if any?

(b) Is any particular stakeholder harmed by the financial vice president's decision?

(c) What should the controller do?

***CA9-7 (Retail Inventory Method and LIFO Retail)** Presented below are a number of items that may be encountered in computing the cost to retail percentage when using the conventional retail method or the LIFO retail method.

1. Markdowns.
2. Markdown cancellations.
3. Cost of items transferred in from other departments.
4. Retail value of items transferred in from other departments.
5. Sales discounts.
6. Purchases discounts (purchases recorded gross).
7. Estimated retail value of goods broken or stolen.
8. Cost of beginning inventory.
9. Retail value of beginning inventory.
10. Cost of purchases.
11. Retail value of purchases.
12. Markups.
13. Markup cancellations.
14. Employee discounts (sales recorded net).

Instructions

For each of the items listed above, indicate whether this item would be considered in the cost to retail percentage under (a) conventional retail and (b) LIFO retail.

USING YOUR JUDGMENT

FINANCIAL REPORTING

Financial Reporting Problem

The Procter & Gamble Company (P&G)

The financial statements of P&G are presented in Appendix 5B or can be accessed at the book's companion website, **www.wiley.com/college/kieso**.

Instructions

Refer to P&G's financial statements and the accompanying notes to answer the following questions.

(a) How does P&G value its inventories? Which inventory costing method does P&G use as a basis for reporting its inventories?

(b) How does P&G report its inventories in the balance sheet? In the notes to its financial statements, what three descriptions are used to classify its inventories?

(c) What costs does P&G include in Inventory and Cost of Products Sold?

(d) What was P&G's inventory turnover ratio in 2009? What is its gross profit percentage? Evaluate P&G's inventory turnover ratio and its gross profit percentage.

Comparative Analysis Case

The Coca-Cola Company and PepsiCo, Inc.

PEPSICO

Instructions

Go to the book's companion website and use information found there to answer the following questions related to **The Coca-Cola Company** and **PepsiCo, Inc.**

(a) What is the amount of inventory reported by Coca-Cola at December 31, 2009, and by PepsiCo at December 26, 2009? What percent of total assets is invested in inventory by each company?

(b) What inventory costing methods are used by Coca-Cola and PepsiCo? How does each company value its inventories?

(c) In the notes, what classifications (description) are used by Coca-Cola and PepsiCo to categorize their inventories?

(d) Compute and compare the inventory turnover ratios and days to sell inventory for Coca-Cola and PepsiCo for 2009. Indicate why there might be a significant difference between the two companies.

Financial Statement Analysis Cases

Case 1 Prab Robots, Inc.

Prab Robots, Inc., reported the following information regarding 2011–2012 inventory.

Prab Robots, Inc.

	2012	2011
Current assets		
Cash	$ 153,010	$ 538,489
Accounts receivable, net of allowance for doubtful accounts of $46,000 in 2012 and $160,000 in 2011	1,627,980	2,596,291
Inventories (Note 2)	1,340,494	1,734,873
Other current assets	123,388	90,592
Assets of discontinued operations	—	32,815
Total current assets	3,244,872	4,993,060

Notes to Consolidated Financial Statements

Note 1 (in part): Nature of Business and Significant Accounting Policies

Inventories—Inventories are stated at the lower-of-cost-or-market. Cost is determined by the last-in, first-out (LIFO) method by the parent company and by the first-in, first-out (FIFO) method by its subsidiaries.

Note 2: Inventories

Inventories consist of the following.

	2012	2011
Raw materials	$1,264,646	$2,321,178
Work in process	240,988	171,222
Finished goods and display units	129,406	711,252
Total inventories	1,635,040	3,203,652
Less: Amount classified as long-term	294,546	1,468,779
Current portion	$1,340,494	$1,734,873

Inventories are stated at the lower of cost determined by the LIFO method or market for Prab Robots, Inc. Inventories for the two wholly-owned subsidiaries, Prab Command, Inc. (U.S.) and Prab Limited (U.K.) are stated on the FIFO method which amounted to $566,000 at October 31, 2011. No inventory is stated on the FIFO method at October 31, 2012. Included in inventory stated at FIFO cost was $32,815 at October 31, 2011, of Prab Command inventory classified as an asset from discontinued operations (see Note 14). If the FIFO method had been used for the entire consolidated group, inventories after an adjustment to the lower-of-cost-or-market, would have been approximately $2,000,000 and $3,800,000 at October 31, 2012 and 2011, respectively.

Inventory has been written down to estimated net realizable value, and results of operations for 2012, 2011, and 2010 include a corresponding charge of approximately $868,000, $960,000, and $273,000, respectively, which represents the excess of LIFO cost over market.

Inventory of $294,546 and $1,468,779 at October 31, 2012 and 2011, respectively, shown on the balance sheet as a noncurrent asset represents that portion of the inventory that is not expected to be sold currently.

Reduction in inventory quantities during the years ended October 31, 2012, 2011, and 2010 resulted in liquidation of LIFO inventory quantities carried at a lower cost prevailing in prior years as compared with the cost of fiscal 2009 purchases. The effect of these reductions was to decrease the net loss by approximately $24,000, $157,000 and $90,000 at October 31, 2012, 2011, and 2010, respectively.

Instructions

(a) Why might Prab Robots, Inc., use two different methods for valuing inventory?

(b) Comment on why Prab Robots, Inc., might disclose how its LIFO inventories would be valued under FIFO.

(c) Why does the LIFO liquidation reduce operating costs?

(d) Comment on whether Prab would report more or less income if it had been on a FIFO basis for all its inventory.

Case 2 Barrick Gold Corporation

Barrick Gold Corporation, with headquarters in Toronto, Canada, is the world's most profitable and largest gold mining company outside South Africa. Part of the key to Barrick's success has been due to its ability to maintain cash flow while improving production and increasing its reserves of gold-containing property. In the most recent year, Barrick achieved record growth in cash flow, production, and reserves.

The company maintains an aggressive policy of developing previously identified target areas that have the possibility of a large amount of gold ore, and that have not been previously developed. Barrick limits the riskiness of this development by choosing only properties that are located in politically stable regions, and by the company's use of internally generated funds, rather than debt, to finance growth.

Barrick's inventories are as follows.

Barrick Gold Corporation

Inventories (in millions, US dollars)	
Current	
Gold in process	$133
Mine operating supplies	82
	$215
Non-current (included in Other assets)	
Ore in stockpiles	$65

Instructions

(a) Why do you think that there are no finished goods inventories? Why do you think the raw material, ore in stockpiles, is considered to be a non-current asset?

(b) Consider that Barrick has no finished goods inventories. What journal entries are made to record a sale?

(c) Suppose that gold bullion that cost $1.8 million to produce was sold for $2.4 million. The journal entry was made to record the sale, but no entry was made to remove the gold from the gold in process inventory. How would this error affect the following?

Balance Sheet		Income Statement	
Inventory	?	Cost of goods sold	?
Retained earnings	?	Net income	?
Accounts payable	?		
Working capital	?		
Current ratio	?		

Accounting, Analysis, and Principles

Englehart Company sells two types of pumps. One is large and is for commercial use. The other is smaller and is used in residential swimming pools. The following inventory data is available for the month of March.

	Units	Price per Unit	Total
Residential Pumps			
Inventory at Feb. 28:	200	$ 400	$ 80,000
Purchases:			
March 10	500	$ 450	$225,000
March 20	400	$ 475	$190,000
March 30	300	$ 500	$150,000
Sales:			
March 15	500	$ 540	$270,000
March 25	400	$ 570	$228,000
Inventory at March 31:	500		
Commercial Pumps			
Inventory at Feb. 28:	600	$ 800	$480,000
Purchases:			
March 3	600	$ 900	$540,000
March 12	300	$ 950	$285,000
March 21	500	$1,000	$500,000
Sales:			
March 18	900	$1,080	$972,000
March 29	600	$1,140	$684,000
Inventory at March 31:	500		

In addition to the above information, due to a downturn in the economy that has hit Englehart's commercial customers especially hard, Englehart expects commercial pump prices from March 31 onward to be considerably different (and lower) than at the beginning of and during March. Englehart has developed the following additional information.

	Commercial Pumps	**Residential Pumps**
Expected selling price (per unit, net of costs to sell)	$1,050	$580
Replacement cost	$ 900	$550

The normal profit margin is 16.67 percent of cost. Englehart uses the FIFO accounting method.

Accounting

(a) Determine the dollar amount that Englehart should report on its March 31 balance sheet for inventory. Assume Englehart applies lower-of-cost-or-market at the individual product level.

(b) Repeat part (a) but assume Englehart applies lower-of-cost-or-market at the major category level. Englehart places both commercial and residential pumps into the same (and only) category.

Analysis

Which of the two approaches above (individual product level or major categories) for applying LCM do you think gives the financial statement reader better information?

Principles

Assume that during April, the replacement cost of commercial pumps rebounds to $1,050 (assume this will be designated market value).

(a) Briefly describe how Englehart will report in its April financial statements the inventory remaining from March 31.

(b) Briefly describe the conceptual trade-offs inherent in the accounting in part (a).

BRIDGE TO THE PROFESSION

Professional Research: FASB Codification

Jones Co. is in a technology-intensive industry. Recently, one of its competitors introduced a new product with technology that might render obsolete some of Jones's inventory. The accounting staff wants to follow the appropriate authoritative literature in determining the accounting for this significant market event.

Instructions

If your school has a subscription to the FASB Codification, go to *http://aaahg.org/asclogin.cfm* to log in and prepare responses to the following. Provide Codification references for your responses.

(a) Identify the primary authoritative guidance for the accounting for inventories. What is the predecessor literature?

(b) List three types of goods that are classified as inventory. What characteristic will automatically exclude an item from being classified as inventory?

(c) Define "market" as used in the phrase "lower-of-cost-or-market."

(d) Explain when it is acceptable to state inventory above cost and which industries allow this practice.

Professional Simulation

In this simulation, you will address questions related to inventory valuation and measurement.

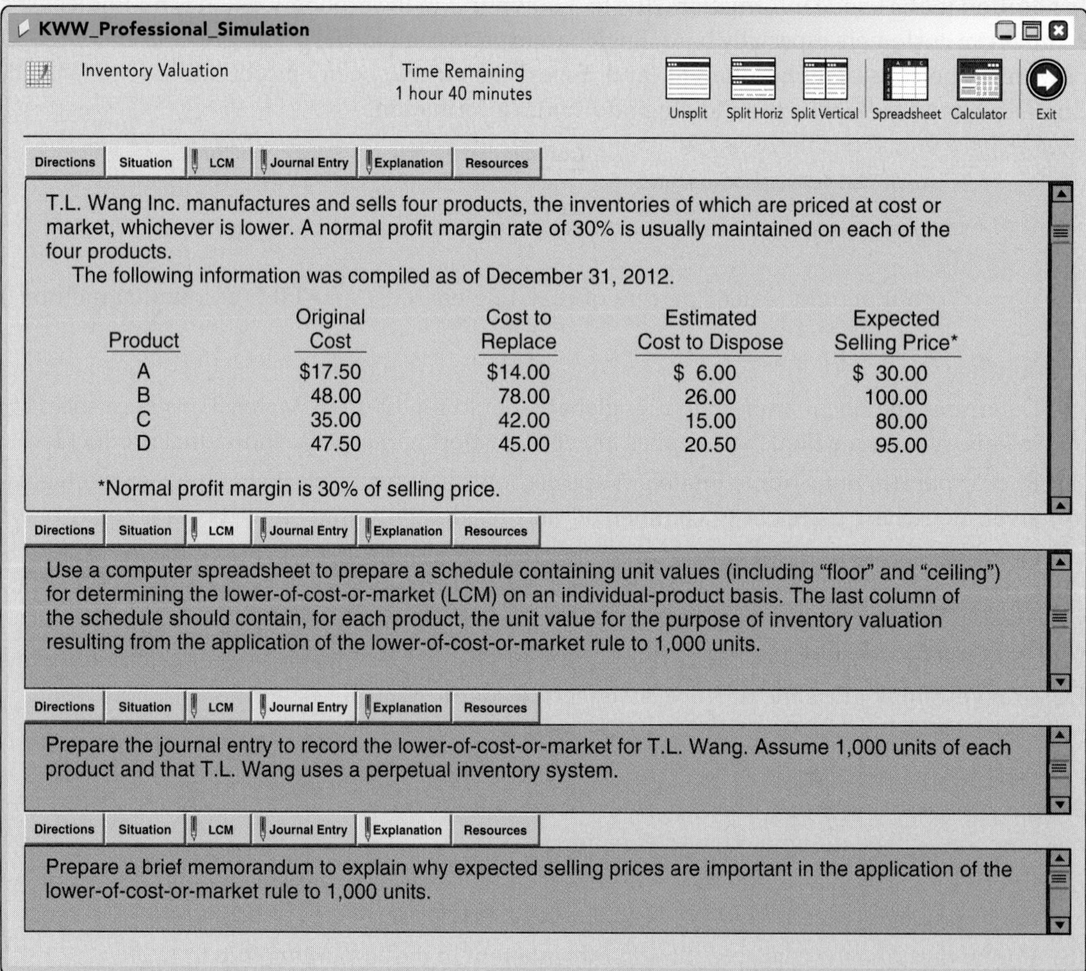

KWW_Professional_Simulation

Inventory Valuation

Time Remaining
1 hour 40 minutes

Unsplit | Split Horiz | Split Vertical | Spreadsheet | Calculator | Exit

Directions | Situation | LCM | Journal Entry | Explanation | Resources

T.L. Wang Inc. manufactures and sells four products, the inventories of which are priced at cost or market, whichever is lower. A normal profit margin rate of 30% is usually maintained on each of the four products.

The following information was compiled as of December 31, 2012.

Product	Original Cost	Cost to Replace	Estimated Cost to Dispose	Expected Selling Price*
A	$17.50	$14.00	$ 6.00	$ 30.00
B	48.00	78.00	26.00	100.00
C	35.00	42.00	15.00	80.00
D	47.50	45.00	20.50	95.00

*Normal profit margin is 30% of selling price.

Directions | Situation | LCM | Journal Entry | Explanation | Resources

Use a computer spreadsheet to prepare a schedule containing unit values (including "floor" and "ceiling") for determining the lower-of-cost-or-market (LCM) on an individual-product basis. The last column of the schedule should contain, for each product, the unit value for the purpose of inventory valuation resulting from the application of the lower-of-cost-or-market rule to 1,000 units.

Directions | Situation | LCM | Journal Entry | Explanation | Resources

Prepare the journal entry to record the lower-of-cost-or-market for T.L. Wang. Assume 1,000 units of each product and that T.L. Wang uses a perpetual inventory system.

Directions | Situation | LCM | Journal Entry | Explanation | Resources

Prepare a brief memorandum to explain why expected selling prices are important in the application of the lower-of-cost-or-market rule to 1,000 units.

The major IFRS requirements related to accounting and reporting for inventories are found in *IAS 2* ("Inventories"), *IAS 18* ("Revenue"), and *IAS 41* ("Agriculture"). In most cases, IFRS and GAAP are the same. The major differences are that IFRS prohibits the use of the LIFO cost flow assumption and records market in the lower-of-cost-or-market differently.

RELEVANT FACTS

- The requirements for accounting for and reporting inventories are more principles-based under IFRS. That is, GAAP provides more detailed guidelines in inventory accounting.
- Who owns the goods—goods in transit, consigned goods, special sales agreements—as well as the costs to include in inventory are essentially accounted for the same under IFRS and GAAP.
- A major difference between IFRS and GAAP relates to the LIFO cost flow assumption. GAAP permits the use of LIFO for inventory valuation. IFRS prohibits its use. FIFO and average cost are the only two acceptable cost flow assumptions permitted under IFRS. Both sets of standards permit specific identification where appropriate.
- In the lower-of-cost-or-market test for inventory valuation, IFRS defines market as net realizable value. GAAP, on the other hand, defines market as replacement cost subject to the constraints of net realizable value (the ceiling) and net realizable value less a normal markup (the floor). IFRS does not use a ceiling or a floor to determine market.
- Under GAAP, if inventory is written down under the lower-of-cost-or-market valuation, the new basis is now considered its cost. As a result, the inventory may not be written back up to its original cost in a subsequent period. Under IFRS, the write-down may be reversed in a subsequent period up to the amount of the previous write-down. Both the write-down and any subsequent reversal should be reported on the income statement. IFRS accounting for lower-or-cost-or-market is discussed more fully in the *About the Numbers* section below.
- IFRS requires both biological assets and agricultural produce at the point of harvest to be reported to net realizable value. GAAP does not require companies to account for all biological assets in the same way. Furthermore, these assets generally are not reported at net realizable value. Disclosure requirements also differ between the two sets of standards. IFRS accounting for agriculture and biological assets is discussed more fully in the *About the Numbers* section.

ABOUT THE NUMBERS

Lower-of-Cost-or-Net Realizable Value (LCNRV)

Inventories are recorded at their cost. However, if inventory declines in value below its original cost, a major departure from the historical cost principle occurs. Whatever the reason for a decline—obsolescence, price-level changes, or damaged goods—a company should write down the inventory to net realizable value to report this loss. **A company abandons the historical cost principle when the future utility (revenue-producing ability) of the asset drops below its original cost.**

Net Realizable Value

Recall that **cost** is the acquisition price of inventory computed using one of the historical cost-based methods—specific identification, average cost, or FIFO. The term **net realizable**

value (NRV) refers to the net amount that a company expects to realize from the sale of inventory. Specifically, net realizable value is the estimated selling price in the normal course of business less estimated costs to complete and estimated costs to make a sale.

To illustrate, assume that Mander Corp. has unfinished inventory with a cost of $950, a sales value of $1,000, estimated cost of completion of $50, and estimated selling costs of $200. Mander's net realizable value is computed as follows.

Inventory value—unfinished		$1,000
Less: Estimated cost of completion	$ 50	
Estimated cost to sell	200	250
Net realizable value		$ 750

Mander reports inventory on its statement of financial position (balance sheet) at $750. In its income statement, Mander reports a Loss on Inventory Write-Down of $200 ($950−$750).

A departure from cost is justified because inventories should not be reported at amounts higher than their expected realization from sale or use. In addition, a company like Mander should charge the loss of utility against revenues in the period in which the loss occurs, not in the period of sale. Companies therefore report their inventories at the **lower-of-cost-or-net realizable value (LCNRV)** at each reporting date.

Illustration of LCNRV

As indicated, a company values inventory at LCNRV. A company estimates net realizable value based on the most reliable evidence of the inventories' realizable amounts (expected selling price, expected costs to completion, and expected costs to sell). To illustrate, Regner Foods computes its inventory at LCNRV, as shown in Illustration IFRS9-1.

ILLUSTRATION IFRS9-1
LCNRV Data

Food	Cost	Net Realizable Value	Final Inventory Value
Spinach	$ 80,000	$120,000	$ 80,000
Carrots	100,000	110,000	100,000
Cut beans	50,000	40,000	40,000
Peas	90,000	72,000	72,000
Mixed vegetables	95,000	92,000	92,000
			$384,000

Final Inventory Value:

Spinach	Cost ($80,000) is selected because it is lower than net realizable value.
Carrots	Cost ($100,000) is selected because it is lower than net realizable value.
Cut beans	Net realizable value ($40,000) is selected because it is lower than cost.
Peas	Net realizable value ($72,000) is selected because it is lower than cost.
Mixed vegetables	Net realizable value ($92,000) is selected because it is lower than cost.

As indicated, the final inventory value of $384,000 equals the sum of the LCNRV for each of the inventory items. That is, Regner Foods applies the LCNRV rule to each individual type of food. Similar to GAAP, under IFRS, companies may apply the LCNRV rule to a group of similar or related items, or to the total of the inventory. If a company follows a group-of-similar-or-related-items or total-inventory approach in determining LCNRV, increases in market prices tend to offset decreases in market prices. In most situations, companies price inventory on an item-by-item basis. In fact, tax rules in some countries require that companies use an individual-item basis, barring practical difficulties.

In addition, the individual-item approach gives the lowest valuation for statement of financial position purposes. In some cases, a company prices inventory on a total-inventory basis when it offers only one end product (comprised of many different raw materials). If it produces several end products, a company might use a similar-or-related approach instead. **Whichever method a company selects, it should apply the method consistently from one period to another.**

Recording Net Realizable Value Instead of Cost

Similar to GAAP, one of two methods may be used to record the income effect of valuing inventory at net realizable value. One method, referred to as the **cost-of-goods-sold method**, debits cost of goods sold for the write-down of the inventory to net realizable value. As a result, the company does not report a loss in the income statement because the cost of goods sold already includes the amount of the loss. The second method, referred to as the **loss method**, debits a loss account for the write-down of the inventory to net realizable value. We use the following inventory data for Ricardo Company to illustrate entries under both methods.

Cost of goods sold (before adjustment to net realizable value)	$108,000
Ending inventory (cost)	82,000
Ending inventory (at net realizable value)	70,000

Illustration IFRS9-2 shows the entries for both the cost-of-goods-sold and loss methods, assuming the use of a perpetual inventory system.

ILLUSTRATION IFRS9-2
LCNRV Entries

Cost-of-Goods-Sold Method			Loss Method		
To reduce inventory from cost to net realizable value					
Cost of Goods Sold	12,000		Loss Due to Decline of Inventory to Net Realizable Value	12,000	
Inventory		12,000	Inventory		12,000

The cost-of-goods-sold method buries the loss in the Cost of Goods Sold account. The loss method, by identifying the loss due to the write-down, shows the loss separate from Cost of Goods Sold in the income statement. Illustration IFRS9-3 contrasts the differing amounts reported in the income statement under the two approaches, using data from the Ricardo example.

ILLUSTRATION IFRS9-3
Income Statement Reporting—LCNRV

Cost-of-Goods-Sold Method	
Sales revenue	$200,000
Cost of goods sold (after adjustment to net realizable value*)	120,000
Gross profit on sales	$ 80,000

Loss Method	
Sales revenue	$200,000
Cost of goods sold	108,000
Gross profit on sales	92,000
Loss due to decline of inventory to net realizable value	12,000
	$ 80,000

*Cost of goods sold (before adjustment to net realizable value)	$108,000
Difference between inventory at cost and net realizable value ($82,000 − $70,000)	12,000
Cost of goods sold (after adjustment to net realizable value)	$120,000

IFRS does not specify a particular account to debit for the write-down. We believe the loss method presentation is preferable because it clearly discloses the loss resulting from a decline in inventory net realizable values.

Use of an Allowance

Instead of crediting the Inventory account for net realizable value adjustments, companies generally use an allowance account, often referred to as the "Allowance to Reduce Inventory to Net Realizable Value." For example, using an allowance account under the loss method, Ricardo Company makes the following entry to record the inventory write-down to net realizable value.

Loss Due to Decline of Inventory to Net Realizable Value	12,000	
Allowance to Reduce Inventory to Net Realizable Value		12,000

Use of the allowance account results in reporting both the cost and the net realizable value of the inventory. Ricardo reports inventory in the statement of financial position as follows.

ILLUSTRATION IFRS9-4
Presentation of Inventory Using an Allowance Account

Inventory (at cost)	$82,000
Allowance to reduce inventory to net realizable value	(12,000)
Inventory at net realizable value	$70,000

The use of the allowance under the cost-of-goods-sold or loss method permits both the income statement and the statement of financial position to reflect inventory measured at $82,000, although the statement of financial position shows a net amount of $70,000. It also keeps subsidiary inventory ledgers and records in correspondence with the control account without changing prices. *For homework purposes, use an allowance account to record net realizable value adjustments, unless instructed otherwise.*

Recovery of Inventory Loss

In periods following the write-down, economic conditions may change such that the net realizable value of inventories previously written down may be *greater* than cost or there is clear evidence of an increase in the net realizable value. In this situation, the amount of the write-down is reversed, with the reversal limited to the amount of the original write-down.

Continuing the Ricardo example, assume that in the subsequent period, market conditions change, such that the net realizable value increases to $74,000 (an increase of $4,000). As a result, only $8,000 is needed in the allowance. Ricardo makes the following entry, using the loss method.

Allowance to Reduce Inventory to Net Realizable Value	4,000	
Recovery of Inventory Loss ($74,000 − $70,000)		4,000

Valuation Bases

For the most part, companies record inventory at LCNRV. However, there are some situations in which companies depart from the LCNRV rule. Such treatment may be justified in situations when cost is difficult to determine, the items are readily marketable at quoted market prices, and units of product are interchangeable. In this section, we discuss agricultural assets (including biological assets and agricultural produce), for which net realizable value is the general rule for valuing inventory.

Agricultural Inventory

Under IFRS, net realizable value measurement is used for inventory when the inventory is related to agricultural activity. In general, agricultural activity results in two types of agricultural assets: (1) biological assets or (2) agricultural produce at the point of harvest.

A **biological asset** (classified as a non-current asset) is a living animal or plant, such as sheep, cows, fruit trees, or cotton plants. **Agricultural produce** is the harvested product of a biological asset, such as wool from a sheep, milk from a dairy cow, picked fruit from a fruit tree, or cotton from a cotton plant.

Biological assets are measured on initial recognition and at the end of each reporting period at fair value less costs to sell (net realizable value). Companies record a gain or loss due to changes in the net realizable value of biological assets in income when it arises. For example, a gain may arise on initial recognition of a biological asset, such as when a calf is born. A gain or loss may arise on initial recognition of agricultural produce as a result of harvesting. Losses may arise on initial recognition for agricultural assets because costs to sell are deducted in determining fair value less costs to sell.

Agricultural produce (which are harvested from biological assets) are measured at fair value less costs to sell (net realizable value) at the point of harvest. Once harvested, the net realizable value of the agricultural produce becomes its cost, and this asset is accounted for similar to other inventories held for sale in the normal course of business. Measurement at fair value or selling price less point of sale costs corresponds to the net realizable value measure in the LCNRV test (selling price less estimated costs to complete and sell) since at harvest, the agricultural product is complete and is ready for sale.

Illustration of Agricultural Accounting at Net Realizable Value

To illustrate the accounting at net realizable value for agricultural assets, assume that Bancroft Dairy produces milk for sale to local cheese-makers. Bancroft began operations on January 1, 2012, by purchasing 420 milking cows for $460,000. Bancroft provides the following information related to the milking cows.

ILLUSTRATION IFRS9-5
Agricultural Assets—Bancroft Dairy

Milking cows		
Carrying value, January 1, 2012*		$460,000
Change in fair value due to growth and price changes	$35,000	
Decrease in fair value due to harvest	(1,200)	
Change in carrying value		33,800
Carrying value, January 31, 2012		$493,800
Milk harvested during January**		$ 36,000

*The carrying value is measured at fair value less costs to sell (net realizable value). The fair value of milking cows is determined based on market prices of livestock of similar age, breed, and genetic merit.
**Milk is initially measured at its fair value less costs to sell (net realizable value) at the time of milking. The fair value of milk is determined based on market prices in the local area.

As indicated, the carrying value of the milking cows increased during the month. Part of the change is due to changes in market prices (less costs to sell) for milking cows. The change in market price may also be affected by growth—the increase in value as the cows mature and develop increased milking capacity. At the same time, as mature cows are milked, their milking capacity declines (fair value decrease due to harvest). For example, changes in fair value arising from growth and harvesting from mature cows can be estimated based on changes in market prices of different age cows in the herd.

Bancroft makes the following entry to record the change in carrying value of the milking cows.

Biological Asset—Milking Cows ($493,800 − $460,000)	33,800	
Unrealized Holding Gain or Loss—Income		33,800

As a result of this entry, Bancroft's statement of financial position reports the Biological Asset—Milking Cows as a noncurrent asset at fair value less costs to sell (net realizable value). In addition, the unrealized gains and losses are reported as other income and expense on the income statement. In subsequent periods at each reporting date, Bancroft continues to report the Biological Asset—Milking Cows at net realizable value and records any related unrealized gains or losses in income. Because there is a ready market for the biological assets (milking cows), valuation at net realizable value provides more relevant information about these assets.

In addition to recording the change in the biological asset, Bancroft makes the following summary entry to record the milk harvested for the month of January.

Milk Inventory	36,000	
Unrealized Holding Gain or Loss—Income		36,000

The milk inventory is recorded at net realizable value at the time it is harvested and an Unrealized Holding Gain or Loss—Income is recognized in income. As with the biological assets, net realizable value is considered the most relevant for purposes of valuation at harvest. What happens to the milk inventory that Bancroft recorded upon harvesting the milk from the cows? Assuming the milk harvested in January was sold to a local cheese-maker for $38,500, Bancroft records the sale as follows.

Cash	38,500	
Cost of Goods Sold	36,000	
Milk Inventory		36,000
Sales Revenue		38,500

Thus, once harvested, the net realizable value of the harvested milk becomes its cost, and the milk is accounted for similar to other inventories held for sale in the normal course of business.

A final note: Some animals or plants may not be considered biological assets but would be classified and accounted for as other types of assets (not at net realizable value). For example, a pet shop may hold an inventory of dogs purchased from breeders that it then sells. Because the pet shop is not breeding the dogs, these dogs are not considered biological assets. As a result, the dogs are accounted for as inventory held for sale (at LCNRV).

ON THE HORIZON

One issue that will be difficult to resolve relates to the use of the LIFO cost flow assumption. As indicated, IFRS specifically prohibits its use. Conversely, the LIFO cost flow assumption is widely used in the United States because of its favorable tax advantages. In addition, many argue that LIFO from a financial reporting point of view provides a better matching of current costs against revenue and therefore enables companies to compute a more realistic income.

IFRS SELF-TEST QUESTIONS

1. All of the following are key similarities between GAAP and IFRS with respect to accounting for inventories *except:*

(a) costs to include in inventories are similar.
(b) LIFO cost flow assumption where appropriate is used by both sets of standards.
(c) fair value valuation of inventories is prohibited by both sets of standards.
(d) guidelines on ownership of goods are similar.

2. All of the following are key differences between GAAP and IFRS with respect to accounting for inventories *except* the:

(a) definition of the lower-of-cost-or-market test for inventory valuation differs between GAAP and IFRS.
(b) average cost method is prohibited under IFRS.
(c) inventory basis determination for write-downs differs between GAAP and IFRS.
(d) guidelines are more principles based under IFRS than they are under GAAP.

3. Starfish Company (a company using GAAP and the LIFO inventory method) is considering changing to IFRS and the FIFO inventory method. How would a comparison of these methods affect Starfish's financials?

(a) During a period of inflation, working capital would decrease when IFRS and the FIFO inventory method are used as compared to GAAP and LIFO.
(b) During a period of inflation, the taxes will decrease when IFRS and the FIFO inventory method are used as compared to GAAP and LIFO.
(c) During a period of inflation, net income would be greater if IFRS and the FIFO inventory method are used as compared to GAAP and LIFO.
(d) During a period of inflation, the current ratio would decrease when IFRS and the FIFO inventory method are used as compared to GAAP and LIFO.

4. Assume that Darcy Industries had the following inventory values.

Inventory cost (on December 31, 2012)	$1,500
Inventory market (on December 31, 2012)	$1,350
Inventory net realizable value (on December 31, 2012)	$1,320

Under IFRS, what is the inventory carrying value on December 31, 2012?

(a) $1,500.
(b) $1,570.
(c) $1,560.
(d) $1,320.

5. Under IFRS, agricultural activity results in which of the following types of assets?

I. Agricultural produce
II. Biological assets

(a) I only.
(b) II only.
(c) I and II.
(d) Neither I nor II.

IFRS CONCEPTS AND APPLICATION

IFRS9-1 Briefly describe some of the similarities and differences between GAAP and IFRS with respect to the accounting for inventories.

IFRS9-2 LaTour Inc. is based in France and prepares its financial statements in accordance with IFRS. In 2012, it reported cost of goods sold of $578 million and average inventory of $154 million. Briefly discuss how analysis of LaTour's inventory turnover ratio (and comparisons to a company using GAAP) might be affected by differences in inventory accounting between IFRS and GAAP.

IFRS9-3 Reed Pentak, a finance major, has been following globalization and made the following observation concerning accounting convergence: "I do not see many obstacles concerning development of a single accounting standard for inventories." Prepare a response to Reed to explain the main obstacle to achieving convergence in the area of inventory accounting.

IFRS9-4 Briefly describe the valuation of (a) biological assets and (b) agricultural produce.

IFRS9-5 In some instances, accounting principles require a departure from valuing inventories at cost alone. Determine the proper unit inventory price in the following cases.

	Cases				
	1	2	3	4	5
Cost	$15.90	$16.10	$15.90	$15.90	$15.90
Sales value	14.80	19.20	15.20	10.40	17.80
Estimated cost to complete	1.50	1.90	1.65	.80	1.00
Estimated cost to sell	.50	.70	.55	.40	.60

IFRS9-6 Riegel Company uses the LCNRV method, on an individual-item basis, in pricing its inventory items. The inventory at December 31, 2012, consists of products D, E, F, G, H, and I. Relevant per unit data for these products appear below.

	Item D	Item E	Item F	Item G	Item H	Item I
Estimated selling price	$120	$110	$95	$90	$110	$90
Cost	75	80	80	80	50	36
Cost to complete	30	30	25	35	30	30
Selling costs	10	18	10	20	10	20

Using the LCNRV rule, determine the proper unit value for statement of financial position reporting purposes at December 31, 2012, for each of the inventory items above.

IFRS9-7 Dover Company began operations in 2012 and determined its ending inventory at cost and at LCNRV at December 31, 2012, and December 31, 2013. This information is presented below.

	Cost	Net Realizable Value
12/31/12	$346,000	$322,000
12/31/13	410,000	390,000

(a) Prepare the journal entries required at December 31, 2012, and December 31, 2013, assuming that the inventory is recorded at LCNRV, and a perpetual inventory system using the cost-of-goods-sold method.

(b) Prepare journal entries required at December 31, 2012, and December 31, 2013, assuming that the inventory is recorded at cost, and a perpetual system using the loss method.

(c) Which of the two methods above provides the higher net income in each year?

IFRS9-8 Keyser's Fleece Inc. holds a drove of sheep. Keyser shears the sheep on a semiannual basis and then sells the harvested wool into the specialty knitting market. Keyser has the following information related to the shearing sheep at January 1, 2012, and during the first six months of 2012.

	Shearing Sheep
Carrying value (equal to net realizable value), January 1, 2012	$74,000
Change in fair value due to growth and price changes	4,700
Change in fair value due to harvest	(575)
Wool harvested during the first 6 months (at NRV)	9,000

Prepare the journal entry(ies) for Keyser's biological asset (shearing sheep) for the first six months of 2012.

IFRS9-9 Refer to the data in IFRS9-8 for Keyser's Fleece Inc. Prepare the journal entries for (a) the wool harvested in the first six months of 2012, and (b) the wool harvested is sold for $10,500 in July 2012.

Professional Research

IFRS9-10 Jones Co. is in a technology-intensive industry. Recently, one of its competitors introduced a new product with technology that might render obsolete some of Jones's inventory. The accounting staff wants to follow the appropriate authoritative literature in determining the accounting for this significant market event.

Instructions

Access the IFRS authoritative literature at the IASB website (*http://eifrs.iasb.org/*). When you have accessed the documents, you can use the search tool in your Internet browser to respond to the following questions. (Provide paragraph citations.)

(a) Identify the authoritative literature addressing inventory pricing.

(b) List three types of goods that are classified as inventory. What characteristic will automatically exclude an item from being classified as inventory?

(c) Define "net realizable value" as used in the phrase "lower-of-cost-or-net realizable value."

(d) Explain when it is acceptable to state inventory above cost and which industries allow this practice.

International Financial Reporting Problem: *Marks and Spencer plc*

IFRS9-11 The financial statements of **Marks and Spencer plc (M&S)** are available at the book's companion website or can be accessed at *http://corporate.marksandspencer.com/documents/publications/2010/Annual_Report_2010.*

Instructions

Refer to M&S's financial statements and the accompanying notes to answer the following questions.

(a) How does M&S value its inventories? Which inventory costing method does M&S use as a basis for reporting its inventories?

(b) How does M&S report its inventories in the statement of financial position? In the notes to its financial statements, what three descriptions are used to classify its inventories?

(c) What costs does M&S include in Inventory and Cost of Sales?

(d) What was M&S's inventory turnover ratio in 2010? What is its gross profit percentage? Evaluate M&S's inventory turnover ratio and its gross profit percentage.

ANSWERS TO IFRS SELF-TEST QUESTIONS

1. b **2.** b **3.** c **4.** d **5.** c

Remember to check the book's companion website to find additional resources for this chapter.

CHAPTER 10

Acquisition and Disposition of Property, Plant, and Equipment

LEARNING OBJECTIVES

After studying this chapter, you should be able to:

1. Describe property, plant, and equipment.
2. Identify the costs to include in initial valuation of property, plant, and equipment.
3. Describe the accounting problems associated with self-constructed assets.
4. Describe the accounting problems associated with interest capitalization.
5. Understand accounting issues related to acquiring and valuing plant assets.
6. Describe the accounting treatment for costs subsequent to acquisition.
7. Describe the accounting treatment for the disposal of property, plant, and equipment.

Where Have All the Assets Gone?

Investments in long-lived assets, such as property, plant, and equipment, are important elements in many companies' balance sheets. As the chart below indicates, major companies, such as **Southwest Airlines** and **Wal-Mart**, recently reported property, plant, and equipment (PP&E) as a percent of total assets ranging from 56 percent up to nearly 75 percent.

However, for various strategic reasons, many companies are now shedding property, plant, and equipment. Instead, they are paying others to manufacture and assemble products—functions they previously performed in their own facilities. Companies are also reducing fixed assets by outsourcing warehousing and distribution. Such logistics outsourcing can cut companies' own costs for keeping and managing inventories, and spare them the need to invest in advanced tracking technologies increasingly required by retailers. In a recent year more than 80 percent of the country's 100 biggest companies used third-party logistics providers. As a result, some companies such as **Nortel** and **Alcatel-Lucent** are decreasing their investment in long-lived assets, as the below chart shows.

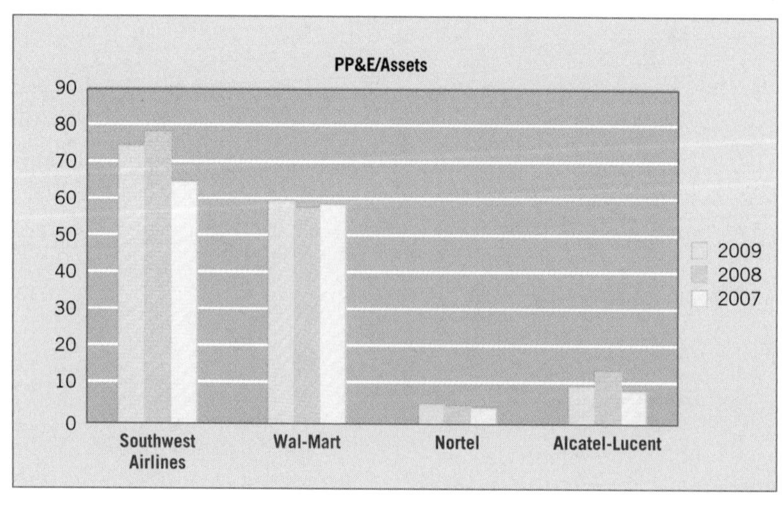

IFRS IN THIS CHAPTER

See the **International Perspectives** on pages 556, 560, 564, 568, and 573.

IFRS Insights related to property, plant, and equipment are presented in Chapter 11.

Nortel is a good example of these strategies. It has sold and outsourced certain facilities in order to reduce its direct manufacturing activities and costs. Nortel also sold its training and headset businesses. Further, it has aggressively outsourced other operations to reduce costs. Reductions in these areas will enable Nortel and other outsourcing companies to concentrate on their core operations and better manage investments in property, plant, and equipment.

Source: Adapted from Chapter 1 in Grady Means and David Schneider, *MetaCapitalism: The e-Business Revolution and the Design of 21st-Century Companies and Markets* (New York: John Wiley and Sons, 2000); and Kris Maher, "Global Goods Jugglers," *Wall Street Journal Online* (July 5, 2005).

PREVIEW OF CHAPTER 10

As we indicate in the opening story, a company like **Southwest Airlines** has a substantial investment in property, plant, and equipment. Conversely, other companies, such as **Nortel**, have a minor investment in these types of assets. In this chapter, we discuss the proper accounting for the acquisition, use, and disposition of property, plant, and equipment. The content and organization of the chapter are as follows.

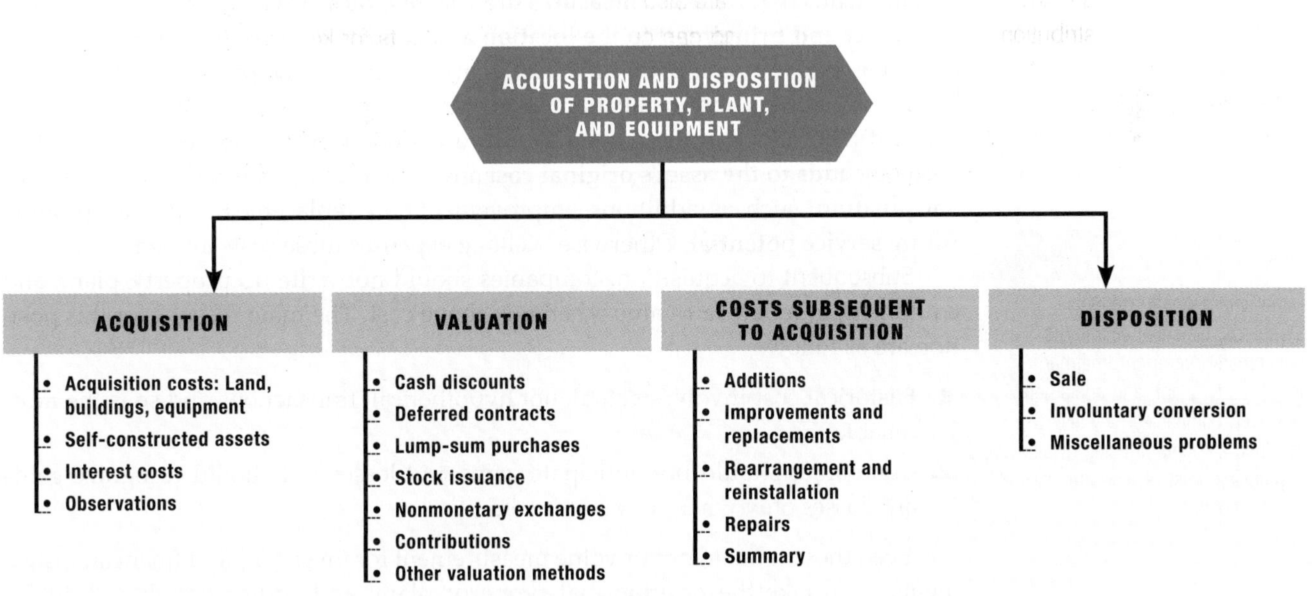

PROPERTY, PLANT, AND EQUIPMENT

LEARNING OBJECTIVE 1
Describe property, plant, and equipment.

Companies like Boeing, Target, and Starbucks use assets of a durable nature. Such assets are called property, plant, and equipment. Other terms commonly used are plant assets and fixed assets. We use these terms interchangeably. Property, plant, and equipment include land, building structures (offices, factories, warehouses), and equipment (machinery, furniture, tools). The major characteristics of property, plant, and equipment are as follows.

1. ***They are acquired for use in operations and not for resale.*** Only assets used in normal business operations are classified as property, plant, and equipment. For example, an idle building is more appropriately classified separately as an investment. Land developers or subdividers classify land as inventory.
2. ***They are long-term in nature and usually depreciated.*** Property, plant, and equipment yield services over a number of years. Companies allocate the cost of the investment in these assets to future periods through periodic depreciation charges. The exception is land, which is depreciated only if a material decrease in value occurs, such as a loss in fertility of agricultural land because of poor crop rotation, drought, or soil erosion.
3. ***They possess physical substance.*** Property, plant, and equipment are tangible assets characterized by physical existence or substance. This differentiates them from intangible assets, such as patents or goodwill. Unlike raw material, however, property, plant, and equipment do not physically become part of a product held for resale.

Underlying Concepts
Fair value is relevant to inventory but less so for property, plant, and equipment which, consistent with the going-concern assumption, are held for use in the business, not for sale like inventory.

ACQUISITION OF PROPERTY, PLANT, AND EQUIPMENT

LEARNING OBJECTIVE 2
Identify the costs to include in initial valuation of property, plant, and equipment.

Most companies use historical cost as the basis for valuing property, plant, and equipment. Historical cost **measures the cash or cash equivalent price of obtaining the asset and bringing it to the location and condition necessary for its intended use.** For example, companies like Kellogg Co. consider the purchase price, freight costs, sales taxes, and installation costs of a productive asset as part of the asset's cost. It then allocates these costs to future periods through depreciation. Further, Kellogg **adds to the asset's original cost** any related costs incurred **after the asset's acquisition**, such as additions, improvements, or replacements, **if they provide future service potential**. Otherwise, Kellogg expenses these costs immediately.[1]

Subsequent to acquisition, companies should not write up property, plant, and equipment to reflect fair value when it is above cost. The main reasons for this position are as follows.

1. Historical cost involves actual, not hypothetical, transactions and so is the most reliable.
2. Companies should not anticipate gains and losses but should recognize gains and losses only when the asset is sold.

INTERNATIONAL PERSPECTIVE

Under international accounting standards, historical cost is the benchmark (preferred) treatment for property, plant, and equipment. However, companies may also use revalued amounts. If using revaluation, companies must revalue the class of assets regularly.

Even those who favor fair value measurement for inventory and financial instruments often take the position that property, plant, and equipment should not be

[1]Additional costs to be included in the cost of property, plant, and equipment are those related to asset retirement obligations (AROs). These costs, such as those related to decommissioning nuclear facilities or reclamation or restoration of a mining facility, reflect a legal requirement to retire the asset at the end of its useful life. The expected costs are recorded in the asset cost and depreciated over the useful life. (See Chapter 13.)

revalued. The major concern is the difficulty of developing a reliable fair value for these types of assets. For example, how does one value a **General Motors** automobile manufacturing plant or a nuclear power plant owned by **Consolidated Edison**?

However, if the fair value of the property, plant, and equipment is less than its carrying amount, the asset may be written down. These situations occur when the asset is impaired (discussed in Chapter 11) and in situations where the asset is being held for sale. A long-lived asset classified as held for sale should be measured at the lower of its carrying amount or fair value less cost to sell. In that case, a reasonable valuation for the asset can be obtained, based on the sales price. A long-lived asset is not depreciated if it is classified as held for sale. This is because such assets are not being used to generate revenues. [1]

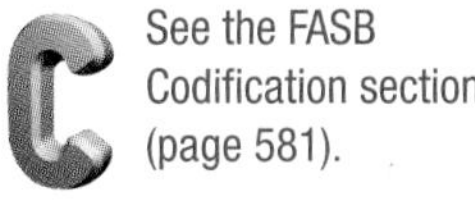
See the FASB Codification section (page 581).

Cost of Land

All expenditures made to acquire land and ready it for use are considered part of the land cost. Thus, when **Wal-Mart** or **Home Depot** purchases land on which to build a new store, its land costs typically include (1) the purchase price; (2) closing costs, such as title to the land, attorney's fees, and recording fees; (3) costs incurred in getting the land in condition for its intended use, such as grading, filling, draining, and clearing; (4) assumption of any liens, mortgages, or encumbrances on the property; and (5) any additional land improvements that have an indefinite life.

Gateway to the Profession

Expanded Discussion of Alternative Valuation Methods

For example, when Home Depot purchases land for the purpose of constructing a building, it considers all costs incurred up to the excavation for the new building as land costs. **Removal of old buildings—clearing, grading, and filling—is a land cost because this activity is necessary to get the land in condition for its intended purpose.** Home Depot treats any proceeds from getting the land ready for its intended use, such as salvage receipts on the demolition of an old building or the sale of cleared timber, as **reductions in the price of the land**.

In some cases, when Home Depot purchases land, it may assume certain obligations on the land such as back taxes or liens. In such situations, the cost of the land is the cash paid for it, plus the encumbrances. In other words, if the purchase price of the land is $50,000 cash, but Home Depot assumes accrued property taxes of $5,000 and liens of $10,000, its land cost is $65,000.

Home Depot also might incur **special assessments** for local improvements, such as pavements, street lights, sewers, and drainage systems. It should charge these costs to the Land account because they are relatively permanent in nature. That is, after installation, they are maintained by the local government. In addition, Home Depot should charge any permanent improvements it makes, such as landscaping, to the Land account. It records separately any **improvements with limited lives**, such as private driveways, walks, fences, and parking lots, as Land Improvements. These costs are depreciated over their estimated lives.

Generally, land is part of property, plant, and equipment. However, if the major purpose of acquiring and holding land is speculative, a company more appropriately classifies the land as an **investment**. If a real estate concern holds the land for resale, it should classify the land as **inventory**.

In cases where land is held as an investment, what accounting treatment should be given for taxes, insurance, and other direct costs incurred while holding the land? Many believe these costs should be capitalized. The reason: They are not generating revenue from the investment at this time. Companies generally use this approach except when the asset is currently producing revenue (such as rental property).

Cost of Buildings

The cost of buildings should include all expenditures related directly to their acquisition or construction. These costs include (1) materials, labor, and overhead costs incurred during construction, and (2) professional fees and building permits. Generally, companies contract others to construct their buildings. Companies consider all costs incurred, from excavation to completion, as part of the building costs.

But how should companies account for an old building that is on the site of a newly proposed building? Is the cost of removal of the old building a cost of the land or a cost of the new building? Recall that **if a company purchases land with an old building on it, then the cost of demolition less its salvage value is a cost of getting the land ready for its intended use and relates to the land rather than to the new building**. In other words, all costs of getting an asset ready for its intended use are costs of that asset.

Cost of Equipment

The term "equipment" in accounting includes delivery equipment, office equipment, machinery, furniture and fixtures, furnishings, factory equipment, and similar fixed assets. The cost of such assets includes the purchase price, freight and handling charges incurred, insurance on the equipment while in transit, cost of special foundations if required, assembling and installation costs, and costs of conducting trial runs. Costs thus include all expenditures incurred in acquiring the equipment and preparing it for use.

Self-Constructed Assets

LEARNING OBJECTIVE 3
Describe the accounting problems associated with self-constructed assets.

Occasionally companies construct their own assets. Determining the cost of such machinery and other fixed assets can be a problem. Without a purchase price or contract price, the company must allocate costs and expenses to arrive at the cost of the **self-constructed asset**. Materials and direct labor used in construction pose no problem. A company can trace these costs directly to work and material orders related to the fixed assets constructed.

However, the assignment of indirect costs of manufacturing creates special problems. These indirect costs, called **overhead** or burden, include power, heat, light, insurance, property taxes on factory buildings and equipment, factory supervisory labor, depreciation of fixed assets, and supplies.

Companies can handle indirect costs in one of two ways:

1. *Assign no fixed overhead to the cost of the constructed asset.* The major argument for this treatment is that indirect overhead is generally fixed in nature; it does not increase as a result of constructing one's own plant or equipment. This approach assumes that the company will have the same costs regardless of whether it constructs the asset or not. Therefore, to charge a portion of the overhead costs to the equipment will normally reduce current expenses and consequently overstate income of the current period. However, the company would assign to the cost of the constructed asset variable overhead costs that increase as a result of the construction.
2. *Assign a portion of all overhead to the construction process.* This approach, called a **full-costing approach**, is appropriate if one believes that costs attach to all products and assets manufactured or constructed. Under this approach, a company assigns a portion of all overhead to the construction process, as it would to normal production. Advocates say that failure to allocate overhead costs understates the initial cost of the asset and results in an inaccurate future allocation.

Companies should assign to the asset **a pro rata portion** of the fixed overhead to determine its cost. Companies use this treatment extensively because many believe that it results in a better matching of costs with revenues.

If the allocated overhead results in recording construction costs in excess of the costs that an outside independent producer would charge, the company should record the excess overhead as a period loss rather than capitalize it. This avoids capitalizing the asset at more than its probable fair value.[2]

Interest Costs During Construction

4 LEARNING OBJECTIVE
Describe the accounting problems associated with interest capitalization.

The proper accounting for interest costs has been a long-standing controversy. Three approaches have been suggested to account for the interest incurred in financing the construction of property, plant, and equipment:

1. ***Capitalize no interest charges during construction.*** Under this approach, interest is considered a cost of financing and not a cost of construction. Some contend that if a company had used stock (equity) financing rather than debt, it would not incur this cost. The major argument against this approach is that the use of cash, whatever its source, has an associated implicit interest cost, which should not be ignored.
2. ***Charge construction with all costs of funds employed, whether identifiable or not.*** This method maintains that the cost of construction should include the cost of financing, whether by cash, debt, or stock. Its advocates say that all costs necessary to get an asset ready for its intended use, including interest, are part of the asset's cost. Interest, whether actual or imputed, is a cost, just as are labor and materials. A major criticism of this approach is that imputing the cost of equity capital (stock) is subjective and outside the framework of a historical cost system.
3. ***Capitalize only the actual interest costs incurred during construction.*** This approach agrees in part with the logic of the second approach—that interest is just as much a cost as are labor and materials. But this approach capitalizes only interest costs incurred through debt financing. (That is, it does not try to determine the cost of equity financing.) Under this approach, a company that uses debt financing will have an asset of higher cost than a company that uses stock financing. Some consider this approach unsatisfactory because they believe the cost of an asset should be the same whether it is financed with cash, debt, or equity.

Illustration 10-1 shows how a company might add interest costs (if any) to the cost of the asset under the three capitalization approaches.

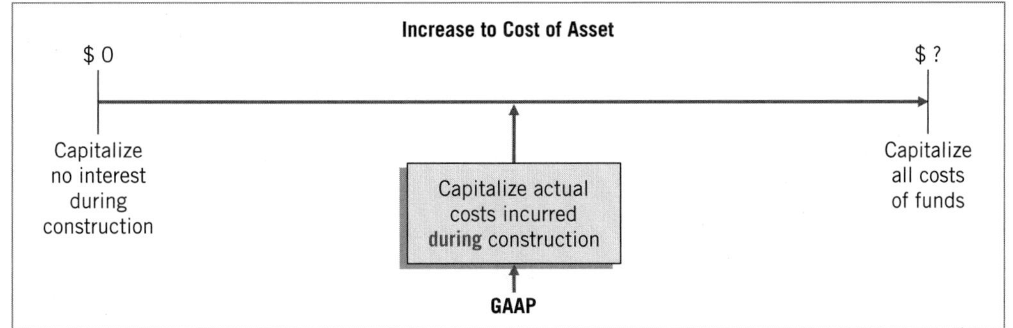

ILLUSTRATION 10-1
Capitalization of Interest Costs

[2]The Accounting Standards Executive Committee (AcSEC), in an exposure draft related to property, plant, and equipment, argues against allocation of overhead. Instead, it supports capitalization of only direct costs (costs directly related to the specific activities involved in the construction process). AcSEC was concerned that the allocation of overhead costs may lead to overly aggressive allocations and therefore misstatements of income. In addition, not reporting these costs as period costs during the construction period may affect comparisons of period costs and resulting net income from one period to the next. See Accounting Standards Executive Committee, "Accounting for Certain Costs and Activities Related to Property, Plant, and Equipment," Exposure Draft (New York: AICPA, June 29, 2001).

GAAP requires the third approach—capitalizing actual interest (with modification). This method follows the concept that the **historical cost of acquiring an asset includes all costs (including interest) incurred to bring the asset to the condition and location necessary for its intended use**. The rationale for this approach is that during construction, the asset is not generating revenues. Therefore, a company should defer (capitalize) interest costs. [2] Once construction is complete, the asset is ready for its intended use and a company can earn revenues. At this point the company should report interest as an expense and match it to these revenues. It follows that the company should expense any interest cost incurred in purchasing an asset that is ready for its intended use.

Underlying Concepts

The objective of capitalizing interest is to obtain a measure of acquisition cost that reflects a company's total investment in the asset and to charge that cost to future periods benefited.

To implement this general approach, companies consider three items:

1. Qualifying assets.
2. Capitalization period.
3. Amount to capitalize.

Qualifying Assets

To qualify for interest capitalization, assets must require a period of time to get them ready for their intended use. A company capitalizes interest costs starting with the first expenditure related to the asset. Capitalization continues until the company substantially readies the asset for its intended use.

Assets that qualify for interest cost capitalization include assets under construction for a company's own use (including buildings, plants, and large machinery) and assets intended for sale or lease that are constructed or otherwise produced as discrete projects (e.g., ships or real estate developments).

Examples of assets that do not qualify for interest capitalization are (1) assets that are in use or ready for their intended use, and (2) assets that the company does not use in its earnings activities and that are not undergoing the activities necessary to get them ready for use. Examples of this second type include land remaining undeveloped and assets not used because of obsolescence, excess capacity, or need for repair.

INTERNATIONAL PERSPECTIVE

Recently, IFRS changed to require companies to capitalize borrowing costs related to qualifying assets. These changes were made as part of the IASB's and FASB's convergence project.

Capitalization Period

The **capitalization period** is the period of time during which a company must capitalize interest. It begins with the presence of three conditions:

1. Expenditures for the asset have been made.
2. Activities that are necessary to get the asset ready for its intended use are in progress.
3. Interest cost is being incurred.

Interest capitalization **continues as long as these three conditions are present**. The capitalization period ends when the asset is substantially complete and ready for its intended use.

Amount to Capitalize

The amount of interest to capitalize is limited to the lower of actual interest cost incurred during the period or avoidable interest. **Avoidable interest** is the amount of interest cost during the period that a company could theoretically avoid if it had not made expenditures for the asset. If the actual interest cost for the period is $90,000 and the avoidable interest is $80,000, the company capitalizes only $80,000. Or, if the actual interest cost is $80,000 and the avoidable interest is $90,000, it still capitalizes only $80,000. In no situation should interest cost include a cost of capital charge for stockholders' equity. Furthermore, GAAP requires interest capitalization for a qualifying asset only if its effect, compared with the effect of expensing interest, is material. [3]

To apply the avoidable interest concept, a company determines the potential amount of interest that it may capitalize during an accounting period by multiplying the interest rate(s) by the **weighted-average accumulated expenditures** for qualifying assets during the period.

Weighted-Average Accumulated Expenditures. In computing the weighted-average accumulated expenditures, a company weights the construction expenditures by the amount of time (fraction of a year or accounting period) that it can incur interest cost on the expenditure.

To illustrate, assume a 17-month bridge construction project with current-year payments to the contractor of $240,000 on March 1, $480,000 on July 1, and $360,000 on November 1. The company computes the weighted-average accumulated expenditures for the year ended December 31 as follows.

ILLUSTRATION 10-2
Computation of Weighted-Average Accumulated Expenditures

Expenditures						
Date	Amount	×	Capitalization Period*	=	Weighted-Average Accumulated Expenditures
March 1	$ 240,000		10/12		$200,000
July 1	480,000		6/12		240,000
November 1	360,000		2/12		60,000
	$1,080,000				$500,000

*Months between date of expenditure and date interest capitalization stops or end of year, whichever comes first (in this case December 31).

To compute the weighted-average accumulated expenditures, a company weights the expenditures by the amount of time that it can incur interest cost on each one. For the March 1 expenditure, the company associates 10 months' interest cost with the expenditure. For the expenditure on July 1, it incurs only 6 months' interest costs. For the expenditure made on November 1, the company incurs only 2 months of interest cost.

Interest Rates. Companies follow these principles in selecting the appropriate interest rates to be applied to the weighted-average accumulated expenditures:

1. For the portion of weighted-average accumulated expenditures that is less than or equal to any amounts borrowed specifically to finance construction of the assets, **use the interest rate incurred on the specific borrowings.**
2. For the portion of weighted-average accumulated expenditures that is greater than any debt incurred specifically to finance construction of the assets, **use a weighted average of interest rates incurred on all other outstanding debt during the period.**[3]

[3]The interest rate to be used may rely exclusively on an average rate of all the borrowings, if desired. For our purposes, we use the specific borrowing rate followed by the average interest rate because we believe it to be more conceptually consistent. Either method can be used; GAAP does not provide explicit guidance on this measurement. For a discussion of this issue and others related to interest capitalization, see Kathryn M. Means and Paul M. Kazenski, "SFAS 34: Recipe for Diversity," *Accounting Horizons* (September 1988); and Wendy A. Duffy, "A Graphical Analysis of Interest Capitalization," *Journal of Accounting Education* (Fall 1990).

Illustration 10-3 shows the computation of a weighted-average interest rate for debt greater than the amount incurred specifically to finance construction of the assets.

ILLUSTRATION 10-3
Computation of Weighted-Average Interest Rate

	Principal	Interest
12%, 2-year note	$ 600,000	$ 72,000
9%, 10-year bonds	2,000,000	180,000
7.5%, 20-year bonds	5,000,000	375,000
	$7,600,000	$627,000

$$\text{Weighted-average interest rate} = \frac{\textbf{Total interest}}{\textbf{Total principal}} = \frac{\$627{,}000}{\$7{,}600{,}000} = 8.25\%$$

Comprehensive Example of Interest Capitalization

To illustrate the issues related to interest capitalization, assume that on November 1, 2011, Shalla Company contracted Pfeifer Construction Co. to construct a building for $1,400,000 on land costing $100,000 (purchased from the contractor and included in the first payment). Shalla made the following payments to the construction company during 2012.

January 1	March 1	May 1	December 31	Total
$210,000	$300,000	$540,000	$450,000	$1,500,000

Pfeifer Construction completed the building, ready for occupancy, on December 31, 2012. Shalla had the following debt outstanding at December 31, 2012.

Specific Construction Debt

1. 15%, 3-year note to finance purchase of land and construction of the building, dated December 31, 2011, with interest payable annually on December 31 — $750,000

Other Debt

2. 10%, 5-year note payable, dated December 31, 2008, with interest payable annually on December 31 — $550,000
3. 12%, 10-year bonds issued December 31, 2007, with interest payable annually on December 31 — $600,000

Shalla computed the weighted-average accumulated expenditures during 2012 as shown in Illustration 10-4.

ILLUSTRATION 10-4
Computation of Weighted-Average Accumulated Expenditures

Expenditures			Current-Year		
Date	Amount	×	Capitalization Period	=	Weighted-Average Accumulated Expenditures
January 1	$ 210,000		12/12		$210,000
March 1	300,000		10/12		250,000
May 1	540,000		8/12		360,000
December 31	450,000		0		0
	$1,500,000				$820,000

Note that the expenditure made on December 31, the last day of the year, does not have any interest cost.

Shalla computes the avoidable interest as shown in Illustration 10-5.

ILLUSTRATION 10-5
Computation of Avoidable Interest

Weighted-Average Accumulated Expenditures	×	Interest Rate	=	Avoidable Interest
$750,000		.15 (construction note)		$112,500
70,000[a]		.1104 (weighted average of other debt)[b]		7,728
$820,000				$120,228

[a]The amount by which the weighted-average accumulated expenditures exceeds the specific construction loan.

[b]Weighted-average interest rate computation:

	Principal	Interest
10%, 5-year note	$ 550,000	$ 55,000
12%, 10-year bonds	600,000	72,000
	$1,150,000	$127,000

$$\text{Weighted-average interest rate} = \frac{\text{Total interest}}{\text{Total principal}} = \frac{\$127{,}000}{\$1{,}150{,}000} = 11.04\%$$

The company determines the actual interest cost, which represents the maximum amount of interest that it may capitalize during 2012, as shown in Illustration 10-6.

ILLUSTRATION 10-6
Computation of Actual Interest Cost

Construction note	$750,000 × .15 = $112,500
5-year note	$550,000 × .10 = 55,000
10-year bonds	$600,000 × .12 = 72,000
Actual interest	$239,500

The interest cost that Shalla capitalizes is the lesser of $120,228 (avoidable interest) and $239,500 (actual interest), or $120,228.

Shalla records the following journal entries during 2012:

	Debit	Credit
January 1		
Land	100,000	
Buildings (or Construction in Process)	110,000	
Cash		210,000
March 1		
Buildings	300,000	
Cash		300,000
May 1		
Buildings	540,000	
Cash		540,000
December 31		
Buildings	450,000	
Cash		450,000
Buildings (Capitalized Interest)	120,228	
Interest Expense ($239,500 − $120,228)	119,272	
Cash ($112,500 + $55,000 + $72,000)		239,500

Gateway to the Profession

Tutorial on Interest Capitalization

Shalla should write off capitalized interest cost as part of depreciation over the useful life of the assets involved and not over the term of the debt. It should disclose the total interest cost incurred during the period, with the portion charged to expense and the portion capitalized indicated.

At December 31, 2012, Shalla discloses the amount of interest capitalized either as part of the nonoperating section of the income statement or in the notes accompanying the financial statements. We illustrate both forms of disclosure, in Illustrations 10-7 and 10-8 (page 564).

ILLUSTRATION 10-7
Capitalized Interest Reported in the Income Statement

Income from operations		XXXX
Other expenses and losses:		
Interest expense	$239,500	
Less: Capitalized interest	120,228	119,272
Income before income taxes		XXXX
Income taxes		XXX
Net income		XXXX

ILLUSTRATION 10-8
Capitalized Interest Disclosed in a Note

Note 1: Accounting Policies. *Capitalized Interest.* During 2012, total interest cost was $239,500, of which $120,228 was capitalized and $119,272 was charged to expense.

WHAT'S IN YOUR INTEREST?

What do the numbers mean?

The requirement to capitalize interest can significantly impact financial statements. For example, when earnings of building manufacturer **Jim Walter's Corporation** dropped from $1.51 to $1.17 per share, the company offset 11 cents per share of the decline by capitalizing the interest on coal mining projects and several plants under construction.

How do statement users determine the impact of interest capitalization on a company's bottom line? They examine the notes to the financial statements. Companies with material interest capitalization must disclose the amounts of capitalized interest relative to total interest costs. For example, **Anadarko Petroleum Corporation** capitalized nearly 30 percent of its total interest costs in a recent year and provided the following footnote related to capitalized interest.

Financial Footnotes
Total interest costs incurred during the year were $82,415,000. Of this amount, the Company capitalized $24,716,000. Capitalized interest is included as part of the cost of oil and gas properties. The capitalization rates are based on the Company's weighted-average cost of borrowings used to finance the expenditures.

Special Issues Related to Interest Capitalization

Two issues related to interest capitalization merit special attention:

1. Expenditures for land.
2. Interest revenue.

Expenditures for Land. When a company purchases land with the intention of developing it for a particular use, interest costs associated with those expenditures qualify for interest capitalization. If it purchases land as a site for a structure (such as a plant site), **interest costs capitalized during the period of construction are part of the cost of the plant, not the land.** Conversely, if the company develops land for lot sales, it includes any capitalized interest cost as part of the acquisition cost of the developed land. However, it should **not** capitalize interest costs involved in purchasing land held **for speculation** because the asset is ready for its intended use.

INTERNATIONAL PERSPECTIVE

IFRS requires that interest revenue earned on specific borrowings should offset interest costs capitalized. The rationale is that the interest revenue earned is directly related to the interest cost incurred on the specific borrowing.

Interest Revenue. Companies frequently borrow money to finance construction of assets. They temporarily invest the excess borrowed funds in interest-bearing securities until they need the funds to pay for construction. During the early stages of construction, interest revenue earned may exceed the interest cost incurred on the borrowed funds.

Should companies offset interest revenue against interest cost when determining the amount of interest to capitalize as part of the construction cost of assets? In general, **companies should not net or offset interest revenue against interest cost.**

Temporary or short-term investment decisions are not related to the interest incurred as part of the acquisition cost of assets. Therefore, companies should capitalize the interest incurred on qualifying assets whether or not they temporarily invest excess funds in short-term securities. Some criticize this approach because a company can defer the interest cost but report the interest revenue in the current period.

Observations

The interest capitalization requirement is still debated. From a conceptual viewpoint, many believe that, for the reasons mentioned earlier, companies should either capitalize **no interest cost** or **all interest costs**, actual or imputed.

VALUATION OF PROPERTY, PLANT, AND EQUIPMENT

> **5 LEARNING OBJECTIVE**
> Understand accounting issues related to acquiring and valuing plant assets.

Like other assets, **companies should record property, plant, and equipment at the fair value of what they give up or at the fair value of the asset received, whichever is more clearly evident**. However, the process of asset acquisition sometimes obscures fair value. For example, if a company buys land and buildings together for one price, how does it determine separate values for the land and buildings? We examine these types of accounting problems in the following sections.

Cash Discounts

When a company purchases plant assets subject to cash discounts for prompt payment, how should it report the discount? If it takes the discount, the company should consider the discount as a reduction in the purchase price of the asset. But should the company reduce the asset cost even if it does not take the discount?

Two points of view exist on this question. One approach considers the discount—whether taken or not—as a reduction in the cost of the asset. The rationale for this approach is that the real cost of the asset is the cash or cash equivalent price of the asset. In addition, some argue that the terms of cash discounts are so attractive that failure to take them indicates management error or inefficiency.

Proponents of the other approach argue that failure to take the discount should not always be considered a loss. The terms may be unfavorable, or it might not be prudent for the company to take the discount. At present, companies use both methods, though most prefer the former method.

Deferred-Payment Contracts

Companies frequently purchase plant assets on long-term credit contracts, using notes, mortgages, bonds, or equipment obligations. **To properly reflect cost, companies account for assets purchased on long-term credit contracts at the present value of the consideration exchanged between the contracting parties at the date of the transaction.**

For example, Greathouse Company purchases an asset today in exchange for a \$10,000 zero-interest-bearing note payable four years from now. The company would not record the asset at \$10,000. Instead, the present value of the \$10,000 note establishes the exchange price of the transaction (the purchase price of the asset). Assuming an appropriate interest rate of 9 percent at which to discount this single payment of \$10,000 due four years from now, Greathouse records this asset at \$7,084.30 (\$10,000 × .70843). [See Table 6-2 (page 357) for the present value of a single sum, $PV = \$10,000\ (PVF_{4,9\%})$.]

When no interest rate is stated, or if the specified rate is unreasonable, the company imputes an appropriate interest rate. The objective is to approximate the interest rate that the buyer and seller would negotiate at arm's length in a similar borrowing transaction. In imputing an interest rate, companies consider such factors as the borrower's credit rating, the amount and maturity date of the note, and prevailing interest rates. **The company uses the cash exchange price of the asset acquired (if determinable) as the basis for recording the asset and measuring the interest element.**

To illustrate, Sutter Company purchases a specially built robot spray painter for its production line. The company issues a $100,000, five-year, zero-interest-bearing note to Wrigley Robotics, Inc. for the new equipment. The prevailing market rate of interest for obligations of this nature is 10 percent. Sutter is to pay off the note in five $20,000 installments, made at the end of each year. Sutter cannot readily determine the fair value of this specially built robot. Therefore, Sutter approximates the robot's value by establishing the fair value (present value) of the note. Entries for the date of purchase and dates of payments, plus computation of the present value of the note, are as follows.

Date of Purchase

Equipment	75,816*	
Discount on Notes Payable	24,184	
Notes Payable		100,000

*Present value of note = $20,000 ($PVF\text{-}OA_{5,10\%}$)
= $20,000 (3.79079); Table 6-4
= $75,816

End of First Year

Interest Expense	7,582	
Notes Payable	20,000	
Cash		20,000
Discount on Notes Payable		7,582

Interest expense in the first year under the effective-interest approach is $7,582 [($100,000 − $24,184) × 10%]. The entry at the end of the second year to record interest and principal payment is as follows.

End of Second Year

Interest Expense	6,340	
Notes Payable	20,000	
Cash		20,000
Discount on Notes Payable		6,340

Interest expense in the second year under the effective-interest approach is $6,340 [($100,000 − $24,184) − ($20,000 − $7,582)] × 10%.

If Sutter did not impute an interest rate for deferred-payment contracts, it would record the asset at an amount greater than its fair value and overstate depreciation expense. In addition, Sutter would understate interest expense in the income statement for all periods involved.

Lump-Sum Purchases

A special problem of valuing fixed assets arises when a company purchases a group of plant assets at a single lump-sum price. When this common situation occurs, the company allocates the total cost among the various assets on the basis of their relative fair values. The assumption is that costs will vary in direct proportion to fair value. This is the same principle that companies apply to allocate a lump-sum cost among different inventory items.

To determine fair value, a company should use valuation techniques that are appropriate in the circumstances. In some cases, a single valuation technique will be appropriate. In other cases, multiple valuation approaches might have to be used.[4]

To illustrate, Norduct Homes, Inc. decides to purchase several assets of a small heating concern, Comfort Heating, for $80,000. Comfort Heating is in the process of liquidation. Its assets sold are:

	Book Value	Fair Value
Inventory	$30,000	$ 25,000
Land	20,000	25,000
Building	35,000	50,000
	$85,000	$100,000

Norduct Homes allocates the $80,000 purchase price on the basis of the relative fair values (assuming specific identification of costs is impracticable) in the following manner.

ILLUSTRATION 10-9
Allocation of Purchase Price—Relative Fair Value Basis

Inventory	$\frac{\$25,000}{\$100,000} \times \$80,000 = \$20,000$
Land	$\frac{\$25,000}{\$100,000} \times \$80,000 = \$20,000$
Building	$\frac{\$50,000}{\$100,000} \times \$80,000 = \$40,000$

Issuance of Stock

When companies acquire property by issuing securities, such as common stock, the par or stated value of such stock fails to properly measure the property cost. If trading of the stock is active, **the market price of the stock issued is a fair indication of the cost of the property acquired. The stock is a good measure of the current cash equivalent price.**

For example, Upgrade Living Co. decides to purchase some adjacent land for expansion of its carpeting and cabinet operation. In lieu of paying cash for the land, the company issues to Deedland Company 5,000 shares of common stock (par value $10) that have a fair value of $12 per share. Upgrade Living Co. records the following entry.

Land (5,000 × $12)	60,000	
Common Stock		50,000
Paid-In Capital in Excess of Par—Common Stock		10,000

If the company cannot determine the market price of the common stock exchanged, it establishes the fair value of the property. It then uses the value of the property as the basis for recording the asset and issuance of the common stock.

[4]The valuation approaches that should be used are the market, income, or cost approach, or a combination of these approaches. The *market approach* uses observable prices and other relevant information generated by market transactions involving comparable assets. The *income approach* uses valuation techniques to convert future amounts (for example, cash flows or earnings) to a single present value amount (discounted). The *cost approach* is based on the amount that currently would be required to replace the service capacity of an asset (often referred to as current replacement cost). In determining the fair value, the company should assume the highest and best use of the asset. **[4]**

Exchanges of Nonmonetary Assets

The proper accounting for exchanges of nonmonetary assets, such as property, plant, and equipment, is controversial.[5] Some argue that companies should account for these types of exchanges based on the fair value of the asset given up or the fair value of the asset received, with a gain or loss recognized. Others believe that they should account for exchanges based on the recorded amount (book value) of the asset given up, with no gain or loss recognized. Still others favor an approach that recognizes losses in all cases, but defers gains in special situations.

Ordinarily companies account for the exchange of nonmonetary assets on the basis of **the fair value of the asset given up or the fair value of the asset received, whichever is clearly more evident**. [5] Thus, companies **should recognize immediately** any gains or losses on the exchange. The rationale for immediate recognition is that most transactions have **commercial substance**, and therefore gains and losses should be recognized.

INTERNATIONAL PERSPECTIVE

The FASB recently changed its accounting for exchanges to converge with IFRS. Previously, the FASB used a "similar in nature" criterion for exchanged assets to determine whether gains should be recognized. With use of the commercial substance test, GAAP and IFRS are now very similar.

Meaning of Commercial Substance

As indicated above, fair value is the basis for measuring an asset acquired in a nonmonetary exchange if the transaction has commercial substance. An exchange has commercial substance if the future cash flows change as a result of the transaction. That is, if the two parties' economic positions change, the transaction has commercial substance.

For example, Andrew Co. exchanges some of its equipment for land held by Roddick Inc. It is likely that the timing and amount of the cash flows arising for the land will differ significantly from the cash flows arising from the equipment. As a result, both Andrew Co. and Roddick Inc. are in different economic positions. Therefore, the exchange has commercial substance, and the companies recognize a gain or loss on the exchange.

What if companies exchange similar assets, such as one truck for another truck? Even in an exchange of similar assets, a change in the economic position of the company can result. For example, let's say the useful life of the truck received is significantly longer than that of the truck given up. The cash flows for the trucks can differ significantly. As a result, the transaction has commercial substance, and the company should use fair value as a basis for measuring the asset received in the exchange.

However, it is possible to exchange similar assets but not have a significant difference in cash flows. That is, the company is in the same economic position as before the exchange. In that case, the company recognizes a loss but generally defers a gain.

As we will see in the examples below, use of fair value generally results in recognizing a gain or loss at the time of the exchange. Consequently, companies must determine if the transaction has commercial substance. To make this determination, they must carefully evaluate the cash flow characteristics of the assets exchanged.[6]

Illustration 10-10 summarizes asset exchange situations and the related accounting.

[5]Nonmonetary assets are items whose price in terms of the monetary unit may change over time. Monetary assets—cash and short- or long-term accounts and notes receivable—are fixed in terms of units of currency by contract or otherwise.

[6]The determination of the commercial substance of a transaction requires significant judgment. In determining whether future cash flows change, it is necessary to do one of two things: (1) Determine whether the risk, timing, and amount of cash flows arising for the asset received differ from the cash flows associated with the outbound asset. Or, (2) evaluate whether cash flows are affected with the exchange versus without the exchange. Also note that if companies cannot determine fair values of the assets exchanged, then they should use recorded book values in accounting for the exchange.

Type of Exchange	Accounting Guidance
Exchange has commercial substance.	Recognize gains and losses immediately.
Exchange lacks commercial substance—no cash received.	Defer gains; recognize losses immediately.
Exchange lacks commercial substance—cash received.	Recognize partial gain; recognize losses immediately.*

*If cash is 25% or more of the fair value of the exchange, recognize entire gain because earnings process is complete.

ILLUSTRATION 10-10
Accounting for Exchanges

As Illustration 10-10 indicates, companies immediately recognize losses they incur on all exchanges. The accounting for gains depends on whether the exchange has commercial substance. If the exchange has commercial substance, the company recognizes the gain immediately. However, the profession modifies the rule for immediate recognition of a gain when an exchange lacks commercial substance: If the company receives no cash in such an exchange, it defers recognition of a gain. If the company receives cash in such an exchange, it recognizes part of the gain immediately.

To illustrate the accounting for these different types of transactions, we examine various loss and gain exchange situations.

Exchanges—Loss Situation

When a company exchanges nonmonetary assets and a loss results, the company recognizes the loss immediately. The rationale: Companies should not value assets at more than their cash equivalent price; if the loss were deferred, assets would be overstated. Therefore, companies recognize a loss immediately whether the exchange has commercial substance or not.

For example, Information Processing, Inc. trades its used machine for a new model at Jerrod Business Solutions Inc. The exchange has commercial substance. The used machine has a book value of $8,000 (original cost $12,000 less $4,000 accumulated depreciation) and a fair value of $6,000. The new model lists for $16,000. Jerrod gives Information Processing a trade-in allowance of $9,000 for the used machine. Information Processing computes the cost of the new asset as follows.

List price of new machine	$16,000
Less: Trade-in allowance for used machine	9,000
Cash payment due	7,000
Fair value of used machine	6,000
Cost of new machine	$13,000

ILLUSTRATION 10-11
Computation of Cost of New Machine

Information Processing records this transaction as follows.

Equipment	13,000	
Accumulated Depreciation—Equipment	4,000	
Loss on Disposal of Equipment	2,000	
Equipment		12,000
Cash		7,000

We verify the loss on the disposal of the used machine as follows.

Fair value of used machine	$6,000
Less: Book value of used machine	8,000
Loss on disposal of used machine	$2,000

ILLUSTRATION 10-12
Computation of Loss on Disposal of Used Machine

Why did Information Processing not use the trade-in allowance or the book value of the old asset as a basis for the new equipment? The company did not use the trade-in allowance because it included a price concession (similar to a price discount). Few individuals pay list price for a new car. Dealers such as Jerrod often inflate trade-in allowances on the used car so that actual selling prices fall below list prices. To record the car at list price would state it at an amount in excess of its cash equivalent price because of the new car's inflated list price. Similarly, use of book value in this situation would overstate the value of the new machine by $2,000.[7]

Exchanges—Gain Situation

Has Commercial Substance. Now let's consider the situation in which a nonmonetary exchange has commercial substance and a gain is realized. In such a case, a company usually records the cost of a nonmonetary asset acquired in exchange for another nonmonetary asset at the **fair value of the asset given up**, and immediately recognizes a gain. The company should use the **fair value of the asset received** only if it is more clearly evident than the fair value of the asset given up.

To illustrate, Interstate Transportation Company exchanged a number of used trucks plus cash for a semi-truck. The used trucks have a combined book value of $42,000 (cost $64,000 less $22,000 accumulated depreciation). Interstate's purchasing agent, experienced in the secondhand market, indicates that the used trucks have a fair value of $49,000. In addition to the trucks, Interstate must pay $11,000 cash for the semi-truck. Interstate computes the cost of the semi-truck as follows.

ILLUSTRATION 10-13
Computation of Semi-Truck Cost

Fair value of trucks exchanged	$49,000
Cash paid	11,000
Cost of semi-truck	$60,000

Interstate records the exchange transaction as follows.

Trucks (semi)	60,000	
Accumulated Depreciation—Trucks	22,000	
Trucks (used)		64,000
Gain on Disposal of Trucks		7,000
Cash		11,000

The gain is the difference between the fair value of the used trucks and their book value. We verify the computation as follows.

ILLUSTRATION 10-14
Computation of Gain on Disposal of Used Trucks

Fair value of used trucks		$49,000
Cost of used trucks	$64,000	
Less: Accumulated depreciation	22,000	
Book value of used trucks		(42,000)
Gain on disposal of used trucks		$ 7,000

In this case, Interstate is in a different economic position, and therefore the transaction has commercial substance. Thus, it **recognizes a gain.**

Lacks Commercial Substance—No Cash Received. We now assume that the Interstate Transportation Company exchange lacks commercial substance. That is, the economic

[7]Recognize that for Jerrod (the dealer), the asset given up in the exchange is considered inventory. As a result, Jerrod records a sale and related cost of goods sold. The used machine received by Jerrod is recorded at fair value.

position of Interstate did not change significantly as a result of this exchange. In this case, Interstate defers the gain of $7,000 and reduces the basis of the semi-truck. Illustration 10-15 shows two different but acceptable computations to illustrate this reduction.

Fair value of semi-truck	$60,000		Book value of used trucks	$42,000
Less: Gain deferred	7,000	OR	Plus: Cash paid	11,000
Basis of semi-truck	$53,000		Basis of semi-truck	$53,000

ILLUSTRATION 10-15
Basis of Semi-Truck—Fair Value vs. Book Value

Interstate records this transaction as follows.

Trucks (semi)	53,000	
Accumulated Depreciation—Trucks	22,000	
Trucks (used)		64,000
Cash		11,000

If the exchange lacks commercial substance, the company recognizes the gain (reflected in the basis of the semi-truck) through lower depreciation expense or when it later sells the semi-truck, not at the time of the exchange.

Lacks Commercial Substance—Some Cash Received. When a company receives cash (sometimes referred to as "boot") in an exchange that lacks commercial substance, it may immediately recognize a portion of the gain.[8] Illustration 10-16 shows the general formula for gain recognition when an exchange includes some cash.

$$\frac{\textbf{Cash Received (Boot)}}{\textbf{Cash Received (Boot) + Fair Value of Other Assets Received}} \times \textbf{Total Gain} = \textbf{Recognized Gain}$$

ILLUSTRATION 10-16
Formula for Gain Recognition, Some Cash Received

To illustrate, assume that Queenan Corporation traded in used machinery with a book value of $60,000 (cost $110,000 less accumulated depreciation $50,000) and a fair value of $100,000. It receives in exchange a machine with a fair value of $90,000 plus cash of $10,000. Illustration 10-17 shows calculation of the total gain on the exchange.

Fair value of machine exchanged	$100,000
Less: Book value of machine exchanged	60,000
Total gain	$ 40,000

ILLUSTRATION 10-17
Computation of Total Gain

Generally, when a transaction lacks commercial substance, a company defers any gain. But because Queenan received $10,000 in cash, it recognizes a partial gain. The portion of the gain a company recognizes is the ratio of monetary assets (cash in this case) to the total consideration received. Queenan computes the partial gain as follows.

$$\frac{\$10{,}000}{\$10{,}000 + \$90{,}000} \times \$40{,}000 = \$4{,}000$$

ILLUSTRATION 10-18
Computation of Gain Based on Ratio of Cash Received to Total Consideration Received

[8]When the monetary consideration is significant, i.e., **25 percent or more** of the fair value of the exchange, both parties consider the transaction a **monetary exchange**. Such "monetary" exchanges rely on the fair values to measure the gains or losses that are recognized in their entirety. **[6]**

Because Queenan recognizes only a gain of $4,000 on this transaction, it defers the remaining $36,000 ($40,000 − $4,000) and reduces the basis (recorded cost) of the new machine. Illustration 10-19 shows the computation of the basis.

ILLUSTRATION 10-19
Computation of Basis

Fair value of new machine	$90,000		Book value of old machine	$60,000
Less: Gain deferred	36,000	OR	Portion of book value presumed sold	6,000*
Basis of new machine	$54,000		Basis of new machine	$54,000

$$^*\frac{\$10,000}{\$100,000} \times \$60,000 = \$6,000$$

Queenan records the transaction with the following entry.

Cash	10,000	
Machinery (new)	54,000	
Accumulated Depreciation—Machinery	50,000	
Machinery (old)		110,000
Gain on Disposal of Machinery		4,000

The rationale for the treatment of a partial gain is as follows: Before a nonmonetary exchange that includes some cash, a company has an unrecognized gain, which is the difference between the book value and the fair value of the old asset. When the exchange occurs, a portion of the fair value is converted to a more liquid asset. The ratio of this liquid asset to the total consideration received is the portion of the total gain that the company realizes. Thus, the company recognizes and records that amount.

Illustration 10-20 presents in summary form the accounting requirements for recognizing gains and losses on exchanges of nonmonetary assets.[9]

ILLUSTRATION 10-20
Summary of Gain and Loss Recognition on Exchanges of Nonmonetary Assets

1. Compute the total gain or loss on the transaction. This amount is equal to the difference between the fair value of the asset given up and the book value of the asset given up.
2. If a loss is computed in step 1, always recognize the entire loss.
3. If a gain is computed in step 1,
   (a) and the exchange has commercial substance, recognize the entire gain.
   (b) and the exchange lacks commercial substance,
      (1) and no cash is involved, no gain is recognized.
      (2) and some cash is given, no gain is recognized.
      (3) and some cash is received, the following portion of the gain is recognized:

$$\frac{\text{Cash Received (Boot)}}{\text{Cash Received (Boot)} + \text{Fair Value of Other Assets Received}} \times \text{Total Gain}^*$$

*If the amount of cash exchanged is 25% or more, both parties recognize entire gain or loss.

Companies disclose in their financial statements nonmonetary exchanges during a period. Such disclosure indicates the nature of the transaction(s), the method of accounting for the assets exchanged, and gains or losses recognized on the exchanges. **[7]**

[9]Adapted from an article by Robert Capettini and Thomas E. King, "Exchanges of Nonmonetary Assets: Some Changes," *The Accounting Review* (January 1976).

ABOUT THOSE SWAPS

What do the numbers mean?

In a press release, Roy Olofson, former vice president of finance for Global Crossing, accused company executives of improperly describing the company's revenue to the public. He said the company had improperly recorded long-term sales immediately rather than over the term of the contract, had improperly booked as cash transactions swaps of capacity with other carriers, and had fired him when he blew the whistle.

The accounting for the swaps involves exchanges of similar network capacity. Companies have said they engage in such deals because swapping is quicker and less costly than building segments of their own networks, or because such pacts provide redundancies to make their own networks more reliable. In one expert's view, an exchange of similar network capacity is the equivalent of trading a blue truck for a red truck—it shouldn't boost a company's revenue.

But Global Crossing and Qwest, among others, counted as revenue the money received from the other company in the swap. (In general, in transactions involving leased capacity, the companies booked the revenue over the life of the contract.) Some of these companies then treated their own purchases as capital expenditures, which were not run through the income statement. Instead, the spending led to the addition of assets on the balance sheet (and an inflated bottom line).

The SEC questioned some of these capacity exchanges, because it appeared they were a device to pad revenue. This reaction was not surprising, since revenue growth was a key factor in the valuation of companies such as Global Crossing and Qwest during the craze for tech stocks in the late 1990s and 2000.

Source: Adapted from Henny Sender, "Telecoms Draw Focus for Moves in Accounting," *Wall Street Journal* (March 26, 2002), p. C7.

Accounting for Contributions

Companies sometimes receive or make contributions (donations or gifts). Such contributions, nonreciprocal transfers, transfer assets in one direction. A contribution is often some type of asset (such as cash, securities, land, buildings, or use of facilities), but it also could be the forgiveness of a debt.

When companies acquire assets as donations, a strict cost concept dictates that the valuation of the asset should be zero. However, a departure from the cost principle seems justified; the only costs incurred (legal fees and other relatively minor expenditures) are not a reasonable basis of accounting for the assets acquired. To record nothing is to ignore the economic realities of an increase in wealth and assets. Therefore, companies use the **fair value of the asset** to establish its value on the books.

INTERNATIONAL PERSPECTIVE

IFRS provides detailed guidance on how to account for contributions and government grants.

What then is the proper accounting for the credit in this transaction? Some believe the credit should be made to Donated Capital (an additional paid-in capital account). This approach views the increase in assets from a donation as contributed capital, rather than as earned revenue.

Others argue that companies should report donations as revenues from contributions. Their reasoning is that only the owners of a business contribute capital. At issue in this approach is whether the company should report revenue immediately or over the period that the asset is employed. For example, to attract new industry a city may offer land, but the receiving enterprise may incur additional costs in the future (e.g., transportation or higher state income taxes) because the location is not the most desirable. As a consequence, some argue that company should defer the revenue and recognize it as the costs are incurred.

The FASB's position is that **in general, companies should recognize contributions received as revenues in the period received.** [8][10] Companies measure contributions at the fair value of the assets received. [9] To illustrate, Max Wayer Meat Packing, Inc. has

[10]GAAP is silent on how to account for the transfers of assets from governmental units to business enterprises. However, we believe that the basic requirements should hold also for these types of contributions. Therefore, companies should record all assets at fair value and all credits as revenue.

recently accepted a donation of land with a fair value of $150,000 from the Memphis Industrial Development Corp. In return Max Wayer Meat Packing promises to build a packing plant in Memphis. Max Wayer's entry is:

Land	150,000	
Contribution Revenue		150,000

When a company contributes a nonmonetary asset, it should record the amount of the donation as an expense at the fair value of the donated asset. If a difference exists between the fair value of the asset and its book value, the company should recognize a gain or loss. To illustrate, Kline Industries donates land to the city of Los Angeles for a city park. The land cost $80,000 and has a fair value of $110,000. Kline Industries records this donation as follows:

Contribution Expense	110,000	
Land		80,000
Gain on Disposal of Land		30,000

In some cases, companies promise to give (pledge) some type of asset in the future. Should companies record this promise immediately or when they give the assets? If the promise is **unconditional** (depends only on the passage of time or on demand by the recipient for performance), the company should report the contribution expense and related payable immediately. If the promise is **conditional**, the company recognizes expense in the period benefited by the contribution, generally when it transfers the asset.

Other Asset Valuation Methods

The exception to the historical cost principle for assets acquired through donation is based on fair value. Another exception is the **prudent cost** concept. This concept states that if for some reason a company ignorantly paid too much for an asset originally, it is theoretically preferable to charge a loss immediately.

For example, assume that a company constructs an asset at a cost much greater than its present economic usefulness. It would be appropriate to charge these excess costs as a loss to the current period, rather than capitalize them as part of the cost of the asset. In practice, the need to use the prudent cost approach seldom develops. Companies typically either use good reasoning in paying a given price or fail to recognize that they have overpaid.

What happens, on the other hand, if a company makes a bargain purchase or internally constructs a piece of equipment at a cost savings? Such savings should not result in immediate recognition of a gain under any circumstances.

COSTS SUBSEQUENT TO ACQUISITION

LEARNING OBJECTIVE 
Describe the accounting treatment for costs subsequent to acquisition.

After installing plant assets and readying them for use, a company incurs additional costs that range from ordinary repairs to significant additions. The major problem is allocating these costs to the proper time periods. **In general, costs incurred to achieve greater future benefits should be capitalized, whereas expenditures that simply maintain a given level of services should be expensed.** In order to capitalize costs, one of three conditions must be present:

1. The useful life of the asset must be increased.
2. The quantity of units produced from the asset must be increased.
3. The quality of the units produced must be enhanced.

Underlying Concepts

Expensing long-lived ashtrays and waste baskets is an application of the materiality constraint.

For example, a company like **Boeing** should expense expenditures that do not increase an asset's future benefits. That is, it expenses immediately ordinary repairs that maintain the existing condition of the asset or restore it to normal operating efficiency.

Companies expense most expenditures below an established arbitrary minimum amount, say, $100 or $500. Although, conceptually, this treatment may be incorrect, expediency demands it. Otherwise, companies would set up depreciation schedules for such items as wastepaper baskets and ashtrays.

DISCONNECTED

What do the numbers mean?

It all started with a check of the books by an internal auditor for **WorldCom Inc.** The telecom giant's newly installed chief executive had asked for a financial review, and the auditor was spot-checking records of capital expenditures. She found the company was using an unorthodox technique to account for one of its biggest expenses: charges paid to local telephone networks to complete long-distance calls.

Instead of recording these charges as operating expenses, WorldCom recorded a significant portion as capital expenditures. The maneuver was worth hundreds of millions of dollars to WorldCom's bottom line. It effectively turned a loss for all of 2001 and the first quarter of 2002 into a profit. The graph below compares WorldCom's accounting to that under GAAP. Soon after this discovery, WorldCom filed for bankruptcy.

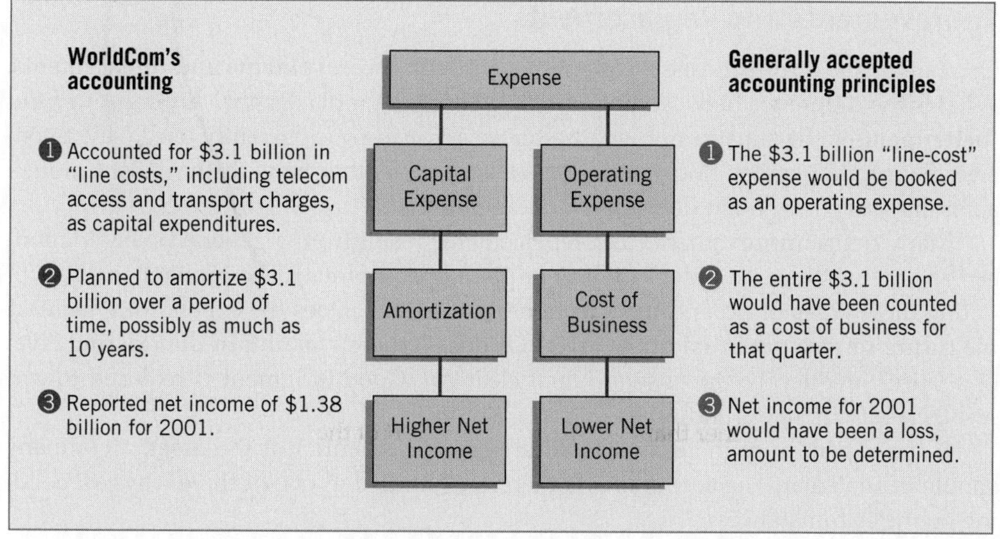

Source: Adapted from Jared Sandberg, Deborah Solomon, and Rebecca Blumenstein, "Inside WorldCom's Unearthing of a Vast Accounting Scandal," *Wall Street Journal* (June 27, 2002), p. A1.

The distinction between a capital expenditure (asset) and a revenue expenditure (expense) is not always clear-cut. Yet, in most cases, **consistent application of a capital/expense policy** is more important than attempting to provide general theoretical guidelines for each transaction. Generally, companies incur four major types of expenditures relative to existing assets.

MAJOR TYPES OF EXPENDITURES

ADDITIONS. Increase or extension of existing assets.

IMPROVEMENTS AND REPLACEMENTS. Substitution of an improved asset for an existing one.

REARRANGEMENT AND REINSTALLATION. Movement of assets from one location to another.

REPAIRS. Expenditures that maintain assets in condition for operation.

Additions

Additions should present no major accounting problems. By definition, **companies capitalize any addition to plant assets because a new asset is created**. For example, the addition of a wing to a hospital, or of an air conditioning system to an office, increases the service potential of that facility. Companies should capitalize such expenditures and match them against the revenues that will result in future periods.

One problem that arises in this area is the accounting for any changes related to the existing structure as a result of the addition. Is the cost incurred to tear down an old wall, to make room for the addition, a cost of the addition or an expense or loss of the period? The answer is that it depends on the original intent. If the company had anticipated building an addition later, then this cost of removal is a proper cost of the addition. But if the company had not anticipated this development, it should properly report the removal as a loss in the current period on the basis of inefficient planning. Normally, the company retains the carrying amount of the old wall in the accounts, although theoretically the company should remove it.

Improvements and Replacements

Companies substitute one asset for another through **improvements** and **replacements**. What is the difference between an improvement and a replacement? An improvement (**betterment**) is the substitution of a **better asset** for the one currently used (say, a concrete floor for a wooden floor). A replacement, on the other hand, is the substitution of a **similar asset** (a wooden floor for a wooden floor).

Many times improvements and replacements result from a general policy to modernize or rehabilitate an older building or piece of equipment. The problem is differentiating these types of expenditures from normal repairs. Does the expenditure increase the **future service potential** of the asset? Or does it merely **maintain the existing level** of service? Frequently, the answer is not clear-cut. Good judgment is required to correctly classify these expenditures.

If the expenditure increases the future service potential of the asset, a company should capitalize it. The accounting is therefore handled in one of three ways, depending on the circumstances:

1. *Use the substitution approach.* Conceptually, the **substitution approach** is correct if the carrying amount of the old asset is available. It is then a simple matter to remove the cost of the old asset and replace it with the cost of the new asset.

   To illustrate, Instinct Enterprises decides to replace the pipes in its plumbing system. A plumber suggests that the company use plastic tubing in place of the cast iron pipes and copper tubing. The old pipe and tubing have a book value of $15,000 (cost of $150,000 less accumulated depreciation of $135,000), and a scrap value of $1,000. The plastic tubing costs $125,000. If Instinct pays $124,000 for the new tubing after exchanging the old tubing, it makes the following entry:

Plant Assets (plumbing system)	125,000	
Accumulated Depreciation—Plant Assets	135,000	
Loss on Disposal of Plant Assets	14,000	
Plant Assets		150,000
Cash ($125,000 − $1,000)		124,000

   The problem is determining the book value of the old asset. Generally, the components of a given asset depreciate at different rates. However, generally no separate accounting is made. For example, the tires, motor, and body of a truck depreciate at different rates, but most companies use one rate for the entire truck. Companies can set separate depreciation rates, but it is often impractical. If a company cannot determine the carrying amount of the old asset, it adopts one of two other approaches.

2. ***Capitalize the new cost.*** Another approach capitalizes the improvement and keeps the carrying amount of the old asset on the books. The justification for this approach is that the item is sufficiently depreciated to reduce its carrying amount almost to zero. Although this assumption may not always be true, the differences are often insignificant. Companies usually handle improvements in this manner.
3. ***Charge to accumulated depreciation.*** In cases when a company does not improve the quantity or quality of the asset itself, but instead extends its useful life, the company debits the expenditure to Accumulated Depreciation rather than to an asset account. The theory behind this approach is that the replacement extends the useful life of the asset and thereby recaptures some or all of the past depreciation. The net carrying amount of the asset is the same whether debiting the asset or accumulated depreciation.

Rearrangement and Reinstallation

Companies incur rearrangement and reinstallation costs to benefit future periods. An example is the rearrangement and reinstallation of machines to facilitate future production.

If a company like **Eastman Kodak** can determine or estimate the original installation cost and the accumulated depreciation to date, it handles the rearrangement and reinstallation cost as a replacement. If not, which is generally the case, Eastman Kodak should capitalize the new costs (if material in amount) as an asset to be amortized over future periods expected to benefit. If these costs are immaterial, if they cannot be separated from other operating expenses, or if their future benefit is questionable, the company should immediately expense them.

Repairs

A company makes ordinary repairs to maintain plant assets in operating condition. It charges ordinary repairs to an expense account in the period incurred, on the basis that **it is the primary period benefited**. Maintenance charges that occur regularly include replacing minor parts, lubricating and adjusting equipment, repainting, and cleaning. A company treats these as ordinary operating expenses.

It is often difficult to distinguish a repair from an improvement or replacement. The major consideration is whether the expenditure benefits more than one year or one operating cycle, whichever is longer. If a major repair (such as an overhaul) occurs, several periods will benefit. A company should handle the cost as an addition, improvement, or replacement.[11]

An interesting question is whether a company can accrue planned maintenance overhaul costs *before* the actual costs are incurred. For example, assume that **Southwest Airlines** schedules major overhauls of its planes every three years. Should Southwest be permitted to accrue these costs and related liability over the three-year period? Some argue that this accrue-in-advance approach better matches expenses to revenues and reports Southwest's obligation for these costs. However, reporting a liability is inappropriate. To whom does Southwest owe? In other words, Southwest has no obligation to an outside party until it has to pay for the overhaul costs, and therefore it has no liability. As a result, companies are not permitted to accrue in advance for planned major overhaul costs either for interim or annual periods. **[10]**

[11]AcSEC has proposed (see footnote 2) that companies expense as incurred costs involved for planned major expenditures unless they represent an *additional* component or the *replacement* of an existing component.

Summary of Costs Subsequent to Acquisition

Illustration 10-21 summarizes the accounting treatment for various costs incurred subsequent to the acquisition of capitalized assets.

ILLUSTRATION 10-21
Summary of Costs Subsequent to Acquisition of Property, Plant, and Equipment

Type of Expenditure	Normal Accounting Treatment
Additions	Capitalize cost of addition to asset account.
Improvements and replacements	(a) **Carrying value known:** Remove cost of and accumulated depreciation on old asset, recognizing any gain or loss. Capitalize cost of improvement/replacement. (b) **Carrying value unknown:** 1. If the asset's useful life is extended, debit accumulated depreciation for cost of improvement/replacement. 2. If the quantity or quality of the asset's productivity is increased, capitalize cost of improvement/replacement to asset account.
Rearrangement and reinstallation	(a) If original installation cost is **known**, account for cost of rearrangement/reinstallation as a replacement (carrying value known). (b) If original installation cost is **unknown** and rearrangement/reinstallation cost is **material** in amount and benefits future periods, capitalize as an asset. (c) If original installation cost is **unknown** and rearrangement/reinstallation cost is **not material or future benefit is questionable**, expense the cost when incurred.
Repairs	(a) **Ordinary:** Expense cost of repairs when incurred. (b) **Major:** As appropriate, treat as an addition, improvement, or replacement.

DISPOSITION OF PROPERTY, PLANT, AND EQUIPMENT

LEARNING OBJECTIVE 7
Describe the accounting treatment for the disposal of property, plant, and equipment.

A company, like **Intel**, may retire plant assets voluntarily or dispose of them by sale, exchange, involuntary conversion, or abandonment. Regardless of the type of disposal, depreciation must be taken up to the date of disposition. Then, Intel should remove all accounts related to the retired asset. Generally, the book value of the specific plant asset does not equal its disposal value. As a result, a gain or loss develops. The reason: Depreciation is an estimate of cost allocation and not a process of valuation. **The gain or loss is really a correction of net income** for the years during which Intel used the fixed asset.

Intel should show gains or losses on the disposal of plant assets in the income statement along with other items from customary business activities. However, if it sold, abandoned, spun off, or otherwise disposed of the "operations of a component of a business," then it should report the results separately in the discontinued operations section of the income statement (as discussed in Chapter 4). That is, Intel should report any gain or loss from disposal of a business component with the related results of discontinued operations.

Sale of Plant Assets

Companies record depreciation for the period of time between the date of the last depreciation entry and the date of sale. To illustrate, assume that Barret Company recorded depreciation on a machine costing $18,000 for 9 years at the rate of $1,200 per year. If it sells the machine in the middle of the tenth year for $7,000, Barret records depreciation to the date of sale as:

Depreciation Expense ($1,200 × $\frac{1}{2}$)	600	
Accumulated Depreciation—Machinery		600

The entry for the sale of the asset then is:

Cash	7,000	
Accumulated Depreciation—Machinery [($1,200 × 9) + $600]	11,400	
Machinery		18,000
Gain on Disposal of Machinery		400

The book value of the machinery at the time of the sale is $6,600 ($18,000 − $11,400). Because the machinery sold for $7,000, the amount of the gain on the sale is $400.

Involuntary Conversion

Sometimes an asset's service is terminated through some type of **involuntary conversion** such as fire, flood, theft, or condemnation. Companies report the difference between the amount recovered (e.g., from a condemnation award or insurance recovery), if any, and the asset's book value as a gain or loss. They treat these gains or losses like any other type of disposition. In some cases, these gains or losses may be reported as extraordinary items in the income statement, **if the conditions of the disposition are unusual and infrequent in nature.**

To illustrate, Camel Transport Corp. had to sell a plant located on company property that stood directly in the path of an interstate highway. For a number of years the state had sought to purchase the land on which the plant stood, but the company resisted. The state ultimately exercised its right of eminent domain, which the courts upheld. In settlement, Camel received $500,000, which substantially exceeded the $200,000 book value of the plant and land (cost of $400,000 less accumulated depreciation of $200,000). Camel made the following entry.

Cash	500,000	
Accumulated Depreciation—Plant Assets	200,000	
Plant Assets		400,000
Gain on Disposal of Plant Assets		300,000

If the conditions surrounding the condemnation are judged to be unusual and infrequent, Camel's gain of $300,000 is reported as an extraordinary item.

Some object to the recognition of a gain or loss in certain *involuntary* conversions. For example, the federal government often condemns forests for national parks. The paper companies that owned these forests must report a gain or loss on the condemnation. However, companies such as **Georgia-Pacific** contend that no gain or loss should be reported because they must replace the condemned forest land immediately and so are in the same economic position as they were before. The issue is whether condemnation and subsequent purchase should be viewed as one or two transactions. GAAP requires "that a gain or loss be recognized when a nonmonetary asset is involuntarily converted to monetary assets even though an enterprise reinvests or is obligated to reinvest the monetary assets in replacement nonmonetary assets." **[11]**

Miscellaneous Problems

If a company scraps or abandons an asset without any cash recovery, it recognizes a loss equal to the asset's book value. If scrap value exists, the gain or loss that occurs is the difference between the asset's scrap value and its book value. If an asset still can be used even though it is fully depreciated, it may be kept on the books at historical cost less depreciation.

Companies must disclose in notes to the financial statements the amount of fully depreciated assets in service. For example, **Petroleum Equipment Tools Inc.** in its annual report disclosed, "The amount of fully depreciated assets included in property, plant, and equipment at December 31 amounted to approximately $98,900,000."

KEY TERMS

additions, 576
avoidable interest, 560
capital expenditure, 575
capitalization period, 560
commercial substance, 568
fixed assets, 556
historical cost, 556
improvements (betterments), 576
involuntary conversion, 579
lump-sum price, 566
major repairs, 577
nonmonetary assets, 568
nonreciprocal transfers, 573
ordinary repairs, 577
plant assets, 556
property, plant, and equipment, 556
prudent cost, 574
rearrangement and reinstallation costs, 577
replacements, 576
revenue expenditure, 575
self-constructed asset, 558
weighted-average accumulated expenditures, 561

SUMMARY OF LEARNING OBJECTIVES

1 Describe property, plant, and equipment. The major characteristics of property, plant, and equipment are as follows. (1) They are acquired for use in operations and not for resale. (2) They are long-term in nature and usually subject to depreciation. (3) They possess physical substance.

2 Identify the costs to include in initial valuation of property, plant, and equipment. The costs included in initial valuation of property, plant, and equipment are as follows.

Cost of land: Includes all expenditures made to acquire land and to ready it for use. Land costs typically include (1) the purchase price; (2) closing costs, such as title to the land, attorney's fees, and recording fees; (3) costs incurred in getting the land in condition for its intended use, such as grading, filling, draining, and clearing; (4) assumption of any liens, mortgages, or encumbrances on the property; and (5) any additional land improvements that have an indefinite life.

Cost of buildings: Includes all expenditures related directly to their acquisition or construction. These costs include (1) materials, labor, and overhead costs incurred during construction, and (2) professional fees and building permits.

Cost of equipment: Includes the purchase price, freight and handling charges incurred, insurance on the equipment while in transit, cost of special foundations if required, assembling and installation costs, and costs of conducting trial runs.

3 Describe the accounting problems associated with self-constructed assets. Indirect costs of manufacturing create special problems because companies cannot easily trace these costs directly to work and material orders related to the constructed assets. Companies might handle these costs in one of two ways: (1) Assign no fixed overhead to the cost of the constructed asset, or (2) assign a portion of all overhead to the construction process. Companies use the second method extensively.

4 Describe the accounting problems associated with interest capitalization. Only actual interest (with modifications) should be capitalized. The rationale for this approach is that during construction, the asset is not generating revenue and therefore companies should defer (capitalize) interest cost. Once construction is completed, the asset is ready for its intended use and revenues can be earned. Any interest cost incurred in purchasing an asset that is ready for its intended use should be expensed.

5 Understand accounting issues related to acquiring and valuing plant assets. The following issues relate to acquiring and valuing plant assets: (1) *Cash discounts:* Whether taken or not, they are generally considered a reduction in the cost of the asset; the real cost of the asset is the cash or cash equivalent price of the asset. (2) *Deferred-payment contracts:* Companies account for assets purchased on long-term credit contracts at the present value of the consideration exchanged between the contracting parties. (3) *Lump-sum purchase:* Allocate the total cost among the various assets on the basis of their relative fair values. (4) *Issuance of stock:* If the stock is actively traded, the market price of the stock issued is a fair indication of the cost of the property acquired. If the market price of the common stock exchanged is not determinable, establish the fair value of the property and use it as the basis for recording the asset and issuance of the common stock. (5) *Exchanges of nonmonetary assets.* The accounting for exchanges of nonmonetary assets depends on whether the exchange has commercial substance. See Illustrations 10-10 (page 569) and 10-20 (page 572) for summaries of how to account for exchanges. (6) *Contributions:* Record at the fair value of the asset received, and credit revenue for the same amount.

6 Describe the accounting treatment for costs subsequent to acquisition. Illustration 10-21 (page 578) summarizes how to account for costs subsequent to acquisition.

 **Describe the accounting treatment for the disposal of property, plant, and equipment.** Regardless of the time of disposal, companies take depreciation up to the date of disposition, and then remove all accounts related to the retired asset. Gains or losses on the retirement of plant assets are shown in the income statement along with other items that arise from customary business activities. Gains or losses on involuntary conversions, if unusual and infrequent, may be reported as extraordinary items.

FASB CODIFICATION

FASB Codification References

[1] FASB ASC 360-10-35-43. [Predecessor literature: "Accounting for the Impairment or Disposal of Long-lived Assets," *Statement of Financial Accounting Standards No. 144* (Norwalk, Conn.: FASB, 2001), par. 34.]

[2] FASB ASC 835-20-05. [Predecessor literature: "Capitalization of Interest Cost," *Statement of Financial Accounting Standards No. 34* (Stamford, Conn.: FASB, 1979).]

[3] FASB ASC 835-20-15-4. [Predecessor literature: "Determining Materiality for Capitalization of Interest Cost," *Statement of Financial Accounting Standards No. 42* (Stamford, Conn.: FASB, 1980), par. 10.]

[4] FASB ASC 820-10-35. [Predecessor literature: "(Predecessor literature: "Fair Value Measurement," *Statement of Financial Accounting Standards No. 157* (Norwalk, Conn.: FASB, September 2006), paras. 13–18.]

[5] FASB ASC 845-10-30. [Predecessor literature: "Accounting for Nonmonetary Transactions," *Opinions of the Accounting Principles Board No. 29* (New York: AICPA, 1973), par. 18, and "Exchanges of Nonmonetary Assets, an Amendment of *APB Opinion No. 29*," *Statement of Financial Accounting Standards No. 153* (Norwalk, Conn.: FASB, 2004).]

[6] FASB ASC 845-10-25-6. [Predecessor literature: "Interpretations of *APB Opinion No. 29*," EITF Abstracts No. 01-02 (Norwalk, Conn.: FASB, 2002).]

[7] FASB ASC 845-10-50-1. [Predecessor literature: "Accounting for Nonmonetary Transactions," *Opinions of the Accounting Principles Board No. 29* (New York: AICPA, 1973), par. 28, and "Exchanges of Nonmonetary Assets, an Amendment of *APB Opinion No. 29*," *Statement of Financial Accounting Standards No. 153* (Norwalk, Conn.: FASB, 2004).]

[8] FASB ASC 958-605-25-2. [Predecessor literature: "Accounting for Contributions Received and Contributions Made," *Statement of Financial Accounting Standards No. 116* (Norwalk, Conn.: FASB, 1993).]

[9] FASB ASC 845-10-30. [Predecessor literature: "Accounting for Nonmonetary Transactions," *Opinions of the Accounting Principles Board No. 29* (New York: AICPA, 1973), par. 18, and "Exchanges of Nonmonetary Assets, an Amendment of *APB Opinion No. 29*," *Statement of Financial Accounting Standards No. 153* (Norwalk, Conn.: FASB, 2004).]

[10] FASB ASC 360-10-25-5. [Predecessor literature: "Accounting for Planned Major Maintenance Activities," FASB Staff Position AUG-AIR-1 (Norwalk, Conn.: FASB, September 2006), par. 5.]

[11] FASB ASC 605-40-25-2. [Predecessor literature: "Accounting for Involuntary Conversions of Nonmonetary Assets to Monetary Assets," *FASB Interpretation No. 30* (Stamford, Conn.: FASB, 1979), summary paragraph.]

Exercises

If your school has a subscription to the FASB Codification, go to *http://aaahq.org/asclogin.cfm* to log in and prepare responses to the following. Provide Codification references for your responses.

CE10-1 Access the glossary ("Master Glossary") to answer the following.

(a) What does it mean to "capitalize" an item?

(b) What is the definition of a nonmonetary asset?

(c) What is a nonreciprocal transfer?

(d) What is the definition of "contribution"?

CE10-2 Herb Scholl, the owner of Scholl's Company, wonders whether interest costs associated with developing land can ever be capitalized. What does the Codification say on this matter?

CE10-3 What guidance does the Codification provide on the accrual of costs associated with planned major maintenance activities?

CE10-4 Briefly describe how the purchases and sales of inventory with the same counterparty are similar to the accounting for other nonmonetary exchanges.

An additional Codification case can be found in the Using Your Judgment section, on page 603.

Be sure to check the book's companion website for a Review and Analysis Exercise, with solution.

Questions, Brief Exercises, Exercises, Problems, and many more resources are available for practice in WileyPLUS.

QUESTIONS

1. What are the major characteristics of plant assets?

2. Mickelson Inc. owns land that it purchased on January 1, 2000, for $450,000. At December 31, 2012, its current value is $770,000 as determined by appraisal. At what amount should Mickelson report this asset on its December 31, 2012, balance sheet? Explain.

3. Name the items, in addition to the amount paid to the former owner or contractor, that may properly be included as part of the acquisition cost of the following plant assets.

(a) Land.

(b) Machinery and equipment.

(c) Buildings.

4. Indicate where the following items would be shown on a balance sheet.

(a) A lien that was attached to the land when purchased.

(b) Landscaping costs.

(c) Attorney's fees and recording fees related to purchasing land.

(d) Variable overhead related to construction of machinery.

(e) A parking lot servicing employees in the building.

(f) Cost of temporary building for workers during construction of building.

(g) Interest expense on bonds payable incurred during construction of a building.

(h) Assessments for sidewalks that are maintained by the city.

(i) The cost of demolishing an old building that was on the land when purchased.

5. Two positions have normally been taken with respect to the recording of fixed manufacturing overhead as an element of the cost of plant assets constructed by a company for its own use:

(a) It should be excluded completely.

(b) It should be included at the same rate as is charged to normal operations.

What are the circumstances or rationale that support or deny the application of these methods?

6. The Buildings account of Postera Inc. includes the following items that were used in determining the basis for depreciating the cost of a building.

(a) Organization and promotion expenses.

(b) Architect's fees.

(c) Interest and taxes during construction.

(d) Interest revenue on investments held to fund construction of a building.

Do you agree with these charges? If not, how would you deal with each of the items above in the corporation's books and in its annual financial statements?

7. Burke Company has purchased two tracts of land. One tract will be the site of its new manufacturing plant, while the other is being purchased with the hope that it will be sold in the next year at a profit. How should these two tracts of land be reported in the balance sheet?

8. One financial accounting issue encountered when a company constructs its own plant is whether the interest cost on funds borrowed to finance construction should be capitalized and then amortized over the life of the assets constructed. What is the justification for capitalizing such interest?

9. Provide examples of assets that do not qualify for interest capitalization.

10. What interest rates should be used in determining the amount of interest to be capitalized? How should the amount of interest to be capitalized be determined?

11. How should the amount of interest capitalized be disclosed in the notes to the financial statements? How should interest revenue from temporarily invested excess funds borrowed to finance the construction of assets be accounted for?

12. Discuss the basic accounting problem that arises in handling each of the following situations.

(a) Assets purchased by issuance of capital stock.

(b) Acquisition of plant assets by gift or donation.

(c) Purchase of a plant asset subject to a cash discount.

(d) Assets purchased on a long-term credit basis.

(e) A group of assets acquired for a lump sum.

(f) An asset traded in or exchanged for another asset.

13. Magilke Industries acquired equipment this year to be used in its operations. The equipment was delivered by the suppliers, installed by Magilke, and placed into operation. Some of it was purchased for cash with discounts available for prompt payment. Some of it was purchased under long-term payment plans for which the interest charges approximated prevailing rates. What costs should Magilke capitalize for the new equipment purchased this year? Explain.

14. Schwartzkopf Co. purchased for $2,200,000 property that included both land and a building to be used in operations. The seller's book value was $300,000 for the land and $900,000 for the building. By appraisal, the fair value was estimated to be $500,000 for the land and $2,000,000 for the building. At what amount should Schwartzkopf report the land and the building at the end of the year?

15. Pueblo Co. acquires machinery by paying $10,000 cash and signing a $5,000, 2-year, zero-interest-bearing note payable. The note has a present value of $4,208, and Pueblo purchased a similar machine last month for $13,500. At what cost should the new equipment be recorded?

16. Stan Ott is evaluating two recent transactions involving exchanges of equipment. In one case, the exchange has commercial substance. In the second situation, the exchange lacks commercial substance. Explain to Stan the differences in accounting for these two situations.

17. Crowe Company purchased a heavy-duty truck on July 1, 2009, for $30,000. It was estimated that it would have a useful life of 10 years and then would have a trade-in value of $6,000. The company uses the straight-line method. It was traded on August 1, 2013, for a similar truck costing $42,000; $16,000 was allowed as trade-in value (also fair value) on the old truck and $26,000 was paid in cash. A comparison of expected cash flows for the trucks indicates the exchange lacks commercial substance. What is the entry to record the trade-in?

18. Once equipment has been installed and placed in operation, subsequent expenditures relating to this equipment are frequently thought of as repairs or general maintenance and, hence, chargeable to operations in the period in which the expenditure is made. Actually, determination of whether such an expenditure should be charged to operations or capitalized involves a much more careful analysis of the character of the expenditure. What are the factors that should be considered in making such a decision? Discuss fully.

19. What accounting treatment is normally given to the following items in accounting for plant assets?

(a) Additions.

(b) Major repairs.

(c) Improvements and replacements.

20. New machinery, which replaced a number of employees, was installed and put in operation in the last month of the fiscal year. The employees had been dismissed after payment of an extra month's wages, and this amount was added to the cost of the machinery. Discuss the propriety of the charge. If it was improper, describe the proper treatment.

21. To what extent do you consider the following items to be proper costs of the fixed asset? Give reasons for your opinions.

(a) Overhead of a business that builds its own equipment.

(b) Cash discounts on purchases of equipment.

(c) Interest paid during construction of a building.

(d) Cost of a safety device installed on a machine.

(e) Freight on equipment returned before installation, for replacement by other equipment of greater capacity.

(f) Cost of moving machinery to a new location.

(g) Cost of plywood partitions erected as part of the remodeling of the office.

(h) Replastering of a section of the building.

(i) Cost of a new motor for one of the trucks.

22. Neville Enterprises has a number of fully depreciated assets that are still being used in the main operations of the business. Because the assets are fully depreciated, the president of the company decides not to show them on the balance sheet or disclose this information in the notes. Evaluate this procedure.

23. What are the general rules for how gains or losses on retirement of plant assets should be reported in income?

BRIEF EXERCISES

2 **BE10-1** Previn Brothers Inc. purchased land at a price of $27,000. Closing costs were $1,400. An old building was removed at a cost of $10,200. What amount should be recorded as the cost of the land?

4 **BE10-2** Hanson Company is constructing a building. Construction began on February 1 and was completed on December 31. Expenditures were $1,800,000 on March 1, $1,200,000 on June 1, and $3,000,000 on December 31. Compute Hanson's weighted-average accumulated expenditures for interest capitalization purposes.

4 **BE10-3** Hanson Company (see BE10-2) borrowed $1,000,000 on March 1 on a 5-year, 12% note to help finance construction of the building. In addition, the company had outstanding all year a 10%, 5-year, $2,000,000 note payable and an 11%, 4-year, $3,500,000 note payable. Compute the weighted-average interest rate used for interest capitalization purposes.

4 **BE10-4** Use the information for Hanson Company from BE10-2 and BE10-3. Compute avoidable interest for Hanson Company.

5 **BE10-5** Garcia Corporation purchased a truck by issuing an $80,000, 4-year, zero-interest-bearing note to Equinox Inc. The market rate of interest for obligations of this nature is 10%. Prepare the journal entry to record the purchase of this truck.

5 **BE10-6** Mohave Inc. purchased land, building, and equipment from Laguna Corporation for a cash payment of $315,000. The estimated fair values of the assets are land $60,000, building $220,000, and equipment $80,000. At what amounts should each of the three assets be recorded?

5 **BE10-7** Fielder Company obtained land by issuing 2,000 shares of its $10 par value common stock. The land was recently appraised at $85,000. The common stock is actively traded at $40 per share. Prepare the journal entry to record the acquisition of the land.

5 **BE10-8** Navajo Corporation traded a used truck (cost $20,000, accumulated depreciation $18,000) for a small computer worth $3,300. Navajo also paid $500 in the transaction. Prepare the journal entry to record the exchange. (The exchange has commercial substance.)

5 **BE10-9** Use the information for Navajo Corporation from BE10-8. Prepare the journal entry to record the exchange, assuming the exchange lacks commercial substance.

5 **BE10-10** Mehta Company traded a used welding machine (cost $9,000, accumulated depreciation $3,000) for office equipment with an estimated fair value of $5,000. Mehta also paid $3,000 cash in the transaction. Prepare the journal entry to record the exchange. (The exchange has commercial substance.)

5 **BE10-11** Cheng Company traded a used truck for a new truck. The used truck cost $30,000 and has accumulated depreciation of $27,000. The new truck is worth $37,000. Cheng also made a cash payment of $36,000. Prepare Cheng's entry to record the exchange. (The exchange lacks commercial substance.)

5 **BE10-12** Slaton Corporation traded a used truck for a new truck. The used truck cost $20,000 and has accumulated depreciation of $17,000. The new truck is worth $35,000. Slaton also made a cash payment of $33,000. Prepare Slaton's entry to record the exchange. (The exchange has commercial substance.)

6 **BE10-13** Indicate which of the following costs should be expensed when incurred.

- **(a)** $13,000 paid to rearrange and reinstall machinery.
- **(b)** $200,000 paid for addition to building.
- **(c)** $200 paid for tune-up and oil change on delivery truck.
- **(d)** $7,000 paid to replace a wooden floor with a concrete floor.
- **(e)** $2,000 paid for a major overhaul on a truck, which extends the useful life.

7 **BE10-14** Ottawa Corporation owns machinery that cost $20,000 when purchased on July 1, 2009. Depreciation has been recorded at a rate of $2,400 per year, resulting in a balance in accumulated depreciation of $8,400 at December 31, 2012. The machinery is sold on September 1, 2013, for $10,500. Prepare journal entries to (a) update depreciation for 2013 and (b) record the sale.

7 **BE10-15** Use the information presented for Ottawa Corporation in BE10-14, but assume the machinery is sold for $5,200 instead of $10,500. Prepare journal entries to (a) update depreciation for 2013 and (b) record the sale.

EXERCISES

2 **E10-1 (Acquisition Costs of Realty)** The expenditures and receipts below are related to land, land improvements, and buildings acquired for use in a business enterprise. The receipts are enclosed in parentheses.

(a)	Money borrowed to pay building contractor (signed a note)	$(275,000)
(b)	Payment for construction from note proceeds	275,000
(c)	Cost of land fill and clearing	10,000
(d)	Delinquent real estate taxes on property assumed by purchaser	7,000
(e)	Premium on 6-month insurance policy during construction	6,000
(f)	Refund of 1-month insurance premium because construction completed early	(1,000)
(g)	Architect's fee on building	25,000
(h)	Cost of real estate purchased as a plant site (land $200,000 and building $50,000)	250,000
(i)	Commission fee paid to real estate agency	9,000
(j)	Installation of fences around property	4,000
(k)	Cost of razing and removing building	11,000
(l)	Proceeds from salvage of demolished building	(5,000)
(m)	Interest paid during construction on money borrowed for construction	13,000
(n)	Cost of parking lots and driveways	19,000
(o)	Cost of trees and shrubbery planted (permanent in nature)	14,000
(p)	Excavation costs for new building	3,000

Instructions

Identify each item by letter and list the items in columnar form, using the headings shown below. All receipt amounts should be reported in parentheses. For any amounts entered in the Other Accounts column, also indicate the account title.

Item	Land	Land Improvements	Buildings	Other Accounts

2 **E10-2 (Acquisition Costs of Realty)** Pollachek Co. purchased land as a factory site for $450,000. The process of tearing down two old buildings on the site and constructing the factory required 6 months. The company paid $42,000 to raze the old buildings and sold salvaged lumber and brick for $6,300. Legal fees of $1,850 were paid for title investigation and drawing the purchase contract. Pollachek paid $2,200 to an engineering firm for a land survey, and $65,000 for drawing the factory plans. The land survey had to be made before definitive plans could be drawn. Title insurance on the property cost $1,500, and a liability insurance premium paid during construction was $900. The contractor's charge for construction was $2,740,000. The company paid the contractor in two installments: $1,200,000 at the end of 3 months and $1,540,000 upon completion. Interest costs of $170,000 were incurred to finance the construction.

Instructions

Determine the cost of the land and the cost of the building as they should be recorded on the books of Pollachek Co. Assume that the land survey was for the building.

2 **E10-3 (Acquisition Costs of Trucks)** Shabbona Corporation operates a retail computer store. To improve delivery services to customers, the company purchases four new trucks on April 1, 2012. The terms of acquisition for each truck are described below.

1. Truck #1 has a list price of $15,000 and is acquired for a cash payment of $13,900.
2. Truck #2 has a list price of $20,000 and is acquired for a down payment of $2,000 cash and a zero-interest-bearing note with a face amount of $18,000. The note is due April 1, 2013. Shabbona would normally have to pay interest at a rate of 10% for such a borrowing, and the dealership has an incremental borrowing rate of 8%.
3. Truck #3 has a list price of $16,000. It is acquired in exchange for a computer system that Shabbona carries in inventory. The computer system cost $12,000 and is normally sold by Shabbona for $15,200. Shabbona uses a perpetual inventory system.
4. Truck #4 has a list price of $14,000. It is acquired in exchange for 1,000 shares of common stock in Shabbona Corporation. The stock has a par value per share of $10 and a market price of $13 per share.

Instructions

Prepare the appropriate journal entries for the foregoing transactions for Shabbona Corporation. (Round computations to the nearest dollar.)

2 3 **E10-4 (Purchase and Self-Constructed Cost of Assets)** Dane Co. both purchases and constructs various equipment it uses in its operations. The following items for two different types of equipment were recorded in random order during the calendar year 2013.

Purchase	
Cash paid for equipment, including sales tax of $5,000	$105,000
Freight and insurance cost while in transit	2,000
Cost of moving equipment into place at factory	3,100
Wage cost for technicians to test equipment	6,000
Insurance premium paid during first year of operation on this equipment	1,500
Special plumbing fixtures required for new equipment	8,000
Repair cost incurred in first year of operations related to this equipment	1,300

Construction	
Material and purchased parts (gross cost $200,000; failed to take 1% cash discount)	$200,000
Imputed interest on funds used during construction (stock financing)	14,000
Labor costs	190,000
Allocated overhead costs (fixed—$20,000; variable—$30,000)	50,000
Profit on self-construction	30,000
Cost of installing equipment	4,400

Instructions

Compute the total cost for each of these two pieces of equipment. If an item is not capitalized as a cost of the equipment, indicate how it should be reported.

2 3 4 **E10-5 (Treatment of Various Costs)** Allegro Supply Company, a newly formed corporation, incurred the following expenditures related to Land, to Buildings, and to Machinery and Equipment.

Abstract company's fee for title search		$ 520
Architect's fees		3,170
Cash paid for land and dilapidated building thereon		92,000
Removal of old building	$20,000	
Less: Salvage	5,500	14,500
Interest on short-term loans during construction		7,400
Excavation before construction for basement		19,000
Machinery purchased (subject to 2% cash discount, which was not taken)		65,000
Freight on machinery purchased		1,340
Storage charges on machinery, necessitated by noncompletion of building when machinery was delivered		2,180
New building constructed (building construction took 6 months from date of purchase of land and old building)		485,000
Assessment by city for drainage project		1,600
Hauling charges for delivery of machinery from storage to new building		620
Installation of machinery		2,000
Trees, shrubs, and other landscaping after completion of building (permanent in nature)		5,400

Instructions

Determine the amounts that should be debited to Land, to Buildings, and to Machinery and Equipment. Assume the benefits of capitalizing interest during construction exceed the cost of implementation. Indicate how any costs not debited to these accounts should be recorded.

3 4 **E10-6 (Correction of Improper Cost Entries)** Plant acquisitions for selected companies are presented below and on the next page.

1. Natchez Industries Inc. acquired land, buildings, and equipment from a bankrupt company, Vivace Co., for a lump-sum price of $680,000. At the time of purchase, Vivace's assets had the following book and appraisal values.

	Book Values	Appraisal Values
Land	$200,000	$150,000
Buildings	230,000	350,000
Equipment	300,000	300,000

To be conservative, the company decided to take the lower of the two values for each asset acquired. The following entry was made.

Land	150,000	
Buildings	230,000	
Equipment	300,000	
Cash		680,000

2. Arawak Enterprises purchased store equipment by making a $2,000 cash down payment and signing a 1-year, $23,000, 10% note payable. The purchase was recorded as follows.

Equipment	27,300	
Cash		2,000
Notes Payable		23,000
Interest Payable		2,300

3. Ace Company purchased office equipment for $20,000, terms 2/10, n/30. Because the company intended to take the discount, it made no entry until it paid for the acquisition. The entry was:

Equipment	20,000	
Cash		19,600
Purchase Discounts		400

4. Paunee Inc. recently received at zero cost land from the Village of Cardassia as an inducement to locate its business in the Village. The appraised value of the land is $27,000. The company made no entry to record the land because it had no cost basis.
5. Mohegan Company built a warehouse for $600,000. It could have purchased the building for $740,000. The controller made the following entry.

Buildings	740,000	
Cash		600,000
Profit on Construction		140,000

Instructions

Prepare the entry that should have been made at the date of each acquisition.

4 **E10-7 (Capitalization of Interest)** McPherson Furniture Company started construction of a combination office and warehouse building for its own use at an estimated cost of $5,000,000 on January 1, 2012. McPherson expected to complete the building by December 31, 2012. McPherson has the following debt obligations outstanding during the construction period.

Construction loan—12% interest, payable semiannually, issued December 31, 2011	$2,000,000
Short-term loan—10% interest, payable monthly, and principal payable at maturity on May 30, 2013	1,600,000
Long-term loan—11% interest, payable on January 1 of each year; principal payable on January 1, 2016	1,000,000

Instructions

(Carry all computations to two decimal places.)

(a) Assume that McPherson completed the office and warehouse building on December 31, 2012, as planned at a total cost of $5,200,000, and the weighted average of accumulated expenditures was $3,800,000. Compute the avoidable interest on this project.

(b) Compute the depreciation expense for the year ended December 31, 2013. McPherson elected to depreciate the building on a straight-line basis and determined that the asset has a useful life of 30 years and a salvage value of $300,000.

4 **E10-8 (Capitalization of Interest)** On December 31, 2011, Hurston Inc. borrowed $3,000,000 at 12% payable annually to finance the construction of a new building. In 2012, the company made the following expenditures related to this building: March 1, $360,000; June 1, $600,000; July 1, $1,500,000; December 1, $1,200,000. Additional information is provided as follows.

1. Other debt outstanding	
10-year, 11% bond, December 31, 2005, interest payable annually	$4,000,000
6-year, 10% note, dated December 31, 2009, interest payable annually	$1,600,000
2. March 1, 2012, expenditure included land costs of $150,000	
3. Interest revenue earned in 2012	$49,000

Instructions

(a) Determine the amount of interest to be capitalized in 2012 in relation to the construction of the building.

(b) Prepare the journal entry to record the capitalization of interest and the recognition of interest expense, if any, at December 31, 2012.

4 **E10-9 (Capitalization of Interest)** On July 31, 2012, Bismarck Company engaged Duval Tooling Company to construct a special-purpose piece of factory machinery. Construction began immediately and was completed on November 1, 2012. To help finance construction, on July 31 Bismarck issued a $400,000, 3-year, 12% note payable at Wellington National Bank, on which interest is payable each July 31. $300,000 of the proceeds of the note was paid to Duval on July 31. The remainder of the proceeds was temporarily invested in short-term marketable securities (debt investments) at 10% until November 1. On November 1, Bismarck made a final $100,000 payment to Duval. Other than the note to Wellington, Bismarck's only outstanding liability at December 31, 2012, is a $30,000, 8%, 6-year note payable, dated January 1, 2009, on which interest is payable each December 31.

Instructions

(a) Calculate the interest revenue, weighted-average accumulated expenditures, avoidable interest, and total interest cost to be capitalized during 2012. Round all computations to the nearest dollar.

(b) Prepare the journal entries needed on the books of Bismarck Company at each of the following dates.

(1) July 31, 2012.

(2) November 1, 2012.

(3) December 31, 2012.

4 **E10-10 (Capitalization of Interest)** The following three situations involve the capitalization of interest.

Situation I

On January 1, 2012, Columbia, Inc. signed a fixed-price contract to have Builder Associates construct a major plant facility at a cost of $4,000,000. It was estimated that it would take 3 years to complete the project. Also on January 1, 2012, to finance the construction cost, Columbia borrowed $4,000,000 payable in 10 annual installments of $400,000, plus interest at the rate of 10%. During 2012, Columbia made deposit and progress payments totaling $1,500,000 under the contract; the weighted-average amount of accumulated expenditures was $900,000 for the year. The excess borrowed funds were invested in short-term securities, from which Columbia realized investment income of $250,000.

Instructions

What amount should Columbia report as capitalized interest at December 31, 2012?

Situation II

During 2012, Evander Corporation constructed and manufactured certain assets and incurred the following interest costs in connection with those activities.

	Interest Costs Incurred
Warehouse constructed for Evander's own use	$30,000
Special-order machine for sale to unrelated customer, produced according to customer's specifications	9,000
Inventories routinely manufactured, produced on a repetitive basis	8,000

All of these assets required an extended period of time for completion.

Instructions

Assuming the effect of interest capitalization is material, what is the total amount of interest costs to be capitalized?

Situation III

Antonio, Inc. has a fiscal year ending April 30. On May 1, 2012, Antonio borrowed $10,000,000 at 11% to finance construction of its own building. Repayments of the loan are to commence the month following completion of the building. During the year ended April 30, 2013, expenditures for the partially completed structure totaled $6,000,000. These expenditures were incurred evenly throughout the year. Interest earned on the unexpended portion of the loan amounted to $650,000 for the year.

Instructions

How much should be shown as capitalized interest on Antonio's financial statements at April 30, 2013?

(CPA adapted)

2 3 5 **E10-11 (Entries for Equipment Acquisitions)** Chopin Engineering Corporation purchased conveyor equipment with a list price of $15,000. Presented below are three independent cases related to the equipment. (Round to nearest dollar.)

(a) Chopin paid cash for the equipment 8 days after the purchase. The vendor's credit terms are 2/10, n/30. Assume that equipment purchases are recorded gross.

(b) Chopin traded in equipment with a book value of $2,000 (initial cost $8,000), and paid $14,200 in cash one month after the purchase. The old equipment could have been sold for $400 at the date of trade. (The exchange has commercial substance.)

(c) Chopin gave the vendor a $16,200 zero-interest-bearing note for the equipment on the date of purchase. The note was due in one year and was paid on time. Assume that the effective-interest rate in the market was 9%.

Instructions

Prepare the general journal entries required to record the acquisition and payment in each of the independent cases above. Round to the nearest dollar.

2 3 **E10-12 (Entries for Asset Acquisition, Including Self-Construction)** Below are transactions related to
5 Impala Company.

(a) The City of Pebble Beach gives the company 5 acres of land as a plant site. The fair value of this land is determined to be $81,000.

(b) 14,000 shares of common stock with a par value of $50 per share are issued in exchange for land and buildings. The property has been appraised at a fair value of $810,000, of which $180,000 has been allocated to land and $630,000 to buildings. The stock of Impala Company is not listed on any exchange, but a block of 100 shares was sold by a stockholder 12 months ago at $65 per share, and a block of 200 shares was sold by another stockholder 18 months ago at $58 per share.

(c) No entry has been made to remove from the accounts for Materials, Direct Labor, and Overhead the amounts properly chargeable to plant asset accounts for machinery constructed during the year. The following information is given relative to costs of the machinery constructed.

Materials used	$12,500
Factory supplies used	900
Direct labor incurred	16,000
Additional overhead (over regular) caused by construction of machinery, excluding factory supplies used	2,700
Fixed overhead rate applied to regular manufacturing operations	60% of direct labor cost
Cost of similar machinery if it had been purchased from outside suppliers	44,000

Instructions

Prepare journal entries on the books of Impala Company to record these transactions.

2 5 **E10-13 (Entries for Acquisition of Assets)** Presented below is information related to Rommel Company.

1. On July 6, Rommel Company acquired the plant assets of Studebaker Company, which had discontinued operations. The appraised value of the property is:

Land	$ 400,000
Buildings	1,200,000
Equipment	800,000
Total	$2,400,000

Rommel Company gave 12,500 shares of its $100 par value common stock in exchange. The stock had a fair value of $180 per share on the date of the purchase of the property.

2. Rommel Company expended the following amounts in cash between July 6 and December 15, the date when it first occupied the building.

Repairs to building	$105,000
Construction of bases for machinery to be installed later	135,000
Driveways and parking lots	122,000
Remodeling of office space in building, including new partitions and walls	161,000
Special assessment by city on land	18,000

3. On December 20, the company paid cash for machinery, $280,000, subject to a 2% cash discount, and freight on machinery of $10,500.

Instructions

Prepare entries on the books of Rommel Company for these transactions.

5 **E10-14 (Purchase of Equipment with Zero-Interest-Bearing Debt)** Sterling Inc. has decided to purchase equipment from Central Michigan Industries on January 2, 2012, to expand its production capacity to meet customers' demand for its product. Sterling issues a $900,000, 5-year, zero-interest-bearing note to Central Michigan for the new equipment when the prevailing market rate of interest for obligations of this nature is 12%. The company will pay off the note in five $180,000 installments due at the end of each year over the life of the note.

Instructions

(a) Prepare the journal entry(ies) at the date of purchase. (Round to nearest dollar in all computations.)
(b) Prepare the journal entry(ies) at the end of the first year to record the payment and interest, assuming that the company employs the effective-interest method.
(c) Prepare the journal entry(ies) at the end of the second year to record the payment and interest.
(d) Assuming that the equipment had a 10-year life and no salvage value, prepare the journal entry necessary to record depreciation in the first year. (Straight-line depreciation is employed.)

5 **E10-15 (Purchase of Computer with Zero-Interest-Bearing Debt)** Napoleon Corporation purchased a computer on December 31, 2011, for $130,000, paying $30,000 down and agreeing to pay the balance in five equal installments of $20,000 payable each December 31 beginning in 2012. An assumed interest rate of 10% is implicit in the purchase price.

Instructions

(a) Prepare the journal entry(ies) at the date of purchase. (Round to two decimal places.)
(b) Prepare the journal entry(ies) at December 31, 2012, to record the payment and interest (effective-interest method employed).
(c) Prepare the journal entry(ies) at December 31, 2013, to record the payment and interest (effective-interest method employed).

5 **E10-16 (Asset Acquisition)** Logan Industries purchased the following assets and constructed a building as well. All this was done during the current year.

Assets 1 and 2

These assets were purchased as a lump sum for $104,000 cash. The following information was gathered.

Description	Initial Cost on Seller's Books	Depreciation to Date on Seller's Books	Book Value on Seller's Books	Appraised Value
Machinery	$100,000	$50,000	$50,000	$90,000
Equipment	60,000	10,000	50,000	30,000

Asset 3

This machine was acquired by making a $10,000 down payment and issuing a $30,000, 2-year, zero-interest-bearing note. The note is to be paid off in two $15,000 installments made at the end of the first and second years. It was estimated that the asset could have been purchased outright for $35,900.

Asset 4

This machinery was acquired by trading in used machinery. (The exchange lacks commercial substance.) Facts concerning the trade-in are as follows.

Cost of machinery traded	$100,000
Accumulated depreciation to date of sale	36,000
Fair value of machinery traded	80,000
Cash received	10,000
Fair value of machinery acquired	70,000

Asset 5

Office equipment was acquired by issuing 100 shares of $8 par value common stock. The stock had a market price of $11 per share.

Construction of Building

A building was constructed on land purchased last year at a cost of $180,000. Construction began on February 1 and was completed on November 1. The payments to the contractor were as follows.

Date	Payment
2/1	$120,000
6/1	360,000
9/1	480,000
11/1	100,000

To finance construction of the building, a $600,000, 12% construction loan was taken out on February 1. The loan was repaid on November 1. The firm had $200,000 of other outstanding debt during the year at a borrowing rate of 8%.

Instructions

Record the acquisition of each of these assets.

5 **E10-17 (Nonmonetary Exchange)** Alatorre Corporation, which manufactures shoes, hired a recent college graduate to work in its accounting department. On the first day of work, the accountant was assigned to total a batch of invoices with the use of an adding machine. Before long, the accountant, who had never before seen such a machine, managed to break the machine. Alatorre Corporation gave the machine plus $320 to Mills Business Machine Company (dealer) in exchange for a new machine. Assume the following information about the machines.

	Alatorre Corp. (Old Machine)	Mills Co. (New Machine)
Machine cost	$290	$270
Accumulated depreciation	140	–0–
Fair value	85	405

Instructions

For each company, prepare the necessary journal entry to record the exchange. (The exchange has commercial substance.)

5 **E10-18 (Nonmonetary Exchange)** Montgomery Company purchased an electric wax melter on April 30, 2013, by trading in its old gas model and paying the balance in cash. The following data relate to the purchase.

List price of new melter	$15,800
Cash paid	10,000
Cost of old melter (5-year life, $700 residual value)	12,700
Accumulated depreciation—old melter (straight-line)	7,200
Secondhand fair value of old melter	5,200

Instructions

Prepare the journal entry(ies) necessary to record this exchange, assuming that the exchange (a) has commercial substance, and (b) lacks commercial substance. Montgomery's year ends on December 31, and depreciation has been recorded through December 31, 2012.

5 **E10-19 (Nonmonetary Exchange)** Santana Company exchanged equipment used in its manufacturing operations plus $2,000 in cash for similar equipment used in the operations of Delaware Company. The following information pertains to the exchange.

	Santana Co.	Delaware Co.
Equipment (cost)	$28,000	$28,000
Accumulated depreciation	19,000	10,000
Fair value of equipment	13,500	15,500
Cash given up	2,000	

Instructions

(a) Prepare the journal entries to record the exchange on the books of both companies. Assume that the exchange lacks commercial substance.

(b) Prepare the journal entries to record the exchange on the books of both companies. Assume that the exchange has commercial substance.

5 **E10-20 (Nonmonetary Exchange)** McArthur Inc. has negotiated the purchase of a new piece of automatic equipment at a price of $7,000 plus trade-in, f.o.b. factory. McArthur Inc. paid $7,000 cash and traded in used equipment. The used equipment had originally cost $62,000; it had a book value of $42,000 and a secondhand fair value of $45,800, as indicated by recent transactions involving similar equipment. Freight and installation charges for the new equipment required a cash payment of $1,100.

Instructions

(a) Prepare the general journal entry to record this transaction, assuming that the exchange has commercial substance.

(b) Assuming the same facts as in (a) except that fair value information for the assets exchanged is not determinable. Prepare the general journal entry to record this transaction.

6 **E10-21 (Analysis of Subsequent Expenditures)** Accardo Resources Group has been in its plant facility for 15 years. Although the plant is quite functional, numerous repair costs are incurred to maintain it in sound working order. The company's plant asset book value is currently $800,000, as indicated below.

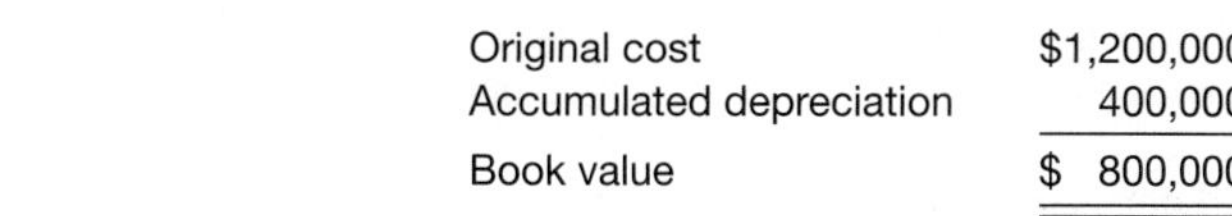

Original cost	$1,200,000
Accumulated depreciation	400,000
Book value	$ 800,000

During the current year, the following expenditures were made to the plant facility.

(a) Because of increased demands for its product, the company increased its plant capacity by building a new addition at a cost of $270,000.
(b) The entire plant was repainted at a cost of $23,000.
(c) The roof was an asbestos cement slate. For safety purposes it was removed and replaced with a wood shingle roof at a cost of $61,000. Book value of the old roof was $41,000.
(d) The electrical system was completely updated at a cost of $22,000. The cost of the old electrical system was not known. It is estimated that the useful life of the building will not change as a result of this updating.
(e) A series of major repairs were made at a cost of $47,000, because parts of the wood structure were rotting. The cost of the old wood structure was not known. These extensive repairs are estimated to increase the useful life of the building.

Instructions
Indicate how each of these transactions would be recorded in the accounting records.

6 **E10-22 (Analysis of Subsequent Expenditures)** The following transactions occurred during 2013. Assume that depreciation of 10% per year is charged on all machinery and 5% per year on buildings, on a straight-line basis, with no estimated salvage value. Depreciation is charged for a full year on all fixed assets acquired during the year, and no depreciation is charged on fixed assets disposed of during the year.

Jan. 30	A building that cost $112,000 in 1996 is torn down to make room for a new building. The wrecking contractor was paid $5,100 and was permitted to keep all materials salvaged.
Mar. 10	Machinery that was purchased in 2006 for $16,000 is sold for $2,900 cash, f.o.b. purchaser's plant. Freight of $300 is paid on the sale of this machinery.
Mar. 20	A gear breaks on a machine that cost $9,000 in 2008. The gear is replaced at a cost of $3,000. The replacement does not extend the useful life of the machine.
May 18	A special base installed for a machine in 2007 when the machine was purchased has to be replaced at a cost of $5,500 because of defective workmanship on the original base. The cost of the machinery was $14,200 in 2007. The cost of the base was $4,000, and this amount was charged to the Machinery account in 2007.
June 23	One of the buildings is repainted at a cost of $6,900. It had not been painted since it was constructed in 2009.

Instructions
Prepare general journal entries for the transactions. (Round to the nearest dollar.)

6 **E10-23 (Analysis of Subsequent Expenditures)** Plant assets often require expenditures subsequent to acquisition. It is important that they be accounted for properly. Any errors will affect both the balance sheets and income statements for a number of years.

Instructions
For each of the following items, indicate whether the expenditure should be capitalized (C) or expensed (E) in the period incurred.

(a) __________ Improvement.
(b) __________ Replacement of a minor broken part on a machine.
(c) __________ Expenditure that increases the useful life of an existing asset.
(d) __________ Expenditure that increases the efficiency and effectiveness of a productive asset but does not increase its salvage value.
(e) __________ Expenditure that increases the efficiency and effectiveness of a productive asset and increases the asset's salvage value.
(f) __________ Ordinary repairs.
(g) __________ Improvement to a machine that increased its fair value and its production capacity by 30% without extending the machine's useful life.
(h) __________ Expenditure that increases the quality of the output of the productive asset.

7 **E10-24 (Entries for Disposition of Assets)** On December 31, 2012, Chrysler Inc. has a machine with a book value of $940,000. The original cost and related accumulated depreciation at this date are as follows.

Machine	$1,300,000
Accumulated depreciation	360,000
Book value	$ 940,000

Depreciation is computed at $72,000 per year on a straight-line basis.

Instructions

Presented below is a set of independent situations. For each independent situation, indicate the journal entry to be made to record the transaction. Make sure that depreciation entries are made to update the book value of the machine prior to its disposal.

(a) A fire completely destroys the machine on August 31, 2013. An insurance settlement of $630,000 was received for this casualty. Assume the settlement was received immediately.

(b) On April 1, 2013, Chrysler sold the machine for $1,040,000 to Avanti Company.

(c) On July 31, 2013, the company donated this machine to the Mountain King City Council. The fair value of the machine at the time of the donation was estimated to be $1,100,000.

7 **E10-25 (Disposition of Assets)** On April 1, 2012, Pavlova Company received a condemnation award of $410,000 cash as compensation for the forced sale of the company's land and building, which stood in the path of a new state highway. The land and building cost $60,000 and $280,000, respectively, when they were acquired. At April 1, 2012, the accumulated depreciation relating to the building amounted to $160,000. On August 1, 2012, Pavlova purchased a piece of replacement property for cash. The new land cost $90,000, and the new building cost $380,000.

Instructions

Prepare the journal entries to record the transactions on April 1 and August 1, 2012.

See the book's companion website, www.wiley.com/college/kieso, for a set of B Exercises.

PROBLEMS

2 **P10-1 (Classification of Acquisition and Other Asset Costs)** At December 31, 2011, certain accounts included in the property, plant, and equipment section of Reagan Company's balance sheet had the following balances.

Land	$230,000
Buildings	890,000
Leasehold improvements	660,000
Equipment	875,000

During 2012, the following transactions occurred.

1. Land site number 621 was acquired for $850,000. In addition, to acquire the land Reagan paid a $51,000 commission to a real estate agent. Costs of $35,000 were incurred to clear the land. During the course of clearing the land, timber and gravel were recovered and sold for $13,000.
2. A second tract of land (site number 622) with a building was acquired for $420,000. The closing statement indicated that the land value was $300,000 and the building value was $120,000. Shortly after acquisition, the building was demolished at a cost of $41,000. A new building was constructed for $330,000 plus the following costs.

Excavation fees	$38,000
Architectural design fees	11,000
Building permit fee	2,500
Imputed interest on funds used during construction (stock financing)	8,500

   The building was completed and occupied on September 30, 2012.
3. A third tract of land (site number 623) was acquired for $650,000 and was put on the market for resale.
4. During December 2012, costs of $89,000 were incurred to improve leased office space. The related lease will terminate on December 31, 2014, and is not expected to be renewed. (*Hint:* Leasehold improvements should be handled in the same manner as land improvements.)
5. A group of new machines was purchased under a royalty agreement that provides for payment of royalties based on units of production for the machines. The invoice price of the machines was $87,000, freight costs were $3,300, installation costs were $2,400, and royalty payments for 2012 were $17,500.

Instructions

(a) Prepare a detailed analysis of the changes in each of the following balance sheet accounts for 2012.

Land	Leasehold improvements
Buildings	Equipment

Disregard the related accumulated depreciation accounts.

(b) List the items in the situation that were not used to determine the answer to (a) above, and indicate where, or if, these items should be included in Reagan's financial statements.

(AICPA adapted)

2 7 **P10-2 (Classification of Acquisition Costs)** Selected accounts included in the property, plant, and equipment section of Lobo Corporation's balance sheet at December 31, 2011, had the following balances.

Land	$ 300,000
Land improvements	140,000
Buildings	1,100,000
Equipment	960,000

During 2012, the following transactions occurred.

1. A tract of land was acquired for $150,000 as a potential future building site.
2. A plant facility consisting of land and building was acquired from Mendota Company in exchange for 20,000 shares of Lobo's common stock. On the acquisition date, Lobo's stock had a closing market price of $37 per share on a national stock exchange. The plant facility was carried on Mendota's books at $110,000 for land and $320,000 for the building at the exchange date. Current appraised values for the land and building, respectively, are $230,000 and $690,000.
3. Items of machinery and equipment were purchased at a total cost of $400,000. Additional costs were incurred as follows.

Freight and unloading	$13,000
Sales taxes	20,000
Installation	26,000

4. Expenditures totaling $95,000 were made for new parking lots, streets, and sidewalks at the corporation's various plant locations. These expenditures had an estimated useful life of 15 years.
5. A machine costing $80,000 on January 1, 2004, was scrapped on June 30, 2012. Double-declining-balance depreciation has been recorded on the basis of a 10-year life.
6. A machine was sold for $20,000 on July 1, 2012. Original cost of the machine was $44,000 on January 1, 2009, and it was depreciated on the straight-line basis over an estimated useful life of 7 years and a salvage value of $2,000.

Instructions

(a) Prepare a detailed analysis of the changes in each of the following balance sheet accounts for 2012.

Land
Land improvements
Buildings
Equipment

(*Hint:* Disregard the related accumulated depreciation accounts.)

(b) List the items in the fact situation that were not used to determine the answer to (a), showing the pertinent amounts and supporting computations in good form for each item. In addition, indicate where, or if, these items should be included in Lobo's financial statements.

(AICPA adapted)

2 3 5 **P10-3 (Classification of Land and Building Costs)** Spitfire Company was incorporated on January 2, 2013, but was unable to begin manufacturing activities until July 1, 2013, because new factory facilities were not completed until that date.

The Land and Building account reported the following items during 2013.

January 31	Land and building	$160,000
February 28	Cost of removal of building	9,800
May 1	Partial payment of new construction	60,000
May 1	Legal fees paid	3,770
June 1	Second payment on new construction	40,000
June 1	Insurance premium	2,280
June 1	Special tax assessment	4,000
June 30	General expenses	36,300
July 1	Final payment on new construction	30,000
December 31	Asset write-up	53,800
		399,950
December 31	Depreciation—2013 at 1%	4,000
December 31, 2013	Account balance	$395,950

The following additional information is to be considered.

1. To acquire land and building, the company paid $80,000 cash and 800 shares of its 8% cumulative preferred stock, par value $100 per share. Fair value of the stock is $117 per share.
2. Cost of removal of old buildings amounted to $9,800, and the demolition company retained all materials of the building.
3. Legal fees covered the following.

Cost of organization	$ 610
Examination of title covering purchase of land	1,300
Legal work in connection with construction contract	1,860
	$3,770

4. Insurance premium covered the building for a 2-year term beginning May 1, 2013.
5. The special tax assessment covered street improvements that are permanent in nature.
6. General expenses covered the following for the period from January 2, 2013, to June 30, 2013.

President's salary	$32,100
Plant superintendent's salary—supervision of new building	4,200
	$36,300

7. Because of a general increase in construction costs after entering into the building contract, the board of directors increased the value of the building $53,800, believing that such an increase was justified to reflect the current market at the time the building was completed. Retained earnings was credited for this amount.
8. Estimated life of building—50 years.
   Depreciation for 2013—1% of asset value (1% of $400,000, or $4,000).

Instructions

(a) Prepare entries to reflect correct land, building, and depreciation accounts at December 31, 2013.

(b) Show the proper presentation of land, building, and depreciation on the balance sheet at December 31, 2013.

(AICPA adapted)

P10-4 (Dispositions, Including Condemnation, Demolition, and Trade-in) Presented below is a schedule of property dispositions for Hollerith Co.

Schedule of Property Dispositions

	Cost	Accumulated Depreciation	Cash Proceeds	Fair Value	Nature of Disposition
Land	$40,000	—	$31,000	$31,000	Condemnation
Building	15,000	—	3,600	—	Demolition
Warehouse	70,000	$16,000	74,000	74,000	Destruction by fire
Machine	8,000	2,800	900	7,200	Trade-in
Furniture	10,000	7,850	—	3,100	Contribution
Automobile	9,000	3,460	2,960	2,960	Sale

The following additional information is available.

Land

On February 15, a condemnation award was received as consideration for unimproved land held primarily as an investment, and on March 31, another parcel of unimproved land to be held as an investment was purchased at a cost of $35,000.

Building

On April 2, land and building were purchased at a total cost of $75,000, of which 20% was allocated to the building on the corporate books. The real estate was acquired with the intention of demolishing the building, and this was accomplished during the month of November. Cash proceeds received in November represent the net proceeds from demolition of the building.

Warehouse

On June 30, the warehouse was destroyed by fire. The warehouse was purchased January 2, 2009, and had depreciated $16,000. On December 27, the insurance proceeds and other funds were used to purchase a replacement warehouse at a cost of $90,000.

Machine
On December 26, the machine was exchanged for another machine having a fair value of $6,300 and cash of $900 was received. (The exchange lacks commercial substance.)

Furniture
On August 15, furniture was contributed to a qualified charitable organization. No other contributions were made or pledged during the year.

Automobile
On November 3, the automobile was sold to Jared Winger, a stockholder.

Instructions
Indicate how these items would be reported on the income statement of Hollerith Co.

(AICPA adapted)

2 4 **P10-5 (Classification of Costs and Interest Capitalization)** On January 1, 2012, Blair Corporation purchased for $500,000 a tract of land (site number 101) with a building. Blair paid a real estate broker's commission of $36,000, legal fees of $6,000, and title guarantee insurance of $18,000. The closing statement indicated that the land value was $500,000 and the building value was $100,000. Shortly after acquisition, the building was razed at a cost of $54,000.

Blair entered into a $3,000,000 fixed-price contract with Slatkin Builders, Inc. on March 1, 2012, for the construction of an office building on land site number 101. The building was completed and occupied on September 30, 2013. Additional construction costs were incurred as follows.

Plans, specifications, and blueprints	$21,000
Architects' fees for design and supervision	82,000

The building is estimated to have a 40-year life from date of completion and will be depreciated using the 150% declining-balance method.

To finance construction costs, Blair borrowed $3,000,000 on March 1, 2012. The loan is payable in 10 annual installments of $300,000 plus interest at the rate of 10%. Blair's weighted-average amounts of accumulated building construction expenditures were as follows.

For the period March 1 to December 31, 2012	$1,300,000
For the period January 1 to September 30, 2013	1,900,000

Instructions

(a) Prepare a schedule that discloses the individual costs making up the balance in the land account in respect of land site number 101 as of September 30, 2013.

(b) Prepare a schedule that discloses the individual costs that should be capitalized in the office building account as of September 30, 2013. Show supporting computations in good form.

(AICPA adapted)

2 4 **P10-6 (Interest During Construction)** Grieg Landscaping began construction of a new plant on December 1, 2012. On this date, the company purchased a parcel of land for $139,000 in cash. In addition, it paid $2,000 in surveying costs and $4,000 for a title insurance policy. An old dwelling on the premises was demolished at a cost of $3,000, with $1,000 being received from the sale of materials.

Architectural plans were also formalized on December 1, 2012, when the architect was paid $30,000. The necessary building permits costing $3,000 were obtained from the city and paid for on December 1 as well. The excavation work began during the first week in December with payments made to the contractor as follows.

Date of Payment	Amount of Payment
March 1	$240,000
May 1	330,000
July 1	60,000

The building was completed on July 1, 2013.

To finance construction of this plant, Grieg borrowed $600,000 from the bank on December 1, 2012. Grieg had no other borrowings. The $600,000 was a 10-year loan bearing interest at 8%.

Instructions
Compute the balance in each of the following accounts at December 31, 2012, and December 31, 2013. (Round amounts to the nearest dollar.)

(a) Land.

(b) Buildings.

(c) Interest Expense.

4 **P10-7 (Capitalization of Interest)** Laserwords Inc. is a book distributor that had been operating in its original facility since 1985. The increase in certification programs and continuing education requirements in several professions has contributed to an annual growth rate of 15% for Laserwords since 2007. Laserwords' original facility became obsolete by early 2012 because of the increased sales volume and the fact that Laserwords now carries CDs in addition to books.

On June 1, 2012, Laserwords contracted with Black Construction to have a new building constructed for $4,000,000 on land owned by Laserwords. The payments made by Laserwords to Black Construction are shown in the schedule below.

Date	Amount
July 30, 2012	$ 900,000
January 30, 2013	1,500,000
May 30, 2013	1,600,000
Total payments	$4,000,000

Construction was completed and the building was ready for occupancy on May 27, 2013. Laserwords had no new borrowings directly associated with the new building but had the following debt outstanding at May 31, 2013, the end of its fiscal year.

10%, 5-year note payable of $2,000,000, dated April 1, 2009, with interest payable annually on April 1.
12%, 10-year bond issue of $3,000,000 sold at par on June 30, 2005, with interest payable annually on June 30.

The new building qualifies for interest capitalization. The effect of capitalizing the interest on the new building, compared with the effect of expensing the interest, is material.

Instructions

(a) Compute the weighted-average accumulated expenditures on Laserwords' new building during the capitalization period.
(b) Compute the avoidable interest on Laserwords' new building.
(c) Some interest cost of Laserwords Inc. is capitalized for the year ended May 31, 2013.
  (1) Identify the items relating to interest costs that must be disclosed in Laserwords' financial statements.
  (2) Compute the amount of each of the items that must be disclosed.

(CMA adapted)

5 **P10-8 (Nonmonetary Exchanges)** Holyfield Corporation wishes to exchange a machine used in its operations. Holyfield has received the following offers from other companies in the industry.

1. Dorsett Company offered to exchange a similar machine plus $23,000. (The exchange has commercial substance for both parties.)
2. Winston Company offered to exchange a similar machine. (The exchange lacks commercial substance for both parties.)
3. Liston Company offered to exchange a similar machine, but wanted $3,000 in addition to Holyfield's machine. (The exchange has commercial substance for both parties.)

In addition, Holyfield contacted Greeley Corporation, a dealer in machines. To obtain a new machine, Holyfield must pay $93,000 in addition to trading in its old machine.

	Holyfield	Dorsett	Winston	Liston	Greeley
Machine cost	$160,000	$120,000	$152,000	$160,000	$130,000
Accumulated depreciation	60,000	45,000	71,000	75,000	-0-
Fair value	92,000	69,000	92,000	95,000	185,000

Instructions

For each of the four independent situations, prepare the journal entries to record the exchange on the books of each company.

5 **P10-9 (Nonmonetary Exchanges)** On August 1, Hyde, Inc. exchanged productive assets with Wiggins, Inc. Hyde's asset is referred to below as "Asset A," and Wiggins' is referred to as "Asset B." The following facts pertain to these assets.

	Asset A	Asset B
Original cost	$96,000	$110,000
Accumulated depreciation (to date of exchange)	40,000	47,000
Fair value at date of exchange	60,000	75,000
Cash paid by Hyde, Inc.	15,000	
Cash received by Wiggins, Inc.		15,000

Instructions

(a) Assuming that the exchange of Assets A and B has commercial substance, record the exchange for both Hyde, Inc. and Wiggins, Inc. in accordance with generally accepted accounting principles.

(b) Assuming that the exchange of Assets A and B lacks commercial substance, record the exchange for both Hyde, Inc. and Wiggins, Inc. in accordance with generally accepted accounting principles.

5 **P10-10 (Nonmonetary Exchanges)** During the current year, Marshall Construction trades an old crane that has a book value of $90,000 (original cost $140,000 less accumulated depreciation $50,000) for a new crane from Brigham Manufacturing Co. The new crane cost Brigham $165,000 to manufacture and is classified as inventory. The following information is also available.

	Marshall Const.	Brigham Mfg. Co.
Fair value of old crane	$ 82,000	
Fair value of new crane		$200,000
Cash paid	118,000	
Cash received		118,000

Instructions

(a) Assuming that this exchange is considered to have commercial substance, prepare the journal entries on the books of (1) Marshall Construction and (2) Brigham Manufacturing.

(b) Assuming that this exchange lacks commercial substance for Marshall, prepare the journal entries on the books of Marshall Construction.

(c) Assuming the same facts as those in (a), except that the fair value of the old crane is $98,000 and the cash paid is $102,000, prepare the journal entries on the books of (1) Marshall Construction and (2) Brigham Manufacturing.

(d) Assuming the same facts as those in (b), except that the fair value of the old crane is $97,000 and the cash paid $103,000, prepare the journal entries on the books of (1) Marshall Construction and (2) Brigham Manufacturing.

2 5 **P10-11 (Purchases by Deferred Payment, Lump-Sum, and Nonmonetary Exchanges)** Klamath Company, a manufacturer of ballet shoes, is experiencing a period of sustained growth. In an effort to expand its production capacity to meet the increased demand for its product, the company recently made several acquisitions of plant and equipment. Rob Joffrey, newly hired in the position of fixed-asset accountant, requested that Danny Nolte, Klamath's controller, review the following transactions.

Transaction 1

On June 1, 2012, Klamath Company purchased equipment from Wyandot Corporation. Klamath issued a $28,000, 4-year, zero-interest-bearing note to Wyandot for the new equipment. Klamath will pay off the note in four equal installments due at the end of each of the next 4 years. At the date of the transaction, the prevailing market rate of interest for obligations of this nature was 10%. Freight costs of $425 and installation costs of $500 were incurred in completing this transaction. The appropriate factors for the time value of money at a 10% rate of interest are given below.

Future value of $1 for 4 periods	1.46
Future value of an ordinary annuity for 4 periods	4.64
Present value of $1 for 4 periods	0.68
Present value of an ordinary annuity for 4 periods	3.17

Transaction 2

On December 1, 2012, Klamath Company purchased several assets of Yakima Shoes Inc., a small shoe manufacturer whose owner was retiring. The purchase amounted to $220,000 and included the assets listed below. Klamath Company engaged the services of Tennyson Appraisal Inc., an independent appraiser, to determine the fair values of the assets which are also presented below.

	Yakima Book Value	Fair Value
Inventory	$ 60,000	$ 50,000
Land	40,000	80,000
Buildings	70,000	120,000
	$170,000	$250,000

During its fiscal year ended May 31, 2013, Klamath incurred $8,000 for interest expense in connection with the financing of these assets.

Transaction 3

On March 1, 2013, Klamath Company exchanged a number of used trucks plus cash for vacant land adjacent to its plant site. (The exchange has commercial substance.) Klamath intends to use the land for a parking lot.

The trucks had a combined book value of $35,000, as Klamath had recorded $20,000 of accumulated depreciation against these assets. Klamath's purchasing agent, who has had previous dealings in the secondhand market, indicated that the trucks had a fair value of $46,000 at the time of the transaction. In addition to the trucks, Klamath Company paid $19,000 cash for the land.

Instructions

(a) Plant assets such as land, buildings, and equipment receive special accounting treatment. Describe the major characteristics of these assets that differentiate them from other types of assets.

(b) For each of the three transactions described above, determine the value at which Klamath Company should record the acquired assets. Support your calculations with an explanation of the underlying rationale.

(c) The books of Klamath Company show the following additional transactions for the fiscal year ended May 31, 2013.

(1) Acquisition of a building for speculative purposes.

(2) Purchase of a 2-year insurance policy covering plant equipment.

(3) Purchase of the rights for the exclusive use of a process used in the manufacture of ballet shoes.

For each of these transactions, indicate whether the asset should be classified as a plant asset. If it is a plant asset, explain why it is. If it is not a plant asset, explain why not, and identify the proper classification.

(CMA adapted)

CONCEPTS FOR ANALYSIS

CA10-1 (Acquisition, Improvements, and Sale of Realty) Tonkawa Company purchased land for use as its corporate headquarters. A small factory that was on the land when it was purchased was torn down before construction of the office building began. Furthermore, a substantial amount of rock blasting and removal had to be done to the site before construction of the building foundation began. Because the office building was set back on the land far from the public road, Tonkawa Company had the contractor construct a paved road that led from the public road to the parking lot of the office building.

Three years after the office building was occupied, Tonkawa Company added four stories to the office building. The four stories had an estimated useful life of 5 years more than the remaining estimated useful life of the original office building.

Ten years later, the land and building were sold at an amount more than their net book value, and Tonkawa Company had a new office building constructed in another state for use as its new corporate headquarters.

Instructions

(a) Which of the expenditures above should be capitalized? How should each be depreciated or amortized? Discuss the rationale for your answers.

(b) How would the sale of the land and building be accounted for? Include in your answer an explanation of how to determine the net book value at the date of sale. Discuss the rationale for your answer.

CA10-2 (Accounting for Self-Constructed Assets) Troopers Medical Labs, Inc., began operations 5 years ago producing stetrics, a new type of instrument it hoped to sell to doctors, dentists, and hospitals. The demand for stetrics far exceeded initial expectations, and the company was unable to produce enough stetrics to meet demand.

The company was manufacturing its product on equipment that it built at the start of its operations. To meet demand, more efficient equipment was needed. The company decided to design and build the equipment, because the equipment currently available on the market was unsuitable for producing stetrics.

In 2012, a section of the plant was devoted to development of the new equipment and a special staff was hired. Within 6 months a machine developed at a cost of $714,000 increased production dramatically and reduced labor costs substantially. Elated by the success of the new machine, the company built three more machines of the same type at a cost of $441,000 each.

Instructions

(a) In general, what costs should be capitalized for self-constructed equipment?

(b) Discuss the propriety of including in the capitalized cost of self-constructed assets:

(1) The increase in overhead caused by the self-construction of fixed assets.

(2) A proportionate share of overhead on the same basis as that applied to goods manufactured for sale.

(c) Discuss the proper accounting treatment of the $273,000 ($714,000 − $441,000) by which the cost of the first machine exceeded the cost of the subsequent machines. This additional cost should not be considered research and development costs.

CA10-3 (Capitalization of Interest) Langer Airline is converting from piston-type planes to jets. Delivery time for the jets is 3 years, during which substantial progress payments must be made. The multimillion-dollar cost of the planes cannot be financed from working capital; Langer must borrow funds for the payments.

Because of high interest rates and the large sum to be borrowed, management estimates that interest costs in the second year of the period will be equal to one-third of income before interest and taxes, and one-half of such income in the third year.

After conversion, Langer's passenger-carrying capacity will be doubled with no increase in the number of planes, although the investment in planes would be substantially increased. The jet planes have a 7-year service life.

Instructions

Give your recommendation concerning the proper accounting for interest during the conversion period. Support your recommendation with reasons and suggested accounting treatment. (Disregard income tax implications.)

(AICPA adapted)

CA10-4 (Capitalization of Interest) Vania Magazine Company started construction of a warehouse building for its own use at an estimated cost of $5,000,000 on January 1, 2011, and completed the building on December 31, 2011. During the construction period, Vania has the following debt obligations outstanding.

Construction loan—12% interest, payable semiannually, issued December 31, 2010	$2,000,000
Short-term loan—10% interest, payable monthly, and principal payable at maturity, on May 30, 2012	1,400,000
Long-term loan—11% interest, payable on January 1 of each year. Principal payable on January 1, 2014	1,000,000

Total cost amounted to $5,200,000, and the weighted average of accumulated expenditures was $3,500,000.

Jane Esplanade, the president of the company, has been shown the costs associated with this construction project and capitalized on the balance sheet. She is bothered by the "avoidable interest" included in the cost. She argues that, first, all the interest is unavoidable—no one lends money without expecting to be compensated for it. Second, why can't the company use all the interest on all the loans when computing this avoidable interest? Finally, why can't her company capitalize all the annual interest that accrued over the period of construction?

Instructions

You are the manager of accounting for the company. In a memo, explain what avoidable interest is, how you computed it (being especially careful to explain why you used the interest rates that you did), and why the company cannot capitalize all its interest for the year. Attach a schedule supporting any computations that you use.

CA10-5 (Nonmonetary Exchanges) You have two clients that are considering trading machinery with each other. Although the machines are different from each other, you believe that an assessment of expected cash flows on the exchanged assets will indicate the exchange lacks commercial substance. Your clients would prefer that the exchange be deemed to have commercial substance, to allow them to record gains. Here are the facts:

	Client A	Client B
Original cost	$100,000	$150,000
Accumulated depreciation	40,000	80,000
Fair value	80,000	100,000
Cash received (paid)	(20,000)	20,000

Instructions

(a) Record the trade-in on Client A's books assuming the exchange has commercial substance.
(b) Record the trade-in on Client A's books assuming the exchange lacks commercial substance.
(c) Write a memo to the controller of Company A indicating and explaining the dollar impact on current and future statements of treating the exchange as having versus lacking commercial substance.
(d) Record the entry on Client B's books assuming the exchange has commercial substance.
(e) Record the entry on Client B's books assuming the exchange lacks commercial substance.
(f) Write a memo to the controller of Company B indicating and explaining the dollar impact on current and future statements of treating the exchange as having versus lacking commercial substance.

CA10-6 (Costs of Acquisition) The invoice price of a machine is $50,000. Various other costs relating to the acquisition and installation of the machine including transportation, electrical wiring, special base, and so on amount to $7,500. The machine has an estimated life of 10 years, with no residual value at the end of that period.

The owner of the business suggests that the incidental costs of $7,500 be charged to expense immediately for the following reasons.

1. If the machine should be sold, these costs cannot be recovered in the sales price.
2. The inclusion of the $7,500 in the machinery account on the books will not necessarily result in a closer approximation of the market price of this asset over the years, because of the possibility of changing demand and supply levels.
3. Charging the $7,500 to expense immediately will reduce federal income taxes.

Instructions

Discuss each of the points raised by the owner of the business.

(AICPA adapted)

CA10-7 (Cost of Land vs. Building—Ethics) Tones Company purchased a warehouse in a downtown district where land values are rapidly increasing. Gerald Carter, controller, and Wilma Ankara, financial vice president, are trying to allocate the cost of the purchase between the land and the building. Noting that depreciation can be taken only on the building, Carter favors placing a very high proportion of the cost on the warehouse itself, thus reducing taxable income and income taxes. Ankara, his supervisor, argues that the allocation should recognize the increasing value of the land, regardless of the depreciation potential of the warehouse. Besides, she says, net income is negatively impacted by additional depreciation and will cause the company's stock price to go down.

Instructions

Answer the following questions.

(a) What stakeholder interests are in conflict?
(b) What ethical issues does Carter face?
(c) How should these costs be allocated?

USING YOUR JUDGMENT

FINANCIAL REPORTING

Financial Statement Analysis Case

Johnson & Johnson

Johnson & Johnson, the world's leading and most diversified healthcare corporation, serves its customers through specialized worldwide franchises. Each of its franchises consists of a number of companies throughout the world that focus on a particular health care market, such as surgical sutures, consumer pharmaceuticals, or contact lenses. Information related to its property, plant, and equipment in its 2009 annual report is shown in the notes to the financial statements below and on the next page.

Johnson & Johnson

1. Property, Plant and Equipment and Depreciation

Property, plant and equipment are stated at cost. The Company utilizes the straight-line method of depreciation over the estimated useful lives of the assets:

Building and building equipment	20–40 years
Land and leasehold improvements	10–20 years
Machinery and equipment	2–13 years

4. Property, Plant and Equipment

At the end of 2009 and 2008, property, plant and equipment at cost and accumulated depreciation were:

(dollars in millions)	2009	2008
Land and land improvements	$ 714	$ 886
Buildings and building equipment	8,863	7,720
Machinery and equipment	17,153	15,234
Construction in progress	2,521	3,552
	29,251	27,392
Less accumulated depreciation	14,492	13,027
	$14,759	$14,365

The Company capitalizes interest expense as part of the cost of construction of facilities and equipment. Interest expense capitalized in 2009, 2008 and 2007 was $101 million, $147 million and $130 million, respectively.

Depreciation expense, including the amortization of capitalized interest in 2009, 2008 and 2007 was $2.1 billion, $2.0 billion and $1.9 billion, respectively.

Johnson & Johnson's provided the following selected information in its 2009 cash flow statement.

Johnson & Johnson

Johnson & Johnson
2009 Annual Report

Consolidated Financial Statements (excerpts)

Net cash flows from operating activities	$ 16,571
Cash flows from investing activities	
Additions to property, plant and equipment	(2,365)
Proceeds from the disposal of assets	154
Acquisitions, net of cash acquired	(2,470)
Purchases of investments	(10,040)
Sales of investments	7,232
Other (primarily intangibles)	(109)
Net cash used by investing activities	(7,598)
Cash flows from financing activities	
Dividends to shareholders	(5,327)
Repurchase of common stock	(2,130)
Proceeds from short-term debt	9,484
Retirement of short-term debt	(6,791)
Proceeds from long-term debt	9
Retirement of long-term debt	(219)
Proceeds from the exercise of stock options/excess tax benefits	882
Net cash used by financing activities	(4,092)
Effect of exchange rate changes on cash and cash equivalents	161
Increase in cash and cash equivalents	5,042
Cash and cash equivalents, beginning of year (Note 1)	10,768
Cash and cash equivalents, end of year (Note 1)	$ 15,810
Supplemental cash flow data	
Cash paid during the year for:	
Interest	$ 533
Income taxes	2,363

Instructions

(a) What was the cost of buildings and building equipment at the end of 2009?

(b) Does Johnson & Johnson use a conservative or liberal method to depreciate its property, plant, and equipment?

(c) What was the actual interest expense incurred by the company in 2009?

(d) What is Johnson & Johnson's free cash flow? From the information provided, comment on Johnson & Johnson's financial flexibility.

Accounting, Analysis, and Principles

Durler Company purchased equipment on January 2, 2008, for $112,000. The equipment had an estimated useful life of 5 years with an estimated salvage value of $12,000. Durler uses straight-line depreciation on all assets. On January 2, 2012, Durler exchanged this equipment plus $12,000 in cash for newer equipment. The old equipment has a fair value of $50,000.

Accounting

Prepare the journal entry to record the exchange on the books of Durler Company. Assume that the exchange has commercial substance.

Analysis

How will this exchange affect comparisons of the return on asset ratio for Durler in the year of the exchange compared to prior years?

Principles

How does the concept of commercial substance affect the accounting and analysis of this exchange?

BRIDGE TO THE PROFESSION

Professional Research: FASB Codification

Your client is in the planning phase for a major plant expansion, which will involve the construction of a new warehouse. The assistant controller does not believe that interest cost can be included in the cost of the warehouse, because it is a financing expense. Others on the planning team believe that some interest cost can be included in the cost of the warehouse, but no one could identify the specific authoritative guidance for this issue. Your supervisor asks you to research this issue.

Instructions

If your school has a subscription to the FASB Codification, go to *http://aaahq.org/asclogin.cfm* to log in and prepare responses to the following. Provide Codification references for your responses.

(a) Is it permissible to capitalize interest into the cost of assets? Provide authoritative support for your answer.

(b) What are the objectives for capitalizing interest?

(c) Discuss which assets qualify for interest capitalization.

(d) Is there a limit to the amount of interest that may be capitalized in a period?

(e) If interest capitalization is allowed, what disclosures are required?

Professional Simulation

In this simulation, you are asked to address questions regarding the accounting for property, plant, and equipment. Prepare responses to all parts.

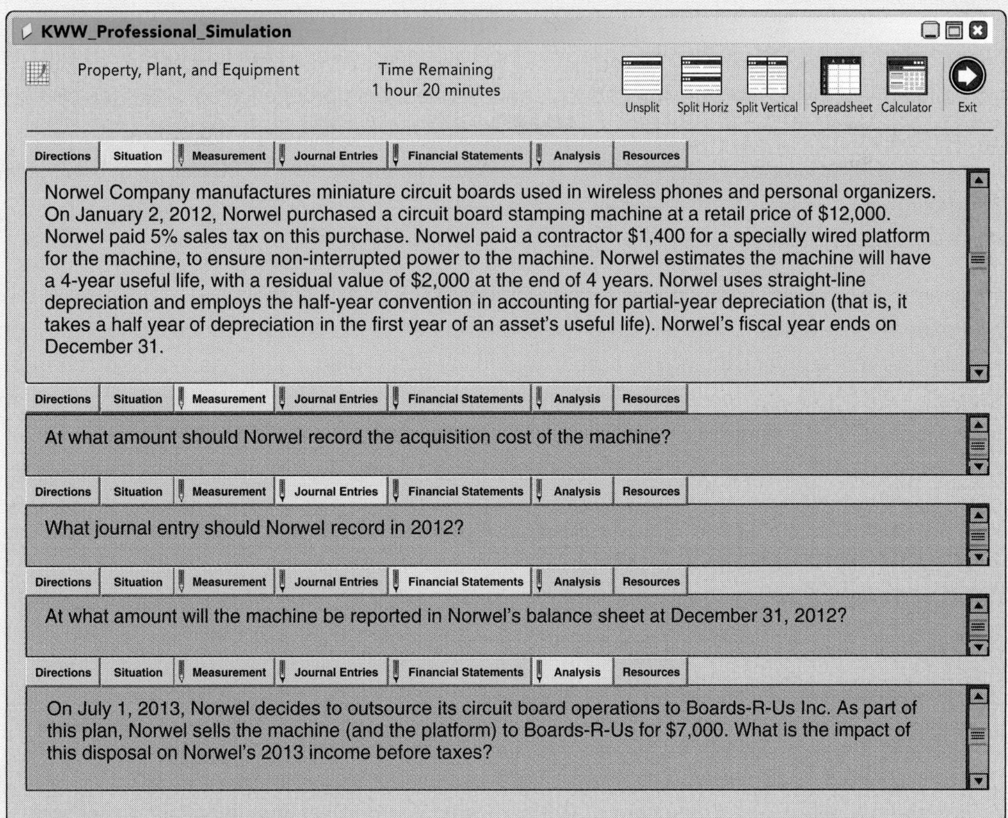

Remember to check the book's companion website to find additional resources for this chapter.

CHAPTER 11

Depreciation, Impairments, and Depletion

LEARNING OBJECTIVES

After studying this chapter, you should be able to:

1. Explain the concept of depreciation.
2. Identify the factors involved in the depreciation process.
3. Compare activity, straight-line, and decreasing-charge methods of depreciation.
4. Explain special depreciation methods.
5. Explain the accounting issues related to asset impairment.
6. Explain the accounting procedures for depletion of natural resources.
7. Explain how to report and analyze property, plant, equipment, and natural resources.

Here Come the Write-Offs

The credit crisis starting in late 2008 has affected many financial and nonfinancial institutions. Many of the statistics related to this crisis are sobering, as noted below.

- In October 2008, the FTSE 100 in the United Kingdom suffered its biggest one-day fall since October 1987. The index closed at its lowest level since October 2004.
- The Dow Jones Industrial Average fell below the 8,000 level for the first time since 2003.
- Germany's benchmark DAX tumbled after the collapse of the proposed rescue plan for **Hypo Real Estate**.
- Tightening credit and less disposable income led to Japanese electronic groups losing value; the Nikkei fell to its lowest point since February 2004.
- The Hong Kong Hang Seng dropped in line with the rest of Asia, closing below 17,000 points for the first time in two years in October and below 11,000 by November 2008.
- Governments have spent billions of dollars bailing out financial institutions.

Although some financial rebound has occurred since October 2008, it is clear that most economies of the world are now in a slower growth pattern. This slowdown raises many questions related to the proper accounting for many long-term assets, such as property, plant, and equipment; intangible assets; and many types of financial assets. One of the most difficult issues relates to the possibility of higher impairment charges related to these assets and the related disclosures that may be needed. Below and on the next page is an example of a recent impairment charge taken by **Fujitsu Limited.**

Impairment Losses (in part)

Due to the worsening of the global business environment, Fujitsu recognized consolidated impairment losses of ¥58.9 billion in relation to property, plant, and equipment of businesses with decreased profitability. The main losses are as follows:

(1) Property, Plant, and Equipment of LSI Business
Impairment losses related to the property, plant, and equipment of the LSI business of Fujitsu Microelectronics Limited totaled 49.9 billion yen. In January, Fujitsu Microelectronics announced business reforms in response to a sharp downturn in customer demand that began last autumn.

(2) Property, Plant, and Equipment of Optical Transmission Systems and Other Businesses
Consolidated impairment losses of 8.9 billion yen were recognized in relation to the property, plant, and equipment of the optical transmission systems business, the electronic components business and other businesses due to their decreased profitability.

IFRS IN THIS CHAPTER

- See the **International Perspectives** on pages 613, 618, 619, and 625.
- Read **IFRS Insights** on pages 653–663 for a discussion of:

—Component depreciation

—Impairments

—Revaluations

Property, Plant, and Equipment of HDD Business (included in business restructuring penses)
pairment losses of 16.2 billion yen have been recognized in relation to the property, plant, and uipment of the reorganized HDD business. These losses are included in business restructuring penses. The impairment loss includes 5.3 billion yen recognized in the third quarter for the scontinuation for the HDD head business.

Impairment losses for property, plant, and equipment for many companies in the next few years will be substantial. Here are some of the questions that will need to be addressed regarding possible impairments.

1. How often should a company test for impairment?
2. What are key impairment indicators?
3. What disclosure are necessary for impairments?
4. How do companies match their cash flows to the asset that is potentially impaired?

Assessing whether a company has impaired assets is difficult. For example, in addition to the technical accounting issues, the environment can change quickly. Reduced spending by consumers, lack of confidence in global economic decisions, and higher volatility in both stock and commodity markets are factors to consider. Nevertheless, for investors and creditors to have assurance that the amounts reported on the balance sheet for property, plant, and equipment are relevant and representationally faithful, appropriate impairment charges must be reported on a timely basis.

Source: A portion of this discussion is taken from "Top 10 Tips for Impairment Testing," PricewaterhouseCoopers (December 2008).

PREVIEW OF CHAPTER 11

As noted in the opening story, both U.S. and foreign companies are affected by impairment rules. These rules recognize that when economic conditions deteriorate, companies may need to write off an asset's cost to indicate the decline in its usefulness. The purpose of this chapter is to examine the depreciation process and the methods of writing off the cost of property, plant, and equipment and natural resources. The content and organization of the chapter are as follows.

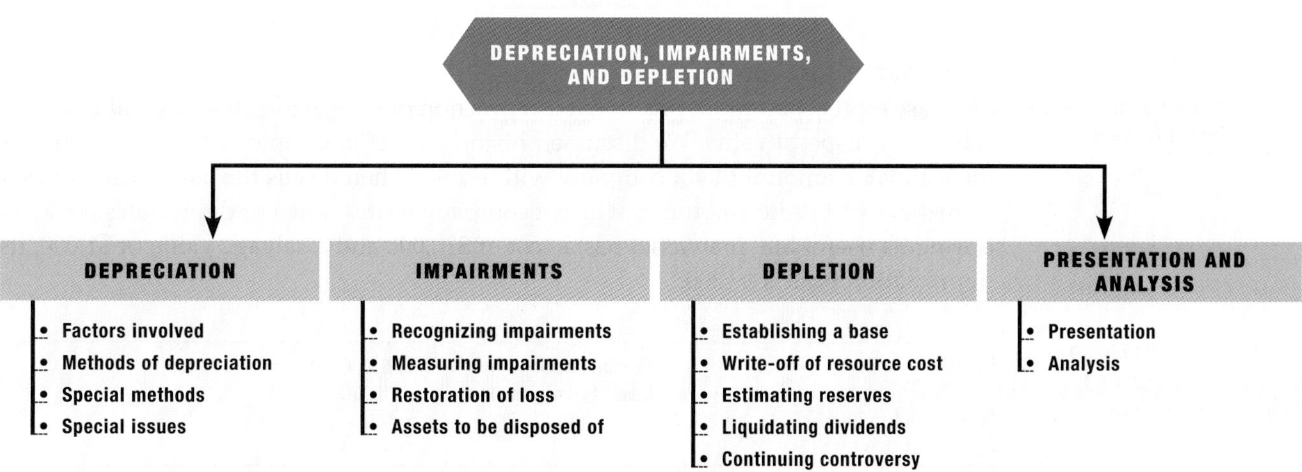

DEPRECIATION—A METHOD OF COST ALLOCATION

LEARNING OBJECTIVE 1
Explain the concept of depreciation.

Most individuals at one time or another purchase and trade in an automobile. The automobile dealer and the buyer typically discuss what the trade-in value of the old car is. Also, they may talk about what the trade-in value of the new car will be in several years. In both cases, a decline in value is considered to be an example of depreciation.

To accountants, however, depreciation is not a matter of valuation. Rather, **depreciation is a means of cost allocation. Depreciation is the accounting process of allocating the cost of tangible assets to expense in a systematic and rational manner to those periods expected to benefit from the use of the asset.** For example, a company like Goodyear (one of the world's largest tire manufacturers) does not depreciate assets on the basis of a decline in their fair value. Instead, it depreciates through systematic charges to expense.

This approach is employed because the value of the asset may fluctuate between the time the asset is purchased and the time it is sold or junked. Attempts to measure these interim value changes have not been well received because values are difficult to measure objectively. Therefore, Goodyear charges the asset's cost to depreciation expense over its estimated life. It makes no attempt to value the asset at fair value between acquisition and disposition. Companies use the cost allocation approach because it matches costs with revenues and because fluctuations in fair value are uncertain and difficult to measure.

When companies write off the cost of long-lived assets over a number of periods, they typically use the term **depreciation**. They use the term depletion to describe the reduction in the cost of natural resources (such as timber, gravel, oil, and coal) over a period of time. The expiration of intangible assets, such as patents or copyrights, is called amortization.

Factors Involved in the Depreciation Process

LEARNING OBJECTIVE 2
Identify the factors involved in the depreciation process.

Before establishing a pattern of charges to revenue, a company must answer three basic questions:

1. What depreciable base is to be used for the asset?
2. What is the asset's useful life?
3. What method of cost apportionment is best for this asset?

The answers to these questions involve combining several estimates into one single figure. Note the calculations assume perfect knowledge of the future, which is never attainable.

Depreciable Base for the Asset

Gateway to the Profession
Tutorial on Depreciation Methods

The base established for depreciation is a function of two factors: the original cost, and salvage or disposal value. We discussed historical cost in Chapter 10. Salvage value is the estimated amount that a company will receive when it sells the asset or removes it from service. It is the amount to which a company writes down or depreciates the asset during its useful life. If an asset has a cost of $10,000 and a salvage value of $1,000, its depreciation base is $9,000.

ILLUSTRATION 11-1
Computation of Depreciation Base

Original cost	$10,000
Less: Salvage value	1,000
Depreciation base	$ 9,000

From a practical standpoint, companies often assign a zero salvage value. Some long-lived assets, however, have substantial salvage values.

Estimation of Service Lives

The service life of an asset often differs from its physical life. A piece of machinery may be physically capable of producing a given product for many years beyond its service life. But a company may not use the equipment for all that time because the cost of producing the product in later years may be too high. For example, the old Slater cotton mill in Pawtucket, Rhode Island, is preserved in remarkable physical condition as an historic landmark in U.S. industrial development, although its service life was terminated many years ago.[1]

Companies retire assets for two reasons: **physical factors** (such as casualty or expiration of physical life) and **economic factors** (obsolescence). Physical factors are the wear and tear, decay, and casualties that make it difficult for the asset to perform indefinitely. These physical factors set the outside limit for the service life of an asset.

We can classify the economic or functional factors into three categories:

1. **Inadequacy** results when an asset ceases to be useful to a company because the demands of the firm have changed. An example would be the need for a larger building to handle increased production. Although the old building may still be sound, it may have become inadequate for the company's purpose.
2. **Supersession** is the replacement of one asset with another more efficient and economical asset. Examples would be the replacement of the mainframe computer with a PC network, or the replacement of the Boeing 767 with the Boeing 787.
3. **Obsolescence** is the catchall for situations not involving inadequacy and supersession.

Because the distinction between these categories appears artificial, it is probably best to consider economic factors collectively instead of trying to make distinctions that are not clear-cut.

To illustrate the concepts of physical and economic factors, consider a new nuclear power plant. Which is more important in determining the useful life of a nuclear power plant—physical factors or economic factors? The limiting factors seem to be (1) ecological considerations, (2) competition from other power sources, and (3) safety concerns. Physical life does not appear to be the primary factor affecting useful life. Although the plant's physical life may be far from over, the plant may become obsolete in 10 years.

For a house, physical factors undoubtedly are more important than the economic or functional factors relative to useful life. Whenever the physical nature of the asset primarily determines useful life, maintenance plays an extremely vital role. The better the maintenance, the longer the life of the asset.[2]

In most cases, a company estimates the useful life of an asset based on its past experience with the same or similar assets. Others use sophisticated statistical methods to establish a useful life for accounting purposes. And in some cases, companies select arbitrary service lives. In a highly industrial economy such as that of the United States, where research and innovation are so prominent, technological factors have as much effect, if not more, on service lives of tangible plant assets as physical factors do.

[1]Taken from J. D. Coughlan and W. K. Strand, *Depreciation Accounting, Taxes and Business Decisions* (New York: The Ronald Press, 1969), pp. 10–12.

[2]The airline industry also illustrates the type of problem involved in estimation. In the past, aircraft were assumed not to wear out—they just became obsolete. However, some jets have been in service as long as 20 years, and maintenance of these aircraft has become increasingly expensive. As a result, some airlines now replace aircraft not because of obsolescence but because of physical deterioration.

ALPHABET DUPE

What do the numbers mean?

Some companies try to imply that depreciation is not a cost. For example, in their press releases they will often make a bigger deal over earnings before interest, taxes, depreciation, and amortization (often referred to as EBITDA) than net income under GAAP. They like it because it "dresses up" their earnings numbers. Some on Wall Street buy this hype because they don't like the allocations that are required to determine net income. Some banks, without batting an eyelash, even let companies base their loan covenants on EBITDA.

For example, look at **Premier Parks**, which operates the Six Flags chain of amusement parks. Premier touts its EBITDA performance. But that number masks a big part of how the company operates—and how it spends its money. Premier argues that analysts should ignore depreciation for big-ticket items like roller coasters because the rides have a long life. Critics, however, say that the amusement industry has to spend as much as 50 percent of its EBITDA just to keep its rides and attractions current. Those expenses are not optional—let the rides get a little rusty, and ticket sales start to tail off. That means analysts really should view depreciation associated with the costs of maintaining the rides (or buying new ones) as an everyday expense. It also means investors in those companies should have strong stomachs.

What's the risk of trusting a fad accounting measure? Just look at one year's bankruptcy numbers. Of the 147 companies tracked by Moody's that defaulted on their debt, most borrowed money based on EBITDA performance. The bankers in those deals probably wish they had looked at a few other factors. Investors should as well.

Source: Adapted from Herb Greenberg, Alphabet Dupe: "Why EBITDA Falls Short," *Fortune* (July 10, 2000), p. 240.

Methods of Depreciation

The third factor involved in the depreciation process is the **method** of cost apportionment. The profession requires that the depreciation method employed be "systematic and rational." Companies may use a number of depreciation methods, as follows.

Underlying Concepts

Depreciation attempts to recognize the cost of an asset to the periods that benefit from the use of that asset.

1. Activity method (units of use or production).
2. Straight-line method.
3. Decreasing charge methods (accelerated):
   (a) Sum-of-the-years'-digits.
   (b) Declining-balance method.
4. Special depreciation methods:
   (a) Group and composite methods.
   (b) Hybrid or combination methods.[3]

To illustrate these depreciation methods, assume that Stanley Coal Mines recently purchased an additional crane for digging purposes. Illustration 11-2 contains the pertinent data concerning this purchase.

ILLUSTRATION 11-2
Data Used to Illustrate Depreciation Methods

Cost of crane	$500,000
Estimated useful life	5 years
Estimated salvage value	$ 50,000
Productive life in hours	30,000 hours

[3]*Accounting Trends and Techniques—2010* reports that of its 500 surveyed companies, for reporting purposes, 488 used straight-line, 10 used declining-balance, 3 used sum-of-the-years'-digits, 17 used an accelerated method (not specified), 16 used units of production, and 10 used group/composite.

Activity Method

> **3 LEARNING OBJECTIVE**
> Compare activity, straight-line, and decreasing-charge methods of depreciation.

The **activity method** (also called the **variable-charge** or **units-of-production approach**) assumes that depreciation is **a function of use or productivity, instead of the passage of time**. A company considers the life of the asset in terms of either the **output** it provides (units it produces), or an **input** measure such as the number of hours it works. Conceptually, the proper cost association relies on output instead of hours used, but often the output is not easily measurable. In such cases, an input measure such as machine hours is a more appropriate method of measuring the dollar amount of depreciation charges for a given accounting period.

The crane poses no particular depreciation problem. Stanley can measure the usage (hours) relatively easily. If Stanley uses the crane for 4,000 hours the first year, the depreciation charge is:

$$\frac{\text{(Cost less salvage)} \times \text{Hours this year}}{\text{Total estimated hours}} = \text{Depreciation charge}$$

$$\frac{(\$500{,}000 - \$50{,}000) \times 4{,}000}{30{,}000} = \$60{,}000$$

ILLUSTRATION 11-3
Depreciation Calculation, Activity Method—Crane Example

The major limitation of this method is that it is inappropriate in situations in which depreciation is a function of time instead of activity. For example, a building steadily deteriorates due to the elements (time) regardless of its use. In addition, where economic or functional factors affect an asset, independent of its use, the activity method loses much of its significance. For example, if a company is expanding rapidly, a particular building may soon become obsolete for its intended purposes. In both cases, activity is irrelevant. Another problem in using an activity method is the difficulty of estimating units of output or service hours received.

In cases where loss of services results from activity or productivity, the activity method does the best to record expenses in the same period as associated revenues. Companies that desire low depreciation during periods of low productivity, and high depreciation during high productivity, either adopt or switch to an activity method. In this way, a plant running at 40 percent of capacity generates 60 percent lower depreciation charges. **Inland Steel**, for example, switched to units-of-production depreciation at one time and reduced its losses by $43 million, or $1.20 per share.

Straight-Line Method

> **Underlying Concepts**
> If benefits flow on a "straight-line" basis, then justification exists for matching the cost of the asset on a straight-line basis with these benefits.

The **straight-line method** considers depreciation a **function of time rather than a function of usage**. Companies widely use this method because of its simplicity. The straight-line procedure is often the most conceptually appropriate, too. When creeping obsolescence is the primary reason for a limited service life, the decline in usefulness may be constant from period to period. Stanley computes the depreciation charge for the crane as follows.

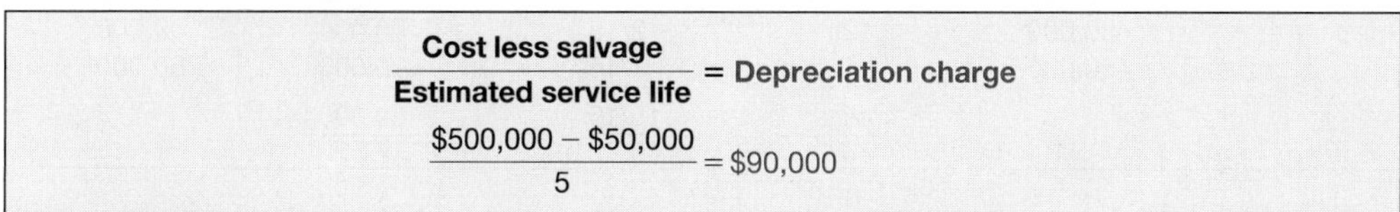

$$\frac{\text{Cost less salvage}}{\text{Estimated service life}} = \text{Depreciation charge}$$

$$\frac{\$500{,}000 - \$50{,}000}{5} = \$90{,}000$$

ILLUSTRATION 11-4
Depreciation Calculation, Straight-Line Method—Crane Example

The major objection to the straight-line method is that it rests on two tenuous assumptions: (1) The asset's economic usefulness is the same each year, and (2) the repair and maintenance expense is essentially the same each period.

One additional problem that occurs in using straight-line—as well as some others—is that distortions in the rate of return analysis (income/assets) develop.

Illustration 11-5 indicates how the rate of return increases, given constant revenue flows, because the asset's book value decreases.

ILLUSTRATION 11-5
Depreciation and Rate of Return Analysis—Crane Example

Year	Depreciation Expense	Undepreciated Asset Balance (book value)	Income (after depreciation expense)	Rate of Return (Income ÷ Assets)
0		$500,000		
1	$90,000	410,000	$100,000	24.4%
2	90,000	320,000	100,000	31.2%
3	90,000	230,000	100,000	43.5%
4	90,000	140,000	100,000	71.4%
5	90,000	50,000	100,000	200.0%

Underlying Concepts

The expense recognition principle does not justify a constant charge to income. If the benefits from the asset decline as the asset ages, then a decreasing charge to income better matches cost to benefits.

Decreasing-Charge Methods

The **decreasing-charge methods** provide for a higher depreciation cost in the earlier years and lower charges in later periods. Because these methods allow for higher early-year charges than in the straight-line method, they are often called **accelerated depreciation methods.**

What is the main justification for this approach? The rationale is that companies should charge more depreciation in earlier years because the asset is most productive in its earlier years. Furthermore, the accelerated methods provide a constant cost because the depreciation charge is lower in the later periods, at the time when the repair and maintenance costs are often higher. Generally, companies use one of two decreasing-charge methods: the sum-of-the-years'-digits method, or the declining-balance method.

Sum-of-the-Years'-Digits. The **sum-of-the-years'-digits method** results in a decreasing depreciation charge based on a decreasing fraction of depreciable cost (original cost less salvage value). Each fraction uses the sum of the years as a denominator (5 + 4 + 3 + 2 + 1 = 15). The numerator is the number of years of estimated life remaining as of the beginning of the year. In this method, the numerator decreases year by year, and the denominator remains constant (5/15, 4/15, 3/15, 2/15, and 1/15). At the end of the asset's useful life, the balance remaining should equal the salvage value. Illustration 11-6 shows this method of computation.[4]

ILLUSTRATION 11-6
Sum-of-the-Years'-Digits Depreciation Schedule—Crane Example

Year	Depreciation Base	Remaining Life in Years	Depreciation Fraction	Depreciation Expense	Book Value, End of Year
1	$450,000	5	5/15	$150,000	$350,000
2	450,000	4	4/15	120,000	230,000
3	450,000	3	3/15	90,000	140,000
4	450,000	2	2/15	60,000	80,000
5	450,000	1	1/15	30,000	50,000[a]
		15	15/15	$450,000	

[a]Salvage value.

[4]What happens if the estimated service life of the asset is, let us say, 51 years? How would we calculate the sum-of-the-years'-digits? Fortunately mathematicians have developed the following formula that permits easy computation:

$$\frac{n(n+1)}{2} = \frac{51(51+1)}{2} = 1{,}326$$

Declining-Balance Method. The declining-balance method utilizes a depreciation rate (expressed as a percentage) that is some multiple of the straight-line method. For example, the double-declining rate for a 10-year asset is 20 percent (double the straight-line rate, which is 1/10 or 10 percent). Companies apply the constant rate to the declining book value each year.

Unlike other methods, the declining-balance method **does not deduct the salvage value** in computing the depreciation base. The declining-balance rate is multiplied by the book value of the asset at the beginning of each period. Since the depreciation charge reduces the book value of the asset each period, applying the constant-declining-balance rate to a successively lower book value results in lower depreciation charges each year. This process continues until the book value of the asset equals its estimated salvage value. At that time the company discontinues depreciation.

Companies use various multiples in practice. For example, the double-declining-balance method depreciates assets at twice (200 percent) the straight-line rate. Illustration 11-7 shows Stanley's depreciation charges if using the double-declining approach.

ILLUSTRATION 11-7
Double-Declining Depreciation Schedule—Crane Example

Year	Book Value of Asset First of Year	Rate on Declining Balance[a]	Depreciation Expense	Balance Accumulated Depreciation	Book Value, End of Year
1	$500,000	40%	$200,000	$200,000	$300,000
2	300,000	40%	120,000	320,000	180,000
3	180,000	40%	72,000	392,000	108,000
4	108,000	40%	43,200	435,200	64,800
5	64,800	40%	14,800[b]	450,000	50,000

[a]Based on twice the straight-line rate of 20% ($90,000/$450,000 = 20%; 20% × 2 = 40%).
[b]Limited to $14,800 because book value should not be less than salvage value.

Companies often switch from the declining-balance method to the straight-line method near the end of the asset's useful life to ensure that they depreciate the asset only to its salvage value.[5]

Special Depreciation Methods

4 LEARNING OBJECTIVE
Explain special depreciation methods.

Sometimes companies adopt special depreciation methods. Reasons for doing so might be that a company's assets have unique characteristics, or the nature of the industry. Two of these special methods are:

1. Group and composite methods.
2. Hybrid or combination methods.

Group and Composite Methods

Companies often depreciate multiple-asset accounts using one rate. For example, AT&T might depreciate telephone poles, microwave systems, or switchboards by groups.

Two methods of depreciating multiple-asset accounts exist: the group method and the composite method. The choice of method depends on the nature of the assets involved. Companies frequently use the group method when the assets are similar in nature and

[5]A pure form of the declining-balance method (sometimes appropriately called the "fixed percentage of book value method") has also been suggested as a possibility. This approach finds a rate that depreciates the asset exactly to salvage value at the end of its expected useful life. The formula for determination of this rate is as follows:

$$\text{Depreciation rate} = 1 - \sqrt[n]{\frac{\text{Salvage value}}{\text{Acquisition cost}}}$$

The life in years is n. After computing the depreciation rate, a company applies it on the declining book value of the asset from period to period, which means that depreciation expense will be successively lower. This method is not used extensively in practice due to cumbersome computations. Further, it is not permitted for tax purposes.

have approximately the same useful lives. They use the **composite approach** when the assets are dissimilar and have different lives. The group method more closely approximates a single-unit cost procedure because the dispersion from the average is not as great. The computation for group or composite methods is essentially the same: find an average and depreciate on that basis.

Companies determine the **composite depreciation rate** by dividing the depreciation per year by the total cost of the assets. To illustrate, Mooney Motors establishes the composite depreciation rate for its fleet of cars, trucks, and campers as shown in Illustration 11-8.

ILLUSTRATION 11-8
Depreciation Calculation, Composite Basis

Asset	Original Cost	Residual Value	Depreciation Cost	Estimated Life (yrs.)	Depreciation per Year (straight-line)
Cars	$145,000	$25,000	$120,000	3	$40,000
Trucks	44,000	4,000	40,000	4	10,000
Campers	35,000	5,000	30,000	5	6,000
	$224,000	$34,000	$190,000		$56,000

$$\text{Composite depreciation rate} = \frac{\$56,000}{\$224,000} = 25\%$$

Composite life = 3.39 years ($190,000 ÷ $56,000)

If there are no changes in the asset account, Mooney will depreciate the group of assets to the residual or salvage value at the rate of $56,000 ($224,000 × 25%) a year. As a result, it will take Mooney 3.39 years to depreciate these assets. The length of time it takes a company to depreciate it assets on a composite basis is called the **composite life**.

We can highlight the differences between the group or composite method and the single-unit depreciation method by looking at asset retirements. If Mooney retires an asset before, or after, the average service life of the group is reached, it buries the resulting gain or loss in the Accumulated Depreciation account. This practice is justified because Mooney will retire some assets before the average service life and others after the average life. For this reason, the debit to Accumulated Depreciation is the difference between original cost and cash received. Mooney does not record a gain or loss on disposition.

To illustrate, suppose that Mooney Motors sold one of the campers with a cost of $5,000 for $2,600 at the end of the third year. The entry is:

Accumulated Depreciation	2,400	
Cash	2,600	
Cars, Trucks, and Campers		5,000

If Mooney purchases a new type of asset (mopeds, for example), it must compute a new depreciation rate and apply this rate in subsequent periods.

Illustration 11-9 presents a typical financial statement disclosure of the group depreciation method for **Ampco-Pittsburgh Corporation**.

ILLUSTRATION 11-9
Disclosure of Group Depreciation Method

Ampco-Pittsburgh Corporation

Depreciation rates are based on estimated useful lives of the asset groups. Gains or losses on normal retirements or replacements of depreciable assets, subject to composite depreciation methods, are not recognized; the difference between the cost of the assets retired or replaced and the related salvage value is charged or credited to the accumulated depreciation.

The group or composite method simplifies the bookkeeping process and tends to average out errors caused by over- or underdepreciation. As a result, gains or losses on disposals of assets do not distort periodic income.

On the other hand, the unit method has several advantages over the group or composite methods: (1) It simplifies the computation mathematically. (2) It identifies gains and losses on disposal. (3) It isolates depreciation on idle equipment. (4) It represents the best estimate of the depreciation of each asset, not the result of averaging the cost over a longer period of time. As a consequence, companies generally use the unit method. Unless stated otherwise, you should use the unit method in homework problems.[6]

Hybrid or Combination Methods

In addition to the depreciation methods already discussed, companies are free to develop their own special or tailor-made depreciation methods. GAAP requires only that the method result in the allocation of an asset's cost over the asset's life in a **systematic and rational manner**.

Gateway to the Profession

Expanded Discussion—Special Depreciation Methods

For example, the steel industry widely uses a hybrid depreciation method, called the **production variable method**, that is a combination straight-line/activity approach. The following note from WHX Corporation's annual report explains one variation of this method.

WHX Corporation

The Company utilizes the modified units of production method of depreciation which recognizes that the depreciation of steelmaking machinery is related to the physical wear of the equipment as well as a time factor. The modified units of production method provides for straight-line depreciation charges modified (adjusted) by the level of raw steel production. In the prior year, depreciation under the modified units of production method was $21.6 million or 40% less than straight-line depreciation, and in the current year it was $1.1 million or 2% more than straight-line depreciation.

ILLUSTRATION 11-10
Disclosure of Hybrid Depreciation Method

DECELERATING DEPRECIATION

What do the numbers mean?

Which depreciation method should management select? Many believe that the method that best matches revenues with expenses should be used. For example, if revenues generated by the asset are constant over its useful life, select straight-line depreciation. On the other hand, if revenues are higher (or lower) at the beginning of the asset's life, then use a decreasing (or increasing) method. Thus, if a company can reliably estimate revenues from the asset, selecting a depreciation method that best matches costs with those revenues would seem to provide the most useful information to investors and creditors for assessing the future cash flows from the asset.

Managers in the real estate industry face a different challenge when considering depreciation choices. Real estate managers object to traditional depreciation methods because in their view, real estate often does not decline in value. In addition, because real estate is highly debt-financed, most real estate concerns report losses in earlier years of operations when the sum of depreciation and interest exceeds the revenue from the real estate project. As a result, real estate companies, like Kimco Realty, argue for some form of **increasing-charge** method of depreciation (lower depreciation at the beginning and higher depreciation at the end). With such a method, companies would report higher total assets and net income in the earlier years of the project.[7]

[6]AcSEC has indicated in an exposure draft that companies should use the unit approach whenever feasible. In fact, it indicates that an even better way to depreciate property, plant, and equipment is to use *component depreciation*. Under component depreciation, a company should depreciate over its expected useful life any part or portion of property, plant, and equipment that can be separately identified as an asset. For example, a company could separate the various components of a building (e.g., roof, heating and cooling system, elevator, leasehold improvements) and depreciate each component over its useful life.

INTERNATIONAL PERSPECTIVE

IFRS requires use of component depreciation.

[7]In this regard, real estate investment trusts (REITs) often report (in addition to net income) an earnings measure, funds from operations (FFO), that adjusts income for depreciation expense and other noncash expenses. This method is not GAAP. There is mixed empirical evidence about whether FFO or GAAP income is more useful to real estate investment trust investors. See, for example, Richard Gore and David Stott, "Toward a More Informative Measure of Operating Performance in the REIT Industry: Net Income vs. FFO," *Accounting Horizons* (December 1998); and Linda Vincent, "The Information Content of FFO for REITs," *Journal of Accounting and Economics* (January 1999).

Special Depreciation Issues

We still need to discuss several special issues related to depreciation:

1. How should companies compute depreciation for partial periods?
2. Does depreciation provide for the replacement of assets?
3. How should companies handle revisions in depreciation rates?

Depreciation and Partial Periods

Companies seldom purchase plant assets on the first day of a fiscal period or dispose of them on the last day of a fiscal period. A practical question is: How much depreciation should a company charge for the partial periods involved?

In computing depreciation expense for partial periods, companies must determine the depreciation expense for the full year and then prorate this depreciation expense between the two periods involved. This process should continue throughout the useful life of the asset.

Assume, for example, that Steeltex Company purchases an automated drill machine with a 5-year life for $45,000 (no salvage value) on June 10, 2011. The company's fiscal year ends December 31. Steeltex therefore charges depreciation for only 6⅔ months during that year. The total depreciation for a full year (assuming straight-line depreciation) is $9,000 ($45,000/5). The depreciation for the first, partial year is therefore:

$$\frac{6\frac{2}{3}}{12} \times \$9{,}000 = \$5{,}000$$

The partial-period calculation is relatively simple when Steeltex uses straight-line depreciation. But how is partial-period depreciation handled when it uses an accelerated method such as sum-of-the-years'-digits or double-declining-balance? As an illustration, assume that Steeltex purchased another machine for $10,000 on July 1, 2011, with an estimated useful life of five years and no salvage value. Illustration 11-11 shows the depreciation figures for 2011, 2012, and 2013.

ILLUSTRATION 11-11
Calculation of Partial-Period Depreciation, Two Methods

	Sum-of-the-Years'-Digits	Double-Declining-Balance
1st full year	(5/15 × $10,000) = $3,333.33	(40% × $10,000) = $4,000
2nd full year	(4/15 × 10,000) = 2,666.67	(40% × 6,000) = 2,400
3rd full year	(3/15 × 10,000) = 2,000.00	(40% × 3,600) = 1,440

Depreciation from July 1, 2011, to December 31, 2011

Sum-of-the-Years'-Digits	Double-Declining-Balance
6/12 × $3,333.33 = $1,666.67	6/12 × $4,000 = $2,000

Depreciation for 2012

Sum-of-the-Years'-Digits	Double-Declining-Balance
6/12 × $3,333.33 = $1,666.67	6/12 × $4,000 = $2,000
6/12 × 2,666.67 = 1,333.33	6/12 × 2,400 = 1,200
$3,000.00	$3,200
	or ($10,000 − $2,000) × 40% = $3,200

Depreciation for 2013

Sum-of-the-Years'-Digits	Double-Declining-Balance
6/12 × $2,666.67 = $1,333.33	6/12 × $2,400 = $1,200
6/12 × 2,000.00 = 1,000.00	6/12 × 1,440 = 720
$2,333.33	$1,920
	or ($10,000 − $5,200) × 40% = $1,920

Sometimes a company like Steeltex modifies the process of allocating costs to a partial period to handle acquisitions and disposals of plant assets more simply. One variation is to take no depreciation in the year of acquisition and a full year's depreciation in the year of disposal. Other variations charge one-half year's depreciation both in the year of acquisition and in the year of disposal (referred to as the **half-year convention**), or charge a full year in the year of acquisition and none in the year of disposal.

In fact, Steeltex may adopt any one of these several fractional-year policies in allocating cost to the first and last years of an asset's life so long as it applies the method consistently. However, **unless otherwise stipulated, companies normally compute depreciation on the basis of the nearest full month.**

Illustration 11-12 shows depreciation allocated under five different fractional-year policies using the straight-line method on the $45,000 automated drill machine purchased by Steeltex Company on June 10, 2011, discussed earlier.

ILLUSTRATION 11-12
Fractional-Year Depreciation Policies

Machine Cost = $45,000	Depreciation Allocated per Period Over 5-Year Life*					
Fractional-Year Policy	2011	2012	2013	2014	2015	2016
1. Nearest fraction of a year.	$5,000[a]	$9,000	$9,000	$9,000	$9,000	$4,000[b]
2. Nearest full month.	5,250[c]	9,000	9,000	9,000	9,000	3,750[d]
3. Half year in period of acquisition and disposal.	4,500	9,000	9,000	9,000	9,000	4,500
4. Full year in period of acquisition, none in period of disposal.	9,000	9,000	9,000	9,000	9,000	-0-
5. None in period of acquisition, full year in period of disposal.	-0-	9,000	9,000	9,000	9,000	9,000

[a]6.667/12 ($9,000) [b]5.333/12 ($9,000) [c]7/12 ($9,000) [d]5/12 ($9,000)
*Rounded to nearest dollar.

Depreciation and Replacement of Property, Plant, and Equipment

A common misconception about depreciation is that it provides funds for the replacement of fixed assets. Depreciation is like other expenses in that it reduces net income. It differs, though, in that **it does not involve a current cash outflow.**

To illustrate why depreciation does not provide funds for replacement of plant assets, assume that a business starts operating with plant assets of $500,000 that have a useful life of five years. The company's balance sheet at the beginning of the period is:

Plant assets	$500,000	Stockholders' equity	$500,000

If we assume that the company earns no revenue over the five years, the income statements are:

	Year 1	Year 2	Year 3	Year 4	Year 5
Revenue	$ -0-	$ -0-	$ -0-	$ -0-	$ -0-
Depreciation	(100,000)	(100,000)	(100,000)	(100,000)	(100,000)
Loss	$(100,000)	$(100,000)	$(100,000)	$(100,000)	$(100,000)

Total depreciation of the plant assets over the five years is $500,000. The balance sheet at the end of the five years therefore is:

Plant assets	-0-	Stockholders' equity	-0-

This extreme example illustrates that depreciation **in no way** provides funds for the replacement of assets. **The funds for the replacement of the assets come from the revenues** (generated through use of the asset). Without the revenues, no income materializes and no cash inflow results.

Revision of Depreciation Rates

When purchasing a plant asset, companies carefully determine depreciation rates based on past experience with similar assets and other pertinent information. The provisions for depreciation are only estimates, however. They may need to revise them during the life of the asset. Unexpected physical deterioration or unforeseen obsolescence may decrease the estimated useful life of the asset. Improved maintenance procedures, revision of operating procedures, or similar developments may prolong the life of the asset beyond the expected period.[8]

For example, assume that **International Paper Co.** purchased machinery with an original cost of $90,000. It estimates a 20-year life with no salvage value. However, during year 6, International Paper estimates that it will use the machine for an additional 25 years. Its total life, therefore, will be 30 years instead of 20. Depreciation has been recorded at the rate of 1/20 of $90,000, or $4,500 per year by the straight-line method. On the basis of a 30-year life, International Paper should have recorded depreciation as 1/30 of $90,000, or $3,000 per year. It has therefore overstated depreciation, and understated net income, by $1,500 for each of the past 5 years, or a total amount of $7,500. Illustration 11-13 shows this computation.

ILLUSTRATION 11-13
Computation of Accumulated Difference Due to Revisions

	Per Year	For 5 Years
Depreciation charged per books (1/20 × $90,000)	$4,500	$22,500
Depreciation based on a 30-year life (1/30 × $90,000)	(3,000)	(15,000)
Excess depreciation charged	$1,500	$ 7,500

International Paper should report this change in estimate in the current and prospective periods. It should not make any changes in previously reported results. And it does not adjust opening balances nor attempt to "catch up" for prior periods. The reason? Changes in estimates are a continual and inherent part of any estimation process. Continual restatement of prior periods would occur for revisions of estimates unless handled prospectively. Therefore, no entry is made at the time the change in estimate occurs. Charges for depreciation in subsequent periods (assuming use of the straight-line method) are determined by **dividing the remaining book value less any salvage value by the remaining estimated life.**

ILLUSTRATION 11-14
Computing Depreciation after Revision of Estimated Life

Machinery	$90,000
Less: Accumulated depreciation	22,500
Book value of machinery at end of 5th year	$67,500

Depreciation (future periods) = $67,500 book value ÷ 25 years remaining life = $2,700

The entry to record depreciation for each of the remaining 25 years is:

Depreciation Expense	2,700	
Accumulated Depreciation—Machinery		2,700

[8]As an example of a change in operating procedures, **General Motors** (GM) used to write off its tools—such as dies and equipment used to manufacture car bodies—over the life of the body type. Through this procedure, it expensed tools twice as fast as **Ford** and three times as fast as **Chrysler**. However, it slowed the depreciation process on these tools and lengthened the lives on its plant and equipment. These revisions reduced depreciation and amortization charges by approximately $1.23 billion, or $2.55 per share, in the year of the change. In Chapter 22, we provide a more complete discussion of changes in estimates.

DEPRECIATION CHOICES

What do the numbers mean?

The amount of depreciation expense recorded depends on both the depreciation method used and estimates of service lives and salvage values of the assets. Differences in these choices and estimates can significantly impact a company's reported results and can make it difficult to compare the depreciation numbers of different companies.

For example, when **Willamette Industries** extended the estimated service lives of its machinery and equipment by five years, it increased income by nearly $54 million.

An analyst determines the impact of these management choices and judgments on the amount of depreciation expense by examining the notes to financial statements. For example, Willamette Industries provided the following note to its financial statements.

Note 4: Property, Plant, and Equipment (partial)

	Range of Useful Lives
Land	—
Buildings	15–35
Machinery & equipment	5–25
Furniture & fixtures	3–15

During the year, the estimated service lives for most machinery and equipment were extended five years. The change was based upon a study performed by the company's engineering department, comparisons to typical industry practices, and the effect of the company's extensive capital investments which have resulted in a mix of assets with longer productive lives due to technological advances. As a result of the change, net income was increased by $54,000,000.

IMPAIRMENTS

5 LEARNING OBJECTIVE
Explain the accounting issues related to asset impairment.

The general accounting standard of **lower-of-cost-or-market for inventories does not apply to property, plant, and equipment**. Even when property, plant, and equipment has suffered partial obsolescence, accountants have been reluctant to reduce the asset's carrying amount. Why? Because, unlike inventories, it is difficult to arrive at a fair value for property, plant, and equipment that is not subjective and arbitrary.

Underlying Concepts

The *going concern concept* assumes that the company can recover the investment in its assets. Under GAAP companies do not report the fair value of long-lived assets because a going concern does not plan to sell such assets. However, if the assumption of being able to recover the cost of the investment is not valid, then a company should report a reduction in value.

For example, **Falconbridge Ltd. Nickel Mines** had to decide whether to write off all or a part of its property, plant, and equipment in a nickel-mining operation in the Dominican Republic. The project had been incurring losses because nickel prices were low and operating costs were high. Only if nickel prices increased by approximately 33 percent would the project be reasonably profitable. Whether a write-off was appropriate depended on the future price of nickel. Even if the company decided to write off the asset, how much should be written off?

Recognizing Impairments

As discussed in the opening story, the credit crisis starting in late 2008 has affected many financial and nonfinancial institutions. As a result of the global slump, many companies are considering write-offs of some of their long-lived assets. These write-offs are referred to as **impairments**.

Various events and changes in circumstances might lead to an impairment. Examples are:

a. A significant decrease in the fair value of an asset.

b. A significant change in the extent or manner in which an asset is used.

c. A significant adverse change in legal factors or in the business climate that affects the value of an asset.

d. An accumulation of costs significantly in excess of the amount originally expected to acquire or construct an asset.

e. A projection or forecast that demonstrates continuing losses associated with an asset.

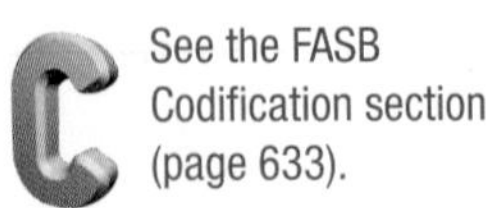
See the FASB Codification section (page 633).

These events or changes in circumstances indicate that the company may not be able to recover the carrying amount of the asset. In that case, a **recoverability test** is used to determine whether an impairment has occurred. **[1]**

To apply the first step of the recoverability test, a company like **UPS** estimates the future net cash flows expected from the **use of that asset and its eventual disposition**. If the sum of the expected future net cash flows (undiscounted) is **less than the carrying amount** of the asset, UPS considers the asset impaired. Conversely, if the sum of the expected future net cash flows (undiscounted) is **equal to or greater than the carrying amount** of the asset, no impairment has occurred.

The recoverability test therefore screens for asset impairment. For example, if the expected future net cash flows from an asset are $400,000 and its carrying amount is $350,000, no impairment has occurred. However, if the expected future net cash flows are $300,000, an impairment has occurred. The rationale for the recoverability test relies on a basic presumption: A balance sheet should report long-lived assets at no more than the carrying amounts that are recoverable.

Measuring Impairments

If the recoverability test indicates an impairment, UPS computes a loss. The **impairment loss** is the amount by which the carrying amount of the asset **exceeds its fair value**. How does UPS determine the fair value of an asset? It is measured based on the market price if an active market for the asset exists. If no active market exists, UPS uses the **present value of expected future net cash flows to determine fair value**.

INTERNATIONAL PERSPECTIVE

IFRS also uses a fair value test to measure the impairment loss. However, IFRS does not use the first-stage recoverability test used under GAAP—comparing the undiscounted cash flows to the carrying amount. As a result, the IFRS test is more strict than GAAP.

To summarize, the process of determining an impairment loss is as follows.

1. Review events or changes in circumstances for possible impairment.
2. If the review indicates a possible impairment, apply the recoverability test. If the sum of the expected future net cash flows from the long-lived asset is less than the carrying amount of the asset, an impairment has occurred.
3. Assuming an impairment, the impairment loss is the amount by which the carrying amount of the asset exceeds the fair value of the asset. The fair value is the market price or the present value of expected future net cash flows.

Impairment—Example 1

M. Alou Inc. has equipment that, due to changes in its use, it reviews for possible impairment. The equipment's carrying amount is $600,000 ($800,000 cost less $200,000 accumulated depreciation). Alou determines the expected future net cash flows (undiscounted) from the use of the equipment and its eventual disposal to be $650,000.

The recoverability test indicates that the $650,000 of expected future net cash flows from the equipment's use exceed the carrying amount of $600,000. As a result, no impairment occurred. (Recall that the undiscounted future net cash flows must be less than the carrying amount for Alou to deem an asset to be impaired and to measure the impairment loss.) Therefore, M. Alou Inc. does not recognize an impairment loss in this case.

Impairment—Example 2

Assume the same facts as in Example 1, except that the expected future net cash flows from Alou's equipment are $580,000 (instead of $650,000). The recoverability test indicates that the expected future net cash flows of $580,000 from the use of the asset are less than its carrying amount of $600,000. Therefore, an impairment has occurred.

The difference between the carrying amount of Alou's asset and its fair value is the impairment loss. Assuming this asset has a fair value of $525,000, Illustration 11-15 shows the loss computation.

Carrying amount of the equipment	$600,000
Fair value of equipment	(525,000)
Loss on impairment	$ 75,000

ILLUSTRATION 11-15
Computation of Impairment Loss

M. Alou records the impairment loss as follows.

Loss on Impairment	75,000	
Accumulated Depreciation—Equipment		75,000

M. Alou Inc. reports the impairment loss as part of income from continuing operations, in the "Other expenses and losses" section. Generally, Alou **should not report this loss as an extraordinary item**. Costs associated with an impairment loss are the same costs that would flow through operations and that it would report as part of continuing operations. Alou will continue to use these assets in operations. Therefore, it should not report the loss below "Income from continuing operations."

A company that recognizes an impairment loss should disclose the asset(s) impaired, the events leading to the impairment, the amount of the loss, and how it determined fair value (disclosing the interest rate used, if appropriate).

Restoration of Impairment Loss

After recording an impairment loss, the reduced carrying amount of an asset held for use becomes its new cost basis. A company does not change the new cost basis except for depreciation or amortization in future periods or for additional impairments.

To illustrate, assume that Damon Company at December 31, 2011, has equipment with a carrying amount of $500,000. Damon determines this asset is impaired and writes it down to its fair value of $400,000. At the end of 2012, Damon determines that the fair value of the asset is $480,000. The carrying amount of the equipment should not change in 2012 except for the depreciation taken in 2012. Damon **may not restore an impairment loss for an asset held for use**. The rationale for not writing the asset up in value is that the new cost basis puts the impaired asset on an equal basis with other assets that are unimpaired.

INTERNATIONAL PERSPECTIVE

IFRS permits write-ups for subsequent recoveries of impairment, back up to the original amount before the impairment. GAAP prohibits those write-ups, except for assets to be disposed of.

Impairment of Assets to Be Disposed Of

What happens if a company intends to dispose of the impaired asset, instead of holding it for use? At one time, Kroger recorded an impairment loss of $54 million on property, plant, and equipment it no longer needed due to store closures. In this case, Kroger reports the impaired asset at the lower-of-cost-or-net realizable value (fair value less cost to sell). Because Kroger intends to dispose of the assets in a short period of time, it uses net realizable value in order to provide a better measure of the net cash flows that it will receive from these assets.

Kroger does not depreciate or amortize assets held for disposal during the period it holds them. The rationale is that depreciation is inconsistent with the notion of assets to be disposed of and with the use of the lower-of-cost-or-net realizable value. In other words, **assets held for disposal are like inventory; companies should report them at the lower-of-cost-or-net realizable value.**

Because Kroger will recover assets held for disposal through sale rather than through operations, it continually revalues them. Each period, the assets are reported at the lower-of-cost-or-net realizable value. Thus, **Kroger can write up or down an asset held for disposal in future periods, as long as the carrying value after the write-up never exceeds the carrying amount of the asset before the impairment.** Companies should report losses or gains related to these impaired assets as part of **income from continuing operations.**

Illustration 11-16 summarizes the key concepts in accounting for impairments.

ILLUSTRATION 11-16
Graphic of Accounting for Impairments

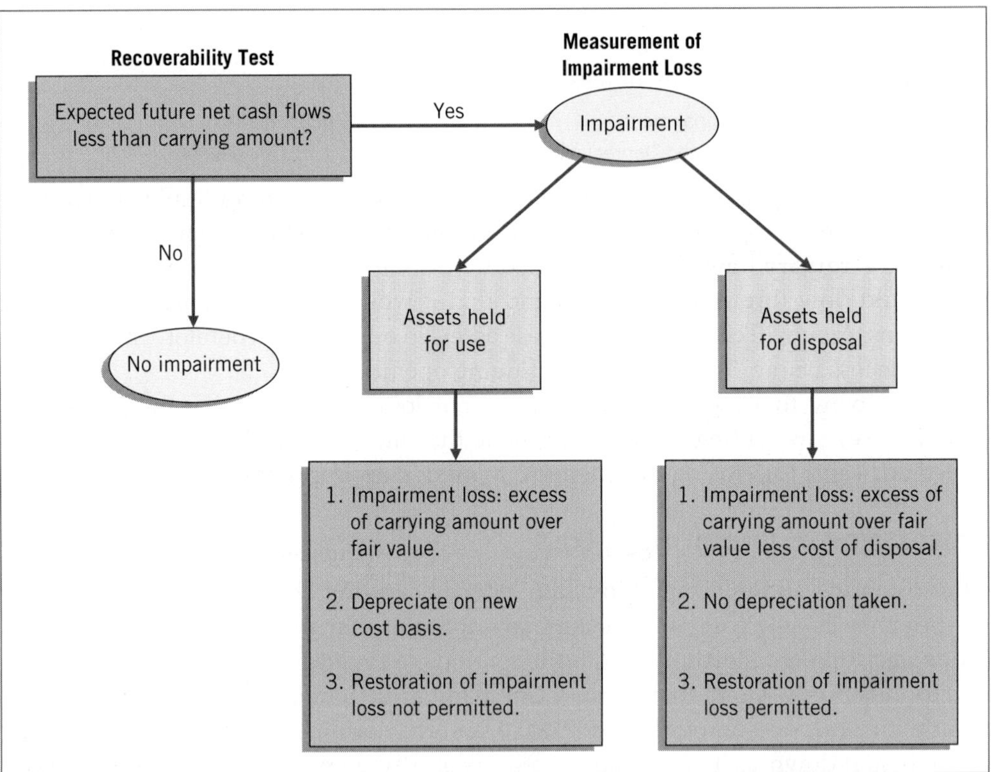

DEPLETION

LEARNING OBJECTIVE 6
Explain the accounting procedures for depletion of natural resources.

Natural resources, often called wasting assets, include petroleum, minerals, and timber. They have two main features: (1) the complete removal (consumption) of the asset, and (2) replacement of the asset only by an act of nature. Unlike plant and equipment, natural resources are consumed physically over the period of use and do not maintain their physical characteristics. Still, the accounting problems associated with natural resources are similar to those encountered with fixed assets. The questions to be answered are:

1. How do companies establish the cost basis for write-off?
2. What pattern of allocation should companies employ?

Recall that the accounting profession uses the term **depletion** for the process of allocating the cost of natural resources.

Establishing a Depletion Base

How do we determine the depletion base for natural resources? For example, a company like **ExxonMobil** makes sizable expenditures to find natural resources, and for every successful discovery there are many failures. Furthermore, it encounters long delays between the time it incurs costs and the time it obtains the benefits from the extracted resources. As a result, a company in the extractive industries, like ExxonMobil, frequently adopts a conservative policy in accounting for the expenditures related to finding and extracting natural resources.

Computation of the depletion base involves four factors: (1) acquisition cost of the deposit, (2) exploration costs, (3) development costs, and (4) restoration costs.

Acquisition Costs

Acquisition cost is the price ExxonMobil pays to obtain the property right to search and find an undiscovered natural resource. It also can be the price paid for an already-discovered resource. A third type of acquisition cost can be lease payments for property containing a productive natural resource; included in these acquisition costs are royalty payments to the owner of the property.

Generally, the acquisition cost of natural resources is recorded in an account titled Undeveloped Property. ExxonMobil later assigns that cost to the natural resource if exploration efforts are successful. If the efforts are unsuccessful, it writes off the acquisition cost as a loss.

Exploration Costs

As soon as a company has the right to use the property, it often incurs **exploration costs** needed to find the resource. When exploration costs are substantial, some companies capitalize them into the depletion base. In the oil and gas industry, where the costs of finding the resource are significant and the risks of finding the resource are very uncertain, most large companies expense these costs. Smaller oil and gas companies often capitalize these exploration costs. We examine the unique issues related to the oil and gas industry on pages 624–625 (see "Continuing Controversy").

Development Costs

Companies divide **development costs** into two parts: (1) tangible equipment costs and (2) intangible development costs. Tangible equipment costs include all of the transportation and other heavy equipment needed to extract the resource and get it ready for market. Because companies can move the heavy equipment from one extracting site to another, companies do not normally include **tangible equipment costs in the depletion base**. Instead, they use separate depreciation charges to allocate the costs of such equipment. However, some tangible assets (e.g., a drilling rig foundation) cannot be moved. Companies depreciate these assets over their useful life or the life of the resource, whichever is shorter.

Intangible development costs, on the other hand, are such items as drilling costs, tunnels, shafts, and wells. These costs have no tangible characteristics but are needed for the production of the natural resource. **Intangible development costs are considered part of the depletion base.**

Restoration Costs

Companies sometimes incur substantial costs to restore property to its natural state after extraction has occurred. These are **restoration costs**. Companies consider **restoration costs part of the depletion base**. The amount included in the depletion base is the fair value of the obligation to restore the property after extraction. A more complete discussion of the accounting for restoration costs and related liabilities (sometimes referred to as asset retirement obligations) is provided in Chapter 13. Similar to other long-lived assets, companies deduct from the depletion base any salvage value to be received on the property.

Write-Off of Resource Cost

Once the company establishes the depletion base, the next problem is determining how to allocate the cost of the natural resource to accounting periods.

Normally, companies compute depletion (often referred to as cost depletion) on a **units-of-production method** (an activity approach). Thus, depletion is a function of the number of units extracted during the period. In this approach, the total cost of the natural resource less salvage value is divided by the number of units estimated to be in the resource deposit, to obtain a **cost per unit of product**. To compute depletion, the cost per unit is then multiplied by the number of units extracted.

For example, MaClede Co. acquired the right to use 1,000 acres of land in Alaska to mine for gold. The lease cost is \$50,000, and the related exploration costs on the property are \$100,000. Intangible development costs incurred in opening the mine are \$850,000. Total costs related to the mine before the first ounce of gold is extracted are, therefore, \$1,000,000. MaClede estimates that the mine will provide approximately 100,000 ounces of gold. Illustration 11-17 shows computation of the depletion cost per unit (depletion rate).

ILLUSTRATION 11-17
Computation of Depletion Rate

$$\frac{\textbf{Total cost} - \textbf{Salvage value}}{\textbf{Total estimated units available}} = \textbf{Depletion cost per unit}$$

$$\frac{\$1{,}000{,}000}{100{,}000} = \$10 \text{ per ounce}$$

If MaClede extracts 25,000 ounces in the first year, then the depletion for the year is \$250,000 (25,000 ounces × \$10). It records the depletion as follows.

Inventory (gold)	250,000	
Gold Mine		250,000

MaClede debits Inventory for the total depletion for the year and credits Gold Mine to reduce the carrying value of the natural resource. MaClede credits Inventory when it sells the inventory and debits Cost of Goods Sold. The amount not sold remains in inventory and is reported in the current assets section of the balance sheet.[9]

Sometimes companies use an Accumulated Depletion account. In that case, MaClede's balance sheet would present the cost of the natural resource and the amount of accumulated depletion entered to date as follows.

ILLUSTRATION 11-18
Balance Sheet Presentation of Natural Resource

Gold mine (at cost)	\$1,000,000	
Less: Accumulated depletion	250,000	\$750,000

For purposes of homework, credit depletion to the asset account.

[9]The tax law has long provided a deduction against revenue from oil, gas, and most minerals for the greater of cost or percentage depletion. The percentage (statutory) depletion allows some companies a write-off ranging from 5 percent to 22 percent (depending on the natural resource) of gross revenue received. As a result of this tax benefit, the amount of depletion may exceed the cost assigned to a given natural resource. An asset's carrying amount may be zero, but the company may take a depletion deduction if it has gross revenue. The significance of the percentage depletion allowance is now greatly reduced, since Congress repealed it for most oil and gas companies.

MaClede may also depreciate on a units-of-production basis the tangible equipment used in extracting the gold. This approach is appropriate if it can directly assign the estimated lives of the equipment to one given resource deposit. If MaClede uses the equipment on more than one job, other cost allocation methods such as straight-line or accelerated depreciation methods would be more appropriate.

Estimating Recoverable Reserves

Sometimes companies need to change the estimate of recoverable reserves. They do so either because they have new information or because more sophisticated production processes are available. Natural resources such as oil and gas deposits and some rare metals have recently provided the greatest challenges. Estimates of these reserves are in large measure merely "knowledgeable guesses."

This problem is the **same as accounting for changes in estimates for the useful lives of plant and equipment**. The procedure is to **revise the depletion rate on a prospective basis**: A company divides the remaining cost by the new estimate of the recoverable reserves. This approach has much merit because the required estimates are so uncertain.

Liquidating Dividends

A company often owns as its only major asset a property from which it intends to extract natural resources. If the company does not expect to purchase additional properties, it may gradually distribute to stockholders their capital investments by paying **liquidating dividends**, which are dividends greater than the amount of accumulated net income.

The major accounting problem is to distinguish between dividends that are a return of capital and those that are not. Because the dividend is a return of the investor's original contribution, the company issuing a liquidating dividend should debit Paid-in Capital in Excess of Par for that portion related to the original investment, instead of debiting Retained Earnings.

To illustrate, at year-end, Callahan Mining had a retained earnings balance of \$1,650,000, accumulated depletion on mineral properties of \$2,100,000, and paid-in capital in excess of par of \$5,435,493. Callahan's board declared a dividend of \$3 a share on the 1,000,000 shares outstanding. It records the \$3,000,000 cash dividend as follows.

Retained Earnings	1,650,000	
Paid-in Capital in Excess of Par—Common Stock	1,350,000	
Cash		3,000,000

Callahan must inform stockholders that the \$3 dividend per share represents a \$1.65 (\$1,650,000 ÷ 1,000,000 shares) per share return on investment and a \$1.35 (\$1,350,000 ÷ 1,000,000 shares) per share liquidating dividend.

Continuing Controversy

A major controversy relates to the accounting for exploration costs in the oil and gas industry. Conceptually, the question is whether unsuccessful ventures are a cost of those that are successful. Those who hold the **full-cost concept** argue that the cost of drilling a dry hole is a cost needed to find the commercially profitable wells. Others believe that companies should capitalize only the costs of successful projects. This is the **successful-efforts concept**. Its proponents believe that the only relevant measure for a project is the cost directly related to that project, and that companies should report any remaining costs as period charges. In addition, they argue that an unsuccessful company will end up capitalizing many costs that will make it, over a short period of time, show no less income than does one that is successful.[10]

The FASB has attempted to narrow the available alternatives, with little success. Here is a brief history of the debate.

1. *1977—The FASB required oil and gas companies to follow successful-efforts accounting.* Small oil and gas producers, voicing strong opposition, lobbied extensively in Congress. Governmental agencies assessed the implications of this standard from a public interest perspective and reacted contrary to the FASB's position.[11]
2. ***1978—In response to criticisms of the FASB's actions, the SEC reexamined the issue and found both the successful-efforts and full-cost approaches inadequate. Neither method, said the SEC, reflects the economic substance of oil and gas exploration.*** As a substitute, the SEC argued in favor of a yet-to-be developed method, **reserve recognition accounting (RRA)**, which it believed would provide more useful information. Under RRA, as soon as a company discovers oil, it reports the value of the oil on the balance sheet and in the income statement. Thus, RRA is a fair value approach, in contrast to full-costing and successful-efforts, which are historical cost approaches. The use of RRA would make a substantial difference in the balance sheets and income statements of oil companies. For example, **Atlantic Richfield Co.** at one time reported net producing property of $2.6 billion. Under RRA, the same properties would be valued at $11.8 billion.
3. ***1979–1981—As a result of the SEC's actions, the FASB issued another standard that suspended the requirement that companies follow successful-efforts accounting.*** Therefore, full costing was again permissible. In attempting to implement RRA, however, the SEC encountered practical problems in estimating **(1) the amount of the reserves, (2) the future production costs, (3) the periods of expected disposal, (4) the discount rate, and (5) the selling price**. Companies needed an estimate for each of these to arrive at an accurate valuation of existing reserves. Estimating the future selling price, appropriate discount rate, and future extraction and delivery costs of reserves that are years away from realization can be a formidable task.
4. ***1981—The SEC abandoned RRA in the primary financial statements of oil and gas producers.*** The SEC decided that RRA did not possess the required degree of reliability for use as a primary method of financial reporting. However, it continued to stress the need for some form of fair value–based disclosure for oil and gas reserves. As a result, the profession now requires fair value disclosures for those natural resources.

INTERNATIONAL PERSPECTIVE

IFRS also permits companies to use either full-cost or successful-efforts approaches.

Currently, companies can use either the full-cost approach or the successful-efforts approach. It does seem ironic that Congress directed the FASB to develop one method of accounting for the oil and gas industry, and when the FASB did so, the government chose not to accept it. Subsequently, the SEC attempted to develop a new approach,

[10]Large international oil companies such as **ExxonMobil** use the successful-efforts approach. Most of the smaller, exploration-oriented companies use the full-cost approach. The differences in net income figures under the two methods can be staggering. Analysts estimated that the difference between full-cost and successful-efforts for **ChevronTexaco** would be $500 million over a 10-year period (income lower under successful-efforts).

[11]The Department of Energy indicated that companies using the full-cost method at that time would reduce their exploration activities because of the unfavorable earnings impact associated with successful-efforts accounting. The Justice Department asked the SEC to postpone adoption of one uniform method of accounting in the oil and gas industry until the SEC could determine whether the information reported to investors would be enhanced and competition constrained by adoption of the successful-efforts method.

failed, and then urged the FASB to develop the disclosure requirements in this area. After all these changes, the two alternatives still exist.[12]

This controversy in the oil and gas industry provides a number of lessons. First, it demonstrates the strong influence that the federal government has in financial reporting matters. Second, the concern for economic consequences places pressure on the FASB to weigh the economic effects of any required standard. Third, the experience with RRA highlights the problems that accompany any proposed change from an historical cost to a fair value approach. Fourth, this controversy illustrates the difficulty of establishing standards when affected groups have differing viewpoints. Finally, it reinforces the need for a conceptual framework with carefully developed guidelines for recognition, measurement, and reporting, so that interested parties can more easily resolve issues of this nature in the future.

Underlying Concepts

Failure to consider the economic consequences of accounting principles is a frequent criticism of the profession. However, the neutrality concept requires that the statements be free from bias. Freedom from bias requires that the statements reflect economic reality, even if undesirable effects occur.

RAH-RAH SURPRISE

What do the numbers mean?

Recent cuts in the estimates of oil and natural gas reserves at **Royal Dutch/Shell**, **El Paso Corporation**, and other energy companies highlight the importance of reserve disclosures. Investors appear to believe that these disclosures provide useful information for assessing the future cash flows from a company's oil and gas reserves. For example, when Shell's estimates turned out to be overly optimistic (to the tune of 3.9 billion barrels or 20 percent of reserves), Shell's stock price fell.

The experience at Shell and other companies has led the SEC to look at how companies are estimating their "proved" reserves. *Proved reserves* are quantities of oil and gas that can be shown ". . . with reasonable certainty to be recoverable in future years. . . ." The phrase "reasonable certainty" is crucial to this guidance, but differences in interpretation of what is reasonably certain can result in a wide range of estimates.

In one case, for example, **ExxonMobil**'s estimate was 29 percent higher than an estimate the SEC developed. ExxonMobil was more optimistic about the effects of new technology that enables the industry to retrieve more of the oil and gas it finds. Thus, to ensure the continued usefulness of RRA disclosures, the SEC may have to work on a measurement methodology that keeps up with technology changes in the oil and gas industry.

Source: S. Labaton and J. Gerth, "At Shell, New Accounting and Rosier Outlook," *New York Times* (*nytimes.com*) (March 12, 2004); and J. Ball, C. Cummins, and B. Bahree, "Big Oil Differs with SEC on Methods to Calculate the Industry's Reserves," *Wall Street Journal* (February 24, 2005), p. C1.

PRESENTATION AND ANALYSIS

Presentation of Property, Plant, Equipment, and Natural Resources

7 LEARNING OBJECTIVE
Explain how to report and analyze property, plant, equipment, and natural resources.

A company should disclose the basis of valuation—usually historical cost—for property, plant, equipment, and natural resources along with pledges, liens, and other commitments related to these assets. It should not offset any liability secured by property, plant, equipment, and natural resources against these assets. Instead, this obligation should be reported in the liabilities section. The company should

[12]One requirement of the full-cost approach is that companies can capitalize costs only up to a ceiling, which is the present value of company reserves. Companies must expense costs above that ceiling. When the price of oil fell in the mid-1980s, so did the present value of companies' reserves, thus forcing expensing of costs beyond the ceiling. Companies lobbied for leniency, but the SEC decided that the write-offs had to be taken. **Mesa Limited Partnerships** restated its \$31 million profit to a \$169 million loss, and **Pacific Lighting** restated its \$44.5 million profit to a \$70.5 million loss.

segregate property, plant, and equipment not currently employed as producing assets in the business (such as idle facilities or land held as an investment) from assets used in operations.

When depreciating assets, a company credits a valuation account such as Accumulated Depreciation—Equipment. Using an accumulated depreciation account permits the user of the financial statements to see the original cost of the asset and the amount of depreciation that the company charged to expense in past years.

When depleting natural resources, some companies use an accumulated depletion account. Many, however, simply credit the natural resource account directly. The rationale for this approach is that the natural resources are physically consumed, making direct reduction of the cost of the natural resources appropriate.

Because of the significant impact on the financial statements of the depreciation method(s) used, companies should disclose the following.

a. Depreciation expense for the period.

b. Balances of major classes of depreciable assets, by nature and function.

c. Accumulated depreciation, either by major classes of depreciable assets or in total.

d. A general description of the method or methods used in computing depreciation with respect to major classes of depreciable assets. **[2]**[13]

Special disclosure requirements relate to the oil and gas industry. Companies engaged in these activities must disclose the following in their financial statements: (1) the basic method of accounting for those costs incurred in oil and gas producing activities (e.g., full-cost versus successful-efforts), and (2) how the company disposes of costs relating to extractive activities (e.g., dispensing immediately versus depreciation and depletion). **[3]**[14]

The 2009 annual report of **International Paper Company** in Illustration 11-19 shows an acceptable disclosure. It uses condensed balance sheet data supplemented with details and policies in notes to the financial statements.

ILLUSTRATION 11-19
Disclosures for Property, Plant, Equipment, and Natural Resources

International Paper Company

Consolidated Balance Sheet (partial)

In millions at December 31	2009	2008
Assets		
Total current assets	$ 7,551	$ 7,360
Plants, properties and equipment, net	12,688	14,202
Forestlands	757	594
Investments	1,077	1,274
Goodwill	2,290	2,027
Deferred charges and other assets	1,185	1,456
Total assets	$25,548	$26,913

[13]Some believe that companies should disclose the average useful life of the assets or the range of years of asset life to help users understand the age and life of property, plant, and equipment.

[14]Public companies, in addition to these two required disclosures, must include as supplementary information numerous schedules reporting reserve quantities; capitalized costs; acquisition, exploration, and development activities; and a standardized measure of discounted future net cash flows related to proved oil and gas reserve quantities. Given the importance of these disclosures, the SEC recently issued a new set of disclosures to help investors better understand the nature of oil and gas company operations. These rules provide updated guidance on (1) estimates of quantities of proved reserves, (2) estimates of future net revenues, and (3) disclosure of reserve information. See SEC Financial Reporting Release No. 78 (Release No. 33-8995), "Modernization of Oil and Gas Reporting" (December 31, 2008).

ILLUSTRATION 11-19
(continued)

Note 1 (partial)

Plants, Properties and Equipment. Plants, properties and equipment are stated at cost, less accumulated depreciation. Expenditures for betterments are capitalized, whereas normal repairs and maintenance are expensed as incurred. The units-of-production method of depreciation is used for major pulp and paper mills, and the straight-line method is used for other plants and equipment. Annual straight-line depreciation rates are, for buildings—2 1/2% to 8 1/2%, and for machinery and equipment—5% to 33%.

Forestlands. At December 31, 2009, International Paper and its subsidiaries owned or managed about 200,000 acres of forestlands in the United States, approximately 250,000 acres in Brazil, and through licenses and forest management agreements, had harvesting rights on government-owned forestlands in Russia. Costs attributable to timber are charged against income as trees are cut. The rate charged is determined annually based on the relationship of incurred costs to estimated current merchantable volume.

Note 7 (partial)

Plants, properties and equipment by major classification were:

In millions at December 31	2009	2008
Pulp, paper and packaging facilities		
Mills	$22,615	$21,819
Packaging plants	6,348	6,485
Other plants, properties and equipment	1,542	1,511
Gross cost	30,505	29,815
Less: Accumulated depreciation	17,817	15,613
Plants, properties and equipment, net	$12,688	$14,202

Analysis of Property, Plant, and Equipment

Analysts evaluate assets relative to activity (turnover) and profitability.

Asset Turnover Ratio

How efficiently a company uses its assets to generate sales is measured by the **asset turnover ratio**. This ratio divides net sales by average total assets for the period. The resulting number is the dollars of sales produced by each dollar invested in assets. To illustrate, we use the following data from the **Tootsie Roll Industries** 2009 annual report. Illustration 11-20 shows computation of the asset turnover ratio.

Tootsie Roll Industries	(in millions)
Net sales	$495.6
Total assets, 12/31/09	838.2
Total assets, 12/31/08	813.5
Net income	53.5

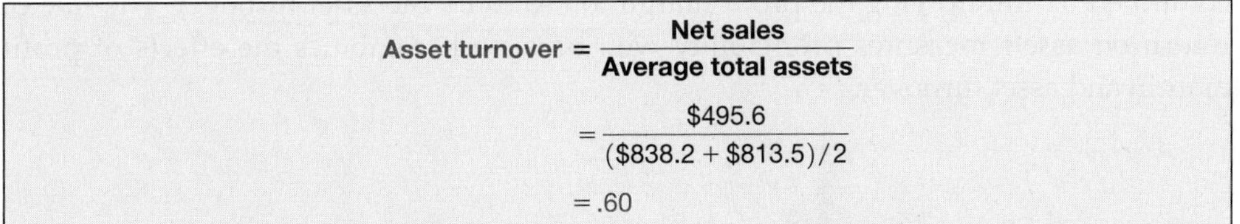

ILLUSTRATION 11-20
Asset Turnover Ratio

The asset turnover ratio shows that Tootsie Roll generated sales of $0.60 per dollar of assets in the year ended December 31, 2009.

Asset turnover ratios vary considerably among industries. For example, a large utility like **Ameren** has a ratio of 0.32 times. A large grocery chain like **Kroger** has a ratio of 2.73 times. Thus, in comparing performance among companies based on the asset turnover ratio, you need to consider the ratio within the context of the industry in which a company operates.

Profit Margin on Sales Ratio

Another measure for analyzing the use of property, plant, and equipment is the **profit margin on sales ratio** (rate of return on sales). Calculated as net income divided by net sales, this profitability ratio does not, by itself, answer the question of how profitably a company uses its assets. But by relating the profit margin on sales to the asset turnover during a period of time, we can ascertain how profitably the company used assets during that period of time in a measure of the rate of return on assets. Using the Tootsie Roll Industries data shown on page 627, we compute the profit margin on sales ratio and the rate of return on assets as follows.

ILLUSTRATION 11-21
Profit Margin on Sales

$$\text{Profit margin on sales} = \frac{\text{Net income}}{\text{Net sales}}$$

$$= \frac{\$53.5}{\$495.5}$$

$$= 10.8\%$$

$$\text{Rate of return on assets} = \text{Profit margin on sales} \times \text{Asset turnover}$$

$$= 10.8\% \times .60$$

$$= 6.5\%$$

Rate of Return on Assets

The rate of return a company achieves through use of its assets is the **rate of return on assets (ROA)**. Rather than using the profit margin on sales, we can compute it directly by dividing net income by average total assets. Using Tootsie Roll's data, we compute the ratio as follows.

ILLUSTRATION 11-22
Rate of Return on Assets

$$\text{Rate of return on assets} = \frac{\text{Net income}}{\text{Average total assets}}$$

$$= \frac{\$53.5}{(\$838.2 + \$813.5)/2}$$

$$= 6.5\%$$

The 6.5 percent rate of return computed in this manner equals the 6.5 percent rate computed by multiplying the profit margin on sales by the asset turnover. The rate of return on assets measures profitability well because it combines the effects of profit margin and asset turnover.

You will want to read the IFRS INSIGHTS on pages 653–663 for discussion of IFRS related to property, plant, and equipment.

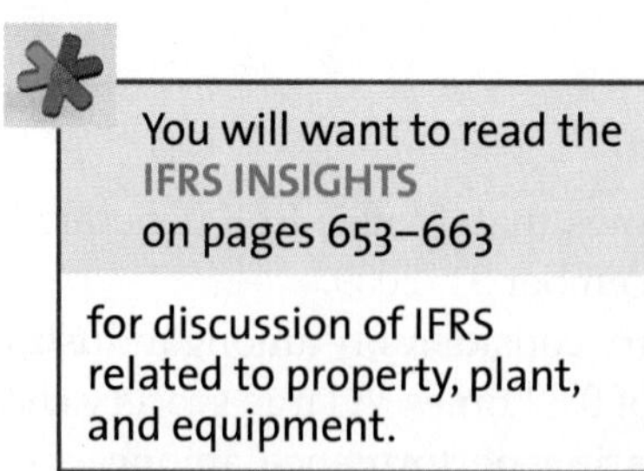

SUMMARY OF LEARNING OBJECTIVES

1 Explain the concept of depreciation. Depreciation allocates the cost of tangible assets to expense in a systematic and rational manner to those periods expected to benefit from the use of the asset.

2 Identify the factors involved in the depreciation process. Three factors involved in the depreciation process are: (1) determining the depreciation base for the asset, (2) estimating service lives, and (3) selecting a method of cost apportionment (depreciation).

3 Compare activity, straight-line, and decreasing-charge methods of depreciation. (1) *Activity method:* Assumes that depreciation is a function of use or productivity instead of the passage of time. The life of the asset is considered in terms of either the output it provides, or an input measure such as the number of hours it works. (2) *Straight-line method:* Considers depreciation a function of time instead of a function of usage. The straight-line procedure is often the most conceptually appropriate when the decline in usefulness is constant from period to period. (3) *Decreasing-charge methods:* Provides for a higher depreciation cost in the earlier years and lower charges in later periods. The main justification for this approach is that the asset is the most productive in its early years.

4 Explain special depreciation methods. Two special depreciation methods are: (1) *Group and composite methods:* The group method is frequently used when the assets are fairly similar in nature and have approximately the same useful lives. The composite method may be used when the assets are dissimilar and have different lives. (2) *Hybrid or combination methods:* These methods may combine straight-line/activity approaches.

5 Explain the accounting issues related to asset impairment. The process to determine an impairment loss is as follows: (1) Review events and changes in circumstances for possible impairment. (2) If events or changes suggest impairment, determine if the sum of the expected future net cash flows from the long-lived asset is less than the carrying amount of the asset. If less, measure the impairment loss. (3) The impairment loss is the amount by which the carrying amount of the asset exceeds the fair value of the asset.

After a company records an impairment loss, the reduced carrying amount of the long-lived asset is its new cost basis. Impairment losses may not be restored for assets held for use. If the company expects to dispose of the asset, it should report the impaired asset at the lower-of-cost-or-net realizable value. It is not depreciated. It can be continuously revalued, as long as the write-up is never to an amount greater than the carrying amount before impairment.

6 Explain the accounting procedures for depletion of natural resources. To account for depletion of natural resources, companies (1) establish the depletion base and (2) write off resource cost. Four factors are part of establishing the depletion base: (a) acquisition costs, (b) exploration costs, (c) development costs, and (d) restoration costs. To write off resource cost, companies normally compute depletion on the units-of-production method. Thus, depletion is a function of the number of units withdrawn during the period. To obtain a cost per unit of product, the total cost of the natural resource less salvage value is divided by the number of units estimated to be in the resource deposit, to obtain a cost per unit of product. To compute depletion, this cost per unit is multiplied by the number of units withdrawn.

7 Explain how to report and analyze property, plant, equipment, and natural resources. The basis of valuation for property, plant, and equipment and for natural resources should be disclosed along with pledges, liens, and other commitments related

KEY TERMS

accelerated depreciation methods, *610*
activity method, *609*
amortization, *606*
asset turnover ratio, *627*
composite approach, *612*
composite depreciation rate, *612*
cost depletion, *622*
declining-balance method, *611*
decreasing-charge methods, *610*
depletion, *606, 620*
depreciation, *606*
depreciation base, *606*
development costs, *621*
double-declining-balance method, *611*
exploration costs, *621*
full-cost concept, *623*
group method, *611*
impairment, *617*
inadequacy, *607*
liquidating dividends, *623*
natural resources, *620*
obsolescence, *607*
percentage depletion, *622(n)*
profit margin on sales ratio, *628*
rate of return on assets (ROA), *628*
recoverability test, *618*
reserve recognition accounting (RRA), *624*
restoration costs, *621*
salvage value, *606*
straight-line method, *609*
successful-efforts concept, *623*
sum-of-the-years'-digits method, *610*
supersession, *607*

to these assets. Companies should not offset any liability secured by property, plant, and equipment or by natural resources against these assets, but should report it in the liabilities section. When depreciating assets, credit a valuation account normally called Accumulated Depreciation. When depleting assets, use an accumulated depletion account, or credit the depletion directly to the natural resource account. Companies engaged in significant oil and gas producing activities must provide additional disclosures about these activities. Analysis may be performed to evaluate the asset turnover ratio, profit margin on sales, and rate of return on assets.

APPENDIX 11A INCOME TAX DEPRECIATION

LEARNING OBJECTIVE 9
Describe income tax methods of depreciation.

For the most part, a financial accounting course does not address issues related to the computation of income taxes. However, because the concepts of tax depreciation are similar to those of book depreciation, and because tax depreciation methods are sometimes adopted for book purposes, we present an overview of this subject.

Congress passed the Accelerated Cost Recovery System (ACRS) as part of the Economic Recovery Tax Act of 1981. The goal was to stimulate capital investment through faster write-offs and to bring more uniformity to the write-off period. For assets purchased in the years 1981 through 1986, companies use ACRS and its preestablished "cost recovery periods" for various classes of assets.

In the Tax Reform Act of 1986 Congress enacted a **Modified Accelerated Cost Recovery System**, known as **MACRS**. It applies to depreciable assets placed in service in 1987 and later. The following discussion is based on these MACRS rules. Realize that tax depreciation rules are subject to change annually.[15]

MODIFIED ACCELERATED COST RECOVERY SYSTEM

The computation of depreciation under MACRS differs from the computation under GAAP in three respects: (1) a mandated tax life, which is generally shorter than the economic life; (2) cost recovery on an accelerated basis; and (3) an assigned salvage value of zero.

Tax Lives (Recovery Periods)

Each item of depreciable property belongs to a property class. The recovery period (depreciable tax life) of an asset depends on its property class. Illustration 11A-1 presents the MACRS property classes.

[15]For example, in an effort to jump-start the economy following the September 11, 2001, terrorist attacks, Congress passed the Job Creation and Worker Assistance Act of 2002 (the Act). The Act allows a 30 percent first-year bonus depreciation for assets placed into service after September 11, 2001, but before September 11, 2004. A follow-up provision enacted in 2003 extended the tax savings to assets placed in service before January 1, 2005. And in 2010, Congress extended bonus depreciation for smaller companies. These laws encourage companies to invest in fixed assets because they can front-load depreciation expense, which lowers taxable income and amount of taxes companies pay in the early years of an asset's life. Although the Act may be a good thing for the economy, it can distort cash flow measures—making them look artificially strong when the allowances are in place but reversing once the bonus depreciation expires. See D. Zion and B. Carcache, "Bonus Depreciation Boomerang," *Credit Suisse First Boston Equity Research* (February 19, 2004).

ILLUSTRATION 11A-1
MACRS Property Classes

3-year property	Includes small tools, horses, and assets used in research and development activities
5-year property	Includes automobiles, trucks, computers and peripheral equipment, and office machines
7-year property	Includes office furniture and fixtures, agriculture equipment, oil exploration and development equipment, railroad track, manufacturing equipment, and any property not designated by law as being in any other class
10-year property	Includes railroad tank cars, mobile homes, boilers, and certain public utility property
15-year property	Includes roads, shrubbery, and certain low-income housing
20-year property	Includes waste-water treatment plants and sewer systems
27.5-year property	Includes residential rental property
39-year property	Includes nonresidential real property

Tax Depreciation Methods

Companies compute depreciation expense using the tax basis—usually the cost—of the asset. The depreciation method depends on the MACRS property class, as shown below.

ILLUSTRATION 11A-2
Depreciation Method for Various MACRS Property Classes

MACRS Property Class	Depreciation Method
3-, 5-, 7-, and 10-year property	Double-declining-balance
15- and 20-year property	150% declining-balance
27.5- and 39-year property	Straight-line

Depreciation computations for income tax purposes are based on the **half-year convention**. That is, a half year of depreciation is allowable in the year of acquisition and in the year of disposition.[16] A company depreciates an asset to a zero value so that there is no salvage value at the end of its MACRS life.

Use of IRS-published tables, shown in Illustration 11A-3, simplifies application of these depreciation methods.

ILLUSTRATION 11A-3
IRS Table of MACRS Depreciation Rates, by Property Class

	MACRS Depreciation Rates by Class of Property					
Recovery Year	3-year (200% DB)	5-year (200% DB)	7-year (200% DB)	10-year (200% DB)	15-year (150% DB)	20-year (150% DB)
1	33.33	20.00	14.29	10.00	5.00	3.750
2	44.45	32.00	24.49	18.00	9.50	7.219
3	14.81*	19.20	17.49	14.40	8.55	6.677
4	7.41	11.52*	12.49	11.52	7.70	6.177
5		11.52	8.93*	9.22	6.93	5.713
6		5.76	8.92	7.37	6.23	5.285
7			8.93	6.55*	5.90*	4.888
8			4.46	6.55	5.90	4.522
9				6.56	5.91	4.462*
10				6.55	5.90	4.461
11				3.28	5.91	4.462
12					5.90	4.461
13					5.91	4.462
14					5.90	4.461
15					5.91	4.462
16					2.95	4.461
17						4.462
18						4.461
19						4.462
20						4.461
21						2.231

*Switchover to straight-line depreciation.

[16]The tax law requires mid-quarter and mid-month conventions for MACRS purposes in certain circumstances.

Example of MACRS

To illustrate depreciation computations under both MACRS and GAAP straight-line accounting, assume the following facts for a computer and peripheral equipment purchased by Denise Rode Company on January 1, 2011.

Acquisition Date	January 1, 2011
Cost	$100,000
Estimated useful life	7 years
Estimated salvage value	$16,000
MACRS class life	5 years
MACRS method	200% declining-balance
GAAP method	Straight-line
Disposal proceeds—January 2, 2018	$11,000

Using the rates from the MACRS depreciation rate schedule for a 5-year class of property, Rode computes depreciation as follows for tax purposes.

ILLUSTRATION 11A-4
Computation of MACRS Depreciation

MACRS Depreciation

2011	$100,000 × .20	=	$ 20,000
2012	$100,000 × .32	=	32,000
2013	$100,000 × .192	=	19,200
2014	$100,000 × .1152	=	11,520
2015	$100,000 × .1152	=	11,520
2016	$100,000 × .0576	=	5,760
	Total depreciation		$100,000

Rode computes the depreciation under GAAP straight-line method, with $16,000 of estimated salvage value and an estimated useful life of 7 years, as shown in Illustration 11A-5.

ILLUSTRATION 11A-5
Computation of GAAP Depreciation

GAAP Depreciation

($100,000 − $16,000) ÷ 7 =	$12,000	annual depreciation
	× 7	years
1/1/11–1/2/18	$84,000	total depreciation

The MACRS depreciation recovers the total cost of the asset on an accelerated basis. But, a taxable gain of $11,000 results from the sale of the asset at January 2, 2018. Therefore, the net effect on taxable income for the years 2011 through 2018 is $89,000 ($100,000 depreciation − $11,000 gain).

Under GAAP, the company recognizes a loss on disposal of $5,000 ($16,000 book value − $11,000 disposal proceeds). The net effect on income before income taxes for the years 2011 through 2018 is $89,000 ($84,000 depreciation + $5,000 loss), the same as the net effect of MACRS on taxable income.

Even though the net effects are equal in amount, the deferral of income tax payments under MACRS from early in the life of the asset to later in life is desirable. The different amounts of depreciation for income tax reporting and financial GAAP reporting in each year are a matter of timing and result in temporary differences, which require **interperiod tax allocation**. (See Chapter 19 for an extended treatment of this topic.)

OPTIONAL STRAIGHT-LINE METHOD

An alternate MACRS method exists for determining depreciation deductions. Based on the straight-line method, it is referred to as the **optional** (elective) **straight-line method**. This method applies to the six classes of property described earlier. The alternate MACRS applies the straight-line method to the MACRS recovery periods. It ignores salvage value.

Under the optional straight-line method, in the first year in which the property is put in service, the company deducts half of the amount of depreciation that would be permitted for a full year (half-year convention). Use the half-year convention for homework problems.

TAX VERSUS BOOK DEPRECIATION

GAAP requires that companies allocate the cost of depreciable assets to expense over the expected useful life of the asset in a systematic and rational manner. Some argue that from a cost-benefit perspective it would be better for companies to adopt the MACRS approach in order to eliminate the necessity of maintaining two different sets of records.

However, the tax laws and financial reporting have different objectives: The purpose of taxation is to raise revenue from constituents in an equitable manner. The purpose of financial reporting is to reflect the economic substance of a transaction as closely as possible and to help predict the amounts, timing, and uncertainty of future cash flows. Because these objectives differ, the adoption of one method for both tax and book purposes in all cases is not in accordance with GAAP.

SUMMARY OF LEARNING OBJECTIVE FOR APPENDIX 11A

KEY TERM

Modified Accelerated Cost Recovery System (MACRS), *630*

8 **Describe income tax methods of depreciation.** Congress enacted a Modified Accelerated Cost Recovery System (MACRS) in the Tax Reform Act of 1986. It applies to depreciable assets placed in service in 1987 and later. The computation of depreciation under MACRS differs from the computation under GAAP in three respects: (1) a mandated tax life, which is generally shorter than the economic life; (2) cost recovery on an accelerated basis; and (3) an assigned salvage value of zero.

FASB CODIFICATION

FASB Codification References

[1] FASB ASC 360-10-05. [Predecessor literature: "Accounting for the Impairment or Disposal of Long-lived Assets," *Statement of Financial Accounting Standards No. 144* (Norwalk, Conn.: 2001).]

[2] FASB ASC 360-10-50-1. [Predecessor literature: "Omnibus Opinion—1967," *Opinions of the Accounting Principles Board No. 12* (New York: AICPA, 1967), par. 5.]

[3] FASB ASC 932-235-50-1. [Predecessor literature: "Disclosures about Oil and Gas Producing Activities," *Statement of Financial Accounting Standards Board No. 69* (Stamford, Conn.: FASB, 1982).]

Exercises

If your school has a subscription to the FASB Codification, go to *http://aaahq.org/asclogin.cfm* to log in and prepare responses to the following. Provide Codification references for your responses.

CE11-1 Access the glossary ("Master Glossary") to answer the following.

- **(a)** What is the definition of amortization?
- **(b)** What is the definition of impairment?
- **(c)** What is the definition of recoverable amount?
- **(d)** What are activities, as they relate to the construction of an asset?

CE11-2 Your client, Barriques Inc., is contemplating a restructuring of its operations, including the possibility of spinning off some of its assets to the original owners. However, management is unsure of the accounting for any impairment on the assets. What does the authoritative literature say about these types of impairments?

CE11-3 Your great-uncle, who is a CPA, is impressed that you are majoring in accounting, but based on his experience, he believes that depreciation is something that companies do based on past practice, not on the basis of any authoritative guidance. Provide the authoritative literature to support the practice of fixed-asset depreciation.

CE11-4 What is the nature of the SEC guidance concerning property, plant, and equipment disclosures?

An additional Codification case can be found in the Using Your Judgment section, on page 652

Be sure to check the book's companion website for a Review and Analysis Exercise, with solution.

Questions, Brief Exercises, Exercises, Problems, and many more resources are available for practice in WileyPLUS.

Note: All asterisked Questions, Exercises, and Problems relate to material in the appendix to the chapter.

QUESTIONS

1. Distinguish among depreciation, depletion, and amortization.
2. Identify the factors that are relevant in determining the annual depreciation charge, and explain whether these factors are determined objectively or whether they are based on judgment.
3. Some believe that accounting depreciation measures the decline in the value of fixed assets. Do you agree? Explain.
4. Explain how estimation of service lives can result in unrealistically high carrying values for fixed assets.
5. The plant manager of a manufacturing firm suggested in a conference of the company's executives that accountants should speed up depreciation on the machinery in the finishing department because improvements were rapidly making those machines obsolete, and a depreciation fund big enough to cover their replacement is needed. Discuss the accounting concept of depreciation and the effect on a business concern of the depreciation recorded for plant assets, paying particular attention to the issues raised by the plant manager.
6. For what reasons are plant assets retired? Define inadequacy, supersession, and obsolescence.

7. What basic questions must be answered before the amount of the depreciation charge can be computed?

8. Workman Company purchased a machine on January 2, 2012, for $800,000. The machine has an estimated useful life of 5 years and a salvage value of $100,000. Depreciation was computed by the 150% declining-balance method. What is the amount of accumulated depreciation at the end of December 31, 2013?

9. Silverman Company purchased machinery for $162,000 on January 1, 2012. It is estimated that the machinery will have a useful life of 20 years, salvage value of $15,000, production of 84,000 units, and working hours of 42,000. During 2012, the company uses the machinery for 14,300 hours, and the machinery produces 20,000 units. Compute depreciation under the straight-line, units-of-output, working hours, sum-of-the-years'-digits, and double-declining-balance methods.

10. What are the major factors considered in determining what depreciation method to use?

11. Under what conditions is it appropriate for a business to use the composite method of depreciation for its plant assets? What are the advantages and disadvantages of this method?

12. If Remmers, Inc. uses the composite method and its composite rate is 7.5% per year, what entry should it make when plant assets that originally cost $50,000 and have been used for 10 years are sold for $14,000?

13. A building that was purchased December 31, 1988, for $2,500,000 was originally estimated to have a life of 50 years with no salvage value at the end of that time. Depreciation has been recorded through 2012. During 2013, an examination of the building by an engineering firm discloses that its estimated useful life is 15 years after 2012. What should be the amount of depreciation for 2013?

14. Charlie Parker, president of Spinners Company, has recently noted that depreciation increases cash provided by operations and therefore depreciation is a good source of funds. Do you agree? Discuss.

15. Andrea Torbert purchased a computer for $8,000 on July 1, 2012. She intends to depreciate it over 4 years using the double-declining-balance method. Salvage value is $1,000. Compute depreciation for 2013.

16. Walkin Inc. is considering the write-down of its long-term plant because of a lack of profitability. Explain to the management of Walkin how to determine whether a write-down is permitted.

17. Last year, Wyeth Company recorded an impairment on an asset held for use. Recent appraisals indicate that the asset has increased in value. Should Wyeth record this recovery in value?

18. Toro Co. has equipment with a carrying amount of $700,000. The expected future net cash flows from the equipment are $705,000, and its fair value is $590,000. The equipment is expected to be used in operations in the future. What amount (if any) should Toro report as an impairment to its equipment?

19. Explain how gains or losses on impaired assets should be reported in income.

20. It has been suggested that plant and equipment could be replaced more quickly if depreciation rates for income tax and accounting purposes were substantially increased. As a result, business operations would receive the benefit of more modern and more efficient plant facilities. Discuss the merits of this proposition.

21. Neither depreciation on replacement cost nor depreciation adjusted for changes in the purchasing power of the dollar has been recognized as generally accepted accounting principles for inclusion in the primary financial statements. Briefly present the accounting treatment that might be used to assist in the maintenance of the ability of a company to replace its productive capacity.

22. List (a) the similarities and (b) the differences in the accounting treatments of depreciation and cost depletion.

23. Describe cost depletion and percentage depletion. Why is the percentage depletion method permitted?

24. In what way may the use of percentage depletion violate sound accounting theory?

25. In the extractive industries, businesses may pay dividends in excess of net income. What is the maximum permissible? How can this practice be justified?

26. The following statement appeared in a financial magazine: "RRA—or Rah-Rah, as it's sometimes dubbed—has kicked up quite a storm. Oil companies, for example, are convinced that the approach is misleading. Major accounting firms agree." What is RRA? Why might oil companies believe that this approach is misleading?

27. Shumway Oil uses successful-efforts accounting and also provides full-cost results as well. Under full-cost, Shumway Oil would have reported retained earnings of $42 million and net income of $4 million. Under successful-efforts, retained earnings were $29 million, and net income was $3 million. Explain the difference between full-costing and successful-efforts accounting.

28. Target Corporation in 2010 reported net income of $2.5 billion, net sales of $63.4 billion, and average total assets of $44.3 billion. What is Target's asset turnover ratio? What is Target's rate of return on assets?

***29.** What is a modified accelerated cost recovery system (MACRS)? Speculate as to why this system is now required for tax purposes.

BRIEF EXERCISES

2 3 **BE11-1** Fernandez Corporation purchased a truck at the beginning of 2012 for $50,000. The truck is estimated to have a salvage value of $2,000 and a useful life of 160,000 miles. It was driven 23,000 miles in 2012 and 31,000 miles in 2013. Compute depreciation expense for 2012 and 2013.

2 3 **BE11-2** Lockard Company purchased machinery on January 1, 2012, for $80,000. The machinery is estimated to have a salvage value of $8,000 after a useful life of 8 years. (a) Compute 2012 depreciation expense using the straight-line method. (b) Compute 2012 depreciation expense using the straight-line method assuming the machinery was purchased on September 1, 2012.

2 3 **BE11-3** Use the information for Lockard Company given in BE11-2. (a) Compute 2012 depreciation expense using the sum-of-the-years'-digits method. (b) Compute 2012 depreciation expense using the sum-of-the-years'-digits method assuming the machinery was purchased on April 1, 2012.

2 3 **BE11-4** Use the information for Lockard Company given in BE11-2. (a) Compute 2012 depreciation expense using the double-declining-balance method. (b) Compute 2012 depreciation expense using the double-declining-balance method assuming the machinery was purchased on October 1, 2012.

2 3 **BE11-5** Cominsky Company purchased a machine on July 1, 2013, for $28,000. Cominsky paid $200 in title fees and county property tax of $125 on the machine. In addition, Cominsky paid $500 shipping charges for delivery, and $475 was paid to a local contractor to build and wire a platform for the machine on the plant floor. The machine has an estimated useful life of 6 years with a salvage value of $3,000. Determine the depreciation base of Cominsky's new machine. Cominsky uses straight-line depreciation.

4 **BE11-6** Dickinson Inc. owns the following assets.

Asset	Cost	Salvage	Estimated Useful Life
A	$70,000	$7,000	10 years
B	50,000	5,000	5 years
C	82,000	4,000	12 years

Compute the composite depreciation rate and the composite life of Dickinson's assets.

4 **BE11-7** Holt Company purchased a computer for $8,000 on January 1, 2011. Straight-line depreciation is used, based on a 5-year life and a $1,000 salvage value. In 2013, the estimates are revised. Holt now feels the computer will be used until December 31, 2014, when it can be sold for $500. Compute the 2013 depreciation.

5 **BE11-8** Jurassic Company owns machinery that cost $900,000 and has accumulated depreciation of $380,000. The expected future net cash flows from the use of the asset are expected to be $500,000. The fair value of the equipment is $400,000. Prepare the journal entry, if any, to record the impairment loss.

6 **BE11-9** Everly Corporation acquires a coal mine at a cost of $400,000. Intangible development costs total $100,000. After extraction has occurred, Everly must restore the property (estimated fair value of the obligation is $80,000), after which it can be sold for $160,000. Everly estimates that 4,000 tons of coal can be extracted. If 700 tons are extracted the first year, prepare the journal entry to record depletion.

7 **BE11-10** In its 2009 annual report, **Campbell Soup Company** reports beginning-of-the-year total assets of $6,474 million, end-of-the-year total assets of $6,056 million, total sales of $7,586 million, and net income of $736 million. (a) Compute Campbell's asset turnover ratio. (b) Compute Campbell's profit margin on sales. (c) Compute Campbell's rate of return on assets (1) using asset turnover and profit margin and (2) using net income.

8 ***BE11-11** Francis Corporation purchased an asset at a cost of $50,000 on March 1, 2012. The asset has a useful life of 8 years and a salvage value of $4,000. For tax purposes, the MACRS class life is 5 years. Compute tax depreciation for each year 2012–2017.

EXERCISES

2 3 **E11-1 (Depreciation Computations—SL, SYD, DDB)** Lansbury Company purchases equipment on January 1, Year 1, at a cost of $518,000. The asset is expected to have a service life of 12 years and a salvage value of $50,000.

Instructions

(a) Compute the amount of depreciation for each of Years 1 through 3 using the straight-line depreciation method.

(b) Compute the amount of depreciation for each of Years 1 through 3 using the sum-of-the-years'-digits method.
(c) Compute the amount of depreciation for each of Years 1 through 3 using the double-declining-balance method. (In performing your calculations, round constant percentage to the nearest one-hundredth of a point and round answers to the nearest dollar.)

2 3 **E11-2 (Depreciation—Conceptual Understanding)** Hasselback Company acquired a plant asset at the beginning of Year 1. The asset has an estimated service life of 5 years. An employee has prepared depreciation schedules for this asset using three different methods to compare the results of using one method with the results of using other methods. You are to assume that the following schedules have been correctly prepared for this asset using (1) the straight-line method, (2) the sum-of-the-years'-digits method, and (3) the double-declining-balance method.

Year	Straight-Line	Sum-of-the-Years'-Digits	Double-Declining-Balance
1	$ 9,000	$15,000	$20,000
2	9,000	12,000	12,000
3	9,000	9,000	7,200
4	9,000	6,000	4,320
5	9,000	3,000	1,480
Total	$45,000	$45,000	$45,000

Instructions
Answer the following questions.

(a) What is the cost of the asset being depreciated?
(b) What amount, if any, was used in the depreciation calculations for the salvage value for this asset?
(c) Which method will produce the highest charge to income in Year 1?
(d) Which method will produce the highest charge to income in Year 4?
(e) Which method will produce the highest book value for the asset at the end of Year 3?
(f) If the asset is sold at the end of Year 3, which method would yield the highest gain (or lowest loss) on disposal of the asset?

2 3 **E11-3 (Depreciation Computations—SYD, DDB—Partial Periods)** Cosby Company purchased a new plant asset on April 1, 2012, at a cost of $774,000. It was estimated to have a service life of 20 years and a salvage value of $60,000. Cosby's accounting period is the calendar year.

Instructions
(a) Compute the depreciation for this asset for 2012 and 2013 using the sum-of-the-years'-digits method.
(b) Compute the depreciation for this asset for 2012 and 2013 using the double-declining-balance method.

2 3 **E11-4 (Depreciation Computations—Five Methods)** Wenner Furnace Corp. purchased machinery for $279,000 on May 1, 2012. It is estimated that it will have a useful life of 10 years, salvage value of $15,000, production of 240,000 units, and working hours of 25,000. During 2013, Wenner Corp. uses the machinery for 2,650 hours, and the machinery produces 25,500 units.

Instructions
From the information given, compute the depreciation charge for 2013 under each of the following methods. (Round to the nearest dollar.)

(a) Straight-line.
(b) Units-of-output.
(c) Working hours.
(d) Sum-of-the-years'-digits.
(e) Double-declining-balance.

2 3 **E11-5 (Depreciation Computations—Four Methods)** Maserati Corporation purchased a new machine for its assembly process on August 1, 2012. The cost of this machine was $150,000. The company estimated that the machine would have a salvage value of $24,000 at the end of its service life. Its life is estimated at 5 years and its working hours are estimated at 21,000 hours. Year-end is December 31.

Instructions
Compute the depreciation expense under the following methods. Each of the following should be considered unrelated.

(a) Straight-line depreciation for 2012.
(b) Activity method for 2012, assuming that machine usage was 800 hours.
(c) Sum-of-the-years'-digits for 2013.
(d) Double-declining-balance for 2013.

2 3 **E11-6 (Depreciation Computations—Five Methods, Partial Periods)** Agazzi Company purchased equipment for $304,000 on October 1, 2012. It is estimated that the equipment will have a useful life of 8 years and a salvage value of $16,000. Estimated production is 40,000 units and estimated working hours are 20,000. During 2012, Agazzi uses the equipment for 525 hours and the equipment produces 1,000 units.

Instructions

Compute depreciation expense under each of the following methods. Agazzi is on a calendar-year basis ending December 31.

(a) Straight-line method for 2012.
(b) Activity method (units of output) for 2012.
(c) Activity method (working hours) for 2012.
(d) Sum-of-the-years'-digits method for 2014.
(e) Double-declining-balance method for 2013.

2 3 **E11-7 (Different Methods of Depreciation)** Jeeter Industries presents you with the following information.

Description	Date Purchased	Cost	Salvage Value	Life in Years	Depreciation Method	Accumulated Depreciation to 12/31/12	Depreciation for 2013
Machine A	2/12/11	$159,000	$16,000	10	**(a)**	$37,700	**(b)**
Machine B	8/15/10	**(c)**	21,000	5	SL	29,000	**(d)**
Machine C	7/21/09	88,000	28,500	8	DDB	**(e)**	**(f)**
Machine D	10/12/**(g)**	219,000	69,000	5	SYD	70,000	**(h)**

Instructions

Complete the table for the year ended December 31, 2013. The company depreciates all assets using the half-year convention.

2 3 **E11-8 (Depreciation Computation—Replacement, Nonmonetary Exchange)** Goldman Corporation bought a machine on June 1, 2010, for $31,800, f.o.b. the place of manufacture. Freight to the point where it was set up was $200, and $500 was expended to install it. The machine's useful life was estimated at 10 years, with a salvage value of $2,500. On June 1, 2011, an essential part of the machine is replaced, at a cost of $2,700, with one designed to reduce the cost of operating the machine. The cost of the old part and related depreciation cannot be determined with any accuracy.

On June 1, 2014, the company buys a new machine of greater capacity for $35,000, delivered, trading in the old machine which has a fair value and trade-in allowance of $20,000. To prepare the old machine for removal from the plant cost $75, and expenditures to install the new one were $1,500. It is estimated that the new machine has a useful life of 10 years, with a salvage value of $4,000 at the end of that time. The exchange has commercial substance.

Instructions

Assuming that depreciation is to be computed on the straight-line basis, compute the annual depreciation on the new equipment that should be provided for the fiscal year beginning June 1, 2014.

4 **E11-9 (Composite Depreciation)** Presented below is information related to Morrow Manufacturing Corporation.

Machine	Cost	Estimated Salvage Value	Estimated Life (in years)
A	$40,500	$5,500	10
B	33,600	4,800	9
C	36,000	3,600	8
D	19,000	1,500	7
E	23,500	2,500	6

Instructions

(a) Compute the rate of depreciation per year to be applied to the machines under the composite method.
(b) Prepare the adjusting entry necessary at the end of the year to record depreciation for the year.
(c) Prepare the entry to record the sale of Machine D for cash of $5,000. It was used for 6 years, and depreciation was entered under the composite method.

2 3 **E11-10 (Depreciation Computations, SYD)** Bosh Company purchased a piece of equipment at the beginning of 2009. The equipment cost $502,000. It has an estimated service life of 8 years and an expected salvage value of $70,000. The sum-of-the-years'-digits method of depreciation is being used. Someone has already correctly prepared a depreciation schedule for this asset. This schedule shows that $60,000 will be depreciated for a particular calendar year.

Instructions

Show calculations to determine for what particular year the depreciation amount for this asset will be $60,000.

2 3 4 **E11-11 (Depreciation—Change in Estimate)** Machinery purchased for $52,000 by Carver Co. in 2008 was originally estimated to have a life of 8 years with a salvage value of $4,000 at the end of that time. Depreciation has been entered for 5 years on this basis. In 2013, it is determined that the total estimated life should be 10 years with a salvage value of $4,500 at the end of that time. Assume straight-line depreciation.

Instructions

(a) Prepare the entry to correct the prior years' depreciation, if necessary.
(b) Prepare the entry to record depreciation for 2013.

2 3 4 **E11-12 (Depreciation Computation—Addition, Change in Estimate)** In 1985, Abraham Company completed the construction of a building at a cost of $1,900,000 and first occupied it in January 1986. It was estimated that the building will have a useful life of 40 years and a salvage value of $60,000 at the end of that time.

Early in 1996, an addition to the building was constructed at a cost of $470,000. At that time, it was estimated that the remaining life of the building would be, as originally estimated, an additional 30 years, and that the addition would have a life of 30 years and a salvage value of $20,000.

In 2014, it is determined that the probable life of the building and addition will extend to the end of 2045 or 20 years beyond the original estimate.

Instructions

(a) Using the straight-line method, compute the annual depreciation that would have been charged from 1986 through 1995.
(b) Compute the annual depreciation that would have been charged from 1996 through 2013.
(c) Prepare the entry, if necessary, to adjust the account balances because of the revision of the estimated life in 2014.
(d) Compute the annual depreciation to be charged beginning with 2014.

2 3 4 **E11-13 (Depreciation—Replacement, Change in Estimate)** Peloton Company constructed a building at a cost of $2,400,000 and occupied it beginning in January 1993. It was estimated at that time that its life would be 40 years, with no salvage value.

In January 2013, a new roof was installed at a cost of $300,000, and it was estimated then that the building would have a useful life of 25 years from that date. The cost of the old roof was $180,000.

Instructions

(a) What amount of depreciation should have been charged annually from the years 1993 to 2012? (Assume straight-line depreciation.)
(b) What entry should be made in 2013 to record the replacement of the roof?
(c) Prepare the entry in January 2013, to record the revision in the estimated life of the building, if necessary.
(d) What amount of depreciation should be charged for the year 2013?

2 3 **E11-14 (Error Analysis and Depreciation, SL and SYD)** Kawasaki Company shows the following entries in its Equipment account for 2013. All amounts are based on historical cost.

Equipment

Date	Description	Amount	Date	Description	Amount
2013			2013		
Jan. 1	Balance	133,000	June 30	Cost of equipment sold (purchased prior to 2013)	23,000
Aug. 10	Purchases	32,000			
12	Freight on equipment purchased	700			
25	Installation costs	2,500			
Nov. 10	Repairs	500			

Instructions

(a) Prepare any correcting entries necessary.
(b) Assuming that depreciation is to be charged for a full year on the ending balance in the asset account, compute the proper depreciation charge for 2013 under each of the methods listed below. Assume an estimated life of 10 years, with no salvage value. The machinery included in the January 1, 2013, balance was purchased in 2011.
   (1) Straight-line.
   (2) Sum-of-the-years'-digits.

2 3 **E11-15 (Depreciation for Fractional Periods)** On March 10, 2014, No Doubt Company sells equipment that it purchased for $240,000 on August 20, 2007. It was originally estimated that the equipment would have a life of 12 years and a salvage value of $21,000 at the end of that time, and depreciation has been computed on that basis. The company uses the straight-line method of depreciation.

Instructions

(a) Compute the depreciation charge on this equipment for 2007, for 2014, and the total charge for the period from 2008 to 2013, inclusive, under each of the six following assumptions with respect to partial periods.

(1) Depreciation is computed for the exact period of time during which the asset is owned. (Use 365 days for the base.)

(2) Depreciation is computed for the full year on the January 1 balance in the asset account.

(3) Depreciation is computed for the full year on the December 31 balance in the asset account.

(4) Depreciation for one-half year is charged on plant assets acquired or disposed of during the year.

(5) Depreciation is computed on additions from the beginning of the month following acquisition and on disposals to the beginning of the month following disposal.

(6) Depreciation is computed for a full period on all assets in use for over one-half year, and no depreciation is charged on assets in use for less than one-half year.

(b) Briefly evaluate the methods above, considering them from the point of view of basic accounting theory as well as simplicity of application.

5 **E11-16 (Impairment)** Presented below is information related to equipment owned by Pujols Company at December 31, 2012.

Cost	$9,000,000
Accumulated depreciation to date	1,000,000
Expected future net cash flows	7,000,000
Fair value	4,400,000

Assume that Pujols will continue to use this asset in the future. As of December 31, 2012, the equipment has a remaining useful life of 4 years.

Instructions

(a) Prepare the journal entry (if any) to record the impairment of the asset at December 31, 2012.

(b) Prepare the journal entry to record depreciation expense for 2013.

(c) The fair value of the equipment at December 31, 2013, is $5,100,000. Prepare the journal entry (if any) necessary to record this increase in fair value.

5 **E11-17 (Impairment)** Assume the same information as E11-16, except that Pujols intends to dispose of the equipment in the coming year. It is expected that the cost of disposal will be $20,000.

Instructions

(a) Prepare the journal entry (if any) to record the impairment of the asset at December 31, 2012.

(b) Prepare the journal entry (if any) to record depreciation expense for 2013.

(c) The asset was not sold by December 31, 2013. The fair value of the equipment on that date is $5,100,000. Prepare the journal entry (if any) necessary to record this increase in fair value. It is expected that the cost of disposal is still $20,000.

5 **E11-18 (Impairment)** The management of Sprague Inc. was discussing whether certain equipment should be written off as a charge to current operations because of obsolescence. This equipment has a cost of $900,000 with depreciation to date of $400,000 as of December 31, 2012. On December 31, 2012, management projected its future net cash flows from this equipment to be $300,000 and its fair value to be $280,000. The company intends to use this equipment in the future.

Instructions

(a) Prepare the journal entry (if any) to record the impairment at December 31, 2012.

(b) Where should the gain or loss (if any) on the write-down be reported in the income statement?

(c) At December 31, 2013, the equipment's fair value increased to $300,000. Prepare the journal entry (if any) to record this increase in fair value.

(d) What accounting issues did management face in accounting for this impairment?

6 **E11-19 (Depletion Computations—Timber)** Hernandez Timber Company owns 9,000 acres of timberland purchased in 2001 at a cost of $1,400 per acre. At the time of purchase, the land without the timber was valued at $400 per acre. In 2002, Hernandez built fire lanes and roads, with a life of 30 years, at a cost of $87,000. Every year, Hernandez sprays to prevent disease at a cost of $3,000 per year and spends $7,000 to maintain the fire lanes and roads. During 2003, Hernandez selectively logged and sold 700,000 board feet

of timber, of the estimated 3,000,000 board feet. In 2004, Hernandez planted new seedlings to replace the trees cut at a cost of $100,000.

Instructions

(a) Determine the depreciation expense and the cost of timber sold related to depletion for 2003.

(b) Hernandez has not logged since 2003. If Hernandez logged and sold 900,000 board feet of timber in 2014, when the timber cruise (appraiser) estimated 5,000,000 board feet, determine the cost of timber sold related to depletion for 2014.

6 **E11-20 (Depletion Computations—Oil)** Federer Drilling Company has leased property on which oil has been discovered. Wells on this property produced 18,000 barrels of oil during the past year that sold at an average sales price of $65 per barrel. Total oil resources of this property are estimated to be 250,000 barrels.

The lease provided for an outright payment of $600,000 to the lessor (owner) before drilling could be commenced and an annual rental of $31,500. A premium of 5% of the sales price of every barrel of oil removed is to be paid annually to the lessor. In addition, Federer (lessee) is to clean up all the waste and debris from drilling and to bear the costs of reconditioning the land for farming when the wells are abandoned. The estimated fair value, at the time of the lease, of this clean-up and reconditioning is $30,000.

Instructions

From the provisions of the lease agreement, compute the cost per barrel for the past year, exclusive of operating costs, to Federer Drilling Company.

6 **E11-21 (Depletion Computations—Timber)** Jonas Lumber Company owns a 7,000-acre tract of timber purchased in 2005 at a cost of $1,300 per acre. At the time of purchase, the land was estimated to have a value of $300 per acre without the timber. Jonas Lumber Company has not logged this tract since it was purchased. In 2012, Jonas had the timber cruised. The cruise (appraiser) estimated that each acre contained 8,000 board feet of timber. In 2012, Jonas built 10 miles of roads at a cost of $8,400 per mile. After the roads were completed, Jonas logged and sold 3,500 trees containing 880,000 board feet.

Instructions

(a) Determine the cost of timber sold related to depletion for 2012.

(b) If Jonas depreciates the logging roads on the basis of timber cut, determine the depreciation expense for 2012.

(c) If Jonas plants five seedlings at a cost of $4 per seedling for each tree cut, how should Jonas treat the reforestation?

6 **E11-22 (Depletion Computations—Mining)** Henrik Mining Company purchased land on February 1, 2012, at a cost of $1,250,000. It estimated that a total of 60,000 tons of mineral was available for mining. After it has removed all the natural resources, the company will be required to restore the property to its previous state because of strict environmental protection laws. It estimates the fair value of this restoration obligation at $90,000. It believes it will be able to sell the property afterwards for $100,000. It incurred developmental costs of $200,000 before it was able to do any mining. In 2012, resources removed totaled 30,000 tons. The company sold 24,000 tons.

Instructions

Compute the following information for 2012.

(a) Per unit mineral cost.

(b) Total material cost of December 31, 2012, inventory.

(c) Total materials cost in cost of goods sold at December 31, 2012.

6 **E11-23 (Depletion Computations—Minerals)** At the beginning of 2012, Callaway Company acquired a mine for $850,000. Of this amount, $100,000 was ascribed to the land value and the remaining portion to the minerals in the mine. Surveys conducted by geologists have indicated that approximately 12,000,000 units of the ore appear to be in the mine. Callaway incurred $170,000 of development costs associated with this mine prior to any extraction of minerals. It also determined that the fair value of its obligation to prepare the land for an alternative use when all of the mineral has been removed was $40,000. During 2012, 2,500,000 units of ore were extracted and 2,200,000 of these units were sold.

Instructions

Compute the following.

(a) The total amount of depletion for 2012.

(b) The amount that is charged as an expense for 2012 for the cost of the minerals sold during 2012.

E11-24 (Ratio Analysis) The 2009 Annual Report of McDonald's Corporation contains the following information.

(in billions)	December 31, 2009	December 31, 2008
Total assets	$30,225	$28,462
Net sales	22,745	
Net income	4,551	

Instructions

Compute the following ratios for McDonald's for 2009.

(a) Asset turnover ratio.
(b) Rate of return on assets.
(c) Profit margin on sales.
(d) How can the asset turnover ratio be used to compute the rate of return on assets?

8 ***E11-25 (Book vs. Tax (MACRS) Depreciation)** Annunzio Enterprises purchased a delivery truck on January 1, 2012, at a cost of $41,000. The truck has a useful life of 7 years with an estimated salvage value of $6,000. The straight-line method is used for book purposes. For tax purposes the truck, having an MACRS class life of 7 years, is classified as 5-year property; the MACRS tax rate tables are used to compute depreciation. In addition, assume that for 2012 and 2013 the company has revenues of $200,000 and operating expenses (excluding depreciation) of $130,000.

Instructions

(a) Prepare income statements for 2012 and 2013. (The final amount reported on the income statement should be income before income taxes.)
(b) Compute taxable income for 2012 and 2013.
(c) Determine the total depreciation to be taken over the useful life of the delivery truck for both book and tax purposes.
(d) Explain why depreciation for book and tax purposes will generally be different over the useful life of a depreciable asset.

8 ***E11-26 (Book vs. Tax (MACRS) Depreciation)** Elwood Inc. purchased computer equipment on March 1, 2012, for $36,000. The computer equipment has a useful life of 10 years and a salvage value of $3,000. For tax purposes, the MACRS class life is 5 years.

Instructions

(a) Assuming that the company uses the straight-line method for book and tax purposes, what is the depreciation expense reported in (1) the financial statements for 2012 and (2) the tax return for 2012?
(b) Assuming that the company uses the double-declining-balance method for both book and tax purposes, what is the depreciation expense reported in (1) the financial statements for 2012 and (2) the tax return for 2012?
(c) Why is depreciation for tax purposes different from depreciation for book purposes even if the company uses the same depreciation method to compute them both?

See the book's companion website, www.wiley.com/college/kieso, for a set of B Exercises.

PROBLEMS

P11-1 (Depreciation for Partial Period—SL, SYD, and DDB) Alladin Company purchased Machine #201 on May 1, 2012. The following information relating to Machine #201 was gathered at the end of May.

Price	$85,000
Credit terms	2/10, n/30
Freight-in costs	$ 800
Preparation and installation costs	$ 3,800
Labor costs during regular production operations	$10,500

It was expected that the machine could be used for 10 years, after which the salvage value would be zero. Alladin intends to use the machine for only 8 years, however, after which it expects to be able to sell it for $1,500. The invoice for Machine #201 was paid May 5, 2012. Alladin uses the calendar year as the basis for the preparation of financial statements.

Instructions

(a) Compute the depreciation expense for the years indicated using the following methods. (Round to the nearest dollar.)
  (1) Straight-line method for 2012.
  (2) Sum-of-the-years'-digits method for 2013.
  (3) Double-declining-balance method for 2012.

(b) Suppose Kate Crow, the president of Alladin, tells you that because the company is a new organization, she expects it will be several years before production and sales reach optimum levels. She asks you to recommend a depreciation method that will allocate less of the company's depreciation expense to the early years and more to later years of the assets' lives. What method would you recommend?

2 3 **P11-2 (Depreciation for Partial Periods—SL, Act., SYD, and DDB)** The cost of equipment purchased by Charleston, Inc., on June 1, 2012, is $89,000. It is estimated that the machine will have a $5,000 salvage value at the end of its service life. Its service life is estimated at 7 years; its total working hours are estimated at 42,000; and its total production is estimated at 525,000 units. During 2012, the machine was operated 6,000 hours and produced 55,000 units. During 2013, the machine was operated 5,500 hours and produced 48,000 units.

Instructions

Compute depreciation expense on the machine for the year ending December 31, 2012, and the year ending December 31, 2013, using the following methods.

(a) Straight-line.
(b) Units-of-output.
(c) Working hours.
(d) Sum-of-the-years'-digits.
(e) Declining-balance (twice the straight-line rate).

2 3 **P11-3 (Depreciation—SYD, Act., SL, and DDB)** The following data relate to the Machinery account of Eshkol, Inc. at December 31, 2012.

Machinery

	A	B	C	D
Original cost	$46,000	$51,000	$80,000	$80,000
Year purchased	2007	2008	2009	2011
Useful life	10 years	15,000 hours	15 years	10 years
Salvage value	$ 3,100	$ 3,000	$ 5,000	$ 5,000
Depreciation method	Sum-of-the-years'-digits	Activity	Straight-line	Double-declining-balance
Accum. depr. through 2012*	$31,200	$35,200	$15,000	$16,000

*In the year an asset is purchased, Eshkol, Inc. does not record any depreciation expense on the asset. In the year an asset is retired or traded in, Eshkol, Inc. takes a full year's depreciation on the asset.

The following transactions occurred during 2013.

(a) On May 5, Machine A was sold for $13,000 cash. The company's bookkeeper recorded this retirement in the following manner in the cash receipts journal.

Cash	13,000	
Machinery (Machine A)		13,000

(b) On December 31, it was determined that Machine B had been used 2,100 hours during 2013.

(c) On December 31, before computing depreciation expense on Machine C, the management of Eshkol, Inc. decided the useful life remaining from January 1, 2013, was 10 years.

(d) On December 31, it was discovered that a machine purchased in 2012 had been expensed completely in that year. This machine cost $28,000 and has a useful life of 10 years and no salvage value. Management has decided to use the double-declining-balance method for this machine, which can be referred to as "Machine E."

Instructions

Prepare the necessary correcting entries for the year 2013. Record the appropriate depreciation expense on the above-mentioned machines.

2 3 **P11-4 (Depreciation and Error Analysis)** A depreciation schedule for semi-trucks of Ichiro Manufacturing Company was requested by your auditor soon after December 31, 2013, showing the additions, retirements,

depreciation, and other data affecting the income of the company in the 4-year period 2010 to 2013, inclusive. The following data were ascertained.

Balance of Trucks account, Jan. 1, 2010	
Truck No. 1 purchased Jan. 1, 2007, cost	$18,000
Truck No. 2 purchased July 1, 2007, cost	22,000
Truck No. 3 purchased Jan. 1, 2009, cost	30,000
Truck No. 4 purchased July 1, 2009, cost	24,000
Balance, Jan. 1, 2010	$94,000

The Accumulated Depreciation—Trucks account previously adjusted to January 1, 2010, and entered in the ledger, had a balance on that date of $30,200 (depreciation on the four trucks from the respective dates of purchase, based on a 5-year life, no salvage value). No charges had been made against the account before January 1, 2010.

Transactions between January 1, 2010, and December 31, 2013, which were recorded in the ledger, are as follows.

July 1, 2010	Truck No. 3 was traded for a larger one (No. 5), the agreed purchase price of which was $40,000. Ichiro Mfg. Co. paid the automobile dealer $22,000 cash on the transaction. The entry was a debit to Trucks and a credit to Cash, $22,000. The transaction has commercial substance.
Jan. 1, 2011	Truck No. 1 was sold for $3,500 cash; entry debited Cash and credited Trucks, $3,500.
July 1, 2012	A new truck (No. 6) was acquired for $42,000 cash and was charged at that amount to the Trucks account. (Assume truck No. 2 was not retired.)
July 1, 2012	Truck No. 4 was damaged in a wreck to such an extent that it was sold as junk for $700 cash. Ichiro Mfg. Co. received $2,500 from the insurance company. The entry made by the bookkeeper was a debit to Cash, $3,200, and credits to Miscellaneous Income, $700, and Trucks, $2,500.

Entries for depreciation had been made at the close of each year as follows: 2010, $21,000; 2011, $22,500; 2012, $25,050; 2013, $30,400.

Instructions

(a) For each of the 4 years, compute separately the increase or decrease in net income arising from the company's errors in determining or entering depreciation or in recording transactions affecting trucks, ignoring income tax considerations.

(b) Prepare one compound journal entry as of December 31, 2013, for adjustment of the Trucks account to reflect the correct balances as revealed by your schedule, assuming that the books have not been closed for 2013.

3 6 **P11-5 (Depletion and Depreciation—Mining)** Khamsah Mining Company has purchased a tract of mineral land for $900,000. It is estimated that this tract will yield 120,000 tons of ore with sufficient mineral content to make mining and processing profitable. It is further estimated that 6,000 tons of ore will be mined the first and last year and 12,000 tons every year in between. (Assume 11 years of mining operations.) The land will have a residual value of $30,000.

The company builds necessary structures and sheds on the site at a cost of $36,000. It is estimated that these structures can serve 15 years but, because they must be dismantled if they are to be moved, they have no salvage value. The company does not intend to use the buildings elsewhere. Mining machinery installed at the mine was purchased secondhand at a cost of $60,000. This machinery cost the former owner $150,000 and was 50% depreciated when purchased. Khamsah Mining estimates that about half of this machinery will still be useful when the present mineral resources have been exhausted but that dismantling and removal costs will just about offset its value at that time. The company does not intend to use the machinery elsewhere. The remaining machinery will last until about one-half the present estimated mineral ore has been removed and will then be worthless. Cost is to be allocated equally between these two classes of machinery.

Instructions

(a) As chief accountant for the company, you are to prepare a schedule showing estimated depletion and depreciation costs for each year of the expected life of the mine.

(b) Also compute the depreciation and depletion for the first year assuming actual production of 5,000 tons. Nothing occurred during the year to cause the company engineers to change their estimates of either the mineral resources or the life of the structures and equipment.

6 **P11-6 (Depletion, Timber, and Extraordinary Loss)** Conan O'Brien Logging and Lumber Company owns 3,000 acres of timberland on the north side of Mount Leno, which was purchased in 2000 at a cost of $550 per acre. In 2012, O'Brien began selectively logging this timber tract. In May of 2012, Mount Leno erupted, burying the timberland of O'Brien under a foot of ash. All of the timber on the O'Brien tract was downed. In addition, the logging roads, built at a cost of $150,000, were destroyed, as well as the logging equipment, with a net book value of $300,000.

At the time of the eruption, O'Brien had logged 20% of the estimated 500,000 board feet of timber. Prior to the eruption, O'Brien estimated the land to have a value of $200 per acre after the timber was harvested. O'Brien includes the logging roads in the depletion base.

O'Brien estimates it will take 3 years to salvage the downed timber at a cost of $700,000. The timber can be sold for pulp wood at an estimated price of $3 per board foot. The value of the land is unknown, but must be considered nominal due to future uncertainties.

Instructions

(a) Determine the depletion cost per board foot for the timber harvested prior to the eruption of Mount Leno.

(b) Prepare the journal entry to record the depletion prior to the eruption.

(c) If this tract represents approximately half of the timber holdings of O'Brien, determine the amount of the extraordinary loss due to the eruption of Mount Leno for the year ended December 31, 2012.

6 **P11-7 (Natural Resources—Timber)** Bronson Paper Products purchased 10,000 acres of forested timberland in March 2012. The company paid $1,700 per acre for this land, which was above the $800 per acre most farmers were paying for cleared land. During April, May, June, and July 2012, Bronson cut enough timber to build roads using moveable equipment purchased on April 1, 2012. The cost of the roads was $250,000, and the cost of the equipment was $225,000; this equipment was expected to have a $9,000 salvage value and would be used for the next 15 years. Bronson selected the straight-line method of depreciation for the moveable equipment. Bronson began actively harvesting timber in August and by December had harvested and sold 540,000 board feet of timber of the estimated 6,750,000 board feet available for cutting.

In March 2013, Bronson planted new seedlings in the area harvested during the winter. Cost of planting these seedlings was $120,000. In addition, Bronson spent $8,000 in road maintenance and $6,000 for pest spraying during calendar-year 2013. The road maintenance and spraying are annual costs. During 2013, Bronson harvested and sold 774,000 board feet of timber of the estimated 6,450,000 board feet available for cutting.

In March 2014, Bronson again planted new seedlings at a cost of $150,000, and also spent $15,000 on road maintenance and pest spraying. During 2014, the company harvested and sold 650,000 board feet of timber of the estimated 6,500,000 board feet available for cutting.

Instructions

Compute the amount of depreciation and depletion expense for each of the 3 years (2012, 2013, 2014). Assume that the roads are usable only for logging and therefore are included in the depletion base.

P11-8 (Comprehensive Fixed-Asset Problem) Darby Sporting Goods Inc. has been experiencing growth in the demand for its products over the last several years. The last two Olympic Games greatly increased the popularity of basketball around the world. As a result, a European sports retailing consortium entered into an agreement with Darby's Roundball Division to purchase basketballs and other accessories on an increasing basis over the next 5 years.

To be able to meet the quantity commitments of this agreement, Darby had to obtain additional manufacturing capacity. A real estate firm located an available factory in close proximity to Darby's Roundball manufacturing facility, and Darby agreed to purchase the factory and used machinery from Encino Athletic Equipment Company on October 1, 2011. Renovations were necessary to convert the factory for Darby's manufacturing use.

The terms of the agreement required Darby to pay Encino $50,000 when renovations started on January 1, 2012, with the balance to be paid as renovations were completed. The overall purchase price for the factory and machinery was $400,000. The building renovations were contracted to Malone Construction at $100,000. The payments made, as renovations progressed during 2012, are shown below. The factory was placed in service on January 1, 2013.

	1/1	4/1	10/1	12/31
Encino	$50,000	$90,000	$110,000	$150,000
Malone		30,000	30,000	40,000

On January 1, 2012, Darby secured a $500,000 line-of-credit with a 12% interest rate to finance the purchase cost of the factory and machinery, and the renovation costs. Darby drew down on the line-of-credit to meet the payment schedule shown above; this was Darby's only outstanding loan during 2012.

Bob Sprague, Darby's controller, will capitalize the maximum allowable interest costs for this project. Darby's policy regarding purchases of this nature is to use the appraisal value of the land for book purposes and prorate the balance of the purchase price over the remaining items. The building had originally cost Encino $300,000 and had a net book value of $50,000, while the machinery originally cost $125,000 and had a net book value of $40,000 on the date of sale. The land was recorded on Encino's books at $40,000. An appraisal, conducted by independent appraisers at the time of acquisition, valued the land at $290,000, the building at $105,000, and the machinery at $45,000.

Angie Justice, chief engineer, estimated that the renovated plant would be used for 15 years, with an estimated salvage value of $30,000. Justice estimated that the productive machinery would have a remaining useful life of 5 years and a salvage value of $3,000. Darby's depreciation policy specifies the 200% declining-balance method for machinery and the 150% declining-balance method for the plant. One-half year's depreciation is taken in the year the plant is placed in service and one-half year is allowed when the property is disposed of or retired. Darby uses a 360-day year for calculating interest costs.

Instructions

(a) Determine the amounts to be recorded on the books of Darby Sporting Goods Inc. as of December 31, 2012, for each of the following properties acquired from Encino Athletic Equipment Company.
(1) Land. **(2)** Buildings. **(3)** Machinery.

(b) Calculate Darby Sporting Goods Inc.'s 2013 depreciation expense, for book purposes, for each of the properties acquired from Encino Athletic Equipment Company.

(c) Discuss the arguments for and against the capitalization of interest costs.

(CMA adapted)

5 **P11-9 (Impairment)** Roland Company uses special strapping equipment in its packaging business. The equipment was purchased in January 2011 for $10,000,000 and had an estimated useful life of 8 years with no salvage value. At December 31, 2012, new technology was introduced that would accelerate the obsolescence of Roland's equipment. Roland's controller estimates that expected future net cash flows on the equipment will be $6,300,000 and that the fair value of the equipment is $5,600,000. Roland intends to continue using the equipment, but it is estimated that the remaining useful life is 4 years. Roland uses straight-line depreciation.

Instructions

(a) Prepare the journal entry (if any) to record the impairment at December 31, 2012.

(b) Prepare any journal entries for the equipment at December 31, 2013. The fair value of the equipment at December 31, 2013, is estimated to be $5,900,000.

(c) Repeat the requirements for (a) and (b), assuming that Roland intends to dispose of the equipment and that it has not been disposed of as of December 31, 2013.

2 3 **P11-10 (Comprehensive Depreciation Computations)** Kohlbeck Corporation, a manufacturer of steel products, began operations on October 1, 2011. The accounting department of Kohlbeck has started the fixed-asset and depreciation schedule presented on page 647. You have been asked to assist in completing this schedule. In addition to ascertaining that the data already on the schedule are correct, you have obtained the following information from the company's records and personnel.

1. Depreciation is computed from the first of the month of acquisition to the first of the month of disposition.
2. Land A and Building A were acquired from a predecessor corporation. Kohlbeck paid $800,000 for the land and building together. At the time of acquisition, the land had an appraised value of $90,000, and the building had an appraised value of $810,000.
3. Land B was acquired on October 2, 2011, in exchange for 2,500 newly issued shares of Kohlbeck's common stock. At the date of acquisition, the stock had a par value of $5 per share and a fair value of $30 per share. During October 2011, Kohlbeck paid $16,000 to demolish an existing building on this land so it could construct a new building.
4. Construction of Building B on the newly acquired land began on October 1, 2012. By September 30, 2013, Kohlbeck had paid $320,000 of the estimated total construction costs of $450,000. It is estimated that the building will be completed and occupied by July 2014.
5. Certain equipment was donated to the corporation by a local university. An independent appraisal of the equipment when donated placed the fair value at $40,000 and the salvage value at $3,000.
6. Machinery A's total cost of $182,900 includes installation expense of $600 and normal repairs and maintenance of $14,900. Salvage value is estimated at $6,000. Machinery A was sold on February 1, 2013.
7. On October 1, 2012, Machinery B was acquired with a down payment of $5,740 and the remaining payments to be made in 11 annual installments of $6,000 each beginning October 1, 2012. The prevailing interest rate was 8%. The following data were abstracted from present value tables (rounded).

Present value of $1.00 at 8%		Present value of an ordinary annuity of $1.00 at 8%	
10 years	.463	10 years	6.710
11 years	.429	11 years	7.139
15 years	.315	15 years	8.559

KOHLBECK CORPORATION
Fixed-Asset and Depreciation Schedule
For Fiscal Years Ended September 30, 2012, and September 30, 2013

Assets	Acquisition Date	Cost	Salvage	Depreciation Method	Estimated Life in Years	Depreciation Expense Year Ended September 30 2012	2013
Land A	October 1, 2011	$ (1)	N/A	N/A	N/A	N/A	N/A
Building A	October 1, 2011	(2)	$40,000	Straight-line	(3)	$13,600	(4)
Land B	October 2, 2011	(5)	N/A	N/A	N/A	N/A	N/A
Building B	Under Construction	$320,000 to date	—	Straight-line	30	—	(6)
Donated Equipment	October 2, 2011	(7)	3,000	150% declining-balance	10	(8)	(9)
Machinery A	October 2, 2011	(10)	6,000	Sum-of-the-years'-digits	8	(11)	(12)
Machinery B	October 1, 2012	(13)	—	Straight-line	20	—	(14)

N/A—Not applicable

Instructions

For each numbered item on the schedule above, supply the correct amount. Round each answer to the nearest dollar.

P11-11 (Depreciation for Partial Periods—SL, Act., SYD, and DDB) On January 1, 2010, a machine was purchased for $90,000. The machine has an estimated salvage value of $6,000 and an estimated useful life of 5 years. The machine can operate for 100,000 hours before it needs to be replaced. The company closed its books on December 31 and operates the machine as follows: 2010, 20,000 hrs; 2011, 25,000 hrs; 2012, 15,000 hrs; 2013, 30,000 hrs; 2014, 10,000 hrs.

Instructions

(a) Compute the annual depreciation charges over the machine's life assuming a December 31 year-end for each of the following depreciation methods.
- **(1)** Straight-line method.
- **(2)** Activity method.
- **(3)** Sum-of-the-years'-digits method.
- **(4)** Double-declining-balance method.

(b) Assume a fiscal year-end of September 30. Compute the annual depreciation charges over the asset's life applying each of the following methods.
- **(1)** Straight-line method.
- **(2)** Sum-of-the-years'-digits method.
- **(3)** Double-declining-balance method.

***P11-12 (Depreciation—SL, DDB, SYD, Act., and MACRS)** On January 1, 2011, Locke Company, a small machine-tool manufacturer, acquired for $1,260,000 a piece of new industrial equipment. The new equipment had a useful life of 5 years, and the salvage value was estimated to be $60,000. Locke estimates that the new equipment can produce 12,000 machine tools in its first year. It estimates that production will decline by 1,000 units per year over the remaining useful life of the equipment.

The following depreciation methods may be used: (1) straight-line; (2) double-declining-balance; (3) sum-of-the-years'-digits; and (4) units-of-output. For tax purposes, the class life is 7 years. Use the MACRS tables for computing depreciation.

Instructions

(a) Which depreciation method would maximize net income for financial statement reporting for the 3-year period ending December 31, 2013? Prepare a schedule showing the amount of accumulated depreciation at December 31, 2013, under the method selected. Ignore present value, income tax, and deferred income tax considerations.

(b) Which depreciation method (MACRS or optional straight-line) would minimize net income for income tax reporting for the 3-year period ending December 31, 2013? Determine the amount of accumulated depreciation at December 31, 2013. Ignore present value considerations.

(AICPA adapted)

CONCEPTS FOR ANALYSIS

CA11-1 (Depreciation Basic Concepts) Burnitz Manufacturing Company was organized January 1, 2012. During 2012, it has used in its reports to management the straight-line method of depreciating its plant assets.

On November 8, you are having a conference with Burnitz's officers to discuss the depreciation method to be used for income tax and stockholder reporting. James Bryant, president of Burnitz, has suggested the use of a new method, which he feels is more suitable than the straight-line method for the needs of the company during the period of rapid expansion of production and capacity that he foresees. Following is an example in which the proposed method is applied to a fixed asset with an original cost of $248,000, an estimated useful life of 5 years, and a salvage value of approximately $8,000.

Year	Years of Life Used	Fraction Rate	Depreciation Expense	Accumulated Depreciation at End of Year	Book Value at End of Year
1	1	1/15	$16,000	$ 16,000	$232,000
2	2	2/15	32,000	48,000	200,000
3	3	3/15	48,000	96,000	152,000
4	4	4/15	64,000	160,000	88,000
5	5	5/15	80,000	240,000	8,000

The president favors the new method because he has heard that:

1. It will increase the funds recovered during the years near the end of the assets' useful lives when maintenance and replacement disbursements are high.
2. It will result in increased write-offs in later years and thereby will reduce taxes.

Instructions

(a) What is the purpose of accounting for depreciation?

(b) Is the president's proposal within the scope of generally accepted accounting principles? In making your decision discuss the circumstances, if any, under which use of the method would be reasonable and those, if any, under which it would not be reasonable.

(c) The president wants your advice on the following issues.

- **(1)** Do depreciation charges recover or create funds? Explain.
- **(2)** Assume that the Internal Revenue Service accepts the proposed depreciation method in this case. If the proposed method were used for stockholder and tax reporting purposes, how would it affect the availability of cash flows generated by operations?

CA11-2 (Unit, Group, and Composite Depreciation) The certified public accountant is frequently called upon by management for advice regarding methods of computing depreciation. Of comparable importance, although it arises less frequently, is the question of whether the depreciation method should be based on consideration of the assets as units, as a group, or as having a composite life.

Instructions

(a) Briefly describe the depreciation methods based on treating assets as (1) units and (2) a group or as having a composite life.

(b) Present the arguments for and against the use of each of the two methods.

(c) Describe how retirements are recorded under each of the two methods.

(AICPA adapted)

CA11-3 (Depreciation—Strike, Units-of-Production, Obsolescence) Presented below and on page 649 are three different and unrelated situations involving depreciation accounting. Answer the question(s) at the end of each situation.

Situation I

Recently, Broderick Company experienced a strike that affected a number of its operating plants. The controller of this company indicated that it was not appropriate to report depreciation expense during this period because the equipment did not depreciate and an improper matching of costs and revenues would result. She based her position on the following points.

1. It is inappropriate to charge the period with costs for which there are no related revenues arising from production.
2. The basic factor of depreciation in this instance is wear and tear, and because equipment was idle, no wear and tear occurred.

Instructions
Comment on the appropriateness of the controller's comments.

Situation II
Etheridge Company manufactures electrical appliances, most of which are used in homes. Company engineers have designed a new type of blender which, through the use of a few attachments, will perform more functions than any blender currently on the market. Demand for the new blender can be projected with reasonable probability. In order to make the blenders, Etheridge needs a specialized machine that is not available from outside sources. It has been decided to make such a machine in Etheridge's own plant.

Instructions

(a) Discuss the effect of projected demand in units for the new blenders (which may be steady, decreasing, or increasing) on the determination of a depreciation method for the machine.

(b) What other matters should be considered in determining the depreciation method? Ignore income tax considerations.

Situation III
Haley Paper Company operates a 300-ton-per-day kraft pulp mill and four sawmills in Wisconsin. The company is in the process of expanding its pulp mill facilities to a capacity of 1,000 tons per day and plans to replace three of its older, less efficient sawmills with an expanded facility. One of the mills to be replaced did not operate for most of 2012 (current year), and there are no plans to reopen it before the new sawmill facility becomes operational.

In reviewing the depreciation rates and in discussing the residual values of the sawmills that were to be replaced, it was noted that if present depreciation rates were not adjusted, substantial amounts of plant costs on these three mills would not be depreciated by the time the new mill came on stream.

Instructions
What is the proper accounting for the four sawmills at the end of 2012?

CA11-4 (Depreciation Concepts) As a cost accountant for San Francisco Cannery, you have been approached by Phil Perriman, canning room supervisor, about the 2012 costs charged to his department. In particular, he is concerned about the line item "depreciation." Perriman is very proud of the excellent condition of his canning room equipment. He has always been vigilant about keeping all equipment serviced and well oiled. He is sure that the huge charge to depreciation is a mistake; it does not at all reflect the cost of minimal wear and tear that the machines have experienced over the last year. He believes that the charge should be considerably lower.

The machines being depreciated are six automatic canning machines. All were put into use on January 1, 2012. Each cost $625,000, having a salvage value of $55,000 and a useful life of 12 years. San Francisco depreciates this and similar assets using double-declining-balance depreciation. Perriman has also pointed out that if you used straight-line depreciation the charge to his department would not be so great.

Instructions
Write a memo to Phil Perriman to clear up his misunderstanding of the term "depreciation." Also, calculate year-1 depreciation on all machines using both methods. Explain the theoretical justification for double-declining-balance and why, in the long run, the aggregate charge to depreciation will be the same under both methods.

CA11-5 (Depreciation Choice—Ethics) Jerry Prior, Beeler Corporation's controller, is concerned that net income may be lower this year. He is afraid upper-level management might recommend cost reductions by laying off accounting staff, including him.

Prior knows that depreciation is a major expense for Beeler. The company currently uses the double-declining-balance method for both financial reporting and tax purposes, and he's thinking of selling equipment that, given its age, is primarily used when there are periodic spikes in demand. The equipment has a carrying value of $2,000,000 and a fair value of $2,180,000. The gain on the sale would be reported in the income statement. He doesn't want to highlight this method of increasing income. He thinks, "Why don't I increase the estimated useful lives and the salvage values? That will decrease depreciation expense and require less extensive disclosure, since the changes are accounted for prospectively. I may be able to save my job and those of my staff."

Instructions
Answer the following questions.

(a) Who are the stakeholders in this situation?

(b) What are the ethical issues involved?

(c) What should Prior do?

USING YOUR JUDGMENT

FINANCIAL REPORTING

Financial Reporting Problem

P&G **The Procter & Gamble Company (P&G)**

The financial statements of P&G are presented in Appendix 5B or can be accessed at the book's companion website, **www.wiley.com/college/kieso**.

Instructions

Refer to P&G's financial statements and the accompanying notes to answer the following questions.

(a) What descriptions are used by P&G in its balance sheet to classify its property, plant, and equipment?

(b) What method or methods of depreciation does P&G use to depreciate its property, plant, and equipment?

(c) Over what estimated useful lives does P&G depreciate its property, plant, and equipment?

(d) What amounts for depreciation and amortization expense did P&G charge to its income statement in 2009, 2008, and 2007?

(e) What were the capital expenditures for property, plant, and equipment made by P&G in 2009, 2008, and 2007?

Comparative Analysis Case

The Coca-Cola Company and PepsiCo., Inc.

Instructions

Go to the book's companion website and use information found there to answer the following questions related to The Coca-Cola Company and PepsiCo, Inc.

(a) What amount is reported in the balance sheets as property, plant, and equipment (net) of Coca-Cola at December 31, 2009, and of PepsiCo at December 26, 2009? What percentage of total assets is invested in property, plant, and equipment by each company?

(b) What depreciation methods are used by Coca-Cola and PepsiCo for property, plant, and equipment? How much depreciation was reported by Coca-Cola and PepsiCo in 2009, 2008, and 2007?

(c) Compute and compare the following ratios for Coca-Cola and PepsiCo for 2009.

(1) Asset turnover.

(2) Profit margin on sales.

(3) Rate of return on assets.

(d) What amount was spent in 2009 for capital expenditures by Coca-Cola and PepsiCo? What amount of interest was capitalized in 2009?

Financial Statement Analysis Case

McDonald's Corporation

McDonald's is the largest and best-known global food service retailer, with more than 32,000 restaurants in 118 countries. On any day, McDonald's serves approximately 1 percent of the world's population. Presented on the next page is information related to McDonald's property and equipment.

McDonald's Corporation
Summary of Significant Accounting Policies Section

Property and Equipment. Property and equipment are stated at cost, with depreciation and amortization provided using the straight-line method over the following estimated useful lives: buildings—up to 40 years; leasehold improvements—lesser of useful lives of assets or lease terms including option periods; and equipment—3 to 12 years.

[In the notes to the financial statements:]

Property and Equipment
Net property and equipment consisted of:

(In millions)	December 31 2009	2008
Land	$ 5,048.3	$ 4,689.6
Buildings and improvements on owned land	12,119.0	10,952.3
Buildings and improvements on leased land	11,347.9	10,788.6
Equipment, signs and seating	4,422.9	4,205.1
Other	502.4	516.8
	33,440.5	31,152.4
Accumulated depreciation and amortization	(11,909.0)	(10,897.9)
Net property and equipment	$ 21,531.5	$ 20,254.5

Depreciation and amortization expense related to continuing operations was (in millions): 2009—$1,160.8; 2008—$1,161.6; 2007—$1,145.0.

[In its 6-year summary, McDonald's provides the following information.]

Cash Provided by Operations

(dollars in millions)	2009	2008	2007
Cash provided by operations	$5,751	$5,917	$4,876
Capital expenditures	$1,952	$2,136	$1,947
Cash provided by operations as a percent of capital expenditures	295%	277%	250%

Instructions

(a) What method of depreciation does McDonald's use?

(b) Does depreciation and amortization expense cause cash flow from operations to increase? Explain.

(c) What does the schedule of cash flow measures indicate?

Accounting, Analysis, and Principles

Electroboy Enterprises, Inc. operates several stores throughout the western United States. As part of an operational and financial reporting review in a response to a downturn in its markets, the company's management has decided to perform an impairment test on five stores (combined). The five stores' sales have declined due to aging facilities and competition from a rival that opened new stores in the same markets. Management has developed the following information concerning the five stores as of the end of fiscal 2011.

Original cost	$36 million
Accumulated depreciation	$10 million
Estimated remaining useful life	4 years
Estimated expected future annual cash flows (not discounted)	$4.0 million per year
Appropriate discount rate	5 percent

Accounting

(a) Determine the amount of impairment loss, if any, that Electroboy should report for fiscal 2011 and the book value at which Electroboy should report the five stores on its fiscal year-end 2011 balance sheet. Assume that the cash flows occur at the end of each year.

(b) Repeat part (a), but instead, assume that (1) the estimated remaining useful life is 10 years, (2) the estimated annual cash flows are $2,720,000 per year, and (3) the appropriate discount rate is 6 percent.

Analysis

Assume that you are a financial analyst and you participate in a conference call with Electroboy management in early 2012 (before Electroboy closes the books on fiscal 2011). During the conference call, you learn that management is considering selling the five stores, but the sale won't likely be completed until the second quarter of fiscal 2012. Briefly discuss what implications this would have for Electroboy's 2011 financial statements. Assume the same facts as in part (b) above.

Principles

Electroboy management would like to know the accounting for the impaired asset in periods subsequent to the impairment. Can the assets be written back up? Briefly discuss the conceptual arguments for this accounting.

BRIDGE TO THE PROFESSION

Professional Research: FASB Codification

Matt Holmes recently joined Klax Company as a staff accountant in the controller's office. Klax Company provides warehousing services for companies in several midwestern cities.

The location in Dubuque, Iowa, has not been performing well due to increased competition and the loss of several customers that have recently gone out of business. Matt's department manager suspects that the plant and equipment may be impaired and wonders whether those assets should be written down. Given the company's prior success, this issue has never arisen in the past, and Matt has been asked to conduct some research on this issue.

Instructions

If your school has a subscription to the FASB Codification, go to *http://aaahq.org/asclogin.cfm* to log in and prepare responses to the following. Provide Codification references for your responses.

(a) What is the authoritative guidance for asset impairments? Briefly discuss the scope of the standard (i.e., explain the types of transactions to which the standard applies).

(b) Give several examples of events that would cause an asset to be tested for impairment. Does it appear that Klax should perform an impairment test? Explain.

(c) What is the best evidence of fair value? Describe alternate methods of estimating fair value.

Professional Simulation

In this simulation, you are asked to address questions regarding the accounting for property, plant, and equipment. Prepare responses to all parts.

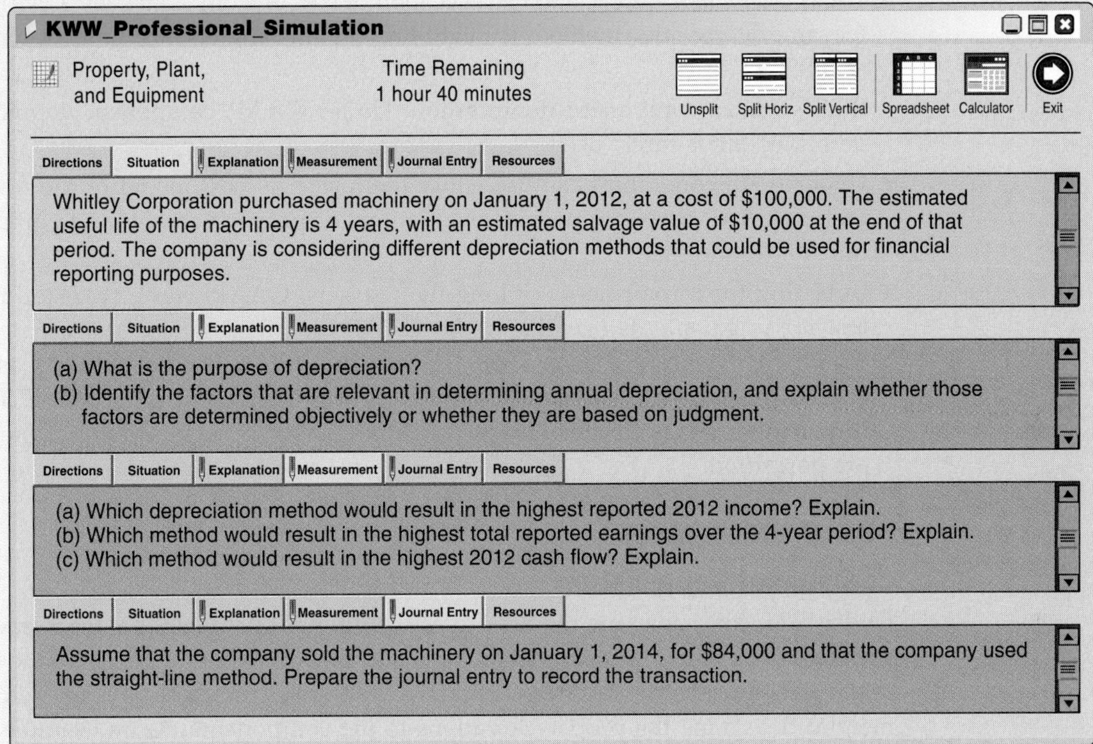

GAAP adheres to many of the same principles of IFRS in the accounting for property, plant, and equipment. Major differences relate to use of component depreciation, impairments, and revaluations.

RELEVANT FACTS

- The definition of property, plant, and equipment is essentially the same under GAAP and IFRS.
- Under both GAAP and IFRS, changes in depreciation method and changes in useful life are treated in the current and future periods. Prior periods are not affected. GAAP recently conformed to IFRS in this area.
- The accounting for plant asset disposals is the same under GAAP and IFRS.
- The accounting for the initial costs to acquire natural resources is similar under GAAP and IFRS.
- Under both GAAP and IFRS, interest costs incurred during construction must be capitalized. Recently, IFRS converged to GAAP.

- The accounting for exchanges of nonmonetary assets has recently converged between IFRS and GAAP. GAAP now requires that gains on exchanges of nonmonetary assets be recognized if the exchange has commercial substance. This is the same framework used in IFRS.
- GAAP also views depreciation as allocation of cost over an asset's life. GAAP permits the same depreciation methods (straight-line, diminishing-balance, units-of-production) as IFRS.
- IFRS requires component depreciation. Under GAAP, component depreciation is permitted but is rarely used.
- Under IFRS, companies can use either the historical cost model or the revaluation model. GAAP does not permit revaluations of property, plant, and equipment or mineral resources.
- In testing for impairments of long-lived assets, GAAP uses a two-step model to test for impairments (details of the GAAP impairment test is presented in the *About the Numbers* discussion). As long as future undiscounted cash flows exceed the carrying amount of the asset, no impairment is recorded. The IFRS impairment test is stricter. However, unlike GAAP, reversals of impairment losses are permitted.

ABOUT THE NUMBERS

Component Depreciation

Under IFRS, companies are required to use **component depreciation**. IFRS requires that each part of an item of property, plant, and equipment that is significant to the total cost of the asset must be depreciated separately. Companies therefore have to exercise judgment to determine the proper allocations to the components. As an example, when a company like **Nokia** purchases a building, it must determine how the various building components (e.g., the foundation, structure, roof, heating and cooling system, and elevators) should be segregated and depreciated.

To illustrate the accounting for component depreciation, assume that EuroAsia Airlines purchases an airplane for $100,000,000 on January 1, 2012. The airplane has a useful life of 20 years and a residual value of $0. EuroAsia uses the straight-line method of depreciation for all its airplanes. EuroAsia identifies the following components, amounts, and useful lives, as shown in Illustration IFRS11-1.

ILLUSTRATION IFRS11-1
Airplane Components

Components	Component Amount	Component Useful Life
Airframe	$60,000,000	20 years
Engine components	32,000,000	8 years
Other components	8,000,000	5 years

Illustration IFRS11-2 shows the computation of depreciation expense for EuroAsia for 2012.

ILLUSTRATION IFRS11-2
Computation of Component Depreciation

Components	Component Amount	÷	Useful Life	=	Component Depreciation
Airframe	$ 60,000,000		20		$3,000,000
Engine components	32,000,000		8		4,000,000
Other components	8,000,000		5		1,600,000
Total	$100,000,000				$8,600,000

As indicated, EuroAsia records depreciation expense of $8,600,000 in 2012 as follows.

Depreciation Expense	8,600,000	
Accumulated Depreciation—Airplane		8,600,000

On the statement of financial position at the end of 2012, EuroAsia reports the airplane as a single amount. The presentation is shown in Illustration IFRS11-3.

Non-current assets	
Airplane	$100,000,000
Less: Accumulated depreciation—airplane	8,600,000
	$ 91,400,000

ILLUSTRATION IFRS11-3
Presentation of Carrying Amount of Airplane

In many situations, a company may not have a good understanding of the cost of the individual components purchased. In that case, the cost of individual components should be estimated based on reference to current market prices (if available), discussion with experts in valuation, or use of other reasonable approaches.

Recognizing Impairments

As discussed in the text, the credit crisis starting in late 2008 has affected many financial and nonfinancial institutions. As a result of this global slump, many companies are considering write-offs of some of their long-lived assets. These write-offs are referred to as **impairments**. The accounting for impairments is different under GAAP and IFRS.

A long-lived tangible asset is impaired when a company is not able to recover the asset's carrying amount either through using it or by selling it. To determine whether an asset is impaired, **on an annual basis, companies review the asset for indicators of impairments**—that is, a decline in the asset's cash-generating ability through use or sale. This review should consider internal sources (e.g., adverse changes in performance) and external sources (e.g., adverse changes in the business or regulatory environment) of information. **If impairment indicators are present, then an impairment test must be conducted.** This test compares the asset's recoverable amount with its carrying amount. If the carrying amount is higher than the recoverable amount, the difference is an impairment loss. If the recoverable amount is greater than the carrying amount, no impairment is recorded.

Recoverable amount is defined as the higher of fair value less costs to sell or value-in-use. **Fair value less costs to sell** means what the asset could be sold for after deducting costs of disposal. **Value-in-use** is the present value of cash flows expected from the future use and eventual sale of the asset at the end of its useful life. Illustration IFRS11-4 highlights the nature of the impairment test.

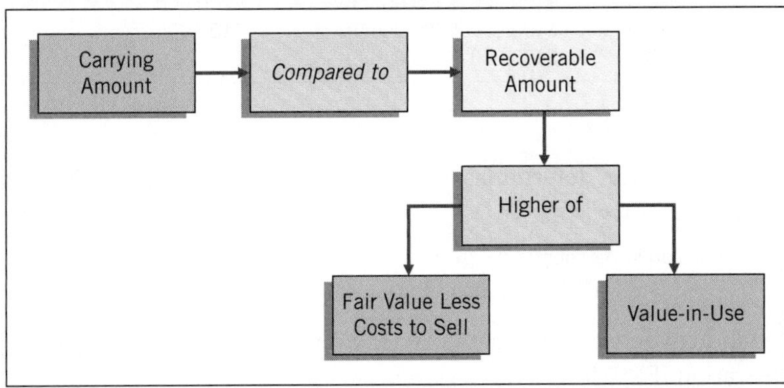

ILLUSTRATION IFRS11-4
Impairment Test

If either the fair value less costs to sell or value-in-use is higher than the carrying amount, there is no impairment. If both the fair value less costs to sell and value-in-use are lower than the carrying amount, a loss on impairment occurs.

Example: No Impairment

Assume that Cruz Company performs an impairment test for its equipment. The carrying amount of Cruz's equipment is $200,000, its fair value less costs to sell is $180,000, and its value-in-use is $205,000. In this case, the value-in-use of Cruz's equipment is higher than its carrying amount of $200,000. As a result, there is no impairment. (If a company can more readily determine value-in-use (or fair value less costs to sell) and it determines that no impairment is needed, it is not required to compute the other measure.)

Example: Impairment

Assume the same information for Cruz Company above except that the value-in-use of Cruz's equipment is $175,000 rather than $205,000. Cruz measures the impairment loss as the difference between the carrying amount of $200,000 and the higher of fair value less cost to sell ($180,000) or value-in-use ($175,000). Cruz therefore uses the fair value less cost of disposal to record an impairment loss of $20,000 ($200,000 − $180,000). Cruz makes the following entry to record the impairment loss.

Loss on Impairment	20,000	
Accumulated Depreciation—Equipment		20,000

The Loss on Impairment is reported in the income statement in the "Other income and expense" section. The company then either credits Equipment or Accumulated Depreciation—Equipment to reduce the carrying amount of the equipment for the impairment. *For purposes of homework, credit accumulated depreciation when recording an impairment for a depreciable asset.*

Reversal of Impairment Loss

After recording the impairment loss, the recoverable amount becomes the basis of the impaired asset. What happens if a review in a future year indicates that the asset is no longer impaired because the recoverable amount of the asset is higher than the carrying amount? In that case, the impairment loss may be reversed.

To illustrate, assume that Tan Company purchases equipment on January 1, 2012, for $300,000, with a useful life of three years, and no residual value. Its depreciation and related carrying amount over the three years is as follows.

Year	Depreciation Expense	Carrying Amount
2012	$100,000 ($300,000/3)	$200,000
2013	$100,000 ($300,000/3)	$100,000
2014	$100,000 ($300,000/3)	0

At December 31, 2012, Tan determines it has an impairment loss of $20,000 and therefore makes the following entry.

Loss on Impairment	20,000	
Accumulated Depreciation—Equipment		20,000

Tan's depreciation expense and related carrying amount after the impairment is as indicated in Illustration IFRS11-5.

ILLUSTRATION IFRS11-5
Carrying Value of Impaired Asset

Year	Depreciation Expense	Carrying Amount
2013	$90,000 ($180,000/2)	$90,000
2014	$90,000 ($180,000/2)	0

At the end of 2013, Tan determines that the recoverable amount of the equipment is $96,000, which is greater than its carrying amount of $90,000. In this case, Tan reverses the previously recognized impairment loss with the following entry.

Accumulated Depreciation—Equipment	6,000	
Recovery of Impairment Loss		6,000

The recovery of the impairment loss is reported in the "Other income and expense" section of the income statement. The carrying amount of Tan's equipment is now $96,000 ($90,000 + $6,000) at December 31, 2013. The general rule related to reversals of impairments is as follows: The amount of the recovery of the loss is limited to the carrying amount that would result if the impairment had not occurred. For example, the carrying amount of Tan's equipment at the end of 2013 would be $100,000, assuming no impairment. The $6,000 recovery is therefore permitted because Tan's carrying amount on the equipment is now only $96,000.

However, any recovery above $10,000 is not permitted. The reason is that any recovery above $10,000 results in Tan carrying the asset at a value above its historical cost.

Revaluations

Up to this point, we have assumed that companies use the cost principle to value long-lived tangible assets after acquisition. However, under IFRS companies have a choice: They may value these assets at cost or at fair value.

Recognizing Revaluations

Network Rail (a company in Great Britain) is an example of a company that elected to use fair values to account for its railroad network. Its use of fair value led to an increase of £4,289 million to its long-lived tangible assets. When companies choose to fair value their long-lived tangible assets subsequent to acquisition, they account for the change in the fair value by adjusting the appropriate asset account and establishing an unrealized gain on the revalued long-lived tangible asset. This unrealized gain is often referred to as **revaluation surplus**.

Revaluation—Land. To illustrate revaluation of land, assume that **Siemens Group** purchased land for $1,000,000 on January 5, 2012. The company elects to use revaluation accounting for the land in subsequent periods. At December 31, 2012, the land's fair value is $1,200,000. The entry to record the land at fair value is as follows.

Land	200,000	
Unrealized Gain on Revaluation—Land		200,000

The land is reported on the statement of financial position at $1,200,000, and the Unrealized Gain on Revaluation—Land increases other comprehensive income in the statement of comprehensive income. In addition, if this is the only revaluation adjustment to date, the statement of financial position reports accumulated other comprehensive income of $200,000.

Revaluation—Depreciable Assets. To illustrate the accounting for revaluations of depreciable assets, assume that **Lenovo Group** purchases equipment for $500,000 on January 2, 2012. The equipment has a useful life of five years, is depreciated using the straight-line method of depreciation, and its residual value is zero. Lenovo chooses to revalue its equipment to fair value over the life of the equipment. Lenovo records depreciation expense of $100,000 ($500,000 ÷ 5) at December 31, 2012, as follows.

December 31, 2012		
Depreciation Expense	100,000	
Accumulated Depreciation—Equipment		100,000
(To record depreciation expense in 2012)		

After this entry, Lenovo's equipment has a carrying amount of $400,000 ($500,000 − $100,000). Lenovo receives an independent appraisal for the fair value of equipment at December 31, 2012, which is $460,000. To report the equipment at fair value, Lenovo does the following.

1. Reduces the Accumulated Depreciation—Equipment account to zero.
2. Reduces the Equipment account by $40,000—it then is reported at its fair value of $460,000.
3. Records Unrealized Gain on Revaluation—Equipment for the difference between the fair value and carrying amount of the equipment, or $60,000 ($460,000 − $400,000).

The entry to record this revaluation at December 31, 2012, is as follows.

December 31, 2012		
Accumulated Depreciation—Equipment	100,000	
Equipment		40,000
Unrealized Gain on Revaluation—Equipment		60,000
(To adjust the equipment to fair value and record revaluation increase)		

The equipment is now reported at its fair value of $460,000 ($500,000 − $40,000). As an alternative to the one shown here, companies restate on a proportionate basis the cost and accumulated depreciation of the asset, such that the carrying amount of the asset after revaluation equals its revalued amount.

The increase in the fair value of $60,000 is reported on the statement of comprehensive income as other comprehensive income. In addition, the ending balance is reported in accumulated other comprehensive income on the statement of financial position in the equity section. Illustration IFRS11-6 shows the presentation of revaluation elements.

ILLUSTRATION IFRS11-6
Financial Statement Presentation—Revaluations

On the statement of comprehensive income:	
Other comprehensive income	
Unrealized gain on revaluation—equipment	$ 60,000
On the statement of financial position:	
Non-current assets	
Equipment ($500,000 − $40,000)	$460,000
Accumulated depreciation—equipment ($100,000 − $100,000)	-0-
Carrying amount	$460,000
Equity	
Accumulated other comprehensive income	$ 60,000

As indicated, at December 31, 2012, the carrying amount of the equipment is now $460,000. Lenovo reports depreciation expense of $100,000 in the income statement and an Unrealized Gain on Revaluation—Equipment of $60,000 in "Other comprehensive income." Assuming no change in the useful life of the equipment, depreciation in 2013 is $115,000 ($460,000 ÷ 4).

In summary, a revaluation increase generally goes to equity. A revaluation decrease is reported as an expense (as an impairment loss), unless it offsets previously recorded revaluation increases. If the revaluation increase offsets a revaluation decrease that went to expense, then the increase is reported in income. **Under no circumstances can the Accumulated Other Comprehensive Income account related to revaluations have a negative balance.**

ON THE HORIZON

With respect to revaluations, as part of the conceptual framework project, the Boards will examine the measurement bases used in accounting. It is too early to say whether a converged conceptual framework will recommend fair value measurement (and revaluation accounting) for property, plant, and equipment. However, this is likely to be one of the more contentious issues, given the long-standing use of historical cost as a measurement basis in GAAP.

IFRS SELF-TEST QUESTIONS

1. Mandall Company constructed a warehouse for $280,000 on January 2, 2012. Mandall estimates that the warehouse has a useful life of 20 years and no residual value. Construction records indicate that $40,000 of the cost of the warehouse relates to its heating, ventilation, and air conditioning (HVAC) system, which has an estimated useful life of only 10 years. What is the first year of depreciation expense using straight-line component depreciation under IFRS?
   (a) $28,000.
   (b) $14,000.
   (c) $16,000.
   (d) $4,000.

2. Francisco Corporation is constructing a new building at a total initial cost of $10,000,000. The building is expected to have a useful life of 50 years with no residual value. The building's finished surfaces (e.g., roof cover and floor cover) are 5% of this cost and have a useful life of 20 years. Building services systems (e.g., electric, heating, and plumbing) are 20% of the cost and have a useful life of 25 years. The depreciation in the first year using component depreciation, assuming straight-line depreciation with no residual value, is:
   (a) $200,000.
   (b) $215,000.
   (c) $255,000.
   (d) None of the above.

3. Which of the following statements is *correct?*
   (a) Both IFRS and GAAP permit revaluation of property, plant, and equipment.
   (b) IFRS permits revaluation of property, plant, and equipment but not GAAP.
   (c) Both IFRS and GAAP do not permit revaluation of property, plant, and equipment.
   (d) GAAP permits revaluation of property, plant, and equipment but not IFRS.

4. Hilo Company has land that cost $350,000 but now a fair value of $500,000. Hilo Company decides to use the revaluation method specified in IFRS to account for the land. Which of the following statements is *correct*?
   (a) Hilo Company must continue to report the land at $350,000.
   (b) Hilo Company would report a net income increase of $150,000 due to an increase in the value of the land.
   (c) Hilo Company would debit Revaluation Surplus for $150,000.
   (d) Hilo Company would credit Revaluation Surplus by $150,000.

5. Under IFRS, value-in-use is defined as:
  (a) net realizable value.
  (b) fair value.
  (c) future cash flows discounted to present value.
  (d) total future undiscounted cash flows.

IFRS CONCEPTS AND APPLICATION

IFRS11-1 Walkin Inc. is considering the write-down of its long-term plant because of a lack of profitability. Explain to the management of Walkin how to determine whether a write-down is permitted.

IFRS11-2 Last year, Wyeth Company recorded an impairment on an asset held for use. Recent appraisals indicate that the asset has increased in value. Should Wyeth record this recovery in value?

IFRS11-3 Toro Co. has equipment with a carrying amount of $700,000. The value-in-use of the equipment is $705,000, and its fair value less costs of disposal is $590,000. The equipment is expected to be used in operations in the future. What amount (if any) should Toro report as an impairment to its equipment?

IFRS11-4 Explain how gains or losses on impaired assets should be reported in income.

IFRS11-5 Tanaka Company has land that cost $15,000,000. Its fair value on December 31, 2012, is $20,000,000. Tanaka chooses the revaluation model to report its land. Explain how the land and its related valuation should be reported.

IFRS11-6 Why might a company choose not to use revaluation accounting?

IFRS11-7 Ortiz purchased a piece of equipment that cost $202,000 on January 1, 2012. The equipment has the following components.

Component	Cost	Residual Value	Estimated Useful Life
A	$70,000	$7,000	10 years
B	50,000	5,000	5 years
C	82,000	4,000	12 years

Compute the depreciation expense for this equipment at December 31, 2012.

IFRS11-8 Tan Chin Company purchases a building for $11,300,000 on January 2, 2012. An engineer's report shows that of the total purchase price, $11,000,000 should be allocated to the building (with a 40-year life), $150,000 to 15-year property, and $150,000 to 5-year property. Compute depreciation expense for 2012 using component depreciation.

IFRS11-9 Brazil Group purchases a vehicle at a cost of $50,000 on January 2, 2012. Individual components of the vehicle and useful lives are as follows.

	Cost	Useful Lives
Tires	$ 6,000	2 years
Transmission	10,000	5 years
Trucks	34,000	10 years

Instructions

  (a) Compute depreciation expense for 2012, assuming Brazil depreciates the vehicle as a single unit.
  (b) Compute depreciation expense for 2012, assuming Brazil uses component depreciation.
  (c) Why might a company want to use component depreciation to depreciate its assets?

IFRS11-10 Jurassic Company owns machinery that cost $900,000 and has accumulated depreciation of $380,000. The present value of expected future net cash flows from the use of the asset are expected to be $500,000. The fair value less costs of disposal of the equipment is $400,000. Prepare the journal entry, if any, to record the impairment loss.

IFRS11-11 Presented below is information related to equipment owned by Pujols Company at December 31, 2012.

Cost (residual value $0)	$9,000,000
Accumulated depreciation to date	1,000,000
Value-in-use	5,500,000
Fair value less cost of disposal	4,400,000

Assume that Pujols will continue to use this asset in the future. As of December 31, 2012, the equipment has a remaining useful life of 8 years. Pujols uses straight-line depreciation.

Instructions

(a) Prepare the journal entry (if any) to record the impairment of the asset at December 31, 2012.
(b) Prepare the journal entry to record depreciation expense for 2013.
(c) The recoverable amount of the equipment at December 31, 2013, is $6,050,000. Prepare the journal entry (if any) necessary to record this increase.

IFRS11-12 Assume the same information as in IFRS11-11, except that Pujols intends to dispose of the equipment in the coming year.

Instructions

(a) Prepare the journal entry (if any) to record the impairment of the asset at December 31, 2012.
(b) Prepare the journal entry (if any) to record depreciation expense for 2013.
(c) The asset was not sold by December 31, 2013. The fair value of the equipment on that date is $5,100,000. Prepare the journal entry (if any) necessary to record this increase. It is expected that the cost of disposal is $20,000.

IFRS11-13 Falcetto Company acquired equipment on January 1, 2011, for $12,000. Falcetto elects to value this class of equipment using revaluation accounting. This equipment is being depreciated on a straight-line basis over its 6-year useful life. There is no residual value at the end of the 6-year period. The appraised value of the equipment approximates the carrying amount at December 31, 2011 and 2013. On December 31, 2012, the fair value of the equipment is determined to be $7,000.

Instructions

(a) Prepare the journal entries for 2011 related to the equipment.
(b) Prepare the journal entries for 2012 related to the equipment.
(c) Determine the amount of depreciation expense that Falcetto will record on the equipment in 2013.

International Reporting Case

IFRS11-14 Companies following international accounting standards are permitted to revalue fixed assets above the assets' historical costs. Such revaluations are allowed under various countries' standards and the standards issued by the IASB. **Liberty International**, a real estate company headquartered in the United Kingdom (U.K.), follows U.K. standards. In a recent year, Liberty disclosed the following information on revaluations of its tangible fixed assets. The revaluation reserve measures the amount by which tangible fixed assets are recorded above historical cost and is reported in Liberty's stockholders' equity.

Liberty International

Completed Investment Properties

Completed investment properties are professionally valued on a market value basis by external valuers at the balance sheet date. Surpluses and deficits arising during the year are reflected in the revalution reserve.

Liberty reported the following additional data. Amounts for **Kimco Realty** (which follows GAAP) in the same year are provided for comparison.

	Liberty (pounds sterling, in thousands)	Kimco (dollars, in millions)
Total revenues	£ 741	$ 517
Average total assets	5,577	4,696
Net income	125	297

Instructions

(a) Compute the following ratios for Liberty and Kimco.

(1) Return on assets.

(2) Profit margin.

(3) Asset turnover.

How do these companies compare on these performance measures?

(b) Liberty reports a revaluation surplus of £1,952. Assume that £1,550 of this amount arose from an increase in the net replacement value of investment properties during the year. Prepare the journal entry to record this increase.

(c) Under U.K. (and IASB) standards, are Liberty's assets and equity overstated? If so, why? When comparing Liberty to U.S. companies, like Kimco, what adjustments would you need to make in order to have valid comparisons of ratios such as those computed in (a) above?

Professional Research

IFRS11-15 Matt Holmes recently joined Klax Company as a staff accountant in the controller's office. Klax Company provides warehousing services for companies in several European cities. The location in Koblenz, Germany, has not been performing well due to increased competition and the loss of several customers that have recently gone out of business. Matt's department manager suspects that the plant and equipment may be impaired and wonders whether those assets should be written down. Given the company's prior success, this issue has never arisen in the past, and Matt has been asked to conduct some research on this issue.

Instructions

Access the IFRS authoritative literature at the IASB website (*http://eifrs.iasb.org/*). When you have accessed the documents, you can use the search tool in your Internet browser to respond to the following questions. (Provide paragraph citations.)

(a) What is the authoritative guidance for asset impairments? Briefly discuss the scope of the standard (i.e., explain the types of transactions to which the standard applies).

(b) Give several examples of events that would cause an asset to be tested for impairment. Does it appear that Klax should perform an impairment test? Explain.

(c) What is the best evidence of fair value? Describe alternate methods of estimating fair value.

International Financial Reporting Problem: *Marks and Spencer plc*

IFRS11-16 The financial statements of Marks and Spencer plc (M&S) are available at the book's companion website or can be accessed at *http://corporate.marksandspencer.com/documents/publications/2010/Annual_Report_2010.*

Instructions

Refer to M&S's financial statements and the accompanying notes to answer the following questions.

(a) What descriptions are used by M&S in its statement of financial position to classify its property, plant, and equipment?
(b) What method or methods of depreciation does M&S use to depreciate its property, plant, and equipment?
(c) Over what estimated useful lives does M&S depreciate its property, plant, and equipment?
(d) What amounts for depreciation and amortization expense did M&S charge to its income statement in 2010 and 2009?
(e) What were the capital expenditures for property, plant, and equipment made by M&S in 2010 and 2009?

ANSWERS TO IFRS SELF-TEST QUESTIONS

1. c **2.** c **3.** b **4.** d **5.** c

Remember to check the book's companion website to find additional resources for this chapter.

CHAPTER

23 Statement of Cash Flows

LEARNING OBJECTIVES

After studying this chapter, you should be able to:

1. Describe the purpose of the statement of cash flows.
2. Identify the major classifications of cash flows.
3. Differentiate between net income and net cash flow from operating activities.
4. Contrast the direct and indirect methods of calculating net cash flow from operating activities.
5. Determine net cash flows from investing and financing activities.
6. Prepare a statement of cash flows.
7. Identify sources of information for a statement of cash flows.
8. Discuss special problems in preparing a statement of cash flows.
9. Explain the use of a worksheet in preparing a statement of cash flows.

Show Me the Money

Investors usually look to net income as a key indicator of a company's financial health and future prospects. The following graph shows the net income of one company over a seven-year period.

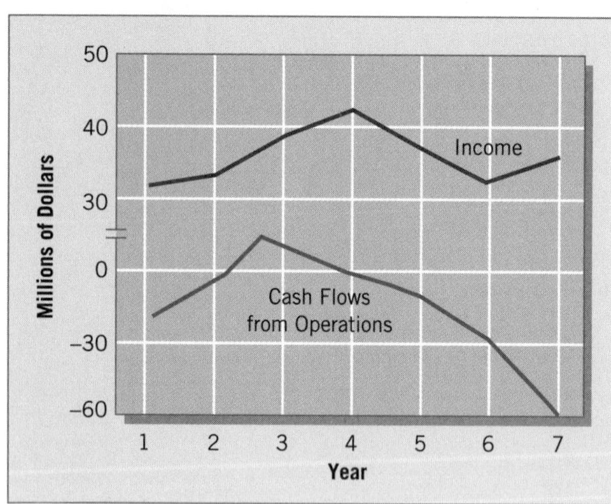

The company showed a pattern of consistent profitability and even some periods of income growth. Between years 1 and 4, net income for this company grew by 32 percent, from $31 million to $41 million. Would you expect its profitability to continue? The company had consistently paid dividends and interest. Would you expect it to continue to do so? Investors answered these questions by buying the company's stock. Eighteen months later, this company—**W. T. Grant**—filed for bankruptcy, in what was then the largest bankruptcy filing in the United States.

How could this happen? As indicated by the second line in the graph, the company had experienced several years of negative cash flow from its operations, even though it reported profits. How can a company have negative cash flows while reporting profits? The answer lays partly in the fact that W. T. Grant was having trouble collecting the receivables from its credit sales, causing cash flow to be less than the net income. Investors who analyzed the cash flows would have been likely to find an early warning signal of W. T. Grant's operating problems.

Investors can also look to cash flow information to sniff out companies that can be good buys. As one analyst stated when it comes to valuing stocks: "Show me the money!" Here's the thinking behind that statement. Start with the "cash flows from operations" reported in the statement of cash

IFRS IN THIS CHAPTER

See the **International Perspectives** on pages 1437, 1439, and 1458.

Read the **IFRS Insights** on pages 1505–1510 for a discussion of:

—Significant non-cash transactions

—Special disclosures

flows, which (as you will learn in this chapter) consists of net income with noncash charges (like depreciation and deferred taxes) added back and cash-draining events (like an inventory pile-up) taken out. Now subtract capital expenditures and dividends. What you're left with is free cash flow (as discussed in Chapter 5).

Many analysts like companies trading at low multiples of their free cash flow—low, that is, in relation to rivals today or the same company in past years. Why? They know that reported earnings can be misleading. Case in point: Computer-game firm **Activision Blizzard** reported net income of $113 million last year. But it did better than that. It took in an additional $300 million, mostly for subscriptions to online multiplayer games. It gets the cash now but records the revenue only over time, as the subscriptions run out. A couple of investment houses put this stock on their buy list on the strength of its cash flows. So watch cash flow—to get an indicator of companies headed for trouble, as well as companies that may be undervalued.

Source: Adapted from James A. Largay III and Clyde P. Stickney, "Cash Flows, Ratio Analysis, and the W. T. Grant Company Bankruptcy," *Financial Analysts Journal* (July–August 1980), p. 51; and D. Fisher, "Cash Doesn't Lie," *Forbes* (April 12, 2010), pp. 52–55.

PREVIEW OF CHAPTER 23

As the opening story indicates, examination of **W. T. Grant**'s cash flows from operations would have shown the financial inflexibility that eventually caused the company's bankruptcy. This chapter explains the main components of a statement of cash flows and the types of information it provides. The content and organization of the chapter are as follows.

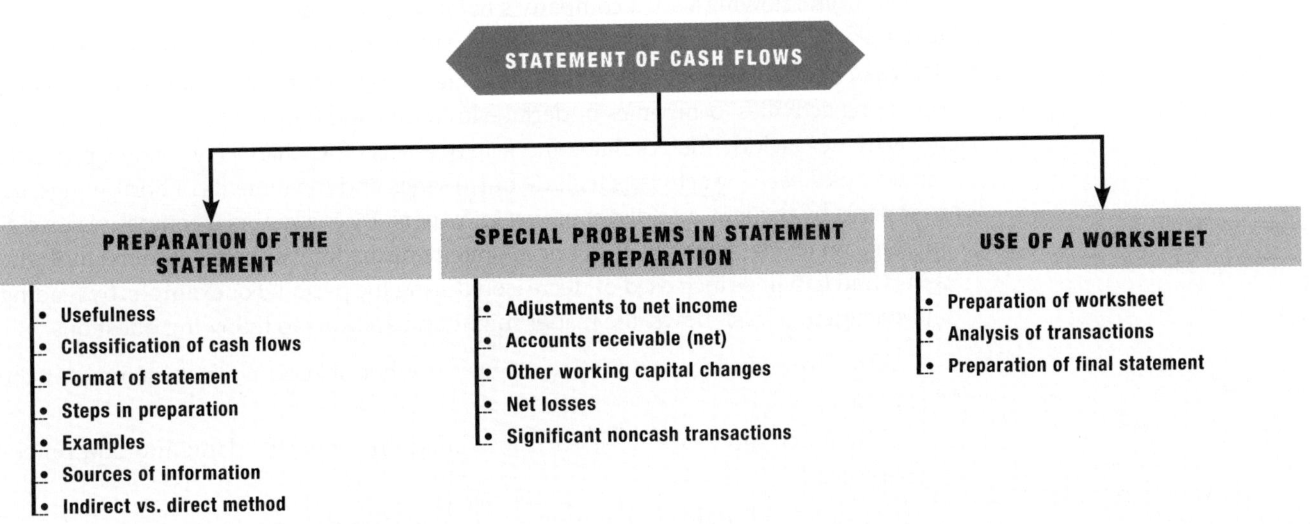

SECTION 1 • PREPARATION OF THE STATEMENT OF CASH FLOWS

LEARNING OBJECTIVE 1
Describe the purpose of the statement of cash flows.

The primary purpose of the **statement of cash flows** is to provide information about a company's cash receipts and cash payments during a period. A secondary objective is to provide cash-basis information about the company's operating, investing, and financing activities. The statement of cash flows therefore reports cash receipts, cash payments, and net change in cash resulting from a company's operating, investing, and financing activities during a period. Its format reconciles the beginning and ending cash balances for the period.

USEFULNESS OF THE STATEMENT OF CASH FLOWS

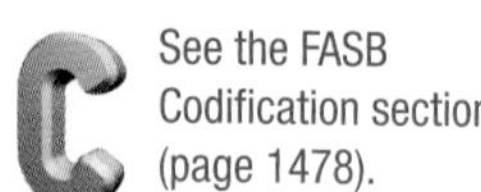
See the FASB Codification section (page 1478).

The statement of cash flows provides information to help investors, creditors, and others assess the following [1]:

1. ***The entity's ability to generate future cash flows.*** A primary objective of financial reporting is to provide information with which to predict the amounts, timing, and uncertainty of future cash flows. By examining relationships between items such as sales and net cash flow from operating activities, or net cash flow from operating activities and increases or decreases in cash, it is possible to better predict the future cash flows than is possible using accrual-basis data alone.
2. ***The entity's ability to pay dividends and meet obligations.*** Simply put, cash is essential. Without adequate cash, a company cannot pay employees, settle debts, pay out dividends, or acquire equipment. A statement of cash flows indicates where the company's cash comes from and how the company uses its cash. Employees, creditors, stockholders, and customers should be particularly interested in this statement, because it alone shows the flows of cash in a business.
3. ***The reasons for the difference between net income and net cash flow from operating activities.*** The net income number is important: It provides information on the performance of a company from one period to another. But some people are critical of accrual-basis net income because companies must make estimates to arrive at it. Such is not the case with cash. Thus, as the opening story showed, financial statement readers can benefit from knowing why a company's net income and net cash flow from operating activities differ, and can assess for themselves the reliability of the income number.
4. ***The cash and noncash investing and financing transactions during the period.*** Besides operating activities, companies undertake investing and financing transactions. *Investing* activities include the purchase and sale of assets other than a company's products or services. *Financing* activities include borrowings and repayments of borrowings, investments by owners, and distributions to owners. By examining a company's investing and financing activities, a financial statement reader can better understand why assets and liabilities increased or decreased during the period. For example, by reading the statement of cash flows, the reader might find answers to following questions:

   Why did cash decrease for **Home Depot** when it reported net income for the period?

   How much did **Southwest Airlines** spend on property, plant, and equipment last year?

   Did dividends paid by **Campbell's Soup** increase?

   How much money did **Coca-Cola** borrow last year?

   How much cash did **Hewlett-Packard** use to repurchase its common stock?

CLASSIFICATION OF CASH FLOWS

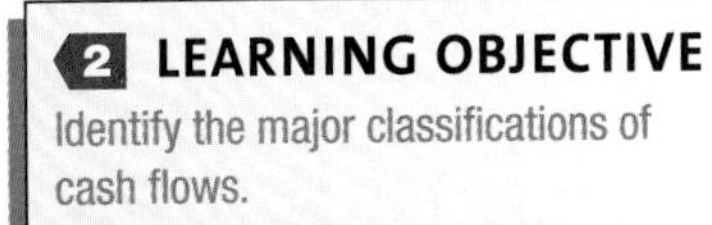

2 LEARNING OBJECTIVE
Identify the major classifications of cash flows.

The statement of cash flows classifies cash receipts and cash payments by operating, investing, and financing activities.[1] Transactions and other events characteristic of each kind of activity is as follows.

1. **Operating activities** involve the cash effects of transactions that enter into the determination of net income, such as cash receipts from sales of goods and services, and cash payments to suppliers and employees for acquisitions of inventory and expenses.
2. **Investing activities** generally involve long-term assets and include (a) making and collecting loans, and (b) acquiring and disposing of investments and productive long-lived assets.
3. **Financing activities** involve liability and stockholders' equity items and include (a) obtaining cash from creditors and repaying the amounts borrowed, and (b) obtaining capital from owners and providing them with a return on, and a return of, their investment.

Illustration 23-1 classifies the typical cash receipts and payments of a company according to operating, investing, and financing activities. The operating activities category is the most important. It shows the cash provided by company operations. This source of cash is generally considered to be the best measure of a company's ability to generate enough cash to continue as a going concern.

ILLUSTRATION 23-1
Classification of Typical Cash Inflows and Outflows

Operating	Income Statement Items
Cash inflows	
From sales of goods or services.	
From returns on loans (interest) and on equity securities (dividends).	
Cash outflows	
To suppliers for inventory.	
To employees for services.	
To government for taxes.	
To lenders for interest.	
To others for expenses.	
Investing	Generally Long-Term Asset Items
Cash inflows	
From sale of property, plant, and equipment.	
From sale of debt or equity securities of other entities.	
From collection of principal on loans to other entities.	
Cash outflows	
To purchase property, plant, and equipment.	
To purchase debt or equity securities of other entities.	
To make loans to other entities.	
Financing	Generally Long-Term Liability and Equity Items
Cash inflows	
From sale of equity securities.	
From issuance of debt (bonds and notes).	
Cash outflows	
To stockholders as dividends.	
To redeem long-term debt or reacquire capital stock.	

INTERNATIONAL PERSPECTIVE

According to IFRS, companies can define "cash and cash equivalents" as "net monetary assets"—that is, as "cash and demand deposits and highly liquid investments less short-term borrowings."

[1]The basis recommended by the FASB for the statement of cash flows is actually "cash and cash equivalents." **Cash equivalents** are short-term, highly liquid investments that are both: (a) readily convertible to known amounts of cash, and (b) so near their maturity that they present insignificant risk of changes in interest rates. Generally, only investments with original maturities of three months or less qualify under this definition. Examples of cash equivalents are Treasury bills, commercial paper, and money market funds purchased with cash that is in excess of immediate needs.

Although we use the term "cash" throughout our discussion and illustrations, we mean cash and cash equivalents when reporting the cash flows and the net increase or decrease in cash.

Note the following general guidelines about the classification of cash flows.

1. Operating activities involve income statement items.
2. Investing activities involve cash flows resulting from changes in investments and long-term asset items.
3. Financing activities involve cash flows resulting from changes in long-term liability and stockholders' equity items.

Companies classify some cash flows relating to investing or financing activities as operating activities.[2] For example, companies classify receipts of investment income (interest and dividends) and payments of interest to lenders as operating activities. Why are these considered operating activities? Companies report these items in the income statement, where the results of operations are shown.

Conversely, companies classify some cash flows relating to operating activities as investing or financing activities. For example, a company classifies the cash received from the sale of property, plant, and equipment at a gain, although reported in the income statement, as an investing activity. It excludes the effects of the related gain in net cash flow from operating activities. Likewise, a gain or loss on the payment (extinguishment) of debt is generally part of the cash outflow related to the repayment of the amount borrowed. It therefore is a financing activity.

HOW'S MY CASH FLOW?

What do the numbers mean?

To evaluate overall cash flow, it is useful to understand where in the product life cycle a company is. Generally, companies move through several stages of development, which have implications for cash flow. As the graph below shows, the pattern of cash flows from operating, financing, and investing activities will vary depending on the stage of the product life cycle.

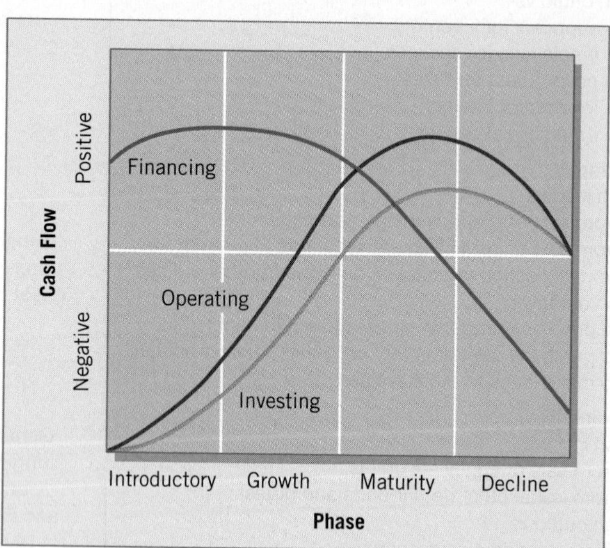

In the introductory phase, the product is likely not generating much revenue (operating cash flow is negative). Because the company is making heavy investments to get a product off the ground, cash flow from investment is negative, and financing cash flows are positive.

[2]Banks and brokers must classify cash flows from purchases and sales of loans and securities specifically for resale and carried at fair value **as operating activities**. This requirement recognizes that for these firms these assets are similar to inventory in other businesses. [2]

As the product moves to the growth and maturity phases, these cash flow relationships reverse. The product generates more cash flow from operations, which can be used to cover investments needed to support the product, and less cash is needed from financing. So is a negative operating cash flow bad? Not always. It depends on the product life cycle.

Source: Adapted from Paul D. Kimmel, Jerry J. Weygandt, and Donald E. Kieso, *Financial Accounting: Tools for Business Decision Making*, 6th ed. (New York: John Wiley & Sons, 2011), p. 628.

What do the numbers mean? (continued)

FORMAT OF THE STATEMENT OF CASH FLOWS

The three activities we discussed above constitute the general format of the statement of cash flows. The operating activities section always appears first. It is followed by the investing activities section and then the financing activities section.

A company reports the individual inflows and outflows from investing and financing activities separately. That is, a company reports them gross, not netted against one another. Thus, a cash outflow from the purchase of property is reported separately from the cash inflow from the sale of property. Similarly, a cash inflow from the issuance of debt is reported separately from the cash outflow from its retirement.

The net increase or decrease in cash reported during the period should reconcile the beginning and ending cash balances as reported in the comparative balance sheets. The general format of the statement of cash flows presents the results of the three activities discussed previously–operating, investing, and financing. Illustration 23-2 shows a widely used form of the statement of cash flows.

ILLUSTRATION 23-2
Format of the Statement of Cash Flows

COMPANY NAME STATEMENT OF CASH FLOWS PERIOD COVERED		
Cash flows from operating activities		
Net income		XXX
Adjustments to reconcile net income to net cash provided (used) by operating activities:		
(List of individual items)	XX	XX
Net cash provided (used) by operating activities		XXX
Cash flows from investing activities		
(List of individual inflows and outflows)	XX	
Net cash provided (used) by investing activities		XXX
Cash flows from financing activities		
(List of individual inflows and outflows)	XX	
Net cash provided (used) by financing activities		XXX
Net increase (decrease) in cash		XXX
Cash at beginning of period		XXX
Cash at end of period		XXX

INTERNATIONAL PERSPECTIVE

Both IFRS and GAAP specify that companies must classify cash flows as operating, investing, or financing.

STEPS IN PREPARATION

Companies prepare the statement of cash flows differently from the three other basic financial statements. For one thing, it is not prepared from an adjusted trial balance. The cash flow statement requires detailed information concerning the changes in account balances that occurred between two points in time. An adjusted trial balance will not provide the necessary data. Second, the statement of cash flows deals with cash receipts and payments. As a result, the company must adjust the effects of the use of accrual accounting to determine cash flows. The information to prepare this statement usually comes from three sources:

1. **Comparative balance sheets** provide the amount of the changes in assets, liabilities, and equities from the beginning to the end of the period.
2. **Current income statement** data help determine the amount of cash provided by or used by operations during the period.
3. **Selected transaction data** from the general ledger provide additional detailed information needed to determine how the company provided or used cash during the period.

Preparing the statement of cash flows from the data sources above involves three major steps:

Step 1. ***Determine the change in cash.*** This procedure is straightforward. A company can easily compute the difference between the beginning and the ending cash balance from examining its comparative balance sheets.

Step 2. ***Determine the net cash flow from operating activities.*** This procedure is complex. It involves analyzing not only the current year's income statement but also comparative balance sheets as well as selected transaction data.

Step 3. ***Determine net cash flows from investing and financing activities.*** A company must analyze all other changes in the balance sheet accounts to determine their effects on cash.

On the following pages we work through these three steps in the process of preparing the statement of cash flows for Tax Consultants Inc. over several years.

FIRST EXAMPLE—2011

To illustrate a statement of cash flows, we use the **first year of operations** for Tax Consultants Inc. The company started on January 1, 2011, when it issued 60,000 shares of $1 par value common stock for $60,000 cash. The company rented its office space, furniture, and equipment, and performed tax consulting services throughout the first year. The comparative balance sheets at the beginning and end of the year 2011 appear in Illustration 23-3.

ILLUSTRATION 23-3
Comparative Balance Sheets, Tax Consultants Inc., Year 1

TAX CONSULTANTS INC.
COMPARATIVE BALANCE SHEETS

Assets	Dec. 31, 2011	Jan. 1, 2011	Change Increase/Decrease
Cash	$49,000	$-0-	$49,000 Increase
Accounts receivable	36,000	-0-	36,000 Increase
Total	$85,000	$-0-	
Liabilities and Stockholders' Equity			
Accounts payable	$ 5,000	$-0-	$ 5,000 Increase
Common stock ($1 par)	60,000	-0-	60,000 Increase
Retained earnings	20,000	-0-	20,000 Increase
Total	$85,000	$-0-	

Illustration 23-4 shows the income statement and additional information for Tax Consultants.

ILLUSTRATION 23-4
Income Statement, Tax Consultants Inc., Year 1

TAX CONSULTANTS INC.
INCOME STATEMENT
FOR THE YEAR ENDED DECEMBER 31, 2011

Revenues	$125,000
Operating expenses	85,000
Income before income taxes	40,000
Income tax expense	6,000
Net income	$ 34,000

Additional Information
Examination of selected data indicates that a dividend of $14,000 was declared and paid during the year.

Step 1: Determine the Change in Cash

To prepare a statement of cash flows, the first step is to **determine the change in cash.** This is a simple computation. Tax Consultants had no cash on hand at the beginning of the year 2011. It had $49,000 on hand at the end of 2011. Thus, cash changed (increased) in 2011 by $49,000.

Step 2: Determine Net Cash Flow from Operating Activities

3 LEARNING OBJECTIVE
Differentiate between net income and net cash flow from operating activities.

To determine net cash flow from operating activities,[3] companies adjust net income in numerous ways. A useful starting point is to understand why net income must be converted to net cash provided by operating activities.

Under generally accepted accounting principles, most companies use the accrual basis of accounting. As you have learned, this basis requires that companies record revenue when earned and record expenses when incurred. Earned revenues may include credit sales for which the company has not yet collected cash. Expenses incurred may include some items that the company has not yet paid in cash. Thus, under the accrual basis of accounting, net income is not the same as net cash flow from operating activities.

To arrive at net cash flow from operating activities, a company must determine revenues and expenses on a **cash basis. It does this by eliminating the effects of income statement transactions that do not result in an increase or decrease in cash.** Illustration 23-5 shows the relationship between net income and net cash flow from operating activities.

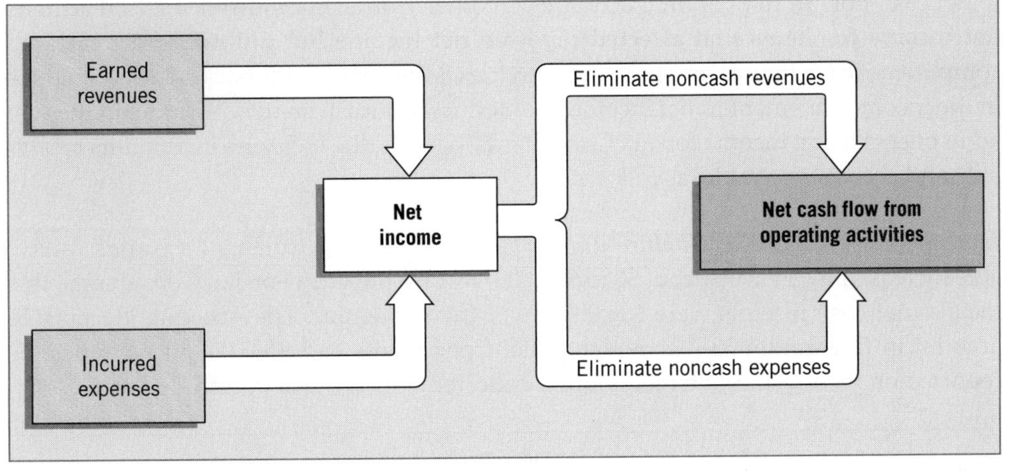

ILLUSTRATION 23-5
Net Income versus Net Cash Flow from Operating Activities

[3]"Net cash flow from operating activities" is a generic phrase, replaced in the statement of cash flows with either "Net cash **provided by** operating activities" if operations increase cash, or "Net cash **used by** operating activities" if operations decrease cash.

In this chapter, we use the term net income to refer to accrual-based net income. A company may convert net income to net cash flow from operating activities through either a direct method or an indirect method. We explain both methods in the following sections. The advantages and disadvantages of these two methods are discussed later in the chapter.

Direct Method

LEARNING OBJECTIVE 4
Contrast the direct and indirect methods of calculating net cash flow from operating activities.

The direct method (also called the **income statement method**) reports cash receipts and cash disbursements from operating activities. The difference between these two amounts is the net cash flow from operating activities. In other words, the direct method deducts operating cash disbursements from operating cash receipts. The direct method results in the presentation of a condensed cash receipts and cash disbursements statement.

As indicated from the accrual-based income statement, Tax Consultants reported revenues of $125,000. However, because the company's accounts receivable increased during 2011 by $36,000, the company collected only $89,000 ($125,000 − $36,000) in cash from these revenues. Similarly, Tax Consultants reported operating expenses of $85,000. However, accounts payable increased during the period by $5,000. Assuming that these payables relate to operating expenses, cash operating expenses were $80,000 ($85,000 − $5,000). Because no taxes payable exist at the end of the year, the company must have paid $6,000 income tax expense for 2011 in cash during the year. Tax Consultants computes net cash flow from operating activities as shown in Illustration 23-6.

ILLUSTRATION 23-6
Computation of Net Cash Flow from Operating Activities, Year 1—Direct Method

Cash collected from revenues	$89,000
Cash payments for expenses	80,000
Income before income taxes	9,000
Cash payments for income taxes	6,000
Net cash provided by operating activities	$ 3,000

"Net cash provided by operating activities" is the equivalent of cash basis net income. ("Net cash used by operating activities" is equivalent to cash basis net loss.)

Indirect Method

The indirect method (or **reconciliation method**) starts with net income and converts it to net cash flow from operating activities. In other words, **the indirect method adjusts net income for items that affected reported net income but did not affect cash**. To compute net cash flow from operating activities, a company adds back noncash charges in the income statement to net income and deducts noncash credits. We explain the two adjustments to net income for Tax Consultants, namely, the increases in accounts receivable and accounts payable, as follows.

Increase in Accounts Receivable—Indirect Method. Tax Consultant's accounts receivable increased by $36,000 (from $0 to $36,000) during the year. For Tax Consultants, this means that cash receipts were $36,000 lower than revenues. The Accounts Receivable account in Illustration 23-7 shows that Tax Consultants had $125,000 in revenues (as reported on the income statement), but it collected only $89,000 in cash.

ILLUSTRATION 23-7
Analysis of Accounts Receivable

Accounts Receivable				
1/1/11	Balance	-0-	Receipts from customer	89,000
	Revenues	125,000		
12/31/11	Balance	36,000		

As shown in Illustration 23-8, to adjust net income to net cash provided by operating activities, Tax Consultants must deduct the increase of $36,000 in accounts receivable from net income. When the Accounts Receivable balance *decreases*, cash receipts are higher than revenue earned under the accrual basis. Therefore, the company adds to net income the amount of the decrease in accounts receivable to arrive at net cash provided by operating activities.

Increase in Accounts Payable—Indirect Method. When accounts payable increase during the year, expenses on an accrual basis exceed those on a cash basis. Why? Because Tax Consultants incurred expenses, but some of the expenses are not yet paid. To convert net income to net cash flow from operating activities, Tax Consultants must add back the increase of $5,000 in accounts payable to net income.

As a result of the accounts receivable and accounts payable adjustments, Tax Consultants determines net cash provided by operating activities is $3,000 for the year 2011. Illustration 23-8 shows this computation.

Net income		$ 34,000
Adjustments to reconcile net income to net cash provided by operating activities:		
Increase in accounts receivable	$(36,000)	
Increase in accounts payable	5,000	(31,000)
Net cash provided by operating activities		$ 3,000

ILLUSTRATION 23-8
Computation of Net Cash Flow from Operating Activities, Year 1—Indirect Method

Note that net cash provided by operating activities is the same whether using the direct (Illustration 23-6) or the indirect method (Illustration 23-8).

PUMPING UP CASH

What do the numbers mean?

Due to recent concerns about a decline in the quality of earnings, some investors have been focusing on cash flow. Management has an incentive to make operating cash flow look good because Wall Street has paid a premium for companies that generate a lot of cash from operations, rather than through borrowings. However, similar to earnings, companies have ways to pump up cash flow from operations.

One way that companies can boost their operating cash flow is by "securitizing" receivables. That is, companies can speed up cash collections by selling their receivables. For example, **Federated Department Stores** reported a $2.2 billion increase in cash flow from operations. This seems impressive until you read the fine print, which indicates that a big part of the increase was due to the sale of receivables. As discussed in this section, decreases in accounts receivable increase cash flow from operations. So while it appeared that Federated's core operations had improved, the company really did little more than accelerate collections of its receivables. In fact, the cash flow from the securitizations represented more than half of Federated's operating cash flow. Thus, just like earnings, cash flow can be of high or low quality.

Source: Adapted from Ann Tergesen, "Cash Flow Hocus Pocus," *BusinessWeek* (July 16, 2002), pp. 130–131. See also Bear Stearns Equity Research, *Accounting Issues: Cash Flow Metrics* (June 2006).

Step 3: Determine Net Cash Flows from Investing and Financing Activities

5 LEARNING OBJECTIVE
Determine net cash flows from investing and financing activities.

After Tax Consultants has computed the net cash provided by operating activities, the next step is to determine whether any other changes in balance sheet accounts caused an increase or decrease in cash.

For example, an examination of the remaining balance sheet accounts for Tax Consultants shows increases in both common stock and retained earnings. The common stock increase of $60,000 resulted from the issuance of common stock for cash. The issuance of common stock is reported in the statement of cash flows as a receipt of cash from a financing activity.

Two items caused the retained earnings increase of $20,000:

1. Net income of $34,000 increased retained earnings.
2. Declaration of $14,000 of dividends decreased retained earnings.

Tax Consultants has converted net income into net cash flow from operating activities, as explained earlier. The additional data indicate that it paid the dividend. Thus, the company reports the dividend payment as a cash outflow, classified as a financing activity.

Statement of Cash Flows—2011

LEARNING OBJECTIVE 6
Prepare a statement of cash flows.

We are now ready to prepare the statement of cash flows. The statement starts with the operating activities section. Tax Consultants may use either the direct or indirect method to report net cash flow from operating activities.

The FASB **encourages** the use of the direct method over the indirect method. If a company uses the direct method of reporting net cash flow from operating activities, the FASB **requires** that the company provide in a separate schedule a reconciliation of net income to net cash flow from operating activities. If a company uses the indirect method, it can either report the reconciliation within the statement of cash flows or can provide it in a separate schedule, with the statement of cash flows reporting only the **net** cash flow from operating activities. [3] Throughout this chapter we use the indirect method, which is also used more extensively in practice.[4] *In doing homework assignments, you should follow instructions for use of either the direct or indirect method.*

Illustration 23-9 shows the statement of cash flows for Tax Consultants Inc., for year 1 (2011).

ILLUSTRATION 23-9
Statement of Cash Flows, Tax Consultants Inc., Year 1

TAX CONSULTANTS INC.
STATEMENT OF CASH FLOWS
FOR THE YEAR ENDED DECEMBER 31, 2011
INCREASE (DECREASE) IN CASH

Cash flows from operating activities		
Net income		$ 34,000
Adjustments to reconcile net income to net cash provided by operating activities:		
Increase in accounts receivable	$(36,000)	
Increase in accounts payable	5,000	(31,000)
Net cash provided by operating activities		3,000
Cash flows from financing activities		
Issuance of common stock	60,000	
Payment of cash dividends	(14,000)	
Net cash provided by financing activities		46,000
Net increase in cash		49,000
Cash, January 1, 2011		-0-
Cash, December 31, 2011		$ 49,000

As indicated, the $60,000 increase in common stock results in a financing-activity cash inflow. The payment of $14,000 in cash dividends is a financing-activity outflow of cash. The $49,000 increase in cash reported in the statement of cash flows agrees with the increase of $49,000 shown in the comparative balance sheets as the change in the cash account.

[4] *Accounting Trends and Techniques—2010* reports that out of its 500 surveyed companies, 495 (99 percent) used the indirect method, and only 5 used the direct method.

SECOND EXAMPLE—2012

Tax Consultants Inc. continued to grow and prosper in its second year of operations. The company purchased land, building, and equipment, and revenues and net income increased substantially over the first year. Illustrations 23-10 and 23-11 present information related to the second year of operations for Tax Consultants Inc.

ILLUSTRATION 23-10
Comparative Balance Sheets, Tax Consultants Inc., Year 2

TAX CONSULTANTS INC.
COMPARATIVE BALANCE SHEETS
AS OF DECEMBER 31

Assets	2012	2011	Change Increase/Decrease
Cash	$ 37,000	$ 49,000	$ 12,000 Decrease
Accounts receivable	26,000	36,000	10,000 Decrease
Prepaid expenses	6,000	-0-	6,000 Increase
Land	70,000	-0-	70,000 Increase
Buildings	200,000	-0-	200,000 Increase
Accumulated depreciation—buildings	(11,000)	-0-	11,000 Increase
Equipment	68,000	-0-	68,000 Increase
Accumulated depreciation—equipment	(10,000)	-0-	10,000 Increase
Total	$386,000	$ 85,000	
Liabilities and Stockholders' Equity			
Accounts payable	$ 40,000	$ 5,000	$ 35,000 Increase
Bonds payable	150,000	-0-	150,000 Increase
Common stock ($1 par)	60,000	60,000	-0-
Retained earnings	136,000	20,000	116,000 Increase
Total	$386,000	$ 85,000	

ILLUSTRATION 23-11
Income Statement, Tax Consultants Inc., Year 2

TAX CONSULTANTS INC.
INCOME STATEMENT
FOR THE YEAR ENDED DECEMBER 31, 2012

Revenues		$492,000
Operating expenses (excluding depreciation)	$269,000	
Depreciation expense	21,000	290,000
Income from operations		202,000
Income tax expense		68,000
Net income		$134,000

Additional Information
(a) The company declared and paid an $18,000 cash dividend.
(b) The company obtained $150,000 cash through the issuance of long-term bonds.
(c) Land, building, and equipment were acquired for cash.

Step 1: Determine the Change in Cash

To prepare a statement of cash flows from the available information, the first step is to determine the change in cash. As indicated from the information presented, cash decreased $12,000 ($49,000 − $37,000).

Step 2: Determine Net Cash Flow from Operating Activities—Indirect Method

Using the indirect method, we adjust net income of $134,000 on an accrual basis to arrive at net cash flow from operating activities. Explanations for the adjustments to net income follow.

Decrease in Accounts Receivable. Accounts receivable decreased during the period, because cash receipts (cash-basis revenues) are higher than revenues reported on an accrual basis. To convert net income to net cash flow from operating activities, the decrease of $10,000 in accounts receivable must be added to net income.

Increase in Prepaid Expenses. When prepaid expenses (assets) increase during a period, expenses on an accrual-basis income statement are lower than they are on a cash-basis income statement. The reason: Tax Consultants has made cash payments in the current period, but expenses (as charges to the income statement) have been deferred to future periods. To convert net income to net cash flow from operating activities, the company must deduct from net income the increase of $6,000 in prepaid expenses. An increase in prepaid expenses results in a decrease in cash during the period.

Increase in Accounts Payable. Like the increase in 2011, Tax Consultants must add the 2012 increase of $35,000 in accounts payable to net income, to convert to net cash flow from operating activities. The company incurred a greater amount of expense than the amount of cash it disbursed.

Depreciation Expense (Increase in Accumulated Depreciation). The purchase of depreciable assets is a use of cash, shown in the investing section in the year of acquisition. Tax Consultant's depreciation expense of $21,000 (also represented by the increase in accumulated depreciation) is a noncash charge; the company adds it back to net income, to arrive at net cash flow from operating activities. The $21,000 is the sum of the $11,000 depreciation on the building plus the $10,000 depreciation on the equipment.

Certain other periodic charges to expense do not require the use of cash. Examples are the amortization of intangible assets and depletion expense. Such charges are treated in the same manner as depreciation. Companies frequently list depreciation and similar noncash charges as the first adjustments to net income in the statement of cash flows.

As a result of the foregoing items, net cash provided by operating activities is $194,000 as shown in Illustration 23-12.

ILLUSTRATION 23-12
Computation of Net Cash Flow from Operating Activities, Year 2—Indirect Method

Net income		$134,000
Adjustments to reconcile net income to net cash provided by operating activities:		
Depreciation expense	$21,000	
Decrease in accounts receivable	10,000	
Increase in prepaid expenses	(6,000)	
Increase in accounts payable	35,000	60,000
Net cash provided by operating activities		$194,000

Step 3: Determine Net Cash Flows from Investing and Financing Activities

After you have determined the items affecting net cash provided by operating activities, the next step involves analyzing the remaining changes in balance sheet accounts. Tax Consultants Inc. analyzed the following accounts.

Increase in Land. As indicated from the change in the Land account, the company purchased land of $70,000 during the period. This transaction is an investing activity, reported as a use of cash.

Increase in Buildings and Related Accumulated Depreciation. As indicated in the additional data, and from the change in the Buildings account, Tax Consultants acquired an office building using $200,000 cash. This transaction is a cash outflow, reported in the investing section. The $11,000 increase in accumulated depreciation results from recording depreciation expense on the building. As indicated earlier, the reported depreciation expense has no effect on the amount of cash.

Increase in Equipment and Related Accumulated Depreciation. An increase in equipment of $68,000 resulted because the company used cash to purchase equipment. This transaction is an outflow of cash from an investing activity. The depreciation expense entry for the period explains the increase in Accumulated Depreciation—Equipment.

Increase in Bonds Payable. The Bonds Payable account increased $150,000. Cash received from the issuance of these bonds represents an inflow of cash from a financing activity.

Increase in Retained Earnings. Retained earnings increased $116,000 during the year. Two factors explain this increase: (1) Net income of $134,000 increased retained earnings, and (2) dividends of $18,000 decreased retained earnings. As indicated earlier, the company adjusts net income to net cash provided by operating activities in the operating activities section. Payment of the dividends is a financing activity that involves a cash outflow.

Statement of Cash Flows—2012

Combining the foregoing items, we get a statement of cash flows for 2012 for Tax Consultants Inc., using the indirect method to compute net cash flow from operating activities.

ILLUSTRATION 23-13
Statement of Cash Flows, Tax Consultants Inc., Year 2

TAX CONSULTANTS INC.
STATEMENT OF CASH FLOWS
FOR THE YEAR ENDED DECEMBER 31, 2012
INCREASE (DECREASE) IN CASH

Cash flows from operating activities		
Net income		$ 134,000
Adjustments to reconcile net income to net cash provided by operating activities:		
Depreciation expense	$ 21,000	
Decrease in accounts receivable	10,000	
Increase in prepaid expenses	(6,000)	
Increase in accounts payable	35,000	60,000
Net cash provided by operating activities		194,000
Cash flows from investing activities		
Purchase of land	(70,000)	
Purchase of building	(200,000)	
Purchase of equipment	(68,000)	
Net cash used by investing activities		(338,000)
Cash flows from financing activities		
Issuance of bonds	150,000	
Payment of cash dividends	(18,000)	
Net cash provided by financing activities		132,000
Net decrease in cash		(12,000)
Cash, January 1, 2012		49,000
Cash, December 31, 2012		$ 37,000

THIRD EXAMPLE—2013

Our third example, covering the 2013 operations of Tax Consultants Inc., is more complex. It again uses the indirect method to compute and present net cash flow from operating activities.

Tax Consultants Inc. experienced continued success in 2013 and expanded its operations to include the sale of computer software used in tax-return preparation and tax planning. Thus, inventory is a new asset appearing in the company's December 31, 2013, balance sheet. Illustrations 23-14 and 23-15 show the comparative balance sheets, income statements, and selected data for 2013.

ILLUSTRATION 23-14
Comparative Balance Sheets, Tax Consultants Inc., Year 3

TAX CONSULTANTS INC.
COMPARATIVE BALANCE SHEETS
AS OF DECEMBER 31

Assets	2013	2012	Change Increase/Decrease
Cash	$ 54,000	$ 37,000	$ 17,000 Increase
Accounts receivable	68,000	26,000	42,000 Increase
Inventory	54,000	-0-	54,000 Increase
Prepaid expenses	4,000	6,000	2,000 Decrease
Land	45,000	70,000	25,000 Decrease
Buildings	200,000	200,000	-0-
Accumulated depreciation—buildings	(21,000)	(11,000)	10,000 Increase
Equipment	193,000	68,000	125,000 Increase
Accumulated depreciation—equipment	(28,000)	(10,000)	18,000 Increase
Totals	$569,000	$386,000	
Liabilities and Stockholders' Equity			
Accounts payable	$ 33,000	$ 40,000	$ 7,000 Decrease
Bonds payable	110,000	150,000	40,000 Decrease
Common stock ($1 par)	220,000	60,000	160,000 Increase
Retained earnings	206,000	136,000	70,000 Increase
Totals	$569,000	$386,000	

ILLUSTRATION 23-15
Income Statement, Tax Consultants Inc., Year 3

TAX CONSULTANTS INC.
INCOME STATEMENT
FOR THE YEAR ENDED DECEMBER 31, 2013

Revenues		$890,000
Cost of goods sold	$465,000	
Operating expenses	221,000	
Interest expense	12,000	
Loss on sale of equipment	2,000	700,000
Income from operations		190,000
Income tax expense		65,000
Net income		$125,000

Additional Information
(a) Operating expenses include depreciation expense of $33,000 and expiration of prepaid expenses of $2,000.
(b) Land was sold at its book value for cash.
(c) Cash dividends of $55,000 were declared and paid.
(d) Interest expense of $12,000 was paid in cash.
(e) Equipment with a cost of $166,000 was purchased for cash. Equipment with a cost of $41,000 and a book value of $36,000 was sold for $34,000 cash.
(f) Bonds were redeemed at their book value for cash.
(g) Common stock ($1 par) was issued for cash.

Step 1: Determine the Change in Cash

The first step in the preparation of the statement of cash flows is to determine the change in cash. As the comparative balance sheets show, cash increased $17,000 in 2013.

Step 2: Determine Net Cash Flow from Operating Activities—Indirect Method

We explain the adjustments to net income of $125,000 as follows.

Increase in Accounts Receivable. The increase in accounts receivable of $42,000 represents recorded accrual-basis revenues in excess of cash collections in 2013. The company deducts this increase from net income to convert from the accrual basis to the cash basis.

Increase in Inventory. The $54,000 increase in inventory represents an operating use of cash, not an expense. Tax Consultants therefore deducts this amount from net income, to arrive at net cash flow from operations. In other words, when inventory purchased exceeds inventory sold during a period, cost of goods sold on an accrual basis is lower than on a cash basis.

Decrease in Prepaid Expenses. The $2,000 decrease in prepaid expenses represents a charge to the income statement for which Tax Consultants made no cash payment in the current period. The company adds back the decrease to net income, to arrive at net cash flow from operating activities.

Decrease in Accounts Payable. When accounts payable decrease during the year, cost of goods sold and expenses on a cash basis are higher than they are on an accrual basis. To convert net income to net cash flow from operating activities, the company must deduct the $7,000 in accounts payable from net income.

Depreciation Expense (Increase in Accumulated Depreciation). Accumulated Depreciation—Buildings increased $10,000 ($21,000 − $11,000). The Buildings account did not change during the period, which means that Tax Consultants recorded depreciation expense of $10,000 in 2013.

Accumulated Depreciation—Equipment increased by $18,000 ($28,000 − $10,000) during the year. But Accumulated Depreciation—Equipment decreased by $5,000 as a result of the sale during the year. Thus, depreciation for the year was $23,000. The company reconciled Accumulated Depreciation—Equipment as follows.

Beginning balance	$10,000
Add: Depreciation for 2013	23,000
	33,000
Deduct: Sale of equipment	5,000
Ending balance	$28,000

The company must add back to net income the total depreciation of $33,000 ($10,000 + $23,000) charged to the income statement, to determine net cash flow from operating activities.

Loss on Sale of Equipment. Tax Consultants Inc. sold for $34,000 equipment that cost $41,000 and had a book value of $36,000. As a result, the company reported a loss of $2,000 on its sale. To arrive at net cash flow from operating activities, it must add back to net income the loss on the sale of the equipment. The reason is that the loss is a non-cash charge to the income statement. The loss did not reduce cash, but it did reduce net income.[5]

[5]A similar adjustment is required for unrealized gains or losses recorded on trading security investments or other financial assets and liabilities accounted for under the fair value option. Marking these assets and liabilities to fair value results in an increase or decrease in income, but there is no effect on cash flows.

From the foregoing items, the company prepares the operating activities section of the statement of cash flows, as shown in Illustration 23-16.

ILLUSTRATION 23-16
Operating Activities Section of Cash Flows Statement

Cash flows from operating activities		
Net income		$ 125,000
Adjustments to reconcile net income to net cash provided by operating activities:		
Depreciation expense	$ 33,000	
Loss on sale of equipment	2,000	
Increase in accounts receivable	(42,000)	
Increase in inventory	(54,000)	
Decrease in prepaid expenses	2,000	
Decrease in accounts payable	(7,000)	(66,000)
Net cash provided by operating activities		59,000

Step 3: Determine Net Cash Flows from Investing and Financing Activities

By analyzing the remaining changes in the balance sheet accounts, Tax Consultants identifies cash flows from investing and financing activities.

Land. Land decreased $25,000 during the period. As indicated from the information presented, the company sold land for cash at its book value. This transaction is an investing activity, reported as a $25,000 source of cash.

Equipment. An Analysis of the Equipment account indicates the following.

Beginning balance	$ 68,000
Purchase of equipment	166,000
	234,000
Sale of equipment	41,000
Ending balance	$193,000

The company used cash to purchase equipment with a fair value of $166,000—an investing transaction reported as a cash outflow. The sale of the equipment for $34,000 is also an investing activity, but one that generates a cash inflow.

Bonds Payable. Bonds payable decreased $40,000 during the year. As indicated from the additional information, the company redeemed the bonds at their book value. This financing transaction used $40,000 of cash.

Common Stock. The Common Stock account increased $160,000 during the year. As indicated from the additional information, Tax Consultants issued common stock of $160,000 at par. This financing transaction provided cash of $160,000.

Retained Earnings. Retained earnings changed $70,000 ($206,000 − $136,000) during the year. The $70,000 change in retained earnings results from net income of $125,000 from operations and the financing activity of paying cash dividends of $55,000.

Statement of Cash Flows—2013

Tax Consultants Inc. combines the foregoing items to prepare the statement of cash flows shown in Illustration 23-17.

ILLUSTRATION 23-17
Statement of Cash Flows, Tax Consultants Inc., Year 3

TAX CONSULTANTS INC. STATEMENT OF CASH FLOWS FOR THE YEAR ENDED DECEMBER 31, 2013 INCREASE (DECREASE) IN CASH		
Cash flows from operating activities		
Net income		$ 125,000
Adjustments to reconcile net income to net cash provided by operating activities:		
Depreciation expense	$ 33,000	
Loss on sale of equipment	2,000	
Increase in accounts receivable	(42,000)	
Increase in inventory	(54,000)	
Decrease in prepaid expenses	2,000	
Decrease in accounts payable	(7,000)	(66,000)
Net cash provided by operating activities		59,000
Cash flows from investing activities		
Sale of land	25,000	
Sale of equipment	34,000	
Purchase of equipment	(166,000)	
Net cash used by investing activities		(107,000)
Cash flows from financing activities		
Redemption of bonds	(40,000)	
Sale of common stock	160,000	
Payment of dividends	(55,000)	
Net cash provided by financing activities		65,000
Net increase in cash		17,000
Cash, January 1, 2013		37,000
Cash, December 31, 2013		$ 54,000

SOURCES OF INFORMATION FOR THE STATEMENT OF CASH FLOWS

7 LEARNING OBJECTIVE
Identify sources of information for a statement of cash flows.

Important points to remember in the preparation of the statement of cash flows are these:

1. Comparative balance sheets provide the basic information from which to prepare the report. Additional information obtained from analyses of specific accounts is also included.
2. An analysis of the Retained Earnings account is necessary. The net increase or decrease in Retained Earnings without any explanation is a meaningless amount in the statement. Without explanation, it might represent the effect of net income, dividends declared, or prior period adjustments.
3. The statement includes all changes that have passed through cash or have resulted in an increase or decrease in cash.
4. Write-downs, amortization charges, and similar "book" entries, such as depreciation of plant assets, represent neither inflows nor outflows of cash, because they have no effect on cash. To the extent that they have entered into the determination of net income, however, the company must add them back to or subtract them from net income, to arrive at net cash provided (used) by operating activities.

NET CASH FLOW FROM OPERATING ACTIVITIES—INDIRECT VERSUS DIRECT METHOD

As we discussed previously, the two different methods available to adjust income from operations on an accrual basis to net cash flow from operating activities are the indirect (reconciliation) method and the direct (income statement) method.

The FASB encourages use of the direct method and permits use of the indirect method. Yet, if the direct method is used, the Board requires that companies provide in a separate schedule a reconciliation of net income to net cash flow from operating activities. Therefore, under either method, companies must prepare and report information from the indirect (reconciliation) method.

Indirect Method

For consistency and comparability and because it is the most widely used method in practice, we used the indirect method in the examples just presented. We determined net cash flow from operating activities by adding back to or deducting from net income those items that had no effect on cash. Illustration 23-18 presents more completely the common types of adjustments that companies make to net income to arrive at net cash flow from operating activities.

ILLUSTRATION 23-18
Adjustments Needed to Determine Net Cash Flow from Operating Activities—Indirect Method

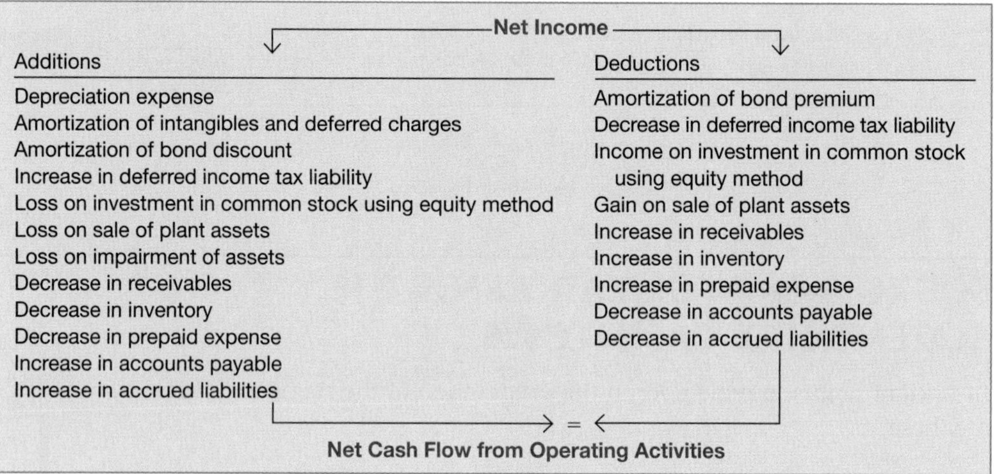

The additions and deductions in Illustration 23-18 reconcile net income to net cash flow from operating activities, illustrating why the indirect method is also called the reconciliation method.

Direct Method—An Example

Under the direct method the statement of cash flows reports net cash flow from operating activities as major classes of *operating cash receipts* (e.g., cash collected from customers and cash received from interest and dividends) and *cash disbursements* (e.g., cash paid to suppliers for goods, to employees for services, to creditors for interest, and to government authorities for taxes).

We illustrate the direct method here in more detail to help you understand the difference between accrual-based income and net cash flow from operating activities. This example also illustrates the data needed to apply the direct method. Emig Company, which began business on January 1, 2012, has the following selected balance sheet information.

ILLUSTRATION 23-19
Balance Sheet Accounts, Emig Co.

	December 31, 2012	January 1, 2012
Cash	$159,000	-0-
Accounts receivable	15,000	-0-
Inventory	160,000	-0-
Prepaid expenses	8,000	-0-
Property, plant, and equipment (net)	90,000	-0-
Accounts payable	60,000	-0-
Accrued expenses payable	20,000	-0-

Emig Company's December 31, 2012, income statement and additional information are as follows.

ILLUSTRATION 23-20
Income Statement, Emig Co.

Sales revenue		$780,000
Cost of goods sold		450,000
Gross profit		330,000
Operating expenses	$160,000	
Depreciation	10,000	170,000
Income before income taxes		160,000
Income tax expense		48,000
Net income		$112,000

Additional Information
(a) Dividends of $70,000 were declared and paid in cash.
(b) The accounts payable increase resulted from the purchase of merchandise.
(c) Prepaid expenses and accrued expenses payable relate to operating expenses.

Under the **direct method**, companies compute net cash provided by operating activities by **adjusting each item in the income statement** from the accrual basis to the cash basis. To simplify and condense the operating activities section, only major classes of operating cash receipts and cash payments are reported. As Illustration 23-21 shows, the difference between these major classes of cash receipts and cash payments is the net cash provided by operating activities.

ILLUSTRATION 23-21
Major Classes of Cash Receipts and Payments

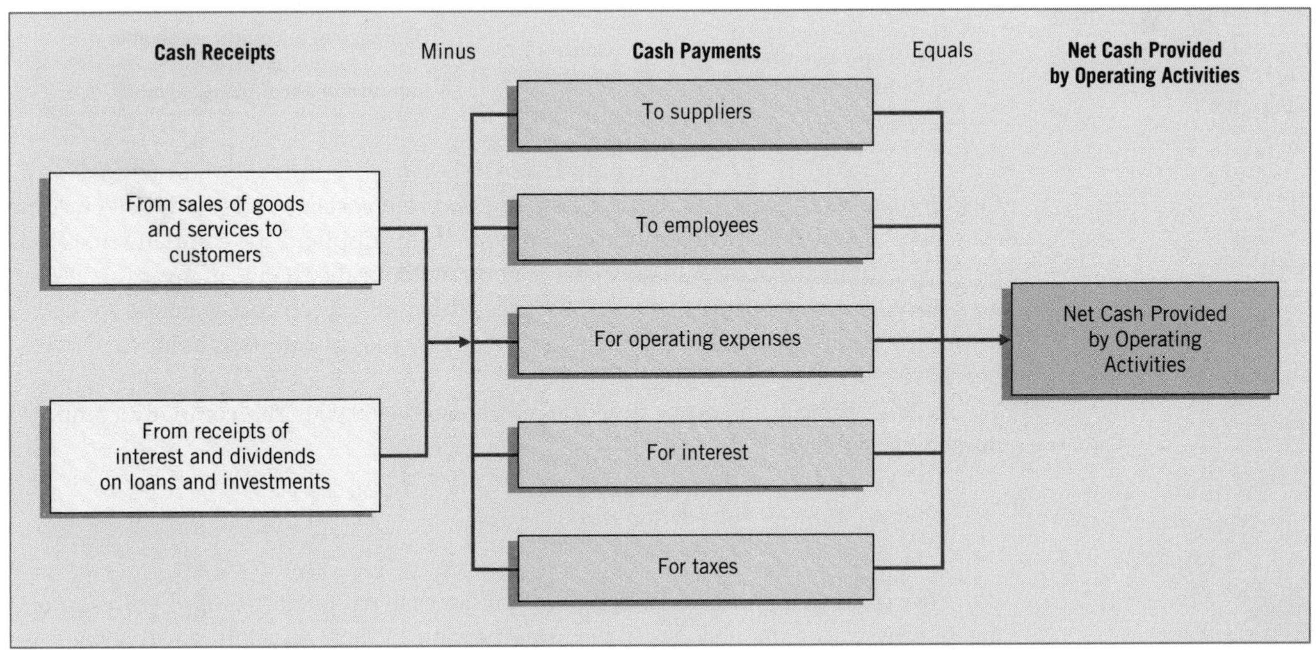

An efficient way to apply the direct method is to analyze the revenues and expenses reported in the income statement in the order in which they are listed. The company then determines cash receipts and cash payments related to these revenues and expenses. In the following sections, we present the direct method adjustments for Emig Company in 2012, to determine net cash provided by operating activities.

Cash Receipts from Customers. The income statement for Emig Company reported revenues from customers of $780,000. To determine cash receipts from customers, the company considers the change in accounts receivable during the year.

When accounts receivable increase during the year, revenues on an accrual basis are higher than cash receipts from customers. In other words, operations led to increased revenues, but not all of these revenues resulted in cash receipts. To determine the amount of increase in cash receipts, deduct the amount of the increase in accounts receivable from the total sales revenue. Conversely, a decrease in accounts receivable is added to sales revenue, because cash receipts from customers then exceed sales revenue.

For Emig Company, accounts receivable increased $15,000. Thus, cash receipts from customers were $765,000, computed as follows.

Sales revenue	$780,000
Deduct: Increase in accounts receivable	15,000
Cash receipts from customers	$765,000

Emig could also determine cash receipts from customers by analyzing the Accounts Receivable account as shown below.

Accounts Receivable

1/1/12	Balance	–0–	Receipts from customers	765,000
	Sales revenue	780,000		
12/31/12	Balance	15,000		

Illustration 23-22 shows the relationships between cash receipts from customers, sales revenue, and changes in accounts receivable.

ILLUSTRATION 23-22
Formula to Compute Cash Receipts from Customers

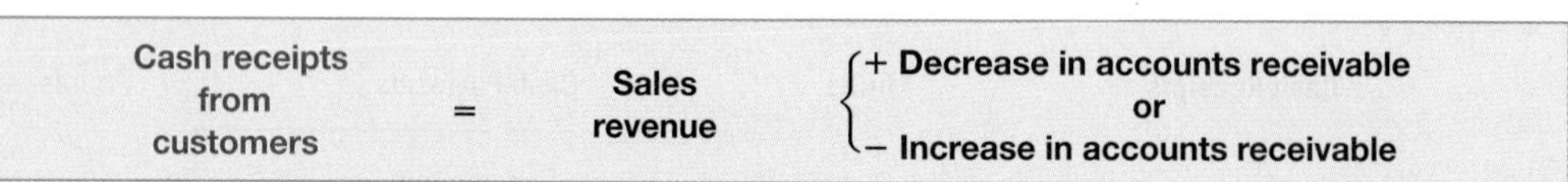

Cash Payments to Suppliers. Emig Company reported cost of goods sold on its income statement of $450,000. To determine cash payments to suppliers, the company first finds purchases for the year, by adjusting cost of goods sold for the change in inventory. When inventory increases during the year, purchases this year exceed cost of goods sold. As a result, the company adds the increase in inventory to cost of goods sold, to arrive at purchases.

In 2012, Emig Company's inventory increased $160,000. The company computes purchases as follows.

Cost of goods sold	$450,000
Add: Increase in inventory	160,000
Purchases	$610,000

After computing purchases, Emig determines cash payments to suppliers by adjusting purchases for the change in accounts payable. When accounts payable increase during the year, purchases on an accrual basis are higher than they are on a cash basis. As a result, it deducts from purchases the increase in accounts payable to arrive at cash payments to suppliers. Conversely, if cash payments to suppliers exceed purchases, Emig adds to purchases the decrease in accounts payable. Cash payments to suppliers were $550,000, computed as follows.

Purchases	$610,000
Deduct: Increase in accounts payable	60,000
Cash payments to suppliers	$550,000

Emig also can determine cash payments to suppliers by analyzing Accounts Payable, as shown below.

Accounts Payable				
Payments to suppliers	550,000	1/1/12	Balance	-0-
			Purchases	610,000
		12/31/12	Balance	60,000

Illustration 23-23 shows the relationships between cash payments to suppliers, cost of goods sold, changes in inventory, and changes in accounts payable.

ILLUSTRATION 23-23
Formula to Compute Cash Payments to Suppliers

Cash payments to suppliers	=	Cost of goods sold	+ Increase in inventory or − Decrease in inventory	+ Decrease in accounts payable or − Increase in accounts payable

Cash Payments for Operating Expenses. Emig reported operating expenses of $160,000 on its income statement. To determine the cash paid for operating expenses, it must adjust this amount for any changes in prepaid expenses and accrued expenses payable.

For example, when prepaid expenses increased $8,000 during the year, cash paid for operating expenses was $8,000 higher than operating expenses reported on the income statement. To convert operating expenses to cash payments for operating expenses, the company adds to operating expenses the increase of $8,000. Conversely, if prepaid expenses decrease during the year, it deducts from operating expenses the amount of the decrease.

Emig also must adjust operating expenses for changes in accrued expenses payable. When accrued expenses payable increase during the year, operating expenses on an accrual basis are higher than they are on a cash basis. As a result, the company deducts from operating expenses an increase in accrued expenses payable, to arrive at cash payments for operating expenses. Conversely, it adds to operating expenses a decrease in accrued expenses payable, because cash payments exceed operating expenses.

Emig Company's cash payments for operating expenses were $148,000, computed as follows.

Operating expenses	$160,000
Add: Increase in prepaid expenses	8,000
Deduct: Increase in accrued expenses payable	(20,000)
Cash payments for operating expenses	$148,000

The relationships among cash payments for operating expenses, changes in prepaid expenses, and changes in accrued expenses payable are shown in Illustration 23-24 (page 1456).

ILLUSTRATION 23-24
Formula to Compute Cash Payments for Operating Expenses

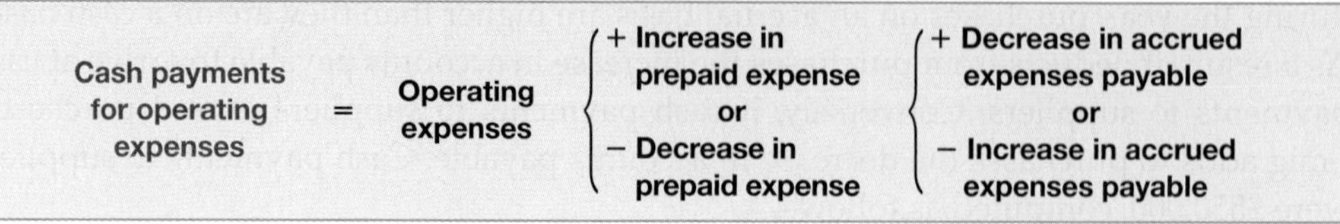

Note that the company did not consider depreciation expense, because it is a non-cash charge.

Cash Payments for Income Taxes. The income statement for Emig shows income tax expense of $48,000. This amount equals the cash paid. How do we know that? Because the comparative balance sheet indicated no income taxes payable at either the beginning or end of the year.

Summary of Net Cash Flow from Operating Activities—Direct Method

The following schedule summarizes the computations illustrated above.

ILLUSTRATION 23-25
Accrual Basis to Cash Basis

Accrual Basis			Adjustment	Add (Subtract)	Cash Basis
Sales revenue	$780,000	−	Increase in accounts receivable	$ (15,000)	$765,000
Cost of goods sold	450,000	+	Increase in inventory	160,000	
		−	Increase in accounts payable	(60,000)	550,000
Operating expenses	160,000	+	Increase in prepaid expenses	8,000	
		−	Increase in accrued expenses payable	(20,000)	148,000
Depreciation expense	10,000	−	Depreciation expense	(10,000)	-0-
Income tax expense	48,000				48,000
Total expense	668,000				746,000
Net income	$112,000		Net cash provided by operating activities		$ 19,000

Illustration 23-26 shows the presentation of the direct method for reporting net cash flow from operating activities for the Emig Company illustration.

ILLUSTRATION 23-26
Operating Activities Section—Direct Method, 2012

EMIG COMPANY
STATEMENT OF CASH FLOWS (PARTIAL)

Cash flows from operating activities		
Cash received from customers		$765,000
Cash payments:		
To suppliers	$550,000	
For operating expenses	148,000	
For income taxes	48,000	746,000
Net cash provided by operating activities		$ 19,000

If Emig Company uses the direct method to present the net cash flow from operating activities, it must provide in a separate schedule the reconciliation of net income to net cash provided by operating activities. The reconciliation assumes the identical form and content of the indirect method of presentation, as shown on the next page.

ILLUSTRATION 23-27
Reconciliation of Net Income to Net Cash Provided by Operating Activities

EMIG COMPANY RECONCILIATION		
Net income		$112,000
Adjustments to reconcile net income to net cash provided by operating activities:		
Depreciation expense	$ 10,000	
Increase in accounts receivable	(15,000)	
Increase in inventory	(160,000)	
Increase in prepaid expenses	(8,000)	
Increase in accounts payable	60,000	
Increase in accrued expense payable	20,000	(93,000)
Net cash provided by operating activities		$ 19,000

When the direct method is used, the company may present this reconciliation at the bottom of the statement of cash flows or in a separate schedule.

Direct versus Indirect Controversy

The most contentious decision that the FASB faced related to cash flow reporting was choosing between the direct method and the indirect method of determining net cash flow from operating activities. Companies lobbied *against* the direct method, urging adoption of the indirect method. Commercial lending officers expressed to the FASB a strong preference in favor of the direct method. In the next two sections, we consider the arguments in favor of each of the methods.

In Favor of the Direct Method

The principal advantage of the direct method is that **it shows operating cash receipts and payments**. Thus, it is more consistent with the objective of a statement of cash flows—to provide information about cash receipts and cash payments—than the indirect method, which does not report operating cash receipts and payments.

Supporters of the direct method contend that knowledge of the specific sources of operating cash receipts and the purposes for which operating cash payments were made in past periods is useful in estimating future operating cash flows. Furthermore, information about amounts of major classes of operating cash receipts and payments is more useful than information only about their arithmetic sum (the net cash flow from operating activities). Such information is more revealing of a company's ability (1) to generate sufficient cash from operating activities to pay its debts, (2) to reinvest in its operations, and (3) to make distributions to its owners. [4]

Many companies indicate that they do not currently collect information in a manner that allows them to determine amounts such as cash received from customers or cash paid to suppliers directly from their accounting systems. But supporters of the direct method contend that the incremental cost of determining operating cash receipts and payments is not significant.

In Favor of the Indirect Method

The principal advantage of the indirect method is that **it focuses on the differences between net income and net cash flow from operating activities**. That is, it provides a useful link between the statement of cash flows and the income statement and balance sheet.

Many companies contend that it is less costly to adjust net income to net cash flow from operating activities (indirect) than it is to report gross operating cash receipts and payments (direct). Supporters of the indirect method also state that the direct method, which effectively reports income statement information on a cash rather than an accrual basis, may erroneously suggest that net cash flow from operating activities is as good as, or better than, net income as a measure of performance.

Special Rules Applying to Direct and Indirect Methods

Companies that use the direct method are required, at a minimum, to report separately the following classes of operating cash receipts and payments:

Receipts

1. Cash collected from customers (including lessees, licensees, etc.).
2. Interest and dividends received.
3. Other operating cash receipts, if any.

Payments

1. Cash paid to employees and suppliers of goods or services (including suppliers of insurance, advertising, etc.).
2. Interest paid.
3. Income taxes paid.
4. Other operating cash payments, if any.

INTERNATIONAL PERSPECTIVE

Consolidated statements of cash flows may be of limited use to analysts evaluating multinational companies. Without disaggregation, users of such statements are not able to determine "where in the world" the funds are sourced and used.

The FASB encourages companies to provide further breakdowns of operating cash receipts and payments that they consider meaningful.

Companies using the indirect method must disclose separately changes in inventory, receivables, and payables in order to reconcile net income to net cash flow from operating activities. In addition, they must disclose, elsewhere in the financial statements or in accompanying notes, interest paid (net of amount capitalized) and income taxes paid.[6] The FASB requires these separate and additional disclosures so that users may approximate the direct method. Also, an acceptable alternative presentation of the indirect method is to report net cash flow from operating activities as a single line item in the statement of cash flows and to present the reconciliation details elsewhere in the financial statements.

NOT WHAT IT SEEMS

What do the numbers mean?

The controversy over direct and indirect methods highlights the importance that the market attributes to operating cash flow. By showing an improving cash flow, a company can give a favorable impression of its ongoing operations. For example, WorldCom concealed declines in its operations by capitalizing certain operating expenses—to the tune of $3.8 billion! This practice not only "juiced up" income but also made it possible to report the cash payments in the investing section of the cash flow statement rather than as a deduction from operating cash flow.

The SEC recently addressed a similar cash flow classification issue with automakers like Ford, GM, and Chrysler. For years, automakers classified lease receivables and other dealer-financing arrangements as investment cash flows. Thus, they reported an increase in lease or loan receivables from cars sold as a use of cash in the investing section of the statement of cash flows. The SEC objected and now requires automakers to report these receivables as operating cash flows, since the leases and loans are used to facilitate car sales. At GM, these reclassifications reduced its operating cash flows from $7.6 billion to $3 billion in the year before the change. So while the overall cash flow—from operations, investing, and financing—remained the same, operating cash flow at these companies looked better than it really was.

Source: Peter Elstrom, "How to Hide $3.8 Billion in Expenses," *BusinessWeek Online* (July 8, 2002); and Judith Burns, "SEC Tells US Automakers to Retool Cash-Flow Accounting," *Wall Street Journal Online* (February 28, 2005).

[6]*Accounting Trends and Techniques—2010* reports that of the 500 companies surveyed, 244 disclosed interest paid in notes to the financial statements, 235 disclosed interest paid at the bottom of the statement of cash flows, 6 disclosed interest paid within the statement of cash flows, and 15 reported no separate amount. Income taxes paid during the year were disclosed in a manner similar to interest payments.

SECTION 2 • SPECIAL PROBLEMS IN STATEMENT PREPARATION

We discussed some of the special problems related to preparing the statement of cash flows in connection with the preceding illustrations. Other problems that arise with some frequency in the preparation of this statement include the following.

8 LEARNING OBJECTIVE
Discuss special problems in preparing a statement of cash flows.

1. Adjustments to net income.
2. Accounts receivable (net).
3. Other working capital changes.
4. Net losses.
5. Significant noncash transactions.

ADJUSTMENTS TO NET INCOME

Depreciation and Amortization

Depreciation expense is the most common adjustment to net income that companies make to arrive at net cash flow from operating activities. But there are numerous other noncash expense or revenue items. Examples of expense items that companies must add back to net income are the **amortization of limited-life intangible assets** such as patents, and the **amortization of deferred costs** such as bond issue costs. These charges to expense involve expenditures made in prior periods that a company amortizes currently. These charges reduce net income without affecting cash in the current period.

Also, **amortization of bond discount or premium** on long-term bonds payable affects the amount of interest expense. However, neither affects cash. As a result, a company should add back discount amortization and subtract premium amortization from net income to arrive at net cash flow from operating activities.

Postretirement Benefit Costs

If a company has postretirement costs such as an employee pension plan, chances are that the pension expense recorded during a period will either be higher or lower than the cash funded. It will be higher when there is an unfunded liability and will be lower when there is a prepaid pension cost. When the expense is higher or lower than the cash paid, **the company must adjust net income by the difference between cash paid and the expense reported** in computing net cash flow from operating activities.

Change in Deferred Income Taxes

Changes in deferred income taxes affect net income but have no effect on cash. For example, Delta Airlines reported an increase in its liability for deferred taxes of approximately $1.2 billion. This change in the liability increased tax expense and decreased net income, but did not affect cash. Therefore, Delta added back $1.2 billion to net income on its statement of cash flows.

Equity Method of Accounting

Another common adjustment to net income is **a change related to an investment in common stock** when recording income or loss under the equity method. Recall that under the equity method, the investor (1) debits the investment account and credits revenue for its share of the investee's net income, and (2) credits dividends received to the investment account. Therefore, the net increase in the investment account does not affect cash flow. A company must deduct the net increase from net income to arrive at net cash flow from operating activities.

Assume that Victor Co. owns 40 percent of Milo Inc. During the year Milo reports net income of $100,000 and pays a cash dividend of $30,000. Victor reports this in its statement of cash flows as a deduction from net income in the following manner—Equity in earnings of Milo, net of dividends, $28,000 [($100,000 − $30,000) × 40%].

Losses and Gains

Realized Losses and Gains

In the illustration for Tax Consultants, the company experienced a loss of $2,000 from the sale of equipment. The company added this loss to net income to compute net cash flow from operating activities because **the loss is a noncash charge in the income statement.**

If Tax Consultants experiences a **gain** from a sale of equipment, it too requires an adjustment to net income. Because a company reports the gain in the statement of cash flows as part of the cash proceeds from the sale of equipment under investing activities, **it deducts the gain from net income to avoid double-counting**—once as part of net income and again as part of the cash proceeds from the sale.

To illustrate, assume that Tax Consultants had land with a carrying value of $200,000, which was condemned by the state government for a highway project. The condemnation proceeds received were $205,000, resulting in a gain of $5,000. In the statement of cash flows (indirect method), the company would deduct the $5,000 gain from net income in the operating activities section. It would report the $205,000 cash inflow from the condemnation as an investing activity, as follows.

Cash flows from investing activities	
Condemnation of land	$205,000

Unrealized Losses and Gains

Unrealized losses and gains generally occur for debt investments and for equity investments. For example, assume that **Target** purchases the following two investments on January 10, 2012.

1. Debt investment for $1 million that is classified as trading. During 2012, the debt investment has an unrealized holding gain of $110,000 (recorded in net income).
2. Equity investment for $600,000 that is classified as available-for-sale. During 2012, the available-for-sale equity investment has an unrealized holding loss of $50,000 (recorded in other comprehensive income).

For Target, the unrealized holding gain of $110,000 on the debt investment increases net income but does not increase net cash flow from operating activities. As a result, the unrealized holding gain of $110,000 is deducted from net income to compute net cash flow from operating activities.

On the other hand, the unrealized holding loss of $50,000 that Target incurs on the available-for-sale equity investment does not affect net income or cash flows—this loss is reported in the other comprehensive income section. As a result, no adjustment to net income is necessary in computing net cash flow from operating activities.

Thus, the general rule is that unrealized holding gains or losses that affect net income must be adjusted to determine net cash flow from operating activities. Conversely, unrealized holding gains or losses that do not affect net income are not adjusted to determine net cash flow from operating activities.

Stock Options

Recall for share-based compensation plans that companies are required to use the fair value method to determine total compensation cost. The compensation cost is then recognized as an expense in the periods in which the employee provides services. When Compensation Expense is debited, Paid-in Capital—Stock Options is often credited. Cash is not affected by recording the expense. **Therefore, the company must increase net income by the amount of compensation expense from stock options in computing net cash flow from operating activities.**

To illustrate how this information should be reported on a statement of cash flows, assume that First Wave Inc. grants 5,000 options to its CEO, Ann Johnson. Each option entitles Johnson to purchase one share of First Wave's $1 par value common stock at $50 per share at any time in the next two years (the service period). The fair value of the options is $200,000. First Wave records compensation expense in the first year as follows.

Compensation Expense ($200,000 ÷ 2)	100,000	
Paid-in Capital—Stock Options		100,000

In addition, if we assume that First Wave has a 35 percent tax rate, it would recognize a deferred tax asset of $35,000 ($100,000 × 35%) in the first year as follows.

Deferred Tax Asset	35,000	
Income Tax Expense		35,000

Therefore, on the statement of cash flows for the first year, First Wave reports the following (assuming a net income of $600,000).

Net income	$600,000
Adjustments to reconcile net income to net cash provided by operating activities:	
Share-based compensation expense	100,000
Increase in deferred tax asset	(35,000)

As shown in First Wave's statement of cash flows, it adds the share-based compensation expense to net income because it is a noncash expense. The increase in the deferred tax asset and the related reduction in income tax expense increase net income. Although the negative income tax expense increases net income, it does not increase cash. Therefore, it should be deducted.

Subsequently, if Ann Johnson exercises her options, Third Wave reports "Cash provided by exercise of stock options" in the financing section of the statement of cash flows.[7]

Extraordinary Items

Companies should report **either as investing activities or as financing activities** cash flows from extraordinary transactions and other events whose effects are included in net income, but which are not related to operations.

[7]Companies receive a tax deduction related to share-based compensation plans at the time employees exercise their options. The amount of the deduction is equal to the difference between the market price of the stock and the exercise price at the date the employee purchases the stock, which in most cases is much larger than the total compensation expense recorded. When the tax deduction exceeds the total compensation recorded, this provides an additional cash inflow to the company. For example, in a recent year Cisco Systems reported an additional cash inflow related to its stock option plans equal to $537 million. Under GAAP, this tax-related cash inflow is reported in the financing section of the statement of cash flows. [5]

For example, assume that Tax Consultants had land with a carrying value of $200,000, which was condemned by the state of Maine for a highway project. The condemnation proceeds received were $205,000, resulting in a gain of $5,000 less $2,000 of taxes. In the statement of cash flows (indirect method), the company would deduct the $5,000 gain from net income in the operating activities section. It would report the $205,000 cash inflow from the condemnation as an investing activity, as follows.

Underlying Concepts

By rejecting the requirement to allocate taxes to the various activities the FASB invoked the cost constraint. The information would be beneficial, but the cost of providing such information would exceed the benefits of providing it.

Cash flows from investing activities	
Condemnation of land	$205,000

Note that Tax Consultants handles the gain at its **gross** amount ($5,000), not net of tax. The company reports the cash received in the condemnation as an investing activity at $205,000, also exclusive of the tax effect.

The FASB requires companies to classify **all income taxes paid as operating cash outflows**. Some suggested that income taxes paid be allocated to investing and financing transactions. But the Board decided that allocation of income taxes paid to operating, investing, and financing activities would be so complex and arbitrary that the benefits, if any, would not justify the costs involved. Under both the direct method and the indirect method, companies must disclose the total amount of income taxes paid.[8]

ACCOUNTS RECEIVABLE (NET)

Up to this point, we assumed no allowance for doubtful accounts—a contra account—to offset accounts receivable. However, if a company needs an allowance for doubtful accounts, how does that allowance affect the company's determination of net cash flow from operating activities? For example, assume that Redmark Co. reports net income of $40,000. It has the accounts receivable balances as shown in Illustration 23-28.

ILLUSTRATION 23-28
Accounts Receivable Balances, Redmark Co.

	2012	2011	Change Increase/Decrease
Accounts receivable	$105,000	$90,000	$15,000 Increase
Allowance for doubtful accounts	(10,000)	(4,000)	6,000 Increase
Accounts receivable (net)	$ 95,000	$86,000	9,000 Increase

Indirect Method

Because an increase in Allowance for Doubtful Accounts results from a charge to bad debt expense, a company should add back an increase in Allowance for Doubtful Accounts to net income to arrive at net cash flow from operating activities. Illustration 23-29 shows one method for presenting this information in a statement of cash flows.

[8]For an insightful article on some weaknesses and limitations in the statement of cash flows, see Hugo Nurnberg, "Inconsistencies and Ambiguities in Cash Flow Statements Under *FASB Statement No. 95*," *Accounting Horizons* (June 1993), pp. 60–73. Nurnberg identifies the inconsistencies caused by the three-way classification of all cash receipts and cash payments, gross versus net of tax, the ambiguous disclosure requirements for noncash investing and financing transactions and the ambiguous presentation of third-party financing transactions. See also Paul B. W. Miller and Bruce P. Budge, "Nonarticulation in Cash Flow Statements and Implications for Education, Research, and Practice," *Accounting Horizons* (December 1996), pp. 1–15; and Charles Mulford and Michael Ely, "Calculating Sustainable Cash Flow: A Study of the S&P 100," *Georgia Tech Financial Analysis Lab* (October 2004).

ILLUSTRATION 23-29
Presentation of Allowance for Doubtful Accounts—Indirect Method

REDMARK CO.
STATEMENT OF CASH FLOWS (PARTIAL)
FOR THE YEAR 2012

Cash flows from operating activities		
Net income		$40,000
Adjustments to reconcile net income to net cash provided by operating activities:		
Increase in accounts receivable	$(15,000)	
Increase in allowance for doubtful accounts	6,000	(9,000)
		$31,000

As we indicated, the increase in the Allowance for Doubtful Accounts balance results from a charge to bad debt expense for the year. Because bad debt expense is a noncash charge, a company must add it back to net income in arriving at net cash flow from operating activities.

Instead of separately analyzing the allowance account, a short-cut approach is to net the allowance balance against the receivable balance and compare the change in accounts receivable on a net basis. Illustration 23-30 shows this presentation.

ILLUSTRATION 23-30
Net Approach to Allowance for Doubtful Accounts—Indirect Method

REDMARK CO.
STATEMENT OF CASH FLOWS (PARTIAL)
FOR THE YEAR 2012

Cash flows from operating activities	
Net income	$40,000
Adjustments to reconcile net income to net cash provided by operating activities:	
Increase in accounts receivable (net)	(9,000)
	$31,000

This short-cut procedure works also if the change in the allowance account results from a write-off of accounts receivable. This reduces both Accounts Receivable and Allowance for Doubtful Accounts. No effect on cash flows occurs. *Because of its simplicity, use the net approach for your homework assignments.*

Direct Method

If using the direct method, a company **should not net** Allowance for Doubtful Accounts against Accounts Receivable. To illustrate, assume that Redmark Co.'s net income of $40,000 consisted of the items shown in Illustration 23-31.

ILLUSTRATION 23-31
Income Statement, Redmark Co.

REDMARK CO.
INCOME STATEMENT
FOR THE YEAR 2012

Sales		$100,000
Expenses		
Salaries	$46,000	
Utilities	8,000	
Bad debts	6,000	60,000
Net income		$ 40,000

If Redmark deducts the $9,000 increase in accounts receivable (net) from sales for the year, it would report cash sales at $91,000 ($100,000 – $9,000) and cash payments for operating expenses at $60,000. Both items would be misstated: Cash sales should be reported at $85,000 ($100,000 – $15,000), and total cash payments for operating expenses should be reported at $54,000 ($60,000 – $6,000). Illustration 23-32 shows the proper presentation.

ILLUSTRATION 23-32
Bad Debts—Direct Method

REDMARK CO.
STATEMENT OF CASH FLOWS (PARTIAL)
FOR THE YEAR 2012

Cash flows from operating activities		
Cash received from customers		$85,000
Salaries paid	$46,000	
Utilities paid	8,000	54,000
Net cash provided by operating activities		$31,000

An added complication develops when a company writes off accounts receivable. Simply adjusting sales for the change in accounts receivable will not provide the proper amount of cash sales. The reason is that the write-off of the accounts receivable is not a cash collection. Thus, an additional adjustment is necessary.

OTHER WORKING CAPITAL CHANGES

Up to this point, we showed how companies handled all of the changes in working capital items (current asset and current liability items) as adjustments to net income in determining net cash flow from operating activities. You must be careful, however, because **some changes in working capital, although they affect cash, do not affect net income**. Generally, these are investing or financing activities of a current nature.

One activity is the purchase of **short-term available-for-sale securities**. For example, the purchase of short-term available-for-sale securities for $50,000 cash has no effect on net income but it does cause a $50,000 decrease in cash. A company reports this transaction as a cash flow from investing activities as follows. **[6]**

Cash flows from investing activities	
Purchase of short-term available-for-sale securities	$(50,000)

What about **trading securities?** Because companies hold these investments principally for the purpose of selling them in the near term, companies should classify the cash flows from purchases and sales of trading securities as cash flows from **operating activities**. **[7]**[9]

Another example is the issuance of a **short-term nontrade note payable** for cash. This change in a working capital item has no effect on income from operations but it increases cash by the amount of the note payable. For example, a company reports the

[9]If the basis of the statement of cash flows is **cash and cash equivalents** and the short-term investment is considered a cash equivalent, then a company reports nothing in the statement because the transaction does not affect the balance of cash and cash equivalents. The Board notes that cash purchases of short-term investments generally are part of the company's cash management activities rather than part of its operating, investing, or financing activities.

issuance of a $10,000 short-term note payable for cash in the statement of cash flows as follows.

Cash flows from financing activities	
Issuance of short-term note	$10,000

Another change in a working capital item that has no effect on income from operations or on cash is a **cash dividend payable**. Although a company will report the cash dividends when paid as a financing activity, it does not report the declared but unpaid dividend on the statement of cash flows.

NET LOSSES

If a company reports a net loss instead of a net income, it must adjust the net loss for those items that do not result in a cash inflow or outflow. The net loss, after adjusting for the charges or credits not affecting cash, may result in a negative or a positive cash flow from operating activities.

For example, if the net loss is $50,000 and the total amount of charges to add back is $60,000, then net cash provided by operating activities is $10,000. Illustration 23-33 shows this computation.

Net loss		$(50,000)
Adjustments to reconcile net income to net cash provided by operating activities:		
Depreciation of plant assets	$55,000	
Amortization of patents	5,000	60,000
Net cash provided by operating activities		$ 10,000

ILLUSTRATION 23-33
Computation of Net Cash Flow from Operating Activities—Cash Inflow

If the company experiences a net loss of $80,000 and the total amount of the charges to add back is $25,000, the presentation appears as follows.

Net loss	$(80,000)
Adjustments to reconcile net income to net cash used by operating activities:	
Depreciation of plant assets	25,000
Net cash used by operating activities	$(55,000)

ILLUSTRATION 23-34
Computation of Net Cash Flow from Operating Activities—Cash Outflow

Although not illustrated in this chapter, a negative cash flow may result even if the company reports a net income.

SIGNIFICANT NONCASH TRANSACTIONS

Because the statement of cash flows reports only the effects of operating, investing, and financing activities in terms of cash flows, it omits some **significant noncash transactions** and other events that are investing or financing activities. Among the more common of these noncash transactions that a company should report or disclose in some manner are the following.

1. Acquisition of assets by assuming liabilities (including capital lease obligations) or by issuing equity securities.
2. Exchanges of nonmonetary assets.
3. Refinancing of long-term debt.
4. Conversion of debt or preferred stock to common stock.
5. Issuance of equity securities to retire debt.

A company does not incorporate these noncash items in the statement of cash flows. If material in amount, these disclosures may be either narrative or summarized in a separate schedule at the bottom of the statement, or they may appear in a separate note or supplementary schedule to the financial statements.[10] Illustration 23-35 shows the presentation of these significant noncash transactions or other events in a separate schedule at the bottom of the statement of cash flows.

ILLUSTRATION 23-35
Schedule Presentation of Noncash Investing and Financing Activities

Net increase in cash	$3,717,000
Cash at beginning of year	5,208,000
Cash at end of year	$8,925,000
Noncash investing and financing activities	
Purchase of land and building through issuance of 250,000 shares of common stock	$1,750,000
Exchange of Steadfast, NY, land for Bedford, PA, land	$2,000,000
Conversion of 12% bonds to 50,000 shares of common stock	$500,000

Or, companies may present these noncash transactions in a separate note, as shown in Illustration 23-36.

ILLUSTRATION 23-36
Note Presentation of Noncash Investing and Financing Activities

Note G: Significant noncash transactions. During the year, the company engaged in the following significant noncash investing and financing transactions:

Issued 250,000 shares of common stock to purchase land and building	$1,750,000
Exchanged land in Steadfast, NY, for land in Bedford, PA	$2,000,000
Converted 12% bonds to 50,000 shares of common stock	$500,000

Companies do not generally report certain other significant noncash transactions or other events in conjunction with the statement of cash flows. Examples of these types of transactions are **stock dividends, stock splits, and restrictions on retained earnings.** Companies generally report these items, neither financing nor investing activities, in conjunction with the statement of stockholders' equity or schedules and notes pertaining to changes in capital accounts.

[10]Some noncash investing and financing activities are part cash and part noncash. Companies should report only the cash portion on the statement of cash flows. The noncash component should be reported at the bottom of the statement or in a separate note.

CASH FLOW TOOL

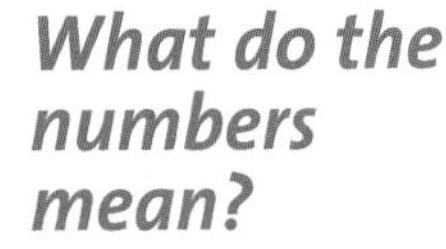

By understanding the relationship between cash flow and income measures, analysts can gain better insights into company performance. Because earnings altered through creative accounting practices generally do not change operating cash flows, analysts can use the relationship between earnings and operating cash flow to detect suspicious accounting practices. Also, by monitoring the ratio between cash flow from operations and operating income, they can get a clearer picture of developing problems in a company.

For example, the chart below plots the ratio of operating cash flows to earnings for **Xerox Corp.** in the years leading up to the SEC singling it out in 2000 for aggressive revenue recognition practices on its leases.

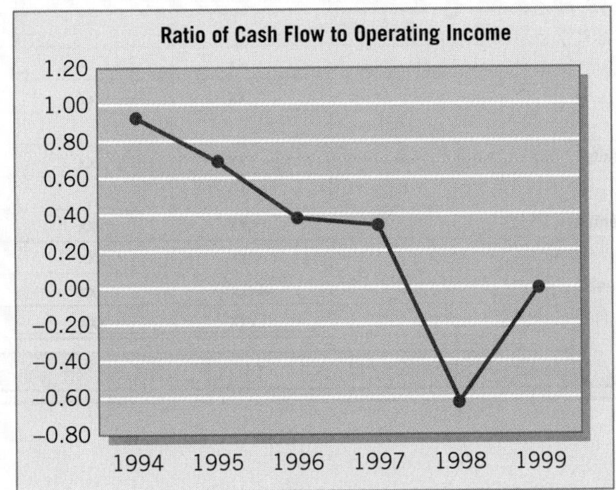

Similar to **W. T. Grant** in the chapter opening story, Xerox was reporting earnings growth in the years leading up to its financial breakdown in 2000 but teetering near bankruptcy in 2001. However, Xerox's ratio of cash flow to earnings showed a declining trend and became negative well before its revenue recognition practices were revealed. The trend revealed in the graph should have given any analyst reason to investigate Xerox further. As one analyst noted, "Earnings growth that exceeds the growth in operating cash flow cannot continue for extended periods and should be investigated."

Source: Adapted from Charles Mulford and Eugene Comiskey, *The Financial Numbers Game: Detecting Creative Accounting Practices* (New York: John Wiley & Sons, 2002), Chapter 11, by permission.

SECTION 3 • USE OF A WORKSHEET

9 LEARNING OBJECTIVE
Explain the use of a worksheet in preparing a statement of cash flows.

When numerous adjustments are necessary or other complicating factors are present, companies often use **a worksheet to assemble and classify the data that will appear on the statement of cash flows**. The worksheet (a **spreadsheet** when using computer software) is merely a device that aids in the preparation of the statement. Its use is optional. Illustration 23-37 (page 1468) shows the skeleton format of the worksheet for preparation of the statement of cash flows using the indirect method.

XYZ COMPANY
Statement of Cash Flows for the Year Ended...

	A	B	C	D	E
		End of Prior Year Balances	Reconciling Items		End of Current Year Balances
1	Balance Sheet Accounts		Debits	Credits	
2	Debit balance accounts	XX	XX	XX	XX
3		XX	XX	XX	XX
4	Totals	XXX			XXX
5	Credit balance accounts	XX	XX	XX	XX
6		XX	XX	XX	XX
7	Totals	XXX			XXX
8	Statement of Cash Flows Effects				
9	Operating activities				
10	Net income		XX		
11	Adjustments		XX	XX	
12	Investing activities				
13	Receipts and payments		XX	XX	
14	Financing activities				
15	Receipts and payments		XX	XX	
16	Totals		XXX	XXX	
17	Increase (decrease) in cash		(XX)	XX	
18	Totals		XXX	XXX	

Sheet1 Sheet2 Sheet3

ILLUSTRATION 23-37
Format of Worksheet for Preparation of Statement of Cash Flows

The following guidelines are important in using a worksheet.

1. In the balance sheet accounts section, **list accounts with debit balances separately from those with credit balances**. This means, for example, that Accumulated Depreciation is listed under credit balances and not as a contra account under debit balances. Enter the beginning and ending balances of each account in the appropriate columns. Then, enter the transactions that caused the change in the account balance during the year as reconciling items in the two middle columns.

   After all reconciling items have been entered, each line pertaining to a balance sheet account should foot across. That is, the beginning balance plus or minus the reconciling item(s) must equal the ending balance. When this agreement exists for all balance sheet accounts, all changes in account balances have been reconciled.

2. The bottom portion of the worksheet consists of the operating, investing, and financing activities sections. Accordingly, it provides the information necessary to prepare the formal statement of cash flows. **Enter inflows of cash as debits in the reconciling columns, and outflows of cash as credits in the reconciling columns.** Thus, in this section, a company would enter the sale of equipment for cash at book value as a debit under inflows of cash from investing activities. Similarly, it would enter the purchase of land for cash as a credit under outflows of cash from investing activities.
3. **Do not enter in any journal or post to any account the reconciling items shown in the worksheet.** These items do not represent either adjustments or corrections of the balance sheet accounts. They are used only to facilitate the preparation of the statement of cash flows.

PREPARATION OF THE WORKSHEET

The preparation of a worksheet involves the following steps.

Step 1. Enter the balance sheet accounts and their beginning and ending balances in the balance sheet accounts section.

Step 2. Enter the data that explain the changes in the balance sheet accounts (other than cash) and their effects on the statement of cash flows in the reconciling columns of the worksheet.

Step 3. Enter the increase or decrease in cash on the cash line and at the bottom of the worksheet. This entry should enable the totals of the reconciling columns to be in agreement.

To illustrate the preparation and use of a worksheet and to illustrate the reporting of some of the special problems discussed in the prior section, we present a comprehensive example for Satellite Corporation. Again, the indirect method serves as the basis for the computation of net cash provided by operating activities. Illustrations 23-38 and 23-39 present the balance sheet, combined statement of income and retained earnings, and additional information for Satellite Corporation.

ILLUSTRATION 23-38
Comparative Balance Sheet, Satellite Corporation

SATELLITE CORPORATION
Comparative Balance Sheet–December 31, 2012 and 2011

	A	B	C	D
1	Assets	2012	2011	Increase or (Decrease)
2	Cash	$ 59,000	$ 66,000	$ (7,000)
3	Accounts receivable (net)	104,000	51,000	53,000
4	Inventory	493,000	341,000	152,000
5	Prepaid expenses	16,500	17,000	(500)
6	Investment in Porter Co. (equity method)	18,500	15,000	3,500
7	Land	131,500	82,000	49,500
8	Equipment	187,000	142,000	45,000
9	Accumulated depreciation—equipment	(29,000)	(31,000)	(2,000)
10	Buildings	262,000	262,000	—
11	Accumulated depreciation—buildings	(74,100)	(71,000)	3,100
12	Trademarks	7,600	10,000	(2,400)
13	Total assets	$1,176,000	$884,000	
14	Liabilities			
15	Accounts payable	$ 132,000	$ 131,000	1,000
16	Accrued liabilities	43,000	39,000	4,000
17	Income taxes payable	3,000	16,000	(13,000)
18	Notes payable (long-term)	60,000	—	60,000
19	Bonds payable	100,000	100,000	—
20	Premium on bonds payable	7,000	8,000	(1,000)
21	Deferred tax liability (long-term)	9,000	6,000	3,000
22	Total liabilities	354,000	300,000	
23	Stockholders' Equity			
24	Common stock ($1 par)	60,000	50,000	10,000
25	Paid-in capital in excess of par—common stock	187,000	38,000	149,000
26	Retained earnings	592,000	496,000	96,000
27	Treasury stock	(17,000)	—	17,000
28	Total stockholders' equity	822,000	584,000	
29	Total liabilities and stockholders' equity	$1,176,000	$884,000	

Sheet1 Sheet2 Sheet3

ILLUSTRATION 23-39
Income and Retained Earnings Statements, Satellite Corporation

SATELLITE CORPORATION
COMBINED STATEMENT OF INCOME AND RETAINED EARNINGS
FOR THE YEAR ENDED DECEMBER 31, 2012

Net sales		$526,500
Other revenue		3,500
Total revenues		530,000
Expense		
Cost of goods sold		310,000
Selling and administrative expenses		47,000
Other expenses and losses		12,000
Total expenses		369,000
Income before income tax and extraordinary item		161,000
Income tax		
Current	$47,000	
Deferred	3,000	50,000
Income before extraordinary item		111,000
Gain on condemnation of land (net of $2,000 tax)		6,000
Net income		117,000
Retained earnings, January 1		496,000
Less:		
Cash dividends	6,000	
Stock dividend	15,000	21,000
Retained earnings, December 31		$592,000
Per share:		
Income before extraordinary item		$2.02
Extraordinary item		.11
Net income		$2.13

Additional Information

(a) Other income of $3,500 represents Satellite's equity share in the net income of Porter Co., an equity investee. Satellite owns 22% of Porter Co.

(b) An analysis of the equipment account and related accumulated depreciation indicates the following:

	Equipment Dr./(Cr.)	Accum. Dep. Dr./(Cr.)	Gain or (Loss)
Balance at end of 2011	$142,000	$(31,000)	
Purchases of equipment	53,000		
Sale of equipment	(8,000)	2,500	$(1,500)
Depreciation for the period		(11,500)	
Major repair charged to accumulated depreciation		11,000	
Balance at end of 2012	$187,000	$(29,000)	

(c) Land in the amount of $60,000 was purchased through the issuance of a long-term note; in addition, certain parcels of land costing $10,500 were condemned. The state government paid Satellite $18,500, resulting in an $8,000 gain which has a $2,000 tax effect.

(d) The change in the Accumulated Depreciation—Buildings, Trademarks, and Premium on Bonds Payable accounts resulted from depreciation and amortization entries.

(e) An analysis of the paid-in capital accounts in stockholders' equity discloses the following.

	Common Stock	Paid-In Capital in Excess of Par—Common Stock
Balance at end of 2011	$50,000	$ 38,000
Issuance of 2% stock dividend	1,000	14,000
Sale of stock for cash	9,000	135,000
Balance at end of 2012	$60,000	$187,000

(f) Interest paid (net of amount capitalized) is $9,000; income taxes paid is $62,000.

The discussion that follows provides additional explanations related to the preparation of the worksheet.

ANALYSIS OF TRANSACTIONS

The following discussion explains the individual adjustments that appear on the worksheet in Illustration 23-40 (page 1475). Because cash is the basis for the analysis, Satellite reconciles the cash account last. Because income is the first item that appears on the statement of cash flows, it is handled first.

Change in Retained Earnings

Net income for the period is $117,000. The entry for it on the worksheet is as follows.

(1)

Operating—Net Income	117,000	
Retained Earnings		117,000

Satellite reports net income on the bottom section of the worksheet. This **is the starting point for preparation of the statement of cash flows (under the indirect method).**

A stock dividend and a cash dividend also affected retained earnings. The retained earnings statement reports a stock dividend of $15,000. The worksheet entry for this transaction is as follows.

(2)

Retained Earnings	15,000	
Common Stock		1,000
Paid-in Capital in Excess of Par—Common Stock		14,000

The issuance of stock dividends is not a cash operating, investing, or financing item. Therefore, **although the company enters this transaction on the worksheet for reconciling purposes, it does not report it in the statement of cash flows.**

The $6,000 cash dividend paid represents a financing activity cash outflow. Satellite makes the following worksheet entry:

(3)

Retained Earnings	6,000	
Financing—Cash Dividends		6,000

The company reconciles the beginning and ending balances of retained earnings by entry of the three items above.

Accounts Receivable (Net)

The increase in accounts receivable (net) of $53,000 represents adjustments that did not result in cash inflows during 2012. As a result, the company would deduct from net income the increase of $53,000. Satellite makes the following worksheet entry.

(4)

Accounts Receivable (net)	53,000	
Operating—Increase in Accounts Receivable (net)		53,000

Inventory

The increase in inventory of $152,000 represents an operating use of cash. The incremental investment in inventory during the year reduces cash without increasing the cost of goods sold. Satellite makes the following worksheet entry.

(5)		
Inventory	152,000	
Operating—Increase in Inventory		152,000

Prepaid Expense

The decrease in prepaid expenses of $500 represents a charge in the income statement for which there was no cash outflow in the current period. Satellite should add that amount back to net income through the following entry.

(6)		
Operating—Decrease in Prepaid Expenses	500	
Prepaid Expenses		500

Investment in Stock

Satellite's investment in the stock of Porter Co. increased $3,500. This amount reflects Satellite's share of net income earned by Porter (its equity investee) during the current year. Although Satellite's revenue, and therefore its net income increased $3,500 by recording Satellite's share of Porter Co.'s net income, no cash (dividend) was provided. Satellite makes the following worksheet entry.

(7)		
Equity Investments (Porter Co.)	3,500	
Operating—Equity in Earnings of Porter Co.		3,500

Land

Satellite purchased land in the amount of $60,000 through the issuance of a long-term note payable. This transaction did not affect cash. It is a significant noncash investing/financing transaction that the company would disclose either in a separate schedule below the statement of cash flows or in the accompanying notes. Satellite makes the following entry to reconcile the worksheet.

(8)		
Land	60,000	
Notes Payable		60,000

In addition to the noncash transaction involving the issuance of a note to purchase land, the Land account was decreased by the condemnation proceedings. The following worksheet entry records the receipt of $18,500 for land having a book value of $10,500.

(9)		
Investing—Proceeds from Condemnation of Land	18,500	
Land		10,500
Operating—Gain on Condemnation of Land		8,000

In reconciling net income to net cash flow from operating activities, Satellite deducts from net income the extraordinary gain of $8,000. The reason is that the transaction that gave rise to the gain is an item whose cash effect is already classified as an investing cash inflow. The Land account is now reconciled.

Equipment and Accumulated Depreciation

An analysis of Equipment and Accumulated Depreciation—Equipment shows that a number of transactions have affected these accounts. The company purchased equipment in the amount of $53,000 during the year. Satellite records this transaction on the worksheet as follows.

(10)

Equipment	53,000	
Investing—Purchase of Equipment		53,000

In addition, Satellite sold at a loss of $1,500 equipment with a book value of $5,500. It records this transaction as follows.

(11)

Investing—Sale of Equipment	4,000	
Operating—Loss on Sale of Equipment	1,500	
Accumulated Depreciation—Equipment	2,500	
Equipment		8,000

The proceeds from the sale of the equipment provided cash of $4,000. In addition, the loss on the sale of the equipment has reduced net income but did not affect cash. Therefore, the company adds back to net income the amount of the loss, in order to accurately report cash provided by operating activities.

Satellite reported depreciation on the equipment at $11,500 and recorded it on the worksheet as follows.

(12)

Operating—Depreciation Expense—Equipment	11,500	
Accumulated Depreciation—Equipment		11,500

The company adds depreciation expense back to net income because that expense reduced income but did not affect cash.

Finally, the company made a major repair to the equipment. It charged this expenditure, in the amount of $11,000, to Accumulated Depreciation—Equipment. This expenditure required cash, and so Satellite makes the following worksheet entry.

(13)

Accumulated Depreciation—Equipment	11,000	
Investing—Major Repairs of Equipment		11,000

After adjusting for the foregoing items, Satellite has reconciled the balances in the Equipment and related Accumulated Depreciation—Equipment accounts.

Building Depreciation and Amortization of Trademarks

Depreciation expense on the buildings of $3,100 and amortization of trademarks of $2,400 are both expenses in the income statement that reduced net income but did not require cash outflows in the current period. Satellite makes the following worksheet entry.

(14)

Operating—Depreciation Expense—Buildings	3,100	
Operating—Amortization of Trademarks	2,400	
Accumulated Depreciation—Buildings		3,100
Trademarks		2,400

Other Noncash Charges or Credits

Analysis of the remaining accounts indicates that changes in the Accounts Payable, Accrued Liabilities, Income Taxes Payable, Premium on Bonds Payable, and Deferred Tax Liability balances resulted from charges or credits to net income that did not affect cash. The company should individually analyze each of these items and enter them in the worksheet. The following compound entry summarizes these noncash, income-related items.

(15)

Income Taxes Payable	13,000	
Premium on Bonds Payable	1,000	
Operating—Increase in Accounts Payable	1,000	
Operating—Increase in Accrued Liabilities	4,000	
Operating—Increase in Deferred Tax Liability	3,000	
Operating—Decrease in Income Taxes Payable		13,000
Operating—Amortization of Bond Premium		1,000
Accounts Payable		1,000
Accrued Liabilities		4,000
Deferred Tax Liability		3,000

Common Stock and Related Accounts

Comparison of the Common Stock balances and the Paid-in Capital in Excess of Par—Common Stock balances shows that transactions during the year affected these accounts. First, Satellite issues a stock dividend of 2 percent to stockholders. As the discussion of worksheet entry (2) indicated, no cash was provided or used by the stock dividend transaction. In addition to the shares issued via the stock dividend, Satellite sold shares of common stock at $16 per share. The company records this transaction as follows.

(16)

Financing—Sale of Common Stock	144,000	
Common Stock		9,000
Paid-in Capital in Excess of Par—Common Stock		135,000

Also, the company purchased shares of its common stock in the amount of $17,000. It records this transaction on the worksheet as follows.

(17)

Treasury Stock	17,000	
Financing—Purchase of Treasury Stock		17,000

Final Reconciling Entry

The final entry to reconcile the change in cash and to balance the worksheet is shown below. The $7,000 amount is the difference between the beginning and ending cash balance.

(18)

Decrease in Cash	7,000	
Cash		7,000

Once the company has determined that the differences between the beginning and ending balances per the worksheet columns have been accounted for, it can total the reconciling transactions columns, and they should balance. Satellite can prepare the statement of cash flows entirely from the items and amounts that appear at the bottom of the worksheet under "Statement of Cash Flows Effects," as shown in Illustration 23-40.

ILLUSTRATION 23-40
Completed Worksheet for Preparation of Statement of Cash Flows, Satellite Corporation

SATELLITE CORPORATION
Worksheet for Preparation of Statement of Cash Flows for the Year Ended December 31, 2012

	A	B	C	D	E	F	G
1		Balance 12/31/11	Reconciling Items–2012 Debits		Credits		Balance 12/31/12
2	Debits						
3	Cash	$ 66,000			(18)	7,000	$ 59,000
4	Accounts receivable (net)	51,000	(4)	$ 53,000			104,000
5	Inventory	341,000	(5)	152,000			493,000
6	Prepaid expenses	17,000			(6)	500	16,500
7	Investment in Porter Co. (equity method)	15,000	(7)	3,500			18,500
8	Land	82,000	(8)	60,000	(9)	10,500	131,500
9	Equipment	142,000	(10)	53,000	(11)	8,000	187,000
10	Buildings	262,000					262,000
11	Trademarks	10,000			(14)	2,400	7,600
12	Treasury stock		(17)	17,000			17,000
13	Total debits	$986,000					$1,296,100
14	Credits						
15	Accum. depr.–equipment	$ 31,000	(11)	2,500	(12)	11,500	
16			(13)	11,000			$ 29,000
17	Accum. depr.–buildings	71,000			(14)	3,100	74,100
18	Accounts payable	131,000			(15)	1,000	132,000
19	Accrued liabilities	39,000			(15)	4,000	43,000
20	Income taxes payable	16,000	(15)	13,000			3,000
21	Notes payable	-0-			(8)	60,000	60,000
22	Bonds payable	100,000					100,000
23	Premium on bonds payable	8,000	(15)	1,000			7,000
24	Deferred tax liability	6,000			(15)	3,000	9,000
25	Common stock	50,000			(2)	1,000	
26					(16)	9,000	60,000
27	Paid-in capital in excess of	38,000			(2)	14,000	
28	par—common stock				(16)	135,000	187,000
29	Retained earnings	496,000	(2)	15,000	(1)	117,000	
30			(3)	6,000			592,000
31	Total credits	$986,000					$1,296,100
32	Statement of Cash Flows Effects						
33	Operating activities						
34	Net income		(1)	117,000			
35	Increase in accounts receivable (net)				(4)	53,000	
36	Increase in inventory				(5)	152,000	
37	Decrease in prepaid expenses		(6)	500			
38	Equity in earnings of Porter Co.				(7)	3,500	
39	Gain on condemnation of land				(9)	8,000	
40	Loss on sale of equipment		(11)	1,500			
41	Depr. expense–equipment		(12)	11,500			
42	Depr. expense–buildings		(14)	3,100			
43	Amortization of trademarks		(14)	2,400			
44	Increase in accounts payable		(15)	1,000			
45	Increase in accrued liabilities		(15)	4,000			
46	Increase in deferred tax liability		(15)	3,000			
47	Decrease in income taxes payable				(15)	13,000	
48	Amortization of bond premium				(15)	1,000	
49	Investing activities						
50	Proceeds from condemnation of land		(9)	18,500			
51	Purchase of equipment				(10)	53,000	
52	Sale of equipment		(11)	4,000			
53	Major repairs of equipment				(13)	11,000	
54	Financing activities						
55	Payment of cash dividend				(3)	6,000	
56	Issuance of common stock		(16)	144,000			
57	Purchase of treasury stock				(17)	17,000	
58	Totals			697,500		704,500	
59	Decrease in cash		(18)	7,000			
60	Totals			$704,500		$704,500	

Sheet1 / Sheet2 / Sheet3

PREPARATION OF FINAL STATEMENT

Illustration 23-41 presents a formal statement of cash flows prepared from the data compiled in the lower portion of the worksheet.

ILLUSTRATION 23-41
Statement of Cash Flows, Satellite Corporation

SATELLITE CORPORATION
STATEMENT OF CASH FLOWS
FOR THE YEAR ENDED DECEMBER 31, 2012
INCREASE (DECREASE) IN CASH

Cash flows from operating activities		
Net income		$117,000
Adjustments to reconcile net income to net cash used by operating activities:		
Depreciation expense	$ 14,600	
Amortization of trademarks	2,400	
Amortization of bond premium	(1,000)	
Equity in earnings of Porter Co.	(3,500)	
Gain on condemnation of land	(8,000)	
Loss on sale of equipment	1,500	
Increase in deferred tax liability	3,000	
Increase in accounts receivable (net)	(53,000)	
Increase in inventory	(152,000)	
Decrease in prepaid expenses	500	
Increase in accounts payable	1,000	
Increase in accrued liabilities	4,000	
Decrease in income taxes payable	(13,000)	(203,500)
Net cash used by operating activities		(86,500)
Cash flows from investing activities		
Proceeds from condemnation of land	18,500	
Purchase of equipment	(53,000)	
Sale of equipment	4,000	
Major repairs of equipment	(11,000)	
Net cash used by investing activities		(41,500)
Cash flows from financing activities		
Payment of cash dividend	(6,000)	
Issuance of common stock	144,000	
Purchase of treasury stock	(17,000)	
Net cash provided by financing activities		121,000
Net decrease in cash		(7,000)
Cash, January 1, 2012		66,000
Cash, December 31, 2012		$ 59,000

Supplemental Disclosures of Cash Flow Information:

Cash paid during the year for:	
Interest (net of amount capitalized)	$ 9,000
Income taxes	$ 62,000

Supplemental Schedule of Noncash Investing and Financing Activities:
Purchase of land for $60,000 in exchange for a $60,000 long-term note.

Gateway to the Profession
Discussion of the T-Account Approach to Preparation of the Statement of Cash Flows

You will want to read **IFRS INSIGHTS** on pages 1505–1510 for discussion of IFRS related to the statement of cash flows.

SUMMARY OF LEARNING OBJECTIVES

1 Describe the purpose of the statement of cash flows. The primary purpose of the statement of cash flows is to provide information about cash receipts and cash payments of an entity during a period. A secondary objective is to report the entity's operating, investing, and financing activities during the period.

2 Identify the major classifications of cash flows. Companies classify cash flows as follows: (1) *Operating activities*—transactions that result in the revenues, expenses, gains, and losses that determine net income. (2) *Investing activities*—lending money and collecting on those loans, and acquiring and disposing of investments, plant assets, and intangible assets. (3) *Financing activities*—obtaining cash from creditors and repaying loans, issuing and reacquiring capital stock, and paying cash dividends.

3 Differentiate between net income and net cash flow from operating activities. Companies must adjust net income on an accrual basis to determine net cash flow from operating activities because some expenses and losses do not cause cash outflows, and some revenues and gains do not provide cash inflows.

4 Contrast the direct and indirect methods of calculating net cash flow from operating activities. Under the direct approach, companies calculate the major classes of operating cash receipts and cash disbursements. Companies summarize the computations in a schedule of changes from the accrual to the cash basis income statement. Presentation of the direct approach of reporting net cash flow from operating activities takes the form of a condensed cash-basis income statement. The indirect method adds back to net income the noncash expenses and losses and subtracts the noncash revenues and gains.

5 Determine net cash flows from investing and financing activities. Once a company has computed the net cash flow from operating activities, the next step is to determine whether any other changes in balance sheet accounts caused an increase or decrease in cash. Net cash flows from investing and financing activities can be determined by examining the changes in noncurrent balance sheet accounts.

6 Prepare a statement of cash flows. Preparing the statement involves three major steps: (1) *Determine the change in cash.* This is the difference between the beginning and the ending cash balance shown on the comparative balance sheets. (2) *Determine the net cash flow from operating activities.* This procedure is complex; it involves analyzing not only the current year's income statement but also the comparative balance sheets and the selected transaction data. (3) *Determine cash flows from investing and financing activities.* Analyze all other changes in the balance sheet accounts to determine the effects on cash.

7 Identify sources of information for a statement of cash flows. The information to prepare the statement usually comes from three sources: (1) *Comparative balance sheets.* Information in these statements indicates the amount of the changes in assets, liabilities, and equities during the period. (2) *Current income statement.* Information in this statement is used in determining the cash provided by operations during the period. (3) *Selected transaction data.* These data from the general ledger provide additional detailed information needed to determine how cash was provided or used during the period.

8 Discuss special problems in preparing a statement of cash flows. These special problems are: (1) adjustments to income (depreciation and amortization, post retirement benefit costs, change in deferred income taxes, equity method of accounting, losses and gains, stock options, extraordinary items); (2) accounts receivable (net); (3) other working capital changes; (4) net losses; and (5) significant noncash transactions.

KEY TERMS

9 Explain the use of a worksheet in preparing a statement of cash flows. When numerous adjustments are necessary, or other complicating factors are present, companies often use a worksheet to assemble and classify the data that will appear on the statement of cash flows. The worksheet is merely a device that aids in the preparation of the statement. Its use is optional.

FASB CODIFICATION

FASB Codification References

[1] FASB ASC 230-10-10-2. [Predecessor literature: "The Statement of Cash Flows," *Statement of Financial Accounting Standards No. 95* (Stamford, Conn.: FASB, 1987), paras. 4 and 5.]

[2] FASB ASC 230-10-45-18 through 21. [Predecessor literature: "Statement of Cash Flows—Exemption of Certain Enterprises and Classification of Cash Flows from Certain Securities Acquired for Resale (amended)," *Statement of Financial Accounting Standards No. 102* (February 1989).]

[3] FASB ASC 230-10-45-31. [Predecessor literature: "The Statement of Cash Flows," *Statement of Financial Accounting Standards No. 95* (Stamford, Conn.: FASB, 1987), paras. 27 and 30.]

[4] FASB ASC 230-10-45-25. [Predecessor literature: "Statement of Cash Flows," *Statement of Financial Accounting Standards No. 95* (Stamford, Conn.: FASB, 1987), paras. 107 and 111.]

[5] FASB ASC 230-10-45-14. [Predecessor literature: "Share-Based Payment," *Statement of Financial Accounting Standard No. 123(R)* (Norwalk, Conn.: FASB, 2004), par. 68.]

[6] FASB ASC 320-10-45-11. [Predecessor literature: "Accounting for Certain Investments in Debt and Equity Securities," *Statement of Financial Accounting Standards No. 115* (Norwalk, Conn.: 1993), par. 118.]

[7] FASB ASC 320-10-45-11. [Predecessor literature: "Accounting for Certain Investments in Debt and Equity Securities," *Statement of Financial Accounting Standards No. 115* (Norwalk, Conn.: 1993), par. 118.]

Exercises

If your school has a subscription to the FASB Codification, go to *http://aaahq.org/ascLogin.cfm* to log in and prepare responses to the following. Provide Codification references for your responses.

CE23-1 Access the glossary ("Master Glossary") to answer the following.

(a) What are cash equivalents?
(b) What are financing activities?
(c) What are investing activities?
(d) What are operating activities?

CE23-2 Name five cash inflows that would qualify as a "financing activity."

CE23-3 How should cash flows from purchases, sales, and maturities of available-for-sale securities be classified and reported in the statement of cash flows?

CE23-4 Do companies need to disclose information about investing and financing activities that do not affect cash receipts or cash payments? If so, how should such information be disclosed?

An additional codification case can be found in the Using Your Judgment section, on page 1504.

Be sure to check the book's companion website for a Review and Analysis Exercise, with solution.

QUESTIONS

1. What is the purpose of the statement of cash flows? What information does it provide?
2. Of what use is the statement of cash flows?
3. Differentiate between investing activities, financing activities, and operating activities.
4. What are the major sources of cash (inflows) in a statement of cash flows? What are the major uses (outflows) of cash?
5. Identify and explain the major steps involved in preparing the statement of cash flows.
6. Identify the following items as (1) operating, (2) investing, or (3) financing activities: purchase of land; payment of dividends; cash sales; and purchase of treasury stock.
7. Unlike the other major financial statements, the statement of cash flows is not prepared from the adjusted trial balance. From what sources does the information to prepare this statement come, and what information does each source provide?
8. Why is it necessary to convert accrual-based net income to a cash basis when preparing a statement of cash flows?
9. Differentiate between the direct method and the indirect method by discussing each method.
10. Broussard Company reported net income of $3.5 million in 2012. Depreciation for the year was $520,000; accounts receivable increased $500,000; and accounts payable increased $300,000. Compute net cash flow from operating activities using the indirect method.
11. Collinsworth Co. reported sales on an accrual basis of $100,000. If accounts receivable increased $30,000, and the allowance for doubtful accounts increased $9,000 after a write-off of $2,000, compute cash sales.
12. Your roommate is puzzled. During the last year, the company in which she is a stockholder reported a net loss of $675,000, yet its cash increased $321,000 during the same period of time. Explain to your roommate how this situation could occur.
13. The board of directors of Gifford Corp. declared cash dividends of $260,000 during the current year. If dividends payable was $85,000 at the beginning of the year and $90,000 at the end of the year, how much cash was paid in dividends during the year?
14. Explain how the amount of cash payments to suppliers is computed under the direct method.
15. The net income for Letterman Company for 2012 was $320,000. During 2012, depreciation on plant assets was $124,000, amortization of patent was $40,000, and the company incurred a loss on sale of plant assets of $21,000. Compute net cash flow from operating activities.
16. Each of the following items must be considered in preparing a statement of cash flows for Blackwell Inc. for the year ended December 31, 2012. State where each item is to be shown in the statement, if at all.
    - **(a)** Plant assets that had cost $18,000 6½ years before and were being depreciated on a straight-line basis over 10 years with no estimated scrap value were sold for $4,000.
    - **(b)** During the year, 10,000 shares of common stock with a stated value of $20 a share were issued for $41 a share.
    - **(c)** Uncollectible accounts receivable in the amount of $22,000 were written off against Allowance for Doubtful Accounts.
    - **(d)** The company sustained a net loss for the year of $50,000. Depreciation amounted to $22,000, and a gain of $9,000 was realized on the sale of available-for-sale securities for $38,000 cash.
17. Classify the following items as (1) operating, (2) investing, (3) financing, or (4) significant noncash investing and financing activities, using the direct method.
    - **(a)** Cash payments to employees.
    - **(b)** Redemption of bonds payable.
    - **(c)** Sale of building at book value.
    - **(d)** Cash payments to suppliers.
    - **(e)** Exchange of equipment for furniture.
    - **(f)** Issuance of preferred stock.
    - **(g)** Cash received from customers.
    - **(h)** Purchase of treasury stock.
    - **(i)** Issuance of bonds for land.
    - **(j)** Payment of dividends.
    - **(k)** Purchase of equipment.
    - **(l)** Cash payments for operating expenses.
18. Stan Conner and Mark Stein were discussing the presentation format of the statement of cash flows of Bombeck Co.

At the bottom of Bombeck's statement of cash flows was a separate section entitled "Noncash investing and financing activities." Give three examples of significant noncash transactions that would be reported in this section.

19. During 2012, Simms Company redeemed $2,000,000 of bonds payable for $1,880,000 cash. Indicate how this transaction would be reported on a statement of cash flows, if at all.

20. What are some of the arguments in favor of using the indirect (reconciliation) method as opposed to the direct method for reporting a statement of cash flows?

21. Why is it desirable to use a worksheet when preparing a statement of cash flows? Is a worksheet required to prepare a statement of cash flows?

BRIEF EXERCISES

5 **BE23-1** Wainwright Corporation had the following activities in 2012.

1. Sale of land $180,000
2. Purchase of inventory $845,000
3. Purchase of treasury stock $72,000
4. Purchase of equipment $415,000
5. Issuance of common stock $320,000
6. Purchase of available-for-sale securities $59,000

Compute the amount Wainwright should report as net cash provided (used) by investing activities in its statement of cash flows.

5 **BE23-2** Stansfield Corporation had the following activities in 2012.

1. Payment of accounts payable $770,000
2. Issuance of common stock $250,000
3. Payment of dividends $350,000
4. Collection of note receivable $100,000
5. Issuance of bonds payable $510,000
6. Purchase of treasury stock $46,000

Compute the amount Stansfield should report as net cash provided (used) by financing activities in its 2012 statement of cash flows.

2 **BE23-3** Novak Corporation is preparing its 2012 statement of cash flows, using the indirect method. Presented below is a list of items that may affect the statement. Using the code below, indicate how each item will affect Novak's 2012 statement of cash flows.

Code Letter	Effect
A	Added to net income in the operating section
D	Deducted from net income in the operating section
R-I	Cash receipt in investing section
P-I	Cash payment in investing section
R-F	Cash receipt in financing section
P-F	Cash payment in financing section
N	Noncash investing and financing activity

Items

_____ **(a)** Purchase of land and building.
_____ **(b)** Decrease in accounts receivable.
_____ **(c)** Issuance of stock.
_____ **(d)** Depreciation expense.
_____ **(e)** Sale of land at book value.
_____ **(f)** Sale of land at a gain.
_____ **(g)** Payment of dividends.
_____ **(h)** Increase in accounts receivable.
_____ **(i)** Purchase of available-for-sale investment.
_____ **(j)** Increase in accounts payable.
_____ **(k)** Decrease in accounts payable.
_____ **(l)** Loan from bank by signing note.
_____ **(m)** Purchase of equipment using a note.
_____ **(n)** Increase in inventory.
_____ **(o)** Issuance of bonds.
_____ **(p)** Retirement of bonds payable.
_____ **(q)** Sale of equipment at a loss.
_____ **(r)** Purchase of treasury stock.

3 4 **BE23-4** Bloom Corporation had the following 2012 income statement.

Sales	$200,000
Cost of goods sold	120,000
Gross profit	80,000
Operating expenses (includes depreciation of $21,000)	50,000
Net income	$ 30,000

The following accounts increased during 2012: Accounts Receivable $12,000; Inventory $11,000; Accounts Payable $13,000. Prepare the cash flows from operating activities section of Bloom's 2012 statement of cash flows using the direct method.

3 4 **BE23-5** Use the information from BE23-4 for Bloom Corporation. Prepare the cash flows from operating activities section of Bloom's 2012 statement of cash flows using the indirect method.

4 **BE23-6** At January 1, 2012, Eikenberry Inc. had accounts receivable of $72,000. At December 31, 2012, accounts receivable is $54,000. Sales for 2012 total $420,000. Compute Eikenberry's 2012 cash receipts from customers.

4 **BE23-7** Moxley Corporation had January 1 and December 31 balances as follows.

	1/1/12	12/31/12
Inventory	$95,000	$113,000
Accounts payable	61,000	69,000

For 2012, cost of goods sold was $500,000. Compute Moxley's 2012 cash payments to suppliers.

6 **BE23-8** In 2012, Elbert Corporation had net cash provided by operating activities of $531,000; net cash used by investing activities of $963,000; and net cash provided by financing activities of $585,000. At January 1, 2012, the cash balance was $333,000. Compute December 31, 2012, cash.

3 4 **BE23-9** Loveless Corporation had the following 2012 income statement.

Revenues	$100,000
Expenses	60,000
	$ 40,000

In 2012, Loveless had the following activity in selected accounts.

Accounts Receivable

1/1/12	20,000		
Revenues	100,000	1,000	Write-offs
		90,000	Collections
12/31/12	29,000		

Allowance for Doubtful Accounts

		1,200	1/1/12
Write-offs	1,000	1,840	Bad debt expense
		2,040	12/31/12

Prepare Loveless's cash flows from operating activities section of the statement of cash flows using (a) the direct method and (b) the indirect method.

3 **BE23-10** Hendrickson Corporation reported net income of $50,000 in 2012. Depreciation expense was $17,000. The following working capital accounts changed.

Accounts receivable	$11,000 increase
Available-for-sale securities	16,000 increase
Inventory	7,400 increase
Nontrade note payable	15,000 decrease
Accounts payable	12,300 increase

Compute net cash provided by operating activities.

3 **BE23-11** In 2012, Wild Corporation reported a net loss of $70,000. Wild's only net income adjustments were depreciation expense $81,000, and increase in accounts receivable $8,100. Compute Wild's net cash provided (used) by operating activities.

8 **BE23-12** In 2012, Leppard Inc. issued 1,000 shares of $10 par value common stock for land worth $40,000.

(a) Prepare Leppard's journal entry to record the transaction.
(b) Indicate the effect the transaction has on cash.
(c) Indicate how the transaction is reported on the statement of cash flows.

9 **BE23-13** Indicate in general journal form how the items below would be entered in a worksheet for the preparation of the statement of cash flows.

(a) Net income is $317,000.
(b) Cash dividends declared and paid totaled $120,000.
(c) Equipment was purchased for $114,000.
(d) Equipment that originally cost $40,000 and had accumulated depreciation of $32,000 was sold for $10,000.

EXERCISES

2 **E23-1 (Classification of Transactions)** Springsteen Co. had the following activity in its most recent year of operations.

(a) Pension expense exceeds amount funded.
(b) Redemption of bonds payable.
(c) Sale of building at book value.
(d) Depreciation.
(e) Exchange of equipment for furniture.
(f) Issuance of capital stock.
(g) Amortization of intangible assets.
(h) Purchase of treasury stock.
(i) Issuance of bonds for land.
(j) Payment of dividends.
(k) Increase in interest receivable on notes receivable.
(l) Purchase of equipment.

Instructions

Classify the items as (1) operating—add to net income; (2) operating—deduct from net income; (3) investing; (4) financing; or (5) significant noncash investing and financing activities. Use the indirect method.

2 3 **E23-2 (Statement Presentation of Transactions—Indirect Method)** Each of the following items must be considered in preparing a statement of cash flows (indirect method) for Granderson Inc. for the year ended December 31, 2012.

(a) Plant assets that had cost $25,000 6 years before and were being depreciated on a straight-line basis over 10 years with no estimated scrap value were sold at the beginning of the year for $5,300.
(b) During the year, 10,000 shares of common stock with a stated value of $10 a share were issued for $33 a share.
(c) Uncollectible accounts receivable in the amount of $27,000 were written off against Allowance for Doubtful Accounts.
(d) The company sustained a net loss for the year of $50,000. Depreciation amounted to $22,000, and a gain of $9,000 was realized on the sale of land for $39,000 cash.
(e) A 3-month U.S. Treasury bill was purchased for $100,000. The company uses a cash and cash-equivalent basis for its cash flow statement.
(f) Patent amortization for the year was $20,000.
(g) The company exchanged common stock for a 70% interest in Plumlee Co. for $900,000.
(h) During the year, treasury stock costing $47,000 was purchased.

Instructions

State where each item is to be shown in the statement of cash flows, if at all.

E23-3 (Preparation of Operating Activities Section—Indirect Method, Periodic Inventory) The income statement of Rodriquez Company is shown below.

RODRIQUEZ COMPANY
INCOME STATEMENT
FOR THE YEAR ENDED DECEMBER 31, 2012

Sales		$6,900,000
Cost of goods sold		
Beginning inventory	$1,900,000	
Purchases	4,400,000	
Goods available for sale	6,300,000	
Ending inventory	1,600,000	
Cost of goods sold		4,700,000
Gross profit		2,200,000
Operating expenses		
Selling expenses	450,000	
Administrative expenses	700,000	1,150,000
Net income		$1,050,000

Additional information:

1. Accounts receivable decreased $310,000 during the year.
2. Prepaid expenses increased $170,000 during the year.
3. Accounts payable to suppliers of merchandise decreased $275,000 during the year.
4. Accrued expenses payable decreased $120,000 during the year.
5. Administrative expenses include depreciation expense of $60,000.

Instructions
Prepare the operating activities section of the statement of cash flows for the year ended December 31, 2012, for Rodriquez Company, using the indirect method.

3 4 **E23-4 (Preparation of Operating Activities Section—Direct Method)** Data for the Rodriquez Company are presented in E23-3.

Instructions
Prepare the operating activities section of the statement of cash flows using the direct method.

3 4 **E23-5 (Preparation of Operating Activities Section—Direct Method)** Norman Company's income statement for the year ended December 31, 2012, contained the following condensed information.

Service revenue		$840,000
Operating expenses (excluding depreciation)	$624,000	
Depreciation expense	60,000	
Loss on sale of equipment	26,000	710,000
Income before income taxes		130,000
Income tax expense		40,000
Net income		$ 90,000

Norman's balance sheet contained the following comparative data at December 31.

	2012	2011
Accounts receivable	$37,000	$59,000
Accounts payable	46,000	31,000
Income taxes payable	4,000	8,500

(Accounts payable pertains to operating expenses.)

Instructions
Prepare the operating activities section of the statement of cash flows using the direct method.

3 4 **E23-6 (Preparation of Operating Activities Section—Indirect Method)** Data for Norman Company are presented in E23-5.

Instructions
Prepare the operating activities section of the statement of cash flows using the indirect method.

3 4 **E23-7 (Computation of Operating Activities—Direct Method)** Presented below are two independent situations.

Situation A:
Chenowith Co. reports revenues of $200,000 and operating expenses of $110,000 in its first year of operations, 2012. Accounts receivable and accounts payable at year-end were $71,000 and $39,000, respectively. Assume that the accounts payable related to operating expenses. Ignore income taxes.

Instructions
Using the direct method, compute net cash provided (used) by operating activities.

Situation B:
The income statement for Edgebrook Company shows cost of goods sold $310,000 and operating expenses (exclusive of depreciation) $230,000. The comparative balance sheet for the year shows that inventory increased $21,000, prepaid expenses decreased $8,000, accounts payable (related to merchandise) decreased $17,000, and accrued expenses payable increased $11,000.

Instructions
Compute (a) cash payments to suppliers and (b) cash payments for operating expenses.

3 4 **E23-8 (Schedule of Net Cash Flow from Operating Activities—Indirect Method)** Messner Co. reported $145,000 of net income for 2012. The accountant, in preparing the statement of cash flows, noted several items occurring during 2012 that might affect cash flows from operating activities. These items are listed below and on page 1484.

1. Messner purchased 100 shares of treasury stock at a cost of $20 per share. These shares were then resold at $25 per share.
2. Messner sold 100 shares of IBM common at $200 per share. The acquisition cost of these shares was $165 per share. This investment was shown on Messner's December 31, 2011, balance sheet as an available-for-sale security.

3. Messner revised its estimate for bad debts. Before 2012, Messner's bad debt expense was 1% of its net sales. In 2012, this percentage was increased to 2%. Net sales for 2012 were $500,000, and net accounts receivable decreased by $12,000 during 2012.
4. Messner issued 500 shares of its $10 par common stock for a patent. The market price of the shares on the date of the transaction was $23 per share.
5. Depreciation expense is $39,000.
6. Messner Co. holds 30% of the Sanchez Company's common stock as a long-term investment. Sanchez Company reported $27,000 of net income for 2012.
7. Sanchez Company paid a total of $2,000 of cash dividends to all investees in 2012.
8. Messner declared a 10% stock dividend. One thousand shares of $10 par common stock were distributed. The market price at date of issuance was $20 per share.

Instructions

Prepare a schedule that shows the net cash flow from operating activities using the indirect method. Assume no items other than those listed above affected the computation of 2012 net cash flow from operating activities.

6 **E23-9 (SCF—Direct Method)** Waubansee Corp. uses the direct method to prepare its statement of cash flows. Relevant balances for Waubansee at December 31, 2012 and 2011, are as follows.

	December 31	
	2012	2011
Debits		
Cash	$ 35,000	$ 32,000
Accounts receivable	33,000	30,000
Inventory	31,000	47,000
Property, plant, & equipment	100,000	95,000
Unamortized bond discount	4,500	5,000
Cost of goods sold	250,000	380,000
Selling expenses	141,500	172,000
General and administrative expenses	137,000	151,300
Interest expense	4,300	2,600
Income tax expense	20,400	61,200
	$756,700	$976,100
Credits		
Allowance for doubtful accounts	$ 1,300	$ 1,100
Accumulated depreciation	16,500	13,500
Trade accounts payable	25,000	17,000
Income taxes payable	21,000	29,100
Deferred income taxes	5,300	4,600
8% callable bonds payable	45,000	20,000
Common stock	50,000	40,000
Paid-in capital in excess of par—common stock	9,100	7,500
Retained earnings	44,700	64,600
Sales revenue	538,800	778,700
	$756,700	$976,100

Additional information:

1. Waubansee purchased $5,000 in equipment during 2012.
2. Waubansee allocated one-third of its depreciation expense to selling expenses and the remainder to general and administrative expenses.
3. Bad debt expense for 2012 was $5,000, and write-offs of uncollectible accounts totaled $3,800.

Instructions

Determine what amounts Waubansee should report in its statement of cash flows for the year ended December 31, 2012, for the following items.

(a) Cash collected from customers.
(b) Cash paid to suppliers.
(c) Cash paid for interest.
(d) Cash paid for income taxes.
(e) Cash paid for selling expenses.

2 8 **E23-10 (Classification of Transactions)** Following are selected balance sheet accounts of Sander Bros. Corp. at December 31, 2012 and 2011, and the increases or decreases in each account from 2011 to 2012. Also presented is selected income statement information for the year ended December 31, 2012, and additional information.

Selected balance sheet accounts	2012	2011	Increase (Decrease)
Assets			
Accounts receivable	$ 34,000	$ 24,000	$ 10,000
Property, plant, and equipment	277,000	247,000	30,000
Accumulated depreciation	(178,000)	(167,000)	(11,000)

	2012	2011	Increase
Liabilities and stockholders' equity			
Bonds payable	$ 49,000	$46,000	$ 3,000
Dividends payable	8,000	5,000	3,000
Common stock, $1 par	22,000	19,000	3,000
Paid-in capital in excess of par—common stock	9,000	3,000	6,000
Retained earnings	104,000	91,000	13,000

Selected income statement information for the year ended December 31, 2012	
Sales revenue	$155,000
Depreciation	38,000
Gain on sale of equipment	14,500
Net income	31,000

Additional information:

1. During 2012, equipment costing $45,000 was sold for cash.
2. Accounts receivable relate to sales of merchandise.
3. During 2012, $25,000 of bonds payable were issued in exchange for property, plant, and equipment. There was no amortization of bond discount or premium.

Instructions
Determine the category (operating, investing, or financing) and the amount that should be reported in the statement of cash flows for the following items.

(a) Payments for purchase of property, plant, and equipment.
(b) Proceeds from the sale of equipment.
(c) Cash dividends paid.
(d) Redemption of bonds payable.

6 **E23-11 (SCF—Indirect Method)** Condensed financial data of Fairchild Company for 2012 and 2011 are presented below and on page 1486.

FAIRCHILD COMPANY
COMPARATIVE BALANCE SHEET
AS OF DECEMBER 31, 2012 AND 2011

	2012	2011
Cash	$1,800	$1,100
Receivables	1,750	1,300
Inventory	1,600	1,900
Plant assets	1,900	1,700
Accumulated depreciation	(1,200)	(1,170)
Long-term investments (held-to-maturity)	1,300	1,470
	$7,150	$6,300
Accounts payable	$1,200	$ 800
Accrued liabilities	200	250
Bonds payable	1,400	1,650
Common stock	1,900	1,700
Retained earnings	2,450	1,900
	$7,150	$6,300

FAIRCHILD COMPANY
INCOME STATEMENT
FOR THE YEAR ENDED DECEMBER 31, 2012

Sales	$6,900
Cost of goods sold	4,700
Gross margin	2,200
Selling and administrative expenses	930
Income from operations	1,270
Other revenues and gains	
Gain on sale of investments	80
Income before tax	1,350
Income tax expense	540
Net income	$ 810

Additional information:

During the year, $70 of common stock was issued in exchange for plant assets. No plant assets were sold in 2012. Cash dividends were $260.

Instructions
Prepare a statement of cash flows using the indirect method.

6 **E23-12 (SCF—Direct Method)** Data for Fairchild Company are presented in E23-11.

Instructions
Prepare a statement of cash flows using the direct method. (Do not prepare a reconciliation schedule.)

6 **E23-13 (SCF—Direct Method)** Andrews Inc., a greeting card company, had the following statements prepared as of December 31, 2012.

ANDREWS INC.
COMPARATIVE BALANCE SHEET
AS OF DECEMBER 31, 2012 AND 2011

	12/31/12	12/31/11
Cash	$ 6,000	$ 9,000
Accounts receivable	62,000	49,000
Short-term investments (available-for-sale)	35,000	18,000
Inventory	40,000	60,000
Prepaid rent	5,000	4,000
Equipment	154,000	130,000
Accumulated depr.—equipment	(35,000)	(25,000)
Copyrights	46,000	50,000
Total assets	$313,000	$295,000
Accounts payable	$ 46,000	$ 42,000
Income taxes payable	4,000	6,000
Salaries and wages payable	8,000	4,000
Short-term loans payable	8,000	10,000
Long-term loans payable	60,000	67,000
Common stock, $10 par	100,000	100,000
Contributed capital, common stock	30,000	30,000
Retained earnings	57,000	36,000
Total liabilities & stockholders' equity	$313,000	$295,000

ANDREWS INC.
INCOME STATEMENT
FOR THE YEAR ENDING DECEMBER 31, 2012

Sales		$338,150
Cost of goods sold		175,000
Gross margin		163,150
Operating expenses		120,000
Operating income		43,150
Interest expense	$11,400	
Gain on sale of equipment	2,000	(9,400)
Income before tax		33,750
Income tax expense		6,750
Net income		$ 27,000

Additional information:

1. Dividends in the amount of $6,000 were declared and paid during 2012.
2. Depreciation expense and amortization expense are included in operating expenses.
3. No unrealized gains or losses have occurred on the investments during the year.
4. Equipment that had a cost of $30,000 and was 70% depreciated was sold during 2012.

Instructions
Prepare a statement of cash flows using the direct method. (Do not prepare a reconciliation schedule.)

6 **E23-14 (SCF—Indirect Method)** Data for Andrews Inc. are presented in E23-13.

Instructions
Prepare a statement of cash flows using the indirect method.

6 **E23-15 (SCF—Indirect Method)** Presented below are data taken from the records of Morganstern Company.

	December 31, 2012	December 31, 2011
Cash	$ 15,000	$ 10,000
Current assets other than cash	85,000	58,000
Long-term investments	10,000	53,000
Plant assets	335,000	215,000
	$445,000	$336,000
Accumulated depreciation	$ 20,000	$ 40,000
Current liabilities	40,000	22,000
Bonds payable	75,000	–0–
Common stock	254,000	254,000
Retained earnings	56,000	20,000
	$445,000	$336,000

Additional information:

1. Held-to-maturity securities carried at a cost of $43,000 on December 31, 2011, were sold in 2012 for $34,000. The loss (not extraordinary) was incorrectly charged directly to Retained Earnings.
2. Plant assets that cost $60,000 and were 80% depreciated were sold during 2012 for $8,000. The loss (not extraordinary) was incorrectly charged directly to Retained Earnings.
3. Net income as reported on the income statement for the year was $59,000.
4. Dividends paid amounted to $10,000.
5. Depreciation charged for the year was $28,000.

Instructions
Prepare a statement of cash flows for the year 2012 using the indirect method.

2 3 5 **E23-16 (Cash Provided by Operating, Investing, and Financing Activities)** The balance sheet data of Wyeth Company at the end of 2012 and 2011 are shown on page 1488.

	2012	2011
Cash	$ 30,000	$ 35,000
Accounts receivable (net)	55,000	45,000
Inventory	65,000	45,000
Prepaid expenses	15,000	25,000
Equipment	90,000	75,000
Accumulated depreciation—equipment	(18,000)	(8,000)
Land	70,000	40,000
	$307,000	$257,000
Accounts payable	$ 65,000	$ 52,000
Accrued expenses	15,000	18,000
Notes payable—bank, long-term	-0-	23,000
Bonds payable	30,000	-0-
Common stock, $10 par	189,000	159,000
Retained earnings	8,000	5,000
	$307,000	$257,000

Land was acquired for $30,000 in exchange for common stock, par $30,000, during the year; all equipment purchased was for cash. Equipment costing $13,000 was sold for $3,000; book value of the equipment was $6,000. Cash dividends of $9,000 were declared and paid during the year.

Instructions

Compute net cash provided (used) by:

(a) Operating activities.
(b) Investing activities.
(c) Financing activities.

6 **E23-17 (SCF—Indirect Method and Balance Sheet)** Ochoa Inc., had the following condensed balance sheet at the end of operations for 2011.

OCHOA INC.
BALANCE SHEET
DECEMBER 31, 2011

Cash	$ 8,500	Current liabilities	$ 15,000
Current assets other than cash	29,000	Long-term notes payable	25,500
Investments	20,000	Bonds payable	25,000
Plant assets (net)	67,500	Common stock	75,000
Land	40,000	Retained earnings	24,500
	$165,000		$165,000

During 2012, the following occurred.

1. A tract of land was purchased for $11,000.
2. Bonds payable in the amount of $20,000 were retired at par.
3. An additional $10,000 in common stock was issued at par.
4. Dividends totaling $9,375 were paid to stockholders.
5. Net income was $30,250 after deducting depreciation of $13,500.
6. Land was purchased through the issuance of $22,500 in bonds.
7. Ochoa Inc. sold part of its investment portfolio for $12,875. This transaction resulted in a gain of $2,000 for the company. The company classifies the investments as available-for-sale.
8. Both current assets (other than cash) and current liabilities remained at the same amount.

Instructions

(a) Prepare a statement of cash flows for 2012 using the indirect method.
(b) Prepare the condensed balance sheet for Ochoa Inc. as it would appear at December 31, 2012.

6 8 **E23-18 (Partial SCF—Indirect Method)** The following accounts appear in the ledger of Popovich Company.

	Retained Earnings	Dr.	Cr.	Bal.
Jan. 1, 2012	Credit Balance			$ 42,000
Aug. 15	Dividends (cash)	$15,000		27,000
Dec. 31	Net Income for 2012		$50,000	77,000

	Machinery	Dr.	Cr.	Bal.
Jan. 1, 2012	Debit Balance			$140,000
Aug. 3	Purchase of Machinery	$62,000		202,000
Sept. 10	Cost of Machinery Constructed	48,000		250,000
Nov. 15	Machinery Sold		$66,000	184,000

	Accumulated Depreciation—Machinery	Dr.	Cr.	Bal.
Jan. 1, 2012	Credit Balance			$ 84,000
Apr. 8	Extraordinary Repairs	$21,000		63,000
Nov. 15	Accum. Depreciation on Machinery Sold	25,200		37,800
Dec. 31	Depreciation for 2012		$16,800	54,600

Instructions

From the postings in the accounts above, indicate how the information is reported on a statement of cash flows by preparing a partial statement of cash flows using the indirect method. The loss on sale of equipment (November 15) was $5,800.

9 **E23-19 (Worksheet Analysis of Selected Accounts)** Data for Popovich Company are presented in E23-18.

Instructions

Prepare entries in journal form for all adjustments that should be made on a worksheet for a statement of cash flows.

9 **E23-20 (Worksheet Analysis of Selected Transactions)** The transactions below took place during the year 2012.

1. Convertible bonds payable with a par value of $300,000 were exchanged for unissued common stock with a par value of $300,000. The market price of both types of securities was par.
2. The net income for the year was $360,000.
3. Depreciation expense for the building was $90,000.
4. Some old office equipment was traded in on the purchase of some newer office equipment and the following entry was made. (The exchange has commercial substance.)

Equipment	45,000	
Accum. Depreciation—Equipment	30,000	
Equipment		40,000
Cash		34,000
Gain on Disposal of Plant Assets		1,000

   The Gain on Disposal of Plant Assets was credited to current operations as ordinary income.
5. Dividends in the amount of $123,000 were declared. They are payable in January of next year.

Instructions

Show by journal entries the adjustments that would be made on a worksheet for a statement of cash flows.

9 **E23-21 (Worksheet Preparation)** Below is the comparative balance sheet for Lowenstein Corporation.

	Dec. 31, 2012	Dec. 31, 2011
Cash	$ 16,500	$ 24,000
Short-term investments	25,000	19,000
Accounts receivable	43,000	45,000
Allowance for doubtful accounts	(1,800)	(2,000)
Prepaid expenses	4,200	2,500
Inventory	81,500	57,000
Land	50,000	50,000
Buildings	125,000	78,500
Accumulated depreciation—buildings	(30,000)	(23,000)
Equipment	53,000	46,000
Accumulated depreciation—equipment	(19,000)	(15,500)
Delivery equipment	39,000	39,000
Accumulated depreciation—delivery equipment	(22,000)	(20,500)
Patents	15,000	-0-
	$379,400	$300,000

	Dec. 31, 2012	Dec. 31, 2011
Accounts payable	$ 26,000	$ 16,000
Short-term notes payable (trade)	4,000	6,000
Accrued payables	3,000	4,600
Mortgage payable	73,000	53,400
Bonds payable	50,000	62,500
Common stock	140,000	102,000
Paid-in capital in excess of par—common stock	10,000	4,000
Retained earnings	73,400	51,500
	$379,400	$300,000

Dividends in the amount of $10,000 were declared and paid in 2012.

Instructions

From this information, prepare a worksheet for a statement of cash flows. Make reasonable assumptions as appropriate. The short-term investments are considered available-for-sale, and no unrealized gains or losses have occurred on these securities.

See the book's companion website, www.wiley.com/college/kieso, for a set of B Exercises.

PROBLEMS

P23-1 (SCF—Indirect Method) The following are Sullivan Corp.'s comparative balance sheet accounts at December 31, 2012 and 2011, with a column showing the increase (decrease) from 2011 to 2012.

COMPARATIVE BALANCE SHEETS

	2012	2011	Increase (Decrease)
Cash	$ 815,000	$ 700,000	$115,000
Accounts receivable	1,128,000	1,168,000	(40,000)
Inventory	1,850,000	1,715,000	135,000
Property, plant, and equipment	3,307,000	2,967,000	340,000
Accumulated depreciation	(1,165,000)	(1,040,000)	(125,000)
Investment in Myers Co.	310,000	275,000	35,000
Loan receivable	250,000	—	250,000
Total assets	$6,495,000	$5,785,000	$710,000
Accounts payable	$1,015,000	$ 955,000	$ 60,000
Income taxes payable	30,000	50,000	(20,000)
Dividends payable	80,000	100,000	(20,000)
Capital lease obligation	400,000	—	400,000
Common stock, $1 par	500,000	500,000	—
Paid-in capital in excess of par—common stock	1,500,000	1,500,000	—
Retained earnings	2,970,000	2,680,000	290,000
Total liabilities and stockholders' equity	$6,495,000	$5,785,000	$710,000

Additional information:

1. On December 31, 2011, Sullivan acquired 25% of Myers Co.'s common stock for $275,000. On that date, the carrying value of Myers's assets and liabilities, which approximated their fair values, was $1,100,000. Myers reported income of $140,000 for the year ended December 31, 2012. No dividend was paid on Myers's common stock during the year.
2. During 2012, Sullivan loaned $300,000 to TLC Co., an unrelated company. TLC made the first semi-annual principal repayment of $50,000, plus interest at 10%, on December 31, 2012.
3. On January 2, 2012, Sullivan sold equipment costing $60,000, with a carrying amount of $38,000, for $40,000 cash.
4. On December 31, 2012, Sullivan entered into a capital lease for an office building. The present value of the annual rental payments is $400,000, which equals the fair value of the building. Sullivan made the first rental payment of $60,000 when due on January 2, 2013.
5. Net income for 2012 was $370,000.
6. Sullivan declared and paid cash dividends for 2012 and 2011 as shown on the next page.

	2012	2011
Declared	December 15, 2012	December 15, 2011
Paid	February 28, 2013	February 28, 2012
Amount	$80,000	$100,000

Instructions

Prepare a statement of cash flows for Sullivan Corp. for the year ended December 31, 2012, using the indirect method.

(AICPA adapted)

P23-2 (SCF—Indirect Method) The comparative balance sheets for Hinckley Corporation show the following information.

	December 31	
	2012	2011
Cash	$ 33,500	$13,000
Accounts receivable	12,250	10,000
Inventory	12,000	9,000
Investments	-0-	3,000
Buildings	-0-	29,750
Equipment	45,000	20,000
Patents	5,000	6,250
	$107,750	$91,000
Allowance for doubtful accounts	$ 3,000	$ 4,500
Accumulated depreciation—equipment	2,000	4,500
Accumulated depreciation—building	-0-	6,000
Accounts payable	5,000	3,000
Dividends payable	-0-	5,000
Notes payable, short-term (nontrade)	3,000	4,000
Long-term notes payable	31,000	25,000
Common stock	43,000	33,000
Retained earnings	20,750	6,000
	$107,750	$91,000

Additional data related to 2012 are as follows.

1. Equipment that had cost $11,000 and was 40% depreciated at time of disposal was sold for $2,500.
2. $10,000 of the long-term note payable was paid by issuing common stock.
3. Cash dividends paid were $5,000.
4. On January 1, 2012, the building was completely destroyed by a flood. Insurance proceeds on the building were $30,000 (net of $2,000 taxes).
5. Investments (available-for-sale) were sold at $1,700 above their cost. The company has made similar sales and investments in the past.
6. Cash was paid for the acquisition of equipment.
7. A long-term note for $16,000 was issued for the acquisition of equipment.
8. Interest of $2,000 and income taxes of $6,500 were paid in cash.

Instructions

Prepare a statement of cash flows using the indirect method. Flood damage is unusual and infrequent in that part of the country.

P23-3 (SCF—Direct Method) Mortonson Company has not yet prepared a formal statement of cash flows for the 2012 fiscal year. Comparative balance sheets as of December 31, 2011 and 2012, and a statement of income and retained earnings for the year ended December 31, 2012, are presented below and on page 1492.

MORTONSON COMPANY
STATEMENT OF INCOME AND RETAINED EARNINGS
FOR THE YEAR ENDED DECEMBER 31, 2012
($000 OMITTED)

Sales		$3,800
Expenses		
Cost of goods sold	$1,200	
Salaries and benefits	725	
Heat, light, and power	75	
Depreciation	80	
Property taxes	19	
Patent amortization	25	
Miscellaneous expenses	10	
Interest	30	2,164

MORTONSON COMPANY
STATEMENT OF INCOME AND RETAINED EARNINGS
FOR THE YEAR ENDED DECEMBER 31, 2012
(CONTINUED)

Income before income taxes	1,636
Income taxes	818
Net income	818
Retained earnings—Jan. 1, 2012	310
	1,128
Stock dividend declared and issued	600
Retained earnings—Dec. 31, 2012	$ 528

MORTONSON COMPANY
COMPARATIVE BALANCE SHEETS
AS OF DECEMBER 31
($000 OMITTED)

Assets	2012	2011
Current assets		
Cash	$ 333	$ 100
U.S. Treasury notes (available-for-sale)	10	50
Accounts receivable	780	500
Inventory	720	560
Total current assets	1,843	1,210
Long-term assets		
Land	150	70
Buildings and equipment	910	600
Accumulated depreciation	(200)	(120)
Patents (less amortization)	105	130
Total long-term assets	965	680
Total assets	$2,808	$1,890
Liabilities and Stockholders' Equity		
Current liabilities		
Accounts payable	$ 420	$ 330
Income taxes payable	40	30
Notes payable	320	320
Total current liabilities	780	680
Long-term notes payable—due 2014	200	200
Total liabilities	980	880
Stockholders' equity		
Common stock	1,300	700
Retained earnings	528	310
Total stockholders' equity	1,828	1,010
Total liabilities and stockholders' equity	$2,808	$1,890

Instructions

Prepare a statement of cash flows using the direct method. Changes in accounts receivable and accounts payable relate to sales and cost of goods sold. Do not prepare a reconciliation schedule.

(CMA adapted)

8 **P23-4 (SCF—Direct Method)** Michaels Company had available at the end of 2012 the information shown below.

MICHAELS COMPANY
COMPARATIVE BALANCE SHEETS
AS OF DECEMBER 31, 2012 AND 2011

	2012	2011
Cash	$ 10,000	$ 4,000
Accounts receivable	20,500	12,950
Short-term investments	22,000	30,000
Inventory	42,000	35,000
Prepaid rent	3,000	12,000
Prepaid insurance	2,100	900
Supplies	1,000	750
Land	125,000	175,000
Buildings	350,000	350,000
Accumulated depreciation—buildings	(105,000)	(87,500)
Equipment	525,000	400,000
Accumulated depreciation—equipment	(130,000)	(112,000)
Patents	45,000	50,000
Total assets	$910,600	$871,100
Accounts payable	$ 22,000	$ 32,000
Income taxes payable	5,000	4,000
Salaries and wages payable	5,000	3,000
Short-term notes payable	10,000	10,000
Long-term notes payable	60,000	70,000
Bonds payable	400,000	400,000
Premium on bonds payable	20,303	25,853
Common stock	240,000	220,000
Paid-in capital in excess of par—common stock	25,000	17,500
Retained earnings	123,297	88,747
Total liabilities and stockholders' equity	$910,600	$871,100

MICHAEL S COMPANY
INCOME STATEMENT AND DIVIDEND INFORMATION
FOR THE YEAR ENDED DECEMBER 31, 2012

Sales revenue		$1,160,000
Cost of goods sold		748,000
Gross margin		412,000
Operating expenses		
Selling expenses	$ 79,200	
Administrative expenses	156,700	
Depreciation/Amortization expense	40,500	
Total operating expenses		276,400
Income from operations		135,600
Other revenues/expenses		
Gain on sale of land	8,000	
Gain on sale of short-term investment	4,000	
Dividend revenue	2,400	
Interest expense	(51,750)	(37,350)
Income before taxes		98,250
Income tax expense		39,400
Net income		58,850
Dividends to common stockholders		(24,300)
To retained earnings		$ 34,550

Instructions

Prepare a statement of cash flows for Michaels Company using the direct method accompanied by a reconciliation schedule. Assume the short-term investments are classified as available-for-sale.

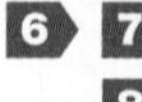

P23-5 (SCF—Indirect Method) You have completed the field work in connection with your audit of Alexander Corporation for the year ended December 31, 2012. The balance sheet accounts at the beginning and end of the year are shown below.

	Dec. 31, 2012	Dec. 31, 2011	Increase or (Decrease)
Cash	$ 277,900	$ 298,000	($20,100)
Accounts receivable	469,424	353,000	116,424
Inventory	741,700	610,000	131,700
Prepaid expenses	12,000	8,000	4,000
Investment in subsidiary	110,500	–0–	110,500
Cash surrender value of life insurance	2,304	1,800	504
Machinery	207,000	190,000	17,000
Buildings	535,200	407,900	127,300
Land	52,500	52,500	–0–
Patents	69,000	64,000	5,000
Copyrights	40,000	50,000	(10,000)
Bond discount and issue cost	4,502	–0–	4,502
	$2,522,030	$2,035,200	$486,830
Accrued taxes payable	$ 90,250	$ 79,600	$ 10,650
Accounts payable	299,280	280,000	19,280
Dividends payable	70,000	–0–	70,000
Bonds payable—8%	125,000	–0–	125,000
Bonds payable—12%	–0–	100,000	(100,000)
Allowance for doubtful accounts	35,300	40,000	(4,700)
Accumulated depreciation—buildings	424,000	400,000	24,000
Accumulated depreciation—machinery	173,000	130,000	43,000
Premium on bonds payable	–0–	2,400	(2,400)
Common stock—no par	1,176,200	1,453,200	(277,000)
Paid-in capital in excess of par—common stock	109,000	–0–	109,000
Retained earnings—unappropriated	20,000	(450,000)	470,000
	$2,522,030	$2,035,200	$486,830

STATEMENT OF RETAINED EARNINGS
FOR THE YEAR ENDED DECEMBER 31, 2012

January 1, 2012	Balance (deficit)	$(450,000)
March 31, 2012	Net income for first quarter of 2012	25,000
April 1, 2012	Transfer from paid-in capital	425,000
	Balance	–0–
December 31, 2012	Net income for last three quarters of 2012	90,000
	Dividend declared—payable January 21, 2013	(70,000)
	Balance	$ 20,000

Your working papers from the audit contain the following information:

1. On April 1, 2012, the existing deficit was written off against paid-in capital created by reducing the stated value of the no-par stock.
2. On November 1, 2012, 29,600 shares of no-par stock were sold for $257,000. The board of directors voted to regard $5 per share as stated capital.
3. A patent was purchased for $15,000.
4. During the year, machinery that had a cost basis of $16,400 and on which there was accumulated depreciation of $5,200 was sold for $9,000. No other plant assets were sold during the year.
5. The 12%, 20-year bonds were dated and issued on January 2, 2000. Interest was payable on June 30 and December 31. They were sold originally at 106. These bonds were retired at 100.9 plus accrued interest on March 31, 2012.
6. The 8%, 40-year bonds were dated January 1, 2012, and were sold on March 31 at 97 plus accrued interest. Interest is payable semiannually on June 30 and December 31. Expense of issuance was $839.
7. Alexander Corporation acquired 70% control in Crimson Company on January 2, 2012, for $100,000. The income statement of Crimson Company for 2012 shows a net income of $15,000.
8. Extraordinary repairs to buildings of $7,200 were charged to Accumulated Depreciation—Buildings.
9. Interest paid in 2012 was $10,500 and income taxes paid were $34,000.

Instructions
From the information given, prepare a statement of cash flows using the indirect method. A worksheet is not necessary, but the principal computations should be supported by schedules or general ledger accounts. The company uses straight-line amortization for bond interest.

3 4 6 8 **P23-6 (SCF—Indirect Method, and Net Cash Flow from Operating Activities, Direct Method)** Comparative balance sheet accounts of Marcus Inc. are presented below.

MARCUS INC.
COMPARATIVE BALANCE SHEET ACCOUNTS
AS OF DECEMBER 31, 2012 AND 2011

	December 31	
Debit Accounts	2012	2011
Cash	$ 42,000	$ 33,750
Accounts Receivable	70,500	60,000
Inventory	30,000	24,000
Investments (available-for-sale)	22,250	38,500
Machinery	30,000	18,750
Buildings	67,500	56,250
Land	7,500	7,500
	$269,750	$238,750
Credit Accounts		
Allowance for Doubtful Accounts	$ 2,250	$ 1,500
Accumulated Depreciation—Machinery	5,625	2,250
Accumulated Depreciation—Buildings	13,500	9,000
Accounts Payable	35,000	24,750
Accrued Payables	3,375	2,625
Long-Term Notes Payable	21,000	31,000
Common Stock, no-par	150,000	125,000
Retained Earnings	39,000	42,625
	$269,750	$238,750

Additional data (ignoring taxes):

1. Net income for the year was $42,500.
2. Cash dividends declared and paid during the year were $21,125.
3. A 20% stock dividend was declared during the year. $25,000 of retained earnings was capitalized.
4. Investments that cost $25,000 were sold during the year for $28,750.
5. Machinery that cost $3,750, on which $750 of depreciation had accumulated, was sold for $2,200.

Marcus's 2012 income statement follows (ignoring taxes).

Sales		$540,000
Less: cost of goods sold		380,000
Gross margin		160,000
Less: Operating expenses (includes $8,625 depreciation and $5,400 bad debts)		120,450
Income from operations		39,550
Other: Gain on sale of investments	$3,750	
Loss on sale of machinery	(800)	2,950
Net income		$ 42,500

Instructions
(a) Compute net cash flow from operating activities using the direct method.
(b) Prepare a statement of cash flows using the indirect method.

3 4 6 8 **P23-7 (SCF—Direct and Indirect Methods from Comparative Financial Statements)** Chapman Company, a major retailer of bicycles and accessories, operates several stores and is a publicly traded company. The comparative balance sheet and income statement for Chapman as of May 31, 2012, are shown on the next page. The company is preparing its statement of cash flows.

CHAPMAN COMPANY
COMPARATIVE BALANCE SHEET
AS OF MAY 31

	2012	2011
Current assets		
Cash	$ 28,250	$ 20,000
Accounts receivable	75,000	58,000
Inventory	220,000	250,000
Prepaid expenses	9,000	7,000
Total current assets	332,250	335,000
Plant assets		
Plant assets	600,000	502,000
Less: Accumulated depreciation—plant assets	150,000	125,000
Net plant assets	450,000	377,000
Total assets	$782,250	$712,000
Current liabilities		
Accounts payable	$123,000	$115,000
Salaries and wages payable	47,250	72,000
Interest payable	27,000	25,000
Total current liabilities	197,250	212,000
Long-term debt		
Bonds payable	70,000	100,000
Total liabilities	267,250	312,000
Stockholders' equity		
Common stock, $10 par	370,000	280,000
Retained earnings	145,000	120,000
Total stockholders' equity	515,000	400,000
Total liabilities and stockholders' equity	$782,250	$712,000

CHAPMAN COMPANY
INCOME STATEMENT
FOR THE YEAR ENDED MAY 31, 2012

Sales	$1,255,250
Cost of goods sold	722,000
Gross profit	533,250
Expenses	
Salaries and wages expense	252,100
Interest expense	75,000
Depreciation expense	25,000
Other expenses	8,150
Total expenses	360,250
Operating income	173,000
Income tax expense	43,000
Net income	$ 130,000

The following is additional information concerning Chapman's transactions during the year ended May 31, 2012.

1. All sales during the year were made on account.
2. All merchandise was purchased on account, comprising the total accounts payable account.
3. Plant assets costing $98,000 were purchased by paying $28,000 in cash and issuing 7,000 shares of stock.
4. The "other expenses" are related to prepaid items.
5. All income taxes incurred during the year were paid during the year.
6. In order to supplement its cash, Chapman issued 2,000 shares of common stock at par value.
7. Cash dividends of $105,000 were declared and paid at the end of the fiscal year.

Instructions

(a) Compare and contrast the direct method and the indirect method for reporting cash flows from operating activities.

(b) Prepare a statement of cash flows for Chapman Company for the year ended May 31, 2012, using the direct method. Be sure to support the statement with appropriate calculations. (A reconciliation of net income to net cash provided is not required.)

(c) Using the indirect method, calculate only the net cash flow from operating activities for Chapman Company for the year ended May 31, 2012.

P23-8 (SCF—Direct and Indirect Methods) Comparative balance sheet accounts of Sharpe Company are presented below.

SHARPE COMPANY
COMPARATIVE BALANCE SHEET ACCOUNTS
AS OF DECEMBER 31

Debit Balances	2012	2011
Cash	$ 70,000	$ 51,000
Accounts Receivable	155,000	130,000
Inventory	75,000	61,000
Investments (Available-for-sale)	55,000	85,000
Equipment	70,000	48,000
Buildings	145,000	145,000
Land	40,000	25,000
Totals	$610,000	$545,000
Credit Balances		
Allowance for Doubtful Accounts	$ 10,000	$ 8,000
Accumulated Depreciation—Equipment	21,000	14,000
Accumulated Depreciation—Buildings	37,000	28,000
Accounts Payable	66,000	60,000
Income Taxes Payable	12,000	10,000
Long-Term Notes Payable	62,000	70,000
Common Stock	310,000	260,000
Retained Earnings	92,000	95,000
Totals	$610,000	$545,000

Additional data:

1. Equipment that cost $10,000 and was 60% depreciated was sold in 2012.
2. Cash dividends were declared and paid during the year.
3. Common stock was issued in exchange for land.
4. Investments that cost $35,000 were sold during the year.
5. There were no write-offs of uncollectible accounts during the year.

Sharpe's 2012 income statement is as follows.

Sales		$950,000
Less: Cost of goods sold		600,000
Gross profit		350,000
Less: Operating expenses (includes depreciation expense and bad debt expense)		250,000
Income from operations		100,000
Other revenues and expenses		
Gain on sale of investments	$15,000	
Loss on sale of equipment	(3,000)	12,000
Income before taxes		112,000
Income taxes		45,000
Net income		$ 67,000

Instructions

(a) Compute net cash provided by operating activities under the direct method.

(b) Prepare a statement of cash flows using the indirect method.

P23-9 (Indirect SCF) Dingel Corporation has contracted with you to prepare a statement of cash flows. The controller has provided the following information.

	December 31	
	2012	2011
Cash	$ 38,500	$13,000
Accounts receivable	12,250	10,000
Inventory	12,000	10,000
Investments	–0–	3,000
Buildings	–0–	29,750
Equipment	40,000	20,000
Copyrights	5,000	5,250
Totals	$107,750	$91,000
Allowance for doubtful accounts	$ 3,000	$ 4,500
Accumulated depreciation—equipment	2,000	4,500
Accumulated depreciation—buildings	–0–	6,000
Accounts payable	5,000	4,000
Dividends payable	–0–	5,000
Notes payable, short-term (nontrade)	3,000	4,000
Long-term notes payable	36,000	25,000
Common stock	38,000	33,000
Retained earnings	20,750	5,000
	$107,750	$91,000

Additional data related to 2012 are as follows.

1. Equipment that had cost $11,000 and was 30% depreciated at time of disposal was sold for $2,500.
2. $5,000 of the long-term note payable was paid by issuing common stock.
3. Cash dividends paid were $5,000.
4. On January 1, 2012, the building was completely destroyed by a flood. Insurance proceeds on the building were $33,000 (net of $4,000 taxes).
5. Investments (available-for-sale) were sold at $1,500 above their cost. The company has made similar sales and investments in the past.
6. Cash and long-term note for $16,000 were given for the acquisition of equipment.
7. Interest of $2,000 and income taxes of $5,000 were paid in cash.

Instructions

(a) Use the indirect method to analyze the above information and prepare a statement of cash flows for Dingel. Flood damage is unusual and infrequent in that part of the country.

(b) What would you expect to observe in the operating, investing, and financing sections of a statement of cash flows of:

(1) A severely financially troubled firm?

(2) A recently formed firm that is experiencing rapid growth?

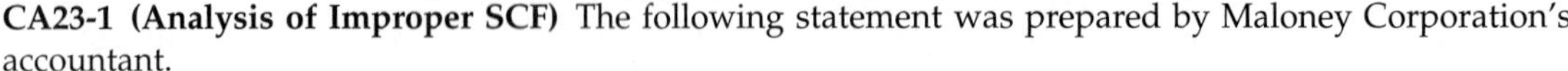

CONCEPTS FOR ANALYSIS

CA23-1 (Analysis of Improper SCF) The following statement was prepared by Maloney Corporation's accountant.

MALONEY CORPORATION
STATEMENT OF SOURCES AND APPLICATION OF CASH
FOR THE YEAR ENDED SEPTEMBER 30, 2012

Sources of cash	
Net income	$111,000
Depreciation and depletion	70,000
Increase in long-term debt	179,000
Changes in current receivables and inventories, less current liabilities (excluding current maturities of long-term debt)	14,000
	$374,000

Application of cash	
Cash dividends	$ 60,000
Expenditure for property, plant, and equipment	214,000
Investments and other uses	20,000
Change in cash	80,000
	$374,000

The following additional information relating to Maloney Corporation is available for the year ended September 30, 2012.

1. Wage and salary expense attributable to stock option plans was $25,000 for the year.
2. Expenditures for property, plant, and equipment $250,000
   Proceeds from retirements of property, plant, and equipment 36,000
   Net expenditures $214,000
3. A stock dividend of 10,000 shares of Maloney Corporation common stock was distributed to common stockholders on April 1, 2012, when the per share market price was $7 and par value was $1.
4. On July 1, 2012, when its market price was $6 per share, 16,000 shares of Maloney Corporation common stock were issued in exchange for 4,000 shares of preferred stock.
5. Depreciation expense $ 65,000
   Depletion expense 5,000
   $ 70,000
6. Increase in long-term debt $620,000
   Retirement of debt 441,000
   Net increase $179,000

Instructions

(a) In general, what are the objectives of a statement of the type shown above for Maloney Corporation? Explain.

(b) Identify the weaknesses in the form and format of Maloney Corporation's statement of cash flows without reference to the additional information. (Assume adoption of the indirect method.)

(c) For each of the six items of additional information for the statement of cash flows, indicate the preferable treatment and explain why the suggested treatment is preferable.

(AICPA adapted)

CA23-2 (SCF Theory and Analysis of Improper SCF) Teresa Ramirez and Lenny Traylor are examining the following statement of cash flows for Pacific Clothing Store's first year of operations.

PACIFIC CLOTHING STORE
STATEMENT OF CASH FLOWS
FOR THE YEAR ENDED JANUARY 31, 2012

Sources of cash	
From sales of merchandise	$ 382,000
From sale of capital stock	380,000
From sale of investment	120,000
From depreciation	80,000
From issuance of note for truck	30,000
From interest on investments	8,000
Total sources of cash	1,000,000
Uses of cash	
For purchase of fixtures and equipment	330,000
For merchandise purchased for resale	253,000
For operating expenses (including depreciation)	170,000
For purchase of investment	95,000
For purchase of truck by issuance of note	30,000
For purchase of treasury stock	10,000
For interest on note	3,000
Total uses of cash	891,000
Net increase in cash	$ 109,000

Teresa claims that Pacific's statement of cash flows is an excellent portrayal of a superb first year, with cash increasing $109,000. Lenny replies that it was not a superb first year—that the year was an operating failure, the statement was incorrectly presented, and $109,000 is not the actual increase in cash.

Instructions

(a) With whom do you agree, Teresa or Lenny? Explain your position.

(b) Using the data provided, prepare a statement of cash flows in proper indirect method form. The only noncash items in income are depreciation and the gain from the sale of the investment (purchase and sale are related).

CA23-3 (SCF Theory and Analysis of Transactions) Ashley Company is a young and growing producer of electronic measuring instruments and technical equipment. You have been retained by Ashley to advise it in the preparation of a statement of cash flows using the indirect method. For the fiscal year ended October 31, 2012, you have obtained the following information concerning certain events and transactions of Ashley.

1. The amount of reported earnings for the fiscal year was $700,000, which included a deduction for an extraordinary loss of $110,000 (see item 5 below).
2. Depreciation expense of $315,000 was included in the income statement.
3. Uncollectible accounts receivable of $40,000 were written off against the allowance for doubtful accounts. Also, $51,000 of bad debt expense was included in determining income for the fiscal year, and the same amount was added to the allowance for doubtful accounts.
4. A gain of $6,000 was realized on the sale of a machine. It originally cost $75,000, of which $30,000 was undepreciated on the date of sale.
5. On April 1, 2012, lightning caused an uninsured building loss of $110,000 ($180,000 loss, less reduction in income taxes of $70,000). This extraordinary loss was included in determining income as indicated in item 1 above.
6. On July 3, 2012, building and land were purchased for $700,000. Ashley gave in payment $75,000 cash, $200,000 market price of its unissued common stock, and signed a $425,000 mortgage note payable.
7. On August 3, 2012, $800,000 face value of Ashley's 10% convertible debentures was converted into $150,000 par value of its common stock. The bonds were originally issued at face value.

Instructions

Explain whether each of the seven numbered items above is a cash inflow or outflow, and explain how it should be disclosed in Ashley's statement of cash flows for the fiscal year ended October 31, 2012. If any item is neither an inflow nor an outflow of cash, explain why it is not, and indicate the disclosure, if any, that should be made of the item in Ashley's statement of cash flows for the fiscal year ended October 31, 2012.

CA23-4 (Analysis of Transactions' Effect on SCF) Each of the following items must be considered in preparing a statement of cash flows for Cruz Fashions Inc. for the year ended December 31, 2012.

1. Fixed assets that had cost $20,000 6½ years before and were being depreciated on a 10-year basis, with no estimated scrap value, were sold for $4,750.
2. During the year, goodwill of $15,000 was considered impaired and was completely written off to expense.
3. During the year, 500 shares of common stock with a stated value of $25 a share were issued for $32 a share.
4. The company sustained a net loss for the year of $2,100. Depreciation amounted to $2,000 and patent amortization was $400.
5. Uncollectible accounts receivable in the amount of $2,000 were written off against Allowance for Doubtful Accounts.
6. Investments (available-for-sale) that cost $12,000 when purchased 4 years earlier were sold for $10,600. The loss was considered ordinary.
7. Bonds payable with a par value of $24,000 on which there was an unamortized bond premium of $2,000 were redeemed at 101. The gain was credited to ordinary income.

Instructions

For each item, state where it is to be shown in the statement and then how you would present the necessary information, including the amount. Consider each item to be independent of the others. Assume that correct entries were made for all transactions as they took place.

CA23-5 (Purpose and Elements of SCF) GAAP requires the statement of cash flows be presented when financial statements are prepared.

Instructions

(a) Explain the purposes of the statement of cash flows.

(b) List and describe the three categories of activities that must be reported in the statement of cash flows.

(c) Identify and describe the two methods that are allowed for reporting cash flows from operations.

(d) Describe the financial statement presentation of noncash investing and financing transactions. Include in your description an example of a noncash investing and financing transaction.

CA23-6 (Cash Flow Reporting) Brockman Guitar Company is in the business of manufacturing top-quality, steel-string folk guitars. In recent years, the company has experienced working capital problems resulting from the procurement of factory equipment, the unanticipated buildup of receivables and inventories, and the payoff of a balloon mortgage on a new manufacturing facility. The founder and president of the company, Barbara Brockman, has attempted to raise cash from various financial institutions, but to no avail because of the company's poor performance in recent years. In particular, the company's lead bank, First Financial, is especially concerned about Brockman's inability to maintain a positive cash position. The commercial loan officer from First Financial told Barbara, "I can't even consider your request for capital financing unless I see that your company is able to generate positive cash flows from operations."

Thinking about the banker's comment, Barbara came up with what she believes is a good plan: With a more attractive statement of cash flows, the bank might be willing to provide long-term financing. To "window dress" cash flows, the company can sell its accounts receivables to factors and liquidate its raw materials inventories. These rather costly transactions would generate lots of cash. As the chief accountant for Brockman Guitar, it is your job to tell Barbara what you think of her plan.

Instructions

Answer the following questions.

(a) What are the ethical issues related to Barbara Brockman's idea?

(b) What would you tell Barbara Brockman?

USING YOUR JUDGMENT

FINANCIAL REPORTING

Financial Reporting Problem

The Procter & Gamble Company (P&G)

The financial statements of P&G are presented in Appendix 5B or can be accessed at the book's companion website, **www.wiley.com/college/kieso**.

Instructions

Refer to P&G's financial statements and the accompanying notes to answer the following questions.

(a) Which method of computing net cash provided by operating activities does P&G use? What were the amounts of net cash provided by operating activities for the years 2007, 2008, and 2009? Which two items were most responsible for the increase in net cash provided by operating activities in 2009?

(b) What was the most significant item in the cash flows used for investing activities section in 2009?

What was the most significant item in the cash flows used for financing activities section in 2009?

(c) Where is "deferred income taxes" reported in P&G's statement of cash flows? Why does it appear in that section of the statement of cash flows?

(d) Where is depreciation reported in P&G's statement of cash flows? Why is depreciation added to net income in the statement of cash flows?

Comparative Analysis Case

The Coca-Cola Company and PepsiCo, Inc.

Instructions

Go to the book's companion website and use information found there to answer the following questions related to **The Coca-Cola Company** and **PepsiCo, Inc.**

(a) What method of computing net cash provided by operating activities does Coca-Cola use? What method does PepsiCo use? What were the amounts of cash provided by operating activities reported by Coca-Cola and PepsiCo in 2009?

(b) What was the most significant item reported by Coca-Cola and PepsiCo in 2009 in their investing activities sections? What is the most significant item reported by Coca-Cola and PepsiCo in 2009 in their financing activities sections?

(c) What were these two companies' trends in net cash provided by operating activities over the period 2007 to 2009?

(d) Where is "depreciation and amortization" reported by Coca-Cola and PepsiCo in their statements of cash flows? What is the amount and why does it appear in that section of the statement of cash flows?

(e) Based on the information contained in Coca-Cola's and PepsiCo's financial statements, compute the following 2009 ratios for each company. These ratios require the use of statement of cash flows data. (These ratios were covered in Chapter 5.)

(1) Current cash debt coverage ratio.

(2) Cash debt coverage ratio.

(f) What conclusions concerning the management of cash can be drawn from the ratios computed in (e)?

Financial Statement Analysis Case

Vermont Teddy Bear Co.

Founded in the early 1980s, the **Vermont Teddy Bear Co.** designs and manufactures American-made teddy bears and markets them primarily as gifts called Bear-Grams or Teddy Bear-Grams. Bear-Grams are personalized teddy bears delivered directly to the recipient for special occasions such as birthdays and anniversaries. The Shelburne, Vermont, company's primary markets are New York, Boston, and Chicago. Sales have jumped dramatically in recent years. Such dramatic growth has significant implications for cash flows. Provided below are the cash flow statements for two recent years for the company.

	Current Year	Prior Year
Cash flows from operating activities:		
Net income	$ 17,523	$ 838,955
Adjustments to reconcile net income to net cash provided by operating activities		
Deferred income taxes	(69,524)	(146,590)
Depreciation and amortization	316,416	181,348
Changes in assets and liabilities:		
Accounts receivable, trade	(38,267)	(25,947)
Inventories	(1,599,014)	(1,289,293)
Prepaid and other current assets	(444,794)	(113,205)
Deposits and other assets	(24,240)	(83,044)
Accounts payable	2,017,059	(284,567)
Accrued expenses	61,321	170,755
Accrued interest payable, debentures	—	(58,219)
Other	—	(8,960)
Income taxes payable	—	117,810
Net cash provided by (used for) operating activities	236,480	(700,957)
Net cash used for investing activities	(2,102,892)	(4,422,953)
Net cash (used for) provided by financing activities	(315,353)	9,685,435
Net change in cash and cash equivalents	(2,181,765)	4,561,525

Other information:

	Current Year	Prior Year
Current liabilities	$ 4,055,465	$ 1,995,600
Total liabilities	4,620,085	2,184,386
Net sales	20,560,566	17,025,856

Instructions

(a) Note that net income in the current year was only $17,523 compared to prior-year income of $838,955, but cash flow from operations was $236,480 in the current year and a negative $700,957 in the prior year. Explain the causes of this apparent paradox.

(b) Evaluate Vermont Teddy Bear's liquidity, solvency, and profitability for the current year using cash flow-based ratios.

Accounting, Analysis, and Principles

The income statement for the year ended December 31, 2012, for Laskowski Manufacturing Company contains the following condensed information.

LASKOWSKI CO.
INCOME STATEMENT

Revenues		$6,583,000
Operating expenses (excluding depreciation)	$4,920,000	
Depreciation expense	880,000	5,800,000
Income before income tax		783,000
Income tax expense		353,000
Net income		$ 430,000

Included in operating expenses is a $24,000 loss resulting from the sale of machinery for $270,000 cash. The company purchased machinery at a cost of $750,000.

Laskowski reports the following balances on its comparative balance sheets at December 31.

LASKOWSKI CO.
COMPARATIVE BALANCE SHEETS (PARTIAL)

	2012	2011
Cash	$672,000	$130,000
Accounts receivable	775,000	610,000
Inventory	834,000	867,000
Accounts payable	521,000	501,000

Income tax expense of $353,000 represents the amount paid in 2012. Dividends declared and paid in 2012 totaled $200,000.

Accounting

Prepare the statement of cash flows using the indirect method.

Analysis

Laskowski has an aggressive growth plan, which will require significant investments in plant and equipment over the next several years. Preliminary plans call for an investment of over $500,000 in the next year. Compute Laskowski's free cash flow (from Chapter 5) and use it to evaluate the investment plans with the use of only internally generated funds.

Principles

How does the statement of cash flows contribute to achieving the objective of financial reporting?

BRIDGE TO THE PROFESSION

Professional Research: FASB Codification

As part of the year-end accounting process for your company, you are preparing the statement of cash flows according to GAAP. One of your team, a finance major, believes the statement should be prepared to report the change in working capital, because analysts many times use working capital in ratio analysis. Your supervisor would like research conducted to verify the basis for preparing the statement of cash flows.

Instructions

If your school has a subscription to the FASB Codification, go to *http://aaahq.org/ascLogin.cfm* to log in and prepare responses to the following. Provide Codification references for your responses.

(a) What is the primary objective for the statement of cash flows? Is working capital the basis for meeting this objective?

(b) What information is provided in a statement of cash flows?

(c) List some of the typical cash inflows and outflows from operations.

Professional Simulation

The professional simulation for this chapter asks you to address questions related to the accounting for the statement of cash flows.

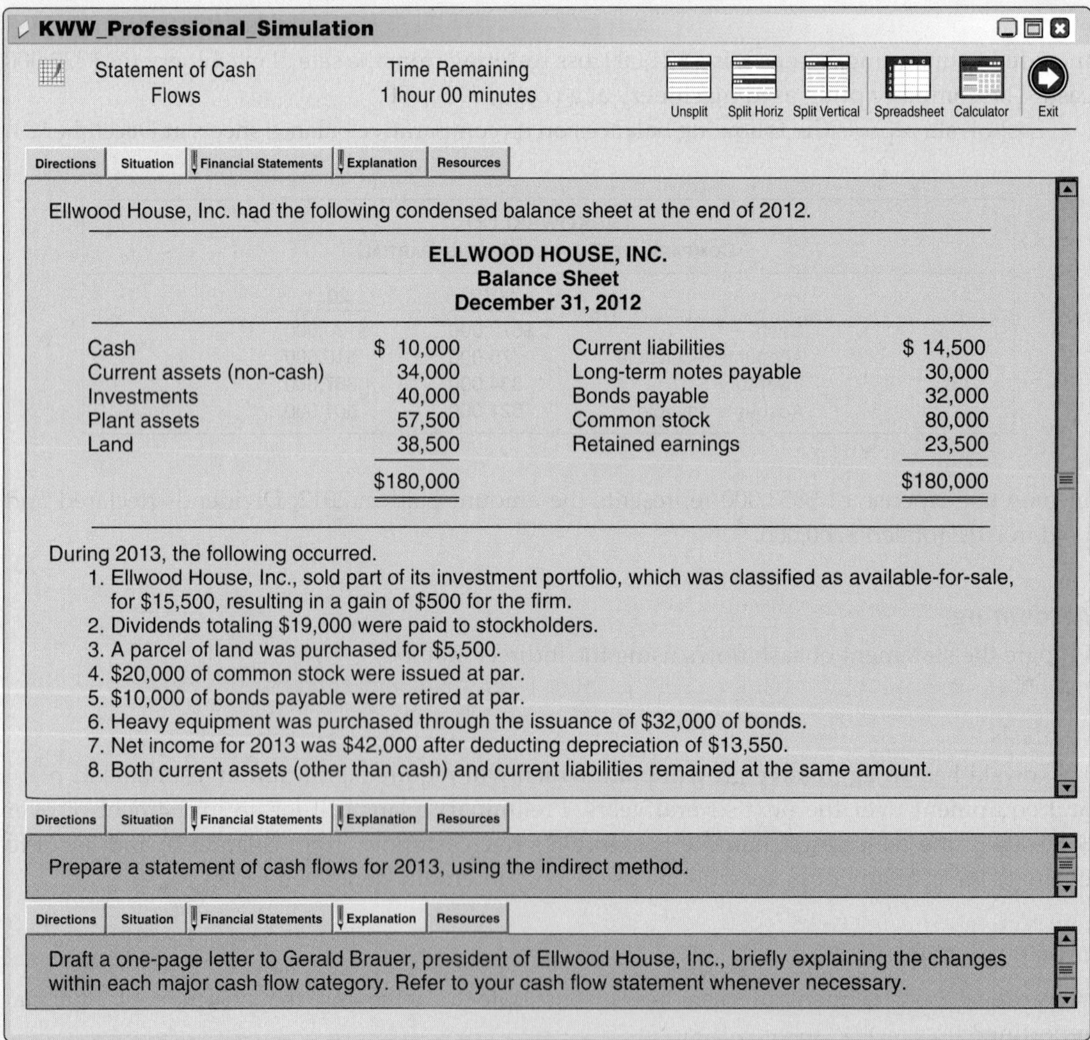

Ellwood House, Inc. had the following condensed balance sheet at the end of 2012.

ELLWOOD HOUSE, INC.
Balance Sheet
December 31, 2012

Cash	$ 10,000	Current liabilities	$ 14,500
Current assets (non-cash)	34,000	Long-term notes payable	30,000
Investments	40,000	Bonds payable	32,000
Plant assets	57,500	Common stock	80,000
Land	38,500	Retained earnings	23,500
	$180,000		$180,000

During 2013, the following occurred.

1. Ellwood House, Inc., sold part of its investment portfolio, which was classified as available-for-sale, for $15,500, resulting in a gain of $500 for the firm.
2. Dividends totaling $19,000 were paid to stockholders.
3. A parcel of land was purchased for $5,500.
4. $20,000 of common stock were issued at par.
5. $10,000 of bonds payable were retired at par.
6. Heavy equipment was purchased through the issuance of $32,000 of bonds.
7. Net income for 2013 was $42,000 after deducting depreciation of $13,550.
8. Both current assets (other than cash) and current liabilities remained at the same amount.

Prepare a statement of cash flows for 2013, using the indirect method.

Draft a one-page letter to Gerald Brauer, president of Ellwood House, Inc., briefly explaining the changes within each major cash flow category. Refer to your cash flow statement whenever necessary.

As in GAAP, the statement of cash flows is a required statement for IFRS. In addition, the content and presentation of a U.S. statement of cash flows is similar to one used for IFRS. However, the disclosure requirements related to the statement of cash flows are more extensive under GAAP. *IAS 7* ("Cash Flow Statements") provides the overall IFRS requirements for cash flow information.

RELEVANT FACTS

- Companies preparing financial statements under IFRS must prepare a statement of cash flows as an integral part of the financial statements.
- Both IFRS and GAAP require that the statement of cash flows should have three major sections—operating, investing, and financing—along with changes in cash and cash equivalents.
- Similar to GAAP, the cash flow statement can be prepared using either the indirect or direct method under IFRS. For both IFRS and GAAP, most companies use the indirect method for reporting net cash flow from operating activities.
- The definition of cash equivalents used in IFRS is similar to that used in GAAP. A major difference is that in certain situations, bank overdrafts are considered part of cash and cash equivalents under IFRS (which is not the case in GAAP). Under GAAP, bank overdrafts are classified as financing activities.
- IFRS requires that non-cash investing and financing activities be excluded from the statement of cash flows. Instead, these non-cash activities should be reported elsewhere. This requirement is interpreted to mean that non-cash investing and financing activities should be disclosed in the notes to the financial statements instead of in the financial statements. Under GAAP, companies may present this information in the cash flow statement.
- One area where there can be substantive differences between IFRS and GAAP relates to the classification of interest, dividends, and taxes. IFRS provides more alternatives for disclosing these items, while GAAP requires that except for dividends paid (which are classified as a financing activity), these items are all reported as operating activities.

ABOUT THE NUMBERS

Significant Non-Cash Transactions

Because the statement of cash flows reports only the effects of operating, investing, and financing activities in terms of cash flows, it omits some **significant non-cash transactions** and other events that are investing or financing activities. Among the more common of these non-cash transactions that a company should report or disclose in some manner are the following.

1. Acquisition of assets by assuming liabilities (including finance lease obligations) or by issuing equity securities.
2. Exchanges of non-monetary assets.
3. Refinancing of long-term debt.
4. Conversion of debt or preference shares to ordinary shares.
5. Issuance of equity securities to retire debt.

Investing and financing transactions that do not require the use of cash are excluded from the statement of cash flows. If material in amount, these disclosures may be either narrative or summarized in a separate schedule. This schedule may appear in a separate note or supplementary schedule to the financial statements.

Illustration IFRS23-1 shows the presentation of these significant non-cash transactions or other events in a separate schedule in the notes to the financial statements.

ILLUSTRATION IFRS23-1
Note Presentation of Non-Cash Investing and Financing Activities

Note G: Significant non-cash transactions. During the year, the company engaged in the following significant non-cash investing and financing transactions:

Issued 250,000 ordinary shares to purchase land and building	$1,750,000
Exchanged land in Steadfast, New York, for land in Bedford, Pennsylvania	$2,000,000
Converted 12% bonds to 50,000 ordinary shares	$ 500,000

Companies do not generally report certain other significant non-cash transactions or other events in conjunction with the statement of cash flows. Examples of these types of transactions are **share dividends, share splits, and restrictions on retained earnings**. Companies generally report these items, neither financing nor investing activities, in conjunction with the statement of changes in equity or schedules and notes pertaining to changes in equity accounts.

Special Disclosures

IAS 7 indicates that cash flows related to interest received and paid, and dividends received and paid, should be separately disclosed in the statement of cash flows. Each item should be classified in a consistent manner from period to period as operating, investing, or financing cash flows. *For homework purposes, classify interest received and paid and dividends received as part of cash flows from operating activities and dividends paid as cash flows from financing activities.* The justification for reporting the first three items in cash flows from operating activities is that each item affects net income. Dividends paid, however, do not affect net income and are often considered a cost of financing.

Companies should also disclose income taxes paid separately in the cash flows from operating activities unless they can be separately identified as part of investing or financing activities. While tax expense may be readily identifiable with investing or financing activities, the related tax cash flows are often impracticable to identify and may arise in a different period from the cash flows of the underlying transaction. Therefore, taxes paid are usually classified as cash flows from operating activities. IFRS requires that the cash paid for taxes, as well as cash flows from interest and dividends received and paid, be disclosed. The category (operating, investing, or financing) that each item was included in must be disclosed as well.

An example of such a disclosure from the notes to **Daimler**'s financial statements is provided in Illustration IFRS23-2.

ILLUSTRATION IFRS23-2
Note Disclosure of Interest, Taxes, and Dividends

Daimler

Cash provided by operating activities includes the following cash flows:

(in millions of €)	2009	2008	2007
Interest paid	(894)	(651)	(1,541)
Interest received	471	765	977
Income taxes paid, net	(358)	(898)	(1,020)
Dividends received	109	67	69

Other companies choose to report these items directly in the statement of cash flows. In many cases, companies start with income before income taxes and then show income taxes paid as a separate item. In addition, they often add back interest expense on an accrual basis and then subtract interest paid. Reporting these items in the operating activities section is shown for Mermel Company in Illustration IFRS23-3.

ILLUSTRATION IFRS23-3
Reporting of Interest, Taxes, and Dividends in the Operating Section

MERMEL COMPANY STATEMENT OF CASH FLOWS ($000,000) (OPERATING ACTIVITIES SECTION ONLY)		
Income before income tax		$ 4,000
Adjustments to reconcile income before income tax to net cash provided by operating activities:		
Depreciation expense	$1,000	
Interest expense	500	
Investment revenue (dividends)	(650)	
Decrease in inventories	1,050	
Increase in trade receivables	(310)	1,590
Cash generated from operations		5,590
Interest paid	(300)	
Income taxes paid	(760)	(1,060)
Net cash provided by operating activities		$ 4,530

Companies often provide a separate section to identify interest and income taxes paid.

ON THE HORIZON

Presently, the IASB and the FASB are involved in a joint project on the presentation and organization of information in the financial statements. With respect to the cash flow statement specifically, the notion of *cash equivalents* will probably not be retained. The definition of cash in the existing literature would be retained, and the statement of cash flows would present information on changes in cash only. In addition, the IASB and FASB favor presentation of operating cash flows using the direct method only. This approach is generally opposed by the preparer community.

IFRS SELF-TEST QUESTIONS

1. Which of the following is true regarding the statement of cash flows under IFRS?
   (a) The statement of cash flows has two major sections—operating and non-operating.
   (b) The statement of cash flows has two major sections—financing and investing.
   (c) The statement of cash flows has three major sections—operating, investing, and financing.
   (d) The statement of cash flows has three major sections—operating, non-operating, and financing.

2. In the case of a bank overdraft:
   (a) GAAP typically includes the amount in cash and cash equivalents.
   (b) IFRS typically includes the amount in cash equivalents but not in cash.
   (c) GAAP typically treats the overdraft as a liability, and reports the amount in the financing section of the statement of cash flows.
   (d) IFRS typically treats the overdraft as a liability, and reports the amount in the investing section of the statement of cash flows.

3. Under IFRS, significant non-cash transactions:
   (a) are classified as operating, if they are related to income items.
   (b) are excluded from the statement of cash flows and disclosed in a narrative form or summarized in a separate schedule.

(c) are classified as an investing or financing activity.
(d) are classified as an operating activity, unless they can be specifically identified with financing or investing activities.

4. For purposes of the statement of cash flows, under IFRS interest paid is treated as:
(a) an operating activity in all cases.
(b) an investing or operating activity, depending on use of the borrowed funds.
(c) either a financing or investing activity.
(d) either an operating or financing activity, but treated consistently from period to period.

5. For purposes of the statement of cash flows, under IFRS income taxes paid are treated as:
(a) cash flows from operating activities unless they can be separately identified as part of investing or financing activities.
(b) an operating activity in all cases.
(c) an investing or operating activity, depending on whether a refund is received.
(d) either operating, financing, or investing activity, but treated consistently to other companies in the same industry.

IFRS CONCEPTS AND APPLICATION

IFRS23-1 Where can authoritative IFRS related to the statement of cash flows be found?

IFRS23-2 Briefly describe some of the similarities and differences between GAAP and IFRS with respect to cash flow reporting.

IFRS23-3 What are some of the key obstacles for the FASB and IASB within its accounting guidance in the area of cash flow reporting? Explain.

IFRS23-4 Stan Conner and Mark Stein were discussing the statement of cash flows of Bombeck Co. In the notes to the statement of cash flows was a schedule entitled "Non-cash investing and financing activities." Give three examples of significant non-cash transactions that would be reported in this schedule.

IFRS23-5 Springsteen Co. had the following activity in its most recent year of operations.

(a) Pension expense exceeds amount funded.
(b) Redemption of bonds payable.
(c) Sale of building at book value.
(d) Depreciation.
(e) Exchange of equipment for furniture.
(f) Issuance of ordinary shares.
(g) Amortization of intangible assets.
(h) Purchase of treasury shares.
(i) Issuance of bonds for land.
(j) Payment of dividends.
(k) Increase in interest receivable on notes receivable.
(l) Purchase of equipment.

Instructions

Classify the items as (1) operating—add to net income; (2) operating—deduct from net income; (3) investing; (4) financing; or (5) significant non-cash investing and financing activities. Use the indirect method.

IFRS23-6 Following are selected statement of financial position accounts of Sander Bros. Corp. at December 31, 2012 and 2011, and the increases or decreases in each account from 2011 to 2012. Also presented is selected income statement information for the year ended December 31, 2012, and additional information.

Selected statement of financial position accounts	2012	2011	Increase (Decrease)
Assets			
Property, plant, and equipment	$277,000	$247,000	$30,000
Accumulated depreciation	(178,000)	(167,000)	(11,000)
Accounts receivable	34,000	24,000	10,000

Selected statement of financial position accounts	2012	2011	Increase (Decrease)
Equity and liabilities			
Share capital—ordinary, $1 par	$ 22,000	$19,000	$ 3,000
Share premium—ordinary	9,000	3,000	6,000
Retained earnings	104,000	91,000	13,000
Bonds payable	49,000	46,000	3,000
Dividends payable	8,000	5,000	3,000

Selected income statement information for the year ended December 31, 2012	
Sales revenue	$155,000
Depreciation	38,000
Gain on sale of equipment	14,500
Net income	31,000

Additional information:

1. During 2012, equipment costing $45,000 was sold for cash.
2. Accounts receivable relate to sales of merchandise.
3. During 2012, $25,000 of bonds payable were issued in exchange for property, plant, and equipment.

There was no amortization of bond discount or premium.

Instructions

Determine the category (operating, investing, or financing) and the amount that should be reported in the statement of cash flows for the following items.

(a) Payments for purchase of property, plant, and equipment.
(b) Proceeds from the sale of equipment.
(c) Cash dividends paid.
(d) Redemption of bonds payable.

IFRS23-7 Dingel Corporation has contracted with you to prepare a statement of cash flows. The controller has provided the following information.

	December 31	
	2012	2011
Buildings	$ -0-	$29,750
Equipment	45,000	20,000
Patents	5,000	6,250
Investments	-0-	3,000
Inventory	12,000	9,000
Accounts receivable	12,250	10,000
Cash	33,500	13,000
	$107,750	$91,000
Share capital—ordinary	$ 43,000	$33,000
Retained earnings	20,750	6,000
Allowance for doubtful accounts	3,000	4,500
Accumulated depreciation on equipment	2,000	4,500
Accumulated depreciation on buildings	-0-	6,000
Accounts payable	5,000	3,000
Dividends payable	-0-	5,000
Long-term notes payable	31,000	25,000
Notes payable, short-term (non-trade)	3,000	4,000
	$107,750	$91,000

Additional data related to 2012 are as follows.

1. Equipment that had cost $11,000 and was 40% depreciated at time of disposal was sold for $2,500.
2. $10,000 of the long-term notes payable was paid by issuing ordinary shares.
3. Cash dividends paid were $5,000.
4. On January 1, 2012, the building was completely destroyed by a flood. Insurance proceeds on the building were $32,000.

5. Equity investments (non-trading) were sold at $1,700 above their cost.
6. Cash was paid for the acquisition of equipment.
7. A long-term note for $16,000 was issued for the acquisition of equipment.
8. Interest of $2,000 and income taxes of $6,500 were paid in cash.

Instructions

Prepare a statement of cash flows using the indirect method.

Professional Research

IFRS23-8 As part of the year-end accounting process for your company, you are preparing the statement of cash flows according to IFRS. One of your team, a finance major, believes the statement should be prepared to report the change in working capital because analysts many times use working capital in ratio analysis. Your supervisor would like research conducted to verify the basis for preparing the statement of cash flows.

Instructions

Access the IFRS authoritative literature at the IASB website (*http://eifrs.iasb.org/*). When you have accessed the documents, you can use the search tool in your Internet browser to respond to the following questions. (Provide paragraph citations.)

(a) What is the primary objective for the statement of cash flows? Is working capital the basis for meeting this objective?
(b) What information is provided in a statement of cash flows?
(c) List some of the typical cash inflows and outflows from operations.

International Financial Reporting Problem: *Marks and Spencer plc*

IFRS23-9 The financial statements of **Marks and Spencer plc (M&S)** are available at the book's companion website or can be accessed at *http://corporate.marksandspencer.com/documents/publications/2010/Annual_Report_2010.*

Instructions

Refer to M&S's financial statements and the accompanying notes to answer the following questions.

(a) Which method of computing net cash provided by operating activities does M&S use? What were the amounts of net cash provided by operating activities for the years 2009 and 2010? Which two items were most responsible for the increase in net cash provided by operating activities in 2010?
(b) What was the most significant item in the cash flows used for investing activities section in 2010? What was the most significant item in the cash flows used for financing activities section in 2010?
(c) Where is "deferred income taxes" reported in M&S's statement of cash flows? Why does it appear in that section of the statement of cash flows?
(d) Where is depreciation reported in M&S's statement of cash flows? Why is depreciation added to net income in the statement of cash flows?

ANSWERS TO IFRS SELF-TEST QUESTIONS

1. c 2. c 3. b 4. d 5. a

Remember to check the book's companion website to find additional resources for this chapter.

NOTES

NOTES

INDEX

N

T